Pro Patria Mori

The 56th (1st London) Division at Gommecourt
1st July 1916

For

Chief Engine Room Artificer 1st Class William MacCormick,
HMS Hannibal
Died in an accident on 29th October 1915
and
4540 Rfn. Charles Robert Tompson,
1/9th London Regt (Queen Victoria's Rifles)
Missing at Gommecourt, 1st July 1916, aged 20

who gave everything

Maj. Ewen MacDonald MacCormick M.C.,
1/20th London Regt (Blackheath & Woolwich) and
1/4th London Regt (Royal Fusiliers)

who gave to his country, his family and his students

PRO PATRIA MORI

The 56th (1st London) Division at Gommecourt
1st July 1916

Alan MacDonald

IONA BOOKS

Copyright © Alan MacDonald 2006 and 2008

British Library Cataloguing In Publication Data
A Record of this Publication is available
from the British Library

ISBN 978-0-9558119-1-3

First edition published May 2006 by Exposure Publishing

Revised edition published July 2008 by Iona Books
and printed by Lightning Source, Milton Keynes

Typeset in 10pt Garamond

Also by Alan MacDonald
*A Lack of Offensive Spirit? The 46ᵗʰ (North Midland) Division
at Gommecourt, 1ˢᵗ July 1916*

Pro Patria Mori
Email: info@gommecourt.co.uk ● website: www.gommecourt.co.uk

Front Cover Photograph:
'C' Company, 1/14ᵗʰ London Regiment (London Scottish) marching through
Pas-en-Artois on their way to the front line and the attack on 1ˢᵗ July 1916.
(Photograph courtesy of Imperial War Museum, Q791)

CONTENTS:

USE OF FOOTNOTES & ENDNOTES

Both footnotes and endnotes are used in this book. Footnotes are marked with Roman numerals (i.e. ⁱⁱ) and normally refer to people or events within the text. Footnotes are to be found at the bottom of the relevant page. Endnotes are marked with ordinary numbers (i.e. ²) and normally refer to sources or information not directly related to events within the text. Endnotes are to be found at the end of each chapter.

MAPS

TABLES

FIGURES

PHOTOGRAPHS

INTRODUCTION TO THE REVISED EDITION

W HEN IT BECAME necessary to re-publish *'Pro Patria Mori'* (for reasons too frustrating to go into here) I decided to take advantage of the lessons I had learned during the researching of its Gommecourt companion volume *'A Lack of Offensive Spirit?'* to considerably update certain aspects of the book. In addition, the research for the second book threw up the need for some corrections to certain aspects of the first book and, rather more crucially, a re-interpretation of some of the conclusions reached about the eventual tragic failure of the attack on Gommecourt on 1ˢᵗ July 1916.

The two key lessons learned from the research into the book about the 46ᵗʰ Division's involvement at Gommecourt were firstly that a huge amount of previously unused information lurked in the personal files of the officers involved in the action. For this book every available officer files was examined and, as a result, several mysteries about the fate of some of the leading personalities of the 46ᵗʰ Division were explained. As a result of this experience I have further investigated the personal files of some 120 56ᵗʰ Division officers whose files I unwisely did not consult for the first edition of the book.

The second lesson was that some local newspapers contain a fabulous wealth of information about the men involved in the Great War. The British Museum's Newspaper Archive at Colindale may not look especially inspiring (it appears to be an architectural second, and slightly poorer, cousin to many London telephone exchanges) but it contains, either as original newsprint or on microfiche, copies of nearly every edition of every newspaper printed in the United Kingdom. For both the journalists and the readers of the time the Great War was an event like no other and the coverage – every word thoroughly warranted – reflects the seismic nature of the cataclysm that befell Europe and the communities of Great Britain between 1914 and 1918. Many of the beautifully bound copies of these newspapers are in increasing danger of disintegration and it is to be hoped that the British Museum either has, or is allocated, the funds to ensure this invaluable resource is preserved so that it continues to be made available to everyone interested in the country's history and society.

Having garnered a large quantity of valuable information from the newspapers of the North Midlands for the 46ᵗʰ Division book I visited Colindale in the expectation that London newspapers would be similarly useful. Oddly, and sadly, I was wrong. The two main London newspapers, *The Evening Standard* and *Evening News*, reported the war in the fashion of national newspapers with barely a mention of the actions of London based Army units. Many of the smaller local newspapers reported the war with some local detail but, with one or two notable exceptions, coverage was sparse. One newspaper, the *West London Press, Westminster & Chelsea News*, carried on as if nothing untoward was happening on the other side of the English Channel, but its reporting of whist drives, mothers meetings and minor local criminality was second to none. In general, therefore, London newspapers were a relatively insignificant source of useful information. That is not to say that the trip to Colindale was time wasted. Whilst there I consulted the *'Territorial Service Gazette'*, a weekly magazine devoted to the activities of all Territorial Force units. Until August 1916 the *'TSG'* was devoted to a variety of topics: casualty lists, changes in Army regulations and, extensively, the recruiting needs of the various units of the Territorial Force. In August, however, its character changed dramatically and it was the casualties suffered at Gommecourt and, most especially, by the 56th Division which drove that change. Essentially, thereafter, the *'TSG'* became a melancholy roll call of ever lengthening casualty lists, plaintive requests from parents and sweethearts for news of the missing, brief biographies of the dead submitted by their families and information from and about Prisoners of War. Also included were page after page of photographs of the missing submitted in the hope that someone might recognise the man and have some news, any news, of the man's fate. It is a sad and sometimes tragic publication but, nonetheless, an invaluable source of information about the members of the Territorial Force. There is a certain London-centric element to it but, as it was distributed to every hospital within the United Kingdom coverage of all T.F. units its extensive and for anyone with an interest in Britain's Territorial units it is an essential resource.

Having started to develop a new research plan, other original sources were revealed that had somehow slipped through the net between 1998 and 2006 when *'Pro Patria Mori'* was originally researched and written. In addition, certain individuals have been very helpful and, although already mentioned in the 'Acknowledgements' section, here I should mention Chris Rippingale for his enormous help on aspects of the London Rifle Brigade, Ralph Whitehead for providing details of the German casualties at Gommecourt, Dick Flory who searched his huge library of School Rolls of Honour for information about 56th Division officers, Simon Jervis for providing many photographs of men who appear in the 'Fallen at Gommecourt' section and Pam and Ken Linge of the excellent 'Thiepval Project' who kindly gave me access to their files.

The result is a substantially expanded book which has grown by some 180 pages. I make no apology for the resulting increased length of a book some already thought excessively long. My aim has always been to record the stories of the men who fought and died at Gommecourt and no-one, however minor their role, deserves to be forgotten or ignored. Because for me the main objective of *'Pro Patria Mori'* has always been to ensure that:

"We Shall Remember Them"

A.M.
June 2008

INTRODUCTION

A S A CHILD I WAS always interested in military and naval history and I spent many happy hours wandering around the Imperial War Museum and Maritime Museum on weekends and in the school holidays. My interests tended towards either the modern – the Second World War in which both my parents had served – or the less recent – the Napoleonic Wars, the English Civil War, the Wars of the Roses to name but a few. The war about which I knew little was the Great War. It was not covered at school and, until BBC2's ground breaking TV programme *'The Great War'* in the mid-60s, little was seen or heard of it in the media. My only dim recollection of anything to do with the war was a dark and somewhat forbidding picture which hung on the wall of my grand-parents' house just down the road from where we lived in South London. It showed a rank of kilted soldiers standing steadfastly under a hail of shot and shell holding back a horde of the enemy. A few men lay wounded or dead and in the background a windmill burned, but the poses of all were heroic: heads up, backs straight, stern resolution on every face. I never thought to ask about what it portrayed. Tucked away in a draw in the little used front room of their house was a neat little, plush-lined box containing a small brass cross with some coloured ribbons attached. On occasion my brother and I would retrieve it and stare at it but not once did we enquire what it meant, what it represented, whose it was.

It was only in the early 1990s, after my father found a small pocket diary amongst the belongings of his father who had died nearly thirty years earlier that my interest in the Great War was fired. The diary contained the brief, scribbled notes of my grandfather's experiences on the Western Front in 1915 and 1916, first at the Battle of Loos and then near Vimy Ridge in the early summer of 1916. Further research showed that he had been a pre-war Territorial with the 1/20ᵗʰ London Regiment (Blackheath and Woolwich) and that he had gone to France in the August of 1915 as a private. Promotion to the rank of sergeant followed within months as casualties opened up the path to promotion and then, in July 1916, he was plucked from the ranks of the battalion's NCOs and gazetted Second Lieutenant in the 1/4ᵗʰ London Regiment (Royal Fusiliers). Within two months his war was over and so, nearly, was his life. Less than two weeks after winning the Military Cross for his actions on the 15ᵗʰ September 1916 near Leuze Wood on the Somme, he was severely wounded by machine gun fire and nearly died. He survived to become a temporary Major and commandant of the military hospital at Osborne on the Isle of Wight. He died in 1962 and I remember him as a large, cheerful, warm but somehow remote presence who oversaw large family occasions from the comforts of his arm chair in the back room that overlooked his rambling garden in Streatham, South London.

Sadly, I never talked to him about his experiences although I doubt whether he would have talked about them much or at all. Everything I know about his war-time exploits come from his diary and from researching his war record at the National Archives. In pursuit of this background, however, I came to be fascinated by the Great War. Visits to Western Front battlefields on the way back from French holidays became the norm and the anguished wail of the children "not another empty field!" when we stopped next to another unremarkable expanse of French cornfield or pasture became a staple of these journeys.

Visits turned to books and the first one I read had a profound impact on my interest in the war. Martin Middlebrook's *'The First Day on the Somme'* affected me deeply and visits to the sites of some of the greatest tragedies described – Thiepval, Beaumont Hamel, La Boiselle, Serre – became an annual pilgrimage. On these journeys, however, one village was always passed by as we rushed off northwards to catch the Calais ferry home.

Gommecourt seemed something of a sideshow and my knowledge of it was dim compared to the rest of the 1st July front. The fate of another relative was to change this. Twenty year old Charles Robert Tompson came from Watford and was a cousin of my mother. In 1914, on the outbreak of war and aged eighteen, he joined up to become a rifleman in the 1/9th London Regiment (Queen Victoria's Rifles). After training in the UK, he was sent to France as a replacement for the hundreds of casualties the battalion had suffered during the hard fighting of 1915. And so, in May 1916, he found himself marching with his mates towards the village of Hebuterne where he spent the next eight weeks working and training for the biggest event of his young life. At 7.30 a.m. on Saturday, 1st July 1916 he climbed out of the British trenches opposite the village of Gommecourt and trudged forward with the rest of the battalion as his division, the 56th (1st London), took part in a diversionary attack designed to deflect attention away from the main Somme offensive. Charles Tompson was never seen again. He is one of the 'Missing of the Somme' whose name is recorded on the massive Thiepval Memorial that sits glowering over the battlefield from the heights above the River Ancre.

And so was born the need to find out what happened to Charles and his friends on that day. How and why did he and hundreds of his mates die? What did they achieve and who was responsible for the decisions that ended with his death and those of so many others? The work has taken six years. It has grown from a desire to know what happened to a determination to write it down, to detail the daily lives and the deaths of the men from London and beyond who fought so bravely on the 'First Day on the Somme'.

Inevitably, in analysing the planning and the outcome of any battle, comment must be made on those in charge of those processes. It is not the job of this book to pass judgement on the overall war-time performance of these men but the author has been drawn inexorably to certain conclusions about the judgement and, in some cases, competence of the Commander in Chief and the Army and Corps commanders involved *at this time and in this battle.*

I have tried to make *'Pro Patria Mori'* a history, a guide and a memorial to the men of the two armies who fought in the little known fields outside the village of Gommecourt on 1st July 1916. It is dedicated to my distant relative Charles Tompson who didn't make it and to my grandfather, who was not there but who knew only too well the terrors, squalor and pain of the Battle of the Somme in the following weeks. I am grateful to them both.

Lastly, we should never forget the personal impact of the battles like that of Gommecourt. For years afterwards, numerous poignant messages appeared in the 'In Memoriam' section of newspapers like *'The Times'.* They served as a tragic reminder of the deep and abiding personal loss felt by so many families. It is perhaps extraordinary to think that the last such message referring to a man of the 56th Division appeared as recently as *'The Times'* of Tuesday, 2nd July 1974, fifty eight years after the event. It refers to a man whose death is recounted in this book. It reads simply:

"In proud and happy memory of my brother,
Sergeant Hugh Victor Hember, London Rifle Brigade,
killed at Gommecourt, 1st July 1916."

ACKNOWLEDGEMENTS

I WOULD LIKE TO THANK the following people for their help and support during the writing of this book.

For help in locating German sources: Eberhardt Kettlitz and Jack Sheldon and for their help in the translation of these documents: David Gregory, Justin Levy, Ralph Whitehead, Theo Penhallurick and Philip A. Heinecke. I must also thank Ralph Whitehead for access to his work on the German Army on the Somme 1914-16 and German casualties at Gommecourt.

For general encouragement and several useful suggestions on the chapter relating to the treatment of casualties: Dr Andrew Bamji, Consultant rheumatologist, Curator of the Gillies Archives and Director of the Elmstead Rehabilitation Unit.

Chris Rippingale for his help with the casualties and prisoners of war of the London Rifle Brigade. Chris has done great work researching the 1/5th London Regt. and I am indebted to him for his willingness to share the fruits of his considerable research.

Several of the photographs in this book come from the collection of Paul Reed who I thank both for the permission to use them and for his general advice on this subject and the battlefields of the Somme.

Simon Jervis also was very generous with images from his collection and many now appear in the 'Fallen at Gommecourt' Section of this book.

Pam and Ken Linge of the excellent Thiepval Project which is seeking to produce a biographical and, where possible, photographic database of the missing of the Somme. They, and their sources, have provided invaluable assistance in fleshing out the backgrounds of many officers and men.

From the other side of the 'pond' I'd like to thank Dick Flory for researching many officers in his substantial library of British School and University Rolls of Honour.

I must thank Richard Davies and the staff at the Brotherton Library, Leeds University for helping with access to, and permission to quote from, documents held by the Liddle Collection. Similar gratitude must be expressed to the staff at the National Archives, Kew, the staff at the Newspaper Archive of the British Museum, Colindale and the Imperial War Museum Library and Photographic Library for their assistance in meeting many requests made over the past year.

I must express my gratitude to the Commonwealth War Graves Commission for giving me permission to use the details drawn from their web site (http://www.cwgc.org/) for the Roll of Honour in the Appendices in this book.

For their general encouragement and interest over a very long time: Ken Lees, John Hartley and all the folk over at the Long, Long Trail web site and its W.W.1. Forum so wonderfully run by Chris Baker and his associates (http://www.1914-1918.net/home.htm).

Also, thanks to Avril Williams and her many guests, all met at her excellent and hospitable guest house at Auchonvillers over the past few summers.

I must also mention the late Iain Kerr for his unstinting help in providing background information to the battalions mentioned in this book.

Finally, for starting me off on this long journey and for expressing his encouragement for the first edition of *'Pro Patria Mori'*, I must thank Martin Middlebrook, whose book *'The First Day on the Somme'* has meant so much to so many World War One enthusiasts such as myself.

***

WHERE POSSIBLE I have attempted to gain permission for the use of the quotations found in this book, however, if I have unknowingly infringed copyright in the writing of this book I would hope that my apologies are accepted.

Photographs, unless otherwise credited, are the author's.

***

I MUST ALSO THANK my much published and much missed late brother Ian whose prowess as a writer inspired me to pursue the idea of writing a book and my parents for so many things but, importantly, those genes which appear to have combined to produce sons who write.

Also thanks to my mother-in-law, Chris Purnell, for so carefully proof-reading the final document.

***

LASTLY, MY GRATITUDE and love go to my wife Helen and our two children, Tom and Kate, who have had to put up with innumerable trips to empty fields in France and to interminable recitals on subjects of interest to only a few World War One enthusiasts. Thank you for helping to make it possible in your different ways.

A. M.
June 2008

1. PLANNING THE 'BIG PUSH'

"In Sir Douglas Haig's plan nothing depended on the capture of Gommecourt."

Military Operations, France and Belgium 1916
Volume I

BY JULY 1ST 1916, Europe had been at war for nearly two years. After the first fluid months, during which the Imperial German Army had so nearly swept to victory, the Western Front had begun to settle into the static squalor of the trenches. France's armies, shattered in the Battle of the Frontiers in the autumn of 1914 and then hurled without thought of cost against the barbed wire, entrenched Maxim guns and artillery of the invader throughout 1915, were now caught in the mincing machine that was Verdun. Their commander, 64-year old Gen. Joseph Jacques Cesaire Joffre, had, with increasing impatience, waited for his British allies to recruit, train and equip an army that would stand comparison with his own in raw numbers if not in experience. With the opening of the Battle of the Somme, that day had at last arrived and Britain was ready to play its full part in shaping the decisive military campaigns in Northern France.

After an early mist, Saturday, 1st July 1916 broke bright and sunny. Following a 65 minute hurricane bombardment involving over 1,500 guns and howitzers, the men of the attacking battalions walked into battle at 7.30 a.m. Sir Douglas Haig, the commander of Britain's first mass 'citizen army', spent the morning reading the early optimistic reports from the front. Their positive tone reflected his own confident expectations. The early entries in his diary on that Saturday suggest little concern about the progress of the 'Big Push':

"A fine sunny morning with gentle breeze from the west and south-west. At first some mist in the hollows. This very favourable because it concealed the concentration of our troops (author: it also made life very difficult for the Royal Flying Corps observers trying to spot targets for the British artillery)....

Reports up to 8 a.m. most satisfactory. Our troops had everywhere crossed the Enemy's front trenches."[1]

By the following morning, the true extent of the calamity that had befallen the men of the Third and Fourth Armies of the B.E.F. was still not entirely clear. Sir Douglas's diary records that one village at the southern end of the front had been taken (Montauban) but then listed a series of reverses in village after village as the narrative moved north. Four battalions, two at the Schwaben Redoubt near Thiepval and two at Serre, were thought to be cut off (what little that was left of them was, in fact, long since back in their trenches). Then, later in the day, the Adjutant-General, Lt. Gen. Fowke, was to report to his commander in chief that casualties were estimated to be over 40,000 – some 33% of all those who had gone 'over the top'. Haig was not to be dismayed. The diary entry read:

"This cannot be considered severe in view of the numbers engaged and the length of front attacked..."[2]

Lt. Gen. Fowke's report was to prove, however, grossly optimistic. As the details of the battalion roll calls from one end of the front to the other were reported the true nature of the catastrophe became apparent. Entries in the War Diaries of the infantry battalions and other units involved on the 1st July 1916 were to show that the British Army had suffered 61,816 casualties[i], over 50% of those who went into action. When the battle officially ended on the wet, cold and windy Sunday, 19th November, the British butcher's bill for the Battle of the Somme stood at 432,000; of which it is estimated that 150,000 were dead and another 100,000 too badly wounded ever to serve again.[3]

It was not meant to be like this.

***

THE IDEA OF A grand joint Anglo-French offensive was born at the Inter-Allied Military Conference held at the ornate chateau at Chantilly, just north of Paris, on the 6-8th December 1915. Attended by representatives of the four main allies - France, Britain, Russia and Italy – a broad agreement was reached on a strategy involving simultaneous offensives on three fronts in the summer of 1916. The armies of France and Britain would work together to drive the Germans from their entrenched positions stretching from the Belgium coast to the Swiss border.

Eleven days later, on the 19th December, Sir Douglas Haig was appointed C-in-C of the British Armies in France, replacing the incompetent and out-of-touch Field Marshal Sir John French who had presided over a series of military setbacks throughout 1914 and 1915. Although Haig had assiduously and successfully undermined French by exploiting his wife's contacts in the Royal household, he and his predecessor had one thing in common: they were both cavalrymen and their love of horses, attachment to the thrill and spectacle of massed cavalry and conviction that the horse still had a vital role to play on the modern battlefield therefore coloured the views of the British Commanders in Chief on strategy and tactics throughout the entire war.

As the New Year loomed, Gen. Joffre wrote to his new counterpart on 30th December proposing a joint offensive on a 60-mile front astride the Somme (from Lassigny in the south to Arras in the north). Although he anticipated that the French would still provide the major component in the attack he expected the British Army to contribute far more than previously. Also, as part of a realignment prior to any such attack, he asked Haig to take over the whole of the French 10th Army's frontage between Ransart and Loos which, at this time, stood between the British Third Army, to the south, and the First Army to the north. Apprised of his ally's intentions, Haig instructed the commander of the British Third Army, Sir Edmund Allenby (another cavalry officer but no friend of Haig's), to prepare a plan of attack on his front which ran from Curlu on the River Somme north to its current junction with the French 10th Army at Ransart. Haig suggested an area between Maricourt and Gommecourt as the appropriate front. Haig was not, however, an enthusiast for a Somme offensive and, in truth, it offered little of strategic value in its immediate vicinity. Its only real significance was that it was the border between the British and the main French

---

i Later revised to just over 57,000 of whom c. 19,000 died. The main factor explaining the discrepancy was the large number of men reported as 'missing', some of whom later returned to their units but most of whom were killed.

armies and, therefore, was the logical location for a joint, as opposed to a co-ordinated, offensive. But, be that as it may, Haig's persistent preference was for a British attack further north towards the Ypres salient. As a result, whilst Allenby's staff pored over plans for the Somme attack, Gen. Sir Herbert Plumer, commander of the Second Army, was instructed to prepare plans for attacks against the Messines-Wytschaete ridge, Lille and the Houthulst Forest north east of Ypres.

Three weeks after making his first proposal for action on the Somme, Joffre visited Haig's H.Q. on the 20th January and made a new proposal for a summer offensive, part of which involved the Third Army making preliminary attacks on a 20,000 yard front on the Somme on 20th April. Three days later this plan was further defined when Joffre suggested two 'wearing down' attacks prior to the main joint offensive. These would both be conducted by the Third Army on the Somme using 15-18 divisions; one starting on 20th April and the other in May. This proposal was flatly rejected by Haig and instead he suggested a series of raids and some preparatory actions away from the main front 10-14 days before the main offensive.

Meanwhile, other organisational changes were in hand within the British command. As the B.E.F. expanded in units and men, Haig had decided to create a Fourth Army which, when in existence, would take over the southern end of the British line with its right flank on the River Somme. Its commander would be Gen. Sir Henry Rawlinson, previously the commander of the Army's IV Corps, and currently in temporary command of the First Army. On the 4th February, Rawlinson gave over command of the First Army to Sir Charles Monro on his return from Gallipoli and, whilst he waited for the formation of his new command, he was asked by Haig to consider options for an attack on the Northern end of British front near Ypres. In addition, he was ordered to collaborate with Allenby on the planning of the Somme offensive. Crucially, Rawlinson, an infantryman by training and experience, held significantly different views from his Commander in Chief on the conduct of offensive operations and, as a result, the planning of the Somme battle became an unequal struggle between the increasingly aggressive and expansive outlook of Haig and the more circumspect and cautious view of his subordinate.

In mid-February, Joffre and Haig reached agreement on a plan for the joint summer offensive. The date of 1st July was agreed as the target for its commencement. In addition, Haig agreed to a partial attack 1-2 weeks earlier to be made by the British Army in the La Bassee-Ypres area. Haig also undertook to take over the whole of the French 10th Army front in early March by which time the Fourth Army would be ready. To fulfil this move, the Third Army would side step to the north with its right now to the north of Foncquevillers and its left on Vimy Ridge. To bridge the remaining gap the First Army was to expand its front to the south to take over the area opposite the German held city of Lens.

On the 19th February the French advised Haig about an impending German attack on the small but emotionally important city of Verdun. It was not clear how significant the offensive would be as intelligence reports also suggested the possibility of attacks elsewhere, however, Haig undertook to speed the take over of the 10th Army front if a substantial attack materialised. At an Army

Commanders' meeting on the same day it was decided to bring forward Third Army's plans for the Somme attack in case it was deemed necessary to relieve pressure on the French. These plans were to become the responsibility of Rawlinson and the Fourth Army when he took over command on 1st March. Two day's later, the German Fifth Army unleashed a hurricane bombardment of unprecedented violence on the threadbare defences of the hills to the north of Verdun and the Meuse. Against all expectations, the French defence held – just. But the storm that had engulfed the French XXX Corps on the 21st February showed no signs of abating and, by 3rd March, Gen. Joffre was convinced that the attack at Verdun was a major German offensive and not a diversionary attack in preparation for another blow elsewhere. With his 10th Army now available for re-assignment, he believed he had sufficient men to resist effectively, nonetheless he appealed to Haig to be ready to launch relieving attacks and to bring forward his plans for the main summer offensive. Italy and Russia were also asked to help detain German divisions on their fronts in order to prevent the further reinforcement of the Verdun offensive.

Between the 2nd and 14th March, Rawlinson's Fourth Army completed its move into the position north of the Somme but on the 8th March, Rawlinson was struck down by a bout of influenza so severe that, on the 17th, he was sent to Nice to recuperate. Throughout this time his staff, led by his Chief of Staff Maj. A A Montgomery, considered their options for an attack across the chalk down land of the Somme, "capital country in which to undertake an offensive", according to Rawlinson after several inspections[4] before his illness. The proposed battlefield had, as its southern border, the languid, marsh-fringed, winding River Somme, an area more normally populated by water fowl, wading birds and ever hopeful fishermen. Now it not only provided an opportunity for the nearby soldiers to swim and wile away the hours when out of the trenches and not on fatigues but it also presented an impassable barrier to both armies providing protection to their flanks in this part of the theatre. North of the river, the countryside was rolling farmland dotted with small villages that often nestled in hollows and whose location was often only given away by the local church spire. Between them the open down land was broken by a series of woods, previously the pre-war preserve of the rural hunter, imbued with that French obsession with massacring small birds and animals. Then, as now, you entered them at your peril. Some were soon to become infamous in the British Army's annals: Trones, Mametz, Delville and High Woods, places of misery and death. Here, the Germans had possession of the higher land and their trenches expertly exploited this advantage using both forward and reverse slopes to maximum effect. Between the Somme and the River Ancre to the north (the Ancre being a miniature version of its southern big brother) these trench lines ran along the western edge of a plateau dominated by the small village of Pozieres, set to become one of the most fought over locations of the entire battle. From the centre of this village, which straddled the arrow straight Roman road from Albert to Bapaume, it was possible to gain observation over miles of territory in all directions. Tiny unexceptional villages lay between it and the British front lines to the west, villages until then unknown to the British public but whose names would become tragically familiar to hundreds of families as the summer of 1916 wore on: La Boiselle, Ovillers, Thiepval, Contalmaison, Fricourt, Mametz,

Guillemont. For a year, German engineers had been able, almost without interruption, to turn these tiny hamlets into little fortresses, linked by miles of trenches and protected by thickets of barbed wire. They had constructed comprehensively defended front and reserve lines and, further back, more trenches were already in preparation giving their defences depth as well as strength. North of the Ancre, the roll call of heavily protected villages continued, more names that would bring misery to men and relatives alike: Beaumont Hamel, Serre and, lastly, Gommecourt. Each had the same advantage of terrain skilfully chosen and powerfully fortified. For anyone attacking along the length of this front, their task would be an uphill one, both literally and metaphorically. Nevertheless, Rawlinson was optimistic, regarding the area as having 'great possibilities'[5].

On the 26th March, Rawlinson received from Lt. Gen. Kiggell, Chief of Haig's General Staff, an outline of the resources in men and artillery he could expect to employ in the forthcoming offensive and, the following day, Joffre wrote to Haig suggesting another plan for a joint attack. For this the front would run from Lassigny in the south to Hebuterne in the north. He had it in mind that the attack north of the Somme should precede that to the south, i.e. the British should attack first and the French only when the Germans were exhausted. Whilst Haig considered Joffre's suggestion, Rawlinson completed his first plan for the Fourth Army offensive which was submitted to Haig on 3rd April[6]. In it, Rawlinson suggested a 20,000 yard front running from Serre to Maricourt. He proposed an initial advance to a depth of 1-3,000 yards depending, to a great extent, on the nature of the preliminary bombardment and the location of the second line of German defences. Thus, he proposed taking the German Second Position to the north of the village of Pozieres but not to the south as the distance would have been too great for effective artillery preparation. This position would be assaulted after a short delay caused by the need to bring up the artillery needed to pound the defences and cut the extensive wire of the German Second Position. Rawlinson also discussed and then discounted a Fourth Army attack on Gommecourt as it:

> "…involves a front of 26,000 yards, which is more than the force available can deal with satisfactorily."[7]

Rawlinson's plan was either prudent, cautious or timid depending on one's perspective but he and Montgomery had been left in something of a strategic vacuum when it came to planning the offensive. Haig had set them no particular short, medium or long term objectives and the plan had been developed on the basis of Rawlinson's and his Corps commanders' instincts as to what was achievable. On the 5th April Haig and Rawlinson met to discuss his 'Bite and Hold' plan designed, as the G.O.C. of Fourth Army wrote, to "kill as many Germans as possible with the least loss to ourselves". At the meeting it became immediately clear that Haig regarded Rawlinson's proposals as unnecessarily cautious, not something that will have surprised Rawlinson as, on the 30th March, he had confided to his diary the comment that:

> "I shall have a tussle with (Haig) over the limited objective for I hear he is inclined to favour the unlimited with the chance of breaking the German line."[8]

Rawlinson was not deeply shocked, therefore, when Haig pressed for deeper advances on either wing, i.e. towards Montauban in the south and on the Serre/Miraumont spur on the northern flank (see maps), as well as the capture of the majority of the German second line with Pozieres as a prime objective.

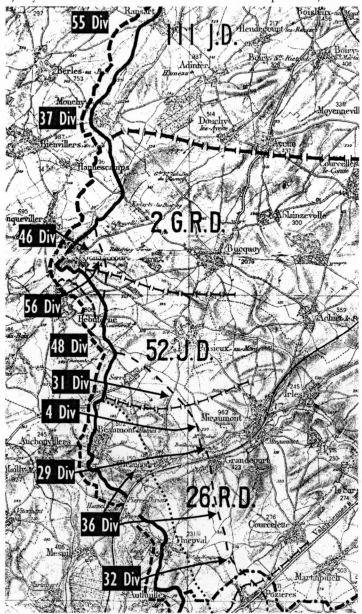

Map I Northern Flank of Offensive – First Day Objectives

▪▪▪▪▪ Rawlinson's original objectives for first day   – – – – – Haig's proposal for revised first day objectives
(Source of original map: 'Schlachten des Weltkrieges', Somme Teil I, Oldenburg)

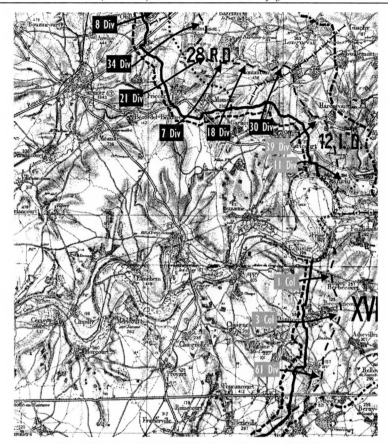

Map 2 Southern Flank of Offensive – First Day Objectives

■■■■■ Rawlinson's original objectives for first day   – – – – – Haig's proposal for revised first day objectives
(Source of original map: 'Schlachten des Weltkrieges', Somme Teil I, Oldenburg)

Rawlinson might have been justifiably piqued, however, when Haig criticised the plan for lacking strategic purpose as this had been notably absent from Haig's initial instructions for the planning of the attack.   Haig then brushed aside Rawlinson's concerns about the ability of the artillery to prepare adequately for a deeper penetration of the German lines and of the difficulties of bringing forward the heavier guns over a much damaged battlefield, instead arguing that the Fourth Army should be prepared to take advantage of the "confusion and disorganisation⁹'" in the defending troops caused by the initial attack. Furthermore, he reinforced the importance of the attack keeping in close contact with the French to the south in order that they might force a passage of the Somme near to Peronne.

Whilst Haig and Rawlinson argued about the emphasis and detail of the Fourth Army's attack, Sir Edmund Allenby and his staff had been investigating ways in which they could assist their southern colleague's venture. Consequently, on 9ᵗʰ April, Allenby sent to Lt. Gen. Kiggell, Haig's Chief of Staff at G.H.Q. options for Third Army's actions in support of the Fourth Army offensive. They were:

1. A diversionary attack on Vimy Ridge;
2. A diversionary attack on the German line between Monchy-au-Bois and Ransart; or
3. A diversion of men and material to the Fourth Army's front[10].

Four days later, Kiggell replied to Allenby's proposals endorsing the attack on the Monchy-au-Bois to Ransart line and detailed plans were requested for the end of May. Allenby was also told to withdraw one or preferably two divisions into reserve either for use in the Monchy attack or for deployment elsewhere. In a further weakening of the Third Army Kiggell confirmed that three divisions were to be withdrawn for use elsewhere during the second half of May.

At the same time, Gen. Plumer had forwarded plans for various offensive options on the Second Army front, as had been requested on 14ᵗʰ January. On 10ᵗʰ April, after considering the various plans, Haig asked him to proceed with that for the capture of the Messines-Wytschaete ridge. Haig also instructed that 20 large mines should be included in the plan. On the same day, he belatedly replied to Joffre's letter of the 27ᵗʰ March concerning the proposed phased Somme offensive. Whilst rejecting the idea of a two stage attack, Haig accepted the limitations of the front proposed, i.e. Lassigny to Hebuterne (exclusive). Northwards the Gommecourt salient would be subject to action taken to hold the Germans in expectation of an attack there.

On the 12ᵗʰ April Haig put into writing in G.H.Q. Letters O.A.D 710 and 710/1 to Rawlinson the essentials he had set out in the meeting of the 5ᵗʰ April. The capture of the Serre-Miraumont spur in the north and Montauban in the south were now deemed prerequisites of the initial advance. In the centre, the taking of Pozieres and the spurs leading towards Beaucourt sur Ancre, Grandcourt and Fricourt were also now crucial elements of the first movement. Through Kiggell, Haig then addressed the issue of the Gommecourt salient:

> "Simultaneous activity against the Gommecourt salient, designed to hold the attention of the enemy's artillery and reserves on that side, is advisable *so far as can be arranged for* (author's emphasis). The Third Army will probably be able to give some assistance of the same nature further to the north."[11]

It would seem from this comment that Haig and the General Staff did not yet envisage a major operation against Gommecourt. The "simultaneous activity" suggested was still to be the responsibility of the Fourth Army and its commander had made it fairly clear that there were insufficient resources for any action of significance. The day after Haig's letters were sent out, Kiggell wrote to Allenby asking for more details for his proposed attack between Monchy and Ransart which Kiggell regarded as having 'great value in conjunction with the Fourth Army attack.'[12] No mention was made of Gommecourt, again underlining the thinking that any operation there was to be of a minor scale.

Lastly, Haig emphasised the potential offensive role of the cavalry, even during the early stages of the attack. Rawlinson was charged to foresee any "probable opportunities" for their use. For the first time, the idea that a clean breakthrough of the enemy's lines was possible had entered the reckoning and Haig was to pursue this line of thought with increasing vigour over the coming weeks.

Haig believed his more distant and difficult objectives (and possibly even more) were attainable as a result of the damage to German morale caused by a "comparatively short intensive bombardment". In addition, he stressed the need for speed of advance after the initial attack stating that "the more the enemy can be pressed while he is shaken the less the need there will be for a long artillery preparation.[13]" Haig's optimism about the efficacy of a 'short and sharp' bombardment seem rooted in the Allies' (somewhat erroneous) appreciation of the effectiveness of the German artillery immediately prior to the Verdun assault and, perhaps, a failure to appreciate the failings of their own artillery preparations in the offensive battles of 1915. On the 4th March Haig had circulated to his four Army commanders a note about the tactics employed in the initial German attack and the defensive and offensive lessons that could be learned. He was clearly impressed by the style of the German Fifth Army's artillery preparations: 1,400 guns and howitzers on an eight mile front had brought down a bombardment of shattering intensity for a relatively brief eight hours. 100,000 shells an hour had rained down on the unfortunate defenders of the trenches in the heights above Verdun. Haig's report read thus:

> "Firstly, the artillery bombardment has been concentrated in one effort, immediately preceding the infantry attack. Little or no time seems to have been devoted to the registration of the heavy artillery and, so far as information goes, the bombardment has been of comparatively short duration but of the greatest intensity."[14]

The reported results also met with Haig's approval:

> "The result of the combination of surprise and an overwhelming artillery preparation was that the infantry appear to have had little more to do in their first advance than *to take possession of ground already practically won by the artillery* (author's emphasis)."[15]

Thus, the doctrine that 'artillery conquers and infantry occupies' established itself in the planning for the summer offensive. Haig's note then went on to draw a series of lessons that could be learned from the German early 'successes' at Verdun. Oddly, at a time when his armies were planning major offensives, Haig spent three pages setting out the defensive lessons. Offensive lessons warranted just three short and rather general paragraphs, one of which suggested that the Verdun artillery programme had already been tried by the Allies and with initial success. And where and under which perspicacious general had this occurred? Why, at Neuve Chapelle on 10th March 1915 when one Douglas Haig was then the commander of the attacking First Army. The attack itself had failed.

But, dangerously, an uncontested belief in the effectiveness of "an overwhelming artillery preparation" had taken root at the highest levels of command and this was to have a significant impact on the nature of the infantry tactics employed when the offensive eventually started. Furthermore, Haig's observation about the lack of target registration conducted prior to the attack on Verdun seems to have filtered through to the artillery programme prior to the opening of the summer offensive. As later War Diaries were to show, many new and inexperienced siege and heavy batteries were given few chances to register their targets with far reaching consequences for the general infantry attack on 1st July.

A week after Haig's letter of the 12th April Rawlinson forwarded to G.H.Q. an amended plan for the assault on the German positions. The paper addressed five key points:

1. Objectives to be taken in the first phase;
2. Including Montauban in the first objectives;
3. The extent of activity possible against Gommecourt;
4. The length of the proposed bombardment; and
5. Plans for a further advance to take the villages of Ginchy and Bazentin le Grand.

In paragraphs 6 to 14 of his response, Rawlinson can be seen to squirm and wriggle in an effort to not too obviously contradict the tactical concepts of his Commander in Chief. One by one he raised objections to what he seemed clearly to think were overly optimistic plans emanating from G.H.Q. – and one by one he knocked down his own perfectly logical arguments in order to get his new proposals to coincide with Haig's wishes. 'Considerable risks' were set aside in view of the 'importance of the object to be attained'. Rawlinson's original plan to 'kill as many Germans as possible' was over taken by the need to achieve a breakthrough to be exploited by Haig's beloved cavalry. And so, in short order, any objections to any of items 1, 2 and 5 listed above were seen off. Only on two issues was Rawlinson prepared to put his foot down: on the length of the initial bombardment and on an attack on Gommecourt. On the bombardment, Rawlinson dutifully recited Haig's new found enthusiasm for a short and intense artillery preparation but then, through clear logic and by explaining that the French intended a long bombardment, Rawlinson re-stated his absolute wish for a three to four day bombardment. Issues of wire cutting in front of both the first and second German lines, the need to cave in the numerous deep dug outs, the requirement for effective counter-battery fire, the undermining of morale resulting from a lack of sleep and food were all forcefully put forward. Nor did Rawlinson ignore the inexperienced nature of much of the artillery on which he would have to rely, stating:

"...with many new gun detachments we cannot expect very accurate shooting in a hurricane bombardment."[16]

On the issue of Gommecourt, Rawlinson was equally forthright:

"I did not include it (Gommecourt) in my original plan of attack because I considered that a 20,000 yards' front was as much as the troops at my disposal could undertake with reasonable hope of success.... There is no doubt that if the attack on the Gommecourt salient could be undertaken as a small independent operation it would be of considerable assistance to my main attack; but I do not consider that the means at my disposal render this possible for me to undertake and I would suggest, as far as this Army is concerned, limiting the activity against Gommecourt to a demonstration in which would be included the discharge of gas and smoke."[17]

Whatever G.H.Q.'s thinking on the bombardment, at least in this last regard, Rawlinson was successful. On reading his response, Haig passed responsibility for the neutralising of the Gommecourt strongpoint to General Allenby's Third Army and on April 21st Kiggell instructed Allenby to prepare a feasibility study for an attack on Gommecourt. Two days later Allenby replied to Kiggell that he could release two divisions for such an attack and stated the number of heavy guns required, which was: eight batteries of 6 in. howitzers, six batteries of 8" or 9.2" howitzers and four 12" howitzers.[18]

***

AS APRIL DREW TO A CLOSE, it became apparent that the French contribution to the attack was no longer certain. On the 21st, Joffre had informed Haig of a reduction in the number of French divisions to be involved in the offensive from 39 to 30, as the open wound that was Verdun began to drain the life blood from the already weakened Army of France. But, no matter, discussions amongst the G.H.Q., Army and Corps staff about the optimal plan for both the main and subsidiary attacks carried on. On May 6th, another meeting between Haig and Rawlinson finalised two of the outstanding issues at stake. Haig had his way over the first day's objectives. Rawlinson now had to plan to take, in one fell swoop, the Serre-Miraumont spur in order to protect his left flank; Pozieres and Contalmaison in the centre; and Montauban on his right flank. Rawlinson, on the other hand, appeared to have won the argument over the length of the bombardment. Indeed, in the G.H.Q. letter of the 16th May that confirmed the content of their discussions, the nature of the artillery preparations was stated in such a way as to satisfy the most cautious exponent of modern siege warfare:

> "As regards the artillery bombardment, it should be of the nature of a methodical bombardment and be continued until the officers commanding the attacking units are satisfied that the obstacles to their advance have been adequately destroyed."[19]

This statement would not have been out of place in the planning of one of Wellington's infamous sieges in the Peninsular – Cuidad Rodrigo or the dreaded Badajoz. There, the opening and clearing of a sufficient breach to allow access to the infantry was, at the very least, a hoped for consequence of the bombardment of a city's defences and any attack was not normally sanctioned unless and until a reasonable chance of success was perceived by the *local* commanders. But, as at the Battle of the Somme, intentions and the end product were rarely one and the same and any plan, depending on co-ordinated timing with the French, had not the flexibility in timing that applied in the Peninsular War. And Haig, by extending, indeed nearly doubling, the area to be taken had necessarily diluted the intensity of the agreed artillery bombardment by a factor of 50% and, by so doing, had reduced the concentration of the available heavy howitzers to the same as was used at the disastrous attack on Aubers Ridge on 8th May 1915. There may have been more of these weapons available by the Summer of 1916 but Haig, by his own decision, had dramatically reduced their potency by insisting on an ambitious plan of attack that his local commander and his subordinates disagreed with privately but felt unable to criticise publicly.

On the 14th May, however, another event threatened to destabilise the plans of the Allies for simultaneous offensives across the three main fronts. Pre-empting any Italian offensive moves, the Austrian Army under Field Marshal Conrad von Hötzendorf launched their own attack in the South Tirol, south east of Trent, and achieved considerable initial success. With its First Army pressed back in disarray some eight miles, Italy appealed to its Allies for help. In particular it looked to Russia to launch its own offensive in the hope that success on that front would demand a withdrawal of Austrian troops to a threatened Eastern Front. Added to the pressure on the French Army at Verdun, the Italian Trentino debacle made a major and early strike in the British sector of the Western Front all the more essential. Joffre announced to Haig that their attack could now take place no later, and perhaps earlier, than the first days of July. A few days later, when Joffre informed Haig of a further reduction in the number of French divisions to be involved in the offensive from 30 to 26, the strains within the French Army became all the more apparent. As the French contribution rapidly dwindled, so Haig's confidence in the entire Somme project seemed on the verge of evaporating. On 27th May, the day after Joffre had visited his H.Q. at Montreuil to explain the scale of French losses at Verdun, G.H.Q. informed Rawlinson that:

> "…as French support for the attack was uncertain, it was not clear whether his attack or that of the Second Army at Messines would start first."

This extraordinary news was further confirmed in G.H.Q. letter OAD 912 from Kiggell to all Army commanders. In it Kiggell re-stated the G.H.Q. view that:

> "It is not certain which of these attacks (i.e. Second Army at Messines or Fourth Army on the Somme) will be launched first."[20]

It is clear that the Second Army's attack on the Messines-Wytschaete ridge was a viable alternative to the attack on the Somme. Plumer had wasted no time in putting his Commander-in Chief's orders into operation and, by the end of May, his engineers and tunnelling companies had driven five miles of galleries under the German positions and filled them with one million pounds of explosive. There was still some work to be done in finishing the infrastructure necessary to support an offensive – roads, railways, ammunition and supply dumps, for example – but these could be finished well within the time scale of an attack on or before 1st July.

Over the next four days, the fate of the Somme offensive seemed to hang in the balance. On 28th May, Gen. Plumer was asked to push forward with plans at all possible speed as his offensive against Messines might still be launched first. On the following day, Haig warned Rawlinson that he might have to attack without French support and that, in these circumstances, the first objective would be the wearing out of the enemy (which, ironically, Rawlinson had wanted to do all along when first invited to prepare a plan for the attack). And, back in London, optimism about the prospects of the offensive were also at a low ebb after Sir William Robertson, Chief of the Imperial General Staff, informed the War Committee not to expect any far-reaching results. The whole saga reached the nadir of its fortunes on 31st May. Joffre and Haig met at Saleux Station near Amiens, and whilst Joffre confirmed the planned start date for the attack still as early July he also advised an increasingly dismayed British C-in-C that the French now could only spare 20 divisions, barely half of what had been expected as recently as 20th April.

Over the next three days, the Fourth Army handed over a section of front between Curlu on the river to Maricourt to the French XXth Army Corps. This now formed the new junction with the French 6th Army and acted as both link with the British and flank guard to the French. It was with this Corps that

Fourth Army had to liaise. The existing plan called for close co-operation between XIII Corps, on the right of the Fourth Army, and XXth Army Corps and, though unit borders were traditionally an area of weakness, this location was to be the exception that proved the rule. With French artillery assistance, XIII Corps was to advance further than any other British element on 1st July and, as a result, the whole emphasis of the attack would switch in the following weeks from the centre to the right of the British battlefield.

Throughout May and early June, preparations for the summer offensive drew on apace. Vast quantities of ammunition and stores were being stockpiled behind the lines and the infantry battalions earmarked for the assault were both training and preparing the ground for the attack. Due to a severe shortage of Labour battalions, only five were available as a consequence of the failure of the British Government to use sensibly the 1.3 million men being trained in the UK, the infantry did rather more labouring than training, much to the dismay of Rawlinson and his subordinates. Realising the need for his New Army battalions to be properly schooled in the arts of offensive warfare, Rawlinson had originally planned for a lengthy training programme but, instead, the men dug, marched and dug again, bearing the wearisome burden of the preparation of such a huge enterprise. In orchards, villages and quarries behind the lines, artillery moved into position, gun positions were constructed, telephone lines laid and 7,000 miles of cable buried, light railways were laid to bring supplies and ammunition to the front and heavy lines were put in place for the super heavy railway-mounted siege guns. There were roads to be metalled and trenches to be dug, ammunition and food dumps to be created in the never ending myriad of activities needed to get an Army ready for action. By the end the men were exhausted and, to the consternation of many officers, inadequately trained. But, no matter, the attack would still go ahead. The only remaining question was when.

On 3rd June Joffre wrote to Haig confirming 1st July as the preferred start date for the offensive to which, in response, Haig asked for twelve day's notice of the attack. On the same day, Kiggell wrote to Gen. Allenby asking for the details of the planned attack on Gommecourt which had been requested at the end of April. The following day, Allenby sent to G.H.Q. a three-page outline for the attack on Gommecourt.

But the 4th June saw another event that seemed to inject the western allies with a much-needed dose of optimism. Gen. Alexei Brusilov, the recently appointed commander of the Russian South West Army Group, had, unlike most of his predecessors, meticulously planned an offensive against the severely weakened Austrian forces on the Carpathian Front. Within days, the front had moved forward by between 40 and 80 miles as exhausted Austrians surrendered in droves. It was a success the Allies urgently needed and it raised both morale and expectations on the Western Front, none more so than at Haig's hilltop headquarters at Montreuil. However, before news of Brusilov's success had reached France, Haig was still hedging his bets over the Somme attack. The day after the four Russian armies had swept over the Austrian defences, Haig was still considering whether to move the G.H.Q. reserve from the Somme to Plumer's Second Army front for the Messines attack. In consequence, Rawlinson was advised that, if his offensive met with considerable opposition, the attack would be closed down in favour of the Messines operation. Haig even went to the lengths of preparing a rough draft of instructions to Gen. Sir Hubert Gough (O.C. G.H.Q. Reserve) to move to the support of the Second Army.

Haig's concerns about the prospects on the Somme must have been still further exacerbated on 6ᵗʰ June when Joffre wrote to Haig in decidedly downbeat terms about their joint offensive. Joffre talked about the need for a battle of attrition - a battle of 'duree prolongee' – and one of limited objectives. He took the view that the German First Position should be the objective (as Rawlinson had first proposed and Haig rejected) and that it was premature to fix any other beyond the Third Position. In this respect, Joffre's views were far closer to those of Rawlinson's than were Rawlinson's to those of his Commander in Chief. After all, Rawlinson's original 'bite and hold' plan and Joffre's battle of 'duree prolongee' were not ones likely to involve the use of many divisions of cavalry. Both Joffre and Rawlinson seemed committed to the 'wearing out' battle – "the killing of as many Germans as possible with the least loss to ourselves" - in which the Germans would be invited to exhaust themselves trying to re-take strongly held and well supported areas of local tactical importance. Haig, however, would only become a late convert to this policy after the failures of the Summer's expansively planned but expensively conducted battles.

But Joffre had another bombshell for Haig which, when detonated, one would imagine might have further undermined his confidence in the Somme attack. The French C-in-C stated quite firmly that, as the number of French divisions to be involved was now reduced from 20 to 12, the role of the French 6ᵗʰ Army's was now to support the British attack. In other words, the original balance of the attack had been reversed. It was now the British Army who would bear the brunt of the Somme offensive whilst the French did what they could in a limited fashion either side of the meandering marshland of the River Somme opposite Peronne.

As June wore on, however, Haig's optimism about the prospects for the attack appeared to grow rather than diminish in spite of the news from elsewhere. On 13ᵗʰ June, against a background of threatening imminent catastrophe around Verdun and of a growing political crisis in Paris, Joffre, through Col. des Vallieres, Head of the French Mission at G.H.Q., pleaded with Haig to bring forward the date of the Somme offensive by a week. The offensive would now start on Monday, 25ᵗʰ June, with the bombardment to start on Tuesday, 20ᵗʰ June. Taking the sudden alteration in his stride, Haig agreed and ordered all preparations to be made ready for a 25ᵗʰ June start. Overall, Col. des Vallieres' desperate request for an early assault seems to have done little to dampen Haig's growing conviction that his Somme attack represented a golden opportunity for a complete rupture in the German front, one that could lead to a return to a war of movement, that could even end the war.

In almost the blink of an eye, events took another turn. The pressure on Verdun was still severe (and would be for another week) but Gen. Petain was, at least, talking with confidence about the eventual outcome. The rumours of Brusilov's sweeping gains were now firm news not just gossip and, in consequence, the political crisis within the French government eased. Eased sufficiently, indeed, for Joffre to return to Haig just three days after the panic ridden plea for a 25ᵗʰ June assault with a new request for a delay to either 29ᵗʰ June or 1ˢᵗ July – Haig, confidence high, swiftly agreed to 29ᵗʰ June.

But, before this further change, on June 15th, in the knowledge that his allies were asking for an urgent advance of the opening of the attack, Haig met with his Army commanders. His diary records, and a G.H.Q. letter to Rawlinson the following day[21] confirmed, that now Haig believed that not only was the taking of the German Second Position almost inevitable but that the total collapse of their defences on the Pozieres ridge a real possibility. And, if this were to happen, Rawlinson was told that:

"..our advance will be pressed forward eastwards far enough to enable our cavalry to push through into open country... Our objective will then be to turn northwards, taking the enemy's lines in flank and reverse."[22]

What Haig was proposing was something not seen since the early days of the war – a great left hook into open country towards Monchy-le-Preux (east of Arras) in which cavalry would roam free destroying German communications and supplies and disrupting attempts to bring up reserves. The end product of this dramatic advance would be the inevitable "capture of the enemy's forces in the re-entrant south of Arras"[23]. No longer was there any talk of keeping in close touch with the French to the south in their attempts to force a crossing of the Somme at Peronne. This plan was the antithesis of Joffre's battle of 'duree prolongee'. This was not attrition, this was a venture of Napoleonic vision and daring which could end the war with a campaign in which his beloved cavalry would play their full and deserved part. Berlin by Christmas, perhaps.

But Haig was not quite ready to stop hedging his bets. The final paragraph in his diary describing the Fourth Army's objectives, and in the G.H.Q. letter, still hinted at a degree of caution. But only a degree. Both documents assumed the taking of the Pozieres ridge between the Ancre and Montauban but, if the German defences then held, Haig was ready to fall back on his preferred plan, the Second Army's attack at Messines, as a preface to a major movement east and north east from Ypres towards Roulers and the Belgian coast. His use of words is interesting bearing in mind what happened on the Somme after 1st July:

"… after gaining our first objective (i.e. the Pozieres ridge) we may find that a further advance eastwards is not advisable. In that case the most profitable course will probably be to transfer our main efforts rapidly to another portion of the British front..."[24]

Gen. Sir Anthony Farrar-Hockley, in his 1964 book 'The Somme', commented:

"…here is the sign that Haig recognised his ability to keep the strategic initiative, to deliver the powerful second blow while the enemy reserves were still flocking to parry the first. The labour was there in the First and Second Armies to complete the road and railway construction and the dumping of ammunition and supplies. The French railway system was adequate to the task of moving swiftly British reserves from Picardy to Flanders. The possibility of an exceptional strategic success was maturing; and it was recognised."[25]

Recognised – and then ignored for reasons that only Sir Douglas Haig could explain. As it turned out, of the first objectives set out in G.H.Q. OAD 12 of 16th June, what was left of Pozieres village, expected to be taken in the first advance, was taken by the Australians on 25th July at huge expense; Thiepval village, another first morning objective, eventually fell on the 26ᵗʰ September; and the Serre-Miraumont spur, the 'hinge' of Haig's great northern sweep, was never taken in spite of another equally hopeless and expensive attack on 13ᵗʰ November. Perhaps the much maligned David Lloyd George was closer to the truth than some modern analysts when he wrote in his 'War Memoirs' that:

> "Haig was constitutionally incapable of changing plans he had once prepared and set his mind on carrying through."[26]

Whatever else was planned, however, the Third Army's operation at Gommecourt was described in the OAD 12 report in downbeat terms as:

> "...misleading and wearing out the enemy and preventing him from sending reinforcements to the scene of the main operations."[27]

The opening of the bombardment was now only a few days away, the batteries in place and the firing plans agreed, when, out of the blue, Haig determined to re-open the arguments about the bombardment but now in a subtly different manner. A G.H.Q. letter from Kiggell to Rawlinson dated 20ᵗʰ June suddenly raised concerns about the planned expenditure of ammunition and the problem of wear and tear on the guns themselves. The letter is worthy of lengthy quotation:

> "...it is not desired to *fetter your discretion* (author's emphasis) in the matter; and it is essential that the artillery preparation should be thorough; but, unless due regard is had to the limitations in the ammunition supply and to the effect on the guns of prolonged and heavy shooting, the continuance of offensive operations during the summer may be seriously prejudiced..."[28]

So, gone was Haig's view stated on May 16ᵗʰ that the artillery preparation should be:

> "...of the nature of a methodical bombardment and be continued until the officers commanding the attacking units are satisfied that the obstacles to their advance have been adequately destroyed."[29]

Now, four days before the bombardment was due to start, a sudden and major concern was the conserving of ammunition and gun barrels for later use rather than the 'adequate' destruction of the German fortified villages, deep dugouts, extensive wire and the German guns.

Haig, through Kiggell, then went on to question certain key elements of Rawlinson's artillery plan. First of all there were the "large number of apparently intense bombardments, some of considerable duration, and amounting in aggregate to 8¼ hours." Rawlinson was invited to 'carefully consider' these sections of the bombardment as:

> "...their value against lightly manned trenches and when not followed by assault, is open to doubt."[30]

Of course, it was not the plan for the heavy artillery to be firing at 'lightly manned trenches'. Although it had been left very much for Corps commanders to determine the best use of the guns and howitzers at their disposal the fact that they were taking on the destruction of heavily fortified positions giving excellent protection to their defenders was well known. Rawlinson had previously noted the German's increasing use of deep dugouts and knew how difficult it would be to destroy them. Confirmation of their existence on the Somme (later confirmed by a raiding party on 8th June) had already come from a German PoW captured on 17th January 1916. This man gave details of a dugout at Ovillers, a village at the centre of the planned attack. Seventeen feet deep and able to sustain a garrison of twelve men in decent conditions and great security this, and dozens of other such dugouts, was the priority target for the heavy howitzers although Rawlinson, writing about similar dugouts at Givenchy in the Summer of 1915, had described the artillery's prospects of burying the dugouts and their occupants as "a matter of chance"[31]. But, be that as it may, aerial photographs taken just before the infantry went over show that the average length of trench had received relatively little attention from the 'heavies'. The various strongpoints, redoubts and the fortified villages had, however, been seriously pounded, so much so that some of the attacking infantry lost their bearings because, highly rehearsed as they were, they could not find any recognisable landmarks in these pockmarked landscapes.

But, to make his point even more forcefully, Haig then questioned "whether a three days' bombardment… is not as effective as one lasting four days."[32] To make disagreement with him more or less impossible, Kiggell finished by stating, on his boss's behalf, that on the argument about the length of the bombardment:

> "…the Commander in Chief understood you agreed with him in the discussion on Sunday last."[33]

Rawlinson was now in a delicate position. His superior was, as near as he could, telling him to reduce the intensity *and* length of a bombardment his staff and that of the various Army Corps had been planning for weeks. He was doing it because of a presumption of success, i.e. the need to conserve guns and shells for 'the continuance of offensive operations during the summer'. Whilst Rawlinson was concerned about his ability to take the objectives he had originally outlined (and which Haig regarded as unduly conservative), Haig was concerned to conserve his artillery for the big strategic campaign to come when the B.E.F. would burst through the German defences and sweep all before them in a march to the north.

What is extraordinary about this is that Haig appeared to be basing his optimistic views about the B.E.F.'s prospects on a misinterpretation of the reasons for the apparent success of the German artillery on the opening day of Verdun. What Haig either did not know, or chose to ignore, was that:

1. The German front at Verdun was only 12,900 yards against the 25,000 yards proposed for the opening of the Somme; and that
2. The British, with some French assistance around Montauban, were to employ 261 medium and heavy howitzers (6 in. or heavier calibres) whilst the German Fifth Army had been able to call upon c. 300 similar weapons.[34]

In other words, while there would be about one medium/heavy howitzer for every 96 yards of front on the Somme, at Verdun there had been one medium/heavy howitzer for only 43 yards of front – more than double the concentration of 'heavies' available to Haig and Rawlinson.

In order for the British to have delivered on the Somme a hurricane bombardment of the intensity delivered at Verdun the British heavy artillery would have needed to fire continuously for nearly eighteen hours (with untold damage to the guns, something Haig was now keen to avoid). Whichever way one looks at it, the British bombardment on the Somme was never going to come close to replicating the 'shock and awe' impact of the Verdun initial bombardment and nor had Rawlinson imagined that it would. His approach had been, therefore, to replicate old-style siege tactics which Haig, in May, had seemed to endorse. Now Haig was backtracking at speed all because of a misunderstanding about the nature of the Verdun bombardment. Lastly of course, in spite of the perceived effectiveness of the Verdun bombardment the Germans were still held up by the French defences and were now threatening to turn the attack into a truly Pyrrhic victory as their casualties began to match those of the city's defenders. The Verdun bombardment had not presaged a breakthrough, the dearest wish of the German local commander, Crown Prince Wilhelm, if not of Falkenhayn, it had merely dragged his men into a long term slugging match which would grind down both sides' armies by its end.

At a meeting on the 21ˢᵗ June, Haig reiterated his concerns about the nature of the bombardment and, under pressure from above, Rawlinson made a concession. On the 19ᵗʰ April, Rawlinson had explained why he thought a long and intense bombardment was necessary. The reasons had included the destruction of the numerous deep dug outs, the need for effective counter-battery fire and the corrosion of German morale as men went for days without sleep and food and under the imminent threat of oblivion. But, under pressure from G.H.Q., Rawlinson conceded that, whilst the overall length of the bombardment would remain the same, he would cancel half of the intense periods of the proposed bombardment.

On the same day, Kiggell issued Haig's final instructions prior to the opening of the bombardment. In addition to the existing assumptions about the probable success of the initial attack, this document set out Haig's thoughts on what would happen "if the first attack goes very well."[35] First of all, the note set out the strength of the German units opposite as ascertained by Army Intelligence. This information stated that there were:

"…only 32 battalions now on the Fourth Army front, and he can make available during the first six days only some 65 additional battalions in all, as reinforcements."[36]

There were, in fact, 39 in the front line or close reserve opposite the Fourth Army and a further twelve opposite the VII Corps at Gommecourt. The War Diary of the 55ᵗʰ Reserve Infantry Regiment, which was to play a major part in the defence of Gommecourt, shows an average strength of 170 rifles per company of which there were four per battalion and, with three battalions per regiment, this would suggest an average regimental strength of some 2,000 men. In other words, in or close to the front line from Gommecourt to Montauban the British faced approximately 35,000 infantry plus machine guns teams and pioneers (who were capable of fighting as infantry) comprising maybe another 5,000 men. In reserve were available, according to G.H.Q., another 45-50,000 men in 65 battalions. Whilst it was accepted wisdom that a small number of troops, well dug in and equipped with adequate numbers of machine guns and with artillery support could hold up a significantly larger force, Haig clearly thought that Fourth Army's superiority in numbers, allied to the strength of the British artillery, would suffice. In this, another lesson from Verdun had either not been learnt or had been ignored. In spite of the overwhelming artillery bombardment that fell on them and the huge superiority of the German infantry once they attacked, two battalions of the 56th and 59th Battalions of Chasseurs a Pied, commanded by Lt. Col. Emile Driant, held out for nearly 48 hours in the Bois de Caures near Verdun. Driant's 1,200 Chasseurs are reputed to have lost at least 50% of their number before the infantry attacked and yet they clung on to their positions grimly, causing delay and concern to the German High Command. If so for the French defenders of Verdun, then why not the same for the Germans on the Somme?

But, this thought seemed not have occurred to anyone at a high level in the B.E.F. and the G.H.Q. letter stressed that, because of the apparent imbalance in resources:

> "We shall therefore have considerable numerical superiority, and prompt action taken to develop a success gained in the assault on the first objective assigned may give great results."[37]

This 'prompt action' was a confirmation and an amplification of Haig's belief, first set out on 16ᵗʰ June, that a complete breakthrough was now possible. The cavalry were to be pushed NE through any gap at the earliest opportunity with the intention of seizing Bapaume and, for this reason, G.H.Q. relinquished command of the 1ˢᵗ and 3ʳᵈ Cavalry Divisions, currently part of the G.H.Q. Reserve, in favour of Rawlinson. Further, Rawlinson was told to support the cavalry with as many troops as he could and that these units, along with the cavalry, would fall under the command of Gen. Sir Hubert Gough. In addition, Rawlinson was told to push due east to the villages of Ginchy and Morval in order to keep in touch with the French to his right. Lastly, Rawlinson was told that the cavalry, by now sitting victorious in Bapaume, were to be relieved at the earliest opportunity. They were then to gallop north (along the path of what is now the A1 autoroute from Paris) in order to take in reverse the German troops to the north of the breakthrough as far as Arras. These troops were to be held in place by another action of the Third Army, an attack towards Blairville for which the 35ᵗʰ Division, then in reserve, had been earmarked and a further attack from the new Gommecourt position towards Bucquoy. Now, there was no talk of moving the offensive to Messines if the Somme attack faced effective resistance. Now there was only talk of breakthrough with images of massed cavalry sweeping across Northern France towards Arras, Douai and beyond.

Quite what happened to so encourage Sir Douglas Haig is not clear. Matters at Verdun were reaching a dangerous climax. After the fall of Fort Vaux at the end of the first week of June, the Germans had pressed on towards the two inner ring forts of Souville and Tavannes. Though Haig could not know it, the crisis of the battle was to occur in two day's time when an assault launched on the 22ⁿᵈ June faltered and stopped short of its objectives. With the outcome of the biggest battle on the Western Front still uncertain, Haig now appeared to have put all his eggs in the Somme basket. Wearing out battles, 'bite and hold', closing down the offensive in favour of attacks at Messines were all removed from the agenda and replaced by a firm belief that the 'Big Push' could be the war winning event of the summer. The following day, as the French Army around Verdun cowered under a new bombardment and gasped and choked in the ghastly and lethal clouds of Green Cross gas[i], Rawlinson briefed his Corps commanders one last time. The contents of OAD 17 were duly passed onto his subordinates. Rawlinson's comments about the letter and the use of cavalry were down beat to put it mildly:

> "I had better make it quite clear that it may not be possible to break the enemy's line and put the cavalry through at the first rush... until we can see what is the [state] of the battle, it is impossible to predict at what moment we shall be able to undertake this [pushing the cavalry through any gap], and the decision will rest in my hand to say when it can be carried out."[38]

As Rawlinson second-guessed his C-in-C and the French clung on by their finger nails at Verdun, the gunners on the Somme stood ready for the opening of the biggest bombardment in the British Army's history. Two days later, in an atmosphere of almost surreal self-confidence, it began.

***

WHILST HAIG AND RAWLINSON wrangled over the methods and objectives of the Fourth Army's attack, Gen. Allenby and his staff had been considering the options for the diversion at Gommecourt, the most westerly possession of the Imperial German Army. Lt. Gen. Kiggell had asked Allenby to report on the feasibility for an attack on Gommecourt on 21st April[39] and, two days later, Allenby replied giving the details of general scheme of attack and the resources needed for its implementation. At this time it was not clear which divisions might be used for the attack and Allenby suggested that, whichever ones were chosen, they should be withdrawn brigade by brigade in order to give time for the other Third Army divisions to reorganise and take over extended areas of the front. Allenby's report did give an indication of the heavy artillery required for a successful attack but his proposal made it clear that the numbers required would denude the rest of his front of heavy guns. To attack Gommecourt, Allenby estimated that he would need:

> Eight batteries of 6 in. howitzers (i.e. 32 howitzers)
> Six batteries of 8 in. or 9.2 in. howitzers (i.e. 24 howitzers)
> Four 12 in. howitzers

He pointed out that the rest of his front would have to be satisfied with having just one 18 pdr field gun for every 250 yards of front but that this should be sufficient unless the Germans reinforced their existing troops[40]. With this outline in G.H.Q.'s hands, Allenby set to identifying the units to be used in the attack and the best plan of action to be employed.

Edmund Henry Hynman Allenby was born on the 23rd April 1861 – St George's Day. There were no obvious military connections in his immediate family, however, he was a descendant of a singularly famous general and cavalryman. On his mother's side he was descended from the marriage of Henry Ireton, a close colleague of Oliver Cromwell, who had commanded the left wing of the Parliamentarian army at Naseby in 1645 and who had fought at Edgehill

---

i An improved version of Chlorine gas, first used against French and Algerian troops north of Ypres on the 22nd April 1915.

and Marston Moor, and Bridget Cromwell, the second daughter of the Lord Protector. It could be said that the cavalry was in his blood and so it proved when he joined the army in 1882. Originally intended for the Indian Civil Service he failed the examination and instead he entered Sandhurst, coming fifth out of 110 successful candidates in the entrance examination. On passing out, he continued the distant family 'tradition' by joining the 6th Royal Inniskilling Dragoons and his formative military years were spent in the dust and heat of Natal and the Transvaal policing bitter disputes between Zulu tribes and their Boer neighbours. In the mid-1890s Allenby returned to England to pass his Staff College exams and to marry Adelaide Mabel Chapman of Salisbury. The Second Boer War saw him return to South Africa where the Inniskillings formed part of Gen. French's[41] cavalry. Here, Allenby led a number of daring manoeuvres behind enemy lines and took part in French's epic march to Kimberley in early 1900, and, by the time the army reached Pretoria, Allenby was the C.O. of the Inniskillings. Heavy fighting continued throughout 1900 and 1901 with Allenby excelling at the war of speed and manoeuvre, experiences that no doubt stood him in good stead when he soundly defeated the Turks in Palestine in 1917 and 1918.

As the war ended with the signing of the Treaty of Vereeniging, Allenby returned home and in 1905 he was given command of the 4th Cavalry Brigade, Eastern Command. Five year's later he became Inspector of Cavalry having been appointed Major General the previous year. The outbreak of war saw him well positioned for senior command and, between October 1914 and May 1915, he was the commander of the B.E.F.'s cavalry in France and Flanders. Although the cavalry performed well in the retreat from Mons and Le Cateau his reputation had taken something of a battering in the advance from the Marne to the Aisne with Haig, in particular, being critical of what he saw as their laggardly performance. The Cavalry Corps' defence of the Messines-Ploegsteert Line in the 1st Battle of Ypres, however, did much to restore his somewhat tarnished reputation. An inarticulate man of stolid almost dour demeanour, Allenby was still able to think what, for some, was the unthinkable. His observation of the battles of Spring 1915, the trenches, barbed wire, massed machine guns and the increasing weight of the artillery, convinced him that cavalry had no part to play on the Western Front. However obvious with hindsight, this was an extraordinary view to be expressed by a cavalryman and it immediately set him in opposition to another taciturn and sometimes tongue-tied general with a cavalry background: Sir Douglas Haig. Haig would continue to believe that cavalry had a future on the modern battlefield even after the war but Allenby's heretical views meant it was no longer possible for him to continue as commander of the Cavalry Corps and thus, on 6th May, he was given control of V Corps then located on the south eastern sector of the Ypres salient.

His was now an infantry command in a static conflict of trenches and siege warfare and, although he could see that the cavalry would play no useful part in breaking the stranglehold of wire and massed firepower, he had no useful insights into what might work. He was, however, a conscientious commander – as far as his superiors were concerned – and followed orders in a most relentless fashion. Throughout the summer and autumn of 1915 his men fought savage battles around Hooge and the Bellewaarde Ridge sustaining heavy casualties especially from gas attacks. But it was his policy of remorseless counter-attacks to regain ground lost which gained him severe notoriety amongst his men. Allenby was neither a popular nor a 'populist' general and his image suffered greatly, with some of his divisional commanders even secretly approaching G.H.Q. with requests for his removal. But Allenby cared little for the views of his juniors and not at all for the suffering of his soldiers. During the Bellewaarde Ridge attacks in June 1915 Allenby had visited the headquarters of the 3rd Division to watch their attack. Watching next to him was the Division's commander, Maj. Gen. Aylmer Haldane. Haldane detested Allenby whom he regarded as arrogant and bullying and was repulsed by his willingness to throw men's lives away in hopeless attacks. Now, as the attack faltered and then failed, Allenby concluded that the best option was to throw yet another Brigade, the 42nd Brigade of the 14th Division, into the mincer. Haldane's observation that this was likely to result in even heavier losses with little profit was met with an extraordinary outburst by Allenby, one that epitomises the still popular image of many British Great War Generals as 'butchers and bunglers':

"What the Hell does that matter?" was Allenby's retort, "There are plenty more men in England!"

"Not like these", was Haldane's terse reply. So outraged was one 3rd Division Staff Officer by Allenby's callous comment that it was later reported he had to be held back by from attacking his G.O.C. During the attack the 3rd Division had suffered the loss of 140 officers and 3,391 men. German losses were less than 500.[42]

With his pre-war nickname, 'The Bull', he now came to embody for many the blinkered, brass hat whose only solution to the problem in front of him was to throw more and more troops into the mincing machine. Together with his notoriously short fuse, these factors made Allenby one of the least popular of generals with his men, a standing he had already managed to achieve with his soon to be Commander in Chief with his views on the use of the cavalry in modern, industrialised warfare. Stories about his yell first, think afterwards approach to his men quickly spread. Some time later, whilst on a tour of the trenches, he came across a man lying in the front line. The fellow was wearing neither his helmet nor his leather jerkin, both of which Allenby had ordered men to wear at all times when in the trenches. In mitigation for this gross and flagrant breach of orders the man was clearly dead, a point not lost on the late soldier's commanding officer. A school teacher in his pre-war life his sarcastic response seems to have been lost on his superior:

"Yes, sir. Disobedience in death is to my mind even graver than disobedience in life. This man has undoubtedly lost his chance of ever going to Heaven."[43]

His popularity reached its lowest ebb during the Battle of Loos in the autumn of 1915 when he was asked to deliver a diversionary attack near Ypres. His selection of the area around Hooge, one of the strongest points in the German lines, led to predictably heavy casualties amongst the men of the 3rd and 14th Divisions when they attacked on 25th September. By the end of the day 4,000 men of the two Divisions had been killed or wounded. Allenby's reputation sank still further.

Plate I Gen. Edmund Henry Hynman Allenby, G.O.C., Third Army
(Photograph courtesy of Imperial War Museum, Q82969)

He was now, however, to be the beneficiary of the internecine warfare being carried on at the highest levels of command. At Court and amongst the Government, Haig was lobbying intensely for the removal of French - and for his promotion to the vacancy. Lords Kitchener and Roberts, meanwhile, favoured Sir Ian Hamilton. What was clear, even to Sir John French, was that his days as C-in-C were numbered and in October, with his last major appointment, he thumbed his nose at his likely successor Haig by giving Allenby command of the Third Army currently holding a quiet part of the front from the Somme to near Arras. It was an area that had seen little action since the early summer of 1915 and in which the German defenders had been able to construct a defensive system of great complexity and strength almost without interference.

Thus, in the Spring of 1916, Allenby came to be asked to attack what was, perhaps, the strongest part of this undisturbed line. Allenby's early cavalry instincts, honed in South Africa, were, wherever possible, to take the line of least resistance, i.e. to exploit areas of enemy weakness rather than attack head-on those of the greatest strength. As an infantry commander, however, his conviction was to follow orders to the letter, whatever he may have thought of them privately. He was not one to sit quietly in meetings, however, and he expressed his feelings forcefully (another factor that irritated his new commander, Haig) but, when decisions had been made, his interpretation of his duty was to follow them to the utmost. It is said that he was far happier in Egypt and Palestine in 1917 and 1918 where there was room for manoeuvre, scope for some strategic and tactical flights of fancy. But, with Gommecourt, there was no such room for manoeuvre either figuratively or literally within the plan set for him by Haig.

On 28ᵗʰ April, Lt. Gen. Sir Thomas D'Oyly Snow, the commander of the VII Corps, was ordered by Allenby to prepare a plan for an attack on the Gommecourt salient. Initially, the timetable given was brief. The offensive was to take place at the end of May. This date was soon revised to the end of June, however, giving the assaulting divisions at least some time to make preparations and get acquainted with the ground.

It was plainly explained by Haig that this was to be a diversionary *attack* rather than a decoy with which to attract German reserves of infantry and artillery. But it was also clear that there was little more to the attack than the prospect of cutting out the small salient, thereby straightening and advancing the line by a few hundred yards. There would be no reserves and, consequently, there could be no exploitation of a successful advance. It was designed simply:

"to assist in the operations of the Fourth Army by diverting against itself the fire of artillery and infantry which might otherwise be directed against the left flank of the main attack near Serre."[44]

Lt. Gen. Snow and his army commander were not without their reservations about this attack. Except in its proximity to Serre and the northern flank of the main assault, Gommecourt had few advantages but many drawbacks as the location for a diversion and Allenby and Snow pointed this out to the Commander in Chief. Their points were these:

1. As a result of previous French attacks on the village, the area had been increasingly heavily fortified. The village, its surrounding woods and the trench lines running north-east and south-east from the Kaiser's Oak, the western most projection of the salient, were riddled with deep dugouts chiselled out of the underlying chalk. These dugouts were, as was later shown, virtually impervious to all but the heaviest weight of artillery shell;

2. No Man's Land was wide, especially on the southern flank of the salient. Here, between the Gommecourt to Puisieux Road and the small village of Hebuterne, nearly 800 metres of gently sloping grassland divided the German and British front line trenches;

3. Furthermore, some 2,000 metres to the south-east of Gommecourt the front lines turned sharply to the south. This meant that German artillery and machine guns in the area surrounding Puisieux could enfilade British trenches and the infantry advance at an almost perfect right angle;

4. On the northern flank, the distance between the front lines was less, some 400 to 500 yards but here, between Gommecourt and Foncquevillers, the nature of the terrain gave the German defenders a good view into the rear areas of the British entrenchments; and lastly,

5. In the rear of the German front lines and on each flank of the planned attack lay many thickly wooded areas and shallow valleys, which concealed dozens of German batteries able to range on the British front and rear lines.

Of course, one other objection could be added to those listed above. Unless some geographical feature physically protects the flanks from interference by defenders not under direct attack, any assault such as this would show two open flanks to the enemy, each susceptible to enfilade fire. In reality, on the Western Front only two such barriers existed - the Channel Coast and the Swiss Border. Any attack would have to accept, therefore, the problem of enfilade fire on each wing. By creating the Gommecourt 'diversion', however, the British assault on the 1st July 1916 gave the Germans four flanks to enfilade; the French one where their assault ended to the South of the River Somme and three British ones. These were at Serre where the main advance was to stop, then 1½ kilometres further north on the right flank of the first attacking division, the 56th (1st

London) Division and then another 3 kilometres further north still where rested the left flank of the second division to be committed to the assault, the 46th (North Midland) Division.

Allenby and Snow were concerned by the strength of the position in front of them and the weakness of their own. So concerned that, according to the Official History[45], they argued an alternative strategy for an attack further north at Arras for which they had already planned[46]. Here the terrain was more favourable, the German positions less well developed and the German forces fewer and of lower calibre. Their argument was this: a diversionary attack with no prospect of exploitation was best delivered against a point of enemy weakness not strength. The more so as they had been given explicit instructions not to attempt to conceal the projected assault. By the very nature of such obvious preparations for an attack, especially on a weak part of the line, German reserves of both infantry and artillery would be drawn to this area of the front. Wherever they came from would weaken the German ability to respond to the main advance further south. They could, therefore, achieve the result desired without exposing their men to unnecessarily heavy casualties.

So went their argument. The Official History, perhaps with the benefit of hindsight, concurs with their views:

"It was, however, asking very much that two divisions new to the ground should attack at two months' notice defences of the strength of Gommecourt, unless a complete surprise without much previous preparation were intended. The enemy salient was in reality a small modern fortress. It required siege operations, or, at any rate as events proved, bombardment by super-heavy guns to destroy its dug-outs, as well as a great amount of trenchwork to get within assaulting distance, besides an ample supply of labour for carrying up stores and munitions.... It seems improbable that G.H.Q. realised the strength - and that strength enormously increased by flanking artillery defence - of the Gommecourt salient. If an attack is to be made merely in order to hold enemy troops and prevent their employment elsewhere, a weak or vulnerable part of the enemy's front should be chosen, not the strongest. Further, Gommecourt was particularly easy of defence, and from the shape of the ground it was a most difficult place from which to disengage troops in the event of partial failure or incomplete success."[47]

Another option discounted by higher authority was to use the heavy and field artillery available to the VII Corps to suppress artillery intervention to the North of the main attack. What if the two divisions allocated to the Gommecourt sector had made all preparations for an attack but, instead, on the day had pinned infantry to their front with demonstrations, smoke, machine gun and trench mortar fire? Then, it could be argued, the Corps and Divisional artillery that was used so desperately to aid the attacking troops, could have profitably spent their time targeting German artillery with effective counter-battery work whilst the field artillery took care of German infantry and trenches on the 1,500 metres of front to the north of Serre.

These arguments found no favour with Haig. The purpose of this attack, in his mind, was not to draw enemy reserves many miles away from the scene of the main advance. No, it was to "(divert) against itself the fire of artillery and infantry which might otherwise be directed against the left flank of the main attack near Serre[48]" and, to his mind, the only way of achieving this was by an all out assault on Gommecourt.

Allenby and Snow set to work reluctantly to plan their attack. After inspecting the ground and reviewing the resources at their disposal their conclusion was that the best plan of attack was to cut out the strongest element of the German position, Gommecourt village and Park, by means of a pincer movement. These two areas would then be reduced by the reserve battalions whilst a new defensive front line was constructed to the east by reversing captured German trenches and by digging new trenches across stretches of what had been No Man's Land. By these means the British front line would advance by about 2,000 yards at its maximum point. Apart from straightening the line, the other advantage of this forward movement would be the improved visibility over areas behind the German lines to the NE and SE given by possession of a point at the top of the ridge that ran from the rear of Gommecourt towards Rossignol Wood and then to Bucquoy.

To mount the attack two experienced Territorial Army divisions were selected: the 46th (North Midland) Division and the 56th (1st London) Division. The North Midlanders, who had spent a fruitless few weeks in Egypt in January and February, had returned to be attached to the XVII Corps north of Arras. The recently formed London division was currently training and resting behind the lines west of Arras and both would need to move south for the purpose of the attack. This they did in early May, taking over the trenches around Gommecourt then occupied by the 37th and 48th Divisions. The 46th (North Midland) Division took up position on the northern face of the Gommecourt salient in front of the small village of Foncquevillers while the 56th (1st London) Division occupied the trenches in front of the large village of Hebuterne which peered through its orchard fringe across a shallow valley at the village of Gommecourt and its park. On their arrival, the 37th Division took up a place to the left of the attack area in front of Hannescamps and Bienvillers-au-Bois whilst the 48th side-stepped south to occupy the gap between the right of the Gommecourt attack and the left of the main attack at Serre.

Worryingly though, at almost every level within the Third Army, concerns were expressed by either senior or junior officers about the quality of the superior officers involved in the planning and organisation of the attack. Allenby was unpopular with Haig for reasons already explained and others were critical of Snow and his handling of VII Corps.

Born on 5th May 1858, Old Etonian Snow[49] had joined the army in 1879 having spent just one year as an undergraduate at St John's, Cambridge. As a 2nd Lieutenant in the 13th Foot (later the Somerset Light Infantry) he first saw service at the end of the Zulu campaign of that year and in 1884 he saw combat in Egypt with the 1st Mounted Infantry Regiment of the Camel Corps in the Nile Expedition of 1884-5, being severely wounded in his second action, the Battle at Gubat. In the 1890s he attended the Staff College at Camberley, a contemporary of Generals Rawlinson and Henry Wilson, and in 1895 he was appointed Brigade Major at Aldershot. He was then promoted Major in the Royal Inniskilling Fusiliers in May 1897. In January 1898 he was given a position on Kitchener's staff during the Sudan campaign. Returning to regimental duties in 1899 he was transferred to the 2nd Northamptonshire Regiment then based in India, an appointment not greatly to his taste, not least because he was prevented from seeing action in the Boer War. To his relief in 1903 he joined the staff of Eastern Command (IV Corps) as Assistant Quarter Master General, progressing to command of the 11th Brigade in 1909 and when the war started he was the G.O.C. of 4th Division during the retreat from Mons, fighting at Le Cateau, the Marne and the Aisne. On the Aisne, he sustained a heavy fall from his horse which necessitated home leave for health reasons. Pressed to return by Kitchener, in November 1914 he was appointed G.O.C., 27th Division although not fully fit to do so. In this capacity he found himself the only divisional general east of the Ypres Canal on 22nd April 1915, the day when the Germans first employed poison gas. His performance in helping to stabilise the line after the collapse of the French troops worst affected by the gas cloud drew praise and he was created a K.B.C. in recognition of this and his other war-time services.

Plate 2 Lt. Gen. Sir Thomas D'Oyly Snow, GOC VII Corps
(Photograph 'The Great World War – A History' ed. Frank A Mumby, Gresham Publishing Co. 1915-17)

He was given command of VII Corps on 15th July 1915. His nicknames were either the obvious 'Snowball' or the rather less kindly 'Slush'. But Snow was not a well man. His fall in September 1914 had left him prone to severe back and leg pains which required regular trips home. One such ten day trip occurred within a few days of the opening of the Battle of the Somme, leaving his staff to carry on the planning of the Gommecourt attack on their own. His position was already under threat and Maj. Gen. S E Hollond, then a G.S.O.2 on Third Army's Staff, would later describe how he had tried to persuade Allenby to sack him because of the "monstrously bad" planning of the Gommecourt attack.

Archibald Home, a cavalryman who had been appointed G.S.O.1 to the 46th Division in early April 1916, was one singularly unconvinced by Snow and his staff. Home first visited the H.Q. of VII Corps when he lunched with Snow and his staff before driving out to inspect the Gommecourt sector and he came away unimpressed, describing Snow as a 'fusser'. His views were further confirmed after what he described as a 'futile' conference at VII Corps H.Q. on Sunday, 14th May:

"It would appear that we make the Scheme (of attack) and Corps sit on – this is quite wrong. The Corps wants ginger badly – it ought to take the thing in hand and issue quite definite orders as to what it wants. They will not take the responsibility – but the only thing left is to do it oneself."[50]

On Wednesday, 24ᵗʰ May another Corps conference took place and Home again felt obliged to put into writing his feelings about Snow's performance:

"Old Snow is very fussy and making points of things we had already done."[51]

Home, however, did not reserve his criticism just for Snow. Though a friend of his divisional commander, Sir Edward Montagu Stuart-Wortley, he viewed the division with a distinctly jaundiced eye. Back in April, when they had occupied trenches near Vimy Ridge, he had been highly critical of the quality of the junior officers in the division who, he felt, were unable to get the men to do what was required. In addition, he had felt that discipline in the trenches was poor. His opinion did not improve as time passed. By the 19ᵗʰ May he had concluded, on the basis of his experience with the 46ᵗʰ Division, that the Territorials were just not up to scratch:

"This whole division wants ginger putting into it from top to bottom!"[52]

Two weeks later the Brigade staff were the targets of his ire:

"Went round some of the trenches with the General – the work is not yet satisfactory. The reason is that the Brigade staffs do not supervise nearly enough."[53]

Brig. Gen. Frank Lyon of VII Corps staff, one of the men implicitly criticised by Home's views in his 14ᵗʰ May diary entry, was no admirer of Stuart-Wortley, calling him a 'worn out man' and Col. J F C Fuller, attached to the 37ᵗʰ Division, described the 46ᵗʰ Division's command and staff work as "absolutely shocking".

Only the newly promoted Maj. Gen. Hull of the 56ᵗʰ Division was a man to attract praise being depicted as a commander of "dash and determination" by Lyon and his division was generally regarded as the best Territorial unit in the B.E.F., if not one of the best of any type.

Hull, however, was but one of four senior officers overseeing the Gommecourt diversion and the other three were all currently the subject of sceptical and often damning appraisal by their fellow officers. Hardly a healthy position when planning an attack so fraught with potential problems and pitfalls.

***

PREPARATIONS FOR THE ATTACK were already well under way when, on 3ʳᵈ June, Kiggell sent Allenby the equivalent of a military 'final demand'. It read:

"With reference to G.H.Q. letters No. OAD 790/1 (paragraph 4), dated 26ᵗʰ April 1916 and OAD 912, dated the 27ᵗʰ May 1916: will you please submit, as early as possible, your project for attack on the Gommecourt salient. It is important that the project should be laid before the C-in-C early next week."[54]

Some might think it extraordinary that a plan of this importance could have developed so far without the C-in-C appearing to know much about it. Already, several thousand yards of new trench had been dug; many new batteries had arrived from the UK; and enormous supplies of food and ammunition were building up behind the lines. In short, the areas from Foncquevillers and Hebuterne westwards were veritable hives of military activity. But, be that as it may, Haig and Kiggell apparently needed to see a written presentation of the plan. It arrived on 4th June[55] and it too was something of a surprise given Allenby and Snow's earlier misgivings. Now, Gommecourt was an excellent place to attack and the prospects were rosy. Either Allenby and Snow had been affected by the general aura of optimism that hung over G.H.Q. through the early summer of 1916 or they had made the sensible professional choice and decided to make the best of a bad job. Their later comments to more junior officers and men as the attack came closer suggests that it was the former rather than the latter which led to the apparent volte-face. Their memorandum stated:

"The position itself is a favourable one to attack for the following reasons:

(a) The position of the Park and village, situated at the apex of the salient, enables a converging attack to be delivered North and South of these points, which should result in the 2 divisions joining hands east of Gommecourt.

(b) Enfilade fire can be brought to bear on both faces of the salient, and on any counter attacks that may be launched from Rossignol Wood, Biez Wood or Pigeon Wood.

(c) The approaches to the villages of Hebuterne and Foncquevillers are screened from the enemy's view and the cellars and numerous trenches in the villages afford shelter.

(d) The villages west of Hebuterne and Foncquevillers and the orchards surrounding the villages afford good cover for artillery positions."[56]

The memorandum then went on to describe the main geographical features affecting the attack. Given their surprising new optimism, only one of these was in the attacker's favour. They were:

In the attack's favour:

The spur of ground running east from Hebuterne towards Puisieux which would protect most of the area to be attacked by the 56th Division from German machine gun fire from the trenches to the south of the spur;

To the attack's disadvantage:

The fact that Gommecourt village and Park commanded all of the ground over which the 56th Division was to attack;

The ridge running from the rear of Gommecourt to Rossignol Wood that overlooked the whole area to be attacked by the 56th Division as well as the majority of the front two lines of British trenches from which this attack were to be launched; and

The valleys on either side of this ridge which "offer(ed) concealment for gun positions and covered approaches for counter attack".

The report then explained that the attack was to be divided into three phases:

- The capture of the first two (or three in the case of the 56th Division) German lines in one bound;
- The advance to the fourth line (on the Gommecourt-Rossignol Wood ridge); and

The two divisions joining hands behind Gommecourt village followed by the mopping up of enemy troops trapped in the village and Park.

The timing of these advances was, in Third Army's original plan, to be left to Snow as VII Corps commander. The concern was, most particularly, the vulnerable position the 56th Division would find itself in if it moved towards its final objectives without a reciprocal movement from the north by the 46th Division. This would, the memorandum stated "leave the former division (i.e. 56th Division) in an unfavourable position."

It would seem that either Haig or Kiggell or, indeed, both were shown a précis of Allenby's proposal. On it were several hand-written notes. The first was opposite the suggestion of a three-phase assault. It read:

"Unless the attack is made in one rush by each division it will probably not succeed – each division will wait for the other…"[57]

The same hand then wrote at the end of the document:

"If the G.O.C. (VII) Corps tries to control and time the various stages in accordance with information which he may receive, the operations will be delayed and success compromised."

In other words, what was clearly realised at the most senior level was that the attack was a high risk concept which depended on both divisions being equally successful within the same time frame. Experience of nearly two years of a war riddled with failures, cock-ups and disasters might have alerted someone to the possibility that the attack on Gommecourt was another of these in the making. If ever there was a war to which the phrase 'what can go wrong, will go wrong' comprehensively applied then this was it. And, as pointed out by Allenby, if things did go wrong, most at risk in the event of a failure would be the 56th Division. But of course, as far as G.H.Q. was concerned the true success of this operation did not rely on the two divisions joining up. Arguably it didn't really matter if they even got into the first German trenches. No, the judgement of its success or failure would be based on applying Haig's clear statement about the true objectives of the attack. If the men from London and the Midlands succeeded in "(diverting) against (themselves) the fire of artillery and infantry which might otherwise be directed against the left flank of the main attack near Serre" then the attack, whatever its local result, would be deemed a success.

The inevitable conclusion is that the attack on Gommecourt was fraught with considerable danger. It was a complex operation in which timing was critical; it was to be launched against possibly the strongest part of the German line on the British Western Front; and it was to be organised in such a way that the Germans would know an attack was coming so that they would reinforce the area with both infantry and artillery. It might be said it was an accident waiting to happen.

The two divisions selected for the attack on Gommecourt were the 'forlorn hope' of the 'Big Push'. Theirs was a desperate sacrificial advance with little practical hope of success, indeed little need of success. It would be one made 'for the greater good'. It made no difference whether they succeeded or failed in their planned advance, so long as they drew enemy fire. And the more the better. The more artillery fire that was directed onto the attacking battalions by German guns north of Serre the more successful would the 'diversion' be. Of necessity of course, the more successful was the diversion then the higher would be the casualties amongst these two divisions.

The true nature of this sacrificial diversion is succinctly summed up by the Official History:

"It must, however, be distinctly borne in mind that in Sir Douglas Haig's plan nothing depended on the capture of Gommecourt.... There was no intention of exploiting the capture of Gommecourt by sending a force southwards from the village to roll up the German line or clear the ridge leading south-east behind it. No troops were provided or available for such a purpose. A success at Gommecourt would merely shorten the British line by cutting off an enemy salient."[58]

So, the success or failure of the attack on Gommecourt was not to be judged by the ability of the attacking troops to take and hold a line of enemy trenches but on the success or otherwise of an assault 1½ kilometres to the South by another division of another Army.

There could be four results of this operation:

1. At best, the Gommecourt salient would fall, German reserves that might otherwise have interfered with the Serre attack would be diverted and the attack on Serre would be, as a result, a success;

2. The action against Gommecourt could fail but the diversion caused would help ensure success against Serre. Haig and G.H.Q. would of course, have regarded this as a success and the sacrifice of the VII Corps as a contribution to 'the greater good';

3. The opposite could happen, success at Gommecourt and failure at Serre. Clearly, by the objectives set for the main plan, this would have to be regarded as a failure as nothing depended on the taking of Gommecourt; and lastly

4. Both attacks could fail. The sacrifice of the diversionary attack would achieve nothing, Serre would not fall and the grand plan for the 'Big Push' would be compromised.

The tragedy of Gommecourt is that it was the fourth outcome that occurred. In the process, 6,800 men of the two attacking divisions became casualties; 40% of whom were either killed or missing presumed dead.

It is against this background that the assault on Gommecourt should be viewed. An assault that, on a day of tragedies, had tragedy compounded by the purely sacrificial nature of the action. A sacrifice that reaped no reward.

ENDNOTES:

1 War Diary of Sir Douglas Haig, Haig Papers, National Library of Scotland
2 Ibid
3 Prior R & Wilson T, The Somme, 2005 page 301.
4 Rawlinson Papers 5201/33/18 National Army Musuem.
5 Letter to Field Marshal Lord Kitchener, 9th March 1916. Rawlinson Letters, National Army Museum.
6 The Somme - Plan for Offensive by the Fourth Army, G.X.3/1.
7 Ibid. para. 17
8 Rawlinson Diary, 30th March 1916
9 G.H.Q Letters (O.A.D 710 and 710/1) to Gen. Sir Henry Rawlinson, 12th April 1916.
10 Third Army memorandum, SGR 33
11 G.H.Q Letters (O.A.D 710 and 710/1) to Gen. Sir Henry Rawlinson, 12th April 1916.
12 GQH Letter (O.A.D. 751) to Gen Sir Edmund Allenby, 13th April 1916.
13 G.H.Q Letters (O.A.D 710 and 710/1) to Gen. Sir Henry Rawlinson, 12th April 1916.
14 Memorandum from Sir Douglas Haig, OAD 522, to Army Commanders, 4th March 1916
15 Ibid.
16 Amended Plan submitted by the Fourth Army to G.H.Q 19th April 1916.
17 Ibid.
18 Sir Edmund Allenby's Memorandum from Third Army, No. SGR 33/1 to G.H.Q, dated 23rd April 1916.
19 G.H.Q Letter OAD 876 to Sir H Rawlinson, 16th May 1916.
20 G.H.Q letter OAD 912
21 G.H.Q Letter OAD 12 to General Sir Henry Rawlinson, 16th June stating the objectives.
22 Ibid.
23 Sir Douglas Haig's War Diary, WO 256/10 National Archives
24 G.H.Q Letter OAD 12 to General Sir Henry Rawlinson, 16th June stating the objectives.
25 Gen Sir A Farrar-Hockley, 'The Somme', 1964, page 79
26 David Lloyd George, 'War Memoirs', page 1425
27 Sir Douglas Haig's War Diary, WO 256/10 National Archives. para. 1
28 G.H.Q Letter OAD 15 to General Sir Henry Rawlinson, 20th June re: shortening the bombardment, para. 2
29 Ibid.
30 Ibid.
31 IV Corps War Diary, June-August 1915, Wo 95/710 National Archives.
32 Ibid.
33 Ibid.
34 Ian Hogg gives the following figures: 24 380-420mm (12"+) howitzers, 2 380mm (15 in.) guns, 128 21cm (8.4") howitzers, 266 105-155mm (4.2"-5.9 in.) howitzers, 150 105-155mm (4.2"-5.9 in.) guns, 247 77-90mm (3.1"-4.2") guns + 600 trench mortars. Quoted from 'The Guns' by Ian V Hogg, pub. 1971, page 113.
35 Note OAD 17, 21st June 1916 of C-in-C's instructions in amplification of OAS 12, issued 16th June 1916.
36 Ibid.
37 Ibid.
38 Report of the Army Commander's Remarks at the Conference held at Fourth Army Headquarters, 22nd June 1916. Fourth Army papers, Vol 6. IWM.
39 G.H.Q letter OAD 790, dated 21st April 1916
40 3rd Army letter to G.H.Q SGR 33/1, dated 23rd April 1916
41 Later Field Marshal Lord French who led the B.E.F. to France in 1914 and commanded until December 1915.
42 Haldane Papers, National Library of Scotland, 14th June 1915.
43 Allenby Papers, Liddell Hart Collection, King's College, London
44 Edmonds, Brig. Gen. Sir James E, Official History of the War: Military Operations, France and Belgium 1916, Volume 1 page 454.
45 Ibid.
46 Contained in Third Army memorandum, SGR 33, April 9th 1916
47 Edmonds, op. cit..
48 Ibid.
49 Snow was the grandfather of two TV personalities, newsreader Jon Snow and his cousin, Peter Snow.
50 Home, Brig. Gen Sir Archibald, The Diary of a World War One Cavalry Officer, 1985 page 107
51 Ibid, page 107
52 Ibid, page 108
53 Ibid, page 107
54 G.H.Q letter OAD 790/2, dated 3rd June 1916.
55 As Third Army memorandum SGR 33/23, 4th June 1916.
56 Ibid.
57 G.H.Q précis of Third Army plan for attack on Gommecourt, undated and unsigned.
58 Edmonds, op. cit.

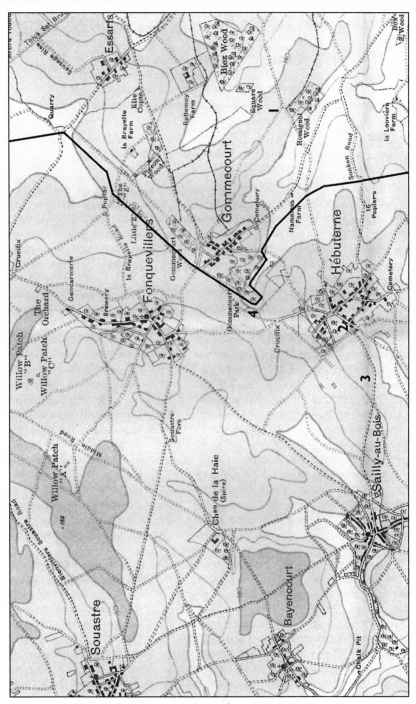

Map 3 Terrain surrounding Gommecourt

Legend: 1 = Point 147 2 = Location of Advanced Dressing Station 3 = Route to & from front line 4 = Kaiser's Oak

2. "THE VERY DEVIL"

> *"Though Gommecourt is not impressive to look at, most soldiers are agreed that it was one of the very strongest points in the enemy's fortified lines on the Western Front. French and Russian officers who have seen it since the enemy left it have described it as 'terrible' and as 'the very devil'.*

John Masefield
Introduction to Edward Liveing's 'Attack'

TO DESCRIBE THE TERRITORY surrounding Gommecourt as 'undulating' almost does the word a disservice. For several kilometres in all directions the land rises or falls by no more than 25 metres in gently extended gradients. Gommecourt itself squats on one of the 'higher' points at just over the 150-metre contour line. The village, previously small and sleepy and small and sleepy now, sits at the conjunction of four low ridges, described in the Official History as forming a St Andrew's Cross or saltire.

One ridge runs north-east from the centre of the Village towards the village of Essarts just under 3 kilometres away (see map, page 33). The three forward German defence lines ran along the forward slope, the top and the reverse slope of this ridge. In front of this ridge and between the two front lines ran a shallow depression dropping barely 5 metres at most. This was to be the area of attack for the 46ᵗʰ Division. On July 1ˢᵗ 1916, much of this depression was covered by thick grass which, in places, concealed both German wire and older, unknown tangles left by the previous French occupants of the poorly constructed trenches.

Another, but slightly lower, ridge runs E.S.E. from the centre of Gommecourt in the general direction of Rossignol Wood, 1¼ kilometres away. Between this ridge (along which ran the German reserve or Switch line) and the British front lines just in front of Hebuterne lay a more pronounced valley than that on the northern front of the salient. Here the land drops by between 10 and 20 metres, reaching its lowest point just in front of Rossignol Wood, just behind the third German trench line. Here, for the most part, the three German trench lines ran along the forward slope of the ridge and, as a result, the British in the remains of the battered village of Hebuterne had observation across all of these lines and the reserve line beyond.

These two ridges join at Gommecourt and, in the angle between them to the east lies another shallow valley. Over this valley no British trench had complete observation and within it lay two woods, Biez Wood (the larger of the two) and Square Wood, as well as Rettemoy Farm. All of these became important locations for German artillery batteries and, as we shall see, attempts to neutralise these batteries were uneasily dependent on R.F.C. aerial and balloon observation.

The third ridge ran SW from Gommecourt, past the western edge of Hebuterne and on to the village of Sailly-au-Bois some 3¾ kilometres distant. From this ridge another, slightly lower one ran through Hebuterne and back in an arc eastwards towards the German lines. The British front lines south of Gommecourt ran along the forward slope of this ridge until they turned sharp south across its brow down towards Touvent Farm (scene of heavy French

34

versus German fighting in June 1915) and the northern flank of the main advance. It was here that the 56th Division was located from early in May 1916. Behind this ridge, the approaches to the front were given some cover from German observation and, in relative safety, this allowed both troops and supplies to leave and enter Hebuterne and the trench system along roads and lanes from the villages to the west where they were billeted.

The 46th Division did not enjoy the luxury afforded to the 56th Division of a relatively unobserved approach to its front line trenches which ran in front of Foncquevillers. The fourth, north-westerly, arm of the saltire runs through that village and, in general, the gradient runs upwards north west on the line from Bienvillers-au-Bois, through Pommier and Humbercamps towards Saulty. Here, as one goes west, heights of 170 metres are reached. But, in between Foncquevillers and the British front line some 500 metres to the east, almost all of the ground was under observation from German positions in Gommecourt and from the ridge running NE to Essarts. As a result, approaches to the front were by means of long and ill-constructed trenches starting deep behind the village. These trenches were liable to flood all too easily, a problem that would turn into a considerable issue for the men of the 46th Division when the day came for them to attack.

For anyone visiting the battlefields of the Somme now it is an education to see the condition of the ground after even the most moderate fall of rain. Surface water accumulates only too easily. The topsoil turns to a sticky, clinging treacle into which boots quickly sink. It is easy to imagine the muddy morass into which trenches would turn and then how they would fill with dark, cold and filthy water after a prolonged downpour or even a sharp shower. Throughout the winter, spring and early summer of 1916 the weather in Picardy was truly awful. Some diarists recall Saturday, 1st July as the first fine day of the summer. This was not quite true, but the other good days were so few and far between that one can understand their selective memory on the subject. Indeed, Maj. Charles Ward-Jackson, a VII Corps staffer, recorded in a letter home to his wife on June 16th 1916:

> *"I have just counted the number of sunny days we have had this year. They only amount to forty-two altogether, an average of not more than seven days a month. Did you ever hear of such a thing!"*[1]

The continuous rain and the cold would make a significant contribution to wearing out the British troops preparing for the attack. For some battalions it would be a more dangerous foe than the soldiers lurking in the trenches on the other side of No Man's Land. Trench foot and fever were only too common amongst men asked to stand for hours in inches, and sometimes feet of water and there was a constant flow of men back down the line to the Casualty Clearing Stations for treatment and rehabilitation. But the unseasonable weather did not kill, at least not immediately, and the direct threat to the well-being of the men came from the complex of trenches and fortifications that glowered at them from the woodland and fields opposite.

The Germans first occupied Gommecourt on the night of the 5th/6th October 1914. Three French territorial divisions were driven out of the village and, three days later, from Monchy-au-Bois away to the north. In spite of counter-attacks neither village could be retaken from the Grenadier Guard Regiments Nrs. 2 and

3 and the front line settled down in much the positions from which the British attacked on 1st July. June 1915 saw further heavy fighting to the south of Hebuterne when the French 2nd Army attempted unsuccessfully to take Serre. They did, however, push the German line back 1,000 metres from a salient to the south of Hebuterne to the positions they still held on 1st July and for months afterwards. But the Germans were alert to the possibility of further attacks and the area surrounding Gommecourt and the lines further south were the subject of furious German engineering activity throughout the next twelve months. That this became a quiet zone of relative inaction made their efforts easier as there was little done to inhibit their work.

On the Allied side of No Man's Land a series of interchanges and adjustments were to take place over the following nine months, the net effect of which was an overall weakening of both the manpower and the trench systems surrounding the Gommecourt salient. Between the 19th and 24th July 1915, soon after the failure of the French attack on Serre, the British 48th (South Midland) Division was inserted into the line, taking over the trenches previously occupied by the 42nd Brigade of the 21st French Division. By the end of the month the Division, with two brigades up, was occupying the line from La Signy Farm, just to the north west of Serre, to in front of Hebuterne. In the area to their left around Gommecourt Park and running away to the north in front of Foncquevillers and Hannescamps, the 56th French Division occupied the line until the beginning of September but then, in the first week of the month, they were replaced by a joint move of the 48th Division, which extended their left and took over the trenches in front of Foncquevillers, and the 37th Division to the north, which extended their right to join up with the South Midland Division.

The length of line the 48th Division now occupied so over-extended their resources that their trenches were, necessarily, only lightly held. The area in front of Foncquevillers in particular suffered from a want of men and attention, with the result that it proved impossible to maintain a continuous length of trench opposite Gommecourt Wood to the north of the village. Instead, the Division resorted to a series of defensive outposts with the intervening trenches being filled with barbed wire. This flimsy system was weakened still further when, on the 13th and 14th February 1916, the Division was asked to take over the trenches to the left currently manned by 112th Brigade of the 37th Division. The winter rains had already undermined the sides of the abandoned trenches, which had collapsed into a tangled mire of mud and rusting barbed wire, and now, with the men stretched paper thin along a great length of line, there was no-one available to do anything to repair the disastrous impact of the elements and months of neglect.

There would be no improvement. On 31st March, the 31st Division of North country Pals battalions moved into the line opposite Serre in preparation for their calamitous assault on the village and, a few days later, Maj. Gen. R Fanshawe, GOC 48th Division was asked to prepare for an assault on the German lines to the south of Gommecourt. The Division's 144th Brigade was earmarked for the job while the other two, the 143rd and 145th Brigades, were ordered to mount dummy attacks. The timetable set was as follows:

8th April – 48th Division ordered to prepare plans;

11th/13th April – new advanced trench dug south of Gommecourt;

21st April – Divisional plans to be finalised; and

30th April – Operation to take place.

The focus of these preparations was all to the south of Gommecourt, along the front soon to be occupied by the 56th Division and, in consequence, no work was put in hand to improve the very poor state of the trenches on what would be the 46th Division's lines. The result would be that the weaker of the two Division's selected for the diversion at Gommecourt would take over by far the worst of the ground, a decision that would have profound consequences for the fate of the entire operation. On 1st May, Maj. Gen. Fanshawe received orders to hand over the lion's share of his Division's front to the 46th and 56th Divisions. The South Midlanders were to hold onto a short stretch of line between the right of the 56th Division and the left of the 31st Division opposite Serre whilst withdrawing two battalions for reserve duties in the attack of the VIII Corps on German lines north of the River Ancre.

With little to bother them during this period of relative calm, the Germans continued to construct their complex of fortifications along the entire Somme front. Small French farming villages became fortresses of concrete and steel. Inter-connected dugouts were sunk 10 to 15 metres deep and given multiple exits so that infantry and machine gunners could unexpectedly spring to the surface, like a jack-in-the-box, to repel an assault. Lines of wide and deep trenches studded with heavily protected machine gun and observation posts and protected by thick belts of wire, stretched back across kilometres of French farmland. The farms themselves became reinforced concrete strong points, loop-holed for rifle and machine gun fire, their cellars, strengthened and improved, offering yet more shell-proof accommodation to the defending infantry.

And nowhere on the British front to be attacked on 1st July was more heavily fortified than Gommecourt. A British trench map of the German defences surrounding the salient gives the positions of well over 120 dugouts, over twenty alone in Gommecourt Park and the grounds of the Chateau. Allenby, Snow and their divisional commanders could, or should, have been under no illusions as to the strength and sophistication of these dugouts. After the shambles of IV Corps' attack on Givenchy on 15th/16th June 1915, in another of Haig's ill-judged and ill-fated battles and as every senior officer failed to take responsibility and instead blamed the troops for their own shortcomings, there was at least one piece of information which should have helped inform the planning of any B.E.F. attack for the foreseeable future. In a IV Corps report on the attack, Rawlinson, then G.O.C. IV Corps, noted that, not only were the German trenches deep and well built, but that the defences had been further strengthened by the use of subterranean, shell-proof dugouts. Rawlinson's report warrants extensive quotation:

"It is evident that … shell-proof dugouts have been constructed some five or six feet below ground level... The moral(e) effect of the heavy shells is neutralised by this form of semi-permanent fortification which the enemy has had ample time to prepare in the last six months in soil very well suited to the purpose at this time of year. I much doubt if any kind of artillery however accurate and well sustained will have the desired effect unless it is sufficient to bury the garrisons in the deep dugouts they have now constructed, *and this is a matter of chance* (author's emphasis)."[2]

If, in six months, the German defenders of Givenchy had managed to construct such defences as these then how much more robust and complex might those be on the Somme where engineers and soldiers had laboured unfettered for over a year in terrain even more conducive to the excavation of secure bolt holes than was the case at Givenchy? And, of course, senior officers already knew exactly what they were up against on the Somme. As previously mentioned, on 17th January 1916, a report had set out the evidence of a Prisoner of War. He had described a dugout at Ovillers la Boisselle soon to be attacked with disastrous consequences by the 8th Division. It was seventeen feet deep and could hold at least twelve men. Then, on 5th June, confirmation of the strength of such dugouts was received from a III Corps raiding party. Able to roam the front and communication trenches, the raiders came back with a chilling description of the strength of the German defences:

"Dugouts are found... in the fire trench and in communication trenches... there is little doubt that these dugouts are connected up to each other."[3]

The officer responsible for the report, Capt. N W R Torr, also attached two plans of the dugouts, one a floor plan and the other a cross-section (see Figures 1 and 2 below. It showed the ceilings of these dugouts to be nearly three times as deep as those at Givenchy - being nearly fourteen feet below the bottom of the trenches and nearly twenty feet below No Man's Land into which they projected. If an experienced officer such as Rawlinson thought that dugouts a mere six feet below ground were difficult to destroy then how much more so would be those buried three times deeper? 'A matter of chance' had become, as the men of the attacking divisions would soon find out, nearly a practical impossibility.

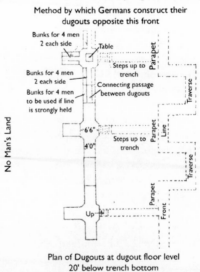

Method by which Germans construct their dugouts opposite this front

Plan of Dugouts at dugout floor level
20' below trench bottom

Figure 1 Floor plan of German dugouts explored on 5th June 1916
Taken from III Corps, Fourth Army, Intelligence Report dated 8th June 1916 of a trench raid conducted on 5th June 1916, (Source: NA WO 157/171)

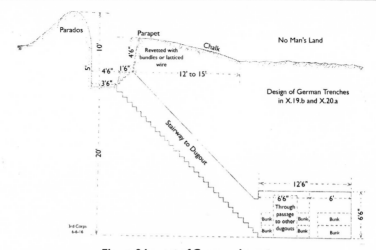

Figure 2 Layout of German dugouts
Taken from III Corps, Fourth Army Intelligence Report dated 8ᵗʰ June 1916 of a trench raid conducted on 5ᵗʰ June 1916, (Source: NA WO 157/171)

But it was not only on the main Somme front that senior officers knew of, or should have known of, the existence of these deep German dugouts. On the night of the 25ᵗʰ November 1915 a large trench raid was mounted by officers and men of 'C' Company, 1/6ᵗʰ Gloucestershire Regt., 144ᵗʰ Brigade, 48ᵗʰ (South Midland) Division. Five officers and 100 men were involved and their objective were trenches at the south east corner of Gommecourt Park. The raiding party was split into three groups:

Left party - 2ⁿᵈ Lt. J M C Badgeley and 25 men;

Right party - 2ⁿᵈ Lt. T T Pryce and 25 men; and the

Reserve party – three officers and 50 men.

As the Left and Right Parties rushed the German wire the 18 pdr field guns of the 3ʳᵈ South Midland Brigade, R.F.A., provided a covering barrage designed to prevent the enemy rushing reinforcements to the spot under attack. Badgeley's party on the left found a belt of thick wire and were rather noisily cutting it when the alerted Germans threw out a volley of grenades. The Gloucesters replied in kind but, with Badgeley being wounded, the men were forced to retire to the reserve party waiting out in No Man's Land. Pryce's party on the right enjoyed greater success, however, and, entering the German trenches, bombed their way along the traverses sending grenades into the openings of the dugouts under the parapet of the German trenches. They also took a prisoner and one wounded German was bundled back across No Man's Land to be interrogated somewhere behind the lines. Casualties were viewed as light: Badgeley and Pryce were both wounded, two men were killed and another 18 slightly wounded. Once officers and men were de-briefed a report was written and sent up to Division by Brig. Gen. G H Nicholson, GOC 144ᵗʰ Brigade. There was a highly revealing section in the Brigadier's report about the condition of the German trenches *and* their front line accommodation, 2ⁿᵈ Lt. Pryce provided the bulk of the information and his final point was tellingly revealed in Nicholson's report:

"(Trenches) very good condition, revetted with rabbit wire and stakes[i]. About 10 ft deep, firing bays for three men each, with good steps leading up to them. Trenches in chalk but not boarded or bricked, with large sump holes[ii]. *Shelters very deep with some spiral staircases. All appeared to be connected with underground passages to each other and back to second line* (author's emphasis)."

It seems a not unreasonable assumption to make that this information was passed through Division, Corps and Army to GHQ. It also seems reasonable to assume that this same information was passed down the chain of command through Third Army, VII Corps and to the 46th and 56th Divisions when they took over the Gommecourt sector. As previously mentioned, trench maps of the German lines in use in the summer of 1916 showed the presence of over 120 dugouts from the front lines back to the reserve and communication trenches. One presumes these dugouts were identified by the observers in either No. 8 Squadron's BE2cs or the kite balloon of No. 5 Kite Balloon Section. It can be assumed, however, that the intelligence existed in British hands from which an accurate picture of the depth and complexity of the system of German dugouts could easily have been deduced. The fact is, however, that this information was either not known, forgotten or ignored as the plans laid by the attacking Divisions and their supporting heavy artillery seems not to have taken it into account

But the deep and interlinked German dugouts were not the totality of the earthworks defending Gommecourt.

Plate 3 German trench and dugout entrance, Gommecourt
(Photograph courtesy of Paul Reed)

---

[i] Rabbit wire was staked along the side of the trench to prevent the sides from collapsing, especially when wet.
[ii] The bottom of the trenches were sometimes covered with duckboards to raise a walkway above any water or mud in the base of the trench or were bricked, often using bricks from the brickfields which were often found in the larger villages in this area. There was one, for example, at the eastern end of Hebuterne and several of the long communication trenches in the British lines near the village had brick floors.

Behind the trench lines lay the farms of La Brayelle at the north end of the 46th Division's front, the heavily fortified and wire-enclosed Rettemoy Farm, 2,000 metres to the east of Gommecourt (both of which still exist), and the long since disappeared Nameless Farm (Bock Farm to the Germans) on the Gommecourt-Puisieux Road. The six woods (Gommecourt Park and Wood, Pigeon Wood, Rossignol Wood, Square Wood and Biez Wood) that lay across the front and rear of the Gommecourt position were all heavily fortified, wired and entrenched. In the early summer of 1916, they were also thickly planted and heavy with leaves. Immediate intelligence as to what lay within these woods was, as a result, difficult to obtain.

On the 46th Division's front the German front line ran north-east along the western edges of Gommecourt Park and village and then two hundred yards in front of the long and narrow Gommecourt Wood. At the northern end of the 46th Division's front two strongpoints, the 'Z' and the 'Little Z' butted out into No Man's Land. These were of significance as they gave German machine gunners the perfect angle to fire almost at right angles into the 46th Division's flank as it moved towards the Wood and village. To the north of these strongpoints No Man's Land, which was for the most part about 350 yards wide, expanded sharply so that, at its extremity, 1,200 yards separated the two armies. Behind the front trench line, another ran parallel about midway between the front line and Gommecourt Wood's edge. In addition, on the front and rear edges of the wood lay two more trench lines with a fifth a further 350 yards back running from the southern end of Gommecourt Wood towards the tiny village of Essarts. Parallel to this last defensive work lay a complex of light railway tracks which ran up from the rear areas and were used to re-supply the men in their forward defences. It would be these trenches that would be occupied by seven companies of the 91st Reserve Infantry Regiment and two companies of the 55th Reserve Infantry Regiment, both of the 2nd Guard Reserve Division, on 1st July.

The poet John Masefield wrote a vivid description of the Gommecourt salient for a review of Edward Liveing's short book 'Attack' in Blackwood's Magazine in 1917. It gives an excellent flavour of the area over which the 56th Division was to attack on 1st July:

"The country in that part is high-lying chalk downland, something like the downland of Berkshire and Buckinghamshire, though generally barer of trees and less bold in its valleys... the chalk is usually well covered, as in Buckinghamshire, with a fat clay. Gommecourt... is hidden... by the tilt of the high lying chalk plateau and by the woodland and orchards round Hebuterne village. Passing through this village... one comes to a fringe of orchard, now deep in grass and of exquisite beauty. From the hedge of this fringe of orchard one sees the Gommecourt position straight in front, with the Gommecourt salient on slightly rising ground, so as to enclose the left flank. At first sight the position is not remarkable. One sees, to the left, a slight rise or swelling in the chalk, covered thickly with the remains and stumps of noble trees, now mostly killed by shell-fire. This swelling, which is covered by the remains of Gommecourt Park, is the salient of the enemy position... Further to the right this rise... contains the few stumps and heaps of bricks that were once Gommecourt village... It is nothing but a gentle rise above a gentle valley. The position is immensely strong in itself, with a perfect glacis and field of fire. Every invention of modern defensive war helped to make it stronger…"⁴

Plate 4 Remains of Gommecourt Church
(Photograph courtesy of Paul Reed)

Plate 5 A German trench in the Gommecourt sector
This is a British photograph taken in early 1917 after the Germans abandoned Gommecourt and retired to the Hindenburg Line. (Photograph courtesy of the Imperial War Museum, Q4912)

On the 56th Division front, the German front line ran round the south side of Gommecourt Park. This alignment gave the defenders several important advantages. Apart from the fact that the Park was thickly wooded[5] and the trees

43

were densely leafed, the boundary of the Park here turned three times at a right angle, twice to the left and once to the right. This meant that two faces of the Park's southern edge looked down the length of the section of No Man's Land across which the 169th Brigade was to attack, giving the defenders the perfect opportunity to take the assaulting infantry in enfilade. British intelligence suggested that two machine guns were located in this part of the Park. One was at the SE corner of the southern-most tip of the Park (at the junction of Fit and Fig trenches) and another in Fig trench facing straight across the 169th Brigade's planned line of attack. The defenders of this sector, known to the Germans as G4 (G4 sector ran along Fish and Firm trenches and was occupied by the 134 men of the 6th Company of the 55th R.I.R with another 26 in close support within the Park.), not only had the cover of the Park to keep them safe but, more significantly, a network of deep dugouts and, according to British intelligence, there were four dugouts at the southern tip of the Park and five in the support line (trenches Fine and Fight). Within these dug outs on 1st July would be 160 men of the 6th Company, 55th Reserve Infantry Regiment.

Sector G5 ran from the western end of Firm trench along the southern edge of the Park to its SE corner. Then the front line turned sharp left and followed the line of the trees to the NE for about 200 metres (Fir trench) at which point the line turned at right angles where the road from Hebuterne meets the edge of the Park and moved out into open fields. This first stretch of trench was known to the British as Fen and from there back to the Firm/Fish junction was sector G5. Its defenders would be 170 men of the 8th Company, 55th R.I.R. and its three machine guns, two of which were near the SE corner opposite the Z Hedge[i] (at the junction of Firm and Fit trenches) and another towards the junctions of Fish and Firm trenches, would dominate this end of the battlefield on 1st July. Four dugouts for the front line men had been built at the SE corner where Fir and Firm trenches met.

The front line then followed a long, shallow arc across the forward slope of a low ridge until it reached the sunken Hebuterne to Puisieux Road some 1,500 metres to the south-east. At this point the line turned due South. It was here that the gap between the Gommecourt attack and the main offensive at Serre started.

The German defenders of this part of the line (from, but not including, sector G5) were drawn from the 170th Regiment of the 52nd Division. Elements of five companies of this regiment held the front and close support lines about 100 metres to the rear. The 2nd Company held the trenches Ferret, Fern and Fever. The 1st Company occupied Fetter and Fate trenches in front of Nameless Farm. The 5th and 6th Companies occupied the Farmyard-Farmer-Farm strongpoint. Behind them, the 3rd Company was split into three, one part holding Feed, another Feud-Fellow and the third the southern flank of the Quadrilateral (Ems trench)[ii]. Two-thirds of the 4th Company were in Fell and Fellow trenches, and the other third was in the Switch line, hidden away in dugouts in Mess trench.

---

i In fact there were three machine guns with the 8th Company located in dug outs in Eel and Fen trenches and the 5th Company had another in close support in a dug out inside Gommecourt Park. The 7th Company, with another two machine guns and 158 men, were located in the southern lines of the Kern Redoubt. In all, therefore, seven machine guns were available to the 55th R.I.R. to defend the area to be attacked by the left wing of the 169th Brigade.
ii Fillet trench, the western face of the Quadrilateral was occupied by 62 men of the 2nd Company of the 55th R.I.R., the other 90 men being part of the garrison of the Kern Redoubt.

The front line troops were kept safe by four deep bunkers in the lines north of the Hebuterne to Bucquoy Road and in another five, grouped together as part of a strongpoint 200 metres north of the Sunken Road. This strongpoint was the main objective of the London Scottish (168ᵗʰ Brigade) and comprised a network of trenches (Farmyard, Farmer and Farm), saps and dugouts forming a rough oval 200 metres at its widest.

Running parallel to the front line was the heavily wired close support line some 100 metres to the rear. Both the front and close support lines were connected to the German third or intermediate line by a series of communication trenches which cut across at right angles at approximately 200 metre intervals. These communication trenches ran back from the front line, up the gentle slope of the ridge to another line of trenches (the Switch Line) about 900 metres to the north. At the Gommecourt end of these entrenchments, the close support line was lightly held. Here, only 50 metres behind the close support line lay the south-eastern edge of the Kern Redoubt. The Kern Redoubt was a large enclosed fortification, which took in most of the eastern end of the village. Serviced by at least sixteen deep dugouts, the redoubt was home to 3½ companies of the 55ᵗʰ R.I.R. Half of the 2ⁿᵈ Company (90 riflemen) was positioned on the northern face, the 1ˢᵗ Company (159 riflemen and one machine gun) was on the western side and the 7ᵗʰ Company (158 riflemen and two machine guns) was to the south. Ready to move in any direction as required was the bulk of the Infantry Pioneer Company (150 riflemen). In total, the redoubt was home to 557 men and five machine guns. Given their location, these troops had the advantage of internal lines and were, as a result, able to move in numbers to either the northern or southern flanks of the salient at speed and under the cover either of the inter-linked dugouts or the complex network of trenches.

Plate 6 Radfahrer Trench running into Gommecourt village
(Photograph courtesy of Paul Reed)

A further 200 metres behind the close support line ran the third or intermediate line, the objective of the right and centre battalions of the British assault. Emerging from the north end of the village this trench line ran just to the north of the Gommecourt-Puisieux Road (also known as Nameless Farm Road to the British as a farm given this name[i] was located about 750 metres along and just to the south of this road). Another 100 metres or so past Nameless Farm this trench line formed a T junction with the Elbe communication trench (Elbe forming the top of the T) only to re-emerge as a distinct third line of trenches at the point where Elbe met the Hebuterne to Bucquoy Road. This line then resumed its path parallel to the front and close support lines but now, instead of there being a 200 metre gap between the close support and intermediate line this gap had closed to 100 metres as it ran behind the Farmyard trench strongpoint.

Another 900 metres beyond this line ran a Switch line that emerged from the western corner of Rossignol Wood and ran along the top of the ridge, eventually disappearing into the rear of Gommecourt village. At its eastern end, this trench was again well endowed with deep dugouts with at least fifteen being built into the trench system just on the reverse slope of the Gommecourt-Rossignol Wood ridge. Here was located the headquarters of the 55ᵗʰ R.I.R. in bunkers in Mere and Meed trenches. They were also occupied, as were more dugouts in Exe trench, by the 162 men of the 10ᵗʰ Company, 55ᵗʰ R.I.R. This location provided the highest viewing point in the German lines and was known as Hill 147[ii]. From this position, it was possible to take observation over the whole area of the 56ᵗʰ Divisions attack and across all of the British lines before they disappeared into Hebuterne. It was from here that the counter-attacks and artillery fire that eventually repulsed the London Division were directed. And from here, further communication trenches ran back into rear positions towards Puisieux to the south east and Bucquoy to the east.

Hill 147 was jointly used by observers of both the infantry and artillery and it was from here that both counter-attacks and devastating artillery fire would be directed on 1ˢᵗ July 1916. The obvious preparations for the attack had not only brought about a reinforcement of the trenches with a fresh infantry division but the many gun positions lying in the farms, woods and hollows to the east of Gommecourt would soon become home to numerous extra batteries. The artillery of the 2ⁿᵈ Guard Division alone had over fifty battery positions prepared for action. They were concealed in places like Rettemoy Farm and Biez Wood and were usually constructed with heavy wooden supports protecting the gun pits which were cunningly camouflaged from aerial observation. To the north of the Gommecourt position lay the large expanse of Adinfer Wood, home to the artillery of the 111ᵗʰ Infantry Division. Here were more field guns and light howitzers, some protected by concrete embrasures, and all were within easy range of the entire Gommecourt salient. Away to the south-east were several hollows surrounding the small town of Puisieux. These too held batteries able to enfilade the entire front of the 56ᵗʰ Division and, although their main responsibility was to help protect the 52ⁿᵈ Infantry Division's position in front of Serre, all of its guns could easily reach, and had been registered on, the British front line trenches and

---

i Bock Farm to the Germans.
ii Hill 147 because the place was on the 147 metre contour line.

No Man's Land in front of Hebuterne. In all, there was more artillery available to support the defenders of Gommecourt than in any other sector of the German line to be attacked on 1ˢᵗ July.

***

THE BRITISH WERE WELL AWARE of the depth, strength and complexity of the trench systems dug by German troops in the months since they had occupied Gommecourt. Contemporary panoramic photographs taken from the British reserve line at the end of May clearly show the matrix of trenches leading across and back from the front line. Highlighted by the chalk spoil hacked out as the Germans dug through the surface clay, these lines snaked and coiled their way up the gentle slope of the ridge opposite for a distance exceeding 1,000 metres.

But this was not the only view the British had over this sector. In the spring of 1916 the R.F.C. had a clear advantage over the opposing air forces and a comprehensive series of aerial photographs was taken over a period of weeks showing exactly the location of all trenches not hidden by the woods. In Army, Corps and Divisional headquarters staff officers pored over composite photographs of the German trench system made from a mosaic of such photographs. So, whilst the depth and solidity of the deep dugouts was not wholly recognised, the obstacle provided by the trenches and the wide wire entanglements before the front and between the support lines had been clearly identified from the air and plans were afoot to neutralise their impact.

But what of the troops occupying these defence systems?

What intelligence the British could gather about the forces opposing them was drawn from the interrogation of soldiers captured during trench raids. By mid-June, it became apparent that the obvious preparations for the assault had already had one effect. The 2ⁿᵈ Guard Reserve Division, which had been held in a reserve position, had been brought into the line between the 52ⁿᵈ and 111ᵗʰ Divisions in early May in order to bolster the Gommecourt defences. In addition, six heavy batteries attached to the division had been brought up and located in positions ready to bombard the British trenches, supply lines and artillery as the offensive drew near. In this respect at least the diversion was working.

The 2ⁿᵈ Guard Reserve Division was a highly experienced unit that had been in action since the early days of the war[i]. Recruited from Westphalia and Hannover, the division started the war as part of von Bülow's Second Army, fighting at Namur, Marbaix, Ribemont and St. Quentin in the initial German advance in the late summer of 1914. The division then fought on the Marne and ended up on the Rheims front after the withdrawal.

In 1915 the division was split up with the 38ᵗʰ Reserve Infantry Brigade (15ᵗʰ and 55ᵗʰ R.I.R.) going into line between Thiescourt and the Oise while the 26ᵗʰ Reserve Infantry Brigade (77ᵗʰ and 91ˢᵗ R.I.R.) went to the Argonne Forest. The division was reunited at the end of April 1915 and sent to the La Bassee sector, fighting at Cuinchy and Givenchy in June and July.

---

[i] The 2ⁿᵈ Guard Reserve Division comprised two brigades, the 26ᵗʰ Reserve Infantry Brigade (15ᵗʰ Infantry Regiment and 55ᵗʰ Reserve Infantry Regiments) and the 38ᵗʰ Reserve Infantry Brigade (77ᵗʰ and 91ˢᵗ Reserve Infantry Regiments). The 77ᵗʰ R.I.R. was in the line beyond the 91ˢᵗ R.I.R. to the north of Gommecourt.

At the beginning of August 1915 the division was sent to rest near Cambrai. In September they occupied the sector at Vingles-Hulluch, south of the La Bassee Canal and on September 25th and 26th they took part in the Third Battle of the Artois. On October 8th parts of the division fought at Loos. The division remained in the La Bassee area until the end of March 1916 when it was sent to Gommecourt area after resting for a month near Tournai.

To the south was the 52nd Infantry Division, formed in March 1915 from regiments recruited around Baden and Magdeburg[i]. It was sent to the line south of Arras and around Monchy aux Bois and Hebuterne where it remained until September 1916. Between the 7th and 13th June 1915 the division was involved in resisting a series of heavy French attacks from SE of Hebuterne in the direction of Serre. The French, in particular, lost heavily with some 2,000 dead and another 9,000 wounded or missing. The ground gained, about 1,000 metres, moved the front lines into the positions from which the 31st Division would attack Serre so disastrously on the morning of 1st July 1916.

When the time came for the assault, British intelligence suggested that the following German units were aligned against the two British divisions:

- On the left, facing the right wing of the 56th Division - the 170th (9th Baden) Infantry Regiment, 52nd Division.

- In the centre, facing the left wing of the 56th Division and the right wing of the 46th Division - the 55th Reserve Infantry Regiment, 2nd Guard Reserve Division.

- On the right, facing the extreme left of the 46th - the 91st Reserve Infantry Regiment, 2nd Guard Reserve Division.

- In reserve, towards Bucquoy, lay the 15th Reserve Infantry Regiment, 2nd Guard Reserve Division.

In all, the three front line regiments represented a strength of nine infantry battalions. In addition, British intelligence had identified a number of other units in the Gommecourt area. Attached to the 2nd Guard Reserve Division were, it was believed:

- 2nd Reserve Uhlan Regiment (Divisional cavalry)
- 20th Reserve Field Artillery Regiment (made up of six 6-gun field gun batteries and one howitzer battery)
- The 7th and 8th Batteries of the 2nd Battalion, 2nd Guard Foot Artillery (15 cm howitzers)
- An unidentified battery of the 2nd Battalion, 6th Reserve Foot Artillery Regiment
- 'A' Battery of the Ersatz Battalion, 9th Foot Artillery Regiment
- 618th Foot Artillery Battery
- 73rd Machine Gun Marksmen Section
- 20th Reserve Minenwerfer Company.

---

i The 52nd Division comprised four regiments: the (9th Baden), 169th (8th Baden) which was in the front line to the south defending the village of Serre, the 66th (3rd Magdeburg) on the front line between the 170th and the 169th Regiments and the 15th Reserve Infantry Regiment in reserve.

The make up of the units attached to the 52nd Division was even more complex. By 1st July, intelligence had identified these units as being attached to this division:

- 103rd and 104th Field Artillery Regiments
- 52nd Foot Artillery Battalion
- 472nd and 692nd Foot Artillery Batteries (12 cm howitzers)
- 406th and 492nd Foot Artillery Batteries
- 381st and 612th Bavarian Foot Artillery Batteries (15 cm howitzers)
- 74th Machine Gun Marksmen Section (6 guns)
- 13th Machine Gun Company (7 guns)
- 13th Machine Gun Company (169th Infantry Regiment) (9 guns)
- Combined 148th and 169th Machine Gun Companies (6 guns)
- 52nd Minenwerfer Company (2 heavy, 4 medium and 12 to 14 light minenwerfers)
- 103rd and 104th Pioneer Companies.

In fact, British Intelligence had seriously underestimated the number of artillery units concentrated in the area around Gommecourt. Although they were aware that some batteries had been moved south from the Arras sector in the days before the attack, they did not realise that the 10th Bavarian Division (in Corps reserve) had released nearly two regiments of Bavarian Field and Foot artillery - the 19th Bavarian Field Artillery Regiment and the 20th Bavarian Foot Artillery Regiment. These were now concentrated in the valleys and woods to the east and south east of Gommecourt ready to support the 2nd Guard Reserve and 52nd Infantry Divisions.

Further to the north, and completely unoccupied except for some desultory smoke demonstrations and fire from the field artillery of the 37th Division, was positioned the 111th Division and its regiments. Rather more important, however, was this division's artillery. This was to pour a torrent of fire onto the 46th Division from its concealed artillery positions in and about Adinfer Wood on July 1st. Adding these batteries to those used by the 2nd Guard Reserve and the 52nd Divisions meant that, during the Gommecourt attack, British artillery was outnumbered by that of the defending German artillery. A fact that was to become of serious consequence as the action on 1st July developed.

ENDNOTES:
1 Ward-Jackson Maj. C L, Letter to his wife, VII Corps, IWM.
2 IV Corps report, dated 21st June 1915
3 Report by Capt. N W R Torr, General Staff III Corps, to Fourth Army. Fourth Army Intelligence Summary 8th June 1916, NA File WO 157/171
4 John Masefield's introduction to Edward Living, 'Attack', 1918.
5 Lt. Col. J F C Fuller, attached to the 37th Division wrote after the war that "the trees around Gommecourt were quite thick and it was impossible to see through them at a distance" (NA file CAB 454/185) and this is confirmed by the adjutant of the London Rifle Brigade, Lt F H Wallis (NA file CAB 45/136).

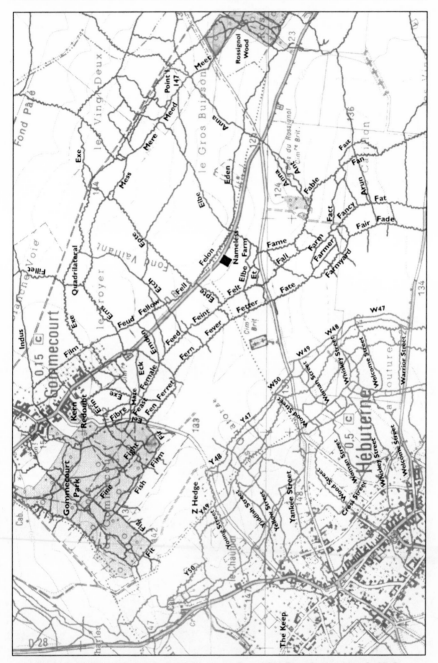

Map 4 British trench maps overlaid on modern IGN Blue Series Map 2407 O

BRITISH TRENCH NAMES AND OTHER LOCATIONS AND THEIR GERMAN EQUIVALENTS

English	German
Anna Trench	Pionier Graben
Arun Trench	Imle Graben
Arun Trench (continued)	Bülow Graben
Eden Trench	Moltke Graben
Elbe Trench	Bock Graben
Elbe Trench (continued)	Schweikert Graben
Ems Trench	Roth Graben
Epte Trench	Becker Graben
Erin Trench	Kürchen Graben
Etch Trench	Lehmann Graben
Exe Trench	Süd Graben
Exe Trench (continued)	Heinzelmännchen Graben
Fig Trench	Walter Allee
Fillet Trench	Riegel Stellung I
Film, Feud, Fellow, Fell & Felon Trenches	Helmut Graben
Indus Trench	Radfahrer Graben
Mess, Mere, Meed and Meet Trenches	Garde Stellung
Nameless Farm	Bock Ferme
Rossignol Wood	Waldchen 125
Square Wood	Birkert Wald

3. "A SMALL MODERN FORTRESS"

"Gommecourt...a small modern fortress. It seems improbable that G.H.Q. realised the strength of the Gommecourt salient."

Military Operations, France and Belgium 1916
Volume I

THE MEN BEING ASKED to attack and take this 'small modern fortress' were two Territorial divisions whose battalions had already seen some hard fighting in the opening years of the war.

The 46ᵗʰ Division was a Territorial Division based on the counties of Staffordshire, Derbyshire, Nottinghamshire, Lincolnshire and Leicestershire and had been the first complete Territorial division to land in France when the Division had crossed from Southampton to Le Havre at the end of February 1915. Within a few days of their arrival, the Division was in general reserve for the attack on Neuve Chapelle on 10ᵗʰ March though, as French and Haig both believed such Divisions needed further training and experience before being committed to action, no part of the division was involved in the ensuing battle. The Division eventually first saw combat at Hooge near Ypres at the end of July 1915.

In the autumn the Division saw serious action late in the Battle of Loos when it was committed to an attack on the heavily fortified Hohenzollern Redoubt. It was a poorly conceived and badly organised attack for which Sir Douglas Haig must shoulder the responsibility and the 46ᵗʰ Division suffered its heaviest casualties of the entire war. In all, 3,763 officers and men were killed or wounded in the assault in an action in which the battalions pressed forward in an effort that was both gallant and futile. Seven battalions each lost more 300 men with the 137ᵗʰ and 138ᵗʰ Brigades being especially badly hit, losing 85% of all those killed and wounded on 13ᵗʰ and 14ᵗʰ October 1915. With the Division still yet to recover from its devastating wounds, it was ordered to Egypt on the 27ᵗʰ December and its units were despatched south to Marseilles by rail. Although some of the battalions spent a few weeks getting a tan and helping to defend the Suez Canal, owing to a shortage of suitable shipping the move was cancelled even while the Leicesters were enjoying themselves onboard the *H.M.T. Aldania*, a former Cunard liner. By the 9ᵗʰ March, the Division was back in the trenches, this time in the Berthonval Sector on Vimy Ridge, where they suffered losses continuously during the frenetic mining and counter-mining that characterised this part of the front. On 20ᵗʰ April the division was withdrawn from the line and some days later it was ordered south to make ready for the 'Big Push'.

It is not clear why the 46ᵗʰ Division was selected for the attack on Gommecourt as nowhere is the decision explained or discussed in existing official documents. What is clear, however, is that the Division was weak numerically and also, because of the severe losses in Company and Platoon officers in October 1915, in terms of the experience of many of its junior battalion officers. The Hohenzollern Redoubt attack had crippled the Division and sown the seeds of the personal antipathy between Sir Douglas Haig and Maj. Gen. Stuart Wortley, G.O.C. 46ᵗʰ Division, that culminated in the abrupt sacking of the Divisional commander within days of the failed attack on Gommecourt. The Division had remained severely weakened throughout the intervening winter and spring, and its enervating time in the unpleasant and dangerous surroundings of Vimy Ridge had done little to repair the weakened fabric of the unit. To make matters worse and for reasons that were never properly understood or explained at the time, the Division was swept by a epidemic of serious diseases which weakened the Division still further. Typhoid, paratyphoid, diphtheria and trench fever were rampant throughout the Division from March to May 1916 and, in spite of several draft of men joining the battalions, the numerical strength of the Division continued to be undermined by this incessant erosion of its strength. Meanwhile, the components that would make up the 56ᵗʰ Division in early 1916 were 'enjoying' a relatively quiet time and continued to do so during the first four months of 1916. They would approach the new offensive rested, trained and reinforced in stark contrast to the 46ᵗʰ Division.

The units making up the 56ᵗʰ (1ˢᵗ London) Division had been in France for many months but the Division was only assembled in its complete form in early 1916. The timetable of their arrival in France is as follows:

Sept 1914	1/14ᵗʰ Londons	1ˢᵗ Brigade, 1ˢᵗ Division
Nov 1914	1/13ᵗʰ Londons	24ᵗʰ Brigade, 8ᵗʰ Division
Nov 1914	1/5ᵗʰ Londons	11ᵗʰ Brigade, 4ᵗʰ Division
Nov 1914	1/9ᵗʰ Londons	13ᵗʰ Brigade, 5ᵗʰ Division
Nov 1914	1/16ᵗʰ Londons	18ᵗʰ Brigade, 6ᵗʰ Division
Jan 1915	1/2ⁿᵈ Londons	G.H.Q. troops then: 17ᵗʰ Brigade, 6ᵗʰ Division
Jan 1915	1/3ʳᵈ Londons	G.H.Q. troops then: Garwhal Brigade, Meerut Division (Feb 19ᵗʰ) 142ⁿᵈ Brigade, 47ᵗʰ Division (Nov 15ᵗʰ)
Jan 1915	1/1ˢᵗ Londons	25ᵗʰ Brigade, 8ᵗʰ Division
Jan 1915	1/12ᵗʰ Londons	G.H.Q. troops then: 84ᵗʰ Brigade, 28ᵗʰ Division (Feb 15ᵗʰ)
Jan 1915	1/4ᵗʰ Londons	G.H.Q. troops then: Ferozepore Brigade, Lahore Division (Feb 19ᵗʰ) 140ᵗʰ Brigade, 47ᵗʰ Division (Nov 15ᵗʰ)
Feb 1915	1/7ᵗʰ Middlesex	23ʳᵈ Brigade, 8ᵗʰ Division
Mar 1915	1/8ᵗʰ Middlesex	88ᵗʰ Brigade, 3ʳᵈ Division

Table 1 Dates of arrival in France of 56ᵗʰ Division battalions

Prior to their arrival in France, six of the battalions had been sent to the Mediterranean; four to Malta[1] and two to Gibraltar[2] but, by early 1915, they were all in France as the huge losses of the B.E.F., especially at First Ypres, were made good. From the start, the battalions that were to make up the division were scattered amongst numerous units, the last to arrive in France being the two battalions of Middlesex 'Terriers' who had spent the winter months basking in the weak sunshine of Gibraltar.

The division's various battalions had been engaged in numerous actions, some suffering horrendous casualties. The 1/14ᵗʰ (London Scottish) were, for a time, attached to the 1ˢᵗ Brigade, 1ˢᵗ Division and had been the first Territorial battalion to see action, at Messines in November 1914. In 1915, they were involved in fighting at Festubert and then in the first big set piece British battle at Loos in September 1915 where they were joined by the 1/3ʳᵈ Londons. In March 1915, the 1/3ʳᵈ Londons and the 1/13ᵗʰ (Kensingtons) fought at Neuve Chapelle. Six of the battalions were heavily involved in the actions comprising the 2ⁿᵈ Battle of Ypres in April and May 1915. The 1/12ᵗʰ (Rangers) London Regiment, for example, suffered 159 fatal casualties during the fighting, being particularly heavily involved in holding back the furious German attacks on the Bellewaarde and Frezenberg ridges in May 1915. The 1/5th (London Rifle Brigade)[i] suffered badly at 2nd Ypres with the 1/8th Middlesex, 1/1st Londons, 1/9th (Queen Victoria Rifles) and 1/4th Londons also spending a desperate time in the 'mincing machine' that was 'The Salient'. The 1/13th (Kensingtons) had suffered most, losing 315 officers and men killed in action since their arrival in France. More than half of these losses were incurred in one day at the Battle of Aubers Ridge on 9th May, 1915. In total, this battalion lost 195 officers and men killed or died of wounds as a consequence of this ill-conceived and ill-executed assault.

All had seen action, suffered casualties and been reinforced by fresh drafts of new volunteers. A small nucleus of each battalion was veteran and experienced, in some cases, very small. The London Scottish, after the experiences at Messines, Loos and elsewhere, had, by May 1916, just fifty men left from the thousand or so who had sailed from Southampton on 15th September 1914. Their experience was not untypical. So severe had been the casualties amongst the Kensingtons and Rangers, for example, that they had been forced to form a composite battalion during the late summer and early autumn of 1915 whilst they waited for the arrival of fresh drafts from their second line battalions back home. The battalions that were to form the new division were, therefore of a different character to that which had left London in 1914 and 1915. The majority of the rank and file were volunteers who had joined up in the autumn of 1914. They were enthusiastic but inexperienced. Some of their officers and N.C.O.s, however, had learned their trade in the battles of 1915 and passing on that knowledge and experience would be critical to any chances of success in the campaigns to come.

Unlike many of the battalions involved on the first day of the Battle of the Somme, the London battalions tended not to have any special local connections with communities in the capital. There was as much a tendency to join a battalion close to where one worked as there was to join one near home. Some of the battalions, the London Rifle Brigade and London Scottish especially, were regarded, not least by themselves, as elite battalions and attracted volunteers from across London and beyond. An analysis of the addresses of the men that died throughout May, June and July 1916 shows that 21% of the London Scottish's casualties came from outside London, nearly twice as many as any other battalion in the division. The L.R.B. , or 'God's Own' as they were jokingly called by men from the rest of the division, appear to have recruited fairly evenly from across the capital but with a slight emphasis on what are now the London Boroughs of Hackney, Waltham Forest and Newham. Other 'local' connections to current London Boroughs were:

1/1st London Regiment – 58% recruited from Camden, Islington and Westminster (Many signed up at the Regimental H.Q. and recruitment office in Handel Street, WC1 near St Pancras Station where were based 'A', 'B', 'C', 'F', 'G' and 'H' Companies. 'D' and 'E' Companies were based south of the river at a drill hall at 15, High Street, Battersea);

1/2nd London Regiment – 48% recruited from Westminster, Southwark, Lambeth and Wandsworth (Regimental H.Q. at 9, Tufton Street, Westminster);

---

[i] The 1/5th London Rifle Brigade suffered 144 fatal casualties during 2nd Ypres.

1/3rd London Regiment – 68% recruited from Enfield, Haringey, Brent, Islington and Camden (Regimental H.Q. at Hampstead Road to the west of Euston Station with volunteers coming from recruitment offices at 207-209, Harrow Road near Paddington, 21, Edward Street near St Pancras and Farringdon Street);

1/4th London Regiment – 53% recruited from Islington and Hackney (Regimental H.Q. in the City Road and recruitment office at 112, Shaftesbury Street, Shoreditch);

1/13th London Regiment (Kensingtons) – 50% recruited from Hammersmith, Kensington and Westminster (Regimental H.Q. at Iverna Gardens in Kensington);

1/7th Middlesex Regiment – 58% recruited from Haringey. The regimental headquarters was at The Elms, Priory Road, Hornsey and the battalion's Companies were based as follows (pre-war these battalions were organised into eight companies, the concentration into four happened in the early part of the war):

A Company – Holly Bush Vale, Hampstead
B Company – The Barracks, Barnet
C Company – The Elms, Priory Road, Hornsey
D Company – Northfield Hall, North Road, Highgate
E Company – Drill Hall, 24, Park Lane, Tottenham
F Company – Drill Hall, Windmill Hill, Enfield, detachment at Enfield Lock
G Company – Drill Hall, 24, Park Lane, Tottenham
H Company – The Elms, Priory Road, Hornsey

1/8th Middlesex Regiment – 66% recruited from Hillingdon, Hounslow and Ealing. The regimental headquarters was at 202a, Hanworth Road, Hounslow and the Companies were based as follows:

A Company – Drill Hall, Sherland Road, Twickenham
B Company – Drill Hall, 114, Ealing Road, Brentford
C Company – 202a, Hanworth Road, Hounslow
D Company – Drill Hall, Featherstone Road, Southall
E Company – Drill Hall, Vine Street, Uxbridge
F Company – Drill Hall, Churchfield Road, Ealing
G Company – Drill Hall, High Street, Hampton Hill
H Company – Drill Hall, Leacroft, Staines

The locations of the other battalions headquarters were as follows:

1/5th London Regiment (London Rifle Brigade) – 130, Bunhill Row, Finsbury.

1/9th London Regiment (Queen Victoria's Rifles) – 56, Davies Street, off Berkeley Street in Westminster.

1/12th London Regiment (The Rangers) – Chenies Street, Bedford Square, Holborn.

1/14th London Regiment (London Scottish) – 59, Buckingham Gate, Westminster.

1/16th London Regiment (Queen's Westminster Rifles) - Queen's Hall, 58 Buckingham Gate, Westminster.

The 1/7th Middlesex was, perhaps, the only battalion with highly localised links and the companies were given names depending on their main recruitment areas as well as the traditional letters. 'A' Company was linked closely with

Hampstead and Highgate, then a mix of fine residential properties around the Heath and the more working class areas of Kentish Town and Highgate. In Highgate it was estimated in 1910 that one in ten of the working population was a railwayman, a prosperous 'working class' occupation. These suburbs fell within the LCC area and were regarded as part of capital. The other companies were drawn from the old county of Middlesex. 'B' Company was based at Enfield, home of the Government Small Arms Factory at Enfield Lock from which came the rifles the men would carry with them into battle. Another influence was the Great Eastern Railway, partly in terms of employment, but mainly because its twopenny return fares allowed working people to travel further to work than had previously been affordable. Consequently, the Enfield and Edmonton areas were mixed middle and working class. To the west, in an area served by the less enlightened London and North Western Railway, lay the more affluent suburbs of Southgate and Barnet (from which, we may surmise, the company's early officer material was more likely to have been drawn). The modern boroughs of Barnet and Haringey provided the battalion with two companies: 'C' Company from Hornsey and 'D' Company from Tottenham. Hornsey was then a predominantly middle class area, drawing on the suburbs of Hornsey itself and Finchley, although at Harringay a working class enclave existed, bordered by Finsbury Park to the south and the King's Cross railway to the west. Tottenham itself was mixed, containing both wealthy residents from Tottenham and Wood Green and working class families in dwellings developed along the strands of the Great Eastern's lines and influenced by its 'liberal' ticket pricing strategies.

Other than this battalion, though, none of the London battalions contained the ingredients that led to such concentrated grief in certain cities and towns once the full extent of the casualties became known. There were no sections made up of local football teams or Boy's Brigade mates or platoons from the same pit or mill or companies from the same tightly knit neighbourhood of back to back terraces. After 1st July, the sorrow would be widespread, families and friends devastated but there would be no long standing commemorations of the dead of the first day on the Somme as were to take place within some communities for decades to come.

***

THE 56TH (1ST LONDON) DIVISION was formed in February of 1916. Their Territorial colleagues of the 47th (2nd London) Division had already fought together as a unit at Loos four months earlier. Now was the opportunity for some of the oldest and proudest Territorial battalions from the Capital to work and fight as one. Most were pleased to be brought together with their pre-war colleagues but one battalion, the London Scottish, raised a metaphorical eyebrow. To move from the elite 1st 'Guards' Brigade[i] of the 1st Division to the 168th Brigade of the 56th Division was seen by the battalion as a decided lowering of status.

The Commanding Officer of this new division, Major General Charles Patrick Amyatt Hull, arrived at the village of Hallencourt between Abbeville and Amiens on the 5th February 1916 for his first meeting with his staff though, a short time

---

i When the time came for the move, the 1st Brigade had lost its Guards battalion, 1st Coldstreams, as part of the reorganisation prior to Loos. The Scottish, however, still liked to refer to their brigade as the '1st Guards'.

later, the fully formed division was to move to an area between Arras and Doullens for training. Hull was a regular of vast experience. He had joined the Royal Scots Fusiliers in November 1887 and progressed through the officer hierarchy to be made Brigade Major of the 11th Brigade in November 1903. He remained at this rank for four years serving also on the 6th and 9th Brigades before spending two years at Staff College emerging as a General Staff Officer, 2nd Grade in 1912. He then moved to the Middlesex Regiment and, on the outbreak of war, he was the C.O. of the 4th Middlesex, leading them through the first battle at Mons and the helter-skelter retreat to the Marne. On 17th November, six days after the climactic action at Nonne Boschen towards the end of the first battle of Ypres, Hull was made Brigadier and given command of the 10th Brigade. He occupied this position until the 4th February 1916, the date he was given command of the newly formed 56th Division, and two days later he was promoted to Major General. Described as a "tall, good looking man with a abrupt manner, but of singular charm"[3], Hull's first meetings were with his staff, led by Lt. Col. J E S Brind[i] of the Royal Artillery. On the 11th, the first Divisional conference was held at which the majority of the officers who would lead the men at Gommecourt first met as a team.

Plate 7 Maj. Gen. Charles Patrick Amyatt Hull, GOC 56th Division
(Photograph 'The Great World War – A History' ed. Frank A Mumby, Gresham Publishing Co. 1915-17)

His three brigade commanders were men of varying experience. The youngest was (Temp.) Brig. Gen. Frank Henry Burnell-Nugent D.S.O., G.O.C. 167th Brigade. He was aged 35 and had been commissioned into the Rifle Brigade in 1899 and served with the mounted infantry in South Africa being severely wounded. Having enjoyed a very brief 'career' as a county cricketer, playing one game for his home county, Hampshire, in 1904, he remained with the regiment until 1915 being wounded during the retreat from Mons. In 1915 he was given command of the 2nd Rifle Brigade having reached the rank of Major. He was

---

[i] Lt. Col. J E S Brind., CMG, DSO, Royal Artillery, was GSO1, 56th Division, between February and October 1916. He was then promoted to GSO1 –Operation at First Army.

appointed Temp. Brigadier General on 5th February 1916 when he took command of the 167th Brigade, his first main command[i].

(Temp.) Brig. Gen. Granville George Loch C.M.G. was appointed to his new rank on the 8th February 1916 when he took command of the 168th Brigade. Forty-five years old, Loch, the son of Gen. F A E Loch CB of the Bombay Staff Corps, had spent his career in the Royal Scots having joined the regiment in 1890. After eighteen years he had reached the rank of Major in a career that seemed somewhat stalled, however, on the outbreak of war he was given command of the 12th Royal Scots (Service) Battalion, (Lothian Regiment) formed in Edinburgh in September 1914. The battalion was attached to the 27th Brigade, 9th Scottish Division and arrived in France in mid-1915 after which they saw action at the Battle of Loos in September 1915.

The new commander of the 169th Brigade was an army man through and through. (Temp.) Brig. Gen. Edward Sacheverell D'Ewes Coke C.M.G. was the eldest son of Maj. Gen. John Talbot Coke of Trusley, Derbyshire who had commanded an infantry brigade in the South African War. Born on 3rd December 1872, Coke had joined the Kings Own Scottish Borderers in 1894 and had risen to be Lt. Col. of the regiment by 1915. His formative military years were spent on the North-West Frontier where he served with the Chitral Force in 1895, being severely wounded at Malakand Pass. He was the brigade signalling officer with the Tirah Expeditionary Force in 1897-8 before returning to the UK to marry Helen Maud A'Deane[ii]. Serving briefly as (Temp) Lt. Col. in the Notts and Derby Regt. in 1915 he returned to the 2nd K.O.S.B later that year before being promoted Temp. Brigadier General on 5th February 1916. His C.M.G was awarded in 1915.

The brigades they were to command were made up entirely of London-based Territorial units, ten from the London Regiment and two Middlesex battalions. In support were four brigades of Royal Field Artillery, three Field Ambulances and a Mobile Veterinary Section and four companies of the Royal Army Service Corps, again all London based. Only the Royal Engineers and the Pioneer battalion were not wholly 'London'. In addition to two London Territorial R.E. Field companies, the 416th Edinburgh Field Company, R.E. was attached to the 169th Brigade and the divisional pioneers were the 1/5th Battalion, the Cheshire Regiment (Earl of Chester's).

Initially, the 56th Division was part of the VI Corps, Third Army. Once formed, the units of the division moved to replace the French XVII Corps in the area around Domart-en-Ponthieu in late February. In mid-March, they moved again to occupy some thirty small towns and villages either side of the River Canche between Doullens and St Pol. In all, they were spread over an area of almost 200 sq. km. At the heart of their vast encampment was the Divisional H.Q. at Le Cauroy. The three brigades and the sundry support units were scattered in all directions. The 167th Brigade's H.Q. was at Rebreuve, six kilometres west of Le Cauroy. The 168th had their brigade base at Manin, eight kilometres north east of Divisional H.Q. and the 169th Brigade headquarters were

---

[i] Brig. Gen. Burnell-Nugent's grandson is Admiral Sir James Burnell-Nugent RN, C-in-C Fleet, recently Second Sea Lord. Burnell-Nugent was removed from command of the 167th Brigade on 27th July 1916. He was subsequently awarded the C.B. and O.B.E.

[ii] Their son, Maj. John Sacheverell A'Deane Coke, Second-in-Command, 7th Battalion The King's Own Scottish Borderers, was killed while trying to evade the Germans after the battle of Arnhem in 1944.

at Houvin-Houvigneul, five kilometres to the north west. Each was surrounded by their infantry battalions, trench mortar batteries, field artillery, Royal Engineers, Field Ambulances and all the other accoutrements that made up the complex organism that is an army brigade in wartime.

Although most elements of the division existed, some had still to be created. Each brigade required a machine gun company and they were formed by seconding some thirty officers and men of each battalion to the new unit. The battalions were still under strength after their losses at Loos and elsewhere and there was some resentment when experienced officers, N.C.O.s and men were snatched from their companies to be the nucleus of the Brigade's Machine Gun Company. Furthermore, the men so chosen were not expert in the ways of the Vickers gun and intensive training was required on the ranges in the rear areas. The expansion of the number of Lewis gun teams, the need for highly trained bombing squads and other specialised units also contributed to the drain of competent and experienced men[i]. But, as a result of this expanded network of brigade and battalion 'specialists', much of March and April was spent in intensive training and practice of the new skills required. The woods and fields of this small part of Picardy, resounded to the crack and rattle of grenades and automatic fire, to shouted orders, the heavy tramp of marching feet and the sound of cursing and swearing aimed at the men's newly issued steel helmet. Poorly balanced, heavy and with no ventilation, the Brodie helmet was regarded by the men as a mixed blessing as they toiled down the narrow country lanes on innumerable route marches. Life was, however, relatively quiet and it had the inestimable virtue of being a long way from the mud and danger of the front line trenches. There were worse ways to spend their time, as the men of the 56th Division were about to find out.

***

WHILE THE INFANTRY TRAINED and the artillery moved their guns into place, the staff officers of VII Corps studied maps, timetables, photographs and intelligence reports. Theories were proposed, knocked down and rebuilt in a slightly modified form. A dismal prognosis for the outcome of the attack was not shared by the staff officers developing the scheme for the attack on Gommecourt. As at nearly all levels of command, they set their faith implicitly in the killing power of the concentration of artillery that was now at their disposal, a concentration of guns and ammunition unprecedented in the British Army's history. As a result, the plan of attack (see map, page 61) that evolved at Third Army's and VII Corps' H.Q.s was a complex one, depending for success on the completion of two independent but inter-dependent actions by the two divisions involved.

What the staff officers decided was that the heavily fortified and densely wooded Gommecourt Park should not be attacked head on. This decision was probably correct given the awful later experiences of assaults on places like Mametz, Trones, Delville and High Woods. Instead, they decided to pinch out the Park by attacking on either flank of the salient, with the 46th Division attacking the north-west flank and the 56th Division the south west one. The two

---

[i] The Westminsters were still losing men to the Trench Mortar Battery in May. 2nd Lt. P C Coote and 12 men were assigned to this duty on 1st May.

divisions were then to join hands on top of the Gommecourt to Rossignol Wood ridge at a place called the Quadrilateral, a rectangular complex of trenches where several important German communication trenches met behind the village itself. Once this had been achieved the troops were then given four major tasks:

1. Several strongpoints were to be constructed with the help of the Royal Engineers and the Divisional Pioneers. These were to be wired and reinforced with machine guns and were to act as bastions in the new front line which would then look down into the rear areas in which lay much of the German artillery;

2. The German trenches linking these bastions were to be reversed so that a new parapet faced the German lines and, in the communication trenches which were now front line trenches, a parapet and parados would be have to be constructed to make them defensible. Where the captured trenches abutted existing German ones, i.e. on either flank, several traverses were to be blown in to prevent encroachment by German bombers;

3. Trenches were to be dug across No Man's land to link the existing British trench systems to the newly captured ones and the trenches on either flank, i.e. from the right of the 56ᵗʰ Division's position and the extreme left of the 46ᵗʰ Division's line, were to be constructed as front line trenches, again with a parapet and parados. These trenches would require wiring and all the other elements needed to prevent easy assault. The other trenches would be used as communication trenches and, initially, those nearest the Park would see the urgent re-supply of the troops required for the fourth task; which was that

4. Once re-supplied with bombs and, after a continuation of the heavy howitzer's bombardment of the Park, men from each Division would start to clear the trenches and dugouts of the Park and village in a methodical manner using the large supplies of bombs that had been brought forward and stored within easy reach of the assembly trenches. Cut-off as they were it was hoped that the majority of the encircled German defenders would surrender but, if not, then the unpleasant task of clearing a heavily defended wooded area would take place yard by yard.

In order to achieve these tasks it would be necessary for successive waves of troops to carry the heavy loads of material that would be needed to transform the trenches and build, wire and equip the new strongpoints and front lines trenches. Later waves would also bring over the stores of ammunition and bombs needed to enable the troops to resist any German counter-attacks as well as overcome any resistance in the Park. While these waves moved forward, other men from the reserve battalions would move out into No Man's Land and start to dig the new communication and front line trenches which would be marked out by small teams of Royal Engineers. Carrying parties would then use the new communication trenches to move material up to the new front line and it was also hoped that the various roads that ran across No Man's Land might be repaired so that wheeled transport could be utilised in the re-supply process. To achieve this, groups of Royal Engineers and Pioneers would blow up the various blocks built across these roads and fill in the stretches of trench that ran across them.

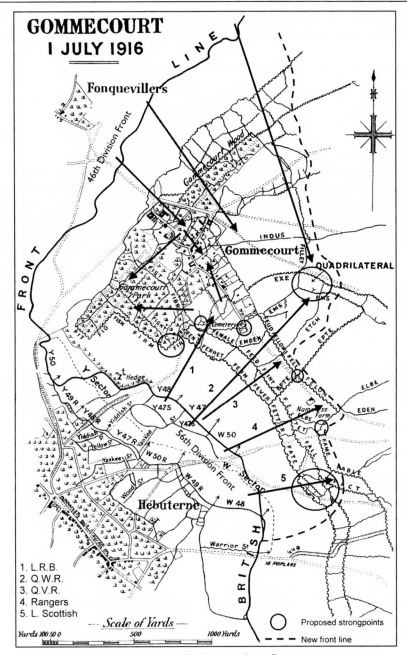

Map 5 VII Corps' plan for the attack on Gommecourt
Original map taken from 'The War History of the 1st Battalion, Queen's Westminster Rifles',
Medici Society, 1923

The timing of these actions was critical. Firstly, it was important that the men newly established within the German positions were re-supplied with food, water, ammunition, etc., and secondly, the artillery programme was designed to march in front of the attacking troops in such a way as to provide a curtain of fire in front of them which would prevent interference from German reserves coming up from the villages in the rear. This would be done by timed and pre-determined 'lifts' at which point the artillery would move from one set of targets to another further into the German lines. Behind this, the troops would occupy an area which the staff expected to be devoid of any form of organised resistance. The key to success was the artillery bombardment. It was first and foremost designed to perform three functions: kill or demoralise the defenders in the front lines; prevent their re-supply and relief; and destroy the German artillery defending Gommecourt. To achieve this Allenby was given more or less the number of heavy guns he had asked for in his original feasibility study. To this were added the field artillery of the two attacking divisions. This impressive array of guns had four tasks: the field guns would cut the wire, the medium and heavy guns would target the German artillery, the long range guns would disrupt re-supply and reliefs and the heavy howitzers would flatten the trenches, destroy the German dug outs and kill their occupants.

Across the whole front line of both the 3rd and 4th Armies the number of guns was some three times the number employed at the B.E.F.'s previous biggest battle at Loos in September 1915. The one drawback of this dramatic increase in capacity was that many of the gunners who were to man this huge concentration of firepower were, until recently, training at home and had never fired a gun in anger. Rawlinson, as has been mentioned, clearly considered this a potential concern but, as the days and weeks drew on to zero hour on 'Z' Day, others seemed not to consider this an issue of much consequence. In truth, the plan devised for the attack on Gommecourt, indeed the plans for the whole offensive, seemed predicated on the idea that the sheer weight of the British bombardment would sweep away all resistance to such an extent that the advancing troops would occupy the German lines with precious little resistance from what was left of the demoralised and exhausted defenders. To again quote Haig's Verdun report the troops would, "take possession of ground already practically won by the artillery".

It was on this basis, and with no allowances made for delays, problems, poor communications, the resistance of the enemy or any other unforeseen eventuality, that the timetables for the attacks of the two divisions and their co-ordinated artillery programmes were determined. Each division was to attack on a two brigade front with each brigade having two battalions up and one in reserve. The fourth battalion in each brigade were given carrying, trench digging and other roles and were to hold themselves in reserve in case of any particular requirement determined by Corps or Division. On the 56th Division's front the two brigades allocated to the attack were the 168th and 169th Brigades, the 168th being on the right and the 169th on the left. Each of the eight battalions involved had a specific task:

168th Brigade

London Scottish – to take and hold the three trench lines of a German stronghold on the rising ground east of Hebuterne called the Farmer/Farmyard stronghold after the names the trenches had been given by the British planners. This area was then to be fortified, the trenches to the south and east leading to the German lines were to be blocked, the new position was to be wired, machine and Lewis gun emplacements constructed and all trenches re-built and reversed.

Kensingtons – to dig a trench from the end of a sap near the end of Welcome Street across No Man's Land to a sap projecting from Farmyard trench. In this they were to be assisted by 143 men from the 1/1st London Regt., 167th Brigade. This trench to be fortified on its southern face and to act as the new front line. Another Company of the battalion was to follow the London Scottish over and act as a clearing party in the German front line. They were to ensure that no surviving German soldiers emerged from the bunkers and interfered with the either the progress of the attack or consolidation of the newly won position.

The Rangers – to attack astride the sunken Hebuterne to Bucquoy Road and to take the first three lines including Nameless Farm. They would maintain contact with the battalions on either flank (London Scottish to their right and the Queen Victoria's Rifles to their left) and help establish a new front line along Fame-Elbe-Felon trenches to a strongpoint to be constructed at the junction of Felon and Epte trenches.

1/4th Londons – to reinforce the Rangers, clear the German front lines and act as carrying parties. Another communication trench was to be dug across No Man's Land in this sector.

169th Brigade

Queen Victoria's Rifles – to take the first three lines of German trenches between Epte and Ems trenches, maintain contact on either wing with the Rangers and the London Rifle Brigade and help establish the strongpoint in the German third line at the Epte trench junction. Three hours after zero, they were to start clearing the eastern end of Gommecourt village (the 1/5th South Staffordshires would perform this role for the 46th Division).

Queen's Westminster Rifles – to pass through the Queen Victoria's Rifles and, turning half left, take Gommecourt cemetery and move up the Etch and Ems communication trenches to the Quadrilateral. Here they were to start preparing a new strongpoint where they would establish two machine guns and await the arrival of the 1/6th South Staffordshire Regiment who would be coming down Fillet trench from the north-west. Etch trench was to be fortified as the new eastern facing front line trench with the assistance of the Royal Engineers and Cheshire Pioneers.

London Rifle Brigade – three companies to advance and take the three lines of trenches between Points 94 (southern corner of Gommecourt Park) and Point 63 (Ferret and Fern junction). With the assistance of two sections from the Cheshires they would establish strongpoints at Point 94 and in the Maze. From the Point 94 strongpoint, three hours after zero, the fourth company would start the process of clearing the bunkers and trenches of the Park.

1/2nd Londons – the reserve battalion would provide carrying parties and lend assistance as and when required.

In addition to the battalions of these two brigades, the 1/1st and 1/3rd Londons of the 167th Brigade were given the job of digging 5 ft. deep communication trenches across No Man's Land. As mentioned, one party of the 1/1st Londons was to help the Kensingtons on the far right of the front and another was to dig one from the end of Wood Street to the end of Elbe trench. The two trenches to be dug by the 1/3rd Londons ran from the right hand end of the 'Z' Hedge to Point 94 and the other was to extend from the end of the sap at Yellow Street to Point 63 at the end of Ferret trench. Between 200 and 300 men were to dig each of these trenches and the rest of the two battalions were to act as carrying parties for stores and R.E. supplies across to dumps to be established in the German front lines. If anything confirms the overwhelming, not to say overweening, confidence of senior officers in the effectiveness of the artillery preparations it was that they expected several hundred men to stand out in No Man's Land digging hundreds of yards of trenches unscathed or, at least, relatively so over several hours. Clearly, even one machine gun surviving the bombardment would be able to scythe down such a static target with horrifying ease and speed and it is difficult to imagine that these men would have been deliberately exposed in such a fashion if senior officers thought this likely to happen. It would seem that, amongst many others, they had not thought of this eventuality.

Meanwhile, whilst their colleagues in the two London battalions were digging away merrily, the two remaining battalions of the 167th Brigade, the 1/7th and 1/8th Middlesex Regt., were to be held in reserve, the 1/7th in The Keep and the 1/8th further back in Sailly.

Every detail of the advance was planned down to the 'nth degree with timings set to the minute so that troops, artillery and supplies would arrive on time at the required locations. Repeated rehearsals over replicas of the German trenches drilled into officers and men every action they should take, every line of trenches they were to occupy, the movement of every box of ammunition and bombs and every roll of wire. Dozens of orders were written, printed, marked secret and distributed. One such, Operation Order No. 1 (Part One), was issued on 26th June by Lt. Col. Bates[i] of the London Rifle Brigade. This covered in detail almost every conceivable aspect of the battalion's planned actions on the day of battle (and those not immediately covered were done so subsequently in Operation Order No. 1 (Part Two), Operation Order No. 2 and Amendments 2 and 3). Communications, synchronising watches, dress, battle surplus, formations, timing of the advance – all this and more were set out in painstaking detail. What is clear from reading these documents, however, is just how much it was anticipated that the troops were going over to *occupy* the German trenches. The L.R.B. was going to attack on a three company front, 'A', 'C' and 'D' from left to right. Each company was to advance in six waves. After the battle surplus, Quartermaster's section, etc., had been discounted, the strength of the battalion was 26 officers and 803 men, in other words, just over 200 men per company. This meant that, after taking away 'B' Company, about 620 officers and men were going to advance in the first six waves. The first wave was slightly reinforced to allow extra men for special details to enter and clear all dug outs, otherwise successive waves were of a similar size. Irrespective of which wave a man was in he was

---

i Lt. Col. Arthur Sydney Bates, DSO, CdeG, TD, 1/5th London Regt. (London Rifle Brigade) was educated at Winchester. He was a Private in the 1st Hampshire Volunteer Battalion between 1896 and 1898 and joined the London Rifle Brigade as 2nd Lt. in March 1900. He was promoted Lieutenant in 1901, Captain in 1905 and Major in 1915. He went to France as OC, 'D' Company. On 16th April 1915 he was promoted to Temp. Lieutenant Colonel commanding the battalion and was in France continuously from November 1914 to August 1916. Invalided home in August 1916 he returned to France commanding first the 3/5th Lancashire Fusiliers and then the 4th Loyal North Lancashire Regt. He was an expert shot, winning various prizes at Bisley, shooting for England in 1907 and was appointed Adjutant of the British Olympic Team in 1908 and the British Empire Team in 1910 and 1913.

ordered to be equipped as follows. In addition to his normal equipment, i.e. uniform, rifle, bayonet, helmet and entrenching tool he carried:

Two bandoliers of small arms ammunition (220 rounds)

Two full water bottles

Mess tin

Mackintosh sheet

Iron ration

Remainder of day's ration

Two smoke helmets

In addition, all N.C.O.s and men (except for scouts, bombers and stretcher bearers) were to carry two Mills grenades and three (empty) sand bags. But this was not to be their only burden. The first wave was also to carry either a billhook or a set of wirecutters or wire breakers; not to cut their way through the wire to get into the German lines but so that they could remove any wire or obstacles for the following waves. As some of this wire would be out in the open it was clearly thought reasonable that these men would be able to stand out in full view in No Man's Land or between the German lines removing wire in order to facilitate the progress of the following waves. Some in the second, third and fourth waves were to carry either a shovel or a pick with which to start reversing the captured trenches and clear any blocks within them caused by the artillery bombardment and, in the third and fourth waves, others were told off to carry trench ladders and bridges. The fifth and sixth waves, which also contained the battalion bombers who were not asked to carry any 'extras', had to manhandle boxes of small arms ammunition (ten each by 'C' and 'D' Companies) and those not thus encumbered were to carry half loads of R.E. stores.

The numbers required to carry this material are instructive. With about 620 officers and men starting out, one can discount the officers and the battalion bombers, scouts and signallers from the carrying parties. This reduces the number of available men to about 560. Allowing for, say, 130 men to go over in the reinforced first wave, this leaves 430 men to carry the listed equipment and stores. The numbers detailed to carry this in each wave were:

2nd Wave (shovels and picks)   74

3rd Wave (shovels, picks, ladders and bridges) 116

4th Wave (shovels, picks, ladders and bridges) 102

5th & 6th Waves (SAA boxes)   40 (rest to carry R.E. stores)

In other words, every man involved in the attack, except for the officers and specialists were to carry over additional equipment and the specialists would have been carrying extra bombs or signalling equipment or Lewis guns and ammunition, etc. The Official History estimates that the total weight carried by each man was 66lbs or more. It goes on to say:

"(this) made it difficult to get out of a trench, impossible to move much quicker than a slow walk, or to rise and lie down quickly."[4]

It would seem apparent that the weight and type of burden was not designed for men who expected a hard fight against experienced troops at the end of their movement across No Man's Land. These loads were intended for men who expected to consolidate a captured position, construct strongpoints and re-build and reverse trenches - but not fight. Of course, when the attack came, much of this material was discarded to litter the battlefield for months to come and would be collected by the battlefield salvage crews in the Spring of 1917. At the same time the fields surrounding Gommecourt would also give up their grim harvest of the dead from 1st July.

---

[1] 1/1st Londons, 1/2nd Londons, 1/3rd Londons and the 1/4th Londons.
[2] 1/7th Middlesex and the 1/8th Middlesex.
[3] Dudley Ward, Maj. C A, The Fifty Sixth Division 1914-1918, 1921 and 1998.
[4] Edmonds, Brig. Gen. Sir James E, Official History of the War: Military Operations, France and Belgium 1916, Volume 1, p. 314

4. MAY 1916

"No civilian population was left in the shattered village; none but soldiers moved through the streets and passed through the broken houses. The great church was in ruins, its gaunt round tower sheltering nothing more than swallows and sparrows and starlings, all of them busy about their nesting."

Hebuterne described in 'The 2/2nds in France'
History of the 2/2nd London Field Ambulance

Monday, 1st May 1916

Third Army weather report: Very fine, rained in the evening

FOR MOST OF THE 56TH DIVISION, the first week of May was the last relaxed and danger-free period they were to experience for many months. Having worked, trained and played hard throughout April, May started with two brigade sports days. On Monday, 1st May, it was the turn of the 168th Brigade. The men congregated at the village of Ambrines, the home of the Rangers, where sprints, tug of war and obstacles course races were enthusiastically entered into by the chosen participants. With battalion pride at stake, the races were cheered heartily by the crowds of men who lined the running track. Julian Bickersteth, a chaplain attached to the 56th Division, wrote home some days later about how pleased he was that the two battalions to which he acted as chaplain, The Rangers and the London Scottish, had shared the honours. Commenting on the excellent health of the men he declared the Division one of the finest Divisions in the Army, a result, he thought, of the generally high levels of education within the battalions:

"... there are still many men in the ranks who have had public school education and practically all the officers are public school or varsity men."[1]

Tuesday, 2nd May 1916

Third Army weather report: Fine but cloudy. Thunderstorms later

THE FOLLOWING DAY it was the turn of the 169th Brigade. Their sports day took place on neutral territory at Frevent, twenty kilometres to the west of their brigade H.Q. There were nine events and, in the trials of speed and strength, the Westminsters excelled. Serenaded by the fifes and drums of the 1/2nd Londons, the same two men, L/Cpl. McMillan and 2nd Lt. N T Thurston, came first and second in the 100 and 200 yards sprints. In a one sided relay race the Westminsters four-man team finished some 200 yards ahead of their rivals in the L.R.B.[i]. The hurdle race was another one-two for the Westminsters with Rifleman Radcliffe getting his nose in front of Rifleman Bodenham[ii] on the

---

[i] Lt, later Capt. Frederick Leycester Barwell, a member of the relay team, was killed in action on Sunday, 29th April 1917, aged 22 having joined No. 40 Squadron., Royal Flying Corps. The son of Leycester and Mabel Barwell of The Red Cottage, Waltham St. Lawrence, Berks, he is buried by the West hedge in Beaumont Communal Cemetery, Pas de Calais, France. 'Freddie' Barwell was killed in a dogfight over Beaumont Hamel in which he single-handedly took on six German aircraft. Flying a new Nieuport 17 aircraft Barwell attacked a group of aircraft from Jasta 5 and was shot down by a pilot names Nathanael for whom this was his 13th victory.
Barwell had been with the Q.W.R.s since their arrival in France on 3rd November 1914. The other members of the team were Cpl. Knudson, Sgt. Owen and Rfn. Bright.
[ii] 3892 Rfn John Bodenham 1/16th London Regt (Queen's Westminster Rifles) died on Saturday, 1st July 1916. His body was never recovered and his name is inscribed on the Thiepval Memorial, Pier & Face 13C

finishing line. Each race was worth points so that an overall Brigade sports champion battalion could be identified and, on the running track, the Westminster's advantage was further reinforced by third places in the Obstacle Race, L/Cpl. Harry Roper carrying the battalion colours, and the Quarter Mile (Rfn. Griffiths[i]). To round off their points scoring, the Westminsters won through to the final of the tug of war, beating the L.R.B. by two pulls to one in the first round[ii]. In the final they met their close rivals, the Q.V.R.s, beating them 2-0 and thus assuring themselves of the overall title in spite of gaining no points in the Cross country and the more obviously military Grenade throwing competition. In spite of their sprinting prowess, the Westminsters only narrowly won the Brigade championship. Finishing first with 32 points, they were chased all the way by the Q.V.R.s with 30. The Q.V.R.s may also have been at something of a disadvantage as the majority of the battalion had marched to Dainville the previous day and spent 'Sports Day' on R.E. fatigues, staying until the 4th May. The L.R.B. with 15 points - mostly, it seems, scored by Lt. Geoffrey 'Curly' Boston DCM who won the 5 mile and ¼ mile races - and the 1/2nd Londons, with a disappointing 5 points, trailed in third and fourth.

The Westminster's victory, though undoubtedly satisfying, came as a surprise to some:

"Our brigade held their sports last week, and to the surprise of us all our battalion won the Brigade Cup. We got 32 points, the Queen Vics got 30 points, the other two battalions got a few points but were nowhere near us, so you see it was very exciting and we won by two points."[2]

It was, however, a proud battalion and a contented C.O. who headed back to their billets at Moncheaux that night. But, the Q.W.R.'s Lt. Col. Shoolbred[iii] also had other things on his mind that day. Whilst the men had been shouting themselves hoarse in encouragement of their mates, orders had been received from G.H.Q. to make ready for a move. The division was switching from the VI to the VII Corps and they would be moving south within days to make ready for a major attack on the German lines in a few weeks.

Whilst the men of these two brigades were enjoying themselves, those of the 167th Brigade were still hard at it. They would be the first brigade to move south to their new positions and they had spent the first two days of the month making ready for the move. The 1/1st Londons were some distance away from base when the orders came through. Dainville, a small village just a couple of kilometres west of Arras, was in the rear area of the 14th Division and various units of the 56th had been sent up the line for a week at a time to work with the 14th Division and to keep up their experience of 'forward areas'. The 1/1st were there now and, in the mid-evening of the 1st May, they had set off on a 28 kilometre march to their 'home' village of Ivergny. Whilst their Fusilier colleagues were hiking westwards, the 1/3rd Londons were 'enjoying' some last minute physical exercise and bayonet practice before an inspection of both kit

---

[i] Two Griffiths from the Westminsters were killed in action on the Somme in September 1916
[ii] The tug of war team was coached by RSM A H Davis, DCM, MSM.
[iii] Lt. Col. R Shoolbred, 1/16th London Regt. (Queen's Westminster Rifles) had been in the regiment since 1888 and was made CO in February 1911. He commanded the battalion from the outbreak of war until 18th October 1916 when he was sent home sick. He returned to command in February 1917 before leaving permanently in August 1917.

and feet. At 11.00 a.m. on the 2nd, they set to cleaning out their billets and tidying up Canettemont in readiness for their departure early the next morning.

Wednesday 3rd March 1916
Third Army weather report: Fine and warm

THE NEXT DAY, whilst the foot sore men of the 1/1st Londons[i] rested briefly before starting their clean-up operation, the 1/3rd Londons were up with the proverbial lark ready to parade at 7.00 a.m. Soon after they were off, swinging down the lanes, to be watched by curious men from the Divisional Ammunition Column as they tramped through Estree-Wamin. The sun was high in a typically clear French summer's day. It was, unusually, very hot, dry and dusty - not the day to be marching with full kit, steel helmet, gas mask, greatcoat, rifle and pack. At Coullemont, just north of the Arras-Doullens road, they halted, brewed tea, eased off their boots and massaged tired feet, lay back and snatched forty winks. They had marched 15 kilometres and, at dusk, they set off to complete the last ten. It was 10.00 p.m. before they arrived in Souastre to be billeted in some of the many huts built here and in neighbouring villages to accommodate the troops in their new concentration area. Already arrived after their slightly shorter journey from Rebreuviette were the men of the 1/8th Middlesex[ii]. The next day, they would both see the front lines south of Gommecourt for the first time.

Thursday, 4th May 1916
Third Army weather report: Very warm and close

THE 1/1ST LONDONS left Ivergny and the 1/7th Middlesex departed Beaudricourt on a similar, if shorter, journey the following day. For the Middlesex men, their journey started at 10.15 a.m. and the route took them through the sleepy villages of Sus-St Leger, Warluzel and Couturelle. At Couturelle they were to stop until dusk in order to avoid observation by any inquisitive German aircraft. In fields and along the banks by the side of the road they rested through the long, warm afternoon until abrupt and urgent calls from officers and N.C.O.s called them to order. A few minutes later, a small convoy of staff cars pulled up next to the battalion and out stepped a senior, red-tabbed officer and his younger and most attentive staff. Lt. General Sir Thomas Snow, commander of the VII Corps, had come a-visiting. After a quick conversation with Lt. Col. King and a swift inspection of some men of the battalion the convoy was back on the road leaving the men to pass the rest of the afternoon in peace and quiet. At 6.30 p.m. they were called to order and the march resumed. Crossing the busy Arras-Doullens road, they swung through Gaudiempre and St Amand, heading south east towards their final destination.

The 1/1st and the 1/7th would take the place of the men of the other two battalions in Souastre late that evening. By that time, the 1/3rd Londons and the 1/8th Middlesex would have been up at the front for several hours. At 2.00 p.m.,

---

[i] Lt. Col. Duncan Vaughan Smith, D.S.O., 1/1st London Regt. (Royal Fusiliers), commanded the battalion from June to October 1916, when he was seriously wounded near Le Transloy on 2nd October, and again from February 1917 to April 1917. Aged 38, he was the son of Mr. and Mrs. Frederick Smith, of 2, Clarence Terrace, Regent's Park, London and was married to Nora E. B. Smith, of Kewferry Lodge, Northwood, Middlesex. He died of wounds suffered during the Battle of Arras on 9th April 1917. He was buried in St. Sever Cemetery, Rouen, grave Officers, B. 5. 26.

[ii] Lt. Col. P L Ingpen, D.S.O., 1/8th Middlesex Regt., was the CO from February to October 1916 and again between March and August 1917 when he was wounded at Langemarck, part of the Third Battle of Ypres. He had previously commanded the 2nd West Yorkshire Regt. leading it at Neuve Chapelle in March 1915.

the 1/3rd had left Souastre to be met by a guide from the Oxford and Buckinghamshire Light Infantry at Sailly. His job was to take the battalion up to Hebuterne and then to conduct them through the maze of old French trenches in front of the village to their assigned positions in the front line. They would be the first battalion of the 56th Division to see the battleground of Gommecourt. As the 1/3rd trudged up the communication trenches opposite Gommecourt Park, the 1/8th followed on to take over the right hand trenches of their new position from the men of the 1/5th Gloucesters.

Already Hebuterne was a war-ravaged village, having been previously occupied by the French when the front line stabilised after the retreats and advances of 1914. A later arrival, Rfn. Frank Hawkings[i] of the Queen Victoria's Rifles gave a description of the village in his diary kept throughout the war:

"It contains a number of innovations instituted by the French when they were here. In the centre of the village they sank a large well which drains the water from about a dozen others. Over this well they erected a petrol pump and in consequence water is pumped up night and day for the troops. They also fixed up a small dynamo beneath a miniature waterfall, and this supplies electric light for all the principle dugouts in the village which, by the way, are large and well beneath the ground. A number of communication trenches radiate out from the centre of the village connecting up to the firing line. In addition to La Calvaire, the three most important are Yellow Street, Yankee Street and Woman Street. The latter owes its name to a certain gruesome discovery. Opposite its entrance is a pool of stagnant, putrid water which was once the village pond. One day two men noticed what looked like a sack near the edge amongst a litter of perambulators, bicycles, pictures, chairs, beds and dead dogs and cats. They drew it out and were horrified to discover that it was the half decomposed corpse of a young woman."[3]

Another description of the village occurs in the history of the 2/2nd City of London Field Ambulance published after the war:

"No civilian population was left in the shattered village; none but soldiers moved through the streets and passed through the broken houses. The great church was in ruins, its gaunt round tower sheltering nothing more than swallows and sparrows and starlings, all of them busy about their nesting. The bell, bearing the date of 1861, had been saved and rested on the ground. Along the main street was a strip of grass, with a double row of lime trees trained and interwoven into leafy screens. At one end of this avenue was the church, at the other a little chapel or shrine beyond which was a pond fringed with tall and ragged birches. The single chamber of the shrine was occupied by an infantry guard, and the altar now held nothing more than soldiers' gear. The communication trenches started from the streets and the firing trenches were only a few hundred yards away."[4]

***

---

[i] 2122 Rfn. Frank Hawkings, 1/9th London Regt. (Queen's Victoria Rifles) was born on 30th June 1898 and enlisted under-age. After recovering from wounds suffered at Gommecourt he was commissioned into the Anson Battalion, 63rd (Royal Naval) Division. He was wounded again on 1st October 1918 and demobilised oin March 1919. He became a tea planter in India before returning to England to grow apples in Somerset. His account of his Great War experiences, *'From Ypres to Cambrai'*, was published in 1974.

THE 167ᵀᴴ BRIGADE had moved first because they were needed near the front to start the enormous task of preparation for the attack. They were to dig miles of new trenches, install complex communications systems, lay railways, metal roads, build supply depots. The other elements of the division would join in these tasks; the workload was too large for just one brigade, but the 167ᵗʰ were to be the workhorses of the division. They would not fight, but they would certainly try to dig their way to victory.

As the men of the 167ᵗʰ moved south, the other brigades carried on with last minute training exercises. Practice attacks in company and battalion strength were mounted on dummy trenches marked out with hundreds of metres of white tape. At their base at Beaufort, the 1/4ᵗʰ Londons had arranged a series of lectures for both officers and N.C.O.s. On the morning of the 4ᵗʰ, Lt. Col. Wheatley, after inspecting the whole battalion, gave a presentation on the essential elements of 'Command' but when the C.O. was called away on other business R.S.M. Harris completed part of his lecture directed at the N.C.O.s. The following afternoon, the Quartermaster, Lt. E S Tomeset, gave a lecture to be followed by Capt. D J Leonard who spoke on 'Offensive Spirit'. At Ambrines, the Brigade commander, Brig. Gen. Loch inspected the Rangers, before they carried on the work of clearing up their billets and the village. They had been ordered to move on the morrow.

Friday, 5ᵗʰ May 1916
Third Army weather report: Hot and close. Rained in the evening

FOR SOME OF THE MEN of the 169ᵗʰ Brigade, the 5ᵗʰ was an altogether more strenuous and nerve-wracking day. For those who had not yet endured a gas attack, this was to be their first opportunity to undergo the experience. Brigade H.Q. had arranged a 'gas demonstration' at Houvin-Houvigneul. The normal process for such a 'demonstration' was for the men to don their gas masks. They would then be made to find their way through a smoke filled room. They would blunder around through the gloom peering through the steamed up goggles, breathing noisily the rubber and sweat tinged air, some fighting against rising panic until they would be grabbed by the lapels by a shouting N.C.O. and dragged out into the clean, fresh air. Though artificial, it gave the men some idea of the problems caused by wearing the cumbersome gas mask - the heat, the restricted vision, the difficulty breathing. Some men of the Westminsters were excused this particular duty. They knew what to expect. On the 19ᵗʰ December 1915, they had been the unintended victims of a gas attack at Potijze in the Ypres salient. 'A' Company, then in the trenches affected, had happily survived with one minor injury – and that a wound in the hand.

While the men of the 169ᵗʰ tasted the terrors of gas, the men of the 167ᵗʰ were getting a sharp reminder of life in the front line trenches, something they had avoided for the last three months. On their arrival near Gommecourt, the 1/3ʳᵈ Londons and the 1/8ᵗʰ Middlesex had gone straight into the front line. They would now resume acquaintance with the Germans, watching them through periscopes and binoculars by day, and flirting with them dangerously during hushed and nervous night-time patrols. They also had to learn to live with the sudden scream and crash of artillery shells ploughing into their positions and the moan and roar of the minenwerfers as their fearful projectiles soared and wobbled across the sky and today this cost the 1/8ᵗʰ Middlesex two men wounded. The minenwerfer, or 'moaning minnie' as they were dubbed by the men, became one of the daily terrors of the front line trenches. Rifleman Barber of the London Rifle Brigade later described their effect both on morale and material:

"When I stated the line was quiet there was one troublesome weapon used by the enemy. It was a large cylinder of metal filled with bits of old iron. They were called minenwerfers and were used as morale breakers. They were shot into the air about 100 feet up and came over with what appeared to be a fuse burning. They only came over at night and the sparks from the burning fuse enabled men to scatter before impact or exploding. On bursting the noise was deafening. Debris collected after a burst revealed the contents to be bits of smashed up bicycles, bedsteads, in fact any old iron. One man was hit by a sprocket wheel from a clock. When one or two came over our artillery opened on Gommecourt Wood [*sic* Gommecourt Park] where it was thought that the weapon was concealed."[5]

On the 5ᵗʰ, whilst the front line companies cowered in scrapes and dug outs under a heavy German bombardment, a draft of one officer and 246 men arrived to bulk up the 1/3ʳᵈ London's numbers. Today, the battalion was lucky. The arrival of reinforcements was not counter-balanced by losses under fire. Two days later, another two officers and 45 men arrived, giving the battalion strength another boost. Behind them, the 1/1ˢᵗ Londons and the 1/7ᵗʰ Middlesex had finished their march at Sailly-au-Bois where they went into Brigade reserve. The following day, 'A' and 'B' Companies of the 1/7ᵗʰ were to take over as garrison of 'The Keep'[i] in Hebuterne.

On the other side of No Man's Land a relief was taking place. The 55ᵗʰ Reserve Infantry Regiment of the 2ⁿᵈ Guard Reserve Division took over the line previously occupied by the 169ᵗʰ Regiment of the 52ⁿᵈ Division. The 2ⁿᵈ Guard Reserve Division had just enjoyed a month's rest after spending many months in the trenches near La Bassee but now they had come to bolster a part of the line that O.H.L., the German high Command, perceived as either on or near to the area most likely to be under threat from the anticipated Allied summer offensive. To the north, towards Monchy, part of the 170ᵗʰ Regiment was relieved by the 91ˢᵗ Reserve Infantry Regiment, also part of the 2ⁿᵈ Guard Reserve Division. This movement represented a serious reinforcement of the area lying between the Monchy-Hannescamps Road to the north and the Serre-Mailly Maillet road to the south. Until this point, the four regiments of the 52ⁿᵈ Infantry Division had manned this 11 kilometre length of line, now instead of stretching their resources thinly they could concentrate their men, machine guns and artillery along slightly less than half of this distance, a considerable enhancement to the defences of both Gommecourt and Serre.

Saturday, 6ᵗʰ May 1916
Third Army weather report: Much cooler

TO THE NORTH, the other brigades were, at long last, on the move. The 168ᵗʰ and the Cheshire Pioneers went first. They had spent 5ᵗʰ May cleaning billets, tidying the village, collecting kit and being inspected. All the things a soldier

---

[i] The Keep was an area at the west end of Hebuterne which contained various brigade and battalion offices and stores. It was also designed to be a defensive stronghold if required.

learns to do when 'moving house'. The next day they started out, the 1/4th Londons at Beaufort and the Kensingtons at Ligneroul moving to Souastre. There, the Cheshires joined them after their route march from Grand Rullecourt.

Plate 8 Lt. Col. J E G Groves, 1/5th Cheshire Regt (Earl of Chester's)

The 1/5th Cheshires was not a happy battalion. Like the London Regiments, they were inheritors of the Victorian Volunteer tradition, having their origins in the Old Chester Volunteers formed in 1860. The 5th Cheshires were then formed by the amalgamation of the 2nd (Earl of Chester's) and the 3rd Volunteer Battalion and, on the formation of the Territorial Force in 1907, became part of a Cheshire Infantry Brigade. When war broke out, the battalion had its headquarters in Chester but soon moved to Cambridge where it took rooms in Magdalene College for its headquarters, the rest of the battalion being billeted in Chesterton on the city's outskirts. It left for France on 14th February 1915 and was attached to the 14th Brigade of the 5th Division. For most of 1915, it was in and out of the trenches near Givenchy and the Ypres Salient before moving, late in the year, to a new and quiet sector of the line abutting the valley of the River Somme. Its C.O. throughout this period and since before the beginning of the war was the 51-year old Lt. Col. J E G Groves. Groves was old for such a position; indeed, in 1917 it was ordered that no one over 35 should be given command of a battalion, such were the stresses, strains and dangers. But somehow, Groves had clung on to his post and was clearly determined to stay there.

Shortly after war broke out, he had been appointed Chairman and Managing Director of the family brewers, Groves and Whitnall. In peacetime, he had been a major benefactor of the Cheshire Volunteers and he obviously viewed the colonelcy as just reward for his fund-raising and personal financial contributions. But the 1/5th Cheshires in wartime was not the same cosy social milieu that Groves had presided over in its pre-war days. Now the officers' mess was full of young men not time serving personal and business friends of Lt. Col. Groves. Most of them were young enough to be his son. They had come straight out of university or from middle and lower ranking white-collar office jobs. They were

73

the sort of people he was used to having do his bidding at Groves and Whitnall or deferring to him in the prosperous family home. There was little sympathy between commander and junior officers and even less between the C.O. and the other ranks. Groves was something of a martinet, a man of petty attitudes with little understanding of the trials facing the men and no inclination to find out. He was rarely seen near the front lines in an active sector, preferring to find a comfortable billet where he and his equally unpopular adjutant could devise excuses for parades and inspections in addition to the heavy physical workload heaped upon the men.

2nd Lt. Tom Heald[i] kept a diary throughout his time in the 1/5th Cheshires. A 25-year old, Shrewsbury School educated solicitor from Southport, he had no time for his C.O., describing him in April 1915 as:

"An absolute coward (he) dare not go to the trenches, (he) also does not know his own mind. A wash out."[6]

Heald's view of Groves was widely shared, and other officers committed to paper scathing comments about his performance and attitudes and their effect on the morale and efficiency of the battalion. Adrian Hodgkin[ii] was another well-educated subaltern in the 1/5th Cheshires to keep a diary. Schooled at Repton and with a chemistry degree from Keble College, Oxford, Hodgkin was a research chemist at Brunner Mond[7] at Winnington in Cheshire. Unlike Heald, who had enlisted in August 1914 as a private and been commissioned in early 1915, Hodgkin had been a Territorial 2nd Lt. since 1910. He had seen Groves in action from his perspective in the Officer's Mess since before the war and his opinion of the man had been steadily eroded. After a particularly tough stint in the Ypres' trenches in the early summer of 1915, the battalion was withdrawn for a week's much-needed rest. Hodgkin wrote on the 24th May:

"The march was a rather hectic performance: the whole of the Officer's Mess Cart was taken up with the C.O.'s baggage, and he had the grace to declare that he didn't much care a damn what happened to the Company's mess boxes… This will give a hint as to the relations existing between him and the other officers. It is a great pity, as the efficiency of the battalion is greatly affected by it."[8]

A third subaltern's diary also made clear the junior officers' dislike and contempt for the C.O. and the equally well-loathed Adjutant. 2nd Lt. George McGowan was a native of Eccles in Lancashire who had lived and worked in London since the beginning of 1914. In 1910 he had joined the 6th Battalion of

---

[i] 2nd Lt. Thomas Claypole Lane Heald, M.C., 1/5th Cheshire Regt., was born in 1889 and was educated at Shrewsbury School. He was promoted Captain in 1916 and wa twice Mentioned in Despatches. [*Source:* Dick Flory: Shrewsbury School Register, Vol. 1, 1798 to 1908; Shrewsbury School Roll of Service, 1914-1918]

[ii] 2nd Lt. Adrian Eliot Hodgkin, M.C., 1/5th Cheshire Regt., was born on 1st October 1890, the son of J Hodgkin. He was educated at Repton School from September 1904 to July 1909 (Shooting VIII, 1907, 08, 09; Crewe Exhibitoner, 1909; Science Scholar) and at Keeble College, Oxford, BA, Honours Chemistry, 1912. He was a lieutenant on the unattached list in 1913 and joined the 5th Cheshires in April 1914. He was promoted Captain in June 1916 and was Acting Major from February 1915 and was awarded the M.C. on 1st January 1919. After the war he worked as a research chemist at ICI. He was a Major in the Royal Engineers at GHQ, France 1939-1940, was promoted Lt-Col and Colonel in 1943 and Brigadier in 1945. He was on the Staff of 21st Army Group, NW Europe. He was awarded an OBE (1945) and an Officer, US Legion of Merit and Officer, Order of Leopold, Belgium. He married Beatrice Nina Robarts in 1921. He was the author of *The Archer's Craft* (1951). [*Source:* Dick Flory: Repton School Register, 1922; Repton School Register, 1933; Old Reptonian War Register, 1914-1919; Repton School Register, 1957; Keble College Register, 1870-1925; Keble College Register, 1870-1970]

the Manchester Regiment from which he was gazetted 2nd Lt. to the 2/5th Cheshires in November 1914. He went out to France with the first line battalion two months later. Two days after Hodgkin's comment was written, McGowan could also report on Groves' petty and demoralising behaviour when, in a fit of pique, the C.O. ordered an unfortunate officer, 2nd Lt. Gamon, and fifty innocent men to march 23 miles to collect some hand grenades inadvertently returned to stores, a job one man and a wagon could equally well have performed.

Matters did not improve and, in August, Heald recorded another vitriolic attack on his C.O.'s behaviour:

> "A day of frightfulness by the C.O. and Adjutant. Drilled all morning and because the C.O. found fault with one of the platoons, all afternoon too. Finally, lecture by C.O. and Adjutant to subalterns in the course of which the C.O. told us (practically) that we should run away when a crisis came. I know who would be the first to run and that would be the C.O. Every soldier in the battalion knows it too, which is very unfortunate from the disciplinary point of view... the silly man thinks he is regarded as the 'Father' of the Battalion."[9]

The acute resentment of the junior officers and men for the behaviour of their C.O. was compounded by his well-known liking for the luxuries of life, always taken well behind the front lines. By October, the battalion had established itself around Maricourt just north of the Somme. Whilst the men made the acquaintance of mud, rats and lice in the trenches, Lt. Col. Groves found himself a more congenial set of surroundings resplendent with carpets, comfy chairs and deep, soft beds. And his food was not a tin of Maconochies hurriedly heated and wolfed down but roast meats, fine wines and, no doubt, post-prandial port and cigars.

But Groves' biggest crime in the eyes of the whole battalion was yet to come. In November, decisions were made that were to devastate the already poor morale of the officers and men. The battles of 1915 had made it clear to all that they were in for the long haul. There would be no quick and easy victories, trench warfare was here to stay and men were needed to dig the B.E.F. to victory. Unfortunately, the 1/5th Cheshires had established an unlooked for reputation for excellence with the pick and shovel. With the General Staff looking for units who could perform the dual role of fighting and forward trench construction, the battalion seemed too good to be true. Consequently, the 1/5th Cheshires were told at the end of November that, for the foreseeable future, they were to become a Pioneer battalion. Apart from the dirty, dangerous and backbreaking nature of the work to which they were now committed, the battalion was quick to understand how much their status had been belittled in the eyes of other Territorial and Regular troops. As far as they could see, no longer a front-line fighting unit, the 1/5th Cheshires now stood only marginally higher in the Army's pecking order than the Labour Battalions that dug and hauled in the rear areas. McGowan described them as becoming "the scavengers of the brigade". Some determined that it was the C.O.'s fault and 2nd Lt. Heald described the battalion as 'on the verge of mutiny'[10].

So, it was a less than happy battalion that found itself attached to the 56th Division as its Pioneers. Led by a C.O. they loathed and ordered to do jobs they had not signed up for, the men of the 1/5th Cheshires approached their new tasks in grim and disaffected mood.

Plate 9 Officers of the 1/5th Cheshire Regiment

Top row (left to right): 2nd Lt. T L C Heald M.C. (B Company), Capt. H Caldecutt (B Company), Capt. W A V Churton D.S.O. T. D. (Major, 2iC), 2nd Lt. N Holmstrom (wounded 10/5/15) & Lt. E J Bairstow (B later A Company) (Photograph taken April 1915)

Bottom row (left to right): Capt. E M Dixon (C Company), 2nd Lt. J D Salmon M.C. (B Company), Capt. O Johnson M.C. (D Company), Capt. H W Glendinning (D Company) & Capt. A H Jolliffe M.C. (C Company) (Photographs taken 1918. Source for all The War Record of the 1/5th (Earl of Chester's) Battalion, The Cheshire Regiment, Philipson & Golder 1920. All ranks given as of 1st July 1916)

On their arrival at their new billets in Souastre, 2nd Lt. Heald of the Cheshires recorded his first impressions of their new home village in his diary:

"Battalion marched to a place called Souastre about four miles from the line. This place is packed with troops, but does not seem to have been shelled. The billets are very scarce here, I share a room with another officer but we have no beds. However, I managed to pinch two wire netting beds. This is quite a small place, in a hollow like all French villages. If you stand clear of a village and look round the country you cannot see a village at all, although in the clumps of trees or woods about two or three miles apart from each other there is invariably a village of which only the church spire is showing."[11]

Spartan though their accommodation was, Heald was lucky in one respect in his choice of new-found home:

"The people in my billet are very decent and their little girl, Georgette, has quite adopted me. She is six. She puts flowers into my room every day."[12]

Whilst the Cheshires got used to their new homes, the London Scottish and the Rangers, based a couple of kilometres further north at Viller-sir-Simon and Ambrines respectively, marched to St Amand, passing through Avesnes-le-Comte, Saulty and Gaudiempre on the way. To avoid congestion on the narrow country lanes south, start times were staggered. The Rangers, with furthest to travel, left Ambrines at 12.45 p.m. After a stop for tea, they arrived in St Amand at 8.30 in the evening. There they were joined by the Scottish, whose cooks had served them tea from the mobile cookers at the side of the road in Couturelle. The Kensingtons, meanwhile, strode into Souastre at 9.00 p.m., having covered the 17 kilometres in just under six hours including the requisite stop to 'brew up'.

Sunday, 7ᵗʰ May 1916
Third Army weather report: Cold and wet. Cleared in the evening

THE FOLLOWING DAY, the 7ᵗʰ, the 169ᵗʰ Brigade packed up their 'old kit bags' and moved south. This time, though, every battalion's destination was the same village, Halloy, five miles due east of Doullens. The brigade was due to concentrate at Estree-Wamin on the southern banks of the small River Canche at 11.00 a.m. and for the 1/2ⁿᵈ Londons this meant leaving Sericourt, their home for the past two months, at nine in the morning. The Victorias left Houvin an hour later, by which time the whole brigade was on the move from the north and west towards the bridges at Estree. Once at Estree, their route took them due south down the long straight road to Beaudricourt, then through Ivergny and the four kilometre 'ramble' through the forest of Lucheux and the small town of the same name with the ruins of its ancient abbey. From there, it was but another three kilometres to Halloy, crossing the busy main Arras-Doullens road a few hundred metres before the village was entered.

Halloy was a small village surrounded by trees with a population of no more than 800. Now it was the temporary home to the majority of the 169ᵗʰ Brigade. The billets here were newly built, canvass covered wooden huts with tarpaulin roofs, erected, so some messages stated, by the men of the 6ᵗʰ King's Liverpools. To the men's dismay, in what was to become a miserable early summer, they were soon to discover that the huts had a major design flaw - the tarpaulin roofs were not waterproof! The accommodation failed to impress Sgt. Thornton Bisgood of the 1/2ⁿᵈ Londons:

> "What an awful hole. Only 4 houses and whole brigade to be billeted in this area. Our battalion billeted in structures very much like large greenhouses, except that walls and roofs were of sacking. The men have no blankets or covers and the rain simply pours through the sacking. It is extremely cold."[13]

Whilst the weather was poor, the outlook on the work front was not much better for the four battalions of the 169ᵗʰ Brigade. They would now spend nearly two weeks in an increasingly muddy and damp environment on an exhausting course of physical training, trench digging, route marches and night-time practices. There would be regular bayonet drills (to fulfil the higher ranks' conviction that cold steel and the élan of the charge would still overcome entrenched infantry and massed machine guns), there were specialist sniper and bombing courses - all the preparations for a major attack to come. And of course, it rained.

The 169th had made their march on a Sunday so, for those battalions of the 56th Division not in the front line, this was the time for Church services. For men of the Church of England, services were held in the village church at Souastre. Roman Catholics congregated at St Amand and used the small church there. For any Jews amongst the men, the trip was somewhat longer. They had a march of ten kilometres before they could attend their services in the hamlet of Grenas. For the men of the Rangers the service was an especially poignant one. The next day would be the first anniversary of their action on Frezenberg Ridge during the Second Battle of Ypres. Nearly ninety officers and men of the battalion had been killed or died of wounds received that day and, on this Sunday nearly twelve months later, the Rangers held a special service in memory of their dead. The following day a memorial parade would be held, before the men marched off to start training for the battalion's greatest trial in battle.

For the 1/4th Londons of the 168th Brigade, Sunday saw a major increase in their strength. Four officers and 214 men of the 2/4th Londons marched into Souastre during the day. These men had just completed the last leg of a long and tiring journey. They were not green, untried volunteers from England, their journey to the Western Front had been long, hard and bitter. On 23rd December 1914, they had embarked at Southampton on the troop ship *'Avon'* and set sail for Malta. But, in late August 1915, they had sailed from the pleasant and unthreatening sunshine of this key strategic island to land at Alexandria in Egypt, from there to be thrown into the last two months of the squalor, filth and danger of the Gallipoli campaign. Arriving at W Beach at Cape Helles on 16th October, the battalion was attached to the Royal Naval Division. There they had clung to the flanks of the precipitate peninsula, losing men to sickness, snipers and shells[i]. It was with huge relief that they sailed for Egypt when the campaign was abandoned and their positions evacuated on 8th January 1916. From Egypt, after spending three months as part of the Minia Force defending parts of the Nile Valley against insurgents, the battalion trans-shipped to Marseilles on board HT *'Transylvania'*, arriving in the south of France on 24th April.

Once at Marseilles they were left to the tender mercies of the French railway system but, for once, the trains ran fairly smoothly and, within two days, they had arrived at Rouen where they were sent to the Bruyeres Camp. Here, the battalion was effectively disbanded, with all but a few officers being ordered to join up with the senior battalion.

On the 7th May, they finally met up with their new colleagues and, over the next two days, they were inspected first by the C.O., Lt. Col. L L Wheatley, and then by the Brigade C.O., Brig. Gen. Loch. To complete their introduction to their new comrades, a battalion concert party would be held on Wednesday night in a large farm outhouse. So popular was the event that many men were turned away through lack of space. But the songs, turns and jokes gave the new, sun-tanned members of the battalion a chance to mix with old stagers, learn about the new characters they would meet over the coming weeks and forget, albeit briefly, the war and its effects.

---

i During their stay at Gallipoli, the 2/4th Londons lost sixteen dead and forty wounded through enemy action. Nearly 160 men died or were evacuated as a result of illness.

Monday, 8th May 1916

Third Army weather report: Cold and stormy with heavy showers

THE 8TH MAY BROUGHT 'all change' for the 167th Brigade. The 1/7th Middlesex relieved the 1/3rd Londons after their brief acclimatising sojourn in the trenches. At the same time, the 1/1st Londons, who had marched up from Bayencourt during the day, relieved the 1/8th Middlesex. 'A' and 'B' Companies were billeted in The Keep at the west end of Hebuterne village and 'C' and 'D' Companies made their way up the communication trenches to the dug outs and 'scrapes' of the front line trenches. Both reliefs were complete by 6.00 p.m. and the pleasure in leaving the sodden trenches would have only been exceeded by the knowledge that the 1/3rd Londons and 1/8th Middlesex had only suffered one casualty, and that man only wounded, since their arrival at the front.

Although the weather for the first few days of May had been quite reasonable this now changed and the trenches quickly became waterlogged. Pte. Atkins of the 1/7th Middlesex remembered the conditions all too well:

"After the first day the rain began to collect in the bottom of the trench and, after about a week's rain, we were standing and living in the flooded trench over our knees. Of course most of us got trench feet and influenza etc., but there were not many of us that went sick. We managed to stick it out and rub along somehow as, by now, we came to take everything as it came. If we had orders to stop in a trench with freezing cold water up past our knees, well, we simply stopped there and made the best of a bad job."[14]

Life for the new battalions was to be somewhat livelier. They had been ordered to actively and aggressively patrol No Man's Land and the 1/7th Middlesex took to this with a will. The night they arrived, a three-man patrol was sent out towards Gommecourt Park. With No Man's Land some 700 metres wide, coming across another small patrol creeping through the wire tangles and shell holes in pitch darkness could be regarded as a chance encounter. But, that night, Lance Corporal Bullock's small patrol ran into a hostile patrol twice their size. The German soldiers drew first blood, a grenade wounding Private Ede, but Bullock and the third man returned fire and were able to withdraw taking their wounded colleague with them.

Tuesday, 9th May 1916

Third Army weather report: Cold and heavy rain

THE NEXT DAY, the 1/7th Middlesex reorganised their dispositions. 'B' and 'D' Companies withdrew into Hebuterne, leaving 'A' and 'C' to man the front line. To help in case of attack two Vickers guns from the Brigade Machine Company were brought up and two medium trench mortars were placed on the left of their positions opposite the Park. These reinforcements seem to have been observed from the German positions because that night, at 11.00 p.m., a medium minenwerfer greeted their arrival with twelve bombs, fired from the depths of the Park. In the hours of darkness, in the wasteland between the lines, the various patrols of both sides managed to avoid one another. Probably only the officers in their respective H.Q.s were disappointed.

From the 9th May onwards, German artillery and mortar activity increased sharply and reached far beyond the trenches in and around Hebuterne. To give the men some support, the 2 in. medium trench mortars of X56 Trench Mortar

Battery relieved the two mortars on the left of the 1/7th Middlesex position and another two were placed in reserve in the village. At the same time, the new Stokes' mortars of the 167th Trench Mortar Battery arrived in Hebuterne.

As night drew on, two officer patrols from the Middlesex made ready in the front lines. One of five men and led by 2nd Lt. Brown, was to investigate a German sap that snaked out from Point 94 at the corner of the Park towards the Gommecourt Road. The other of 2nd Lt. Weston and eight men, was to reconnoitre other saps that stretched out towards the Z Hedge from Fig and Fish trenches. Both patrols went through the wire at 8.45 p.m. and were both soon in trouble. Half way across No Man's Land lay the odd shaped Z Hedge and a German patrol twenty strong was already there, watching and waiting for their British counterparts. Brown's party was the first to be challenged. Surprised and outnumbered, they withdrew hurriedly to the sanctuary of their wire and the cover of the Vickers guns. A few moments later, Weston's men came across the same patrol. Three hand grenades were thrown at their enemy before a volley of stick grenades and rifle fire sent them scurrying for home carrying a wounded man, Private Godfrey, with them.

Wednesday, 10th May 1916
Third Army weather report: Fine. Cold wind.

FOR THE MEN of the 167th Brigade this was a time of constant nervousness as they learned to tell the sound of different munitions, tried to guess their likely targets and took desperate evasive action when necessary. For two days they were lucky. In spite of persistent artillery and mortar fire, only one man was caught by an explosion and he was dug out unharmed from a collapsed trench. All the while, the 1/1st patrolled their sections of trench and worked on improving them where possible. Further back, the 1/3rd were busy digging new communication trenches both day and night.

Thursday, 11th May 1916
Third Army weather report: Fine and warm

THEIR FIRST CASUALTIES occurred on the 11th May when working parties of both battalions were caught in a morning 'strafe' by the German guns. One man from the 1st Londons, Private Harry Foster of Southwark[i], died immediately. Two more survived a long and painful ambulance journey across the rutted country roads only to succumb to their wounds at a Casualty Clearing Station in Doullens[ii]. In addition, 2nd Lt. Lister of the 1/3rd Londons and another man were wounded.

While the 167th Brigade were getting re-acquainted with the disciplines and dangers of working in the front line, the division's other two brigades had been working and training hard. The morning after the night before's well attended concert party, the 1/4th Londons were hard at it. A working party of 200 was sent from Souastre to Pas-en-Artois for tree cutting. Wood was needed in large

---

[i] 5142 Pte H Foster, 1/1st London Regt (Royal Fusiliers) died on Thursday, 11th May 1916. He is buried in Hebuterne Military Cemetery, grave I. H. 15.
[ii] The other dead were:
3979 Pte William Hunt from Lambeth is reported in the 1/3rd War Diary as having died of wounds on 11th May. He is listed in 'Soldiers Died', but nothing can be found in the Commonwealth War Graves Commission records.
3748 Pte C Hedges 1/1st London Regt (Royal Fusiliers) died of wounds on Friday, 12th May 1916. He is buried in Doullens Communal Cemetery Extension No.1, grave II. C. 4. He lived in Islington, North London.

quantities: for railway sleepers for the lengths of new track to be laid to gun positions and for the light railways used to supply the front line villages; for strengthening the emplacements of the heavy artillery; and for revetments and dug outs in the trenches at the front. Another 250 men were sent to Henu to work in the local chalk quarries. Massive volumes of stone were essential as foundations for the new roads and railways spreading, like the tentacles of an octopus, across the lush, green French countryside. Closer to the front, the London Scottish were regretting their reputation as excellent diggers. They were being kept busy digging miles of communication trenches about Hebuterne before returning each night, tired and muddy, to their billets in St Amand. And if they weren't digging, they were training. Route marches, PE, bayonet practice - anything and everything other than practice the flexible forms of attack that might help when they came to face the enemy. It would be like this for the next eight weeks, back breaking and exhausting work followed by hair raising and dangerous stints in the trenches. As there was no-one else available to do the labouring there would be precious little time for rest and relaxation before the planned attack. The men would go 'over the top' wearied by their unrelenting efforts.

Friday, 12ᵗʰ May 1916
Third Army weather report: Fine and warm.

THIS SLOW ATTRITION by shellfire carried on over the next week. On the 12ᵗʰ, Lt. Parry[i] and six men of the 1/3ʳᵈ were wounded as the working parties carried on digging and extending the network of communications trenches spreading around and through Hebuterne, and the 1/1ˢᵗ were lucky to lose only two men wounded when a ration party was hit by shrapnel. Over the next two days, three men of the 1/3ʳᵈ would succumb to their wounds[ii]. Luckier still was 'B' Company, 1/7ᵗʰ Middlesex. They sat under a 300-shell bombardment in the morning but without reporting one casualty.

On the afternoon of the 12ᵗʰ May, after another route march for the Kensingtons and after the 1/4ᵗʰ's Lewis gun teams had been inspected by the Brigadier on the firing ranges, the two battalions cheered on their soccer teams in a tightly fought 1-1 draw. The spectators of both battalions drifted away afterwards wondering whether sporting honour would be settled in two day's time on the Brigade 'rugby field'. There was no such light relief for the Scottish and the Rangers. The Scottish just kept on digging whilst the Rangers had working parties out cutting trees and quarrying chalk by 7.45 in the morning. In the afternoon, 'B' and 'D' companies marched off to Mondicourt for duties at this important railhead east of Doullens.

---

[i] Lt. William Norman Maule Parry,, 1/3ʳᵈ London Regt. (Royal Fusiliers) died of wounds 19ᵗʰ August 1917 whilst a German prisoner of war. Aged 20, he was the son of the late Rev. John Parry and Louisa Flora Parry of London. He is buried in Harlebeke New British Cemetery, grave: XI.D.13.
[ii] The men of the 1/3ʳᵈ Londons to die were:
2269 Pte Sydney Edward Harris died of wounds on 13ᵗʰ May 1916. He is buried in Hebuterne Military Cemetery, grave II.R.3
3456 Pte Frederick Charles Ryan died of wounds on 13ᵗʰ May 1916. He is buried in St Amand British Cemetery, grave, I.A.5.
4634 Pte William Reed died of wounds on 14ᵗʰ May 1916. He is buried in St Amand British Cemetery, grave, I.A.13.

Saturday, 13ᵗʰ May 1916

Third Army weather report: Cold, rained all day

ON THE 13ᵀᴴ, it was the turn of the minenwerfers. On an otherwise quiet day, two men were killed and two wounded by the 'moaning minnies'ⁱ. The night, however, was anything but quiet. The B Company of the 1/7ᵗʰ Middlesex were determined to give the 'Z' Hedge a thorough going over. The field artillery were asked to shell the hedge at 11 p.m. at which point a patrol led by the intrepid L/Cpl. Bullock was to go and investigate. 11 p.m. came and the sharp crack of 18 pdrs could be heard from behind the village, then the shells whined overhead to explode loudly deep in Gommecourt Park – nearly three hundred yards off target! Hurried phone calls were made to the divisional artillery and a new time of midnight set for the bombardment. This time the shells fell smartly into the hedge and, as they did, fourteen men slipped out of the trenches and through the British wire. Five men were sent into the Gommecourt Road to act as a covering party and the rest, led by Bullock, approached the corner of the hedge. Six Germans then appeared and a brief fight ensued resulting in one German soldier being killed. An attempt to recover the body was thwarted when the patrol found three feet of barbed wire on the far side of the hedge and any further action was prevented when they came under fire from more Germans lined up along the stretch of the hedge that ran parallel to the road. Having achieved all they could, Bullockⁱⁱ led his men back to the sanctuary of the British lines.

Even on the weekend the work for the 168ᵗʰ Brigade was unrelenting. On Saturday 13ᵗʰ it was working parties and training all round. The 1/4ᵗʰ at least got to use the baths in the morning but, at 8.00 p.m., 'A' and 'B' Companies were out digging yet again. This time, a cable trench for the complex telephone system being laid to connect each headquarters with every other headquarters, and from these headquarters to the front. But, even though the work was hard men still found the time to write a quick letter home. One such was 5644 Pte Richard Edgar Cecil Bryden of B Company, London Scottish. The 20-year old had arrived in France on 22ⁿᵈ November 1915 and he wrote to his mother and his four sisters regularly at their home 30 Norwich Road in Forest Gate. Today's subject matter, apart from the normal requests for more socks and a cake or two, was about the conflict overhead:

"Dear Mother

.... The only sign practically of war are the aeroplanes. Every now and again they are shelled, it is seldom a German one comes across. Ours fly up and down and prevent any crossing. One tried yesterday and was chased back by the sentry who worked his machine gun although they were nearly two miles apart. Of course it did not hit but it served its purpose." [15]

ⁱ 4030 Pte F Elston 1/3ʳᵈ London Regt (Royal Fusiliers) died on Saturday, 13ᵗʰ May 1916. He is buried in Hebuterne Military Cemetery, grave II. R. 1. He was born and lived in Islington, North London.
5026 Pte Richard Massy 1/1ˢᵗ London Regt (Royal Fusiliers) died on Saturday, 13ᵗʰ May 1916, aged 19. He was the son of Francis Joseph and Louise Emistone Massy of 60, Mervan Rd., Brixton, London. He is buried in Hebuterne Military Cemetery, grave Sp. Mem. 16.
ⁱⁱ Cpl R Bullock was awarded the Military Medal for his actions at this time.

Sunday, 14ᵗʰ May 1916
Third Army weather report: Dull and cold

ON SUNDAY, those that could attended religious services and, in the afternoon, in a field on the outskirts of Souastre, sporting honour was settled between the 1/4ᵗʰ and the Kensingtons. A rugby match (officers only of course) was played and the Kensingtons emerged victorious by one try to nil. They were becoming the battalion to beat in the 168ᵗʰ Brigade. But the need to dig was never very far away and, by Sunday evening, all of the battalions were hacking away at the soil and shovelling for all they were worth.

The German artillery marked the Lord's Day with an intense bombardment of Hebuterne and the trenches. The British lines were pounded by 15cm and 10.5cm high explosive whilst 77mm shrapnel whined and fizzed through the air. Under the strafe, three men from the 167ᵗʰ Brigade died and a fourth was injured[i].

In their trenches the 1/7ᵗʰ Middlesex wanted another bash at the 'Z' Hedge. An R.F.A. barrage was put down on the hedge and the fringe of the park just before midnight and two patrols were sent out towards either end of the hedge. The right patrol was to mount a demonstration in an effort to draw out any German patrol manning the hedge and at about 12.30 a.m. in order to mimic a typical night time skirmish, two bombs were thrown, a shot fired and a whistle blown. In the meantime, eight men under 2ⁿᵈ Lt. Forbes had slipped out of No. 3 sap to the left of the hedge and moved around the end of it onto the 'German' side of the hedge. It was a fruitless venture. There was no German patrol, no signs of work or wire, just a plaintive letter from a young German girl from Berlin enquiring about the death of her fiancé.

Monday, 15ᵗʰ May 1916
Third Army weather report: Dull, rained in the morning.

THE WEATHER, never very good at the best of times, now took a turn for the worse and on the morning of the 15ᵗʰ, a party of the 1/4ᵗʰ Londons despatched to the Henu quarries for digging fatigues returned early to their billets. It was too wet even for the Army. But the others still dug; cable trenches, communication trenches, dug outs - whatever the staff planners needed. One small party from the 169ᵗʰ Brigade, however, did get 'out from under' on this day. 2ⁿᵈ Lt. R G T Groves of the 1/2ⁿᵈ Londons and five men were packed off to the Third Army Trench Mortar School to be trained in the use of the new Stokes mortar. After that, they would join up with the 169ᵗʰ Trench Mortar Battery; ready to learn about the special tasks planned for them when the 'Big Push' came.

Some men, however, were able to sample the more pleasant side of Army life in Northern France. Pte. H T Clements and some of his chums in the 1/2ⁿᵈ Londons were given passes for Doullens:

---

i 3364 Pte Henry William Bennion 1/3ʳᵈ London Regt (Royal Fusiliers) died of wounds on Sunday, 14ᵗʰ May 1916, aged 18. From Kilburn, he was the son of Henry and Matilda Bennion of 63, Walterton Rd., Paddington, London. He is buried in Doullens Communal Cemetery Extension No.1, grave II. C. 3.

5200 Pte R Prentice 1/1ˢᵗ London Regt (Royal Fusiliers) died on Sunday, 14ᵗʰ May 1916. He is buried in Hebuterne Military Cemetery, grave II. G. 1. He lived in Islington, North London.

5172 Pte Edward William Wingett Willis 1/1ˢᵗ London Regt (Royal Fusiliers) died on Sunday, 14ᵗʰ May 1916, aged 20. He was the son of Edward Henry and Florence Catherine Lucas Willis of 28, Henry St. Gloucester and lived in Westminster. He is buried in Hebuterne Military Cemetery, grave II. H. 1.

"Walked into Doullens along the railway line. Quite a decent time and a decent time usually consists of walking around the town looking at the shops and buying odds and ends; a haircut; a shave; and going into a good confectioners and eating innumerable pastries of the richest kind. In the evening, a good dinner with, if you were very lucky, a bottle of Bass. If not some good wine, liqueurs and coffee. We managed to get a ride on an ASC lorry back."[16]

On this day, though. the German gunners rested. All was quiet as a draft of sixty men marched in to join up with the 1/1st Londons at Hebuterne, meanwhile the rest of the battalion got ready to move out the following day. Back at Bayencourt, the 1/3rd prepared to move up the lines to relieve the 1/7th Middlesex from their stint in the trenches. For six days straight, the German guns concealed in the woods and valleys to the east had strafed the British lines. Now the silence of the guns was almost unnatural, but a relief none the less. Due to be relieved the following day and in the trenches and the shell battered billets in Hebuterne the men of the 1/7th Middlesex and the 1/1st Londons collected their belongings and talked about the chances for relaxation and rest in the rear villages. There was an estaminet in Souastre to be sampled. A chance for beer, thin, but beer nonetheless. Maybe a big plate of ham, eggs and 'pommes frites' could be obtained. There were baths at Sailly; a wash, clean clothes, a spot of de-lousing all seemed in the offing.

The men of the 55th Reserve Infantry Regiment were anticipating similar creature comforts. They had spent ten days in the front line, getting used to the complex trench systems, the deep dugouts and the routines of front line life. Now they would get a week's rest in Haplincourt just to the east of Bapaume while the 169th Regiment from the neighbouring 52nd Division took their place. Well out of the reach of even the most powerful British guns they could relax and prepare themselves for the attack they knew was imminent. After a week in their rest billets they would go back into reserve on the 22nd May – but that was a whole week away and the men looked forward no further than being clean, well fed and safe, even if it was for only a few days.

Tuesday 16th May 1916
Third Army weather report: Fine and warm.

AT VII CORPS HEADQUARTERS in the imposing chateau in Pas, Brig. Gen. Frank Lyon, GSO1 to Lt. Gen. Snow, was this morning finalising a memorandum that would shortly be falling on the desks of Major Generals Hull and Stuart Wortley. The memorandum concerned each Division's plans for the attack on Gommecourt and set down certain criteria which they must meet. It also set a date by which both Divisions must return to Corps HQ their detailed operational programmes for the attack. This date was Monday, 25th May.

At Pas thought was being given to the artillery's role in the attack and Lyon's memo required that each Division supply the details of two essential elements which would allow the Commander of the Royal Artillery and his staff to prepare the necessary fire plans to support the infantry's objectives. To achieve this, each Division was required to answer two key questions:

1. which German trenches would the Divisions be able to capture 'in one bound'; and

2.	the best course of action to be taken for any further advance.

Lyon reminded both Divisional Generals of the limitations of the planned attack. The intention was not to 'pierce the enemy line' but to cut out the Gommecourt salient and, by threatening to so do, draw enemy forces away from the main attack to the south. Consequently, the Divisional Staffs needed to plan on the basis that there were no reserves to help with the attack and no need to plan for any exploitation of success. Success would be judged by the gaining of a specific amount of territory and the success of the neighbouring attacks of the main Somme offensive.

Lyon then went on to refer to the philosophy of the attack, one very much drawn by Allied Generals from the perceived success of the initial German attacks on Verdun (which had had a great effect of Haig). This was summed up in the final paragraph of Lyon's memo:

"The objective of the first bound should therefore be restricted to occupying the ground that is won by the artillery."

The last phrase, "occupying the ground that is won by the artillery", suggests that there was a belief in an almost empirical relationship between the weight of shell dropped on a given zone of enemy occupation and the results achieved in terms of death, destruction and the collapse of enemy morale. If sufficient heavy guns with an sufficient supply of shell could be brought to bear on the German lines, so this line of thinking went, then success was almost inevitable. And now, of course, the British Army had at its disposal more guns and more ammunition than at any time in its history. What was now needed was a calculation to show how much ground could be saturated with sufficient high explosive to guarantee the results required. The resulting slice of territory would then have been "won by the artillery" and the infantry would simply be able to advance, mop up and occupy – objective achieved, job done.

Leaving to one side the uncomfortable fact that the Germans at Verdun, even after their murderous initial bombardment, were, three months on, still fighting to gain objectives anticipated with the first few days, this theory of 'artillery conquers, infantry occupies' had taken such a strong grip on Allied planners that an unreal sense of optimism permeated down through layer after layer of the Army, from GHQ down to Brigade, and sometimes further. The consequences for the main Somme offensive was a completely unrealistic expectation of success, and in Haig's mind, even of breakthrough – a rupture of the German lines through which cavalry and then infantry would burst into the open, unspoilt fields of Northern France. At Gommecourt, meanwhile, it led to the belief that a realistic plan was a pincer movement in which two Divisions would sweep across four lines of German defences before joining hands behind the village and park, thereby capturing all the men trapped within. This was a time when, during a battle, communications between a battalion's headquarters and its men on the other side of No Man's Land was at best slow and at worst impossible. The idea, therefore, that two Divisions, attacking independently but each dependent for their success on the other also achieving their objectives, could somehow co-ordinate their actions in such a move was asking a lot of planning and execution and, in addition, would demand a huge slice of good luck. Once the infantry went 'over the top' control of the attack would be very much out of the hands of the Generals and their Staffs. The more so at Gommecourt as it was clear there were no reserves with which to either reinforce success or bolster failure. It would, therefore, be up to the men of each Division involved to succeed with a plan that was timed to the minute and in which any delays or setbacks on one front would be equally disastrous on the other.

***

AWAY FROM THE REFINED CALM of Lyon's room at the chateau in Pas, the bombardment, when it hit at 12.30 a.m., was sudden, heavy and unexpected. It fell mainly on 'A' and 'B' Companies of the 1/1st Londons on the right of the British line near to the Hebuterne to Puisieux Road. The Lewis gun post there was struck and gun and team rendered hors de combat. For two hours, fountains of black smoke and flashes of orange fire smothered the trench line with the men of the 1/7th Middlesex now cowering under its weight. To add to the scrambling panic, gas shells were thudding dully into the soil around them. Men were transfixed by indecision; run to avoid the shelling or pause to pull on the gas mask? Could a moment's hesitation be fatal? When they were done, the German gunners would have set to breakfast in their dug outs and bunkers. In the British lines, the call for stretcher-bearers was a desperate clamour as men dug frantically to free their buried mates or tried to staunch the pulsing flows of blood. Nine men died where they stood or in the nearby Aid Post[i]. Later that day, their bodies were taken to be buried in the ever-growing cemetery on the south side of Hebuterne village. Thirteen more were wounded and another gassed. Fortunately for the gassed man, the shell filling was tear gas not poison. It was a very fine sliver of silver in a dark, funereal cloud.

The German gunners had already got their hand in earlier in the day with a battering of C/281st Brigade's battery position in front of Sailly. Between 9.00 a.m. and 11.45 a.m. about 200 5.9 in. high explosive shells had blanketed the gun pits, damaging one gun and the dugouts. So severe was the pounding that the whole battery position was moved back further down the road towards Sailly. Lt. Nathan, BSM Bush and Sgt. Bath did well to keep the battery nearly in one piece and organised the withdrawal to the new position. Apart from the damage and the hard work involved the unit was lucky to avoid any casualties but the Hun artillery had made a clear point. They were not to be taken lightly.

---

[i] The men of the 1/1st London Regt (Royal Fusiliers) who died on Tuesday, 16th May 1916 were all buried in Hebuterne Military Cemetery. They were:
118 Pte Horatio Walter Baron, 'B' Coy., aged 26. He was the son of Horatio Walter and Rebecca Baron and the husband of Dorothy May Baron of 73, Harrison St., Gray's Inn Rd., London. He was a native of Clerkenwell, London. grave II. I. 1.
4599 Pte William Edward Buckland, aged 23. He was the son of John and Ellen Buckland of Charlbury, Oxon and lived in Brentwood in Essex. grave II. I. 4.
1977 Pte Frederick Thomas Charles, A Coy., aged 19. He was the son of Frederick and Emma Charles of 43, Mortimer Rd., Kensal Rise, London. grave II. I. 7.
4151 Pte James Coutts, A Coy., aged 19. He was the son of Hendry Smellie Coutts and Louise Coutts of 3, William St., Hampstead Rd., London. grave II. G. 4.
4775 Pte Sydney Arthur Coventry, aged 21. He was the son of Henry George and Emily Jane Coventry of 38, Ackroyd Rd., Honor Oak Park, London. grave II. I. 2.
4516 Pte Joseph William Gutteridge of Hackney. grave II. I. 5.
2237 Pte Joseph Henry Hall of St Pancras. grave Sp. Mem. 1.
1365 Pte Wilfred Lawrence Rowe, aged 21. He was the son of Henry and Isabella Rowe of 122, King's Rd., Camden Town, London. grave II. H. 3.
3547 L/Cpl Christopher Stoddard of Finsbury. grave II. G. 3.

In the morning, the men of the 1/3rd completed their cleaning up at Bayencourt, checked their kit and got ready to move forward. At Sailly, the 1/8th Middlesex did the same. By 6.00 p.m., the battered trenches of the 1/1st Londons had been taken over by the 1/8th Middlesex and the 1/3rd Londons had occupied the trenches and billets of the 1/7th Middlesex on the left wing of the divisional position. In the evening twilight, the subdued members of 'A' and 'B' Companies of the 1/1st marched back to their new billets in Sailly, their cushy life in reserve of just a few days ago an increasingly distant memory.

Wednesday, 17th May 1916
Third Army weather report: Fine and warm

THE NEXT FEW DAYS were spent in the routine monotony of life behind the lines. Training and fatigues, fatigues and training; the hours crawled past. Scattered across the rolling, green countryside groups of men in khaki were marching for the sake of marching, sticking sand bags with sharpened bayonets, straining and grunting through special 'Swedish' PE drills. Sergeant Majors and their acolytes screamed instructions, exhorted men to greater efforts and instructed men to 'kill' the sandbags as if they really meant it. Elsewhere, men dug as if their lives depended on it. Shallow trenches for cables in the rear areas, six foot deep trenches for deeper cabling towards the front, communication trenches, fire trenches, dug outs, gun emplacements, roads, railways - there was no end of the need to dig. Others were loading and unloading, stacking and re-stacking from lorries and trains and wagons. Artillery shells and charges, small arms ammunition, hand grenades, mortar shells, barbed wire (various), wooden stakes and metal pickets, spades, picks, axes, tinned foods, powdered foods, iron rations, medicines, splints, dressings - there was an almost endless list of stores and a seemingly endless supply of them to shift. There were few breaks in the schedule for the men to enjoy themselves and relax. On the 17th, the London Scottish organised a brigade sports day for the 168th Brigade at St Amand, and on the next day, the Kensingtons confirmed their sporting supremacy with a 3-1 win over the Scottish in a well-supported football match. And the officers of the Kensingtons weren't finished yet. On Friday the 19th, they took on and beat the Brigade H.Q. at cricket, making them unbeaten in all sports played.

The British were not the only ones reinforcing their positions. On the night of the 16th/17th May sixteen guns from three batteries of the 20th Reserve Field Artillery Regiment took up position to be followed by another six guns on the following night. Eight of these guns were placed in three neighbouring emplacements either side of a trench to the north east of Essarts. From south to north, the 2/20th Battery placed two guns in Position 506; and 1/20th Battery located two in Position 507 and another four in Position 505. A short distance to the south east along the aptly named Artillerie Graben, 2/20th dug in its remaining four field guns. To the north, mid-way between Ferme de Quesnoy and the corner of Adinfer Wood, 8/20th Battery placed four guns in Position 500b. On the night of the 17th/18th a fourth battery of the 20th R.F.A.R, the 3/20th, brought its guns up to two battery positions, 501 and 530, opposite Hannescamps. They key to the positioning of all of these batteries was that they would be in position to fire, in enfilade, the length of the 46th Division's front and these guns, supported by those of the 111th Division hidden away in Adinfer

Wood, would play a key role in the defence of Gommecourt Wood when the attack took place.

In all, these guns represented a significant addition to the artillery defences of the 2nd Guard Reserve Division but they also helped to reinforce the artillery build up taking place south of Bucquoy that would be used against both the 31st Division at Serre and the 56th Division at Gommecourt. Already, two batteries of the 104th Field Artillery Regiment, the 1st and the 3rd, had been able to move south to new positions covering both of these division's fronts. More would follow as the 20th R.F.A.R continued to move its batteries into the positions in the woods and valleys to the east of Gommecourt. There they would find a considerable number of other batteries with guns with a wide variety of calibres:

- In Position 1, on the edge of Adinfer Wood, was half a battery of the 5/2nd Guard Foot Artillery Regiment;
- In Position 6, just east of the field guns of the 1/20th R.F.A.R, were the 15cm howitzers of the 3rd Battalion of the 2nd Bavarian Landsturm Foot Artillery Regiment;
- Position, or Stellung, 7 just to the south was home to the captured Russian 15cm howitzers of the 706th Foot Artillery Battery;
- The 9cm guns of the 692nd Foot Artillery Battery were dug in at Stellung 509, 1,000 yards east of Essarts; and finally,
- In and about Rettemoy Farm, in Stellung 513, were five captured Belgian field guns.

The positioning of all of these guns was significant. With the German High Command still convinced that any British attack was likely to fall north of Gommecourt, perhaps at Monchy, these guns could be employed to help repulse any such attack from that direction was well as anything aimed at Gommecourt. And these would not be the only artillery reinforcements to arrive in the 2nd Guard Reserve Division sector. More would come in June, making the defences, already strong, stronger still.

Thursday, 18th May 1916
Third Army weather report: Very fine and warm

BACK IN HÉBUTERNE the 167th Brigade had claimed what the 56th Divisional History described as 'first blood'. At 11.30 p.m. on the night of the 18th May, a German patrol approached the British wire at the end of No. 3 sap to the left of Y sector, a position held by the 1/3rd Londons. In the front line the local commander, Capt. Bernard Christmas, was enjoying a late evening meal with Capt. Fripp, the C.O. of X56 Trench Mortar Battery. They were chatting away by candle light in Christmas's dugout when a sergeant came to tell him that a brief but vicious firefight was ongoing in the sap head. Buckling on his revolver, Christmas excused himself, promising to be back in a few minutes. The next Fripp saw of his host was when he was rushed past on a stretcher bleeding badly from severe stomach wounds inflicted by a German grenade. The clash had left two casualties on either side. One wounded and one dead German warrant officer, identified as being from the 169th Regiment of the 52nd Division, were later brought into the British lines by a patrol. Capt. Christmas and the wounded German officer with whom he had fought in single combat were rushed to the nearest Aid Post and treated as best as the orderlies could, but they were both in need of more specialist attention than they could offer. Taken on stretchers to the Advanced Dressing Station at the rear of Hebuterne they were placed carefully in an ambulance. Then the long and painful journey across the bumpy French roads started. The plan would have been to get them to the care and expertise of one of the Casualty Clearing Stations at Doullens, twenty kilometres away. Both men survived for less than half the journey, dying in or near Henu, the H.Q. of the 56th Division.

Chaplain Bickersteth conducted the ceremony twelve hours later, laying to rest Capt. Christmas[i] and the German officer in the same cemetery. Both men were buried with full military honours with the escort accompanying both Englishman and German to their graves. For some of the escort, men from Capt. Christmas's company, it was all too much as Bickersteth recalled:

"Two lads in the escort found the whole thing too much for them. I think they belonged to the Captain's company, but they collapsed before the end of the service." [17]

Capt. Christmas's grave still looks along the line of the sixteen other British soldiers whose last resting place this is. His epitaph reads: "There is no death, the stars go down to rise upon another shore."

Friday, 19th May 1916
Third Army weather report: Very fine and warm

Saturday, 20th May 1916
Third Army weather report: Very fine and warm.

THE 167TH BRIGADE SPENT another three days in the trenches. Thankfully, they were quiet with little shelling and only some sporadic machine gun fire. At night, the 1/3rd sent out patrols into No Man's Land. A favourite area to investigate was a crooked hedge lying equidistant from the British front lines and the German trenches around Gommecourt Park. Its shape gave it its name - the Z Hedge. Most nights, about 9.00 p.m., a patrol would move cautiously out of the British lines and creep silently down the slope towards the line of bushes. They would stay out in No Man's Land for an hour or two before slipping back through a gap in the wire into the sanctuary of the trenches.

For the battalions behind the lines digging was the order of the day, for day after day. So great was the demand for labour that on the 20th, every man of the 1/4th Londons, from the front line infantry to the bandsmen and battalion transport were sent out digging. Digging communication trenches, digging dugouts, digging cable trenches, digging, digging, digging.

---

[i] Capt. Bernard Lovell Christmas, 1/3rd London Regt (Royal Fusiliers), died on Friday, 19th May 1916, aged 23. Born on 23rd December 1892, and was the younger son of Mrs. S. F. Christmas of 26 Queen's Road, Beckenham and the late Mr. A. G. Christmas of 'Tankerton', Clapham Park, London. He was educated at the Abbey School, Beckenham and Repton and joined the Artists' Rifles in August 1914. He was commissioned in November 1914 into the 4/3rd Londons and went with them to Malta, Sinkat in the Sudan and Gallipoli. He was invalided home in October 1915 having been gazetted Captain the previous August. He arrived in France in March 1916. He is buried in Henu Churchyard. [*Additional source*: Dick Flory: Repton School Register, 1922; Repton School Register, 1933; Old Reptonian War Register, 1914-1919; Artists Rifles Regimental Roll of Honour and War Record, 1914-1919]

Sunday, 21ˢᵗ May 1916
Third Army weather report: Very fine and warm

ON THE 21ˢᵀ it was all change. The battalions of the 167ᵗʰ Brigade were relieved from the positions they had held for over two weeks. On the left, the London Rifle Brigade relieved the 1/3ʳᵈ Londons. The L.R.B. and the Queen Victorias had left Halloy in the early morning of the 20ᵗʰ, arriving in temporary billets in St Amand at 10.00 p.m. that night. They completed their journey in searing heat the following day, losing a man to shelling within hours of their arrivalⁱ. Two companies of the L.R.B. went straight into the front line. The other two, plus two from the Q.V.R.s found billets in Hebuterne and the Keep at the western end of the village. The remainder of the Q.V.R. stayed in Sailly along with the battalion headquarters. On the right, the Kensingtons relieved the 1/8th Middlesex. On the extreme right, where the trenches cut across the Hebuterne to Puisieux Road, 'A' Company under Major Dickens occupied W47 and W48 sectors. Two Lewis guns were positioned in the trenches to help ward off any intrusion from the lines opposite. To their left, in W49 and W50 sectors, 'B' Company, Capt. Whitty, with another pair of Lewis guns settled down to 'enjoy' life in the front line. Behind them were two platoons each of 'C' Company (Capt. Ware) in Warwick trench and 'D' Company (Capt. Taggart) in the Biron dug outs. The other four platoons were billeted in the village and the Keep.

Across the whole divisional area, it was like a giant game of musical chairs as battalions chased one another from one village to another. The 1/3ʳᵈ and the 1/1ˢᵗ Londons made their way to new billets in St Amand where they would be based for the rest of the month. The 1/2ⁿᵈ Londons had left Halloy on the 19ᵗʰ and were now at Souastre, just down the road from the other two City of London regiments. To take their place, the London Scottish had, at long last, been relieved of their digging duties and had been packed off along with the Rangers to the Halloy huts to start the process of rehearsing the forthcoming attack. There they joined up with the Westminsters who had been at Halloy since the 6ᵗʰ May and who would stay there until the end of the month. As ever, the cooks and their cookers trundled along behind the ranks of marching men, ready to supply tea on the line of march (if circumstances allowed). For the cooks of the London Scottish, home for the next twelve days was to be an orchard in which to cook and a nearby barn for sleeping accommodation. Facilities here were poor and every day, the water carts had to undertake three six-mile round trips to the nearest water supply. To add to the men's irritation, some of the cookers were taken away to be repaired (presumably in readiness for the big advance to come) and cooking was done over "a trench fire made with iron bars and bricks"¹⁸ – no easy task with the unseasonably inclement weather conditions.

Although a long way from the front and apparently well out of harm's way, the Westminster's had suffered a steady toll from sickness and trench foot which wore away at their strength. By the end of the month, 10% of the battalion strength of 714 (at 1ˢᵗ May) had reported sick for one reason or another. Thankfully, though, the battalion's numbers were made up by a draft of 10

ⁱ 9410 Rfn Cecil Thomas Hugh Myddelton, 1/5ᵗʰ London Regt (London Rifle Brigade), died of wounds on Sunday, 21ˢᵗ May 1916, aged 21. He was the son of Mr. R. F. and Mrs. A. C. K. Myddelton of Colne Mead, Rickmansworth, Herts and a native of St. Margarets, Twickenham. He is buried in St. Amand British Cemetery, grave I.A.6.

officers and 223 men from the 2/2nd Londons who had seen service in the Dardanelles.

Halloy may not have been shelled, gassed or machine-gunned by the enemy but it was still a less than healthy place to be - at least, that is, until the last few days of the month when the weather turned with a welcome hot and sunny interlude. A letter from 1681 Rifleman Wally Mockett to his chum Charlie Miller back at 23 Wandle Road, Upper Tooting, South London, written at this time, also shows how those with initiative could turn even the most inhospitable locations into a haven of serenity and sanity:

"We have had a very nice time for the last seven days. We have a mess of our own (there are six of us that run it), we pay the good lady of the house 17 francs a week between us. For that amount, she lets us have a room in which we can have our meals and she lets us use her crockery. In the evenings we borrow a gramophone and about fifty records, very good ones, then we sit in the garden and put the gramophone on a table and then we put on the records. In this way we have some decent evenings. The weather has been lovely, it is very hot. I think I prefer the heat to the rain."[19]

The 1/4th Londons had the shortest move of all, a two kilometres saunter down the lane from Souastre to Bayencourt. But, by the evening of the 21st, the rotation was complete and, with but a couple of exceptions, the battalions would stay where they were until the end of the month. For some, the next few days would be the most difficult and dangerous time they had experienced so far in 1916. And it all revolved around a plan. A plan that General Hull and his staff had been mulling over for some weeks.

Plate 10 56th Division's H.Q. at Henu

When the attack came, a number of problems would face the attacking troops. Of most concern to the senior officers was the distance between the opposing front lines. At its widest, No Man's Land was some 700 metres across. The ground was open and devoid of cover and it gently sloped forward from either front line into a gentle valley across which the British troops would have to toil.

Gen. Snow, VII Corps, and Major General Hull, C.O. 56ᵗʰ Division, determined that a new front line trench would have to be dug some 3-400 metres in advance of the existing line. This would still leave No Man's Land wider than they would have liked but, with the time and manpower available, this was the best they could achieve. The question was: how to dig this line as quickly as possible without incurring heavy casualties?

Hull's solution was a bold initiative, one so out of character with the usual cautious approach to such problems that its sheer audacity might catch the enemy unawares and ill-prepared to respond. On the other hand, the plan proposed exposing a complete brigade to enemy fire without cover in the middle of No Man's Land over three nights. There was clear potential for disaster, but Hull saw no other way forward if the new trench line was to be ready in time for the proposed assault on 29ᵗʰ June. In the drawing room of the magnificent 17ᵗʰ Century chateau on the western edge of the otherwise unprepossessing village of Henu, Hull and his staff set to the task of planning the operation. A start date was fixed of Wednesday, 25ᵗʰ May (for outline of proposed trench digging see map on page 99).

Monday, 22ⁿᵈ May 1916
Third Army weather report: Very hot in the morning. Rained and cooler in the afternoon.

THE ROTATION of the battalions around the 21ˢᵗ May had been done to allow the plan's participants to be in place. The job of digging the new trench fell to the men of the 167ᵗʰ Brigade. They had not been selected to go over the top during the attack and so the potentially dangerous task of digging the new line fell to them. Their withdrawal from the front line did not, therefore, signal any lessening in their workload. The 1/1ˢᵗ and 1/3ʳᵈ Londons had both withdrawn to St Amand on the 21ˢᵗ, arriving at 8.00 p.m., and the following day they immediately set to practising the various tasks required - as if they had never dug or wired a trench before in their lives! The difference was though, that the operation to dig the new trench was to take place in the middle of the night. As far as was possible, it was to be done silently, and, rather than a few men of a working party working on a short stretch of trench, there would be some 3,500 troops involved digging a length of trench nearly two kilometres long to which had to be added communication trenches, each 300 metres long.

Cover for the operation was to be supplied principally by the London Rifle Brigade on the left, with the Kensingtons keeping look out on the far right of the line. As the 167ᵗʰ Brigade practised, these two battalions prepared for the dig and actively patrolled No Man's Land at night. German shelling on the 22ⁿᵈ was intermittent, a few 77mm shrapnel shells sent over to keep British heads down.

In his billet, Pte Cecil Bryden of the London Scottish was again writing to his mum. Concerned for her youngest son's well being she had sought out and purchased a body shield in the hope that it might protect him in any fighting to come. Cecil was happy enough to receive it, even if he felt that such assistance would not be needed:

"....I received the shield OK and was very surprised at its neatness and the lightness of same... the fellows think it will be very serviceable. At the same time I think it rather improbable that it will be called upon to prove its toughness, but one never knows."[20]

But Cecil had more to report on than the receipt of his new shield. Capt. Lindsay, 'B' Company's O.C., had conducted a little research study into the make up and plans of some of his men:

"Today we were asked the following questions by our company commander:

Who came from an office (70 out of 82)
Who proposed to go back to the office after the war (60 out of 82)
Who proposed to go to Canada   )
Who proposed to go to Australia   ) 10
Who proposed to go to East Africa   )
We wonder why? So you see, our battalion is 80% Commercial, I wonder if this means anything?"

Lindsay's little study is revealing and shows how much regiments like the London Scottish had drawn upon well-educated white collar workers when the need came to top up the ranks on the outbreak of war.

Tuesday, 23ʳᵈ May 1916
Third Army weather report: Fine, cooler.

THE NEXT DAY the trench mortars joined in with a few ineffective bombs. Casualties were restricted to one unlucky member of the L.R.B.[i] killed and six others wounded during a patrol near the Z Hedge.

Wednesday, 24ᵗʰ May 1916
Third Army weather report: Cooler. Rain in the afternoon.

THIS MORNING was the Corps headquarters conference which so alarmed Lt. Col. Home, GSO1 of the 46ᵗʰ Division, that he recorded in his diary:

"Old Snow very fussy and making points of things we had already done, but he must be humoured."[21]

Third Army was, appropriately, taking an interest in the planning of the attack and had asked VII Corps to forward a break down of the works being put in hand by the two attacking Divisions. In response, VII Corps forwarded a paper, GCR 237/19, which listed the details of the enormous workload being undertaken. The contents of the note were listed under six headings:

1. Reconnaissance and digging of sections of enemy trenches to be attacked, for practice purposes -
   a. Ground in the back portion of the Corps Area has been requisitioned near Lucheux and Halloy and sections of German 1ˢᵗ Line system of trenches have been marked out and are being dug for practicing the troops taking part in the operations. The digging of these trenches was begun on 22ⁿᵈ May and will be completed by 27ᵗʰ instant;
   b. One Brigade of 46ᵗʰ and one of 56ᵗʰ Divisions at a time is billeted in the back area to dig and practise on these trenches.
2. Organization of trenches for attack:
   a. Main communication trenches leading up to the front line are being deepened. Dumps in the forward lines and the digging of assembly trenches have not yet been started.

---

[i] 1658 Rfn Percy Randolph Smith, 1/5ᵗʰ London Regt (London Rifle Brigade), of Woodford, East London, died on Tuesday, 23ʳᵈ May 1916. He is buried in Hebuterne Military Cemetery, grave IV. D. 1.

3. Signal Service:

   a. A Corps scheme for buried cable lines has been prepared to serve both infantry and artillery requirements, and the work of digging 6' trenches to take the wires is .5 completed. This main system of cables includes all main lines as far forward as Advanced Infantry Brigade Headquarters or roughly to within from 800 yards to 1000 yards of our present front line trenches.

4. Artillery preparations. Divisional artillery:

   a. Of the 20 new battery positions to be prepared 17 are .5 dug.

   b. Ammunition dug-outs for 800 rounds per gun are under construction.

5. R.E. arrangements:

   a. Water supply principally at Hebuterne and Foncquevillers is being increased both by pipe and well supply. (The well) at Foncquevillers has been surveyed but not commenced;

   b. 6000 additional hut shelters have been erected in the area Henu-Souastre-Humbercamp;

   c. Position of forward dumps for tools for Labour battalions for rapid repair of roads, in event of an advance, selected also for forward dumps of road metal.

6. Administrative:

   a. Roads. Considerable improvements carried out and new lorry roads opened. Work proceeding on certain tracks and deviations required and also on sidings to enable horse transport to be temporarily parked off roads in event of traffic congestion;

   b. Divisional refilling points prepared which are now ready for reception of ammunition. Dumping of ammunition up to the limited amounts sanctioned by Third Army now in progress;

   c. Work on railway yard and road for advanced railhead at La Bazeque commenced;

   d. Proposals regarding Decauville[i] line submitted and work commenced;

   e. Medical. Position of all Advanced Dressing Stations, Main Dressing Stations and Field Ambulances settled. Hut shelters erected at two different positions each for one Field Ambulance for use during operations.

In addition, the paper also listed other matters still in the planning stage. There would be a need for the creation of huge dumps for food, water and ammunition, barbed wire cages for the large number of prisoners of war that were anticipated and the infantry would also be needed in large numbers to help with the construction of the numerous gun positions required by the heavy and field artillery batteries. In all the workload for the next five weeks was huge and the men would have little or no time to rest up before going into action.

***

AT THE SHARP END today was a busier one all round. All over the divisional area, drafts of reserves were arriving from England and elsewhere; some fresh

---

[i] A Decauville was a narrow gauge light railway used to bring stores, ammunition, etc., close to the front line. Both sides used these extensively with one German line running into the rear of Gommecourt Wood. An example of this sort of train exists and can be ridden at the south end of the Somme. It is called the 'P'tit train de la Haute-Somme' and it, and the Narrow Gauge Railway Museum, can be found at Froissy, 3 km South of Bray-sur-Somme

and untried troops others, like the men from the 2/2ⁿᵈ Londons, with experience of fighting the Turks at Gallipoliⁱ. Not all went to their brother battalions and for some there was acute frustration. Though they greeted 130 men from the 2/4ᵗʰ London Regt on 24ᵗʰ May, the battalion also had to look on with some annoyance when another 100 men from their second line battalion marched past en route to the Kensingtons. Things would look up, though, when eight officers from the 2/4ᵗʰ arrived, two of them, Capts Arthur and Stanham, veterans of the mobilisation of August 1914.

German machine guns joined the artillery and mortars in giving the new arrivals an unwelcome greeting. Overall, casualties on the 24ᵗʰ were marginally worse than the day before. Two 19-year old riflemen from the L.R.B. were killedⁱⁱ and six wounded along with two fusiliers of the 1/4ᵗʰ Londons and five men of the Kensingtons.

That night, the L.R.B. scouted the Z Hedge. It was to be incorporated into the new front line and it was important that there were no concealed German outposts that might disrupt the coming operations. At 1.30 on the morning of the 25ᵗʰ, the L.R.B.'s Intelligence Officer reported the Hedge clear of the enemy and a party of fifteen men, led by Lt. Clode-Baker, crept forward to occupy it. Before they went, the Lieutenant checked with each man that all maps, papers and personal letters had been left behind. There should be nothing on their person that might help German Intelligence deduce the reasons for their presence in the vicinity of Hebuterne. The Lieutenant and his men would now spend a damp and anxious 16 hours lying behind a low bank with just scrubby bushes for cover, ready to deny the Hedge to any German patrol rash enough to approach to near.

Thursday, 25ᵗʰ May 1916
Third Army weather report: Fairly fine. Rained in the evening.

THE BATTALIONS of the 167ᵗʰ Brigade had now spent two nights practising for the task in hand. One of these men was Private W. Miller of 'C' Company, 1/1st Londons. He was an old Gallipoli-hand and had arrived in Northern France from the Middle East in April. This was to be his first real experience of action on the Western Front. But tonight, it was his turn to lie out in a muddy French field for five hours. His not to reason why.

"Marched five or six miles to St Amand. There are some 9.2 inch guns here. They make a hell of a noise. We are in 'C' Company. We in 'C' Company are to go out covering and wiring some new firing line one day this week. I am on covering. We are practising it tonight at 6. Went out this evening and laid in field from 8 to 1. Came home and got in just as it got light. Slept till 10."[22]

ⁱ The drafts were: 110 other ranks from the 2/16ᵗʰ Londons, 150 other ranks from the 2/1ˢᵗ Londons, 130 other ranks from the 2/4ᵗʰ Londons, 223 other ranks from the 2/2ⁿᵈ Londons joined 1/16ᵗʰ Londons and 200 other ranks 2/2ⁿᵈ Londons joined the 1/12ᵗʰ Londons. A draft of 78 other ranks joined the 1/9ᵗʰ Londons on the 23ʳᵈ.

ⁱⁱ 1256 Rfn Eric Alfred White, 1/5ᵗʰ London Regt (London Rifle Brigade), died on Wednesday, 24ᵗʰ May 1916, aged 19. He was the son of Mr. and Mrs. A. C. White of 93, Plough Rd., Rotherhithe. He is buried in Hebuterne Military Cemetery, grave IV. D. 3. His epitaph reads: "Our deeds still travel with us from afar, and what we have been makes us what we are."

2547 Rfn Ellis George Young, 1/5ᵗʰ London Regt (London Rifle Brigade), died on Wednesday, 24ᵗʰ May 1916, aged 19. He was the only son of George and Emily C. Young of 31, Torbay Rd., Paignton, Devon. He lived in Enfield, Middx. Riflemen White and Young are buried next to one another in Hebuterne Military Cemetery, graves IV.D.3. and IV.D.2.

Practice over, on the afternoon of the 25th May, they marched up from Souastre and St Amand to be ready to move forward as dusk fell. Apart from the four battalions of the Brigade, 'B' Company of the 1/5th Cheshire Regiment, the Divisional pioneers, and the 2/1st London Field Company of the Royal Engineers commanded by Major Johnstone were also to take part.

The plan as devised by General Hull and his staff was this. First, covering parties from various battalions would move out into No Man's Land to ensure no interference from German patrols. Then, on the first night, small parties, each led by a Royal Engineers officer, would mark out the proposed line of the new trench using pegs and jute twine. The following night, the pegging and taping parties would be first out again, to ensure their work had not been interfered with and to mark out more elements of the new position. When this job had been done, the digging parties would emerge from the cover of the trenches to work furiously during the hours of deepest darkness. Behind them, wagons carrying empty biscuit tins were to drive up and down the ruined streets of Hebuterne to drown out, as far as possible, the sounds of the work. The work was scheduled to run over three nights with the first night dedicated solely to the task of marking the new lines. What concerned senior officers most was the reaction of the Germans when they saw the results of the digging. It was impossible to conceal. The white chalk spoil alone would betray the activity and, it was thought, ensure a high level of retaliation during the day and of interference during the night. Thankfully, the pilots of the R.F.C. had achieved a fair degree of air superiority over the front lines and it was hoped that a lack of aerial observation would prevent the German artillery accurately registering the new trench. But all they could do now was cross their fingers and hope for the best. One way or another the trench had to be dug if the planned attack was to have any hope of success. They had devised their plan and would have to stick with it, although many, like 2nd Lt. Heald of the Cheshires, faced the forthcoming days with trepidation:

"I am going with 'B' Company to help dig a new trench in front of our present line some 400 yards nearer the German trench. I think there will be something like 5,000 men out. If the Germans spot us there will be hell to pay.[23]"

At about 5.30 p.m., the covering parties started up the long communication trenches towards the front line. Capt. Somers-Smith of the L.R.B. led a party of 110 men from 'A' and 'B' Companies whilst other parties from the 1/3rd Londons, led by 2nd Lts. Knight and Maunsell, and 80 men from the 1/1st Londons under 2nd Lt. Campbell also started through the muddy trenches. As they left for their allotted posts, thirty men under 2nd Lt. Pogose relieved Clode-Baker's contingent at the Z Hedge. They would be relieved by another 15-man team from the L.R.B., led by Lt. Bromiley[i] at 1.30 a.m., thereby continuously occupying the Hedge. In the front line, ready to reinforce if required, were Lt.

---

[i] Lt. Bertram Bromiley, 1/5th London Regt. (London Rifle Brigade), was educated at Colfes Grammar School between 1894 and 1898. He joined the 15th London Regt (Civil Service Rifles) on 30th August 1914 and was commissioned into the 3/5th London Rifle Brigade on 16th January 1915. He went to France on 24th December 1915, returning to England on 5th July 1916. He was Assistant Adjutant between 5th May and 5th July 1916. He returned to France in May 1917 having been promoted Captain and briefly commanded the battalion in September 1917. He was gassed at Moeuvres in 1917 and Mentioned in Despatches in May 1918. [*Additional sources: Dick Flory: Colfe's Grammar School and The Great War 1914-19*]

Wills and an additional twenty men. It had been determined that this feature had to be denied to the enemy throughout the exercise, by which time it would be incorporated into the new lines.

Behind the covering parties came the pegging and taping parties, usually of two officers and three or four other ranks. The line to be marked out had been organised into four sectors from right to left - 'A', 'B', 'C' and 'D'. The right flank of A sector rested on the Hebuterne to Puisieux Road and ran to a point 100 yards east of the fork in the Hebuterne to Bucquoy Road. This area was the responsibility of the 1/1st Londons. 'B' sector carried on from this point some 400 yards north west to map reference K.10.b.4.6. and was the sector where the 1/8th Middlesex would work. Next came the 1/3rd London's sector. This carried on from the left flank of sector 'B' and ran for 450 yards to the Hebuterne to Gommecourt Road. From here, the new line to be dug by the 1/7th Middlesex ran for 690 yards from the road along the zigzag line of the Z Hedge to the head of No. 4 sap near the north end of Hebuterne village (see map page 99).

Major F D Samuel was in overall charge of the 1/3rd Londons taping party which was led by Capt. Arthur Agius and Lt. H A Scott[i] R.E. Six days before the first trench marking started, 2nd Lt. Scott, had already spent several hours out in No Man's Land surveying the area to be dug. He had concluded that the new line had to be slightly further up the slope of the shallow valley, i.e. nearer the existing British trenches. His reason was sound, the ground further out looked liable to waterlogging, but the effect was to widen No Man's Land on the 169th Brigade's front to nearly 450 yards compared with 300 yards in the 168th Brigade's area. When the taping party arrived at the front, they found that men from 'B' Company of the L.R.B. covering party had cut five gaps through the British wire as the plan required. It was about 10.00 p.m. on a particularly dark and wet night when they left the security of the trenches. Capt. Agius has left a description of that night's activities, which is reproduced in Lyn Macdonald's 'Somme'[24]:

> "Our lines were about eight hundred yards from the Germans. We … were told we were to go out and build a complete new trench system, four hundred yards in front and four hundred yards nearer the Germans, which sounded absolute madness. So, I went out with our Brigade-Major [*sic*] one night from a forward sap and we went on for a quarter of a mile, just the two of us, with a soldier carrying a sandbag full of chalk. After taking various measurements and compass directions, we dumped all this chalk and made a cairn of it. (It was chalk country, so it wouldn't be noticed.) We covered the German side with grass so that they shouldn't see the cairn and then we had to work to our left until we came to a road that ran out of our lines (the Hebuterne to Gommecourt Road). The landmark there was a hawthorn bush that was in full blossom (this was the middle of May) and that made a very convenient point for a marker. It took some doing to lay out a complete front line with traverses and so on. But, in the hours of darkness, we marked all this out with string and pegs."

---

i Lt. Henry Arthur Scott, 512th (1/1st London) Field Coy., Royal Engineers, died on Sunday, 8th April 1917, aged 26. He was the son of Amelia Tanswell Scott of Amison House, East Molesey, Surrey and the late Frederick Scott. He is buried in Agny Military Cemetery, Pas de Calais, France, grave G. 46.

In this sector, the operation was trouble-free[i] and by three in the morning, all the men of the taping and covering parties were back inside the British lines. They then started to work their way back down the sodden and slimy communication trenches towards the relative comforts of their billets in Hebuterne and Sailly.

In 'D' sector, the taping party also worked quietly and effectively without hindrance from any German patrols. 2nd Lt. D E Clerk R.E. was working with the 1/7th Middlesex here and they had the longest stretch of trench to mark out, some 690 yards. On the first night, under the command of the long serving Capt. S. H. Gillett[ii], they successfully marked an extension of 80 yards from the head of No. 4 sap, 650 yards of front line and 40 yards of communication trench before returning to the safety of their lines.

In A sector, on the right, things had not run so smoothly. The taping party of the 1/1st Londons consisted of Lt. J T F Henderson R.E. and 2nd Lts. Johnson and Barr with three other ranks. Accompanied by the covering party, they left Hebuterne via Wood Street for a point in the front line known locally as the Crows Nest at 8.30 p.m. but they met a working party coming down the same communication trench and, in the mud and gathering gloom, were much delayed. They did not arrive at the Crows Nest until midnight, well behind schedule, and there they found to their dismay that the wire was not cut and the covering party, who had pressed ahead in an effort to make up time, were waiting in the British trenches for their arrival. To make matters worse, when 2nd Lt. Campbell and the men of the covering party eventually found a narrow gap in the wire, they ran almost immediately into a German patrol. A brief but savage scrap ensued which left Campbell[iii] and five of his men wounded. Private Miller, clearly a subscriber to the 'What can go wrong, will go wrong' school of soldiering, describes the venture with a combination of impatience and resignation.

"At about five this evening we got orders on covering, to get ready, full pack, destination not known. We marched up to Sailly-au-Bois, the village about two miles behind the line. Went up in drill order almost at once. Rained all time. Went to Hebuterne across open ground where there were a lot of batteries, at last got out into firing line about 10. Waiting in trench to about 11.30. Told we were to go out and cover for pegging out new trench.

---

i The LRB covering party suffered one casualty, Lt. Sawbridge being wounded.

ii Capt. Sydney Harold Gillett M.C. had been an officer since 1911, serving with the Highgate detachment. After serving on the Somme, Capt. Gillett broke down under the strain of operations and returned to the UK where he undertook instructional duties. He was later mentioned by the Secretary of State for War for his valuable services in August 1918. He was awarded the M.C. in January 1916 for his part in covering the retirement of a patrol on 25th August 1915 near Givenchy. A chartered accountant, he was elected Lord Mayor of London in 1958 and was created Baronet of Bassishaw Ward in the City of London, in 1959. Born on 27th November 1890, he died on 21st September 1976, aged 85.

iii 2nd Lt. Walter Stanley Campbell MC, 1/1st London Regt. (Royal Fusiliers) was wounded in the right hand and was evacuated on 3rd June from Calais to Dover. The bullet entered the front of the hand causing a comminuted fracture of the 5th Metacarpal. He was admitted to Princess Henry of Battenberg's Hospital in Hill Street, Mayfair and was declared fit for General Service on 10th August. Born on 29th September 1888, he was the son of Mr. J A and Mrs. Jane Campbell of Toorak, Melbourne, Australia and was educated at Melbourne Grammar School. He lived at 54, Cambridge Terrace near Hyde Park and came to England in order to join up, attesting 6193 Private in the Inns of Court OTC on 13th October 1915. 2nd Lt. Campbell was killed in an attack on Spectrum trench near Le Transloy on Saturday, 7th October 1916. His body was never found and his name is inscribed on the Thiepval Memorial, Pier & Face 9D & 16B. His older brother, 765 Pte, later 2nd Lt. Donald Gordon Campbell, 51st Battalion, Australian Infantry, was killed at Mouquet Farm on 3rd September 1916, aged 31. His body was never found and his name is inscribed on Australian National Memorial at Villers-Bretonneux.

Started to go out and got shot out by German patrol just outside our wire. I had not got outside.

Campbell (Lieutenant) and some three or four wounded. I flopped down in mud and went in again after more messing about, went back to Sailly. Got there about 3.30 or four. Slept till 11. About 4 p.m. shells came over. Ran to a cellar place in back."[25]

Still hoping to be able to achieve something that night, 2nd Lt. Henderson led his party to the head of Woman Street but here, again, there was no gap in the wire and, with dawn breaking, the operation was abandoned for the night with no work done. The casualties were helped down the communication trenches to the battalion Aid Posts and the taping party trudged mournfully back to their distant billets with nothing achieved.

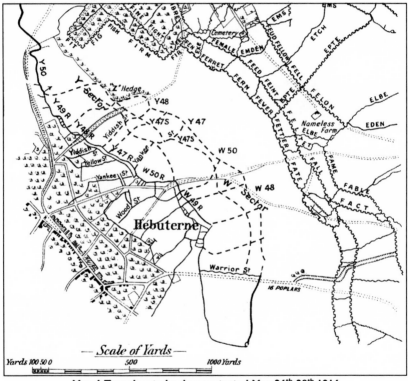

Map 6 Trenches to be dug or started May 26th-28th 1916
Dotted lines indicate main assembly and communication trenches. Another trench called the 'Boyau de Service' was dug immediately behind the new front line trench along its entire length.

The efforts in 'B' sector presented a similarly sorry tale. 2nd Lt. E L Martin of the 2/1st London R.E. had reported to the battalion H.Q. of the 1/8th Middlesex and joined up with their taping party led by Capt. Peake. Their first problem came with the guide supplied to lead them through the maze of trenches that criss-crossed Hebuterne. In a wet and pitch black night, it was easy for even those most familiar with the trench system to mistake a turning and lose their way. The guide did exactly that. When they did find the correct trench, it proved to be the same one being used by the 1/1st Londons - Wood Street. Then, they ran into the same 170 strong working party coming down the line as 2nd Lt. Henderson's unhappy team. They too found the wire uncut on their arrival, three hours later, at the front and signs of a hostile patrol close by. But, Peake and Martin persevered. They worked their way along the trenches until another exit was found but, as they got ready to move out, the men of their covering party were seen retiring up the slope towards the wire and, a few minutes later, the first grey light of dawn could be seen above the German lines to the east.

The first night of the operation had proved a true 'curate's egg'. On the left, everything was ready for the working parties to start digging but, on the right, the taping parties would have to start again from scratch. They would also have to keep their fingers crossed that the Germans had not been alerted to something big happening under their noses. If more large German patrols were found the following night, then the whole operation might be compromised. It was unpalatable food for thought as the men marched back to their daytime billets.

Friday, 26th May 1916
Third Army weather report: Fine, rather cold.

FRIDAY 26TH MAY was to be the first night of the 'big dig'. At 4.00 p.m., the battalions of the 167th Brigade marched out of their 'home' villages and started towards Hebuterne across the plain beyond Sailly. Unfortunately for one of the units not involved in the operation, this large-scale troop movement was spotted from one of two balloons the Germans had up to the rear of Gommecourt. The news of 'enemy activity' was sent down to the artillery and, as the columns arrived at Sailly, a heavy bombardment fell on the village and its surroundings. Sailly was the home of the headquarters of the Queen Victorias and of two of its companies. The battalion history describes the events that followed:

> "Col. Dickins, Major Sampson, Capt. Andrews, the Adjutant, and Capt. Clarke, the M.O., occupied a cottage owned by a couple of ancients, man and wife. They had just finished lunch and were enjoying a smoke or writing letters home when suddenly a flight of shells burst all around the cottage; three fell in the front garden and four others in the back, none of them many yards away. One shell fell about four yards only from the open front door, causing a lot of damage to the cottage, bringing down most of the tiles and chipping the walls with flying fragments, and doing considerable harm to the walls, ceilings, and appointments inside. The dust was so thick that for some time it was impossible to see what had really happened, but when it had settled down a bit it was found that none of the inmates was harmed. This was remarkable, considering the number of pieces of shell and splinters that were flying in all directions. In the village one shell burst by 'D' Company's Sergeants' Mess, killing or wounding four of its members. Sergt. Redgell[i], the sergeant cook, was later found killed in the village."[26]

Private Hawkings of the Queen Victorias was also caught in the strafe:

> "I was startled by four high velocity shells which came shrieking overhead and burst near the church. I hesitated, but had decided to go on when

---

[i] 1541 Sgt Percival John Redgell, 1/9th London Regt (Queen Victoria's Rifles), died on Friday, 26th May 1916. He is buried in Hebuterne Military Cemetery, grave IV.G.3.

several more arrived and burst a little nearer. I then turned to walk back, but quickly broke into a run as shells began bursting all round, filling the air with smoke, bricks and tiles. I pelted up the street, and rushed into my cottage and billet just as a heavy swan shrapnel burst overhead, with a terrific crash. There was no one in the house, but I quickly found my way into a cellar. Then a 5.9 crashed into the garden and the fumes entering by the cellar grating became so stifling that I was obliged to leave it. At that moment the shelling ceased as suddenly as it had begun, and I walked out into the street, where I found an enormous change had been wrought in the five minutes or so since the first shells came over. The walls of some houses had fallen across the pavement into the road, while others were large holes, and over all the buildings clouds of red dust and black smoke rose in the still air. Among the heaps of masonry we found the mutilated bodies of 28 men of whom very few were still alive. The dead included Redgell, the sergeant cook."[27]

The nearest dressing station was the one at Hebuterne and the wounded men were rushed along the track to the rear of the village[i]. It was too late for two of the Sergeants and they were buried next to one another in the fast-growing cemetery at the rear of the village. Another twenty-two members of the battalion were wounded.

The usually 'lucky' 1/7ᵗʰ Middlesex were also caught up in the strafe on Sailly. They had left Souastre at 3 p.m. and were marching through Sailly at 4.30 p.m. when the strafe hit. Although they had lost only three men wounded whilst out digging in No Man's Land the previous night, on this occasion, some distance from the front, they suffered nearly sixty casualties[28] including one of their best scouts, 2381 Pte. John Farleigh[ii].

The infantry were not alone in suffering from this sudden bombardment. Either side of the road were arrayed the field guns and howitzers of the 56ᵗʰ Division's four artillery brigades. For several days they had been harassing the German lines with shrapnel and high explosive and now it was their turn to be caught in a strafe. The results were seen by Pte. Arthur Boyd of the 2/1ˢᵗ London Field Ambulance who were based in Sailly:

"After a vigorous morning's shelling from the enemy, he succeeded in causing casualties on the plain between Sailly and Hebuterne. When I reached the scene with a friend I got my first vision of how ghastly and repulsive a thing is war! We found three of four men buried beneath the debris of timber and corrugated iron which had formed some slight

---

[i] The casualties were
4112 L/Sgt Harold Wilton Stephenson, 1/9ᵗʰ London Regt (Queen Victoria's Rifles), died on Friday, 26ᵗʰ May 1916, aged 30. He was the son of the Rev. W. W. and Emma Stephenson of 29, Garfield Rd., Scarborough. Born in India, he was buried in Hebuterne Military Cemetery, grave IV.G.1.
2673 L/Sgt Frank Hubert Stone, 1/9ᵗʰ London Regt (Queen Victoria's Rifles), died on Friday, 26ᵗʰ May 1916, aged 24. He was the son of Francis R. and Sarah Stone of 33, Vestry Road, Camberwell, London. Segt Stone was educated at Alleyn's School, Dulwich. A keen footballer, he was captain of the Old Silverdalians F.C. He joined the Q.V.R. on the outbreak of war and went to France with the battalion in November, 1914. Capt. Lindsey-Renton wrote to his father: "No cheerier soul could have been found in the British Army. No matter what discomforts or what dangers surrounded him, he was always cheerful, always had a bright smile and a cheerful word for everybody." He is buried in Hebuterne Military Cemetery, grave IV.G.2.
[ii] 2381 Pte John Thomas Farleigh, 1/7ᵗʰ Middlesex Regt., died on 26ᵗʰ May 1916. Aged 23, he was the son of Joel Farleigh of "Le Chalet," Elder Avenue, Wickford, Essex. He is buried in Hebuterne Military Cemetery, grave II.M.2.

protection for the artillerymen. One of these, in great pain, was being extricated, whilst the Field ambulance medical officer was preparing to address the wounds. Close by was another site which sickened me. An artillerymen[i] had been buried deep in the ground beyond hope of recovery but one of his legs fully dressed with boot and puttees projected from a wall of earth."[29]

At about 7.00 p.m., the men of the digging parties again arrived in their assembly positions in and around the village, to be greeted by some light artillery and mortar fire. From 7.30 p.m. onwards, the covering and taping parties started to make their way down the communication trenches towards the front lines. First to leave were the men of the 1/1st Londons under 2nd Lt. Johnson and Capt. Peake's group from the 1/8th Middlesex. They were to dig the new trench on 'A' and 'B' sector and had the furthest to travel from the assembly points in the western end of the village and the most work to complete after the fiasco of the night before. Private Miller of the 1/1st Londons briefly recounted their night's work and a lucky near miss in his diary:

> "Parading about 4.15 to go up for real job this evening. Went over top about 9.15, about dusk. Two parties to stop in trench and hold it tomorrow went out first. They found a German patrol. One shot ensured Germans ran. Two of us wounded -- rifle and bomb. Was just outside our wire when this happened. Went on and got in position by about 10. Were there until about 1.45 - about 11.30 they sent over whizz bangs which burst just behind our new line."[30]

On the left, the men of the 1/3rd Londons started to filter through the five gaps in the wire cut by the L.R.B. the night before at 8.30 p.m. There they were joined by the 'tapers' and 'peggers' of the 1/7th Middlesex who were ready to mark out the new communication trench that was to become Young Street. They had been preceded by the covering parties of an officer, an N.C.O. and ten men who had been told to get as close as possible to the German lines and to bayonet anyone who tried to leave their trenches.

At the same time, a party took over responsibility for the Z Hedge from Lt. Bromiley's chilled and stiff team. Fifteen minutes later, the covering party of the 1/1st Londons set out from the head of Woman Street, their route to the front, to ensure their part of No Man's Land was clear of the enemy. At Lone Tree, a position just to the south of Hebuterne to Bucquoy road, a German patrol was encountered and, as per instructions, they were silently rushed and routed with the bayonet. The action again delayed progress on the right and it wasn't until 9.45 p.m. that the taping parties were able to start work on marking out the new lines.

By this time, on the left, the digging parties of the 1/3rd Londons and 1/7th Middlesex were already in position and at 10.00 p.m. they set to work, the 1/3rd losing one man on their way up the trenches[ii]. The Middlesex men used three trenches to reach No Man's Land: on the right, 'B' Company moved up York

---

[i] The only RFA casualty on this day was 1269 Gnr Harry William Kennard, A Battery, 282nd Brigade, RFA. Aged 23, he was the son of Ernest and Emma Kennard of 74, Sistova Rd., Balham, London. He is buried in Hebuterne Military Cemetery, grave IV.G.5.

[ii] 1423 Pte Harry Reuben Holmes, 1/3rd London Regt (Royal Fusiliers), died on Friday, 26th May 1916. He is buried in Hebuterne Military Cemetery, grave II.R.2.

Street; 'A' and 'C' Companies in the centre proceeded up Yule Street; and on the left, 'D' Company trekked up Yussuf Street. At the front line, a party under Lt. Ashby had marked the exits with white boards and tape. By 10 minutes after ten, all companies were reported as being at work.

But there were problems again on 'B' sector. Peake's small team from the 1/8th Middlesex were at the head of Wood Street by 9.00 p.m. but, unbelievably, the wire was still not cut and it was another two hours before he and 2nd Lt. Martin of the Royal Engineers were out in No Man's Land marking out the trenches to be dug. Digging eventually started at 10.50 p.m. in A sector but it was not until 11.25 p.m. that Capt. Peake led the 1/8th Middlesex out to start digging in 'B'.

Each digging battalion was specially equipped for the night and forty picks and 330 sharpened shovels were brought up from the billets by each one. The sharpened shovels, wrapped around with one of three sandbags the men carried so as to avoid noise, proved to be a great help in starting the digging in near silence. With the ground wet from the continuous rain, the shovels sliced effectively and quietly into the turf beside the white tape that had now been laid alongside the twine to clearly mark the lines to be dug. Behind the digging parties came the carrying and wiring parties. About 100 men per battalion were detailed for these tasks. They were to collect French and barbed wire, screw posts and sandbags from dumps near every gap in the wire. The wiring parties then moved out into No Man's Land in front of the digging parties and started the task of securing the wire defences of the new position. The sandbags were used to build barricades across the three roads that cut through the new trench lines. Capt. Agius describes the scene on the 1/3rd London's front:

> "We taped the whole of this thing out and, as soon as we'd finished running the white tape across it, marking all the traverses and every inch of the line, and every angle and turn, the troops filed in and started to dig like billy-o. We had more than five hundred men out there and we dug that whole length of trench in two nights. What a job that was!"[31]

Whilst the men dug frantically, aware that at any moment they could be scythed down by machine gun fire and slaughtered by shrapnel and high explosive, behind them the plans to cover their activities swung into action. Cartloads of empty biscuit tins were ridden noisily along the cobbled streets of Hebuterne, the rattling designed to smother the sounds of pick and shovel on the chalk sub-soil. Further back, the entire VII Corps heavy artillery along with some 4.5 in. howitzers of the divisional R.F.A. were poised to bring a hurricane of fire down on any German batteries or machine guns that tried to molest the men in No Man's Land. But the night was calm and by 1.30 a.m., the working parties had started to withdraw to their own lines, using the white boards placed near the gaps in the wire as beacons for their safe return.

In general, apart from the delays on the right, the night of the 26th/27th had gone well. In A sector the 1/1st Londons had made a good start on the main trench and Lts. Johnson and Henderson had spent an hour between quarter to one and 1.45 p.m. taping out the line of a support trench. Next door, a large amount of ground had been broken along a long stretch of the new line and 2nd Lt. Martin had spent time reconnoitring the path of a support trench. The 1/3rd Londons in 'C' sector had been lucky. The Royal Engineer officer, 2nd Lt. Scott, had investigated a series of old rifle pits strung out across No Man's Land and had decided that they could be joined up and converted into a new communication trench (Yellow Street), saving the men hours of digging. He had also marked out another communication trench (Yiddish Street) which ran from the head of Sap No. 2 to a point to the east of the Gommecourt Road where the Hawthorn bush was in full bloom. This point was known as the May Bush bank. On the far left, the front line had been started along its whole length and a new 220 yard communication trench (Young Street) had been taped and pegged from No. 3 sap to the Z Hedge. On the 1/7th Middlesex's sector, a complete fire trench had been dug and a double row of French wire strung out along three-quarters of its length.

By 2.30 a.m., all of the men from the covering parties were back inside the wire and by 4.00 a.m. they were back in their billets in Sailly, Hebuterne and St Amand. Behind them were left small parties of men who were to occupy the new trenches and the barricades during the day. Two parties of sixteen men under 2nd Lts. E A Brown[i] and W A Whyman[ii] covered the area of the 1/7th Middlesex's endeavours. On the 1/3rd front, an officer, an N.C.O., ten men and a Lewis Gun plus two telephone operators occupied one post. In the 1/1st London's sector, there were two barricades to man and each one was covered by a party of the same size[iii]. The trenches and barricades they occupied were already of impressive dimensions. The trench had been dug to a depth of three feet and was also three feet wide. The sandbag barricades were three to four feet high, being six feet wide at the base and four feet wide at the top. Furthermore, two thirds of the new line had been wired.

As daylight crept across the landscape, the men in the outposts waited with some trepidation for the reaction of the Germans when they saw the obvious signs of the huge project undertaken. It was not necessary to dig down very far before the chalk was reached and, across the whole Somme battlefield, any new trench was betrayed by the line of chalk spoil that made up the parapet and parados. But German reaction was surprisingly trivial. A few bombs from a heavy minenwerfer plummeted into the thinly held trenches. The odd shell ploughed into the turf as the artillery started to register the new lines. Other than that, their activity was limited to some sporadic longer-range fire. In a tragic irony the 1/3rd Londons, who had stood so exposed for four hours in No Man's Land, were to suffer most of their casualties once back in their quarters at Sailly. A stray shell ploughed into one of the covering party's billets, leaving two men so severely wounded they were immediately sent to the rear. Neither survived[iv].

---

i 2nd Lt. Brown was wounded on 4th July 1916.
ii 2nd Lt. William Arthur Whyman, 1/7th Middlesex Regt., was killed in action on 16th September 1916. He is buried in Combles Communal Cemetery Extension, grave VII. D. 21.
iii The parties were led by Lt. Westlake and 2nd Lt. Selden.
Lt. Geoffrey Arthur Westlake, 1/1st London Regt. (Royal Fusiliers), was killed in an attack on Spectrum trench near Le Transloy on Saturday, 7th October 1916. His body was never found and his name is inscribed on the Thiepval Memorial Pier & Face 9D & 16B. Born on 2nd October 1891, he was the son of Arthur Ulysses Westlake of 19, Hill View Road, Orpington, Kent and lived at 5, Baring Road, Lee, Kent. Educated at Dulwich College, he worked for Samuel Westlake and Sons, a timber merchant. He attested as 355 Private in the Honourable Artillery Company on 22nd February 1909 and was commissioned into the 1/1st Londons on 2nd February 1915. He went to France in October 1915 and was promoted Lieutenant in in December 1915. He was later appointed Battalion Machine Gun Officer.e
iv 1943 Pte James Henry Brown, 1/3rd London Regt (Royal Fusiliers), died of wounds on Saturday, 27th May 1916. A resident of Marylebone, he was the son of Mrs. E. J. Brown of 9, Venables St., Edgware Rd., London. He is buried in St. Amand British Cemetery, grave I. A. 8.

But, in total, the night's work and the shelling of the following day left remarkably few casualties given that for four hours over 3,000 men had been working in the open just a few hundred yards in front of the German lines. Across the whole division, there were 63 casualties for the entire day. For the 1/1ˢᵗ Londons one officer, 2ⁿᵈ Lt. Gibson, was wounded and 21-year old Private Eric Taylorⁱ died of wounds the following day. Another 15 men were wounded. The 'lucky' 1/7ᵗʰ Middlesex lost no-one during the digging and the 1/8ᵗʰ Middlesex just four men wounded.

Saturday, 27ᵗʰ May 1916
Third Army weather report: Fine

AT 9.00 A.M., 2ⁿᵈ LT. MARTIN of the Royal Engineers and Major Blewitt, the Brigade Major of the 167ᵗʰ Brigade, went out to inspect the work in 'B' sector. There had been more problems here than anywhere else and there was some concern about the ability of the 1/8ᵗʰ Middlesex to complete the work in time. By noon, the two officers were back in the Brigade H.Q. to discuss the situation with the Brigadier and his staff. Martin and Blewitt were convinced the work could be completed as long as the arrangements for the night ran smoothly. Access to No Man's Land needed to be assured and aggressive patrolling by the covering party was essential. With these provisos, the conference broke up and the officers went away to complete preparations for the coming night.

For the working troops the day was spent catching up on their sleep, having a decent meal and wondering whether they would be exposed to the dangers of No Man's Land for a third successive night. Private Miller of the 1/1ˢᵗ Londons had struggled back to his billet in Sailly in the early hours:

> "Got to Sailly about three. Tea, breakfast and bed till 11. Wonder if got to be out tonight. More shells over about dinner time. Heard some guns knocked out. Got orders to pack up, thought going back, soon after orders to go in again."[32]

The 167ᵗʰ Brigade's battalions set off as usual in the early afternoon for the journey back to Hebuterne. This time, however, there was even greater concern about how the enemy might react to the sudden overnight appearance of a new trench. It seemed inconceivable to some that they would let the work carry on unmolested and there was an expectation that Saturday night would be vastly more difficult and dangerous than Friday had proved to be. To prevent German aircraft from helping their artillery to register the new lines, the R.F.C. mounted sufficient patrols to prevent any over-flying of the new trenches. Additionally, aerial photographs were forwarded to divisional H.Q. so that General Hull and his staff could see the progress made so far.

For the night's work, the procedure was to be as for the night before, and the battalions paraded behind Hebuterne at about 5.00 p.m. before they set off up the communication trenches to their allotted positions. As before, the covering parties were in full fighting kit with one day's rations. The digging parties carried

---

142 L/Cpl Albert Edward Hulstrom, 1/3ʳᵈ London Regt (Royal Fusiliers), died of wounds on Saturday, 27ᵗʰ May 1916, aged 29. He was the son of Otto Albert and Emma Hulstrom of Hoxton and had served 16 years with the Royal Fusiliers. He is buried in Louvencourt British Cemetery, Somme, France grave Plot I. Row C. grave 44.
ⁱ 4532 Pte Eric Albert Taylor, 1/1ˢᵗ London Regt (Royal Fusiliers), died of wounds on Sunday, 28ᵗʰ May 1916, aged 21. He was the son of James Richard and Elizabeth Alice Taylor. Born at Bolton, he lived in Manor Park, London. He is buried in Hebuterne Military Cemetery, grave II.H.6.

their rifles, loaded with 10 rounds and an additional bandolier of SAA. The wiring parties, given the loads they had to carry, went unarmed. In order to make up for the lost time on the right flank, the 1/1st Londons and the 1/8th Middlesex started to move out into No Man's Land 45 minutes before the left flank battalions. In A sector, the covering party of the 1/1st Londons was at the top of Woman Street by 8.30 p.m. and fifteen minutes later, the covering party passed through the gaps in the wire and spread out across No Man's Land. Lt. Henderson R.E. taped out the line of the new communication trench to be dug and, by 9.45 p.m., the digging parties were ready to start. Capt. Peake and 2nd Lt. Martin had started to tape the new support lines at 9.00 p.m. and, after thirty minutes, Peake returned through the wire to call up the digging parties. Sixty minutes later, they were joined in No Man's Land by the working parties of the 1/3rd Londons and 1/7th Middlesex.

In addition to deepening the front line trench to 4 ft. 6 in. and adding a fire step, the men were also to dig some 600 yards of support trench to a depth of 3 feet, another 1,000 yards of communication trench to a depth of between 2 ft. 6 in. and 4 ft. and finish the existing barricades. 2nd Lt. Martin had also to supervise the building of another barricade where the support line crossed the Bucquoy Road and he and four R.E. sappers stayed with the men of the 1/8th Middlesex to complete the job. Lastly, across the whole length of the new line the wiring parties had to complete their essential task.

The Divisional Pioneers, the 1/5th Cheshires, had the job of improving a communication trench started the night before. For them, the previous night had been relatively quiet. An artillery duel away to the right had covered the noises of digging in their sector and their luck had even extended to the one man hit by a stray bullet being saved by his new Brodie helmet. This night was to be more eventful, however, as 2nd Lt. Heald recorded the next day in his diary:

"Last night we had a much worse time. We had support lines to dig and the top of our communication trench to finish. Fritz was uncannily quiet at first. He let us get well out and then he hailed shrapnel shells and machine gun bullets on us for about ten minutes. The air was one mass of bursting shells. Luckily we had a little cover. I was just spacing our men out to dig when it started. The trench was about two feet deep. We had no one hit which seemed to me absolutely marvellous. Our helmets are splendid. Our men dug like they have never done before... They gave us four or five more of these bursts of fire. I was very lucky the last time. I had picked up a shovel, when they started. The trench was enfiladed. I got down as low as possible and put the shovel in front of me. A shell burst in the air about three yards off and pieces came all round but I was not touched... Everybody got mixed up in the trench and we had a job to sort them out. We got home quite safely after about as exciting a night as I have ever had."[33]

Again, to cover the sound of the digging, the biscuit tins were hurried up and down the lanes of Hebuterne and behind them, the heavy artillery awaited orders to fire at a moment's notice. Every now and then, one of the howitzers sent off a shell into the German lines to distract their attention and provide extra background noise.

Five minutes after the left-hand battalions started to dig a German machine gun started a seemingly idle traverse of the British positions. Shortly after, intermittent shelling started up from field guns dug in north of Puisieux. Again, it was the work of the 1/8th Middlesex in 'B' sector that was most inconvenienced with Capt. H E Martin[i] being amongst those seriously wounded, a shell fragment entering his lung. He was hurried to the No. 19 Casualty Clearing Station where, two days later, Maj. Don conducted a rib resection. He survived the operation to be evacuated to one of the main Hospitals on the coast at Le Treport. He did not survive, dying three week's later, and was buried in the growing cemetery in the town his committal conducted to the keening cries of the swooping and soaring seagulls.

In No Man's Land itself, German patrols were more active than on the previous nights but, whenever encountered, they seemed reluctant to engage the larger British covering parties and they slunk away into the night. To keep German heads down, the heavies lobbed a few shells at the best registered of known targets but, in general, retaliation was restrained so as to avoid an all-out artillery duel. It was the battalions on the right whose work was again the most disrupted by enemy action and, at about 2.00 a.m., as the working parties made their way back through the gaps in the wire, a brief burst of heavy shelling fell amongst the men queuing to get through. Even so, casualties were still mercifully light amongst the 2,500 men who had been digging so earnestly within point blank range of German Mausers, Maxims and Mortars.

Worst hit were the 1/1st Londons in A sector. Private Miller recorded the details with understated brevity:

"While waiting in the end of Woman Street, Col.[34] said got to be done tonight or would be another night (God forbid). Went out and all much same as last night. Bit hotter maybe. Potter[ii] killed and some more casualties, about 40. Got back safely. Slept till 12."[35]

---

[i] Capt. Horace Edmund Martin, 1/8th Middlesex Regt., died of wounds on 19th June 1916. Aged 24 he was the son of John Jeffery and Katherine Wells Martin of Linslade, Bucks., B.A. Cantab. He is buried in Le Treport Military Cemetery, Plot 2. Row O. grave 14.

[ii] 3146 Pte Stanley Edwin Teall Potter, 1/1st London Regt (Royal Fusiliers), died on Saturday, 27th May 1916. A resident of Islington, N London, he is buried in Hebuterne Military Cemetery, grave II.G.6.

In all, the battalion suffered ten dead[i] and one officer[ii] and 23 men wounded. Such simple statistics conceal what would have been a world of suffering for the men involved. One such was a 19-year old private from Walthamstow in East London. George Blum was caught by a shrapnel blast and several fragments pierced his abdomen. It was an excruciatingly painful wound but not immediately fatal although there was little hope of recovery. Cleaned and dressed at the Advanced Dressing Station on the edge of Hebuterne, Blum clung to life for hours, surviving the agonizing journey by ambulance over the rutted French roads back through Sailly and on towards the Casualty Clearing Stations at Doullens. At some time on the 28th Blum was brought by ambulance to the reception marquee at No. 19 Casualty Clearing Station where his wounds were assessed and an urgent operation scheduled. Major A Don R.A.M.C. had already had a busy day of it, operating on seven men in the operating marquee in front of ward block 'A' over the previous twenty four hours. He had already lost two men to multiple shell wounds and, on inspecting the young Fusilier, he must have approached this last operation on his roster with a feeling of despair. The shrapnel had torn through Blum's lower abdomen perforating his intestine and bladder. There was little to be done except clean the wound, administer as much morphine as was needed to ease his patient's agony and wait for him to die.[iii]

During the night the 1/3rd Londons suffered three fatalities and another nine men wounded. The officer, Lt. Knight[iv], and seven men were wounded and, with

---

[i] 2193 L/Sgt Henry Buffham, 1/1st London Regt (Royal Fusiliers), died on Saturday, 27th May 1916. He was the son of Mrs. Buffham of 36, Bassett St., Kentish Town, London. He is buried in Hebuterne Military Cemetery, grave II.G.7.

5180 Pte Lionel Hicks, 1/1stLondon Regt (Royal Fusiliers), died on Saturday, 27th May 1916. He was the son of M E and the late George Hicks of 14, High Street, Mitcham, Surrey. His body was never found and his name is inscribed on the Thiepval Memorial, Pier and Face 9D and 16B. His brother, 5191 Pte W Hicks, 1/1st London Regt., was killed in action on 5th June 1916.

1725 Pte Stanley Harry Parry Hose, 1/1st London Regt (Royal Fusiliers), died on Saturday, 27th May 1916, aged 20. He was the son of William Ernest Arthur and Charlotte Hose of Penge, London and lived in Battersea. He is buried in Hebuterne Military Cemetery, grave II.G.2.

5326 Pte Ernest Lawrence, 1/1st London Regt (Royal Fusiliers), died on Saturday, 27th May 1916, aged 20. He was the son of Ernest and Annie Lawrence of 1 18, Farrant Avenue, Wood Green, London. He is buried in Hebuterne Military Cemetery, grave II.I.8.

4890 Pte Harry Rhein (alias Day), 1/1st London Regt (Royal Fusiliers), died on Saturday, 27th May 1916. Aged 19, he was the son of Henry and Louisa Rhein of 14, Cumberland Market, Regent's Park, London. His body was never found and his name is inscribed on the Thiepval Memorial, Pier & Face 9D & 16B

1283 Pte Charles Harold Sporle, 1/1st London Regt (Royal Fusiliers), died on Saturday, 27th May 1916. A resident of Battersea, his body was never found and his name is inscribed on the Thiepval Memorial, Pier & Face 9D & 16B

5322 Pte Bert Wright, No. 12 Platoon, C Company, 1/1st London Regt (Royal Fusiliers), died on Saturday, 27th May 1916. A resident of Wood Green, he is buried in Gommecourt British Cemetery No. 2, grave II.C.30.

4301 Pte George Wright, 1/1st London Regt (Royal Fusiliers), died on Saturday, 27th May 1916. A resident of Islington, he is buried in Hebuterne Military Cemetery, grave II.H.9.

[ii] 2nd Lt. Ronald Burrell Ind Scott, 1/1st London Regt (Royal Fusiliers), recovered from his wounds but died on Saturday, 9th September 1916, aged 20. He was the son of the Rev. Edward Battyll Scott and Ellen Louisa Scott of The Vicarage, Market Rasen, Lincs. Native of South Tottenham, London. He is buried in Delville Wood Cemetery, Longueval, Somme, France grave XXIV. A. 10.

[iii] 5201 Pte George Blum, 1/1st London Regt (Royal Fusiliers), died of wounds on Sunday, 28th May 1916, aged 19. He was the son of Gebhard and Anna Blum of 73, Somerset Rd., Walthamstow, London. He is buried in Doullens Communal Cemetery Extension No. 1, grave I.C.4.

[iv] 2nd Lt. Edgar Frederick Knight, 1/3rd London Regt (Royal Fusiliers), died of wounds on Sunday, 28th May 1916, aged 24. He was the eldest son of Daniel and Emily Stewart Knight of Grahamstown, South Africa. He was educated at Kingswood College, Grahamstown and served in German SW Africa under Gen. Botha. He came to London in November 1915 and was commissioned into the 1/3rd London Regt, going to the front in March 1916. His father was the Mayor of Grahamstown when the Duke and Duchess of York visited South Africa. He is buried in St. Amand British Cemetery, grave I.A.10.

dawn making movement difficult, they were left out in the new trench until the following night. The wait for the young lieutenant and two of his men proved fatal. They were to die of their wounds on Sunday night at the dressing station at St Amand. The Kensingtons, holding the W sector trenches on the right, lost one man under the bombardment[i] and a Lt. Pelegrett was wounded.

Sunday, 28ᵗʰ May 1916
Third Army weather report: Fine and warm

ON THE NIGHT of the 28ᵗʰ May the London Rifle Brigade were relieved by the Queen Victoria's Rifles and went to billets in Bayencourt. Two companies of the Q.V.R.s had taken over the front line and the detached outposts from the L.R.B. earlier in the evening of the 28ᵗʰ, 'D' Company being given the task of occupying these posts, two in the Z Hedge and one, on the right, at the Maybush at the head of Yiddish Street. Just after dark, a guide moved off at the head of three teams of Victorias. The first outpost was on the left of the Z Hedge and here, Lt. Ogilvie and his men and their Lewis gun took position for the night. The next team, led by Lt. A C Rumsey, was to have been dropped of at the second outpost at the right hand end of the hedge but, by mistake, the guide took both the remaining parties to the Maybush. And here they would have remained had not Capt. Lindsey-Renton decided to check on their whereabouts. Leaving Lt. Hodgson and his men at the Maybush, the intrepid Captain led Rumsey's group back along the shallow trenches to the Gommecourt-Hebuterne road and the outpost on the right of the Z Hedge. At about 10.15 he set off back to battalion headquarters when a sudden and heavy bombardment crashed into the area around the new trench line. He, and a number of others, took refuge in part of the newly dug trenches but several men were wounded and, by the end of the night, three Q.V.R.s of 'D' Company were killed[ii] and 14 wounded. Undismayed by his near miss, Capt. Lindsey-Renton returned to the outpost line later in the night only to be caught once more by a sudden eruption by the German guns. This time, he was trying to get through the British wire and it was only the safety of a shallow trench that protected him and another Q.V.R. officer from injury. Capt. Leys Cox had also been out inspecting the battalions dispositions and now, he and his brother officer spent a windy ten minutes with their noses pressed firmly into the muddy soil as the night was lit up by shells bursting on either side of them[iii].

3182 Sgt James Frederick Norman, 'A' Coy., 1/3ʳᵈ London Regt (Royal Fusiliers), died of wounds on Monday, 29ᵗʰ May 1916, aged 22. He was the son of James and Elizabeth Norman of 22, Lewis Rd., Southall, Middx., and lived in Paddington, London. He is buried in St. Amand British Cemetery, grave I.A.11.

4692 Pte Harry Frank Daines, 1/3ʳᵈ London Regt (Royal Fusiliers), died of wounds on Sunday, 28ᵗʰ May 1916. He was the nephew of Mr. A. Sayers of 7, Railway St., Caledonian Rd., King's Cross, London. He is buried in St. Amand British Cemetery, grave I.A.12.

[i] 1762 Pte Herbert Green, 1/13ᵗʰ London Regt (Kensingtons), died on Saturday, 27ᵗʰ May 1916. A resident of Wood Street, North London, he is buried in Hebuterne Military Cemetery, grave III.L.1.

[ii] 3627 Rfn Henry George East, 1/9ᵗʰ London Regt (Queen Victoria's Rifles), died on Sunday, 28ᵗʰ May 1916. A resident of Queen's Park in NW London, he is buried in Hebuterne Military Cemetery, grave IV.G.6.

4789 Rfn Horace George William Glover, 1/9ᵗʰ London Regt (Queen Victoria's Rifles), died on Sunday, 28ᵗʰ May 1916. A resident of Lambeth he is buried in Hebuterne Military Cemetery, grave IV.G.7.

2392 Rfn Charles Albert Cade, 'D' Coy., 1/9ᵗʰ London Regt (Queen Victoria's Rifles), died on Monday, 29ᵗʰ May 1916, aged 37. He was the son of Thomas and Mary Cade. Born in Bristol he was a resident of Bayswater. He is buried in Hebuterne Military Cemetery, Pas de Calais, France grave IV. G. 4.

[iii] In the period from 17ᵗʰ-31ˢᵗ May, German field artillery from the Reserve-Feldartillerie-Regiment 20 alone fired 4,150 field gun rounds and 800 light field howitzer rounds.

In the W Sector on the right, the 1/4th Londons relieved the Kensingtons who withdrew to Bayencourt on the night of the 28th. 'A' Company (Capt. A R Moore) took up position on the division's extreme right with 'B' Company (Maj. S Elliott) to their left. 'D' Company (Capt. Giles) were in the support trenches and 'C' Company (Capt. Long) occupied billets in the village. The men were not there just to guard against German trench raids, huge amounts of digging were required: a new trench immediately behind the front line (later called the 'boyau du service), a support line (the WS line) and communication trenches to connect them all to the old front line (the WR line). More work was needed on wiring the front line, digging dugouts for Aid shelters, company headquarters, ammunition stores and signal offices, preparing positions for mortars and machine guns. The toil was never ending.

Monday, 29th May 1916
Third Army weather report: Fine and warm

FOR THE 1/4TH LONDONS the shellfire testing the Q.V.R.s was also a severe trial. At 1 a.m. on the morning of the 29th a burst of artillery and mortar fire crashed down on their sector. 'B' Company's Maj. S. Elliott, an officer of vast experience who had left England with the unit in 1914 as the battalion's Machine Gun Officer, was buried in a trench and rushed to hospital with severe concussion, never to return to front line action. Three other men were killed or mortally wounded[i] and twelve others wounded as the battalion suffered its heaviest casualties of their time opposite Gommecourt.

The new trenches were full of men busily deepening and strengthening the assembly and communication trenches and they presented a decent target to the German guns. The London Rifle Brigade alone had 500 men on working parties in front of the Hebuterne, all well within range of the artillery and trench mortars opposite. On this and the following night, when working parties were continually under fire, some splendid work was done by various N.C.O.'s. Sgt. H. C. Munnings of the Queen Victoria's, who rose later to be a R.S.M., gained the Military Medal for his handling of the men under heavy shell-fire when out on wiring and covering parties. But they were not without losses. 3923 Rfn. Henry Green[ii] and one of his mates were wounded. Green survived long enough to reach the Casualty Clearing Stations at Doullens, a long ambulance ride away to the west, but there he died of his wounds. His gravestone is just one of 1,335 World War One headstones that stand in serried ranks in front of the Cross of Sacrifice under the trees in this quiet corner of the cemetery.

The men of the 167th Brigade had been given Monday off after the efforts of the previous three nights. But it was just one day off. There was still too much to do and for the next two nights, working parties four and five hundred strong would be hard at it improving the work already done.

---

i 895 Pte Henry Kirby, 1/4th London Regt (Royal Fusiliers), was killed on 28th May 1916. He is buried in Hebuterne Military Cemetery, grave III. A. 7
2721 Pte James Henry Lemon, 1/4th London Regt (Royal Fusiliers), was killed on 28th May 1916. Aged 29, he was the son of George and Ellen Lemon of 66, Jane St., Commercial Rd., London. Born at Cork. He is buried in Hebuterne Military Cemetery, grave IV. A. 1
3335 L/Cpl Eric Stanley Shinkfield, 1/4th London Regt (Royal Fusiliers), died of wounds on 30th May 1916. Aged 17, he was the son of Henry James and Julia A. Shinkfield of 23, Trossacks Rd., East Dulwich, London. He is buried in Hebuterne Military Cemetery, grave III. A. 8
ii 3923 Rfn Henry Peter Green, 1/9th London Regt (Queen Victoria's Rifles), died of wounds on 29th May 1916. A resident of Marylebone he is buried in Doullens Communal Cemetery Extension No. 1, grave I.C.5.

Tuesday, 30th May 1916
Third Army weather report: Fine and warm

THE GERMAN ARTILLERY was at it again during the afternoon of the 30th May. Starting just after midday the bombardment built in intensity until, just before 3 p.m., the Queen Victorias issued an SOS signal in the belief that the bombardment presaged an infantry attack in their sector. Nothing was to materialise but the German guns were persistent and, two hours later, they increased their length and dropped several shells in the vicinity of the battalion H.Q. of the 1/4th Londons which was sheltered in dugouts beneath a flour mill in Hebuterne. Thirty one casualties were suffered, thankfully none fatal.

During the night, Capt. A. R. Williamson[i] of the 1/7th Middlesex was severely wounded by a shell as he was carrying out a reconnaissance of Gommecourt Park. This was a preliminary to a large scale raid on Gommecourt Park (for which a full sized model of the area had been marked out) but, shortly after, the raid was abandoned as likely to be too costly for the intelligence gathered.

On the same night Sgt. A. J. Wilson, also of the Queen Vics, won another M.M. for his work on the night of May 30th/31st, when out with a covering party which was heavily shelled and suffered a number of casualties. As these occurred he so distributed the men that they still covered all the men at work; he also brought in all his casualties. It was owing to the example he showed that the covering parties carried on, thus allowing the working parties to continue their important work. The casualties suffered that night brought the total Q.V.R. casualties since 26th May to 14 killed and 59 wounded of whom nearly half had occurred on Tuesday afternoon and evening. Under the heavy bombardments brought down on the Q.V.R. five men had been killed, another two died of wounds and 17 were wounded[ii].

The night time shelling also fell on the 1/2nd Londons, newly arrived in Hebuterne, as Sgt. Bisgood recalled:

"Our H.Q. dugouts are splendid. The Orderly Room is 15 feet below surface and fitted with electric light and telephone, the walls are papered. The first shell over seemed remarkably near our billets, and I went up to see if anyone was hit; was just making for a shattered house when over came another, missing me by about 3 feet, and exploding right over against the wall, where an R.G.A. boy was standing, the poor chap got the full dose and called out for aid, so I had to stop to pick him up, no easy job. Having

---

i Capt. Arthur Ross Williamson, 1/7th Middlesex Regt (Highgate detachment), had been an officer in the regiment since 1902. After his injuries, he returned to the regiment in June 1917 but lasted only a month before being forced to return to the regiment's base.

ii The men of the 1/9th London Regt (Queen Victoria's Rifles) to die on Tuesday, 30th May 1916 were:

2449 Rfn. Sidney Charles Davis. Aged 25, he was the son of Harry & Emily Davis; husband of Ellen Frances Prince (formerly Davis) of 63, Darwin Buildings, Darwin St., Walworth, London. He is buried in Hebuterne Military Cemetery IV. H. 4.

3005 L/Cpl. Geoffrey Damarel Gidley. Aged 20, he was the son of George & Annie Maud Gidley of "Katha," Colbert Avenue, Thorpe Bay, Essex. He died of his wounds and is buried in Doullens Communcal Cemetery Extension No.1 I. C. 10

3853 Rfn. Eric Arnold A Good. He died of his wounds and is buried in Doullens Communcal Cemetery Extension No.1 I. C. 11

3656 Rfn. Thomas Lionel Howard . He is buried in Hebuterne Military Cemetery IV. H. 5

3458 Rfn. Frank Marshall. Aged 19, he was the son of Malcolm Clifton Marshall & Eliza Marshall of "Linden Lea," Courthouse Rd., Maidenhead. He is buried in Hebuterne Military Cemetery IV. H. 2

4270 Rfn. William Charles Parish. He is buried in Hebuterne Military Cemetery IV. H. 7

1768 Cpl. Harold John Strangward. He is buried in Hebuterne Military Cemetery IV. H. 3

huddled him up to me I managed to fall into a dugout, at the same time over came a hurricane of shells. I thought the end had come. I was smothered in blood from head to foot yet had no scratch myself. The poor chap I had with me had 3 pieces out of his body, each the size of my fist. I fixed him best I could and waited for ambulance. This chap[i] however only lasted an hour or so."[36]

Wednesday, 31ˢᵗ May 1916
Third Army weather report: Fine and warm

WEDNESDAY SAW MORE of the same from the German guns with the 1/4ᵗʰ Londons H.Q. again being a target. Lt. H B A Balls, later to become the battalion Quartermaster, was wounded in the strafe and one man was killed with three others wounded, one mortally. Another man, the H.Q. sentry from the day before, also died of his wounds at a C.C.S in Doullens[ii]. The Queen Victoria's run of bad luck was not at an end either. Under another 'strafe' their bad week came to an end with another three dead and five wounded bringing their total to 81 in just six days[iii]. But the German guns were not the only way that battalion strength was eroded. The Queen's Westminsters, who at no time had been within range of even the longest German guns, suffered 12% 'wastage'[iv] purely through sickness and injury suffered as they laboured well behind the lines at Halloy and the Mondicourt railhead.

The Rangers and the London Scottish, meanwhile, were passing their time indulging in practice attacks across the rehearsal ground at Hurtebise Farm. Today they spent the day working on signalling systems between the infantry and the observers in the R.F.C.'s BE2c. To make is more realistic some smoke was released in an attempt to replicate the likely conditions of the attack itself. The results were discouraging and definitely food for thought for the planners. Verey lights sent up through the smoke could be seen but the aerial observers found it impossible to determine the precise locations from which they were fired. Yellow flares were then lit but they disappeared without trace when mixed with the thick, coloured, obscuring clouds from the smoke candles. Signallers were also due to take over Venetian blinds with which Morse code signals could be flashed either to the British held trenches or to the aircraft overhead. The only problem to emerge from this element of the plan was that the observers in the BE2cs simply

---

i 47047 Gnr Harold Allen, 16ᵗʰ Siege Bty died of wounds on 30ᵗʰ May 1916. He is buried in Hebuterne Military Cemetery, I.T.1

ii 4832 Pte Charles Edward Wallis, 1/4ᵗʰ London Regt. (Royal Fusiliers), died on 31ˢᵗ May 1916. Aged 18, he was the son of Charles and Catherine Wallis of 158, Bridge Road, Glebe Point, Sydney, Australia. He is buried in Hebuterne Military Cemetery, grave III.A.6.

2889 Pte Arthur Stanley Last, 1/4ᵗʰ London Regt. (Royal Fusiliers), died of wounds on 31ˢᵗ May 1916. He was the son of Mr. W. Last of 31, Dundee Rd., Plaistow, London. He is buried in St. Amand British Cemetery, grave I.A.14

3255 Pte Lawrence Braham Claridge, 1/4ᵗʰ London Regt. (Royal Fusiliers) died of wounds on 31ˢᵗ May 1916. Aged 34 he was the son of George Frederick and Frances Claridge of 6, Grove Rd., Leighton Buzzard, Beds. He was on the staff of the Anglo-South American Bank at Chile at outbreak of war. He is buried in Doullens Communal Cemetery Extension No.1, grave I. C. 14

iii The 1/9ᵗʰ London Regt (Queen Victoria's Rifles) casualties on Wednesday, 31ˢᵗ May 1916 were:

3590 Rfn. Sidney Herbert Fox. Aged 18, he was the son of William & Alice Rose Fox. He is buried in Hebuterne Military Cemetery IV. H. 6.

2800 Cpl. Arthur Frank Ives. Aged 21, he was the son of F. & Kate Ives of 32, Hazelbury Rd., Silver St., Edmonton, London. He is buried in Hebuterne Military Cemetery IV. H. 8.

3561 Rfn. George Herbert Morrison. Aged 21, he was the son of George & Ada Lucy Morrison of 19, Wolseley Rd., Crouch End, London. He is buried in Hebuterne Military Cemetery IV. G. 8

iv 84 men went sick out of a battalion strength of 714 at the beginning of May.

could not see them. Back to the drawing board, then, on the subject of aerial co-operation and communication for the Corps and Divisional Staffs.

***

MEANWHILE, ON THE GERMAN SIDE of No Man's Land the increasingly obvious preparations opposite had not gone unnoticed and moves were already in hand to repel what was clearly coming. The Reserve-Feldartillerie-Regiment 20 had the main responsibility for supporting the 2nd Guard Reserve Division with its field guns and light howitzers. As the preparations opposite gathered pace, the regiment had sent a series of requests to the General der Artillerie of A.O.K.2 for the return of two detached batteries of eight guns, and, on May 30th, these both returned. No. 3 Battery was assigned quarters in the village of Ervillers and No. 5 Battery went to the neighbouring village of Mory, both some 5 kilometres east of Gommecourt.

The artillery organisation of the 2nd Guard Reserve Division's sector was split into two groups: Gruppe Nord, commanded by Major Barnstedt, and Gruppe Süd, C/O Major Niederstein. Gruppe Nord, assisted by the divisional artillery of the 111th Infantry Division to the north, had the responsibility for defensive and offensive fire on the sector north of Gommecourt, i.e. from Monchy down to the area to be attacked by the 46th (North Midland) Division. Gruppe Süd, if necessary with the support of the artillery of the 52nd Infantry Division to the south (including Serre), mainly covered the front to be assaulted by the 56th (London) Division but had the additional responsibility of assisting their neighbours to the south.

Over the preceding months, nearly fifty battery positions had been constructed in the divisional sector. Not all of these were occupied and, in order to confuse British Intelligence, batteries sometimes swapped positions or moved to previously empty dugouts. These precautions were not entirely essential as, by 17th June, Third Army Intelligence believed they had identified just fifteen battery positions with another three unconfirmed, this in spite of the fact that the R.F.C. had air superiority on the Western Front throughout this time. Twelve of these batteries were believed to be 77mm field gun batteries, two were 105mm light howitzer batteries and the other a 150mm heavy howitzer battery. On the 52nd Infantry Division's front a further fifteen batteries capable of hitting the 56th Division's front and rear areas had been identified (seven 77mm batteries, three 105mm batteries, two 150mm batteries and three more unspecified howitzer batteries).

When Battery 3/20 returned to the Gommecourt area it was split between two battery positions, numbers 501 and 530 (about a kilometre behind the German lines opposite Hannescamps and part of Gruppe Nord), with two guns in each. The guns in position 530 relieved two from Battery 2/20 which moved to position 534a, a few hundred metres east of Essarts (and the only position of the three identified by British Intelligence by the middle of June).

Battery 5/20 became part of Gruppe Süd. It's planned location, at the western end of Biez Wood, was occupied by a battery from Feldartillerie-Regiment 104 and, for tactical reasons, this unit could not be moved. Instead, it was decided to construct a new position, position 543, and its commander, Hauptmann der Reserve Schmidt, reconnoitred a new location at the south east corner of Biez

Wood where Hebuterne Trench crossed the Hebuterne to Bucquoy Road. From here the range to the centre of Hebuterne was just 2,500 metres.

Hauptmann der Reserve Schmidt wrote a report of the construction of the position for the Reserve-Feldartillerie-Regiment 20's regimental history:

"The construction and establishment of the new position here did not generally differ much from the other positions occupied by the regiment. To distract any enemy attention from it, it was adapted to our rear-area trench system in such a way that it seemed to be a part of it from a distance. The gun emplacements were built one after the other starting from the right and occupied as soon as they were completed; cover for the men, an officers' dugout, telephone exchange and ammunition bunkers were built alongside. We were helped by a digging party from another unit which, I might interject at this point, worked very hard to bring up ammunition when firing activity picked up one day at the end of June. Leutnant Büsing, who was a member of the battery at that time, was mainly responsible for supervising the construction work. When the enemy preparatory fire began at the end of June, all guns had been brought into their emplacements and work had been completed to range them in on the parts of the enemy front that could be reached.

Since the battery was located quite far forward, it was able to operate quite effectively. From Height 147, where I and the battery troop were guests in the regimental command post of R.I.R. 55, observation was extensive, particularly to the left. Battery firing activity was often very lively during the battle; it was particularly used for a lot of disruptive fire, etc."[37]

In spite of the best efforts of the R.F.C. and the British artillery, batteries such as 5/20 were to cause major damage throughout June and played a significant role in the defeat of the London Division's attack on 1ˢᵗ July. And, as the weeks went by and the preparations for the assault became, as planned, increasingly obvious more artillery was moved into the area surrounding Gommecourt, resulting in one of the highest concentrations of German guns anywhere on the Somme front. However, many of these guns were brought down from the north, around Arras, rather than, as G.H.Q. hoped, being removed from the area to the south where the main axis of the Great Push was located. The strengthening defences of Gommecourt were not weakening German defences elsewhere on the Somme front, they were coming, instead, from the areas that Generals Allenby and Snow had suggested as the better place for a diversionary attack.

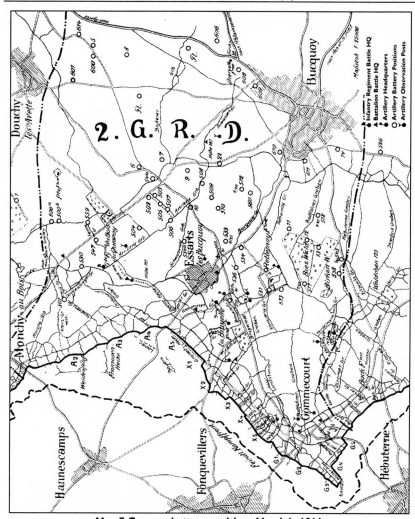

Map 7 German battery positions May-July 1916

(*Source:* Das Reserve-Feldartillerie-Regiment Nr. 20 im Weltkriege 1914-18 by Georg Büsing, published by Göhmann, Hannover 1932)

Battery	Position	Battery	Position
5/2nd Guard Foot Artillery (half)	I	2/19	508
3rd Battn 2/Bavarian Landsturm Foot Artillery 4xsFH93	6	692nd Foot Artillery Battery 9cm	509
706th Foot Artillery Bty 15cm Russian	7	6/20	512
236th Battery 10cm	11	3 x Belgian 5.7cm	513
?	12	7/20	517
8/221	500a	9/20	518
8/20 four guns	500b	3/20	530
3/20	501	4/19	533
1/19	502	3/19	534
1/20 four guns	505	4/20	536
2/20 two guns	506	5/20	543
1/20 two guns	507	3/221	547
2/19	508	2 x Belgian 8.7cm	Rettemoy Fme

NOTES:
Casualties not mentioned in existing footnotes:

9th May 1916
1/7th Middlesex Regiment.
Neate 2381 Pte John Thomas Aged 23 Son of John & Annie Neate of 4, Ruby Terrace, Hammond Road, Southall, Middlesex Hebuterne Military Cemetery II.V.1

12th May 1916
1/1st London Regiment (Royal Fusiliers).
Hedges 3748 Pte Charles Doullens Communal Cemetery Extension No.1, II. C. 4

13th May 1916
1/1st London Regiment (Royal Fusiliers).
Massy 5026 Pte Richard Aged 19 Son of Francis Joseph & Louise Emistone Massy of 60, Mervan Rd., Brixton, London Hebuterne Military Cemetery Sp. Mem. 16.

15th May 1916
Royal Engineers.
Close 3254 Spr. Charles Henry 513th (2/2nd London) Field Coy RE Aged 27 Husband of Ellen Payten (formerly Close) of 62, Summerley, Earlsfield, London. Hebuterne Military Cemetery II. F. 1.
Prichard 2079 Spr. David Thomas 513th (2/2nd London) Field Coy RE Aged 31 Son of Arthur William Morgan Prichard of Coalway Lane End, Coleford, Glos Hebuterne Military Cemetery II. F. 2

17th May 1916
1/8th Middlesex Regiment.
Shackell TF2313 Pte Reginald John Aged 18 Son of Mrs. Jessie Preedy, (formerly Shackell) of 35, Church Rd., Southall, Middx St Sever Cemetery, Rouen A. 21. 3.

18th May 1916
1/7th Middlesex Regiment.
Hodson 5290 Private A J Aged 19 Son of John R. & Minnie S. Hodson of 205, North Hill, Highgate, London. Hebuterne Military Cemetery II. M. 1

19th May 1916
1/7th Middlesex Regiment.
Christmas 2167 L/Cpl Arthur Albert Aged 20 Son of Arthur & Esther Nellie Christmas of 19, Lansdowne Rd., Dalston Doullens Communal Cemetery Extension No. 1, II. C. 13
Young 1553 Serjeant Wilfrid Martin Aged 25 Son of Edgar & Rosina Matilda Young of Tottenham, London Doullens Communal Cemetery Extension No. 1, II. C. 12

21st May 1916
1/8th Middlesex Regiment.
Carpenter TF2111 L/Cpl William Jesse Frederick Aged 19 Son of William Charles & Alice Carpenter of Hillingdon, Middx Doullens Communal Cemetery Extension No. 1, II. C. 16

25th May 1916
1/1st London Regiment (Royal Fusiliers).
Penney 2440 Pte Arthur Aged 23 Son of Thomas Frederick & Sarah E. Penney of 150, Brooke Rd., Stoke Newington, London. Native of Lower Edmonton, London.   Hebuterne Military Cemetery II. H. 8
Reardon 4449 Pte William John Warlincourt Halte British Cemetery, Saulty I.D.6

Royal Field Artillery.
Savoury 81393 Dvr James Edward D Bty., 282nd (1/3rd London) Bde St. Amand British Cemetery I. A. 7

26th May 1916
1/1st London Regiment (Royal Fusiliers).
Loader 3211 L/Cpl Alfred Hebuterne Military Cemetery II. I. 6
Rasey 1389 L/Cpl Harold Son of Mrs. M. Rasey of 57, Bathurst Gardens, Willesden, London   Couin British Cemetery I.A.19
Royal Field Artillery.
Kennard 1269 Gnr Harry William, C Bty., 282nd (1/3rd London) Bde Aged 23 Son of Ernest & Emma Kennard of 74, Sistova Rd., Balham, London Hebuterne Military Cemetery, IV. G. 5.

27th May 1916
Royal Engineers.
Strachan 1778 Spr. James, 416th (1/1st City of Edinburgh) Field Coy RE Aged 20 Son of James & Agnes Strachan of 85, Holyrood Rd., Edinburgh Doullens Communal Cemetery Extension No.1, I. C. 2

29th May 1916
Royal Garrison Artillery.
Baker 66590 Gnr Charles John Joseph, 102nd Siege Bty Aged 24 Son of Charles John & Kate Baker of Holly Cottages, Hatchet Lane, Wirfield, Windsor. Bavincourt Communal Cemetery, France 5

Childs 56480 Bombardier Harry, 102nd Siege Bty Aged 36 Husband of Margaret Mary Childs of 28, Ashley Rd., Forest Gate, London. Doullens Communal Cemetery Extension No.1 I.C.8.

Mulcahy 27358 Gnr William, 102nd Siege Bty Doullens Communal Cemetery Extension No.1, I.C.13

30th May 1916
1/5th Cheshire Regiment (Earl of Chester's).
Jones 1882 Pte. Hugh Hebuterne Military Cemetery II. C. 1.
Royal Field Artillery.
Parry 1103 Bombardier Thomas, Y56th Trench Mortar Bty Aged 31 Son of Thomas George William & Louisa Parry; husband of Lydia Ann Parry of Deanshanger, Stony Stratford, Bucks Doullens Communal Cemetery Extension No.1 I. C. 12

31st May 1916
Royal Engineers.
Leach 2426 Cpl Francis Leonard, 513th (2/2nd London) Field Coy RE Hebuterne Military Cemetery II. F. 3

ENDNOTES:
1 Bickersteth, John (editor), The Bickersteth Diaries 1995, page 79.
2 Mockett 104354 Rifleman Wally (Stretcher bearer), 1/16 Londons (Queen's Westminster Rifles). Letter from to his friend Charlie Miller of 23 Wandle Road, Upper Tooting, dated 12th May 1916. Liddle Collection, Leeds University.
3 Hawkings Frank, From Ypres to Cambrai, The Elmfield Press 1973
4 The Second-Seconds in France: The Story of the 2/2nd City of London Field Ambulance, 1920.
5 Barber, Rfn H, 1/5th London Rifle Brigade from a document held at the Liddle Collection, Leeds University.
6 Wolff, Anne, Subalterns of the Foot, 1992, page 48.
7 Now part of ICI.
8 Wolff, op cit, page 68.
9 Ibid, page 92.
10 Ibid, page 128.
11 Ibid, page 142.
12 Ibid.
13 Bisgood 3254 Sergeant Thornton Henry, 1/2nd Battalion, London Regiment (Royal Fusiliers). Unpublished diary.
14 Atkins, Pte A L, 1/7th Middlesex Regt, IWM.
15 Bryden, Pte. R E C, 1/14th London Regt., (London Scottish), Papers, IWM.
16 Clements Pte (later Lt.) H T, 1/2nd London Regiment, Diary, IWM.
17 Bickersteth, John (editor), The Bickersteth Diaries 1995, page 82.
18 Dolden, A Stuart, Cannon Fodder, Blandford Press 1980.
19 Mockett 104354 Rifleman Wally (Stretcher bearer), 1/16 Londons (Queen's Westminster Rifles). Letter to Charlie Miller dated 30th May 1916. Rifleman Mockett was later made a Prisoner of War. Liddle Collection, Leeds University.
20 Bryden, Pte N E C op cit.
21 Home, op. cit. page 108.
22 Miller Pte W, 1/1st London Regt Diary, Liddle Collection, Brotherston Library, Leeds University.
23 Wolff, op. cit., page 143.
24 Macdonald, Lyn, Somme, 1983 and 1984 page 32.
25 Miller Pte W, 1/1st London Regt Diary, Liddle Collection, Brotherston Library, Leeds University.
26 Keeson, Maj. C A C, Queen Victoria's Rifles,1792-1922, 1923
27 Hawkings Frank, From Ypres to Cambrai, 1973
28 According to 'The History of the Seventh Middlesex' by Lt Col E J King though this figure is not given in either the battalion's War Diary nor the 56th Division's monthly casualty returns.
29 Boyd, Pte A, 2/1st London Field Ambulance, Liddle Collection, Leeds University.
30 Miller Pte W, 1/1st London Regt Diary, Liddle Collection, Brotherston Library, Leeds University..
31 Macdonald, op. cit. page 32.
32 Miller Pte W, 1/1st London Regt Diary, Liddle Collection, Brotherston Library, Leeds University.
33 Wolff, op. cit., page 144
34 Lt Col. E G Mercer C.M.G., T.D. He commanded the 1/1st Londons from January to June 1916.
35 Miller Pte W, 1/1st London Regt Diary, Liddle Collection, Brotherston Library, Leeds University.
36 Bisgood 3254 Sergeant Thornton Henry, 1/2nd Battalion, London Regiment (Royal Fusiliers). Unpublished diary.
37 Büsing, Georg „Das Reserve-Feldartillerie-Regiment Nr. 20 im Weltkriege 1914-18"1932 Büsing was a Leutnant in the regiment at the time of the attack on Gommecourt.

5. JUNE 1ST TO JUNE 23RD

"Raining hard this morning. Trenches getting rather uncomfortable, not much doing. New front line taking the water rapidly... Our chaps have just recovered the remnants of the four boys who were buried in front on the 4th, they were literally torn to pieces, poor devils, and we had to bury them in Hebuterne cemetery and we could not tell who was who."

Sgt T H Bisgood
1/2nd London Regiment

Thursday, 1st June 1916
Third Army weather report: Fine & warm. Rain: 0mm. Temp. 73-51° F

THE FINE WEATHER of the last week in May continued into early June but with no let up in the workload for the men. The Queen Victorias were coming to the end of their stint at the front but were still working without a break on improving the trenches from which they were due to attack in four week's time. German artillery activity, which was on the increase since the digging of the new front line, meant that time spent digging in the shallow and unrevetted new trenches was always going to be hazardous and so it proved on the first day of June. With two companies at work in the trenches a heavy bombardment fell on the men and, for the fifth day out of the last six, the stretcher bearers were called into frantic action. Twenty-one year old Rifleman White[i] was killed outright and another seventeen men were wounded, one to die later in the day of his wounds at a Casualty Clearing Station in Doullens[ii].

At No. 19 C.C.S., the unit's C.O., Lt. Col. Thompson R.A.M.C., was putting his name to the return for admissions and evacuations for May. No. 19 was one of six Casualty Clearing Stations supporting the men opposite Gommecourt and several divisions on either side of the salient. The returns give an excellent insight into the 'wastage' suffered by the units either in, or working behind, the front lines. In total, 1,092 officers and men had been admitted in May of whom two were sick for every one wounded.

May 1916	Sick		Wounded	
	Officers	Men	Officers	Men
Week 1	20	155	1	107
Week 2	11	123	2	20
Week 3	19	141	0	28
Week 4	16	176	6	141
Week 5	6	81	1	38
Total	72	676	10	334
Died	1	2	0	26
To Base Hospitals	51	568	9	290

Table 2 Admissions to No 19 Casualty Clearing Station, May 1916

---

[i] 2544 Rfn Alfred White, 1/9th London Regt. (Queen Victoria's Rifles), was killed in action on Thursday, 1st June 1916, aged 21. He was the son of Frederick John and Alice Hannah White of 136, Eastcombe Avenue, Charlton, London. He is buried in Hebuterne Military Cemetery, grave IV. G. 9.
[ii] 2548 L/Cpl Lawrence George Hemsley, 1/9th London Regt. (Queen Victoria's Rifles), died of wounds on Thursday, 1st June 1916, aged 22. He was the son of William and Ellen Hemsley and lived in Twickenham. He is buried in Doullens Communal Cemetery Extension No.1, grave I. C. 15.

Assuming No. 19 C.C.S. to be typical of the other stations in the sector then nearly 7,000 men would have passed through their hands in a month when no real action took place. Skin diseases were a major cause of wastage and the War Diary for the 26th General Hospital at Etaples recorded in today's entry that 372 out of 1,003 patients were victims of skin complaints. Equally worrying was the growth in mental cases, a problem made worse by the inadequate infrastructure for the evacuation of soldiers somewhat crudely described as 'lunatics'.

It should be noted that 80% of the sick were then evacuated to Base and other hospitals showing that the conditions complained of by the men were, in the main, of a reasonably serious nature. Little evidence, then, of shirking here as the plans for the big offensive came together. But for some men, especially within the 46th Division, the nature of the sickness sweeping the units was of a serious and worrying nature. In the final week of May eight men stricken by variants of the Typhoid family had been hospitalised: one was suffering from Typhoid, four from Paratyphoid A and three more from Paratyphoid B; and in one day alone, 31st May, fifteen trench fever cases were admitted. These were serious conditions requiring weeks and sometimes months from which to recover – and some men never returned. For an already weak Division these losses, and the prospect that there were men defiantly staying in the ranks to keep faith with their mates and their unit who should have been in hospital, was a worrying matter and detailed investigations were being conducted in an effort to identify the source of these infections.

***

THE RANGERS AND THE LONDON SCOTTISH completed their first stint at the Halloy practice grounds on the 1st June and, the following day set off on the long march east, the Rangers to Sailly-au-Bois and the Scottish to Souastre. These two battalions would replace the 1/4th Londons and the Kensingtons in the W Sector. The Rangers would be based at Sailly for five days, each night providing working parties in the new trenches, as preparation for the attack gathered momentum. Sailly was within easy reach of the German guns and, every day, one or two men were wounded by shrapnel[i] from shells lobbed hopefully in the village's direction. The Scottish were billeted in huts of corrugated iron and canvass in Souastre overnight before continuing their journey to the front line. The roofs of the huts had been camouflaged in an effort to prevent them being spotted by the prying eyes of the observers in German aircraft that occasionally overflew the area.

Friday, 2nd June 1916
Third Army weather report: Fine & warm. Rain: 0mm. Temp. 69-44° F

THE WEATHER MAY STILL HAVE BEEN SET FAIR but the Q.V.R.'s luck in the trenches was not to improve on the last two days of their work in the front lines. On Friday, two men were wounded and then, on their final day, they gratefully bid farewell but not without bitter memories.

On Friday, 2nd June, the 1/4th Londons were given orders to get their kit together and, as the men of the London Scottish took over their billets in Hebuterne, they marched westwards on a pleasant summer's afternoon. At Bayencourt, they stopped for a rest and tea before resuming the 'scourge' to

---

i One officer (2nd Lt. H G Brown) and 6 other ranks from the Rangers were wounded in this period.

Souastre where they were to be billeted for the night. It was to be the last dry day for nearly two weeks. The next day, through light rain, they continued their march to the west through the villages of Henu and Pas-en-Artois until they reached Halloy and the divisional practice grounds. For the Scottish, on the other hand, it was to be the beginning of five arduous days in the trenches, working day and night under continuous threat of bombardment by trench mortars or heavier German artillery. Stopping only to pick up rations at Bayencourt, the battalion cooks followed the men up to Hebuterne where they set up the field kitchens to supply the men billeted in the village as well as those in the trenches. Meals and the ubiquitous brew of tea were prepared and fatigue parties were given the arduous and dangerous task of carrying the heavy 'dixies' up to the front line platoons. Even for the cooks, Hebuterne was not a place for the unwary:

> "We occasionally had a walk round in the evenings, but this had to be done very wary as the Germans had a nasty habit of suddenly sweeping the village with machine gun fire. One night MacPherson, a fellow cook, was standing on the cooker attending to the Dixies when a machine gun bullet ricocheted off the cooker chimney. Much too close for his liking!"[1]

Saturday, 3rd June 1916
Third Army weather report: Warm & dull. Rain: 1.6mm. Temp. 63-40° F

ON SATURDAY THE WEATHER STARTED TO TURN. The temperature dropped and some light rain fell on June 3rd. And, as the rain fell so did the German shells. Again the Q.V.R.s were caught, losing one rifleman killed[i] and another two wounded. Since their rotation in the front lines had started the battalion had suffered 99 casualties: sixteen dead, four died of wounds and 79 wounded (they reached an unwanted century when a another rifleman was wounded on 4th June). Only light relief was gained from the news that Lt. Col. Dickins[ii] had been "Mentioned in Dispatches" for the second time.

At the end of the day the battalion was relieved by 'B' and 'D' Companies of the Q.V.R. to the great relief of adjutant Major Sampson:

> "We came out of the trenches last night, and were very glad to do so. We have only moved into dug-outs a short distance back, and the men are doing various jobs, but it is easier work as it is done in daylight and with very few, if any, casualties. The thing we all want is a good night's rest and that we hope for tonight. I think I said we had been digging a new trench which had annoyed the Hun. I don't think there is now any harm in my saying that what we have done is to go forward into No Man's Land and help ourselves to a piece of it, 1400 yards long and 500 in depth. The result has been great artillery activity on both sides and our men have had to dig under shell-fire at night, in the open, which is very trying. Most of them are rather shaken, as they have been shelled off and on, and sometimes very

---

[i] 4030 Rfn Walter West, 1/9th London Regt. (Queen Victoria's Rifles), was killed in action on Saturday, 3rd June 1916. A resident of Hoddesdon, he is buried in Hebuterne Military Cemetery, grave IV. H. 9.
[ii] Lt. Col. Vernon William Frank Dickins, D.S.O., 1/9th London Regt. (Queen Victoria's Rifles) was the CO of the battalion between May 1915 and November 1916. A pre-war Territorial he had been a Captain in 1908 when the Territorial Force was organised. He was promoted Temp. Lt. Col on 6th June 1915 and was awarded the D.S.O. on 13th January 1916. Sent home as a result of ill-health he was appointed CO of the Divisional Training School for Officers at Colchester. He was re-appointed CO of the 1/9th Londons in 1921.

heavily, for a week. Some of the men are rather jumpy, but on the whole it is distinctly a fine piece of work and we are by way of being the heroes of it, as, though other battalions have been engaged, we have had the dirty end of the stick. However, the Hun had a worse time in many ways as he is thoroughly frightened; and our gunners have sent him some tokens of their esteem and affection."[2]

One of the batteries being 'thoroughly frightened' was No. 5 Battery of Reserve Feldartillerie Regt 20 in their newly constructed dugouts south of Biez Wood. Their commander, Hauptmann der Reserve Schmidt, wrote after the war:

"Unfortunately, its position was discovered soon after it began firing. Despite great caution, this was unavoidable, since enemy aircraft were in the air from early in the morning until nightfall, day in and day out, and we still had to range in every gun most comprehensively. The battery's position now became disastrous, as - particularly on the sunken road - it was always easy to find, even after the position had been completed and was hardly visible even from near by when it had been covered with wire mesh.

Judging by the energy expended in trying to destroy it, the battery seems to have become quite a nuisance to the enemy. Already while ranging the guns in, it was simultaneously bombarded by three enemy batteries on two occasions. This resulted in the complete destruction of two guns and considerable damage being caused to a third; the fourth gun was also soon surrounded by large craters. The destroyed guns were replaced straight away; the emplacements were rebuilt again in one night using beams prepared in the pioneer park."[3]

***

ALTHOUGH ALL OF THE BATTALIONS of the 56th Divisions laboured intensely over the preparations for the attack, the true work horses were the men of the 167th Brigade. It was they who had dug the new advanced trench in May, and it would be they who would work without a rest for the whole of June. If they were not based in Hebuterne, working on the front line trenches, they were either in the rear villages digging, moving stores and mending roads or back at Halloy repairing and preparing the practice areas for the assault battalions. For the first two weeks of June, the 1/1st Londons and the 1/3rd Londons shared St Amand as a base, supplying working parties wherever they were needed. The exertions were relentless, the weather poor, the ground heavy to work often, and especially in the front lines, hot food and drink was in short supply. Thankfully, though, casualties from enemy activity were light. But that didn't stop the Tommies grumbling; after all, they'd volunteered to fight the Germans not dig their way across Northern France!

And it was not just the 'other ranks' who complained about the conditions and unrelenting physical effort. Even subalterns were not above a quiet gripe, especially in their letters home. 2nd Lt. Arthur Batho[i] of the 8th Middlesex was a

---

[i] 2nd Lt. Arnold Capel Batho, 8th Middlesex Regt., was killed in action on Sunday 15th September 1916, aged 25. He was the second son of the late W. J. Batho and Mrs Edith Batho of 2, Cresswell Road, East Twickenham. He went on to become the 8th Middlesex's Battalion Signalling Officer. Educated at the Stanley Home School, Maragte and Bancroft's School, Woodford, Essex, pre-war he was an Assistant master at St Cuthbert's School, Malvern. An enthusiastic member of the Boy Scouts movement he was a Scoutmaster in Malvern with the 3rd (St Cuthbert's) Malvern Link Troop and St Stephen's, Twickenham. A pre-war Territorial he re-enlisted on the outbreak of war,

regular correspondent with his mother, Edith, in salubrious East Twickenham and his sister, Kathleen in the quiet rural backwater of Stamford in Lincolnshire. He was a pre-war Territorial of four years service who had re-enlisted in 1914. Wounded the following year and invalided home, on his recovery he was commissioned into the Middlesex Regiment. Passed fit by a Medical Board, he returned to the front in January 1916 were he found the work hard and life dull:

> *Kathleen Batho*
> *Brazenose*
> *Stamford*
> *Lincs*
>
> *3rd June 1916*
>
> *Dear Kathleen,*
>
> *Our daily existence has been nothing but working parties.*
>
> *You needn't complain of Stamford being dull, in this place our only break in the monotony is the arrival of a German shell, so personally I prefer to remain monotonous.*
>
> *Here, while actually in the line we have to stand to arms an hour before dawn every day. That means 1:30 a.m. this time of year. I have seen so many sunrises since I came out here, I never want to see another one. Tomorrow being Sunday I find I am due for a working party unless they decide to give us a rest, a most unlikely happening, so far I have been either marching or in the trenches for the last six Sundays. The only exception was last week when we got back from digging a new front line in front of our old positions and only 250 yards from the Bosch (sic) at five o'clock in the morning. I went to bed and slept until well after midday so, I fancy, did everyone else.'*[1]

Each night, 400 men of the L.R.B. marched from Bayencourt to Hebuterne to continue the work on the new front line. They would form part of the many working parties from various battalions given the task of improving existing trenches, digging new ones and preparing dugouts for machine guns, mortars, aid posts and headquarters.

Until 3rd June, the 1/2nd Londons were based in Hebuterne village itself then, as the rain started to fall, they relieved the Queen Victoria's Rifles in the trenches. 'B' and 'D' Companies were sent out to occupy the trenches in the Y Sector whilst 'A' and 'C' Companies stayed in billets in Hebuterne. As the men snaked their way up the communication trenches to the front, they were greeted by a minenwerfer strafe from the trenches opposite.

***

BACK IN PAS, LT. GEN. SNOW was completing the composition of a report to Allenby outlining the plans for the attack on Gommecourt. Snow had received the two Divisions' plans on 25th May and had spent the intervening time reviewing and amending them. Now he sent on his observations about the Gommecourt operation for Allenby and his Staff to consider. Snow outlined the guiding principle behind the operation in his opening paragraph:

"The plans for the forthcoming operations by the VII Corps are based on the understanding that the role of the Corps was to extend the left of the

---

was wounded and commissioned into the 8th Middlesex. He returned to France in January 1915. He is buried in Combles Communal Cemetery Extension, Somme, France, grave VI. B. 19.

main attack by the Fourth Army and to divert artillery fire to itself which might otherwise be directed against the main attack."

Snow then confirmed his understanding that there would be no reserves available support the attack but he went on to set out his reasons why he believed Gommecourt to be a favourable location for an attack. His primary reason for this statement was that, with the German trenches being at a right angle around the village, it would be possible for the heavy and field artillery to enfilade, i.e. fire along the length of, the German trenches with guns from the south west bombarding the trenches on the northern front (46th Division) and others from the north west pummelling the 56th Divisions front to the south of Gommecourt.

Next, Snow proposed that the attack should follow the same timetable as for the main offensive of the Fourth Army to the south. It was important, so it was thought, for the attack to appear to be part of a co-ordinated Somme attack and the men of the VII Corps would go 'over the top' at the same time as their colleagues to the south on the day selected for the attack.

Snow then turned to the detail of the Gommecourt attack. The attack was to be in three phases. The first phase would see the 56th Division over-run three lines of German lines from a German strongpoint on the right to the edge of Gommecourt village and park on the left. At the same time, the 46th Division was to have moved up to and through Gommecourt Wood. Fighting through the woods on the Somme would soon become frighteningly familiar to many men of the B.E.F. and their experiences would reveal just how difficult a task it was to dislodge a determined defender from these dense thickets. At Gommecourt, however, it was anticipated that the 46th Division would achieve their objective on the eastern side of the wood after an hour's fighting. There would then be an hour's pause whilst reserves and supplies were brought forward and the artillery adjusted their sites onto new targets in the German fourth line whilst all the while bombarding Gommecourt Park and its occupants.

The third phase would see the two Division's close the trap around the rear of the village thereby cutting off any German troops encircled in the Park. Then, whilst the pioneers and engineers worked to construct strongpoints in the newly captured trenches and turn communication trenches into fighting trenches, squads of bombers would move into the Park to destroy or capture the remaining enemy soldiers. That, at least, was the theory.

The completion of the later phases of the 56th Division's attack were entirely dependent on one thing: the ability of the 46th Division to reach the eastern side of Gommecourt Wood. If they failed to reach this line or were long delayed in arriving there then, according to Snow's memo:

"... (the third) phase will have to be put off and form a later operation."

Quite what this meant was not clear. Were the 56th Division to be left in their exposed initial objectives then they would be, in Snow's own words, "(in an) unfavourable position". The longer they were there the more susceptible they would be to counter-attack from three sides and the reason for this was simple: having attacked to cut out a salient they would have created their own by their incursion into the German lines. And there was some reason to think that, even in senior officers' minds, there might well be some delay in the 46th Division reaching the far side of Gommecourt Wood. Maj. Gen. Stuart Wortley had already expressed some concerns about the ability of his men to take the eastern fringe of Gommecourt Wood in one bound. In front of the wood the terrain was an awkward proposition for the wire cutting batteries of 18 pdrs and he had suggested that his attack be broken into two sections, with the ridge to the north of Gommecourt Wood being taken before the main attack on and through the wood. In essence, this was a fourth phase in an already complex operation and, perhaps, warning bells should have been ringing at VII Corps over this proposed change. But Snow seemed unperturbed by this uncertainty over the timing of the plan and , indeed, felt that, once the troops actually reached their second phase positions the battle would, essentially, be over as the Germans in the village and park, threatened with encirclement would swiftly surrender rather than fight.

Snow's appreciation of the plans were, therefore, hedged around with some uncertainties as to the precise timings of the attack but the prevailing sense of optimism seemed undaunted by some yawning gaps in the plans for the Gommecourt attack.

Sunday, 4ᵗʰ June 1916
Third Army weather report: Dull morning, rained afternoon. Rain: 1.2mm.
Temp. 64-50° F

GEN. ALLENBY HAD SPENT the past few days working with his Staff on Lt. Gen. Snow's plan for the assault on the Gommecourt salient and a brief digest of the proposal had been forwarded to GHQ for their consideration. Snow's three part phased programme was set out with little comment by Allenby. He did, however, point out the dangers to the 56ᵗʰ Division if the 46ᵗʰ Division's attack failed wholly or in part and, in view of this, he suggested that the penultimate phase of the attack, the joining hands of the Divisions prior to the assault on Gommecourt village and Park, should take place at Snow's command rather than allow the two Division's to move into position according to a pre-arranged timetable which, however successful the attack, would almost inevitably vary on each front. There was some sense to this and, for Allenby, the danger most involved the 56ᵗʰ Division. If either Division pressed their advance too far forward whilst the other lagged behind or failed entirely then the successful Division faced being lodged in an uncomfortably narrow salient deep within enemy lines. The prospects then would be bleak for the men literally at the sharp end of this salient. The counter argument to Allenby's suggestion, however, was that communications across a battlefield from headquarters to the most advanced troops once the attack went in ranged from difficult to impossible. Timetabled advances, therefore, properly co-ordinated with the heavy and field artillery barrages, were, it was thought at GHQ, the most likely means by which an attack might be successfully prosecuted. Haig and Rawlinson had already argued the toss about phased attacks on the main front with Rawlinson proposing such a means of attack. Haig was unpersuaded however and it seemed probable that the response from on high to Allenby's thoughts was likely to be the same. At their headquarters, Allenby and Snow awaited the CinC's response.

On the 4ᵗʰ, services were held in churches and chapels throughout the divisional areas. These services were voluntary but many were well attended. Chaplain, and honorary Captain, Bickersteth was particularly busy this Sunday. His three services were conducted in a crypt twenty feet beneath the shattered streets of Hebuterne, each one full to overflowing with more than 100 men crowded into the small cruciform cellar. Other denominations also prayed and sang to the accompaniment of a creaking harmonium with a Catholic mass, a Presbyterian and a Wesleyan Service all taking place that day.[5]

Later, after Bickersteth had ministered to the spiritual needs of his men, the Germans again tried to disrupt the work on the new front line they had all helped to dig. Another salvo of minenwerfers was sent rolling and tumbling across the sky. One hit a section of trench occupied by men of the 1/2nd Londons, burying seven men and wounding nine others (including 2nd Lt. H G Guildford). 2nd Lt. W L Stone was a shell shock victim of the strafe - another who could no longer stand the sound of the plummeting bomb, the desperate scramble for safety, the shuddering shock of the explosion and the sound, smell and sight of dead and dismembered men. Sgt. Bisgood's diary recalls the awfulness of the 'Moaning Minnie's' impact on the trenches and the men in them:

> "Our front line is getting hell from the German Minenwerfer. This machine and its projectiles are our chief horror, as at night you can observe the bomb travelling through the air on account of the fuse which burns almost like a faulty star shell. One of these has smashed our parapet killing outright three of our boys and burying a corporal and 3 others. Shall be unable to get these latter out until tomorrow morning. Fear they will be dead, impossible to tell damage in the dark. We are still engaged working at high pressure on the new front line."[6]

Six of the buried men of the 1/2nd Londons were killed[i] with another dying of his wounds[ii] and, far away, one private from the 1/1st Londons[iii] died of his wounds in a hospital overlooking the Channel at Etaples as the subterranean church services went on. Most of the men were buried in the fast-growing cemetery at the rear of Hebuterne village, just north of the Sailly Road. It backed onto the Advanced Dressing Station and was surrounded by trees from the apple orchards that surrounded the village. The dead from May and June were buried in lines and, unusually, they were grouped together by regiment. As the only Church of England padre near the front it fell to Capt. Bickersteth to preside over the internments. He faced another ten days or so of danger and the sadness of conducting funeral services in the orchard that now served as a cemetery to the nearby A.D.S. But, in spite of this, the padre found life at the front a strangely uplifting experience:

---

[i] The following men of the 1/2nd London Regt were killed on Sunday 4th June, 1916:

4659 Pte William Case. A resident of Greenwich he is buried in Hebuterne Military Cemetery, grave IV. A.3.

1254 Pte Arthur Church, aged 24. He was the son of Mr. and Mrs. Church of 85, Harlesden Gardens, Willesden, London. He is buried in Hebuterne Military Cemetery, grave IV. A. 4.

4558 Pte Henry Fisher. A resident of Tooting he is buried in Hebuterne Military Cemetery, grave IV. A. 8.

1409 Pte George William Hatchard. Born in Fulham and a resident of Westminster, he is buried in Hebuterne Military Cemetery, grave IV. A. 5.

4964 Pte Thomas Milsom. Born and living in Westminster, he is buried in Hebuterne Military Cemetery, grave IV. A. 2.

4636 Pte Claude Charles Young, aged 18. A member of 'A' Company he was the son of William and Ellen Young of 62, Turner Building, Millbank Estate, Millbank, Westminster, London. He is buried in Hebuterne Military Cemetery, grave IV. A. 7.

[ii] 3010 Cpl Joseph Edward Smith, 1/2nd London Regt., died of wounds on Monday 5th June, 1916. Aged 19 he was the son of David and Alice Smith of 38, Bromar Road, Denmark Hill, Camberwell, London. He is buried in Hebuterne Military Cemetery, grave IV.A.6.

[iii] 1675 Pte Walter Stanley Green, 'A' Company, 1/1st London Regt., died of wounds on Sunday 4th June, 1916, aged 21. He was the son of Reginald and Amy Green of 17, Ilex Rd., Church Rd., Willesden, London. He is buried in Etaples Military Cemetery, grave V.E.1A

"I wouldn't have missed this experience for the world. It is a privilege to be allowed to share (the men's) dangers."[7]

On the 3ʳᵈ June the London Rifle Brigade. had swapped places with the Queen's Westminster Rifles and, with the exception of 'D' Company who were sent off to be billeted in Mondicourt, returned to Halloy. From the 4ᵗʰ onwards their work alternated between fatigues for the Royal Engineers and practice attacks. Almost every day they practised their attack on the dummy trenches until every man could find his objective with his eyes shut. On Monday, 5ᵗʰ they were joined on the practice grounds by the 1/4ᵗʰ Londons (who had been allowed a rest and attended Church services on the 4ᵗʰ) and together they started to churn up this bit of French countryside still further until its once green and gold cornfields were a mass of mud.

Before the change over, the Q.W.R.s had spent an arduous few days at Halloy. Every day, a regular flow of men had reported to the M.O., and it was the weather that was mainly to blame. The summer of 1916 was turning into one of which the British could be proud. From the 3ʳᵈ to 14ᵗʰ June it rained. Daytime temperatures barely crept above 60° F and, at night, they fell as low as 37° F, cold enough in sheltered places for a decent frost. The training camp at Halloy became a morass. Even here, sixteen kilometres behind the front line, the roads were inches deep in mud. The practice attacks were carried out in slush and mud and it came as a relief to the men to leave Halloy. Conditions were so bad that the Q.W.R. suffered 85 cases of 'trench foot', normally a front-line condition, when using the practice trenches. Trench foot was a debilitating condition that had first been identified during Napoleon's invasion of Russia in 1812. It was caused by a combination of the cold and wet. Standing ankle deep in cold water in a muddy trench were the perfect circumstances in which to contract 'trench foot'. In these conditions, the feet would swell, become red, blistered and severely painful. If left untreated, the nerves would be damaged and the foot would go numb. In these circumstances, the only option was evacuation. Treatment consisted of elevating the affected foot, moderate warmth... and time. In most cases, the foot would heal and the sufferer would return to the ranks. In serious cases, where nerve damage was severe, gangrene could set in and then amputation was the only course of action. But, whatever its causes, 'trench foot' was not supposed to occur in men training behind the lines!

So, it was with some relief that the Westminster's trudged across the rolling Picardy countryside to the small village of Bayencourt, 4½ kilometres to the west of Hebuterne. Here, at least, they would get a day's rest before they would be called upon to provide working parties for the next four days to help complete the new front line trenches that 167ᵗʰ Brigade had started nearly two weeks earlier. Rfn. Percy Jones recalled their time at Bayencourt in his diary:

"We moved again two days ago, thro' Pas and Henu to Bayencourt, about 3 miles from the trenches. Here we are billeted in a sort of outhouse, the floor of which is made of broken concrete and pitted with large holes about two inches deep, so it makes an almost ideal bed! Our waterproof capes have now been withdrawn as well as the blankets. We have been up to the trenches each night, thro' Sailly au Bois to Hebuterne. This small town has been very badly battered but as it is sheltered by a hill it is used extensively for troops and material. We drew tools from an R.E. dump in a ruined house and proceeded thro' a complicated system of communication trenches to the old front line. Our present work consists of improving and strengthening this front line, and digging communication trenches back to the old front lines. These are real trenches, sometimes twelve feet deep and very wide, quite different from our sand bag barricades in Flanders."[8]

Jones wasn't the only man to feel displeased at the absence of his water proof and blankets. The decision to collect them in mid-May was one made according to an Army timetable and not related to the actual weather conditions. It was such decisions as these that failed to endear staff officers to the ordinary soldier:

"The Army have called in all the blankets and Macintoshes so that now we have to sleep with only our jackets and overcoats over us. At first it was rather cold and consequently we got very little sleep but now we are getting used to it and manage to sleep all right."[9]

Rfn. Jones also commented on the dangers of working in the front line trenches as well as the 'unsocial hours' of much of their work:

"The Germans' great stunt here is the minenwerfer and machine-gun combination. The minenwerfers certainly go off with a terrific explosion and are causing rather a lot of casualties. You can see the brutes coming, (by day, a black blob, by night a fiery tail of sparks) but not accurately enough to dodge them. They have got the range of our front line nicely and put their bombs in or very near the trench. The first night up was a terrible muddle. Nobody seemed to know the trenches or where we had to work, and the whole time was spent in drifting about trenches in single file, with interminable waits. Shortly after midnight, the Germans opened up with a combined strafe of minenwerfers and artillery which our people were not slow to answer. About half our men were fresh to trench life, but they behaved very well."

"We generally parade at Bayencourt at about 7 p.m. march to the trenches and dig or carry until dawn, and return to the billet by three or four o'clock when it is broad day-light. We have a cup of tea and a biscuit, and turn in till 9 o'clock when we wake up for breakfast. During the morning anyone who can dodge the various duties sleeps till dinner time."[10]

Blamed for the 'terrible muddle' in the trenches that night was a new and inexperienced young subaltern for whom this was his first experience in the front line trenches. 2nd Lt. C E Moy[i] had only recently arrived in France and he viewed his responsibilities as well as his personal safety with great concern.

"The men paraded at the given hour. I arrayed myself in the Burberry with my revolver in the holster at its waist belt – here my heart sank again to think that I might have to use it in anger before the night was out. I slung my gas helmet (gas respirators had not yet been invented) over my shoulder put a large flask of whisky in my pocket; donned my tin hat. Screwing my courage right up to the bursting point I then grasped my walking stick and

---

i 2nd Lt. Cecil Eric Moy, M.C., 1/16th London Regt. (Queen's Westminster Rifles) lived at 24, Criffel Avenue, Streatham Hill, London. He was in reserve during the attack on Gommecourt but was wounded on 19th September 1916 near Leuze Wood by shrapnel and was evacuated to England for hospital treatment. He recovered to rejoin the battalion.

set out to show a bold front to the men. Giving the order to move off and waving to the other Company officers I set my face for the first time towards the great adventure. The last touch was given by the Colonel who was waiting at the crossroads to wish us good luck."

"For the first part of the journey we stuck to the road, soon passing through a village of awful repute - Sailly-au-Bois - I rejoiced to get through it because on the previous night the 2nd Londons had twelve sergeants killed when a shell landed smack in the middle of their mess. So along the road until we came to within a mile of the line; branched off onto a track made of duckboards, which lay behind the 18 pdr gun positions. The ground round about was pitted with shell holes, and the track itself had been hit in many places. The guns were firing occasionally, but not to any great extent -- so far there had not been anything to trouble us."

"On we went until we came to what had once been the village of Hebuterne, the walls of the houses had been almost raised to the ground, none of them being higher than four or five feet; it had been transformed into a Keep. In front, about 1000 yards away, I could make out a ragged fringe of trees - Gommecourt Wood."[11]

At this point, things started to go wrong for the inexperienced Moy. With the trenches full of men from different battalions, some going up the line and some down, and with many of the guides still finding their way around the maze of trenches it was only too easy for things to go wrong – and this night they did.

"After preceding along the zigzag trench in single file for 200 yards or so, a message came up from the sergeant at the back to the effect that we were walking too fast in front and they were losing touch in the rear. We moved on at a snail's space, but the same message kept on coming up and then it was reported that touch had been lost. I decided not to wait, and left a man behind to tell the other half of the party when it did turn up, which way we had gone. After about half an hour's very slow walking through reserve and support trenches, we arrived in the front line; got out of it by means of steps; and proceeded through the barbed wire entanglements to a spot some hundred yards out in No Man's Land, where the position of the new trenches to be dug was indicated by a line of white tape. Between us and the enemy trenches still 300 yards away was a body of men called a covering party - placed there to prevent any attempt to interfere with us on the part of the Hun."

"Although I had only half of the number of men left that I started out with, under the instructions of the guide I spaced them out along white tape and gave the order to commence work. I sent a men to see if he could find the missing portion of my party, but he came back to report that the trenches were chock a block with men of all kinds of regiments, guides had lost their way and utter confusion prevailed everywhere. I decided to let the matter rest for the moment, and strolled slowly along the line of digging men. Nothing could be heard save the chink of a pick on the stone; the soft fall of excavated earth. The dim line of figures bending and heaving silently and regularly showed that the night's work was in full swing."[12]

To compound Moy's problems, the Germans decided to take a hand in the high speed education of this front line novice:

"Suddenly there was a dull "wumph" - and a trail of sparks shot up into the air from the German lines. I was about to make the acquaintance of a minenwerfer (mine thrower) nicknamed 'rum jars' by our men on account of its shape. The sparks continued for a while and then disappeared as the abomination reached its highest point of flight and started to descend. Terror gripped me. You can't see it – that's the devil of it. You know it is there above you somewhere. In a few seconds a great tearing explosion shook the earth and bits of metal pinged like lost souls through the night. It had fallen some hundred yards to our right."

"By this time my men had dug about a foot of the new trench and I at once ordered them to lie in it, doing the same myself. Soon the air became thick with the awful flaming tails of the 'rum jars' and the noises of the tearing explosions. Mercifully they stayed over to the right of us. After 15 minutes they stopped and we commenced work again. I was now not nearly so confident as I had been, and held myself in readiness for a second quick jump into the shallow trench."

"Soon the necessity for the jump came. This time I was introduced to a fresh form of frightfulness. There was a sudden shrill scream and something burst directly behind us on our old front line. It was the smallest type of shell used by the Germans, a 77 mm, otherwise known as a 'whizz bang'. The first was quickly followed by a whole covey of others, and we once more sought refuge in our trench. They came over thick and fast, mostly at the old front line, but some fell short, and one took away the parapet a yard from me. My impression now was that the whole thing was a horrible nightmare - it all seemed unreal and theatrical; theatrical is the best word for it. The smell of cordite exactly the same as when a pistol is fired in the theatre; the flashes of exploding shell like fake lightning in a storm scene on the stage. The reality soon became evident when the ominous order for stretcher bearers was passed down the line. Thank heaven none of my men had been hit; the message was from another Company who were working on my left. I learnt afterwards that 'A' Company had three men wounded."[13]

Moy's eventful introduction to the terrors of the trenches was nearly over. All he had to do now was find the rest of his men:

"At 1:30 a.m., when we had dug our new trench to the depth of roughly three feet, we packed up work. Once more led by our faithful guide we returned, via the trenches, to Hebuterne. When we reached the village I counted my lambs and found that instead of 100 only 47 were present. An officer of 'D' Company, Iveson, came up to me when I was in the last stages of fright, wondering what had happened to the remainder, and told me that he had found them early in the night, and would I go and relieve him of them - I did so, very thankfully! We returned our tools to The Keep, and started on our home journey, which we accomplished without further excitement."[14]

Although he and his men came away unscathed there were, for Moy at least, repercussions for temporarily 'mislaying' his 53 men.

"On the following afternoon, the colonel once more sent for me and explained that entirely owing to my leaving half my party in the trenches the previous night, they had become jammed and prevented the 200 men of 'C' and 'D' companies from doing any work at all. He did not blame me much because he knew it was due to inexperience and could soon be remedied, however he made me go up again that night."[15]

Monday, 5th June 1916
Third Army weather report: Rain. Rain: 2.6mm. Temp. 63-48° F

THE FOLLOWING DAY was relatively quiet. Every now and then a 77mm shell would shriek overhead making the men crouch and duck, turning their new metal helmets in the direction of the aerial explosion in the hope they would be protected from a flying shard of shrapnel. The rain of the two previous days became somewhat heavier on the 5th, making the dangerous work in the trenches even more unpleasant as the soldiers moved through the mud and slime.

From the 4th to the 8th June, on which day the Q.V.R. was relieved by the London Scottish, it was in reserve in Hebuterne Keep. On the last-mentioned date it returned to Halloy, where it was employed in 'Attack Practice' until June 13th when two companies went to Sailly-au-Bois and the other two to Hebuterne. Sgt. C K Sim in his diary wrote that the attack was practised on a replica of the German system of trenches at Gommecourt; the Q.V.R. and the L.R.B. led the attack. His platoon led for 'C' Company and had to capture three lines of German trenches. "Got wet through during this affair and again in the afternoon while on digging fatigue."[16] He further mentioned that Sgt. F. H. C. Hickman had been awarded the Military Medal and L/Cpl. E. E. Eames the D.C.M.

Tuesday, 6th June 1916
Third Army weather report: Rained very heavily all night and morning. Cleared in the afternoon. Rain: 7.4mm. Temp. 57-37° F

TUESDAY, 6TH JUNE was the middle day of three spent by the 1/4th Londons and the Kensingtons rehearsing for the attack on the Halloy practice grounds. The ground was sodden from heavy overnight rain and the men plodded through the sticky mud of the farmland. As usual, these rehearsals were subject to inspection by senior officers and their staff officers and, the following day, no less than the Army Commander, Gen. Allenby, was present to watch the men struggle in serried ranks across the beaten down corn. Afterwards, and accompanied by Maj. Gen. Hull and Brig. Gen. Loch, Allenby inspected the 1/4th Londons and expressed himself more than satisfied with their conduct in the front lines and with their performance in the practice.

For 'B' and 'D' Companies of the 1/2nd Londons the day was distressing and unpleasant. Sgt. Bisgood's diary recorded the filthy weather, which was beginning to make the front line trenches a most inhospitable place. And there was still the disagreeable but essential task of recovering what was left of the men buried by the minenwerfer strafe two days before:

"Raining hard this morning. Trenches getting rather uncomfortable, not much doing. New front line taking the water rapidly. 6 p.m. instructed to meet draft of 20 from Gallipoli (my own old boys); met them and brought them up under heavy straffing. Got through without any mishaps. Our chaps have just recovered the remnants of the 4 boys who were buried in front on the 4th, they were literally torn to pieces, poor devils, and we had to bury them in Hebuterne cemetery and we could not tell who was who."[17]

At last out of the line, the Q.V.R. looked back on their experiences which, for many of the newer recruits, had been their first time under fire. The battalion had suffered steadily since their arrival at Hebuterne on the 26ᵗʰ May. Twenty men had been killed and another eighty wounded and, in the last week, most of the fatal incidents had affected No. 14 Platoon of 'D' Company. From the relative safety of one of the cellars in 'The Keep' on the western edge of Hebuterne, 3621 Rfn. Reginald Davis wrote home describing the events of the past few days:

> "From the day we entered the trench till now has been one series of heavy bombardment, an absolute rain of shells everywhere – a whole week of it. How so many came out alive I don't know.
>
> We lost four killed in our platoon, including one of my section, a splendid chap, cool and jolly. Three of us went to see him buried yesterday – we had a short service. His brother is with us, a boy of eighteen and is naturally very cut up. We have now sixteen graves where there were none a fortnight ago. Ten whom I knew personally are gone – such is war.
>
> All of us have had a shaking up. To many it has been their first real dose of real grim warfare, and it has been a sore trial for us to lie out in front with shells bursting all round and no cover. The natural tendency is to run back to the trench and get under cover. However, I managed to pull through, and feel more confident of myself…"[18]

Pte. Davis was rewarded for his greater confidence by the award of a stripe and, two days later, the new Lance Corporal and his mates set to further practices of their attack over the muddy corn fields at Halloy.

Wednesday, 7ᵗʰ June 1916
Third Army weather report: Fine (sic). Rain: 7.7mm. Temp. 63-39⁰ F

THE 1/2ᴺᴰ LONDONS swapped their companies over on the 6ᵗʰ June so that 'A' and 'C' Companies now occupied the trenches and 'B' and 'D' had some respite from the rain in their battered billets in Hebuterne. Pte (later Lt.) H T Clements was a member of a 1/2ⁿᵈ Londons Lewis Gun Team and he and his two mates, Frank Schofield and Webb, had been out all night acting as a screening party for the men still working on the new trenches. As the day wore on they started to look forward to their relief and a spot of hot food. They were in for a little frustration:

> "We were relieved rather late and when we got back to the dug out the fellows hadn't brought our tea and bacon along. In consequence, felt bad tempered when we had to go and get it ourselves from the cooker in the village, however, I had a good night's sleep."[19]

The weather had broken in earnest now and, from the 6ᵗʰ to the 8ᵗʰ, an inch of rain fell. The water collected in the bottom of the trenches making the need for proper precautions against trench foot all the more necessary. Keeping the men's feet dry was well nigh impossible but generous applications of whale grease and, whenever possible, changing into a dry pair of the three pairs of socks they were required to have helped ease the problem. Feet and boots were regularly inspected to ensure, as far as was possible, that proper care was being taken to avoid the crippling condition. But, however hard they tried officers and N.C.O.s could not prevent a steady stream of men reporting to the MO with trench foot and other serious conditions.

Thursday, 8th June 1916
Third Army weather report: Fine (!). Rain: 8.5mm. Temp. 62-45° F

ON THE 8TH JUNE, the Rangers marched the two kilometres from Sailly to Hebuterne to take their turn 'at the front', relieving the London Scottish in the front line trenches of the W sector. Leaving at 3 p.m., the battalion marched by companies along the duckboard walkway that ran along the shallow valley between the two villages. On either side, dug in behind sand-bagged emplacements, were several 18 pdr batteries of the Divisional Field Artillery. The relief was complete by midnight with 'A' and 'B' Companies occupying the new front and support lines, 'C' Company settled into the scrapes and dugouts of Cross Street, the old support line, whilst 'D' Company and the Regimental H.Q. took over billets in the cellars of the ruins of Hebuterne. Being that bit nearer to the German guns, and being within range of their machine guns and mortars, had an immediate impact on their casualty rate.

The 8th June also saw the L.R.B. given a brief break from fatigues and practice attacks. General Hull, the 56th Division's commander (who the day before had watched the 1/4th Londons practice their attack along with General Allenby and Brigadier General Loch), appeared before the paraded battalion and presented medals to several worthy recipients. An M.C. went to Capt. Johnston and D.C.M.s to then Corporal but now Lt. Boston and Sgt. Lindsay. Unfortunately, this day was the wettest of a sodden week's worth. So, it was with some despondency that the battalion was told off for another parade the following day. Thankfully, though, the 9th proved drier (though not totally dry!) and the inspection by the Right Hon. Sir Charles Wakefield, the Lord Mayor of London, and General Hull made a welcome break from the new task of digging more practice trenches in the Halloy mudbath. Speeches were made by the notable worthies and the men dispersed afterwards for much needed rest. The following day, the rain came down like stair rods the whole day, the temperature fell and the men of the L.R.B., joined by the 1/4th Londons, carried on digging in the glutinous mud of Halloy. No rest for the wicked!

Friday, 9th June 1916
Third Army weather report: Fine. Rain: 0.3mm. Temp. 64-37° F
Saturday, 10th June 1916
Third Army weather report: Dull & raining. Rain: 9.4mm. Temp. 61-42° F

TWO DAYS AFTER the arrival of the Rangers, and just after a re-distribution of the battalion's companies, a minenwerfer strafe caught a party of 'D' Company. At night, by watching carefully the fiery tail of the projectile, it was often possible to dodge and dive into another stretch of trench in order to avoid the shattering blast. On this occasion, Lt. Meo was standing outside the trench watching the flight of the incoming bomb, ready to order his men to scramble to a safe place when the 'minnie' exploded prematurely in mid-air. The young lieutenant was killed along with 21 year old Rfn. Arthur Jenner from Kentish Town[i]. Two other Riflemen were wounded.

Sunday, 11th June 1916
Third Army weather report: Dull and wet. Rain: 1.5mm. Temp. 62-43º F

THIS MORNING CORPS AND DIVISIONAL STAFFS met at Pas to consider certain revisions for the programme of attack prepared by Brig. Gen. Lyon. VII Corps Staff had been considering a suggestion from 46th Division that their attack should be phased, with the 139th Brigade on the left taking the ridge between Gommecourt and Pigeon Woods before the attack of the 137th Brigade on Gommecourt Wood went in. Their concern was the difficulty in cutting the wire immediately in front of the Wood but their suggestion introduced the uncertainty of a fourth phase into an already complex plan. Snow and his Staff had concluded, however, that the 46th Division's attack should be made with the Brigades attacking simultaneously and now they brought forward the proposed timings for the three phases of the assault. The first phase was to be completed at Zero + 20 minutes. An hour would then pass whilst the freshly captured lines were consolidated and fresh troops and supplies were brought up. During this period, three communication trenches would be dug across No Man's Land to allow easy access to the old German trenches. At Zero + one hour and 20 minutes the assault on the 2nd objectives was to take place. This mainly involved the 46th Division pushing through Gommecourt Wood to take Oxus Trench, ready to push onto the Quadrilateral and the junction with the Londoners pushing northwards. Again, after the taking of these new positions, there would be another pause. Certain key points were to be turned into strongpoints, trenches needed to be properly blocked to prevent counter-attacks and, again, reserves of men, ammunition, food and water needed to be brought up for the final phase – the cutting off of Gommecourt village and Park. This phase was to start at Zero + two hours and 30 minutes at which point the two Divisions were to link up at the Quadrilateral to the east of Gommecourt, thereby cutting off the German garrison of the village and Park. They would then be invited to surrender and, if they refused, then the elimination of their position would start.

That, then, was the plan. All that remained, except for fine tuning of the Divisional programmes, was the detail of the Corps and Divisional artillery schemes which were required to be at VII Corps' headquarters in four days' time. The Divisional Staff then motored back to their headquarters to continue work on their individual responsibilities.

***

---

[i] The Rangers suffered 29 casualties from the 8th to 13th June, two of them fatal. Two officers were casualties: Lt. Meo was killed on the 10th and 2nd Lt. B G Coffin was wounded on the 12th June. Lt. Meo and Rfn Jenner are buried side by side in Hebuterne Military Cemetery, graves III.D.1. and III.D.2.
Lt. Giovanni Battista Meo, 1/12th London Regt (The Rangers), died on Saturday, 10th June 1916. Born on 4th September 1890, he was the son of mixed Italian/Irish parents: Gaetano G F and Agnes Meo of 39, Downshire Hill, Hampstead, London. He was educated at St Mary's Lodge, Hastings and Wellington House, Hampstead. He attested 2277 Private in the 3/12th London Regt., (The Rangers) on 1st September 1914 and was commissioned in December 1914. He is buried in Hebuterne Military Cemetery, grave III.D.1.
3825 Rfn Arthur James Jenner, 1/12th London Regt (The Rangers), died on Saturday, 10th June 1916, aged 21. Born on 6th October 1895. He was the son of Frederick and Maria Jenner of 14, Crogsland Rd., Chalk Farm, London. Employed by the Aylesbury Diary Company at their Finchley branch he enlisted on 12th May 1915 and went to France on 7th November 1915. He is buried in Hebuterne Military Cemetery, grave III.D.2.

THE RANGERS' WORKING PARTIES were subject to intermittent strafes by minenwerfers and artillery as they worked in the rain that fell continuously until their relief on the 13th and on Sunday, 11th June it was the turn of 'A' and 'B' Companies to suffer. Some ten men were wounded, including L/Cpl. Hopkins of 'B' Company who was badly wounded in the head by a piece of shrapnel. At this time, the communication trenches were too narrow to allow a stretcher to reach the front line so Hopkins had to endure a five-hour journey down the sodden and slippery trenches with the bearers carrying him with sandbags under his arms and knees. Fortunately, he was saved by an emergency operation in the Dressing Station on the southern outskirts of Hebuterne before being sent on to No. 19 Casualty Clearing Station which he reached the following day. He was immediately sent onwards by ambulance train to the 2nd Canadian General Hospital at Le Treport where he remained until 18th June when he was sent to Le Havre, loaded onto the hospital ship *'Lanfranc'* and despatched to Southampton. For the next three months he was first in the VA Hospital in Torquay and then the VA Hospital at Plympton but L/Cpl Hopkins never recovered from his injuries and he was discharged from the Army on 26th March 1917.

For the London Scottish, this was not the start of a well-earned rest. Withdrawing only as far as The Keep in the village of Hebuterne, they continued to provide working parties 24 hours a day. Three companies were given night time duties and the fourth was used during the day. This arrangement was to last until the 21st June, just eight days before the scheduled date for the attack. There was no chance that the battalions would be refreshed and fully fit before they went 'over the top'. As this was a diversionary attack, there was no question of the division being given help with the multifarious tasks involved in mounting a major attack. The men would work, dig and then fight. And eat, if the enemy allowed it. Again the battalion cooks went where the infantry went, finding billets in a damaged farmhouse. But, as ever, Hebuterne was not a safe place to:

"On 8th June the battalion was relieved by the Rangers, and moved to The Keep in the village. This was the end part of the village, in which the roads and byways had been barricaded and strongly defended by machine guns. Our horses arrived and drew our cooker into The Keep so that we could be with company. In addition to our equipment we carried with us three cane bottom chairs we had 'scrounged' in the village. We found a billet in a shell shattered farmhouse, and soon after our arrival a big shell whizzing over our heads, and a large piece fell in the midden about ten yards away."

"Profiting by previous experience, we placed the cooker behind a brick wall to avoid being hit by machine gun bullets which had a habit of whistling past us as we were working. The mud was so thick that we obtained three trench boards from the Royal Engineers dump to place round the cooker. Trench boards were similar to a wooden ladder with slats to allow the water to drain off and so did not get buried in the mud."

"The Germans artillery was very lively, and every now and then 'strafed' the village. The machine gun fire also made it decidedly unsafe at times to venture out of the billet. One shell hit 'D' Company's billet (called The Grand Hotel) and four of them were wounded. One Sunday we received a shock for we were calmly sitting at tea when the Germans put some 5.9

inch shells over our billet. The first two shells skimmed the roof, and the third landed in the garden behind. We decided to shift and went along to the sergeants billet where there was a cellar."[20]

***

WHILST THE L.R.B. had been parading in front of the Lord Mayor, the Queen's Westminsters had taken over the Hebuterne trenches from the 1/2nd Londons. Three companies of the 1/2nd Londons ('A', 'B' and 'D') withdrew to Bayencourt after their relief by the Westminsters, marching through pouring rain on the way to their new billets. 'C' Company stayed in Hebuterne to provide extra manpower for the next two days, the rest of the battalion gratefully had two days rest before their next move and another round of exhausting fatigues.

Meanwhile, 'A' and 'B' Companies of the Q.W.R. moved straight into the front lines and 'C' and 'D' Companies found billets amongst the ruins of the village. For 2nd Lt. Moy and the other officers of 'B' Company nights were spent away from their men in a wrecked house in Hebuterne village. They took it in turns to go up to the trenches occupied by their men to ensure all was well. The accommodation was neither salubrious nor safe (but considerably better than a corner of some sopping, stinking trench).

"Inside, in a room about ten feet square, with thick mud on the floor, we found Whitmore and the other Company officers. Whitmore said that as there was no dugout accommodation in the line we should all sleep there but go out at frequent intervals to see if our men were alright. By this time it was nearly midnight, and having had a meal of bully beef and hot cocoa, six of us laid down in the mud on the floor for a little sleep whilst the two others went out to patrol the line."

"I fell asleep and after what seemed like two minutes was awakened by a terrific crash followed immediately by the terrible scream of a man in agony. A voice in the darkness shouted, "stretcher bearer, quick!" Horne got up and rushed out to see what was the matter, another shell whistled over and exploded... another... Horne came back to report that the man was not badly hurt - a splinter in his shoulder, a red hot splinter of a shell can be very painful. Other shells crashed round; lifted; whistled farther back; ceased. The sinking feeling in the pit of my stomach diminished."

"The time was now 3 a.m., time to get ready to "stand to". Having carried out this procedure, I returned once more to headquarters for breakfast, consisting of fried bacon, bread and tea. At 8 a.m. I went back to my platoon; saw that their rifles were clean and that they had taken off their boots and rubbed their feet to prevent a very prevalent complaint - Trench Feet; put them on to clean some of the mud out of the trench."[21]

Monday, 12th June 1916
Third Army weather report: Wet & stormy. Rain: 4.4mm. Temp. 53-44° F

ON THE 11TH AND 12TH JUNE, the L.R.B. were allowed to attack the trenches they had so painstakingly dug over the previous days. The rain persisted and the temperature plummeted. The 11th being a Sunday, the 1/4th Londons from the 168th Brigade were given time off from their working parties to attend religious services before being inspected in the drizzle by General Hull and the ubiquitous

Lord Mayor of London. The Christian services took place in the small Halloy Church, whilst the Jewish members of the battalion went to the nearby village of Grenas for their religious observation. For the Lord Mayor his day was not yet done. In a staff car he set off eastwards and by 2 p.m. was in St Amand where he found the tired men of the 1/3rd Londons lined up for his inspection.

On the 12th, alongside the Q.V.R.s and the 169th Brigade's Machine Gun Company and Trench Mortar Battery, a full-blown rehearsal took place. Watched by Army, Corps, Division and Brigade 'red tabs' through a dense smoke screen, the battalion marched across the Halloy morass 'taking' the 'enemy's' trenches exactly to programme. Satisfied, the generals and their staff retired to their chateau H.Q.s for dinner and drinks where, over a fine, vintage cognac, a cigar or two might be puffed. In the huts at Halloy, the soaking, mud encrusted men shivered. The daytime temperature had barely crept above 50° F. 'Flaming June' had slunk across the Channel to haunt the British.

On the morning of the 13th, word spread that deliverance was at hand. One more successful 'attack' was achieved, before the L.R.B. broke camp and marched off in the pouring rain for the relative 'comfort' of Bayencourt. A terse comment in the battalion's War Diary sums up the men's feelings about their experience at Halloy:

> "During the past week," the diarist wrote, "the weather could not have been worse as it has pelted with rain, making the huts miserable and hampering all operations."[22]

Even billets in broken down farm buildings within range of the German guns seemed an attractive proposition after Halloy! They were joined on the line of march by the 1/4th Londons who were also heading to Bayencourt. For the Fusiliers, this was their last visit to Halloy. As a supporting battalion, their rehearsals had been less detailed than those of the assaulting troops and now they faced nearly two weeks of digging, wiring, cabling, moving stores and all the other tasks needed before such a grand enterprise as 'The Big Push'. In Hebuterne they would join up with their 168th Brigade colleagues, The Rangers, who had been occupying the front line since the 8th June and were now nearly half way through a stint in the trenches. There had been a steady erosion of their strength by enemy action: one officer and one 'other rank' killed and another sixteen men wounded. Today would add another nine to the roll call of the wounded, 2nd Lt. B G Coffin and eight men falling victim to the shelling of the trenches, one dying in one of the Casualty Clearing Stations at Doullens[i].

For the next two days, the L.R.B. were given some relief from the energy sapping digging, marching and general fatigues. Parties were sent up to Hebuterne but those left behind were able to take some time off before their next stint in the front lines.

The L.R.B.'s billets at Halloy were taken over by the 1/1st Londons who were joined, three days, later by the 1/3rd Londons. They were not there to rest or rehearse but to work. 'Enjoying' several days of dry weather, working parties

---

i 2428 Rfn Alfred Herbert Ellis, 1/12th London Regt (The Rangers), died of wounds on Tuesday, 13th June 1916. Aged 19, he was the son of Herbert Liddell Ellis and Louise Elizabeth Ellis of Anerley, London. He is buried in Doullens Communal Cemetery Extension No. 1, grave II.B.7.

were sent out to the practice grounds to prepare them for the full scale dress rehearsals due to start the following week.

***

THE 10TH AND 11TH had been relatively quiet for the Q.W.R. with more men reporting sick than were killed or wounded by enemy activity. Things became more interesting, however, on the evening of the 12th. In the rain and cold, the companies swapped positions and then three patrols were sent out into No Man's Land to collect samples of German wire and to check various saps running out from the edge of Gommecourt Park for machine gun emplacements. The three patrols[i] brought back several samples of very thick wire but, in the dark and wet, they could find no trace of the saps.

One man, however, was having fun. Nineteen year old Jack Engall, a second lieutenant from the Queen's Westminsters seconded to the 169th Brigade Machine Gun Company, had found a way of keeping himself entertained, encouraging the men in the front line *and* irritating the Germans. He called it 'peppering Peter' or 'little strafes on Peter'. He explained what this meant in a letter to a young lady, Miss N Locke, at home in West London:

"In plain English I've been popping off my little machine gun – just an hour's strafe at night and another first thing in the morning… I tell you, it's some feeling to sit down at a gun and pop off at 'Brother Fritz' knowing you are probably causing him as much annoyance as his M.G.s cause you – which is saying a good deal! It bucks you up no end and then, when you shut him up, you feel the war is practically won. It's absolutely great. I never realised I could be so bloodthirsty. And aren't the men in the front lines pleased when you stop 'Brother Fritz's' M.G.s? Well, not slightly! When I opened fire for the first time - I was given the honour of doing the first strafing our MG Company has done - they nearly fell on my neck and kissed me because they'd been having hell; Boches firing M.G.s with absolutely no return at all. And the feeling of the man who presses the trigger, well it's absolutely heavenly and it makes a real man of you. And to think these should be the feelings of your meek and gentle old Jack. Ah well, this fearful war is responsible for lots of dreadful things."[23]

Tuesday, 13th June 1916
Third Army weather report: Cold & wet. Rain: 5.1mm. Temp. 56-47º F

FOR THE 1/2ND LONDONS work resumed on the 13th. After a short two-kilometre march north to Souastre, they were billeted in the houses and large barns of the village where they were re-joined by 'C' Company. There, they were joined by the men of the Rangers who had been relieved in the trenches by the Kensingtons. Although they were there to work, a billet in Souastre had one major advantage, for here was the home of the 'Bow Bells', the Divisional Concert Party. Occupying one of the old barns in the village, the 'Bow Bells' put on a show of sorts most nights after the men had eaten. The Rangers regimental history recalls:

---

[i] They comprised Lt. Webb (see below) and Sgt. Davis of 'D' Company; Lt. Wagner (attached from the 1/2nd Londons), Cpl. Townsend and Rfn Wernham; and Lt. Westmoreland and Lt. Page (attached from the 38th Central Indian Horse).

Lt. (later Capt.) Musgrave Maitland Webb, 1/16th London Regt (Queen's Westminster Rifles), died on Monday, 18th September 1916, aged 24. He was killed in an attack on the Combles-Ginchy Road east of Leuze Wood. He was the son of Florence M. Webb of Westfield, Hatch End, Middx., and the late Mr. W. R. Webb. He is buried in Combles Communal Cemetery Extension, Somme, France, grave VII.G.19.

"There was one song in the show, as it was played then, that had more encores than any others, and that was 'My Old Kentucky Home' rendered and clog-danced to by Mark Leslie. Even now when a barrel-organ comes round and plays that song beneath the windows of any 1916 member of the 56th Division, his memory will travel quickly back to the old barn at Souastre, the smoke from pipes rising on the warm air, and the laughing faces of his 'pals' around him; he will smile at the recollection of that pleasant interlude in a life of toil and danger, but he will sigh when he realises how many of those laughing companions have since 'gone west'."[24]

Plate 11 An old barn in Souastre
This was the sort of barn used by the men as billets and for entertainment. Some even had roofs!

For the next six days the Rangers and the 1/2nd Londons were detailed to bury the many miles of cables needed for the complex telephone communication system required to link Battalion, Brigade, Division, Corps, Army, R.F.C., Artillery and every other H.Q. and observation post together. Much of the cable had already been buried but the last stretch, joining Sailly-au-Bois to Hebuterne, still needed doing. Every morning at 7.30 they would march out to dig, returning each afternoon at 4.30. It was tough, unrelenting work. Mostly, cables were buried from advanced brigade H.Q. to the near end of the communication trenches. Ideally, the cables were to be buried six feet deep, as experience showed such depth to be proof against direct hits of anything less than an 8 in. shell. From there, they ran either along the sides of the C.T.s or were buried a few inches in the bottom. The men were lucky that the weather during this period was the best for the whole month with hardly any rain and temperatures that were warm but not too high to make the arduous work even more taxing. Some men of the 1/2nd Londons were spared the slog of the daily cable laying, but only to face tasks equally back breaking. From the 14th to the 16th, 2nd Lt. A E Wiggs marched No. 7 Platoon into Hebuterne each day to help the 169th Brigade Machine Gun Company prepare their specially dug and protected emplacements from which they would lay down covering fire on the day of the attack and, on the 16th, 2nd Lt. Groves took a small party to assist the 169th Trench Mortar Battery in a similar task. In this work they were assisted by a party from 1/3rd Londons and two of them, 2269 Pte Sydney Harris[i] and 3456 Pte Charles Ryan[ii] of No. 8 Platoon, 'C' Company, 1/3rd Londons, were busy digging a trench mortar pit for one of the new Stokes mortars. The pit was in the front line (and would soon prove an unpopular feature, attracting as it did considerable German 'interest' when it started into action) and Harris and Ryan had managed to dig a hole some eight feet deep. It was, perhaps, for this reason that they did not hear or were unable to move in time when the shout went up that a minenwerfer had been fired from the lines opposite. The 'minnie' ploughed into the British parapet and the explosion buried both men. It too several hours hard digging to retrieve the bodies. Harris was dead but Ryan must have shown some signs of life because he was buried at St Amand. Sydney Harris, however, was buried the following day in the cemetery behind the Advanced Dressing Station in Hebuterne, a party from the Kensingtons in attendance to give him full military honours in farewell.

Whatever their task, the labours of the Rangers and the 1/2nd Londons were relentless and the appreciation that something big was in the offing grew, although the hope was that they were just preparing the way for others:

"The battalion – 'A', 'B' and 'D' Companies (of the 1/2nd Londons) come up every night from Bayencourt, strengthening the line and making assembly trenches. We know that a big attack is coming off shortly but do not know who is to make it. The general idea seems that the 56th are getting things prepared and will hold the line until the evening of the attack when we shall be relieved."[25]

The Kensingtons faced a ten day tour of the front lines. The relief of The Rangers had been delayed until after midnight as a result of some unwanted interference from a German mortar and a machine gun but, unscathed, the forward companies, 'A' and 'B', got into the front lines trenches in W sector. 'C' Company stayed in close support in the old front line trenches and 'D' Company occupied the somewhat more comfortable and secure lodgings of Biron dugouts within Hebuterne village. The next five days would be spent cleaning up and deepening the communication trenches in preparation for their use by the attacking battalions in two weeks time.

Wednesday, 14th June 1916
Third Army weather report: Dull & cold. Rain: 0.5mm. Temp. 60-47° F

THE WORKLOAD for all of the battalions was unremitting. It mattered little whether the unit was earmarked to be involved in the forthcoming attack, in the absence of any special labour units to do the digging and carrying, the infantry had to get on with the job. On 14th June, the 1/4th Londons embarked on a two-

---

[i] 2269 Pte Sidney Edward Harris, 1/3rd London Regiment (Royal Fusiliers) was killed on 13th June 1916. Aged 21, he was the son of Sydney & Alice Alexandra Harris of 7 Castle Road, Isleworth, Middlesex. He was buried in Hebuterne Military Cemetery, grave II.R.3. His officer, Lt. Davison, wrote to his parents describing Harris as: "Always a keen and intelligent solider, I had marked him out for the next vacancy for an NCO". His brother Herbet Harris was also a member of the 1/3rd Londons.

[ii] 3456 Pte Frederick Charles Ryan, 1/3rd London Regiment (Royal Fusiliers) was killed on 13th June 1916. He was the son of Mr J C Ryan of 16 Bertram Street, Upper Holloway, London. He was buried in St Amand Military Cemetery, grave I.A.15.

week night time work schedule of harsh intensity which, if the attack went in on the day planned, would give them just 24 hours in which to recover and be ready to act as the support battalion in the 168ᵗʰ Brigade's assault. Every night for two weeks, between 9 p.m. and 5 a.m., the 1/4ᵗʰ marched three miles to their workplaces and three miles back to their billets when their labours were done. 280 men were seconded to the 2/2ⁿᵈ London Field Company R.E., 140 joined up with the 1/5ᵗʰ Cheshires and another 140 were at the disposal of the Brigade Signal Officer for cable trench digging. It was hard and unpopular work, done mainly in pouring rain and under threat of imminent harm from machine gun, minenwerfer and artillery.

The Queen's Westminsters, meanwhile, were in the front lines where the jobs of the men from 'A' and 'B' Companies of the Q.W.R. were not restricted to aggressive night time patrolling in No Man's Land. They also had a role to play in preventing German patrols from getting too close to the newly constructed trench. Advanced posts had been constructed by the Z Hedge opposite Gommecourt Park and, at all times of day, these exposed positions were occupied by small numbers of men accompanied by their officers. On 14ᵗʰ June, 2ⁿᵈ Lt. Moy drew the short straw.

"The orders I received were to hold 'D' and 'E' posts; with the dread words added "at all costs", for 24 hours. We were not to be aggressive, but if the enemy attacked we were to do the best we could until support arrived. 'D' and 'E' posts were two strongpoints 400 yards in advance of our line, behind the Z hedge. I took over the positions at 4:00 in the afternoon. With half my platoon - 25 men - I held 'D' post, and sent the other half, under Luscombe, to hold E - 500 yards away on my right. The posts were connected by telephone, and there was also a wire back to battalion headquarters."

"The enemy was evidently unaware that the trenches were occupied because for the rest of the day he did not trouble us in any shape or form. At 10.00, accompanied by Bannister, my batman, I went across to 'E' post. Luscombe reported all well and I made my way back. I decided that sleep that night was impossible and sat on a box in the trench to await events."

"At midnight, very much on the 'qui vive', we heard slight sounds in front of us, which stealthily advanced until we thought that the people who made them were going to fall in our trench. When they got to the hedge they stopped and we heard a muttered conversation in German. Apparently deciding that the trenches were empty they proceeded along the other side of the hedge and so missed spotting us. The sounds gradually died away as the patrol passed down to the right. A few minutes later shots rang out from E post, evidently Luscombe had not been as fortunate as I had. Soon there came a telephone call and Luscombe informed me that the patrol had walked right on top of them and had started back at once for their own trenches. He had fired to prevent them getting away with the information, but did not know if he had hit anyone."

"Of course, after this I prepared for an attack at any moment, but the remainder of the night passed away without anything materialising. We were soon to see, however, the results of the knowledge the enemy had gained. At 6.00 in the morning, the enemy started sending over shell after shell from the dreaded Minenwerfer at the luckless 'E' post. The morning grew hideous with the sounds of their terrible triple crashes. After five minutes of it, Luscombe rang through to tell me one had fallen right in the trench and killed three men. A moment later he said two more were killed, what was he to do? I ordered him to abandon the post and close his men up to my position. I rang through to battalion headquarters to tell them what I had done and they ordered me to send them back to their post at once. What the hell was I to do? At that moment, Martin, who had come up from Hebuterne voluntarily to see how I was getting on, arrived - I was never so pleased to see anyone in my life. He and I went down to 'E' post to see what could be done. We met Luscombe and his men halfway, and took them along with us. The shelling had subsided and we went right back to the post, (where) I was introduced to the effect of modern projectiles."

"The trenches were battered almost beyond recognition and looked a shambles. One of the dead men was just a bloody heap, while another had both legs blown clean off[i]. The walls of the trenches were reeking with blood. At these sights most of my nervousness disappeared, I was filled with rage and thirsty for some of the enemy's blood. I turned to the telephone operator and told him to get me onto the artillery. In ten minutes I was through and, indicating the place from where the enemy had been firing, asked for retaliation. I had not long to wait - in a few moments there were a series of cracks and booms behind us, and our shells started to fly over at the enemy's gun position. I soon had the satisfaction of seeing it lifted off the face of the earth. The gunfire continued for a while – black earth fountains shot up all along the enemy trenches then ceased as suddenly as they had begun. I thanked the artillery, and expressing the hope that he would not be troubled further, left Luscombe and proceeded back to my own position with Martin. Before we went, we administered morphine to the more badly wounded, and sent them down. There were 12 casualties."[26]

Thursday, 15th June 1916
Third Army weather report: Rained in the morning. Rain: 0mm. Temp. 60-47° F

SOME INEXPERIENCED officers were coming to terms with what it was to live and lead in the front line trenches, under fire, in appalling conditions and with your men depending on your decisions and choices. 2nd Lt. Percy Simmonds of the Q.V.R. was a man of deep Christian convictions and, convinced of the

---

i No definite information can be found as to the identities of these two men but I believe them to be two men who joined the QWR as part of the May draft from the 2/2nd Londons. Another man, 2942 Pte Cyril Roper Bradbury, had died of wounds the day before whilst attached to the QWR. He is recorded on the Commonwealth War Graves Commission sites as being part of the 2/2nd Londons. Aged 25, he was the son of Son of Edwin and Sarah Elizabeth Bradbury of Woodville, Derbyshire. He served in Malta, Egypt, Gallipoli and France. He is buried in Doullens Communal Cemetery Extension No.1, Somme, France, grave II. B. 6. I believe the other men to be:
2627 Pte George William Arthur Bower, 2/2nd London Regt (Royal Fusiliers) attached 1/16th London Regt (Queen's Westminster Rifles), of Westminster who died on Wednesday 14th June 1916. He is buried at Hebuterne Military Cemetery, Pas de Calais, France grave: IV. J. 2.
2466 Pte Bernie Culf, 'B' Coy, 2/2nd London Regt (Royal Fusiliers), attached 1/16th London Regt (Queen's Westminster Rifles) died on Wednesday 14th June 1916. Aged 26, he was the son of Martha Jane Culf of Highbury, Earls Colne, Essex, and the late S. J. Culf. He is buried at Hebuterne Military Cemetery, Pas de Calais, France grave: IV. J. 1.

rightness of his country's cause, he had left Mansfield College, Oxford to join up. He had been a member of the OTC at Queen's College, Oxford and now thought it his duty to play an active part in the war. He had arrived in France from the regimental base at Fovant Camp near Salisbury at the beginning of March and, in a letter home, he described how he was now bringing his own style of leadership to his platoon in 'A' Company of the Queen Victorias:

"I mustn't give you news, censorship is very strict. I have had my baptism of fire and know what it is to lie out in the open with my head down in grass wondering whether the next whizz bang or machine gun bullet is coming just that little bit nearer. But more and more it is my conviction that it is life not death that is to be feared. Not rum but our 'Easter Hope' will, I believe, take me over the parapet as it has done before. But how to live the eternal life in the midst of battle in such a time, this is the real battle. The men in my platoon are a fine lot. Of course I have made many blunders as an officer and I don't think I shall ever become an officer in the way of army discipline but I feel that as a platoon we are a united family and will stick to each other through thick and thin. One's successes and failures and those of others give heaps of material for a dissertation on leadership. You know what I mean: the fussy man who can't delegate responsibility without wearing himself and everyone else out by attempting to supervise and interfere with the job."[27]

The weather was now beginning to adversely affect the health of the men and, in his entry for today, the ADMS of the 56ᵗʰ Division recorded that 25 men had reported sick with trench foot in the past few days. As a result, the ADMS had applied for a supply of frostbite grease from the Quartermaster General's stores and this was now supplied to the battalions working in the sodden front line trenches. The availability of the grease would be too late, however, to prevent an outbreak of illness as, over the next week, the sick rate more than tripled compared to the previous seven days[i].

Friday, 16ᵗʰ June 1916
Third Army weather report: Fine. Rain: 0mm. Temp. 63-44° F

MAJ. CHARLES WARD-JACKSON[ii] was the Town Major in Pas and, in between finding suitable accommodation for Divisional Generals and other essential tasks such as indulging in a spot of fly fishing with his chums on various Staffs, Charles liked to write lengthy letters home to his wife. Typically British, his focus was on the weather:

"The weather is still bitterly cold...it is perfectly beastly. I have just counted the number of sunny days we have had this year. They only amount to forty-two altogether, an average of not much more than seven days a month. Did you ever hear of such a thing?"[28]

Ward-Jackson was also drawn into mentioning an important change in senior Corps' personnel. Brig. Gen. Fox, VII Corps Commander, Royal Artillery, the man in charge of the Siege and Heavy Batteries even now starting to register targets in the German lines, was to be sent home. Fox, "such a dear" according to Ward-Jackson, was being sent home to be replaced by Brig. Gen. Ross

---

i 121 men reported sick between 9ᵗʰ and 15ᵗʰ June with 373 reporting sick from the 16ᵗʰ to the 22ⁿᵈ June.
ii Maj. Charles L Ward-Jackson, Camp Commandant VII Corps, was born in 1869. He joined the 3ʳᵈ Yorkshire Regt. in 1888 transferring to the 1/1ˢᵗ Yorkshire Hussars in 1892, serving in South Africa. In 1907 he left the regiment and joined the National Reserve. He became part of VII Corps' Staff in July 1915.

Johnson[i], an officer with 30 year's experience in the Royal Artillery. Ross Johnson and Brig. Gen. Buckle, Commander VII Corps Heavy Artillery, would now jointly take responsibility for the crucial role the big guns would play in the outcome of the attack.

Meanwhile, from another office in Pas, Operation Order No. 16 had been issued by the Staff of VII Corps. It contained two key elements: an Intelligence appreciation of the German forces currently concentrated around Gommecourt; and the final version of the plan for the attack to come. The Intelligence report was sadly out of date. The 2nd Guard Reserve Division had been in place for a month but its presence would not be ascertained for another four days. The current assessment was that the salient was still defended by an over-stretched 52nd Infantry Division, with two regiments, the 169th and 170th Regiments, occupying the long front line section from Monchy au Bois down to Serre with the 66th Regiment in reserve. Supporting the infantry it was estimated that there were just five heavy and twelve field artillery batteries organised in three groups at Le Quesnoy Farm, Biez Wood and Puisieux. This appraisal of the strength of the German guns behind Gommecourt was woefully short of the mark. After the battle there were some estimates that, taking into account the flanking fire of the 111th Division's batteries in and about Adinfer Wood to the north, as many as 63 German batteries had fired in defence of the Gommecourt salient – four times the number identified by VII Corps Intelligence Officers just two weeks before the attack was due.

The bulk of Operation Order No. 16, however, concerned the final version of the plan for the assault on the salient. Haig's concerns about the number of phases proposed had been taken on board and, as a result, there were now but two elements as well as a change in timings which would dramatically shorten the whole operation. In spite of the concerns of the men on the spot the 46th Division was now to take the complex of trenches on the left of their attack, the Little Z, the ridge between Pigeon and Gommecourt Woods and Gommecourt Wood itself in one bound. There would then be a slight pause before the troops on the right moved to take the southern end of Oxus trench. The 56th Division was to take the three lines of German trenches from the Farmer-Farmyard strongpoint on the right to the southern edge of Gommecourt village on the left also in one bound and, at the same time, the Queen's Westminster Rifles, would push through the lead battalions on the left to take the Quadrilateral. At Zero + 30 elements of the 137th Brigade to the north and the 169th Brigade to the south were to advance down Fill and Fillet trenches respectively in order to cut off the garrison within Gommecourt village and Park.

The time allowed for the first phase of the operation was a bare thirty minutes, a significantly shorter time than proposed in VII Corps' first proposal. Given the lack of experience the British Army had in fighting through wooded areas it was asking an enormous amount of the 46th Division to take three lines of German trenches *and* the whole of the Gommecourt Wood in just thirty minutes.

---

[i] Brig. Gen. later Maj. Gen. Cyril Maxwell Ross Johnson C.B., C.M.G., D.S.O. was born on 29th January 1868. He joined the Royal Artillery from the Royal Military Academy in 1886. He saw service in the Boer War during which, as a Captain, he saw action at Vaal Krantz, Tugela Heights, Zand River and Diamond Hill. He was awarded a D.S.O. for his services. He was promoted Lieutenant Colonel in June 1914 and went to France with the BEF in August. In May 1915 he was appointed GOC, Royal Artillery with the 48th (South Midland) Division. In March 1916 he was appointed CRA, I Corps before transferring to VII Corps.

Furthermore, if they failed in whole or in part or were significantly delayed in reaching their objectives, then the 56ᵗʰ Division, as Allenby had identified, would be in a badly exposed position occupying a deep and narrow salient within strongly held enemy territory. Clearly, though, Haig and his Staff officers had determined that a more or less constant movement forward was both achievable and carried less risk than an operation that relied on co-ordinated timed movements by different units separated by a strongly held, fortified village. It may be that increasing confidence in the destructive power of the British heavy artillery had persuaded senior officers that there would be little resistance to the advance and, in consequence, the debate about the plan for the Gommecourt became a mini replica of the main Somme advance in which, again, Haig's confidence overcame his junior Generals' more circumspect and cautious approach. In this case, though, Allenby and Snow were substitutes for Rawlinson. So, instead of a phased advance in which areas taken were reinforced and consolidated prior to a further advance, the attack would see the attacking troops sweep over and through the various obstructions at great speed.

There were two issues here that should have concerned Staff officers at all levels. The first was that, in order to protect the rear of the advancing lead elements, the troops designated for the clearance and consolidation of the captured trenches needed to follow on closely, otherwise there was a danger that the leading men could be attacked from the rear and, potentially, cut off. The second issue that should have exercised the planners was what would the enemy's tactics be in defence of Gommecourt? It is not clear that much time was spent analysing this part of the coming battle and, indeed, no document suggesting ways in which the Germans might try to disrupt the attack can be identified amongst existing official documents. Neither are there any 'what if?' style papers that discuss what might go wrong and methods of solving any problems that might then arise. Sod's Law - 'what can go wrong will go wrong' – was simply not on the agenda at G.H.Q. or, subsequently, at Third Army and VII Corps headquarters once the plan had been approved by the highest authority.

The final part of Operation Order No. 16 set out the general scope of the artillery plan for the attack and the various ploys, such as smoke and gas discharges, which, it was hoped, would draw German troops out into the open to be battered by the heavy guns. Lastly, the scheme for the release of smoke on Z Day itself and the communications systems which would link the Divisions, VII Corps and the observers in the R.F.C. aircraft that would be in the air continuously throughout the bombardment and the attack were set out.

In all, Operation Order No. 16 contained a lot of detail for the Divisional Staffs to digest and would generate a lot of work in order to incorporate the many changes that now were needed to the existing plan. With just two weeks to go before the attack was due it was asking an awful lot of everyone involved to ensure that the plan was in good order. The much-maligned Staff officers would earn their corn in late June.

***

AFTER THEIR SHORT BREAK in Bayencourt, the men of the London Rifle Brigade. arrived back in the trenches at Hebuterne, relieving the Westminsters. More deep, thick, red mud greeted them. The Westminsters had been living in that mud for a week, and it was taking a debilitating toll on the men's health.

Every day, more and more men reported sick until, on the 14th and 15th June, nearly 50 men were up in front of the M.O. with various ailments such as trench foot. Ironically, given the hideous weather, 'Summer Time' was officially adopted on June 14th, the clocks going forward from 11 p.m. to 12.0.

This sick rate fell dramatically once the Westminsters stopped living, as well as working, in the trenches. Although, during the five days spent in Bayencourt, working parties were sent back to Hebuterne and the squalor of the trenches, sleeping in dry conditions helped to reduce the sick rate to about 2 men a day[i].

The diary of Rfn. Percy Jones of the Q.W.R. recalls the appalling weather and the shambles of the trenches vividly:

"We have moved up to the trenches, and have slept in a cellar in Hebuterne or in the front line. An enormous amount of work is being put in on this sector of the Front. Trenches and dug-outs are being built as fast as possible, and guns are brought up every night. We put in all the time constructing the new system of trenches in front of the old front line."

"The weather has been truly awful, like midwinter, and the trenches have got quite as bad as in the old 1914 days. Once again we are knee deep in thick stodgy MUD and other sections contain several feet of water. We are at present holding the new front line for 48 hours. It was pouring in torrents and coming back we found Calvaire (a communication trench) nearly waist deep in water. We were of course soaked to the skin, and glad to think we were at least going to sleep in a cellar where the other boys had built a huge fire."

"For the last two days our section has been the centre outpost in the new front line. The weather has been bad and in these new trenches there are no dug-outs or any sort of shelter. We have passed each night sitting on the firing platform in the pouring rain, and yarning about old times, "Gus" Dyson[ii] has left the cooks and come back to us to try for a stripe again."

"The Germans keep very busy with their minenwerfers and machine-guns. They do not seem to have located our outpost, but have discovered the one on our right and caused several casualties."[29]

For the L.R.B. it was now time to live in the trenches. Although wet and muddy, they were fortunate that the rain stopped and the temperatures rose steadily. At night, they worked on the new front line trenches. Communication trenches had been dug out to them and these had to be duck boarded and the wire in front strengthened. Whenever possible, the Germans interfered with frequent bombardments, heavy minenwerfers being the their favourite weapon. On their first night back (the 16th June), Capt. Johnston was rewarded for his newly received Military Cross by a wound that would keep him out of action beyond 1st July.

---

[i] Casualties for the Queen's Westminster Rifles for the month of June were: 4 other ranks killed, 25 other ranks wounded, 123 other ranks sick, 6 other ranks other reasons: a total of 158. On May 31st, the battalion's strength was 29 officers and 938 other ranks (total 967). On June 30th, battalion strength was 44 officers and 922 other ranks (total 960) after reinforcements of 15 officers and 142 other ranks were received.

[ii] 3280 Rfn Augustus Sydney Dyson, 'B' Coy., 1/16th London Regt (Queen's Westminster Rifles), died on Saturday, 1st July 1916, aged 30. He was the son of Annie Maria Dyson of 46, Lambert Rd., Brixton Hill, London and the late Joseph Dyson. His body was never found and his name is inscribed on the Thiepval Memorial, Pier & Face 13C.

The Kensingtons were half way through their term in the front line trenches. 'D' and 'C' Companies were now in the front lines having relieved the other two companies on the night before. After a day and night spent working on the communication trenches trying to clear the mud and water that was pooling the length of the lines a patrol slipped away into No Man's Land near to the Bucquoy Road. Lying in wait for them was a larger German patrol and, in a rush, they were on them. The Kensingtons retreated back up the slope to the security of their own lines but a roll call back in the trenches found them to be two short with both men thought to have been captured by the enemy. One man, however, disappeared forever and Pte. Robert Creighton's name would be added to the lengthening list of the 'Missing of the Somme'.[i]

Saturday, 17th June 1916
Third Army weather report: Fine, cold. Rain: 0mm. Temp. 66-47° F

AS THE WEATHER slowly improved (no rain fell from the 15th to the 18th June) so enemy activity increased and, the following night, six other ranks got their tickets home after an argument with a minenwerfer. The huge bombs from the minenwerfers were a constant cause of concern to the men in the trenches but, unlike the fast moving shells from the 7mm field gun, they did, at least, have a chance to avoid their massive explosions if they were alert and lucky. Pte Cecil Bryden of the London Scottish wrote to his mum in Forest Gate about the trials and tribulations caused by the 'Moaning Minnies':

"Dear Mother

.... On 10th June we left the Bomb School and rejoined the battalion who were now engaged in digging trenches, after having had six days in the trenches, during which time 5 men were killed and 70 wounded. Most of the damage is caused by minenwerfers, affectionately called 'Minnies'. They are a trench mortar torpedo weighing about 200 lbs. They are fired into the air and go about ½ a mile high and fall with a graceful curve into our trenches, (with luck) fortunately, in daytime they can be seen, firstly one hears a dull thud as it is fired and then we watch it rise and nearly 1 minute after it falls, observed all the time, this gives us ample time to clear round the traverse out of harms way. At night time, they look like a rocket having a trail of sparks behind (from the fuse). When they explode the chief damage is to the trench itself. They were very fond of sending a few on our newly dug trenches to keep us busy. However, when they had sent over about five a battery of 18 pounders were roused and they would return the compliment with interest, generally making the Germans pack up for the night." [30]

Sunday, 18th June 1916
Third Army weather report: Fine & warm. Rain: 0mm. Temp. 65-36° F

IN THE EARLY HOURS of the 18th, a German raiding party slipped across No Man's Land and attempted to bomb the L.R.B.'s outposts. In a brief exchange of fire, the German's came off worst, leaving behind one dead but unidentifiable bomber on the fringe of the British wire.

Further behind the lines, the men of the 1/3rd Londons were entertained by a vicious dogfight in the skies above Pas en Artois. Four British aircraft had engaged three German ones and, to the accompaniment of anti-aircraft fire, the

---

i 4117 Pte Robert Creighton, 1/13th London Regt. (Kensingtons), died on Friday, 16th June 1916. His body was never found and his name is inscribed on the Thiepval Memorial, Pier & Face 9D, 13C & 12C.

Londoners watched as two of the German aircraft were brought crashing to the ground. As day wore on working parties moved up from Sailly to Hebuterne to carry on with the myriad of tasks required before the attack. A party of the 1/1st Londons were in the trenches when they were caught by one of the short sharp strafes that were unleashed irregularly by the German artillery. One man was killed[i]. The 1/2nd Londons had been spending the previous four days burying telephone cables deep in the trenches and had another five days of this back-breaking work to look forward to. Every day they marched up from Souastre, 400 men at a time, to dig out narrow furrows in the bottom of the communication trenches within which to lay the cable and, all the while, they would keep a weather eye on the German trenches, ever alert for the scream of the shrapnel or the moan of the minenwerfer. Over the next four nights the shouts to warn of an incoming shell were urgently yelled and men dropped their shovels and picks and dived for the bottom of the trench waiting for the crack of the shell and the whine of the shrapnel balls. Then they would get back to their feet, brush themselves down and look around to ensure that everyone was standing. On three nights out of the four one man was down and each was to find their final resting place amongst the ranks of rough crosses in the cemetery behind the A.D.S.[ii]

Monday, 19th June 1916
Third Army weather report: Dull, some rain. Rain: 3.1mm. Temp. 61-34° F

THE NEXT NIGHT, before they packed off and headed west for another round of rehearsals at Halloy, German shells ploughed into two of the Rangers' last working parties. The men were out in front of the trenches improving the barbed wire defences when the shells landed. Nine men in the group were hit and 2nd Lt. Phillips and two other ranks[iii], one nineteen years old and the other twenty, were killed and another officer, Capt. Withers Green was seriously wounded. The fatal casualties were made up to four later when one of those wounded, 25 year old Rfn. Robert Anderson, died at a Casualty Clearing Station in Doullens[iv]. Back in the village, a party of the 1/1st Londons were on parade

---

[i] 5375 Pte Thomas Burr, 1/1st London Regt., died on Sunday, 18th June 1916. He is buried in Hebuterne Military Cemetery, grave II.H.7.

[ii] The casualties of the 1/2nd Londons on these three days were:
5114 Pte George Rayner was killed on Sunday 18th June 1916. He is buried in Hebuterne Military Cemetery, grave IV.J.2.
3082 Pte Edwin Herbert Cannon was killed on Monday, 19th June 1916. He is buried in Hebuterne Military Cemetery, grave III.D.4.
3223 Pte Frederick August Dietert (alias Dicker) was killed on Wednesday, 21st June 1916. He is buried in Hebuterne Military Cemetery, grave III.D.5.

[iii] 2nd Lt. Arthur Blakeway Phillips, 1/12th London Regt (The Rangers), died on Monday, 19th June 1916, aged 32. He was the son of Richard Blakeway Phillips and Isabel Mary Phillips of Brome Cottage, Meole Brace, Shrewsbury and a native of Hanwood, Salop. He is buried in Hebuterne Military Cemetery, grave III.D.7. His epitaph reads: "Beyond the sea of death love lives. Yesterday, today and forever."
4479 Rfn Harold Tracey Cooper, 1/12th London Regt (The Rangers), died on Monday, 19th June 1916, aged 20. He was the son of Eliza Cooper of 34, Westbourne Rd., Forest Hill, London, and the late James C. Cooper. He is buried in Hebuterne Military Cemetery, grave III.D.3.
4264 Rfn Frederick White, 1/12th London Regt (The Rangers), died on Monday, 19th June 1916, aged 19. He was the son of Frederick and Caroline White of 39, Camellia St., Wandsworth Rd., South Lambeth, London. He is buried in Hebuterne Military Cemetery, grave III.D.6.

[iv] 2714 Rfn Robert Frederick Anderson, 1/12th London Regt (The Rangers), died on Monday, 19th June 1916, aged 25. He was the son of Alfred and Emily Anderson of Stepney, London; husband of Madeline Maud Anderson of

prior to making their way up the trenches to work when they too were caught by the sudden German bombardment. L/Cpl. Houghton was severely wounded and survived into the next day before dying of his wounds[i].

But not all was gloom and doom. The Divisional Concert Party, the Bow Bells, performed to another packed house with, this time, a special guest of honour. Lt. Gen. Snow, G.O.C. VII Corps was in attendance although, according to his personal diary, the 'Pierrots', as he called them:

> "...bore me... (but) last night were really very good but too long. Of course, being a London division, all the performers were professionals and it was quite as good as a London performance. Two men or boys took women's parts and one had one of Marie Lloyd's dresses which she had sent out. Very odd being at a performance which might well have been a London Music Hall and hearing the guns firing outside."[31]

Although the men and their commanders might have been having an enjoyable time away to the east events were occurring that would have a significant impact on the outcome of the attack due in just over a week. With the preparations for the attack so intentionally obvious the command of the German XIV Corps was moving further reinforcements into the area opposite Gommecourt and Serre. Already the power of the artillery had been enhanced by the arrival of the 20ᵗʰ Reserve Field Artillery Regt., and today this strength was further augmented by the arrival of elements of two Bavarian artillery regiments, the 19ᵗʰ Field Artillery Regt and the 20ᵗʰ Foot Artillery Regt. These units, associated with the only reserve division on the Somme, the 10ᵗʰ Bavarian Division, had been brought up to Bapaume on the 13ᵗʰ June from an area SE of Cambrai. Now they were being deployed along the northern front of the offensive from north of Bucquoy to south of Puisieux. They were there to defeat any attacks on Gommecourt or Serre. Theses reinforcements were deployed as follows:

Iˢᵗ Section, 19ᵗʰ F.A.R north of Bucquoy: 1ˢᵗ Battery, 19ᵗʰ F.A.R and 2/20ᵗʰ Foot Artillery Regt attached to the northern group of the 20ᵗʰ Reserve Field Artillery Regiment and the 3ʳᵈ Battery attached to the southern group;

IIⁿᵈ Section, 19ᵗʰ F.A.R south of Bucquoy and Puisieux: 4ᵗʰ Battery under the command of the northern group of the 52ⁿᵈ Inf. Div., the 5ᵗʰ under the middle group and the 6ᵗʰ under the southern group.

These dispositions required some movement of battery positions in order to accommodate the new comers:

2/20ᵗʰ R.F.A.R moved from Stellung 508 to 430a;

4/20ᵗʰ R.F.A.R moved up to occupy Stellung 536 just south of Essarts;

1/19ᵗʰ and 2/19ᵗʰ F.A.R occupied Stellung 502 and 508 respectively; and

3/19ᵗʰ F.A.R replaced 4/19ᵗʰ F.A.R in Stellung 533 with the 4ᵗʰ Battery moving the short distance to Stellung 534.

74, Dersingham Avenue, Manor Park, London. He is buried in Doullens Communal Cemetery Extension No.1, Somme, France, grave II. B. 9.
i 1417 L/Cpl Charles Henry Houghton, 1/1ˢᵗ London Regt., died of wounds on Tuesday, 20ᵗʰ June 1916. Aged 20, he was the son of Mrs B A Houghton of 48, Strathville Road, Earlsfield, London. He is buried in Hebuterne Military Cemetery, grave II.1.9.

Further south, three batteries of the 20th R.F.A.R were preparing to move into three positions around Biez Wood, further strengthening the southern flank of the salient.

The overall command of the 19th Bavarian Field Artillery Regt was put at the disposal of the command of the 52nd Field Artillery Brigade, 52nd Infantry Division. The commander of the 19th F.A.R was an experienced artillerymen, Oberst von Belli, who had fought in the battles around Arras in 1915 (as commander of the Reserve Field Artillery Regiment 5). His immediate demand to 52nd Field Artillery Brigade on arrival was for a considerable increase in the amount of ammunition immediately available in and around the battery positions, a request that was fully complied with. And while the new gunners found their billets and positions the 55th Reserve Infantry Regiment returned from their relief and period in reserve near Bapaume. It was clear that the attack could happen at any moment and the men of this regiment were to be in the front line to face it.

Tuesday, 20th June 1916
Third Army weather report: Cold in morning, warmer later. Rain: 0.7mm.
Temp. 68-36° F

IT WAS NOT ONLY THE GROWTH in the numbers of German guns behind the lines that showed that the German High Command was well aware of the imminence of a major operation against the Gommecourt salient, the German air force was also more active than previously. German pilots had been used to aerial dominance on the Western Front and for some nine months, between the summer of 1915 and the spring of 1916, the Fokker Eindekker had been the 'King of the Skies' above France and Flanders, giving rise to its description in the British Press as the 'Fokker Scourge'. The Fokker E.I., to give it its more precise name, had come into service in the summer of 1915 and had caused a sensation. Given the popular image of all Great War aircraft being bi- or even tri-planes the E.1. was, unusually, a monoplane. But even this curious profile was not the main reason for its unparalleled domination of the skies. For this aspect one has to look at the unique positioning of its forward firing machine gun which was placed directly in front of the pilot and immediately behind the propeller. Bullet damage to the propeller was avoided by the use of 'synchronization gear' which allowed the bullets to pass between the rotating blades without damaging them. The positioning of the gun gave the German Eindekker pilots a considerable advantage over Allied aircraft that depended for both defence and attack on guns located on stands and fired to front or rear by the observer.

It was not until a new, faster and better armed generation of Allied aircraft started to arrive in Spring 1916 that the weaknesses of Eindekker were exposed and command of the skies was wrestled from German pilots' hands. The Fokker's flaws were its slow speed of just 81 mph and a poor rate of climb of 325 ft. per minute and three new Allied aircraft had it beaten in both departments - as well as forward firing guns. The British DH2 and FE2b and the French Nieuport XI contributed to a total turn of the tables on the previously invincible Fokkers. The two British aircraft were both 'pusher' designs: the DH2 was de Havilland conceived and Airco built with a top speed of 93 mph and a rate of climb of 545 ft. per minute; and the FE2b (Farman Experimental 2) was built by the Royal Aircraft Factory with a top speed of 91½ mph. Both were armed with forward firing Lewis guns. The real step forward was the Nieuport XI, a French fabricated, single-seater aircraft armed with a single Lewis gun, a top speed of 104 mph and a rate of climb of 656 ft. per minute. Against such opponents the Eindekker was a dead duck and, through spring and early summer 1916, Allied aircraft assumed command of the skies over the muddy trenches below[i].

The Allies' aerial superiority allowed some of the now obsolete aircraft which had previously been 'Fokker Fodder' to find a new role on the Western Front. One such aircraft was the BE2c (the 'Blériot Experimental'), a two person, slow but highly stable aircraft. The aircraft was strangely configured with the observer/gunner sitting under the top wing and in front of the pilot, with the result that, to fire to the rear, the observer had to stand and shoot over the head of the pilot. It was an odd and unwieldy arrangement and necessary because the BE2c was often flown with a pilot only and he had to sit over the aircraft's centre of gravity. With a top speed of just 72 mph, a dismal rate of climb of 325 ft. per minute and a range of 200 miles the BE2c was no match for an Eindekker, but its inherent stability, which made it a sitting target for the Fokkers, also made it an excellent platform for aerial observation and photography when escorted by a DH2, FE2b or a Nieuport XI. As a result, the 18 BE2cs of No. 8 Squadron of the 12th (Corps) Wing, III Brigade, R.F.C., were now in great demand by the artillery to spot both the fall of their shells and the location of enemy batteries and other units.

No. 8 Squadron was based at an airfield at La Bellevue[ii] which lay just to the west of the Casualty Clearing Stations at Warlincourt Halte on the Arras to Doullens Road. The aircraft of the squadron originally arrived at their first French base at St Omer on 15th April 1915, having come into being just two week's before at Brooklands near Weybridge in Surrey. Things started very much as they were to carry on. A dozen aircraft had taken off into the wind in north Surrey and one by one they had either crashed or wandered off course – and then crashed. One came down and was wrecked south west of Brooklands at Gosport, when it was hoping to land at St Omer, south east of Brooklands and the other side of the English Channel. Two more crashed at Folkestone and, just up the coast, a third was forced down at Dover with engine trouble. Though an inauspicious start to the squadron's life on the Western Front it was not at all an unusual situation for inexperienced pilots who had spent most of their time in the air stooging sedately around the Home Counties to find themselves anywhere but their intended objective. It was not until 25th April that all of the personnel and all of the aircraft had assembled at St Omer and, once done, they became the first squadron to arrive in France fully equipped with the BE2c. Sadly, the squadron did not have long to wait before suffering its first fatality. On the 26th April, 42-year old 2nd Lt. Frederick Polehampton was killed[iii] in BE2c 1758 in yet another flying accident and by the end of the month the number of aircraft had been halved to just six.

---

[i] The Germans regained air superiority in August-September 1916 when new aircraft, primarily the Albatros D.I and D.II, and the Halberstadt D.II appeared, and, most importantly, were organised into dedicated fighter units, the Jagdstaffeln.

[ii] Now a French Airforce base.

[iii] 2nd Lt. Frederick William Polehampton, No. 8 Squadron, R.F.C. formerly 15th Hussars, was killed on 26th April 1915. Aged 42, he was the son of the late Rev. E. and Mrs. Polehampton, of Hartfield, Sussex and husband of Kate Eunice Polehampton, of 10, Dorset St., Marylebone, London. He was buried at Longuenesse (St. Omer) Souvenir Cemetery, grave I. A. 89.

After St Omer, the squadron moved to the Ypres salient before spending time to the south at Loos in the autumn of 1915. They then headed south to La Bellevue in preparation for the 'Big Push' where they came under the command of Maj. Patrick Henry Lyon Playfair. Playfair was born on the 22ⁿᵈ November 1889 and joined the Royal Flying Corps from the Royal Field Artillery in August 1912, initially being attached to No. 4 Squadron based at Farnborough. He gained his RAeC Certificate (No. 283) at Weybridge on 3ʳᵈ September 1912 and went to France with No. 4 Squadron in August 1914. He was promoted to command B Flight, No. 11 Squadron on 27ᵗʰ January 1915 and had been promoted Major and given command of No. 8 Squadron on 12ᵗʰ January 1916[i], an airman of some experience. For the month of May his pilots experienced little opposition to their slow and stately flights over No Man's Land and the German front line trenches. Things began to change as the signs of activity increased behind the British lines and German aircraft started to make more and more daring incursions into Allied airspace. One of these flights had spotted the model of the Gommecourt trenches dug at Hurtebise Farm near Henu and over which the 168ᵗʰ and 169ᵗʰ Brigades had repeatedly rehearsed their attacks. And, while their pilots tried to ascertain as much as possible about the plans of the British Army, the German anti-aircraft defences did their level best to prevent the British observers from spotting anything of interest, like new battery positions. In May observers on the 46ᵗʰ Division's front had noted a new type of German ack ack gun that fired incendiary shells and the reinforced anti-aircraft weaponry behind Gommecourt scored a notable success today. At 9.55 a.m. BE2c 2488 lumbered across the ground at La Bellevue before bouncing into the air on a mission to spot for the 56ᵗʰ Division's field gunners. The pilot was 26-year old 2ⁿᵈ Lt. David Williamson Stewart Paterson, R.F.C. and, sitting in his draughty perch in the front seat, the observer, 2ⁿᵈ Lt. John Cooke, Durham Light Infantry attached to the R.F.C., peered over the side looking out for the explosion of the 18 pdr shells hundreds of feet below. The characteristics that made the BE2c such a good observation platform, steadiness and stability, also made it a predictable target for the gunners on the ground and, just before noon, Paterson flew slap into a angry blast of Hun ack ack. Given the fragile nature of the aircraft there could be only one result and the shattered remains of the men and their plane were found near Puisieux. The bodies of Paterson and Cooke were recovered and buried by their German adversaries in Achiet le Grand cemetery.

***

LATER IN THE DAY the German Maxims joined in the fun, spraying the British parapets whilst the minenwerfers rolled, end over end, across the sky trailing a shower of sparks before they gouged into the earth sending shock waves rippling through the ground. One such bomb caught an unlucky party of L.R.B.s on the night of the 20ᵗʰ, killing two and wounding four riflemen[ii]. After five gruelling

---

[i] Maj., later Air Vice Marshal, Sir Patrick Henry Lyon Playfair KBE, CB, CVO, MC, was promoted to command of the 13ᵗʰ (Army) Wing, R.F.C. in August 1916. He stayed in the RAF after the war and, in 1939, went to France again, this time commanding the Advanced Air Striking Force which supplied the bomber component that supported the BEF in Northern France. In August 1940 he was appointed Officer Commanding, Air Forces in India. He died on 23ʳᵈ November 1974.
[ii] The fatal casualties were:
2098 Rfn Frank Henry Clements, 1/5ᵗʰ London Regt (London Rifle Brigade), died on Tuesday, 20ᵗʰ June 1916, aged 17. He was the son of Frank and Alice Clements of 'Fairlight', Dover Rd., Upper Walmer, Kent.

days, the London Rifle Brigade were to be relieved by the 1/7ᵗʰ Middlesex. The War Diary commented that "Men and officers (are) greatly exhausted". They slept that night in St Amand before rejoining their brigade comrades in the mud of the Halloy practice grounds.

Behind the men toiling in the front lines the rear areas were now reaching a fever pitch of activity as the opening day of the bombardment drew ever closer. Maj. Ward-Jackson of the VII Corps staff wrote to his wife describing the scene around Pas-en-Artois:

> *"Everywhere there are troops; under every bank there are horses; Field Ambulance Hospitals are everywhere; huge howitzers on railway trucks lurk stealthily in orchards; telegraph wires on flimsy stakes like hop poles cross each other in every direction and make a sort of aerial entanglement overhead.... Countless streams of G.S. wagons pass the end of this street on their way, laden with great logs of poplar, to the dugouts for the guns, and as for ammunition convoys, they never cease day or night.'*[32]

On the other side of the line, in anticipation of an imminent attack, artillery reinforcements were being put in place:

"At 11 a.m. on 20 June, the newly created 9ᵗʰ Battery of R.F.A.R. 20 (light field howitzers) arrived at Achiet le Grand railway station. It had been created by the Ersatz-Abteilung (replacement battalion) of A.R. 66 from soldiers of that unit in Lahr-Dinglingen, as well as from men of the 2ⁿᵈ and 4th Batteries of our regiment and was under the command of Oberleutnant der Reserve Melling as battery commander. Platoon commanders were Leutnant der Reserve Rolffs, Leutnant der Reserve Behrens and Feldwebel-Leutnant Weldin. The battery was quartered in Courcelles and also received its gas protection equipment there. The drivers and horses that the battery was still lacking were assigned by taking further men from the 2ⁿᵈ and 4ᵗʰ Batteries of our regiment.

On the same day, Light Field Ammunition Column III was brought up to full strength by absorbing the rest of A.M.K 421. Hauptmann der Landwehr Mostert was appointed commander - the unit was quartered in Ervillers.

At the southern exit of Courcelles to Achiet le Grand, the division had had a large ammunition depot built where ordnance and regimental personnel worked. There was a smaller depot on the east side of Ablainzeville. A gun belonging to 9./20 was taken to Position 518, east of Biez Wood, on 21ˢᵗ June. The position was badly dilapidated and needed a lot of hard work to return it to serviceable condition. The other three guns came into operation on 26 June. The observation post of 9./20 was on a platform in the northern part of Essarts les Bucquoy. The battery belonged to Gruppe "Süd" (headquarters at Rettemoy Farm)."[33]

Clearly, the obvious preparations for the assault were persuading the German High Command to concentrate yet more artillery in the Gommecourt sector. But again, these were not guns drawn from further south by the 'diversion' but

---

2289 Rfn Harold Ernest Abraham, 1/5ᵗʰ London Regt (London Rifle Brigade), died on Tuesday, 20ᵗʰ June 1916, aged 19. He was the son of Ernest and Nellie F. Abraham of 71, Westbury Rd., Walthamstow, Essex. They are buried next to one another in Hebuterne Military Cemetery, graves IV.D.4 and 5.

instead from reserves and Ersatz battalions back home. Such actions were, however, either missed or ignored by senior members of VII Corps staff. At the end of his 20ᵗʰ June letter to his wife, Maj. Ward-Jackson jovially recorded the cheerful opinion of one Maj. Bowles, a staff officer to the newly appointed Brig. Gen. Ross Johnson D.S.O., the 48-year old G.O.C. of VII Corps Royal Artillery:

"Maj. Bowles… thinks the Boches will move of and we shall waste all our shells. A nice prospect!"[54]

Wednesday, 21ˢᵗ June 1916
Third Army weather report: Fine, much warmer. Rain: 0mm. Temp. 68-45° F

TODAY ORDER NO.11 WAS ISSUED by Third Army's headquarters. It set out an overview of the aims and objectives of both VII Corps' operation at Gommecourt and the general offensive further south. It explained that Fourth Army was expected to have reached a line Montuaban-Pozieres-Grandcourt-Serre, an ambitious target for the first day. To assist in this task, especially north of River Ancre, the Third Army's main purpose, set out in the second paragraph, was clear. It was:

"… to prevent the German forces on its front from sending reinforcements southwards."

The attack at Gommecourt was not the only way in which Third Army was to achieve this end. Allenby's forces were made up of three Corps and his front ran from Hebuterne to Vimy Ridge and Third Army's overall plan encompassed five separate engagements from Roclincourt to the north of Arras down the Gommecourt but only the latter would commence at the same time as the main offensive. The others would take place at times to be decided upon locally at Corps' level and were designed to pin German units on their existing fronts rather than to break the German line, although gaining any 'ground of tactical value' was not to be discounted. The planned attacks were:

VII Corps – Gommecourt (46ᵗʰ and 56ᵗʰ Divisions) and Monchy-au-Bois (37ᵗʰ Division);

VI Corps – north of Ficheux and at Beaurains; and

XVII Corps – the salient north of Roclincourt.

Only at Gommecourt was there a specific set of instructions, i.e. to stop German forces from interfering in the attack north of the Ancre and to pinch out the Gommecourt salient. Elsewhere, though, orders were somewhat vague and left very much to local interpretation. As a result, for example, 37ᵗʰ Division, on the immediate left of the 46ᵗʰ Division, restricted its activities to large scale raids supported by field artillery barrages and the release of smoke. The fact that here the two front lines were over 1,000 yards apart in places - and that no effort had been made to close this gap - readily convinced the local German commanders that there was no significant threat to their positions. When the time came, therefore, the 111ᵗʰ Division was content to allow several of its batteries to join in with the destruction of the North Midlanders' attack with the actions of the British 37ᵗʰ Division being regarded as obvious feints rather an a genuine threat.

***

ON THE SAME DAY as the L.R.B. withdrew to the relative comfort of St Amand, the Westminsters left Bayencourt and marched off westwards to the practice grounds at Halloy. Over the 20th and 21st they were joined en route by their colleagues from the attacking battalions of the 168th Brigade: the Rangers and the London Scottish. The Rangers departed first, with 'C' and 'D' Companies leaving Souastre for Halloy on the 20th. At noon the following day, 'A' and 'B' Companies followed on, marching by way of the duck-board tracks to Sailly and then along the screened road to Bayenourtⁱ. Resting in a field to the west of Souastre, they then continued their march by way of Pas, where VII Corps had their headquarters, to arrive in Halloy at 6 p.m. that evening.

At the same time, the London Scottish were relieved at Hebuterne by the men of the 1/1st Londons. The London Scottish had been 'digging' without a break for three weeks, through foul weather and fair. Exhausted though they must have been, on their last night 'C' Company put in what their Regimental History describes as a "record performance":

> "Eighteen of its men began and completed in 3½ hours a short communication trench, 44 yards long, 4½ feet deep, and 2¾ feet wide - more than 91 cubic feet of earth per man. According to the textbooks, 80 cubic feet is the task for a man working for *4 hours* in a narrow trench."[35]

The Kensingtons were the other battalion of the 168th Brigade to be relieved and they were replaced by the 1/8th Middlesex who were set for a torrid time over the next six days. But the Kensingtons left the trenches minus one man for whom the imminent threat of action had become too much. Pte. Hubbard of the London Scottish witnessed the event:

> "I was twenty yards from one of the Kensingtons last week when he shot himself through the foot just to get back to England and out of it. Of course he will get about 84 days field punishment for it after the wound has healed."[36]

The Queen Victorias were also coming to the end of their stint in the trenches at Hebuterne and were to march to Halloy the next day. Exhibiting the concern for his men that seems typical of many of the new officers plucked from less disciplined civilian life and given sudden responsibility in Britain's new army, 'A' Company's 2nd Lt. Simmonds was clear about the need for his men to get a rest:

> *"Dear Mother,*
>
> *All is well. We have just finished our fatigues up in the trenches and leave here this evening for a certain place about twelve miles away (Halloy) where we are due to rest for a few days. I have written to you from this place to which we are going. It is where the huts are with the sand bag roofs which don't keep the rain out. I do hope the men will get some real rest, they want it badly. This has been the programme up here: work of a strenuous kind from 10 til 2 p.m. under a certain amount of fire most of the time and often other work during the afternoon. Keeping us up for ten days on end wants some doing. Personally, I have never felt better in my life but I possess that lucky habit, as you know of sleeping at all sorts of queer times so I just drop off when the spare half hours occur. And then, an officer's job is more a matter of responsibility and direction than sheer bodily labour, although we often keep ourselves as a sort of reserve to work in places where things are a bit more tired than usual.'*[37]

ⁱ This road was visible from German positions and screens were erected to prevent observation of traffic along it

The next day, on their arrival at Halloy after a particularly arduous night-time route march, Simmonds was again making his men his first priority with a successful search for some clover to make beds for his men.

Thursday, 22nd June 1916
Third Army weather report: Fine and very warm. Rain: 0mm. Temp. 77-48º F

THE MEN WERE, by now, exhausted and the men of the three battalions already at Halloy were given the 22nd June off, all except an unlucky 200 of the Westminsters, who were told off for Corps fatigues in preparation for the hard work of rehearsal to come. Late in the day, their 169th Brigade colleagues, the L.R.B. , arrived. They had sweated their way over from St Amand to join in with the preparations for the final dress rehearsals for the attack. Whilst others marched and laboured, the rest of the battalions sunned themselves and relaxed as the temperatures soared into the high seventies. It had barely rained for a week, the weather was balmy and the war seemed a thousand miles away. There was an Army canteen in the village and several estaminets where it was possible to buy 'Bubbly', Veuve Clicquot at 9 francs the bottle, and cheap vin ordinaire and beer. For once, Halloy was the place to be.

From the 20th to the 22nd, the billets and jobs done at the front by the battalions now in Halloy were taken over by the 167th Brigade. All four battalions were based in Hebuterne and the front line trenches, with the exception of 'A' and 'B' Companies of the 1/3rd Londons who were billeted at Sailly-au-Bois. The intensity of the preparatory work was now at fever pitch and the men, who had worked without respite all month, were reaching the final stages of exhaustion. At least until the 21st, the weather had been dry and comfortably warm but, on the 22nd, as they toiled under metallic blue skies, the temperature soared to 77° F. Sweltering in shirt sleeves, they dug, carried, hauled, dragged and lifted like navvies.

Further to the rear another German air raid disrupted life briefly. A flight of Gothas appeared over St Pol, headquarters of the Third Army, and dropped their bombs on the railway station and the nearby houses. Several soldiers were killed and wounded in the attack but one small house was also bombed. Within it was a family of refugees from the battered front-line town of Arras. The head of the family was killed and his baby grandson fatally injured whilst in the arms of his mother. Severely wounded was a little ten year old girl, Azenia, who was wounded in the neck and nearly lost her right hand. Gen. Allenby had been down to inspect the damage and it was now that he intervened. He made a somewhat unlikely soldier with his love of children, animals, botany and literature. Allenby was a parent, his only son Michael[ii] was in France with T Battery of the Royal Horse Artillery, and he had a reputation for befriending local children wherever he was based. Now, he took little Azenia under his wing, helping her to celebrate her birthday with cake and strawberries, sweets and a doll. Army surgeons saved part of her hand and he later arranged for her to be

---

[i] The London Scottish were billeted in huts at Pas-en-Artois and marched into Halloy each day for the rehearsals.
[ii] Lt. Horace Michael Hynman Allenby M.C., T Battery, Royal Horse Artillery, died of wounds on 29th July 1917 near Nieuport, Belgium. He was 20. He was hit in the head by a shell splinter and died five hours later in the 1st Canadian Casualty Clearing Station. Allenby and his wife received the news of their son's death a month after their arrival in Egypt. He had been awarded the M.C. for his actions in bringing in a wounded man from No Man's Land under heavy fire in September 1916 on the Somme. Lt. Allenby is buried in Coxyde Military Cemetery, grave II.D.1.

sent to a home for war-injured children in Paris. It is reported that he had visited her just prior to the lifting of the final hurricane bombardment in the early hours of Saturday, 1st July, bringing her pastries and staying for a quiet chat[38]. By that time, there was little more he could do to affect the outcome of the 'diversion'. But such concern for a little French girl would do nothing to improve his standing with his men. When he was not in the front lines berating his men for not wearing their helmets or for less serious infractions to Army rules, he was known to be enjoying life far to the rear with his pleasant chateau, French cook, fine wines and diverting walks in 'his' garden with an aristocratic French lady, Baroness de le Grange. It is, perhaps, the archetypal image of the selfish, callous, remote and out of touch First World War General on whom the caricature Gen. Melchett in Blackadder might well have been based.[39]

Friday, 23rd June 1916
Third Army weather report: Warm & thundery. Some rain. Rain: 14.1mm.
Temp. 79-54° F

FRIDAY, 23RD JUNE dawned muggy, warm and wet. Thunder was in the air. As the temperature climbed into the high seventies, the humidity rose with it. Towering thunderheads glowered across Northern France and, at 3 p.m., the weather could hold back no longer. As the thunder drowned out the sound of the guns and lightning flashed across the darkening sky, the rain came down in torrents. Overhead, the drama of Second Lieutenants Jardine and Pape's wild balloon ride was about to start. Beneath it, in the trenches in front of Hebuterne, the battalions of the 167th Brigade were labouring over final preparations before the bombardment started the following day. Soon they were soaked to the skin and covered with mud as the trenches began to fill with water. Within a short time 14 mm (¾ in.) of rain had drenched ground already sodden with unseasonable downpours over the previous months[i]. By now, the fine clay that overlaid the chalk beneath was saturated. It could absorb no more. Water and clinging mud filled the trenches to knee height. The work of the 1/8th Middlesex ground to a standstill in the cloudburst. And for the 1/7th Middlesex it set the seal on a dismal day. First, 'A' Company had been hit by a sudden strafe which wounded Capt. Moody and five of his men. Then an unlucky man, Pte. Stedall of 'D' Company, was accidentally killed and later, Pte. Case of 'B' Company was to be killed out on patrol. So, this torrential downpour was the last thing the men in the trenches needed.

Pte. H T Clements, a Lewis gunner with the 1/2nd Londons, was returning to his billet after fatigues in Hebuterne, he wrote in his diary:

"We had just got in at 3.30 p.m. when the storm, which had been gathering since mid-day broke. The observation balloon at St Amand broke loose and drifted over our billet and disappeared. Several chaps stripped and went out in the rain and had a bath. I put my head outside and washed my hair. It was the most torrential rain I've seen in France. In the trenches the water was knee deep in thirty minutes or less."[40]

Around Halloy, the assault battalions had been spared the worst of the weather. The 169th Brigade had been given another day's rest prior to a series of

---

[i] Since the beginning of February, 376 mm (15 in.) had inundated the area of the Somme. This was some 110 mm (4½ in.) more than the seasonal average for the area.

dress rehearsals. They sheltered from the storm in the huts, read and wrote letters home, smoked, slept and gossiped. For the men of the 168th Brigade, however, this would be the first day of three devoted to intense last-minute rehearsals for the attack. The others would be done alongside the 169th Brigade in full divisional rehearsals but today, just the Rangers and the Scottish plodded across the flattened cornfields, weighed down by some of the newly issued paraphernalia needed for the assault. On the day itself, in addition to their rifle and steel helmet, this was to include:

- Rolled groundsheet
- Water bottle
- Haversack containing mess tin, towel, shaving kit, extra socks, message book, the unconsumed portion of the day's ration, extra cheese, one preserved ration and one iron ration
- two gas masks and tear goggles
- Wirecutters
- Field dressing and iodine
- 220 extra rounds of ammunition
- 2 sandbags
- a shovel or a pick
- 2 Mills grenades (for the use of trained bombers)[41]

Whilst others worked, for the officers of the Queen Victoria Rifles, however, this Friday promised to be a night of high jinx. Pooling all their resources from the hampers and packages sent from home, they were determined to enjoy themselves at least one more time. Being officers and being from a London regiment had certain advantages. Relatives and friends tended to frequent the better emporia of the West End. In consequence, their food 'parcels' were rather grander than the mere name suggests. And tonight they would eat, and drink, royally. They would toast their King and his Empire, their regiment and its traditions. The war, the filthy, wet trenches and the enemy could be a million miles away as far as they were concerned. Tonight was a night to celebrate!

The Dinner menu was suitably long and suitably French:

Hors d'oeuvres Saint Germain
Turbot boulli sauce Anchois
Rognons sautes au pommes puree
Jambons braise aux Epinards
Aloyan de Boeuf rotis a l'Anglais
Pommes nouvelles au beurre et Haricots Verts
Asperges Vertes du beurre fondu
Compote de Fruits Chantilly
Scotch Woodcock
Café
Dessert
Sherry, Champagne, Port or Sherry, Whiskey and Soda
Toasts:
The King
The Regiment - Lt. Col. V W F Dickins D.S.O. V.D.
The Bounce - Maj. S J M Sampson

The mess cooks had excelled themselves: fish, kidneys, ham and beef, a variety of vegetables, desserts, coffee and a bountiful supply of alcohol. Then the toasts and speeches - it would be a night few would forget and even fewer would be able to remember long:

"A memorable dinner took place at Halloy while the battalion was training there. About forty officers assembled in a big hut on the evening of June 23rd. It was a sort of "send off" for the "Great Push" which it was expected would take place within a day or two. Menu cards were passed round and autographed by all present. Contrary to Mess custom a few speeches were made wishing success to the battalion in the approaching battle and altogether a very pleasant evening was spent. Sixteen of the signatories of the menus figured in the casualty list for July 1st, and the cards are now highly prized by the fortunate survivors as a melancholy souvenir of their former companions."[42]

NOTES:

Casualties not mentioned in existing footnotes:

3ʳᵈ June 1916
1/4ᵗʰ London Regiment (Royal Fusiliers).
Parsons 4920 Pte James Thomas Aged 35 Boisguillaume Communal Cemetery I. E. 7A.

5ᵗʰ June 1916
1/3ʳᵈ London Regiment (Royal Fusiliers)
Hicks 5191 Pte Rowland William, 1/1ˢᵗ London Regiment died of wounds at No. 19 Casualty Clearing Station. Aged 26, he was the son of M E and the late George Hicks of 14, High Street, Mitcham, Surrey. He is buried in Doullens Communal Cemetery Extension No. 1, grave I.C.19. His brother, 5180 Pte Lionel Hicks, 1/1ˢᵗ London Regt., had been killed in action on 27ᵗʰ May 1916.

6ᵗʰ June 1916
1/14ᵗʰ London Regiment (London Scottish).
Morrison 3992 Cpl. Stuart Aged 23 Brother of Miss E. M. Morrison of 244, Burrage Rd., Plumstead, London. Native of Plumstead, London Hebuterne Military Cemetery III. G. 1

7ᵗʰ June 1916
1/14ᵗʰ London Regiment (London Scottish).
Cranwell 5170 Pte Edmund Percy Aged 19 Son of William James & Elizabeth Cranwell of 11, Brooklands Rd., Bletchley, Bucks. Hebuterne Military Cemetery III. G. 5

9ᵗʰ June 1916
1/14ᵗʰ London Regiment (London Scottish).
Paton 5173 Pte Hugh Cochrane Elsmore Aged 20 Son of Mr. J. E. Paton of 31, Woodside, Wimbledon, London Hebuterne Military Cemetery III.G.4
Stevenson 4154 L/Cpl. James William Balfour Aged 24 Son of William & Eliza Stevenson of Holland, Stronsay, Orkney Hebuterne Military Cemetery III. G. 3
10ᵗʰ June 1916
Royal Garrison Artillery.
Truswell 48800 Gnr Joseph, 68ᵗʰ Siege Bty Aged 26 Son of Joseph & Jane Truswell of 46, Redoubt St., Radford, Nottingham St. Sever Cemetery, Rouen, , A. 18. 41

11ᵗʰ June 1916
1/13th London Regiment (Princess Louise's Kensington).
Terry 4107 Pte James Aged 29 Son of Thomas & Jane Terry of Brentford, Middx Doullens Communal Cemetery Extension No.1II. B. 3
Royal Field Artillery.
Hammond 825 Act Bdr Archibald Walter, A Bty., 282ⁿᵈ (1/3ʳᵈ London) Bde Aged 23 Son of Francis James & Alice Hammond of 47, Bounds Green Rd., Wood Green, London. Hebuterne Military Cemetery, IV. K. 1

13ᵗʰ June 1916
1/14ᵗʰ London Regiment (London Scottish).
Robinson 6438 Pte Ralph Aged 21 Son of Mrs. E. A. Robinson of 14, Azalea Terrace North, Sunderland, & the late Mr. B. A. Robinson. Hebuterne Military Cemetery III. G. 7

14th June 1916
1/3rd London Regiment (Royal Fusiliers)
Reed 4634 Pte William Aged 19 Son of Edward A & Rebecca A Reed of 12 Rudolph Road, Kilburn, London. St Amand Military Cemetery I.A.13
1/5th Cheshire Regiment (Earl of Chester's).
Beesley 1303 Pte. Laurence Charles Hebuterne Military Cemetery II. C. 2

15th June 1916
1/14th London Regiment (London Scottish).
Gunston 4944 Pte Edward George Hebuterne Military Cemetery III. G. 8
Morris 2996 Sgt. Archibald James Aged 22 : Son of Martin & Emma Kate Morris of "Oaklands," Harrow Rd., Wembley, Middx Hebuterne Military Cemetery III. G. 9

17th June 1916
1/5th Cheshire Regiment (Earl of Chester's).
Brandreth 1994 Pte. Albert Hebuterne Military Cemetery II. C. 3
Royal Engineers.
Cunnington 147158 Cpl W M, 5th Special Brigade RE Aged 25 Son of George M. and Mary Cunnington, of Newcastle-on-Tyne. Hebuterne Military Cemetery II. F. 4.

18th June 1916
1/5th Cheshire Regiment (Earl of Chester's).
Brookes 1787 L/Sgt Henry Aged 26 Son of Mrs. Taylor of Lynn, Cheshire Le Treport Military Cemetery Plot 2. Row K. Grave 3B
Royal Engineers.
Cranford 3259 Spr. Walter. 513th (2/2nd London) Field Coy RE Hebuterne Military Cemetery II. P. 5.

19th June 1916
1/16th London Regiment (Queen's Westminster Rifles).
Ablewhite 3044 Sgt. Sidney Aged 35 Son of James & Mary Jane Ablewhite of 19, Wembley Park Drive, Wembley, Middx. Native of Boston, Lincs. 2/2nd Londons att 1/16th Londons. He served in Malta, Egypt, Gallipoli and France. Hebuterne Military Cemetery IV. J. 3

23rd June 1916
1/7th Middlesex Regiment.
Case 5160 Private Cecil John Aged 17 Son of Frederick John & Eliza Case of Station Rd., Potters Bar, Middx. Hebuterne Military Cemetery II. M. 4.
Stedall 3795 Private Alfred Joel Aged 20 Son of Rose Amy Stedall of 119, Rucklidge Avenue, Harlesden, London, & the late Alfred Stedall. Hebuterne Military Cemetery II. M. 3.

ENDNOTES:
1 Dolden, A Stuart, Cannon Fodder, 1980
2 Keeson, Maj. C A C, Queen Victoria's Rifles,1792-1922, 1923 page 141
3 Büsing, Georg „Das Reserve-Feldartillerie-Regiment Nr. 20 im Weltkriege 1914-18"1932
4 Batho 2nd Lt. Arthur, 1/8th Middlesex Regt., Papers, The Liddle Collection, Leeds University.
5 Bickersteth, John (editor), The Bickersteth Diaries 1995 page 86.
6 Bisgood 3254 Sergeant Thornton Henry, 1/2nd Battalion, London Regiment (Royal Fusiliers). Unpublished diary.
7 Ibid.
8 Jones Rfm P H 1/16th London Regt (Queen's Westminster Rifles), Papers, IWM.
9 Mockett 104354 Rifleman Wally (Stretcher bearer), 1/16 Londons (Queen's Westminster Rifles). Letter dated 12th
May 1916 from to his friend Charlie Miller in Upper Tooting. The Liddle Collection, Leeds University.
10 Jones Rfm P H 1/16th London Regt (Queen's Westminster Rifles), Papers, IWM.
11 Moy, 2nd Lt. C E, Unpublished papers, Liddle Collection, Leeds University.
12 Ibid
13 Ibid
14 Ibid
15 Ibid
16 Keeson, Maj. C A C, Queen Victoria's Rifles,1792-1922,.1923, page 143
17 Bisgood 3254 Sergeant Thornton Henry, 1/2nd Battalion, London Regiment (Royal Fusiliers). Unpublished diary.
18 Hodder, Williams J E (editor), One Young Man, Hodder and Stoughton, 1917. The 'one young man' in the book
is L/Cpl Reginald Davis who is given the pseudonym of Sydney Baxter by Hodder Williams.
19 Clements, Pte H T, 1/2nd Battalion, London Regiment (Royal Fusiliers). Papers, IWM.
20 Dolden, A Stuart, Cannon Fodder, 1980
21 Moy, 2nd Lt. C E, Unpublished papers, Liddle Collection, Leeds University..
22 Bisgood 3254 Sergeant Thornton Henry, 1/2nd Battalion, London Regiment (Royal Fusiliers). Unpublished diary.
23 Engall 2nd Lt. John Sherwin Letter from 13th June 1916, IWM
24 Wheeler-Holohan, Capt. A V & Wyatt, Capt. G M C Wyatt, The Rangers Historical Records: From 1859 to the
conclusion of the Great War, 1921
25 Clements Pte (later Lt.) H T, 1/2nd London Regiment, Diary, IWM.
26 Moy, 2nd Lt. C E, Unpublished papers, Liddle Collection, Leeds University. Note: the QWR battalion War Diary
only records two men dead and two wounded for the 14th June 1916.
27 For his friends: letters of 2nd Lt. P.G. Simmonds of Mansfield College, Oxford, who was killed in action on the
Somme, July 1st, 1916, IWM
28 Ward-Jackson, op. cit,
29 Jones Rfm P H 1/16th London Regt (Queen's Westminster Rifles), Papers, IWM
30 Bryden, Pte N E C, 1/14th London Regt. (London Scottish)
31 Snow Maj. Gen Sir Thomas D'Oyly, 20th June 1916 entry in personal diary, IWM.
32 Ward-Jackson Maj. C L, Letter to his wife, VII Corps, IWM..
33 Büsing, Georg „Das Reserve-Feldartillerie-Regiment Nr. 20 im Weltkriege 1914-18"1932
34 Ibid.
35 Lindsay, Lt. Col. J H, The London Scottish in the Great War, 1925 p. 101.
36 Hubbard Pte A, London Scottish, Papers, IWM
37 For his friends: letters of 2nd Lt. P.G. Simmonds of Mansfield College, Oxford, who was killed in action on the
Somme, July 1st, 1916, IWM
38 Savage, R, Allenby of Armageddon, Bobbs-Merrill, 1926 page 144-5.
39 Allenby was, of course, to go on to win sweeping victories against the Turks in Egypt and Palestine, liberating
Jerusalem and Damascus and rehabilitating his reputation most effectively.
40 Clements Pte (later Lt.) H T, 1/2nd London Regiment, Diary, IWM.
41 Edmonds, Brig. Gen. Sir James E, Official History of the War: Military Operations, France and Belgium 1916,
Volume 1 p. 313.
42 Keeson, Maj. C A C, Queen Victoria's Rifles,1792-1922,.1923

6. THE ARTILLERY PROGRAMME

"I should be much obliged if I could be informed whether I have touched my wire target or not as up to present I have had no means of judging what effect my shooting has done."

Major H Mayne
68th Siege Battery

GIVEN THE STRENGTH of the defences to be attacked, it was clear that any offensive plan would depend substantially on VII Corps ability to concentrate a heavy artillery bombardment on the German defences. Some siege and heavy batteries were already in place but not enough to undertake the artillery plan that the Corps staff had in mind. As a result, orders were sent out to a number of batteries both in France and back in the UK to get ready to move to the Gommecourt front. The batteries due to arrive in the Gommecourt sector were:

From VI Corps:
No. 6 howitzer, Royal Marine Artillery (1st/2nd June)
One section of 50th Siege Battery (31st May/1st June)
68th Siege Battery (5th June)
116th Heavy Battery (30th/31st May)
From XVII Corps:
11th Siege Battery (2nd/3rd June, but did not arrive)
131st Heavy Battery (21st May)
From England:
73rd and 74th Siege Batteries[i] (arrived 7th May)
101st Siege Battery (27th May)
88th, 91st, 93rd, 96th Siege Batteries, 133rd & 135th Heavy Batteries (29th May)
94th Siege Battery (31st May)
95th Siege Battery (30th May-2nd June)
98th, 102nd and 103rd Siege Batteries (landing Le Havre, 27th May)

The overwhelming majority of the additional batteries were still training back in England in the Spring of 1916. Many had not fired a round in anger and for them, the complexities of accurate bombardment and barrage fire were, as yet, unknown.

---

[i] The 73rd and 74th Siege Batteries were part of two Brigades of South African artillery made up of five Batteries that were formed in Capetown in August 1915. The five batteries were reorganised in October 1915 as the: 71st (Transvaal), 72nd (Central and Diamond Fields East, Griqualand West), 73rd (Cape Peninsula), 74th (Eastern Cape Province, Port Elizabeth) and 75th (Natal) Siege Batteries. The 71st, 72nd and 75th were grouped together in the Northern & Central South African Siege Brigade and the 73rd and 74th Batteries became the Cape Province South African Siege Brigade and later the 50th Heavy Artillery group before becoming part of the 19th Heavy Artillery Group on 7th May 1916. The two original commanders of the 73rd and 74th Siege Batteries failed to survive the war: Maj. Walter Brydon, DSO, 73rd (South African) Siege Battery, was killed on 12th April 1918. Aged 38, he was the son of Jenny Hay Brydon of Richmond House, 36, Blessington Rd., Lewisham, London and the late William Walter Brydon. He was a native of Whiteabbey, Belfast. He was buried in Noeux-Les-Mines Communal Cemetery Extension, grave IV. B. 16.
Major William Henry Pickburn, 74th (South African) Siege Battery died of wounds on 13th November 1916. Aged 42, he was the son of George Henry and Isabel Pickburn of Staffordshire. He had previously lived in Brisbane, Queensland and Witbank, Transvaal, South Africa. He was Mentioned in Despatches. He is buried in Etaples Military Cemetery, grave I. A. 67. [*Source for all:* Carl Hoehler]

The experience of a young gunner, 2ⁿᵈ Lt. John Eldridge[i], was typical. Eldridge, previously a university student, passed out of Woolwich in October 1915 and was commissioned on 27th October. He was posted to 57 Company R.G.A. T.A. manning the coastal defences at Milford Haven. A few weeks were spent learning the rudiments of coastal defence artillery using some 6 inch coast defence guns and 12 pdr anti-torpedo boat guns before he was sent to Lydd in Kent for a month's course at the Siege Artillery School. There he learnt about emplacing 6 inch howitzers, gun drill and observing the fire of batteries. At the end of the course he was posted to 90ᵗʰ Siege Battery R.G.A. based at Harwich. Eldridge described what he found there:

"The battery consisted of 6 officers and about 160 other ranks. Half the battery were Essex Territorials and half Durham men, mostly miners, together with a sprinkling of regular N.C.O.s and gunners. Our major was a regular, an ex-Instructor in Gunnery; our captain was a Cornwall Territorial; the two senior subalterns were Special Reserve Officers, one from Bangor College of the University of Wales, one from Oxford. Then there was a ranker officer, an ex-Assistant Instructor in Gunnery, and myself, newly fledged from 'the shop'. The two senior subalterns were to command and train the two gun sections; the ranker, ex A.I.G., was to train the Battery Commander's assistants and command personnel; and I took on the signallers and observation duties. I passed as a 2ⁿᵈ class Signaller."[1]

Just before Christmas the battery moved to Cooden Camp at Bexhill on Sea, where several other batteries were also training and then in March he returned, this time with the battery, to Lydd for final training and live firing. The weapons used were not those they were to employ in France as all modern guns had been sent to the front. As a result, the men of the battery practised on a series of obsolete Boer War era guns: 15 pounder BL field guns, 8 inch rifled muzzle loading howitzers and 1898 pattern 9.45 inch Austrian Skoda howitzers, eight of which had been bought in 1900 for the siege of Pretoria in the Boer War but never used. The nearest they came to using a gun they were actually to fire on the Western Front was when they were allowed one shoot from some 6 inch 30 cwt BL siege howitzers just being replaced in service.

They didn't see the guns they were actually going to use until May 1916. After moving to Bristol they were issued with four 9.2 inch Mk 1 howitzers[ii] along with all of their stores, signalling equipment, telephone cable, observation instruments and ammunition (80 rounds a gun). Battery transport consisted of four caterpillar tractors (one per gun to pull the three elements of the gun in a train), thirty three Thorneycroft 3 ton lorries for stores and ammunition (20 rounds of ammunition to a lorry), a Daimler car and four Douglas motor-cycles (two with side cars). The battery's transport was manned by men of the Army Service Corps, two officers and 40 to 50 other ranks. Such was the nature, training and experience

---

[i] Later Sir John Eldridge. He was born in Chiswick in 1898 and was educated at Herne Bay College before attending Northampton Polytechnic (later the City University of London) where he read engineering (1914). In 1944 he was the Commander R.A. of the 56ᵗʰ Division's artillery in Northern Europe. The details of his experiences come from a typescript and an interview conducted by Peter Liddle in July 1979. Both are held at the Liddle Collection at Leeds University.
[ii] The gun on the R.A. Memorial at Hyde Park Corner is a faithful representation of the 9.2 inch BL Mk 1 siege howitzer but without the earth box.

of many of the heavy artillery units that were to be transported to France to support the 1st July attacks[i].

The first logistical problem was to get the men, the guns and the ammunition into place. At the beginning of May, the 101st Siege Battery was based at Fareham in Hampshire. They had been working hard to get to grips with their new 26cwt 6 in. howitzers. These guns had been designed and approved in early 1915 and significant numbers of them had only started to appear in the autumn. On the 9th May, orders were received for the battery to get ready for a rapid move. Six days later their allocation of the new howitzers arrived along with the necessary stores and equipment and, on the 18th, Capt. Dwerryhouse and twelve men left camp en route for France. Their job, as advanced guard, was to survey the site the battery had been given, to sort out billets and generally prepare the ground for the main body of the battery. Two days later, the battery made the short march to Southampton, leaving the guns and stores to follow on behind, and they boarded the *S.S. Caeserea* along with the men of the 88th Siege Battery and detachments from the R.F.C. and the R.E. At 4.30 p.m., the *Caeserea* slipped her moorings and headed off down the Solent towards the open sea and France. Thankfully, the Channel was millpond smooth for the next 36 hours. The next day, after their long crossing of the English Channel, the men of the two batteries disembarked at Rouen just before midnight and marched to the Mechanised Transport Rest Camp in the hills above the historic town. There they waited until, on the 23rd, the guns, the lorries and the stores arrived from England. The following day, the equipment was inspected and the 101st found some of their motor bikes had been damaged in transit. Whilst the men set to repairs, the officers stared at maps and studied orders. They had now to make their way towards Gommecourt.

Unlike some of the luckier batteries who moved by rail, the 101st were to make their way by road. On the 26th, the men of the battery set out. The weather was fine and warm, the roads straight, dusty, undulating, busy and bumpy. It was a tired bunch of amateur artillerymen who arrived at their temporary billets late in the day, having travelled a distance of some 51 miles. The following day, the journey was longer still. After slogging across the French countryside for another 56 miles, the exhausted men arrived at the small village of Authieule, a regular artillery staging post east of the important railhead at Doullens. Some equipment had been damaged in transit, with three sight brackets broken as a result of the constant banging and crashing on the uneven and pot-holed roads. The next day was easier by the previous days' standards, but still involved an eleven-mile hike eastwards along the valley of the Authie to the small village of Bienvillers. This was to be their base for the next month and, after a days' rest, the men of the battery set to work preparing the position of the battery.

Behind them the 88th Siege Battery was treading an equally weary road. Their war diary sets out in detail the route taken on the battery's snail like progress through NW France:

26th May	.	0800	Start to leave Camp
		0810	Clear Camp
		0910	Reach top of hill outside Rouen

---

i 90th Siege Battery did not arrive in France until 16th June when the men landed at Le Havre from Folkestone. The guns and motorised transport embarked at Avonmouth.

	0920	Halted
	1015	Reached Isneauville
	1025	Leave Isneauville
	1135	Arrive Vieux Manoir (14 km)
	1145	Leave Vieux Manoir
	1240	Passed St Martin Osmonville (8 km)
	1315	Halted 1 km north of St Martin Osmonville
	1430	Resumed journey
	1730	Reached top of hill above Neuchatel (13 km)
	1900	Arrived Callengeville (13km) stopped for night
27ᵗʰ May	0715	Start to leave Callengeville
	0720	Cleared Callengeville
	0800	Arrive Foucarmont (4 km)
		FWD breaks down, one-hour delay
	1000	Arrive crossroads in Haute Foret d'Eu (6 km)
		Half hour delay
	1110	Passed Blangy (7 km)
	1300	Dinner just north of St Maxent (10 km)
	1410	Resume journey
	1515	Arrive Abbeville (14 km)
	1615	Leave Abbeville
	1915	Arrived Bernaville (25 km)
28ᵗʰ May	0700	Resume journey
	0905	Reach railway crossing NW of Doullens (16 km). Proceed through Doullens.
	1045	Arrive Authieule (3 km). Park.
	1800	Leave for gun positions
	2100	Arrive Sailly-au-Bois (18 km)

There would be no rest for the tired gunners of the 88ᵗʰ Siege Battery. The next morning they were up early, if not bright, and the task of preparing their battery position started. They would be at it for weeks.

At Bienvillers, six kilometres to the north, the next week would be a hectic one for the officers and men of the 101ˢᵗ Siege Battery. As they would be within range of the more powerful German guns, dug outs 14 ft. deep were constructed for the officers and men serving the guns. A shell magazine 10 ft. deep, 20 ft. feet long and 7 ft. wide was hacked out of the soil. Here, 360 of the 100lb shells would be stored for immediate use. Wooden trolley lines were laid from the guns to the magazine and from the guns to the road so that the unwieldy shells could be run up to the howitzers with relative ease. Next came the communications systems. A telephone exchange and central control system were placed 61 ft. deep in a nearby chalk mine. At the mouth of the chalk mine, a sandbag hut was built to house a wireless, a telephone and speaking tube. Finally, everything was camouflaged to prevent observation by German aircraft. Some cover was already available from the heavily laden trees and all exposed equipment was camouflaged by painted rabbit wire slung over the guns and the limbers.

Further to the east, on the British front line trenches, a detachment of the Battery re-built an Observation Post (or OP) taken over from the 74ᵗʰ South African Battery. The OP was needed for the Battery's Forward Observation Officer (or FOO). When the Battery was in action, the FOO would watch from the OP spotting the fall of shell and phoning through corrections for length and direction of fire. The OP of the 101ˢᵗ was not totally satisfactory. Although it gave a good view over their targets, it had not proved possible to conceal it and the men and officers whose job it would be to occupy the OP knew that they would be a prime target of the German artillery when the action started.

The guns were finally put in position by 4ᵗʰ June and two days later, four weeks after they received their initial orders to be ready to move, they started the process of registering the howitzers on the targets they had been allocated in the VII Corps bombardment plan. With the FOO watching carefully for the fall of shot from the OP and, if possible, a British BE2c flying overhead to spot from the air, single rounds were fired at specific locations. Adjustments were made for errors in direction and for shots falling long or short. When shells appeared to be hitting the target, the details of direction and elevation were recorded and attention was turned to the next target.

In 1916, such range finding was still a relatively crude affair and would have remained so had senior British artillery officers had their way. Only three years before, at a meeting held at the Royal Artillery Institution, a Capt. J E W Headlam had proposed making allowances for meteorological conditions: wind speed, direction and the like. In spite of the fact that the range of a large artillery piece could vary by as much as 1,000 yards from one day to another depending on the weather conditions[2] his superiors greeted this revolutionary suggestion with incredulous laughter. In June of 1915, Lt. Col. Brooke-Popham of the R.F.C. had asked Major General Du Cane, the G.H.Q. Artillery Adviser, whether the details of wind velocity at various altitudes taken each morning at 10.00 a.m. would be of any use. He was sent away with a flea in his ear, Du Cane stating: "we cannot make any use of this information"[3].

Thankfully, however, not all officers were so blinkered. But it was not an artillery officer who persuaded G.H.Q. of the significance of wind speeds and direction when the artillery were in action. It was a Royal Engineer, Major E Gold, who, after several months of study, produced conclusive evidence that these elements were of significance. A report sent to G.H.Q. in March 1916 resulted in a directive dated 12ᵗʰ April stating that, in future, Met reports giving wind speed and direction at 2,000 ft. and 4,000 ft. would be issued at 9.00 a.m. and 3.00 p.m. every day. In a wonderful British compromise, however, the directive stated that the Met report would provide the data for only 3,000 ft. if the weather was either foggy or cloudy. Two weeks before the assault, a third report for 7.00 a.m. was added to the process and altitudes of 200 ft. and 500 ft. were added for the use of the Field Artillery.[i]

So, with this information, added to that gained from the registration process, the batteries set to the task of preparing for the heaviest and most prolonged bombardment the war had yet seen. There was, however, one element about which the artillery could do little - the quality of the shells. Since the 1915 shell crisis, the formidable energies of David Lloyd George had been unleashed on the fledgling British munitions industry. The impact had been dramatic. Production had soared and, as could be seen at the railheads and in the ever-growing dumps behind the lines, supplies of artillery ammunition were growing by the day. But, quantity was one thing, quality quite another. In a few weeks time, those men of

---

[i] Continuing improvements took place throughout the war. In August, air temperatures at specified heights were added. In January 1917, the times were altered and the shell's time of flight replaced altitude. From 2ⁿᵈ March, reports were issued six times a day. In March 1918, barometer readings at mean sea level were added along with a formula each battery had to use to adapt the data to their height above sea level.

the attacking battalions who made it into the German lines would be shocked by the enormous number of unexploded shells of all calibres they would find littering the battlefield. The main problem was the lack of reliable fuses; too many either fell out in flight or simply failed to detonate on impact. Whilst mass-production had led to an improvement in numbers, poor workmanship, poor materials and corner cutting by profiteering businessmen meant that quality was poor. To further exacerbate the problem, the shells themselves were variable in size to an unacceptable degree. During the Somme bombardment, for example, some of the 100lb shells for the modern 6 in. howitzers were found to vary in length by as much as 4 in. The consequent effect on ballistics and, therefore, accuracy can only be guessed at. Dropping shells onto a specified target was a work of art, even for the best-trained and most experienced gun team. Attempting this with defective ammunition, inadequate data and with no experience made the job something of a lottery for a large number of the new batteries digging themselves in on the VII Corps front.

But there was another significant problem for some of the batteries due to play a significant role in the bombardment. The 103rd Siege Battery was based and trained at Aldershot. Their equipment was two 12 in. railway-mounted howitzers that had only been introduced into the R.G.A. armoury in March 1916. With the guns and their carriages weighing in at over 57 tons, these monsters were not easy machines to service and the June bombardment would be their first time in action. But their role was vital. Along with the other heavy and super-heavy howitzers, these guns had the task of collapsing the deep, reinforced bunkers that the German defenders of Gommecourt had been furiously constructing for more than a year. This job would have proved difficult enough, given the strength of the targets and the inadequacies of the British ammunition, but it would have been made somewhat easier if the gun teams had been able to spend some time getting the feel of the guns and their vagaries. But time was not available. The 103rd Battery finally left Aldershot at 5.30 on the morning of the 28th May, arriving by train at Southampton Station at 8.00 a.m. The next morning, the men of the Battery marched to the Docks where H.M. George V inspected them, and one of their guns. The two howitzers were then embarked on the *S.S. Deventia* whilst the men crossed the Channel to Le Havre in the *S.S. Queen Alexandra*. Both ships disembarked on the morning of the 30th and, for the next five days, the men and the guns waited in the Docks Rest Camp awaiting further orders.

On the morning of the 5th June, the men of the battery crowded into wagons for the long and slow rail journey to Doullens. They spent the night at Authieule before the Battery's personnel split into two detachments. One, the right half section, marched off to the village of Humbercamps and the other, the left half section, made their way across country to St Amand. On the next day, the stores arrived at the two villages on the special railway spurs that had been laid by men of the 1/2nd Londons and the Royal Engineers at the end of May. The men then set to work preparing the position, installing communications, excavating dug outs and magazines. The guns themselves arrived in the deep of the night of the 15th/16th June so as to avoid enemy aerial observation. To further ensure that they were not spotted, the rails ran into the heart of the villages and the St Amand gun was eventually located in the tree-sheltered back garden of a small house. One hundred of their 750lb shells arrived with each gun and, on the night of the 19ᵗʰ/20ᵗʰ June, another 82 were brought by rail to each position.

Plate 12 The 12 in. railway howitzer of 103ʳᵈ Battery RGA at Humbercamps
(Photograph courtesy of Imperial War Museum, Q40)

It was not until the 23ʳᵈ June that the guns fired. At 3.30 p.m., the right half section at Humbercamps lifted their first shell by crane into the loading tray. The shell was then rammed into place followed by a 31½ lb bagged modified cordite charge. The twelve-foot long barrel was slowly raised to the correct elevation and the percussion firing mechanism activated. Men standing behind these guns said they could see the huge shell as it arced up into the sky. From being the size of a cricket ball it swiftly became a dot and then disappeared. The first shell fired was aimed at La Brayelle Farm. Another followed some minutes later. They were both reported as hits. The left half section swung into action in St Amand at 4.00 p.m. Their two shells were aimed at Rettemoy Farm. But that was to be it. The next day, the 24th June, was U Day, the first day of the bombardment. The 103rd Battery wasn't involved on the first day but on V-Day, the 25th, their huge guns lumbered into action with the aim of pulverising the German dugouts in the salient. Between them, they had fired just four rounds as rehearsal for their crucial role.

For other batteries concentrating in the VII Corps area, life was far from trouble free. One such was the 102nd Siege Battery R.G.A. who were also based in England when the call came for them to move to Northern France. They were at Portsmouth, familiarising themselves with their old 30 cwt 6 in. howitzers when the orders arrived. They were to proceed to Southampton on the 18th May. Their camp was hurriedly cleared, the guns made ready for the move and equipment and supplies checked, stacked and loaded for the off. An advance party of Capt. I P Smith[i] and fourteen men left for Le Havre on the 16th and the guns and stores left by train for Avonmouth. With them went a detachment of twelve men led by 2nd Lt. J A B Menzies. At 11.00 a.m. on the 18th, the men of the Battery marched out to Southampton Docks. The C.O., Major W Duncan, leading a party of three officers[ii] and 125 other ranks. At 6.30 p.m. they embarked on the *S.S. King Edward*, having been rejoined by 2nd Lt. Menzies and eight men from the Avonmouth party. They had returned after seeing the guns and stores safely embarked on the *S.S. Avenden*. The *King Edward* docked in Le Havre at two in the morning but the men were allowed to stay on board until 7.00 a.m. when they disembarked and marched to the Dock Rest Camp. After a day's rest, the next four days were spent in travelling to Bienvillers via Rouen, Doullens and Authieule. The journey was long not because they had to travel by road, as was the case with the 101st Siege Battery. For the 102nd, most of the journey was made by rail but the French railway system, overloaded and creaking at the seams often made an escargot look rapide. Much time was spent in the cramped wagons waiting whilst other equipment was loaded and other trains departed. The men of the 102nd sat for three hours in a train at Le Havre waiting to leave for Rouen. Then, the journey of only 50 miles took five and a half hours to complete. On the 23rd, having arrived at the Rive Gauche, Rouen at seven in the morning, they were back on a train for Doullens at eight in the evening. Again they waited, this time for an hour, before the train drew slowly from the station. This time, the 95-mile journey took 9 hours and 40 minutes - and even then, their journey was not complete. After de-training, there was a two hour route march to the billets in Authieule. It was a tired and stiff Battery that greeted their guns when they arrived at 5.00 p.m. that evening. The following day they set off for Bienvillers.

---

[i] Acting Major Isham Percy Smith D.S.O., 102nd Siege Bty., Royal Garrison Artillery, died on Friday, 30th November 1917 during a German counter-attack at the Battle of Cambrai. He was aged 27. He was the son of the late Maj. Gen. Percy Smith, R.E., and of Ethel Smith (nee Saunders) of 'Hinton', Aldeburgh, Suffolk. He is buried in Villers Hill British Cemetery, Villers-Guislain, Nord, France. grave II.A.II.
[ii] Lt. E A Anson, 2nd Lts. F B Thomson and A H Davis.

The next few days were busy ones for the men of the 102nd. They not only had to prepare their own gun positions at Bienvillers but they also took over responsibility for the guns of the 15th Siege Battery which were emplaced at Berles and Berneville. Whilst Capt. Smith and fifteen men marched off to Berles to take over the right section of the 15th and Lt. Anson led fifteen men to take over the 15th's left section at Berneville, Major Duncan and the 100 remaining men set to work at Bienvillers. A small party was sent up the line to prepare an OP, and a spot at the Hebuterne end of Yussuf trench, opposite Gommecourt Park, was selected.

At noon on the 29th an unfortunately accurate long-range shot ploughed into the men's billets in Bienvillers. Six men were wounded, three seriously. Gunners Baker and Mulcahy and Bombardier Childs were rushed by ambulance through the villages of Pommier and Humbercamps towards the main Arras to Doullens railway and the Casualty Clearing Stations at Doullens. Baker, gravely wounded, didn't make it. He died at the small hamlet of L'Arbret by the side of the railway line. His badly wounded colleagues were hurried onwards to Doullens. There, Mulcahy and Childs succumbed to their wounds. They were later buried together in the grounds of the Doullens Communal Cemetery[i].

A few days later, Capt. Smith and his detachment at Berles were able to extract some small revenge for their late comrades. On the 3rd June, they registered a target in the German lines and the next day fired 31 of their 100lb Lyddite-filled shells in support of a trench raid. But, even then, life did not run entirely smoothly. To the men's frustration, a buffer cylinder cracked on No. 2 gun during the operation. On the 6th, Lt. Anson at Berneville, a small village 5 km to the west of Arras, handed his two guns on to the 11th Siege Battery and then marched off down the arrow straight Arras-Doullens road to collect two of that battery's guns currently parked up at Mondicourt. At Berles, however, Capt. Smith and his men were assuaging their anger still further with another 54 round 'hate', deposited on the German lines.

At Bienvillers, the rest of the Battery was labouring hard to complete preparations for the position they would occupy during the bombardment to come. By the 14th, the platforms had been laid for Nos. 1 and 2 guns. The next day guns Nos. 137 and 171 arrived. Whilst work carried on preparing the positions for Nos. 3 and 4 guns, the back breaking task of mounting the other two took place. The 1896 pattern 30-cwt 6 in. howitzer was a versatile beast. Left on its two-wheel carriage it could fire its 100lb shells nearly 5,000 metres at an elevation of 35°. It could, however, be transformed into a proper siege howitzer by the removal of the wheels and axle and by the addition of a 'Siege, carriage, top'. This allowed for plunging fire at an angle of 70°; the sort of fire deemed necessary by the Artillery planners to destroy the German trenches and dugouts and have fatal consequences for their occupants. On the 16th, Nos. 1 and 2 guns started the process of registering their targets around Gommecourt.

---

i 66590 Gunner Charles John Joseph Baker, 102nd Siege Bty., Royal Garrison Artillery, died on Monday, 29th May 1916. Aged 24, he was the son of Charles John and Kate Baker of Holly Cottages, Hatchet Lane, Wirfield, Windsor. He is buried in Bavincourt Communal Cemetery, Pas De Calais, France, grave 5.
56480 Bombardier Harry Childs, 102nd Siege Bty., Royal Garrison Artillery, died on Monday, 29th May 1916, aged 36. He was the husband of Margaret Mary Childs of 28, Ashley Rd., Forest Gate, London. He is buried in Doullens Communal Cemetery Extension No.1, grave I.C.8.
27358 Gunner W Mulcahy, 102nd Siege Bty., Royal Garrison Artillery, died on Monday, 29th May 1916. He is buried in the Doullens Communal Cemetery Extension No.1, grave I.C.13.

From in front of Hebuterne, in the OP at the end of Yussuf Street, the Battery's FOO advised on the accuracy of their shooting. On the 18th, a BE2c from 8 Squadron R.F.C., circled overhead, trying to spot the fall of the 102nd's shells. On the 19th they were joined by Nos. 3 and 4 guns and, for the next five days, 102nd Siege Battery sought to accurately measure distance, direction, elevation, the effects of wind speeds, the variation in charges and all the other variables that might make their firing a success. Then, on the 23rd, they fell silent. They would next fire in anger on the 25th June, V-Day, in the planned five-day bombardment programme.

***

THE BOMBARDMENT of which they were to be part was effectively split into three elements:

1. Bombardment - the destruction of trenches, strong points and bunkers by the heavy and super-heavy howitzers;
2. Counter-battery - the destruction of the German artillery capability by the heavy and medium guns and howitzers; and
3. Wire-cutting - mainly by medium guns and howitzers, field artillery and heavy mortars.

To deliver the necessary weight of shell, twenty-four batteries of siege and heavy artillery had been brought together in four Heavy Artillery Groups under VII Corps overall direction. In addition, Corps could command the use of the two attacking divisions' field artillery of 18 pdr guns and 4.5 in. howitzers. In total, therefore, ranged against the defences of Gommecourt were:

56 howitzers (6 in. or heavier)

32 howitzers (4.5 in. R.F.A.)

27 guns (4.7 in. or heavier)

96 18 pdr guns (R.F.A.)

211 artillery pieces all told. To this can be added the divisional trench mortar batteries (four per division each totalling twelve 2 in. and two 240 mm heavy mortars) and the brigade light trench mortar batteries (eight 2 in. Stokes Mortars per brigade or 24 per division) as well as certain elements of the 37th Division's artillery who helped bombard some targets from the northern flank of the attack.

This concentration of firepower had to deal with some 20,000 metres of trenches, perhaps half this length of wire, twelve identified strong points (including most of Gommecourt village and the central areas of Gommecourt Park and Wood), the four villages of Essarts, Bucquoy, Ablainzeville and Achiet-le-Grand and the artillery positions etc., at Rettemoy Farm and in Pigeon, Biez, Square and Rossignol Woods, etc. When put into this context, the concentration of "one heavy gun per 47 yards (of front), with a field gun per 27 yards[4]" looks less formidable. Indeed, if one removes the 18 pdrs from the equation (wholly used for wire cutting) then the task of trench bombardment alone given to the remaining 115 heavy and medium guns and howitzers is put in a completely different perspective. For this part of the operation, each gun on average would have had to deal with 180 metres of trench. Now, whilst some of this fire would have taken a trench in enfilade (so that only direction mattered, as firing either short or long would still put the shell in the trench) it still required the shell to drop in or near to a target no more than 5 metres wide from a range of 5,000 metres and more. But not all targets could be so bombarded. Some batteries were firing face on to their trench targets and so here distance was of key importance - when aiming at their 5 metre wide target, a miss was as good as a mile. If one adds into the mix the problem of observation failures and dud shells then the problem became still greater.

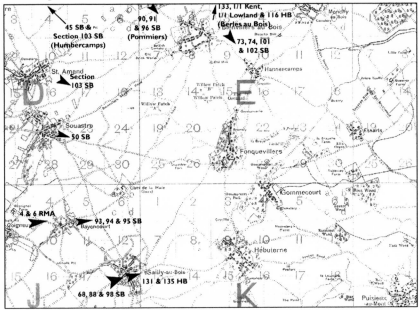

Map 8 Location of R.G.A. batteries

Legend: 19th H.A.G. – Bienvillers 16 x 6 in. howitzers; Pommier 12 x 9.2 in. howitzers; Humbercamps 1 x 9.2 in. railway gun & 1 x 12 in. railway howitzer; St Amand 1 x 12 in. railway howitzer
35th H.A.G. – Sailly au Bois 12 x 6 in. howitzers; Bayencourt 12 x 9.2 in. howitzers; West of Bayencourt 2 x 15 in. howitzers
39th H.A.G. – Sailly au Bois 8 x 60 pdrs
48th H.A.G. – Berles au Bois 12 x 4.7 in. guns & 4 x 60 pdr guns

In these circumstances, it is remarkable that on some parts of the 56th Division's front the German trenches had been so badly damaged as to become unrecognisable. This proved a mixed blessing, however, as it meant that much-needed cover for the attacking troops from counter-attack and retaliatory artillery fire was lacking in these places. Additionally, in one location, it led to the attacking troops moving well forward of their allotted objectives because they could not recognise the trench layouts from the models over which they had so painstakingly practised over in the preceding weeks.

As the artillery plan was developed, however, these problems were, as yet, unknown. During May and June a detailed bombardment programme was put together which, senior officers believed, would leave the defenders of Gommecourt either dead or so dazed as to be unable to defend themselves. They were utterly convinced the attack would be a walk over.

As previously mentioned, twenty-four siege and heavy batteries were at the disposal of Brigadier General C R Buckle, VII Corps Heavy Artillery G.O.C. These batteries were divided in four Heavy Artillery Groups (H.A.G.s): 19th H.A.G., 35th H.A.G., 39th H.A.G. and 48th H.A.G.. In broad terms, the first two groups were tasked to bombard trenches, strong points and villages, whilst the latter two groups were given the main responsibility for counter-battery work (this reducing still further the number of weapons firing at trenches and strongpoints). In addition to the batteries of the H.A.G.s, the 4.5 in. howitzers of the divisional artillery were also used for bombardment and counter-battery work from time to time.

19th Heavy Artillery Group, comprised 8½ Siege Batteries:

- 73rd, 74th and 101st Siege Batteries each of four 6 in. howitzers (26 cwt version)
- 102nd Siege Battery made up of four 6 in. howitzers (30 cwt 1896 version)
- 90th, 91st and 96thi Siege Batteries each of four 9.2 in. howitzers
- 103rd Siege Battery of two 12 in. howitzers
- 45th Siege Battery (Right section) of one 9.2 in. gunii

A further 2,000 metres beyond Bienvillers were the twelve 9.2 in. howitzers, placed around the village of Pommier. 1,500 metres due west of Pommier, in the village of Humbercamps, was the one 9.2 in. gun and one of the two 12 in. howitzers. Two kilometres to the south of Humbercamps, at St Amand, the second 12 in. howitzer was located. These last three guns were, therefore, firing on the defences of Gommecourt at a minimum range of 7,500 metres (4.7 miles); the equivalent of bombarding the House of Commons from the north end of Hampstead Heath.

The two 12 in. howitzers were monstrous guns (see photograph page 120). Mounted on an eight-wheel railway truck, they had been run on specially constructed branch railways into their home villages. Here, cunningly camouflaged, they were to lob their 750lb shells onto the deep dugouts surrounding Gommecourt. Designed by the Elswick Ordnance Company on Tyneside, the 12 in. BL Mk I Railway Howitzers and their carriages weighed nearly 58 tons. The one in St Amand provided entertainment for the men waiting to attack the German lines these guns were supposed to pulverise.

"The 12 inch gun in the back garden is a source of considerable interest," wrote Private Jones of the Queen's Westminster Rifles. "It is on a special railway line, very cunningly screened from aeroplanes and is indeed a monster. This is the first time I have seen a shell en route for the enemy trenches. Standing directly behind the gun it is possible to see the shell travelling up into the heavens - a black speck, no bigger than a cricket ball."[5]

The 9.2 in. gun, based at Humbercamps, was also railway mounted (see photograph page 120). An Elswick adaptation of the naval guns in use for coastal defence and in the obsolete Armoured cruisers of the Grand Fleet (which suffered so badly at Jutlandiii), these guns had a range of up to a maximum range of about 15,000 metres. Propelled by a 120lb bagged Cordite charge, their 380lb shells would be used to reach deep into the enemy rear, seeking out German

---

i The 96th Siege Battery took over the guns and positions of the 62nd Siege Battery. The 96th Siege Battery was formed on 1st January 1916 at Pembroke Docks by three officers and 90 men from the Glamorgan Territorials and 64 RGA recruits from the Docks. It was commanded by Maj. C H M Sturgis and arrived in France on 24th May.

ii One gun, not two as in the Official History. This battery had been in France since 1st September 1915.

iii Nine Armoured cruisers mounting 9.2 in. guns were built for the Royal Navy between 1906 and 1908. Three of them, HMS Black Prince, HMS Warrior and HMS Defence were sunk at Jutland.

batteries, disrupting supplies and bombarding billets in supposedly safe French villages. The 45th Siege Battery was one of the more experienced units in the gun lines opposite Gommecourt. Since September 1915 the right section had been at Ypres sending their huge shells into the German lines behind Sanctuary Wood and it wasn't until 11 a.m. on the 13th June that they were ordered south. On the morning of the 14th the gun, two ammunition wagons and three others for the men and stores set off to Hazebrouck via Steenwerck where they joined up with other sets of wagons pulling the left section of the battery and half of the 18th Siege Battery. After nearly six hours they arrived at St Pol and the next day the men and store wagons moved via Doullens to Humbercamps.

Plate 13 A 9.2 in. Railway Gun just after firing
(Photograph courtesy of the Imperial War Museum, Q98)

Their main position was in an orchard with a road lined by tall oak trees running at right angles to the front. Although the cover provided by the trees was excellent, the curve of the railway line along which they would operate was not so good. Half a dozen tall trees were in the way and would need felling and one section of the curve was useless as it only covered areas behind the British lines. The railway lines themselves were also only camouflaged, after work by the Railway Construction Company of the Monmouth R.E., for the last two hundred yards before the orchard. Work was now put in hand to build a 15 ft. deep dugout whilst the men from the Monmouth R.E. Company ballasted the line prior to the arrival of the gun. At 5 a.m. on the morning of the 19th June, the 24 ton gun on its 36 ton carriage rolled slowly into its berth under the orchard's trees. Around it work continued apace. A dugout was needed for the wireless and its 2nd Air Mechanics R.F.C. operators, ammunition and cartridges had to be unloaded and stored and the main dugout completed. On the 21st and 22nd, the men set to clearing and felling trees with eight of the tall oaks coming down and many of the orchard's trees having upper branches lopped. Work continued on the dugouts and a shelter for the gun team was constructed. Meanwhile, details of their arcs of fire were sent up from 19th H.A.G. as well as instructions that, for counter-battery purposes, they would be under the command of the 35th H.A.G. Their arduous work carried on for another two days, by which time many of the lighter guns had started their part of the bombardment, and it wasn't until 7.15 a.m. on 'V' Day, 25th June, that the gun fired its first unregistered shots; three shells in fifteen minutes soaring on their way towards Bucquoy 12,000 yards away as the whole of the Battery's complement looked on.

35th Heavy Artillery Group (C.O. Lt. Col. H G Brett) was made up of seven Siege Batteries of the R.G.A. and two 15 in. howitzers from the Royal Marine Artillery (Guns No. 4 and No. 6). The Group was made up as follows:

- Nos. 4 and 6 guns R.M.A. 15 in. howitzers
- 93rd, 94th and 95th Siege Batteries each of four 9.2 in. howitzers
- 88th and 98th (Canadian) Siege Batteries each of four 6 in. howitzers (26 cwt version)
- 68th Siege Battery made up of four 6 in. howitzers (30 cwt 1896 version)
- 50th Siege Battery (left section) made up of two Mk VII 6 in. guns

These batteries arrived in the area throughout late May and early June:

21st May – 93rd Siege Battery (Bayencourt)
23rd May – 95th Siege Battery (Bayencourt)
28th May – 88th Siege Battery (Sailly au Bois)
1st June – 50th Siege Battery (between Souastre and Bayencourt)
6th June – 68th Siege Battery (half, remainder arrived 15th June, Sailly au Bois)
8th June – 94th Siege Battery (Bayencourt)
9th June – 98th (Canadian) Siege Battery (Sailly au Bois)

These batteries and guns were mainly concentrated in the villages to the west and south west of Gommecourt. At Sailly-au-Bois, 4,000 metres to the south west of their intended targets, were grouped the three 6 in. batteries (68th, 88th and 98th (Canadian)). At Bayencourt, 5,000 metres WSW of Gommecourt, the 9.2 in. howitzers of 93rd, 94th and 95th Siege Batteries prepared to lob their shells onto the trenches in the salient.

The 9.2 in. howitzers were the 'cruiserweights' of the Royal Garrison Artillery, weighing in at a 'mere' 14 tons. Designed at the instigation of Maj. Gen. Sir Stanley von Donop, who first proposed such a weapon in 1908, their design and proving had been completed just before war began in July 1914 and a prototype, nicknamed 'Mother', first saw service at Neuve Chapelle. These were guns that needed a lot of preparation before action started. The guns travelled in three sections: 5 tons plus of barrel and breech; 5 tons 10 cwt of cradle and recoil system; and 4 tons 5 cwt of platform. But before these huge systems had been put in place, the gun's detachment had more work to do. First, large wooden supports had to be put in place on which the gun platform would sit. The rear beam was laid at right angles to the line of fire and measured 1½ ft by 1 ft by 10 feet long. Two more longitudinal beams (20 feet long by 1 ft by 1 ft) ran forward[i]. Then, in order to stop the gun rearing up from the ground when fired at low elevation, a huge metal box was attached to the front of the gun platform. This box was then filled with 9 tons of earth to act as a counter-weight against the

---

[i] Repeated firing at any degree of traverse could displace, damage or sometimes split these beams and replacements were always to hand. Later in the war they were replaced by steel supports.

recoil of the gun. When it fired its 290lb, Amatol filled shells, they were capable of a range of 9,000 metres, so that the German positions nearly as far as Puisieux would have been within range. In all, there were 24 of these guns ranged against Gommecourt and it was planned that they play an important role in neutralising the village's considerable defences. And so they might have, but for some strange thinking on the part of the Army Staff.

The problem for these batteries was to be a distinct lack of opportunity to accurately register their targets. The 94ᵗʰ Siege Battery had been in France since the 30ᵗʰ May. The men had embarked in Folkestone late in the morning to arrive in Boulogne at 2.15 p.m. They slept overnight in the St Martin's Camp on the heights above the port. They next day, their guns, lorries, caterpillars and supplies arrived in the *S.S. Hunsgate* from Avonmouth under the command of 2ⁿᵈ Lt. Lush[i]. They were to be disembarked and parked up pending their onward journey. This was done with great care so as to avoid a repeat of an incident at Avonmouth when one of the gun parts slipped as it was being winched aboard. The resulting damage to a battery lorry unfortunately parked below was severe.

It was 8.00 a.m. on the 5ᵗʰ June before they moved again. The battery's personnel mounted the lorries and set off south east towards Doullens. The guns and their caterpillar tractors left by train later the same day. At 6.00 p.m. the men arrived in the tiny village of Ruisseauville where they were to be billeted for the night. After nearly ten hours travelling across bumpy French roads in lorries that bucked and juddered on the slightest pothole or rut, the men were tired and stiff, their bones ached and they were hungry. Behind them, the guns were trundling slowly across the French countryside, lashed to creaking and rattling railway wagons. They next saw one another in the mid-evening of the following day. The men had risen early and were on the road by six but it was 3.30 p.m. when they turned into the artillery park at Authieule. Meanwhile, the guns had arrived at Doullens at 11.00 a.m. where they were heaved off the railway wagons, hooked up to their caterpillars and sent on their way eastwards on the 3 kilometre journey to meet the rest of the battery. Ten and a half hours after their arrival at Doullens, the tractors crawled into Authieule. The caterpillars were living up to their name[ii]. At 8.00 a.m. on the 7ᵗʰ June, the men and the guns set off on the last stages of their tortuous journey. The men and the lorries arrived in Bayencourt at 2.30 p.m. where the lorries were unloaded and then packed on their way to the H.A.M.T.[iii] Park at Mondicourt, 12 kilometres to the rear. The guns and the tractors creaked into the Caterpillar Park at Henu late that evening. The 8ᵗʰ was spent exploring the battery position in an orchard on a small road leading west from Bayencourt Church. Work started on the complex preparations for shelters, communications, storage and camouflage. The following day, the tractors crawled out of Henu on the last leg of the journey. They only had another 4 kilometres to travel and their arrival was timed to be covered by darkness. In pouring rain, Nos. 2 and 4 guns arrived and the

---

[i] 2ⁿᵈ Lt., later Brigadier, Maurice Lush was born on the 23ʳᵈ November 1896 in Ryde, on the Isle of Wight. He was educated at Holland House Preparatory School, Hove and Tonbridge where he was a member of the Tonbridge OTC. In April 1915 he joined the Royal Marine Artillery and in December 1915 he was transferred to 94ᵗʰ Siege Battery, RGA then based at Teignmouth.

[ii] The C.O. of the 93ʳᵈ Siege Battery, also equipped with 9.2 in. BL Howitzers, remarked in the War Diary that the tractor drivers appeared not to have had any training driving with the guns attached.

[iii] Heavy Artillery Mechanical Transport

strenuous task of mounting the guns began. The next evening, Nos. 1 and 3 guns appeared and the wet, exhausted gun teams set to work assembling the huge guns by the light of spluttering lamps. The start of the bombardment was now only two weeks away and yet there was still much work to be done. The War Diary of their sister battery, the 93rd Siege Battery, gives some idea of the huge workload undertaken before these guns could be fired[i]. Over a three-week period, this battery excavated ten dugouts and four shell shelters. The dugouts were 14 ft deep and had dimensions of 15 ft. by 8 ft. by 6 ft. It was estimated that they would resist the impact of a 5.9 in. (15 cm) howitzer shell. The shell shelters, designed to hold 200 shells each, were less deep and supposedly able to resist a 4.2 in. (10.5 cm) shell.

By the 15th, the 94th were ready to start registering their targets and, to hand were 500 9.2 in. shells. But, herein lay a bizarre contradiction to be found at the heart of the Staff's planning of the Gommecourt attack. Haig required that the infantry's preparations be as obvious to the Germans as possible. In this way, he hoped that reserves would be drawn away from the rest of the front, especially in the area around Serre. On the other hand, the artillery seems to have been ordered to keep their preparations secret. Thus, many of the big 'siege' guns were brought in overnight to avoid detection from the air. And, in the case of the 94th Siege Battery, they were then allowed to register only six targets "in order not to show unusual activity". This strange piece of thinking on the part of the Staff sets the seal on the sacrificial nature of the Gommecourt attack. A large proportion of the artillery now ranged against the Gommecourt salient was either new to the area, new to their weapons or both. Many batteries had only recently arrived in France and had no experience of precision firing. And yet, the only hope of success for the attacking troops was if these heavy howitzers destroyed a large proportion of the German artillery defending Gommecourt and smashed a significant number of the deep bunkers that the Staff knew existed in large numbers. It was there that the defenders lurked, ready to counter-attack in numbers, not in the trenches which were more easily attacked and destroyed. To do this, the inexperienced gunners needed to accurately register targets with the aid of both aerial and ground observation. But this was denied to them by the order "not to show unusual activity". The effects of this decision were then compounded by the nature of the weather, the failure of adequate aerial co-operation and the two-day postponement of Z Day. The consequences for the infantry were profound and, for many, fatal.

To the west of the twelve 9.2 in. howitzers grouped around Bayencourt, and 6,000 metres WNW of Gommecourt, were the two huge 15 in. R.M.A. howitzers (of which more later) and the two Mk VII 6 in. guns of the 50th Siege Battery[ii] in Souastre. These last guns, although part of an H.A.G. mainly devoted to bombardment work, were also utilised for interdicting the villages deep in the rear of enemy lines and, from time to time, for counter-battery work. In this task, they were joined by between two and four of the 9.2 in. howitzers and the same number of modern 6 in. howitzers.

---

[i] The 93rd Siege Battery had arrived in France on the 5th May, crossing from Folkestone to Boulogne. The guns and lorries left Avonmouth near Bristol (where they had been training for the past month) on the same day and arrived in France on the 8th. The four guns were mounted by the 27th May and they spent the next three weeks preparing the position.
[ii] 50th Siege Battery arrived in France in October 1915.

The Mk VII 6 in. guns were huge and heavy. Over 23 feet long and weighing in at over 25 tons, these guns were adapted coastal defence weapons sent out to France in 1915. With a range of 12,000 metres, they fired a 100lb shell filled, normally, with either Amatol or Lyddite. On occasions, however, they were also used to fire the very limited supply of gas shell at the disposal of VII Corps artillery. The shells were of the 'SK' variety, filled with Ethyl Iodoacetate. SK was not the poison gas of popular World War One mythology but a lachrymatory or tear gas used to disable rather than kill. It got its name from having been developed at Imperial College in their laboratories behind the Albert Hall in South Kensington. The left section of 50th Siege Battery had moved down from their positions at Dainville near Arras at the end of May being stored at Authieule from the 1st to the 9th June. In the meantime, the men cleaned up their new battery position and created an Observation Post in the old French Wagram trench mid-way between Hebuterne and Colincamps. On the night of the 9th, both guns were brought up to Henu in the expectation that No. 1 could be installed the following day but man-handling nearly 24 tons of gun in the wet was not a good idea and the weather prevented any action that day. No. 1 gun was eventually got into position on its platform on the evening of the 11th June but the problems of trying to move these heavyweights in adverse weather was highlighted when No. 2 gun became stuck the following night and work was abandoned at 5.30 a.m. the following morning to be completed that night with a great deal of sweat and muscle power.

Although under the administrative control of 35th H.A.G., 50th Siege Battery came under the tactical control of 39th H.A.G. and its jobs were long distance interference with communications, strafing of the villages thought to contain the German infantry reserves and counter-battery work. Between the 11th and the 14th, 240 of their 100lb shells were brought up and, whilst an ammunition dump, huts and shelters were constructed, the officers spent two days in conferences with the O.C.s of 39th and 35th H.A.G.s at which their targets and priorities were discussed. 50th Siege Battery was one of the few batteries to have a reasonable chance to register their guns and to iron out any problems with their equipment and position before the bombardment started. On the 16th nine unobserved rounds of Amatol HE were fired at Le Quesnoy Farm on the north side of the Gommecourt salient and then they engaged a German battery with a further fourteen rounds with the aid of R.F.C. observation. They finished pleased with themselves. The next day was 'work' not 'fun' with the main concern being the completion of the ammunition dump. On the 18th, the guns fired 24 rounds at Rettemoy Farm, home to three German battery positions but, again, most of the day and all of the 19th were spent in improving the positions, laying telephone lines and bringing up five day's worth of iron rations. From the 20th to the 23rd the gunners had a fine time targeting the observation balloon teams behind the German lines and their attached anti-aircraft batteries. Three times they forced balloons down and followed this up with a quick few rounds of shrapnel aimed at the nearby AA batteries. This activity was not to go unopposed, however, as their location too had been noticed and over 'U' and 'V' Days German 15cm field guns retaliated in the early evening, causing some minor damage to No. 2 gun but considerable consternation to its team. From 'V' Day onwards, the two guns spent their time firing at Ablainzeville, Achiet le Grand and Bucquoy in the mornings and being targeted on likely German batteries in the afternoon.

39th Heavy Artillery Group was normally made up of two 60-pdr batteries (131st Heavy and 135thi Heavy Batteries, each of four 60 pdr guns). The 60 pdr was a 1904 design based on Army experience in South Africa. Capable of delivering its shrapnel or 6lbs of Amatol (i.e. 6lbs of explosive to 60lbs of shell) out to a range of 12,000 metres, they were mainly used for counter-battery work and the bombardment of the four rear villages. On occasion they were joined by two or four 6 in. howitzers of the 74th Siege Battery as well as the guns of the 45th and 50th Siege Batteries and two 4.5 in. howitzers from each of 'D' section, 232 Battery R.F.A. and 'D' section, 280 Battery R.F.A. (divisional artillery). The 131st and 135th Batteries fired from positions just in front of the 6 in. howitzers of 35th H.A.G. in the village of Sailly-au-Bois.

Finally, 48th Heavy Artillery Group was made up four batteries located near to the village of Berles-au-Bois 5,000 metres to the north of Gommecourt. Here, three 4-gun 4.7 in. gun batteries (133rd Heavy, 1/1st Kent Heavy, 1/1st Lowland Heavy Batteries) and the 116th Heavy Battery (four 60 pdr guns) fired onto the northern flank of the Gommecourt defences.

The 116th Battery mainly assisted the 19th H.A.G. in bombardment work, although some time each day was spent on counter-battery work. Although the 116th had been in France since July 1915, they had spent all of that time equipped with 4.7 in. guns. It was not until the 19th June, five days before the bombardment was due to start, that the C.O., Major O R Swayne D.S.O. oversaw the swapping of this equipment for the more modern 60 pdrs. The next few days were spent in frantic efforts to get their guns ready for action. Four days were spent filling various dumps with 2,040 of the new guns' shells. The guns themselves were dragged into position on the night of the 22nd/23rd June and the following night, the last refinements were added in the shape of the guns' oscillating sights. With no time for registration, the battery swung into action the following day, firing a mixture of Lyddite and shrapnel deep into the Gommecourt salient.

Oddly, the 133rd (Co. Palatine) Heavy Battery, which had been shipped out from Southampton on H.M.T.S. *City of Benares* on 26th May, had brought out with it four 60pdr Mk 1 guns which it had spent a month getting used to back in England. On their arrival at Bienvillers they then had to do the opposite to the 116th Battery as they swapped their nice new 60 pdrs for four obsolete 4.7 in. guns previously the property of the 14th Heavy Battery. The end product of this transaction was, at least, that they took over a working battery position with its guns in place and, as a result, were able to open fire with their first ever 'live' shoot at 6 p.m. on the evening of 1st June. The battery's target was to be, in the main, the great expanse of Adinfer Wood within which were concealed numerous batteries attached to the 111th Division and between 1st and 5th June they lobbed 124 shells into the centre of the wood. On two days they had the help of a BE2c flying overhead to observe the fall of shot and, on these occasions, they managed to get just over half of the 82 shells fired within 25 yards of the target. From then onwards the battery's activity was low key to say the least with just nineteen

---

i The 135th Heavy Battery took over the guns and position of the 114th Heavy Battery.

shells being fired over an eleven day period until, on the 17th June, they had a registration shoot supposedly with aerial observation but, unfortunately, the R.F.C. observer failed to spot the fall of nearly half of the shoot. As two of the four guns were trying to target German battery positions behind Essarts this was most regrettable.

The twelve 4.7 in. guns barely participated in all but three days of the bombardment and on July 1st itself. These guns were obsolete and were based on an 1895 design for naval and coastal guns that had been converted for Army use by Capt. Percy Scott R.N. during the Boer War. With a range of just 10,000 yards and a shell of only 46½lbs containing just 4lb of Amatol or 6¾lbs of Lyddite these guns were of little practical use in demolishing the German defences and were used, albeit infrequently, for bombardment on rear villages and lines of supply and communication but their main task, for which they were thoroughly unsuited, was the demolition of German artillery positions.

Some of the batteries had, at least, spent some time in the area getting to know terrain and their elderly guns. The 1/1st Lowland Heavy Battery had been in or around the area since their arrival in France in February 1916. Mobilised immediately war was declared they had spent many months training near to Stirling before being ordered to join the B.E.F. They had been sent to Berles-au-Bois at the beginning of May and had spent a week preparing positions for their guns until, on the 15th, they were ordered to take over the positions currently occupied by the 116th Heavy Battery. It wasn't until the 24th June that they started registering their targets and firing on designated targets on 'night lines'.

Table 3 below shows the number of rounds per gun allocated for each day of the originally planned bombardment. In general, each of the first four days showed little or no variation in the number of shells to be fired and only on 'Y' Day was there due to be a significant increase in tempo though this was negated when the two extension days were inserted into the programme.

Gun type	Rounds per day per gun/howitzer						Rounds remaining
	U Day	V Day	W Day	X Day	Y Day	Z Day	
Guns							
4.7 in.	0	0	0	70	100	150	97
60 pdr*	166	166	166	120	100	150	100
60 pdr†	140	140	140	120	100	150	100
6 in. Mk VII	20	20	20	20	20	30	60
6 in. Mk VII CB	10	20	20	20	20	70	
9.2 in.	0	30	40	40	40	50	50
Howitzers							
6 in. (26 cwt)	0	30	30	30	111	220	34
6 in. (30 cwt)	0	205	205	205	248	200	86
6 in. CB‡	20	25	25	25	50	- Zero 50 + Zero 100	0
9.2 in.	0	50	50	50	70	180	0
9.2 in. CB+	20	20	20	20	50	+ Zero 50	0
12 & 15 in.	0	30	40	40	40	50	50

Table 3 Rounds per gun/howitzer per day in original Heavy Artillery programme
* 116th Heavy Battery   † 131st & 135th Siege Batteries
‡ 6 in. howitzers allocated for counter battery work: U 4, V 2, W 2, X 2, Y 2, Z 2 before Zero, 4 after
+ 9.2 in. howitzers allocated for counter battery work: U 4, V 2, W 2, X 2, Y 2, Z 2 after Zero

Table 4 shows the total number of rounds to be fired by each type of gun with just over 14,000 due to be fired by the guns and a further 28,500 coming from the howitzers giving a combined total of just under 43,000. It should be noted, however, that of the 14,400 shells fired by the guns, 95% were to be fired by the 4.7 in. and 60pdr guns all of which were unable to reach the German heavy artillery and which also delivered a small charge of explosive of around 6lbs which were unlikely to do significant damage to the well established and protected German gun positions unless by way of a direct hit on a gun. The 6 in. howitzers were all also out of range of the German heavies which left the task of destroying these guns to the 720 shells fired by the 6 in. Mk VII guns and 9.2 in. howitzers seconded to counter battery work plus some of the 200 rounds fired by the 9.2 in. railway gun.

Gun type	Total number of rounds to be fire per day						Total per gun	Rounds
	U Day	V Day	W Day	X Day	Y Day	Z Day	type	remaining
Guns								
4.7 in.	0	0	0	840	1,200	1,800	3,840	1,164
60 pdr*	664	664	664	480	400	600	3,472	400
60 pdr†	1,120	1,120	1,120	960	800	1,200	6,320	800
6 in. Mk VII	40	40	40	40	40	60	260	120
6 in. Mk VII CB	20	40	40	40	40	140	320	0
9.2 in.	0	30	40	40	40	50	200	50
Total guns	1,844	1,894	1,904	2,400	2,520	3,850	14,412	2,534
Howitzers								
6 in. (26 cwt)	0	600	600	600	2,220	4,400	8,420	680
6 in. (30 cwt)	0	1,640	1,640	1,640	1,984	1,600	8,504	688
6 in. CB‡	80	50	50	50	100	500	830	0
9.2 in.	0	1,200	1,200	1,200	1,680	4,320	9,600	0
9.2 in. CB+	80	40	40	40	100	100	400	0
12 & 15 in.	0	120	160	160	160	200	800	200
Total howitzers	160	3,650	3,690	3,690	6,244	11,120	28,554	1,568
Grand total	2,004	5,544	5,594	6,090	8,764	14,970	42,966	4,102

Table 4 Rounds to be fired per day by type of gun (Heavy Artillery programme)
* 116th Heavy Battery   † 131st & 135th Heavy Batteries
‡ 6 in. howitzers allocated for counter battery work: U 4, V 2, W 2, X 2, Y 2, Z 2 before Zero, 4 after
+ 9.2 in. howitzers allocated for counter battery work: U 4, V 2, W 2, X 2, Y 2, Z 2 after Zero

On June 16th Brig. Gen. C R Buckle, G.O.C. VII Corps Heavy Artillery, issued the definitive bombardment programme with an associated map showing the areas of responsibility for the various heavy batteries. It also included those field batteries that were to be included in the heavy artillery programme and the wire cutting and bombardment programme for the field artillery. An updated version taking into account the two extension days was circulated on the 28th June.

The heavy guns' bombardment fell broadly into three segments:

1. The bombardment of trenches in the three main German lines plus Exe trench and the western edge of Rossignol Wood and the area around La Brayelle Farm which took place in six hour periods. These were conducted by the 6 in., 9.2 in., 12 in. and 15 in. howitzers;

2. Short (i.e. 3 minutes or less) but intense shoots at one of the four villages in the rear thought to contain German billets and supplies: Bucquoy, Ablainzeville, Essarts and Achiet le Grand. These involved the 4.7 in., 6 in., 9.2 in. and 60pdr guns as well as, on occasions, some 4.5 in. R.F.A., 6

in. and the 12 in. howitzers and, on the short range bombardment of Essarts, an 18 pdr battery of the 46th Division; and

3. Short but intense bombardments by the heavy howitzers at unpredictable times of day timed in the hope that they might catch German reliefs in the trenches or to interrupt attempts at re-supplying the front lines.

The allocation of the heavy howitzers on the 56th Division's front was as follows:

Targets	Batteries
The southern edge of Gommecourt Park from Fit to Fir also Fight and Fine	91, 98 & 102 Siege Batteries
The German front three lines from Gommecourt Park to Farmer-Farmyard stronghold (exclusive) including Nameless Farm	73 & 91 Siege Batteries
Trenches surrounding Farmer-Farmyard stronghold	73, 74 & 91 Siege Batteries
Farmer-Farmyard stronghold	74 & 103 Siege Batteries & 15 in. R.M.A. howitzers
The Maze, Cemetery and Village	103 Siege Battery & 15 in. R.M.A. howitzers
Trenches linking the areas above	68, 73, 91, 93, 94 & 95 Siege Batteries
Exe and Epte communication trenches including Mess, Mere, Meed and Meet	68 & 94 Siege Batteries
Ems, Etch, Elbe and Anna communication trenches	Divisional howitzers
The Quadrilateral	68 & 94 Siege Batteries

Table 5 Siege Battery targets on 56th Division front

'V' Day was the only day when one of the intense howitzer bombardments did not take place but from 'V' through to 'X' days some 3,000 howitzer rounds of various weights fell on the German lines along with another 292 during the intense bombardments which fell at 10.22 a.m. on 'W' Day and 7.02 a.m. on 'X' Day. The programme for the villages was:

'V' Day: Bucquoy 7.15 p.m. – 249 rounds from 35 guns and howitzers of various sizes fired in three minutes. Ablainzeville 9 a.m. - 30 rounds from the 6 in. and 9.2 in. guns.

'W' Day: Essarts 7 a.m. – 168 rounds from 8 guns (mainly field howitzers and 18 pdrs) fired in three minutes. Achiet le Grand – 12 rounds from the 6 in. guns fired during the day.

'X' Day: Achiet le Grand – 12 rounds from the 6 in. guns fired during the day.

'Y' Day was planned to be the most intense day of the bombardment with the heavy howitzers firing nearly 5,500 shells but, with the postponement of the attack and the inclusion of the two extension days, these shells had to be fired over three days rather than one and a series of half bombardments at four to six hour intervals was introduced. It is clear, however, that nothing like the total planned for 'Y' Day was fired during 'Y'-'Y2' Days, a failure which gave the defenders of the salient much needed respite from the punishing bombardment as well as an opportunity to repair wire and trenches and re-supply the men in the front line dugouts.

'Z' Day was to be split into three sections. In the hours before 6.25 a.m. the heavy howitzers were to fire 3,580 shells at the front line and communication trenches, the village and the strongpoints. The guns were to play on the rear villages. At 6.25 a.m. the intense bombardment started and, in 65 minutes, the 6 in. howitzers were due to fire 3,840 shells, the 9.2 in. howitzers 3,120 and the super heavies 60. Thereafter, they fired at a slow and steady rate at predetermined targets unless otherwise advised. The long guns were, during these phases to be firing at the villages and targeting German batteries with R.F.C. assistance.

Throughout this time, the field howitzers, 18 pdrs and the heavy trench mortars of both divisions had the task of wire cutting (18 pdrs), front line bombardment (all), night-time interdiction of known tracks, roads and communication trenches (18pdrs and howitzers). They also had a programme of short intense bombardments, sometimes on their own and sometimes with the heavies. The 56th Division's original programme is set out in Table 6 below:

	U Day	V Day	W Day	X Day	Y Day	Z Day
Wire (shrapnel)	5,500	5,500	5,500	5,500	5,500	
Night lines (shrapnel)	2,000					
Bombardment & Night lines		4,000 S	4,000 S	3,140 S	5,000 S	-06.25
		5,000 HE	3,120 HE	5,000 HE	5,160 HE	900 S
		604 4.5"	400 4.5"	500 4.5"	804 4.5"	1,100 HE
		100 TM	100 TM	100 TM	100 TM	700 4.5"
Intense bombardments			1500 S	2,000 S	3,000 S	06.25-07.30
			1,800 HE	3,000 HE	3,500 HE	3,360 S
			400 4.5"	800 4.5"	850 4.5"	6,000 HE
						2,300 4.5"
						200 TM
Bucquoy		96 4.5"			96 4.5"	

Table 6 Original 56th Division Field Artillery Programme

Note: S = 18 pdr Shrapnel   HE = 18 pdr High Explosive.   4.5 in. = High Explosive from 4.5 in. howitzers. TM = 2 in. Trench Mortars

The total allotment of shells for the bombardment from 'U' Day up until Zero hour on 'Z' Day was:

18 pdrs   90,080 rounds

4.5 in. Howitzers   7,545 rounds

After Zero hour, the field artillery of the 56th Division had available another:

18 pdrs   78,320 rounds

4.5 in. Howitzers   12,921 rounds

The allocation of shells for the 46th Division was broadly similar but with slightly less used prior to Zero hour and slightly more available afterwards.

The introduction of the two extension days did not undermine the intensity of the field artillery bombardment to the same extent as it did the heavy artillery. The expenditure for 'Y', 'Y1' and 'Y2' was reduced to 13,000 18 pdr shells per day (39,000 total) from 22,000 as originally planned for 'Y' Day alone and the field howitzers were to fire 800 shells per day (2,400 total) as against 1654 for 'Y' Day alone. This reduced the volumes of shells available for 'Z' Day but, as it turned out, this would prove academic. Eight days continuous use proved too much for many of the 18 pdrs and there were reports of equipment failures from early on July 1st. The numbers of shells available may have been unprecedented in British military history but, because of this, no-one had any experience of the workings of such an intense and prolonged bombardment and how rapidly the guns would break down under the strain.

But there were other reasons why the bombardment did not achieve what was expected of it. Much has been made of the heavy and relentless weight of the British artillery bombardment over the seven days prior to the assault on July 1st. For the first time, there were few limits on the volume of shells each battery could fire. After the shell crisis of 1915, the efforts of Lloyd George as Minister of Munitions had borne fruit - in quantity if not in quality. It is estimated, therefore, that nearly 1.7 million shells of all sizes were fired during the preliminary bombardment and on July 1st itself along the whole Somme front.

Of course, it is well known that many of these shells failed to detonate. As modern day travellers to the Somme will know, even now, ninety years after the event, hundreds of unexploded shells are removed from the area each year by special French Bomb Disposal squads. The exact proportion of shells which failed to explode can only be guessed at, but comments made by observers both during the bombardment and on Z Day itself testify to the large numbers of dud mortar and artillery shells that could be found littering the battlefield. At Gommecourt, many of these were to be found in the German wire.

Perhaps less well known, however, is that much of the shelling done was fired unobserved either because the weather was too poor to allow for aerial observation or because retaliatory firing made observation by the F.O.O.s[i] difficult or impossible. In consequence, much of the heavy artillery fire from the few weapons capable of penetrating the deep bunkers or the reinforced emplacements was fired blind with little or no correction. Accuracy was not, sometimes, just marginally askew. Often the big guns and howitzers were 'off' by hundreds of metres - and they had no way of knowing how badly out they were.

A further problem was that few, if any, batteries managed to fire the weight of ammunition that the artillery programme called for. In some way, this may be linked to the problem of the weather. If targets could not be observed then was there any point in firing at them? Because of the lie of the land, certain targets could only be observed from the air and, given the prevailing weather conditions through the last week of June, many targets went unobserved resulting in much blind firing and, as will be shown later, great unhappiness amongst the artillerymen.

Crucial to the success of the assault was the destruction of the numerous deep bunkers and redoubts the Germans had constructed since their occupation of the village. The 15 in. and 12 in. super heavy howitzers were mainly to be used for the destruction of these key strong points. Their targets were from north to south:

- La Brayelle Farm
- A group of bunkers to the rear of the Z (north end of 46th Division sector)
- A group of bunkers in Fortress trench 500 metres behind the middle of the German front line opposite the 46th Division
- A group of bunkers in the centre of Gommecourt Wood
- Gommecourt village
- Gommecourt Chateau and the bunkers surrounding it
- A group of bunkers in the centre of Gommecourt Park
- The south east corner of the Maze and a group of nearby bunkers
- A group of bunkers surrounding the Cemetery

---

[i] FOO - Forward Observation Officer - an artillery officer from a particular battery located at or near the front line. Usually in communication with his battery via telephone, these officers had the task of monitoring and correcting the accuracy of the artillery's fire.

- The Farmyard/Farm/Farmer strongpoint at the southern end of the line to be attacked.

Initially, these four guns had ten targets to destroy over a period of four days (i.e. before the postponement added two extra days to the bombardment period; they were not due to fire on U Day, the first day of the bombardment) with an ammunition allowance of 150 shells per gun or 600 in total. So, on average, each of these targets would receive 60 12 in. or 15 in. shells. As a result of the postponement, another 160 shells were added to the total, twenty per day for each gun, but these were all concentrated on the Village and Gommecourt Wood leaving the other targets to the spare capacity of the lighter howitzers. The bombardment plan allowed, therefore, for a total of 760 shells to be fired by the super heavies, 30 per gun on V Day, 40 per gun on W to Y Day and 20 per gun on Y1 and Y2 days. For Z Day itself, the day of the assault, each gun was allocated 65 shells to last the day with 50 each to be fired before zero hour at 7.30 a.m. This gave an overall pre-zero hour bombardment total of 960 shells to be fired by the super heavy howitzers. That, at least, was the plan. Unfortunately, for a variety of reasons, none of the super heavies achieved the required rate of fire. Nor they did they always achieve the required accuracy.

Nos. 4 and 6 guns R.M.A. formed No. 1 Sub Group of the 35th H.A.G. and were the heaviest weight guns available on the VII Corps front. The guns were strange misfits, owing their existence to the private enterprise of the Coventry Ordnance Works, and their presence in Northern France to the First Lord of the Admiralty, Winston Churchill. The Coventry Works had designed and built the 9.2 in. howitzers which had first arrived in France in November 1914 and, after the success of this equipment, had, on their own initiative, decided to build something altogether bigger and more powerful. Thus was born the 15 in. BL Siege Howitzer. In order to gain acceptance within the military establishment, a Coventry Ordnance director, Admiral Bacon, exploited his connections with the Admiralty to effect an introduction to the Ordnance Board of the Army. Churchill, as was his wont, intervened. Spotting an opportunity for the Navy to get embroiled in the action on the Western Front, as well as sensing a good story for the press, Churchill manned the first gun with a team of Royal Marine artillerymen and sent them, post haste, to France. They would be followed by another eleven of the 10 ton 15 cwt behemoths.

Thus, in rainy weather in villages up to 10,000 metres behind the lines, could be found detachments of Royal Marines in sou'westers labouring over their sadly, under-powered, unwieldy and unloved howitzers. Underpowered, because their range was barely more than that of the 6 in., 8 in. and 9.2 in. howitzers now ranged along the front from Gommecourt to the Somme. Unwieldy, because the barrel and breech alone weighed three times that of a 9.2 in. howitzer, making them a swine to move and emplace. Unloved, because the Army had not been consulted about them, had not ordered them and, as they soon made clear, did not want them. Churchill's enthusiasm for his Royal Marine Artillery soon waned and the twelve howitzers were turned over to the Army. When approached by the Director of Artillery for further information about these unwanted 'gifts' the Ordnance Board commented acidly "These equipments were obtained by the Navy in direct negotiation with the manufacturers, and the Board was not consulted. In view of the poor range achieved, it is felt that these weapons are a waste of money and material." The guns were left to roam Northern France like some dying family of dinosaurs. They were declared obsolete and scrapped as soon as possible at the end of the war.[6]

Plate 14 A 15 in. R.M.A. Howitzer being readied for action
(Photograph courtesy of the Imperial War Museum, Q 36)

In mid-May, No. 4 gun was sitting, dismounted and under cover, in the village of Saulty, mid-way between Arras and Doullens. Its confrere, No. 6 gun, was emplaced at Dainville, two kilometres due west of Arras. While a detachment from No. 4 gun made ready at Souastre, Major A P Liston-Foulis, the Battery commander, ordered other men to construct an OP in front of Hebuterne. At the end of the month, No. 4 gun was transported down narrow, congested lanes the 5 km. to Henu, the 56th Divisions H.Q., and the crew of No. 6 were given orders to dismount their gun and ready it for a move south. Each gun needed a heavy, stable platform to be laid. Tracks had to be run to them to move the cumbersome 1400lb shells. The work for the gun teams was arduous, the days were long. The mounting of No. 4 gun was eventually completed on the 2nd June and that of No. 6 by the 8th. The following days saw the filling of the ammunition magazine with 222 shells and the same number of the 55lb modified Cordite bag charges. On the 18th, target registration started, with No. 6 gun tossing a few of its heavyweight projectiles at Gommecourt cemetery. But such was the scramble to be ready, that work on the communications system was only finished two days before the bombardment was due to start. On the 24th June, the worn out Royal Marine artillerymen took a much-needed breather. They would have little rest for the next seven days.

The guns had a vital job to do. The two 15 in. R.M.A. howitzers had to hurl their 1,400lb shells between 6,000 and 7,000 metres onto their targets round Gommecourt. The shells themselves contained 200lb of Amatol, a mixture of TNT and ammonium nitrate, a cheap fertiliser additive. The low proportion of high explosive to total shell weight (1:7) was a function of the huge stresses put on the shell casing as it was propelled up the 12½ feet of howitzer's rifled barrel. To survive the violent explosion of the 55lbs of bagged cordite that acted as propellant and the rapid rotation of the polygrooved rifling, the casing of the shell had to be of thick steel. Even so, premature explosions of shells, either in the barrel or within a few feet of the muzzle were not unknown. However, once the shell had left the gun on its long journey, rising at a maximum 45° angle, the function of the shell casing changed. Now, it was a weapon of random fearfulness. With the Percussion Nose Fuze 100 set to explode on impact, the case would rupture, hurling huge shards of hot metal in a lethal radius around the point of impact. The case was designed as a man killer, not as something to burrow into the earth before its explosion sent destructive waves of concussion through the sub-soil, because on contact was when the 100 fuze detonated. Produced at high speed in 1914 (it went from design to production in ten days), the fuze had a poor record, made worse by the failings of manufacturers either maximising profit or unable to produce them to the needed tolerances.

With the fuze going off on impact, the Amatol itself would detonate not much below ground level, sending showers of mud and debris into the air as well as the thick black smoke that was the call sign of TNT. But, as John Keegan has pointed out in 'The Face of Battle':

> "Out of the 12,000 tons weight of shell delivered on to the German-occupied area (by the heavy guns and howitzers), only about 900 tons represented high explosive. And the greater part of that small explosive load was dissipated in the air, flinging upwards, to be sure, a visually impressive mass of surface material and an aurally terrifying shower of steel splinters but transmitting a proportionately quite trifling concussion downwards towards the hiding places of the German trench garrisons. Each ten square yards had received only a pound of high explosive, or each square mile about thirty tons."[7]

But, in spite of the obvious shortcomings of their shells, these howitzers were the ones that it was hoped would do real damage to the deep bunkers in which the German defenders hid and, because of this, they had been given a vital role to play in the destruction of the enemy's defensive capability.

The records of No. 6 gun R.M.A. show, however, that, in addition to the shortcomings of the ammunition, this gun at least was also unable to meet the requirements of the firing programme. Indeed, it was only on 'Z' Day itself that No. 6 gun exceeded the planned expenditure of ammunition. Table 7 below shows the performance of No. 6 gun R.M.A.:

Overall, over the six days of the bombardment prior to the assault, this heavy howitzer fell 53 rounds short of its planned expenditure of 255 shells, a shortfall of over 20%. To make matters worse, on two of these days ('X' Day and 'Y2' Day) the platform moved causing the gun to slew. As a result, its shells fell as much as 150 metres off target. On these two days a further 34 shells were fired (13% of the planned total). In all, this meant that a third of the planned weight of 15 in. shells due to fall on the Gommecourt defences from this gun either was not fired or may have been fired substantially off target. In addition, an unknown proportion of the shells would have failed to explode.

Day	Shells fired	Shell Allowance	Difference
V	30	30	0
W	34	40	-6
X⁺	24	40	-16
Y	26	40	-14
Y1	5	20	-15
Y2*	10	20	-10
Z	73	65	+8
Totals	202	255	-53

Table 7 Shells fired by No. 6 Gun, R.M.A. during bombardment
+ Out of action part of the day, platform slewing
* Gun slewing means shots up to 150 yards off

Records do not show the detailed performance of No. 4 gun R.M.A., except that the War Diary of the 35ᵗʰ H.A.G. states that first the gun's Observation Post was knocked out by enemy fire on the 26ᵗʰ June ('X' Day) and that both guns platforms started to move towards the end of the bombardment. Consequently, it must be the case that a minimum of one in six of the 15 in. shells planned to devastate German strong points and bunkers either was not fired, missed by a wide margin or failed to explode. The probability is that this failure rate was considerably higher.

The performance of the two 12 in. howitzers of 103ʳᵈ Siege Battery R.G.A. was better than that of No. 6 gun R.M.A. but still fell 20% short of the planned weight of shell required by the Corps artillery programme. The particular problem with these guns was that the shortfall occurred on the last three days of the bombardment (Y, Y1 and Y2 Days). On these days, barely half of the planned 12 in. shells fell on their targets. Their programme is set out in Table 8 below:

Day	Actual number of shells fired per day		Total	Total in	Shortfall
	Humbercamps Right Half Battery	St Amand Left Half Battery	fired	plan	
V	30	30	60	60	0
W	35	39	74	80	-6
X	41	39	80	80	0
Y	18	18	36	80	-44
Y1	10	10	20	40	-20
Y2	15	14	29	40	-11
Z	45*	47*	0	100	-8
Total	149	150	299	480	-89

Table 8 Performance of 103ʳᵈ Siege Battery, R.G.A. during bombardment
* To be fired before zero hour. The guns were then programmed to fire once every ten minutes

On these figures, if one assumes that No. 4 gun R.M.A. performed in a similar fashion to its brother No. 6 gun, then of the 960 15 in. and 12 in. shells due to land on the 10 identified targets between V Day and 7.30 a.m. on the morning of the 1ˢᵗ July some 250 (or 26%) were either never fired or missed their target by an unacceptably wide margin (i.e. 150 metres). In addition, others would have failed to explode. In these circumstances, it is not surprising that the German defenders deep in their bunkers, although deafened, shaken and even frightened, were not killed or disabled in larger numbers.

The 9.2 in. and 6 in. howitzer batteries spent most of their time trying to demolish trenches and strong points in the first three German lines and along the Fillet/Fill trench line running around the back of Gommecourt which was to be the new British front line after the attack.

The 46ᵗʰ Division front was bombarded by the 88ᵗʰ, 93ʳᵈ, 96ᵗʰ and 101ˢᵗ Siege Batteries who took on the targets of La Brayelle Farm, The Z and the Little Z and the trenches connecting all three, as well as the three front lines as far south as the Foncquevillers Road and the Fortune-Force-Form-Forehead-Fortress-Fill-Fillet support line and the western most end of the Oxus communication trench. In addition, 93ʳᵈ and 96ᵗʰ Siege Batteries struck at the northern edge of Gommecourt Village from the Foncquevillers Road to the junction of Film and Exe trenches.

The area surrounding Gommecourt Village, Chateau and Park was allotted to the super heavy howitzers, the 9.2 in. howitzers of 91ˢᵗ and 95ᵗʰ Siege Batteries and the 6 in. howitzers of 73ʳᵈ, 98ᵗʰ (Canadian) and 102ⁿᵈ Siege Batteries.

On the 56ᵗʰ Division front, 73ʳᵈ Siege Battery (6 in. howitzers, 26 cwt) was given the task of hitting the front and close support lines from Gommecourt Park to the Sunken Road. The 73ʳᵈ were one of the few batteries to have been in position for some time and, what is more, they had spent nearly a month registering their targets on the 56ᵗʰ Division's front. On the other hand, the battery needed plenty of practice. They had only mobilised at Fort Fareham on the 16ᵗʰ April 1916 and, within two weeks, were on the boat from Southampton to Le Havre. The men started work on the battery's position at Bienvillers on 8ᵗʰ May and four days later the guns of No. 1 section were in place. They were followed, on the 21ˢᵗ, by No. 2 section. Two of these guns actually fired during the 56ᵗʰ Division's epic trench digging operation at the end of May, loosing off two rounds on the night of the 26ᵗʰ/27ᵗʰ May. They then spent the next four weeks in target registration, a luxury afforded to few of the batteries now concentrating around Gommecourt.

When it came to the bombardment, they were to be helped in the pounding of Nameless Farm and the Farmyard strong point by 91ˢᵗ Siege Battery's 9.2 in. howitzers and by 74ᵗʰ Siege Battery (also 6 in. howitzers, 26 cwt) at the eastern end of the attack area. The vicinity of the Cemetery and the eastern edge of the Maze were to be flattened by a combination of the super heavies, the 9.2 in. howitzers of 91ˢᵗ and 94ᵗʰ Siege Batteries and the 1895 pattern 6 in. howitzers of 68ᵗʰ Siege Battery. These three last batteries were also given the task of taking on the communication trenches of Exe, Ems, Epte and the line of trenches running along the top of the ridge into Rossignol Wood (Mess, Mere, Meed and Meet).

The 68ᵗʰ Siege Battery (1896, 30cwt 6 in. howitzers) was another of the recent arrivals in the Gommecourt area. Mobilised in October 1915, the battery's personnel was made up of Regular R.G.A. and Pembroke T.A. R.G.A. in equal portions. They had arrived in France on the 1ˢᵗ April at Le Havre and then spent two months on the Arras front, refining their skills. On 2ⁿᵈ June, the Right Half Section started south to their new positions at Sailly and the guns arrived on the night of the 7th/8th June after two days of hard digging in pouring rain. Their new location was in an apple orchard on the north side of the village and it had to be made ready swiftly for the bombardment to come. In continuing heavy downpours, dugouts were hacked out of the chalk, cables laid and Observation Posts established. Their first day of firing was the 16th and their registration shots were short. The following day, as the Left Half Section started their second day of digging in, they were assisted by some aerial observation. Then it was working parties one day and registration shoots the other. On the 23rd, the final work was completed on the dugouts and ammunition recesses. Two days later, at five in the morning, their part in the bombardment began.

The 91st Siege Battery was another battery of importance to the 56th Division as they were to spend most of their time bombarding the trenches to be attacked. They were mobilised to overseas service on 4th May 1916 having just completed working up on the ranges at Lydd in Kent. While the guns left from Avonmouth at the end of May the men crossed from Folkestone and they saw one another again in Boulogne on 29th May before moving to their new home at Pommier, north west of the salient. The first two weeks were spent preparing their positions, installing the guns and constructing an OP at the end of Yussuf trench immediately to the south of Gommecourt Park. On the 14th a registration shoot was attempted on some German trenches at the southern end of the Farmer-Farmyard strongpoint. It was clear that a bit of practice was required as only one round out of nineteen fired got an OK from the observers. Two days later they had another go, this time with aerial observation. They managed to get a third of their shells within 25 yards of the target. Work on the battery position and attempts at R.F.C. observed shoots went on with results slowly improving as the days wore on. When the bombardment started, the battery C.O., Maj. Christian, seemed pleased enough with their results, especially on the 26th June, 'W' Day, when he recorded in the unit diary:

"3 excellent counter-battery shoots – 3 batteries being wiped out."

If only all of the other guns on counter-battery work had been so successful! But, if it appeared to be too good to be true (and it probably was) then the battery came down to earth with a bang on 'Y' Day when a shell exploded prematurely in the barrel of No. 2 gun wrecking both gun and carriage. Fortunately, none of the crew were injured but they were a gun short until late on the 30th when a replacement sent over from 90th Siege Battery arrived just in time for 'Z' Day.

'Y' Day was also notable for one other event which, for an hour, rendered one howitzer from 98th (Canadian) Siege Battery unusable. In retaliation for their persistent bombardment, some German guns sent over a few shells in the general direction of Sailly au Bois. Missing their targets they nevertheless caused consternation when a swarm of angry bees, disturbed by the nearby explosions, vented their fury on the unsuspecting gunners. It took an hour to clear them from around the now quiet howitzer but, later that day, the gunners took their revenge with a quick raid on the beehives so, at least for that night, there was honey for tea.

***

THE PATTERN OF BOMBARDMENT for the 9.2 in. and 6 in. howitzers was to be as follows. They all started firing on V-Day, the second day of the bombardment, with the daily ammunition allowance per gun set out below:

	U	V	W	X	Y	Y1	Y2	Z*	Totals
6 in. 26 cwt	0	30	30	30	111	40	60	220	521
6 in. 30 cwt	0	205	205	205	248	40	60	220	1183
9.2 in. how	0	50	50	50	70	0	0	180	400

Table 9 Daily ammunition allowance for 9.2 in. and 6 in. howitzers U-Z Days
* prior to zero hour.

Given that two of the batteries (91st and 74th Siege Batteries) were, from time to time, diverted onto counter-battery work with the 39th H.A.G. and the 48th H.A.G. respectively, the quantity of ammunition available for the bombardment element of the artillery programme is set out in Table 10 below:

	U	V	W	X	Y	Y1	Y2	Z*	Total
6 in. all	0	1,882	1,960	1,960	3,560	1,120†	1,680†	5,780	27,542
9.2 in. how	0	1,200	1,200	1,200	1,680			4,320	

Table 10 Total rounds per day available to 9.2 in. and 6 in. howitzers U-Z Days
* prior to zero hour. † not all available guns fired

In addition to the trench and strong point bombardment included in the table above, some of the 6 in. howitzers were diverted at specific times of day for longer distance shelling of the rear villages. These were done in conjunction with the heavy and medium guns and some of the divisional howitzers.

As with the super heavy howitzers, not all batteries experienced a trouble free time in the field.

For a start, there was the weather. 39th Heavy Artillery Group records the weather during the seven days of the bombardment as follows: U and V-Days - raining, W, X and Y days - fair, Y1 and Y2 days - raining. Apart from the deadening effect on the shells of soft ground, the main cause for concern here was the inability of the aerial observers, either in balloons or aircraft, to adequately report the accuracy of the shelling. This of course, applied to both the bombardment and the counter-battery work.

Then, again, there was the problem of actually delivering the required weight of shell.

102nd Siege Battery comprised four of the old 1895 pattern, 30 cwt, 6 in. howitzers. It was based at Bienvillers-au-Bois with the other 6 in. howitzer batteries of 19th H.A.G.. According to the ammunition allowances for this battery, it should have fired 820 shells per day on V, W and X Days and 992 on Y Day. According to the Battery War Diary[8], these volumes were not achieved once. On V Day 767 shells were fired (94% of allocation), on W Day 464 shells were fired (57% of allocation), on X Day 749 shells were fired (91% of allocation) and on Y Day 470 shells were fired (47% of allocation). On the extension days of Y1 and Y2, 132 and 320 shells respectively were fired, a fraction of the intensity levels set for the previous days. This failure to perform would have been of distinct importance for the 56th Division. This battery was due to fire at targets from the SW corner of Gommecourt Park all along the front line to the Sunken Road, taking on targets allocated to the 73rd, 74th and 101st Siege Batteries in the original programme. Overall, between V and Y days 102nd Siege Battery fired 71% of its ammunition allocation. Even if one includes the shells fired on

Y1 and Y2 Days, the battery still only fired 84% of its allocation before Z Day, a deficit of over 550 6 in. howitzer shells on a front of 1,500 metres. Of course, in addition, a significant proportion of those fired would have missed and/or failed to detonate.

94th Siege Battery of 9.2 in. howitzers was given the task of bombarding The Maze and the communication trenches of Exe, Ems, Epte and the line of trenches running along the top of the ridge into Rossignol Wood (Mess, Mere, Meed and Meet). Each of its four guns had an ammunition allocation of 50 shells per day from V to X Days inclusive and 70 for Y Day. On Z Day their allocation was 180 shells per gun. In practice, however, the guns fell short of their allowance on every day except one and, in total, fired 16% fewer shells than planned. As the Official History identifies the 9.2 in. shells as being especially prone to mis-fires then it would be reasonable to assume that a minimum of a quarter of the 9.2 in. howitzer programme either was not fired or failed to explode. Given observation and other problems it is also reasonable to assume that a proportion of those that were fired and exploded missed by a significant margin. So, like the super heavy howitzers, the 9.2 in. howitzers were failing in their vitally important allotted tasks. But what may have been worse was the fact that these guns seem almost to have ceased firing on the last three days of the bombardment. 94th Siege Battery's actual firing programme is shown in Table 11 below.

	U	V	W	X	Y	Y1	Y2	Z	Totals
94th Siege Battery	0	191	192	206	75	0	59	628	1351
Original programme	0	200	200	200	280	0	0	720	1,600
Shortfall	0	-9	-8	+6	-205	0	+59	-92	-249

Table 11 Planned and actual rounds fired by 94th Siege Battery, R.G.A. U-Z Days

Not only was its anticipated weight of shell reduced by 63% on Y Day (presumably to provide spare capacity for the two day extension to the bombardment caused by the weather), this battery failed to fire at all on Y1 Day and fired only 59 shells on Y2 Day. Whilst it is not possible to be precise about the volume of shells fired by the 68th Siege Battery, which shared 91st Siege Battery's targets, comments in the battery's War Diary suggest a substantial falling off of intensity in the last three day's bombardment:

"Y Day   Ceased firing 1400 hrs
Y1 Day   3 small half hour bombardments?"

In addition, the battery had a premature burst in No. 2 gun on V Day (a not infrequent problem caused by defective ammunition) which must have resulted in a reduction in weight of shell fired for at least one day, if for no other reason than that 5 men were wounded by the explosion.

This diminution of effort over the last three days of the extended bombardment, as well as the problems of defective ammunition, are reinforced by the War Diary of the 91st Siege Battery. This battery was, from time to time, either wholly or partially diverted to counter-battery work under the control of 48th H.A.G.. But, whatever its role and for whatever reason, it had a reduced workload towards the end of the artillery programme:

"Y Day   Premature explosion put one gun out of action.   Gun
             borrowed from 90th SB.

Y1 Day   Quiet. One battery wiped out.
Y2 Day   Quiet"[10]

The 73rd Siege Battery Diary makes this laconic comment about the last three days of the extended bombardment:

"Bombardment relaxed owing to postponement of Z Day."

Whilst the 50th Siege Battery Diary states:

"Y1 Day   Pretty quiet all day.
Y2 Day   Quiet all day."[11]

The War Diary of the 35th H.A.G., which covered seven siege batteries and the two R.M.A. 15 in. howitzers recorded:

"Y Day   Only a little firing
Y1 Day   Altogether a quieter day; only isolated half-hour shoots
Y2 Day   In the morning of the 30th more isolated shoots took place... high wind made shooting difficult."[12]

The loss of a 6 in. howitzer from 88th Siege Battery on 'Y' Day, hit on the wheel and turned over, did nothing to improve the mood of the gunners who spent nearly three days twiddling their thumbs and doing little to prevent the German defenders of Gommecourt to repair their trenches and wire. Indeed, according to the 55th R.I.R.'s diary, the lessening of the bombardment seems to have been particularly noticeable on the 46th Division's front. This factor, when allied to Stuart-Wortley's request that the front line trenches should *not* be bombarded on 'Z' Day (he wanted to use them for his own troops), might explain why even those few troops who did manage to enter the German positions were often attacked from the rear by men issuing from unblocked dugouts in these same trenches.

Commenting after the war on the draft of the Official History, Lt. Colonel J H H Jones, Brigade Major of the VII Corps artillery wrote:

"Reference Y1 and Y2 days, (the reduction in the bombardment) was unfortunate, as it must have given time for the enemy to repair his lines to some extent."[13]

So, not only did the artillery programme fail to deliver the weight of shell that VII Corps staff had decided was necessary to successfully flatten the defences and collapse the German bunkers and dugouts, the 'relaxation' of the bombardment gave German working parties the opportunity to repair and replace wire, clear trenches of debris and generally get key parts of their defensive system back into some sort of shape.

Let us now move on to the issue of the counter-battery programme. The effectiveness or otherwise of the counter-battery programme would be crucial to the prospects of success for the assault. As one of Haig's main aims was to draw enemy artillery fire away from Serre and on to the attack at Gommecourt, if the strategic objective of the assault were to succeed then, by definition, a disproportionate weight of enemy artillery would fall on the attacking troops. Suppressing this fire was a key both to the tactical success of the operation, i.e. cutting out the salient, and to the reduction of casualties amongst the infantry.

The task of counter-battery work fell mainly to the 39th and 48th Heavy Artillery Groups based at Sailly-au-Bois and Berles-au-Bois respectively. 39th

H.A.G. comprised two batteries of 60 pdr guns from two batteries (131st and 135th Heavy Batteries) and 48th H.A.G. was made up of four batteries, three of obsolete 4-gun 4.7 in. guns and one of 60 pdrs (133rd Heavy, 1/1st Kent Heavy, 1/1st Lowland Heavy Batteries and 116th Heavy Battery). In addition, from time to time, the counter-battery groups had the use of some of the modern 6 in. howitzers, the Mk VII 6 in. guns, the 9.2 in. gun and some 9.2 in. howitzers. Lastly, three batteries of 4.5 in. R.F.A. howitzers were available for this work. However, even these weapons were not available for counter-battery work all day. At irregular intervals on V, W, X and Y Days some guns were required to bombard the four rear villages. Even though these bombardments were brief, usually three minutes, each one used up ammunition that might otherwise have been used on other work.

The four 4.7 in. guns of the 133rd Heavy Battery had been allocated a total of 280 shells for 'X' Day, 400 for 'Y' Day and 600 for 'Z' Day, however, they started firing on the evening of the 'U' Day, 24th June, with their targets mainly being German battery positions on the northern edge of the salient. Their bombardments, given their previous accuracy of about 50% within 25 yards, were not exactly intense, and the weight of shell fired not likely to do enormous damage to the well dug-in German guns. They fired at the same two sets of co-ordinates, however, one in front of Le Quesnoy Farm and the other just west of Douchy-les-Ayettes, for three days in an effort to make up in quantity what they perhaps lacked in quality. Quite what happened next in 133rd Heavy Battery's programme is inexplicable (see Table 12 below).

Its four guns were supposed to have smothered German battery positions around Essarts, Le Quesnoy Farm and Little Farm with 632 shells, with a further 48 reserved for the early morning bombardments of Bucquoy. Instead, although Bucquoy was hit on 'X' and 'Y' days with twenty rounds on each occasion, the guns only a managed to fire 179 shells over four days at the selected battery positions. On 'Z' Day they fired less than half of their allowance of 600 shells of which twenty crashed around the crossroads in the middle of Bucquoy and the rest were aimed at a variety of assumed battery positions. There is no explanation for this significant shortfall in counter-battery activity which can only have given the German gun teams much needed respite from the bombardment nor is there any explanation given as to why the battery should have ceased firing soon after each gun had fired ten rounds at battery position 544 at 1.10 p.m. on 1st July. Within a few hundred yards of position 544 were ten other positions of which nearly half were definitely known to British intelligence. One can only wonder why 133rd Battery were not asked to attack these positions with the hundreds of unused rounds that were stacked within reach of the guns.

Day	U	V	W	X	Y	Y1	Y2	Z	Total
Fired	24	12	24	78	44	12	85	267	546
In programme	0	0	0	280		400		600	1280
Difference	+24	+12	+24	-202		-259		-333	-794

Table 12 Planned and actual rounds fired by 133rd Heavy Battery 24th June-1st July

The war diary of the 48th H.A.G. records the various trials and tribulations they experienced in trying to achieve some sort of superiority over the artillery opposite. 'U' Day was meant to be a quiet day with only some light 'night line' firing into the villages taking place. Any attempts to do much during the day were ruined by the poor weather, which made R.F.C. observation impossible; the need for the 116ᵗʰ Heavy Battery to calibrate its guns and set correct fuze settings for its shells; and by the extraordinary fact that there was a shortage of 4.7 in. shells just five days before the attack was scheduled to start!

25ᵗʰ June, 'V' Day, did not start auspiciously. In the early morning there was a smoke demonstration designed to test the readiness of the German defences and, hopefully, to draw out into the open some of the concealed battery positions. This was achieved in an area south of Le Quesnoy Farm where five German battery positions were established near a trench running behind a line of trees. 116ᵗʰ Heavy Battery was called into action by the R.F.C. but, after a short while, the wireless in the BE2c went 'west' and the aircraft had to return the base. In the afternoon, the 116ᵗʰ fired off eighty rounds at the same target but it was the 91ˢᵗ Siege Battery and its 9.2 in. howitzers which had the big success of the day. Fifteen shells were fired at a position just to the south of Biez Wood and the balloon observers spotting for them had the pleasure of witnessing a large explosion when the second shell hit the target. For the rest of the day, the 116th Heavy Battery fired at a variety of targets near Adinfer Wood, into Bucquoy and Essarts. The 91ˢᵗ Siege Battery was called up again to assist with another battery position and another 25 rounds were sent over south of Le Quesnoy Farm. For the 4.7 in. guns it was another quiet day with only some minor night line work to keep them occupied.

'W' Day was another busy day for the 116ᵗʰ Heavy Battery as they fired at intervals from 6.17 a.m. to 7.30 p.m. During the day, the guns fired 192 shells at battery positions and targets of opportunity but, because of the poor weather, the fall of only two shells was observed. The rest were fired 'off map' in the hope that they might reach their targets. 91ˢᵗ Siege Battery again chipped in with 27 rounds fired under aerial observation of which a third were observed as being on target. Helping with the action, were the 4.5 in. howitzers of the D/123 Battery from 37ᵗʰ Division which fired off 78 shells in four shoots at Adinfer Wood with all targets having been located by sound bearing. Sound ranging was a science in embryo and the British version was a development of a French system designed by Lucien Bull of the Institut Marey in Paris. Loosely, a number of microphones recorded the report of a gun firing and the different time delays recorded by the microphones allowed the plotting of intersecting circles which gave the position of the gun. Many problems had to be overcome to refine this system and a 2ⁿᵈ Lt. W L Bragg, later Sir Lawrence Bragg, was given the task of developing the British version. His team spent many hours devising a robust system near Kemmel Hill and, with the help of a Cpl. Tucker, previously a member of the Physics Department at Imperial College, a sufficiently sensitive microphone was developed which could pick up the relatively low frequency sound of a gun or howitzer firing. This system of sound ranging became so effective in 1917 that the German High Command issued an order that guns should fire in groups rather than singly as the British sound ranging equipment was so accurate in identifying gun positions. As it turned out, the German order was pointless as, by then, Bragg's system was so sensitive it could identify individual guns almost irrespective of how many were firing.[14]

Tuesday, 27ᵗʰ June was 'X' Day in the timetable and, for the first time, the 4.7 in. batteries came to the party. The day dawned bright and early for the artillery group's gunners and at 6 a.m. they were sending twenty shells a battery into the heart of Bucquoy in the hopes to catching a relief or a ration party going up the line. With the weather building up to a storm, the firing in the morning was mainly by sound ranging and all of the batteries took turns in firing at what were thought to be German battery positions. For the Lowlands, Kent and 133rd Heavy Batteries these would be the first day-time shoots of the bombardment and, on one of the few occasions when their shots were observed, accuracy was somewhat lacking; the Kents firing thirty shells at German battery position 504, starting at 11.04 a.m. of which only three were on target. As the day drew on, all of the batteries, including the field howitzers of D/123 and the 9.2 in. howitzers of 91st Siege Battery, engaged in a rehearsed bombardment of positions from Adinfer Wood through Little Farm and either side of Le Quesnoy Farm. Nearly 200 shells swept the landscape in a six-minute hurricane bombardment.

At 8.15 a.m. on the morning of 'Y' Day a message came down from Brig. Gen. Buckle, G.O.C. VII Corps Heavy Artillery, that an attempt was to be made to destroy as many German batteries as possible, firing off map. The programme started at 12.15 p.m. with the 116th Battery sending over 102 rounds aimed at the some of the more distant German heavy batteries dug in to the west of the Bucquoy to Ayette road. Thirty five minutes later the 91st Siege Battery joined in, firing forty rounds at the cluster of batteries to the south of Le Quesnoy Farm but at 2 p.m. the order came to close down the bombardment as the whole attack had fallen victim to the weather and was postponed for 24 hours. Further desultory firing resumed at after 4 p.m. but the weather was poor, 'misty and drizzle all day' according to the 35th H.A.G.'s diary, and gusting wind made firing something of a lottery. The disappointing results of 116th Battery's shoot at a observation post in Ferme Graben underlined the difficult nature of the conditions; of forty five rounds fired, not one was observed as hitting its target.

The low levels of activity by 48th H.A.G. on 'Y1' Day emphasised the general reduction in intensity on the first of the two additional days. Apart from a few rounds in the morning no firing at all took place before 2.20 p.m. when D/123 engaged a German battery in Adinfer Wood and again at 4.35 p.m. Apart from a dozen rounds from the 116th Battery in the early evening and the programmed 'night lines' firing of all batteries, the only other guns to be active were the heavy howitzers of 91st Siege Battery who pounded the unfortunate occupants of German battery position 508 east of Essarts. According to the R.F.C. observer, nine of the sixteen shells hit their targets. But this was one of nearly sixty battery positions defending Gommecourt and, in the grand scheme of things, was of minor significance.

On the morning of 'Y2', the final day of the bombardment, word came down from VII Corps that each gun would be able to fire 50 rounds during the course of the day. At mid-day this was increased to 100 rounds per gun. In consequence, all batteries fired almost continuously from 10 a.m. to midnight. All four batteries of the 48th H.A.G. fired in excess of 200 shells during the day, a lot by the previous day's standards but still less than the 400 round per battery limit set by the G.O.C., VII Corps artillery. At 5.20 p.m. an intense bombardment was laid upon six key sites west and south of Le Quesnoy Farm with 487 shells being fired in six minutes. Throughout the day, over 1,100 rounds were fired by 48th H.A.G. guns at eighteen targets, however of these just thirty came from the 9.2 in. howitzers of 91st Siege Battery, the weapons most likely to do serious damage to the enemy's gun positions.

Day	116th HB	Lowland	Kent	133rd HB	91st SB	D/123	Total
V	223	0	0	0	40	0	263
W	224	0	0	0	47	108	379
X	131	68	124	46	21	100	490
Y	147	20	30	0	40	0	237
Y1	12	0	0	0	16	157	185
Y2	277	220	228	220	30	157	1132
Total	1014	308	382	266	194	522	2686

Table 13 Counter battery rounds fired by 48th H.A.G. batteries

Table 13 above shows the total number of rounds fired by 48th H.A.G., one of two dedicated counter-battery artillery groups supporting the attack. The total allowance for all guns and howitzers involved in this attack, excluding D/123 field howitzer battery, was just over 4,100 rounds. Barely half of these rounds were fired and the 48th H.A.G. war diary records how inaccurate some of the shooting was or how much was fired more in hope than expectation given the lack of adequate observation because of the weather. Certainly, none of the German artillery units involved indicate either heavy casualties or large numbers of guns put out of action. It would seem that, except for the occasional intervention of the 91st Siege Battery, 48th H.A.G.'s counter-battery programme had been 'much ado about nothing'. Indeed, it is even possible that the 'much ado' might have been 'not very much ado' as the 48th H.A.G. Diary records 133rd Heavy Battery as having fired 200 rounds on 'Y2' Day while the Battery's war diary mentions only 85 shells as having been fired. In other words, the shortfall in rounds expended by 48th H.A.G. on its crucial counter-battery programme may have been even greater than the numbers appear to show.

The long-range guns, most of which had vital counter-battery targets, also failed to deliver the programmed expenditure of ammunition. The Right section of 45th Siege Battery (one 9.2 in. gun based at Humbercamps) fired less than 40% of its allocation and hardly any of that at a German battery. 50th Siege Battery (two Mk VII 6 in. guns firing from Souastre) fired on V-Day (the only day for which details exist) 54 of its allocation of 80 shells, i.e. only two thirds of its allowance.

The 9.2 in. railway gun of the 45th Siege Battery was the heaviest, long range weapon at the disposal of VII Corps' counter-battery group. It had arrived late, firing its first shells on the morning of 'V' Day, and had suffered niggling irritations thereafter. In the early afternoon of 'W' Day, it had started a registration shoot at a suspected 10.5cm howitzer battery in Fork Wood on the Puisieux to Bucquoy Road. Firing at 11,600 yard range the guns fired short with HE and only a switch to AP (armour piercing) shell increased the range. During the night, the railway track had to be re-ballasted by the R.E. as the stresses on the lines had led to unevenness. On 'X' Day, a five round shoot in the early morning at Bucquoy required a 30° correction and then they sent over twenty unobserved shells in the direction of the trenches and dugouts at the north west corner of Rossignol Wood. Although they had no idea how effective their efforts might be, the local effects of the gun's concussion was quickly obvious. The gun team's shelter started to collapse and a house thirty yards in front of the gun began to disintegrate. Thankfully, its occupants were long since gone. The weather was so poor on 'Y' Day that it was felt safe to run the gun out into the open as any form of aerial observation on either side was next to impossible. In the morning, the gun sent over three shells aimed at Bucquoy and another twenty at Ablainzeville at what was described as a 'slightly unfavourable range of 12,400 yards'. That was their firing for the day and the afternoon was spent unloading and stacking another fifty of the 380lb shells and the rebuilding of the gun team's shelter which, again, was threatening to fall in. The next day was due to have been 'Z' Day but for the weather, instead the next two days were the extension days of the bombardment, 'Y1' and 'Y2', and again the gun was used on anything but counter-battery work. At 4.35 p.m. on 'Y1' the south west corner of Rossignol Wood was the target with nine hits in and around the edge of the wood being observed. Again the track became unstable and the night was spent by the Monmouth Royal Engineers re-packing the line. On 'Y2' it was broadly the same. Twenty shells were directed at Rossignol Wood with eleven landing on or within 20 feet of its edge and later ten rounds were fired at Ablainzeville. Within the originally planned bombardment programme, the heaviest of the guns supposedly available for counter-battery work had fired just five shells at a known German battery position and several of those were known to have fallen short. The western fringe of Rossignol Wood had been peppered, however, unlike Biez Wood just to the north, this was not an area crammed full of artillery indeed, as of 17th June, Army Intelligence had not identified *any* battery positions there. Extraordinarily, the Battery's instructions, as set by Maj. Anley of 39th H.A.G., were to 'silence enemy batteries' with a minimum of five shells to be aimed at any identified battery position. On 'Z' Day itself, when the need to suppress the German artillery was at a premium, this gun was to fire 50% of its day's allocation of sixty shells at the village of Bucquoy and all of this before Zero hour. The other thirty shells were to be fired at the direction of the R.F.C. observers, however, no matter how pressing the need, the battery was told it *had* to reserve fifty shells from its supply for use after Z Day. Just how accurate these shells might have been if fired, however, was anyone's guess. The 9.2 in. gun Mark X only had an average lifespan of just 500 rounds and, by 'Z' Day the gun was nearly 50% through its useful life with consequent issues for accuracy caused by barrel and other component wear[i]. As it turned out, the gun fired 65 shells between the hours of 6 a.m. and 11.45 p.m. only ten of which were aimed at a location in which German guns were known to lurk – Biez Wood. What effect they had is unknown, however, as no-one observed the fall of even one shell during the entire day.

As already hinted at, these problems of the weight and intensity of the bombardment and the counter-battery programme were compounded by the failure of the aerial observation programme to deliver to the batteries the necessary information for the accurate correction of range and direction.

---

[i] Guns had a much shorter life span than howitzers. 'Artillery Development in the Great War', a post-war paper written by Lt. Gen. Sir Noel Birch, CB, Colonel Commandant, Royal Artillery (The Army Quarterly, October 1920) gave the average life spans of heavy artillery of different natures as:
6 in. Gun, Mark VII – 1,500 rounds
6 in. Howitzer, 26 Cwt – 10,000 rounds
9.2 in. Gun, Mark X – 500 rounds
9.2 in. Howitzer, Mark 1 – 7,000 rounds

The War Diary of the 68th Siege Battery gives a clear indication of the problems encountered by the heavy artillery in their attempts to neutralise the German defences that resulted from the breakdown of artillery/R.F.C. co-operation. These breakdowns were caused primarily by the weather, but other failures intervened to exacerbate an already poor situation. It is worth quoting the comments of Major H Mayne, the C.O. of the right half battery of the 68th Siege Battery at some length:

"V Day

Fire was opened at 5 a.m. by the right half battery of 68 Siege Battery. There was a low ground mist which made observation impossible. Targets EXE from FEN-FERRET to FENS (sic: Feast?) to FEMALE had to be taken on blind. Searching and sweeping fire was carried out.

9.00 a.m. to 10.30 a.m. the right half was firing over 88 Siege Battery area under orders from OC, 88 Siege Battery. This area could not be seen from our area. During this shooting No 2 gun had a premature which caused 5 casualties, all wounded.

10.30 a.m. to 12 noon the trenches were supposed to be taken on under aerial observation.... I waited till 10.50 a.m. when I opened fire with both sections blind searching and sweeping.... I opened fire again blind at 11.45 a.m.

Under the above conditions I am unable to say what effect my shooting had on the enemy trenches.

Firing as per programme was carried out this afternoon, the whole of it was aerial. During the wire cutting I only received one G signal for my first round... I got no other signals so cannot say how much wire was cut as the shoot was wholly blind. In the next shoot I was supposed to get aerial calls at 5.20 p.m., 5.30 p.m., 5.40 p.m., 5.50 p.m. and 6.00 p.m. The only one I got was at 6.00 p.m. I got 3 observations from the planes getting an OK[i]. The remainder of the shoot was blind.

W Day

The programme of W day has been carried out. With reference to the wire cutting this had to be done blind, no aerial observation being available and I am dissatisfied with my shooting, not knowing whether I am near the wire or not.

The second series was also done blind but one point had been registered with an OK. The remainder of the target had no observations given....

On the 2 days shooting my 6 aerial targets have practically all been blind shooting, as I have not received any satisfactory observations. I should be much obliged if I could be informed whether I have touched my wire target or not as up to present I have had no means of judging what effect my shooting has done.

The programme as detailed was carried out from 12 noon to 3.30 p.m.

---

[i] When observed from the air, a 'clock' code was used to correct firing with the details being sent by wireless to RFC operators attached to the battery. The system worked like this: an imaginary clock was placed on the target with the centre of the clock the target. 12 o'clock was due north, 3 o'clock east, six o'clock south and 9 o'clock west. A direct hit on the target would be sent down as 'OK'. Twenty five yards from the target was signalled as 'Y', 50 yards was 'A', 100 yards 'B', 200 yards 'C', etc. For example, if the aircraft reported 'B6' then the shell had fallen 100 yards south of the target.

Both targets were visible for visual observation. The target engaged from 12 noon to 2.00 p.m. was rather a difficult one as the observation post line was being heavily shelled and made observation difficult and many rounds were unobserved.

During the time that the battery was in action 8 high explosive shrapnel burst about 50 yds behind the battery rather high up and 8 more burst in line with the battery in line with the church.

X Day

The programme as laid out of was carried out in full. All the shooting had to be done blind as aeroplane observation was impossible and I am unable to state what the effect of my fire has been up to the present time, all my shooting has been done blind. At 8.00 a.m. this morning about 20 150 mm shells fired into Sailly.... Some of the shell splinters fell on right half battery position. No casualties occurred in the battery.

The bombardment as per programme was carried out this afternoon. The shooting appeared to be good, a good many rounds getting into the trenches. No hostile artillery fire came near the battery position.

Y Day

The firing programme was carried out in full this morning. No observations were possible owing to the heavy mist and rain. It is impossible to say what the result of the shooting has been. Since 12 noon, no firing has been carried out in accordance with instructions.

Y1 Day

7.00 a.m. to 7 30 a.m. Firing was carried out today.... and with great success. Observation was easy and good effects were obtained. Was to have been by aerial observation on north-west corner of Gommecourt Wood. I waited till 1.45 p.m. when I got a telephone message to stay that wireless instrument had broken down and plane had returned."[15]

The problems alluded to in the 68th Siege Battery's report of the failures of the aerial co-operation with No. 8 Squadron R.F.C. are reinforced by comments from other batteries. The 101st Siege Battery (four 6 in. howitzers based at Bienvillers-au-Bois) was some 4,000 metres from its targets. Although its FOO obtained good reports for them for their front line targets (The Z, the Little Z, the Gommecourt Barrier and the SW corner of Pigeon Wood), it depended on the R.F.C. for observation over rear areas (Forehead, Fortress and Fill trenches and La Brayelle Farm). Its War Diary comments:

"Visual targets good but only once got results from aerial observations that could be relied upon."[16]

Again, after the war Lt. Colonel J H H Jones, Brigade Major of the VII Corps artillery, commented:

"The heavy artillery groups involved in counter battery work received many locations from the aeroplane observers. All, as far as I can remember, were indefinite and many were outside the range of the 60 pdrs and 6 in. howitzers of these groups. So indefinite were they that one group commander did not engage any enemy batteries and the other, though they fired, did not consider that they could have produced much effect."[17]

It would be unfair of course, to give only the artillery's point of view on the failures of aerial observation. The work of aerial observation fell to No. 8 Squadron R.F.C. and to No. 5 Kite Balloon Section.

The History of the R.F.C. gives an assessment of the usefulness of balloons and aircraft for the task required of them before and during July 1st.

"The balloon appears to have been the better for the purpose of reporting the general situation and the general artillery activity. Both by day and night the observer was able to keep the Artillery Group Commander informed as to the situation, whence hostile shelling was coming, what places were being most heavily shelled, the centres of greatest activity, the presence of gas, and the rough direction of its movement. As regards ranging, the aeroplanes were the more successful and conducted shoots under weather conditions that rendered observation for the balloon impossible. Aeroplanes located many more flashes than the balloon during daylight, but none at night. The balloon was able to report the direction of flashes at night, and in some cases to identify the battery owing to the observer's intimate knowledge of the ground. The advantage of the telephonic communication of the balloon over the wireless of the aeroplane was very apparent."[18]

Unfortunately, however, the balloon used for observing over the Gommecourt lines fell victim to an extraordinary incident on the day before the bombardment began. At 3 p.m. on the afternoon of Friday 23rd June, a violent thunderstorm broke over the British front on the Somme. On the Fourth Army front two balloons were struck by lightning and destroyed and a third was severely damaged, landing empty just behind Hebuterne. On the Third Army front, the fate that befell the balloon of No. 5 section was altogether more dramatic. The balloon, containing Second Lieutenants J W Jardine and G. D. S. M. Pape, was wrenched away from the winch and, within seconds, was being whipped eastwards towards the German lines. At the same time, the balloon rapidly gained height. As the two officers desperately destroyed their maps, notes and photographs, the balloon crossed the front line to the north of Monchy-au-Bois, five kilometres north of Gommecourt. By now, the balloon had reached an altitude of 13,000 feet and was being battered by thunder and lightning as well as a violent snowstorm. Just as the two observers were preparing to be flung far over the German lines the wind backed dramatically and the balloon was sent lurching uncontrollably westwards, back over the British lines.

For the occupants the drama was far from over. When the storm first struck the balloon, the pilots' parachutes (only balloon observers carried parachutes at this time) were shaken from their cases to hang open below the basket. Second Lt. Jardine had quickly cut himself free, however, Lt. Pape remained caught up with his, unable to free himself as the balloon rose dragging the parachute behind it. With the turn westwards the balloon began to lose height just as dramatically as it had been gained. Pape, still attached, was now snatched out of the basket as the parachute opened above the balloon itself. Far from being able to safely float to earth, Pape was now in an even more dangerous position. The ropes of the parachute and the ropes of the balloon had become entwined and, as Pape looked down from his precarious position, he could see flames from the gas valve above the basket start to lick around the fabric of the balloon itself. The balloon, heavy with snow and now rapidly deflating, would have plummeted to earth, with fatal consequences for Second Lt. Jardine had not Pape made an extraordinarily courageous decision. Realising that it was now the parachute that was holding up the balloon, he tied it securely to the balloon's guy ropes and together they all - parachute, balloon and observers - landed safely in a British artillery emplacement to the west of Arras, nearly 20 kilometres from where they had started.

Both officers were badly shaken by the experience, Pape suffering severe frostbite because of the extreme cold. Jardine, displaying a nice degree of sang-froid, stated he expected to be fit for action within a week. This incident displayed more than just the courage, and luck of two fortunate junior officers. It gives an indication of the unreliability of the weather in the first half of 1916 that was to have grave consequences for the attack on Gommecourt and elsewhere.

Aircraft were provided by No. 8 Squadron, part of the 12th (Corps) Wing, III Brigade, R.F.C. The squadron was based at La Bellevue, a small village on the Doullens to Arras Road[19]. Commanded by Major P H L Playfair, it was equipped with eighteen B.E.2.c aircraft, a two person aircraft with a pilot and observer/gunner. The squadron was divided into four flights: 'A', 'B', 'C', and 'D', which were given the following duties:

'A' and 'B' Flights.	Counter battery work
'C' Flight.	Observation of trench bombardment by heavy howitzers
'D' Flight.	Contact patrol work in co-operation with the infantry

During U, V, W, X, Y, Y1, and Y2 days 'D' Flight pilots, observers and machines were used to assist 'C' Flight.

The weather reports from the squadron give some indication of the problems they and the artillery faced:

- U day. Raining in the early morning; clearing about 9.00 a.m. Showers with low clouds all day.
- V-day. Low clouds.
- W day. Rain and low clouds.
- X day. Clouds were very low in the early morning, but lifted slightly later. There were occasional showers of rain during the day.
- Y day. Clouds very low all day, with frequent showers.
- Y1 day. Low clouds on the morning, over cast all day.
- Y2 day. Wind west, about 40 mph. Over cast in the morning, clearing in the evening.

Only on July 1st itself did the weather clear to give a fine, warm and sunny day. 8 Squadron's description was: "Clouds were very low in the early morning and up to about 9.30 a.m. The remainder of the day was fine with a fairly strong wind." Of course, this meant that during the time of the preliminary bombardment, which started in the early hours and grew into an unprecedented intensity for the sixty five minutes prior to zero hour at 7.30 p.m., observation was poor. The northern French weather again conspired against the R.F.C. and the artillery. And the poor, bloody infantry.

In the week before Z day, No. 8 Squadron had three main functions: counter-battery work, observing trench bombardment and photography.

Counter-battery work, in particular, seemed to suffer from the problems caused by the weather. The squadron commander's report on the operation highlights this fact:

"V day. Counter battery work.
One machine patrolled the Corps front for this work from 4.40 a.m. until 9.50 p.m. A large number of hostile batteries were seen active from about 6.00 a.m. to 6.30 a.m. The co-ordinates of these were sent by wireless to the headquarters of the counter battery groups in whose area the flashes were seen. *Owing to low clouds, observation of the effect of our fire was very difficult (author's emphasis here and forward)s.*
W day. Counter battery work.
One machine patrolled the Corps front from 4.25 a.m. till 9.25 p.m. Nine batteries were seen to start firing when the discharge of smoke started. These were specially noted, and communicated to the artillery. Many other hostile batteries located, *but rain and low clouds prevented a real observation of the fire on most of them.* Of those engaged four were seen to be silenced.
X day. Counter battery work.
One machine patrolled the Corps front for this work from 9.00 a.m. until 9.10 p.m. A number of hostile batteries were seen active and reported by wireless to the head quarters of the counter battery group concerned. Several of our own batteries were also called up by wireless to engage some of these, *but clouds rather hampered observation.* 5 batteries were seen to be silenced.
Y Day. Counter battery work.
Owing to the low clouds it was not possible to send out machines for this work before 5 p.m. No hostile artillery activity was observed between that hour and dusk.
Y1 day. Counter battery work
One machine patrolled the Corps front for this work from 4.40 a.m. until 9.35 p.m. A number of hostile batteries were seen active and their positions communicated by wireless to the artillery. *Low clouds interfered with observation of fire in most cases.* Three hostile - which were ranged on and silenced.
Y2 day. Counter battery work.
A machine patrolled the Corps front for this work from 3.00 p.m. until 8.55 p.m. Very little hostile artillery activity was observed." [20]

The Official R.F.C. History hints at the trouble the weather would cause to the assaulting troops:

"Every hour of bad weather that kept aeroplanes away from the front brought respite to some German battery, and the full effect of the lost hours must be borne by the infantry when they advanced to the assault. No one realised this better than the airmen. Pilots flew in and under the low clouds and took advantage of every bright interval to continue their work of helping the artillery to destroy the enemy guns, but the grey days took their toll of flying time, and the effect on the day of attack, although it cannot be estimated, was none the less important." [21]

One incident exemplifies the lengths the squadron's pilots went to and the sacrifices they made in their efforts to pinpoint enemy batteries for destruction by the artillery. On the morning of Y1 Day, June 29th, BE2d[i] No. 5763 piloted by 2nd Lt. Charles Vaisey flew low over the German lines towards Bucquoy in an attempt to locate and report back on an active hostile battery. His aircraft was jumped by three German planes that appeared suddenly from a cloud. In the ensuing dogfight, Vaisey was hit in the back by machine gun fire from a Fokker. Unconscious, he slumped forward onto the joystick, sending the aircraft into a steep dive. 2nd Lt. C. M. Pickthorn, his observer, realising something was amiss and seeing his pilot slumped in the front cockpit, partially climbed out of his seat and pushed Vaisey back into position. 2nd Lt. Vaisey then regained consciousness and, whilst his observer radioed ahead for a doctor, flew his aircraft back to La Bellevue, making a perfect landing.

Maj. Ward-Jackson described what happened in a letter home to his wife:

"A wonderfully brave thing happened yesterday. One of our pilots was shot from above in the air by a Fokker. The bullet entered his back and pierced his intestines. The poor fellow of course fell forward and the machine began to dive. The observer clambered out on the wing and fixed up the connection at the pilot's seat for the dual control, clambered back and took charge of the machine. But, of course, he was an inexperienced driver. However, he managed to guide the machine back to our Aerodrome and when near clambered back to the pilot's seat and changed the connection and handed over the guidance of the machine once more to the pilot who was nearly fainting. He managed to pull himself together and made an absolutely successful landing in the Aerodrome and then collapsed."[22]

In a letter to his father, the observer 2nd Lt. Pickthorn[ii], who had only been appointed as a Flying Officer (Observer) on 25th June 1916, later wrote:

"He was badly hit almost in the first burst of fire from the three hostile machines which attacked us. At first I thought he was all out – but somehow he pulled himself together and brought the machine some eight to ten miles back to the aerodrome, where he made a perfect land. God knows how he did it – for he was in awful pain."[23]

2nd Lt. Vaisey[iii] died two days later in hospital on the same day that so many young men would perish in the fields below the skies he had flown and fought in. He was buried at Warlincourt Halte cemetery, a few hundred metres off the end of the runway at La Bellevue. Each morning, as they took off and turned into the

[i] Basically a BE2c equipped with a larger gravity tank for extended flying time.

[ii] Lt. Charles Edward Murray Pickthorn, Army Service Corps att. Royal Flying Corps, was born on 20th September 1895 the son of Edith Maud B Pickthorn of 79, Edith Road, West Kensington. He was educated at Bristol Grammar School and Aldenham School and lived at 40, Endsleigh Gardens, Ilford. He had spent two years in the Trinidad Light Horse before the war and was a sugar planter. He was commissioned into the ASC on 8th February 1915 and was promoted Lieutenant on 1st June 1916. He was appointed (Temp.) Major in the R.F.C. on 8th January 1918 and Squadron Commander on 20th March 1918, having been made a Flight Commander 21st March 1917. He was Mentioned in Despatches on 4th January 1917 and awarded the MC on 26th April 1917. The citation in the London Gazette reads: "For conspicuous gallantry and devotion to duty in attacking hostile aircraft, and in carrying out difficult reconnaissances. On one occasion, although wounded, he continued his combat and brought down a hostile machine. On two other occasions he brought down hostile machines in flames."

[iii] 2nd Lt. Charles Thomas Hinton Vaisey, Royal Flying Corps, died on Saturday 1st July 1916 of wounds received on 29th June whilst piloting BE2d 5763. He was aged 30. The son of Mr. T. F. and Mrs. L. H. Vaisey of Norden Cottage, Combe Down, Bath he lived in Winslow, Bucks. Educated at Trent College, Derbyshire he was sheep farming in Australia when war broke out. He joined the RFC in 1915. He is buried in Warlincourt Halte British Cemetery, Saulty, Pas de Calais, France, grave I.E.8. His epitaph is the last two lines from Tennyson's 1889 poem *'Crossing the Bar'* and reads: "To see my pilot face to face when I crost the bar". Tennyson wrote the poem three years before his death and requested it be placed as the last entry in any posthumous collections of his work.

sun rising above the mist and clouds in the east, his fellow pilots would fly over the grave of their dead colleague.

Efforts to improve the artillery's registration on key trenches and strong points were also hampered by the continuous low cloud and rain. Because of the large number of batteries and targets involved, a timetable was agreed between the artillery planners and the R.F.C. so that batteries firing at a particular time at a particular target could be identified. It was hoped that this would allow for accurate correction information to be fed back to the batteries. Major Playfair clearly thought that the plan worked satisfactorily[i]. The comments made by the C.O. of the 68th Siege Battery and others quoted earlier suggests otherwise.

Major Playfair's report suggests that, in reality, the measure was something of a 'curate's egg'. On the infrequent occasions when the weather was remotely decent the timetable system sometimes worked, however, as reports elsewhere suggest, the weather, equipment failures and system breakdowns too often left the artillery firing blindly into the murk of a damp Picardy summer.

"**U day.** Trench registration. A few points were registered for 90th Siege Battery, 19th Heavy Artillery Group.

V-day. Trench bombardment. The two machines, one to work with each heavy artillery group, were out from 5.30 a.m. to 8 p.m.

W day. Observation of trench bombardment. Two machines were up from 5.35 a.m. until 7.40 p.m. for this work, 178 observations were given.

X day. Observation of trench bombardment. Two machines employed on this work from 8.50 a.m. to 7.50 p.m. Low clouds made observation difficult but numerous corrections were sent down during the day.

Y Day. Observation of trench bombardment. No notes of any activity.

Y 1 day. Observation of the trench bombardment. This was only carried out during three periods of half an hour's duration each. 37 observations were sent down.

Y2 day. Observation of trench bombardment. The little that there was to do of this work was successfully carried out."[24]

W Day, 26th June, seems to have been the most successful day for the aerial observers of No. 8 Squadron and their brief squadron history records the following:

"On the 26th June the squadron made eight trench flights. They engaged thirteen targets and silenced ten hostile batteries, on one of which two direct hits with 12 in. howitzers were obtained. In addition 168 observations were sent down to the heavy howitzers firing at enemy trenches. On the following day the artillery carried out heavy wire cutting bombardments and Capt. A. H. Morton successfully observed the effect of

---

[i] "The scheme was found to work very satisfactorily, and, owing to the large amount of shelling going on, was probably the only method which could have been used with any hope of success. The artillery liaison officer was found of great assistance in arranging this work. The main point of the scheme was that our batteries had to fire at given times on arranged trenches, on receiving the signal from the aeroplane. If this signal was not received within two minutes of the fixed time, the battery had to fire off the map, and the observer had to wait until the time fixed for the next battery or target came round. From 5 to 20 minutes were usually allotted to each target for the aerial observation, according to the importance of the target, and after that the battery had to fire in its own time without aerial observation. One or two observations were usually found to be sufficient to get a battery onto its target, but as many observations as possible were given in the allotted time." National Archives, Kew file WO 95/360

these operations in front of Gommecourt Wood, descending to 500 feet in order to obtain the required information."[25]

However, reference back to Major Mayne of the 68th Siege Battery suggests a different story:

"W Day

The programme of W day has been carried out.... I am dissatisfied with my shooting, not knowing whether I am near the wire or not.... I should be much obliged if I could be informed whether I have touched my wire target or not as up to present I have had no means of judging what effect my shooting has done."[26]

Clearly, even on good days, there was a good deal of 'hit and miss' about the R.F.C./artillery co-operation. There was no question in the minds of senior officers, however, that the bombardment had done its job. From Corps staff down to battalion commanders, all were convinced that the attack would be a walk over. This confidence was passed on to the rather more sceptical infantry. Some of them, however, had seen this all before. They were not so convinced.

***

THE ROLE of the Royal Field Artillery batteries attached to the two attacking divisions was principally that of cutting the extensive barbed wire strung out across No Man's Land in front of the German front line and also in belts before the second and third lines. It was not an easy task and one which required accurate firing and acute observation. The best way of cutting wire was a topic that had occupied the thinking of both senior artillery and infantry officers since the beginning of static trench warfare in the winter of 1914-15. In November of 1915 four 18 pdr guns of the 72nd Battery, R.F.A. had been set up in the dunes in front of Calais and a series of test firings were undertaken against a set of targets designed to replicate different formats of German wire and front line trenches. The targets consisted of two belts of wire 20 feet deep with a gap between them of ten yards. Ten yards behind the wire was a sandbag parapet, 4 ft. 6 in. high in the centre and ten feet thick, with, behind part of the target, a sandbag parados. The guns were to fire three different sorts of shells at the targets at two ranges: 2,700 and 3,400 yards. The shells used were: timed shrapnel, high explosive fused to burst on impact and high explosive with a delayed action fuse. The results of the test were clear: well timed shrapnel was the only method currently available that in any way cut wire with some efficiency; indeed, shrapnel was the only round which actually cut the wire with the high explosive shells having barely any effect except for some damage to the wire's supports.

But, even with shrapnel, the range at which the guns fired was crucial. In the test, the 18 pdrs, when fired at a range of 2,700 yards, cut a narrow gap about two yards wide through the front line of wire and about five yards wide in the second belt. To achieve this, 120 rounds were fired. The second series of shrapnel fired at a range of 3,400 yards had barely any effect on the wire even though this time 150 rounds were fired. Clearly, therefore, there was not only an optimum height at which the shells should detonate but an optimum range at which they should be fired. Whilst the range could be gauged with some reasonable precision the setting of the fuse to explode at the correct height was something of a lottery. The main issue here was the 'error' of the gun (caused by barrel wear, the stability of the platform, human and instrument error, etc.,). The trials at Calais involving the high explosive fired showed that the effect of this 'error' could be considerable: the '100% zone', i.e. the area in which every shell fired from one gun at the same target would fall, was about 120 yards in length at a range of 3,000 yards. The net effect of these trials was that, at a range greater than 2,500 yards, to be sure of cutting any wire a very large number of shells had to be fired at a particular target. Just how many will be shown later.[27]

In June, G.H.Q. issued 'Artillery Notes Number 5' which discussed the effectiveness of various methods of wire cutting[28]. Highly favoured was the 2 in. trench mortar fitted with the Newton fuse. Experiments with this had proved very successful with tests showing that one round per 10 square yards would successfully cut barbed wire. This was, of course, under test conditions, and, when taking into account variables like high wind, state of the ground, poor observation and difficult firing conditions this was raised to something like five rounds. Relying on the 2 in. mortar to cut wire was not, however, an option. The tests providing the figures mentioned had been conducted at a range of just over 300 yards. The 2 in. mortar was a front line weapon and, as such, subject to effective counter-measures from German artillery and their own mortars which made the use of the static front-line mortar for wire cutting an adjunct to the 18 pdr's shrapnel rather than a substitute.

For the 18 pdr guns the recommendations were detailed. The paper stated that the optimum range for the use of shrapnel in wire cutting was between 1,800 and 2,400 yards. This was in line with the Calais tests and, again as these tests had indicated, the G.H.Q. paper stated that, though wire could be cut at up to 3,500 yards "more time and a considerable increase in the amount of ammunition are required". The paper further recommended that, before firing a wire cutting bombardment, the guns were overhauled and carefully calibrated, in addition, a good steady platform for the gun was required. Observation of the fall of the shot was also vital. G.H.Q. recommended that two F.O.O.s should watch the wire cutting: one as far forward as possible and to the flank to watch for range and the height of the shell burst; and another further back to correct for the line. The paper's sixth point concerning the use of the 18 pdr for wire cutting showed the narrow margins within which the gunners had to operate. The paper concluded that the optimum burst of shell was on the front edge of the barbed wire and about four feet above the ground. Bursting even five yards short meant that the shrapnel discharge would have little effect on the wire. The suggested methods for the firing of an 18 pdr battery was that they should first seek to create a gap and then work to steadily enlarge it. As the guns fired it was also necessary to reduce their elevation as the barrels got hot and regular pauses were necessary to allow the barrels to cool. In other words, the young officers in charge of the guns had many things to consider if they were to cut effectively the bristling wire now facing the infantry. They also had to keep a close eye on the availability of ammunition and fuses so as to ensure a steady bombardment of the enemy's wire. Lastly, the paper addressed the issue about how much ammunition was actually needed to do the job the infantry needed. Their 'rough rule' was to allow 1/3rd the number of hundreds of yards in the range for each yard of front" but this, of course, depended on the depth and type of wire to be cut and took no account of the accuracy of the bombardment in both range and height of burst.

206

A factor that was not yet appreciated, at least by the field gunners on the ground, was that there was another variable that needed to be considered. This certainly applied to the 4.5 in. howitzers and may well have affected the performance of the 18 pdrs too. The OC of D/280th Battery, the field howitzer battery of the 280th Brigade, RFA., wrote in the unit War Diary on 30th June 1916 about problems they had experienced with the various propellant charges used during the bombardment and the battle. There were thee types of propellant charge: NCT, Cordite and Ballistite[i]; and the experiences was that the first two had a range of some 100 yards *less* than Ballistite. Even this variation, however, was not consistent, making accurate firing extremely difficult. Writing after the war, Maj. Gen. A G L McNaughton[ii], by then Chief of the General Staff in Canada but, at the time, the Counter Battery Staff Officer of the Canadian Corps whose work would help with the capture of Vimy Ridge in April 1917, explained the numerous difficulties these three propellant charges created as well as other factors reducing the effectiveness of the field artillery:

"As the war went on, we got more and more ammunition, but we suffered considerably from lack of standardization. In the early summer of 1915, we had four different types of shrapnel in our limbers at the same time, with a variation of range between them of anything up to 400 yards. In 1916 in the 4.5 howitzers, we had three types of propellant in use simultaneously – Cordite, Ballistite and N.C.T. – all with different temperature and moisture coefficients, and all giving results varying in a most obscure way with the wear of the howitzer. Charges originally shipped in lots of similar manufacture got mixed up on the Lines of Communication; shell varied in weight; driving bands were of many varieties; the battery officers had in any event to make corrections for:

Temperature of air and change.

Barometer.

Velocity and direction of wind.

Wear of gun.

Type of shell and fuze.

When the already difficult task was further complicated by lack of standardization in propellant, driving band and shell, the task of exact shooting became almost impossible, and by 1918 the lack of standardization was recognized as one of the serious limiting factors in the tactical employment of artillery."[29]

***

THE FIELD ARTILLERY OF THE 56TH DIVISION was organised in four brigades, the 1/1st to 1/4th London Brigades R.F.A. In early May these brigades were re-designated 280th to 283rd Brigades, R.F.A. Between them, the four brigades

---

[i] NCT - nitrocellulose tubular stabilized with diphenylamine – is an American propellant. Cordite (MD) is a combination of nitroglycerine, gun cotton and acetone with added mineral jelly to reduce barrel wear. Ballistite, invented by Nobel in 1888, was a combination of 40% nitroglycerine and 60% nitrocellulose. NCT has the disadvantage of being hygroscopic, i.e. it attracts water, which adversely affects the reliability of its ballistics. It is, as a result, less easy to store than, say, Cordite. It does, however, result in less barrel wear.

[ii] Maj. Gen. A G L McNaughton was the commander of the First Canadian Army in 1942 and Minister for National Defence in 1944.

comprised twelve batteries of 18 pdr guns (48 guns) and three batteries of 4.5 in. howitzers (12 howitzers). They were distributed into three groups:

- Northern Group under Lt. Col. Southam (called 'Southart' for short and affiliated to 169ᵗʰ Brigade at zero hour on 1ˢᵗ July) which comprised B/280, C/280, A/283 (18 pdrs), D/282 (4.5 in. howitzers) plus A/280 which joined from the Wire-Cutting Group at Zero hour on 1ˢᵗ July;
- the Southern Group under Lt. Col. Macdowell ('Macart', affiliated to 168ᵗʰ Brigade) made up of A/281, B/281, C/281, 109 (18 pdrs) and D/281 (4.5 in. howitzers); and a
- Wire Cutting Group under Lt. Col. Prechtel ('Peltart') comprising: A/282, B/282, C/282, C/283, A/280 (18 pdrs), D/280 (4.5 in. howitzers). A/280 joined the Northern Group at Zero hour on 1ˢᵗ July.

These batteries followed the division to the Hebuterne area but their arrivals were spread over several weeks with A/280 and B/280 being the last to arrive from the vicinity of Arras on the 3ʳᵈ June. By then, the majority of the batteries had prepared their positions and 281ˢᵗ Brigade was the first to start firing, beginning to register their targets from mid-May onwards. The length of time it took to set up a field battery position was considerable. It was not just a case of turning up with the guns, pointing them in the right direction and opening fire as the War Diary of the D/280 Howitzer Battery shows. Before they could fire a shot they first dug four gun pits, constructed four 8ft by 20 ft dug outs, built a telephone exchange and wireless ground station as well as dug two ammunition pits each capable of holding 2,000 rounds. Lastly there was the accommodation for the officer commanding the battery. By 25ᵗʰ May, all of this had been done by the hard-working men of the Battery and a stockpile of 3,600 shells had been accumulated and stored in the pits. All of this labour was greeted four days later by a 77mm shrapnel shell which put No. 1 gun out of action if only for two or three hours. Overall, preparing these positions could take anything between two to three weeks depending on conditions. The weather and transport difficulties served to extend rather than shorten the process for the 56ᵗʰ Division's field batteries and half of them were not completely ready until ten days or less before the attack was due to take place.

Prior to the assault itself, the five 18 pdr batteries of the Wire Cutting group were dedicated to demolishing the wire in front of Hebuterne although others joined in as time allowed. Still preparing their positions as late as 14ᵗʰ June the batteries were widely distributed (see map above) with some used to fire head on into the wire and some used to enfilade the wire from the W.N.W. from positions south of Foncquevillers. Using all of the time available then Batteries of this crucial artillery group then spent the next nine days registering their targets, finishing the day before the bombardment was due to start.

Closest to the German lines was half of 'C' Battery, 283ʳᵈ Brigade whose two 18 pdrs were concealed in one of the orchards that fringed the northern side of Hebuterne. They were to fire over open sites, targeting especially the wire and defences of the German position at Point 94 on the S.E. corner of Gommecourt Park. Behind them, dug into back gardens and orchards on the southern side of the village were the 4.5 in. howitzers of 'D' Batteries of 280ᵗʰ and 281ˢᵗ Brigades. These weapons could range into the German-held woods and rear areas and, for part of the time, some were used in the counter-battery programme that was later to prove so ineffective.

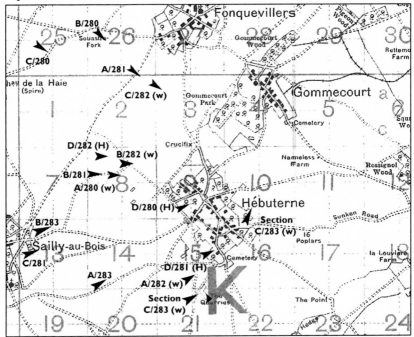

Map 9 Location of Field Artillery batteries
Legend: (w) = Wire Cutting group (H) = 4.5 in. Howitzer battery

The rest of 56th Division's field artillery was distributed over a wide area:

A/282 Battery and the other half of C/283 Battery were dug in just west of the Hebuterne to Auchonvillers road at a range of about 2,000 yards from the German front lines, both being designated as wire cutting batteries;

Grouped together in a fold of the land about 1,500 yards west of the centre of Hebuterne (and about 2,500 yards from the German lines) were the 18 pdrs of A/280, B/281 and B/282 Batteries and the howitzers of D/282 Brigade. A/280 and B/282 Batteries were part of the wire cutting group;

Either side of the road from Sailly to Hebuterne and 500 yards from the centre of the aforementioned village were the two 18 pdr batteries, C/281 and B/283. These guns were just over 3,000 yards from the nearest German trenches; and

Four more batteries were ranged in echelon to the W.N.W. of the German lines in positions designed to take the enemy's position in enfilade. The nearest battery, C/282, part of the wire cutting group, was about 1,700 yards from Point 94, the closest point to the guns which was to be attacked on 1st July and the furthest battery was C/280 which had to fire at a range of 3,000 yards to hit the same position. B/280 and A/281 were somewhere in between the other two, with ranges of between 2,000 and 2,500 yards respectively.

In other words, all of the wire cutting group were just about firing from within the recommended ranges of G.H.Q.'s Artillery Notes issued just a few day's before the bombardment opened, i.e. between 1,800 and 2,400 yards. The failures to cut the wire in front of the centre to the right of the attack cannot, therefore, be explained by the 18 pdrs firing at inappropriate ranges.

The scheduled volume of shrapnel to be used to cut the wire was, in the original five day programme, 27,500 shells; with 5,500 to be fired on every day by the five batteries involved, i.e. 1,100 per battery or 275 per gun. Each of the wire cutting 18 pdrs were scheduled, therefore, to fire 1,375 shells prior to the assault. Applying G.H.Q.'s 'rule of thumb' for the number of shells required to cut wire it can be seen that these numbers were on the low side given the length of line to be attacked. The length of line to be assaulted was approximately 1,600 yards in length. As the guns were firing from an average of about 2,100 yards the formula would be:

21 (i.e. 21 'hundred' yards) ÷ 3 = 7 (i.e. shells per yard of front)

1,600 x 7 = 11,200 shells

At face value, therefore, an allowance of 27,500 shells, two and half times the number suggested by the simple application of the 'formula' for wire cutting, would appear more than adequate for the task. There are, however, several other issues to take into account. Firstly, the field guns had more than one belt of wire to cut. Not only was the wire in front of the German first line to be effectively cut, they also had the task of slicing paths through the wire in front of the second German line. In addition, the formula could take no account of the ability of German defenders to repair and replace the wire. Here, the over-weaning confidence of senior officers in the ability of the heavy artillery to kill, wound and demoralise the occupants of the German trenches came into play. In spite of repeated evidence drawn from patrols that showed German working parties to be highly active at night rebuilding and repairing their defences, there was no adaptation to the bombardment plan which might have disrupted these works. Certainly, the other field artillery batteries had the task of bombarding the German front line trenches, though previous tests had shown 18 pdr high explosive shells to have little effect on trenches, but these tasks were shared with the need to bombard communication trenches, tracks and roads. For the last four days of the scheduled bombardment between 8,000 and 10,000 18 pdr shells, split approximately equally between shrapnel and high explosive, were fired at various hours of the day and night in the hope of interfering with German reliefs, stopping food and other supplies reaching the forward areas and generally disrupting the efforts of the defenders to maintain their positions in decent order. Whilst this volume of shellfire, to which was added the variably timed intense 40-minute bombardments comprising anything between 1,700 and 4,600 shells of various denominations, might terrorise the more nervous German in his deep dugout and make movement up and down the trenches a tricky proposition, the British Army's own tests, including those at Calais at the end of 1915, had clearly shown that they had little practical effect on the fabric of the trenches or would have to be detonated most precisely over a trench occupied by soldiers if serious casualties were to be caused.

In general terms, as German casualty figures would later show, the field artillery's bombardment of the front line trenches and communication trenches was an exercise 'full of sound and fury, signifying nothing'. The wire cutting achieved more but, as the unfortunate infantry were to find out, it was patchy for a combination of the reasons given: inadequate weight of shell, firing and gun error and defensive repairs achieved by the resolute defenders of the salient[i].

And there was another factor to consider, one which was to come in to play most significantly on the day of the attack itself. As Lt. Col. Southam of the 280th Brigade would say after the war when commenting on the draft of the Official History's description of Gommecourt: "Artillery officers, from the highest downward, were generally ignorant of the limitations of this equipment, never having had so much ammunition at disposal before."[30] Southam recorded the effects of these 'limitations' in his Brigade's War Diary:

"28th June, 'Y' Day – Guns of the group showing signs of the strain and requiring constant attention of artificers. Great demand for inner and outer springs.

30th June, 'Y2' Day – Guns showing increasing signs of strain and temporarily going out of action. New parts to replace damaged (principally inner and outer springs) in constant demand and fitted as obtained."

These problems would have affected all batteries whatever their roles. For those guns being used for wire cutting the implications were ominous. Just at the time when the greatest accuracy – of range, direction and height of burst – was in demand the guns were beginning to fail. Two of the Brigade War Diaries provide daily ammunition expenditure records, the 281st and 282nd Brigades but they both refer to the bombardment groups which had been created specifically for the attack. Thus the numbers are for the 'Macart'[ii] group, based on 281st Brigade, and the 'Peltart'[iii] group, based on 282nd Brigade. Table 14 below shows the sharp reduction in activity on the two extension days of the bombardment (though 'Macart' group's last numbers seem more notional than accurate). The fire plans were to climax on the day before the assault, 'Y' Day, but there was a dramatic reduction with the two groups cutting their activity by 40%. Of course, these were also days on which the Heavy Artillery reduced its firing, all of which conspired to give the defenders of Gommecourt time to reorganise and repair.

Day	Macart Group	Peltart Group	Total
U Day	1,050	1,675	2,725
V Day	4,602	4,334	8,936
W Day	5,530	4,768	10,298
X Day	7,056	4,094	11,150
Y Day	8,893	4,283	13,176
Y1 Day	5,300	2,753	8,053
Y2 Day	5,300	2,512	7,812
Total	37,731	24,419*	37,731

Table 14 Rounds fired by Macart & Peltart groups during preliminary bombardment
* Peltart Group fired 95% shrapnel and 5% high explosive

---

[i] Interestingly, the wire cutting programme for the 46th Division was far less intensive than that of the 56th Division. The original programme allocated 22 battery 'days' for wire cutting (against 25 'day's for the 56th Division) using less than half of the shrapnel allocation of the 56th's wire cutting group. Whereas the 56th Division allocated 27,500 rounds for wire cutting, the 46th Division allocated just 10,790 shrapnel plus 1,500 Newton-fused 2 in. mortar shells (possible because No Man's Land was, in general, narrower on the 46th Division's front). Many of the attacking men of the North Midlands division found the wire uncut and suffered accordingly. *Source*: NA file WO 95/811
[ii] Macart Group: A/281, B/281, C/281, 109 (18 pdrs) and D/281 (4.5 in. howitzers)
[iii] Peltart Group: A/282, B/282, C/282, C/283, A/280 (18 pdrs), D/280 (4.5 in. howitzers).

'Peltart' group comprised the batteries earmarked for wire cutting. Their allocation for this purpose had been 27,500 rounds and the total fired was some 10% less than that allowed for in the VII Corps programme. If, as suggested above, the original allocation was on the low side given the length and depth of wire to be cut then this 10% reduction, allied to the likelihood that a significant and increasing proportion of the rounds fired would have burst outside the acceptable parameters (i.e. at the front edge of the barbed wire and about four feet above the ground), must have resulted in a degree of patchiness in the overall results. Given the energetic efforts of the defenders to repair the wire after every day's bombardment then it can easily be seen why there would a fair amount of uncut or only partially cut wire along the 56th Division's front. As it turned out, the wire along nearly two thirds of the line was at best partially cut and, in some places, there were no gaps at all.

This problem was eventually identified on the evening of the 30th June, the night before the attack was due to go in. Every afternoon firing was suspended between 4.00 and 4.30 p.m. while a BE2c of No 8 Squadron took aerial photographs of the whole salient. Analysed by R.F.C. Intelligence Officers these revealed lengths of uncut wire, especially in the centre of the attack in the area where The Rangers were due to attack. It was very late in the day for anything to be done about this problem and last minute efforts to remedy the situation failed with serious and often fatal consequences for the men involved.

These R.F.C. photographs taken on the eve of the attack have survived (see photographs pages 120, 120 and 120) and they warrant some close attention. The four taken over the area to be attacked by the 56th Division exhibit similar characteristics:

1. Extensive scouring marks in the earth in front of the German lines where the shrapnel used for wire cutting has scraped lines in the soil;
2. Surprisingly little damage to the majority of front line and communication trenches (even after seven days of heavy artillery fire); and
3. A concentration of shell holes in the strongpoints which were the focus of attack, i.e. the Farmer-Farmyard strongpoint on the right the objective of the London Scottish and the Maze on the left, to be taken by the London Rifle Brigade.

What struck the author about the photographs on first viewing was just how little damage had been done to the German trenches. For anyone used to seeing the aerial photographs showing the overlapping crater fields from later in the Battle of the Somme, these aerial shots do not give the expected impression of a zone that has been subject to a prolonged and heavy bombardment by heavy howitzers. Admittedly there was the hurricane bombardment still to come in the hour immediately preceding the assault but even this bout of shelling would have been concentrated on the strongpoints and could have had little impact on the trenches in between. Certainly, descriptions of the condition of the strongpoints by men who arrived there showed that many trenches were unrecognisable, often nothing but an irregular line of shell holes. This would prove a mixed blessing as the men of the attacking battalions found these locations difficult to defend against counter-attack. In short, therefore, the heavy artillery's impact on the German defences was, like the wire cutting, patchy and, even where concentrated, not always beneficial to the infantry.

One other factor stands out, especially in the photograph of the area around the Maze. Several of the largest shell craters are clearly filled with water, as good an indication as anything of the volumes of rain that had drenched and softened the ground throughout June. And the softening of the ground had also contributed to rendering the heavy shells of the howitzers less effective. Their explosions of smoke and debris contained showers of mud as the energy of the explosion was mostly either dissipated upwards in a gout of flame and a plume of black smoke or absorbed by the saturated ground. That the damage shown in the aerial photographs appeared relatively small is, perhaps, not altogether surprising when one considers that, according to John Keegan:

"Each ten square yards had received only a pound of high explosive, or each square mile about thirty tons.[31]"

Such concentrations were unlikely to cause major damage to the Germans lurking in their deep dug outs, uncomfortable, frightened and hungry though they may have been. But dead they certainly were not.

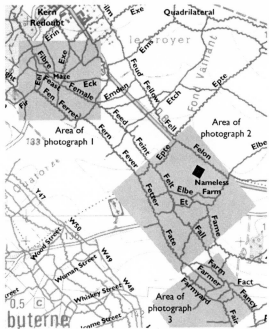

Map 10 Map showing areas covered by aerial photographs
The map shows the areas covered by the aerial photographs to be found on pages 214, 215 and 216

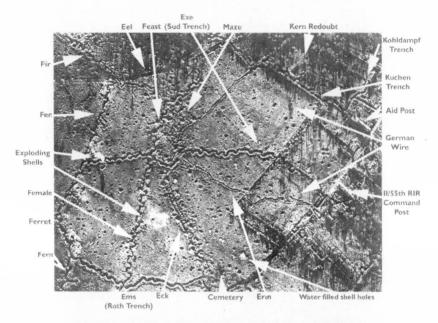

Plate 15 Aerial photograph of the trenches around The Maze

Photograph taken by BE2c of No. 8 Squadron, RFC in the early evening of Friday, 30th June 1916. This is the area attacked by the London Rifle Brigade. The edge of Gommecourt Park can be seen along the top edge, left side. The concentrations of shell holes can be seen in the trenches of The Maze and along Eck Trench otherwise there is limited damage to the trench systems. The last men to be driven out of the German trenches were surrounded in Ferret and Fen Trenches on the left of the photograph. This photograph covers an area of about 250 metres top to bottom and 350 metres left to right. (Photograph Crown Copyright),

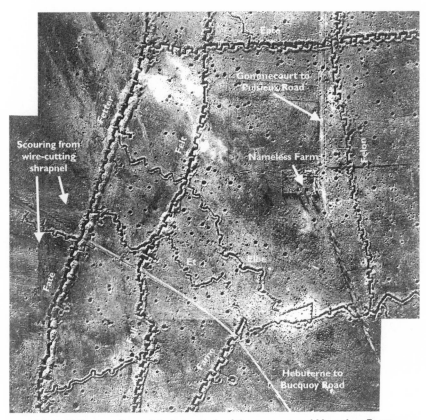

Plate 16 Composite aerial photograph of the area around Nameless Farm
Photograph taken by BE2c of No. 8 Squadron, RFC in the early evening of Friday, 30th June 1916. This is the area attacked by The Rangers who attacked either side of the Hebuterne to Bucquoy Road. The Victorias and Westminsters attacked the area beyond Epte Trench at the top of the photograph. As can be seen, there is relatively little damage to the trenches and hardly any to Nameless Farm. On the left can be seen the marks made by the scouring effect of 18 pdr shrapnel used to cut the German wire. It was here that The Rangers encountered uncut wire with disastrous results. This photograph covers an area of about 450 metres top to bottom and 350 metres left to right. (Photograph Crown Copyright)

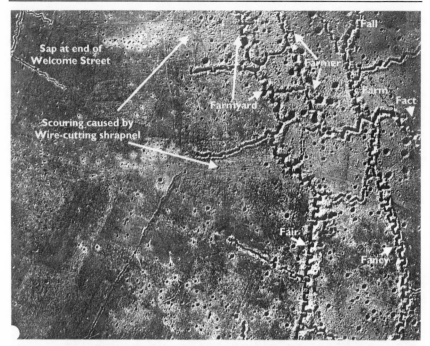

Plate 17 Aerial photograph of the Farmer-Farmyard stronghold

Photograph taken by BE2c of No. 8 Squadron, RFC in the early evening of Friday, 30th June 1916. This is the area attached by the London Scottish. There is some heavy howitzer damage to Farmyard and Farmer trenches but otherwise their shells fell between the trenches not in them. The area in the bottom left of the photograph is the part of No Man's Land across which 'A' and 'B' Companies attacked with part of 'A' Company losing their way in the thick smoke. These men found themselves in front of uncut wire at the bottom of the photograph and suffered heavy casualties. This photograph covers an area of about 250 metres top to bottom and 350 metres left to right. (Photograph Crown Copyright)

ENDNOTES:
1 Eldridge, Sir John Papers, Liddle Collection, Leeds University
2 Birch, Lt Gen Sir Noel, CB, Colonel Commandant, Royal Artillery 'Artillery Development in the Great War', (The Army Quarterly, October 1920)
3 Du Cane
4 Edmonds, Brig. Gen. Sir James E, Official History of the War: Military Operations, France and Belgium 1916, Volume 1 Footnote page 460.
5 Jones Rfm P H 1/16th London Regt (Queen's Westminster Rifles), Papers, IWM.
6 I V Hogg and L F Thurston, 'British Artillery Weapons and Ammunition 1914-18' 1972.
7 Keegan, John, The Face of Battle, 1976. Page 239.
8 NA WO 95/227
9 NA WO 95/480
10 NA WO 95/477
11 50th Siege Battery Diary NA WO 95/476
12 War Diary 35th Heavy Artillery Group, NA WO 95/390
13 From letter dated 3rd June 1929. NA CAB/45/185
14 Farndale, Gen. Sir Martin, History of the Royal Regiment of Artillery, Western Front 1914-18, 1986 Annex L, p 374 'Sound Ranging in France'.
15 68th Siege Battery RGA NA WO 95/480
16 NA WO 95/227
17 Jones, Lieutenant Colonel J H H, Brigade Major of the VII Corps artillery,
18 Jones, H A, The war in the air : being the story of the part played in the Great War by the Royal Air Force. Volume 3. page 194.
19 Now a French Airforce base.
20 NA WO 95/360
21 Jones, H A op. cit.. Vol 3.
22 Ward-Jackson, *Letter to his wife 30th June 1916*, IWM
23 The Times, Saturday, July 8th 1916.
24 8th Squadron RFC NA, AIR/1/688/21/20/8
25 Ibid.
26 68th Siege Battery RGA NA WO 95/480
27 CDS 93 Report on Experimental Firing with 18pdr Shrapnel and High Explosive at Calais, November 1915, issued by the General Staff at General Headquarters.
28 Artillery Notes Number 5, Wire Cutting, June 1916, issued by the General Staff at General Headquarters.
29 McNaughton, Maj. Gen A G L, 'The Development of Artillery in the Great War', The Field Artillery Journal, May-June 1930, page 259.
30 Lt Col L A C Southam's comments on the draft of the Official History, CAB 45/137 NA.
31 Keegan, John, The Face of Battle, 1976. Page 239.

7. THE BOMBARDMENT: U DAY TO Y2 DAY

"The fact is that this attack is based entirely on the supposition that there will be no Germans left alive to oppose us, and that we shall suffer no casualties. On paper, the plans are A1, but if the Germans obstinately refuse to die and make way for us, our scheme will become impractical."

Rfn. Percy Jones
Queen's Westminster Rifles

U Day, Saturday, 24th June 1916
Third Army weather report: Warm but showery. Rain: 2.2mm. Temp. 71-51° F

SATURDAY, 24TH JUNE, WAS U DAY and the bombardment began. The crack and bark of the field and medium artillery filled the air in an arc from Berles-au-Bois in the north to Hebuterne in the south. The weight of the heavy and super heavy pieces would be unleashed the following day. Again, the day dawned damp. In the morning, squally showers left over from the previous day's deluge, swept across the front line depositing another 2 mm of unwelcome rain on the front-line trenches and troops below. These troops were, as before, the men of the 167th Brigade: the 1/7th and 1/8th Middlesex.

On the day the bombardment began the 1/7th Middlesex suffered only slightly from the half-hearted German retaliation with just 2 other ranks wounded. These losses were more than compensated for, however, with the arrival of a 100-man draft from 2/7th Middlesex, its depot battalion.

As the 1/8th Middlesex busied themselves in the trenches they, too, suffered only lightly from German artillery. Shell splinters wounded four other ranks as hostile batteries replied in a desultory fashion. On the other side of No Man's Land, the 55th R.I.R., defending Gommecourt village and Park (some of the main targets for the heavy artillery), suffered casualties of one man wounded and recorded that most of the artillery fire was in the form of shrapnel, usually required for wire cutting.

Back in Halloy it was the turn of the 'other ranks' to enjoy themselves and Pte. Hawkings went into Doullens in the morning to buy beer for a concert to be held that night. Doullens was a town with some history[1]. Set in a fold in the hills at the junction of the Grouche and Authie rivers, the town had avoided the ravages of this war. To the south east of the town, however, was a reminder of earlier conflicts. For the best part of 250 years, Doullens had stood on the border between France and the Spanish Netherlands and, to defend it during the many conflicts that swept across this part of north western Europe from the 15th Century onwards, a citadel in the style of Vauban had been built. It was there to defend a prosperous market town which still boasted l'Eglise St Pierre, a 13th Century church in the Romanesque style, and a 14th Century Belfry which, until twenty years earlier, had been the Town Hall. An imposing redbrick, three-storey Hotel De Ville that dominated the skyline of the town centre now took that role.

Doullens had greeted many high-ranking officials over the centuries. Cardinal Richelieu had visited in 1640 whilst his troops besieged Arras during the French Wars of Religion. On April Fools' Day, 1678, Louis XIV and the Dauphin had stayed in the Belfry in the Rue du Bourg. In 1915, Marshal Joffre had lived some months in a large house in what was to be re-named after the war the Rue Clemenceau. Now Doullens was awash with men in khaki. A major railhead for the Arras and Somme fronts, the site of several Casualty Clearing Stations and a tempting watering hole for any soldier with a few francs to spend, the streets were choked with transports and the pavements heaved with men in uniform. Hawkings was just one amongst many as he and the driver sloshed their way back from the Brasserie, as the rain set in again.

It fell on the men of the 168th and 169th Brigades as they plodded their way in serried ranks across the cornfields of Halloy. They were 'rehearsing' again their 'taking' of the Gommecourt trenches. To describe the movements as an attack would be wrong. An 'occupation' would be more correct. The men, moving precisely to timetable, walked across 'No Man's Land', moved left, right or forward to their assigned objectives, raised signboards to indicate their progress with no enemy to hinder their sedate progress. To some of the men, the process seemed unreal, based on false optimism about the effect of the bombardment just starting. To many officers, from Army down to battalion, it seemed a reasonable representation of what would happen on Z Day. The German defences would be flattened, the enemy soldiers incapacitated - dead or dazed. It would be a question of mopping up and consolidation. The problem of 'Sod's Law' - what can go wrong, will go wrong - seemed not to have entered anyone's head, well no-one above the rank of Lt. Colonel.

The battalion history of the Q.V.R. reflected on these practices and their attention to detail. It also makes an acid comparison between these elaborate but over-confident rehearsals and the shambles of so many attacks later in the Somme campaign:

"The preparations for the attack were the best rehearsed of any that the Q.V.R. did. *Instead of, as often occurred afterwards, hardly anyone knowing anything of the work to be done, every single man in the battalion knew all about the attack and what was expected of him.* Everything possible was done to ensure success. To enable companies to be identified and to avoid confusion by men getting into the wrong trench, or staying in one when they should go forward, each company wore distinguishing colours on their shoulder-straps. Coloured boards on poles were issued to be waved to show the artillery and others in rear how far the troops had reached. Every trench in the system to be attacked was given a name, and maps with the names on were distributed widely; notice boards with these names painted on were carried, to be hoisted when the trench was captured, to facilitate men knowing where they were."[2]

It was not only on the British side of No Man's Land that planning, training and organisation were in full swing. Even as the first day of the bombardment got under way, German artillery units were planning for the assault and for their reaction to the bombardment. A large scale attack had been anticipated ever since the digging of the new trenches at the end of May and German staff officers had been working diligently ever since then on reaction and contingency plans. That they were working on the right lines was confirmed when a British soldier was made prisoner on the 24th:

"Strong enemy activity in extending his trench system and driving saps forward, uninterrupted aerial activity and systematic ranging-in of his artillery with only a few shots, avoiding any effective fire, were ever stronger indicators of an impending major attack.

In view of this situation, our defence work continued at fever pitch: artillery emplacements were reinforced, they were expanded so that they could serve as infantry support positions in the event of any set-backs, all installations were concealed, ammunition was stored safely, all lines and levels of effectiveness were improved. The fire distribution plans were kept up to date taking into consideration all reinforcements that arrived, protection was checked, permanent observation posts were established in the fighting trenches, and signalling was systematically organised for the event that the telephones failed.

Fall-back positions were prepared, decoy positions and screens were set up to deceive the enemy.

Firing activity ranged from worthwhile targets, to retaliatory fire on settlements and identified enemy batteries. Ranging-in exercises were conducted with the help of our flying detachment, however, good results were seldom achieved and exercises mostly had to be cancelled due to the low number of aircraft available and enemy superiority in the air.

A British soldier captured near Gommecourt on 24th June revealed that the British attack was imminent. On our part, all leave was cancelled and everyone on leave was ordered to return to the unit."[3]

The soldier mentioned in the 20th R.F.A.R's history was Pte. Victor Wheat, a member of the 5th North Staffordshires which was due to be the support battalion to their sister battalion, the 6th North Staffordshires during the attack. Pte. Wheat had been a member of a wiring party that had gone out on the night of the 23rd/24th June. Badly wounded by machine gun fire he had wandered into the German lines by mistake and, in a severely weakened state had told his interrogator that the attack was due in the early hours of the 27th. Though inaccurate, this information put the defences on full alert, an alert confirmed by the start of the heavy bombardment. Locally, the true importance of Wheat's statement was not that an attack was due, the defenders of Gommecourt were well aware of that and had been made so by the obvious preparations in front of them, rather the importance lay in what Wheat told his interrogators about the tactics to be employed. Feeble through shock and loss of blood, Wheat gave away the details of the two Division attack on Gommecourt. The report of the interrogation stated:

"Gommecourt was to be by-passed to its north and south. The assault was to be pushed forward to the wood behind the fourth trench... it had all been rehearsed about four days ago in an area of trenches near a copse behind the lines at St Leger (*Author's note:* by the 46th Division)."[4]

As a result General von Süsskind, the commander of the 2nd Guard Reserve Division had a clear idea as to the nature of the threat being mounted against his position. He knew, and was thus able to plan for the fact, that the British attack was to be a pincer movement, avoiding most of Gommecourt Park and village and attacking only the 'wings' of the salient. His defensive plans could be adapted accordingly.

V Day, Sunday, 25ᵗʰ June 1916
Third Army weather report: Dull & warm. Rain: 0mm. Temp. 72-54° F

THE WEATHER ON SUNDAY, 25ᵀʰ JUNE was kinder with early sun. Cloud built up as the day drew on but no rain fell and the temperature climbed to a pleasant 72 degrees. On the German side of the front line, however, things were hotting up. V Day, the second day of the bombardment, was the day the heavy and super-heavy howitzers joined the fray. The huge shells of the 6 in., 9.2 in., 12 in. and 15 in. howitzers lurking in the orchards and amongst the houses of the villages to the west began to smash into their targets around Gommecourt throwing up plumes of smoke, debris and mud. But this increase in intensity provoked a severe German response. 1/7ᵗʰ Middlesex were fortunate - only 4 other ranks were wounded. Their colleagues from the 1/8ᵗʰ Middlesex in the neighbouring trenches were not so lucky. Here 7 other ranks were killed in the counter-bombardment and another 25 were wounded. In addition, 22 other ranks became casualties (five fatal) in the other two battalions of the brigade, the numbers being equally split between the 1/1ˢᵗ and 1/3ʳᵈ Londonsⁱ.

For others, further back from the front line, the damage done by the British heavy howitzers was not just to the enemy's lines. Pte H T Clements of the 1/2ⁿᵈ Londons had the day off and hoped to enjoy a wash and brush up, but one of the 'Grannies', the huge 15 in. howitzers, was uncomfortably close to his billet:

"Had a day off so I got a biscuit tin full of water and had a bath in an old shed. I had just finished when the 15" howitzers behind the basin went off and nearly knocked the barn down. I got covered in mud and dust. The Town Crier, a weird object half soldier and half civilian, kept coming round and informing the people that if they wished to evacuate the village our people would lend them a lorry to put their goods in. This was in case the village is shelled during the attack. Our billet is a very old barn. The drawback is that there is a 15" howitzer just behind it so that whenever the gun is fired the billet nearly falls over and all the accumulated dust of years falls down on us and our food. The great thing at present is to get Heinz Baked Beans in small tins at the canteen and cook them over a candle for breakfast. They are quite good with fried bacon. We know now definitely that our brigade is attacking with ourselves as brigade reserves, with eight companies of the 5ᵗʰ, 9ᵗʰ and 16ᵗʰ as the first line of attack. The attack is to take place Thursday morning. We are all a bit anxious as a lot are sure to 'go west'. Everyone is confident of the result but we are not looking forward to it with pleasure as we all know what hell these big attacks are."[5]

In the morning, back in Halloy, watched by their divisional general, the assaulting battalions trudged patiently through the mud, over-running shallow,

---

ⁱ Two men of the 1/1ˢᵗ Londons died of their wounds, one surviving the long ambulance trip to the C.C.S. at Warlincourt:
2440 Pte Arthur Penney died of wounds on 25ᵗʰ June 1916. Aged 23, he was the son of Thomas Frederick and Sarah E Penney of 150, Brooke Road, Stoke Newington, London. He is buried in Hebuterne Military Cemetery, II.H.8.
4449 Pte William John Reardon is buried at Warlincourt Halte British Cemetery, Saulty, grave I.D.6.

mock trenches and consolidating with uncannily accurate timing essential strongpoints. Later in the day, whilst cleaning up after their exertions, the London Scottish had a foretaste of wars to come. They had returned to their billets in Pas-en-Artois, a village set in the steep and heavily wooded valley of the Authie, when, at noon, a flight of German aircraft droned overhead. They dropped a number of bombs which, though missing them, the redbrick Hotel de Ville, the large church and the splendid manor house set back from the road to Henu, somehow managed to wound a French woman in the local estaminet.

Nearby, Julian Bickersteth was conducting one of the last Sunday services before the attack to come and he wrote home later about how five German aircraft had dropped their bombs in a nearby field in the middle of his service. Unsurprisingly, as the service was outdoors, the men's attention somewhat wandered as the bombs exploded in a shower of mud and plumes of smoke a few hundred yards away but, some moments later, after a rousing rendition of 'God Save the King', the assembled men marched off spiritually uplifted and none the worse for wear. There was, however, a special solemnity about the day's service as it would be the last before the offensive began. There was an awareness that this might be a man's last chance to make his peace with his God in the presence of a priest and hundreds took the opportunity to be confessed. As Bickersteth wrote home later:

"At least these men have tried to prepare themselves to meet their God."[6]

For the attacking battalions it was now time to decide which officers and men would be withdrawn from coming action. It was policy to hold back a nucleus that would form a cadre around which the unit could be re-formed in the event of heavy casualties. In the Q.W.R., 2ⁿᵈ Lt. Moy was amongst the lucky ones, though others found an alternative route to avoiding battle.

"On the eve of all battles a selection of officers who would not take part in it was made. The aim was that in the event of the battalion been wiped out these would form the nucleus of a new one. I have already stated that we had a superfluity of officers, so it is easily understood that to risk their lives would be ridiculous and unnecessary. The selection was duly made. The second in command of the battalion and second-in-command of all companies together with 11 other officers would be left out. I was one of the lucky ones. As was usual before all battles, Whitmore went sick and the command of 'B' Company was given to Capt. Cockerill. The other officers of 'B' Company who were left out beside myself were Martin and Bell. The Colonel explained to us that it was no disgrace to be singled out and we should probably all have quite enough battles in the near future. I don't mind admitting that I felt no sign of sorrow on being selected."[7]

For the officers and men of the Reserve Feldartillerie Regt 20 things were also hotting up. On the 24ᵗʰ, their main activity had been in fire support for the 52ⁿᵈ Infantry Division around Serre. But now, they came under direct attack themselves and, in spite of the pleas of the infantry, pursued the strategy decided upon by the local artillery commander. Rather than try to answer blow for blow, he had concluded that a programme of restraint was in order. He believed the British were trying to identify more German gun positions in order to increase the effectiveness of their counter-battery fire. He, on the other hand, wished to withhold the true extent of the artillery available behind Gommecourt until the attack actually went in. In this respect, he comprehensively out-thought the Generals opposite:

"Strong enemy artillery activity continued on 25th June. The enemy released gas near Serre and to the north, Gruppe Süd provided support in the form of steady fire. Firing on trenches in the division's sector increased in the course of the day. From 10-11 a.m., Bucquoy was subjected to heavy fire, just as the inhabitants were being evacuated, as was Ablainzeville; this was answered with a strong bombardment placed on Bienvillers and Foncquevillers, as well as on the enemy trenches in order to relieve the infantry. To ensure co-operation between the two groups, Gruppe Süd sent a liaison officer to Gruppe Nord; there was continuous contact with the artillery of 111. I.D. to the right; it reinforced our fire.

Although the infantry always demanded stronger artillery fire for obvious reasons, the artillery commander issued orders to maintain a certain level of restraint, as the British seemed, in the first stage of their preparatory fire, to be trying to tempt us to fire in defence so that they could identify our positions, to induce us to expend a lot of ammunition, to find our batteries by aerial observation and to wear down our gas protection prematurely. On 1 July, this initial restraint proved to have been correct, as the British did not expect the concentrated barrage we launched at the decisive moment when they attacked. It simply defeated them.

Unforgettable for anyone who saw it was the sight at 5 p.m. on 25th June, when all tethered balloons of 14. Reserve-Korps were simultaneously attacked by aircraft firing incendiary ammunition. Six of the nine balloons at the front were shot down. Leutnant der Reserve Brinkmann from our regiment, who was serving as an observer in the balloon of 2. G.R.D., was killed when it was shot down in flames.

Our battery positions did not remain unscathed, either. Two men from 2. G.F.R., belonging to the staff of Major Matschke who was in command there, were killed at the command post of Gruppe Nord; Vizewachtmeister Scharnitzki was killed at 7./20, a gun was rendered unserviceable by a direct hit at 5./20."[8]

For the German infantry the increase in both the weight and intensity of the bombardment was obvious. Under the approving gaze of a number of R.F.C. aircraft, heavy howitzer shells had started to crash into the trenches and special treatment was given to the Kern Redoubt in the heart of Gommecourt village. The long guns of the British Heavy Artillery Groups also started to seek out their targets deep behind the front lines. Either side of lunch, Bucquoy and Essarts were subject to heavy shelling and, much to the chagrin of the men of the 12th Company of 55th R.I.R., a field-cooker fell victim to one of these long range pot-shots. More significantly, the regiment lost one man killed and another eleven wounded under the bombardment. This was, as was the case every day, less than the casualties suffered by the British infantry under the German retaliatory fire. In the 56th Division sector alone twelve men were killed and three officers and fifty two men were wounded.

W Day, Monday, 26th June 1916
Third Army weather report: Fine & warm in the morning. Heavy rain later.
Rain: 7.1mm. Temp. 70-56° F

ON MONDAY (the 26th), the weather took a turn for the worse. From lunchtime, persistent rain set in which lasted through the night leaving the men of the 167th Brigade damp and miserable in their trenches and dugouts. In all, a further 7 mm of rain was deposited across the battlefield. The trenches filled still further with filthy water, the mud became more glutinous and, to add to the soldiers' misery, German retaliation became more serious. The programme for W Day called for a feint attack with smoke over the enemy's lines including some dummy assault preparations on the 37th Division's front between Essarts and Monchy. The Germans took the smoke to be gas and called up heavy artillery support in anticipation of an attack. Back towards Bucquoy the III Battalion, 55th R.I.R. was ordered to stand to, just in case.

At least one VII Corps staff officer was impressed by the speed and efficiency of the German response, although, with only two days to go before the expected launching of the offensive, he seems not to have drawn the most obvious conclusions about the 'effectiveness' of the British artillery preparation. Maj. Ward-Jackson wrote to his wife:

> *"(The Germans) are wonderful indeed. One never finds a flaw in their staff work or their Army management and Intelligence Department. But we are hoping before we have done with this bombardment there will not be quite as much kick left in them as there is now for they are sticking it out in a way which nobody but they or we would do."*[9]

1/7th Middlesex had been charged with the smoke demonstration at 10.15 a.m. and, in response, the Germans put down a barrage on the front-line trench that blew in most of the parapet and killed 10 men and wounded 28. In addition, the battalion lost two officers: Capt. Moody and 2nd Lt. Sherlock wounded[i]. It was not just the smoke that had attracted German interest. Just prior to the smoke demonstration 169th Brigade Trench Mortar Battery, which had brought up ammunition and prepared a location for their Stokes mortars the night before, fired off a rapid salvo under the direction of Lt. Nathan. As they fired, the range and direction were checked by the Battery C.O., Capt. Coote. They had just finished and were taking their dismantled guns back down Yellow Street when the German retaliation shrieked overhead. Coote and his men sensibly sought refuge in a dug out in the communication trench. When the strafe seemed over they continued back into the village and headed for their billets. Their relief at escaping unscathed was short-lived, however, as a short time later, four 15cm shells ploughed into the yard behind the officers' mess. 2nd Lt. M L Price[ii], attached to the trench mortar battery from the 1/7th Middlesex, was killed along

---

[i] A battalion signaller, L/Cpl Jones was awarded the Military Medal for keeping his signal station open all through the day, although it was in an exposed part of the line and under continual heavy shellfire.

[ii] 2nd Lt. Montagu Leonard Price, 1/7th Middlesex Regt., died on Monday, 26th June 1916, aged 22. 2nd Lt. Price was the fourth son of Alfred T Price of Montreal and Mrs Hettie Price of South Woodford then resident at 14, Manor Rd, Westcliff-on-Sea, Southend-on-Sea, Essex. He was educated at Grovers' Company's School and Paradise House, Clissold Park. Aged 17, he went to Canada for health reasons but returned after seven months for an operation. On the outbreak of war he applied for a commission and, whilst waiting, joined the 4th Royal Fusiliers. He was gazetted in June 1915 and in April 1916 he was seconded to the trench mortar batteries. His eldest brother, Editor of the Malay Mail, Kuala Lumpur, served in the Malay Rifle Volunteers. Another brother was with the Royal Fusiliers. His father worked for 'The Times' for 33 years. He is buried in Hebuterne Military Cemetery, grave II.M.7.

with six other men of the 169th Battery. Another ten men from the 167th Trench Mortar Battery were wounded and Lt. Nathan was sent to hospital suffering from shell shock. It was the last time the trench mortar battery would fire in the bombardment. They attracted too much retaliation to make their efforts worthwhile.

Whilst the 1/7th Middlesex suffered, so did their fellow battalions. 1/8th Middlesex lost 5 men killed and 3 officers[i] and 25 wounded[ii] on W Day and the 1/1st Londons suffered casualties of 2 officers[iii] and 6 men wounded, two fatally[iv]. The 1/3rd Londons had five men from a working party led by 2032 Cpl. Frank Wells killed by a minenwerfer out in the trenches during the night. Wells's body would never be found[v]. In addition, Maj. Geard[vi] of the R.F.A. and two of his men[vii] were suffocated when their dugout was destroyed by a shell and an Edinburgh Royal Engineer officer, Captain Duncan Galloway Smith[viii], died of wounds with two of his men being killed and another five wounded. In all, the 56th Division lost two officers killed and six wounded and fifteen other ranks killed, ten missing and seventy eight wounded. If nothing else, the period of the bombardment would show up the massive strength of the German fortifications and the relative weakness of the newly dug and, to them, purely temporary trenches of the Londoners. For, opposite them, the casualties of the 55th R.I.R.

---

i Lt. L W Easman, 2nd Lt. Wilkinson and Lt. J D G Louch

ii In total, the 1/8th Middlesex lost 26 men killed or died of wounds on 26th June 1916. Some may have come from the casualties suffered by the 167th Brigade Trench Mortar Battery to which the battalion had seconded men earlier in the year.

iii 2nd Lt. H E Williams and 2nd Lt. R Selden.
2nd Lt. Harold Edward Williams, 1/1st London Regt., was killed in action between 7th and 8th October 1916, aged 30. He was the son of Edwin and Florence Williams of 'Latimers', Beaconsfield, Bucks. He volunteered in August, 1914 for Service in South Africa but was rejected, he resigned his post in the Standard Bank, Rhodesia, in 1916; paid his passage home and enlisted. His body was never recovered and his name is inscribed on the Thiepval Memorial, Pier and Face 9D and 16B.

iv 3211 L/Cpl Alfred Loader is buried in Hebuterne Military Cemetery, grave II.1.6.
1389 L/Cpl Harold Rasey was the son of Mrs M Rasey of 57, Bathurst Gardens, Willesden, London. He is buried in Couin British Cemetery, grave I.A.19.

v The men of the 1/3rd London Regt (Royal Fusiliers) killed on the night of Monday, 26th June 1916 were:
1733 Pte George J Engwell. He is buried in Hebuterne Military Cemetery, grave II. R. 8
5130 Pte William Francis George Hand. Aged 19, he was the son of Edward & Clara Hand of 61, Earlsmead Rd., Kensal Rise, London. He is buried in Hebuterne Military Cemetery, grave II. R. 9
1157 Sgt John Herbert Jordan. He is buried in Hebuterne Military Cemetery, grave II. R. 4.
1156 Cpl Frederick John Noel Aged 23 he was the son of John & Lydia Noel of 15, Wolseley Rd., Wealdstone, Middlesex. He is buried in Hebuterne Military Cemetery, grave II. R. 5
2032 Cpl Frank Wells, B Company. Born and raised in St Pancras. His body was never found and his name is inscribed on the Thiepval Memorial Addenda Panel.

vi Major Walter Leslie Geard, C Bty, 282nd Bde RFA, was killed in action on Monday, 26th June 1916, aged 39. Born on 20th December 1876, he was the younger son of Henry and Evelyn J Geard of 8, Ardwick Road, Hampstead; husband of May Victoria Geard. Educated at the City of London School and Dover College. He served with the Rand Rifles in the South African War and entered the Territorial Force as a 2nd Lt. in January 1909. His body was never recovered and his name is inscribed on the Thiepval Memorial, Pier and Face IA and 8A. [*Additional source:* Dick Flory: City of London School Magazine, December 1916; The History of the 53rd (London) Medium Brigade, Royal Artillery; Dover College Register, 1871 to 1924]

vii 1032 Gnr William Frederick Freeman, C Bty, 282nd Bde RFA, was killed in action on Monday, 26th June 1916, aged 22. He was the son of William Charles and Annie Freeman, of 105, Roding Rd., Clapton, London. His body was never recovered and his name is inscribed on the Thiepval Memorial, Pier and Face IA and 8A.
1627 Gnr Frederick Thomas Thompson, C Bty, 282nd Bde RFA, was killed in action on Monday, 26th June 1916, aged 20. He was the son of Thomas and Isabella Thompson, of 28, Dock Cottages, High St., Poplar, London. His body was never recovered and his name is inscribed on the Thiepval Memorial, Pier and Face IA and 8A.

viii Capt. Duncan Galloway Smith, 1/1st City of Edinburgh Field Coy, RE, was killed in action on Monday, 26th June 1916, aged 26. A Civil Engineer, he was the son of Harold Duke Smith of Ivy Cottage, Ivybridge, South Devon. He married Florence Ethel Smith on 21st August 1915 and their son, Kenneth Hay Duke Smith, was born on 5th April 1916. He was initially buried in St Amand cemetery but was re-buried in Couin British Cemetery, grave I.B.2.

were again lighter – 90% lighter - with just one man killed and ten wounded. But they were lucky, a 9.2 in. howitzer shell managed to penetrate one of the deep dug outs but, like so many, it failed to explode. And to make themselves feel luckier still, the regimental strength was increased by a draft of 165 men from the Field Recruit Depot.

Plate 18 Major Walter Leslie Geard, C Bty, 282ⁿᵈ Bde R.F.A. killed 26ᵗʰ June 1916

In all probability, the 3ʳᵈ Battalion of the 15ᵗʰ Reserve Infantry Regiment (who were to play an important part in the defence of the Gommecourt salient on 1ˢᵗ July) suffered more heavily behind the lines than the 55ᵗʰ R.I.R. did in the trenches. On the 24ᵗʰ June, the four companies of the battalion had been moved forward, the 10ᵗʰ and 11ᵗʰ Companies to Logeast Wood and the 9ᵗʰ and 12ᵗʰ Companies to Achiet le Grand. During the night of the 24ᵗʰ/25ᵗʰ June the battalion was ordered to move forward again to relieve the men of the Recruit Company of the 169ᵗʰ Infantry Regiment in the second position to the south of Puisieux. Later, as they were moving through the deserted town of Puisieux they were spotted by an observer in a BE2c of No. 8 Squadron, R.F.C. A Leutnant Ebeling reported:

"Day dawned [on the 26ᵗʰ June]. A British aviator cruised in circles above us. Three companies had already disappeared into Puisieux. Suddenly a signaller dashed out of a dugout and shouted: 'The village is about to be fired on!' Too late! Immediately afterwards a hail of heavy shells came down on the 10ᵗʰ, 11ᵗʰ and 12ᵗʰ Companies. Only the 9ᵗʰ was spared and that was because it was last on the march by a wide margin and had not yet arrived at the village. The pilot had informed his artillery about the battalion. His radio message had been intercepted by our signallers. Unfortunately it took some time to translate. In proportion to the huge weight of fire which came down the casualties were quite bearable."[10]

***

FOR THE ATTACKING BATTALIONS, W Day was the time for the final 'dress rehearsal' for the attack. At Halloy, sixteen kilometres to the west, the 169ᵗʰ Brigade went through their routines for the final time across the replica trenches that had been dug across the rich French farmland. General Allenby, Lt. General

Snow, Maj. General Hull and the three brigade commanders were there to watch as the men walked over from the 'British' trenches to occupy their German 'objectives' under cover of a perfect smoke screen. The Generals were utterly convinced of the value of these exercises and that, on the day, events would turn out in exactly this fashion. These were not inexperienced, untried men. Snow and Hull had both been successful, in very trying circumstances, during the aftermath of the first German gas attack at the Second Battle of Ypres at the end of April 1915. Hull, in particular, was regarded highly for the manner in which he had organised a disparate force, made up of units from six divisions, to launch a counter-attack at St Julien which had effectively stopped the German advance in its tracks. Snow had made his name at Le Cateau in August 1914 where he had commanded the 4th Division in its obdurate defence against Von Kluck's repeated assaults. Neither, however, had been involved at the only major *offensive* battle since Second Ypres, the Battle of Loos in September 1915.

So, in spite of the fact that they had no previous experience of a major preliminary artillery bombardment, their certainty in the effectiveness of the artillery preparations brooked no argument. This certainty, which was shared by senior officers the length of the front, was very much based on the success of the initial German bombardment at Verdun which had been much analysed by the Allies. Their conclusions called for a far greater concentration of firepower than had been available at Loos, however, on the British front in particular the imbalance between heavy howitzers and guns and field guns was to prove a major obstacle to the demolition of the German defences. But this was not yet appreciated and their message to the men was one of fulsome confidence in the ability of the artillery to flatten the trenches and strongpoints on the other side of No Man's Land.

L/Cpl. Sidney Appleyard of the Queen Victoria Rifles, whose battalion would go over in the first wave, heard their reassuring words:

"The smoke bombs were sent over just before the commencement and the attack was carried out quite satisfactorily and all the positions carried quite easily, but of course we had no opponents on this occasion. However we were informed by all Officers from the Colonel downwards that after our tremendous artillery bombardment there would be very few Germans left to show fight."[11]

Other private soldiers, however, tended towards a more jaundiced view. Rifleman Percy Jones of the Queen's Westminster Rifles was one such. His battalion was to go over in support of the London Rifle Brigade. and the Queen Victoria Rifles on Z Day and, on the 26th, he dutifully practised the attack with his mates under the watchful eye of the Generals and their staff:

"We parade in our "front line" and take "enemy trenches" several times a day. Excellent practice, could anything be simpler? It is a fine sight to see 4,000 men advancing as if on parade and capturing in half-an-hour a model of the enemy trenches at Gommecourt. The country chosen is quite different from that of Gommecourt Wood, and I honestly believe that the practical value of the manoeuvring is nil."[12]

Rifleman Jones was either a cynic or a realist depending on your view. As one who was to go 'over the top', he certainly harboured no illusions about his prospects and he swallowed the reassuring words of the senior commanders with a large sprinkling of salt:

"General Snow and his staff are busy telling us that we shall have practically no casualties because all the Germans will have been killed by our artillery barrage. There is nothing like the truth! The fact is that this attack is based entirely on the supposition that there will be no Germans left alive to oppose us, and that we shall suffer no casualties. On paper, the plans are A1, but if the Germans obstinately refuse to die and make way for us, our scheme will become impractical... Nearly all the boys have no faith in the carefully drawn up plans of attack and consolidation, but they are all determined to go on until something stops them."[13]

Their practice over, the Queen's Westminster Rifles packed up and began the ten kilometre march through Pas-en-Artois and Henu towards Souastre. There, they turned north along the narrow, winding road, up and over the low rise that separated Souastre from the shell-ravaged village of St Amand. Just before the village entrance, stood the forbidding, gothic mausoleum of the Famille Masclef. Obviously a dynasty of some power and influence in the area, now its solid doors and darkened windows only served to remind the marching men of their own mortality amidst the dangers and uncertainties to come. At St Amand, they were to await the final orders to advance. The men were soon billeted in the ruined houses and shops and equally soon became acquainted with the large and very noisy 12 in. howitzer of the 103rd Siege Battery that was hidden in a back garden. Every hour the surrounding buildings shook and rattled as the huge gun sent its shells in a high parabola over the 7,500 metres to their targets around Gommecourt.

Rifleman Jones' cynical view of the effectiveness of the British bombardment was born out by the level of German artillery activity:

"Our trenches were already subjected to heavy fire in the early hours of 26th June, with even heavier fire on the northern sector of 52. I.D. and particularly at Thiepval. The enemy barrage was reported to stretch from La Bassée to the Somme. At around 5 a.m. clouds of gas drifted into sectors X and G with continued artillery fire, and at 11.15 a.m. another stronger gas attack was launched from the enemy trenches in sectors 17, 18 and further south. Gruppe Süd, supported by Gruppe Nord, fired a blocking barrage in that direction, which was soon reduced to steady fire, since our infantry was in a full state of readiness to defend and there was no infantry attack. The regiment gave orders for Gruppe Nord to fire at the gas stores in Foncquevillers which were revealed by a prisoner; this was successful and strong white clouds of smoke rose. The retaliatory fire that soon hit Bucquoy was answered by Gruppe Nord, which fired at the enemy's rear-area quarters.

At around 4.30 p.m., the enemy fire grew to become very strong, and was answered with a steady barrage with the support of 111. I.D. When the enemy moved his fire forward, our own fire was increased. During the night, there was continuous firing on the rear-area lines and settlements, which made ammunition replenishment difficult, however, without causing any interruptions.

The 7th Battery (located at the eastern most point of Biez Wood) lost one Unteroffizier (killed), three men (wounded) and a gun."[i]

Later that evening, Maj. Ward-Jackson, the VII Corps staff officer earlier so impressed by the German efficiency and resolve, dined with the officers of 'B' Company of the London Scottish, amongst them the C.O., Major Francis Lindsay. Ward-Jackson would later write movingly of his reaction to the news of the fate of Lindsay and his men and in a letter to home, written on the 27th June, he described their differing views of the probable outcome of the battle to come:

"It was odd to see the different demeanours of the officers. Some consoled themselves that the Huns would do nothing to stop them at first and that another battalion would push past them when once they had got into the Boche trenches. Others thought they would be stopped by the barrage. Others said that they meant getting on and putting an end to the show."[14]

X Day, Tuesday, 27th June 1916
Third Army weather report: Warm & stormy. Rain: 1.3mm. Temp. 67-50° F

TUESDAY, 27TH JUNE was X Day in the schedule and it rained constantly. Maj. Ward-Jackson wrote that the front line trenches were now "simply rivers"[15] and Lt. Gen. Snow wrote: "Buckets of rain in the night and this morning. It really is vile weather"[16]. The 1/8th Middlesex War Diary described the trenches as 'waterlogged' and the problems of soldiers having to work up to their knees in cold water was now causing health problems. Many cases of 'bad feet' were reported in both of the Middlesex battalions. Pte. William Franklin recorded his unit's purgatory in the trenches in his diary:

"June 22nd to 26th

Thought that I was living in hell. The weather was awful, thunderstorms etc., and, owing to the amount of water in trenches most of us had swollen feet. Including trench feet cases our casualties were about 250. (Were) relieved by 4th London and go to Henu. Owing to the terrible condition of the men we were taken on ambulances."[17]

When, eventually, the 1/8th Middlesex were relieved by 1/4th Londons (168th Brigade) and were able to march out to their billets at Henu and Souastre they had lost 209 officers and men during the period from the 21st-27th June. Of these 119 were wounded (including 3 officers, with Lt. C A Wilkinson being wounded on the 27th), 27 were dead or missing believed dead and 63 had been evacuated sick, mostly suffering from trench foot. Nor did the severity of the German counter-bombardment let up. The enemy shelling of the W and WR lines was incessant and what was left of the trench parapet, after the previous days' shelling and the effects of the heavy rain, was blown in.

The 1/7th Middlesex, who still had another day in the trenches before they were relieved[ii], suffered another forty casualties: 3 officers wounded (2nd Lt. Weston, 2nd Lt. W A Whyman and 2nd Lt. Pidsley), 5 men killed and 31 wounded.

---

[i] Another battery, the 517th Foot Artillery Battery also based in Biez Wood was also hit several times on 26th June.
[ii] Although parts of the battalion were relieved in the front line trenches of the Y49 and Y50 sectors by 'D' Company, 1/3rd Londons.

Casualties amongst the 1/1st Londons were 16[i] (including an officer, 2nd Lt. E M Gibson), the 1/3rd Londons had ten men killed and the 1/4th Londons had one man killed and one officer and one man wounded. The ten casualties from the 1/3rd Londons lie next to one another in the military cemetery behind the farm building that hosted the Advanced Dressing Station on the road to Sailly. In addition, reports were sent in to the Divisional Adjutant of two more R.F.A. officer casualties - one dead[ii] and one wounded[iii] - and a further 8 other ranks killed and 19 wounded[iv]. The dead officer was Lt. John Ball of the 281st Brigade. Sent forward to operate as a Forward Observation Officer or F.O.O. his observation post (O.P) was hit and he was killed. O.P.s were a favourite target of the German gunners and much appreciated by their infantry as by disrupting the FOO's work the gunners reduced the efficiency of the British artillery. And, while the men in the British trenches suffered, by contrast the men of the 55th R.I.R. in the trenches opposite lost just one man killed and four wounded.

Plate 19 Lt. J J B Ball, 281st Brigade, R.F.A. killed 27th June 1916

---

[i] One officer wounded, three other ranks dead and one missing, nine other ranks wounded, two of whom died of wounds. A full list of casualties is given at the end of chapter.

[ii] Lt. John Joseph Barry Ball, 281st Brigade, RFA, was killed in action on Tuesday, 27th June 1916, aged 22. He was born on 6th August 1893, the only son of Dr and Mrs James Barry Ball, 12 Upper Wimpole Street. He was educated at Wimbledon College; St. Stanislaus College, Mons and University College, London, passing his Engineering Matrix in September 1912. He enrolled in the University of London OTC on 24th October 1912 and served for two years. He was commissioned into the 2nd County of London Brigade, RFA TF on 20th October 1914. He went to France on 2nd October 1915. He was killed by a shell whilst acting as a Forward Observation Officer. He is buried in Hebuterne Military Cemetery, grave IV.K.5. [*Assitional sources:* Dick Flory: University College London, University College Hospital and Medical School, A Record, 1914-1919, Vol. 1 Abbati to Lintott; University of London OTC Roll of War Service 1914-1919]

[iii] 2nd Lt. Richard Brenton Westmacott, 280th Brigade, RFA, was born on 20th May 1893, the son of Denham William Westmacott. He was educated at Sutton Valence School and at Magdalen College, Oxford, from 1911-1914, BA, 1914, MA, 1919. He served as a Lieutenant in the RGA and RFA and also with the Ministry of Munitions and from 1920-1922 was an Army Coach with Messrs. Carlyle & Gregson of 5, Lexham Gardens. He was Sub-Director of English School for Boys, Mexico City from 1922-1925 and then employed by City of Vancouver High School, Victoria, British Columbia from 1927 to 1958. [*Source:* Dick Flory: The Magdalen College Record, 1934; The Magdalen College Record, 1966]

[iv] From various units: 2 wounded from each of Z56 and V56 Trench Mortar Batteries, 1 wounded from 280th Brigade, RFA, 2 wounded from the Divisional Ammunition Column, 1 dead and 7 wounded from No 2 Coy, 5th Battalion, Special Brigade RE., six dead and seven wounded from the 1/3rd Londons and one dead and two wounded from the 5th Cheshires (one attached from 4th Cheshires). Four of the 1/3rd Londons men and one of the 1/5th Cheshires died of their wounds. A full list of casualties is given at the end of this chapter.

Conditions in the British trenches were now appalling. The rain was coming down in torrents, filling the trenches to thigh height in places. Many of the men were exhausted and not fit for action and wounded men were drowned in the trenches where they fell. The supply system to the front trenches had broken down because of the weather and the German shelling. There was no means of providing hot food or drink, and worst of all, for 3 days and nights the incessant shelling had made sleep all but impossible.

The 1/4th Londons, having relieved the 1/8th Middlesex, deployed their companies throughout the whole of the W Sector. The VII Corps artillery was pounding the trenches opposite them and, on the whole, German retaliation was light, however, at 7.45 p.m. a heavy salvo came crashing down on the W and WR lines, blowing in 'D' Company's H.Q. dugout. Capt. Eric Giles[i], an experienced company commander who had been with the battalion since the start of the war, was seriously wounded. He died nearly three week's later. Capt. H G Stanham, who had been selected to remain as one of the 'battle surplus' officers for the attack, was put in charge of Giles' men.

They would not have known it, but the men suffering in the trenches and slogging their way through the mud on what passed for roads would have been pleased to hear that they were not the only ones having to endure the filthy weather and the dangers of unsuspected artillery strafes. Behind the German lines, the men of the 15th Reserve Infantry Regiment were now spread out either side of Puisieux; the 3rd Battalion to the south west and the 2nd Battalion to the east. The men of the 3rd Battalion were stretched out across the second position between Puisieux and Serre. Their trenches too were full of water and the men, with the help of engineers from 104th Pioneer Regiment and the 1st Bavarian Pioneer Regiment, were given the task of clearing out the mud, wiring their positions and deepening and improving dugouts. Thirty men from 12th Company were given the dangerous task of constructing a new battery position for a section of the 19th Bavarian Field Artillery Regiment which had been suffering persistent shelling. But it was the men of the 2nd Battalion who suffered from the long distance shelling of rear areas that was a daily part of the bombardment programme. The 2nd Battalion had been moved forward from Achiet le Grand to Achiet le Petit on the 24th but the shelling soon proved sufficiently dangerous that the men were forced to move out of the village and into the surrounding fields. Before that, the 6th and 8th Companies lost between them one dead and four wounded but it was the 5th Company which was most heavily punished. At roll call, a shell ploughed into the waiting ranks and nine men were killed instantly and another twelve wounded. This was enough for the local commanders and the 6th and 7th Companies were told to march some distance up the Courcelles road to find suitable lodgings and the 5th and 8th Company withdrew to Achiet le Grand, the 8th occupying the somewhat macabre surroundings of the local cemetery. However, it had also been decided that the 6th and 8th Companies would later move forward to support the men of the 3rd Battalion and, in order to be in a position to control his forward troops in what they knew to be an

---

i Capt. Eric Giles, 1/4th London Regt (Royal Fusiliers), died of wounds received on 27th June on Sunday, 16th July 1916, aged 23. He was the second and oldest surviving son of Urban and Margaret Giles, Hillcrest, Arkley, Barnet. He was a graduate of Pembroke College, Cambridge. He is buried in Le Treport Military Cemetery, Seine-Maritime, France. grave Plot 2, Row 0, grave 11.

imminent attack, the C.O. of 15ᵗʰ R.I.R., Oberstleutnant Schwarz, moved into an old command post of the 66ᵗʰ Infantry Regiment on the south west edge of Puisieux on the Serre road.

***

AFTER THEIR REHEARSALS across the cornfields at Halloy the previous day, the rest of the assaulting battalions set off east to their pre-attack billets in the network of small villages five or six kilometres west of Gommecourt. The Queen Victoria's Rifles marched the ten kilometres to join the Queen's Westminster Rifles in St Amand. There they were to be billeted until the day before the attack. Morale was high amongst the men. The intensive and detailed training, the optimistic assessments of the higher ranks, the mass of artillery they marched past or saw in action every day had given the less experienced men a confidence and bravado not shared by the old stagers and soon lost in the murderous mire of the Somme.

'D' Company of the Q.V.R. had been selected as the battalion reserve and, for some, this was an outrageous slight on their capabilities:

> "It had to be pointed out to them that somebody had to be kept in reserve and that as a matter of fact theirs would be the worst job, as by the time their turn came the enemy's barrage would certainly be down, whereas the first line might get across No Man's Land in comparative safety. As a matter of fact when their time did come it was apparent that no man could get across and live. A number of officers and N.C.O.'s had to be left behind as "Battle Surplus". They were all much upset about it and begged that they might be allowed to go over."[18]

It was with spirits high that they swung down the country roads, past streams of horse and motorised transport moving supplies to the front. As they strode out, they raucously sang their favourite marching songs. The words of "Blighty Land" and "I want to go home", sung by a few hundred khaki-clad Londoners, couldn't compete with the roar of the artillery from around the villages to their front. But still, they sang the words with feeling:

When first I joined the Army not so very long ago,
I said "I'd fight the foe and help Sir Douglas Haig you know",
I've been in France just sixteen months, and fighting now as yet
I haven't seen a German, all I've seen is mud and wet.
Tomorrow when the officer asks, "What would you like to do?"
I'm going to stand right up and say "If it's all the same to you"

(Chorus)
I want to go 'ome, I want to go 'ome.
I don't want to go in the trenches no more,
Where the whizz-bangs an' shrapnel they whistle an' roar.
Take me over the sea,
Where the Alleyman can't get at me;
Oh, my! I'm too young to die! I want to go 'ome.
From measles I have suffered and had twelve attacks of flu,
And Meningitis too, but then no one ever knew.
The rain and mud has given me, the 'Meditus' of the spine,
I get it every time they ask me to go up the line.

I've got rheumatism of my hair, a dislocated face,
I think it's really, really time, that some one should take my place.
(Chorus)
I want to go 'ome, I want to go 'ome...

When the Q.V.R. joined their brigade colleagues in the battered village word soon got round that the following day they would march the short distance to Souastre. There they would store their packs, collect extra ammunition and bombs and prepare for the march to the front line. According to the plan, Z Day was to be Thursday, June 29ᵗʰ. And according to the plan, by now the German trenches would be flattened, the German artillery destroyed and the German infantry dead or disabled. There is no doubt that the Generals, the Colonels and many officers believed this. Somehow, the common soldier seemed better informed. The Queen's Westminster Rifles' Rifleman Jones' assessment of the situations is so accurate that one wonders why he was not on the Corps staff. Alternatively, we must ask the question: why were the Corps staff not as well briefed as this one shilling a day private soldier?

"As I have already mentioned we mostly hold the view that the plans have been based entirely on the supposition that our artillery barrage will have killed all the Germans within about three miles of Gommecourt. We know however, that the Germans have dugouts 40 feet deep, and I do not see how even the stiffest bombardment is going to kill them all off. Nor do I see how the whole of the enemy's artillery is going to be silenced."[19]

The L.R.B., on their arrival from Halloy, were due to be billeted in the woods near St Amand but the weather was so poor that they moved into Souastre to find shelter in any buildings left with walls and a roof. Their brigade colleagues, the 1/2ⁿᵈ Londons were also billeted in Souastre. In the afternoon, Capt. Handyside, C.O. of 'C' Company, paid out five francs each to the men for biscuits and chocolate and other 'necessities'. Pte. Clements, a member of 'C' Company, remembered Handyside as "rather eccentric - without fear but a bit womanish. He had a premonition that he would not see the end of the war." But, taking his five francs, he and his mates set off to enjoy the evening.

"During the evening Scho (Pte. Frank Schofield), Wright, Phipps and myself wandered down to St Amand, bought our chocolate and then got five bottles of white wine. Those were followed by champagne. By the time we got back to the billets we were all decidedly messy. In Souastre we found that the battalion had all decided to make a night of it - their last night in comparative peace. Everybody was singing and the noise continued until well after midnight."[20]

The London Scottish and the Rangers, with further to march to get to their assembly trenches on the far right of the line, were billeted in Bayencourt, three kilometres further forward than the 169ᵗʰ Brigade battalions. This they shared with the twelve 9.2 in. howitzers of the 93ʳᵈ, 94ᵗʰ and 95ᵗʰ Siege Batteries, R.G.A. Their relentless fire every five minutes or so made sleep either by day or night practically impossible. Furthermore, being that bit nearer the front meant being that bit nearer the German artillery and the Rangers immediately started suffering shrapnel casualties from the shells lobbed hopefully in their direction[i]. That night, as the rain still fell and the British artillery fired along their 'night lines', the 1/7th Middlesex sent out two patrols, one under Lt. Forbes and the other under Lt. Moxon, to see what effect the shelling was having on the German wire and trenches. Both patrols left from the top of New Woman Street (where the new front line crossed the Hebuterne to Bucquoy Road) to examine the wire on the trenches in front of Nameless Farm (Fetter and Fate trenches). The two patrols returned at half past midnight bringing with them samples of the wire. They had been unable, however, to find their way through the wire and into the German lines. But their presence had been detected. Just as the men returned and slipped back into the safety of the British lines, the Germans sent up a red flare followed by two more red flares. In response, the German artillery concentrated a fifteen minute barrage on the British W lines around Lone Tree just to the south of the Bucquoy Road.

Y Day, Wednesday, 28th June 1916
Third Army weather report: Warm, several heavy storms. Rain: 9.7mm. Temp. 64-47° F

Y DAY STARTED badly when, early on the morning of the 28th, four high explosive and one shrapnel shell straddled a howitzer close by the billets of 'B' Company, The Rangers. Cpl. Frank Goldsmith[ii], a popular N.C.O. in the company, was hit by shell fragments in the neck and back and killed instantly and four other men were wounded.

This unhappy incident was witnessed by Rifleman R J Mason:

"We were under occasional shellfire, but at breakfast time on this extra day's rest a heavy shell fell just outside our barn and inflicted quite a number of casualties. A corporal was killed and quite a few were wounded. Another chap fell into a well and could not be rescued owing to the absence of the right tackle for the job despite civilian aid."[21]

Nearby, Capt. Wightwick, OC 'B' Company, and 2nd Lt. Liveing[iii], OC No. 5 Platoon, had been inspecting the nose cone of a German shell which had struck the wall of their billet when they were advised of Goldsmith's death. Both officers went to attend to the wounded but Liveing was unable to look at the shattered body of an N.C.O. they had all come to value over the past ten months.

---

[i] The Rangers lost 1 killed and 12 wounded on the 27th and 28th June. A full list of casualties is given at the end of chapter.

[ii] 2322 Cpl Frank Walter Morgan Goldsmith, 'B' Coy, 1/12th London Regt. (Rangers), was killed on Wednesday, 28th June 1916 aged 21. He was the son of William Morgan Goldsmith and Ellen Ada Goldsmith of 79, Hampton Rd., Forest Gate, London and lived in Hastings, Sussex. He is buried in St. Amand British Cemetery, Pas de Calais, France, grave I. B. 14.

[iii] 2nd Lt. Edward George Downing Liveing, 1/12th London Regt. (The Rangers) was born on 24th March 1895, the third of four children of Henry George Downing and Margaret Liveing. He was educated at Bradfield and St. John's College, Oxford. After recovering from his wounds he went to Palestine and then to Egypt where was appointed the Assistant to the Military Censor 1918-19. He wrote an account of Gommecourt, *Attack on the Somme. An Infantry Subaltern's Impressions of July 1st 1916* which was published by Heinemann in 1918. After the war, he worked for the BBC between 1924 and 1937, and again during the Second World War. He was the first Middle East director of the BBC and established an office in Cairo in 1943. After the war he wrote several commercial histories, e.g. 'Adventure in Publishing', a history of the Ward Lock publishing house, and was a contributor to Blackwood's magazine and The Fortnightly Review. He married Gladys Constance Baker in 1923 and she pre-deceased him, dying in 1959. He died on 31st January 1963. His grandfather, Edward Liveing, was the Registrar of the Royal College of Physicians until 1909 and was famous for a text on Megrim (Migraines) as well as being a noted Victorian physician. [*Sources* various including Matthew J Brosnan, 'The Tactical Development of the 56th (London) Division on the Western Front 1916-18']

On Wednesday, 28ᵗʰ June, it rained yet again, enough for the decision to be taken to postpone the whole offensive for 48 hours. For several hours in the morning the rain was heavy (10 mm fell), making life and work in the trenches increasingly treacherous. The temperature also dropped to an unseasonable 64 degrees and, as the clouds did not lift all day, the men, wet through by lunchtime, had to spend another day working in cold clothes made heavy by rain and the clinging mud. No sun warmed their backs or helped to dry them out.

Before the news came through of the postponement, the attacking battalions readied themselves for the coming fight and some C.O.s took the opportunity to give their men a talk about what was to happen. Lt. Col. Attenborough of the 1/2ⁿᵈ Londons took an interesting tack in his pre-battle speech, as Pte Clements latre recalled:

> "Spent the morning cleaning up the billet and getting our fighting order ready. In the afternoon we stored our packs in an old barn and then paraded for the inspection by the colonel who made us a speech. He said he wouldn't talk bosh about patriotism. Probably we were a bit fed up with England and her petty quarrels, strikes, etc. We were all fed up with the war and wanted to get it over and the only way is to beat the Boche properly. He knew we would do our job properly, etc. Marching back to the billet we heard that the attack had been postponed for forty eight hours and soon we were all excitedly speculating what had happened. We were all more or less disappointed as it means two day's more waiting. We drew our packs again and went up to Hebuterne to relieve the 7ᵗʰ Middlesex who had been badly knocked by the bombardment. Each morning they have sent over smoke bombs which have made the Germans think they were attacking. They have lost over 300. B and D Companies went into the line but we were in support in the village. The gun section got a house and Phipps, Scho, Webb, Milne and I got a cellar, quite clean and dry. It was quite impossible to sleep as our guns kept up the bombardment and the din certainly is the limit."[22]

For the lucky 1/8ᵗʰ Middlesex it was a rest day, safe in their billets four and five kilometres behind the front line. For the 1/7ᵗʰ Middlesex it was their day for relief from the purgatory of the trenches. The physical condition of the battalion's men was serious. Since the 24ᵗʰ, they had been soaked to the skin, and standing continuously knee-deep and sometimes thigh deep in water. Their C.O., Col. King[i], had reported to Brigade H.Q. that his men were exhausted and no longer fit for action and that a complete rest of at least 24 hours was essential. That night they were relieved by 'B' Company of the 1/2ⁿᵈ Londons[ii] (169ᵗʰ Brigade) and the battalion was ordered back to the billets at Souastre, a march of some three kilometres. Afterwards, Col. King wrote of his men:

> "So utterly exhausted were the men that large numbers of them collapsed as they came out of the trenches, and had to be carried back in wagons, which the division had sent forward in anticipation of their condition."[23]

---

i Lt. Col. Edwin James King, C.M.G., 1/7ᵗʰ Middlesex Regt. was a pre-war Territorial and CO of the battalion from the beginning of the war until November 1916 and again from February to May 1917, twice being sent home sick. Knighted after the war he wrote the history of the battalion.

ii 'B' Company, 1/2ⁿᵈ Londons took over Y47/48 sectors from the 1/7ᵗʰ Middlesex. 'A' and 'C' Companies were billeted in Hebuterne and 'D' Company relieved the 1/3ʳᵈ Londons in Y49/50 sectors.

In these five days, the 1/7th Middlesex had lost 148 men: 16 killed (including 1 officer), 84 wounded (including 4 officers) and 48 sent to hospital sick. 'A' Company - the Hampstead and Highgate men (O/C Lt. W G Woodroffe[i]) - had suffered the most severely, having 47 men killed or wounded. It had been holding the worst part of the line and, of the men who were left, 75 were quite unable to walk. During this trial by fire and water, a Private J H Ward[ii] especially distinguished himself. Ward was a stretcher-bearer and, during the battalion's time in the line, he had carried out no less than 30 wounded men of different units, in most cases under heavy shellfire, and in all cases through thick mud and deep, cold water.

Plate 20 Lt. Col. E J King, 1/7th Middlesex Regt

Conditions did not improve for the battalions that took their place. During the afternoon, as came the rain, so came the German counter-bombardment. At 3.45 p.m. the Germans placed a heavy barrage on the WR line and Hebuterne. An area on the northern edge of Hebuterne about the Woman Trench/Cross Street junction came in for particular attention. The Germans were looking for a half battery of 18 pdr field guns (C/283 Battery R.F.A.) that had been hidden in the trees on the edge of the village. It had been positioned so as to fire at nearly point blank range flat into the German lines and they were causing considerable damage to German trenches and wire around the south east corner of Gommecourt Park and the Maze (they were never located). In addition, German machine guns 'searched' the British front lines hoping to disrupt working parties and cause casualties amongst the unwary. The 1/4th Londons can, perhaps, count themselves as lucky. Throughout this onslaught, they lost only 2 men

i Subsequently promoted, Capt. Walter Gordon Woodroffe (Croix de Guerre with Palm, France), 1/7th Middlesex Regt., died on Saturday, 16th September 1916 after his battalion was engaged in an attack on Bouleaux Wood. He was 22. The son of Walter Henry and Mildred M. Woodroffe of 5, Bedford Row, High Holborn, London he is buried in Bronfay Farm Military Cemetery, Bray-Sur-Somme, Somme, France, grave: II. D.4.

ii Pte Ward is described as "one of the bravest men who ever served in the 1/7th Middlesex". He gained a bar to his Military Medal, and also the Distinguished Conduct Medal, and finally died of wounds only 6 days before the Armistice. 200186 Corporal J H Ward DCM, M.M, 1/7th Middlesex Regt., died on Tuesday, 5th November 1918. He is buried in Sebourg British Cemetery, Nord, France, grave B. 10.

killed[i] and 2 officers[ii] and 11 other ranks wounded. The 1/1st Londons and 1/3rd Londons were equally fortunate, suffering just 4 casualties and 11 respectively. Reported casualties for the day were: 2 officers wounded, 4 other ranks killed, 1 other rank missing and 50 other ranks wounded. Under the supposedly devastating British bombardment the 55th R.I.R. had just eight men wounded.

Meanwhile, other German artillery was pounding the north end of W47 at its junction with Welcome Street. They were after the six Stokes trench mortars located here which were being used to wear away at the wire and trenches of the Farmyard strongpoint, a key point of attack for the London Scottish. On the 56th Division front, wherever the Stokes mortars were located, there followed heavy German retaliation. Indeed, on the Y lines of the 169th Brigade front, the post-battle report states:

"Advanced dumps of S.A.A., grenades, water and rations were provided in this 'boyau' (a service trench), but they were not a success, as in every case they were buried by shell fire before the opportunity to use them arose. This was partly due to Stokes mortars having fired a great number of rounds from our front trenches; this drew a very heavy retaliatory fire from the enemy's artillery."[24]

As the battalions in the front lines shivered and soaked, the assaulting troops were making ready for the attack they still thought to be due the following morning. The battalions of the 169th Brigade marched into Souastre to dump their packs in several large barns in the village. In return, they collected two extra ammunition bandoliers and three bombs. They then returned the short distance to St Amand, some to have a hot meal. For the Queen's Westminster Rifles it was bully beef and potatoes. Other battalions, though, complained of short rations. L/Cpl. Sidney Appleyard of the Queen Victoria's Rifles was bitter in his condemnation:

"Our rations were also very poor and the bread issued of one loaf per platoon (about 24 men), which was really disgraceful seeing that the next few days would in all probability find us existing on our emergency rations and one usually expects a fattening before the killing."[25]

Private Arthur Hubbard of the London Scottish was having, to his mind, a particularly bad time of it:

"I have to go over with the first batch and assist in cutting the barbed wire which hasn't been destroyed by our artillery during the past few days heavy bombardment. We have spent a most miserable time during our supposed

---

[i] 1982 Pte Willie Smith Hick, 1/4th London Regt (Royal Fusiliers), died on 28th June 1916. His body was never found and his name is inscribed on the Thiepval Memorial, Pier and Face 9 D and 16 B

4291 Pte Thomas Charles Weller, 1/4th London Regt (Royal Fusiliers), died on 28th June 1916. Aged 17, he was the son of Mr. J. C. and Mrs. L. S. Weller of 65, Cleves Rd., East Ham, London. Born at Bethnal Green, London. He is buried in Hebuterne Military Cemetery, grave III. A. 3.

[ii] Lt. W A Stark and 2nd Lt. J W Price. Price had joined the battalion from the 2/4th London Regt. on 7th May 1916 and Stark joined from the same battalion on the 14th May.

Lt. William Atkins Stark, 1/4th London Regt. (Royal Fusiliers) was born on 9th January 1896 and lived at 29, Downs Park Road, Hackney. He was educated at the Central Foundation School, Cowper Street, Islington and worked as a bank clerk. He was commissioned in September 1914 into the 2/4th London Regt. and went to Malta, Egypt and Gallipoli. He returned from Egypt on 23rd April 1916. He was knocked unconscious by a shell explosion and partially buried. He was evacuated to England suffering from shell shock on 17th July on the recommendation of a Medical Board held at Harfleur. He returned to France with the 2/4th London Regt., 58th Division, and was wounded by a gun shot wound to the knee on 20th September 1917 and again evacuated to England.

rest. Last Saturday and Sunday night we were standing up all night owing to the heavy downfall of rain and everyone has got drenched through to our skins. It is a wonder that none of us are suffering from severe colds and so on and then they expect you to do your very best on the top of it and short rations as well."[26]

Whilst most men waited for the orders to move forward, others, for example the battalion bombers, were working hard to be ready for the off. Grenades needed to be fused - a tricky and potentially dangerous task in the dry – but doing this work in the pouring rain added to the risk. The process was this: the base plate of the Mills grenade was unscrewed and set to one side; the grenade pin was checked and oiled; the detonator was then put gently into its small hole and the base plate screwed back into place. It was not unknown for grenades to go off without warning and the arming of bombs was usually conducted well away from the main body of the men. But, however carefully done, accidents happened and, on the 27th, the L.R.B. fell victim to such an occurrence. The bombs having been armed, a carrying party was sent off towards Hebuterne to have them ready to be collected on the eve of the attack. For whatever reason, two of the grenades were unstable and exploded amongst the men without warning. One man was killed instantly[i] and nine others wounded. They were the L.R.B.'s first casualties for a week and the accident seemed an ill omen to the colleagues of the dead and wounded.

Soon after, word came through that the attack had been postponed for two days. The weather had done its worst. The battalions retraced their steps to Souastre to retrieve their packs. The rest of the day was spent mulling over the reasons for the delay, in half-hearted rifle inspections and, for the curious, in watching the gun team load and fire the monster railway-mounted howitzer that lurked in that French back garden. For the men, the delay was a something of a relief. Lt. Col. Shoolbred of the Queen's Westminsters wrote after the war:

"To our brigade, at any rate, this postponement was a god-send. The men were quite worn out, and they mostly slept solid for the two days in billets in St Amand."[27]

Another Commanding Officer had other things to worry about. During the day, Maj., now Temp. Lt. Col., W H W Young[ii] arrived at the H.Q. of the Kensingtons with orders to take command with immediate effect. Both Young and his predecessor, Lt. Col. H Stafford, were more than a bit perplexed by the timing of the change over, indeed Stafford was apparently unaware that he was due to be replaced. Whilst Young started to get to grips with a battalion, which, but for the weather, would have gone into action the following day, Stafford set off for 168th Brigade's H.Q. with the intention of finding out the reason for his sudden replacement. No explanation for this decision has been found but it seems possible that 168th Brigade's G.O.C., Brig. Gen. Loch, may have had a hand in affairs. Suffice to say that Lt. Col. Young did not last long either, being replaced in October. This was not the end of the changes in command of the

---

[i] 2474 Rfn Ralph Richard Benton Coe, 1/5th London Regt (London Rifle Brigade), died on Wednesday, 28th June 1916, aged 18. He was the son of William Coe of 50, Swan St., Borough, London. He is buried in Hebuterne Military Cemetery, grave IV.D.6.
[ii] Lt. Col. W H W Young, 1/13th London Regt. (Kensingtons) commanded the battalion from 27th June 1916 to 26th October 1916. He had previously been an officer in the 7th Leicestershire Regt.

Kensingtons which had no less than nine different C.O.s between June 1916 and the end of the war.

As night drew in it was the turn of the 1/4th Londons to send patrols out into No Man's Land. At about 11 p.m., one patrol set out across one of the widest parts of this desolate territory. Slipping out of a sap at the head of Welcome Street, they headed across 400 metres of shell-pocked grassland towards the southern corner of the Farmyard strongpoint. Thirty minutes later they found a large German working party at the junction of Farmyard and Farm trenches. They were busily repairing the heavily damaged trenches and wire that were the special targets of the super-heavy howitzers of the VII Corps artillery. The working party was too large to challenge and the patrol moved away on other business. Forty minutes later, at ten past midnight, another patrol approached the same trench junction. The officer in charge was a 2nd Lt. W H Webster[i]. Slowly and quietly he peered over parapet and discovered the same working party similarly engaged. This time, however, his patrol was challenged. Immediately, the night sky was bright with flares as the Germans sent warnings to its artillery and machine guns. As they burst into action, Lt. Webster and his patrol decided discretion was the better part of valour and they retired across No Man's Land taking advantage of the many shell holes for cover.

Further to the north, on the front to be attacked by the Rangers on Z Day, two more patrols were sent out from New Woman Street to examine the German trenches and wire. As before, the message came back that here, even after five days heavy bombardment by the Corps and Divisional artillery, the wire was not completely cut. This information makes it all the more extraordinary that the 56th Division War Diary recorded on the 28th June:

> "Wire reported satisfactorily dealt with in first and second German lines. In third line gaps have been cut but require widening... number of guns employed by (Germans) did not appear to be large."

So, not only were British intelligence apparently believing what they wanted to believe about the state of the German wire they were also being fooled by the tactic of concealing the true strength of the artillery ranged against them in the woods and hollows behind the German lines.

Y1 Day, Thursday, 29th June 1916
Third Army weather report: Stormy. Rain: 0.7mm. Temp. 65-52º F

Y1 DAY, THURSDAY, 29TH JUNE, was the first 'extension' day of the bombardment and a better day than most. There was some light drizzle but nothing like the downpours of previous days. It was not sunny, the constant overcast saw to that, and the temperature stayed stubbornly in the mid-sixties, well below the normal average for a June day in Picardy.

---

[i] 2nd Lt. Walter Henry Webster, D.S.O., 1/4th London Regt. (Royal Fusiliers) was aged 20 and lived at Devonshire House, Devonshire Road, Harrow on the Hill. He attested Private in the 25th Cyclist Battalion, London Regt., on 29th August 1914 and was commissioned into the 4/4th Londons on 26th November 1915. 2nd Lt. Webster was awarded the D.S.O. as a result of an act of extraordinary courage in mid-January 1917 whilst the 1/4th Londons were in the line near Laventie. A medium trench mortar shell landed on the edge of a trench full of men and would have caused severe casualties had not 2nd Lt. Webster grabbed the shell and thrown it into a nearby crater where it immediately exploded. He was killed on the night of the 9th/10th February 1917 near La Bassee during a German trench raid in which he had been taken prisoner. He was buried in Rue-Petillon Military Cemetery, Fleurbaix, grave I. J. 14.

For the two Middlesex battalions it was a day of much needed rest. In their billets at Henu and Souastre they could, at least, get dry, keep warm and eat. Sleeping could have been another matter, however, for Souastre was the home of the two huge 15 in. R.M.A. howitzers and the two Mk VII 6 in. guns of the 50ᵗʰ Siege Battery. For reasons explained elsewhere, however, the 15 in. howitzers fired infrequently on both Y1 and Y2 days and the Mk VIIs fired hardly at all. So, the exhausted men would have been able to sleep soundly between the occasional sudden roar and heavy vibration that followed the howitzers' firing.

For the attacking battalions, Y1 Day was an anti-climax, but few complained. Instead of the 'Big Push' with its anticipated confusion, chaos and casualties, the morning was spent in last minute bayonet and bombing practice. In the afternoon, the men were left more to their own devices. The Queen Victoria's Rifles organised a cricket match in St Amand. There were few interruptions to play caused by the firing of the garden howitzer. Only ten of its huge shells were sent over on Y1 Day. The gun team was, no doubt, grateful for the much-needed relief to aching muscles and deafened eardrums. Few of them, though, gave thought to the relief given to the German defenders of Gommecourt or to the opportunities they now had to creep out of their bunkers to repair blown-in parapets and replace damaged wire.

For the 1/4ᵗʰ Londons on the right of the front line it seemed as though it would be a quieter day all round. In the early hours, German machine guns from the Sunken Road had raked their trenches from time to time, keeping the occupants on their toes. But, as Y1 was an 'extra' day not planned for in the bombardment programme, the British barrage was reduced by the need to conserve ammunition. Seemingly in response, there was also less German shelling during the day. They still sought out the well-concealed field battery in the trees near the Woman and Cross Street junction, however, and between 6.30 and 7.30 in the morning they bombarded the lines and communication trenches of the W sector. Twelve hours later their shelling resumed and the day ran down with an irregular exchange of fire. The 'quiet' day ended with 28 men of the 1/4ᵗʰ needing attention for wounds, though none proved fatal.

On the left of the line, opposite Gommecourt Park, the 1/3ʳᵈ and 1/1ˢᵗ Londons had another busy day. They were lucky too when it came to casualties. Shrapnel caught a working party at Sailly but only 4 men from the 1/3ʳᵈ were wounded and, for the 1/1ˢᵗ, the day ended with only 3 men needing attention from the M.O.

But again, London casualties heavily outweighed those of their enemy. The 55ᵗʰ R.I.R. occupying Gommecourt village, the Kern Redoubt and Gommecourt Park, some of the most heavily bombarded areas of the front, again appreciated the work put into their deep dugouts. Only four men were wounded during the day. Total London casualties were, as usual, significantly greater: 1 officer wounded[i], 4 other ranks killed, 2 other ranks missing and 58 other ranks wounded.

As darkness fell, another night patrol was sent out from the W50 trenches opposite Nameless Farm to examine the wire running north from the Bucquoy Road. As with previous patrols, this one again reported that the wire on this part

---

i 2ⁿᵈ Lt. V S Davies, 1/5ᵗʰ Cheshire Regt attached V56 Trench Mortar Battery.

of the Rangers' front was insufficiently cut. There were gaps but they were narrow and, to get through, the men would have to bunch and slow down presenting perfect targets for well-placed machine guns. As the men crept back through the gaps in the British wire, the Germans opened up a midnight barrage as a reminder of their presence and to show that little went unnoticed on this front.

Another trench raid was planned for the night of the 29th June. This one was to be conducted by men of the 167th Brigade on the far left of the 56th Division's front. At 9.15 p.m. a party of twenty men led by 2nd Lt. P R Henri, 1/3rd Londons, rendezvoused at the H.Q. of 'D' Company in the Keep at the north end of Hebuterne village. Six of the men were equipped with rifles and bayonets and the rest with bayonets, bludgeons and twenty bombs per man. To help identify themselves in the dark they had white arm badges on each arm. Soon they were moving up Yellow Street communication trench, crossing the old front line, before entering a sap dug out into No Man's Land at 10.45 p.m., a journey of about 1,000 metres.

Their objective was the German line at the junction of Fir and Firm trenches – Point 94 as it was known because of its map co-ordinates. Here the German trenches turned away from the British lines at a near right angle at the south east corner of Gommecourt Park and continued to fringe the Park until it met the Hebuterne to Gommecourt Road where they struck out, over open countryside, SE towards the Sunken Road some 2,000 metres away. No Man's Land here was 300 metres wide and, to reach their target, they were forced to crawl and creep across the battered landscape, through heaped-up coils of German wire, towards a re-entrant whose two faces were both thought to contain one or more machine gun posts. The patrol was fortunate - it was the Germans who were caught unawares. A working party was out amongst the wire and repairing the trenches. Lt. Henri's patrol were soon amongst them, dropping bombs into the trench and using their bayonets and bludgeons as if in some savage medieval battle. Within minutes it was all over, the working party was put to flight and, as ordered, a prisoner was bundled at bayonet point back across to the British lines. The patrol suffered four casualties and was safely back in their trenches by midnight.

The prisoner turned out to be from the II/55th Regiment of the 2nd Guard Reserve Division and its 8th Company held the line at the point of the raid and the frightened and dishevelled captive was soon describing to Divisional intelligence officers the conditions of the German defenders. His words would have brought great comfort to the commanders and staff of the attacking units. It presented an image of a battalion under great stress and, possibly, close to collapse after the huge bombardment it had endured. A 56th Division report quotes from his interview as follows:

"The morale of the regiment is very low. Officers have been drinking heavily since the bombardment began and one officer was killed through exposing himself when drunk. The prisoner complained of the quantity and quality of food. They rarely got meat."[28]

His words would have borne out the view commonly held from Army commander down to the battalion colonels. Little could survive the British bombardment. Those who lived through it would be in no fit state to defend themselves. The assault would be a walk over.

At the same time, little notice was taken of a second raid that night. It failed. The German wire was not cut.

Y2 Day, Friday, 30th June 1916
Third Army weather report: Cool & windy. Rain: 0mm. Temp. 69-41° F

FRIDAY, 30TH JUNE was Y2 Day, the second extension day of the bombardment and, for the first time in five days, it did not rain. A gusty 40 mph westerly wind helped in a small way to dry out the sodden landscape but did not help with the accuracy of the heavy artillery although, again, it was muted compared to the previous days' frantic activity. At 7.00 a.m. the Germans shelled the 1/4th Londons in W sector heavily. In the afternoon they lengthened their range, dropping shells on to the WR lines and again they sought out the elusive battery near the Woman Street and Cross Street junction. And, to keep the Tommies' heads down, German machine guns played along the parapet at random intervals. Casualties amongst the Fusiliers were moderate, two men were killed[i] and another 21 wounded, however, one of the men wounded the night before died of wounds at the Main Dressing Station at Couin[ii].

On the left, 'A' and 'B' Companies of the 1/3rd Londons moved up to Hebuterne from Sailly-au-Bois and occupied the Y48 and Y49 reserve lines. At the same time, command of the battalion changed hands with Major F D Samuel[iii] taking over as C.O. from Lt. Col. A E Maitland. The 1/1st Londons carried on with last minute preparations, suffering four casualties for their pains.

For the 1/7th Middlesex, their quiet time was soon over. They had the task of being the most advanced portion of the reserve and were to assemble in the group of trenches at the north end of Hebuterne known as 'The Keep'. And so, after a mere day's rest at Souastre, the 7th Middlesex moved forward again at midnight, arriving at the trenches west of 'The Keep' at 2 p.m. on June 30th. For the 1/8th Middlesex life was somewhat easier - back at Henu, they faced only an inspection.

On the other side of No Man's Land there was still frantic activity going on behind the lines. The men of the 15th R.I.R. were still hard at it around Puisieux. The new regimental command post at the south-west corner of the town still needed proper communications back to 52nd Division's H.Q. at Bihucourt. Several kilometres of telephone cable were being laid and 5th and 7th Companies were given the job of digging a trench for the cable. They were assisted in this task by a reinforced Signals platoon from 9th Company who also had to be continuously available to repair any breaks in the cable caused by the artillery fire that was reaching deep behind German lines. All the while, detachments of the 12th Company were again helping the 19th F.A.R to build and repair some of the many battery positions lurking in the woods and valleys of the countryside

---

i 1385 L/Cpl George Frederick Skipp, 1/4th London Regt. (Royal Fusiliers), died on 30th June 1916. He is buried in Hebuterne Military Cemetery, grave IV. B. 8
2872 Pte George Windle, 1/4th London Regt. (Royal Fusiliers), died on 30th June 1916. He is buried in Hebuterne Military Cemetery, grave IV. M. 18
ii 4329 Pte Frederick William Crawley, 1/4th London Regt. (Royal Fusiliers), died of wounds on 30th June 1916. Aged 21 he was the son of John William and Florence Crawley of Stoke Newington. He is buried in Couin British Cemetery, grave I. B. 18.
iii Maj., later Lt. Col., F D Samuel, D.S.O., T.D., 1/3rd London Regt. (Royal Fusiliers) was a pre-war Territorial and commanded the battalion from June to September 1916, being wounded near Combles on 12th September, and from March 1917 to March 1918. When the 1/3rd and 2/3rd Londons were merged in January 1918 he left to command the 40th Royal Fusiliers in Palestine.

around Puisieux. Huge efforts were made to bring up ammunition and bombs and the transport teams were constantly bringing up wagon loads of material for distribution to the troops. 3,500 hand grenades were brought up the 3rd Battalion's positions and ammunition dumps and other supplies were positioned in easy reach to enable well-armed counter-attacks to be mounted in whatever direction proved necessary. Casualties amongst the men were regular but were insufficient to significantly upset progress. Getting supplies through to the men in the front lines might be proving problematical but, less than a mile behind these battered positions, battalion after battalion were preparing for the attack and were in confident mood.

***

FOR THE ATTACKING BATTALIONS of the 169th Brigade the time had come to march back to Souastre, to dump their packs as before and to collect their extra SAA and bombs. There was then nothing to do but wait. They would not move out until the middle of the evening and so the time was spent in composing letters home, seeking out friends and in spending their last few francs in Souastre's estaminet. Small groups gathered to chat, drink champagne and weak beer and sing favourite songs. Percy Jones' diary paints a poignant picture of the last night he and his mates in the Queen's Westminster Rifles would share together:

> "We met in the little cafe last night and sang the old songs, perhaps for the last time. Everyone turned up.. We are good friends, true friends, because the trials of trench life have made us know one another, because we have held money, food, shelter and clothing in common and shared all that we have had. We hope to meet again in a day or two, but it is quite certain that in the meantime, some of us will have "gone west". You cannot have an omelette without breaking eggs, and we shall not take Gommecourt Wood without losing lives. Who will go? Who can say? I have only one wish - that nothing happen to Billy Green[i]. He is only eighteen, he is always cheerful, he can always make others cheerful, and that is the sort of man we want in the trenches."[29]

Nearby, Rifleman Arthur Schuman and his friends in the London Rifle Brigade waited for orders to move forward. One of his mates made a gloomy but sadly accurate prognostication:

> "The day before, somewhere behind the line, billeted in an empty room of a partly wrecked, derelict building were seven or eight of us. One of the boys named Slaughter (nicknamed 'Bessie' after a well-known actress of that time) said, "Well boys, this time tomorrow we'll be pushing up daisies" - how right he was. I never saw any of that lot again."[30]

Another Rifleman was preparing himself in a rather more practical manner. Rfn. Henry Russell had already equipped himself with a phial of morphine tablets he had 'liberated' from the body of a Medical Officer who he had helped bury. Now he bought a large bottle of Worcester Sauce which was immediately

---

[i] 3935 Rfn Billy Green, 1/16th London Regt (Queen's Westminster Rifles), was killed in action on July 1st 1916, aged 18. His body was never found. His name is inscribed on the Thiepval Memorial, Pier 13, Face C. Only one of Percy Jones's 7th Platoon came back uninjured.

emptied, washed out and filled with rum. Perhaps he had heard that the usual rum ration, doled out from large earthenware jars just before the men went 'over the top', was to be substituted with a rather less invigorating pea soup.

All the while, back in Hebuterne, men of the 1/2ⁿᵈ Londons were waiting for the lead battalions of the 169ᵗʰ Brigade to arrive and take up position in the assembly trenches. Then they would follow on ready to fulfil their role as Brigade reserve. Pte Clements and the rest of his Lewis gun team had spent the day carrying trench bridges and ladders up to the front and, at 6 p.m., had stored their packs in a cellar in 'The Keep' at the west end of Hebuterne. Now they waited and worried about the day to come:

> "Everything is now ready: Lewis gun and ammunition, rifles, bayonets all thoroughly clean. Each man has been given a barbed wire cutter and sandbags to carry. The men who go over have also spades stuck in the back of their equipment and five or six bombs each. We have the gun's spare parts and ammunition. All night we sat in the cellar, sometimes singing to keep cheerful and other times taking each other's home address, reading letters and looking at photos and other little things. Sleep was impossible owing to the terrific din. We were all anxious for none of us wanted to 'go west' and all expect to have the wind up but we are afraid of being afraid. This was the worst part. Every few minutes seemed an hour. All thinking of the past, what was the future to bring – death or Blighty?"³¹

Somewhere else in Hebuterne confusion reigned in the 167ᵗʰ Trench Mortar Battery. Its commander, Capt. Oliver, was already in trouble. A week earlier he'd had the temerity to express his reservations about the relatively new Stokes mortars to the Brigade Major of 169ᵗʰ Brigade. This officer was less than impressed by Oliver's views telling him, in no uncertain terms: "I don't give a blast for your opinion." At 7.30 p.m. on the 30ᵗʰ, Oliver's life took another turn for the worse. He received orders that his battery was to be split amongst the two attacking brigades, No 1 Section was to be attached to 169ᵗʰ Brigade and No. 2 Section to the 168ᵗʰ Brigade. Capt. Oliver now set out to find Capt. Coote of the 169ᵗʰ Trench Mortar Battery to make arrangements for the following day. By the time he met him, at 11.30 p.m., it was clearly impossible for the 167ᵗʰ TMB to prepare emplacements and get forward the necessary ammunition. As a result, Capt. Coote decided that 167ᵗʰ Brigade Trench Mortar Battery should not fire in the final bombardment, meaning there would be three less Stokes mortars firing on the brigade front at Zero hour on Z Day. It was a disgruntled Capt. Oliver who shared Coote's billet in Hebuterne that night.

Whilst Capt. Oliver was in Hebuterne trying to clarify his orders, three kilometres away the London Scottish and the Rangers were moving out of Souastre en route to the front line via 'Blue Track'. Having passed through Bayencourt, The Rangers were about a quarter of the way to Sailly-au-Bois when orders came to let the London Scottish pass through. The evening was now quiet, the guns at rest temporarily. The men lit pipes and cigarettes and joked with the grey-kilted men on the march. Amongst the resting soldiers lay 2ⁿᵈ Lt. Edward Liveing, C.O. of No. 5 Platoon of 'B' Company, The Rangers. As they waited, he found himself reciting the words of a prayer first spoken by Sir Jacob Astley, a Royalist cavalry officer, before the Battle of Newbury in 1643:

"Lord, I shall be very busy this day. I may forget Thee, but do not Thou forget me."[32]

His father had written the prayer on a card he had sent to Liveing in his last letter from home. Now he repeated it to himself over and over, like a protective mantra. His men were similarly reflective as they waited their turn to move forward to the battle zone:

"My men were rather quiet. Perhaps the general calmness was affecting them with kindred thoughts, though an Englishman never shows them. On the left stood the stumpy spire of Bayencourt Church just left by us. On the right lay Sailly-au-Bois in its girdle of trees. Alongside the valley which ran out from behind Sailly-au-Bois, arose numerous lazy pillars of smoke from the wood fires and kitchens of an artillery encampment. An English aeroplane, with a swarm of black puffs around it betokening German shells, was gleaming in the setting sun. It purred monotonously, almost drowning the screech of occasional shells which were dropping by a distant Chateau. The calm before the storm sat brooding over everything."[33]

For the men, laden with extra equipment, the tension was beginning to build. The thunder of the guns did nothing to calm their nerves:

"All around us were guns blazing away day and night which was not very restful to the nerves. But we were what is usually referred to as "fresh troops". That expression could only apply to the time of leaving the billets for every man was so cluttered up with battle equipment when moving forward that exhaustion soon struck home. Everyone was festooned with extra bombs, rifle ammunition, wirecutters, sandbags, rations and all sorts of "going away to stay" necessities. Conversation, to say the least, was not very elevating and neither was it all in King's English. There was also the anticipation that many might not see tomorrow's evening; to be cut off from the thoughts of the future does not make one talkative when only the immediate present is one's concern.

Each man had his set task in the platoon section and knew the exact part to be carried out in the attack which had been practised many times over dummy enemy trenches dug in the back areas. Yes, there was no lack of preparation and sound administration beforehand. Though optimism prevailed everywhere, beneath it all there was the ever-evident feeling that all could not go according to plan, and that the number of casualties would determine everything. Some of us would be unlucky as always; might be me."[34]

Capt. Bickersteth, the 56ᵗʰ Divisional chaplain attached to The Rangers, was on the march with them. Starting out at 8 p.m. this battalion and the London Scottish, the two lead battalions of the 168ᵗʰ Brigade, marched by Company down the tracks towards Hebuterne. Bickersteth passed from platoon to platoon chatting cheerfully to the men who responded to their padre in kind. But there was a serious and sombre side to their conversations as, man by man, they handed him final letters, valuables and other items 'to be sent in case of my death'.[35]

Plate 21 The London Scottish on the their way to Hebuterne

It is believed that the two officers behind the pipe band are Lts. A G Douglas and H C Lamb. Leading 'A' Company behind them is Capt. Conrad Sparks who would play a leading role in the London Scottish attack. (Photograph courtesy of Imperial War Museum, Q 790)

As they marched through the damp, evening air, Bickersteth and Major Francis Lindsay, the C.O. of 'B' Company, London Scottish, talked about the events to come. They knew one another through Bickersteth's work as chaplain. Church service was not compulsory and attendance depended very much on either an individual's faith or on an officer taking the lead amongst his men. Major Lindsay had been one such officer and had helped the Church of England chaplains in their work with the battalion. Lindsay was a pre-war mainstay of the London Scottish and the son of a well-connected family. His father was at Court where he undertook the role of Clarenceux King of Arms.[36]

Lindsay had married some years before the war and he and his wife Helen had two children, John Stewart, who had celebrated his sixth birthday on the 14th April, and Katherine Frances, just six months old. Katherine had been conceived in the Spring of 1915, nearly five months after Lindsay had been severely wounded in the head by shrapnel on the 14th November at Gheluvelt during the fighting of the First Battle of Ypres. Invalided home, Lindsay's recovery from such a severe wound had been slow and he had spent the next seventeen months either in hospital or in the well-appointed family home in Emperor's Gate, South Kensington. During that time, he had seen his daughter born, had been gazetted temporary Major on 13th January 1916 and helped plan and then attended the

---

i Lt. Allen Grant Douglas, 1/14th London Regt. (London Scottish), was killed in action on 30th November 1917. He had been promoted Temporary Captain on 18th October 1916. He is buried in Moeuvres Communal Cemetery Extension, grave III. C. 3.

celebrations of his son's sixth birthday. At the end of April came news that the Medical Board had deemed him fit for action and, on 30ᵗʰ April, he had rejoined his battalion, just in time for its move to the lines near Gommecourt.

Now, as the Major and the Chaplain walked together through the gathering darkness, he talked wistfully about the home he had so recently lived in and about little John Stewart Lindsay, the six-year old he had left behind in London and who prayed for his father's safe return every night:

"The Major and I talked of many things, of the coming battle mostly and how it would go. He spoke of his wife and child and told me of the joy he had in his little boy's faith and of the wonder of his childish prayers. He lay bare to me something of the intense happiness of his home life, and went on to say how confident he felt he would come through safely. 'The faith of my little boy is so real. He prays every night for my safety. God could not disappoint a faith like that'."[37]

Behind them, the Kensingtons were getting ready to leave their billets at Souastre. At 8.25 p.m. they started eastwards towards Gommecourt, stopping only to pick up tools, grenades, etc., at Bayencourt. Ten minutes in front of them marched the London Rifle Brigade.. It was nearly four hours later when the advanced elements began to arrive at their assembly trenches to the east of Hebuterne. Between 1.15 a.m. and 3 a.m. on July 1ˢᵗ the men slowly filed into the trenches either side of W47R and W48R and readied themselves for the 'off'.

At St Amand 2ⁿᵈ Lt. Moy watched his colleagues from the Q.W.R. march out to battle with a deep sense of foreboding.

"Of the officers of 'B' Company taking part all except Cockerill were very nervous. Horne least so than any, Strange very, Thomas a wreck (as I should have been), and Luscombe, who took over my platoon, resigned. The men, in comparison, seemed quite cheery.

At last the order came to move off, we who had been left out stood at the crossroads to see them go. First came 'A' Company, led by Swainson, singing "Here we are again"; at its tail marched Teddy Bovill who waved as he passed. Then came my own Company with Cockerill at its head, the men cracking jokes. Next came 'C' Company with Mott smiling away and Yates and Negus looking thoughtful. Last came 'D' Company with Glasier leading them in a bored fashion and Ivesen like a ghost; the men sang "Old Roger Ruin", and we listened til the sound died away in the distance.

Away they went out into the roaring and flashing night, up the well-defined track marked with tape on each side to the assembly trenches we had dug before Gommecourt - 900 of the finest types of men who ever landed in France and all trained to the minute.

The remainder of us - wishing now that we could have gone with our friends - packed up our belongings and moved over to the village of Souastre, where all the reserve officers of the brigade were to stay until such time as they were required. At Souastre, we reported to OC Reserve Officers, who allotted us tents, hidden beneath the trees of an orchard, in which to spend the night. We turned the gramophone on in an abortive attempt to cheer ourselves up; enjoyed an alfresco dinner; turned in."[38]

At 9.30 p.m., the Queen Victoria's Rifles moved out of Souastre, east in the direction of Gommecourt. The horizon was bright with explosions and the flash of guns firing. The Queen Victorias had left Souastre cheerfully, still under the influence of their last drinks together. But, shortly after leaving the village, they halted in a field to await their turn on the cross-country route into the rear of Hebuterne. The interlude gave the men a chance to reflect on what was to happen in ten hours time and that night and over the preceding days the officers and men of all battalions had been composing letters home, many to be their last. Some spoke in emotional or sentimental terms, others confirmed their firm beliefs in the good of what they were about to do, others seemed oblivious to the imminent danger they faced. For a man as devotedly religious at 2ⁿᵈ Lt. Percy Simmonds of the Q.V.R.s his last letter home was determinedly matter of fact, as if he was intent on calming any fears that he was about to do anything difficult or dangerous:

"My Dear Mother,

Many thanks for parcel received last night containing three cakes and writing pads all of which have disappeared with amazing like rapidity. Also for parcel today with Phosphorene which should be very useful for nervy people up in the trenches this time. But please only send lime juice powder or tablets or some stuff like that. The lemonade tablets are very expensive because one tablet only makes about one glass of lemonade.

All is well. The weather is trying hard to be like mid-summer ought to be, so we all hope the trenches will soon dry up. Meanwhile those trench waders I bought are quite good. Though not absolutely water proof they are mud proof.

My Mackintosh has been stolen. Not by anybody in this regiment but I have ordered one of those long army waterproof capes, price 15 shillings and a penny through the Ordnance.

Love to you all,

Your loving son Percy."

The following morning Percy Simmonds, as yet untried in battle, would take his men over with the leading companies of his battalion in his first major attack.

The night-time temperature had fallen to barely 40° Fahrenheit and, as the chill started to set in, so too did apprehension about the battle to come. When, at about 10.30 p.m., the Queen Victoria's Rifles set off again it was through fields and by farm tracks that they travelled. The villages on the way, Bayencourt and Sailly-au-Bois and the roads leading from them to Hebuterne, were well registered by the German guns and, that night, they were pounding them with a vengeance. The enemy seemed to have sniffed that something big was in the air. Private Frank Hawkings described their march in his diary as he sat in the trenches in front of Hebuterne waiting for the off:

"Today's my birthday, and anyone will concede that is hardly an appropriate time to have one. We suddenly got orders to move this afternoon. Our packs had been taken to Souastre and stored in some old barns, but we are well loaded all the same. Every man carries 200 rounds of ammunition, three hand grenades, three sandbags, wire cutters, rockets and flares, a signboard and 48 hours rations. We marched via Souastre and Bayencourt and reach the plane (sic) between Sailly au Bois and Hebuterne at dusk.

Here we were greeted by a salvo of 5.9s and made a slight detour to avoid the shelling. The roar of the artillery was deafening. Hebuterne, which was reached at about 8 p.m., was being shelled and we could see the village of Colincamps in flames on our right."[39]

As they neared Hebuterne, the German shelling became more intense. Such was the congestion in the village, as men from the different units tried to find their way to their appointed positions, that they were made to wait their turn on the outskirts and in the fields between Sailly and Hebuterne. Edward Liveing's platoon was one such:

"We were about 400 yards from the outskirts of Hebuterne, when I was made aware of the fact that the platoon in front of me had stopped. I immediately stopped my platoon. I set the men down along a bank, and we waited - a wait which was whiled away by various incidents. I could hear a dog barking, and just see two gunner officers who were walking unconcernedly about the battery positions and whistling for it. The next thing that happened was a red flash in the air about 200 yards away, and pinging noise as bits of shrapnel shot into the ground roundabout. One of my men, S. (the poor chap was killed next day), called to me: "Look at that fire in Sailly, sir!" I turned round and saw a great yellow flare illuminating the sky in the direction of Sailly, the fiery end of some barn or farm building, where a high explosive had found its billet."[40]

After a nervous fifteen minute wait, the Rangers moved off into the heart of the village, there to collect the extra tools and equipment that was needed for the advance on the morrow. In a damaged out house were rolls of wire of different sorts, digging implements and the like which were distributed around the platoons – additional burdens to slow them in their trek across No Man's Land in only a few hours time. Once every man had collected his load, the platoons set off one by one, turning first into Wood Street which ran at right angles north off the main street of the village. Here, the communication trench had a floor of bricks, no doubt 'borrowed' from the brick field that had occupied the eastern end of the village in pre-war days. Passing through an orchard, fragrant with the smells of ripening fruits, the Rangers turned right into Cross Street, sheltered by a line of trees that fringed the orchard. The next turn was left into Woman Street which set out across more open terrain towards the old front line and beyond to the new trenches so laboriously dug at the end of May. German shells were now beginning to fall uncomfortably close to the trenches until, turning a bend in the trench, Liveing and his men came across the results of a direct hit. The trench had been blown in and the dead and wounded littered the scene. They were men of Capt. Wyatt's 'A' Company and, as Liveing asked about the state of the trenches ahead he could hear one of Wyatt's subalterns, 2nd Lt. Monier Williams[i] reassuring one of the wounded, telling him: "It's all right, old chap. It's all over

---

[i] 2nd Lt. Clarence Faithfull Monier Williams, 1/12th London Regt. (The Rangers) attested as 1986 Private in the 5th East Surrey Regt. on 10th August 1914. He was commissioned into The Rangers on 26th April 1915. In January 1917 he was seconded to the Foreign Office at the direct request of Arthur Balfour, the Foreign Secretary. He was discharged from the Army, with the rank of Lieutenant, on the grounds of ill-health on 21st February 1919. He later worked for the Department of Overseas Trade as a Senior Intelligence Officer and was awarded the MBE in June 1934. He was the grandson of Sir Monier and Julia Monier Williams (nee Faithfull), KCIE. Monier Monier Williams (died 1899) was the Boden Professor of Sanskrit at Oxford University and produced a Sanskrit-English dictionary that is still in print.

now". Pressing against the sides of the trench, the men passed by the stretcher bearers already doing their work.

To the Ranger's left a small patrol, led by 2nd Lt. Jerry Pogose of the London Rifle Brigade, had left their trenches at 11.00 p.m. and was now out in No Man's Land carefully checking the state of the German wire along the eastern edge of Gommecourt Park. His report, that the wire, whilst not swept away, had been cut sufficiently to allow reasonably free access to the German trenches meant that the Bangalore torpedoes being held at the ready for emergency wire cutting would not be needed, at least not on this part of the Division's front.

Z Day, Saturday, 1st July 1916. Midnight to 5.00 a.m.

THE DAMAGE DONE to the trenches was now beginning to slow progress to the front. No. 5 Platoon of the Rangers found New Woman Street already blocked by another direct hit that had killed three men and wounded several. Passage was impossible and so Liveing and some of his men climbed out of the trench and moved over open ground towards the junction of New Woman Street and the Support Line. By now midnight had passed and still they were not in position. The Support Line had been heavily hit and resembled little more than a string of vaguely connected shell holes. Here, Liveing found a Royal Engineer officer and his team of smoke-bombers who pointed him in the direction of the sunken Hebuterne-Bucquoy Road. By 1 a.m., Liveing had his men in position. Not the correct position, but the nearest he could find to it. They occupied a length of trench and some shell holes and were soon joined by the men of No. 8 Platoon who were equally lost in the dark and dismal landscape. Lastly, the Lewis gunners arrived and found a bit of ruined trench nearby. By 4.30 a.m. they were all in place. A thin line of grey was beginning to show on the eastern horizon and, whilst they waited, a sergeant from No. 8 Platoon went amongst them with a flagon of rum.

Rfn. Mason of the Rangers remembered the tedium of the journey up the packed communication trenches as they left the village behind and headed towards their assigned positions:

"It was always a tedious journey going up into the line and the night before the attack was no exception for everyone was on the move. After leaving Hebuterne church we crossed the little high street into the communication trench (Woman Street) where there was much congestion back and forth. Slowly the warm summer night wore on and the shelling by both sides continued but our casualties were light and by 4 a.m. all companies were in position."[41]

On their left, the Queen Victoria's Rifles were having an equally difficult task in reaching their positions:

"Eventually we entered Yellow Street and proceeded in the direction of the fire trench, but we were bombarded so much en route that it has taken us until 1 a.m. to get here. The bombardment has now died down and things are fairly quiet. Some men have been sent out to place iron pipes containing dynamite under the German wire[i]. These are to be fired

---

[i] Bangalore torpedoes.

electrically tomorrow morning. Am feeling dreadfully tired, so I'm going to try to snatch a little sleep, though I don't expect to be very successful."[42]

Overall, it took the Queen Victoria's Rifles until 2 a.m. to reach their appointed positions on the right of the 169th Brigade front. They were lined up over a depth of three trench lines between Wood Street on the right and Yankee Street on the left. Now, all they could do was jam their helmets down tight on their heads, crouch in the bottom of the trench with their chums, pray that a shell wouldn't land in their traverse - and wait.

For the men of the 167th Trench Mortar Battery the confusion was even greater, with men and officers separated in the maze of muddy trenches. Apart from the Stokes trench mortars[i] themselves each gun team and their special carriers were carrying 40 rounds per gun. With the congestion and chaos in the trenches it was bad enough for a heavily encumbered infantryman to make their way forward but for the TMB it was even worse as the Battery War Diary makes clear:

"The first difficulty which showed itself was getting into the appointed place of assembly. The next difficulty was keeping contact whilst waiting the time for attack. The gun teams, when they had lost their officers, were unaware of the time when the attack was to take place."[43]

***

AT 1.45 A.M., AS THE MEN WAITED in their cramped and damp accommodation, Divisional Headquarters received a disturbing report from No. 8 Squadron, R.F.C. Their intelligence officers had spent the night poring over the aerial photographs taken the afternoon before. Their conclusions were worrying and were contained in a report with an attached map. It showed that the German wire in front of Ferret, Fever and Fetter trenches had either been repaired or had not been properly cut. Both explanations were worrying because either suggested a failing in the artillery preparations. If Germans were alive and working in the front trenches then neither they nor their morale had been destroyed by the heavy artillery. If the wire was not cut, then the field artillery preparation had not worked properly. Urgent messages were sent to the 56th Divisional Artillery and 169th Infantry Brigade. On the 168th Brigade front, The Rangers, whose left company ('D' Company) was to attack Fetter trench, were apparently left to discover this problem for themselves. Lt. A F D Darlington was an officer in the 'D' Battery, the 4.5 in. howitzer battery of the 283rd Brigade R.F.A.. His post-war explanation for the failure to adequately cut the wire was emphatic:

"It is easy to be wise after the event... at that time we had no really efficient means of cutting the many square miles of wire entanglements protecting the German lines. Shrapnel, to be effective, had to burst low which meant that threequarters of the shells burst on percussion (*author*: i.e. hit the ground rather than in the air)... it was extremely expensive and almost useless."[44]

---

[i] The Stokes mortar consisted of a 51 in. barrel of 3 in. diameter which weighed 43lbs, a base plate (weight 28lbs) and a bipod to support the tube (37lbs): total 108lbs. Each mortar shell weighed 11lbs.

The right hand battalion of the assault, the London Scottish, was already in position by 11 p.m. on the 30th June. 2nd Lt. Harold Calder[i] and the battalion scouts went out to examine the wire in front of the Farmyard trench strongpoint. They had been assured that all the wire was adequately cut and so they were disconcerted to find it uncut for over 100 yards from the right. They had come equipped to deal for the eventuality, however, and, with the assistance of two men from the 1st London Field Company, R.E., two 20 ft. long Bangalore torpedoes were successfully exploded under the wire to clear gaps for the assault. Further to the left, the patrols found the wire cut but, north of the Hebuterne to Bucquoy road (i.e. Fetter trench), they confirmed the R.F.C. information that the wire was still uncut. When the patrols returned at 1.30 a.m., the London Scottish sent a message to the Macart (Southern) Group R.F.A. asking for their 18 pdrs to fire a wire cutting shrapnel bombardment in an effort to clear their front thoroughly.

In possible retaliation for the British efforts to destroy their wire protection, German guns opened an intense bombardment on the 168th Brigade's assembly trenches at 2.45 a.m. The Rangers, on the left of the position, were especially badly hit and part of the battalion was forced to withdraw from their assembly trenches. They retreated into the trenches occupied by the 1/4th Londons, the support battalion, causing congestion and confusion amongst the ranks of both units.

By 3.30 a.m. the 168th Brigade with its machine gun company and light trench mortar battery, with 'C' Company, 5th Cheshire Regiment (Pioneers) and No. 1 Section, 2/2nd Field Company, Royal Engineers attached, was in its assembly areas and the problems with the Rangers had been resolved. On the left, in the W48 and W47 front line trenches and supports, the Rangers waited for the off. Behind them, ready to move forward in support were the men of the 1/4th Londons. By 3.40 a.m. the Rangers had reported to brigade headquarters, erroneously as it turned out, that all the wire to their front (both British and German) was cut. On the right, the lead companies of the London Scottish were deployed in W50 and W49 trenches and their supports. The 1/13th London Regiment, in addition to supporting the Scottish, had a reinforced company of 180 men assembled in an area on the immediate right of the London Scottish. Their job was to dig a fire trench joining up the Brigade's right flank at the head of Welcome Street with a German sap projecting SW from Farmyard trench. This was to form the new defensive right flank.

The assaulting battalions of the 169th Brigade had found their way to the front through the tortuous maze of communication trenches that spread out in front of Hebuterne and towards Gommecourt by 3 a.m. At 5 a.m., as they waited apprehensively for Zero hour, many in the Brigade were supplied with mugs of hot pea soup. With the temperature having plummeted to an unseasonable chill the soup came as a welcome relief as the men huddled uncomfortably in the

---

i 2nd Lt. Harold Joseph Calder, 1/14th London Regt. (London Scottish), was born on 7th January 1890. He was the oldest of the ten children (four girls and six boys, the youngest of whom was four years old) of Sarah Annie Calder of 58, Leicester Rd., East Finchley, London, and the late Alexander Calder. Educated at the Stanley Commercial Science and Art Centre he was an accountant. He had joined the London Scottish before the war being discharged in January, 1913 in order to go to Argentina. He rejoined the 3/14th Battalion as 4441Private on 2nd March 1915 and was promoted Corporal before he was commissioned into the 3/14th London Scottish on 3rd October 1915. He was killed in action on Monday, 18th September 1916 during a patrol near Leuze Wood. He is buried in Guillemont Road Cemetery, Guillemont, Somme, France, grave XV. J. I.

damp and muddy trenches. As the minutes slipped by it was mostly quiet on the left of the British lines but, overhead, British artillery shells rumbled and screamed their way towards the German lines. In the main, German retaliation was feeble but one shell, at least, struck a target. Two trench mortars and their teams, due to go forward to make a smoke barrage up Etch and Ems trenches during the assault, were knocked out. Further back, Pte Clements and his Lewis gunners were making themselves ready:

"As soon as it was light we made some tea and had breakfast. Then we took the gun and ammunition to the section of Cross Street between Yellow Street and Yankee Street. About six we had some hot soup and were given a sandwich each. I spoke to (Company) Sgt. Maj. Loates for a few minutes... Then we took up our position in Cross Street. All the time the din was terrific, shells bursting everywhere. It was a beautiful summer morning and some of the boys had picked roses and fastened them in their tunics."[45]

On the right flank and in the centre, however, the German artillery was pounding the British positions from the front lines back down the communication trenches and into Hebuterne. For ninety minutes, from 4.00 a.m. onwards, German artillery hammered the 168th Brigade trenches and those occupied byn the Queen Victorias with 15 cm and 10.5 cm Howitzers. 2nd Lt. Raymond Bennett[i], 'C' Company, Queen Victoria's Rifles, wrote after the war that, as a result, casualties had been "fairly heavy" whilst the men waited in the trenches[46]. As a result, by 5.08 a.m., the bombardment was considered sufficiently severe for the Divisional H.Q. to ask for help from the VII Corps artillery Counter battery group. Forty minutes later they reported that they were engaging five batteries in Biez Wood and one in Fork Wood.

The batteries may have been engaged but they were certainly not being put out of action. Nor had they all been identified. German artillery casualties, as with the infantry, had been remarkably light, a testimony to the solid construction of their dug outs and battery positions. The commander of Reserve Feldartillerie Regt. 20 was well satisfied with his regiment's performance:

"Thanks to the strong construction of our positions, the damage caused by the enemy bombardment was generally light, despite the fact that many shots were on the right side of and landed in the vicinity of the attacked batteries. Our losses in June were: 1 officer, 1 Vizewachtmeister[ii] killed, 5 men wounded. The hard work had paid off!

The following field artillery ammunition was fired in June:

---

[i] 2nd Lt. Raymond Bennett, 1/9th London Regt. (Queen Victoria's Rifles) was born on 30th July 1889, he was the son of George and Mary Ellen Bennett of 19, Market Place, Stockport where his father was the local chemist. Educated at James Leah's Boys' School, 1, Longshut Lane West, Stockport he lived neaqrby at 'Laurel Bank, Longshut Lane West and was an ophthalmic optician. He had gone to South Africa and had enlisted in Hartigan's Horse as a trooper along with 2nd Lt. Douglas Ord-Mackenzie (also QVR) and they had come to England when the regiment was disbanded in May 1915. Hartigan's Horse was raised in the Eastern Cape Province by Lt. Col. M M Hartigan, Deputy Commissioner of the South African Police, Eastern Division, Cape Province and was disbanded, along with the Southern Command of the South West Africa Field Force, after the successful campaign in what is now Namibia. On his return to England he lived with his parents at McAulay House, Davenport Crescent in Stockport. He was commissioned into the 3/9th battalion on 13th October 1915.
[ii] Vice Sergeant Major.

Field gun rounds: 16,106 (including 3,806 on 26 June and 4,518 on 27 June).

Light field howitzer rounds: 3,384 (621 on 26 June, 468 on 27 June).

After the enemy had bombarded our positions with gas and heavy shells and created an incalculable field of craters over a period of seven days and nights using huge quantities of ammunition of all calibres, up to and including the heaviest which we did not have, he expected to reap the success of the fire that was designed to wear us down - and was badly disappointed."[47]

The problem was that the disappointment would not become obvious until after the men had gone 'over the top' on 1st July. Until that point, from Army General down to Brigade commander, everyone believed that the defenders of Gommecourt were teetering on the brink of collapse. To all concerned, 1st July was the day of 'The Big Push' but, as every red-tabbed officer agreed, only a little one was going to be needed to shove the Germans over the edge.

NOTES:
Casualties not mentioned in existing footnotes:

25th June 1916
1/3rd London Regt (Royal Fusiliers)
1950 Pte Gilbert James Faricy. Son of Mr. J. Faricy of 53, Victoria Crescent, South Tottenham, London. St. Amand British Cemetery I. B. 16
4172 Pte Charles Garner. Brother of Mrs. A. Bull of 22, St. Gabriel St., Newington Butts, London. St. Amand British Cemetery I. B. 17
4765 Pte Edward James (Eddie) Place. Aged 17 Son of Alfred George Henry & Mary Place of 68, Drayton Rd., Harlesden, London. Native of Cardiff. St. Amand British Cemetery I.A.16
1/8th Middlesex Regiment
TF2233 Pte Edward Bailey. Aged 22 Son of Mr. & Mrs. A. Bailey of 10, Edgell Rd., Staines, Middx Thiepval Memorial, Pier and Face 12D and 13B
Royal Field Artillery
104232 Gnr Syme Wood Bernard, 281st (1/2nd London) Bde. Aged 23 Son of Andrew & Eliza Bernard of Hawburn House, Hallpark, Sauchie, Alloa, Clackmannanshire. St. Amand British Cemetery I.B.15
2037 Gnr F C Darton, X 56th Trench Mortar Bty. Hebuterne Military Cemetery, IV. K. 3
6631 Gnr George Fernie, 56th Div. Ammunition Col., Royal Field Artillery. Aged 20 Son of George Fernie of 24, Sutherland St., Kirkcaldy. Couin British Cemetery I. A. 13
2250 Drvr William Richards, 56th Div. Ammunition Col., Royal Field Artillery. Aged 29 Son of James & Emily Richards of 17, Rock St., Swansea. Couin British Cemetery I. A. 14
1092 Bombardier Albert Rodney, X 56th Trench Mortar Bty Aged 20 Son of Mrs. Esther Rodney of 42, Wilmington Square, Clerkenwell, London. Hebuterne Military Cemetery, IV. K. 2.

26th June 1916
1/4th London Regt (Royal Fusiliers)
4622 Pte George Albert Lewis Aged 26 Son of Mrs. Lewis of 11, Blackthorn St., Devons Rd., Bow, London. Hebuterne Military Cemetery III. A. 2
4739 Pte Robert Frederick Stokes. Hebuterne Military Cemetery III. A. 4
1/7th Middlesex Regiment
2312 Serjeant George Ernest Andrewes. Aged 24 Son of George W. & Jemima Andrewes of 1, Almond Rd., Tottenham, London. Hebuterne Military Cemetery II. M. 6.
TF/1389 Corporal Edward Frank Damant Aged 24 Son of Edward Damant of 56, Falmer Rd., West Green, Tottenham, London. Thiepval Memorial, Pier and Face 12D and 13B
2381 Private John Thomas Farleigh Aged 23 Son of Joel Farleigh of 'Le Chalet', Elder Avenue, Wickford, Essex. Hebuterne Military Cemetery II.M.2
2400 Private Jack Fleming. Gommecourt British Cemetery No. 2, II. B. 5.
1458 Private George Healey Son of Mrs. A. R. Healey of 38, Rook St., Poplar, London. Couin British Cemetery I. B. 3.
2427 Serjeant Charles Wellsteed Hughes Aged 23 Son of Charles Wellsteed Hughes & Agnes Sarah Hughes of London. Hebuterne Military Cemetery II. L. 5.

1743 Serjeant Herbert Page Aged 24 Son of Herbert & Mary Page of 18, Denzie Rd., Neasden Lane, Willesden, London. Hebuterne Military Cemetery II. M. 5.

5260 Private Stanley Edward Parmenter Aged 21 Son of Sidney L. Parmenter of 131, Salisbury Rd., Barnet. Hebuterne Military Cemetery II. M. 9.

2867 Private Albert Peary Aged 20 Son of H. J. & R. J. Peary of Tottenham, London. Doullens Communal Cemetery Extension No. 1, II. B. 19.

3320 Serjeant Edward James Perry Aged 27 Son of Elizabeth Perry of 88, Hampton Rd., Forest Gate, London, & the late Thomas H. Perry. Native of Seaton, Devon. Hebuterne Military Cemetery II. L. 4.

2nd Lt. Jack Price Aged 22 Son of Alfred & Hettie Price of 14, Manor Rd, Westcliff-on-Sea, Southend-on-Sea, Essex. Hebuterne Military Cemetery II.M.7.

1/8th Middlesex Regiment (Men listed as Thiepval Memorial found on Pier and Face 12D and 13B)

TF4135 Pte William Barnes. Aged 19 Son of Frederick N. & Annie Barnes of 15, Ravenscourt Avenue, Hammersmith, London. Gommecourt British Cemetery No. 2, II. G. 27

TF5344 Pte Ernest Blackwell. Aged 24 Son of Maria Blackwell of 8, Fern Grove, Feltham, Middx. Hebuterne Military Cemetery Sp. Mem. 8

TF3478 Pte Sidney Bowker. Aged 31 Son of William & Annie Bowker of 2, Osborne Rd., Hounslow, Middx. Thiepval Memorial

TF3479 Pte Edward Dennis Bristow. Aged 19 Son of Fred Dennis Bristow of 2, St. Dunstan's Villas, Bath Rd., Cranford, Middx, & the late Lily Bristow. Thiepval Memorial

TF2400 Pte Frederick Thomas Brown. Aged 18 Son of James William & Susannah Emma Brown of 66, Gould Rd., Twickenham, Middx. Hebuterne Military Cemetery II. U. 2

TF3835 Pte Frank Spencer Collison. Thiepval Memorial

TF5089 Pte Edward Cozens. Thiepval Memorial

TF4840 Pte Herbert Henry Crook. Aged 26 Son of Edwin & Annetta Crook of 18, Coningsby Rd., Ealing, London. Thiepval Memorial

TF3497 Pte Mortimer Downing. Aged 19 Son of John R. & Alice Downing of 1, Woodfield Avenue. Ealing, London Thiepval Memorial

TF5214 Pte William Eggleton. Son of Elizabeth Eggleton of The Square, Longford, Yiewsley, Middx, & the late John Eggleton. Thiepval Memorial

TF4981 Pte George Evans. Thiepval Memorial

TF4833 Pte Reginald Fredericks Aged 18 Son of William Henry & Carrie Fredericks of 157, Haliburton Road, St Margarets, Twickenham, Middlesex. Thiepval Memorial

TF3428 Pte Frederick Joseph Gamgee Aged 17 Son of Joseph Hayes Gamgee & Louisa Gamgee of 34, Cross Street, Hampton Hill, Middlesex. Hebuterne Military Cemetery II.S.1.

TF3512 Pte Lionel Percy Gulliver Aged 20 Son of Sydney & Annie Gulliver of 444, London Road, Isleworth, Middlesex. Hebuterne Military Cemetery II.U.6.

TF5236 Pte J. Victor Hawkins   Aged 23 Son of Mrs L Hawkins of Remony Cottage, Iver Heath, Uxbridge, Middlesex. Hebuterne Military Cemetery II.U.5.

TF1877 Pte Thomas F Hazell Aged 23 Son of Mr & Mrs Hazelll of Southall; husband of Mrs A Hazell of 2, Havelock Road, Southall, Middlesex. Hebuterne Military Cemetery II.U.3.

TF2778 Pte Samuel George William Hendy Aged 19 Son of George William & Alice Amy Hendy of 29, Chaucer Road, Acton, London. Thiepval Memorial

TF2955 Pte John Humphries Aged 20 Son of Frank Humphries of 33, Balfour Road, Ealing, London. Thiepval Memorial

TF4266 Pte Thomas Jones Aged 18 Son of Mrs Alice Todd of 15 River Side, Little Britain, Uxbridge, Middlesex. Couin British Cemetery I.B.1.

TF3614 Pte Ernest Davis Mault Aged 18 Son of David & Alice Mault of 3, Wharncliffe Villas, Lower Boston Road, Hanwell, Middlesex. Thiepval Memorial

TF3582 Pte Arthur Moorshead Aged 18 Son of Mrs Jessie Deleenaer (formerly Moorshead) of 37 Balfour Road, West Ealing, London and Alexander Deleenaer (stepfather). Thiepval Memorial

TF2756 Pte Harold Oliver Aged 21 Son of Harold Oliver of 16, Thornfield Road, Shepherd's Bush, London. Hebuterne Military Cemetery Special Memorial 9

TF3540 Pte Frederick Packard Aged 21 Son of William & Annie Packard of 178, Linkfield Road, Isleworth, Middlesex. Couin British Cemetery I.B.4.

TF5308 Pte William Peverill Hebuterne Military Cemetery II.U.4.

TF2378 Pte George Taylor Hebuterne Military Cemetery II.U.7.

TF4797 Pte Joseph James Way Hebuterne Military Cemetery II.T.1.

Royal Engineers
1388 Spr W J Cowler, 1st London Division Signal Coy, R.E. Son of E. and J. Cowler, of Holmesdale, Woolacombe, Devon. Mailly Wood Cemetery, Mailly-Maillet I. P. 13.

Royal Garrison Artillery
2393 Sgt William Rawlings, 96th Siege Battery RGA   Aged 39 Father of Leslie Rawlings of Osbournby, Sleaford, Lincs St. Amand British Cemetery, I. B. 1

Royal Marine Artillery
RMA/12656 Gnr D E Gowney. Aged 19 Son of David James Gowney & Alice Katherine Gowney of The Ranche, Hardway, Gosport, Hants. Hebuterne Military Cemetery, IV. K. 4

27th June 1916
1/1st London Regt (Royal Fusiliers) (Men listed as Thiepval Memorial found on Pier and Face 9D and 16B)
1814 Pte Henry John Golding. Thiepval Memorial
5358 Pte William John Charles Johnson. Thiepval Memorial
5503 Pte William Julian. Hebuterne Military Cemetery II. G. 11
4423 Pte William John Charles Newton. Hebuterne Military Cemetery II. H. 2
5265 Pte Arthur Relfe. Thiepval Memorial
4551 Pte Cecil John Ticehurst. Thiepval Memorial
1/3rd London Regt (Royal Fusiliers)
1858 Pte John William Barnett. Hebuterne Military Cemetery II. Q. 2.
4016 Pte Frederick Devereux Aged 21 Son of Mr. & Mrs. Francis Merall Devereux of 27, Crawford Buildings, Crawford St., Marylebone, London. Hebuterne Military Cemetery II.Q.8
1445 Pte Frederick Robert Guilford. Hebuterne Military Cemetery II. Q. 6.
5054 Pte George Herbert. Hebuterne Military Cemetery II. Q. 4
3209 Pte William John Land. Hebuterne Military Cemetery II. Q. 5
3279 Pte William Edward Ripley. Hebuterne Military Cemetery II. Q. 4
4727 L/Cpl. William Schonbeck. Hebuterne Military Cemetery II. R. 6.
3488 Pte Frederick James Sherwood. Hebuterne Military Cemetery II. Q. 3
1644 Pte John Smith. Hebuterne Military Cemetery II. R. 7.
3654 Pte Arthur Edward Walker Aged 19 Son of William James & Emily Walker of 48, Penshurst Rd., South Hackney, London. Hebuterne Military Cemetery II. Q. 1
1/7th Middlesex Regiment
5317 Pte Charles Harold Ackland. Son of George & Annie Ackland of London; husband of Agnes Partlin (formerly Ackland) of 174, Albion Rd., Stoke Newington, London. Hebuterne Military Cemetery II. M. 8.
2662 Pte Cyril Barton. Couin British Cemetery I. A. 18.
5431 Pte David H Campbell. Aged 25 Son of Malcolm & Alice Campbell of 15, Brunswick Rd., West Green Rd., South Tottenham, London. Born at Cambridge Heath, London. Hebuterne Military Cemetery II. L. 2.
5491 Pte Thomas George Chandler. Hebuterne Military Cemetery II. L. 1.
TF/5637 Private John Thomas Holt   Thiepval Memorial, Pier and Face 12D and 13B
1/8th Middlesex Regiment.
TF3966 Pte Charles Alexander Claridge Aged 25 Husband of A L Mansfield (formerly Claridge) of 2, Glebeland Gardens, Shepperton, Middlesex. Couin British Cemetery I.A.20
TF3177 Cpl Ernest Harding Aged 22 Son of Jesse & Alice Harding of 20, Rectory Lane, Ditton Hill, Surbiton, Surrey. Hebuterne Military Cemetery II.T.2
TF2958 Thomas Walter Herbert Ozard Aged 21 Son of Thomas John & Edith Ozard of 28, Pope's Lane, South Ealing, London. Thiepval Memorial Pier and Face 12 D and 13 B
1/5th Cheshire Regiment
1434 Sgt. A E Pye. Aged 23 Son of Mrs. Kate Florance Pye of 51, Paradise St., Northwich, Cheshire. Hebuterne Military Cemetery II. C. 5
4/1786 Cpl. Ernest Wharton. Aged 23 Son of Thomas Wharton of Birkenhead Hebuterne Military Cemetery II C 4
Royal Marine Artillery
RMA/10120 Gnr F C Rolph Aged 32 Louvencourt Military Cemetery Plot 1. Row B. Grave 44.

28th June 1916
1/5th London Regt (London Rifle Brigade)
2474 Rfn. Ralph Richard Benton Coe. Aged 18 Son of William Coe of 50, Swan St., Borough, London. Hebuterne Military Cemetery IV.D.6.
333 Rfn. Frederick James Hill. Aged 29 Son of Mr. & Mrs. Sidney Frederick Hill of Norwood, London. Ste. Marie Cemetery Div. 19. GG. 3

29th June 1916
1/2nd London Regt (Royal Fusiliers)
2218 Pte William Arthur Bennett. Aged 23 Son of William Clayton Bennett of 76, Park Rd., Rochdale, & the late Eva Bennett. Native of Ashwood, East Grinstead. Hebuterne Military Cemetery IV. A. 11
1/3rd London Regt (Royal Fusiliers)
3677 Pte Francis Connolly, A Company. Thiepval Memorial, Pier and Face 9D and 16B
1/12th London Regt (The Rangers)
3887 Rfn. George Francis Walls. Aged 22 Son of Frederick and Lucy Mary Walls, of 28, Trehern Rd., East Sheen, London. Couin British Cemetery I. B. 9.
Royal Field Artillery
1183 Sgt William Benjamin Badham, X 56th Trench Mortar Bty   Aged 33 Son of Benjamin Charles Badham. Hebuterne Military Cemetery, IV. K. 6
2342 Gnr Colin Campbell, B Bty., 282nd (1/3rd London) Bde Aged 19 Son of Robert & Amy R. Campbell of 32, Vincent Rd., Wood Green, London. Couin British Cemetery I. B. 8

30th June 1916
1/1st London Regt (Royal Fusiliers)
5314 Pte Henry Thomas James. Aged 20 Son of Henry Thomas & Anna James of 36, William St., Hampstead Rd., London. Hebuterne Military Cemetery II. I. 10

1/12th London Regt (The Rangers)
471255 Rfn. James Prayle. Aged 19 Brother of Mrs. Parlair, of 77, Arcadia St., Poplar, London. His body was never found and his name is inscribed on Thiepval Memorial, Pier and Face 9C

ENDNOTES:

[1] On the 26th March 1918, during the crisis of the German Spring Offensive, the Hotel de Ville at Doullens was the site of the meeting between Haig and Milner and, on the French side, Foch, Petain, Poincare and Clemenceau at which Foch was made Supreme Commander of the of the Allied forces in France and Flanders. A stain glass window in the 'Commandement Unique' Hall commemorates the event.

[2] Keeson, Maj. C A C, Queen Victoria's Rifles,1792-1922, Constable and Co.1923

[3] Büsing, Georg „Das Reserve-Feldartillerie-Regiment Nr. 20 im Weltkriege 1914-18" Göhmann, Hannover 1932

[4] Sheldon, Jack, *The German Army on the Somme*, page 131, taken from an unpublished source in the Kriegsarchiv München, ref 8 RIR Bd 4.

[5] Clements Pte (later Lt.) H T, 1/2nd London Regiment, Diary, IWM.

[6] Bickersteth, John (editor), The Bickersteth Diaries Leo Cooper 1995, page 92.

[7] Moy, 2nd Lt. C E, Unpublished papers, Liddle Collection, Leeds University.

[8] Büsing, Georg „Das Reserve-Feldartillerie-Regiment Nr. 20 im Weltkriege 1914-18" Göhmann, Hannover 1932

[9] Ward-Jackson Maj. C L, Letter to his wife 27th June 1916, VII Corps, IWM.

[10] Forstner, Kurt Frhr. v. „Das Königlich – Preussische Reserve-Infanterie-Regiment Nr. 15" Sporn Zeulenroda 1931

[11] Appleyard Rfn S W, 1/9th London Regt (Queen Victoria's Rifles), Papers, IWM

[12] Jones Rfm P H 1/16th London Regt (Queen's Westminster Rifles), Papers, IWM.

[13] Ibid.

[14] Ward-Jackson Maj. C L, Letter to his wife 27th June 1916, VII Corps, IWM.

[15] Ward-Jackson Maj. C L, Letter to his wife 28th June 1916, VII Corps, IWM.

[16] Snow, Maj. Gen Sir Thomas D'Oyly, entry in personal diary 27th June 1916, IWM.

[17] Franklin 240481 Pte William Frederick, 1/8th Middlesex, Diary, IWM. Pte Franklin died of wounds at No. 24 General Hospital, Etaples on 5th May 1917.

[18] Keeson, Maj. C A C, Queen Victoria's Rifles,1792-1922, Constable and Co.1923

[19] Jones Rfm P H 1/16th London Regt (Queen's Westminster Rifles), Papers, IWM.

[20] Clements Pte (later Lt.) H T, 1/2nd London Regiment, Diary, IWM.

[21] Mason, Rfn. R J, 1/12th London Regt (The Rangers). Document held by the Liddle Collection, Leeds University

[22] Clements Pte (later Lt.) H T, 1/2nd London Regiment, Diary, IWM

[23] King Lt Col, 1/7th Middlesex Regt.

[24] 169th Brigade report, NA WO 95/2957

[25] Appleyard Rfn S W, 1/9th London Regt (Queen Victoria's Rifles), Papers, IWM

[26] Hubbard Pte A, London Scottish, Papers, IWM

[27] Henriques Maj. J Q, The War History of the First Battalion, Queen's Westminster Rifles 1914-1918, Medici Society 1923

[28] 56th Division report, NA WO 95/2931

[29] Jones Rfm P H 1/16th London Regt (Queen's Westminster Rifles), Papers, IWM.

[30] Schuman Rfn A, 1/5th London Rifle Brigade. From a document held at the Liddle Collection, Leeds University.

[31] Clements Pte (later Lt.) H T, 1/2nd London Regiment, Diary, IWM

[32] Liveing Edward G, Attack, MacMillan 1918, republished by Strong Oak Press 1986

[33] Ibid.

[34] Mason, Rfn. R J, 1/12th London Regt (The Rangers). Document held by the Liddle Collection, Leeds University

[35] Bickersteth, John (editor), The Bickersteth Diaries Leo Cooper 1995

[36] Clarenceux King of Arms is one of the three subordinate English Kings of Arms. Clarenceux's province has always been the southern part of England, and at least from the sixteenth century has included all England from the River Trent southwards. He is the senior of the two provincial 'Kings' and his name was taken in honour of the Duke of Clarence, third son of Edward III. His official coat of arms, in use circa 1500 were: Argent a Cross Gules on a chief Gules a lion passant guardant crowned with an open crown Or.

[37] Bickersteth, John (editor), The Bickersteth Diaries Leo Cooper 1995

[38] Moy, 2nd Lt. C E, Unpublished papers, Liddle Collection, Leeds University.

[39] Hawkings Frank, From Ypres to Cambrai, The Elmfield Press 1973

[40] Liveing Edward G, Attack, MacMillan 1918, republished by Strong Oak Press 1986

[41] Mason, Rfn. R J, 1/12th London Regt (The Rangers). Document held by the Liddle Collection, Leeds University

[42] Hawkings Frank, From Ypres to Cambrai, The Elmfield Press 1973

[43] 167th Trench Mortar Battery, NA WO 95/2950

[44] Darlington Lt A F D M.C., MA, D/283 Brigade, RFA. Papers IWM

[45] Clements Pte (later Lt.) H T, 1/2nd London Regiment, Diary, IWM

[46] Bennett, 2nd Lt R, 1/9th London Regt. NA CAB 45/132

[47] Büsing, Georg „Das Reserve-Feldartillerie-Regiment Nr. 20 im Weltkriege 1914-18" Göhmann, Hannover 1932.

8. Z DAY: 0500 - 0730

"Just over the trenches, almost raising the hair on one's head... swished the smaller shells from the French .75 and English 18 pdr batteries. They gave one a sensation of being under a swiftly rushing stream. The larger shells kept up a continuous shrieking overhead, falling on the enemy's trenches with the roar of a cataract."

2nd Lt. E H Liveing
1/12th Londons (The Rangers)

Z Day, Saturday, 1st July 1916
Third Army weather report: Early mist, fine & warm. Rain: 0mm. Temp. 76-48° F

A S THE SUN ROSE ON JULY 1ST the ground was still covered by mist. It clung to the woods and sank damply into the valleys that cut across the battlefield. The BE2cs of No. 8 Squadron were already in the air. Just after 5.00 a.m. they had rumbled and bumped their away across the airfield at La Bellevue and, with only 16 km to fly, they were over Gommecourt before the half hour. The observers would have peered intently over the side of the cockpit looking for signs of active hostile batteries but, again, the weather came to the assistance of the German artillery. With such a mist obscuring the ground, the R.F.C. could do little to help the men in the trenches below.

Around 5.30 a.m. the shelling eased on the right battalions of the 168th Brigade, however, shelling was still persistent on the left. By 6.10 a.m., 'B' Company of the Rangers reported about 20 casualties, including some amongst the bomb throwers who were to help create the smoke screen just before Zero hour. Five minutes later, 'A' Company of the Rangers reported that it had only 5 smoke bomb throwers left.

For the artillery it was now just ten minutes before the intense bombardment was due to start. In the previous few hours, the gun teams had been working feverishly to load and fire but now they were to re-double their efforts, as the last frantic hour of the seven-day bombardment was to begin. For all of the guns, from the closest, the 18 pdr field guns 1,000 metres in front of Gommecourt Wood, to the most distant, the 12 in. and 15 in. super-heavy howitzers some seven kilometres to the west, this was to be the most intense bombardment of the war so far.

For the Divisional artillery, the 18 pdrs and 4.5 in. howitzers, 11,660 rounds of shrapnel and high explosive had been allocated for the 65 minutes of the bombardment. They would have to fire at an average of about three rounds a minute. In addition, trench mortars were to drop another 200 rounds into the trenches and wire a few hundred metres away. The Corps heavy artillery, covering both divisional fronts, had an equally onerous task. The 6 in. howitzers were to deliver 3,540 shells onto their targets, firing at nearly two rounds a minute. The 9.2 in. howitzers had to achieve a similar rate of fire if they were to drench the Gommecourt defences with 3,120 of their 290lb shells[i]. And the four

---

[i] The 94th Siege Battery managed to fire 100 rounds per gun in 65 minutes, a remarkable feat. This rate of fire was not to be achieved again as the damage to the guns' buffers and recuperators caused by overheating was significant. The 96th Siege Battery's guns fired: No. 1 120 rounds, No 2 114 rounds and Nos. 3 and 4 90 rounds each. It was reported that "Oil boiled in the buffers of all guns." [*Source:* Historical Record of the 96th Siege Battery RGA]

super-heavies had sixty rounds to load and fire, at a super-human rate of one every four minutes. The gun teams were to fire as many of their allocation as possible before the pre-arranged 'lifts' to the German support lines began at Zero hour.

At 6.25 a.m. it began. If the previous days' bombardment had been awe-inspiring to those observing it then this final 65 minutes was earth-shattering. All the more so, as the two previous days had been relatively quiet because of the need to eke out ammunition supplies over two extra days. In the woods, large trees were uprooted and dismembered, their limbs sent flying through the air in a halo of leaves and splinters. Trenches and wire disappeared beneath the weight of the bombardment. Plumes of dirt and debris erupted into the sky where the heavier shells landed. Shells from the lighter ordnance screamed overhead, some bursting in the air to send a cone of shrapnel flying into wire entanglements, others ploughing the soil into ragged furrows. A cloud of smoke and dust soon covered the German lines, through which could be seen only dimly the flash of more explosions as the artillery warmed to their task.

Waiting to go over as part of the Rangers' third wave, 2nd Lt. Liveing and his men felt as well as saw the effects of the brutal bombardment:

"Just over the trenches, almost raising the hair on one's head (we were helmeted, I must say, that was the feeling), swished the smaller shells from the French .75[i] and English 18 pdr batteries. They gave one a sensation of being under a swiftly rushing stream. The larger shells kept up a continuous shrieking overhead, falling on the enemy's trenches with the roar of a cataract, while every now and then a noise as of thunder sounded above all when our trench mortar shells fell amongst the German wire, blowing it to bits, making holes like mine craters, and throwing dirt and even bits of metal into our own trenches."[1]

Others, like Rfn. Mason, sought safety in the bottom of the trenches, waiting for the signal to go over, listening to the cacophony of the guns and seeking solace in soup, prayers and chocolate:

"At 6.30 the shelling reached a peak hitherto inexperienced, both sides thereby publicly claiming the forthcoming attack to the world at large and the suffering infantrymen in particular. An hour to go! We sat in the bottom of the crowded narrow trench and had some rum issued and also soup, both out of petrol tins direct from the spout for other utensils were ungetatable. Shells bashed in the trench, casualties were cleared and men moved away from the spots exposed to the enemy machine guns. My platoon officer was next to me on one side, with his back towards me and at his request I handed him chocolate from his haversack, the conversation was little and no-one felt particularly bright under the stress of the bombardment. He was a very pleasant parson's son, about 25, popular and courageous. I guessed he was saying his prayers for I was. The hope of earthly help had passed for it seemed by the din that hell had descended upon us all, but there was still worse to come when we were out in the open and machine guns by the hundred added their chatter to the inferno."[2]

---

[i] There were no French 75mm field guns involved at Gommecourt.

Away to Mason's right, 2nd Lt. Robert White, 'A' Company, London Scottish, had been waiting anxiously for the off after a long and difficult journey to the front and now he sat chatting with two of his sergeants, Kirkpatrick and Beattie. Some of the men in his platoon had never experienced the sound and fury of even a small bombardment and, for at least one man, the experience of this cacophony of noise was just too much:

"Up to 2.30 a.m. struggling up CTs overloaded with gear... About 4 a.m. rations turned up - had been held up. The hot soup turned out to be cold soup in petrol cans which had not been cleaned. In other words greasy petrol. My batman made up some cocoa and produced some food. About 7 a.m. the bombardment commenced giving one that sinking feeling akin to sea sickness, word came down - one man fainted. Went to see him and found that he was one of the seven men who had been posted to our platoon out of the draft. Felt sorry for them for it must have been some shock to encounter such convulsions so soon. Gave him some of the cocoa and warmed him up a bit."

But, for those men brave enough to peer carefully over the tops of the trenches, the sight of the lines opposite must have been re-assuring. Now, perhaps, even the cynics might believe that the attack really would be a walkover. Could anything or anyone survive such brutal punishment?

Deep in their bunkers, there must have been German soldiers asking the same question. Where the super-heavy shells landed, around the Maze and the Farmyard strongpoint, the entrances to dugouts were blown in, the trenches flattened out beyond recognition and the wire scattered. The detonation of this mass of shells sent deep tremors through the chalk. Dust drifted down from the ceilings. The walls vibrated, groaned and shook. Equipment fell off shelves and racks. In some, the electricity was cut and the lights went out, leaving the cowering men in pitch darkness. The harsh chemical smell of Lyddite and Amatol caught at their throats. The noise was deafening. Men trembled, wept, prayed. But the dugouts held. The months spent by the troops and their engineers digging deep into the chalk, reinforcing the ceilings with metal and concrete, creating multiple entrances and linking the bunkers one to another, were, in this these moments of trial, justified. Through these labours they survived. They had endured the bombardment and lived through it. But, when the British guns lifted, they would be ready, with rifles, bombs and machine guns.

About halfway through this hurricane bombardment, the German guns retaliated, dropping a concentration of shells on the centre and left of the British trenches. Lt. Col. Bates of the London Rifle Brigade reported that 2 wounded officers and 52 other ranks had passed the advanced battalion headquarters within ten minutes of the attack going in, most caused by the German guns. How many dead L.R.B. men lay dead in the assembly trenches was not known. The Queen Victoria's Rifles lost nearly 40 killed and wounded in one company and, to their rear, the assembly trenches of the 1/2nd Londons were heavily shelled. Cowering under the sudden strafe was Private Hawkings:

"About 7.00 a.m., the enemy suddenly dropped a barrage on our trench, blowing it in and causing many casualties. Dazed by the perpetual crashes we crouched in the bottom of the trench, half buried under the debris which fell around us. This barrage accounted for close on 40 killed and wounded in the company. I was struck by two pieces of shrapnel on the upper part of my left arm and on my shrapnel helmet: but escaped with a bruise on my arm and a dent in my helmet, plus of course, a splitting headache."[3]

Pte. T M Fribbins observed the effect of this strafe on No. 4 Platoon who were crowded into a communication trench when a shell burst on the edge wounding a friend of his, Alf Fenner:

"He was wounded at Hebuterne on Saturday, July 1st, at about ten minutes to seven in the morning previous to the attack on Gommecourt Wood (*sic:* Gommecourt Park). He was standing in a small communication trench leading to our first line trench when he was wounded – apparently in the head, as the blood was running down his face. A shell had burst in front of our parapet, wounding about a dozen men of which Fenner was one. I was standing about 25 yards away and when he passed me he was able to walk and made a remark that he had got 'a nice little Blighty'. He was making for the advanced dressing station about 150 yards away, and that is the last I saw of him."

Either the wound was more serious than Fenner or Fribbins[i] suspected or the wounded man was hit again because 4479 Pte Alfred Fenner of the 1/2nd London Regt. died sometime on Saturday, 1st July, to be buried in the cemetery behind the A.D.S. in Hebuterne[ii].

Some of this barrage also hit Liveing's No. 5 Platoon of the Rangers immediately to their right:

"We must be giving them hell", I said, "as I don't think they are sending much back."

"I don't think much, sir", he replied.

I hardly think we believed each other. Looking up out of the trench beyond him, I saw huge, black columns of smoke and debris rising up from our communication trench. Then, suddenly, there was a blinding crash just by us. We were covered in mud which flopped out of the trench, and the evil-smelling fumes of Lyddite. The cry for stretcher-bearers was passed hurriedly up the line again. Followed crash after crash, and the pinging of shrapnel which flicked into the top of the trench, the purring noise of flying nose caps and soft thudding sounds as they fell into the parapet...

The men were behaving splendidly. I passed along the word to 'Fix swords'."[4]

The smoke screen was due to commence at 7.25 a.m., five minutes before the men went over the top. For some reason, smoke was released from the Z hedge on the extreme left of the line, four minutes early at 7.21 a.m. The smoke screen was to comprise two elements, mortar bombs for longer distance smoke and

---

[i] Pte T M Fribbins, 'A' Company, 1/2nd London Regt. was wounded on Saturday, 1st July 1916 and evacuated to a hospital in Sleaford.

[ii] 4479 Pte Alfred Fenner, No. 4 Platoon, 'A' Company, 1/2nd London Regt. was killed on Saturday, 1st July 1916. He was buried in Hebuterne Military Cemetery, grave IV. B. 6

hand smoke bombs thrown by detachments of the 167th Brigade. It was some hand smoke bombs thrown by the 167th Brigade men that went too early.

Both in the front line and to the rear, German observers noted this smoke and an alert was sent down to the troops that an attack was imminent. But an even more obvious signal that something major was about to happen had occurred five minutes earlier. Some five miles to the south, near the village of Beaumont Hamel, 40,600lbs of ammonal were detonated in a huge mine under what was known as Hawthorn Ridge. Filmed by cameraman Geoffrey Malins for Gaumont Pictures the film has become one of the enduring images of World War One. From an anonymous, barren slope a huge plume of smoke, earth and debris suddenly erupts silently into the air. Silently on 1916 film but in reality with a roar some say was heard on the other side of the English Channel. The sight and sound was all that was needed to alert everyone on both sides of the front that something major was about to happen. For the defending troops, it was a ten minute warning to get themselves into position. Ten minutes extra to get their machine guns into position, to bring up boxes of ammunition and stick grenades and for the artillery to load and make ready to fire. Quite why the British generals opposite Hawthorn Ridge thought giving ten minute's notice of the attack was a good idea is anyone's guess. Originally, the local Corps commander, Lt. Gen. Sir Aylmer Hunter-Weston, had wanted the mine set four hours before Zero hour. The intention was to take the resulting crater and then let the Germans think that was all that was intended. But, given the British track record in attacking mine craters, G.H.Q. was having none of it. Then, in some hugely unhappy compromise resulting, it is thought, from a Divisional staff officer's concern that falling debris might injure the attacking troops, a time of 7.20 a.m. was agreed. Whatever the explanation, now everyone knew the 'Big Show' was on.

North of Hebuterne, British machine guns opened up barrage fire covering the final objectives at the same moment and five minutes later the proper smoke screen was started. Smoke bombs from 4 in. Stokes Mortars (No. 2 Company, 5th Battalion, Special Brigade, R.E.[i]) were sent into the German lines and, at the same time, smoke candles were lit in the front trenches. On either flank, six mortars were used to send over the smoke bombs while another twelve were used to blanket certain key areas. Soon a slowly moving veil of smoke hung along the whole front[ii]. So asphyxiating were the concentrated fumes that a large number of Germans put on their gas masks.

At 7.30 a.m. the artillery lifted as one and began to move onto their pre-arranged targets in the German support and reserve lines. At the same time, all along the front, the infantry got to their feet or climbed out of the trenches and began to move across the thick, rank, yellowing grass of No Man's Land. Behind them, the follow-up waves moved forward across the open areas between the various British trenches, slowing down only to cross the numerous wooden bridges that had been laid across them to help the men on their way. Soon, across the whole length of the front, six long lines of soldiers were surging

---

[i] 'E' Section was attached to the 169th Brigade with twelve mortars, four each at the top of the three main communication trenches: Yiddish, Yellow and Yankee. 'G' Section was with the 168th Brigade with four at the end of Woman Street, six at the end of Welcome Street and four in Warrior Street. The ones in Warrior provided the flank screen and the ones on Welcome were to cover the Farmer-Farmyard strongpoint.
[ii] The wind speed at ground level at 7.26 a.m. was just over 2 mph.

forward down the slopes towards the German lines. As they left, the reserve companies and the support battalions started to move along the communication trenches designated for 'up' traffic. In the battalion, brigade, divisional, Corps and Army headquarters, commanding officers and their staff sat back and awaited news. There was a quiet confidence about the outcome but, as they now knew, there was little more they could do to affect the result of the battle ahead. They had laid their plans, now it was up to the junior officers and men of the infantry to see them through to success.

The most disastrous battle in the long history of the British Army had begun.

ENDNOTES:

1 Liveing Edward G, Attack, MacMillan 1918 and 1986
2 Mason, Rfn R J, The Rangers, from a document held at the Liddle Collection, Leeds University.
3 Hawkings Frank, From Ypres to Cambrai, 1973.
4 Liveing Ibid.

9.   Z DAY: 0730 - 0830

"It was really magnificent the way every man, cool and collected, strolled out through quite a stiff barrage to the tape I had laid down 150 yards out during the night. The smoke lifted for a few seconds when we were out and I noticed the men were inclined to bunch on the right. I shouted an order and they shook out as if they were on Wimbledon Common."

2ⁿᵈ Lt. R E Petley
1/5ᵗʰ Londons (London Rifle Brigade)

GERMAN RETALIATION was instant. From field guns and medium and heavy howitzers hidden in the woods and hollows to the east, a heavy barrage crashed down on the British first and second lines and the communication trenches. Rifleman Frank Jacobs of 'C' Company of the London Rifle Brigade described the barrage as "wicked" with heavy shrapnel shells exploding overhead at twenty yard intervals[1]:

"They put (a barrage) in No Man's Land, one over the front line, one over the reserves and others right along the communication trenches."

The leading waves had anticipated this response, however, and had already moved out into the relative safety of No Man's Land. On the left, a couple of minutes before Zero hour proper, the first two waves of 1/5ᵗʰ (London Rifle Brigade) and 1/9ᵗʰ (Queen Victoria's Rifles) Londons started to advance 'steadily'[i] towards the German lines. They then disappeared into the thick smoke.

The first waves of the Queen Victoria's Rifles and the London Rifle Brigade quickly got across No Man's Land and into the first German trenches. But not without casualties from the growing German barrage and machine gun and rifle fire from those defenders who had managed to make it into the trenches from their deep fastnesses underground. 1471 Rfn. Arthur Schuman of the London Rifle Brigade was in one of the leading waves of 'A' Company on the far left of the Division's attack:

"Whistles blew[ii] at 7.30 a.m. - up the scaling ladders - under the cover of a smoke screen the advance started towards the German lines. The smoke-screen began to lift. Officers led the way, most of whom dropped immediately. Machine guns seemed to crackle from every direction. I kept my head down as low as possible, helmet tilted to protect my eyes, but I could still see men dropping all around me. One on my left clutched his stomach and just collapsed. Another a yard to my right slumped onto his knees. The din was terrific, stifling any screams. Entangled wire had to be negotiated. Just one opening, on which the German fire was rapid and most accurate. Not many of us got through."[2]

Rfn. Jacobs provided a description of the advance in a letter to his local newspaper, the Hackney and Stoke Newington Gazette, written from his hospital

---

[i] Lt. Col Dickins, commanding officer of the Queen Victoria Rifles, saw his men disappear. After the war he wrote (27ᵗʰ July 1929): "The advance was carried out "calmly and slowly," says the Queen Victoria Rifles history, "steadily" says that 56ᵗʰ Division history. Any other pace was out of the question in view of the width of no man's land and the various impedimenta carried by the assaulting troops."
[ii] This is a false memory from Rfn Schuman. Unusually, whistles were not used by the 56ᵗʰ Division on 1ˢᵗ July 1916.

bed somewhere in rural Hampshire. His observations reinforced the concerns about the quality of some of the heavy howitzer shells which should have destroyed the German trenches, dugouts and troops:

"The place was nothing but a mass of shell hole, some small, some huge. Huge 9.2 shells lay there unexploded and the whole place and been smashed to atoms. The German first line was but a ditch and, as we expected, there were very few Germans there. These held up their hands crying 'Kamerad, kamerad' and some were taken prisoner and some were shot."[3]

2122 Rfn. Frank Hawkings of the Q.V.R. was one of the first of his battalion into No Man's Land:

"Sharp to the minute at Zero hour (7:30 a.m.), we erected our ladders, and climbed out into the open. Shells were bursting everywhere, and through the drifting smoke in front of us we could see the enemy's first line from which grey figures emerged and hurled hand grenades. We moved forward in long lines, stumbling through the mass of shell holes, wire and wreckage, and behind us more waves appeared.

As we neared the enemy line, a low-flying shrapnel shell burst right over my head, completely deafening me. I ducked and slipped head first into a shell hole. Simultaneously several more shells burst close around. We must have been in the midst of the Hun barrage. I felt a sharp pain in my back, and my next recollections are of a medley of Hun's and Q.V.R.s at close quarters with bombs and bayonet. The tide of battle rolled on as our fellows forced their way to the Hun trench, and when I recovered my wits, I found myself bleeding profusely from the wound in my left forearm. There was also a patch of blood on my breeches from the wound in my back. I was by this time completely dazed and half deafened, but had sufficient sense left to appreciate in which direction lay our old front line."[4]

Another anonymous member of the Q.V.R., a man from Harborough in Leicester, later wrote:

"We left our trenches under cover of a terrific artillery fire from our own guns and a barrage of fire from the German trenches and guns, and also machine gun fire from them, and also under cover of a tremendous cloud of smoke which we threw out. At about 7.30 in the morning we went over in waves at about 40 yards interval. I was in the second wave, and we walked to the German trenches as if on parade. Several of my pals got hit going over, and when we got there we found all the German sentries had been killed by our artillery fire, and the rest were in their dugouts, which, by the way, are about 30 feet deep. Well, our job was to bomb these dug-outs. After bombing several of them, to our amazement about 30 of them came up out of one of them. They had no equipment, nor rifles, and shouted, 'Kamerade!'. Well, we soon packed them off over the top to our own trenches. Meanwhile, the German barrage of fire was so terrific that several of those prisoners were hit by their own fire in their endeavours to get to our lines."

For some men the battle was all too brief. The unlucky ones were killed or mortally wounded by the German barrage that fell on the British trenches within minutes of the attack starting. Others, like 1471 Sgt Cecil Sim of the Victorias, were luckier. A Blighty wound and a swift passage home:

"I was wounded in the left hand just as I had got on our parapet. Felt a bit dazed owing to a big 'crump' having burst unpleasantly close just before. Didn't twig much that happened, but had sense enough to hop off quickly to the dressing station in Wurzel Street where Doctor Clarke bandaged the wound and told me I should have to lose a finger. Walked to Sailly, got a private motor to clearing hospital at Couin and lorry from there to the railhead clearing hospital at Warlencourt."[5]

By 3ʳᵈ July Sim was a happy man. He had landed in Southampton and was out of the war. To add to his sense of well-being the award of the Military Medal for his general service followed on in the autumn.

4511 Rfn. Charles Richards[i] was another man hit as the waves moved across No Man's Land and it was clear he could go no further. He had gone over with his close friend 4507 Rfn. Herbert Parsons by his side and now he watched his 41 year old mate move away through the smoke, silently wishing him well. It was the last he saw of him, his body would not be recovered until the following spring and was buried in one of the small cemeteries which would soon spring up along No Man's Land[ii].

Behind them assaulting troops Pte Clements of the 1/2ⁿᵈ Londons was waiting with his mates in Cross Street on the orchard lined fringe of Hebuterne:

"A few minutes later men came streaming along all bleeding, some with faces that only looked masses of flesh, others with shattered arms – all horrible sights. Then some prisoners came along. Some were injured and all looked dazed. One of our fellows had been chewing some cheese when a big German came along. He offered it to the man who muttered something and then wolfed it in a second. Of course, the sight of prisoners cheered us up a lot. Every now and then a signaller would come along and would be eagerly questioned: 'How are things going?' 'Jolly good, in the third line, bombing towards the fourth'. Then Coleman came along and told me Harry Deane[iii] has gone. I did sentry with him on the gun mounting sheds in Malta."[6]

Out in No Man's Land the intensity of the artillery fire impressed itself on another young soldier, this time a rifleman with the 1/5ᵗʰ Londons – the London Rifle Brigade. Fifty years after the attack, 2614 RFn. Noel Lockhart recalled the experience:

i 4511 Rfn. Charles Sydney Richards, 1/16ᵗʰ London Regt. (Queen's Westminster Rifles), was evacuated to Ward E, County of London War Hospital, Epsom, Surrey from where he wrote to the Territorial Service Gazette. He was later commissioned into a battalion of the London Regiment [*Source:* TSG, 19ᵗʰ August 1916]

ii 4507 Rfn. Herbert Parsons, 1/16ᵗʰ London Regt. (Queen's Westminster Rifles) was killed on Saturday, 1ˢᵗ July 1916. Aged 41, he was the son of George Henry & Catherine Parsons of 'Maytrees', South Ealing and husband of Florence Edith Parsons of 14A, Northcote Avenue, Ealing, London. He was buried in Gommecourt British Cemetery No. 2, grave I. B. 16

iii 1907 Pte Henry Russell Deane, 1/2ⁿᵈ London Regt. (Royal Fusiliers) was killed on Saturday, 1ˢᵗ July 1916. He was buried in Hebuterne Military Cemetery, grave IV. B. 1.

"I was so young - silly that. I actually called out to a friend "Don't panic, Hill". The moment we went over the top all hell was let loose it seemed. I remember feeling that there was not enough air to breathe - so many shells were bursting. Small bodies of men simply disappeared when a shell burst near them."[7]

To Lockhart's right, Rifleman Mason of the Rangers was experiencing the same combination of confusion, fear and doubt tempered by the ingrained discipline of the well-rehearsed and rigidly trained soldier:

"Word was passed along to get ready to go; then the whistles went and everyone was glad to get on the move, hoping this would relieve the tedium and tension. And up the scaling ladders and through the holes in the front of the trench went eager men to form up in line in the open with 400 yards to go to reach the enemy. No doubt every man was trembling with a mixture of fear, noise and the long sitting in a cramped position. It was impossible for any man to be his normal self in such circumstances which are difficult to describe. Everyone partaking had geed himself up for this surge forward and speculated what it would be like and now here was realisation in a manner far worse than expected even if no one had anticipated a picnic, that theory and practice are always poles apart, no matter how well planned the former might be. To say the least, mental concentration was impaired, and the automatic soldier moved forward over the rough ground if he survived long enough."[8]

For all of the attacking battalions the thickness of the smoke screen was initially comforting - after all, no-one could see through it to fire accurately and some of the early German machine gun fire on either flank was certainly high. But, as they moved further down the gentle slope into the shallow depression between the opposing lines, the sheer density of the smoke started to cause almost as many problems as it solved. For a start, the smoke was thicker than in any of the practice attacks made on the dummy trenches back in the mud at Halloy. Seeing any distance, either straight ahead or to left or right, was impossible. Officers and N.C.O.s attempted vainly to keep their men together, to keep the lines straight, to stop the men bunching. With the volume of noise created by the artillery of both sides, voice commands were all but useless except for those officers and men next to one another. The other forms of command, by gesture or hand signal, were now made redundant by the smoke. The waves started to break up and small groups of men would blunder forward, hoping their sense of direction was true. But, with every explosion or chattering burst of machine gun fire, each group would move to left or right to avoid the danger. Every few yards, a figure would loom dimly through the smoke and gesture to the men to move onwards, down the gentle incline.

In the 168ᵗʰ Brigade, both attacking battalions adopted the same formation. Each battalion went forward on a front 400 metres wide, the four companies side by side. They advanced in four lines, one platoon from each company in every line, and with the lines sixty-five metres behind the other. A line consisted of about 200 officers and men with a gap of two or three paces between each one. From right to left the London Scottish companies were 'A', 'C', 'B' and 'D' and on the Rangers' front 'A' to 'D' alphabetically. Standing in their trenches away to the south, the Acting Adjutant of the 1/5th Royal Warwickshires, Maj. Charles Carrington, was watching for the action to start. The smoke from the screen had already drifted some way into No Man's Land and they could just see the ground across which the London Scottish would start to advance:

"Someone shouted 'there they go' and I looked to the left and there they were, the London Scottish, running forward across the 3 or 400 hundred yards of green grass between our village and Gommecourt Wood (sic). Then they vanished into the smoke and then there was nothing left but noise. After this we saw nothing and we knew nothing."[9]

The London Scottish right and right centre companies ('A' and 'C' Companies) had left their trenches early to collect along a tape which had been placed in No Man's Land overnight. Here, the British front line veered away from the German lines and the tape was designed to bring the London Scottish on to the correct line of attack. In spite of this, 'A' Company of the London Scottish (C.O. Capt. H C Sparks) immediately hit a problem. With the smoke screen so much thicker than in practice and without the gentle slope of the valley to guide them towards the German lines, it was even harder to keep direction here. On the far right, No Man's Land was 100 metres wider than to their left and 'A' Company's line of attack was at an angle of about 45° to the left of the face of their own front line, across the brow of a low, flat ridge that projected out from the eastern fringes of Hebuterne village. In the smoke and confusion the lead platoon, No. 2, lost its bearings and drifted off to the right, followed by most of No. 3 Platoon. They groped their way forward in the dense smoke, no doubt wondering where their colleagues to their left had gone. At some point, they would have emerged from their protective smoke screen, 250 metres away to the south of their intended attack, near to the Hebuterne to Puisieux Road. In the trenches in front of them were lined the men of the 6th Company, 170th Regiment commanded by Leutnant der Reserve Roser. The Londoners would have seen the tops of their helmets as the defenders mounted the firestep. Even above the thunder of the bombardment and the answering fire of the German guns, they might have heard the orders to fire yelled in German. To the right, stretching away across the undulating countryside towards Serre were the trenches occupied by the III/66th Regiment under Hauptmann Trenk[i] and these trenches too were manned in anticipation of an attack. The gunner of at least one Maxim positioned near to the sunken road swung the barrel of his gun towards the isolated troops. It is possible that the men of the 1/5th Royal Warwicks, who were manning the trenches to the south of the attack, saw the two platoons stumble out of the smoke. Saw them turn and look at one another as they realised they were in the wrong place. Watched them as they ran along the thick, uncut German wire trying to find some way forward. Heard the urgent hammer of the German Maxim guns. Saw the men fall. Of the 100 or so men of Nos. 2 and 3 Platoons, 'A' Company, The London Scottish, who left their trenches that morning, only one officer, 2nd Lt. Allan Petrie of No. 3 Platoon, and five men eventually found their way to their objective, the Farmyard stronghold.

---

[i] Hauptmann Trenk was killed in action on the 15th July 1916.

To their left, No. 1 and No. 4 Platoons had better fortune. Coming up to the German line, they too ran into uncut or partially cut wire and, again, here was evidence of the failure of the six-day bombardment as the previous night's patrols had shown the German defenders to be capable of sending out repair parties. They were neither dead nor dazed but ready to defend themselves and the damaged wire had clearly been repaired and replaced. A frantic search eventually showed up a lane cut in the wire to allow German patrols access to No Man's Land. Here, the density of the smoke screen was a blessing not a curse and, under its protection, these platoons found their way into the devastated German lines near the junction of Fair and Farmyard trenches. The 5th Company of the 170th Regiment held this sector. For six days, the super-heavy and heavy howitzers of VII Corps' artillery had targeted them. In anticipation of an attack, the front lines here were only lightly held and 'A' Company of the Scottish rapidly forced the German garrison back across the strong point, wounding the 5th Company's C.O., Leutnant der Reserve Mülhausen, in the process. In the confusion, the 52nd Minenwerfer Company was forced to abandon their mortars and spent the rest of the day fighting as infantrymen. The occupants of one dug out, led by Leutnant der Reserve Steib[i], held on grimly as the Londoners swept round their position but, otherwise, resistance was feeble as the defenders melted away and sought refuge.

2nd Lt. White had been waiting with his men of the 3rd wave to move forward:

"Nearer 7.25 gave orders to fix bayonets. Very tense moments, every nerve in the body seemed to be quivering. Ready, Go! I have no rifle just a light cane and my revolver. I mounted the steps and immediately forgot my fears. On each side of me stretched my platoon with rifles at the high port, in front just an outline of the 2nd wave disappearing into the smoke cloud. One very close shell burst disturbed my complacency especially when I realised that there were big gaps in my platoon, my sergeant (Sgt Kirkpatrick) had gone.

Still we go on and the air is getting .... with the heat of shell bursts, the ground is strewn with occasional forms. Now we seem to be at the wire, there isn't much left of it but it is lying about loose. I am suddenly awakened to the fury of war by the sight of several of the leading wave lying in a heap obviously caught by MG fire. I snatch up one of the vacant rifles and bandoliers and go on.... Just in time see half left about 10 paces off a big German is aligning the sights of a MG on us. I immediately drop on my knees and fire, several other shots are fired simultaneously laying out the team of three. I have a feeling that fear made my knees collapse but it made my firing position steadier (Sgt Beattie put the MG out of action with a pick[ii]). Now we see occasional grey caps of men who have been passed over by the leading waves or have come up from dugouts." [10]

At H-Hour, as the London Scottish moved off, 'C' and 'D' Companies of the 1/13th (Kensingtons) London Regiment moved forward into the empty trenches and a trench clearing party, comprising two platoons of 'B' Company and two

---

i Leutenant der Reserve Steib was killed in action on the 31st July 1916
ii Sgts Kirkpatrick and Beattie survived the attack.

sections of bombers led by Lt. William Penn[i] and 2nd Lt. Percy Pike[ii], followed the London Scottish over to the German lines. Behind them, two men from the 1/1st City of Edinburgh Field Company R.E. were to have gone out into No Man's Land to mark out the new trench to be dug from between Whiskey and Welcome Streets to the end of a German sap in Farmyard trench. Then the Kensington's trench digging company should have gone to work but the hostile barrage on the trenches and between the lines was already so intense that Major W H Young, the Kensingtons C.O., asked for and received permission for his men to stay in the trenches for the time being.[iii]

Plate 22 Lt. William Penn of the Kensingtons with his first wife Jane

Following, on both the London Scottish's and The Ranger's front, came two small parties from the Royal Field Artillery. Made up of an officer and two men these were the Forward Observation Officer (FOO) parties of the Macart artillery group. Led by Lt. Gerald B Wolfe on the Scottish's front and 2nd Lt. J A E Friend on The Rangers' front, they carried with them field telephones, one mile of ladder wire and rations for two days. The intention was that they should set up a position in the advanced headquarters of the two battalions within the German lines and be able then to call down supporting field artillery fire as requested. The 'ladder wire', designed exactly as it sounds, was an attempt to reduce the prospect of the wire being cut by shell fire or shrapnel, i.e. if one side of the ladder was cut then the signal could still be maintained on the other. Each

---

[i] Lt. William A Penn, 1/13th London Regt. (Kensingtons) was born on 28th September 1876 in Doncaster and lived at 62, Albany Mansions, Albert Bridge Road, Battersea prior to going to France. He was the second son of the late M Penn of 21, Queen Adelaide Road, Penge, a Weslyan Minister. A journalist, he wrote a book on tobacco called 'The Soverane Herbe', published in 1901 by Grant Richards. He first married Jane Hartley who lived under the name Winifred Penn and with whom he had three daughters. On his return from France he took up with a lady who became his second wide, Margaret Penn, by whom he had a daughter in January 1918 and a son sometime later. By now an alcoholic, he subsequently abandoned Margaret and her children who were both put up for adoption. He died on 24th July 1948 at Mile End Hospital where, ironically, his third daughter by his first marriage had seen less than four year's old. Margaret Penn wrote a semi-autobiographical trilogy after the war describing her meeting with Penn before he went to France (in the second volume 'The Foolish Virgin') and their subsequent marriage. (in 'The Young Mrs Burton'. The first volume about her upbringing is entitled 'Manchester Fourteen Miles'). Margaret Penn died in 1982. [*Source:* Ralph Howard-Williams, grandson of William and Margaret Penn].
[ii] Both officers were to be wounded during the attack and Pike became a prisoner of war.
[iii] Another pair of 1/1st City of Edinburgh men were to have marked up a similar trench running from Wood Street to the junction of Fetter and Elbe trenches but they too were unable to enter No Man's Land because of the German barrage.

battalion had some field guns allocated to their front and they were given nicknames to describe each supporting battery: for the London Scottish they were 'Ashgun' and 'Nicgun'[i]; for The Rangers it was 'Fishgun'; and, to be allocated as required, 'Jackgun' and 'Dymhow'. Waiting anxiously for the first feedback from these advanced parties were two officers in a control Observation Post (OP). Here, Lt. G M Hamilton and 2nd Lt. W G White[ii] were aided by two headquarters telephonists and two others linked to 'Ashgun' and 'Nicgun'. The Rangers' OP was called OPH and was manned by 2nd Lt. R St John Carr and two telephonists from the 'Fishgun' battery. Lastly, at OPZ, two officers co-ordinated the actions of 'Jackgun' and 'Dymhow'. They were 2nd Lt. E G P Nathan and 2nd Lt. W G Fowler who worked with two 'Jackgun' telephonists and one from 'Dymhow'. Thses officers and their men would now sit and wait for messages from the two parties who should be swiftly established in the captured German lines. They would wait all day. They would hear nothing.

Within a few minutes of the attack going in, requests for extra bombs and small arms ammunition began to filter back from the London Scottish, 300 metres away in the German trenches. Carrying parties of the 1/13th London Regiment were organised by Capt. Francis Ware and sent forward, using for cover a sap that had been dug out from the front lines for some 75 metres. Although the enemy was firing blind into the still dense smoke screen, the range and lines of fire were well known and yard perfect. Hardly a man got further than a few yards before they were cut down by the high explosive, shrapnel and machine gun fire that now filled No Man's Land.

On the Brigade's left, the Rangers also disappeared into the smoke as they moved forward to the assault. 2nd Lt. Edward Liveing commanded the 5th Platoon, 'B' Company and was due to go over in the Rangers' third wave:

"It was just past 7.30 a.m. The third wave, of which my platoon formed a part, was due to start at 7.30 plus 45 seconds - at the same time as the second wave in my part of the line. The corporal got up, so I realised that the second wave was assembling on the top to go over. The ladders had been smashed or used as stretchers long ago. Scrambling out of a battered part of the trench, I arrived on top, looked down my line of men, swung my rifle forward as a signal, and started off at the prearranged walk."

"A continuous hissing noise all around one, like a railway engine letting off steam, signified that the German machine-gunners had become aware of our advance. I nearly trod on a motionless form. It lay in a natural position, but the ashen face and fixed, fearful eyes told me that the man had just fallen. I did not recognise him then... The scene that met my eyes as I stood on the parapet of our trench for that one second is almost indescribable. Just in front the ground was pitted by innumerable shell-holes. More holes opened suddenly every now and then. Here and there a few bodies lay about. Farther away, before our front line and in No Man's Land, lay more. In the smoke one could distinguish the second line

---

[i] These names reflected the surnames of the various battery commanders. The 'gun' batteries referred to the 18pdr field guns and 'Dymhow' was the battery of 4.5 in. field howitzers.

[ii] 2nd Lt. William Gurney White, 281st Brigade, Royal Field Artillery, was killed in action on 23rd September 1916 near Leuze Wood. Aged 28, he was the son of Mr and Mrs Baglin White and the husband of Dagny M White, of 102, Plaistow Lane, Bromley, Kent. He was buried in Grove Town Cemetery, Meaulte, grave I. E. 2.

advancing. One man after another fell down in a seemingly natural manner, and the wave melted away. In the background, where ran the remains of the German lines and wire, there was a mass of smoke, the red of the shrapnel bursting amid it. Amongst it, I saw Captain H.[i] and his men attempting to enter the German front line. The Boches had met them on the parapet with bombs. The whole scene reminded me of battle pictures, at which in earlier years I had gazed with much amazement. Only this scene, though it did not seem more real, was infinitely more terrible. Everything stood still for a second, as a panorama painted with three colours - the white of the smoke, the red of the shrapnel and blood, the green of the grass."[11]

Battalion to attack astride the Hebuterne to Bucquoy Road			
D Company	**C Company**	**B Company**	**A Company**
Front line (1st Wave) No. 13 Platoon Snipers & Observers	No. 10 Platoon	No. 5 Platoon Bombing squad from No. 7 Platoon	No. 1 Platoon Bombing squad from No. 4 Platoon Snipers & Observers
Boyau de Service (2nd Wave) No. 14 Platoon	No. 9 Platoon Snipers & Observers	No. 6 Platoon Snipers & Observers	No. 2 Platoon Lewis Gun Team
Support Line (3rd Wave) No. 15 Platoon Tools, etc.,	No. 11 Platoon Tools, etc.,	No. 7 Platoon Tools, etc., (less Bombers)	No. 3 Platoon Tools, etc.,
Reserve Line (4th Wave) No. 16 Platoon Tools, etc., Lewis gun teams	No. 12 Platoon Tools, etc., Lewis gun teams	No. 8 Platoon Tools & sandbags (less Bombers) Lewis gun teams	No. 4 Platoon Tools, etc., (less Bombers) Lewis gun team
(5th Wave) Napier Street Company HQ	Company HQ	Company HQ	Company HQ
(6th Wave) Battalion bombers, Trench pioneers & Carrying parties			

Figure 3 The Rangers' attack plan
Source: NA file WO 95/2954

As the first waves of the Rangers walked steadily away through the British wire, the 1/4th London Regiment came forward and occupied the front line system: 'A' Company (Capt. A R Moore) on the right, 'C' Company (Capt. J T Sykes) on the left and 'D' Company (Capt. H G Stanham) in reserve. There they waited for further orders except for two platoons of 'B' Company commanded by 2nd Lts. L R Chapman[ii] and H G Hicklenton (the rest of 'B' Company were to

---

[i] Capt. Richard Lennard Hoare, 'C' Company, 1/12th London Regt (The Rangers).
[ii] 2nd Lt. Leslie Rougier Chapman, 1/4th London Regt. (Royal Fusiliers), was born on 7th September 1890. He lived at Woodborough Lodge, Woodborough Road, Putney. He was educated at St Paul's School, where he was a member of the OTC, and was a member of the London Stock Exchange with Chapman, Wolff & Co. He attested 1223 Private in the Honourable Artillery Company on 9th August 1914 and was commissioned into the 1/4th Londons in September 1914. He ended the war at GHQ in France.

be used as carrying parties and held in general reserve). These men formed the fifth, trench clearing wave of the assaulting column and their task was to clear German dugouts and collect prisoners in order to prevent them from attacking the earlier waves from the rear. The two platoons had been made up to a strength of one officer, three N.C.O.s and 36 men organised into four sections: clearing, bombing, blocking and communication and should have played a crucial role in the clearing and securing the captured German trenches. Standing in the assembly trenches, however, they had already suffered 26 casualties, a third of the men, during the earlier bombardment, one of whom was 2nd Lt. Howard Hicklenton[i], blown up by a shell and knocked unconscious. Later in the day, only ten men from these two platoons were to return to the British trenches and their other officer, 2nd Lt. Leslie Chapman, lay wounded with a machine gun bullet wound to his arm.

Because of the heavy German bombardment in this sector, the Companies of the 1/4th Londons found the trenches greatly damaged and the WS Line, to be occupied by 'D' Company under Capt. Hugh Stanham, was especially badly hit. This Company was stretched out behind 'A' and 'C' Companies and such was the damage to the trenches that Stanham was immediately concerned about his ability to communicate with his two platoon commanders, 2nd Lts George Davis and Bryan Yeoman. He thus took up a central position in the hope that this would allow him to keep in touch with his subalterns but communication within 'D' Company, between all three Companies and with Battalion HQ was to prove increasingly difficult as the day went on.

Together, the lead elements of the London Scottish and the flank companies of the Rangers entered the German front line within five minutes. Casualties in the main were remarkably light, the Rangers suffering just a few on the left from machine gun fire from the direction of Gommecourt. On their right things were different and, although 'A' Company found the front line German trenches empty, they lost three out of five officers in the process of crossing No Man's Land. Crossing Fate Trench they moved forward towards Fall, the German second line. As they fanned out (the width of The Rangers final objective was 600 yards but they started from a line 400 yards wide), a group of Germans emerged from a dugout in Fall and threw bombs at the advancing men. On their right, however, the London Scottish had already swept over the German second line and, noticing this minor counter-attack, dispersed the Germans with a well directed volley of Mills grenades. The survivors retreated down Fall Trench but, at about the same time, machine gun fire from Nameless Fire began to sweep the area. Short of the German second line and with their left wing in the air, the survivors of 'A' Company went to ground, some using the shell holes for cover others jumping into Elbe, the long communication trench that snaked back up the hill in front of them. Capt. George Wyatt, 'A' Company's commander, realising that an advance across the open was suicide, organised a bombing party which attempted, under cover of a Lewis gun team placed in a turn in the trench, to bomb up Elbe towards the junction of Felt and Fall trenches in the German second line. A short distance up Elbe their progress was halted by a party of

i 2nd Lt. Howard George Hicklenton, 1/4th London Regt. (Royal Fusiliers) was born in 1897 and lived at 64, Weston Park, Crouch End, London, N8. He joined the battalion from the 2/4th Londons on 14th May 1916. From 1st August to 6th November 1919 he was OC, 344th Prisoner of War Company. He died on 13th October 1971

German bombers who had erected a barricade and were now busily lobbing their stick grenades into the traverses occupied by the Rangers. With their advance stalled and it being impossible to determine the local tactical situation, Capt. Wyatt[i] clambered up the sticky side of the trench and poked his head above the edge in an effort to observe the lie of the land. Within seconds he fell back, seriously wounded and, for a time, 'A' Company's assault lost impetus as the men, and the surviving officer, 2nd Lt. Wilfrid Parker[ii], reorganised and tried, unsuccessfully, to establish contact with 'B' Company who, by now, should have been pressing forward on their left to deal with the defences around Nameless Farm and its venomous machine guns.

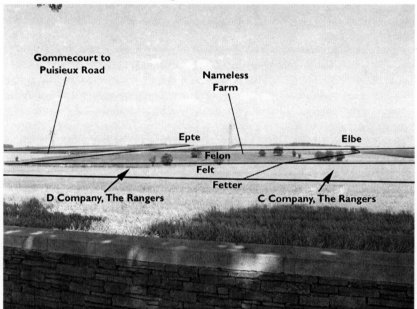

Plate 23 Left wing of Rangers' attack, as seen from Gommecourt Cemetery No. 2

The reason why there was no support on 'A' Company's left was that, in the centre of their attack, the Rangers' advance had already stalled. 2nd Lt. Liveing had seen this from the British parapet. Their difficulties had begun within yards of leaving the trenches as their own wire had not been properly cut leaving only narrow avenues through which the men had to queue. Then, on reaching the German front line, the R.F.C.'s warnings about the uncut wire proved horribly accurate. 2nd Lt. Taplin, Sgt. King and a few others found their way through the thick belt of German wire but their advance then foundered on volleys of rifle

---

i Capt. George Montague Griffith Wyatt, 1/12th London Regt. (The Rangers) was born on 5th December 1887. Educated at Berkhamstead School, he lived at 23, Carlingford Road, Hampstead and was a solicitor. He was commissioned into The Rangers in March 1911 and promoted Lieutenant on 12th November 1911. He was then promoted Captain on 4th September 1914. Sent to France he was wounded and repatriated on 5th May 1915. Promoted Major in 1919 he stayed with the Territorial Force Reserve after the war.

ii 2nd Lt. Wilfrid Grosvenor Parker, 1/12th London Regt. (The Rangers) was born on 12th August 1876 in Rio de Janeiro. The son of the late Thomas Edward and Sarah Parker of 31, Kingscourt Road, Streatham, London, he was educated at Sir Walter St John's Grammar School in Battersea and was employed as a clerk. He was commissioned into the 2/12th London Regt. in June 1915 having previously been 676 Private in the 23rd (Service Battalion), Royal Fusiliers (Sportsmen's), joining on 6th October 1914.

and machine gun fire and a hail of bombs from the German front line. Albert Taplin was never seen again.[i]

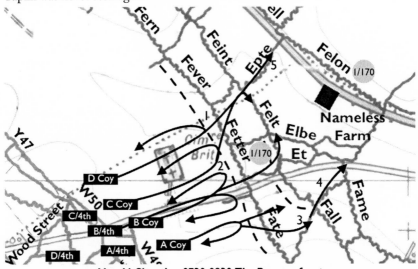

Map 11 Situation 0730-0830 The Rangers front

Legend: 1 – Maj. Jones, D Coy, killed   2 – 2nd Lt. Liveing, B Coy, wounded
3 – Capt. Wyatt, A Coy, wounded   4 – 2nd Lt. Parker's party bomb Germans
5 – Mixed group of Rangers fight up Epte trench

- - - - Lines of uncut wire

As the hostile machine gun and artillery fire grew in intensity, the following waves of the battalion forgot their instructions to walk steadily across No Man's Land. Abandoning their cumbersome burdens, the lines broke up into small groups of men hurrying forward, coalescing then separating, avoiding wire obstacles and deep shell holes, trying to find the lines of least resistance:

"We had been told to walk. Our boys, however, rushed forward with splendid impetuosity to help their comrades and smash the German resistance in the front line. What happened to our materials for blocking the German communication trench, when we got to our objective, I should not like to think. I kept up a fast walking pace and tried to keep the line together. This was impossible. When we had jumped clear of the remains of our front line trench, my platoon slowly disappeared through the line stretching out. For a long time, however, Sergeant S., Lance-Corporal M., Rifleman D, whom I remember being just in front of me, raising his hand in the air and cheering, and myself kept together. Eventually Lance-Corporal M., was the only one of my platoon left near me, and I shouted out to him, "Let's try and keep together." It was not long,

---

[i] 2nd Lt. Albert William Taplin, 1/12th London Regt (The Rangers), was killed on Saturday, 1st July 1916. Born on 8th June 1892, he was the son of William James and Sarah Taplin of 12, North Side, Paddington, London and lived at 12, Wharf House, North Wharf Road, Paddington. He was educated at Paddington Technical Institute and was employed as an Assistant Registrar in the Public Trustee Office, Clement's Inn in The Strand. He attested 3021 Private in the London Scottish on 2nd September 1914 being promoted Corporal and Lance Sergeant and was a member of No. 5 Platoon, 'B' Company. He was commissioned into the 3/12th London Regt. in October 1915. His body was never found and his name is listed on the Thiepval Memorial, Pier and Face 9C. In his will, dated 16th June 1916, he left his medals to his fiancée Miss M Bluck.

however, before we also parted company. One thing I remember very well about this time, and that was that a hare jumped up and rushed towards and past me through the dry, yellowish grass, its eyes bulging with fear."

"We were dropping into a slight valley. The shell-holes were less here, but bodies lay all over the ground, and a terrible groaning arose from all sides. At one time we seemed to be advancing in little groups. I was at the head of one for a moment or two, only to realise shortly afterwards that I was alone."[12]

Under the weight of the German barrage and intense machine gun fire now coming from the earthworks surrounding Nameless Farm, the supporting waves of the Rangers were melting away. They had already suffered heavily in their own trenches whilst waiting for the order to attack and now, as No Man's Land heaved and rocked with explosions and was swept from end to end by relentless Maxim fire, they lost touch with the men in front. Some stopped and fired into the German trenches, but the advance faltered as officers and N.C.O.s became victims of the terrible cross-fire from machine guns to the left and front. 2nd Lt. Liveing had approached the still solid rolls of barbed wire outside the German lines but could go no further:

"I came up to the German wire. Here one could hear men shouting to one another and the wounded groaning above the explosions of shells and bombs and the rattle of machine-guns. I found myself with J(osephs), an officer of 'C' company, afterwards killed while charging a machine gun in the open[i]. We looked round to see what our fourth line was doing. My company's fourth line had no leader. Captain W(ightwick)[ii], wounded twice, had fallen into a shell-hole, while Sergeant S[iii] had been killed during the preliminary bombardment. Men were kneeling and firing. I started back to see if I could bring them up, but they were too far away. I made a cup of my mouth and shouted, as J(osephs) was shouting. We could not be heard. I turned round again and advanced to a gap in the German wire. There was a pile of our wounded here on the German parapet."[13]

Within a few minutes Liveing was wounded in the hip:

"Suddenly I cursed. I had been scalded in the left hip. A shell, I thought, had blown up in a water-logged crump-hole and sprayed me with boiling water. Letting go of my rifle, I dropped forward full length on the ground. My hip began to smart unpleasantly, and I felt a curious warmth stealing down my left leg. I thought it was the boiling water that had scalded me. Certainly my breeches looked as if they were saturated with water. I did not know that they were saturated with blood."

---

i 2nd Lt. J Josephs, 1/12th London Regt (The Rangers).
ii Capt. Humphrey Wolseley Wightwick, M.C., 1/12th London Regt (The Rangers). Educated at Harrow and Oriel College, Oxford, he was a pre-war Territorial, promoted Lieutenant on 2nd September 1914. He was a barrister. He went to France with the battalion on 24th December 1914 and was later promoted to Temp. Major. After being attached to the Tank Corps he was employed as an Instructor until being sent to the Staff College at Cambridge in July 1917. He was later attached to the Adjutant General's Staff as a Deputy Assistant Adjutant General. His M.C. was gazetted on 23rd April 1918.
iii There was only one Sergeant from The Rangers with a surname beginning with an 's' killed on 1st July and that was 1986 Sgt. Thomas Shimmell, however, he is mentioned later as being one of the men who actually managed to penetrate the German lines..

So I lay, waiting with the thought that I might recover my strength (I could barely move) and try to crawl back. There was the greater possibility of death, but there was also the possibility of life. I looked around to see what was happening. In front lay some wounded; on either side of them stakes and shreds of barbed wire twisted into weird contortions by the explosions of our trench-mortar bombs. Beyond this nothing but smoke, interspersed with the red of bursting bombs and shrapnel.

From out this ghastly chaos crawled a familiar figure. It was that of Sergeant K— (*author's note:* it has not proved possible to identify this NCO), bleeding from a wound in the chest. He came crawling towards me.

"Hallo, K—," I shouted.
"Are you hit, sir?" he asked.
"Yes, old chap, I am," I replied.
"You had better try and crawl back," he suggested.
"I don't think I can move," I said.
"I'll take off your equipment for you."

He proceeded very gallantly to do this. I could not get to a kneeling position myself, and he had to get hold of me, and bring me to a kneeling position, before undoing my belt and shoulder-straps. We turned round and started crawling back together. I crawled very slowly at first. Little holes opened in the ground on either side of me, and I understood that I was under the fire of a machine-gun. In front bullets were hitting the turf and throwing it four or five feet into the air. Slowly but steadily I crawled on. Sergeant K— and I lost sight of one another. I think that he crawled off to the right and I to the left of a mass of barbed wire entanglements."[14]

The rest of his day would be spent crawling, staggering and dragging himself back across the bloody shambles of No Man's Land in search of medical help. The 'pile of our wounded' noticed by Liveing near a gap in the German wire was being caused by a machine gun aimed relentlessly on this one spot. Man after man attempted to brave the gap, hardly any succeeded. The Rangers' regimental history records the names of a few men thought to have got through. One was 1986 Sgt. Thomas Shimmell[i], the sergeant of No. 5 Platoon who Liveing had several times had to restrain from going over early "to take on the whole f*cking German Army". Two brothers, Cpl. and Rfn. Mason, also made it and they would be the sole unwounded survivors of 2nd Lt. Liveing's No. 5 Platoon. And there was 1889 Cpl. Walter Tombleson and three other men who were the lone survivors of a group of twelve men who tried to rush this fatal gap in the wire. Others found some small safety in shell holes on the British side of the German wire and attempted to return fire with rifles and a Lewis gun. Behind them, Liveing and dozens of other wounded men started on their tortuous paths back

---

[i] 1986 Sgt Thomas Shimmell, 1/12th London Regt (The Rangers), was killed on Saturday, 1st July 1916. Aged 32, he was the Son of Frederick Shimmell of 92, Overstone Rd., Hammersmith, London and the husband of Caroline Elizabeth Pauline Caterer (formerly Shimmell) of The King's Head, West Drayton, Middx. He was a salesman for the Gas, Light and Coke Company. His body was never found and his name is inscribed on the Thiepval Memorial, Pier and Face 9C.

towards what was left of the British front line, whilst the attack of the Rangers' collapsed on the uncut wire spotted too late by the R.F.C.'s Intelligence Officers.

Plate 24 2nd Lt. Joseph Josephs, 1/12th London Regt. (The Rangers)

'C' Company, the centre left element of the attack, had also been hung up on uncut wire. Led by Capt. Richard Hoare[i], who was killed by shrapnel in front of the German lines, the men desperately sought a passage through the German wire and into the relative safety of the German trenches but a hail of rifle fire and bombs was thinning their ranks by the minute. Those that did get through found themselves a target for the garrison of Nameless Farm to their immediate front. A nineteen year old subaltern, 2nd Lt. Joseph Josephs, determined that attack was the *only* means of defence and charged across the open towards a machine gun nest. His body now lies in Gommecourt Cemetery No. 2[ii]. The few men of 'C' Company still standing were in an untenable position. Both flanks were 'in the air', all of their officers were either dead or wounded and, directed by L/Cpl. Saville, their remaining Lewis gun had fired all of its available ammunition. Headless and defenceless the men recoiled across No Man's Land to the 'safety' of the assembly trenches. L/Cpl. Saville was not finished, however. Collecting some Lewis gun magazines he and 4011 Rfn. Frederick Bartleman set off back towards Fetter trench where they engaged several machine guns until their panniers were empty.[iii]

---

i Capt. Richard Lennard Hoare, 1/12th London Regt (The Rangers), was killed on 1st July 1916, aged 33. He was the third son of William and Laura Hoare of Summerhill, Benenden, Kent. He was born in 1883 and educated at Lambrook, Berks, Eton and Sandhurst. Commissioned into the Royal West Kent Regt in 1902 he left the Army and joined the British-American Tobacco Company working in Bristol, Burma, Karachi and Durban. He then joined the family firm of Hoare, Gothard and Bond, coal factors. He joined the 12th Londons as a subaltern in 1914. He was wounded at St Julien in April 1915, rejoining the regiment in March 1916. He was promoted Captain in August 1915. He took over the company previously commanded by his cousin, Maj. V R Hoare (killed at St Eloi, February 1915), which was made up of members of the Regent Street Polytechnic. He is buried in Gommecourt British Cemetery No. 2, grave I. C. I. [*Additional sources:* Dick Flory: Eton School Register, Part VII, 1899-1909; Etonians Who Fought in the Great War, 1914-1919]

ii 2nd Lt. Joseph Josephs, 1/12th London Regt (The Rangers) was killed on Saturday, 1st July 1916, aged 19. He was the son of David and Siebiene Josephs of 206, Willesden Lane, London and lived at 72, Highbury New Park, North London. He is buried in Gommecourt British Cemetery No. 2, Hebuterne, grave I.C.4.

iii L/Cpl Saville and Rfn Bartleman returned from this trip and joined men of 1/4th Londons who tried to get across later in the day. For their actions both men were awarded the Military Medal. Promoted to Lance Corporal, Frederick Bartleman was killed on 19th September 1916 near Leuze Wood. His body was never found and his name is inscribed on the Thiepval Memorial, Pier and Face 9 C.

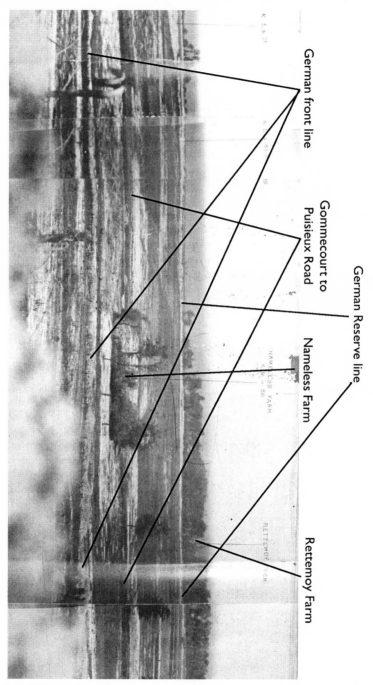

Plate 25 Area of The Rangers' attack (Third Army Artillery Panorama 20th May 1916)

The fourth company to advance was 'D' Company on whose left were the men of the Queen Victoria Rifles of the 169th Brigade. Again, the uncut wire proved a horrendous obstacle to any progress and heavy machine gun fire from their left made progress nigh impossible. 2nd Lt. William Davey[i] was killed trying to lead a way through the wire and, in frustration at their inability to get forward, the few remaining men of the leading waves of 'D' Company fired into the German bombers now standing head and shoulder above their parapet as they tried to throw their bombs into their attackers' ranks. After ten minutes of this furious fire fight barely a man of the first three waves was uninjured. Two of the wounded were 3707 Rfn. Alfred Davis[ii] and 3895 L/Cpl. Reginald Benson[iii] who were part of the Company's bombing squad. Davis was the first to go down, shot through the thigh and, within a few seconds, Benson was also hit. As they lay together out in the open Benson started to crawl back towards the British lines and told Davis to do the same. But Davis was more seriously hit and could not use his leg at all. Thigh wounds were extremely dangerous injuries, especially if the femur was broken, and, if the femoral artery was severed, then death through exsanguination was almost certain unless a tourniquet was immediately applied. Seeing Davis's condition Benson told him to try to find a shell hole and there wait for the stretcher bearers. The Lance Corporal then started on his painful journey back to the relative safety of the trenches but feared for the fate of his companion, wrting later that:

"Even if he had been able to crawl back it was quite a toss up whether he could have reached our lines, as ther was a very heavy shell fire going on."[15]

Coming up with the fourth wave was the Company C.O., Maj. Lewis Jones. He now had but eight men with him and together they rushed a twenty yard gap in the wire whilst two Lewis gun teams attempted to suppress the German bombers with fire from two shell holes. But the withering machine gun fire proved well nigh impenetrable and Major Jones[iv] fell fatally wounded two yards from the German parapet. Only one man of the eight led by Jones made it into the German trenches. Rfn. Perkins was immediately grabbed by two Germans

---

i 2nd Lt. William Roy Davey , 1/12th London Regt (The Rangers), died on Saturday, 1st July 1916. He was born on 14th June 1897 and he was the oldest son of William Henry and Jessie Florence Louisa Davey of 5, Hillcrest Villas, Grove Avenue, Hanwell. He was educated at Acton and Chiswick Polytechnic, Turnham Green and was a bank clerk. He attested 2478 in the 3/2nd County of London Yeomanry (Queen's Westminster Dragoons) on 21st April 1915 and was commissioned into 3/12th London Regt. on 9th December 1915. He was buried in Gommecourt British Cemetery No. 2, grave VI. A. I. 2nd Lt. Davey wrote a will on 23rd May 1916 in which he left all of his personal effects to his parents except for "a sum of money to provide my sweetheart Dorothy Alice Glover with a memento of our true and never broken friendship and also she shall have any article she shall particularly treasure including any medal to which I am entitled."

ii 3707 Rfn. Alfred William Davis, No. 13 Platoon, D Company, 1/12th London Regt. (The Rangers) was killed on Saturday, 1st July 1916. He was the son of Mr G W F Davis, of 26, Banyard Rd., Bermondsey, London. He was buried in Gommecourt British Cemetery No. 2, grave I. D. 4.

iii 3895 L/Cpl. Reginald Benson, No. 13 Platoon, D Company, 1/12th London Regt. (The Rangers) was wounded on Saturday, 1st July 1916 and was evacuated to Boscawen Ward, Croesnewydd Military Hospital, Wrexham.

iv Major Lewis Farewell Jones, 1/12th London Regt (The Rangers), died on Saturday, 1st July 1916, at the age of 31. He was the son of the late George Farewell Jones and Anna Louisa Jones of Brentley, Mitcham, Surrey. Maj. Jones was single and lived at 13 Queen Anne's Gate. He had been previously wounded at the Second Battle of Ypres on 8th May 1915 when he was hit four times, twice by bullets and twice by shrapnel. The last news of the Major came from Rfn R L Robinson who was taken prisoner by the Germans. He stated that Maj. Jones was last seen between the British and German front lines and that he was found dead by a German Red Cross team. He is buried in the London Cemetery and Extension, Longueval, Somme, France. Joint grave 9.J.12.

but, hitting them in the face with a Mills bomb, he made good his escape, keeping any pursuers heads down by the more traditional use of the grenade directly afterwards. Of the first four waves of 'D' Company, just 3 N.C.O.s and nine riflemen, including the fortunate Perkins[i], made it back to the British trenches.

The attack of the Rangers had collapsed. Here and there, scattered elements were fighting in the fringes of the German position but otherwise the men were either casualties or back in their assembly trenches. The machine gunners in Nameless Farm were now able to concentrate their fire elsewhere and the German defenders could start to infiltrate the British positions both to left and right. Almost all of this disaster could be laid at the door of the uncut wire in front of Fetter and Fate trenches. Quite why the wire here was so inadequately dealt with is unknown. But the consequences of the failure of the field artillery to cut the wire in the centre of the attack would prove calamitous to every British solider still fighting in the German lines.

∗∗∗

THE 169TH BRIGADE attack was narrower than that of the 168th Brigade. The two front line battalions, the Queen Victoria's Rifles on the right and the London Rifle Brigade. on the left, each operated on a front just 250 metres wide. There was only space for 'C' and 'A' Companies of the Queen Victoria's Rifles to go forward immediately and each company attacked in four lines of platoons, 'A' on the right and 'C' on the left. These two companies provided the first three waves of five to go over. The fourth wave comprised three sections of battalion bombers, a platoon of the 1/5th Cheshires and eight R.E. sappers. 'B' Company, led by Capt. Philip Houghton[ii], four platoons of the 169th Trench Mortar Battery, under Lt. Edward Lane[iii] of the Q.V.R., and half a section of signallers made up the 5th wave. 'D' Company was to move up behind the attacking companies and then wait in the front line trenches for further orders.

Capt. Lindsey-Renton[iv], OC 'D' Company, watched the attacking companies leave their trenches:

---

[i] Rfn A Perkins was awarded the DCM for his actions on 1st July 1916.

[ii] Capt. Philip Squarey Houghton, 1/9th London Regt (Queen Victoria's Rifles), died on Saturday, 1st July 1916. Born on 11th April 1893, he was the only son of Philip Arthur and Leonie Mabel Houghton of Aldeburgh, Suffolk. He was educated at Brunswick, Haywards Heath, Charterhouse (Weekites House) and University College, Oxford. He lived at Hook Hill Cottage, near Woking, Surrey. He enlisted on 26th August 1914 and was gazetted 2nd Lt. in the QVR in September 1914 and went to France on 4th November 1914. He was promoted to Lieutenant in July 1915 and Captain in May 1916. His body was never found and his name is inscribed on the Thiepval Memorial, Pier and Face 9C. [*Additional Sources:* Pam & Ken Linge, Thiepval Project]

[iii] Lt. Edward Alfred Joseph Aidan Lane, 1/9th London Regt (Queen Victoria's Rifles), died on Saturday, 1st July 1916. He was born on 9th July 1886 and was one of two sons of the late Patrick Chaudeau Bernard Lane, deputy conductor of the choir of the Church of the Sacred Heart, Edgehill, and Catherine Mary Ann Frances Lane of 60, Westbourne Park Villas, London. Educated at College of the Sacred Heart, Wimbledon, he was a Second Lieutenant in the 19th Middlesex Volunteer Battalion (Bloomsbury Rifles) between 1907 and 1908. He attested 19921 Guardsman in the 4th Grenadier Guards on 18th September 1914 but was commissioned into the 3/9th London Regt. in March 1915. He was wounded in the thigh in July 1915. He married Blanche Stormouth Lane on 3rd October 1907 and their daughter, Eileen Ogilvy Lanes, was born on 12th May 1909. They lived at 'Amhurst', 21, Ditton Road, Surbiton. His body was never found and his name is inscribed on the Thiepval Memorial, Pier and Face 9C.

[iv] Capt., later Major, R H Lindsey-Renton, D.S.O., 1/9th London Regt. (Queen Victoria's Rifles) commanded the battalion for three months at the end of 1916. He was awarded the D.S.O. in February 1919, the Belgian Croix de Guerre and was Mentioned in Despatches four times. Educated at New Collge, Oxford he passed the Law Tripos in 1909. A pre-war Territorial he was promoted Lieutenant on 23rd June 1912. He was married to Frances Edith Lindsay-Renton

"At 7.30 the attack commenced, the front line men advancing over the top just as though they were on parade, calmly and slowly while the reserve men stood up on the parapet cheering them on. It was truly a weird sight as the troops gradually disappeared in the smoke."[16]

As 'A' and 'C' Companies were lost in the thick smoke screen, 'B' Company came up behind them using the wooden bridges to cross their trenches to speed themselves forward. As with the later waves of all of the attacking battalions, by the time they arrived in No Man's Land the German barrage was beginning to build in strength and fury and many men of both 'B' Company and the Trench Mortar battery were lost before they had even reached the German wire. The Trench Mortar Battery was trying to take their guns over to help the infantry. The gun teams of Nos. 7 and 8 mortars soon reported that they were unable to get over or had become separated. The teams of Nos. 5 and 3 mortars managed to negotiate No Man's Land and No. 3 was to take some part in the action. No. 2 mortar and its team were effectively wiped out by shell fire. It was not an auspicious debut for the Stokes mortar teams of the 56th Division.

Plate 26 Capt. R H Lindsey-Renton, D Company, Queen Victoria's Rifles

Behind the Queen Victoria's Rifles, and ready to follow them over, lay the Queen's Westminster Rifles, 'A' Company on the right, 'B' company on the left again in columns of platoon each line 70 metres apart. 'C' Company, together with the headquarters bombers, followed in similar formation. 'D' Company (Capt. Glasier), which had assembled in the old R line, was to move forward almost immediately the front companies had moved out, ready to reinforce or take up material for consolidation. The men started to take casualties as soon as they put their heads above the parapets and 3595 Rfn. Richard Beck[17], No. 2 Platoon, recalled seeing one of two brothers from No. 1 Platoon, 4068 L/Cpl Harry Roper[i], who had come third in the Brigade Sports' Day Obstacle Race back

---

[i] 4068 L/Cpl Harry Ernest Roper 1/16th London Regt (Queen's Westminster Rifles) died on Saturday, 1st July 1916, aged 23. He was the son of Henry Charles and Kate Roper of 16, Lammas Park Rd., Ealing, London. His body was never found and his name is inscribed on the Thiepval Memorial, Pier & Face 13C

on 2nd May, lying severely wounded just in front of the British trenches. His brother, 4067 L/Cpl Donald Roper, was to survive though badly wounded[i]. Most of the wire had been pretty well destroyed but the warnings from the R.F.C. about the wire in front of Fern and Fever trenches proved correct. To make matters worse, the wire in front of the second line trenches, Feed and Feint, was also imperfectly cut. Now, as the men bunched at the gaps in the wire, at least two machine guns firing from the right caused a number of casualties amongst the Queen Victoria's Rifles and the Queen's Westminster Rifles. One Maxim was dug in near Nameless Farm and the other was in the front line at Fever trench, thirty yards to the south of the Etch trench junction. Both of them were protected from direct attack by the coils of uncut wire noted by R.F.C. intelligence. One party of the Queen's Westminster Rifles under Lieut. J J Westmoreland[ii] fanned out along the edge of the wire and used the opportunity to fire into the German front line defenders causing heavy losses. The rest of the men waited in line to pass through narrow gaps in the wire and presented excellent targets for the German machine gunners and many fell. Amongst them were 'B' Company's C.O., Capt. George Cockerill[iii], who fell critically wounded, one of the platoon commanders, 2nd Lt. William Strange[iv] who was killed. They were all shot down trying to cross Fern trench, the German front line. Crossing the trenches was supposed to have been made easier by bridges that were to have been laid over them, however, none of them made it across No Man's Land. By now, Rfn. Beck[v] of the Q.W.R.s was waiting outside the German wire with other members of No. 2 Platoon, sheltering from the machine gun fire that was sweeping the gaps in the German wire. Their OC, 2nd Lt. John Daniel[vi], then noticed something and rose to his knees to point it out. Behind him was 2472 Rfn. William Armitage and he got up to see what was the cause of Daniel's interest. Almost immediately, a machine gun bullet drilled its way through

---

[i] 4067 L/Cpl Donald G Roper was evacuated to No. 1 General Hospital, Etretat where he needed an operation. He survived the war.
[ii] 2nd Lt. J J Westmoreland, 1/16th London Regt. (Queen's Westminster Rifles) enlisted as 9037 Rifleman in the 1/5th London Regt. (London Rifle Brigade) and was later promoted L/Cpl. He went to France with the L.R.B. on 4th November 1914. He was commissioned into the Q.W.R. on 22nd July 1915.
[iii] Capt. George Edward Cockerill, 'B' Company, 1/16th London Regt (Queen's Westminster Rifles), died of wounds whilst a German prisoner on the 3rd July 1916 aged 38. The son of George Edward and Edith Cockerill of London, he is buried in Vaulx Hill Cemetery, grave reference I C 15.
[iv] 2nd Lt. William Frederick Strange was attached to 'B' Company, 1/16th London Regt (Queen's Westminster Rifles) from the 2/2nd Londons, having been one of the officers from the disbanded 2/2nd Londons who had recently returned from Gallipoli and Egypt. He was born on 16th January 1889 and was the son of Joseph James and Mary Ann Strange of St Dunstan's School. He was educated at St Dunstan's College and was a managing clerk living at 142, Inderwick Road, Stroud Green. For three years he was in the 1st Cadet Battalion, King's Royal Rifle Corps. He attested 3208 Private in the 1/12th London Regt. (The Rangers) on 11th August 1914 and was commissioned into the 4/2nd London Regt. in August 1915. His body was never found and his name is inscribed on the Thiepval Memorial, Pier and Face 9 D and 16 B.
[v] 3595 Rfn. Richard Beck, 1/16th London Regt (Queen's Westminster Rifles), was himself wounded and was evacuated to Bed 41, Queen's A1 Ward, Graylingswell Hospital, Chichester from where he wrote to the Territorial Service Gazette with news of his colleagues. He was later transferred to the Labour Corps.
[vi] 2nd Lt. John Daniel, 2/3rd London Regt. (Royal Fusiliers) att. 1/16th London Regt. (Queen's Westminster Rifles) was born on 14th December 1894, the son of Hector and Agnes Daniel of Heilbron in the Orange Free State. He was educated at Grey College, Bloemfontein and was a head clerk in an attorney's office. He enlisted in the Heilbron Commando and the 14th Mounted Rifles in South Africa being promoted Sergeant and seeing action in the campaign in German South West Africa before being commissioned into the 4/3rd London Regt. (Royal Fusiliers) in October 1915. He was transferred into the QWR when the 2/3rd Londons were disbanded in May 1916. He had applied to transfer to the RFC in April 1916 but his wounds delayed this move. On his recovery he was attached to the RFC in November 1917 and then the RAF with No. 54 Squadron at Harlaxton near Grantham and then with No. 92 Squadron.

Daniel's shoulder to smash directly into Armitage's face. Beck recalled later that Armitage gave a shout before collapsing full length. He died at once[i].

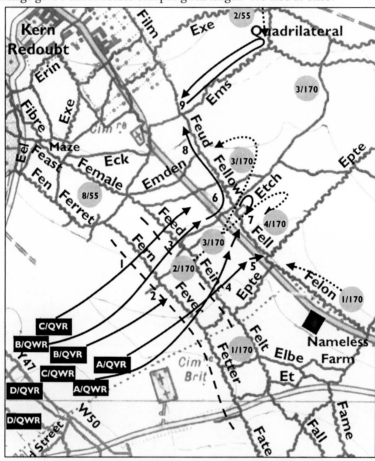

Map 12 Situation 0730-0830 Queen Victoria's Rifles front

Legend: 1 – Capt. Mott, C Coy Q.W.R., killed   2 – Capt. Cockerill, B Coy Q.W.R., wounded
3 – 2nd Lt. Engall, 169 MGC, killed   4 – Capt. Swainson, A Coy Q.W.R., killed
5 – Lewis gunner & Cpl. Ratcliffe, 5th Cheshires   6 – 2nd Lts. Yates and Negus, B Coy Q.W.R., killed
7 – 2nd Lt. Simmonds, A Coy Q.W.R., killed   8 - 2nd Lt. Upton, Q.W.R., leads bombers
9 – 2nd Lt. Arthur, 5th Cheshires, and Q.W.R. party advance to Quadrilateral

- - - - Lines of uncut wire

For some, though, the battle with the enemy was already over and now began a battle for survival. Frank Hawkings, wounded by shrapnel in the initial thrust, was desperately clawing his way back towards the British lines:

"I next found myself sliding head first into the old line upon a heap of mangled bodies. Here, I endeavoured to pull myself together and to bandage up my arm. A half a dozen other fellows wounded like myself, soon joined me, and together we started off for the dressing station.

---

i 2472 Rfn. William Henry Marshall Armitage, 1/16th London Regt (Queen's Westminster Rifles), was killed on 1st July 1916. He is buried in Gommecourt British Cemetery No. 2, I. A. 18

284

Progress was slow however, owing to the fact that the trench was wrecked in many places, and was choked with corpses. As we moved along, I tried to stop the flow of blood from my arm by using my handkerchief as a tourniquet. Eventually we found the dressing station, crowded with wounded, on the outskirts of Hebuterne. While I was waiting to be attended to, I suddenly felt giddy and fainted away. When I recovered, Capt. Clarke, the doctor, was trying to rouse me. He soon bandaged me up, and off I went through the village to find the Field ambulance."[18]

For his erstwhile colleagues, as they scrambled into what was left of the first line of German trenches, came the first of the many unpleasant discoveries for the attacking troops. The deep dugouts had clearly been hardly scratched by the bombardment. Some entrances had been blown in where heavy shells had landed on or near them but every dugout had more than one entrance. And now, as the barrage lifted back into the reserve lines, the defenders of this sector, N1, tried to rush to the surface to help repel the attack. N1 sector was manned by men of the 2nd Company of the 170th Regiment (9th Baden). In the confusion of the bombardment, made worse by the heavy smoke screen that obscured everything to their front, the men of the 2nd Company were either caught emerging from their dug outs or were still deep below ground awaiting orders. Within a few minutes, their commander, Leutnant Bahl, was wounded and the defences overwhelmed. Those not killed, wounded or captured retreated headlong up Etch trench to take cover and re-group in and around the third line at Feud and Fellow. The men of a platoon of the 3rd Company, occupying the German second line, went with them. Many of the prisoners were herded back into the dugouts rather than be sent back across No Man's Land through the devastating barrage now being dropped by their own artillery. The history of the Queen's Westminsters suggests that many of these men then re-armed themselves and attacked the British troops from the rear as they pressed towards the third German line.

Plate 27 Capt. Hugh Mott, 1/16th London Regt (Queen's Westminster Rifles)
(Photograph 'The Sphere', 20th March 1919)

The second unpleasant revelation for the attackers was that the wire between the first, second and third German lines was not properly cut in places. Again, German machine guns in the reserve lines on the slope behind, were trained on the gaps ready to cut the infantry down as they queued patiently to get through the wire. It was here that Capt. Francis Swainson[i], commanding 'A' Company, Queen's Westminster Rifles, was killed shortly after leaving the second line German trench (Feint). A short time after, Capt. Hugh Mott[ii], commanding 'C' Company, was killed while trying to enlarge a gap in the wire between the second and third German lines. Within a few minutes, therefore, all three commanders of the attacking companies of the Queen's Westminster Rifles were lost and with them, some of the direction and impetus of the attack. 95 C.S.M. Donald G C Hawker of 'B' Company had been made acting Company Sergeant Major for 'C' Company and went over with Capt. Mott. He saw his officer fall and, as direction broke down amongst the men of the Company, he collected a party and advanced to the low bank that ran along the far side of the Gommecourt to Nameless Farm road.

Plate 28 Rfn. Allan Paling, Queen's Westminster Rifles, killed 1st July 1916

During this advance one German bullet did for two Westminsters. 2828 Rfn. Allan Paling[iii] and his mate 2533 Rfn. Sydney Burridge[iv] were attacking on the right of the battalion's front and were subject to severe rifle and machine gun fire, some coming from the guns concealed about Nameless Farm. They had crossed the first line of German trenches when they were both hit simultaneously. Paling was only slightly wounded in the shoulder and he helped the more severely wounded Burridge, applying the little bottle of iodine and field dressing to the

---

[i] Capt. Francis Gibbon Swainson M.C., 'A' Company, 1/16th London Regt (Queen's Westminster Rifles), was killed on 1st July 1916. He was the younger son of Mrs Eliza Prowse Swainson of 'Rosebank', Knowsley, Prescot, Lancs, and the late G A Swainson. He lived at 101, Lee Road, Blackheath, Kent. His body was never found and his name is inscribed on the Thiepval Memorial, Pier 13 Face C.
[ii] Lt. (temp. Capt) Hugh Fenwick Mott M.C., 'C' Company, 1/16th London Regt (Queen's Westminster Rifles), was killed on 1st July 1916, aged 22. Single, he was the eldest of five children of Alfred Frederick and Katherine Mary Mott of The Holt, Reigate, Surrey and was educated at Hillside, Reigate, Marlborough College and Oriel College, Oxford. About to start his second year at Oriel College, Oxford when war broke out, he was commissioned in September 1914 and went to the front on 24th January 1915. Slightly wounded once he was awarded the Military Cross in the Birthday Honour's, June 1916. His colonel wrote: "He was gallantly leading his company in the attack when he was hit, absolutely leading them into the enemy trench". His body was never found and his name is inscribed on the Thiepval Memorial, Pier 13 Face C. [*Additional Source:* Pam & Ken Linge, Thiepval Project]
[iii] 2828 Rfn. Allan Clayton Paling, 1/16th London Regt. (Queen's Westminster Rifles) was killed on 1st July 1916. Aged 22, he was the son of Francis & Margaret Paling of 142, Westbourne Grove, Notting Hill, London. His body was never found and his name is inscribed on the Thiepval Memorial, Pier 13 Face C.
[iv] 2533 Rfn. Sydney Walter Burridge, A Company, 1/16th London Regt. (Queen's Westminster Rifles) was wounded on 1st July 1916 and was evacuated to Ward 9, Scottish Red Cross Hospital at Bellahouston, Glasgow.
286

wound. Paling then turned his attention to the other wounded men lying in and around the trench, helping who he could. Later, when it was clear that the soldiers fighting further forward were hard pressed by German counter attacks, Paling picked up his rifle and told Burridge that he was "going off to do his bit to help the boys". He was never seen again.

Soon, what was left of the six companies of the Queen Victoria's Rifles and Queen's Westminster Rifles had pushed forward to take cover there. Here, at least, they had some protection from the fierce rifle and machine gun fire from the German third line (Fell and Fellow trenches) a few yards ahead and to the left, from the reserve line that ran along the top of the low ridge 450 metres away and from the fringes of Gommecourt Park. They were further helped on the right by the courageous work of an anonymous Lewis gunner from the Q.W.R. who, with 3354 Cpl. Leonard Ratcliffe M.M., 1/5th Cheshire Regt., acting as observer, kept at bay the Germans pressing in from behind Nameless Farm down Felon Trench. For twenty minutes this man kept up a steady fire, necessarily exposing himself to the enemy, until he was felled by a German bullet[i]. C.S.M. Hawker too fell victim to the cross-fire sweeping the men crowding along the northern side of the sunken road. Walking to the flank to ascertain the next possible move, Hawker was shot through the neck and windpipe and started to bleed heavily through the mouth and nose. 1191 Sgt. A D H Courtenay, who had recently joined the Westminsters from the 2/2nd Londons, took command of Hawker's party while the badly wounded Sergeant Major struggled back towards the German front line in search of medical treatment. On the way, he was wounded twice more and he lost consciousness through loss of blood in the enemy trench. He would be out cold for several hours.

No. 12 Platoon of the Westminsters was following behind the leading waves and went over laden with equipment for the consolidation of the newly captured German trenches. 2540 L/Cpl. Arthur Read[ii] went over with his chum 4345 Rfn. Norman Drown and, apart from their rifles, they were also carrying shovels, bombs and Read, a heavy coil of barbed wire which Drown offered to help carry. They were approaching the men crowded in front of the German third line where such a slow moving target inevitably was targeted and Read was hit. Unable to carry on Drown helped him into a nearby stretch of trench and out of immediate harm's way. Drown was concerned about Read's condition and offered to stay and help but Read told him to carry on with the rest of the platoon. Having ensured Read was comfortable Drown hefted the barbed wire coil onto his shoulder and set off towards the fighting in the German third line. At some time during the day 23-year old Norman Drown was killed, his body never to be found.[iii]

---

[i] The whole of No. 1 Lewis Gun Team of the Queen's Westminster Rifles became casualties. 2380 Cpl James F Warrilow was made a Prisoner of War and Rfn. H H Heyworth, V J Love, P R Young and J David were all killed. [*Source:* Territorial Service Gazette, 19th August 1916, page 95]

[ii] 2540, L/Cpl Arthur G Read, att. from 2/2nd London Regt. to C Company, 1/16th London Regt. (Queen's Westminster Rifles) was wounded on 1st July 1916 and was evacuated to Hut 21, C Camp, Convalescent Camp, Alnwick, Northumberland.

[iii] 4345 Rfn. Norman Frank Drown, 1/16th London Regt. (Queen's Westminster Rifles) was killed on Saturday,. 1st July 1916. Aged 23, he was the son of Frank & Fanny Amelia Drown of 44, Selsdon Rd., West Norwood, London. His body was never found and his name is inscribed on the Thiepval Memorial, Pier 13 Face C.

The attackers were now faced with elements of three companies of the I/170th Regiment, commanded by Hauptmann Wulff. Two platoons of Oberleutnant der Reserve Reinicke's 3rd Company were spread out along Fellow trench and, to their left, another two platoons of the 4th Company, commanded by Leutnant Itt, occupied Fell. Scattered along the length of the German line, and trying desperately to catch their breath after their precipitate withdrawal, were the remnants of the 2nd Company. The swift ejection of the men of the 170th Regiment from their front line trenches immediately set alarm bells ringing at Regimental H.Q. Assistance was desperately needed and the closest men in support were the reserves of the 55th Reserve Infantry Regiment. An hour after the attack started, a desperate appeal for help was on its way with reports of a "gas attack against Sector North at 9.05"[i], an attack on Sector 19 at 9.15 a.m. and the collapse of the left wing of the 55th R.I.R.'s position in Sector G5 in front of the Maze at 9.30 a.m.[19]

The Victorias and the Westminsters had swept over two lines of trenches and routed elements of two companies of German defenders but, being where they were was one thing, moving forward was another. Already casualties amongst officers and N.C.O.s had been severe (indeed no officers and only one sergeant returned from this position at the end of the day) and communication back across to the German front line and beyond was well nigh impossible. The plan had been for men from each of the lead battalion's Signal Sections to go over early in the attack. They would set up signal stations in the front line from which messages could be sent back to a Report Station in the British lines. These messages would then be transmitted back to Battalion H.Q. and beyond. The hope was that these messages could be sent by telephone and the parties of signallers were sent over with Venetian lamps and shutters as well as D3s - telephone sets - and cable which they were supposed to unroll across No Man's Land. These land lines had also been dug into the bottom of several communication trenches which ran to the battalion and then brigade headquarters but, in the heavy German barrage, these lines were amongst the first to be cut. The methods of communication were, therefore, reduced to two: simple messages flashed by Venetian lamps or longer, written messages sent by runner. On the right hand side of the 169th Brigade's front the problem was compounded by the fact that the Queen Victoria's signallers didn't get across. Due to cross with the fifth wave, they were caught by the curtain of shell fire blocking No Man's Land. A member of one of the two parties, Rfn. Newman, recalled later:

"Six battalion signallers in two parties of three had been detailed to take up positions in the newly dug take-off trench in No Man's Land with instructions to advance after the fifth wave of bombers, one platoon of Cheshires plus eight sappers. We were to establish cable and visual posts in the German front or second line. A Lance Corporal was in charge of each party. We carried lamps and shutters as well as D3s, telephone instruments, and cable... As men rose to the parapet and our own barrage lifted from the German front lines a terrific fire was concentrated by German guns on

---

[i] German time was an hour in advance of British time so the times given in 170th Regiment's report are, respectively, 8.05, 8.15 and 8.30 a.m. B.S.T.,

the assembly trenches and No Man's Land and German machine guns poured an unslackening hail of lead into the advancing troops. Three waves went over. We waited in vain for the fourth. The confusion and smoke were too great to see what was, in fact, happening. L/Cpl. Yapp, in charge of my party, decided to wait a little in the hope of the bombardment lessening. After some time, L/Cpl. Taylor with his two signallers, (L/Cpl.) Dawkes and Dixon, decided, despite the murderous fire, to attempt to cross. They clambered out of the trench but had not gone ten yards when Taylor and Dawkes were blown to pieces and Dixon was wounded. Dixon managed to crawl back to the trench[i]. We waited in the hope of successfully attempting the crossing. How our portion of the trench escaped destruction was a miracle. On either side it was flattened."[20]

Deprived of their signallers, the Westminsters sent off several men with messages for Battalion H.Q. Only one runner who set off from their position survived to return to the British lines. At 8.30 a.m., 1580 Rfn. John Orchard[ii], a Q.W.R. signaller, arrived breathless at Battalion H.Q. after a harrowing, scrambled journey across the devastation that was now No Man's Land. He could point to his unit's position, lined up along the low embankment. He could explain their predicament. He reported that the Q.W.R. and Q.V.R. were losing heavily. His C.O., listening anxiously, could do little about it. He was to hear no more from his men now crouched behind the bank of the sunken road as not one messenger lived to cross No Man's Land. One man of the Queen's Westminsters did display extraordinary bravery in a vain attempt to establish some form of communication with his colleagues in front of the third German line. 1136 Sgt. Leonard Harrow[iii], the signalling sergeant, tried to get a roll of 'rabbit-wire' across No Man's Land but the intense German shelling forced him back into the British trenches.

As the infantry's forward movement faltered and their timetable slipped, the British heavy and field artillery were firing according to the pre-set programme of lifts, moving further and further away from the men they were trying to help. The 18 pdrs of the Divisional artillery were firing fastest and hardest. But within a short time, the first indication of the limitations of their guns became apparent. As early as 7.44 a.m. a report had came through to Brig. Gen. Elkington[iv], C.O. 56th Division Artillery, that one gun was out of action because of a jammed

---

i L/Cpl Dixon recollects the death of his friend L/Cpl Taylor somewhat differently. He states that they made a series of dashes forward from shell hole to shell hole before L/Cpl Taylor was shot and killed. L/Cpl Dixon recalls several unsuccessful efforts to reach the body of his friend before he was himself shot in the left arm. He crawled back to the British trenches about the middle of the day. [*Source*: Queen Victoria's Rifles 1792-1922, Maj. C A Cuthbert Keeson V.D., Constable & Co. 1923]

ii 1580 L/Cpl John Harold Orchard M.M., 1/16th London Regt (Queen's Westminster Rifles), was awarded the Military Medal for his conduct on 1st July 1916. He was killed in action on 14th August 1917 at Glencorse Wood near Ypres. His body was never found and his name is inscribed in the Ypres (Menin Gate) Memorial, Panel 54.

iii 1136 Sgt., later Lt., Leonard Phillip Harrow DCM, 1/16th London Regt (Queen's Westminster Rifles), was killed in action on 28th August 1918 at the Battle of the Scarpe. Harrow, then the battalion Signalling Officer, had landed with the battalion in 1914 and was commissioned in the field on 13th December 1916. Aged 25, he was the son of Philip and Gertrude Harrow of London and husband of Maude Mary Harrow of 44, Flanders Rd., Bedford Park, London. He was a clerk with J V Drake & Co of Mincing Lane. He attested 1136 Private in the battalion on 29th November 1909 and was promoted Corporal in May 1915 and Lance Sergeant in November. He was awarded the DCM on 14th January 1916 and promoted Sergeant in February. He is buried in Bucquoy Road Cemetery, Ficheux, grave VI. F. 2.

iv Brig. Gen. R J G Elkington, C.M.G., D.S.O., was the GOC of the 56th Division's artillery from February 1916 to the end of the war. He was a pre-war Regular artillery officer and had served with 3rd Division at Mons.

289

cartridge. It was to be the first of many. Nine minutes later another message came through that three guns of the Macart Southern Artillery Group were out of action. The enemy was not to blame, however. The guns' springs had broken through their intensive use.

Whilst the Divisional barrage was weakening, the German counter-barrage was building in intensity. It not only targeted the British front line trenches and No Man's Land, it also sought out the Observation Posts where the artillery's Forward Observation Officers were located and the hardened machine gun emplacements from which a barrage was being placed on the German reserve and communication trenches. By 7.45 a.m. word filtered back to 168th Brigade H.Q. that, although all the machine guns were firing, the German artillery was getting the range. Shellfire around the emplacements was heavy.

Throughout this, the men of 2nd Company, 5th Battalion, Special Brigade, R.E. were trying to maintain the smoke screen in order to blind the German machine gunners. The cloud gradually thinned but in the hollow in front of the village and Nameless Farm it lingered for forty five minutes whilst on the far right, in Warrior Street the men of N. 20 Sub-section carried on firing their smoke bombs for 65 minutes. But their locations, at the ends of the main communication trenches were prime targets for the German artillery. No. 14 Sub-section at the end of Yellow Street had two mortars buried and ten out of sixteen men became casualties and No. 21 Sub-section in Woman Street lost six men and one mortar. No. 15 Sub-section at the end of Yankee Street were to have taken two mortars over to help the 169th Brigade and one officer and thirty men had been provided by the Brigade to act as a carrying party. The mortar party, led by 2nd Lt. Roberts, had to move up to the front line from the boyau de service but before they even moved off, twenty two men of the carrying party had been hit and, by the time they reached the front line, six of the remaining eight were wounded. With only four rounds left, there was only one sensible decision to make and the advance was abandoned.

***

ON THE EXTREME LEFT were the three attacking companies of the London Rifle Brigade, 'D' Company on the right, 'C' Company in the centre and 'A' Company on the left. 'B' Company stayed in reserve. Each company went across in six waves, with the first wave having lined up in No Man's Land on a tape that had been laid the night before by a team led by 2nd Lt. Rex Petley of 'D' Company. He was one of only a few officers to survive the attack of the London Rifle Brigade and observed later:

"It was really magnificent the way every man, cool and collected, strolled out through quite a stiff barrage to the tape I had laid down 150 yards out during the night. The smoke lifted for a few seconds when we were out and I noticed the men were inclined to bunch on the right. I shouted an order and they shook out as if they were on Wimbledon Common."[21]

Coming to the German front lines, they had found that the heavy howitzers had done their job well. The wire was flattened, the trenches little more than a series of shell holes and the entrances to the dugouts had been effectively blown in. This sector of the line, G5, was held by the 170 men of the 8th Company of the 55th R.I.R. On the left of their position, by the end of Exe trench, two platoons were overrun as they tried desperately to climb the rubble-choked stairs of their dugouts. In the centre, the Company commander Leutnant der Reserve Holländer gathered his men about him and, organising blocks at the western end of Feast, a few yards into the Park along Fight and just beyond Point 94 where Firm met Fir, held positions on the fringe of Gommecourt Park either side of where the Hebuterne to Gommecourt road cut the German lines. But there was a hole between the left flank of 8/55ᵗʰ R.I.R. and the right flank of 2/170ᵗʰ Regt and, by 7.50 a.m., 2ⁿᵈ Lt. Petley and his platoon from 'D' Company had exploited this. The hole was mainly caused by the actions of a party of seven 'D' Company bombers under L/Cpl. H G F Dennis as 776 Cpl. Roland Ebbetts testified afterwards. Entering the German lines at the left end of Fern trench they bombed their way along Ferret trench to the bottom of Exe trench. On their way, they met and killed a dozen members of two German bombing parties and lobbed grenades down the stairs of any dugouts to which they came. Turning up Exe towards the village they found the communication trench empty and, on reaching what was left of Eck, they turned right and started to consolidate their positions. Eck had been reduced to a series of holes by the bombardment but, with the help of men from the following waves, Ebbetts[i] and a 'D' Company wiring party soon managed to get five rolls of concertina wire and three strands of barbed wire into place along the remains of Eck trench facing towards the Maze and the Village itself. A Lewis gun was placed at the left end of the trench (the second Lewis gun failed to arrive) in order to fire towards the road and the NE edge of the Park and a German machine gun on the fringes of the Park was put out of action. By 7.50 a.m. Ebbetts reported that most of 'D' Company was at work in Eck trench working hard to consolidate their new position with the Company commander, Capt. Bernardo de Cologan, and 2ⁿᵈ Lt. Horace Smith[ii] joining Petley. To their left front they could see a party of 'C' Company bombers trying to bomb their way up Erin trench towards the heart of Gommecourt village but their job was to hold Eck trench and they set to the task with enthusiasm. Apart from a few German snipers firing at 100 metres' range from the Park to the left and The Cemetery to the right, the only troops available to interfere with their efforts were parts of the Jäger Pioneer Company of the 55ᵗʰ R.I.R. and the Pioneer Platoon of Vice Feldwebel Korthaus, (4ᵗʰ Company of the 10ᵗʰ Pioneer Battalion). These men lined the trenches concealed by hedges and trees on the SE side of the Kern Redoubt and stopped any further advance by the L.R.B. with harassing rifle and grenade fire.

Whilst De Cologan, Petley, Smith and their men dug in and dodged and ducked the enemy fire, others started to erect the signboards that had been carried forward to the trenches to indicate they had been captured. Back in the British lines, the reserve battalion, the 1/2ⁿᵈ Londons, had seen the signs go up

---

[i] The brother of 776 Cpl. Roland F Ebbetts, 784 Cpl. Sidney Arthur Ebbetts, also of 'D' Company, 1/5ᵗʰ London Regt. (London Rifle Brigade) was killed on 1ˢᵗ July 1916. Aged 25, he was the son of Charles Frederick and Harriett H. Ebbetts, of 30, Wormholt Rd., Shepherd's Bush, London. His body was never found and his name is inscribed on the Thiepval Memorial, Pier and Face 9 D.

[ii] 2ⁿᵈ Lt. Horace Smith, 1/5ᵗʰ London Regt. (London Rifle Brigade), was the son of Rose Alice Smith, of 'Braemar', Montem Lane, Slough, Bucks, and the late Frederick Percy Smith. He was educated at Manchester and Eton College Choir School. He enlisted in the 2/5ᵗʰ London Rifle Brigade and was commissioned into the 3/5ᵗʰ Battalion on 28ᵗʰ May 1915. He joined the 1/5ᵗʰ London Rifle Brigade on 19ᵗʰ January 1916. He rejoined the battalion on 21ˢᵗ September 1916 and was killed in action on the 8ᵗʰ October 1916. His body was never found and his name is inscribed on the Thiepval Memorial, Pier and Face 9D.

just after 8 a.m. First in Fir, Fen and Ferret, then Feast and Female. Things seemed to be going well! For 'D' Company of the 1/5th Londons, events were progressing quite smoothly. The company was in contact with the Q.V.R. to its right and 'C' Company to its left. It was as it should be. The Company commander, Capt. de Cologan, sent confident and optimistic reports back down Exe trench to the front line where, at the junction of Fen and Ferret trenches, Capt. John Somers-Smith had established the battalion's forward H.Q.

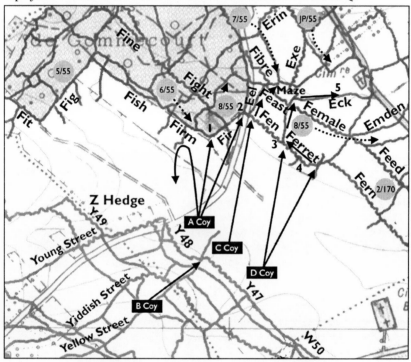

Map 13 Situation 0730-0830 London Rifle Brigade front
Legend: 1 – Point 94, 2nd Lt. Doust, A Coy, killed   2 – Rfn. Reynolds' Lewis gun position
3 – Capt. Somers-Smith 's Forward H.Q.   4 – L/Cpl. Dennis, D Coy, and bombers
5 – 2nd Lt. Petley, D Coy

The centre company, 'C' Company, had advanced approximately along the line of the Hebuterne to Gommecourt Road crossing the German front line at Fen trench. From there, they pushed forward up the slope towards the village and the Maze. At Feast trench, some German soldiers emerged from a deep dugout to be bombed, shot or captured. 'C' Company then pushed forward another few metres to what had been the southern edge of the Maze, utilising what was left of Exe trench for cover. Here, the heavy howitzers had done effective work in demolishing the trenches and 1621 L/Cpl. John Foaden of 'C' Company described what they found:

"On reaching the Maze, which was little more than large shell holes, I bore to the left and took shelter in a large shell hole. I was rather uncertain whether my position was correct but Capt. Harvey arrived and confirmed it as being so. There were about ten men at this point, which we held and

292

commenced to consolidate at once. Snipers were very busy and killed one and wounded two during the first two minutes."[22]

Rfn. Jacobs later testified to the accuracy of the German snipers:

"They sniped us with rifles and machine guns with wicked persistency and man after man was got in this way. Well, we hung on."[23]

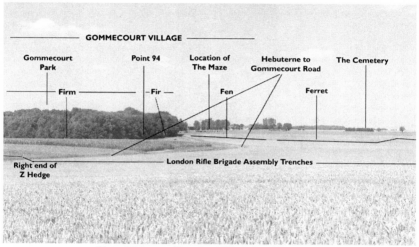

Plate 29 Area of London Rifle Brigade's attack

The sniper fire was coming from the Park to their left and the remains of the village straight ahead. And here, in spite of the rapid advance and the seemingly easy occupation of the planned objectives, the evidence was clear. Although the trenches had been badly damaged and almost flattened in places, the German soldiers had survived in their dugouts and were now coming out to fight hard. In many ways, such damage to the trenches was a real disadvantage to the attacking troops. With the trenches flattened, there was now nowhere to go for protection from the growing storm of machine gun and rifle fire and the barrage that the German artillery was even now bringing down on their own front lines. On this part of the L.R.B.'s front the opposition was being provided by the 158 men of the 7th Company of the 55th R.I.R., who had emerged from their bunkers on the south side of the Kern Redoubt to join in the defence of their positions. Led by their commander, Hauptmann der Reserve Brockmann, they had been ordered by the C.O. of the II/55th R.I.R., Hauptmann der Landwehr Minck, to drive the British out of the German positions. This proved impossible, and so the men set to digging in on a front of 100 metres, just in front of the remains of the Redoubt's trenches. There they sniped - and waited for reinforcements from the reserve companies. Ten minutes later, at about 7.50 a.m., Hauptmann Minck issued more orders. 7th Company's attack in the general direction of Süd (Exe) Trench was confirmed and, with all telephone lines cut by the bombardment, a runner was sent to Regimental H.Q. at Point 147. He carried orders for the 10th Company who were in reserve in the Switch Line. They were to move forward into the SE flank of the Kern Redoubt to support the 7th Company. The message arrived in the H.Q., 2,000 metres away, two and a half hours later.

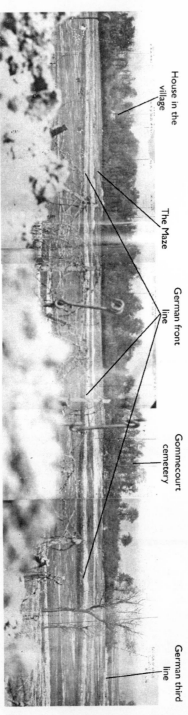

Plate 30 London Rifle Brigade front (Third Army Artillery Panorama, 20th May 1916)

On the far left, 'A' Company of the London Rifle Brigade had the job of taking the corner of Gommecourt Park where Firm and Fir trenches met nearly at right angles. This junction was designated Point 94 on British trench maps because of its map co-ordinates. In the dense smoke some men of the first wave on the extreme left of the attack drifted off line, in the same way that 'A' Company of the London Scottish would lose their way at the other end of the front. This error gave the German defenders the impression that an attack was being mounted on the long southerly face of the Park around Firm and Fish trenches. This sector of the German defences, G4, was held by 134 men of the 6th Company, 55th R.I.R. and their heavy rifle fire, aided by machine gun fire from the 5th Company to their right (in Fig trench), dealt with the small groups of L.R.B. men who emerged haplessly from the smoke screen in front of the trees.

At Point 94 515 Sgt. Walter Lilley of 'A' Company later reported that, although the thick wire had been well cut, it had piled up into coils and mounds, treacherously barbed, and it still presented an obstacle to the advancing infantry. As a result, the 2nd wave had caught up with the 1st wave by the time the leading men had forced their way through and into the German trenches. Soon, however, at this south eastern corner of the Park the British troops had established a tenuous foothold in the German trenches, but there were casualties on both sides in the brisk firefight that developed. The company commander, Capt. Guy Cholmeley[i], who had been wounded as he left the assembly trenches, had taken his men over but then, along with the wounded 2nd Lt. Bernard Pocock[ii], he had struggled back to the British lines to report that the initial advance had gone well.

Below ground Gerfreiter Füchte, the commander of No. 8 gun of the 73rd Machine Gun Marksmen Section, and his team had been waiting in their dugout for a chance to emerge. When Füchte reached the parapet, he saw Second Lt. Charles Doust[iii] emerge from the smoke still blanketing the area. Füchte

---

[i] Capt. Guy Hargreaves Cholmeley, 1/5th London Regt. (London Rifle Brigade), was born on 18th September 1889, the son of Lewin Charles Cholmeley of 19 Hamilton Terrace, NW. He was educated at Eton and Magdalen College, Oxford where he gained a 3rd in Modern History. He was a member of the Eton R.V.C. and Oxford University O.T.C. Before the war he served as a Solicitor's Articled Clerk at Frere, Cholmeley & Co. He joined the London Rifle Brigade as a 2nd Lt. in 1913 and was promoted Lieutenant in 1914, going to France in November. He was invalided home on 20th February 1915 returning to France on 17th July 1915. He was invalided home again on 3rd July 1916, having been severely wounded at Gommecourt, and later rejoined the 3/5th London Rifle Brigade and subsequently was an Instructor with the Officer Cadet Battalion. He married Sylvia Katherine, daughter of Rev. Canon Sydney Cooper, Rector of Upper Heyford, Banbury in 1915; she died in 1941 and they had two daughters. In 1922 he lived at 25 Hamilton Terrace, NW. In 1944 he married Stephany Cooper, the sister of his first wife and they had a son and a daughter. He died on 10th November 1958. [*Additional source:* Dick Flory: Eton School Register, Part VII, 1899-1909; Etonians Who Fought in the Great War, 1914-1919; The Magdalen College Record, 1934; The Magdalen College Record, 1955; The Magdalen College Record, 1966]

[ii] 2nd Lt. Bernard Langdon Elliott Pocock, 1/5th London Regt. (London Rifle Brigade), was born on 25th May 1895, the son of Frederick Augustus and Florence Julia Pocock of 47, Strathblaine Road, Battersea. He was educated at Emanuel School and Bancroft's School, Woodford Green, Essex. An assurance clerk with the Northern Assurance Co., he lived at 'Avondale', 20, West Side, Wandsworth Common. He attested 1796 Private in the 15th County of London Regt. (Civil Service Rifles) on 23rd February 1914 and was commissioned into the 3/5th London Rifle Brigade on 24th March 1915, joining the 1/5th Battalion on 23rd December 1915. He was promoted to Lieutenant on 1st June 1916. After returning to the Battalion he was injured in a Brigade Rugby match in November 1918, losing two front teeth and damaging his left knee.

[iii] 2nd Lt. Charles Bowden Doust, 1/5th London Regt (London Rifle Brigade), died on Saturday, 1st July 1916. The oldest son of Charles Henry and Laura Doust of Inglehurst, Shortlands, Kent and formerly 'Tregothnan', Rydal Place, Streatham, he was born on the 26th October 1887. He was educated at Dulwich College, where he joined the Cadet Force. In 1903 he went to Germany where worked in a textile factory at Hiblersdorf from 1904 to 1905 and then to Paris, France where he was employed in a commercial house from 1906-1909. He then became a Colonial Merchant's Assistant (to his father) in 1910. He and his younger brother joined the regiment on 6th August 1914 at

immediately shot Doust in the head and the 2nd Lieutenant, who had survived a head wound at Second Ypres, was killed instantly. Killing Doust was Füchte's last act as he was himself killed by a grenade thrown by one of Doust's men now led by Sgt. Lilley. His action, however, allowed the rest of his team to move their machine gun to a position in the edge of the Park where they could bring it into action to the great discomfort of the hard pressed Londoners.[24]

Plate 31 2nd Lt. Charles Bowden Doust, 1/5th London Regt. (London Rifle Brigade)
(Photograph: Dulwich College Roll of Honour)

Behind the leading waves, however, machine gun fire caught the follow-up waves of 'A' Company who had clambered out of the trenches and the Boyau de Service in order to follow their colleagues across. A Lewis gunner, 4845 Rfn. Tom Short, recalled the ranks being "raked with machine gun fire". Another rifleman, Henry Russell, dived into a shallow shell hole to avoid the scything bullets. There he was joined by an L.R.B. officer, thought to be 2nd Lt. Archibald Warner[i] who had only arrived in France on the 27th May. The two men then had a rapid discussion about what they should do next. Russell's swiftly aligned himself with Falstaff and concluded that 'the better part of valour is discretion', although he put it rather more succinctly, advising the officer that any further advance would be suicidal. Russell's suggested that they remain there and attempt to pick off any Germans rash enough to expose themselves above the parapet. In the smoke they had lost their bearings and now had no real idea where they were except for the fact that they were somewhat surrounded. Raising themselves above the edge of the crater to ascertain their whereabouts only invited a bullet between the eyes. On reflection, though, Warner decided that their orders to go on at all costs must be complied with but, on standing, the

Bunhill Row and went to the front in November 1914. He was badly wounded in the head by shrapnel on 6th May 1915 during the Second Battle of Ypres, being evacuated to the UK on the Hospital Ship 'Oxfordshire' on the 8th May. Previously promoted L./Cpl in February 1915, he was gazetted 2nd Lt. into the 3/5th London Rifle Brigade on the 16th August 1915, joining the 1/5th on 25th March 1916. He was single. His body was never found and his name is inscribed on the Thiepval Memorial, Pier 9, Face D. His brother, Norman Shellibeer Doust transferred from the LRB to the RFC on 4th March 1916 and was discharged on 8th August 1917. He died of pulmonary tuberculosis on 20th June 1918. [*Additional Sources:* Pam & Ken Linge, Thiepval Project. Dick Flory: Dulwich College War Record, 1914-1919; Dulwich College Register, 1619-1926]
i Russell called the officer Lt. Wallace but no such officer was a member of the London Rifle Brigade.

32-year old officer was "riddled with bullets"[i]. Russell, discretion overwhelmed by a foolhardy gallantry, followed the dead officer's example and tried to move forward but was also hit:

"... having observed his action, I felt that I must do the same. I, therefore, stood up and was immediately hit by two bullets and dropped down... I must say that this action had a profound effect on me in later years. I had thought that a man who could stand up and knowingly face practically certain death in these circumstances must be very brave. I found out that bravery hardly came into it. Once the decision was made to stand up I had no further fear. I was not bothered at all though I believed I would be dead within seconds and would be rotting on the ground, food for the rats next day. I did not even feel appreciably the bullets going through..."[25]

Plate 32 2nd Lt. Archibald Warner, 1/5th London Regt. (London Rifle Brigade)
(Photograph Croydon Roll of Honour)

In the German trenches meanwhile 'A' Company pressed forward. Blocks were built in the eastern ends of Firm and Fight trenches, and a Lewis gun was set up at the junction of Fir and Fen to provide covering fire against persistent bombing attacks from the Park. The gun was manned by a young rifleman, 2173 Rfn. David Reynolds[ii], and his behaviour caught the attention of one of 'A' Company's sergeants, 9849 Sgt. Herbert Frost:

---

[i] 2nd Lt. Archibald Warner, 1/5th London Regt. (London Rifle Brigade), was killed on 1st July 1916. The son of John and the late Alice Warner of Waddon House, Croydon, Warner was born on 13th February 1884. His father was an iron founder. Educated at Whitgift School, Leighton Park School, Reading and Queen's College, Cambridge, he was articled to Messers Trinder, Capron & Co., London, solicitors, joining Messers Bennett and Ferris when he qualified. A keen sportsman he had been captain of the Queen's College boat. He married Norah Elizabeth Goodbody, youngest daughter of Mr J Perry Goodbody of Inchmore, Clara, King's County, Ireland, on 15th September 1914 and they lived at 'Penarth',. North Road, Carshalton. He attested as 3997 Private in the 3/28th London Regt. (Artists' Rifles) on 4th June 1915 and served with them until October. He was commissioned into the 3/5th London Regt. on 29th October 1915 and joined the 1/5th London Regt. in France on 27th May 1916. He is buried in Hebuterne Military Cemetery, grave IV.D.7. His brother, 8050 Sgt Evan Warner, 1/5th London Regt. (London Rifle Brigade), was killed on 11th December 1914 and is buried in Lancashire Cottage Cemetery, grave I. C. 8
[ii] 2173 Rfn David Reynolds, No. 2 Platoon, A Company, 1/5th London Regt (London Rifle Brigade), died on Saturday, 1st July 1916, aged 18. He was the son of Mr. and Mrs. Reynolds of 7, Comus Place, Old Kent Rd., London. His body was never found and his name is inscribed on the Thiepval Memorial, Pier 9, Face D.

"Another who helped greatly was a youngster working the Lewis gun posted in our trench. He kept so cool and never hesitated to expose himself."²⁶

Other members of 'A' Company started to clear Eel trench to the right in order to link up with 'C' Company in Feast and the Maze. It was unwise to show yourself for even the briefest period, however, lest a German sniper get your range. 1520 Rfn. Frederick Imeson[i] of 'A' Company and 2741 Rfn. Frederick Klein[ii] were walking along the German parapet in front of Gommecourt Park looking for a place to get into the security of the trench and it was Klein who drew the short straw, hit in the head and killed instantly by a sniper lurking amongst the shattered tree stumps and waiting for a target such as this. Klein's body was left in the German lines when the men were forced to withdraw in the evening, and so was the body of his best mate, 2751 Rfn. Arthur Davis[iii], another 56ᵗʰ Division man whose name would eventually be listed on the Thiepval Memorial to the Missing. In the meantime, the surviving men of the battered 8ᵗʰ Company of the 55ᵗʰ R.I.R. withdrew a few yards into the dense undergrowth, harrying their enemy with rifle fire and sporadic bomb attacks. There they were joined by men of the 6ᵗʰ Company hurrying down Firm trench to their assistance.

Behind the L.R.B., however, affairs were taking a turn for the worse. The German barrage was now rising to an intensity not seen anywhere else on the Somme battlefront that day. One of the first groups to suffer in their attempts to breach the curtain of fire that had been dropped across No Man's Land was a party of 20 men from 'A' Company, 1/2ⁿᵈ Londons. They went over with the 3ʳᵈ wave carrying trench mortar bombs for the men of the 169ᵗʰ Trench Mortar Battery who had been sent forward to reinforce the position. Led by 2ⁿᵈ Lt. John Sanders[iv] his twenty men were reduced to just eight by the time they reached the German lines. Some of the ammunition was delivered, however of what value this was is moot. A report written after the attack suggested little or none:

"The 169 TMB finished at the end of the day without any guns complete. These guns in an advance, owing to the weight of gun and ammunition, from this experience seem to have no value as, when one part gets forward, the other parts are missing. The carrying of ammunition by ammunition parties does not seem satisfactory as they do not know the officers or men they have to follow, the consequence being touch is lost almost at once in a rush. The weight carried and the improvised method of carriage made the position more difficult."²⁷

2233 Sergeant Robert Lovett Mallett of the No. 1 Platoon, 'A' Company, 1/2ⁿᵈ Londons was one of the men who tried to get across:

---

[i] 1520 Rfn. Frederick G Imeson, 1/5ᵗʰ London Regt. (London Rifle Brigade) was wounded on Saturday, 1ˢᵗ July 1916. He was evacuated to Bed 746, Ward 13, 1ˢᵗ Eastern General Hospital in Cambridge.
[ii] 2741 Rfn. Frederick Henry Klein, 1/5ᵗʰ London Regt. (London Rifle Brigade) was killed on Saturday, 1ˢᵗ July 1916. His body was never found and his name is inscribed on the Thiepval Memorial, Pier 9, Face D.
[iii] 2751 Rfn. Arthur Davis, 1/5ᵗʰ London Regt. (London Rifle Brigade) was killed on Saturday, 1ˢᵗ July 1916. His body was never found and his name is inscribed on the Thiepval Memorial, Pier 9, Face D.
[iv] 2ⁿᵈ Lt. John William Sanders, 1/2ⁿᵈ London Regt. (Royal Fusiliers), joined the 2/2ⁿᵈ London Regt. in Alexandria on 8ᵗʰ February 1916 and was one of ten officers of the battalion who transferred to the 1/2ⁿᵈ Londons when their battalion was disbanded in June 1916. He was wounded on 16ᵗʰ August 1917 at 3ʳᵈ Ypres, returning to the battalion in April 1918.

"My battalion moved into the front-line via Yellow communication trench. During a temporary halt in Yellow trench a shell exploded some way ahead of me killing and wounding about 11 men, many just in front of me. Private Harry was almost decapitated by a splinter.

Although the front-line had scaling ladders it was in a bad state and in many places ladders were not needed. I carried two spare bandoliers of ammo, 2 Mills bombs and two Stokes mortar bombs and wirecutters.

I did not reach the German wire, a shell burst near me and I was wounded in the face and mouth. I struggled back to the front-line by which time I was practically blind, which remained several days and was taken over by the R.A.M.C. and taken to a field casualty station."[28]

Back in the Boyau de Service eleven men of No 1 Section of the 167th Trench Mortar Battery spent the day under murderous shell fire preparing Stokes mortar shells and putting them in sandbags ready for onward transit to the mortar sections in the German lines. It was a fruitless and dangerous task. Not one of the shells was sent forward as no carrying parties returned from the attack and, because no-one knew where the guns were, there was little point in wasting men in speculative trips over No Man's Land. Taking the Stokes mortars into the enemy's lines was an idea whose time had, perhaps, not yet come.

Within just fifteen minutes of the attack going in, 167th Brigade H.Q. was noting despondently that it had become practically impossible to send forward reinforcements or ammunition or to keep up communication because of the intensity of the barrage. From the right, a plaintive message was sent from 168th Brigade H.Q. to Division:

"Considerable hostile artillery fire. Can increased counter battery fire be produced?"[29]

To the rear of the London Rifle Brigade, No Man's Land was some 350 metres wide. But it was as wide and forbidding as a storm-tossed ocean to the reserves waiting in the British trenches. One of the units waiting to do their job was the 1/3rd Londons. Their task mirrored that of the Kensingtons on the far right flank and two companies under Major Samuel were to dig two communication trenches across No Man's Land so that reserves and supplies could get over in relative safety. One, 'C' trench was to be dug from the end of Yellow Street to the junction of Fen and Ferret trenches and the other, 'D' trench, from the 'Z' Hedge to Point 94 at the junction of Fir and Firm. Before they started, two men from the 1/1st City of Edinburgh Field Company had the perilous task of marking the lines of the trenches across No Man's Land. The job of marking out 'C' was given to L/Cpl. Elder and Sapper Pratt. Pratt was wounded by a shell splinter but Elder carried on and successfully completed the trace. Then, as he stood on the parapet of the German trenches he was blown into the entrance of a German dugout by a nearby shell blast. Undismayed, Elder calmly trotted down the remaining stairs and ran off a quick sketch of the dug out which was later passed on to the 56th Division's commander of the Royal Engineers. He spent the rest of his time fetching and carrying bombs for the infantrymen around him - just another normal day on the Western Front! To his left, Cpl. Murray and Sapper Gillies also managed to mark their trench and then they waited for the men of the 1/3rd Londons to start digging.

The 3rd Londons had already suffered badly in their trip towards the front line and had started to take casualties as soon as they entered the communication trenches. Capt. Arthur Agius[i] had not experienced anything approaching the ferocity of the German barrage that was falling on the British trenches:

"the shellfire was absolutely appalling. They were simply pouring shells down. We just couldn't get across. We didn't even get as far as the trench we'd dug, well, there was no trench left. It was all hammered to blazes. We got just about as far as our old line and then it became quite impossible. The company in front of me said, "It's no use. We can't get over.""

We got orders to try to make our way back to the village. This young officer, such a nice chap, jumped out of the trench to try to organise the men, pass the word and get them moving to the communication trench, and he was promptly killed. Just disappeared in an explosion. The whole of the valley was being swept with machine-gun fire and hammered with shells. We got the men organised as best we could - those of us who were left. So many gone, and we'd never even got past our front line trench! And then we found we couldn't get back. The trenches were indescribable! We were simply treading on the dead. Eventually my Sergeant and I got out on top - we were at the back of the company. I heard a shell coming. I remember thinking "Imagine just imagine hearing a single shell in the middle of all this din!" It burst just above my head. The Sergeant was blown one way and I was blown the other. He was killed. I don't know how I got back. I simply don't know how I got back. It was murder."[30]

Agius had been severely shocked by the experience:

"I was shell-shocked, I suppose, At any rate, I wasn't much use- rather inclined to cry, if anything. In fact, I couldn't stop and, being rather young, I was somewhat ashamed of it. But it had been a total shambles."[31]

Some men of the leading companies of the 3rd Londons had reached the front line and three times they bravely tried to complete their task. Whenever the men left the security of the trenches they were shot down within a few metres by machine gun and rifle fire from the eastern face of Gommecourt Park that ran at right angles to the British line of attack. 2nd Lt. Stewart Angus[ii] and L/Cpl.

---

[i] Capt. Arthur Joseph John Paul Agius MC, 1/3rd London Regt., (Royal Fusiliers) was born on 28th April 1893, the son of Edward Tancred and Concepta Maria Agius. His father was a ship owner. He was educated at Downside where he was in the OTC and was a solicitor's articled clerk with A G Gibson of 21, Leadenhall Street, London, EC. He was commissioned into the 3rd Londons in March 1911 being promoted Lieutenant in April 1913 and Temporary Captain in May 1915. His MC was gazetted on 1st January 1917 and he commanded the battalion for three weeks in 1916. He was twice Mentioned in Despatches and was demobilised on 1st March 1919 and lived at 'Redfern', Ash Vale, Surrey. [*Additional sources:* Dick Flory: Downside and the Great War, 1914-1919; Record of Services of Solicitors and Articled Clerks 1914-1918]

[ii] 2nd Lt. Stewart Angus, 1/1st City of Edinburgh Field Coy, RE, died on Saturday, 1st July 1916. Born on 7th July 1890 in Paraguay, he was the only surviving son of Mary Wilson Angus of 9, Muswell Rd., London, and the late David Angus, M. Inst. C.E. A.M.I.C.E., B.Sc. (Engineering) Edinburgh University. Educated at Edinburgh Academy and a graduate of Edinburgh University (where he was in the OTC between 1909 and 1912), Angus was on the engineering staff of the Buenos Aires Great Southern Railway, Argentina but returned on the outbreak of war, being commissioned into the 1/1st City of Edinburgh Works Company, R.E. in April 1915. He went to Egypt in December 1915 before joining the 56th Division in April 1916. His body was buried where he fell but was not found later and his name is inscribed on the Thiepval Memorial, Pier and Face 8A and 8D

George Hogg[i] from the Edinburgh engineers were there to supervise the dig and they were both killed. Major Samuel did his best to encourage his men but was let down by one of the company commanders involved. 252024 Pte. S A Newman, 1/3rd Londons, recorded this loss of nerve in his diary:

"I am sorry to state that Capt. Noel[ii], then in command of my company, was in a shocking funk despite the fact that he was wearing a steel body shield. He evidently valued his own life before those of his men seeing that he attempted to get in the rear of his command by walking on the backs of his own men. Fortunately, (Maj. Samuel) came along and prevented him acting foolishly."[32]

But their job was impossible. Anyone who entered No Man's Land was likely to be hit within thirty metres of the parapet. As with the Kensingtons, the task was suspended.

Plate 33 2nd Lt. Stewart Angus, 1/1st City of Edinburgh Field Company, R.E.
(Photograph: De Ruvigny's Roll Of Honour)

The German machine gunners firing from Gommecourt Park knew the range of the British lines to the metre. Before the war, the French estimated that one machine gun firing at a known range (and the range here would be described as 'close') had the firepower of 150-200 riflemen. The difference was that one machine gun and its team was more accurate than 200 inexpert soldiers, less prone to nerves or to indecision about which target to select, in short, it was less 'human'. At a range of less than 500 metres, one gun could concentrate something like 600 rounds a minute into an oval less than 150 metres in length. This oval was called 'the effective zone'. On the left, the German guns were

---

[i] 1858 L/Cpl George Allan Hogg, 1/1st City of Edinburgh Field Coy, RE, died on Saturday, 1st July 1916. Aged 28, he was the son of the late John and Barbara Hogg; husband of Jane Hogg of 9, South Elgin St., Edinburgh. He is buried in Serre Road Cemetery No. 1, I. B. 58.

[ii] Capt. Emile Valentine Noel, 1/3rd London Regt. (Royal Fusiliers) was born on 13th February 1891, the son of Ludovic Henri, a Foreign Provision Merchant of 7, Soho Square, and Susanna Amy Noel of 45, Compayne Gardens, Hampstead. He was educated at Laleham College, Margate and Handelschute, Leipzig. He was commissioned into the 3rd Londons on 13th October 1910, promoted Lieutenant on 6th June 1911 and Captain on 2nd September 1914. He went to France in December 1914 and was shot through the body at Neuve Chapelle on 20th March 1915. He lived at 29, Harvard Court, Honeybourne Road, West Hampstead. He was returned to the Army from the RAF after going absent without leave for four days in late November 1918 and was demobilised on 21st March 1919.

firing almost at right angles to the British line so, here, the 150-metre long 'effective zone' ran along the length of the trench line and thirty metres or so either side of it. Each machine gun bullet entered the 'effective zone' on a gentle parabolic curve from muzzle to ground. At some point in the zone, the bullet entered what was called 'the dangerous space'. The 'dangerous space' was the area in which the bullet was travelling between 1.85 metres above the ground (the average height of a man) and ground level. At the range the Germans Maxims were firing, the 'dangerous space' in the 'effective zone' was over 50 metres long. So, in other words, in an area 150 metres long by 60 metres wide, 600 rounds a minute (from one gun) would travel through the zone for 50 metres at a height where they might meet a target. On average, with one gun firing, something like 4 machine gun bullets would travel through each square metre of the 'effective zone' in the 'dangerous space' every sixty seconds.

So, for a soldier of the 1/3ʳᵈ Londons to get thirty metres across No Man's Land, he would have to move through an area in which four machine gun bullets per square metre a minute would pass. In other words, to avoid being hit, he would have to evade 120 bullets in all from just one machine gun. This number could have been reduced if the men had been able to sprint through the hail of machine gun fire, but the 1/3ʳᵈ Londons were there to dig a trench. It took a man three minutes to dig just one cubic foot of earth. As he stood there digging, twelve bullets from one gun would pass through the space he was occupying. And here, there was more than one gun firing. To look over the parapet was to invite disaster; to stand in the open and dig was suicidal. The task set for the 1/3ʳᵈ Londons was impossible.

For the men of the Edinburgh R.E. company, these were not the only tasks that proved not only impossible but costly. In the plan, four forward R.E. dumps were to be created in the German front lines and eight sappers were given the task of leading the carrying parties over. Not one left the trenches but in the 'Z' Hedge, which was subject to intermittent but heavy artillery fire, 2ⁿᵈ Cpl. Robert Glover, in charge of the move to No. 8 Dump at Point 94, was killed[i].

***

AT THE OTHER END of the line, the Kensington's stared out at the pall of smoke that still covered No Man's Land. The London Scottish and half a company of their own battalion had disappeared into the gloom twenty minutes earlier and, since then, they had heard nothing. The Kensington's C.O., Major Young, decided that matters could drift no further. He ordered a patrol lead by Lt. George Beggs[ii] to be sent out to find the assaulting troops and report on what was happening. Within a few yards of the parapet, Beggs found himself alone in the smoke and confusion of No Man's Land, his patrol lost somewhere behind. But Beggs persevered. Keeping faith with his own sense of direction, tripping and ducking as the ground around him heaved and shook from German shell

[i] 2012 2ⁿᵈ Cpl Robert Glover, 1/1ˢᵗ City of Edinburgh Field Coy, RE, died on Saturday, 1ˢᵗ July 1916. His body was never found and his name is inscribed on the Thiepval Memorial, Pier and Face 8A and 8D

[ii] Lt. George Arthur Beggs, 1/13ᵗʰ London Regt. (Kensingtons) attested 2040 Private on 10ᵗʰ August 1914. He had previously been a member of the London Rifle Brigade Cadet Corps. He lived at 12, Addison Crescent, Kensington and then 8, Carlton Mansions, Holland Park Gardens, London. He was wounded on 9ᵗʰ May 1915 and evacuated to England joining the 3/13ᵗʰ Battalion in September. After recovering from his wound suffered on 1ˢᵗ July he was attached to the 13ᵗʰ (Reserve) Battalion, London Regt. at the end of October.

explosions, he eventually stumbled into the ruins of a German trench. There, men of the London Scottish greeted him. Farmyard trench, at least, was taken. Armed with this information, Beggs turned and set off back across No Man's Land to tell his C.O. The Lieutenant was lucky as well as brave. He got back, one of the few men to make this tortuous return journey unscathed. But the word was sent back from battalion to brigade and division: The Scottish had made it. The strongpoint was theirs. At the same time, confirmation was received from another source. A VII Corps FOO had somehow seen the Scottish enter the German positions at 7.48 a.m. Farmyard, Farmer and Farm trenches of the strong point were all occupied. To their left, at the same time as the intrepid Lt. Beggs was setting off on his dangerous odyssey, a runner arrived back from the Rangers forward positions. The word was encouraging (if sadly inaccurate). All four waves were across and into the German front line. The 1/4th Londons were in the British front lines ready to assist. So far, so good.

Across nearly the whole front, it appeared that the attacking infantry had swept over the German front and support lines. In most places, they were now moving onto the third line. Only in front of Nameless Farm was progress held up. The uncut wire in front of the first (Fever and Fetter trenches) and second lines (Feint and Fell) had allowed time for the German defenders to rush to the surface. There, directed by their commander, Leutnant Franz Kremp, the men of the 1st Company, 170th Regiment had occupied what was left of the trenches, had moved out into shell holes and were now putting up stiff resistance to the Rangers as they pushed forward. Machine guns were then brought up from the cellars below Nameless Farm and these began to sweep across the open fields to their front and right. Organised rifle fire began to increase at about 8 a.m. and any British troops close enough were likely to be showered with stielhandgranate - the infamous 'potato-masher' stick grenade. Instead of pushing forward towards the farm, the Rangers naturally inclined away from trouble and pushed left and right, leaving a hole in the middle of the advance. A tactical problem the Germans would exploit later in the day.

***

ON THE FAR RIGHT the London Scottish were busy consolidating their gains and establishing defensive positions. No. 1 and No. 4 platoons of 'A' Company had found their way through the wire and entered the south end of Farmyard trench. The Company commander, Capt. Sparks, moved up the short communication trench linking Fair and Fancy trenches and established the company H.Q. Two Lewis guns covered the ground to the south and south east with excellent fields of fire across the top of the ridge and down the slope to the Sunken Road. After some time, they were joined by the one officer and five men who were all that remained of No. 2 and No. 3 platoons.

Led by Lt. John Villa, No. 1 Section, 2/2nd Field Company, Royal Engineers had gone over with the Scottish. Their task was to build blocks in the trenches to the south and in the communication trenches in order to prevent German counter-attacks. Their first job was to block the front line trench, Fair. Whilst a party under 3548 Cpl. William Bain[i] held the top end of Fair trench, a bombing

---

[i] 3548 Corporal William Bain, 1/14th London Regt (London Scottish), died on Saturday, 1st July 1916, aged 25. He was the son of Mr J P Bain of 'Ortinola', Maracas Valley, St. Joseph, Trinidad, British West Indies, and the late Mrs

party led by Lance Corporal Aitken pushed beyond the block in an effort to drive the enemy back. Typically, a bombing party would consist of eight men. In charge, as here, would be an N.C.O. Two specially trained men would throw the bombs with another two acting as bomb carriers. Another two, armed with rifle and bayonet, would push forward just ahead of the bombing team. Their job was to rush into the bombed section of trench to finish off or drive out whoever remained. The eighth man was a reserve in case of casualties. Armed with the 1½ lb Mills grenade, the bombers were trained to land at least half of their bombs in an area of trench 3 yards long and just over 1 yard wide at a range of 30 yards. Set with a fuse of five seconds, the Mills was a vicious fragmentation device. British Army tests showed that anyone within ten yards of an exploding grenade would almost certainly be hit by at least one shrapnel fragment. Within twenty-five yards, it would cause casualties amongst one in four and at thirty yards, one in ten. At thirty-five yards distance most soldiers should be safe unless they were unlucky enough to be hit by the spinning base plate of the bomb. Bombing was a dangerous, 'cat and mouse' game. Technique, bravery and luck were needed in equal measure. At this stage, the advantage fell to Lance Corporal Aitken and his men. As they pushed down Fair, the Germans, men of the 6th Company of the 170th Regiment led by Leutnant der Reserve Thum[i], fell back. Behind Aitken's party, the Royal Engineers were busy constructing their trench block. Four traverses were blown in and two barricades with wire built. They then moved off under heavy rifle and artillery fire to continue their work in Fancy and Fact trenches.

Other men pushed up past the company H.Q. A party led by 2nd Lts. Arthur Speak[ii] and Allan Petrie[iii] took Farm trench and, with the help of the R.E., blocked the north end of Fancy. The lieutenants then started to organise a perimeter defence and set the men to reversing the firesteps in the captured trenches. Snipers were established in good positions to pick off any one unwise enough to interfere and contact was made with 'B' Company to the left in a communication trench that connected Farm and Fable trenches.

'C' Company to the left swept straight over the German front and support lines. First into the enemy lines was No. 11 platoon, followed by No. 12 and the company commander Major Claud Low D.S.O. Here the trenches had been nearly obliterated in places as 2nd Lt. White of the neighbouring 'A' Company observed:

M R F Bain. His body was never found and his name is inscribed on the Thiepval Memorial, Pier and Face 9 C and 13 C.

i Leutenant der Reserve Thum was killed in action later in the day.

ii 2nd Lt. Arthur Aitchison Speak M.C., 1/14th London Regt (London Scottish), arrived in France in April 1916. He was the elder son of Mr Arthur and Mrs Speak of Vinovia, Bishop Auckland. He married Victoria Stillingfleet White in 1919.

iii 2nd Lt. Allan Strachan Petrie, 1/14th London Regt (London Scottish), died on Monday, 11th September 1916 from wounds received the day before, in an attack near Leuze Wood. He was aged 25. He was the son of Andrew and Annie Petrie of 21, Bonnybank Rd., Dundee. He is buried in Guillemont Road Cemetery, Guillemont, Somme, France. grave VIII. H. 5. Born on the 25th April 1891, he was educated at Clepington and Morgan Academy. The son of a grocer's warehouseman, he became a bank clerk in the Dundee branch of theNational Bank of Scotland. He was attested private in the London Scottish on 28th August 1914, later being promoted to L/Cpl. On the 25th September 1915 he was wounded near Hulluch during the Battle of Loos. He was commissioned into the 3/14th London Scottish in December 1915.

"No trenches to be seen just a conglomeration of craters joining each other some with dugout shafts leading from them still intact. Passing one of these a wounded Corporal (Brown[i]) places himself at the entrance with two bombs ready to deal with any signs of life below."[33]

In one of these shell holes White found a badly wounded German and there then occurred one of those disagreeable episodes barely excusable even in the heat of battle:

"In another shell hole I find a wounded Hun lying on his back, holding up his hands, pleads for mercy. I make to pass on Major L (Low) appears out of the mist, takes in the situation, shouts 'kill him'. No, I can't kill a defenceless man whose eyes I can see, my batman has done it and I hate him for it."[34]

White then moved on from the place of execution to the aid of some Royal Engineers:

"Carry on. I seem to be almost alone, only an occasional man dodging here and there. See three or four men, REs, gesticulating. I forget at this distance of time what they did but I gathered that they were covered by some Huns in a crater, lobbed a Mills into the crater and went on."[35]

In the smoke and chaos, the consequence of the lack of recognisable land marks was that the first two platoons of 'C' Company crossed Farm trench without realising it and arrived at Fable, which they took after a stiff fight with the garrison of the 5th Company, 170th Regt. The previously mentioned Major Low, O.C. 'C' Company, was now wounded in the shoulder by a piece of shrapnel and he fell into Fable trench bleeding heavily. Behind him, No. 9 and No. 10 Platoons, led by Lt. H C Lamb, ran into a party of Germans who were late in leaving their dugouts and a brief shower of grenades from the company bombers eliminated this threat and the men carried on forwards. By the time they arrived, Major Low had recovered somewhat, but not enough to resume command of 'C' Company and Lt. Lamb assumed control. Before Major Low[ii] was carried back to the doctor (and before he was hit again by shrapnel, this time in the leg), he and Lamb conferred hurriedly over a trench map. Looking around at the smashed up ground, they agreed that they were in Farm trench and that, therefore, their final objective, Fable, was still ahead. Without realising their error, Lamb re-organised the company and, with two platoons, moved forward in an effort to find and take what they thought was their final objective. Still surrounded by thick smoke, they moved across the open, down the gentle slope towards the Gommecourt to Puisieux Road some 250 metres ahead. After about 100 metres the smoke cleared and a dangerous panorama unfolded before them. 300 metres to their left was Nameless Farm, still held by its defenders and in a position to enfilade the Scottish's ground with machine gun and rifle fire at near point blank range. To their front, some 500 metres away on the top of the ridge, was the German reserve line, bristling with machine guns firing down into the

---

[i] Cpl Brown survived the attack.
[ii] Major Claud Low D.S.O., T.D., 1/14th London Regt. (London Scottish) enlisted in the London Scottish on 9th November 1902 and was commissioned on 14th May 1906. He went to France in September 1914 as a Captain. He was promoted Major on 1st June 1916. He rejoined the battalion on 21st April 1917 towards the end of the Battle of Arras as second in command. He was wounded again on 23rd August 1918 and did not return to the battalion.

valley. And snaking up the slope was Elbe communication trench which, even now, was filling with German troops bent on furious counter-attack.

Lamb and his men were dangerously exposed. Almost immediately, 2nd Lt. Donald Kerr[i], the only other remaining 'C' Company officer, was shot and killed. Coolly, Lamb organised a fighting withdrawal to the comparative safety of Fable trench. As one section opened covering fire, another would withdraw up the slope. After what must have seemed an eternity, Lamb and his men were able to drop back unscathed into the trenches and shell holes of the 'strongpoint' to join their colleagues.

Lamb's excursion into unknown territory had been witnessed by 2nd Lt. White:

"Got up to the only piece of trench seen so far. I realise that there was a big stretch of ground beyond without trenches which meant that someone has gone too far. I could see them bombing towards the right along a trench a long way in front. Gathered a party together around a LG (Lewis Gun) and made a position. Met Maj. Low wounded through chest said to him 'I'm afraid they've gone too far'. He replies, 'I'm afraid so, would you mind fixing up the this pad some way' indicating his field dressing. I don't remember now what I actually did but it helped in some way. Then saw stragglers from the line in front coming tumbling in. Decided to hold this position. Have a good look round at it and think it good if we can obtain some ammunition."

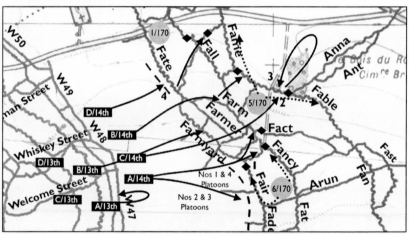

Map 14 Situation 0730-0830, London Scottish front

Legend: I – Location of first trench block and Lewis gun.   2 – Maj. Low, C Coy, wounded
3 – Scene of Lt. Lamb's advance and retreat   4 – Lt. Brown Constable, D Coy, killed
- - - - Lines of uncut wire   ◆ Trench blocks

---

i 2nd Lt. Donald Kerr, 1/14th London Regt (London Scottish), died on Saturday, 1st July 1916, aged 25. He was born on 28th June 1891 in Pitlochry, the youngest of three children of James John and Anne Kerr of 'Struan', 140, Albert Rd., Crosshill, Glasgow. He went to Glasgow University in 1908 studying Latin, Mathematics, Physics and Chemistry. He won a Chemistry prize in 1910 and a First Class Certificate in Advanced Chemistry in 1912 and graduated MA with 2nd Class Honours in Mathematics and Physics. He was awarded a BSc in Chemistry in 1913 and became a teacher before working for Clerical Medical and General Insurance as a trainee actuary. He attested 4229 Private in the 2/14th London Regt. before being commissioned in December 1915. He went to France in May 1916. His body was never found and his name is inscribed on the Thiepval Memorial, Pier and Face 9 C and 13 C. [*Additional Sources:* Pam & Ken Linge, Thiepval Project]

By now, German artillery from the direction of Rossignol Wood, realising their own front line was lost, had started to drop a barrage onto the Farmyard strongpoint. Casualties were mounting at a worrying rate and, by the time 'C' Company had started to block Fact and Fable trenches (about 7.55 a.m.) to prevent attacks from the right, only Lieut. Lamb and about sixty men remained unwounded. All of the other officers and senior N.C.O.s were either dead or wounded.

As 'C' Company consolidated, behind them in Farmyard trench, the men of the Kensingtons 'clearing party' were mopping up. They had suffered badly from the German barrage as they had been the last to leave the British trenches but, once in the German lines, they set to the task of trench clearing with relish. Prisoners were rounded up and some sent back across No Man's Land. Others were herded back down into their dugouts pending the outcome of the battle. After the battle there might well have been more prisoners to count in the cages had some not been killed by their own barrage crossing back to the British lines. Others died in even less happy circumstances. According to one private soldier (Pte. Arthur Hubbard of No. 11 Platoon, 'C' Company, London Scottish), the attacking troops were under orders not to take prisoners. In a letter home, written from a ward in the East Suffolk Hospital in Ipswich six days after the assault, he describes how he shot three wounded Germans soldiers who were trying to surrender:

"We had strict orders not to take prisoners no matter if wounded. My first job when I had finished cutting some of their wire away was to empty my magazine on three Germans that came out of their dug outs bleeding badly and put them out of their misery. They cried for mercy but I had my orders, but they had no feeling whatever for us poor chaps. Soon after that I was waiting for more excitement when one of them huge shells burst a few yards away... '[36]

Led by No. 8 Platoon, 'B' Company under Major Francis Lindsay, had occupied their objective by 7.45 a.m. They had gone forward through the smoke unable to see either company to left or right. As with 'C' Company, the German trenches here had almost been levelled and they had been abandoned by their defenders who had retreated to their second line. When the pursuing London Scots caught up with them a vicious hand to hand fight broke out. Sgt. Henry Smith of No. 8 Platoon recalled the bitter nature of the encounter:

"Tremendous hand to hand fighting and here I killed my first German – shot him clean through the forehead and sent his helmet spinning in the air. Just afterwards I killed two more. Bombs and bullets by the thousand and the ground blowing up under our feet... Our platoon commander, Lt. Curror[i], killed and all other N.C.O.s of No. 8 either killed or wounded... went into the third line, having driven the Huns back further... I killed three more Germans here, making my total bag six."[37]

---

[i] 2nd Lt. William Edwin Forrest Curror, 1/14th London Regt. (London Scottish), died on Saturday, 1st July 1916. He was born on 2nd January 1882 and was the son of John and Annie Forrest Curror of 34, Chancellor Rod, West Dulwich, formerly of Elie in Fife. Educated at Dorking High School he was an engineer and lived at 16, Vaughan Gardens, Ilford. He attested 103 Private in the London Scottish on 1st April 1908 and was a Company Sergeant Major in the 3/14th Battalion when he was commissioned in September 1915. He is buried in Gommecourt British Cemetery No. 2.

Following up, the rest of 'B' Company set to the task of reversing what was left of the trench and blocking their section of Fame trench, all the while coming under fire from the eastern end of Felon trench near Nameless Farm. German bombing parties from the 6th Company, 170th Regiment attempted to interrupt their progress but L/Cpl Thoms with a Lewis gun, well positioned but not well supplied with ammunition[i], helped to hold them off.

On the left, 'D' Company, commanded by Lt. John Brown Constable who strolled into action brandishing a walking stick, lost direction in the thick smoke screen that lingered across No Man's Land. As they moved down the slope between the opposing lines, No. 13 Platoon quickly lost their officer, Lt. Greig[ii], who was wounded within thirty yards of the British wire. The men of No. 13 Platoon were then held up by uncut wire and by bombers and snipers in Fate trench. Lt. Brown Constable was moving forward with the second wave, No. 14 Platoon, and, along with No. 15 Platoon behind, he managed to find a passage through the wire and into the German front line. This was the point where the sectors of the 1st and 5th Companies of the 170th Regiment met and such junctions, where command and control are at their weakest, are always fragile spots in any defensive system. This point was no different and, exploiting the frailty, 'D' Company pushed into the German trenches and started to attack the left wing of the 1st Company's position.

Here, a communication trench ran back from Fate to Fall trench. Parties of all three platoons of 'D' Company now started the dirty and dangerous task of bombing up the German traverses but they left their C.O., Lt. Brown Constable, dead hit somewhere in the German first line. 6546 Pte. George Robinson saw the Lieutenant die, hit on the right side of the forehead by a piece of shrapnel[iii]. Some men managed to bomb all the way up Fate trench until they briefly made contact with some of the Rangers who were here pinned down in front of Nameless Farm. Others worked their way up the communication trench and into the support line, Fall, suffering heavy casualties all the while from both rifle fire and stick grenades. Where resistance was particularly stubborn, one of the company bombers used the tactic of last resort. 4611 Sgt. Edward Gurney[iv] climbed out of the trenches and ran over the open, bullet-swept ground to drop his grenades amongst the German defenders. He was killed in the act. By such

---

[i] The Lewis gun used a 47-round drum. L. Cpl. Thoms had just three of them.
[ii] Capt. Roy Scott Greig, 1/14th London Regt (London Scottish) was born on 26th May 1894, the son of the late John Andrew and Annie Greig of 2, Ravenna Road, Putney. He was educated at Kent Coast College in Herne Bay and was an insurance clerk. He attested 1448 Private in the London Scottish in March 1911 and went to France with the battalion in September 1914, fighting at Messines. Promoted Lance Corporal, he was commissioned into the 3/14th London Scottish in August 1915. On his return to France after being wounded he was attached to the 6th Cameron Highlanders and was reported wounded and missing on Thursday, 28th March 1918. His body was after found and he is buried in Cabaret-Rouge British Cemetery, Souchez, Pas De Calais, France, grave XXIV.
[iii] Lt. John Cecil Brown Constable, 1/14th London Regt (London Scottish), died on Saturday, 1st July 1916, aged 26. He was the son of the Rev. Albert Edward and Clara Emily Brown Constable of 'Greet', Mottingham, London. Born in Allahabad, Uttar Pradesh, India, Brown Constable went on to become a Civil Engineer. He lived at 'Beverley', Frant Road, Tunbridge Wells, Kent. He was attested Private in the London Scottish on 2nd September 1914. His mother Clara was still writing to the War Office for news of her son in March 1917. Robinson, in a letter to Brown Constable's mother, wrote that he had died instantly and that he (Robinson) had placed the Lieutenant's body in a shell hole. In 1919, in a letter to Maj. Claud Low of the London Scottish a member of the 170th IR, by the name of Schneyer, wrote, "Amongst others, I buried an English officer who had entered the storm with a walking stick" (letter from Liddle Collection, Leeds University). This is believed to have been Lt. Brown Constable. He is believed buried in Gommecourt British Cemetery No. 2, Hebuterne, grave II.G.26.
[iv] 4611 Sgt Edward Ernest Gurney, 1/14th London Regt (London Scottish), died on Saturday, 1st July 1916. His body was never found and his name is inscribed on the Thiepval Memorial, Pier and Face 9 C and 13 C.

bravery was progress slowly made. Eventually though, and however hard they tried, they could get no further forward. Fall trench was blocked, leaving Germans to their left in the trench and to their front in Fame trench, 100 metres away.

The final platoon, No. 16, met disaster in their own trenches. The last to leave, they were waiting for the signal to advance when a German salvo crashed down amongst the men. Hardly a man remained unscathed, 2nd Lts. Cecil Woodcock and George Prebble[i] were both wounded and their Lewis guns were destroyed.

***

BY 8 A.M., THE GENERAL SITUATION in the German lines was this:

Unknown to the staff and men of the 56th Division, the attack of the 46th Division was over in all but name. Although plans for new attacks were to occupy the attentions of the Corps and 46th Divisional Staff and, rather more significantly, large sections of the Corps Heavy Artillery, for many fruitless hours, little more would happen in front of Foncquevillers that might divert attention away from the attack on the southern side of the salient. They did not know it but the Londoners were on their own.

But, as far as the 56th Division was concerned, it appeared that there was, after just half an hour, every reason for the Divisional and Brigade Staff to feel some satisfaction.

On the right, the London Scottish were established in the Farmyard strongpoint. They had held off some aggressive bombing attacks down the adjacent trenches but, with the help of the Royal Engineers, they were blocking and reversing trenches, establishing Lewis gun positions and consolidating their exposed position. Behind them, though, communication with the Kensingtons was tenuous and much-needed supplies of SAA and grenades were proving difficult to get across. But a few prisoners had been taken and the first slightly wounded of them to arrive in the British lines somewhat forlornly passed the Kensingtons' advanced battalion headquarters at 8.25 a.m.[ii] The Adjutant was able to make a swift enquiry as the prisoner passed by and ascertained that he was a member of the 170th Infantry Regiment who had been born on 7th February 1893. So clearly not just the elderly reservists that some senior officers had been predicting.

On their left, the Rangers were having problems. The wire had either been repaired or was poorly cut and casualties had been heavy in some of the attacking companies. On their right, they had made contact with the London Scottish in the front line German trenches and on the left, they were in touch with the Queen Victoria's Rifles and Queen's Westminster Rifles. In the centre, however, the failure to break through to Nameless Farm was causing severe problems. This fiercely held German strongpoint was driving a wedge into the heart of the British advance as troops moved away to left and right in an effort to avoid the heavy machine gun and rifle fire pouring from it.

---

i 2nd Lt. George Wilson Prebble, 1/14th London Regt. (London Scottish) was born on 14th June 1895 and was the son of Jonathan and Agnes Eliza Noble Prebble of Craigebank, Beacontree Avenue, Walthamstow. He was educated at Sir George Monoux Grammar School, Walthamstow and was a clerk. He attested 3153 Private in the London Scottish on 14th August 1914 and was commissioned in December 1915.
ii He was a member of the 170th Infantry Regiment who had been born on 7th February 1893.

To the left of the Rangers, the Queen Victoria's Rifles and Queen's Westminster Rifles had become mixed up as they pushed through the first three German lines. Again, the fire from Nameless Farm had pushed the axis of the Queen Victoria's Rifles' attack to the left and now, together with the men of the Queen's Westminster Rifles, they were lining the bank on the northern side of the Gommecourt to Nameless Farm Road. Here they waited, as the few unwounded officers decided how they could push on towards the final objective, the Quadrilateral.

On the far left, the London Rifle Brigade had fought their way into the south eastern corner of Gommecourt Park and were into the Maze and on either side of the Cemetery. Bombing parties were preparing to work their way up the communication trenches on the edge of the Village. Consolidation work was in hand.

In many respects, the attack had gone well. The hole in the centre around Nameless Farm was a problem and the mopping up operations in the front lines were still going on but, otherwise, most initial objectives had been taken, and taken quickly. The problems lay to the rear. As the attacking troops looked over their shoulders in an effort to catch sight of the reserves flooding over No Man's Land they would have been dismayed at the picture that greeted them. Across its whole width and length, No Man's Land was a boiling and heaving mass of explosions. The 2nd Guard Reserve Division alone had eighty guns and howitzers at its disposal. On July 1st, they fired nearly 23,000 shells as the attacks of the 46th and 56th Divisions were made. The 46th Division's assault was soon over and this allowed the German gunners to concentrate their fire on the Londoner's attack. In addition to the 2nd Guard Reserve Division, the guns of the 52nd Division, from the south, and 111th Division, from the north. were also pounding the British lines and, as the attack on Serre foundered, the German guns around Puisieux switched targets towards Gommecourt. In all, it is probable that some 200 German guns were concentrating their fire, at some stage, on the 56th London Division. No other troops on 1st July experienced such an overwhelming counter-barrage as did the 56th Division. In its intensity, it was virtually impenetrable.

*** *

WITH MOST IMMEDIATE OBJECTIVES taken, the battalion with a job still to do was the Queen's Westminster Rifles. Their final objective was the Quadrilateral, a rough rectangle of trenches near the flat top of the ridge that ran between Gommecourt village and Rossignol Wood. The Quadrilateral was bordered by Exe and Ems communication trenches running east to west and Fillet and Etch trenches running north to south. It was at this point that the two attacking divisions were due to link up and to create the new front line facing to the east. The way to the Quadrilateral was up Ems and Etch trenches and as the mixed companies of the Queen Victoria's Rifles and Queen's Westminster Rifles lay in the sunken road to the west of Nameless Farm officers from both battalions started to reorganise their men for the move forward.

The road in 1916 bore little resemblance to the modern metalled one. Visitors today will find a gently curving stretch of tarmac with a slight bank on its northern side. In 1916 the road, like so many in the area, lay some two metres below the level of the neighbouring fields. As a result, whilst it gave the attacking troops decent cover from rifle and machine gun fire, it also meant that, to move forward, the men would have to scramble up a steep and muddy slope before being able to move on. Although the German third line was barely 20 metres beyond the road, the slight delay caused by the need to get up the bank might prove fatal to anyone who attempted an attack over the open. Just looking over the lip of the slope invited a bullet between the eyes. But, for the attackers there was another problem. To their right, 200 metres away, was the stronghold of Nameless Farm, which lay just to the south of the road. The German infantry, who were holding out against attacks from the Rangers, were also able to fire straight down the road into the flank of the Queen Victoria's Rifles and Queen's Westminster Rifles. It was a bullet from this direction that killed Capt. Robert Cunningham[i], C.O. of 'A' Company, Q.V.R.s. The only remaining officer of 'A' Company was now the inexperienced 2nd Lt. Percy Simmonds, a man who had never before led his men into battle. With him were the Company Sergeant Major and three other Sergeants: Wilson, Lewis and Telfer.

As the attack faltered, the remaining officers of the Westminsters had collected a group of men either side of the point where Etch trench cut across the road and then ran back to the third line. The senior surviving subaltern was 2nd Lt. James Horne of 'B' Company. He had with him four platoon commanders from the battalion: 2nd Lt. Arthur Yates and 2nd Lt. Arthur Negus, both of 'B' Company, 2nd Lt. Douglas Upton[ii] of 'C' Company and 2nd Lt. Edward Bovill of 'A' Company. They hurriedly conferred, shouting above the din of explosions and the snap and chatter of rifle and machine gun fire. There was only one decision: they could not go back and they would not stay where they were. There was only one course of action, to move forward. The five young lieutenants gathered their men, moved to the lip of Etch trench and dropped into it. Here, Etch trench ran straight into the third German line between Fellow and Fell trenches. This communication trench was not traversed, it presented just a gentle curve to right and left before coming to the junction. Preceded by a shower of Mills grenades, this mixed group of Westminsters rushed up the trench, driving the defenders in front of them. At the junction of Etch and Fellow a group, led by 2nd Lts. Yates and Negus turned left into Fellow and proceeded to bomb their way along the trench. After 10 yards Yates[iii] was hit and killed. A few yards further on, the already wounded

---

[i] Capt. Robert William Cunningham, 'A' Company, 1/9th London Regt (Queen Victoria Rifles), died on Saturday, 1st July 1916, aged 24. He was the son of the late Robert and Mary Cunningham. Capt. Cunningham was a government clerk and lived at 137, Kings Road, Kingston Hill. He was attested private in the 6th East Surreys on 18th March 1909, aged 17 years and 5 months. He then transferred to the Kensingtons being promoted L./Cpl in July 1910, Cpl in July 1914 and Lance Sergeant on 7th August 1914. He was commissioned into the Queen Victoria's Rifles on 16th January 1915. His body was never found and his name is inscribed on the Thiepval Memorial, Pier 9 Face C.

[ii] Lt. Upton is described as missing believed dead in a number of documents. In fact he was wounded and made prisoner by the Germans.

[iii] 2nd Lt. Arthur Gerald Vavasour Yates, 'C' Company, 1/16th London Regt (Queen's Westminster Rifles), died on Saturday, 1st July 1916. He was the third of six children of Col. Hercules Campbell Yates (Chairman of the Cheshire County Quarter Sessions) and Annie Yates of the Lower Beech, Tytherington, Macclesfield, Cheshire. He was educated at Macclesfield Grammar School (now The King's School) where he was in the school's cricket and football 1st XIs. He left school in 1903 to take up articles with Blunt and Brocklehurst, solicitors and qualified in 1909. He played cricket for Macclesfield Cricket Club. He attested 2162 Private in the 28th London Regt (Artists Rifles) on 2nd September 1914 before being commissioned into the Queen's Westminsters on 2nd July 1915. He went to France on 16th March 1916. His body was never found and his name is inscribed on the Thiepval Memorial, Pier 13 Face C. [*Additional Sources:* Pam & Ken Linge, Thiepval Project]

Negus[i] was hit again and killed outright. But, whatever their losses, the Queen's Westminster Rifles were, at last, in the enemy's third line.

To their right, an act of individual initiative and extraordinary bravery broke the deadlock in front of Fell trench. The act was witnessed by 2361 Sgt. Gilbert Telfer of No. 1 Platoon, Queen Victoria's Rifles:

"Quite on his own initiative, Lance Corporal Packer[ii], the bombing corporal of No. 1 Platoon, who led on our trek up the trenches, although wounded in the ear, rushed forward and bombed the Germans, followed instantaneously by several others, causing the occupants of the German third line to slacken their fire for a few seconds, and with the help of the Queen's Westminster Rifles the third line was rushed and taken."[38]

The British troops were now in the third German line, either side of Etch trench, the route to their final objective. The men spread out along the trenches in all directions in order to make contact with the battalions to left and right and to push forward towards the Quadrilateral. To the right, the men of 'A' Company of the Q.V.R. fanned out, some, under Sgt. Telfer, in an attempt to counter the withering cross fire they were suffering from the direction of Nameless Farm and Felon trench. 2nd Lt. Simmonds, their only remaining officer, was leading another party in an effort to bomb up Etch. For a man unused to battle, Simmonds' composure and confidence were extraordinary. Although only with the Q.V.R. since March he had made a tremendous impression on everyone. Even allowing for understandable hyperbole, his men later gave ample testimony to his courage and concern for their well being: "He was worshipped by all the boys in his company" (Rfn. Mitchell); "He was the pluckiest officer we had out there" (Rfn. Durston); and from 1061 Sgt. Maj. Edward Pulleyn:

"He was as cheery and cool as he was when we were taking part in rehearsals for the attack. I assure you it was impossible to find a more brave, gentlemanly and popular officer. He was absolutely loved by his platoon all of whom he looked after and treated extraordinarily well."

This remarkable, self-effacing officer was now waving his swagger stick in an effort to encourage his men forward. Rfn. Mitchell saw his end:

"He was organising a party of bombers in a communication trench before storming the German third line when a sniper's bullet hit him."

Simmonds was killed instantly[iii]. 'A' Company's last officer was gone.

---

[i] 2nd Lt. Arthur George Negus, 'C' Company, 1/16th London Regt (Queen's Westminster Rifles), died on Saturday, 1st July 1916. He was aged 27. 2nd Lt. Negus was the only son of Mr E M and Mrs C J Negus of 16 Clevedon Road, Norbiton, Surrey. He was married to Ethel Mary Negus and lived at Trevena, Manorgate Road, Kingston Hill. His body was never found and his name is inscribed on the Thiepval Memorial, Pier 13 Face C.

[ii] Cpl Fred G Packer was awarded the Military Medal for his actions on 1st July 1916, the award being posted in the London Gazette on 1st September 1916 along with seven other men from the Q.V.R.s who were all awarded the M.M. He was discharged from the Army in March 1918 as a result of wounds.

[iii] 2nd Lt. Percy Grabham Simmonds, 'A' Company, 1/9th London Regt (Queen Victoria's Rifles), died on Saturday, 1st July 1916. Born on 4th July 1886 at Southend-on-Sea he was the son of Harry and Eliza May Simmonds of 'Naunton', Holland Road, Clacton-on-Sea and the grandson of the late Thomas Dowsett JP, first Mayor of Southend. A graduate of London University and Queen's College, Oxford, where he was a member of the OTC, he was a Theology student at Mansfield College, Oxford, before he joined the QVR. He became a Sunday School teacher, ran a club for boys and was a superintendent of a school in Saffron Walden. He was commissioned into the 3/9th London Regt. in August 1915. His body was never found and his name is inscribed on the Thiepval Memorial, Pier and Face 9C.

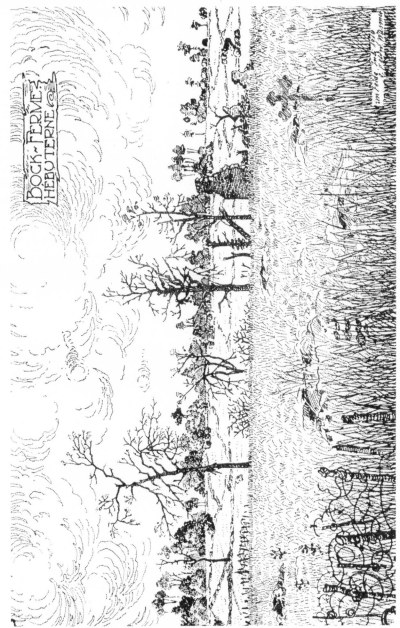

Plate 34 Sketch of Bock or Nameless Farm
(Courtesy of Paul Reed)

The sketch, done by a Vizefeldwebel Wasmer in July 1916, shows Bock (Nameless) Farm from behind the trench that linked Epte and Elbe trenches about half way up the slope behind the German third line trench, Felon. The trees in the background are the orchards and woods that fringed the north side of Hebuterne. The Rangers would have attacked from the trenches on the slope opposite. The panorama shows the excellent field of fire Nameless Farm and the support trenches had over The Rangers' frontage.

To Simmonds' left, 2nd Lt. Upton of the Queen's Westminster Rifles led a bombing party of Q.W.R.s towards Gommecourt cemetery, clearing Fellow and then Feud trenches. A German bombing party held them up for a while as they neared the Cemetery, but their aggression pushed the defenders back towards the village. Behind them, as they went, sign boards were erected in the captured trenches and, when they saw this, the men still lining the Nameless Farm Road left the security of the bank and, coming over the open, dropped into the newly secured trenches.

Whilst 2nd Lt. Upton was making progress to the left, a small bombing team pushed up Etch. 24 C.S.M. Charles Froome[i] of 'B' Company, 2549 L/Cpl. Douglas Newton, 2513 Rfn. Albert Clark[ii] and another bomber of the Queen's Westminster Rifles tried to bomb up the long communication trench, but they met strong parties of German bombers coming the other way and were driven back. To stop the enemy's advance, and to prevent any counter-attacks from the right, these men, with the assistance of some Cheshire pioneers and of the Royal Engineers sappers, blocked Etch and Fell trenches. Whilst the work was done, 2nd Lt. Horne and the only remaining Lewis gunner[iii] gave covering fire. L/Cpl. Newton was last seen defending the barrier, throwing bombs at the oncoming German bombers when the rest of the men were forced to withdraw later in the afternoon[iv].

Behind them, and giving weight to the covering fire, was a Vickers machine gun. It was one of two that had been carried across No Man's Land and had been brought into action by a team led by 2nd Lt. John Engall (Queen's Westminster Rifles attached to 169th Infantry Brigade Machine Gun Company). They had come over with 'A' Company, Queen's Westminster Rifles. 2nd Lt. Engall and his men got their gun as far as the junction of Etch, Feed and Feint in the German support line. Four of the gun team had already been put out of action getting to this spot and Engall and the sole remaining member of the team had to set up and work the gun. Engall fired whilst his colleague fed the machine gun and spotted targets. At some point during the morning, the 19-year old Engall was hit in the head and killed[v]. Like so many, his body was never found. Another member of the Machine Gun Company to meet the exact same fate was

---

[i] 24 CSM Charles William Froome DCM, 'B' Company 1/16th London Regt (Queen's Westminster Rifles), died on Saturday, 1st July 1916. Aged 44, Froome had been in the battalion for over 20 years. He was the son of Charles William and Catherine Mary Froome and the husband of Fanny Elizabeth Froome of 26, Raymond Avenue, West Ealing, London. He is buried in Gommecourt British Cemetery No.2, Hebuterne, grave II. H. 27.

[ii] 2513 Rfn. (later Sgt.) Albert E Clark, 1/16th London Regt (Queen's Westminster Rifles), was awarded the M.M. for his conduct on 1st July 1916. He was killed in action on 28th March 1918. His body was never found and his name is inscribed on the Arras Memorial, Bay 10.

[iii] Thought to be 550612 Rfn Leonard Fairclough, 1/16th London Regt (Queen's Westminster Rifles), who died on Saturday, 1st July 1916. Aged 29, he was the Son of Abraham and Emily Fairclough of 14, Rumsey Rd., Stockwell, London. He is buried in Gommecourt British Cemetery No.2, Hebuterne, grave III. J. 17.

[iv] 2549 L/Cpl Douglas Newton, 1/16th London Regt (Queen's Westminster Rifles), died on Saturday, 1st July 1916. His body was never found and his name is inscribed on the Thiepval Memorial, Pier 13 Face C.

[v] 2nd Lt. John Sherwin Engall, 1/16th London Regt (Queen's Westminster Rifles) attd., Machine Gun Corps (Inf), died on Saturday, 1st July 1916, aged 19. He was the third of four children of John Benjamin Sherwin Engall and Edith Mary Engall of 62, Goldsmith Avenue, Acton, London. Educated at St Paul's School (where he spent two years in the Cadet Corps attached to the 10th Middlesex), Engall was a chartered accountant. He was attested as a rifleman into the Q.W.R. on the 3rd September 1914 and was gazetted 2nd Lt. on 15th January 1915. He went to France on 15th January 1915 and was seconded to the Brigade Machine Gun Company in March 1916. His body was never found and his name is inscribed on the Thiepval Memorial Pier and Face 5 C and 12 C. His older brother Capt. Walter Sherwin Engall served with the Army Service Corps. [*Additional Sources:* Pam & Ken Linge, Thiepval Project]

3223 Rfn. Arthur Claridge from the Queen Victorias. He and another from the Victorias, Rfn. Robert Manning[i], had met up with Rfn. George Bristow of the Queen's Westminsters who was in another section of the company and together they arrived in the German second line ready to work whatever guns were available. Soon after, however, a German bombing attack developed on their position and Claridge, putting his head above the trench to observe the attack, was immediately shot through the head and killed instantly[ii]. Bristow was himself wounded but managed to get back to the British lines late in the day[iii].

The task of consolidating the gains made fell to the men of 'A' Company, 1/5th Cheshires, the Divisional Pioneers. Its platoons followed the assaulting battalions across No Man's Land ready to set to work reversing trenches, building trench blocks and establishing defensive strong points. No. 4 Platoon was commanded by Lt. Bass and went over on the right behind 'C' Company of the Queen Victoria's Rifles and Queen's Westminster Rifles. Their job was to consolidate the Cemetery but, in the confusion and the smoke, some of the men lost contact with their unit, a not uncommon problem on 1st July. Instead, they joined the later waves of infantry in dealing with parties of Germans who had come up from their dugouts and were now causing trouble in the front line. 1460 Pte Joe Brown of No. 4 Platoon described what happened in these first confused minutes:

"We followed up 'C' Company of the Q.V.R. We went over the parapet and got to the German front line and we couldn't see anything of the Q.V.R. so we started letting into the Germans. Then we got to the second line and started letting into the Germans again but Mr Bass stopped us and told us to get into the trench and await orders. We got into the 2nd line trench and sat down. Mr Bass took the first man (*author's note:* 1527 Pte John Clifford) and told him to come with him. Whilst Mr Bass was away we set at work reversing the parapet. Sergt. Lanceley went up to the 3rd line to 2nd Lt. Arthur and then we went up to the 3rd line and attached ourselves to 2nd Lt. Arthur. We started cutting a piece out of the traverse or block for the Q.V.R. and we placed a man on guard in the communication trench. Whilst he was on guard some Germans came up. We cut the piece out and went down the trench and helped to pass bombs up. We then had orders to retire. I never saw Mr Bass after he had taken the man away. He went up to report to Capt. Cox of the Q.V.R."

The recollections of another member of No. 4 Platoon, 2382 Pte Henry Lancashire, suggests that No. 4 Platoon split up in 2nd Lt. Bass's absence, with the majority following Sgt. Lanceley up to the 3rd line to join 2nd Lt. Arthur:

---

[i] Rfn. R J Manning, 1/9th London Regt. (Queen Victoria's Rifles) att. 169th Machine Gun Company was wounded on Saturday, 1st July 1916. He was shot through the right cheek, the bullet exiting behind his left ear. He was evacuated to the Highbury Hall VAD Hospital in King's Heath, Birmingham. Manning lived in Barnsbury, Islington. Highbury Hall had formerly been the home of the politician Joseph Chamberlain and became Worcestershire VAD 30 Hospital on 28th May 1915. VAD stands for Voluntary Aid Detachment.

[ii] 3223 Rfn. Arthur Henry Claridge, 1/9th London Regt. (Queen Victoria's Rifles) att. 169th Machine Gun Company, was killed on Saturday, 1st July 1916. Aged 27, he was the son of the late John H & Emily Claridge of St. Dunstan's House, Fetter Lane, London. His body was never found and his names was inscribed on the Thiepval Memorial, Pier and Face 9C.

[iii] Rfn. George Bristow, 1/16th London Regt. (Queen's Westminster Rifles) att. 169th Machine Gun Company was wounded on Saturday, 1st July 1916. He was evacuated to F Ward in the War Hospital, Huddersfield.

"I went over with the platoon and lost them in the smoke. I got into the first wave with the Q.V.R. and Q.W.R. and opened fire on bombing parties of Germans in the first German trench. I was in a shell hole with a Q.V.R. We got the order to advance and got bombed again so we got down and opened fire near the German front line trench. I looked to my right and saw Lieut. Bass with Private Clifford going over some high ground near the German 2ⁿᵈ line. I made my way to him and found Clifford waiting. He said that Lieut. Bass was reporting to Capt. Cox of the Q.V.R. Lieut. Bass came back and gave orders to three of us who were there to make a fire step in a trench running through the Cemetery (*Author's note:* Eck trench). As we were digging, some bombers passed along and one accidentally dropped a bomb which exploded. Lieut. Bass was hit in the eye and Clifford was wounded[i]. We bandaged them up but could not stop Lieut. Bass bleeding and I went to find someone to report to[ii]. An officer of the Q.V.R. said, 'come along with me'. We found Capt. Cox and reported what had happened."[39]

Plate 35 Lt. Philip Burnet Bass, 1/5ᵗʰ Cheshire Regt.
(Photograph: De Ruvigny's Roll Of Honour)

By this stage it seems that Private Lancashire and one or two others had become completely detached from the rest of No. 4 Platoon. Attaching himself to the Victorias, he spent the rest of the day fetching and carrying bombs and keeping a look-out for German attacks. The rest, including 2057 Sgt. Harold Lanceley[iii] and Pte Joe Brown, made their way forward along the network of

---

[i] 1527 Pte John Clifford, 1/5ᵗʰ Cheshire Regt., died on Saturday, 1ˢᵗ July 1916. His body was never found and his name is inscribed on the Thiepval Memorial, Pier and Face 3 C and 4 A.

[ii] Lt. Philip Burnet Bass, "A" Coy. 1/5ᵗʰ Cheshire Regt., died on Saturday, 1ˢᵗ July 1916, aged 21. He was the son of Col. Philip de Salis Bass, C.M.G., and Mrs. Frances Edith Bass of 33 Cumberland Mansions, West End Lane, NW6, his family reputedly being part of the Bass Brewery family. He was born on the 11ᵗʰ January 1895 in St Helier, Jersey and was educated at the Imperial Service College, Windsor and Pembroke College, Oxford. He joined the Oxford OTC and was commissioned into the 5ᵗʰ Cheshires on 5ᵗʰ November 1914 and was promoted temporary Lieutenant on 1ˢᵗ March 1916. He arrived on the Western Front on 3ʳᵈ May 1915. Bass lived at 28 Liverpool Road, Chester. His body was never found and his name is inscribed on the Thiepval Memorial: Pier and Face 3 C and 4 A.

[iii] 2057 Sgt Harold Lanceley, 1/5ᵗʰ Cheshire Regt., attested 2057 Private in the 5ᵗʰ Cheshire Regt. on 6ᵗʰ April 1914 aged 22. He lived at Woodhead Cottage, Timperley. He went to France on 14ᵗʰ February 1915 and was promoted Cpl. on 11ᵗʰ June. He was slightly wounded in a bombing accident on 23ʳᵈ October in an incident when one

trenches to their assigned locations and, initially under the direction of 2nd Lt. Arthur, set to work creating a trench block in one of the communication trenches running up the slope – the direction from which the German counter-attacks would all too soon come. 'A' Company had reached all of its objectives except the distant Quadrilateral, the point near which the attacking troops of the 56th and 46th Divisions were due to meet.

Plate 36 2057 Sgt. Harold Lanceley, I/5th Cheshire Regt., wounded I st July 1916
(Photograph: Ian Sant, Harold Lanceley's grandson)

Behind them, 2nd Lt. Edward Andrews[i], commanding No. 1 Platoon of the 5th Cheshires, was hit before reaching the German first line, but struggled forward with his men. 1711 Sgt. John Robinson was the platoon sergeant and he took 1464 Sgt. George Ogden up to the 3rd German line where they found Cpl. Ratcliffe of No. 2 Platoon and soon the rest of the men came up to start work on a strong point running through Ems trench to the Cemetery. While they were working, a call came down for more bombers and a Sgt. Jones started along but was shot in the back of the head. As his name does not appear in the list of fatalities one can only assume he somehow survived.

1878 Cpl. Harold Wolfenden of No. 2 Platoon wrote a personal report of the action. His platoon was to follow the Westminsters to the Quadrilateral and then to consolidate Indus and Fillet trenches. His commentary shows graphically the confusion amongst the attacking troops caused by the crossing of No Man's Land in the smoke and then the chaotic state of the German lines when they arrived. It also hints at the problems caused by the over-rehearsal of the troops before the battle:

---

sergeant was killed and eight other men wounded. He was promoted Sgt. on 23rd March 1916. He was reported missing on 1st July 1916 but this was later changed to wounded when he returned to the trenches. He had suffered shrapnel wounds to the head and back and had a broken nose. He was evacuated to No. 43 Casualty Clearing Station and then No. 16 Hospital, Le Treport. He was evacuated from Le Havre on board the *'Salta'* and sent to Cardonald Hospital, Glasgow. He was given a temporary commission in the 3rd Reserve Bn., Cheshire Reg, before being gazetted 2nd Lt. in the 5th South Wales Borderers on 26th February 1918. He married Jane Royle on the 30th March before returning to France on 22nd April 1918. He left the Army on 31st January 1919 and eventually returned to work at Clibrans Nurserymen, Hale, Cheshire before becoming senior foreman at Birken Farm, Ashley. He died in 1972 [*Source:* Ian Sant, his grandson]
i 2nd Lt. Edward I Don Andrews had only joined the battalion on 26th June 1916 from the 3/5th Cheshire Regt.

"It was about 8.0 o'clock when we went over. We set out towards the German Lines and turned to the right as we had rehearsed. We reached the German first line having lost about five men. Stretcher Bearer S. Clarke stayed behind bandaging these men. We got to the 2nd line which was full of Q.V.R. so we could not get in. We lost about 12 men here and Clarke came up and commenced bandaging these. We had to stay outside the trench but we looked about to find our way. Then Sgt. Boardman[i] said "Come on boys, I've got it". We then went along a communication trench and eventually reached a point where the trench branched off to the left and right and also went straight on (Officer's note: Cpl. Wolfenden, states that the trench on the left front was Fillet and the communication trench Ems)."[40]

Unfortunately, Cpl. Wolfenden and the rest of No. 2 Platoon were nowhere near Fillet trench. They were, in fact, in Fellow trench and the communication trench was Etch. In the chaos, they believed that they had advanced 700 metres further than was the case. Unable to get further forward, they set to work on what they now thought was the Quadrilateral. They had actually only got as far as the German third line:

"My platoon had to go on up Fillet but we found the bombers in front of us consisting of Q.W.R. with some Q.V.R. We could not get on and we could not reach the point where we were to work. My party, therefore, joined No. 1 Platoon and worked on the Quadrilateral. We blocked off the trench leading to the right (*author's note:* Fell trench) a distance of about 15 yards from the junction then we went on consolidating. Corporal Ratcliffe found a Lewis gun in the Quadrilateral and fired on any Germans he could see, also snipers. Some of the Q.W.R. and Q.V.R. went to the left after reaching the junction. There were two Officers of the Q.W.R.[ii]. dead at this point."[41]

Like their colleague Private Lancashire near the Cemetery, Cpl. Wolfenden and the remainder of No. 2 Platoon now resorted to aiding the assortment of Q.V.R.s and Q.W.R.s by collecting and carrying bombs. Soon, they would be under serious attack. Cpl. Ratcliffe, who had earlier spotted for a Q.W.R. Lewis gunner, had taken the man's gun after he was sniped and killed and, under instructions from an officer of the Q.V.R., used it to keep the Germans in Felon trench at bay. In ninety minutes he used up six magazines. The magazines had been collected by 2736 Pte. John Mugan and he stayed with Ratcliffe until seriously wounded by the increasingly heavy machine gun fire coming in from their right[iii]. After a while, a specialist Lewis gunner and his No. 2 came along so Ratcliffe handed over the gun and the remaining four magazines and set to building an emplacement from which the gunners could more safely operate. He stayed there, passing up magazines and bombs until the position became untenable and the withdrawal began.[42]

---

[i] 1244 Sgt Edwin Boardman, 1/5th Cheshire Regt., died on Saturday, 1st July 1916, aged 24. He was the son of Edward and Edith Boardman of 7, Broom Rd., Hale. Cheshire. He is buried in Gommecourt British Cemetery No. 2, Hebuterne, grave II. K. 13.

[ii] 2nd Lieuts. Yates and Negus of 'B' Company, Queen's Westminster Rifles.

[iii] 2736 Pte John Mugan, 1/5th Cheshire Regt., died on Saturday, 1st July 1916. A native of Altrincham, his body was never found and his name is inscribed on the Thiepval Memorial, Pier and Face 3C and 4A.

Behind 'A' Company, 'B' Company of the Cheshires (who were attached to the 167th Brigade for the day) plus a platoon of 'D' Company[i] were given various tasks in preparation for the general advance to take over the German positions. 2nd Lt. Frank Davies[ii], who had replaced 2nd Lt. Heald[iii] who had been sent to Doullens with a temperature of 103° the day before, went over in front of his platoon but was killed by machine gun fire soon after he entered No Man's Land. The leading men were also killed or wounded and the remainder of the platoon was held up. 2nd Lt. Wilbraham Smith[iv] was ordered to go over behind the 1/3rd Londons when they started to dig their two communication trenches across No Man's Land. As described, this task had proved impossible and, as a result, 2nd Lt. Smith with his platoon waited all day in the reserve trenches. The other two platoons, however, had important jobs to do in the British front lines. Where the roads from Hebuterne to Gommecourt and Bucquoy crossed the newly built front line trenches, barricades had been built across them and the trenches dug behind. In order for supplies and the reserve battalions to move up quickly, these barricades had to be removed and the trenches behind them bridged. These tasks were allotted to 55 men from No. 14 Platoon, 'D' Company led by 2nd Lt. Henry Glendinning and No. 7 Platoon, 'B' Company, commanded by 2nd Lt. John Salmon, with the assistance from five men of the 1/1st Edinburgh Field Company, R.E. Glendinning's men and his three Edinburgh engineers followed the last waves of the Rangers from the Reserve lines towards the front. They made their way down the sunken Hebuterne-Bucquoy Road and succeeded in removing the front line barricade and bridging the road. Behind them, two more parties of Cheshires and Royal Engineers had two barricades at the Wood Street/Bucquoy Road crossing to remove. Their casualties quickly mounted as the barrage intensified, and they were forced to withdraw on several occasions before returning to their assignment. Eventually, their task became impossible and, unable to complete their work, they withdrew reluctantly to the reserve lines. Behind them they left the bodies of two Edinburgh men, L/Cpl. John Reid and Spr. William Leuchars[v], killed under the relentless shelling. No. 14 Platoon had suffered between 25 and 30 casualties.

---

i 'D' Company (minus No. 14 Platoon) and the specialists of the 1/5th Cheshires stayed in Divisional reserve at Souastre under Lt. E M Dixon.

ii 2nd Lt. Frank Arnold Davies, 1/5th Cheshire Regt., died on Saturday, 1st July 1916. He was born on 20th December 1892, the son of a cotton salesman. Educated at Bebington and Port Sunlight Technical Institute he became a clerk. Single, he lived at Mountfield, Lower Bebington, Cheshire. He was attested private (no. 2092) in the 6th/Kings Liverpool Regiment on the 31st August 1914 and was gazetted 2nd Lt. into the 3/5th Cheshires on the 21st January 1916. He joined the battalion in France on 30th May 1916. He is buried in Gommecourt British Cemetery No. 2, Hebuterne. grave III. B. 7.

iii Heald was sent to Le Havre on one of the first Ambulance Trains used to evacuate the wounded of 1st July. He returned quickly to the battalion and went on to win the Military Cross and to be Mentioned in Despatches.

iv 2nd Lt. Wilbraham Fremantle Smith, 1/5th Cheshire Regt., died on Thursday, 28th September 1916 from wounds received in an attack on Combles. He had joined the battalion from the 3/5th Cheshire Regt. on 26th June 1916 having previously served with the Cheshire Yeomanry. He is buried in Grove Town Cemetery, Meaulte, Somme, France, grave I. K. 2.

v 422599 L/Cpl John Thomas Reid, 1/1st City of Edinburgh Field Coy, RE, died on Saturday, 1st July 1916. Aged 46 he was the son of John and Agnes Reid of 194, Rose St., Edinburgh. His body was never found and his name is inscribed on the Thiepval Memorial, Pier and Face 8 A and 8 D

1409 Spr William Leuchars, 1/1st City of Edinburgh Field Coy, RE, died on Saturday, 1st July 1916. Aged 21 he was the son of Alexander and Georgina Leuchars of 24, Colville Place, Edinburgh. He is buried in Hebuterne Military Cemetery, grave IV. M. 59.

To the left, 2ⁿᵈ Lt. Salmon and his men had more luckⁱ. They had three sets of barricades to remove and trenches to bridge and three parties of fifteen Cheshires plus their engineer advisers succeeded in blowing up each barricade on the Hebuterne-Gommecourt Road with gun cotton charges. They then went on to successfully bridge all trenches to the front line. Should a full advance be possible, the road was now clear for reserves and supplies to get forward quickly along what was left of the road.

Plate 37 Lt. Edgar Williamson MC, London Rifle Brigade att. 169ᵗʰ Trench Mortar Battery

On the far left, behind 'B' Company of the Cheshires, two trench mortars from 169ᵗʰ Trench Mortar Battery were to go forward with each of the first wave battalions and another four with the Queen's Westminster Rifles. They were to be set up and used to defend the new front line when the 56ᵗʰ Division joined up with the 46ᵗʰ Division in the flat open space behind Gommecourt village. As recounted, the Stokes mortars sent across with the Victorias and Westminsters fared badly and the same fate befell the gun teams on the L.R.B. front. The whole of one carrying party was caught in the open by the German barrage and was either killed or wounded. One gun with ten or twelve rounds got across but was not used. Four other guns or parts of guns got across with twelve rounds. 2ⁿᵈ Lt. Edgar Williamson of the L.R.B. had been posted to the Trench Mortar Battery in April. The 22 year old Williamsonⁱⁱ was a soldier of some experience. He had been in France for eighteen months and now, in spite of his relative youth, he rallied the men around him and managed to set up one of the mortars

---

ⁱ 2ⁿᵈ Lt. John Duncan Salmon, 1/5ᵗʰ Cheshire Regt., survived the war though not unscathed. In October 1915, whilst out in No Man's Land with a wiring party, he had been shot through both hands. He returned to the 1/5ᵗʰ Cheshires from the 3/5ᵗʰ Cheshires on 30ᵗʰ May 1916.
ⁱⁱ Lt. Edgar Rowe Williamson M.C., 1/5ᵗʰ London Regt (London Rifle Brigade), was the son of William Rowe Williamson and Emma Rowe Williamson of 33, Vincent Rd., Croydon. He was aged 22 and was educated at Repton. Williamson joined the 2/5ᵗʰ London Rifle Brigade on 15ᵗʰ September 1914. and joined the 1/5ᵗʰ Battalion in January 1915. He was commissioned on the 9ᵗʰ February 1915, rejoining the 1/5ᵗʰ on 7ᵗʰ January 1916. He was promoted Lieutenant on 18ᵗʰ January. He was posted to the 169ᵗʰ Brigade Trench Mortar Battery on 6ᵗʰ April 1916. He was killed on Sunday 10ᵗʰ September 1916 during an attack near Leuze Wood. He had been wounded in both legs and was being carried by two stretcher bearers when last seen. Neither he nor the stretcher bearers were seen again and it was assumed they had been killed by a shell. His body was never found and his name is inscribed on the Thiepval Memorial, Pier and Face 9 D.

and bring it into action. He and his men managed to fire four rounds at a German bombing party but, in the confusion, no-one could say where the shells landed and what good, if any, they did but, nonetheless, Williamson was awarded the M.C. for his actions on the 1st July. The citation reads:

"For conspicuous bravery at Gommecourt on 1st July 1916 whilst employed in the 169th Infantry Brigade TM Battery. He took charge of a section which had lost its officer and did fine work in reconnoitring, bombing and rallying straggling men".

Before being ordered back to headquarters Williamson, having escaped to the British lines, was seen in charge of a Lewis gun.

The fates of the trench mortars that went forward were unremittingly gloomy. By 9.30 a.m. Cpl. Wright and Rfn. Golding were reporting that Nos. 7 and 8 mortars had been unable to get across No Man's Land. It would have come as no surprise to Capt. P C Coote, the OC of 169th Trench Mortar Battery, when L/Cpl. Wells reported that, having been separated from the carrying party, he been unable to find No. 7 mortar as it was not where it should have been. Towards the end of the day, 4376 Rfn. Cecil Hollingham[i] carried the mounting of No. 5 gun back, the only part of the mortar to return to the lines. The other guns fell into German hands when attempts to destroy them were hampered by the presence of wounded men in the same trench.

***

AFTER THE INITIAL apparent success, many of the problems experienced by the right battalions of the 169th Brigade were caused by the failure of the assault on Nameless Farm. The attack of the Rangers had hit numerous obstacles. Uncut wire, vigorous front line defence, heavy fire from the support trenches had all contributed to delay and confusion in the battalion's ranks. The initial reports had talked optimistically about all of the attacking waves getting into the German lines with some ease. By 8 a.m., however, a different picture began to emerge. Soon after the men had disappeared down the slope into the smoke screen, the German barrage had crashed into No Man's Land. The men of the 1/4th Londons who now occupied the British front line watched with grave concern as the curtain of high explosive and shrapnel swept the ground in front. To get up in support, they would have to find a way through this fearful scene. Communication with the attacking troops was already extremely difficult and the messages the runners brought back were worrying. Just after 8 a.m., two messages were received that caused concern to the Rangers' C.O., Lt. Col. Bayliffe. The first came from an officer of 'A' Company on the right. This message stated that the Rangers were held up between the German first and second lines, pinned down in the uncut wire by heavy fire from Nameless Farm and by German shelling. The second message was more worrying still. At 8.05 a.m., a runner breathlessly reported that 'A' Company, or at least parts of it, was back in the British lines. The Colonel sent 2nd Lt. Downs from his battalion H.Q. in the old British front line trench down New Woman Street to find and re-

---

i 4376 L/Cpl Cecil Percy Hollingham, 1/16th London Regt. (Queen's Westminster Rifles) att. 169th Trench Mortar Battery was killed on 10th September 1916. Aged 20, he was the son of John and Kate Mary Hollingham, of 'Nepcote', Church Lane, Southwick, Sussex. He his body was never found and his name is inscribed on the Thiepval Memorial, Pier and Face 13C.

organise these men. He was instructed to take them forward again, only this time it would have to be through the German bombardment. Lt. Downs found the remains of 'A' Company in the wreckage of the Boyau de Service, just behind the main front line. This trench was already a mess. Before the bombardment, six Stokes mortars had been located there in special dugouts. They had been used to pound the German frontlines and wire and they had attracted heavy counter-battery fire from the German guns. Some of these mortars had now been dismantled in an effort to get them forward for use in defence of the new positions, but the German artillery still had the range and the Boyau was nearly as unhealthy a place to be as the German trenches.

Five minutes later came more bad news. With the loss of their C.O., Maj. Jones, and his officers 'D' Company of the Rangers had recoiled, overwhelmed by the ferocity of the vicious fusillade of machine gun and Mauser fire. Cowering as if from a heavy storm, large numbers had retreated up the slope to the uncertain safety of their own lines. By ten past eight, Lt. Col. Wheatley of the 1/4th Londons was reporting the shattered remains of most of 'D' Company back in the trenches.

For the wounded, the journey back across No Man's Land was terrifying and dangerous. Apart from the continuous high explosive and shrapnel fire sweeping the shallow valley they had to cross, the Germans had positioned a machine gun to fire down the length of the sunken Hebuterne to Bucquoy Road on either side of which the Rangers had attacked. 2nd Lt. Liveing, badly wounded in the hip and bleeding heavily, was trying to get back to the relative safety of the British trenches and needed to negotiate this perilous place. It was not easy:

"I fell down into a sunken road with several other wounded, and crawled up over the bank on the other side. The Germans had a machine-gun on that road, and only a few of us got across. Someone faintly called my name behind me. Looking round, I thought I recognised a man of 'C' company. Only a few days later did it come home to me that he was my platoon observer. I had told him to stay with me whatever happened. He had carried out his orders much more faithfully that I had ever meant, for he had come to my assistance, wounded twice in the head himself. He hastened forward to me, but, as I looked round waiting, uncertain quite as to who he was, his rifle clattered on to the ground, and he crumpled up and fell motionless just behind me[i]. Shortly afterwards I sighted the remains of our front line trench and fell into them."[43]

For a fit and alert soldier, the British trenches would have looked a shambles, rendered unrecognisable by shellfire within a few minutes of the attack going in. To a wounded and disorientated man, confused by the chaos around him and dizzy through loss of blood, the scene made little sense. Only the basic instinct for self-preservation helped him now:

"At first I could not make certain as to my whereabouts. Coupled with the fact that my notions in general were becoming somewhat hazy, the trenches themselves were entirely unrecognisable. They were filled with earth, and

---

[i] 1791 Rfn Charles William Dennison, 1/12th London Regt (The Rangers), was killed on Saturday, 1st July 1916, aged 19. The son of Henry John and Emma Jane Dennison of 151, Osborne Rd., Forest Gate, Essex, his body was never found and his name is listed on the Thiepval Memorial, Pier and Face 9C.

about half their original depth. I decided, with that quick, almost semi-conscious intuition that comes to one in moments of peril, to proceed to the left (to one coming from the German lines). As I crawled through holes and over mounds I could hear the vicious spitting of machine-gun bullets. They seemed to skim just over my helmet. The trench, opening out a little, began to assume its old outline. I had reached the head of New Woman Street, though at the time I did not know what communication trench it was."

"A signaller sat, calmly transmitting messages to Battalion Headquarters. A few bombers were walking along the continuation of the front line…"[44]

Behind him, in spite of Liveing's experience of an attack gone badly wrong, it was only in the centre of the Rangers attack that any progress had been made, but even here, resistance had been fierce. A Cpl. Jackman of 'B' Company told an R.F.A. Observation Officer back in the trenches that they had got to the first German wire. "Our bombers threw a few bombs, the Germans got up threw bombs and opened fire with a machine gun," he reported. However, even as Jackman was making his report, the centre companies of the Rangers were driving their enemy out of Fetter and Fate trenches. Giving ground slowly, the men of the 170th Regiment were forced back up Epte communication trench to the left of Nameless Farm and Elbe and Et trenches which, here, ran diagonally across the face and then to the right of the fortified farm. Reaching these trenches' junctions with the German second line (Felt trench), parties of 'B' and 'C' Companies turned inwards from either flank. Traverse by traverse, what remained of the German garrison was compressed into a few yards of trench. There they succumbed to grenades, bullets and, in a final fearful rush of dread and panic, to the jabbing bayonets of their stern faced assailants. Other parties of the Rangers advanced carefully up the communication trenches to the left and right of Nameless Farm. On the right, a party got as far as the junction of Elbe and Fame trenches and on the left, some intrepid Rangers fought their way up Epte trench to the sunken Nameless Farm Road. Here they made contact with a machine gun team from the Queen Victoria's Rifles. But in the centre, as the Maxim guns around the farm swept the fields in front of them, movement was impossible. Any attack across the open invited disaster. The much-depleted Rangers sought protection against the German barrage now hitting Felt trench hard and awaited orders.

By 8.15 a.m., just forty five minutes after the men had gone 'over the top', it was becoming clear to Brigade and Divisional headquarters that matters were amiss. 168th Brigade's headquarters were in a small trench between Woman and Whiskey Streets, just behind the old front line (W48R). A few yards in front was the Rangers' Battalion H.Q. and the 1/4th Londons were a 100 metres away in Woman Street. Next to Brigade H.Q. was an observation post from which R.F.A. officers peered grimly across the lines towards the area around Nameless Farm. Messages had already been sent back to Division that the Rangers' assault had stalled in front of Felon trench. In response, instructions were sent down to Lt. Col. Macdowell, commanding the Southern Group R.F.A., asking him to bring back his 18 pdr's barrage to the German third line. By 8.15 a.m. this was being done, but minus yet another gun put out of action with a jammed cartridge.

Ten minutes later, the problems with the two flank companies of the Rangers became known to Maj. Gen. Hull at Division. He was told that Brigade believed 'B' and 'C' Companies had a foothold in Fetter and Fate and that two companies of the 1/4th Londons were to go over as reinforcements. It is unlikely that Gen. Hull could have understood what this simple message implied about the fate of the two reinforcing companies. Although the reports of the strength of the German barrage had arrived at Division, few could have conceived of its relentless ferocity and power. Whilst the British heavy and field artillery was unequally split between the staged bombardment of trenches and strong points and counter-battery work, the Germans ignored the British artillery. Their tactics were simple: cut the attacking troops off from their supplies and reinforcements then destroy them in the German front line trenches.

***

To the Rangers' left, the Queen's Westminster Rifles were pushing forwards towards their final objective. Back in the British lines, observers from the 1/2nd Londons had seen the signboards going up in Feed and Feint and, after a delay, in Fellow trench too. But, equally well, they could see the gap between the right of the Queen Victoria's Rifles and the left of the Rangers and the problems being caused around Nameless Farm and Epte communication trench. As the clock drew round to half past eight, a mixed team of Queen's Westminster Rifles[i] completed the capture of Feud trench and reached the junction with Ems trench. Now, if they could fight their way up this 250 metre length of trench they would be in the Quadrilateral. There, they would meet and greet the North Midlanders as they came down Fillet trench to the north. The junction would be complete, their job done.

1799 Sgt. Walter Nichols was now in charge of the Queen's Westminster Rifles' Headquarters bombers section, their O.C. Lt. Philip Spencer-Smith[ii], having been wounded crossing the second German line (Feed). He and some of his section together with an assortment of others, 1687 Cpl. Reginald Townsend[iii] and 2036 L/Cpl. William Ide (2/2nd Londons attached to Queen's Westminster Rifles) of 'C' Company, Cpl. Hayward, 'B' Company, and 2755 Rfn. Frederick Stow, 'D' Company, started to push along Ems. They were joined by a second lieutenant of the 1/5th Cheshires, believed to be 32-year old 2nd Lt. George Arthur from Halifax in West Yorkshire. Lt. Arthur led his motley team up the length of Ems trench. The further they progressed, the further they moved away

---

[i] Men of 'B' Company, Q.W.R. (among them 2969 Corporal F E Hayward, 1/2nd London Regiment attached Queen's Westminster Rifles), 'C' Company and of the headquarters bombers.
[ii] Severely wounded, 2nd Lt. Philip Spencer-Smith, BA, became a German prisoner of war. Born on 28th February 1882, he was the son of Charles Spencer-Smith of The Dower House, Woldhurstlea, Ifield, Sussex and lived at 51, Palace Street, Westminster. He was educated at Christ's College, Brecon and Queen's College, Cambridge. He was a Mathematics teacher and had taught in Frankfurt (1905-08) and at the United Services College (1908-09) and Giggleswick School (1910-14). He had three brothers:
Capt. Charles Owen Spencer-Smith, 1/16th London Regt. (Queen's Westminster Rifles) att. 16th King's Royal Rifle Corps, was killed on 3rd August 1917 aged 37. He is buried in Godewaersvelde British Cemetery, grave I. C. 13.;
2nd Lt. Martin Spencer-Smith, 1/16th London Regt. (Queen's Westminster Rifles) was killed on 10th September 1916. His body was never found and his name is inscribed on the Thiepval Memorial, Pier and Face 13 C.; and
Rev. Arnold Patrick Spencer-Smith was the photographer on the Shackleton Antarctic expedition of 1914-17. He died of heart failure brought on by scurvy on 9th March 1916. Cape Spencer-Smith on White Island is named after him.
[iii] 1687 Cpl Reginald F Townsend, 1/16th London Regt. (Queen's Westminster Rifles), was awarded the Military Medal for his actions on 1st July 1916.

from the frantic shelling of the front line German trenches. Here, behind Gommecourt village itself, the British artillery had moved on in the expectation that the position was soon to be occupied by their own troops. The German artillery was concentrating on their front lines and left the long communication trenches alone so that reinforcements could move up quickly and safely. So, as this small band eased slowly and carefully along Ems trench, they entered a zone of relative and eerie calm. Eventually they reached the Quadrilateral (and achieved the deepest penetration of the enemy lines anywhere around Gommecourt on 1st July). Looking back whence they came, they would have seen a complete panorama of the 56th Division's attack. The complex tracery of the trenches picked out in white chalk against the lush grass and deep, red clay. The bright, orange flashes and black smoke from the German shells as they smashed into the shallow valley behind them. Small darting figures in khaki and field grey, like toy soldiers in the distance. All to a soundtrack of the deep roar of the artillery, the continuous hammering of machine guns and the sharp crack of grenades. It would have been an extraordinary scene.

But Arthur's team was not the only one to be heading for the Quadrilateral at that time. Half of the 2nd Company of the 55th R.I.R. was waiting in reserve in Fillet trench north of the Quadrilateral and they were now moving down the communication trench from their dugouts. The two parties collided in a flurry of furious bombing contests as each side sought the advantage. But the German bombing party was larger, better armed and, crucially, carried more bombs than their opponents. The issue was never seriously in doubt. Having exhausted their small supply of grenades, the Queen's Westminster Rifles retreated reluctantly down Ems trench, Lt. Arthur acting as a one-man rearguard. In the confusion, Lt. Arthur and the men of the Queen's Westminster Rifles became separated, leading to reports that he had been killed, fighting a lone battle against overwhelming odds, somewhere deep in the German lines[i]. Other eyewitnesses from his own platoon, however, place him back in the German front lines several hours later, just before they were evacuated in the afternoon[ii]. Wherever 2nd Lt.

---

[i] 2nd Lt. George Stuart Arthur, 'A' Company 1/5th Cheshire Regt., was killed on 1st July 1916, aged 32. He was the son of Samuel and Louisa Arthur of 24, Heath Crescent, Halifax. Arthur was born in Clifton (Bristol) on 24th August 1883. His family moved to West Yorkshire when he was young and he was educated at Heath Grammar School, Halifax. A draper, he had a shop at 5, New Street, Huddersfield. He attested Private on the 14th September 1914. He was promoted corporal and acting sergeant on 9th December 1914 and was gazetted 2nd Lt. on 6th March 1915. He joined the battalion in France on 5th June 1916 from No. 4 Entrenching Battalion. His body was presumably found in post war battlefield clearances and his parents were still writing to the War Office for news about him as late as 27th May 1918. He is believed buried at Gommecourt British Cemetery No. 2, Hebuterne, grave III.C.15.

[ii] Lt. Arthur's story is movingly told in Martin Middlebrook's 'The First Day on the Somme', Penguin, 1971. He writes the story as suggested by the war records of the Queen's Westminster Rifles. However, in a personal eyewitness statement written soon after the attack, 1878 Corporal Wolfenden of No. 2 Platoon, "A" Company, 1/5th Cheshires states:

"Corporal Ratcliffe and myself carried down a wounded man to the German front line and when we got there we were ordered to mount the fire step. The trench was very crowded and I only saw one Officer, 2nd Lt. Arthur. We saw the Germans following down the communication trench and started firing at them. Soon after this the order was passed down 'every man for himself'".

From this account, it would seem likely that 2nd Lt. Arthur was one of the many men killed in their attempts to regain the safety of the British lines during the afternoon and evening withdrawals.

There is also a report of a second party, this time made up of men from the Queen Victoria's Rifles, reaching the Quadrilateral. Lt. Col L A C Southam, 280th Brigade RFA, in his comments on the draft of the description of the attack on Gommecourt for the Official History, recounts how a sergeant reported on 2nd July that he had led a small party that had been driven out of the Quadrilateral [*Source:* CAB 45/137 National Archives]. Southam also states that he met several times a Pte Jeynes, later commissioned, who stated he was wounded in the head in the Quadrilateral and was carried back unconscious all the way to the British lines. One should treat these accounts with

Arthur finally met his fate, however, the attack he led on the Quadrilateral was to be the first and last.

ENDNOTES:

[1] Jacobs, Rfn F W, 1/5ᵗʰ London Rifle Brigade. Hackney and Stoke Newington Recorder, 28ᵗʰ July 1916..

[2] Schuman, Rfn Arthur, 1/5ᵗʰ London Rifle Brigade. From a document held at the Liddle Collection, Leeds University.

[3] Jacobs, op. cit.

[4] Hawkings Frank, From Ypres to Cambrai, 1973

[5] Keeson, Maj. C A C, Queen Victoria's Rifles,1792-1922, .1923, page 167

[6] Clement, Pte H T, 1/2ⁿᵈ London Regt. Papers, IWM.

[7] Response to a questionnaire author Martin Middlebrook sent out prior to writing 'The First Day on the Somme'. Held at the Liddle Collection, Leeds University.

[8] Mason, Rfn R J, The Rangers. From a document held at the Liddle Collection, Leeds University.

[9] Carrington, Maj. C, 1/5ᵗʰ Royal Warwickshire Regt. Recorded interview, IWM.

[10] White, Capt. R, 1/14ᵗʰ London Regt., (London Scottish). Papers, IWM.

[11] Liveing Edward G, Attack, MacMillan 1918 and 1986

[12] Ibid.

[13] Ibid.

[14] Ibid.

[15] Territorial Service Gazette, 9ᵗʰ September 1916, page 132.

[16] Keeson, Maj. C A C, Queen Victoria's Rifles,1792-1922, .1923

[17] Territorial Service Gazette, 19ᵗʰ August 1916, page 95

[18] Hawkings Frank, From Ypres to Cambrai, 1973

[19] Wiβmann, Oberst von, Das Reserve Infanterie Regiment Nr. 55 im Weltkreig, Berlin

[20] Newman, Rfn C T, 1/9ᵗʰ Londons (Queen Victoria Rifles, Unpublished papers, IWM.

[21] The History of the London Rifle Brigade 1859-1919. 1921

[22] Ibid.

[23] Jacobs, op. cit.

[24] Wiβmann, Oberst von, Das Reserve Infanterie Regiment Nr. 55 im Weltkreig, Berlin

[25] Russell, Rfn H, 1/5ᵗʰ London Regt. (London Rifle Brigade). Unpublished papers, IWM

[26] The History of the London Rifle Brigade 1859-1919, 1921

[27] War Diary of the 169ᵗʰ Brigade Trench Mortar Battery NA WO 95/2963

[28] From a Martin Middlebrook questionnaire used to collect information for his book 'The First Day on the Somme'. Liddle Collection

[29] 168ᵗʰ Brigade War Diary, NA WO 95/2951

[30] Agius, Capt. A, 1/3ʳᵈ London Regt. Unpublished papers, IWM

[31] Ibid.

[32] Newman, Pte S A, 1/3ʳᵈ London Regt. Unpublished papers, IWM.

[33] White, 2ⁿᵈ Lt R op. cit.

[34] Ibid.

[35] Ibid.

[36] Hubbard, Pte A, London Scottish Papers, IWM

[37] Sgt Henry Smith quoted in The London Scottish in the Great War, 2001

[38] Keeson, Op. Cit. page 168

[39] 1/5ᵗʰ Cheshire Regt. War Diary, NA WO95/2943

[40] Ibid.

[41] Ibid.

[42] Churton, Lt. Col. W A V, The War Record of the 1/5ᵗʰ (Earl of Chester's) Battalion, The Cheshire Regiment August 1914-June 1919, 1920

[43] Liveing Edward G, Attack, 1918 and 1986

[44] Ibid.

some scepticism firstly because the QVR were not ordered to advance to the Quadrilateral, that was the Q.W.R.s task, and secondly because, as previously recounted, men from the 1/5ᵗʰ Cheshires thought they that had arrived at this location when they were actually several hundred yards away. It is, of course, possible that the sergeant Southam mentions is the same 1799 Sergeant W G Nicholls of the QWR who was part of 2ⁿᵈ Lt. Arthur's party of which Pte Jeynes may well have been a member.

10. Z DAY: 0830 - 1200

"As soon as we advanced over 'No Man's Land' the Germans opened a very deadly machine gun fire, which laid a good number out. On we went and it seemed marvellous how the pieces missed us, for the air appeared to be alive with missiles. At last, after advancing about 30 yards I was struck in the thigh by a bullet the force of which knocked me over."

L/Cpl. Appleyard
1/9th Londons (Queen Victoria's Rifles)

EVEN AS THE SMALL PARTY of Queen's Westminster Rifles scrambled back down Ems trench, some of them might have wondered where were the men of the 46th Division? If the attack to the north of the village had gone to plan, the Londoners should have met soldiers from the North Midlands not a large and aggressive band of Germans. At 56th Division H.Q., information about the attack to their left was sparse but not wholly discouraging. A call from the 46th Division at 8.30 a.m., reported that the 6th South Staffs, the right battalion of the right brigade (137th Brigade), was held up in the British advanced trench. To their left, the 6th North Staffs were thought to have reached the German front line but were now pinned down. On the left wing of the attack, affairs seemed to have progressed better. The 139th Brigade's waves had been watched as they crossed the German front lines. Now they could be seen at the north west corner of Gommecourt Wood. At 46th Division, it was supposed that they had reached the German third line. If the reinforcements could get across, success was still possible. The 56th had to hold what they had captured and be ready for another push towards the Quadrilateral.

Unknown to the men of the 56th Division and, it seems, to the senior officers of both attacking divisions, the assault of the North Midlanders was already almost over. It had floundered on the German wire and then been destroyed by the flanking artillery fire from the 111th Division's guns in Adinfer Wood and by the artillery of the 2nd Guard's Reserve Division. The few men that made it into the German lines were quickly hunted down and either killed, captured or expelled by the men of the 91st Reserve Infantry Regiment. Within minutes of the attack going in the German artillery programme swung into action. Gruppes Nord and Süd placed a steady barrage on No Man's Land and the British front lines according to the prepared "Gommecourt" fire plan; Gruppe Süd using direct observation from their position at Point 147 and Gruppe Nord's fire, which it was unable to observe due to smoke until 9.45 a.m., being directed by telephone. Two batteries behind Biez Wood fired gas shells to suppress supporting fire from the 46th Divisional field artillery batteries near Foncquevillers whilst the 15cm heavy howitzers of a Bavarian Foot Artillery battery fired at identified observation posts in order to disrupt British artillery support. In all, 28 field guns and 22 howitzers from the 2nd Guard's Reserve Division alone poured their fire on the men of the 46th Division. Unsurprisingly, German positions were declared clear of the enemy after just two hours.

***

FOR THE LONDON RIFLE BRIGADE on the far left of the attack holding on to what they had was already beginning to prove difficult in spite of initial early successes. By Gommecourt Park, in the front line trenches of Fir and Fen, damage to the entrances of the dugouts had prevented many of No. 8 Company, 55th R.I.R., from manning the fire trench in time. The London Rifle Brigade had been on them as they clambered up the steep wooden stairs, weighed down with rifles, machine guns, grenade and ammunition boxes. They came face to face with the attacking troops and, for many, surrender was the only option. Disarmed, some were herded back into their dugouts, others were collected at bayonet point until an escort party could be found. At 8.30 a.m. they were sent dashing across No Man's Land dodging their own bombardment[i]. For the men of the 1/2nd Londons watching from their own battered trenches, there was a certain grim satisfaction in seeing German soldiers tormented by the same gun fire that was making their lives so miserable.

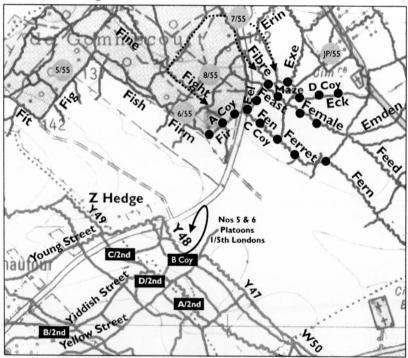

Map 15 Situation 0830-1200 London Rifle Brigade front

Legend: ● Location of L.R.B. companies in German lines.
Nos. 5 & 6 Platoons, B Company, L.R.B. advanced c. 9.00 a.m.

But now, in the fringes of the Park, the London Rifle Brigade was heavily engaged. 'A' Company's success in driving the defenders of No. 8 Company

---

[i] The 169th Brigade estimated some ninety captured Germans were sent back although the 55th R.I.R.'s own records show that the number missing was less than thirty. The War Diary of the 1/2nd Londons does record: "8.35 a.m. Germans surrendering caught by own barrage in no man's land." It is quite possible that a large number of captured Germans were killed or wounded out in No Man's Land and their bodies were recovered during the unofficial truce that occurred on Sunday, 2nd July.

from Point 94 only served to bring the German defensive barrage down on their heads. As the shells ploughed into the trenches and sent vicious splinters whirling from shattered trees, 'A' Company and 'C' to their right became involved in a bitter bombing battle with No. 7 Company, 55th R.I.R. No. 7 Company had emerged from its bunkers in the Maze and its men were now filtering down Fibre and Fight trenches, using the remains of the Park for cover. The fight was at close range - intense and vicious. As the German infantry stabilised their position in the Park, two machine guns started to rake the London Rifle Brigade's lines. One, brought up from a dugout by No. 7 Company swept the battlefield from a strong point in the south of the village. Another fired into the Park from the front line trench, Firm. As casualties mounted, a message was got back across to Lt. Col. Bates, in the London Rifle Brigade's battalion H.Q., that reinforcements and supplies, especially of grenades, were urgently needed.

'B' Company was the reserve company. After the main attack had gone in, they had moved forward from their positions in the old front line, across the trench bridges supplied, to occupy the front line at the head of Yiddish and Yellow Streets. In the German front lines, their company commander, Capt. Robert Somers-Smith, had gone forward to take control of the men now fighting hard in the fringes of the Park and in front of the village. Seeing that 'A' Company was struggling to subdue the dozens of German bombers in the Park, he sent a section of the battalion bombers to their aid and, just before 9 a.m., sent a runner back to 'B' Company in the British lines ordering No. 5 Platoon with supplies of bombs to cross over to Point 94. The same fate befell this platoon as had befallen the 1/3rd Londons in their disastrous attempt to dig their trenches across No Man's Land. Swept by continuous machine gun fire from their left and battered by the savage artillery bombardment no one got more than a few yards. Those that could move crawled back to the relative safety of the trenches or rolled into shell holes away from the vicious patter of bullets. Colonel Bates was watching the attack from the Battalion H.Q. in Yiddish Street and, although No. 5 Platoon's mission had failed completely, he knew nothing of this. At 9.15 a.m., Bates received another note from Somers-Smith explaining that he had ordered No. 6 Platoon from 'B' Company to be sent forward with more bombs. These men had met with the same appalling fate.

1923 Rfn. Gerald Fitzsimons[i] had gone over with the attacking waves and, now wounded, was heading back down the British communication trenches to the Aid Post. As he crawled along looking for help a carrying party from No. 6 Platoon trudged past loaded with bomb boxes. Led by Cpl William Writer, Fitzsimons also recognised 2191 Rfn. Thomas Hooke and 2195 Rfn. Eric Ayton and these three men along with 2148 L/Cpl. George Swan and 2218 Rfn. George Golding and the rest of the party carried on towards the front line and their desperate effort to reinforce and re-supply the men fighting hard in the German lines. As they moved across No Man's Land they came to a piece of ground about 100 yards from their objective that was being swept by two machine guns. Whilst they crouched and waited for an opportunity to move on a series of shrieks alerted them to the imminent arrival of some dreaded 'whizz bangs' – 77mm shrapnel shells. The carrying party, laden as they were with twenty bombs

---

[i] 1923 Rfn. Gerald Fitzsimons, 1/5th London Regt. (London Rifle Brigade) was wounded on Saturday, 1st July 1916. He was evacuated to Ward 2a, 4th Scottish General Hospital in Glasgow.

apiece, scrambled awkwardly for cover and it seemed, at first, that their luck was in. The first three shells were duds and ploughed harmlessly into the earth nearby but the fourth came in low and its explosion 'absolutely blew (Hooke) to atoms", according to 2195 Rfn. Ayton who was only a few feet in front of the unfortunate Hooke[i]. Somehow, Ayton was only slightly wounded in the thigh by the explosion, as was an officer, possibly 2nd Lt. George Clode-Baker[ii], just to Hooke's rear. If this was Clode-Baker then his deliverance would be short-lived. Five months later the 22-year old subaltern was identified by 1416 Sgt. Albert Farmer as having been seen lying about fifty yards from the German trenches shot through the wrist and eye. Nor would Cpl Bill Writer[iii], L/Cpl. Swan and Rfn. Golding return, all lost somewhere in the battered landscape of No Man's Land. The sad remains of Hooke, Clode-Baker and Writer would not be recovered until the Spring of 1917, after the German withdrawal to their new strongholds to the east. Of the two Georges, Golding[iv] and Swan[v] there was no sign.

Plate 38 Rfn George Golding and L/Cpl George Swan, killed 1st July 1916

Ignorant of the fate of these platoons it was still not clear to Col. Bates that it would be impossible to get anyone or anything across to his battalion because of the flanking fire of the German machine guns in Gommecourt Park. He believed that the two platoons of 'B' Company were already in the German trenches and, as a result, sent two runners to order the rest of 'B' Company forward. Neither man arrived, victims of the punishing artillery fire falling on the L.R.B.'s front

---

[i] 2191 Rfn. Thomas Hooke, No. 6 Platoon, B Company, 1/5th London Regt. (London Rifle Brigade), was killed on Saturday, 1st July 1916. Aged 20, he was the son of Thomas & Marion Hooke of 'Moy Mir', 18, Carew Rd., Wallington, Surrey. He was buried in Gommecourt British Cemetery No. 2, grave II. H. 8.

[ii] 2nd Lt. George Edmund Clode Baker, 1/5th London Regt. (London Rifle Brigade), was killed on 1st July 1916. Aged 22, he was the oldest of five children of George & the late Winifred Clode-Baker of Holmfields, Reigate, Surrey. He was born in London and was educated at Uppingham School. He lived at 'The Chestnuts', Croydon Road, Beddington. He attested 2455 Rifleman in the London Rifle Brigade on 3rd September 1914, transferring to the Inns of Court O.T.C. in December. He was commissioned into the 3/5th London Rifle Brigade on 7th February 1915, joining the 1/5th in France on 24th December 1915. He is thought to lie in Gommecourt British Cemetery No. 2 and his name is on the Special Memorial C.6.

[iii] 26 Cpl. William Cecil Writer, No. 6 Platoon, B Company, 1/5th London Regt. (London Rifle Brigade), was killed on Saturday, 1st July 1916. Aged 21, he was the son of Thomas Augustus Writer of 69, Seymour Gardens, Ilford, Essex. He was buried in Gommecourt British Cemetery No. 2, grave III. B. 21.

[iv] 2218 Rfn. George Golding, No. 6 Platoon, B Company, 1/5th London Regt. (London Rifle Brigade), was killed on Saturday, 1st July 1916. He was the son of Mrs M Peppercom of 1, Victoria Villas, Victoria Road, New Barnet. His body was never found and his name is inscribed on the Thiepval Memorial, Pier and Face 9 D

[v] 2148 L/Cpl. George James Swan, No. 6 Platoon, B Company, 1/5th London Regt. (London Rifle Brigade), was killed on Saturday, 1st July 1916. His body was never found and his name is inscribed on the Thiepval Memorial, Pier and Face 9 D

lines. The news that 'A' Company were struggling to establish their position on the edge of the Park was noted, however, and Divisional H.Q. was called with request for an artillery barrage to be brought down along Hauser trench which ran at right angles into the Park from the junction of Fish and Firm trenches.

Back in the Park, the frenetic bombing fights continued. Supplies of Mills grenades were beginning to run short[i] and men were despatched to search the captured German dugouts for supplies of stick grenades. Each man of the London Rifle Brigade had taken three grenades across in the attack but, within ninety minutes, most of these had been used up such was the intensity of the battle. The hand grenade, or 'bomb', was the weapon of choice in hand-to-hand trench warfare and, to the chagrin of many a pre-war officer, the rifle had become something of an encumbrance to the average infantrymen[ii]. The old professional B.E.F., effectively killed off within a few months of the beginning of the war, was famed for the rapid and accurate rifle fire which had so stunned von Kluck's men at Mons, but that was a different type of warfare. Now it was a question of bombing from traverse to traverse, showering a section of trench with grenades irrespective of the number of defenders involved. Then came the mad rush to occupy the stretch of trench attacked and then, maybe, the rifle, or rather more the bayonet, had some use as the wounded or stunned defenders were despatched before the process began again. It was a crude but reasonably effective way of moving through a trench system but it depended on there being a large and reliable supply of bombs available to the attackers. Incredibly, almost any supply of bombs at all had nearly been denied the attacking waves. Such was High Command's confidence in the obliterating effect of the bombardment that they had not felt such supplies necessary until officers like Lt. Col. Bates put in a special plea for his men 'just in case'. To the huge frustration of all concerned, three hundred metres away, in carefully prepared dugouts in the Boyau de Service just behind the British front and in the old front lines, was such a supply. Here there were hundreds of boxes of grenades containing nearly 10,000 Mills bombs. 330 boxes were in the Boyau, ready to be brought over to help with the attack. 500 more were stacked in the old front line to be hurried across partly to help repel counter-attacks once the positions had been taken but mainly to be used in the anticipated mopping up of Gommecourt Village and Park. Each box contained 12 Mills bombs and each bomb weighed 1½lbs. Now these boxes were desperately needed by the men in the German trenches. With the storm of machine gun and rifle fire that swept the ground between the British lines and Point 94 in Gommecourt Park it was almost impossible for one man to get across unscathed however lightly armed and quick. For one or two men to run the gauntlet of Maxim and Mauser fire whilst carrying an unwieldy 25lb wooden box was suicidal. The men of the London Rifle Brigade must make do with what they could find.

---

[i] Colonel A S Bates, commanding officer London Rifle Brigade, wrote in June 1929:
"It had been so impressed upon us that the attack was to be a walk over that the commanding officer obtained leave for each man to take 3 bombs into action, but not without some difficulty as the higher authorities fostered the idea that the attack would be a walk over."
[ii] There was another possible consequence of this reliance on bombs. Lt. Col Southam, 280ᵗʰ Brigade RFA after the war suggested that a large number of men discarded their rifles in order to throw their bombs and that, when these had been used up, they were essentially defenceless. CAB 45/137 National Archives

Meanwhile, the desperate bombing battle amongst the shattered ruins of the edge of Gommecourt Park carried on apace and every few minutes another wounded Rifleman would stagger or crawl away from the fight towards the front lines. There, stretcher bearers were doing their best for the growing crowd of injured men who sheltered in the bottom of the trench or who were carried down into the undamaged German dugouts. One such man was 2969 Rfn. Fred Shackell. He had been slightly wounded in the initial advance but, at about noon, he was wounded again and could no longer continue to fight. He joined a small group of wounded and they helped one another back down to the front line and there awaited events and, where possible, dressed one another's wounds. Whilst he was there Shackell saw his friend 2939 Rfn. Fred Mulligan hurrying along the trench in the direction of the advanced battle headquarters Somers-Smith had established in the German front lines. Shackell asked his mate what was up and he told him that things were going badly in the Park and he had a message to that effect to pass on to a senior officer. With that, Mulligan disappeared into the next traverse and that was the last Shackell[i] ever saw of him – another man to vanish without trace in the fields around Gommecourt.[ii]

To the right of 'A' and 'C' Companies, 'D' Company were having a somewhat easier time. 2nd Lt. Rex Petley had moved from left to right along Eck trench, encouraging his men to dig in and to prepare for the attacks on the Village and the Park that were scheduled for later in the day. Although slightly wounded in the shoulder during his travels, Petley was content. Casualties were few and German activity low. Here, at least, things seemed to be going well. They had reached their objectives and now waited to hear of other developments, in particular that the Westminsters and South Staffs had met in the Quadrilateral and the trap door had slammed shut on the German garrison in Gommecourt Village and Park. Then, on reaching the right of his position near to the Cemetery, Petley received the first unwelcome news:

> "A Queen Victoria Rifles man came and reported that he had lost touch with his regiment and that only about a dozen of his men were on our right, also that they were being bombed."

Another 'D' Company subaltern, 2nd Lt. Horace Smith, sent back with the man to help organise the small band of Queen Victoria's Rifles, found the men and their dying platoon commander, Lt. Cyril Fleetwood[iii]. Petley sent a runner down Eck and Exe trenches to advise Capt. Somers-Smith in the London Rifle Brigade's forward H.Q. in the front line between Fen and Ferret. Clearly, there were still groups of Germans active in the front line areas and a party of headquarters bombers were sent off to deal with them.

---

i 2969 Rfn. Frederick Shackell, 1/5th London Regt. (London Rifle Brigade), was wounded on Saturday, 1st July 1916 and was evacuated to Purley Military Hospital, Brighton Road, Purley.
ii 2939 Rfn. Frederick Herbert Mulligan, No. 3 Platoon, A Company, 1/5th London Regt. (London Rifle Brigade), was killed on Saturday, 1st July 1916. He was the son of Mrs Mulligan of 39, Talbot Road, Tottenham. His body was never found and his name is inscribed on the Thiepval Memorial, Pier and Face 9D.
iii Lt. Cyril Percy Fleetwood, 1/9th London Regt. (Queen Victoria's Rifles), died of wounds on 12th July 1916 in German hands. Aged 33, he was the son of George and Mary Fleetwood and lived at 88, Chetwynd Road, Highgate. Before the war Fleetwood was a civil servant and was a scoutmaster with the 57th North London Troop, Boy Scouts. On the outbreak of war he joined Royal Naval Air Service and served in their Anti-Aircraft Corps but transferred to the Inns of Court OTC, attesting 5061 Private on 3rd July 1915 before being commissioned into the 3/9th London Regt. on 4th October 1915. He died in Kriegslazarett No 1 in Le Cateau and was originally buried in the German Ehrenfriedhof. He is now buried in Le Cateau Military Cemetery, grave III. B. 3

***

FIVE HUNDRED METRES TO THE RIGHT of Lt. Petley's position, the Rangers were still no further forward. Brig. Gen. Loch was in his Brigade H.Q. just behind the old British front line. The position gave good views over his Brigade's front and, with discretion being the better part of valour, also had a deep dugout into which one could retreat if necessary. It was necessary now and Loch, his Brigade Major Philip Neame V.C.[i], his young artillery liaison officer, the Brigade Orderly Sergeant, Harry Coates of the London Scottish, and a team of assorted signallers, runners, orderlies and telephonists now huddled together underground as the invisible German guns swept the trenches above them. Communication to the front was already reduced to the use of runners as the German high explosive had rapidly cut most of the wires laid in the base of the communication trenches which led to the battalion H.Q.s further forward. Contact to Division and Corps to the rear was meant to be by telephone but Loch's team of telephonists was already struggling to hear and be heard as the noise of explosions and the poor quality of the lines hindered their work.

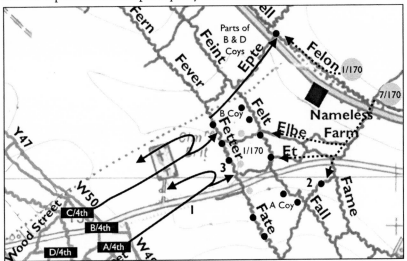

Map 16 Situation 0830-1230 Rangers front

Legend: ● Location of Rangers' companies in German lines. Location of elements of the 1/170th Regiment.
A & C Companies, 1/4th Londons advanced c. 9.00 a.m.
1= Capt. A R Moore, 1/4th Londons mortally wounded   2 = 2nd Lt. Parker's position
3= 2nd Lts. Blunn & Fanghanel wounded

As the walls of the dugouts shuddered and bucked under the repeated concussions of the German guns, Loch had digested the news about The Rangers and had ordered two companies of the 1/4th Londons forward as reinforcements. They were to join with the remnants of the Rangers' 'A' and 'D' Companies in an effort to move the attack forward, sweeping over Nameless Farm to their objective in Felon trench. The order to advance was sent by runner up Woman Street. To help with the attack, the Macart group of the R.F.A. was to bombard Felon trench and the western end of Fame until 8.45 a.m. when the attack was to

---

i Neame, a Royal Engineer, had won his V.C. for his actions at Neuve Chapelle in 1915.

go in. The Brigade's machine guns in their reinforced emplacements were also to give general overhead covering fire, but at 8.40, one of them jammed and there was a furious rush as a reserve gun was brought up and made ready for action. With two minutes to go, a runner from the front appeared, breathless, at the entrance to Brigade H.Q. The messenger, Rfn. Livesey of the Rangers, reported that the reinforcing troops were still in the British trenches. The severity of the German bombardment was now so great that any movement up or down the wreckage of the British trenches was painfully slow and fraught with danger. Everywhere the parapets had been blown in and the sides collapsed. The glutinous mud was like a thick treacle, slowing progress still further. And now the lines were choked with wounded men streaming back from the forward trenches or slumped, unable to move, wherever they could find shelter. Closer to the front, where men had been caught by shellfire in the assembly trenches, getting forward meant climbing over piles of bodies. Back in his battalion H.Q. in a dugout off Woman Street, Col. Wheatley of the 1/4ᵗʰ Londons prepared the orders for his two front companies, 'A' and 'C', to go over. The support company, 'D' Company, was then to move forward to the front line and await further orders. At about 8.45 a.m., six runners were given copies to distribute to the officers awaiting orders and they set off by various routes to find them. They had 400 metres to travel. After ten minutes, Col. Wheatley despatched another two men, one to each company commander. Of the eight men sent, one returned, having failed to locate 'C' Company, the 1/4ᵗʰ's left Company. The other seven died somewhere between H.Q. and the front line, their messages undelivered, victims of the German barrage.

In his battalion H.Q., Col. Bayliffe of the Rangers was also sending messages up and down the communication trenches. Just before nine o'clock his runners made contact with both Col. Wheatley to his rear and the waiting troops in the front line. His message to Wheatley stated that the Rangers would go over as soon as the 1/4ᵗʰ London's companies arrived in the front trenches. The message to the front told the men to attack as soon as the reinforcing companies arrived. As the two companies of the 1/4ᵗʰ Londons had been there for some time, the officers took Bayliffe's order as directions for an immediate advance. In spite of the storm of explosions to their front, the Rangers and one and a half companies of Fusiliers left their trenches and hurried forward as fast as they could. By five past nine, the survivors of the crossing were to be seen dropping into Fetter, the German front line trench. Their arrival was confirmed when a runner from 'B' Company of the Rangers struggled in from No Man's Land. His other news was that his company was held up in Felt trench by the volume of machine gun and rifle fire from Nameless Farm and Felon trench.

The men of the 1/4ᵗʰ Londons were left leaderless as soon as they reached the German front line. 'A' Company had temporarily taken some shelter in the sunken Hebuterne-Bucquoy road that ran diagonally across their front. The company C.O., Capt. Arthur Moore[i], along with his senior subaltern, 2ⁿᵈ Lt.

---

[i] Capt. Arthur Robert Moore M.C., 1/4ᵗʰ London Regt (Royal Fusiliers), died on Saturday, 1ˢᵗ July 1916, aged 32. He was the son of Sir John Moore, M.D., F.R.C.P.I., D.L., Physician to H.M. The King in Ireland, and Lady Moore of 40, Fitzwilliam Square, Dublin. A Barrister-at-Law, he was awarded an M.A. at the University of Dublin. Gazetted Aug., 1914. Capt. Moore had previously been mentioned in despatches and was awarded the Military Cross for his actions at the Battle of Neuve Chappelle on 12ᵗʰ March 1915. He received his award from the King at Buckingham

Achbigh Blunn, then went forward to check their position. Moore had already been hit before he left the assembly trenches and was wounded again as he approached the German lines. Realising he could no longer effectively lead the Company he called over Blunn and told him to carry on. Moore insisted that it was only an arm wound although Blunn thought it more serious, but he had to leave his company commander to lead the men into the German lines. In fact, the bullet had crashed through his left elbow and on into his side. Moore was brought back into the sunken road where he was attended by C.S.M. Edwards, who quickly determined the wound fatal. With Blunn still out towards the German lines, Edwards advised the platoon commander, 2nd Lt. Frederick Fanghanel, that their C.O. was dying at which point Moore opened his eyes and sobbed. Blunn was now waving the men forward and there was nothing to be done except leave Moore in the shelter of the sunken road where, it must be assumed, he died[i]. By now Blunn had pushed close to the German first line and was signalling to Fanghanel to bring the men on. Blunn then jumped into the German trenches and was immediately hit in both legs by fragments from a German bomb. Fanghanel, C.S.M. Edwards and the only three men to make it to the German lines, Sgt. Knight and Ptes. Dunn and Barr (both slightly wounded), rushed to his aid but Fanghanel was hit as he passed through the last line of German wire about six yards from the trenches. He was severely wounded in the stomach, collapsing a few yards from the German parapet. Edwards dressed Blunn's wounds and then helped the other men drag the semi-conscious Fanghanel into the trench where Edwards set to dressing his wound in a shelter in the trench. It soon became apparent that there were numerous Germans nearby and, with every member of the small party now wounded, there was little to do but surrender when a German officer called on them to give up. Blunn and Fanghanel were carried into a nearby dugout where, within a few minutes, Fanghanel died[ii]. Edwards was allowed to take his identity disc, cigarette case and wallet which he entrusted to Blunn and then, after pausing to gently lay the body out, Edwards, 2nd Lt. Blunn and the others were taken off to become prisoners of war along with three other men[iii].

Only eighteen men of 'A' Company returned after the attack. The two platoons of 'C' Company to go across also suffered heavily and two subalterns perished in the attack: 2nd Lt. Thomas Moody[iv] and 2nd Lt. Frederick Bradford[i]

Palace on the 20th May 1916, six weeks before his death. His body was never found and his name is inscribed on the Thiepval Memorial, Pier and Face 9 D and 16 B.

i The War History of the Fourth Battalion, the London Regiment by Grimwade paints a rather more heroic picture of Moore being last seen, revolver in hand and blood pouring from his back, pushing deep into the German lines. The description given in the text comes from an eyewitness letter from C.S.M. H W Edwards written whilst a prisoner of war in a camp at Minden. National Archives WO374/48507.

ii 2nd Lt. Frederick Charles Fanghanel, 1/4th London Regt (Royal Fusiliers), was reported missing on Saturday, 1st July 1916, aged 26. He was the son of Paul Gustav Adolf and Clara A. Fanghanel of 'Ravendale', Shaa Rd., Acton, London. He attested 415 Private in the Public Schools Battalion, Middlesex Regt., on 11th September 1914. His body was never found and his name is inscribed on the Thiepval Memorial, Pier and Face 9 D and 16 B.

iii CSM H W Edwards, 1/4th London Regt. (Royal Fusiliers) was made a prisoner of war and was sent to a German prisoner of war camp (Kriegsgefangenlager) at Minden along with a large number of 56th Division PoWs, including many from the London Rifle Brigade..

iv 2nd Lt. Thomas Moody, 1/4th London Regt (Royal Fusiliers), died on Saturday, 1st July 1916. Aged 27, he was the second of three children of Thomas Riley Moody of 40, Cassland Road, London, E9 and lived at 94, Madrid Road, Castelnau, Barnes. He went to France on 6th January 1915. He was kicked in the mouth by a horse on 16th April, 1915 at Estaires and was evacuated to England, being declared fit for General Service in October 1915. His body was never found and his name is inscribed on the Thiepval Memorial, Pier and Face 9 D and 16 B. [*Additional Sources:* Pam & Ken Linge, Thiepval Project]

being two more to disappear forever on this day. What was left of the company was later brought out of action by C.S.M. Davis who was awarded the D.C.M. for his efforts. The uncompromising artillery barrage across their front, which had led to the effective destruction of the advancing companies of the 1/4ᵗʰ Londons, was again the subject of urgent calls from 168ᵗʰ Brigade H.Q. At 9.03 a.m. they called Division asking for increased counter-battery fire to stop the hail of 15cm howitzer shells now coming from the area between Puisieux and Serre. Division promised to pass on the request to VII Corps Heavy Artillery but there was little respite from the constant hammering the trenches and men were receiving.

***

TO THE LEFT OF THE RANGERS, the position of the Queen's Westminster Rifles and Queen Victoria's Rifles had assumed an air of almost unreal calm. Certainly, German shells still shrieked and howled over their heads from their positions in Biez Wood and Rettemoy Farm but, to their immediate front, little was going on. The bombing party that had pursued 2ⁿᵈ Lt. Arthur and his team down Ems trench had seemed satisfied with driving them out of the Quadrilateral and had now disappeared. Reports showed Ems and Etch communication trenches to be empty, but they would not be empty much longer. At the H.Q. of the 170ᵗʰ Regiment the C.O., Major von Ihlenfeld, was about to send two companies forward. Their job was to mount a counter-attack down Epte trench towards the junction between the left of the Rangers and the right of the mixed group of Q.V.R.s and Q.W.R.s. Orders were sent out at 8.45 a.m. and the men of the 9ᵗʰ and 10ᵗʰ Companies (commanded by Oberleutnant Scheld and Leutnant der Reserve Voelkle) started to move along the long communication trenches through Rossignol Wood heading for the top of Epte. At the same time, the hard-pressed men of the II/55ᵗʰ R.I.R. had sent back urgent requests for help to Oberstleutnant von Laue[ii] in the regimental Reserve Battle Headquarters in a bunker on Hill 147 in Meed trench. At his immediate disposal was the 10ᵗʰ Company, 55ᵗʰ R.I.R. One hundred of them were waiting to be called forward from their dug outs in Exe, Mince and Mix trenches (Riegel Stellung II) and another sixty were further forward in Fillet and Fill (Riegel Stellung I). These men were ordered to advance to the support of the men defending the Kern Redoubt. To get there from Riegel Stellung II meant a journey of nearly 1,500 metres along the length of Indus trench into the rear of the village. Laden with hand grenades carried in stout canvass bags around their necks, the 10ᵗʰ Company set off to aid their comrades. Further to the east were the three other companies that, together with the 10ᵗʰ, made up the III/55ᵗʰ R.I.R. commanded by Major Tauscher. The 11ᵗʰ Company was in Regimental reserve and was nearest. They were put on alert and made ready to move forward. Two thousands metres to the east, in front of Bucquoy, were the 12ᵗʰ and 9ᵗʰ Companies and they, together with their battalion commander and several

---

[i] 2ⁿᵈ Lt. Frederick Reith Campbell Bradford, 1/4ᵗʰ London Regt (Royal Fusiliers), died on Saturday, 1ˢᵗ July 1916, aged 19. He was the son of Archibald Campbell Bradford and Clara Sophia Bradford of 'Alverstoke', 68, Derby Rd., Woodford, Essex. He attested 2924 Private in the 2/4ᵗʰ London Regt. on 1ˢᵗ October 1914 and was promoted Corporal four days later and Acting Lance Sergeant at the end of the month. He was commissioned on 19ᵗʰ January 1915 and joined the Battalion in France on 7ᵗʰ May 1916. His body was never found and his name is inscribed on the Thiepval Memorial, Pier and Face 9 D and 16 B.

[ii] Oberstleutnant von Laue was killed in action on the 13ᵗʰ November 1916.

machine guns, started the long trek up the Hebuterne Graben and then Zitzewitz Graben towards the rear of Rossignol Wood. South west of Puisieux another regiment was preparing to react to the appeals for aid. There were seven companies of the 15th R.I.R. waiting for orders in the German second position and, at around 9 a.m., pleas for help arrived from both the 170th I.R. opposite Hebuterne and the 169th I.R. defending Serre. The situation on the 170th I.R.'s front seemed more serious and two companies, the 10th and 11th, were sent forward down the long communication trenches that led from the outskirts of Puisieux towards Rossignol Wood. The regiment's 9th Company, meanwhile, went south to Serre. As they moved off, the 7th and 8th Companies moved up from reserve to take their places along with a Recruit Company of the 169th I.R. Lastly, the 8th Company of the 77th R.I.R. was placed at the disposal of the 55th R.I.R. and brought forward to billets on the edge of Bucquoy ready to move in which ever direction was required.

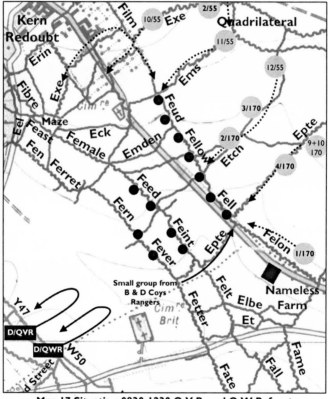

Map 17 Situation 0830-1230 Q.V.R. and Q.W.R. front

Legend: ● Location of Q.V.R. & Q.W.R. companies in German lines.
D Company, Q.V.R. advanced c 9.30-10.00 a.m. D Company, Q.W.R. advanced c. 11.15 a.m.

The elements for a powerful counter-attack were being put in place, but none of this was visible to the British observers in front of Hebuterne. From the British lines observers searching for signs of enemy activity in and around the Quadrilateral saw nothing. Further to the south, however, the concentration of

German reserves was seen by lookouts of the 1/5ᵗʰ Royal Warwickshire Regiment (143ʳᵈ Brigade, 48ᵗʰ South Midland Division). This brigade occupied the stretch of line between the attack on Gommecourt to the north and the attack on Serre to the south. From their positions, columns of men from the III/55ᵗʰ R.I.R. could be seen moving westwards from Bucquoy towards an area of dead ground behind Point 147. Maj. Charles Carrington of the Royal Warwicks personally called VIII Corps artillery with a request for battery fire to be brought to bear on the assembling German reinforcements but he was told that the area was not in their area of responsibility. Carrington then called the battalion H.Q. of the London Scottish, immediately to his left, advising them of the threat gathering some 1,500 yards away. Their call to VII Corps artillery for artillery intervention was also rejected, apparently for the same reason. Consequently, Tauscher's three companies of reinforcements were able to assemble and then march the two miles across the plain from Bucquoy to the dead ground behind Point 147 unmolested except for a few desultory rifles shots. By 11 a.m., they would be ready to be deployed in a series of counter-attacks that would help crush the 56ᵗʰ Division's attack.[1]

Meanwhile, Brig. Gen. Coke of the 169ᵗʰ Brigade read the reports and, at 9.10 a.m., decided it was time to crack on. Lt. Col. Shoolbred of the Queen's Westminster Rifles was instructed to send a platoon forward with supplies of bombs. They were also to take written orders for the Companies already in the German lines to use these new supplies in attacks up Ems, Emden and Etch to the Quadrilateral. The General also wanted reports on how the attack progressed. In spite of the massive hostile barrage, Coke was confident that these jobs could be done.

'D' Company was the Westminster's support unit and, by the time the General's order arrived at 9.20 a.m., they had been standing in their trenches under a constant and terrible bombardment for nearly two hours waiting for instructions. Only one officer remained unwounded. The Company C.O., Capt. Philip Glasier[i], was wounded and 2ⁿᵈ Lts. Cecil Stubbs[ii] and Frederick Farley[iii], two officers recently attached from the disbanded 2/2ⁿᵈ Londons, were either dead or mortally wounded. In addition, the senior N.C.O., 26 C.S.M. Herbert

---

[i] Capt. Philip Mannock Glasier, D.S.O., OC 'D' Company, 1/16ᵗʰ London Regt. (Queen's Westminster Rifles) was later promoted to Lt. Colonel. As the C.O. of the 1/16ᵗʰ London Regt (Queen's Westminster Rifles), he was killed by a shell on 2ⁿᵈ June 1918 near Tilloy. Glasier had joined the battalion in 1911 and had been in France since November 1914. He was wounded at Hooge in June 1915, rejoining in October 1915 and his wounds at Gommecourt kept him away from France until November 1916. He took command of the battalion in August 1917 fighting at Third Ypres, Cambrai and Gavrelle in March 1918. Three times Mentioned in Despatches he was awarded the D.S.O. for his actions at Cambrai. Aged 28, he was the youngest son of the late Capt. and Mrs. G. H. Brougham Glasier of Edgecombe Hall, Wimbledon Park, London. He joined his father's firm of chartered surveyors becoming a partner in 1911. He is buried in Dainville British Cemetery, grave I. E. 1.

[ii] 2ⁿᵈ Lt. Cecil Arthur Stubbs, 2/2ⁿᵈ London Regt att. 1/16ᵗʰ London Regt (Queen's Westminster Rifles), died of wounds on 2ⁿᵈ July 1916 at No. 43 Casualty Clearing Station. Aged 22, he was the son of Arthur and Martha Ann Stubbs of 26, Grafton Rd., Worthing, Sussex. He is buried in Warlincourt Halte British Cemetery, Saulty, grave II. D. 1.

[iii] 2ⁿᵈ Lt. Frederick Albert Farley, 2/2ⁿᵈ London Regt att. 1/16ᵗʰ London Regt (Queen's Westminster Rifles), was killed on 1ˢᵗ July 1916. Born on 19ᵗʰ January 1891, he was the son of Arthur Albert and Frances Eleanor Farley of 11, Warleigh Rd., Brighton, Sussex. He was educated at Rugby Road School, Brighton and Brighton Technical College and was a mechanical engineer working for the London, Brighton and South Coast Railway Company. He attested 1466 Trooper in the Sussex Yeomanry on 23ʳᵈ January 1912 and was commissioned into the 4/2ⁿᵈ London Regt. in September 1915. His body was never found and his name is inscribed on the Thiepval Memorial, Pier and Face 9 D and 16 B.

Masson[i], was dead. 1704 Sergeant Harold Ironmonger[ii] tried to get his platoon over, his men laden with all the bombs they could carry. But, as with almost every other attempt to get across, the Sergeant's gallant band could make no headway. The machine gun fire and artillery barrage were impassable and Ironmonger withdrew the few men not hit. Undaunted, Ironmonger collected together the few remaining men of his platoon and tried again. This time Sgt. Ironmonger was wounded and the effort again failed in the face of overwhelming firepower. By the end of the day, just four men survived from Ironmonger's platoon.

***

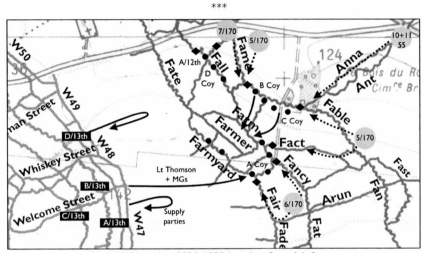

Map 18 Situation 0830-1230 London Scottish front

Legend: Advance by A Company, Kensingtons c. 9.15-930 a.m.
           Advance by D Company, Kensingtons c. 10.00 a.m.
           Lt. Thomson & M.G.s advance c. 10.20 a.m.

           • Positions of British troops ◆ Trench blocks

ON THE FAR RIGHT OF THE ATTACK, the London Scottish were reviewing their position. At 9.15 a.m., Battalion H.Q., just behind W47R trench, received news from Capt. Worlock in the front line that twenty German prisoners had survived the journey across No Man's Land and were at the head of Welcome Street, ready for removal to the cages. Estimates of casualties also filtered back. When the battalion had gone over there had been 804 officers and men (including medical staff and stretcher-bearers)[iii]. The casualty reports from the four companies were as follows:

'A' Company: 1 officer and 50 other ranks
'B' Company: 50 other ranks
'C' Company: 3 officers and 80 other ranks
'D' Company: No message

---

[i] 26 CSM Herbert Montgomery Masson D.S.O., 1/16th London Regt (Queen's Westminster Rifles), was killed on 1st July 1916. His body was never found and his name is inscribed on the Thiepval Memorial, Pier and Face 13C.
[ii] 1704 Sergeant Harold Edward Ironmonger, 1/16th London Regt (Queen's Westminster Rifles), was awarded the Military Medal for his conduct on 1st July 1916.
[iii] The London Scottish's total strength on the morning of 1st July was: 23 officers and 811 soldiers plus one officer and 36 medical staff and stretcher-bearers - 871 all ranks. Of these 5 officers and 62 other ranks were not ordered to go over to the German lines.

'D' Company's problems getting through the German wire, their bitter bombing battles in Fate and Fall and the disaster that befell No. 16 platoon in the assembly trenches had left them without an officer or N.C.O. to make a report. The C.O., 2nd Lt. Brown Constable, was already dead or dying somewhere in a German trench and to all intents and purposes, 'D' Company had ceased to exist. In addition, nearly two platoons of 'A' Company had disappeared into the smoke during the initial advance and an unknown number of them were lying dead or wounded a hundred metres or more to the south of the Farmyard position. Overall, after 1¾ hours, the London Scottish had already suffered close to 50% casualties. And now they were running out of bombs and ammunition.

Plate 39 Lt. Col. B C Green, London Scottish

The Kensingtons had already tried to get supplies over from the dumps at the top of Whiskey and Welcome Streets. There, 84 boxes of Mills grenades (1,000 grenades) and 10,000 rounds of S.A.A. had been stored. Further back, at these trenches' junctions with the old front line, another 125 boxes of bombs (1,500 grenades) and 20,000 rounds of S.A.A. were ready and waiting. Some boxes of grenades had been carried over by a party of Kensingtons led by Capt. Ware, but more were desperately needed. Lt. Col. Green of the London Scottish ordered a bombing squad of one N.C.O. and ten bomb carriers forward at 9.15 a.m. Half an hour later, another team was ordered forward, this time of one N.C.O. and 20 bomb carriers. Like their predecessors, they disappeared into the maelstrom of No Man's Land, slipping out of the sap head at the end of Welcome Street. Then, at 10 a.m., a third, and larger, party was sent forward: a bombing squad, six bomb carriers and three Lewis Gun teams. In all, 59 N.C.O.s and men were sent forward with supplies. Just three men arrived in the Farmyard stronghold. The rest were either killed or wounded by the barrage and most of the supplies and equipment lost with them.

As the clock moved round to 9.30 a.m., the scattered remains of 'D' Company of the London Scottish were established in the middle of Fall. About fifty metres to their left, a few men of the Rangers' 'A' Company held the western end of the trench. 'B' Company of the Rangers was pinned down in Felt trench in front of Nameless Farm. Between them, parties of German bombers were active; attacking the trench blocks hurriedly built when both companies had ceased

340

moving forward. They were also attacking the left flank of the Scottish position in Fame trench and, at about this time, Major Lindsay made the decision to withdraw the men of 'B' and 'C' Companies from their exposed position into Farm and Fall trenches. There they set to improving their positions and blocking the trenches to the left.

Plate 40 Lt. Col. A D Bayliffe, 1/12ᵗʰ London Regt (The Rangers)

On the left of the Rangers' position, small groups of 'B' and 'D' Companies pushed up Epte trench to the left of the Farm, reaching the junction with Felon at about 10 a.m. but, once the men had got to the junction of Felon and Epte, the attack stalled from want of leadership as every officer was long since dead or wounded. An attack down Felon would have given the Rangers the chance of taking Nameless Farm from the rear but no one took the initiative and the leaderless men dug in, building trench blocks and making ready to repel counter-attacks. On the right flank, 'A' Company of the Rangers, decimated by machine gun fire from Nameless Farm as they got into the German lines and across to the end of Fall trench, was reduced to less than twenty men. After the wounding of their C.O., Capt. Wyatt, command of the company had passed to 2ⁿᵈ Lt. Parker. Unable to move forward because of a trench block behind which lurked a team of German bombers, Parker, after a period of reorganisation, had led a party of men who rushed and captured the block, driving the enemy bombers back up Elbe trench. That was the limit of their possible advance. With their numbers so small and being incapable of moving forward and reluctant to withdraw, Parker's men tried to fortify their short section of trench. There they awaited developments and kept their heads down. Parker, the one remaining officer of 'A' Company in the German lines, briefed a runner with a plaintive message:

> "More bombs were needed urgently if the position was to be held. Reinforcements would be appreciated."

It was approaching half past ten when the runner struggled into the Rangers battalion H.Q. As the dugout rocked from the tremors of nearby shell detonations, Lt. Col. Bayliffe[i] ordered bomb-carrying parties to go over. Then, shouting into the telephone to be heard above the din, the message was sent to the Brigade H.Q. in the trench behind. The line to the London Scottish H.Q. was also still working and they were told of the predicament of the Rangers' right company and of what was being done to help them. Lastly, with the shellfire unrelenting, a desperate call was sent through to the Royal Artillery brigade headquarters. Somewhere, a German 10.5cm howitzer had their range to the metre. Could the artillery do something to silence the damn thing?

The failure of the Rangers and the London Scottish to link up in the area around Elbe and Et communication trenches was now causing problems. These two trenches provided a useful passage for any German counter attacks from the area of Rossignol Wood and, as the trenches had not been properly cleared, parties of German infantry were causing difficulties to both battalions. To bridge this gap in the British lines, 'D' Company of the Kensingtons was sent forward at 10 a.m. Their task was to secure Fate, Fall and Farm trenches and link up with 'D' Company of the Scottish to the right and 'A' Company of the Rangers to the left. Within five minutes of going over the top, all three officers became casualties and the heavy machine gun fire and the still unsurpressed artillery decimated the company. Capt. Ernest Tagart, the commander of 'D' Company, was wounded, 2nd Lt. William Mager[ii] was killed and 2nd Lt. Norman Parry[iii] was severely wounded. Led by the inexperienced 2nd Lt. Henry Pilgrim, a 21-year old who had only arrived in France on 31st May, the few men left standing of 'D' Company struggled back into the front line. The hole in the British line went unfilled. More than an hour later the remains of 'D' Company of the Kensingtons were still sheltering in the battered front line trenches. With all of its officers dead or wounded, it took some time for the remaining N.C.O.s to re-organise the shattered company. Someone then realised that H.Q. should be told about the failure of the attack and a runner was despatched down the shambles of Welcome Street.

At 10.30 a.m. Sgt. Jones of 'B' Company arrived at battalion headquarters with news from the German trenches. Casualties amongst the clearing parties were heavy, already about 50%. Amongst the officers Jones had somehow managed to bring the severely wounded Lt. Penn back to the battalion Aid Post; 2nd Lt.

---

[i] Lt. Col. A D Bayliffe, CMG, TD, 1/12th London Regt. (The Rangers) commanded the battalion from its arrival in France at the end of December 1914 to March 1918. A pre-war Territorial Bayliffe was twice Mentioned In Despatches and was awarded the Italian Military Order of Savoy (Cavalier) in May 1917.

[ii] 2nd Lt. William George Mager, 1/13th London Regt. (Kensingtons), died on Saturday, 1st July 1916. Born in St Pancras on the 4th October 1882 he lived at 63 Guildford Street, Russell Square. Educated at Kings College in the Strand he went on to become a civil servant at the Board of Education. He first enlisted in the 12th Middlesex Civil Service Volunteer Rifles on the 25th February 1904. He was then attested private in the 15th County of London Battalion on the 2nd April 1908, being promoted to L/Cpl in January 1913, Cpl in April 1913 and sergeant in June 1914. On the 22nd December 1914 he was discharged from the 15th Londons and commissioned 2nd Lt. in the Kensingtons. Single, on his death his sole surviving relative was his sister, Mrs Kate Albrecht. He is buried in Hebuterne Military Cemetery, grave IV.M.51.

[iii] 2nd Lt. Norman Ernest Parry, 1/13th London Regt. (Kensingtons) was born on 14th September 1894, the son of Ernest Henry and Beatrice Francis Parry of The Grange, London Road, Thornton Heath, Surrey. He was educated at the Chateau de Prangins in Switzerland and Dulwich College where he was a member of the OTC and played rugby for the 1st XV and cricket for the 3rd XI. He was articled to Septimus Gillatt of Wederell, Trenow and Gillatt, chartered accountants of Finsbury. He attested as 2041 Private in the Honourable Artillery Company on 7th September 1914 and went to France in January 1915. He was wounded at Ypres on 16th June and repatriated. He was commissioned into the 3/13th London Regt. in November 1915. After the war he lived at 22 Lyndale Ave, Finchley Road, NW 2. [*Additional sources*: Dick Flory: Dulwich College War Record, 1914-1919; Dulwich College Register, 1619-1926]

Sydney Ball[i] was wounded; but 2nd Lt. Percy Pike[ii] was thought to be still standing. To add to their woes, the Kensingtons over in the German lines had run out of bombs.

It wasn't until 11.15 a.m. that word reached the Kensington's battalion H.Q. in Welcome Street that what was left of 'D' Company was still in the British lines and that 2nd Lt. Mager was dead and 2nd Lts. Parry and Clark were wounded. Whilst 'A' and 'C' Companies continued to send small carrying parties out into the relentless German barrage in futile attempts to get supplies across No Man's Land the Lewis guns of 'B' Company were sent up to the reserve trench, W47R, to bolster the defences of the sector. And as more men were committed the casualties continued to rise. Word came into headquarters at 11.45 a.m. that 2nd Lt. George Bryer[iii] had fallen victim to the hurricane of explosions that was wiping the British trenches off the face of the map.

At the Kensingtons' headquarters Capt. Montgomery Harris[iv] of 'B' Company was the nearest available senior officer and he was sent down the communication trenches to rally the remnants of 'D' Company and any other men he found in the front lines. He was also given orders to take them forward again. When he arrived, he found just twenty shocked and dazed survivors. One look at the curtain of shellfire that smothered No Man's Land convinced him that it would be impossible for anyone to get across to assist the Rangers and Scottish. So, leaving 2nd Lt. Pilgrim to make the best of things, Capt. Harris set off to make the return journey down 500 metres of wrecked trench to advise his C.O., Major Young, and to ask for further orders.

At the same time, another attempt was made to reinforce the London Scottish, this time with two Vickers machine guns. They were needed to prevent counter-attacks that were expected to come from Rossignol Wood, down Anna communication trench, and from the area of the Sunken Road to the south. Orders were sent from Brigade H.Q. and, led by Lt. Frederick Thomson, the two machine gun teams waiting in the front line set off at 10.20 a.m. from the end of a sap in No Man's Land. They were headed in the direction of the junction of Farmyard and Fair trenches and it took them an eternity to get there.

---

[i] 2nd Lt. Sydney Arthur Ball, 1/13th London Regt. (Kensingtons) lived at 29, Dafforne Road, Upper Tooting. On 15th May 1917 he was seconded to the Port and Transit Executive Committee of the Admiralty and was promoted Captain as part of the Transport Workers Battalion.
[ii] 2nd Lt. Percy Reginald Pike, 1/13th London Regt. (Kensingtons) was born on 28th November 1888. He was married to Rae Pike of 25, Vespan Road, Shepherd's Bush and had three daughters: Irene Jessie, Gwendoline Dora and Rae Dorothy. Employed as a cashier by W & G du Cros Ltd, he had previously been a member of the Middlesex Volunteer Rifle Corps and the Civil Service Cadets. He attested 1498 Private in the Kensingtons on 11th November 1913, was embodied on 5th August 1914 and later promoted Sergeant. He was commissioned in April 1916.
[iii] 2nd Lt. George Percival Bryer, 1/13th London Regt., (Kensingtons) was born on 18th May 1892 the son of J Bryer of Salthouse. He was educated at Gresham's School between 1906 and 1909. He attested 3308 Private in the Kensingtons on 10th November 1914 aged 21. He was commissioned in July 1915. After recovering from his wounds he was transferred to the Reserve Battalion of the Kensingtons in November 1916 and the No. 12 Labour Company, Royal West Surrey Regt., in April 1917. Aged 22 and an artist, he lived at 90, Musard Flats, West Kensington having been in the OTC at Gresham's School for two years. [*Additional source:* Dick Flory: History and Register of Gresham's School]
[iv] Capt. (later Major) Montgomery Reader Harris, MC, 1/13th London Regt. (Kensingtons) was born in 1884. He was the son of the late Reader Harris KC, founder of the Pentecostal League, and before the war he was a solicitor. He was a widower. He was blown up by a shell on 15th August 1917 at Ypres which rendered him unconscious for some time. Although he carried on for 24 hours he found he could no longer stand. Diagnosed with severe shell shock he was also found to be partially deaf in both ears. He was discharged from the Army on 18th April 1919. He married Millicent Damaris Turner, daughter of Sir Skinner and Lady Turner after the war. Sir Skinner Turner was a judge of HBM Supreme Court for China.

As they departed, Lt. Col. Green was sending an urgent message back up the lines via Divisional H.Q. to the VII Corps artillery. All morning, three German batteries of 10.5 cm and 15 cm guns had been pounding the W47 front line trench, the machine gun emplacements in W48 reserve trench and the extreme right of the London Scottish position in Fair and Fancy trenches. Green had a good idea where these batteries were located and he wanted them dealt with urgently. One was near Serre and, now that the attack of the 31st Division had collapsed in disarray, they were joining with the bombardment of the Londoner's attack. Another was hidden in a shallow valley near Puisieux and the third was in Fork Wood just to the North of that town. Silencing these guns would immeasurably help the process of consolidation and the bringing up of supplies and reinforcements. Could it be done promptly?

Messages like this poured into the VII Corps artillery H.Q. all day. Recording their contents and locating probable targets on maps was one thing. Dealing with their appeals was another matter entirely. Covering an area over five kilometres square No. 8 Squadron had just one aircraft flying above the lines, spotting for the artillery and reporting back either by radio or by dropping messages at a pre-arranged drop zone. But, even as the sun shone and the early morning mist and clouds burnt away, the observer in the BE2c found identifying German batteries a problem. And then, even if they did make a positive identification and the message was correctly relayed to the appropriate battery, another question arose: could the guns reach these targets?

Counter-battery work had mainly been seconded to the 60pdr and 6 in. guns with some of the 6 in., 9.2 in., 12 in. and 15 in. howitzers joining along with various 4.5 in. howitzer batteries of the R.F.A. The problem was that only the guns, with their relatively light weight delivery of high explosive, could reach into the rear areas near to Bucquoy and Puisieux where a large number of German howitzer batteries were located. For example, in and around the triangle of roads joining Bucquoy, Douchy les Ayette and Ayette were ten battery positions almost all of which could only be reached by the 9.2 in. railway mounted gun at Humbercamps and the fourteen 6 in. and 60pdr guns; and for some of them the range was extreme. Of course, this all might have been academic as there was no certainty that British Intelligence even knew that these positions existed. Two weeks before the attack took place, they had 'identified' just 21 of the 58 battery positions within the 2nd Guard Reserve Division sector and none of these were in the Bucquoy-Douchy-Ayette triangle. Additionally, there were the German batteries firing into the Gommecourt salient from other divisional sectors, the 111th Infantry Division to the north and the 52nd Infantry Division to the south. The 111th Division had a large concentration of artillery in Adinfer Wood, a large thickly sown area of woodland measuring some 3kms by 2kms. These guns easily had the range of the whole salient and the only interference to their activities came from the field artillery of the 37th Division as Third Army had effectively denuded itself of heavy artillery for the Gommecourt bombardment. The problem with the guns of the 52nd Infantry Division was that they were mainly in another Corps' sector. VIII Corps was attacking Serre and Beaumont Hamel and, as their attacks collapsed along the entire Corps front, their heavies were not interested in firing at anything other than German batteries bombarding their own men. Unlike the German artillery, co-operation between different commands was not high on the list of priorities and, anyway, as Gommecourt was a diversion, VIII Corps staff might have been forgiven for asking what was the point in diverting their artillery to support a diversion!

And there was an additional problem. Some German batteries, perhaps those most easy to spot, had been given special treatment in the preliminary bombardment and VII Corps artillery seem to have assumed that such batteries must now be hors de combat. They were wrong and had grossly underestimated the resilience and morale of the German gunners. One of these supposedly 'defunct' batteries was No. 5 Battery of Reserve Feldartillerie Regiment 20 at position 530 just south of Biez Wood. Here, their four 77mm field guns had been subject to repeated attacks and, as a result, two had been destroyed and a third badly damaged. But the guns had been replaced and the dugouts rebuilt. As the regimental history somewhat gleefully recounts:

> "On 1st July, the battery, which had had a hard time until then, remained largely untouched by enemy fire; the enemy must have assumed that the battery had already been taken care of. In reality, it succeeded in taking part in the battle with all force."

To make matters worse, the 18 pdrs of the R.F.A. were also having trouble. The gunners, stripped to the waist and dripping with sweat, had been loading and firing continuously since the intense bombardment began at 6.25 a.m. They were feeling the strain and so were the guns. At 9.55 a.m., the whole of A/283 Battery, located in a shallow valley some 1,500 metres SW of Hebuterne, stopped firing. The men were tired but, more importantly, key components of the 18 pdr guns were failing and it would take them half an hour to make the necessary repairs. The main problem was the guns' buffer springs which were an essential part of the recoil process and acted with a hydraulic system to return the barrel to its firing position. The stress of constant action, not only on July 1st but on the previous seven days, had weakened the springs, some of which were of dubious quality anyway. The heat generated by constant firing had lowered the viscosity of the buffer oil in the hydraulics, putting more and more strain on the springs alone. Something had to give and, from 10 a.m. onwards, it was the springs. By 11.30 a.m., the problem was so widespread that the rate of fire from the divisional artillery had started to slacken dramatically. There was no shortage of ammunition but, if the guns were to keep firing throughout the rest of the day, the rate of fire had to be slowed. It was an impossible dilemma for the officers in charge but then the broken springs started to force their hand.

In spite of these problems, some of the German batteries were effectively targeted, but these seem to have been those that arrived last and had the least amount of time to camouflage and reinforce their positions. Two batteries of the 19th Bavarian Field Artillery Regt. had been in place for just twelve days. No. 3 Battery, commanded by Leutnant von Kraft, was dug on a road side near Essarts and No. 4 Battery near the road by Fork Wood, south of Bucquoy. No. 3 Battery's position was described as 'makeshift'[2] and had clearly been noticed by observers in either a BE2c or a balloon. Their position was pounded but, in spite of this effort, not too much damage was done with four men wounded, one fatally[i]. No. 4 Battery, under Leutnant der Reserve Adam, was to suffer most. Their battery position was between Bucquoy and the Ziegelwäldchen (Fork Wood). It was very close to the road and partially visible from Hebuterne. Given its visibility it soon became a prime target, to such an extent that, at about 11.00 a.m., it was put out of action. Two guns were hit, one by four heavy-calibre direct hits and another by two. Although wounded, Leutnant der Reserve Adam continued to fire from the last usable gun while the rest of the battery's men still standing tried to sort out the shambles around them and organise medical help for the wounded. Two men in particular stood out and, as a result, Uffz. Burkhard and Gefr. Militzer were both later promoted for conspicuous gallantry in the face of the enemy. Battery commander, Lt. Adam, was awarded the Iron Cross, 1ˢᵗ class, the first Battery Officer of the 19ᵗʰ F.A.R to receive this prestigious medal.

No. 4 Battery's particular problem was that they had been spotted by a British aircraft and, because the R.F.C. had almost total local air superiority, there was little that some desultory anti-aircraft fire and the defiant but out-gunned German pilots could do to drive them away. The bane of their existence, a BE2c from No. 8 Squadron R.F.C., spent his time circling at no more than 200 metres spotting the fall of shot for the British counter-battery guns. On one of the few occasions that a German aircraft dared to challenge the British pilots it was chased down to nearly ground level without any of the AA guns being able make even one hole in the canvass of the chasing plane. The concentration of fire on No. 4 Battery made re-supply a problem and the ammunition wagons were only brought up to the positions one at a time. Even then, the men unloading the shells and cartridges were strafed by the British aircraft which also interfered with the evacuation of the wounded. Even when moved to the nearby field ambulance the wounded were not safe. The first party of casualties from No. 4 Battery had only just reached the Northern Group's field ambulance, near to the Ziegelwäldchen and next to the 6ᵗʰ Battery, 103ʳᵈ Field Artillery Regiment's position, when the telephone dug-out, where the wounded were being taken, collapsed as a result of direct-hit. There was frantic activity as every available man tried to rescue the buried men and, amazingly, they were all rescued alive. As the rescue went on, however, two guns from the nearby 6ᵗʰ Battery, 103ʳᵈ F.A.R were hit and put out of action. Nonetheless, in spite of the heavy bombardment aimed at the 19ᵗʰ F.A.R's two positions, casualties overall were extremely light, two men killed and fifteen wounded, suggesting that the guns being used against these positions were of insufficient calibre to do serious damage to even these 'makeshift' emplacements.

***

BACK IN THE TRENCHES opposite Gommecourt Park, the 1/2ⁿᵈ Londons were watching developments uneasily. From their position, they could see the L.R.B.'s ongoing battle for the perimeter of the Park and they could tell that progress had stalled. Then, at 10.15 a.m., they saw the first signs of renewed activity around the Cemetery. A German bombing party was coming down Ems trench towards the area where the Q.W.R. were established in Feud. These were the men of the

---

[i] The men were Kanonier Ortmeier, Gefreiter Wimmer, Unteroffizier Maas, Vize-Wachmeister Hafner; Uffz. and Geschützführer Kuchler. The latter was seriously wounded and died in a field hospital on 6ᵗʰ July.

11th Company of the 55th R.I.R led by Leutnant der Reserve Stolper. Having been brought up from regimental reserve, the commander of the III/55th R.I.R., Major Tauscher, had sent them forward with instructions to attack down Ems. A few minutes later the 12th Company (Hauptmann der Landwehr Winkelmann) had arrived from Brigade reserve near Bucquoy and they had followed the 11th along Ems trench only to turn left at Etch trench. They were to move down the slope towards the centre of the trenches now held by the Westminsters and Victorias. Following along behind these two companies came the men of the 9th Company, breathless and sweating after their long hike up the communication trenches from in front of Bucquoy.

On the left, at Point 94, the L.R.B. had a problem. However hard they tried, they could not penetrate the Park. Into its still dense undergrowth numerous German trenches snaked and coiled. And from the security of their deep dugouts in the Maze and in the heart of the Park itself, German reserves were now using these trenches to press 'A' Company fiercely. Securing Point 94 was an important element of the Divisional plan. Once it had been secured, it was intended that the Pioneers and the Royal Engineers should construct a strong point from which would be launched the final clearing operations of the Village and Park. These final operations were timed to start three hours after Zero hour. That was in only thirty minutes time and 'A' Company had barely got beyond the tree line.

Two other strongpoints were to be constructed on the L.R.B.'s front. The southern edge of the Maze and the area around the Cemetery, where Eck and Ems trenches met, were the sites of the other two and, at both, German aggression was building as the men of the 10th Company, 55th R.I.R. arrived in support. In addition, the strong attacks of the 11th Company, 55th R.I.R. down Ems trench from the direction of the Quadrilateral, supported by machine gun fire from Erin trench near to the village, were beginning to detach the Westminsters and Victorias on the right from the L.R.B.'s increasingly tenuous hold on Eck. If the link between the battalions were broken, matters would rapidly deteriorate. The L.R.B.'s officers looked anxiously to the right. Where were the other battalions?

Although the Westminsters still had an important objective to take, the Queen Victorias had taken all of theirs by 9.30 a.m. and a runner got a message back to their battalion H.Q. with the news. Elements of 'B' Company set to the task of consolidating their hold on Feed trench in the Germans second line while further forward, the Westminsters and a mixed group from 'B' and 'C' Company worked with the Pioneers to make Feud and Fellow trenches secure. The problem was not with holding their own objectives; it was in the failure of the Rangers to the right to achieve theirs. German bombing parties of the 7th Company, 170th Regiment were now appearing in growing numbers and had found ways to infiltrate back into the front line areas, bypassing the flimsy defences of the badly weakened Rangers. As elsewhere, a severe shortage of grenades was being felt.

The programme for the assault indicated that it was time for three sections of Q.V.R. bombers from the battalion reserve, 'D' Company, to go forward along with members of the battle police, needed to control and corral German prisoners. The chaos and congestion in the communication trenches was so great, however, that the orders to advance took an hour to arrive in the front lines. As the runners were forcing their way through the muddy and bloody disorder of the trenches, observers were watching counter-attacks developing along the Brigade front. Large groups of German bombers, men of the 11ᵗʰ and 12ᵗʰ Companies of the 55ᵗʰ R.I.R., could be seen converging on the junction of Ems and Epte communication trenches up on top of the ridge at about 10 a.m. and a short time later, a bombing fight could be seen developing near to the Ems-Feud junction.

It was clear that supplies were needed with increasing desperation by the men in the German lines. But, because of the delay in receiving orders and because they had to move up from the reserve line, it wasn't until 10.30 a.m. that the carrying party, led by 2ⁿᵈ Lt. Douglas Ord-Mackenzie, stepped over the parapet. Each man was heavily laden with 24 of the 1½ lb. Mills bombs and to slow them down even further they had to negotiate the almost uncut British wire as here the attacking waves of the Q.V.R. had moved out in front of the wire whilst the final bombardment was still ongoing.

L/Cpl. Appleyard described what happened next:

> "As soon as we advanced over 'No Man's Land' the Germans opened a very deadly machine gun fire, which laid a good number out. On we went and it seemed marvellous how the pieces missed us, for the air appeared to be alive with missiles. At last, after advancing about 30 yards I was struck in the thigh by a bullet the force of which knocked me over. The only thing to do was to crawl back, and this I did and explained things to Captain Renton. Knowing that a good number had been hit, I decided to crawl out on top again and give any assistance that might be required. My efforts were fruitless for the only man left out had been shot through the head and killed instantly."[3]

Such was the intensity of machine gun fire that, within a few minutes, half the carrying party had been hit. As with the Westminsters' earlier attempt, the much-needed supply of bombs failed to get through. Another attempt to cross was then made by Lt. Thomas Hodgson's platoon of 'D' Company. It met with the same fate as Ord-Mackenzie and his men. A few men did get through, however, one of these being the newly promoted 3621 L/Cpl. Reginald Davis of No. 14 Platoon who had been put in charge of the 'Battle Police':

> "I was in charge of the 'Battle Police' that day, and we had to accompany the bombers. We started over the top under heavy fire and many were bowled over within a few minutes.
>
> Lanky of limb, I was soon through the barbed wire and came to the first trench and jumped in. Some seven of us were there and, as senior N.C.O., I led the way along the trench. One Hun came round the corner, and he would have been dead but for his cry, "Kamerad, blessé." I lowered my rifle, and making sure he had no weapon, passed him to the rear and led on."[4]

As 2ⁿᵈ Lt. Ord-Mackenzie and his men recovered from their ordeal a runner, Rfn. Coventry, appeared with a message for the officers of the Q.V.R. in the German trenches. Having experienced what is was like to be exposed to the machine gun and artillery fire sweeping No Man's Land, Ord-Mackenzie consulted Coventry and together they peered across the ground over which he was to travel. Just then, a young rifleman of the L.R.B., 647 Rfn. Charles Hudson[i], collapsed into the trench shouting that he had two messages brought across from the German lines. Hudson had volunteered to carry this message across the 400 yards of fire-swept ground between the lines but, about half way across, a bullet had hit him in the back, piercing his stomach and then being diverted to exit through his left thigh. Ord-Mackenzie read and signed for the messages, two of very few written messages to make it back to the British trenches. Hudson, who said he was the third runner to attempt the crossing, was determined to take his messages to L.R.B. battalion H.Q. as instructed but before he would let him go, Ord-Mackenzie examined his injury. The stomach wound was severe and the sort that was often (and was in this case) fatal, but the young man was unwavering in his desire to see the messages in his C.O.'s hand. As one of the messages answered the question posed in Rfn. Coventry's note, Ord-Mackenzie ordered Coventry to help Hudson down the communication trenches to his battalion's H.Q. Ord-Mackenzie[ii], in a report written after the battle and passed to Lt. Col. Bates of the L.R.B., stated:

"Rfn. Coventry asserts that Rfn. Hudson displayed great courage and fortitude throughout, and I should like to call attention to the fact that his first thought, when he met me, was for his duty and not for himself."

22-year old Charles Hudson would die seven days later in hospital at Le Treport, his grieving parents at his bedside. His valour would go unrecognised.

***

THE COMPLETE BREAKDOWN of the reinforcement process was now having a severe impact on the course of the action. German bombing parties supported by a light minenwerfer emerged from the Village (10th Company, 55th R.I.R.) and others forced their way down Ems trench (11th Company, 55th R.I.R.). By 10.45 a.m., they had driven a wedge between the left platoon of the Q.V.R. and the rest of the battalion. Fighting their way into the Cemetery, the German infantry now threatened the positions of all three battalions of the 169th Brigade. The network of trenches here was so complex that it was possible for almost any position to be outflanked once the British line had been broken. And now, as 11 o'clock approached, the centre of the 169th Brigade's front had nearly caved in and was in danger of destabilising the entire position. Six men of 'C' Company of the

---

i 647 Rfn Charles Henry Hudson, 1/5th London Regt (London Rifle Brigade), died of wounds on 7th July 1916. Aged 22, he was the son of Charles Ernest and Ellen Hudson of 28, Norwich Road, Forest Gate. He had been awarded a B.Sc. by London University and had just been awarded a scholarship to West Hame Technical Institute when war broke out. His parents travelled to be by his side, arriving two days before he died. He had not been expected to survive to see them and had dictated a letter for them to a clergyman before they arrived. He died at 2.20 a.m. on the morning of Monday, 7th July. He is buried in Le Treport Military Cemetery, Plot 2. Row L grave 6. Ord-Mackenzie, Coventry and Lt. Col Dickins of the QVR all endorsed the account of Charles Hudson's bravery. Lt. Col Bates strongly advocated some sort of award but this was refused by higher authorities. He had previously been wounded at Ypres in spring 1915.

ii 2nd Lt. Douglas Allan Ord-Mackenzie, 1/9th London Regt (Queen Victoria's Rifles), died on 24th September 1916 in fighting near Bouleaux Wood. Aged 28, he was the son of the late Mr. W. H. and Mrs. C. Ord Mackenzie of Albert Square, Bowdon, Cheshire. He was educated at Sedbergh and trained as an engineer working for Messers Stewarts and Lloyds Ltd., South Africa. He joined Hartigan's Horse at East London on the outbreak of war and served in the South West Africa campaign as a trooper. When the regiment was disbanded he travelled to England at this own expense and was commissioned into the QVR in October 1915 along with 2nd Lt. Ralph Bennett. He went to the front in March 1916 being slightly wounded twice. His body was never found and his name is inscribed on the Thiepval Memorial, Pier and Face 9C.

Westminsters, Sgt. H A London, L/Cpl. F E Wright and Rfn. Fraser, Lakeman, Pinnell and H R Wallis, drove back the approaching Germans of 11/55th R.I.R. in the vicinity of the junction of Feud and Ems and then fought a dogged 90-minute action from behind a trench barricade until they had run out of bombs and become isolated[i].

Across the whole of the 169th Brigade front the supply of both British and captured German grenades was fast running out. In addition, the Lewis guns' ammunition supplies were severely depleted and had to be used sparingly. The close quarter action prevented the R.F.A. from doing anything to assist. Those machine guns that had been brought over had been mostly silenced and the Stokes mortars that had arrived were either incomplete or ineffective.

At 10.45 a.m., a message arrived at the L.R.B.'s forward H.Q. at the junction of Fen and Ferret trenches. The left platoon of the Victorias which had become detached from the rest of the battalion by the German attacks down Ems and into Feud trenches was now the only unit protecting the right of the L.R.B. and they were under fierce bombing attacks. Almost as if this was a signal, the German assault along the whole battalion front from the Cemetery to Point 94 increased to a new pitch of ferocity. It was like an animal sensing a weakness in its prey and going for the kill. The Germans seemed to have recognised that the balance had swung decisively in their favour. They could see that behind the British, No Man's Land was being swept by a hurricane of high explosive and shrapnel. Surely, no supplies or reserves could get through such a wall of explosions? The more experienced men of the 55th R.I.R. would also have recognised a reduction in the number of grenades being used by the British troops. The most alert would have recognised their own stick grenades being used against them. Whilst some would have cursed as they ducked and scrabbled to avoid them, the officers and N.C.O.s would have sensed a certain desperation in this form of defence. Their enemy was running out of bombs. When there were none left, they would be defenceless. The tide of battle was running in their favour. Victory was but a matter of time.

***

As the British front began to crumble, more desperate efforts were being made to re-supply the men with bombs. At about 11.15 a.m., led by 1013 Sgt. Henry Couper[ii], the last two platoons of 'D' Company of the Queen's Westminster Rifles set off, festooned with bags of bombs. A few minutes later, the last survivors of the doomed attempt were back in the trenches, their mates lying dead or wounded within a few yards of the parapet, victims of the barrage and vicious machine gun crossfire.

A few hundred yards to the right, opposite Nameless Farm, the trench pioneers of the 1/4th Londons had started forward at 10.45 a.m. on a similar task. They were laden with equipment and supplies to be used for the consolidation of the captured trenches. Their fate was the same as that of every brave but futile attempt to re-supply the men the other side of No Man's Land.

---

[i] Fraser was reported missing but survived and Lakeman and Pinnell were both wounded.
[ii] 1013 CSM Henry William Couper M.M., 1/16th London Regt. (Queen's Westminster Rifles), died of wounds on 11th June 1917. He is buried in Fulford Cemetery, Fulford near York, grave G.3. He was awarded the Military Medal for his conduct on 1st July 1916.

Just behind them, two volunteer runners, Privates Whitehead and Buckingham from the 1/4th, slipped across the front line. When Brig. Gen. Loch called for men to find out what was going on around Nameless Farm, these two had stepped forward. Loch was anxious for any information about the progress of the Rangers and this was the only method at his disposal. Hopefully, one man at least would survive the trip there and back.

Back at the Rangers' H.Q. various messages came in and orders flooded out. 2nd Lt. Higgins, the Rangers' Bombing officer, arrived at 11.30 to ask why seventy men of the 1/4th Londons were still in the Boyau de Service and the support trench. Surely, they should have gone forward to assist the men in the German lines? A message was sent down the trenches to the Fusiliers' H.Q. asking what the men were doing there. The reply came back that Brigade H.Q. thought it best for the men to stay in the trenches for the time being at least. But reinforcements were still desperately needed and, as the time crawled towards noon, it was decided to send over two Vickers guns from the Brigade Machine Company. They were to make their way to the Felon-Epte junction, there to reinforce the team of Rangers and to help repel the counter-attacks that were thought to be imminent. As the runner made his way up Woman Street to alert the two machine gun teams, the pace of the German bombardment still had not slackened. Again, the artillery liaison officer at the Rangers' H.Q. phoned the Royal Artillery brigade headquarters. His message was blunt: 'find that German howitzer and do something about it'.

In an orchard on the western side of Hebuterne, D/280 battery was lobbing its 4.5 in. shells at some distant targets to the east. It was receiving the requests for counter-battery fire from the nearby infantry and had passed them on. In the battery's log for the day, a note was taken of these pleas for help:

"11.30 - 12.15 constant messages as to heavy barrages by guns apparently firing from direction of Rossignol Wood (H[eavy].A[rtillery]. Liaison informed)".

They awaited orders to re-direct their fire towards these troublesome batteries. The orders did not come. In the German batteries, the artillerymen waited anxiously for the scream of plunging shells from the British medium and heavy howitzers and guns. They waited, but nothing happened. German ammunition supplies were replenished with wagons and lorries moving up to the battery positions in full view of the British trenches. Lorries laden with shells drove up to Rettemoy Farm unmolested. The weight of the German bombardment went unchecked. What was the VII Corps Heavy Artillery doing?

***

FOR NEARLY TWO HOURS, Major General Hull had been reading reports from the 169th Brigade H.Q. about the absence of men, from either side, in and around the Quadrilateral. At 11 a.m., an R.F.A. observation post had reported the area clear of troops. At the same time they reported (correctly) that the German third line to the left of Nameless Farm was in British hands and that signboards had gone up in most of the observed trenches.

A few minutes later, a message from the No. 8 Squadron BE2c over-flying the battlefield confirmed the OP reports about the absence of activity in the

Quadrilateral. The dropping of the message from the aircraft was seen by 2nd Lt. Moy as he waited near Souastre for news of the attack:

"At 11:30 a.m., after three hours of agony, an aeroplane came back flying low; it dropped a message gay with ribbons – 'Quadrilateral free of enemy. Why doesn't infantry take it?'"[5]

Keen to grasp the opportunity that seemed to be presenting itself, Hull's staff phoned the 169th Brigade H.Q. issuing orders requiring that the men push up Ems and Etch trenches in order to occupy this essential objective. Other orders were phoned through to the Artillery H.Q. Hull wanted the barrage now being placed on the Quadrilateral to be lifted so that the Westminsters could push up the communication trenches and occupy their objective without falling victim to 'friendly fire'.

For a few minutes, matters appeared to be progressing satisfactorily. Another R.F.A. report suggested that British troops were moving up Etch trench in the direction of the Quadrilateral. Hull was encouraged; the much-delayed link-up with the 46th Division could still be achieved. By 11.20 a.m., however, these optimistic thoughts were put to one side. Within minutes of one another, reports from the O.P.s made it clear that no-one was moving towards the Quadrilateral and, from 46th Divisional H.Q., came news that all progress with what was left of their attack had ceased, foundering on yet more undiscovered, uncut wire and the relentless pounding of the German defensive barrage. Another call was put into the Artillery: resume the bombardment of the Quadrilateral. If the British could not have it, then the Germans were to be denied it too. But, with the northern flank of Gommecourt secure, 2nd Guard Reserve Division's Artillery Gruppe Nord switched its attention to the London Divisional front. Gruppe Süd, along with the 103rd and 104th Field Artillery Regiments of the 52nd Field Artillery Brigade around Puisieux and Miraumont, had been pounding this sector for hours now with both rolling and static barrages. Their job was to ensure nothing got across No Man's Land – in either direction. They were succeeding admirably.

ENDNOTES:
[1] Taken from an extract of 'The Defence of Gommecourt 1st July 1916' by Maj. C E Carrington, 1/5th Royal Warwickshire Regt., found in the battalion's National Archive file WO95/2755.
[2] Nörr, Hermann „Das K. B. 19. Feldartillerie-Regiment" 1930
[3] Appleyard Rfn S W, 1/9th London Regt (Queen Victoria's Rifles), Papers, IWM
[4] Hodder, Williams J E (editor), One Young Man, 1917
[5] Moy, 2nd Lt. C E, Unpublished papers, Liddle Collection, Leeds University.

11. Z DAY: 1200 - 1430

"I have, as far as I can find, only 13 left besides myself. Trenches unrecognisable. Quite impossible to hold. Bombardment fearful for last two hours. I am the only officer left. Please send instructions."

Major C C Dickens
1/13th Londons (Kensingtons)

B Y MID-DAY the 56th Division had been fighting on their own for over three hours. On the other side of the village, utter chaos still reigned in the trenches of the 46th Division. No-one, from the lowliest private up to Maj. Gen. Stuart-Wortley and beyond, appeared to have the slightest idea about what was to happen next. Gen. Hull and his staff were anxious to know whether the pressure on their men was to be relieved by another attack on the northern face of the salient. Of course, if there was no realistic chance of such an attack then it was clear that the operation had failed and, as the 56th Division could not achieve VII Corps' objectives on their own, rather than reinforce failure, the Division should be looking at ways of extricating their hard-pressed men. There was no particular need to sustain the attack on their own as, with the collapse of the attack on Serre, the 'diversion' had also failed. As a result, Hull looked for clarification of 46th Division's intentions. He had already been told that a new attack was planned for 12.15 p.m. but now, two minutes before this was due to occur, a message came through advising him that there was a delay of an hour.

Although there were no fresh troops available for this assault Stuart-Wortley still considered it reasonable to ask the shattered battalions of the 137th and 139th Brigades to reorganise, re-supply and go back into action. Lt. Gen. Snow, who was visiting 46th Division's H.Q., agreed and messages were sent to elements of the VII Corps Heavy Artillery to be ready to assist. Tragically for the Londoners stranded in the German trenches, the chances of any effective resumption of hostilities by the 46th Division were remote in the extreme. The surviving men of the attacking battalions were now badly mixed up and, because of the very heavy casualties amongst the gallant officers who had tried to get their men forward, there was a complete loss of direction and control. Within the trenches themselves reorganisation was next to impossible. Already knee deep in mud and, in places, under several feet under water, they were now clogged with crowds of wounded, confused and lost men. To make matters even worse, the over-rehearsed men now found it difficult to adapt to new orders:

"...the men had been carefully trained for weeks to play definite parts in the assault, and it was not easy to make them realise that these roles must now be forsaken and something different done. For instance, a party told off to carry concertina wire could not for some time be got to understand that they must drop their loads and help to form an attacking wave."[1]

Officers were sent up from 137th Brigade H.Q. to help but they, and men carrying supplies, were severely delayed by the acute congestion in the dreadfully dilapidated communication trenches. On the 139th Brigade front the reasons for delay were somewhat different. Some brave souls of the Sherwood Foresters had made it into the German positions on the extreme left of the assault, around the

Z and Little Z strongholds. Although nothing had been seen of them since 11 a.m., Brig. Gen. Shipley, G.O.C. 139th Brigade, was concerned to support them but, given the conditions, he felt it necessary for another smoke screen to be laid across his front before reinforcements could go forward. There were no smoke bombs to be had and so another delay was caused whilst supplies were located and brought forward. At 1.15 p.m., the time the previously postponed attack was due to go in, another delay was announced, this time to 2.45 p.m. Forty minutes later, 56th Division would be told that this time was no longer possible and that 3.30 p.m. was the new hour set for the advance (and even this timetable would eventually be abandoned). Writing after the war, Brig. Gen. Lyon of the VII Corps staff would remark about the 46th Division's inability to deliver a new attack at Gommecourt:

> "It... made me realise a fact... that once an attack has failed it was absolutely impossible to improvise a new one."[2]

Given the number of failed attacks over the past twenty two months this revelation suggests that Lyon, was something of a slow learner. Sadly, at senior level, he was not alone in being educationally backward in the dynamics and mechanics of the offensive.

As delay piled on delay the consequences of this chaos would be fatal for hundreds of men of the 56th Division. Whilst the prospect for success still existed (at least in the minds of VII Corps and 46th Divisional staff) the 56th Division not only had to keep on fighting, it had to keep on trying to reinforce its increasingly tenuous lodgement in the German lines. For several hours parties of brave men would struggle out of their trenches in an effort to reach their beleaguered colleagues. Each one would be mown down by machine guns or pulverised by the German artillery.

And so, just after twelve, two machine gun teams struggled across the parapet just to the north of the Bucquoy Road with their Vickers Mk I machine guns. Each gun with its tripod weighed 73 lbs. to which had to be added the weight of the ammunition and water for the cooling jacket. The gun was broken down into two parts. The main gunner, No. 1 in a team of six, carried the tripod. This weighed 40 lbs. The No. 2 carried the gun itself (it weighed 33 lbs.) and, when it was set up, he would supervise the belt feed of the ammunition. Nos. 3 and 4 carried the ammunition whilst No. 4 also took responsibility for the water jacket. Each ammunition box carried a 250-round belt and weighed 22 lbs. and, at best, between them they might have struggled forward with five of them (1,250 rounds equalled just 2½ minutes continuous firing). Nos. 5 and 6 of the team were to be used as scouts and range-takers but here, they would almost certainly have been weighed down with extra ammunition boxes and with petrol cans of water for the journey across No Man's Land. There was a certain urgency to their mission now. Observers in an observation post next to 168th Brigade H.Q. could see large bands of Germans (from the 9th Company, 55th R.I.R.) moving down Epte trench towards the Rangers' position at Felon. The extra firepower of the two machine guns might just turn the tide. They might even then be used to suppress the German Maxims in Nameless Farm that were causing the remnants of the Rangers and the 1/4th Londons so much trouble. But, as the men dragged their loads across the first few yards of No Man's Land, the relentless shellfire and scything bullets of the German machine guns caught them. They were moving

354

too slowly to get anywhere, and those that were not quickly hit, struggled back into the trenches, their equipment lost.

At the junction of Felon and Epte trenches, the men of the Rangers could see the tops of countless German helmets[i] in the long communication trench (the 12th and 9th Companies, 55th R.I.R). They were all moving down the slope towards their position. An attack was imminent. When it came, it was preceded by a flurry of stick grenades to which the Rangers could barely reply, so scarce were their supplies of Mills bombs. They had no alternative but to withdraw towards the German second line, where men of 'B' Company were still holding Felt. It was a hasty and ragged retreat and only the intervention of some 18 pdr shells from the R.F.A. delayed the enemy's progress. By 12.30 p.m. 168th Brigade H.Q. was reporting the loss of the Felon-Epte junction to Division. They also confirmed that their two lead battalions, the Rangers and the London Scottish, had lost contact. They were fighting their own isolated actions. The 1/1st Londons were available to 168th Brigade as a reserve and Hull instructed Brig. Gen. Loch to bring them from their positions in Hebuterne with the hope that they might be able to bridge the gap between the two battalions.

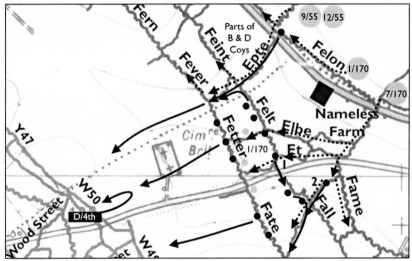

Map 19 Situation 1230-14.30 Rangers front

Legend: ● Location of Rangers' companies in German lines. ⬤ Location of elements of the 1/170th Regiment.
D Company, 1/4th Londons advance c. 1.00 p.m.
1 = 2nd Lt. Harper's party   2 = 2nd Lt. Parker's party

Back in the Observation post near the Brigade H.Q. the situation looked bad. The attack down Epte had very nearly driven a wedge through the British position all the way to the front line. The Germans were only 150 metres short of splitting the British assault in two. It was plain that the Rangers' position was fast becoming untenable. Both wings were exposed to attack - they were barely in touch with either the London Scottish on the right or the Queen Victorias on

---

[i] The steel 'coal scuttle' style helmets were just being introduced at this time and Maj. Philip Neame V.C., Brigade Major of the 168th Brigade, remarked that the bombing parties who counter-attacked during the day were the first men he had seen wearing this design.

the left. Men and supplies were urgently needed if they were to hold. But the constant German barrage made that well nigh impossible and, at 12.45 p.m., Lt. Col. Bayliffe reported to Brigade that there was still no sign of the enemy artillery fire slackening. In spite of that, Bayliffe ordered another carrying party across. One more team of runners set off towards the front lines to pass on the order. Eventually, at 1.20 p.m., C.S.M. Brown and a team of bomb carriers climbed out of the trenches laden with bombs and, shoulders hunched against the storm of shrapnel and bullets, they set off towards 'C' Company's position in Felt trench.

In the trenches on the left of the 168th Brigade's front line position, the 1/4th Londons were losing men steadily to the relentless battering of the German bombardment. The new trenches, so painstakingly dug by the men of the 167th Brigade, had the virtue of moving the British front line forward 350 metres and, by doing so, had reduced the gap between the opposing lines by half. But the effort put into digging the communication trenches out to the new line, the need to wire the positions and to dig machine gun and mortar emplacements had meant that the new lines had not been reinforced and revetted in any significant way. Consequently, the heavy shellfire did disproportionate damage to the trenches and they gave little protection to the troops taking shelter in them. As a result, the reserve companies of the 1/4th Londons were suffering badly, taking casualties every few minutes from the German howitzers pounding the lines. The brutal barrage across No Man's Land had also prevented the 1/4th Londons reinforcing company from getting over to the German lines in support of the Rangers. At 11.50 a.m., a message was received at battalion H.Q. from Capt. Arthur Moore. Timed at 9.05 a.m. it stated that his company was still in its preliminary battle position in W49 trench. As Moore's men should have gone across some time before, a patrol was dispatched down Woman Street to find out the reason for the delay. When the two men, 3267 L/Cpl. Harold Hyde[i] and 4151 Pte. Horace Lear[ii], arrived at the stretch of trench just to the south of the Bucquoy Road, they were told that Capt. Moore's company had indeed gone forward, probably just after Moore's last message was sent. They had disappeared into the forest of black smoke and orange flashes. As previously recounted, this was the last that was seen of Capt. Moore and many of his company.

***

THERE IS SOME CONFUSION about the time what was left of the two machine gun teams sent forward to the London Scottish arrived. They had been despatched at 10.20 a.m. and both of the guns had got over, but not before Sgt. Strachan had gone back out into No Man's Land to help bring the second gun in. The No. 1 in the team, 4135 Cpl. Ralph Millingen, had been hit and he was crawling towards the German trenches, dragging his Vickers gun with him, when

---

[i] 3267 Pte Harold Edward Hyde, 1/4th London Regt (Royal Fusiliers), was awarded the Military Medal as a result of this action. Recommended for a commission he was killed on 9th September 1916 near Bouleaux Wood. His body was never found and his name is inscribed on the Thiepval Memorial, Pier and Face 9D and 16B.

[ii] 4151 Pte Horace Victor Lear, 1/4th London Regt (Royal Fusiliers), was killed on 7th October 1916 during the Battle of Le Transloy Ridge. Aged 19, he was the son of Clara Helen Lear of 20, Driffield Rd., Roman Rd., Bow, London, and the late John Lear. His body was never found and his name is inscribed on the Thiepval Memorial, Pier and Face 9D and 16B.

Strachan arrived to help[i]. Casualties amongst the gun teams, however, meant only one gun could be brought into action. Thomson and his men took up position at the southern end of the strongpoint near the junction of Fair and Farmyard trenches facing towards the trenches occupied by the 6th Company, 170th Regiment. Here, they could cover the open expanse of rolling countryside that ran to the south east. Any attempts by the Germans to bomb up Fair or Fancy or to bring up reserves via the Sunken Road or Arun trench could now be covered.

But they could only be covered so long as there was enough ammunition, and by noon that was starting to run short. Another poor soul was selected as a runner and ordered by Lt. Thomson to get a message through: "bring up MG ammunition urgently". In spite of the shell swept No Man's Land (the batteries from Serre, Puisieux and Fork Wood had not been silenced), he got back and, just after one in the afternoon, a carrying party with fifteen boxes of ammunition set off for Lt. Thomson's position. At about the same time, a bomb carrying party of one officer and fifty men of the Kensingtons left the front line. The journey was desperately slow and dangerous for both groups. Their route took them almost along the skyline, excellent targets for any German rifleman or machine gunner watching from the Sunken Road or the trenches to the south. As they scrambled and ducked, dragging their loads with them, the sharp crack and chatter of small arms aimed at them from the right would have joined with the constant crash of artillery shells from the German's hidden batteries. Some of the machine gun ammunition got through, but the Kensington's party suffered badly. Just five boxes of bombs (60 grenades in all) arrived in the Farmyard trenches. The fifty-man team that set off would probably have been carrying a box each. Those that got there had taken nearly an hour to cover the 400 metre stretch of ground.

Only half a company of the Kensingtons had actually left their lines and they were now helping the London Scottish defend the Farmyard strongpoint. The other 3½ companies were cowering in the British trenches, victims of a fearful and continuous battering from German 15 cm and 10.5 cm howitzers. Even though less than ⅛th of the battalion was in close touch with the Germans, the casualties were increasing at a frightening rate. Already, one third of the officers were either killed or wounded. In addition to the three officers from 'D' Company, 2nd Lt. Charles Sach[ii] was dead and Lt. Penn, and 2nd Lts. Bryer, Beggs and Ball were wounded. Another three were to die[iii] and five more were to be wounded before the day was out.

***

<hr>

[i] Both Millingen and Strachan were awarded the Military Medal for their actions on 1st July 1916. Cpl Ralph Edwin Millingen was later transferred to the Machine Gun Corps and commissioned into the Tank Corps.

[ii] 2nd Lt. Charles Burleigh Sach, 1/13th London Regt. (Kensingtons), died on Saturday, 1st July 1916, aged 19. He was the elder son of Charles Frederick and Emily Hannah Sach of 155, Victoria St., Westminster, London. Single, he was born on 18th May 1897 and was educated at the City of London School. He became an insurance clerk with the Clerical, Medical and General Assurance Company in St James's Square, living at 76, Lebanon Gardens in Wandsworth. He attested 6101 Private in the Inns of Court OTC on 15th September 1914 and was commissioned into the 3/13th London Regt. (Kensingtons) on the 24th December 1915. He went to the front on May 25th 1916. His body was never found and his name is inscribed on the Thiepval Memorial, Pier and Face 9 D 9 C 13 C and 12 C. [*Additional sources:* Dick Flory: City of London School Magazine, December 1916; The Inns of Court O.T.C. during the Great War]

[iii] The three that died were: Capt. Francis Henry Ware (see footnote page 372), 2nd Lt. Henry Bastick Pilgrim (see footnote page 390) and 2nd Lt. Noel Olliffe Compton Mackenzie.

BY NOON, THE PRESSURE on the L.R.B. was almost intolerable. Covered by machine guns set up within the Village, heavy bombing attacks were converging on either end of Eck trench. At the Cemetery end of the trench, the 11ᵗʰ Company of the 55ᵗʰ R.I.R. was pressing hard down Ems and Emden. At 12.30 p.m. a bombing party from the 11ᵗʰ Company collided with a mixed party of L.R.B.s and Q.V.R.s and their advance was held up for some thirty minutes. In the centre and on the left of Eck, the 10ᵗʰ, the Pioneers and parts of the 7ᵗʰ Company, 55ᵗʰ R.I.R., were threatening the British position down Exe, Erin and Fibre trenches. In the park, the rest of the 7ᵗʰ Company led by Hauptmann der Reserve Brockmann plus the 8ᵗʰ and 6ᵗʰ Companies were now inching forward through the trees from Hauser Graben showering the men of 'A' Company, L.R.B. with stick grenades. For the British, this was most galling. Almost every Mills bomb and stick grenade they could find had already been used up.

In Eck, Capt. de Cologan, the C.O. of 'D' Company, realised that if he and his men stayed there they would be cut off. Orders were passed along and the men moved to the left towards the junction with Exe trench in order to keep in touch with the rest of the battalion. In the confusion caused by the attacks, however, the orders did not reach everyone. 2ⁿᵈ Lt. Petley and his platoon, along with a small group of Victorias and Westminsters, were left behind in Eck trench.

Back in the 169ᵗʰ Brigade H.Q., the apparent failure to move towards the Quadrilateral was causing Brig. Gen. Coke considerable frustration. Peering through binoculars from the observation positions, his staff officers had repeatedly commented on the emptiness of the position and of the trenches leading to it. Confirmation of this fact was brought in the shape of messages from the observer of a No. 8 Squadron BE2c. Armed with this intelligence, a number of runners had been sent forward with messages exhorting the Victorias and Westminsters to move aggressively up Ems trench, but, to date, all forms of communication had failed. Coke now turned to the men of the reserve battalion, the 1/2ⁿᵈ Londons, and called for volunteer runners. Incredibly, four men stepped forward and, at 12.35 p.m. they set off by different routes in an effort to get forward to the men who could be seen in the German third line. Coke's rather tetchy message read:

"R.F.C. observers repeatedly report Ems, Etch and the Quadrilateral empty of Germans. Push on bombings parties at once and occupy Quadrilateral whilst opportunity offers. Barrage on Quadrilateral lifts at 1.30 p.m. Ends."

Of the four men who set out, two made it across No Man's Land. 4248 Cpl. Frederick Werner and 6332 L/Cpl. Arthur Boyceⁱ, having somehow survived the carnage between the opposing lines, then set off to find the officers in charge of the two battalions. Werner reached the Q.W.R.s in the German lines and looked for an officer to whom to deliver his message. The most senior man he could find was the seriously wounded C.S.M. Donald Hawker of the Westminsters who was lying in the German front line trench. Hawker had been joined at about 2.00 p.m. by Sgt Courtenay and some twenty men who had been driven out of the German third and then second lines by counter-attacks coming in from the right where the Rangers attack had completely collapsed. Courtenay had advised

---

ⁱ 6332 L/Cpl. Arthur R Boyce was attached to the 1/16ᵗʰ London Regt. (Queen's Westminster Rifles) from the 2/2ⁿᵈ London Regt.

Hawker that his men had run out of supplies of both bombs and small arms ammunition and asked the now conscious Hawker what they should do. Hawker had just suggested building a trench block to their right and to start collecting weapons, bombs and ammunitions from the dead and wounded when Werner arrived breathlessly in the trench after a journey of, it seems, over two hours from Brigade Headquarters. Werner's message was addressed to 'Any Officer' but there were none nearby and so Hawker assumed responsibility for reading and responding to the contents. The instruction to move forward to take the German third and fourth line was clearly an impossibility but, as Werner volunteered to go back with a reply, Hawker had someone write a message to Brig. Gen. Coke acknowledging receipt of his message and making a request for immediate support. Ignoring the dangers and the long odds that he would survive, Cpl. Werner headed back off through the German wire. He was not seen alive again[i]. Boyce, meanwhile, had met some men of the Queen Victorias as they left the German front line trenches and about to make the dangerous journey back to the British lines. He was told that the whole battalion was on the move. The attack had failed. They were retreating. In this event, Boyce's message seemed somewhat irrelevant and he too turned and hurried back to his own lines. His message for the Brigadier General would not be well received[ii].

Even more dismaying for the General was the news from the divisional artillery. The problem of broken buffer springs was now so widespread that a large proportion of the 18 pdrs and some of the 4.5 in. howitzers were temporarily out of action. In total, the 56ᵗʰ Division had 48 field guns and 12 howitzers at their disposal. They had been split into three groups: the Northern Group[iii] (commanded by Lt. Col. Southam), the Southern Group[iv] (commanded by Lt. Col. Macdowell) and the Wire-Cutting Group[v] (commanded Lt. Col. Prechtel). In broad terms, The Northern Group (known as Southart) looked after the attack of the 169ᵗʰ Brigade, with its targets ranging between Fit trench on the left to Fever trench on the right. The Southern Group (Macart) fired on the 168ᵗʰ Brigade front from Nameless Farm to the Sunken Road. The Wire-Cutting Group (Peltart) was to be used for longer ranging fire into the rear areas and acted independently of the attacking Brigades. Each group comprised four 18 pdr batteries and one 4.5 in. howitzer battery (although two of Peltart's howitzers were on call for Corps directed counter-battery work). In the period of the seven-day bombardment, these sixty guns had fired 126,404 shells. The 18 pdrs had fired an average of 340 shells per day for seven days. Now, at a crucial time, the gunners and their guns were beginning to wear out. At 12.05 p.m., Southart reported that only 13 guns out of twenty were firing. All of the 18 pdrs of A/280 and C/280 batteries were in action but only four guns from the other three batteries. There is every reason to believe that the Macart and Peltart

---

[i] 4248 Cpl Frederick Stevens Werner M.M., 1/2ⁿᵈ London Regt (Royal Fusiliers), died on Saturday, 1ˢᵗ July 1916. Aged 22, he was the son of Louis George and Dorothy S. Werner. He was born at Clifton, Cincinnati, Ohio, U.S.A. He is buried in Bienvillers Military Cemetery, grave XXI. G. 9.
[ii] Both Boyce and Werner were awarded the Military Medal for their actions.
[iii] Northern Group (Southart): B/280, C/280, A/283, D/282 plus A/280 which joined from the Wire-Cutting Group at Zero hour.
[iv] Southern Group (Macart): A/281, B/281, C/281, D/281, 109.
[v] Wire Cutting Group (Peltart): A/282, B/282, C/282, C/283, A/280, D/280. A/280 joined the Northern Group at Zero hour.

groups were experiencing the same difficulties. Just when the infantry needed their support most, a third of the field artillery was out of action[i].

Observers in the 169th Brigades reserve lines now watched as large groups of German troops moved along the Switch line on the ridge opposite and then disappeared down Epte, Ems and Etch trenches. It was clear that another major counter-attack was imminent. German attacks had already punched a hole between the L.R.B. and the combined Q.W.R./Q.V.R. lines around the Cemetery, now they seemed intent on driving all three battalions out of the third German line. At 12.30 p.m. the attack started. At the junction of Fellow and Etch trenches, the attack came from three directions. German bombing teams were pressing in from the left. To the right, they had come up behind the trench block hurriedly built by the Cheshires some hours before. Corporal Ratcliffe had kept possession of the Lewis gun he had used to good effect earlier in the day and now he turned it on the Germans massing in Fell trench. To their front, more bombers were thrusting down Etch. The imbalance in the supply of grenades was the decisive factor. All along the line, the Londoners gave ground. In Feud and Fellow trenches, 2nd Lt. James Horne of 'B' Company, Q.W.R., had spent the whole morning organising and directing his men. They had worked frantically to reverse the trenches and tried building blocks in the communication trenches when it became clear that they were no longer on the offensive. They had ransacked dugouts for supplies of German bombs but, now, even they were all used up. Horne had even taken over a Lewis gun when all the team had been killed or wounded, using the ammunition supply sparingly to keep the German bombers and snipers at bay. Now, as he watched the counter-attack develop, he decided that withdrawal to the next line of German trenches was the only sensible option, to do otherwise risked being cut off and overwhelmed. He gave the orders to withdraw and, as his men backed down the short stretch of Emden trench towards the German second line (Feed), 2nd Lt. Horne and some Lewis gunners covered their retreat. One by one they were picked off by the advancing Germans until only he remained to fire the gun and protect the retreating men. It was whilst doing this that he was hit and killed[ii]. His friend, 2nd Lt. Moy, wrote later:

> "Horne apparently did a VC stunt, holding up the enemy by Lewis gun fire until the ammunition was exhausted, then throwing bombs, then firing his revolver until he was killed."[3]

Lt. Col. Shoolbred agreed that his young subaltern's courage deserved official recognition[iii]:

---

[i] In a report written by Brig. Gen. Elkington, G.O.C. 56th Division Artillery he wrote:
"It seems obvious that before such operations a liberal supply of springs and all spare parts should be collected at places close to the Division in action... this had not been done and there were many cases of guns being out of action through delay in supply of springs, etc. This had the effect of putting extra strain on other guns... and resulting in further breakdowns."
[ii] 2nd Lt. James Anthony Horne, 1/16th London Regt. (Queen's Westminster Rifles), died on Saturday, 1st July 1916, aged 23. He was the son of the Rev. Joseph White Horne and Katherine Grace Horne of 8, Stradmore Gardens, Kensington, London. At University studying for the priesthood he enlisted on the outbreak of war and joined the battalion at Ypres in November 1915. He is buried in Gommecourt British Cemetery No. 2, grave Sp. Mem. C.5
[iii] Horne's brave sacrifice would go officially unrecognised.

"The honour of the Victoria Cross would not have been more than his bravery and leadership merited. The few survivors spoke of him and his conduct throughout the day in terms of glowing admiration."[4]

Horne's death left just two junior officers in charge of the remnants of the Westminsters. 2nd Lt. Edward Bovill had been wounded in the nose very early in the morning. He was now the senior officer from 'A' Company still standing. 2nd Lt. Upton was the only remaining officer of 'C' Company. Between them, they gathered their men and prepared for the next and imminent onslaught. In Ferret trench, in the German front line, 3218 Rfn. Eric Long[i] was working a Venetian shutter in a desperate effort to get messages across to the other side of No Man's Land. His message was picked up by a low flying BE2c of the R.F.C. at around 1 p.m. The message was soon to be replicated by the signallers of the L.R.B. from the fringes of Gommecourt Park. It simply read: 'SOS Bombs, SOS Bombs'. As the message flickered out a general attack broke across what was left of the British positions. The Germans were moving in for the kill.

***

THE L.R.B.'S POSITION WAS NOW GRAVE. Lt. 'Curly' Boston and the battalion bombers had fought for every inch of trench; they had fought heroically and none more so than 1176 Cpl. Horace Cowlin. Cowlin led his section of bombers into the German trenches and had been engaged in fierce exchanges with the Germans pressing from the Park. He was about to throw a Mills grenade when a bullet struck his wrist sending the 'live' bomb tumbling into the bottom of the crowded trench. There was no time to shout a warning and, in the noise and confusion, it was doubtful whether anyone would have heard. And, anyway, what could the nearby men do? The trench was packed with bombers with little room to move let alone find a safe place in which to take cover. Cowlin knew this and did not think twice. With thought only for the safety of his men he dived onto the bomb, smothering its detonation. He was killed instantly.[ii]

Plate 41 1176 Rfn Horace Cowlin, London Rifle Brigade, killed 1st July 1916

---

i 3218 Rfn. Eric D Long, 1/16th London Regt. (Queen's Westminster Rifles), was awarded the Military Medal for his actions on 1st July 1916.
ii 1176 Cpl Horace Cowlin, A Company, 1/5th London Regt. (London Rifle Brigade) was killed on Saturday, 1st July 1916. Aged 35, he was married with two children and had been a jeweller in Ilford High Road before he enlisted in November 1914. There is a weather-shelter erected to his memory today in Valentine's Park at Ilford. His body was never found and his name is inscribed on the Thiepval Memorial, Pier and Face 9 D.

Cowlin was not the only brave man from 'A' Company to die that day in the furious but increasingly one sided bombing battle taking place on the fringe of the Park. 2796 Rfn. Norman Crabb was one of a party of men including 1520 Rfn. Fred Imeson[i] and 2745 Rfn. Arthur Richardson[ii] trying desperately to keep the German bombers at bay. After the battle, the wounded Imeson and Richardson both wrote to Norman Crabb's distraught sister describing the heroic death of her brother. Richardson's description read:

'We were occupying a German trench we had taken at Gommecourt close to our machine gun (note: probably a Lewis Gun) which was covering a wood through which German bombing parties were constantly attacking us. One of these parties were (sic) bombing us – a serious danger to our position – when Rfn. Crabb climbed out of the trenches with some bombs and succeeded in driving them off with loss. He nearly got back safely when a bomb must have exploded near him, his tin hat went flying, and we pulled him back in the trench, hoping he was only wounded but to find that he had given his life in the act of saving many of our lives. We laid him reverently in the trench, covering him over, but being driven out of that trench the same evening we regretted having to leave the body of such a brave comrade behind. I trust the knowledge of his having died in such a noble way will give you strength to bear this great loss.'

According to Imeson, Crabb's fatal wound was a piece of shrapnel to the neck which must have severed at major artery as he described Crabb's death as "almost instantaneous". The gallant rifleman's body was never found.[iii]

Plate 42 2796 Rfn. Norman Crabb, London Rifle Brigade, killed 1st July 1916

But now their bombs were all thrown. Boston had then forced some German prisoners to fetch German grenades from their dugouts, and he had kept the prisoners working all day until even the generous supply of some 300 stick

---

i 1520 Rfn. Frederick G Imeson, A Company, 1/5th London Regt. (London Rifle Brigade) was wounded on Saturday, 1st July 1916 and was evacuated to Bed 746, Ward 13, 1st Eastern General Hospital in Cambridge.
ii 2745 Rfn. Arthur G Richardson, A Company, 1/5th London Regt. (London Rifle Brigade) was wounded on Saturday, 1st July 1916 and was evacuated to the VAD Hospital, Newton Abbott, Devon.
iii 2796 Rfn. Norman Frank Crabb, A Company, 1/5th London Regt. (London Rifle Brigade), was killed on Saturday, 1st July 191. Aged 26, he was the son of Thomas & Martha Crabb of 72, Parchmore Rd., Thornton Heath, Surrey His body was never found and his name was inscribed on the Thiepval Memorial, Pier and Face 9 D

grenades was used up and he was himself twice badly wounded[i]. In this work he was ably assisted by 660 Sgt. Percy Dyer, the battalion Bombing Sergeant who, for his efforts, was awarded the Military Medal. Col. Bates wrote about him:

> "My bombing Sergeant, who, with three others, is the only survivors of my Battalion Bombers. He behaved with great gallantry throughout the action at Gommecourt. After all our own grenades had been thrown he organised the collection of German grenades, of which a very large number were used."[5]

But now, pressed from all sides, their bombs all used up, their only hope was that somehow reserves and supplies could get be brought across. But, if they were to be effective, they were needed now, before their position became utterly hopeless. Somehow, this had to be communicated to the men waiting in the British lines.

When they had gone over, some battalion signallers had gone over with the early waves. Now they were established along the battalion front with the Venetian shutters they had so painstakingly carried with them across No Man's Land. They had only been taken as a precaution against emergencies – an emergency such as this. The first message flickered out from the base of Exe trench at 12.49 p.m.[ii] and was sent by 1220 L/Cpl Victor Lewis Fowle of the London Rifle Brigade. Fowle was in charge of the battalion's visual signalling party and had originally been ordered to set up a position at Point 94 but the fighting here was too fierce and he moved to the right to a position at the end of Exe trench before starting to send his vital message. It was picked up by an R.F.A. observer, spotting for his 18 pdr section dug in on the north side of Hebuterne. Four minutes later, the same message was seen flashing from Fibre trench on the western side of the Maze. Then, at a few minutes past one o'clock, the same flickering lights and the same desperate message was seen from Ferret trench. In the Z Hedge, No. 15 Platoon, 1/3ʳᵈ Londons under Lt. Johnson and a machine gun team were lying waiting and observing the southern end of Gommecourt Park. Just before 1 p.m., as they were watching the desperate flickering of the signals from the corner of the park, a salvo of German shells crashed down onto their concealed positions. By the end of the day, only Johnson and one man were left unscathed. For what seemed like an age, the dim

---

[i] Lt. Geoffrey Greenwood Boston DCM, 1/5ᵗʰ London Regt. (London Rifle Brigade), was educated at Weymouth College and lived at 'Monfode', Furze Lane, Purley. He was a clerk with Duncker, Joly and Collins. He attested 9497 Private on 6ᵗʰ February 1914, joining 'A' Company. He went to France in November 1914. Promoted Lance Corporal on 26ᵗʰ September 1914, he was commissioned in the field on 8ᵗʰ May 1915. He was awarded the DCM for conspicuous bravery at the 2ⁿᵈ Battle of Ypres (London Gazette, 14ᵗʰ January 1916). Promoted Lieutenant on 9ᵗʰ August, he was appointed Bombing Officer on 26ᵗʰ October 1915. Boston was severely wounded at Gommecourt and was gazetted out of the Army on 26ᵗʰ February 1918 as a result of his wounds with the honorary rank of Captain. He was recommended for, but did not receive, an award for his conduct at Gommecourt. The recommendation read:
"This officer behaved with the utmost gallantry and organised all the bombing attacks in Gommecourt Park which materially helped the companies who were endeavouring to consolidate there. He personally compelled the enemy to collect and supply him with a large number of their own bombs which were used with good effect by our men. He was severely wounded in two places."
[ii] 1220 L/Cpl Victor Lewis Fowle of the 1/5ᵗʰ London Regt (London Rifle Brigade) was awarded the Military Medal for his actions on 1ˢᵗ July 1916. The citation in the London Gazette of the 1ˢᵗ September 1916 read:
"This NCO was in charge of the visual signalling party sent across with the assaulting troops on July 1ˢᵗ, 1916. He attempted to establish his station as arranged at point 94, but found this was impossible. He then moved to the base of Exe, where he established his station, and, using his Venetian blind, got the 'S.O.S. bombs' message through to me (Lt. Col. Bates). He behaved with coolness and gallantry throughout the action." [*Source*: Chris Rippingale]

lights blinked on and off, each an imploring plea for deliverance. The message was of twenty-five short and long flashes. They all started the same: ··· --- ···. The watching officers and men in the British trenches all understood the international sign for help: S.O.S. Only those familiar with Morse code understood the rest of the message and the others turned to them for translation. As each group of lights was read, each letter was whispered: B-O-M-B-S. "S.O.S. Bombs, S.O.S. Bombs" was the despairing message from the German lines just 350 metres away. In the British lines the men looked towards Gommecourt in grim impotence. And, in the German trenches, the men of the London Rifle Brigade were throwing their last bombs.

In the L.R.B.'s H.Q. Col. Bates was desperate for accurate information. Looking about he found two battalion runners waiting for orders. The same note was scribbled twice and one each given to Rfn. Arthur Hollis and the other man. They were told to find either Capt. Somers-Smith or Capt. de Cologan and get back as soon as humanly possible. Hurrying off down what was left of the Hebuterne to Gommecourt road they headed towards Fen trench. Hollis' fellow runner was soon wounded in the wrist but Hollis carried on, reaching the German lines where the message was passed to an L.R.B. sergeant. He then turned back and somehow reached the partial sanctuary of the British lines, sustaining an injury on the way. But he had nothing useful to report because there was nothing that could be done.

***

BY 1.00 P.M. THE WITHDRAWAL from the German third line became general. The collapse of the Rangers position around Nameless Farm meant that German troops were now pouring down Epte trench and were outflanking the men of the 169ᵗʰ Brigade. As another forlorn attempt by fragments of the Queen's Westminster Rifles to reinforce and re-supply broke down within yards of the British lines, positions in the third line were abandoned. Because of the pressure from their right caused by the breakthrough at Epte, the remains of the Q.V.R.s, Q.W.R.s and a few Rangers retired diagonally to the left, heading towards Ferret trench in the German front line. It seems that the men in the support trenches moved first and the most advanced withdrew when it became clear they were in danger of being cut-off from flank and rear. Because the German artillery had now also heavily bombarded the trenches there was, in places, little to be gained by trying to follow their shattered path. Some men made the decision to go over ground and many were caught in the open by German machine guns now set up on the edges of Gommecourt village. Capt. Leys Cox, the most senior Q.V.R. officer in the German trenches and known to officers and, behind his back, the men as 'The Bantam', had been trying to send runners across No Man's Land for some time with requests for help and explanations of their position. The last one to reach the Q.V.R.'s advanced HQ at 12.20 p.m. read:

"To O.C. Q.V.R.

Reached third line German trenches. Cannot get in touch with Rangers. Q.W.R. still in third line German trench with us. Boches still very active. Barrage would help beyond third line. Bombs required urgent.

Leys Cox"

One by one the runners had left the battered German trenches and one by one they had been knocked over. Eventually, Cox's batman, 2218 Rfn. Percy Armitage stepped forward and was given his Captain's note. He slipped over the German parapet and headed off up the gentle slope towards the British lines. At about the same time, another runner, 1421 Rfn. Lawrence Collins from 'B' Company, was also attempting the crossing of this lethal patch of ground. That both succeeded and survived is remarkable, though Armitage was wounded in the attempt, and their bravery was recognised with the award of the Military Medal[i]. Their news, though, was the same: the Q.V.R. could no longer hold their position. They were pulling back towards the German front lines.

***

AT THE SAME TIME, the bombardment on the front lines either side of the Bucquoy Road had rendered the positions of the 1/4th Londons untenable. Capt. Stanham[ii], the C.O. of 'D' Company, sent a message to battalion H.Q. saying his unit had suffered 50% casualties - what should he do? The reply was not the one he anticipated. He was told to send a bombing squad over with as many grenades as they could carry. A few minutes later, another small group of men, weighed down with bombs, climbed the ladders into No Man's Land. They hunched their shoulders against the metal storm of bullets, shrapnel and shell splinters and set off stoically for the German lines. Not one got across. Every man was killed or wounded.

Back at battalion H.Q., an order was received from Brigade. Something needed to be done to bridge the gap between the Rangers and the London Scottish. The advance of the Kensingtons had foundered within yards of their own trench. No matter, now the 1/4th Londons should send a company forward to achieve what the Kensingtons could not. Everything told the officers at the Fusilier's H.Q. that it could not be done, but the order was there. Every effort would be made to comply. A runner was found, the order was written, and he set off down the blasted and wrecked trenches to deliver his unwelcome news.

Further back, 168th Brigade H.Q. was trying to put together another, somewhat more ambitious, plan to stabilise their front. The 1/1st Londons, allocated to the brigade by Division, were going to be the key to success. One company was to try to plug the gap between the Scottish and the Rangers either side of Elbe trench and another was to cross opposite Epte and drive up the communication trench in order to re-establish contact with the Q.V.R. and Q.W.R. to their left. Like so many plans it looked good on paper. Nothing would come of it and the battalion would remain in the reserve trenches around Cross Street as an insurance against the Germans taking advantage of the chaos to launch a sneak attack on the British positions.

---

[i] Rfn Collins was later awarded the Russian Cross of St George, 4th Class.
[ii] Capt. Hugh G Stanham, TD., 1/4th London Regt. (Royal Fusiliers) joined from the 2/4th London Regt. on 14th May 1916. he went on to become Lt. Col. of the battalion in the late 20s and was promoted full Colonel in 1931, retiring in 1934. He was elected a Fellow of the Royal Institute of British Architects in 1939.

To their right Major Cedric Dickens[i], the C.O. of 'A' Company of the 1/13th Kensingtons, had been in the front line trenches almost since the battle began. His company had been detailed to dig a communication trench across to the German lines, linking the head of Whiskey Street to a German sap that projected from the middle of the Farmyard strong point. Within minutes of the attack going in it had become clear that the job was simply impossible. The company had, instead, occupied the front line trenches and, from time to time, tried to answer the increasingly desperate requests for ammunition and reinforcements that were sent back by runner by the London Scottish. He had now spent six hours watching the trenches destroyed and his men maimed and killed by the thunderous bombardment of the German howitzers. Now, of 'A' and 'C' Companies, just 50 men remained. At just after 1 p.m., Major Dickens sent 2nd Lt. Dawes back to headquarters with a dispirited message back to Battalion H.Q.:

"Shelling fearful. Trench practically untenable, full of dead and wounded. Very few men indeed left. Must have instructions and assistance."

Plate 43 Maj. C C Dickens, I/I3th London Regt. (Kensingtons)
(Photograph 'The Great War', volume 8)

The shelling certainly was 'fearful'. Peltart, the independent group of field artillery batteries, had reported to 56th Division H.Q. at 1.10 p.m. that the German barrage was:

"As heavy if not heavier than at any other time this morning."[6]

And it was under this ferocious bombardment that the Kensingtons were forced to stand, wait and suffer. Their frustration was intense. Certainly, their colleagues in the attacking battalions were suffering heavy casualties but they, at

---

[i] Major Cedric Charles Dickens, 1/13th London Regt. (Kensingtons), died on Saturday, 9th September 1916 in an attack near Ginchy. His body was never found and his name is inscribed on the Thiepval Memorial, Pier and Face 9 D 9 C 13 C and 12 C. There is a special memorial to Major Dickens between Ginchy and Bouleaux Wood near where he was last seen. He was born on 8th March 1889, the son of Sir Henry Dickens KC., and Lady Dickens of 8, Mulberry Walk, Chelsea, London and the grandson of the author, Charles Dickens. Dickens was educated at Eton and Trinity Hall, Cambridge before being commissioned into the Kensingtons on 20th April 1909. Single, he qualified as a solicitor in March 1913 and was Managing Clerk in the firm of Coward, Hawksley, Sons and Chance, 30 Mincing Lane, E C. He had been wounded previously by a rifle bullet at La Bassee on 22nd February 1915. [*Additional source*: Dick Flory: Eton School Register, Part VII, 1899-1909; Etonians Who Fought in the Great War, 1914-1919; Eton College Chronicle, 5 October 1916; Record of Services of Solicitors and Articled Clerks 1914-1918]

least, had got to grips with the enemy. Only half a company of the Kensingtons had seen such action. The bulk of their dead and wounded were being caused by an enemy they could not see, let alone reach. Somewhere, a few thousand metres behind some low hills to the east, teams of German gunners were pouring a continuous rain of high explosive onto the heads of the Kensingtons. They could only sit there and take it. And their casualties were mounting at a most alarming rate. Extraordinarily, by the end of the day, this battalion, whose men had barely seen a German all day, would suffer 59% casualties – more than the Rangers who had led the attack on the 168th Brigade's left.[i]

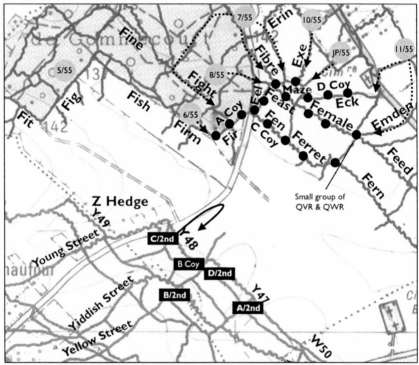

Map 20 Situation early afternoon London Rifle Brigade front
Legend: C Company, 1/2nd London Regt. advance c. 1.30 p.m.

By 1.30 p.m., men were leaving the German front lines and heading, as best they could, for the safety of the British lines. All the way, they were chased by the relentless machine gun fire pouring from the Park. Such was the speed of collapse of the British position that concerns arose not just about the safety of the men still in the German lines but about whether the momentum of the German counter-attacks might sweep across No Man's Land and into the British trenches. So, when, at about 1.30 p.m., a party of about two platoons fell back to the British trenches, they were collected together and made to man the fire step along with anyone else still fit to fight. When news arrived at the Westminsters' battalion H.Q. that the attack was collapsing, orders were sent for every available

---

[i] The percentage casualties for the battalions were: Queen's Westminster Rifles 73%, London Scottish 71%, London Rifle Brigade 67%, Queen Victoria's Rifles 66%, Rangers 58%, Kensingtons 59% and the 1/4th Londons 51%.

man to collect in Cross Street, ready to move forward whenever needed. Runners, H.Q. staff, signallers, anyone who could fire a Lee Enfield were turned out and made ready. As they did so, another group of men was thrown into the furnace of No Man's Land. 'D' Company of the reserve battalion, the 1/2nd Londons, were ordered over to reinforce the men now collecting in Ferret trench. They collected their supply of bombs and made ready for the ordeal.

At the same time, the desperate pleas for help from the men of the L.R.B. had been passed to Brigade H.Q. There, Brig. Gen. Coke weighed up his options. They were few. All calls for effective counter-battery work to help reduce the power and weight of the German barrage had failed to achieve the required results. The Stokes mortars had either been put out of action or dismantled and taken across to the German lines, there to be lost. All the covering fire he could organise was from the 169th Machine Gun Company's reserve guns in the WR line. At 1.30 p.m. they were ordered to be ready to provide overhead covering fire when the 1/2nd Londons moved forward. At the same time, messages were sent by Lt. Col. Attenborough of the 1/2nd Londons to his companies to prepare for action. 'D' Company, Capt. Robert Sneath[i], was to go over with bombs. They were to take them to Ferret trench from where they could be distributed to all three attacking battalions in the adjacent trenches. 'C' Company, Capt. Handyside, was to move left in support of the L.R.B. They were ordered to get across to Fen trench and support the men now fighting in Fir, Feast and Female. 'A' Company, Capt. Garland, was to advance on the right of the Brigade front. They were to get into Fern and Fever trenches to support the Q.V.R. and the Q.W.R. With luck, they might make contact with any Rangers still active to the left of Nameless Farm. Such a juncture would help stabilise the front and stop the German bombing parties outflanking the attacking battalions. 'B' Company, Capt. Kellett, was to stay in the Y47 and Y48 trenches as a reserve.

On paper, it looked a viable plan. Reality, however, was another matter. 'C' Company of the 1/2nd Londons had been in reserve in Cross Street when their OC, Capt. Percy Handyside, ordered the men up to the front line trenches. Pte. Clements and his Lewis gun team laboured along the muddy and congested trenches:

"We went up the old line and then to Sap 2 which we went along. Everywhere the trenches were blown in and fellows lay everywhere, some dead. At the top of the sap one chap was half buried, terribly mangled but still living. Others in a like condition were dead all over the place. When we were told to go up I had a touch of 'wind'. Going along the 'commo' trench I got so I didn't care. During a stoppage in Sap 4 Ted Walters said we should have to send somebody back for ammunition and 'Scho' and I volunteered but, in less than half an hour, 'Scho'[ii] was killed and Ted and I wounded. Reaching the top of the sap, we deployed in No Man's Land now, for the time being, ours. The Captain (Capt. P J A Handyside) spoke to me and said, 'Hot work, Clements'. A moment later he got up and said,

---

[i] Capt. Robert Ernest Foster Sneath, M.C., 1/2nd London Regt. (Royal Fusiliers), was a pre-war Territorial, commissioned on 19th October 1912 and promoted Lieutenant on 29th July 1913, and was given command of D Company in May 1915 . He was a graduate of Cambridge University where he was in the OTC. He took command of the battalion in August 1917, leading it through the Battle of Cambrai.
[ii] 2304 Pte Frank Schofield, 1/2nd London Regt. (Royal Fusiliers), was killed on Saturday, 1st July 1916. He is buried in Bienvillers Military Cemetery, XXI. J. 6

'You go now Grainger[i], don't sport for shellfire'. Up we jumped and tore along. Now the machine guns were cracking like hell. We drifted down. A fellow near asked me if I'd help him back. He was wounded in the legs. 'No', I yelled, 'take off your equipment and crawl'. It was rotten. Then the Captain jumped up and yelled, 'Come along boy'. I hesitated for a fraction of a second in the comparative safety of a shell hole then said to myself, 'Come out of that you bloody coward', jumped up and ran on. This took the merest fraction of time. After running a short distance, a perfect hail of shells met us but we still kept on but only a few now. And then I found myself alone. Then I saw a trench ahead and wondered if I should reach it alive. I didn't feel a pain, rather numb in fact but my one hope was that if I were to be killed it would be outright. After dropping into the trench which was only two foot deep I crawled up and down to see if anyone was there but I could only find dead. Feeling rather lost I looked over the top and, at the same time, got a terrific punch on the jaw and saw the blood dripping onto my equipment. Thank heaven I'm wounded. My first thought then was how to get back. I took my equipment off and took a bottle of rum out of my haversack, had a stiff dose which immediately got into my head. Then by running, crawling, walking and dodging I got back into our own line. How it was that I wasn't hit I don't know – pure luck.'[7]

Once 'C' Company left the relative safety of the trenches, they were immediately assailed by heavy machine gun fire from both the Park and Nameless Farm. A few moments later, the redoubled efforts of the German artillerymen, plunged into their ranks. Capt. Handyside was hit within fifteen yards of the parapet. Undaunted, he crawled forward, encouraging his men to get on until a nearby shell burst wounded him mortally. He died the following day[ii]. His men did their best to live up to their Captain's example. They moved forward into the holocaust until all the officers were hit, until staying above ground became more than mortal men could bear. Within less than five minutes it was all over. 'C' Company, 1/2nd Londons had ceased to exist. About fifty survivors of the attack crawled back into the British lines after dark. No one got over[iii].

The intensity of the artillery fire in No Man's Land was later testified to by Rfn. Henry Russell of the London Rifle Brigade. Russell had been wounded earlier in the day two thirds of the way across to the German lines. He had followed the example of 2nd Lt. Archibald Warner in trying to get forward from a

---

i 2nd Lt. John Scott Grainger, 1/2nd London Regt (Royal Fusiliers), was killed on Saturday, 1st July 1916, aged 27. Born on 17th November 1889, he was the third son of Thomas Alexander and Marion Grainger of 122, Main St., Tweedmouth, Berwick-on-Tweed. He attested 2019 Private in the 4th (TF) Queen's Own Cameron Highlanders and was commissioned into the 2/2nd Londons on 16th January 1915, serving in Malta, Gallipoli and Egypt before transferring to the 1/2nd Londons in early June. His body was never found and his name is inscribed on the Thiepval Memorial, Pier and Face 9 D and 16 B. [*Additional Sources:* Pam & Ken Linge, Thiepval Project]

ii Capt. Percy James Alexander Handyside, 1/2nd London Regt (Royal Fusiliers), died from his wounds on Sunday, 2nd July 1916. Born on 10th December 1878, he was the son of James Handyside of Redcourt, Pyrford, Surrey. He was a merchant in the Brazilian trade. Known in the battalion as 'Uncle' he married Dorothy Handyside (nee Hampshire) on 20th May 1916, six weeks before his death. They were married in Pyrford Parish Church and lived at Hill View, Pirbright in Surrey. Born in St Petersburg, Russia on 10th December 1878 he was educated by a private tutor in Stuttgart and at a college in Bruges. He was commissioned into the 2nd Londons on 7th October 1913 and was promoted Captain on 21st April 1915. Originally interred in Gommecourt No. 4 Cemetery his body was moved in the post-war cemetery concentrations and he is now buried in Gommecourt British Cemetery No. 2, Hebuterne, grave II.L.II.

iii After the war, Sir Charles Wakefield, the Lord Mayor of London in 1916, who had visited the battalions of the 56th Division shortly before the attack, compared the advance of the 1/2nd Londons to the Charge of the Light Brigade.

shell hole but Warner had been immediately killed and Russell hit twice within a few seconds. Looking for a 'better hole', Russell had crawled some distance before dropping into another crater already occupied by the severely wounded 1498 Rfn. Archibald Norris. Norris told Russell of his wound: the bullet had hit him in the middle of the back, then hitting one or more bones had tumbled upwards, exiting through his left ear. His internal injuries must have been severe and the pain and blood loss considerable but still the man talked, rather optimistically in Russell's view, about whether they might end up in the same hospital. Such discussions were brought to a premature halt when a heavy barrage started to fall about them:

> "For those who do not know the meaning of the word 'barrage', I should explain that barrage, or 'tir-de-barrage' to give it it's full name, was a method of fire originated by the French Army and copied by the Germans and ourselves. The idea was not to fire at given targets but to put down a carpet of fire mathematically calculated to hit everything over a given area so that nothing could survive there."[8]

Russell had summed up the German artillery plan succinctly – lay an impenetrable curtain of fire along No Man's Land to prevent any movement either to or from the captured German trenches. Both men soon fell victim to the German gunners when a shell exploded on the rim of their crater. The badly wounded Norris[i] was killed instantly and Russell was "virtually emasculated". Lying in the shell hole, No Man's Land a carpet of explosions, Russell concluded that his situation was hopeless and that, even in the event of a miraculous escape, his new wounds rendered him unfit for anything in the world. His wounds were appalling: his left arm was torn and the bone shattered, his left thigh and right leg were cut and gashed and "strips of flesh" hung from his abdomen. With his prospects bleak, Russell decided to end it all but could not decide on the best method. He had three options: detonate a Mills grenade he had in his pocket; consume the large number of morphine tablets he had previously found on the body of a doctor about to be buried; or drink the contents of a Worcester Sauce bottle full of rum he had concealed in his haversack in the hope that the resulting increase in bleeding would soon see him off. Russell discounted the grenade option for the rather illogical reason that "it would only be doing what the Germans were already attempting to do". The morphine overdose proved impossible as the tube containing them had been lost sometime during the attack. This left the rum and Russell downed the lot. It did not have the desired effect:

> "… it did me no harm at all. It probably made me slightly merry and bright and rather stupefied. It also probably caused me to drop off to sleep… I came to the conclusion, when I had recovered my senses, that, in spite of my condition, it was still worthwhile making a serious effort to save myself."[9]

371 Rfn. Henry Russell somehow survived, but his wounds were such that he took no further active part in the Great War.

***

---

[i] 1498 Rfn. Archibald William Norris, 1/5ᵗʰ London Regt. (London Rifle Brigade), was killed on Saturday, 1ˢᵗ July 1916. Aged 22, he was the son of Henry & Annie Norris of 'Elmslie', Bourne End, Bucks He was buried in Gommecourt British Cemetery No. 2, Special Memorial B. 17.

CONCERN WAS NOW GROWING about the possibility of a German attack on the British trenches on the 168th Brigade front, at least in the minds of the Brigade's staff. This was viewed as such a serious possibility that signallers, runners, servants and even shell-shock cases were collected together as a reserve in case of trouble. These thirty-two men under Capt. Harris of the Kensingtons' 'B' Company and 2nd Lt. Dawes, 'stood to' in the old front line. From where they were, they could see that the trenches in front of them had practically ceased to exist. Somewhere out there, in the ruins of the front line, Major Dickens was in despair:

"Sap absolutely impassable owing to shell fire. Every party that enters it is knocked out at once. Captain Ware has been wounded somewhere there. I have just crawled to the end of it with Scottish machine gun party. Could not find him. One of the Scottish had his hand blown off. Our front line is in an awful state. Two more men killed and one wounded. Estimate casualties to 'A' and 'C' Companies at least 25 killed and 5 wounded. Impossible to man large lengths of our front line."

Twenty five minutes later Major Dickens sent another despondent message to his battalion H.Q.:

"I have, as far as I can find, only 13 left besides myself. Trenches unrecognisable. Quite impossible to hold. Bombardment fearful for last two hours. I am the only officer left. Please send instructions."

The message took 45 minutes to travel 400 metres. It arrived with another that confirmed that 2nd Lt. Mackenzie had been killed[i].

Unknown to Dickens, the unfortunate Capt. Ware, O.C. 'C' Company, was dead, not wounded. Ware was a popular Company commander, fortyish, slightly greying, tall and well built, he made a good impression on his men and had a penchant for giving out chocolate whilst on his rounds in the trenches. He was killed by shell fire leading his men into No Man's Land laden with bombs for the London Scottish.

His only surviving relatives were his brother Charles and sister Florence and, in the absence of any definitive information about his fate, she set to finding out what she could from the men who had served with her brother, many of whom were now in hospital recovering from wounds suffered on 1st July. The first to respond was 3995 Pte Albert Phillips who wrote to Miss Ware at her Hampstead home from his bed in Ward 5, Lord Derby's War Hospital in Warrington. Writing on the 24th July, Phillips told how he had been in Ware's 'C' Company for twelve months and had trained under him in Richmond Park and Tadworth. He then told how the Captain had set off with some other officers to take bombs to the London Scottish but, within a short distance, the whole group was hit and fell to the ground. Phillips and a few others led by a sergeant then tried themselves to get across and they passed Ware's body. Phillips was one of the few to arrive in the Scottish's trenches and, as he returned to the British lines, he was hit in the thigh by a machine bullet and his battle was ended.

---

i 2nd Lt. Noel Olliffe Compton Mackenzie, 1/13th London Regt. (Kensingtons), died on Saturday, 1st July 1916. He was the son of W O C Mackenzie and Geraldine Oliffe Augusta Mackenzie of 36, Park Village East, Regent's Park, NW1. A medical student, Mackenzie was attested private in the R.A.M.C. on 4th October 1914 and was attached to the 54th Field Ambulance. He was gazetted 2nd Lt. in the Kensingtons on 25th February 1915. His body was never found and his name is inscribed on the Thiepval Memorial, Pier and Face 9 D 9 C 13 C and 12 C.

On the 31st July two further reports were forward to Miss Ware from the British Red Cross. From his hospital bed in Le Treport, 4356 Pte Cecil Pert told how he had accompanied Ware up the sap as part of the carrying party and had seen him hit by shrapnel. Carrying on, Pert then found the German barrage impenetrable and returned to Capt. Dickens to report on Ware's fate and to tell him where he was lying, on which news Dickens declared he would find him and bring him in. Pert was then wounded and was unable to give any further information about the fates of either Ware or Dickens. 4193 Pte Richard Allibone, 'C' Company, also in hospital at Le Treport, was the provider of gloomy hearsay. His evidence was heard from a Pte Williams who had been the servant to 2nd Lt. Pike, the OC of No. 10 Platoon, 'C' Company, but Williams report was definite: he had seen Capt. Ware lying dead in the sap.

Just over two weeks later 4162 Pte Edwin Williams wrote to Miss Ware directly. His letter left no doubts:

"... I think that nothing at all has been heard of our old dear Captain Ware since July 1st and I expect I must have been the last man to come across (him)... I met Captain Ware after the attack and I could not fetch him round any way as I shook him and spoke to him but could see no signs of life so I gave up all hopes and one of my comrades said that he was killed right enough but if there had been any life left in Captain Ware I should have willingly brought him in to the dressing station. I am sorry we have lost one of the best officers in the battalion."[10]

It would seem that Miss Ware was still not yet convinced by the evidence provided and on 3rd September she enquired again of the Red Cross about the fate of her brother. The reply came on 7th September and was a report from 3402 Pte Stanley Earthy lying in a hospital in France. Though again partial hearsay, Earthy's report seems, like that of Pte Williams, unambiguous:

"Cpl Maslyn (author's note: actually Maslen), C Coy, X Pltn. was with the Capt. when he was killed. Capt. Ware was in charge of a bombing party carrying bombs to the London Scottish. On the 1st July just after he came back Cpl. Maslyn showed me Capt. Ware's body lying about 20 yards from our trench but the barrage of fire was so intense that it was impossible to get the body in. Cpl. Maslyn was killed 4 days later in a bombing raid. Capt. Ware was also my Company Commander and I knew him well, a very fine officer about 40, medium coloured hair, tinged grey, fairly tall, well built."[11]

For some reason, undoubtedly a symptom of the rigid British class system, officers too often failed to accept the evidence of other ranks as conclusive and thus gave false hope to grieving relatives. So it happened here. On two occasions, Lord Lucan, on behalf of the British Red Cross, whilst assuring Miss Ware of "our sympathy in your anxiety", appended comments to these men's reports that "information from Privates always needs verifying" (Pert's and Allibone's evidence) and "we have so many instances of men being mistaken in describing what they have seen" (Earthy). Thus it was that she continued to solicit further information in the months to come with a Pte C Porton writing from yet another hospital in France on 22nd September that Capt. Ware had first been wounded by a shell and then afterwards killed.

---

i 2479 Cpl. Alfred John Maslen, 1/13th London Regt. (Kensingtons), was actually killed on 17th July 1916. Aged 20, he was the son of Alfred John and Norah Maslen, of Francis Cottages, Knaphill, Woking, Surrey. His body was never found and his name is inscribed on the Thiepval Memorial, Pier and Face 9 D 9 C 13 C and 12 C.

It was not until a letter was written to Florence Ware on the 4th November 1916 from the Auxiliary Military Hospital at Primrose Bank in Burnley by 1945 Pte. Ernest Hurcomb of the Kensingtons that the family at last appeared to accept his death. Hurcomb recounted how, sometime in the mid-morning of 1st July, the gallant 43-year old Captain Ware[i] had met his end:

"He (Hurcomb) saw Ware in a trench when a shell from a German trench mortar exploded where the officer was standing and after the explosion he could see nothing of Capt. Ware."

***

ACROSS IN THE GERMAN LINES, the position of the 169th Brigade was falling apart. Lts. Bovill and Upton of the Westminsters had withdrawn their men to the junction of Female and Feed trenches in the German second line. As some men searched frantically amongst the dead and wounded for supplies of bombs and ammunition, the others tried their best to fend off the twin German attacks down Emden trench and from the direction of the Cemetery. The enormous pressure of the constant bombing attacks was too much to resist and, at 1.45 p.m., their defences failed. There was only one line of retreat, down the 100 metres of Ems trench to the front line. The rapidly dwindling band dragged themselves down the short winding stretch of trench. Those that could carried their wounded colleagues.

Plate 44 Cpl. Alfred Maidment, Queen Victoria's Rifles, killed 1ˢᵗ July 1916

A small rearguard, using what ammunition they still had left, held the enemy at bay but behind them they had left a dedicated bunch of unarmed men who, ignorant of the tide of battle, were doing their best to help the dozens of wounded men who had sought their urgent help. Two of the rearguard were men of the bombing section of 'B' Company, Queen Victoria's, and the survivor, 4408 Rfn. Frederick Ratcliff[ii], described what happened:

[i] Capt. Francis Henry Ware, 1/13th London Regt. (Kensingtons), died on Saturday, 1st July 1916. Born on 12th September 1873 he was the youngest of three children of Charles T aand Frances Ware of 11, Philimore Gardens, Kensington. Educated at Mr C A Ford's School, Potton and Winchester (between 1886 and 1891) he went to Trinity College, Cambridge where he took the Law Tripos, graduating as BA and LLB in 1894. HE went into practice with Messers Foster, Spicer and Foster of 7, Queen's Street Place, London, E.C. Capt. Ware was single and lived at 5, The Pryors, East Heath Road, Hampstead. Having previously served in a Volunteer Rifle Corps he was commissioned early in the war and went to France in September 1915. He was survived by this brother Charles Martin and his sister Florence Mary Ware. His body was never found and his name is inscribed on the Thiepval Memorial, Pier and Face 9 D, 9 C, 13 C and 12 C. [*Additional Sources:* Pam & Ken Linge, Thiepval Project]

[ii] 4408 Rfn. Frederick Charles Ratcliff survived the battle relatively unscathed but did not survive the war. He was killed on 31st August 1918 and was buried in Bac-Du-Sud British Cemetery, Bailleulval, grave I. F. 17. Aged 19 (and, therefore, just 17 at the time of the attack on Gommecourt), he was the son Mr. F Ratcliff and Emily (his wife), of London. He suffered from shell shock after the attack and was transferred from the boming section to the Buglers.

"Cpl. Maidment was in charge of the bombing section and I was a member... and I was with him all day... we had to retire and, to let our boys get back, Maidment and I went up the communication trench towards the German second line to try to stop them. As the communication trench had been blown in we must have been seen going up for, as we were passing round the buttress they threw two bombs and Cpl. Maidment said, 'run for your life, kid' and, of course, I went. Maidment passed me and I saw he had been hit in the right buttock, but it was not at all a serious wound. He passed back along the German first lines to try and get back to our own lines. This was about 3 p.m. and I think he was hit again going across No Man's Land."

Alfred Maidment did not survive the trip, dying alone somewhere in No Man's Land.[i]

1681 Rfn. Wally Mockett was a stretcher bearer with 'B' Company of the Queen's Westminsters and he had gone across with the attacking troops to take care of the wounded. Given the ferocity of the fighting and the danger to the wounded men of trying to treat them out in the open the stretcher bearers had made use of a German dugout in the second line of German trenches. Earlier in the day, 4334 Rfn. Herbert Burley, part of No. 1 Lewis Gun Team of the Queen's Westminsters, had made it to the German third line and there his team had engaged the enemy. To do this meant that the man firing the gun had necessarily to expose his head in order to see his targets. Burley was the man with his finger on the Lewis Gun's trigger and he had been firing his gun at about noon when a bullet smashed through his neck and chin. With the Germans pressing hard and the men around him starting to withdraw Burley abandoned his gun and set off down a communication trench towards the second line of trenches. There he found Mockett and several other stretcher bearers working feverishly to dress wounds. Burley was taken down the steps of the dugout where Wally Mockett dressed his wounds which, according to Burley, were "more numerous than serious". Many of the other inhabitants of the dugouts were more seriously wounded and were unable to move and so, when the order came to evacuate the second German line, they had to be abandoned. Burley[ii] set off with the others towards the front line but Mockett and the other stretcher bearers stayed with their patients to be taken as Prisoners of War along with their charges. Wally Mockett would spend the rest of his war as a PoW at a camp at Giessen[iii], a university town in Hesse.

At about the same time as the withdrawal back to the German front line, a patrol from the 1/4th Londons returned to their trenches south of the Bucquoy Road from Fate trench. 3130 Pte. Henry Whitehead and 3662 Pte Walter

---

[i] 8422 Cpl. Alfred Sydney Maidment, No. 8 Platoon, B Company, 1/9th London Regt. (Queen Victoria's Rifles) was killed on Saturday, 1st July 1916. He was the son of Mrs Maidment of 27, Lanark Villas, Clifton Road, Paddington His body was never found and his name was inscribed on the Thiepval Memorial, Pier and Face 9C.

[ii] 4334 Rfn. Herbert D Burley, 1/16th London Regt. (Queen's Westminster Rifles), was wounded on Saturday, 1st July 1916. He was evacuated to Hut 18, C Division, Military Convalescent Hospital, Woodcote Park, Epsom. His brother, 2829 Sgt Ernest Leonard Burley, 1/19th London Regt. (Queen Victoria's Rifles) was reported missing on 1st July but was later confirmed as killed. He was aged 27. Ernest and Herbert Burley were the sons of Edmund and Hannah Burley, of 5A, Fieldhouse Rd., Balham, London.. Ernest Burley's body was never found and his name was inscribed on the Thiepval Memorial, Pier and Face 9C.

[iii] A satellite camp of the notorious Buchenwald concentration camp was located at Giessen during World War II.

Buckingham[i] had set out on their perilous journey just before 11 a.m. They had crept past shell holes, through shattered wire entanglements and past the bodies of dozens of dead and wounded Rangers and Fusiliers, until they entered the German lines and sought out their colleagues in the warren of trenches, saps and alleys. They found two small groups of Rangers, each with a leavening of Kensingtons and Queen Victorias who were separated from their units. The first, under 2nd Lt. Harper, was at the junction of Et and Felt trench, almost directly in front of Nameless Farm. Harper confirmed that there were no British troops in front of him and that any hold on the German third line around Nameless Farm had been relinquished. He also complained of the urgent need for more bombs; Germans were to his front in both Et and Elbe trenches and, without bombs, they would find it difficult to hold them off. Fifty metres to his right, the Fusiliers found another small party, commanded by 2nd Lt. Parker of 'A' Company, The Rangers. He and his twelve men were holding a section of Fall trench where it crossed the Bucquoy Road. Parker asked that his position be reported to his commanding officer. He too asked for more bombs before the Fusilier patrol turned back. One man was detached from the patrol to act as a runner. As he neared the British lines, he found some more Fusiliers doggedly going in the opposite direction. They were a bombing section ordered up in an effort to plug the growing gap between the Rangers and the Scottish. Their rather optimistic orders were for them to consolidate the hold on Fall and Fame trenches and then to bomb up Elbe communication trench in an effort to get at the rear of Nameless Farm. But, as the runner jogged past them, those still on their feet turned back as the ground around them erupted from another salvo of German shells. As they fell back into their trenches, the Rangers' bombing officer, 2nd Lt. Higgins, had been watching their efforts. He could see that their venture had been gallant but forlorn. He turned and pushed past the muddied and bloodied men in the wrecked trench and started back towards his battalion's H.Q. His report, delivered at 2 p.m., would be stark: "it was quite impossible to cross the barrage on our front line trench". Further forward movement was hopeless.

But, even as Higgins dragged his feet through the thick mud and over the bodies and debris that now filled Woman Street, Parker and Harper, the two Rangers' subalterns, and their small groups of desperately tired men had been forced to retire. The German attacks down Et and Elbe had proved too powerful. They were unable to resist the showers of stick grenades; they had nothing to resist with! Using what bombs they could recover from the dead and wounded that filled the trenches and losing men step by step, they fell back slowly down Fall trench. After 50 metres, they entered a 150 metre long section of communication trench that led back to the German front line at the east end of Fate trench. Traverse by traverse they were bombed backwards until they reached the front line. Now, behind them, was the expanse of No Man's Land, wracked its length and breadth by furious German artillery fire. They could go no further. The small group of Rangers, Kensingtons and Fusiliers fanned out along a short stretch of Fate trench, determined to sell their lives and their modest piece of German trench dearly.

---

[i] Pte W Buckingham and Pte H Whitehead were both awarded the Military Medal for their actions. Whitehead was later commissioned.

The battle was all but over for the Rangers. At 2.20 p.m., an hour after he set out with his carrying party, Company Sergeant Major Brown returned to report it was quite impossible to get through the German barrage. Men from the attacking companies and from the 1/4ᵗʰ Londons trickled back across No Man's Land, scrambling from shell hole to shell hole until reaching the relative safety of the British trenches. All the while, in the German lines, individuals and small groups were hunted down by the men of the 170ᵗʰ Regiment and shot, bombed or, if lucky, captured. By ten past three it was done. Officers in the 168ᵗʰ Brigade Observation Post saw the last men leave in a frantic dash for the nearest cover. They mustered what covering fire they could manage from the machine guns still in action from their emplacements in W48R trench and called down some artillery fire on the relinquished German trenches.

ENDNOTES:
[1] Edmonds, Brig. Gen. Sir James E, Official History of the War: Military Operations, France and Belgium 1916, Volume 1 page 468
[2] CAB 45/135 NA
[3] Moy, 2ⁿᵈ Lt. C E, Unpublished papers, Liddle Collection, Leeds University.
[4] Henriques Maj. J Q, The War History of the First Battalion, Queen's Westminster Rifles 1914-1918, 1923
[5] Source: Chris Rippingale
[6] 56ᵗʰ Division War Diary NA WO 95/2931
[7] Clements Pte (later Lt.) H T, 1/2ⁿᵈ London Regiment, Diary, IWM.
[8] Russell, Rfn H, 1/5ᵗʰ London Regt. (London Rifle Brigade), papers, IWM.
[9] Ibid.
[10] Ware, Capt. F H, 1/13ᵗʰ London Regt. (Kensingtons), personal file NA WO374/71892
[11] Ibid.

12. Z DAY: 1430 - 1630

"I am faced with three alternatives:
a. to stay here with such of my men as are alive and be killed;
b. to surrender to the enemy;
c. to withdraw such of my men as I can.

Either of the first two alternatives is distasteful to me. I propose to adopt the latter."

Capt. H C Sparks
1/14ᵗʰ Londons (London Scottish)

BY 2.30 P.M., GERMAN BOMBING ATTACKS were increasing in both frequency and violence on both flanks of the weakening London Scottish position. The 5ᵗʰ Company, 170ᵗʰ Regiment, the German garrison of the Farmyard strongpoint, had been steadily reinforced as the day went on. The 6ᵗʰ Company had, since the beginning of the battle, been pressing 'A' Company in Fair and Fancy trenches on the southern flank. In the centre, three groups of Pioneers from the 103ʳᵈ Pioneer Company[i] had joined the action, possibly coming down the appropriately named Pionier Graben (Anna Trench). On the northern flank of the strongpoint, the 7ᵗʰ Company had come down Elbe trench and was now infiltrating the positions of the Scottish in the maze of trenches around Fame, Et and Fall. And, if this was not enough, the 8ᵗʰ Company of the 170ᵗʰ Regiment, led by Oberleutnant Krumbiegel, was poised to bomb their way down Fable and Fact trenches having moved up from Rossignol Wood along Arun trench.

Behind them, in the shelter of Rossignol Wood, four more companies were made ready for the assault. The last two companies of the 170ᵗʰ Regiment, the 11ᵗʰ and 12ᵗʰ, were joined by the 10ᵗʰ and 11ᵗʰ Companies of the 15ᵗʰ R.I.R., a force of nearly 600 men. Leutnant Petersen of the 15ᵗʰ R.I.R. later recalled:

"Clouds of gas (*author's note:* smoke, no gas was used) covered the ground, darkening the sun. Men of the 77ᵗʰ were hurrying in assault order along the road to Gommecourt. All was haste and urgency. The barrels of the remaining undamaged guns were being cooled, then once more they gave it all they had got. At Copse 125 (Rossignol Wood), we were given our orders from the commander of 2ⁿᵈ Battalion, 170ᵗʰ I.R. and received hand grenades, rifle and machine gun ammunition. The 11ᵗʰ Company was to eject the Tommies, who had forced their way into N3 and N2."[1]

The men sheltered in the complex of trenches that criss-crossed through the wood as last minute artillery preparations were put in hand. In addition to the batteries near Serre, Puisieux and in Fork Wood, a light field howitzer was deployed in the open, the better to pound the few remaining men of the London Scottish in their tattered trenches. The state of the 56ᵗʰ Division's field artillery made this less of a risk than at first glance it would seem if the experience of one artillery support group was anything to go by. At twelve o'clock, only thirteen of the twenty 18 pdrs and howitzers of the Southart Group supporting the 169ᵗʰ

---

[i] These three groups were led by Vizefeldwebel Peter and Unteroffiziers Brandt and Kleinau. Peters and Brandt were both killed in the subsequent fighting.

Brigade had been in operation. Although some of these had been brought back into action, the general wear and tear on barrels and buffer springs was catching up with them again. By 3.45 p.m., only eight guns were still firing - 40% of the total available. Three 18 pdrs from A/280 Battery were firing from a position 1,000 metres to the west of Hebuterne and another 18 pdr from C/280 Battery was firing at Gommecourt Park from a range of 3,000 metres. Only four other guns from the three other batteries were in action. Over the next half an hour, another six pieces came back into service but now they were firing slowly as orders came from Divisional H.Q. to conserve ammunition in case of a German counter-attack. Post-war comments suggest that the Macart Group supporting the 168th Brigade were experiencing the same problems. Except for the intervention of the Corps heavy artillery, the battalions of the 56th Division were now almost without any form of artillery support and German reserves could now pour forward almost unmolested. So, unaffected by counter-battery fire, the German howitzer in front of Rossignol Wood proceeded to lob its shells at 1,200-metre range into the heart of the Farmyard strongpoint. After a brief five-minute bombardment, the infantry went in. Lt. Kaiser led the attack of the 11th Company, 15th R.I.R.:

> "When the company arrived at Copse 125 at 2.00 p.m., I was ordered by the commander of the 2nd Battalion (170th I.R.) to clear out the enemy who were occupying the trench in N3, together with two saps and the communication trench to the second trench. I called for artillery [fire]. As soon as the howitzers opened up, we began our attack against the totally levelled trench at about 3.00 p.m. (2 p.m. B.S.T.), but we made no progress at all when we attempted to use the rolling up procedure. Instead we went up over the parapet and parados and attacked across country with hand grenades. At that the enemy pulled back rapidly and some Tommies surrendered."[2]

Already, more than half of the London Scottish strength had been killed or wounded[i]. As the position of the Rangers on their left collapsed, German bombers from the 7/170th I.R. took advantage of their forced withdrawal to drive down Elbe trench into Fame. At the same time, the bombing parties coming down Anna trench from Rossignol Wood were making Fable trench difficult to hold and threatened the men in Fame from the other flank. Fame and part of Fall were held by elements of 'B' and 'C' Companies, commanded by 2nd Lt. White. The attacks from Elbe forced the men to withdraw to their right and then down a short communication trench into Fall. But the German advance was brought up short by covering fire from two Lewis guns, well placed in Fall trench to the rear. One of the guns was fired by Lance Cpl. Thoms, the same Lewis gunner who had caused great execution in German ranks when the attack was but fifteen minutes old.

On the right, yet more hostile bombing parties from the 6/170th and 8/170th were building pressure on the positions at the head of Fair and Fancy trenches. And it was here that the German guns were concentrating their fire. What was left of 'A' Company, along with others from 'C' Company held the line. Corporals Bain and Fairman still held the trench block at the top of Fair trench

---

[i] 1.30 p.m. Estimated casualties 1/14th Londons: 5 officers and 400 other ranks.

but a new block made in the southern face of the strong point between Fair and Fancy was destroyed by shelling. Behind them, under orders from Lt. Speak, a new fire trench was made in a communication trench between Farm and Farmyard and the work on reversing Farm trench carried on apace. This work was given covering fire by two Lewis guns and by Lt. Thomson and his Vickers gun. While his men fired the gun, Thomson sniped with a German Mauser abandoned in the initial attack. All the while, Lance Corporal Aitken and a team of snipers picked off enemy bombers whenever opportunities arose. But, in spite of their best efforts, the weight of shellfire and the pressure of the counter-attacks told. Covered by the heavy and light machine guns, the blocks at the end of Fair and Fancy were reluctantly given up and a new front line established in Lt. Speak's new fire trench.

Plate 45 Maj. Francis Howard Lindsay, 1/14ᵗʰ London Regt. (London Scottish)

2ⁿᵈ Lt. White of 'A' Company had been involved in holding parts of the Farm trench and, apart from a lack of men with which to man properly his section of trench. He had reported his position to the advanced headquarters in a German dugout and was now rushing to and from his position to those behind in the German first and second line trenches in an effort to ensure that his back was being covered by the mixture of Kensingtons and London Scottish established there. With one officer, presumably of the Kensingtons, more than anxious to retire he constantly had to check regularly to see whether his position was being exposed by the withdrawal of these supporting troops. And, all the while, he could see the enemy's bombing parties advance through the network of trenches to front and right with little red triangular flags marking their progress.

"Hill Young[i] starts work on this corner. I go back to where Company HQ should be and find it established in a dugout. Leave all my equipment,

---

[i] 3405 L/Sgt James Hill Young, 1/14ᵗʰ London Regt. (London Scottish), was commissioned in July 1917 and joined No. 35 Squadron of the RFC. He died from wounds on 17ᵗʰ January 1918 in German hands. He had been flying with 2ⁿᵈ Lt. Thomas Alexander Urwin in Armstrong Whitworth FK 8 B283 on 12ᵗʰ January. The airmen were on an Artillery Patrol when they were shot down behind German lines. Ltn Ludwig Hanstein of Jasta 35 was credited with a victory south of Nauroy; it was the of 15ᵗʰ of his eventual 16 victories before he was killed in action on 21ˢᵗ March. Lt. Young is buried in Premont British Cemetery, grave V. A. 24. Then aged 30, he was the son of James Young and the husband of Anna Frances Young, of 4, Lansdowne Terrace, Eastbourne. He was born in Londonderry. 2ⁿᵈ Lt. Urwin died from his wounds on 15ᵗʰ January.and is also buried at Premont in grave III. AA. 19.

including sporran, except revolver which I have slung loosely at my side on a webbing strap. Meet Maj. Lindsay and Capt. Sparks, describe the position held and they go off towards the right when Lindsay was shortly afterwards killed.

Investigating trenches to left showed them to be empty for a considerable distance but short of men and cannot stretch out much more. Make trench block in front, instruct party of mixed troops to make ditto in old German front line. Experience the disagreeable necessity of trying to make a windy officer (of another regiment thank goodness) see reason why he should not retire past a certain point. Twice I go back by way of …. (?) to find that they have retired and left my rear unguarded.

All day back and forward watching these two corners. See the German bombing parties come down the CTs from Gommecourt. With the regular explosions of heavy stuff in front. A little triangular red flag stuck on the corner of each traverse making the limit of advance of their own men… the little red flags advance steadily and methodically towards us … we have no ammunition except what we have brought with us and has thinned down to nothing. We cannot make a bombing fight for it for we've no bomb supply therefore it would be better to keep them at arms length with rifle fire. The left position is good for this and I get a good fire point prepared but will the block behind us be held? I don't think so at least the men there must remain if it is hot. Some commotion behind, find they are in touch with bombers and have retired past my trench."³

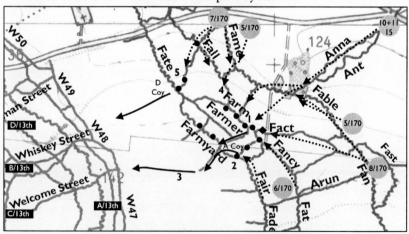

Map 21 Situation afternoon London Scottish front

Legend: 1 = Maj. Lindsay killed 2 = Retreat to new fire trench 3 = Withdrawal in which Lt. Thomson killed
4 = L/Cpl. Thoms and Lewis gun 5 = 2ⁿᵈ Lt. Parker's party withdraw to front line before capture

● Positions of British troops ♦ Trench blocks

As the London Scottish's perimeter contracted with the loss of Fame, Fair and Fancy trenches, their problems were compounded by the previously mentioned loss of the commander of 'B' Company and the battalion's senior officer in the German lines. Maj. Francis Lindsay had just conferred with 'A' Company's Capt. Sparks. They had agreed the new defensive line and sent orders for the necessary adjustments. A sniper had been creeping ever closer to the position and had already accounted for several men and, as Maj. Lindsay was making his way back to his own position in Fall trench, the sniper shot him in the head and he was killed instantly[i]. The heart felt prayers of his little boy back in South Kensington had not saved him. His men took the time to lie his body at the bottom of the trench and cover him with a waterproof sheet in the forlorn hope that it would be found and decently buried by the Germans.

At this loss, Capt. Sparks took command. The battalion's history describes his actions thus:

"The better to direct the fighting, he was often seen standing and moving on the unbroken ground between the trenches. But he seemed to have a charmed life and was never hit."

As John Keegan writes in his book 'The Face of Battle':

"(this) conduct… would have attracted admiration at Waterloo and, when displayed on a First World War battlefield, beggars powers of eulogy."[4]

Guided by Sparks' heroic example, the London Scottish perimeter held. Just.

***

BEHIND THEM, THE PLUNGING FIRE of the German howitzers around Puisieux was still shattering the trenches the London Scottish had left seven hours earlier. At 2.30 p.m., a German high explosive shell ploughed into Woman trench directly outside the front of the 1/4th Londons headquarters. Fourteen men were waiting in the traverse into which the shell fell. Of these, seven were killed and another seven wounded. After frantic digging at the entrance of the dugout, Lt. Col. Wheatley, the commanding officer, Major Moore, the adjutant, and the signalling officer, 2nd Lt. Victor Donaldson[ii], were freed from the clinging mud but both Moore and Donaldson were wounded. By this time, the casualties of the 1/4th Londons were estimated at 10 officers and 300 other ranks, more than half of a battalion most of which had not left their own trenches.

500 metres to the right, the Kensington's battalion H.Q. was in Welcome Street, designated the 'down' trench for the day's activities. Fifty metres behind them, was a special emplacement concealing a 240-mm heavy trench mortar of the V56 Trench Mortar Battery. Every few minutes, with a roar and cloud of

---

[i] Capt. (Temp. Major) Francis Howard Lindsay, 1/14th London Regt (London Scottish), died on Saturday, 1st July 1916, aged 40. Born on 9th March 1876, he was the fourth of seven children of William Alexander Lindsay Esq, K.C., Windsor Herald (1894 to 1919) and later Clarenceux King of Arms, and Lady Harriet Lindsay. Born in London in 1876 he was educated at Malvern and Clare College, Cambridge. He went on to become a junior examiner at the Scotch Education Department. He married Helen Margaret Lindsay (nee MacDougall, eldest daughter of the late Colonel Stewart MacDougall of Lunga) of 7, Emperor's Gate, South Kensington, London in April 1910. They had three children: John Stewart (born 14th April 1910, died 5th August 1943 from wounds whilst an Italian Prisoner of War), David William (born 24th March 1914, died 16th June 1914) and Katherine Frances (born 26th December 1915). He was severely wounded in November 1914. His body was never found and his name is inscribed on the Thiepval Memorial, Pier and Face 9 C and 13 C.
Major Lindsay was mentioned in Despatches: "This officer, having gallantly led his company to its objective under very heavy fire, by his personal bravery, example and devotion, organised his bombing and blocking parties, and as far as possible consolidated the position. Though the artillery, machine gun and sniping fire was very heavy, he at all times exposed himself fearlessly and by his splendid example and courage held the position until killed."
[ii] 2nd Lt. Victor Cecil Donaldson, 1/4th London Regt. (Royal Fusiliers) was aged 19 and lived at 45, Fountayne Road, Stoke Newington. He was the eldest son of Cllr E Donaldson of Dalston Lane. After recovering he joined the 3rd (Reserve) Battalion, London Regt., at Hurdcott Camp, Salisbury. He then joined the ASC being attached to No 1 Reserve Mechanical Transport Depot, Grove Park, Lee, SE London. He went back to France with the ASC (MT) where he was attached to the 125th (South African) Siege Battery RGA.

smoke, it sent its 190 lb. projectile wobbling skyward towards German positions 1,000 metres away. Everywhere was a chaos of shouts and curses, the cries of the wounded, the shattering crash and tremor of high explosive. At 3 p.m., through this scene of total confusion staggered an exhausted runner from the front lines. He carried Major Dickens' message sent forty-five minutes previously. His note told of the shambles at the front, the heavy casualties, the relentless shelling - and it asked for instructions. Major Young took the only reasonable decision on a day when nothing was remotely reasonable. He ordered Maj. Dickens and his thirteen men back to the reserve lines and, once there, the Major was to organise whoever he found for defence. The only men of the Kensingtons still left in the British front line now was the tiny and rapidly dwindling party of men from 'D' Company led by young Henry Pilgrim. Cowering in W48 his handful of men had been left to occupy 100 metres of now unrecognisable trench for over three hours since Capt. Harris had briefly appeared in order to ascertain the local situation. In the absence of contrary orders they stayed where they were in the blasted and shattered landscape, dying where they stood.

Behind the Kensingtons, the Cheshires attached to 168th Brigade had been experiencing a frustrating time of it. Threequarters of 'C' Company waited for orders all day in Cross Street on the edge of Hebuterne. For sixteen hours, they were under constant shell fire as the German artillery sought out the nearby R.F.A. 18 pdr section, the adjacent machine gun emplacement and the Y56 and V56 trench mortar positions. The second in command of the Company, Lt. Archibald Jolliffe, later recalled the time spent under the bombardment. There was a steady flow of wounded men to deal with and direct to the Aid Post and the Advanced Dressing Station. But, with all of this going on, there was still plenty of time to read, 'Pickwick Papers' was his choice, exchange views with the men about what was going on and lastly to watch idly the antics of a plump grey rat as it scurried around the trench.

Only No. 9 platoon of 'C' Company was ordered to do anything – even though it proved a pointless waste. Led by Lt. Henry Leigh they had moved up to the front line trenches earlier in the day but, once there, a party led by 2333 Sgt. Richard Prince became separated from Leigh and the rest of the platoon by a party from 'A' Company of the Kensingtons. As a result, Prince was not aware of the fact that, at about 2.30 p.m., Leigh and his men had been told to re-inforce the London Scottish in the Farmyard strong point. As Leigh and his men struggled up the battered communication trenches to the front line, Prince received an order from the Brigade Major to return to their assembly trench near Warrior Street. Leigh's party was, meanwhile, hurrying up the sap that ran deep into No Man's Land. At the end of the sap there was no alternative but to attempt to cross the shell swept expanse of blasted ground between the two lines and, in spite of the ferocious barrage to their front, they stepped out gamely, shoulders hunched against the storm. As they reached the tattered edges of the German wire a runner with another order caught them up. The original instruction was countermanded as it seemed clear that the London Scottish position in the German lines was soon to be evacuated. Leigh turned his men about and, still under heavy artillery and machine gun fire, the platoon toiled back to rejoin the rest of the Company in Cross Street amongst the orchards on the north side of the village. To add injury to insult, at some point in this abortive advance, a shell blew off Lt. Leigh's right arm, two inches above the elbow. The rest of the arm would be amputated later in the day but, luckily, he survived to see out not only this World War but the next one as well[i]. But 'C' Company had suffered heavily for all of its unavailing efforts. They suffered sixty-three casualties without once coming into direct contact with the enemy. A bad enough day at anyone's office.

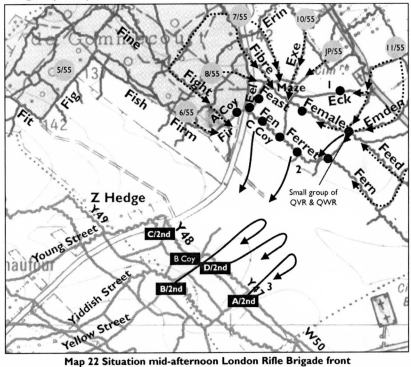

Map 22 Situation mid-afternoon London Rifle Brigade front

Legend: A, B & D Companies, 1/2nd Londons advance 2.00-3.00 p.m. B Company, L.R.B. in front line
1 = 2nd Lt. Petley's party 2 = Withdrawal starts 3 = Capt. Garland, A Company, 1/2nd Londons killed

BACK ON THE BATTLEFIELD, one by one, the companies of the 1/2nd Londons had tried to go to the aid of their colleagues in the German lines in front of Gommecourt. At 3 p.m., Capt. James Garland took 'A' Company over the top in yet another forlorn attempt at reinforcement. Their objectives were Fern and Fever trenches into which the Q.V.R.s and Q.W.R.s had disappeared some hours before. Within a few yards, a rifle bullet killed Garland[ii]. Every officer and

---

i Lt. Henry Raymond Leigh, 1/5th Cheshire Regt. was born on 10th June 1893. He was educated at Bedford Grammar School and, on leaving school, he went into the Worsted spinning industry being employed by J J Baldwin & Partners at the Clarkebridge Mills in Halifax, W. Yorkshire. He lived at Grove House, Stafford Avenue, Halifax. Lt. Leigh eventually married on 31st March 1962, dying in Harrogate on 6th December 1974, aged 81. His widow, Mrs B Leigh, survived him. He was attested Private into the 5th Cheshires on 17th September 1914 and was rapidly gazetted 2nd Lt. the following month.

ii Capt. James Richard Garland BSc., AKC, 1/2nd London Regt (Royal Fusiliers), died on Saturday, 1st July 1916, aged 23. He was the only son of Richard Edmund and Olive May Garland of 162, All Souls Avenue, Willesden, London. Garland had graduated from King's College, London where he had been a member of the O.T.C. for two years before the war. He was commissioned into the 3/2nd Londons on 23rd August 1914 and arrived in France in July 1915. He was promoted to Captain on 14th March 1916. Garland was well known in the parish of St Lawrence in

practically every N.C.O. was either killed or wounded as they tried desperately to go to the aid of their comrades[i].

3 C.S.M. James Macrow described their effort in a letter after the war:

"At 2 p.m. Capt. Garland received the order to draw three grenades per man and attack a portion of the trench to the right of our position. We proceeded up the communication trench at the rear of the new front line. We took a long time owing to the number of wounded trying to get back to the dressing station. At the last minute Capt. Garland gave me the orders to remain in the trench and see that everyone went over. I am very glad to say that not a single man needed any urging on. The men had to dig holes in the sides of the trenches and climb eight feet up to get on the top and throw their rifles up before they could get up. No sooner had the men started than the Germans opened a murderous machine-gun fire and increased artillery fire which had been going on all morning. Before all the men had got over, others came tumbling back with two, three, four and, in two cases, five wounds."[5]

Of the five officers, six sergeants and 91 men who Garland led into action with 'A' Company that afternoon only ten returned unwounded. Every officer was a casualty and only one sergeant, Sgt C S Taylor, and six others ranks returned to report to C.S.M. Macrow[ii]. After dark, thirty five wounded men from the company returned from No Man's Land under cover of night. Next to them, 'B' Company tried three times to leave the trenches and get forward to Fetter trench. Three times they were cut to pieces by 7.62 mm machine gun bullets and hot shards of shrapnel. 'D' Company had, meanwhile, taken some time to reach the front lines, such was the chaos and congestion in the battered communication trenches. In his forward H.Q. the 1/2nd Londons' C.O., Lt. Col. Attenborough[iii], had watched the destruction of half of his battalion and, after a long and tortuous journey, Capt. John Kellett[iv], 'B' Company's C.O., arrived to update him on the conditions further forward. Attenborough needed little telling before he sent a message to Brig. Gen. Coke stating that any further action by his battalion would just be a waste of valuable men. At 3.15 p.m., Brig. Gen. Coke referred this statement to Division and the answer came back to abandon all further attempts at reinforcement. Securing the front line against possible German counter-attacks was now the priority. To the relief of all concerned, all further attacks were called off and the men were held in the dubious comfort of the front lines to await

---

Brondesbury and s memorial service was held for him. He is buried at Gommecourt British Cemetery No. 2, Hebuterne, grave III.H.I.

i As an example of the incredible efforts made by the 1/2nd Londons to get across to assist their colleagues it should be noted that twelve officers and 244 other ranks were either killed or later died from wounds received or were wounded on 1st July 1916. Most of these men fell within a few yards of the British trenches and it is not known whether any member of the battalion got into the German lines. One should also note the possible confusion caused in the lists of casualties as a result of men from the disbanded 2/2nd Londons being attached to other battalions, especially the Queen's Westminsters, but still appearing in the casualty lists of the 1/2nd Londons. In the Roll of Honour where such attachments are known they are mentioned.

ii 'A' Company, 1/2nd London Regt., including the trench mortar bomb carrying party led by Lt. Sanders, lost five officers, six sergeants and 124 other ranks on 1st July 1916.

iii Lt. Col. J Attenborough, 1/2nd London Regt. (Royal Fusiliers), commanded the battalion from December 1914 to April 1917. He was a pre-war Territorial and solicitor. He left the battalion on 28th April 1917 due to ill-health.

iv Capt., later Lt. Col. John Philip Kellett, D.S.O. and Bar, M.C., 1/2nd London Regt. (Royal Fusiliers) was a pre-war Territorial who commanded the battalion between April and August 1917, when he was wounded at Glencorse Wood (Third Battle of Ypres) and January to October 1918. He was promoted Captain on 7th July 1915 and was awarded the M.C. in June 1916, the first D.S.O. in July 1918 and the Bar on 27th-28th September for his conduct during the Battle of the Canal du Nord. He was promoted Colonel in 1932 having become a Regular after the war. He was appointed a GSO2 in the Indian Army in 1933 and made CO of the 1st Wiltshire Regt. in August 1939. He married Evelyn Tingle in October 1941 and died in January 1959.

further orders[i]. Although Coke had now been given the 1/3rd Londons there was nothing he could do with the extra resources. Throwing them into the inferno of No Man's Land was no longer an option. Keeping a force in hand capable of defending their own trenches was now the priority and they, and the 1/7th Middlesex who had been kept in reserve in the Keep for the whole day, stayed in the reserve trenches. But, even there, they were not immune and casualties mounted, with a number of officers and men falling victim to the German shells which began to reach more deeply into the village as the attack collapsed.

Plate 46 Lt. Col. J Attenborough, I/2nd London Regt.

By now, the remains of the L.R.B., Q.W.R., Q.V.R. and the Cheshires were compressed into some 400 metres of German front line trench. It stretched from Fir on the left, through Fen and Ferret to Fern on the right. In these broken and battered trenches some 200 men of the four battalions defended themselves from the constant stream of bombing attacks from both flanks and down the three communication trenches to their front. Whilst a defence of sorts was mounted, the few remaining officers knew that survival could only be ensured by an evacuation of the position. Just before 3.30 p.m., a small group was sent out to attempt an escape. They were unable to get through the massive German barrage. Those not killed or wounded struggled back to the German trenches. They were cut off.

By 3.30 p.m. the beleaguered London Scottish were the only men of the 168th Brigade left alive in the German lines. The withdrawal of most of the Rangers and the Fusiliers meant that both flanks were now in the air. It was only a matter of time before the intolerable pressure of the continuous bombing attacks and the constant and heavy shelling overwhelmed their position. 2nd Lt. White's position was now so precarious that he hurried off to consult with Capt. Sparks:

---

[i] There is a strange report from an RFA observer in the official reports. It reads: "The second Londons successfully got across No Man's Land with hardly any casualties (the Germans appear to have been caught napping or to have been temporarily out of ammunition). They seem to have made headway towards Fibre and the South-East outskirts of Gommecourt Village but then appeared to run out of bombs and were seen to be being heavily bombed and retiring." This bears no resemblance to any known attack at any time during the afternoon on the 169th Brigade front. Whatever the RFA officer thought he saw, it was not the 2nd Londons attacking Gommecourt Village.

"I see Hill Young, advise him to watch that direction (*author's note*: believed to be the left of the battalion's position) and personally go to consult Capt. Sparks. See Sparks who decides that under the circumstances it would be better to evacuate as many of the wounded as possible. All capable of walking told to hop it. Meanwhile, Young's party are retiring down and towards the German front line. I happen to be standing beside a man who is excitedly firing at the enemy. He shouts 'here they come the cowards, they are wearing steel helmets off our boys'. I jumped to the awful conclusion that he was firing at the party under Hill Young and jumped up to make sure when, crack!, my energetic rifleman has gone."[6]

Capt. Hubert Sparks of 'A' Company was the senior surviving officer of the London Scottish in the German lines. Writing hurriedly on a scrap of paper, he sent one last runner on the dreadful journey back across No Man's Land to his battalion H.Q. When it arrived at 4 p.m., it was passed to Col. Green. It read:

"I am faced with this position. I have collected all bombs and small arms ammunition from casualties - everyone has been used. Owing to the enemy's continued barrage fire none can be brought to me. I am faced with three alternatives:

a) to stay here with such of my men as are alive and be killed;
b) to surrender to the enemy;
c) to withdraw such of my men as I can.

Either of the first two alternatives is distasteful to me. I propose to adopt the latter."

As the able bodied men manned a rough perimeter for the final acts of defence, the wounded who could move were ushered towards the German front lines. 2nd Lt. White later described the situation their gallant 'last stand':

"It would be difficult to imagine a more heroic setting for a battle picture, in a trough of trench and shell holes are gathered the remains of 'A' Company, all facing outwards. (Lt.) F S Thomson and his MG are in position in a little sap. Sparks stands in the centre giving orders for the retiral."[7]

In the British lines all eyes turned to the trenches opposite. For twenty minutes, nothing happened. Then, whilst the officers and men of the London Scottish and the Kensingtons craned for a view from the British lines, small groups of men appeared in No Man's Land, running, crawling and scrambling their way to safety.

On the southern edge of the Farmyard strongpoint, a German sap stretched 100 metres out into No Man's Land. This had given some cover for the withdrawal. At Capt. Spark's instruction, 2nd Lt. Gavin had supervised the collection of the walking wounded and, in small groups, he had sent them out from the end of the sap for the perilous journey back to their own lines. Meanwhile, the final acts were taking place in the German lines. As the wounded made a scramble for safety the few remaining officers and men readied themselves for the dash across No Man's Land. 2nd Lt. White was with them and remembered those final moments:

"An officer of a trousered regiment in his panic for unrestricted freedom for the run home asks me to cuts his equipment off, this I do with my Skean-dhu. Wounded have been passing out of the sap head for some time now, then we withdraw those few who remain looking outwards, we are not yet being followed in the trench. Feeling that there is no more to be done I turn and joining (2nd Lt) A Petrie and (Lt.) F S Thomson also leave the sap head. We agree to separate, 'F S' goes left, Petrie right and I go ahead. There are many shots being fired at me. I can see them spurt on the ground ahead but I've got 300 yards to go."[8]

Lt. Frederick Thomson, his gun team mostly dead, disabled the Vickers gun and abandoned it at the head of Fancy trench. He then set off to withdraw, along with the battered remains of the battalion, carrying the German Mauser he had picked up along the way. But the Lieutenant, who had survived so much, failed to make it back. Turning to fire one last shot with his rifle, he was hit eighty metres from the German trenches. He died alone somewhere in No Man's Land[i]. Cpl. Forsyth, an 'A' Company Lewis gunner, left the German trenches just behind Thomson but was delayed when a wounded man asked for his water bottle. He then paused to pick up a discarded bucket of Lewis gun ammunition and had now lost sight of the officer. Seeing many men being hit by the withering machine gun fire he decided to sprint from shell to shell hole in 20 yard dashes and it was when he was about to dive into another crater that he saw Thomson lying in the open. He dropped into a nearby hole and called out to the officer. Getting no reply he tried to crawl out to him but was continually shot at by a sniper who ripped the heel off one boot with one shot and pierced his mess tin with another. But Forsyth was close enough to see that Thomson had received a large and fatal head wound, an explosive bullet through the right temple Forsyth thought, and so he left him and continued his escape to safety.

To his right, 2nd Lt. White was leading a charmed life:

"My neck feels as though it had a 6 ft regulation target pasted on it. I feel that they are all shooting at it. Still walking I must have charmed life, conscious of others also walking beside me. One, Thoms[ii] with his LG. Hear a cry and see the LG thrown forward. I don't know if he is hit."[9]

The evacuation went on until only Capt. Sparks and four N.C.O.s were left in the German lines. Sparks, 3286 Sgt. Carl Latham[iii] and 4946 Sgt. Robert Leggat[iv] and 3474 Cpl. C H Fairman and 2568 Cpl. Stanley Weston, with one Lewis gun, held the line until the men were all away. Then it was their turn. Firing a few last, Parthian shots, they put their heads down and made a dash for it. Both of the Sergeants would die making this last sprint to safety. To avoid the furious

[i] Lt. Frederick Stanley Thomson, 1/14th London Regt (London Scottish) attd. 168th Machine Gun Company, died on Saturday, 1st July 1916, aged 34. The son of the late W E S Thomson (Admiralty Registry and Treasury) he had been a civil servant in the Admiralty Registry and lived at 50, Hilldrop Road, Camden Road, Middlesex. His body was never found and his name is inscribed on the Thiepval Memorial, Pier and Face 5 C and 12 C

[ii] L/Cpl Thoms, a Lewis gunner, survived.

[iii] 3286 Sgt. Carl Stanley Latham M.M., 1/14th London Regt (London Scottish), died on Saturday, 1st July 1916. His body was never found and his name is inscribed on the Thiepval Memorial, Pier and Face 9 C and 13 C

[iv] 4946 L/Sgt Robert Leggat, 1/14th London Regt (London Scottish), died on Saturday, 1st July 1916, aged 28. He was the son of James Leggat of 'Duncarnock', Dumbreck, Glasgow. His body was never found and his name is inscribed on the Thiepval Memorial, Pier and Face 9 C and 13 C.

German barrage they dived into the same crater and were there killed by an enemy shell.

Plate 47 Sgt Carl Latham, London Scottish, killed 1st July 1916

Capt. Sparks[i] got fifty metres before falling into a shell hole and was lying there when he saw White still wandering across No Man's Land:

"Hear a voice crying 'here man, lie down or you'll be killed'. I lie down in the shell hole and find myself with Capt. Sparks and Drake[ii]. We arrange ourselves in a form resembling the I(sle) O(f) M(an) Coat of Arms, Drakes' head to Sparks' feet and I am facing Sparks. Up to this point I had been taking life very seriously but began to see the humour of the situation. The shell hole was very shallow and only just hid the three of us from view when we lay so arranged on our sides. Heavy calibre shells were now falling and each one seemed to shake up the hole to such an extent that we effected to find ourselves wholly under observation....

Just before this a heavy body (fell) in on top of us, Sgt McKenzie of 'B' Coy looking for (cover). Sparks said here if you know of a better hole go to it which he did by rolling into the next one. Sparks lay with his revolver in his hand all the time just about one inch from my nose and rather disturbed me by falling asleep. Waking later he found that his leg had cramped (lucky for me it wasn't his trigger finger).

It was promising dusk now and I decided to make a series of hops across whilst I saw the way. We agreed to try. Drake and I both got up and ran but the shots which chased us were fair warning to Sparks who waited until they had forgotten us. After several rushes and plunges both Drake and I

---

[i] Capt. Hubert Conrad Sparks was later promoted to Colonel and awarded the C.M.G. (1st January 1919), the D.S.O. (25th August 1916), the M.C. (3rd June 1916) and the Croix de Guerre (9th December 1916). He was twice mentioned in despatches (4th January 1917 and 20th December 1918). Born on the 14th February 1874, the son of E A Sparks, he was educated at Repton, Sparks was a consulting engineer with offices in Moorgate and a house on Putney Hill. Joining the Reserve in 1914, Sparks started the war as a Sergeant and was gazetted 2nd Lt. on 19th December 1914. Two days later he was wounded in the leg near Givenchy having seen action at Messines, First Ypres and La Bassee. Promoted Lieutenant Colonel he became Assistant Director of Labour at G.H.Q on 2nd January 1917. He was promoted full colonel on 20th February 1918. He died on 15th October 1933. [*Additional source:* Dick Flory: Repton School Register, 1922; Repton School Register, 1933; Old Reptonian War Register, 1914-1919; Repton School Register, 1957]

[ii] It has not been possible to identify this man but it is assumed he was either Sparks' batman or a senior sergeant.

388

tumbled into our old front line. Drake's dismay that his beloved OC was not following was indeed touching."[10]

Having reached safety, Drake now wanted to go back for Sparks but White persuaded him it was too risky and that he should have faith in Sparks' luck which had seemed boundless throughout the day. They then made their way through the wreckage of the forward trenches, which White described as 'horrible', before arriving at the advanced battalion HQ. There the news that Sparks was safe, although still hiding in a shell hole in No Man's Land, was some little cheer on a day of disaster. White's record of the day ends with an understandably brief comment: "Large rum toddy, lie down."[11] Sparks, meanwhile, waited for another four hours until the coming darkness and a general cease-fire made it safe to return[i].

As the Scottish withdrew the strongpoint was overrun by the men of the 170ᵗʰ I.R. and the 15ᵗʰ R.I.R. Lt. Kaiser of the 11ᵗʰ Company, 15ᵗʰ R.I.R. described the final moments:

"Our soldiers performed brilliantly. Within half an hour and to the sound of continuous shouts of *'Hurra'* the trench was cleared.

We captured a machine gun and an American quick firing rifle[ii]. Leutnant Stollberg was lying out front, shot through the stomach. Feldwebel Piepertz was killed and Vizefeldwebel Strohmeyer was wounded. Other casualties were three dead, six wounded and three missing. We were able to liberate a good many members of 170ᵗʰ I.R. who were still in the dugouts. One officer and sixty men, mostly from the London Scotch Regt. [*sic*] were taken prisoner. The artillery fired very well and very accurately. Everything was under control."[12]

***

FOR THE SURVIVING MEN of the 1/4ᵗʰ Londons cowering in the remains of the front trenches life was now impossible. The trenches were a shambles of dead and dying men. Movement was nearly impossible. There was no prospect of anyone getting over to the German lines. The question was: would anyone get back from them? At 3.30 p.m., the battalion C.O. asked Brigade H.Q. for permission for the men to withdraw to the relative safety of the reserve lines and, fifteen minutes later, permission was given. A runner was sent to inform the forward companies of the news of their withdrawal and Colonel Bayliffe of the Rangers was telephoned with the news a few minutes later. An hour passed before the twenty remaining men of 'D' Company, 1/4ᵗʰ Londons, staggered into

---

[i] One of the subalterns of the London Scottish who failed to return was 2ⁿᵈ Lt. Ralph Adair Brown. The 21-year old was the fourth of five brothers who joined up during the War. The son of George T. and Mary A. Brown, of Manor Hurst Palmerston Rd., Bowes Park, London, formerly of Abroath, his body was never found and his name his inscribed on the Thiepval Memorial, Pier and Face 9 C and 13 C. Brown was on the staff of Messers Guthrie & Co, East India Merchants and attested Private in the London Scottish in September 1914. He was commissioned in 1915 and went to France on 25ᵗʰ May 1916.

His older brother served in Salonika, and the next oldest was commissioned into the Royal Navy as a surgeon. The three youngest all enrolled in the London Scottish and all three were commissioned but the third brother, Atholl S Brown, was so severely wounded in 1915 he was invalided out of the Army. The two youngest, Ralph and Lindsay were twins, with Ralph the older by a few minutes. They were identical to the extent that the Army insisted that Ralph grow a moustache so that they could be told apart. The twins arrived in France in May 1916, Ralph to die at Gommecourt and Lindsay, later awarded the M.C. for gallantry at Bullecourt in 1917, to be dangerously wounded at Combles in September 1916. [*Additional Sources:* Pam & Ken Linge, Thiepval Project]

[ii] Presumably a Lewis gun.

the WR lines and slumped in shock in whatever space they could find. Capt. Stanham, their commander, explained to Col. Wheatley that this was all that remained of the Company. The rest of his men were lying dead and wounded in the forward trenches. They had never left their lines. They had died where they stood under the inexorable weight of the German barrage.

At 3.45 p.m., Major Dickens and his baker's dozen of Kensingtons arrived back at the reserve lines. They had, under orders, abandoned the front lines to the dead and wounded. The Major reported to his C.O. and then set off to try to organise a defence line along the WR line. If the Germans tried to take advantage of the chaos in the British lines to launch a follow-up attack then here, at least, they would be ready for them. But, alone and almost forgotten in the front lines, 2ⁿᵈ Lt. Pilgrim and his men were still holding on tenaciously to the left of the Kensingtons' position. Just after 4 p.m. Pilgrim sent one of his few remaining men down the choked and shattered communication trenches asking for instructions. He had seven men left, they were trying to hold the remains of a trench 100 metres long, what should he do? There seems to have been no answer forthcoming from Battalion H.Q. as Pilgrim and his last six men were still in W48 trench at 7 p.m. when an unlucky artillery shell struck the trench and killed the resolute Henry Pilgrimⁱ. His body now lies in Hebuterne Military Cemetery, a young man who stood the test of battle but on whom fortune failed to smile that day.

The whole of the 168ᵗʰ Brigade's front line was now an abandoned wreck. Five week's work of digging had been reduced to a shattered charnel house by the uncompromising weight of the German bombardment. It would be weeks before the lines were re-dug and re-occupied and many never were. In the meantime, the able bodied waited to repel any German attacks and the stretcher-bearers and medical orderlies struggled with near impossible task of bringing aid to the wounded and comfort to the dying. Behind them, the 1/1ˢᵗ Londons 'stood to' in the reserve lines and sensibly ignored a 56ᵗʰ Divisional order issued at 4 p.m. to:

"… secure a line as far forward as possible with advanced posts in German front line."

At 56ᵗʰ Division's H.Q. notice was at last given that the 46ᵗʰ Division could not attack again. The information came too late for Gen. Hull to respond in any useful way. His men had been pointlessly killed and wounded for over four hours while VII Corps and 46ᵗʰ Division conjured plans out of thin air, using men who did not exist to launch attacks that were impossible. Of course, throughout that time, key elements of the VII Corps Heavy Artillery had been kept busy preparing the way for these non-existent attacks and several companies of the 56ᵗʰ Division had been sacrificed in futile attempts to re-supply men who might otherwise have been evacuated from their clearly hopeless positions. The heavies were now directed to bring their fire back to the German third line in a pointlessly overdue attempt to disrupt the flow of German reinforcements coming up from Bucquoy and Puisieux. Bizarrely, the guns of the counter-

---

ⁱ 2ⁿᵈ Lt. Henry Bastick Pilgrim, 1/13ᵗʰ London Regt. (Kensingtons), died on Saturday, 1ˢᵗ July 1916. Aged 22 and single, he was the son of Mrs Fanny Pilgrim of 277, Norwood Road, SE24 and Albert Ezra Pilgrim. He is buried in Hebuterne Military Cemetery, grave IV.B.14.

battery groups were also told to join in on this barrage line thus allowing the German gunners even greater freedom to pound the British lines with unfettered ease.

ENDNOTES:
1 Forstner, Kurt Frhr. v., Das Königlich – Preussische Reserve-Infanterie-Regiment Nr. 15
2 Ibid.
3 White, 2nd Lt R, 1/14th London Regt. (London Scottish), Paper, IWM.
4 Lindsay, Lt. Col. J H, The London Scottish in the Great War
5 Gray, Maj. W E, 2nd City of London Regiment (Royal Fusiliers) in the Great War
6 White, 2nd Lt R, op. cit.
7 Ibid.
8 Ibid.
9 Ibid.
10 Ibid.
11 Ibid.
12 Forstner, Kurt Frhr. v., op. cit.

13. Z DAY: 1630 - 1930

"Sergeant Robinson brings me verbal orders to withdraw which of course we reluctantly must obey... Should like some hot dinner when we get back."

2nd Lt. Rex Petley
1/5th London Rifle Brigade

ON THE 168TH BRIGADE front there was a slight but detectable slackening of the German artillery fire once the last of the London Scottish had been ejected from the Farmer-Farmyard strongpoint. On the slopes in front of Rossignol Wood, parties of Germans could be seen advancing over the open. They did this with impunity. Those R.F.A. batteries still in action had been told to reserve fire in case of a German attack and requests to VII Corps for a barrage from the heavies had not been complied with. In the shattered trenches efforts were being made to collect and organise survivors. With the Rangers having lost all of their officers in the attacking waves, Lt. Col. Bayliffe sent his Bombing and Signalling Officers down the communication trenches from Battalion H.Q. to see what they could do. The few men left were led back to Napier trench in the orchards around Hebuterne and two companies of the 1/1st Londons trudged past them to take up defensive positions in the WR line.

To their left the fighting continued. On top of the hill behind Gommecourt German bombers could be seen massing around the Indus-Fillet junction in preparation for a move down Exe and Ems towards the remnants of the 169th Brigade. They did not progress unscathed, however. The forward section of C/283 Battery, R.F.A. dug in on the northern fringe of Hebuterne was one of the few R.F.A. batteries still firing and, just before 6 p.m., they had the small satisfaction of catching a party in the open. Otherwise, the German bombers filtered down the numerous communication trenches and pushed forward in numbers from both the village and the park, pressing back the remaining men of the L.R.B. and the other intermingled battalions. There was little that could be done to stop them.

As the front of the 169th Brigade collapsed all about him, 2nd Lt. Rex Petley had been fighting hard in his little corner of Eck trench. Since early in the afternoon, German bombers had been pressing down from the now over run Cemetery and at 2 p.m., 2nd Lt. Petley and his mixed bunch of Londoners were forced to give ground:

"I found myself in a sort of Cul de sac and managed to get into the main trench, if it can be so-called, by making each man crawl singly over a big mound of earth while we kept the Huns on our right down with bombs and sniping. As soon as we were all over we turned this mound into a barricade and managed easily enough to hold the Germans back. I then went along to the left to find Capt. de Cologan but could find no trace of the rest of 'D' Company nor 'C' Company. I at once sent a message back to advanced headquarters asking for more bombs and men."[1]

Petley's runner never arrived at the headquarters at the top of Exe trench less than 150 metres away. Earlier, two different runners from his company commander, Capt. de Cologan, had failed to make the reverse journey. They were to have told Petley to withdraw down Eck trench into new positions around Feast and Female. They did not arrive and, without orders, Petley was not about to retire voluntarily. And, by now, he was becoming more than a little frustrated by the failure of anyone to come to his support. Although nearly surrounded by hostile infantry, Petley could see no reason why he should stop fighting. All he needed was a few more bombs. Petley's 4 p.m. message to his senior officers contained an understandable if misplaced edge of irritation:

> "I sent a message to you about 2 hours ago to the effect that I am holding onto Eck with about 40 men including a dozen Queen Victoria Rifles and one Queen's Westminster Rifle and that I wanted more bombs. Quite out of touch to right and left. Have held off Germans on our right with barricade. It is quite absurd to lay here at night as we are."[2]

Nearly half an hour passed before he received a reply. The runner was Signalling Sergeant F S Robinson and he had verbal orders from Capt. De Cologan for Petley to fall back. Lt. Petley accepted the inevitable and gave instructions for his small party to withdraw to their left towards Exe trench and the rest of the battalion. Robinson was sent off with the bulk of the men, including Rfn. Arthur Schuman and the twin brother corporals, the Ebbetts, and with a brief message for Petley's company commander. Clearly, the Lieutenant could see no real justification for leaving his little bit of German trench:

> "Sergeant Robinson brings me verbal orders to withdraw which of course we reluctantly must obey. Sergeant Robinson is bringing all the men down to you and Sergeant Austin and I are trying to get Sergeant Olorenshaw. Should like some hot dinner when we get back."[3]

Plate 48 Rfn Frank Hollingham, London Rifle Brigade, killed 1st July 1916

2099 Rfn. Frank Hollingham and 2722 Rfn. Arthur Wood[i] from No. 15 Platoon, 'D' Company, were two of the men manning Eck trench and they had spent a nervous time dodging the German snipers who had steadily picked off men from their vantage points on the edge of the village. Here they had been joined by 4427 Rfn. Jack Manning from the Queen's Westminsters who had probably withdrawn down the battered trench from the cemetery when German counter-attacks had driven the men out some hours before. When the time came for them to withdraw Wood saw Hollingham lying in a recess in the side of what

---

[i] Rfn Arthur E Wood was evacuated to The Priory Military Hospital at Frimley in Surrey.

was left in the trench and Manning later reported he had been shot in the head. Assuming him to be dead Wood and Manning set off towards safety but Hollingham was still alive although severely wounded. He was later found by the advancing Germans and taken off for medical treatment. He survived for a fortnight before succumbing to his wounds at a German Field Ambulance at Caudry, where his body now lies[i].

Petley had planned to bring some of the wounded men out of the trench with him, one of whom was Sgt. Sidney Olorenshaw who had been hit early in the day as 'D' Company arrived in Eck trench[ii]. But, as soon as they moved away from their trench block, they were showered with bombs by a German party coming down Female trench to their rear and were forced to leave the wounded riflemen behind. Again in danger of being cut-off, the Lieutenant and two N.C.O.s, 1703 Sgt. Henry Austin and Cpl. Thorpe, acted as a rear guard to their retreating fellows. They accounted for several German bombers while the men in front found a tortuous route back to the front line. Finding direct access to Fen and Ferret trenches blocked, Petley's gallant band circled round to the left, to the point where Fibre trench joined the Maze. By now, as the clock passed five, they were being pursued by no less than four different bombing parties and, from here, the quickest route was over the top. Having only lost two or three men in his fighting withdrawal, Petley was reluctant to lose more in a madcap dash across the open, but the net was tightening and his options were few. They set off in small groups, bobbing and weaving through the hail of machine gun fire that tracked them. Petley and Austin were amongst the last to leave the trench and, finding a nearby shell hole, they used its shelter to give some covering fire to the others as they ran. There they stayed until a grenade burst next to them in the hole. Petley received a few fragments in the legs but Austin seemed to have been more seriously wounded although still able to move. Using the smoke from the explosion as cover they both ran for it, but in different directions. Austin was never seen again[iii].

While Petley[iv] and his men tried to find a way back to the German front lines, another group of L.R.B. men, this time from 'C' Company, were facing a similar dilemma: how to rejoin the rest of the battalion without taking unnecessary risks. Ten men, led by 1621 L/Cpl. John Foaden, had arrived near the western end of Feast trench early in the day and had spent an uncomfortable time in a large shell hole which they had unsuccessfully tried to consolidate with sandbags. They had

---

[i] 2099 Rfn. Frank Vincent Hollingham, 1/5th London Regt. (London Rifle Brigade) died of wounds on 14th July 1916 in German hands. He was buried in Caudry Old Communal Cemetery, grave A.14.

[ii] 88 L/Sgt. Sydney Harold Olorenshaw, 1/5th London Regt. (London Rifle Brigade) died of his wounds on 18th July 1916. Aged 27, he was the husband of Muriel Olorenshaw of 'Northcote', Woodlands Avenue, Rhos-on-Sea, Colwyn Bay. A prisoner of war he is buried in Le Cateau Military Cemetery grave, IV. A. 10.

[iii] 1703 Sergeant Henry Austin, 1/5th London Regt (London Rifle Brigade), died on Saturday 1st July 1916. His body was never found and his name is inscribed on the Thiepval Memorial, Somme, France, Pier and Face 9 D.

[iv] 2nd Lt. Reginald Edmund Petley M.C.., 1/5th London Regt. (London Rifle Brigade), was born on the 12th August 1892 in Weybridge, Surrey. Educated at St Annes, Redhill, he worked for the United River Plate Telephone Company, London Wall Buildings, Finsbury Circus. He later moved with his mother, Amy, to live at 'Ormesby', Langley Road, Beckenham in Kent. Petley was attested Private in the L.R.B. on the 23rd February 1911 at the age of 18 years and six months. He was promoted Lance Corporal on the 5th August 1914, Sergeant on the 6th September 1915 and gazetted 2nd Lt. on the 24th January 1916. He was promoted Lt. on the 24th July 1917 and disembodied on the 26th April 1919. The citation for his M.C. appeared in the London Gazette on 25th August 1916 and read: "For conspicuous gallantry in action. He reached and consolidated his objective, and, when the rest of the troops had been forced to withdraw, he refused to go without his wounded, and finally had to fight his way back. He was himself wounded on the return journey." [*Source*: Chris Rippingale]

tried to fight off the unwarranted attentions of bombers and snipers from the Park with their Lewis gun but they had become so cut off from the rest of the company that they had no idea that the majority of them had retired to the front line trenches (Fen and Ferret) early in the afternoon.

Plate 49 Rex Petley in 1923 after he rejoined the L.R.B.

At about 4 p.m. 8838 Sgt. Hugh Hember found them and advised them to retire, however, as there was no communication trench down which to withdraw, Foaden pointed out that the men would have to scramble out of the hole and across the open space towards Fen. Laden down with their Lewis gun and the heavy ammunition panniers which Foaden was loath to leave behind, such a move was tantamount to suicide given the volume of machine gun fire coming from the Park's tree line. Hember and Foaden agreed to wait until dusk. The approach of a German bombing party down Fibre trench meant waiting was no longer an option. Foaden, manning the Lewis gun, fought off three successive advances by the German bombers but eventually pressure told and the small group from 'C' Company withdrew into the warren of trenches and crater field of shell holes that was the Maze. They soon found themselves in another shell hole created by one of the super heavy howitzers and there, after a consultation between Hember and Foaden, it was decided to abandon the Lewis gun and the packs of ammunition they had brought over (they had been part of the 5th wave that had brought forward supplies and equipment for the consolidation of the position). The Lewis gun was made inoperable and the party, some fifteen strong, prepared to withdraw. Now, the occasional but potentially lethal instability of the Mills bomb came into play. Between them, the men had just two bombs left but, just as they were preparing to leave their hole, one exploded, fatally wounding Sgt. Hember and injuring five others. For Foaden[i] and the rest there was nothing for it, they could not carry the wounded and their only hope was to find the rest of the Company and hope to bring up reinforcements. Circling around the north edge of the Maze they entered Exe trench and, having

---

[i] 1621 L/Cpl. John Henry Foaden was awarded the Military Medal for his efforts on 1st July 1916. The citation in the London Gazette of the 1st September 1916 read:
"This NCO behaved with great courage and gallantry in charge of a Lewis gun on July 1st, 1916. He was cut off, but fought his way back, inflicting severe casualties on the enemy. He reported to me very clearly on his return. He destroyed his gun before his return over the open, as he found it impossible to bring it with him." [*Source:* Chris Rippingale]

some idea as to which way they should be heading, turned right passing the junction with Feast and Female trenches. Here they encountered another German bombing party coming down Female and their last grenade was used to hold them off briefly. They were now within reach of their beleaguered colleagues who were being pressed into Firm, Fen and Ferret trenches by attacks from all sides. Their journey, which had started at 4 p.m., had taken over an hour. They had travelled not much more than 200 yards.

Plate 50 Rfn. Vernon Gillbard and Rfn. Harold Langham, killed 1st July 1916

It is here that we must also recount a much disputed but, nevertheless, disturbing report from 1311 Rfn. Raymond Parker. Parker was part of 'A' Company and had been fighting hard all day on the edge of Gommecourt Park. They were in danger of being over run when, at about 2.30 p.m., a party of bombers appeared in timely fashion. Amongst these new arrivals were 2409 Rfn. Vernon Gillbard and 1985 Rfn. Cyril Brett. Before the two parties could join up a German bombing party appeared between them and a sharp scrap ensued. Although the enemy were driven off, both groups of L.R.B.s suffered casualties but Parker later testified that neither Gillbard nor Brett were amongst the wounded. At 4.00 p.m. the pressure from the German bombing parties became too intense and, in the absence of any grenades with which to retaliate, the order came down to withdraw. Parker had become separated from Gillbard and Brett and was able to make a successful getaway and the last he saw of this two friends was in a party he estimated at about thirty strong which was now surrounded by German troops. He was convinced they were in the process of surrendering. He later identified two other soldiers in the captured group as 3037 Rfn. Thomas Gasston and 2222 Rfn. Harold Langham. That was the last Parker saw of them.

In October, he wrote to Cyril Brett's father explaining what had happened. The reason for the letter was that Mr Brett had not heard anything from his son who, it was presumed, was a Prisoner of War along with Gillbard, Gasston and Langham, all of whom were unwounded when last seen. Parker later insisted that he had observed these men laying down their weapons and that they had clearly been in the process of surrendering when surrounded. The problem was that not one of the men's families had heard anything from them and it was not until Parker's comments first appeared in the *Territorial Service Gazette* of 4th November that concerns about the fate of these men grew. The anxious parents of Gasston and Langham wrote to the *TSG* and explained that all efforts to trace their sons had failed. They had contacted the German Red Cross, the Red Cross in Geneva and Berne and even the King of Spain in an effort to trace their boys but all to no effect. Members of Parliament were contacted and questions asked in the House of Commons, all in the belief that these men were being held incommunicado by the dreaded Hun for some unknown reason. The rather more distressing and suspicious fact was that all four of the men named were dead, their bodies never to be found. Whether Parker was mistaken in his recollection or whether these men had been shot out of hand by the Germans of the 55th R.I.R. will never be known, but their possible summary 'execution' in the middle of battle is an unhappy mirror to the actions of some British soldiers earlier in the day when they too reported shooting wounded and unarmed Germans in the initial stages of the assault.[i] Perhaps the men had tried to escape or maybe the attacking troops simply did not wish to be encumbered by such a large party of potentially hostile prisoners. Whatever the truth, the fate of these men would remain a sad and unresolved mystery.

***

ALL THE WHILE, THE REMNANTS of the 169th Brigade still trapped in the German front lines, were taking casualties. Pressure from the right and down Ems and Etch trenches had forced them to abandon Fern and most of Ferret trenches to the 11/55th and 12/55th R.I.R. By 4.45 p.m., behind hastily built blocks in a stretch of trench no more than 200 metres long, about 100 men fought desperately to hold off the German attacks. To their left, the 6/55th and 8/55th R.I.R. crowded in from the Park. To their front, the 7/55th, 10/55th and 55th R.I.R. Jäger Pioneers were bombing their way down Exe and Eel. From the German rear, the last remaining light minenwerfer of the 6th Guards Minenwerfer Company tossed its bombs a few hundred metres into the tightly packed trenches.

In the absence of most of their officers, Sgts. Lilley, Frost[ii] and Munday had been desperately holding on in Fir trench. They had already fought off a strong bombing attack by men of the 6/55th R.I.R. late in the afternoon and, with their reserves of Mills and German stick grenades exhausted, Sgt. Lilley[iii] recognised it was only a matter of time before they were overrun. Around 6.00 p.m. the sergeant set off to find a senior officer to advise him of their tenuous state of their position and, in Fen, he found Capt. de Cologan. De Cologan had been watching the 169th Brigade's position collapse and seen two parties of men dash into No Man's Land in an attempt to escape the showers of bombs being flung into every stretch of British held trench. Other men from all three attacking battalions were now crowding into a rapidly shortening stretch of German front line trench. They were essentially defenceless. Without any grenades their only

---

[i] Lt. Col. A S Bates, CO of the 1/5th London Regt. (London Rifle Brigade), whose men were involved in this 'surrender', was seriously exercised by the suggestion that his men would have capitulated en masse in such a way and repeatedly denied that any similar reports of this event had reached him. Of course, this does not necessarily mean that these men were not shot in the act of surrendering but there is no third party confirmation which might prove or disprove Parker's report. There is no mention of this incident in the London Rifle Brigade's regimental history.

[ii] 9849 Sgt Herbert Frost, 1/5th London Regt. (London Rifle Brigade) had gone to France on 4th November 1914. He was seriously wounded on 1st July 1916 and did not return to the battalion [*Source*: Chris Rippingale]

[iii] 515 Sgt. Walter Morris Lilley, 1/5th London Regt. (London Rifle Brigade) was awarded the D.C.M. for his conduct on 1st July 1916. The award was gazetted in the London Gazette of 22nd September 1916 and read:
"For conspicuous gallantry in organising snipers and keeping back enemy bombers until compelled, by overwhelming numbers, to retire. After all the officers had been killed or wounded, he assumed command of the company, and by his fine behaviour inspired all ranks with confidence". [*Source*: Chris Rippingale]

option was to go above ground in an effort to shoot the enemy bombers but anyone brave enough or desperate enough to try this almost inevitably fell victim to one of the many German snipers ringing their position. In the British lines, their mates could do nothing but watch. Further back, appeals for artillery intervention were reluctantly turned down. Such was the concern at H.Q. about a German attack on the British lines, that the artillery had been told to conserve ammunition in case it were needed to repel an assault. All across the length of the line reserves, stragglers and any unwounded men who had somehow returned from the attack were being collected and given lengths of trench to defend. The 167ᵗʰ Brigade was also bolstering the line. The 1/1ˢᵗ Londons and 1/3ʳᵈ Londons were in the reserve trench and the 1/7ᵗʰ Middlesex were close by in the Keep. Behind the lines the 1/8ᵗʰ Middlesex had started to move forward from Souastre, but, at the same time, such was the confusion about the precise details of the situation that at 4.42 p.m. 169ᵗʰ Brigade H.Q. instructed the 1/2ⁿᵈ Londons to be ready to push two companies over to the German lines at dusk in order to consolidate the German lines overnight!

It was approaching 5.30 p.m. when Petley eventually fell into the German front line trenches. There, he found a number of officers and about seventy men of the L.R.B., the Westminsters and the Victorias. He recognised Capts. Harvey[i] and Somers-Smith and his own company commander, Capt. de Cologan. The wounded Capt. Cox from the Queen Victoria's Rifles was there, as well as 2ⁿᵈ Lts. Bovill and Upton from the Westminsters. This small band were being heavily bombed from the right, along Ferret trench, whilst other attacks pressed in from the Park and the area of the Maze. A defensive line of sorts was put together using what ammunition they had and whatever could be collected from the dead and wounded of both sides. Shortly afterwards possibly the last of all of the runners who had tried to cross No Man's Land arrived at the Q.V.R.'s battalion H.Q. Rfn. Morris, a slight young man, appeared filthy and sweating to report on the imminent collapse of the 169ᵗʰ Brigade's position. After being given a drink he sat down and cleaned his rifle as if it were the most natural thing in the world to do after such perilous exertions.

With the two sides now in such close proximity artillery support was no longer possible. The speed of the German attack slowed - there was an inevitability about the result that made men less keen to risk themselves. Machine guns were manoeuvred into position to enfilade the British position. Trench mortars were brought up and prepared for action and, towards 7 p.m., they started to lob their bombs in ponderous arcs towards the short line of British-held trench. By this time, the intervention of the British field artillery had almost ceased. Three-quarters of the 56ᵗʰ Division's guns and howitzers had long since finished their day's work. Their equipment was either out of order or they had been ordered to stop firing whilst H.Q. watched to see what the Germans would do next. All of

---

i Capt. Bernard Sydney Harvey, 1/5ᵗʰ London Regt (London Rifle Brigade), died on Saturday, 1st July 1916, aged 27. He was the younger son of the late Walter Sydney and Florence Harvey of 24, Westbourne Terrace Road, later 9, Vale Court, Maida Vale, London. Educated at St Andrew's, Eastbourne, Malvern College, and Trinity College, Oxford; he was a member of the Oxford University O.T.C. and Captain of the Trinity College Rowing Eight between 1907 and 1910. On leaving Oxford he became assistant master at St Andrew's, Eastbourne. He was commissioned into the 2/5ᵗʰ London Rifle Brigade on 23ʳᵈ September 1914 and he joined the 1/5ᵗʰ Battalion in France in December 1914. He was promoted Lieutenant and then Captain in 1915. His body was never found and his name was inscribed on the Thiepval Memorial, Pier and Face 9 D. [*Additional Sources:* Pam & Ken Linge, Thiepval Project]

the field guns of 281ˢᵗ and 282ⁿᵈ Batteries had been out of action for most of the afternoon although the Southart group, which at 3.45 p.m. had been reduced to eight out of twenty guns, was now able to bring fourteen guns to bear and they were firing just over the heads of the men in the front German trenches[i].

By 7 p.m., seventy survivors were compressed into a short stretch of Fen and Ferret trenches. Some had already made a dash into No Man's Land, seeking the shelter of a nearby shell crater, others were now dead or wounded, hit by fragments from the persistent bombing attacks crowding in on them from all sides or from the minenwerfer shells being lobbed at short range. From the British trenches a concentration of Germans could be seen lurking behind the Cemetery waiting for orders to advance and, at 7.15 p.m., an urgent message was sent to both Corps and Divisional artillery for a rapid intervention. Severe pressure was now coming from the left, from the men of the 55ᵗʰ R.I.R. who had emerged from the Park, and, unable to hold them back, the last few yards of Fen were given up. The remaining officers led desperate efforts to block off the short stretch of Ferret trench that was now their only refuge.

Plate 51 Rfn. Archibald Froment, Queen Victoria's Rifles, killed 1ˢᵗ July 1916

Rfn. Ratcliff of the Q.V.R.s who, with Cpl. Maidment, had earlier made a desperate and fruitless attempt to stem the German advance from the second line was now waiting for orders in the German front line trench. On his arrival he found an old chum from his training days at Sheen, 4280 Rfn. Archie Froment, sitting on the firestep. Ratcliff and Froment had been billeted together in the vicarage at Sheen the previous December and now they passed the time of day:

"Ratcliff said: 'What do you think of this, Arch? I reckon it will be every man for himself' and Froment replied, 'It's a bit of a devil, Ratty'... As you know we had to retire at 7.40 p.m. and he (Froment) was hit getting back... I lay in a shell hole until dusk when I managed to get back safely."[4]

---

[i] Totals of ammunition fired by the Southart RFA Group of 1ˢᵗ July 1916:

	A	AX	BX	Totals
A/283	1,001	796	0	1,797
A/280	1,903	1,529	0	3,432
B/280	1,966	716	0	2,682
C/280	1,753	700	0	2,453
D/280	0	0	1,587	1,587
Totals	6,623	3,741	1,587	11,951

A = shrapnel, AX = high explosive (18 pdr), BX = high explosive (4.5 in. howitzer)
These batteries had fired continuously for 14 hours and 20 minutes since the start of the intense bombardment at 6.25 a.m.

Sadly, Froment[i] would not enjoy Ratcliff's continuing good luck and was to be killed in the desperate escape about to be mounted by the survivors in the German front line trench. And like so many, his body would never be found. As time wore on, the number of defenders was steadily eroded so that, by 8.20 p.m., there were but thirty men able to carry on the defence of their small stretch of line. Capt. Somers-Smith[ii] and Lt. Petley of the L.R.B., Capt. Leys Cox of the Q.V.R., 2nd Lt. Arthur of the Cheshires and 2nd Lt. Teddy Bovill of the Q.W.R. were amongst the last men still holding out, and with the majority of the men clear, they decided their time had come. Together with a small group of others they prepared a final rearguard action whilst the rest of the men got ready to escape. Jettisoning anything that might slow them down, each of the remaining men drew breath, wished their neighbour good luck and bade farewell to the wounded men they must leave behind. On a command, they clambered across the parapet and sprinted as fast they were able for the nearest shell hole. Immediately, the German machine guns started their infernal chattering from both left and right. Many fell, others gratefully gained cover.

Plate 52 Capt. John Robert Somers-Smith M.C. (London Rifle Brigade)
(Photograph Ruvigny's Roll of Honour, Volume 2)

Rfn. Arthur Schuman of the L.R.B was among the group that made their dash for safety:

---

[i] 4280 Rfn. Archibald Walter Froment, No. 5 Platoon, 'B' Company, 1/9th London Regt. (Queen Victori'a Rifles) was killed on Saturday, 1st July 1916. He was the son of Mrs Froment of 7, Begnold Road, Forest Gate. His body was never found and his name is inscribed on the Thiepval Memorial, Pier and Face 9 C.

[ii] Capt. John Robert Somers-Smith M.C., 1/5th London Regt (London Rifle Brigade), died on Saturday, 1st July 1916. He was aged 29. He was the only surviving son and the youngest of four children of Robert Vernon and Mary Gertrude Somers-Smith of Bur Lea, Hersham. Born on 15th December 1887 he was educated at Eton (Eton College Volunteers 1903-6) and Magdalen College, Oxford (Oxford University OTC) being Captain of Boats at both. married Marjorie Duncan on 25th July 1914 and his son, Henry, was born on the 5th May 1915. A solicitor working at 5 Kensington Square Mansion, Young Street, W, he lived at The Barn, Walton on the Hill, Epsom in Surrey and was gazetted 2nd Lt. in the L.R.B. in March 1909. Promoted Captain in June 1914, he went to the front on 3rd November 1914 with the LRB and was awarded the M.C. at Second Ypres. The Times obituary described him as having "a genius for friendship" and Lt. Belcher V.C., previously sergeant in B Company, described him as "The best Captain the London Rifle Brigade ever had". His body was never found and his name is inscribed on the Thiepval Memorial, Pier 9, Face D. His brother, 2nd Lt. Richard Willingdon Somers-Smith, 7th KRRC, was killed at Hooge on 30th June 1915 and is buried in Bedford House Cemetery, enclosure No. 2, grave VI. A. 27. [*Additional Sources:* Pam & Ken Linge, Thiepval Project. Dick Flory: Eton School Register, Part VII, 1899-1909; Etonians Who Fought in the Great War, 1914-1919; Record of Services of Solicitors and Articled Clerks 1914-1918: Fifty Years of Sport: Eton, Harrow and Winchester]

"I hardly waited for the order, but it came - 'Every man for himself'. I did not wait to argue - over the top I went like greased-lightning - surviving a hail of bullets. I immediately fell flat. Then trying to imagine I was part of the earth, I wriggled along on my belly. Dead, dying, wounded, feigning death, who knows? The ground was covered with them. I sped from shell-hole to shell-hole. Never had I run faster. It was snipers, machine guns and shrapnel all the way. About half-way across, I rolled into a shell-hole and fell on top of a badly wounded German in a pitiable state. All he said was 'Schlecht, Schlecht' which means bad. I don't know what made me do it, but I gripped his hand and sped on. I often think that someone above was looking over me through that act of kindness. When I finally scrambled into our front-line trench I was greeted by our Adjutant, Capt. Wallis, and R.S.M. Macveagh who both solemnly shook my hand. I was told that only twenty had returned so far."[5]

Rfn. Jacobs of 'C' Company, L.R.B., was another to make a break for safety:

"It was either a bolt back with a sporting chance of getting through or surrender. We turned tail and made a blind bolt… The moment we did so they turned a veritable hail of fire on us from machine guns and rifles. I got caught in the wire and sprawled headlong, tore myself free and they got caught again. Once more I disentangled myself and then plunged into a shell hole and stopped there. How I got as far as there I know not for men were falling like flies. None who kept on with this rush for our line got through."[6]

Plate 53 Rfn. Shirley Harris, Queen's Westminster Rifles, killed 1st July 1916

Rfn. W J Poole, No. 4 Platoon of the Queen's Westminsters, was one of a mixed group of Westminsters and Victorias crowded into the German front line waiting for the order to abandon the position. He later reported from his bed at Littlehampton Red Cross Hospital the fate of the men near him. Poole had been a bomber and one of his section colleagues was 4060 Rfn. Shirley Harris. Harris had been slightly wounded earlier in the day but, though fit enough to make a run for it, he was caught in the cross fire which scythed through the fleeing men. Harris died somewhere in No Man's Land and his body was never found[i]. 4214 Rfn. Arthur Bolt would not be one to try to reach the British lines. He had been

---

[i] 4060 Rfn. Shirley Woodbine Harris, 1/16th London Regt. (Queen's Westminster Rifles) was killed on Saturday, 1st July 1916. He was the son of Mr F Harris of 11, Sidney Avenue, Bowes Park, London. His body was never found and his name is inscribed on the Thiepval Memorial, , Pier 9, Face D.

shot in the stomach and Poole saw him lying fatally wounded in a German traverse. Readying himself for the off he took a few moments to comfort the anguished Bolt but it was clear that the wounded man could not last much longer[i]. Poole then started to climb out of the trench and it was not a moment too soon as German troops suddenly rushed into the traverse seeming to take prisoner 4431 Rfn. Reginald Small of No. 8 Platoon and four men from the Queen Victorias. Small, however, was later found to have died in the last few moments of the battle[ii].

Two other Westminsters were also waiting, wounded, in the front line. 3708 Rfn. Reginald Knott of 'A' Company had been attached to the Headquarters bombers and had been wounded earlier in the day in the advance towards the German third line. He had then spent a long afternoon dragging himself back towards the first line in the hope of receiving some medical treatment. His rests had been frequent and time was also spent sheltering from the storm of rifle and machine gun fire coming from the right where the Rangers' attack had long since collapsed. He eventually crawled into the German front line where stretcher bearers and others were dressing the wounds of a number of men. As he waited his turn 2380 Rfn. James Warrilow, an old 'A' Company chum, wandered past. He had discarded his helmet and jacket and was clearly in great distress with his right arm badly injured. Knott called out to him but he seemed not to hear and, instead, joined the queue for treatment. Having had his arm put in a sling he moved off down the trench as if oblivious to the carnage around him. The wounded that could walk or crawl were now ordered out into No Man's Land in preparation for the withdrawal and Knott[iii] found himself a convenient shell hole from which he would inch his way to safety during the night. Of Warrilow there was no sign and it seems that he was taken prisoner by the Germans when they overran this stretch of trench.

Plate 54 Cpl. Ernest Matthey, Queen Victoria's Rifles, killed 1st July 1916

---

[i] 4214 Rfn. Arthur James Bolt, 1/16th London Regt. (Queen's Westminster Rifles) was killed on Saturday, 1st July 1916. Aged 20, he was the son of William & Mary Bolt of 30, High St., Wimbledon, London. His body was never found and his name is inscribed on the Thiepval Memorial, , Pier 9, Face D.
[ii] 4431 Rfn. Reginald Robert Small, 1/16th London Regt. (Queen's Westminster Rifles) was killed on Saturday, 1st July 1916. His body was never found and his name is inscribed on the Thiepval Memorial, , Pier 9, Face D.
[iii] 3708 Rfn. Reginald Frederick Knott, A Company, 1/16th London Regt. (Queen's Westminster Rifles), was wounded on Saturday, 1st July 1916. He was evacuated to Boscawen Ward, Croesnewydd Hospital in Wrexham. He returned to the battalion and died on 8th June 1917. By then aged 24, he was the son of Albert George and Fanny Louisa Knott, of 'Hurley', Bellfield Avenue, Harrow Weald, Middx.. He was buried in Hampstead Cemetery, grave E. 2. 61. Unusually, his brother, 2207 Cpl. Ralph Miles Knott, also of the Queen's Westminsters, is buried in the same cemetery in grave F. 1. 53. He died on 17th October 1915.

4189 Rfn. Edward Hall, No. 7 Platoon, 'B' Company, Queen Victoria's Rifles, was another man waiting for the off and along side him was one of his mates from 'B' Company, 26-year old 1004 L/Cpl. Ernest Matthey from Bayswater. These two nearly left it too late as German bombers suddenly appeared at the end of their traverse just as they scrambled over the parapet. But, like so many, having survived all day Matthey's luck now ran out in the last few minutes of the fight. He was caught by some of the still vicious barbed wire that littered the ground. The more he struggled the more he became entangled and soon he was a sitting target for some German rifleman. He did not miss[i]. Hall's luck was still in, at least for a short while, but it did not hold for long. A rifle bullet hit his hand, going through and into his water bottle and then into his hip. Unable to move he was forced to lie out amongst the bodies and debris waiting for some form of help. He struggled into a nearby shell hole and sheltered there but could not move further because of his wounds. Two days later he was found by a German patrol and made a Prisoner of War. He had, unlike so many, survived.

Plate 55 Capt. Bernard Sydney Harvey, 1/5ᵗʰ London Regt. (London Rifle Brigade)

Behind them the rear guard of Somers-Smith, Harvey, Petley, Leys Cox, Arthur, Bovill and the rest now threw away their weapons and headed for the nearest shell hole. The three Captains, John Somers-Smith, Bernard Harvey and Harold Cox[ii] were all killed in the withdrawal, their bodies never to be found. Somewhere in No Man's Land the gallant 2ⁿᵈ Lt. Arthur also met his fate, his body to be retrieved the following spring. Better fortune attended Lt. Petley[iii], whose path the day before must have been crossed by several lucky black cats. He was hit in the knee but survived to collapse into a shell hole where he stayed

---

[i] 1004 L/Cpl. Ernest Matthey, 'B' Company, 1/19ᵗʰ London regt. (Queen Victoria's Rifles) was killed on Saturday, 1ˢᵗ July 1916. Aged 26, he was the son of Mr Albert & Mrs Fanny Matthey of 21, Westmoreland Rd., Bayswater, London. His body was never recovered and his name is inscribed on the Thiepval Memorial, Pier and Face 9 C.

[ii] Capt. Harold Edward Leys Cox, 1/9ᵗʰ London Regt (Queen Victoria's Rifles), died on Saturday, 1ˢᵗ July 1916, aged 29. He was the Son of Edward William Cox of 28, Madeley Rd., Ealing, London. His body was never found and his name is inscribed on the Thiepval Memorial, Pier and Face 9 C. Leys Cox was educated at St George's, Windsor Castle and St Paul's. He joined the QVR in 1909 and was promoted Captain in August 1914. His brother, Maj. R H Woodruff Cox OBE T.D. also served in the battalion.

[iii] On the 24ᵗʰ March 1918, 2ⁿᵈ Lt. Petley was wounded in the lung by a sniper's bullet and captured by the Germans during their Spring offensive. He was transferred first to a German hospital (Kriegs Lazarett) at Ytres and then moved to Germany. He was repatriated via Copenhagen in 1919 returning to work at the United River Plate Telephone Company. He resigned his commission after a dispute with the War Office over a disability pension.

until night fell. In his report, Lt. Petley told of an incident that occurred in No Man's Land at about 9.45 p.m.:

"About the twilight, a German came out to us, and as I saw his Red Cross I prevented our men from firing. He came up, saw I had been roughly dressed, and went nearer to our own lines to attend to one of his own men. Some of our men got up to go and he shouted out and stopped one of their machine guns. I think his action showed pluck and decency and augurs well for our wounded which we have had to leave behind."

Petley then crawled back to the British lines after a general cease-fire fell across the battlefield. Capt. de Cologan, Rex Petley's commander in 'D' Company in the London Rifle Brigade, and the wounded 2nd Lt. Upton[i] of the Westminsters were two of those taken prisoner when the Germans eventually overran the last few yards of trench. Others were left dying in the trenches and the German dugouts whence they had been carried. Amongst those fatally wounded were Capt. Houghton and 2nd Lt. Norman Meeking[ii] both of 'B' Company of the Q.V.R. Meeking was later carried down into a German dugout along with the wounded 2647 Rfn. Walter Cane of the Q.V.R.s, where he was also seen by another soon-to-be Prisoner of War 2475 Rfn. Harry Courteen. Both men, then held at Langensalza Camp, later testified to the severity of Meeking's wounds and Cane reported that the officer had died soon after.

To the left, another group of men, led by the surviving N.C.O.s of 'A' Company of the L.R.B., Sgts. Lilley, Frost and Munday, made a desperate dash for safety from Point 94 which they had steadfastly held for over twelve hours against repeated German bombing attacks. Frost was hit in the head to add heavy bleeding to the extensive bruising he had received from an explosion earlier in the day, but the three of them survived to make the return journey. Behind them they left the bodies of many colleagues - men of all ranks like 2nd Lt. Charles Bowden Doust and the fearless 18-year old Lewis gunner from the Old Kent Road, 2173 Rfn. David Reynolds, No. 2 Platoon, 'A' Company.

One of the last to leave the German lines was 2nd Lt. Edward Bovill of 'A' Company, 1/16th Queen's Westminster Rifles. Before the war a wealthy corn merchant with offices in the City and a devout, church-going man from Surrey, Bovill had been wounded in the face as he left the safety of the trenches but he had gone forward with his men nonetheless. He had been one of the small group of Q.W.R. platoon commanders who had kept their battalion's attack from failing after the company commanders had all been killed. Throughout, he had led his dwindling band of men gallantly and aggressively. Now he found himself

---

i 2nd Lt. Douglas Field Upton, M.C., 2/2nd London Regt, att. 1/16th London Regt. (Queen's Westminster Rifles) was awarded the M.C. for his gallantry at Gommecourt (London Gazette, 3rd September 1918). He enlisted in the 5th East Surrey Regt. before being commissioned into the 3/2nd London Regt. on 16th January 1915. He went to Egypt with the 2/2nd London Regt. before being attached to the Queen's Westminsters when the battalion returned to France and was disbanded in May 1916. He was made a Prisoner of War but repatriated and was seconded to the Royal Engineers. He was later promoted Captain and returned to the 2nd Londons on 23rd May 1919.

ii 2nd Lt. Normam Arthur Meeking, 1/9th London Regt (Queen Victoria's Rifles), died on Saturday, 1st July 1916. He was born on 26th May 1892, the son of Thomas Arthur and Gertrude Mary Meeking of 'Rocheford', King Edward Road, New Barnet. His father was a tea merchant. He was educated at King's School, Canterbury and was he was employed in the London Office of Entre Rios Railways Co, Ltd, River Plate House, Finsbury Circus, E. C. He was commissioned on 1st March 1915 into the 2/9th London Regt. having been No. Z 24 Ordinary Seaman, Royal Naval Volunteer Reserve, London Division and part of the Nelson Battalion of the Royal Naval Division. He was a nephew of a Captain in the Queen Victorias. His body was never found and his name is inscribed on the Thiepval Memorial, Pier and Face 9C. [*Additional source:* Dick Flory: King's School Canterbury Register, 1859-1931]

scurrying from shell hole to shell hole, until eventually he moved into the lee of the slight rise that gave protection from the machine guns firing from the cover of the Park. His escape was nearly complete. The last few yards took him through the graveyard of the 1/2nd Londons who had been slaughtered as they tried in vain to reinforce the men of the 169th Brigade in front of Gommecourt. Their bodies now littered the gentle slope up which the lieutenant crawled and scrambled. Bullets still whistled and sang close by. Grass and earth were flung into the air by their impact. From what was left of the British front line trenches, men peered anxiously, each one charting his tortuous progress, each one encouraging him onwards to safety. By the time the lieutenant reached the British parapet, his journey of 300 metres had taken fully half an hour. Hands reached out to meet him; cheerful voices greeted his safe return. As he stepped into the trench and safety, a bullet from some unknown weapon in the German lines slammed into the lieutenant's body. Surrounded by his despairing colleagues, 2nd Lt. Edward Henry Bovill of 'Buckland', Betchworth in Surrey died before medical aid could help him[i].

Plate 56 2nd Lt. Edward Bovill, 1/16th London Regt. (Queen's Westminster Rifles)
(Photograph Harrow Roll of Honour)

ENDNOTES:
[1] The History of the London Rifle Brigade 1859-1919, 1921
[2] Ibid.
[3] Ibid.
[4] Territorial Service Gazette, 9th September 1916, page 132.
[5] Schuman Rfn A, 1/5th London Rifle Brigade. From a document held at the Liddle Collection, Leeds University and the IWM
[6] Jacobs, Rfn F W Hackney and Stoke Newington Recorder, 28th July 1916.

[i] 2nd Lt. Edward Henry Bovill, 'A' Company, London Regt. (Queen's Westminster Rifles), died on Saturday, 1st July 1916. He was the elder and only surviving son of Mr and Mrs J. Henry Bovill of 'Buckland', Betchworth in Surrey, his younger brother, 2nd Lt. J Eric Bovill, 6th Dragoon Guards (The Carabiniers) was killed on 23rd January 1916 and is buried in Vermelles British Cemetery, grave III. A. 1. Born in April 1887 he was educated at Summerfields, Oxford, Harrow and Pembroke College, Cambridge. He was gazetted on the 9th August 1915 and went to the front in March 1916. Bovill was a wealthy City corn merchant with offices in Mark Lane, EC1. In his will, he left £32,207 (approximately £1.2 million in today's money). A codicil to his will stated: "In case I am killed I want to give the parish of Buckland a new organ. I want a good one, so please spend up to £500 on it. If necessary, spend another £500 on it" (£500 in 1916 was the equivalent of some £18,300 now). His body was lost and his name is inscribed on the Thiepval Memorial, Pier 13 Face C. [*Additional Sources:* Pam & Ken Linge, Thiepval Project]

14.   Z DAY: THE EVENING AND BEYOND

"I have very bad news for you, gentlemen. Your Regiment has done splendid work today, but unfortunately your casualties are very heavy. You have one officer and 150 men left, please join them and do what you can for them."

Brig. Gen. Coke, OC 169ᵗʰ Brigade
addressing the 'surplus' officers of
the 1/16ᵗʰ Queen's Westminsters

A S THE FINE SUMMER'S EVENING wore on the guns of both sides gradually fell silent. But the air was not still. Replacing the thunder of the artillery and the vicious chatter of the machine guns was a lesser though more harrowing sound. Across the fields and in the shattered remains of the trenches on both sides of No Man's Land, hundreds of men lay wounded and dying. In their agony they now filled the air with their shrieks and moans. There were desperate cries for help, for water, often they called out for the tender ministrations of their mothers. Men swore and wept and prayed. Those that could crawled to find shelter, in a shell hole perhaps, or struggled towards the remains of the British trenches. If they were able, they would use their field dressing to cover the most serious of their wounds. It had been a hot day and, for many, thirst became a most pressing problem. Unknown dozens died within reach of their trenches or in the shambles of the front line trenches for lack of help.

In the British trenches, battered though they were, stretcher bearers sought out the wounded but care had to be taken as any movement was likely to bring down machine gun or artillery fire in an instant. The front trenches, the ones so gallantly dug at the end of May, lay in ruins. The wounded and dead were scattered every few yards and to get help to the injured or bring them back down to the aid posts, the stretcher bearers often had to walk on the bodies of their dead colleagues. 3254 Sgt. Thornton Bisgood of the 1/2ⁿᵈ Londons recalled the scenes of devastation in the British lines:

> "Passing along Young Street I came along a tableau of three of my chums, one standing, one sitting (headless) and the other lying, all three had been hit by the same shell. In the dusk in Yiddish Street I stumbled over something and bending down to my horror found it was a mans head, so as to save some other chaps a similar shock I tried to pick up the offending napper but found that it was rigid as the whole body was beneath the ground and it remained there the whole night and part of the next day. In Yellow Street I was clutched at and caught by a hand protruding from the side of the trench, all that was visible was a hand and arm, the sleeve showed it to be an officer (1ˢᵗ Lt.) of the L.R.B.'s."[1]

What was left of the British battalions were now back in the reserve line, those in front having been abandoned to the dead, the wounded and the medical staff. There was still concern amongst senior officers that the Germans would take advantage of the chaos in front of Hebuterne to launch their own attack across No Man's Land and so every able bodied man, and even some that weren't, were pressed into service in the trenches, waiting for an attack that never came.

Behind the lines, the officers who had been kept behind, the 'battle surplus' who would form the nucleus of the unit in the case of severe casualties, were being rushed to the front. At Souastre the officers of the 169th Brigade had been waiting for news of the attack. By now they were aware that casualties had been heavy and that all was not well, but the full scale of the disaster was not yet apparent. At 6.15 p.m. a runner arrived from Brigade H.Q. with a message that stated: "all reserve officers will report to brigade headquarters in Hebuterne forthwith". There were sixteen officers and their servants at Souastre and, for the next thirty minutes, all was a frantic scramble for helmets, revolvers, gas masks. Non-essential equipment was packed and dumped in the village and, just before 7 p.m. they started off up the tracks through Sailly and then across the plain to Hebuterne. The closer they got to the village the greater was the damage. Sailly had been bombarded and was on fire and the field guns arrayed behind Hebuterne had also been targets of the German guns. Smoking shell holes pockmarked the landscape. Overloaded ambulances rushed past and the bloodied walking wounded struggled along the wooden tracks towards Sailly and beyond to Couin.

Hebuterne was a smouldering ruin. The houses that had remained before the battle were now piles of bricks and match-wood. The great church was irrevocably smashed. A haze of dust and smoke hung over everything and, at intervals throughout the village, lay the huddled bodies of the dead. The officers and their men sought out the H.Q. of 169th Brigade. 2nd Lt. Moy recalled the moment when the dreadful news of the fate of their battalion was given to them:

"General Coke's slim figure loomed out of the darkness and he started to speak, "I have very bad news for you, gentlemen. Your Regiment has done splendid work today, but unfortunately your casualties are very heavy. You have one officer and 150 men left, please join them and do what you can for them." At those words my heart sank into my boots; judging by the expressions on the other people's faces they were feeling the same as I was. We saluted the general, and started off to the trenches."[2]

Moy and his fellow officers started up what remained of the communication trenches and soon came upon a group of three men, two supporting the bloodied and unconscious figure of a third. The badly wounded man, shot in the back and through both hands, was Moy's friend 2nd Lt. Frederick Thomas[i] who had looked so wretchedly nervous when the battalion marched out of St Amand the evening before. The increasingly horrified Q.W.R. officers carried on until they arrived at the old front line trenches. There they found the remains of the battalion – shocked, exhausted and covered in mud and blood. There was nothing much to be done that night. Roll calls and reorganisation could wait and so, leaving them to sleep under the care of an officer and some of the batmen, the rest of the party pushed up to the new front line trenches from where, just over twelve hours earlier, the great attack had been launched with such high hopes. The scene was deeply shocking even to officers with some experience of death and destruction in the trenches:

---

i 2nd Lt. Frederick Stanley Thomas, 1/16th London Regt., (Queen's Westminster Rifles) lived at 41, Almeric Road, Clapham Common, London. Aged 27, he had joined the Army on 21st November 1914 first going to France on 5th May 1916. Although later promoted Captain he spent the rest of the war at home not having recovered from his wounds.

"The same sight met our gaze on every side; dead men and blood. On until we came out into No Man's Land. Here the sight was indescribable. Dead and dying Englishman and Germans were lying in heaps; some writhing, some moaning and screaming, some lying still. We spent the remainder of that night getting in the ones who were still alive."[3]

Searching amongst the dead and wounded, they came across a body lying on a stretcher. It was 2nd Lt. Teddy Bovill, who had so nearly made it back across No Man's Land when the German lines were evacuated, but who died within a few seconds of safety. As the hours wore on, Moy would learn of the fate of the other officers of 'B' Company who gone 'over the top' on that Saturday morning: Capt. George Cockerill had been severely wounded and lay in the German trenches[i]; 2nd Lt. James Horne had died doing 'a VC stunt' as he covered the withdrawal of his men from the German third line; 2nd Lt. William Strange, the recent arrival from the 2/2nd Londons, had been killed with no-one to mark the place of his passing; and 2nd Lt. Henry Luscombe, the 2/3rd Londons' officer who had taken Moy's place at the head of his platoon for the attack, had been knocked unconscious be a shell explosion early in the day[ii]. Every officer except one from 'B', 'C' and 'D' Companies of the Queen's Westminsters was a casualty and nearly 600 men of the battalion were either dead, wounded or missing.

At 168th Brigade's Forward H.Q. Brig. Gen. Loch and Maj. Philip Neame V.C. surveyed the wreckage of their attack and contemplated the ruin of their command. For Loch the loss seemed overwhelming. He had gone as far forward as reasonably possible to stay in touch with his men and he had spent much of the day begging and pleading VII Corps for effective heavy artillery counter-battery fire. He could see the carnage being caused amongst his men by the German guns at first hand. He just had to step out of his dugout to see the shattered bodies of soldiers killed where they stood in what was left of the trenches. And he could not understand why the artillery support for the attack had been so feeble. Its failure was killing and maiming his men and he took it badly. As the day drew to a close, Neame, Loch's Brigade Major, decided it was time for his general to retire to a safer position. Sgt Coates, who had stood alongside them under the terrific German barrage, was ordered to accompany Loch to the rear and he later described their journey and the impact the Brigade's destruction had on Loch:

"He was like a man in a dream. It was terrible to see him like that, because he was quite a chatty old boy, always talking about his little daughter, and friendly, though he could be severe sometimes. The Old Man was a daredevil, a real fighter... I'm sure the Old Man was shell-shocked. I know he was! He was broken. He made no objection to coming with me. He didn't say a word. He just got up very, very slowly and, in a break in the shelling, we went off... the line was absolutely broken and the trenches

---

i He would die in a German hospital two days later.
ii 2nd Lt. (later Lt.) Henry Luscombe, 2/3rd London Regt. att. 1/16th London Regt. (Queen's Westminster Rifles) was born on 11th November 1891 and was the son on of Mr. and Mrs. George Luscombe of 25, Princes Road, Holland Park Avenue, London. He was educated at Saunders Road School and was a solicitor's clerk with Chandler, Somers and Boulton, living at 'The Lawn', Vicarage Road, East Sheen. He attested Private in the 1/9th London Regt. (Queen Victoria's Rifles) on 6th October 1913 and went to France with the battalion in November 1914. He was commissioned into the 4/3rd London Regt. in December 1915. He was killed in action on 11th April 1917 and is buried at London Cemetery, Neuville-Vitasse, grave I. B. 27.

were all knocked in and chaps buried underneath. We were treading over dead bodies and all sorts of things going along. We just struggled back as best we could."⁴

Joining the stream of casualties that was flowing across the plain to Sailly, Coates and Loch struggled back the two kilometres to the village and the main Brigade H.Q. Here they each found a corner in the cellar in which to silently reflect on the disaster and the shattering loss of officers and men, friends and colleagues.

What was happening on the ground, however, appeared not to have been reported to VII Corps headquarters. At 7.30 p.m., as the last men were struggling back from in front of Gommecourt village over what remained of the British parapet, VII Corps staff were demanding that 56ᵗʰ Division press home their 'success'. They still seemed to think that the 46ᵗʰ Division, which had been back in their trenches since mid-morning, was capable of linking up with the 56ᵗʰ behind Gommecourt:

"7.30 p.m. 56ᵗʰ Division to take advantage of darkness to support troops still in German front line. Develop success hitherto gained - particular attention to left flank with a view to joining hands with 46ᵗʰ Division and then clearing Gommecourt Park."⁵

Twenty minutes later they issued another order which bore no relationship to any reality the men back in the trenches knew:

"7.50 p.m. Support troops in German front line, who on no account should withdraw. At 0230 attack towards Gommecourt Park."⁶

That senior officers should have lost touch so completely with the facts as they were at the front should come as no surprise. Battalion commanders had effectively lost contact with their men as soon as they crossed the parapet and they were only a few hundred yards from the front line. With the forward telephone lines mainly cut by the German artillery fire, messages had to be sent by runner from battalion to brigade before anything could be wired to division or VII Corps H.Q. Sometimes these journeys took hours to complete and, too often, the runners fell victim to the torrent of shells that fell on Hebuterne and messages went undelivered. It is still remarkable, however, that barely twelve hours after the attack had gone in, events at VII Corps H.Q. were running something like eight to ten hours behind what was happening on the ground.

Still further behind the lines at Pas, Gen. Allenby was waiting anxiously for news of the assault and by late evening it was confirmed that the men of the 56ᵗʰ Division were all back in their lines. As aerial observation had confirmed that the 46ᵗʰ Division had now 'lost' the few bits of line they had only briefly occupied during the early hours of the attack it was clear that the whole operation had failed – at least in terms of taking Gommecourt. Indeed, it should have been clear to Allenby that the whole diversionary operation had failed too. In a hand written note sent to G.H.Q. on the night of 1ˢᵗ July, he reported that his neighbour at VIII Corps, Gen. Hunter-Weston, had intended, but then cancelled, an attack on Serre at 2 a.m. on the morning of the 2ⁿᵈ July, so clearly the Serre attack had collapsed as well. But Allenby reported that he too had planned a renewal of the attack timed for 2.30 a.m. This attack was to somehow replicate the original plan with both divisions attacking the flanks of the salient and joining hands behind Gommecourt. Hunter-Weston's proposal, unrealistic though it was, was at least conceived on the basis that it was thought there were men of the 31ˢᵗ Division fighting in Serre and that an attempt should be made to make contact with them. Sensibly, this plan was abandoned at 9.50 p.m. Allenby's plan beggars belief. First of all there were only two battalions plus elements of two more in the 56ᵗʰ Division which had not suffered significant casualties and on the 46ᵗʰ Division's front it had proved impossible to re-organise the men in daylight, quite how they were to do this in the dark defies all explanation. Then those men remaining were to be asked to fight their way through German trenches packed with reinforcements, through artillery barrages that had got stronger as the day went on and then find their way through battered and unrecognisable trenches to locations no British soldier living had ever seen. And the troops to be asked to do this were the ones that had not been trained to do this job. Allenby's letter at least shows that Lt. Gen. Snow had seen the light:

> "My intention was to attack at 2.30 a.m. on the original plan, the 2 divisions joining hands behind Gommecourt, but the G.O.C. VII Corps (Snow) does not now think this attack has any chance of success. If, however, this attack were necessary to ease pressure elsewhere or to co-operate with the VIII Corps attacking Serre, I would carry it out regardless of casualties, but the general situation does not appear to demand this sacrifice."[7]

It was Allenby's willingness to sacrifice his men in hopeless causes that had led to his unpopularity in his previous commands. He clearly saw no point in trying to improve people's opinions of him now. And his reading of the situation seems still to be most perplexing. Having earlier in the note mentioned that six companies of Sherwood Foresters had entered the German lines around the Little Z on the extreme left of the 46ᵗʰ Division's attack he now proposed that the Division mount a two battalion night-time attack in order to withdraw these men. The issue here, as far as Allenby's reading of the situation is concerned, is that earlier in the same note he had written that "...airman report that there are only Germans there (i.e. Little Z) now". Thankfully, like all of the other attempts to renew the attack, this utterly pointless exercise was cancelled.

As it turned out, however, the decision to ignore Allenby's plan for a renewed attack had been pre-empted by the two Divisional commanders in an extraordinary, and high risk, display of independent decision making. The 46ᵗʰ Division's War Diary reports a meeting of the two defeated Generals in the mid-evening. It should be noted that the time to which the Diary refers is some ten minutes before that at which the order for the cancellation of the renewed attack was even issued by Third Army HQ:

> "9:40 p.m. GOC (Stuart Wortley) and GSO1 (Thorpe) motored to see GOC 56ᵗʰ Division (Hull). GOC, 46ᵗʰ Division explained his plan of attack to take place at midnight. GOC 56ᵗʰ Division said he had orders from the Corps for all commanders who had just visited him that at 2.30 a.m. he was to attack again his left flank. The object of the attack was to help the 46ᵗʰ Division. Both GOCs agreed that any attack 56ᵗʰ Division could make would in no way help 46ᵗʰ Division. Their sole object was to extricate 5ᵗʰ and 7ᵗʰ Sherwoods and there could be no idea of 46ᵗʰ and 56ᵗʰ Divisions joining hands. As 46ᵗʰ Division attack must take place as early

as possible and time had been approved by Corps commander, 56th Division would be immediately informed of its progress. Unless GOC, 56th Division could see a way to help 46th Division he would not make the attack ordered."

In essence, Hull and Stuart Wortley had privately concluded that the joint attack ordered by the Army commander was both impractical and pointless and that, therefore, Allenby's order should be ignored. Stuart Wortley was still of the conviction that some men of the 5th and 7th Sherwoods were trapped in the German lines and that he had a responsibility to attempt a rescue. The evidence that, in fact, those few men in the lines in front of Gommecourt Wood had long since been killed or captured had either not been collated or had been incorrectly interpreted and so Stuart Wortley planned to send the 1/5th Lincolns, a battalion from his reserve Brigade, the 138th Brigade, across No Man's Land just before midnight in an effort to contact and then extract these men.

Hull was going to do nothing apart from clear the wounded away and reorganise his shattered and exhausted battalions. Both Generals appreciated, in a way that more senior officers further back clearly either could not or did not want to, that there was absolutely no way that the operation to cut off Gommecourt could be renewed. With the resources available, barely one and a half Brigades across the two Divisions, any plan to attack a German positions full of troops on high alert was only a recipe for more heavy casualties from which nothing could possibly be gained. And so, before any official word came down from on high that the attack should be cancelled Stuart Wortley and Hull took their own decision in plain defiance of their Corps and Army commanders. This was a brave decision and, thankfully, one borne out by the soon communicated Third Army order to cancel the operation.

It would not be the end of the slaughter, though. The 1/5th Lincolns struggled into place in the British front lines and, as Saturday drew into Sunday, in a shambolic advance in which, for a time, the men out in No Man's Land lined up facing the wrong way, they wandered into the German wire and were cut down by machine gun and rifle fire. In a few chaotic minutes one officer was killed, another died later of wounds and a third was wounded. In addition, eleven N.C.O.s and Other Ranks were killed and 34 more wounded. Again it was a junior General, Brig. Gen. Kemp of 138th Brigade, who first saw the light and abandoned the operation. And then the dying stopped.

***

EARLIER, AT 8 P.M., THE 1/2ND LONDONS had reported that the last man had been seen leaving the German lines. Anyone else still there was either dead or a prisoner of war. By 8.30 p.m., 169th Brigade H.Q. was reporting up the line that all of its men capable of so doing had left the German lines. Twenty minutes later, another message confirmed the fact and stated that:

"… no men capable of movement remained in the German line."[8]

At 9.15 p.m. on the evening of 1st July, 56th Divisional H.Q. ordered the 167th Brigade forward to relieve those men of the attacking battalions still manning the trenches and, about thirty minutes later, the majority of the guns finally fell silent. But VII Corps was still not finished with its demands on the men of the 56th Division. Just after half past ten, VII Corps instructed 56th Division to send out several raiding parties in order "to ascertain the situation on its front". The 'situation on its front', as any member of the Division could have told any staff officer were one nearby, was that the German trenches were teeming with men, all on the alert for any movement in the British lines. Their machine gun teams and gun crews were on stand by to repel any further attacks or interfere with any reinforcements moving up to Hebuterne. But orders are orders and, just after 11 p.m., the 1/7th Middlesex, who had spent most of the day sitting in 'The Keep' at the western end of Hebuterne awaiting instructions, sent out two strong patrols so that the staff could have confirmed what the men already knew. Their journey through the abattoir of No Man's Land must have been especially harrowing. They were not there to bring help to the hundreds of wounded men they must have passed and their urgent pleas for help had to be disregarded. No, instead of bringing aid to the wounded they were to contribute to their number. Twenty-seven men under Lt. William Whyman headed off towards Gommecourt Park under cover of the darkness that now enveloped the battlefield and another twenty men under the Lt. Patrick Forbes moved towards the trenches to the right. Both parties found the trenches full and the Germans on the 'qui vive' and they were chased back across No Man's Land by heavy machine gun and rifle fire. Lt. Forbes' party, in particular, suffered several casualties and getting them back in was a problem they could have surely done without.

Across the rest of the front line, attacking battalions were slowly relieved and sent to the rear. The 1/8th Middlesex took over the trenches from The Rangers but the men of Q.W.R. slept on until, at about 2.00 a.m., the Germans put down a sharp bombardment on the village hoping, presumably, to catch men in the open as the reliefs went on. 2nd Lt. Moy, who had spent the previous day in the safety of Souastre, was now saved by his new Brodie helmet when a piece of shrapnel put a dent in it and rendered him unconscious but otherwise uninjured.

Men, many severely wounded, crawled and hauled themselves into the British lines throughout the night. Rfn. Jacobs of the London Rifle Brigade had found a temporary home in a shell hole after his frantic dash for freedom. He shared his hole with three wounded men and sat for some two hours in a pool of blood and water as the firing died away around them. Exhaustion got the better of them and every man dozed off in spite of the imminent danger from shells and mortar bombs which were still dropping from time to time. As darkness fell the quartet crept out of their shelter and scrambled back to safety, there to find the remnants of their battalions. Jacobs was stunned to find just three men left from his platoon and eighteen able bodied men from the whole of 'C' Company.

Rfn. Henry Russell, also of the L.R.B., who had who had become happily inebriated after consuming a Worcester Sauce bottle full of rum out near the German lines, started for home from his bolt hole in a shell crater at about 11 p.m. His first problem was to decide which way to go. Looking around he concluded that he should crawl towards a fire on a nearby hill top on the basis that he had walked down a slope towards the German lines therefore going back up a slope must deliver him into British hands. The journey seemed interminable with barbed wire and shell holes obstructing him every few yards. Around him the wounded and dying kept up a long and desperate lament with cries for water, help and, from the most desperately injured, heart rending calls for the tender care of their mothers. At last, Russell was challenged *in English* by two men in an advanced post. Before he slipped into unconsciousness they promised Russell they would return with a stretcher but, when he came too as the sun started to rise over the horrors of the battlefield, he found himself abandoned. With no one to be seen, Russell started to crawl along the bottom of the trench, having to clamber over the cold bodies of the dead from the day before, before deciding that his dwindling energies were best spent shouting for help. At last his luck changed. A man from one of the Middlesex battalions was out giving aid to a seriously wounded officer and he heard Russell's desperate cries. He was then man-handled down a communication trench, through the wrecked heart of Hebuterne to the Advanced Dressing Station. There he was given some coffee and several injections while he waited for a vacancy in an outgoing ambulance.

While Russell was lurking out in No Man's Land, efforts were made to bring in the wounded and one officer, Capt. Wallis of the L.R.B. who had impotently watched the destruction of his battalion from the British lines, was determined to help who he could. His initial concern was for an officer who, it was reported, was lying wounded close to the German wire. Having badgered Lt. Col. Bates into allowing him to go in search of 2nd Lt. Jerry Pogose, Wallis slipped out of the battered trenches into the shambles of No Man's Land. There he found the badly wounded Pogose and brought him in unaided although, tragically, the 21 year old subaltern would die from his wounds the next day at the Main Dressing Station at Couin. But Wallis was not finished. His search had revealed several more wounded men and, time after time, he went out, eventually bringing in fourteen men in all. Amongst those he met was the wounded 811 Rfn. Gilbert Elleson from 'C' Company. Elleson had spent hours sheltering with 1067 L/Sgt. William Marlborough and 1576 Cpl. Bernard Waddington in a shell hole just outside the German trenches but a grenade had exploded wounding all three. Marlborough was the most seriously injured and passed out as a result of the pain and loss of blood. At about midnight the other two roused Marlborough and set out on the agonising and dangerous journey back across No Man's Land. Elleson assisted the fading Marlborough and behind them Waddington, suffering from some twenty wounds of varying severity including one which left a metal fragment in his skull, dragged himself slowly along. Having cleared the German wire Waddington ordered Elleson to go on and find some stretcher bearers. It was on this trip that he came across Wallis out looking for casualties but the Captain was on his own and he advised Elleson to do what he could for his wounded colleagues. Elleson, with little thought for his own safety, returned to the German wire and spent the next three hours searching for Marlborough[i] and Waddington until the approaching dawn forced him to abandon his search. Waddington eventually managed to crawl into the British lines where he was found by some stretcher bearers and hurried off to the Dressing Station. Marlborough's body was recovered when the battlefield was cleared in the Spring of 1917. For his bravery and devotion to his men Wallis was awarded the first of three Military Crosses[ii], Elleson's bravery went unrewarded[i].

[i] 1067 L/Sgt. William George Marlborough, 1/5th London Regt. (London Rifle Brigade), was killed on Saturday, 1st July 1916. Aged 24, he was the son of Florence Phillis Marlborough of 157, Thorold Rd., Ilford, Essex, & the late William James Marlborough. He was originally buried in Gommecourt British Cemetery No. 3, being moved to Cemetery No. 2, grave III. C. 13 when the 56th Division's dead were concentrated in a single cemetery.

[ii] Capt. Ferdinand Howship Wallis, 1/5th London Regt. (London Rifle Brigade), was educated at Doncaster and Priscas Grammar School. He enlisted as Private 8852 in O Company of the London Rifle Brigade in January 1899,

At the end of 1916 Elleson wrote to L/Sgt. Marlborough's distraught sister, her brother being still listed as 'missing'. He set out in detail the trio's painful and desperate experiences in No Man's Land on the night of 1st July:

"Dear Miss Marlborough,

Your letter of 25th inst. is the first I have had from you so I am afraid the other must have gone astray somehow. I am very sorry you have had no news of your brother and I sincerely wish I could give you some information that would be of comfort to you. I deeply regret I can tell you no more than Cpl Waddington must have done because he was the last, as far as I know, to be with your brother.

Sgt Marlborough, Cpl Waddington and myself were together taking shelter in a shell hole on the evening of 1st July. Your brother was wounded in the arm and in the leg. We stayed in the hole until after darkness had set in and then helped each other to crawl out. We managed to get through the German barbed wire but your brother and Waddington were too exhausted to move further. As I was the least injured they implored me to carry on back to our lines which must have been some 250 yards away and pick up stretcher bearers. I did not want to leave them but, being unable to help them myself, I thought it best to go forward and get assistance. I reached our front line and met Capt. Wallis who was out looking for wounded. I told him what had happened and he said it was impossible to get stretcher bearers and told me to do my best without. I decided to return to the two I had left behind and try to get them in somehow. I reached the German barbed wire again but could not find them anywhere. I searched thoroughly for them crawling in front of the wire for more than three hours but with no success. I began to think that, having rested, they must have determined to move on. I was obliged to give up the search for daylight and the vigilance of a German sentry drove me on.

There was no news of his return but that might easily happen particularly as he might have reached another part of our line then in charge of a different battalion. Then again, he might have been picked up by some German patrols which were about which has been the case with many of our men. But now that so much time has past with no news of him I fear that he must have been hit again by one of the shells which were still falling heavily.

Please forgive me if my letter appears to be callous or unfeeling but I have endeavoured to tell you all I know. What I have told you cannot be of much use to relieve the terrible suspense of anxious waiting you have so long endured. I feel very deeply for you and I wish I could tell you more or, rather, could have done more. I sincerely trust that some information will come that will afford you a little of the relief you so longingly seek.

Rfn Ellison."

Ordinary soldiers also played their part in bringing aid to the wounded. 2822 Rfn. Arthur Edington of the London Rifle Brigade had been a clergyman before

serving to 1907. He re-enlisted in March 1909 and served continuously to the end of the war. He lived at 8, St John's Road, Hendon and was the manager of Greenshields and Company's London office. He was commissioned on 11th February 1915 and promoted to Lieutenant on 1st June 1916. He was appointed Adjutant on 7th April 1916, remaining in that post until 12th September 1916. He commanded the battalion for the last four months of 1917. He was awarded an M.C. for his conduct at Gommecourt, a bar to the M.C. at 3rd Ypres and a second bar on 5th November 1918. After the war he went to Montreal where he joined the Head Office staff of Greenshields. The London Gazette citation for his Gommecourt M.C. appeared on 25th August 1916 and read:
"For conspicuous gallantry during operations. He went out alone immediately after dark, and under considerable fire, brought in unaided one wounded officer and fourteen men of other ranks."
i Neither Waddington nor Elleson returned to active service as a result of their wounds.

joining the Army and had arrived in France on the 12th March 1916. Edington was a stretcher bearer and had already spent an exhausting day dragging his heavy loads down the congested communication trenches to the middle of Hebuterne, there to be transferred onto the wheeled stretchers for the short journey to the Advanced Dressing Station on the edge of the village on the Sailly road. Again, his devotion to the wounded meant there was no respite and, throughout the night, he carried on his life saving work. For his dedication and courage he was rewarded the Military Medal.[i]

One of the men seen lying out in No Man's Land was the prolific correspondent with his mother back in Norwich Road, Forest Gate, 5644 Pte Richard Edgar Cecil Bryden, 'B' Company, London Scottish. His older brother, 6524 Pte William McNaught Bryden of No. 10 Platoon, 'C' Company, had volunteered to carry ammunition boxes across behind the attacking waves and, though encumbered by the heavy cases, he had survived to return to the shattered British trenches. On his way across No Man's Land Bill Bryden had come across the body of his beloved younger brother. Writing in 1998 his daughter, Mary Lawton, recalled the circumstances of this dreadful discovery and the life-time impact it had on her father:

"When he saw Cecil dead his mates kept him going and he suffered afterwards as he felt he had not been certain he was dead, but of course the infantry were not allowed to stop to help comrades who had fallen. I don't think there was any real doubt but it was an added nightmare for Dad to the end of his days."[9]

When Bill eventually returned to the shattered British trenches he sought out his C.O., Lt. Col. Green, and begged to be allowed to find and bury Cecil but his body could not be found and his name is now one of the tens of thousands inscribed on the Thiepval Memorial. The body shield sent by his mum to protect Cecil Bryden had not saved him after all.[ii]

And it was not only the fighting men who risked their lives to bring aid to the wounded in No Man's Land. The Padre of the 1/4th Londons, the Rev. Reginald Palmer who had joined the battalion in February 1916 as their first chaplain in France, organised search and carrying parties who brought in many of the wounded who were stranded, unable to move, out in the carnage between the lines. For his sterling work he was awarded the Military Cross.

***

JULY 2ND WAS ANOTHER SUNNY SUMMER'S DAY and, while the battalions at the front kept to the task of recovering the dead and wounded from the trenches, the

---

[i] The citation for the Military Medal awarded to 2822 Rfn. A F H Edington, 1/5th London Regt. (London Rifle Brigade), read:
"This rifleman, who is a clergyman, acted as a stretcher bearer. He volunteered to go to all parts of the trenches throughout the day, in spite of the very heavy shell-fire. During the day and night of July 1st, 1916, he helped to bring in many wounded from exposed places, who would probably have died had they not been brought in quickly." Edington was discharged from the Army on 13th December 1916.

[ii] 5644 Pte Richard Edgar Cecil Bryden, 1/14th London Regt. (London Scottish), was born on 26th April 1896 at 44, Tredegar Square, Bow, the son of John Bryden (b. 1854) and Louisa Bryden (nee Richards). The family lived at 41, and 41 Tredegar Square and then moved to 30, Norwich Road, Forest Gate in 1915. He and his elder brother, 6524 Pte William McNaught Bryden (born 13th June 1894), were educated at Coopers Company School, Tredegar Road in Bow. Cecil Bryden joined 'B' Company, London Scottish on 22nd November 1915. Bill Bryden joined No. 10 Platoon, 'C' Company, London Scottish in May 1916. Cecil Bryden's body was never found and his name is inscribed on the Thiepval Memorial, Pier and Face 9 C and 13 C.

battalions behind the lines started a series of depressing roll calls. Some once proud battalions had been reduced to less than two hundred men. By platoon and company they stood in thin, ragged lines and those still present quietly answered to their names. Where definite knowledge of the fate of a comrade was known this too was marked down in the register. The figures made truly dreadful reading.

On the 168th Brigade front, all four battalions had sent men into the German trenches whilst those that remained behind had stood for hours under a persistent and awful barrage. The London Scottish had lost the most. On the 30th June, the battalion could call upon 23 officers, 811 men plus the Medical Officer and 36 other medical staff and stretcher bearers – a total of 24 officers and 847 men. Five officers and 62 other ranks were withdrawn as 'battle surplus' leaving 18 officers and 749 men to go 'over the top'. The medical staff and stretcher bearers were mainly left in the trenches though some went over with the attacking infantry. According to the War Diary, at roll call on 2nd July, 9 officers, 236 other ranks and 21 medical staff answered their names (see Table 15 below). This included the officers and men of the 'battle surplus'. Their losses (dead, wounded and missing) were 14 officers, 575 other ranks and 15 medical staff – a total of 604[i] or 77%[ii] of those actively involved.

	Company	A	B	C	D	HQ	Total
In attack on 1st July	Officers	3	2	1	0	3	9
	M.O.	-	-	-	-	1	1
	Warrant Off.	-	-	-	-	1	1
	Sergeants	1	2	0	2	2	7
	Corporals	4	2	3	1	-	10
	Other Ranks	44	44	64	53	44	249
	Total	52	50	68	56	51	277
Not in attack on 1st July	Officers	2	2	2	2	2	10
	Warrant Off.	-	1	-	1	-	2
	Sergeants	3	3	2	-	1	9
	Corporals	-	-	1	1	1	3
	Other Ranks	2	2	2	2	1	9
	Total	59	58	75	62	56	310

Table 15 Strength of London Scottish after the attack

The officer casualties were:

Killed:

Capt. F H Lindsay, OC 'B' Company

Lt. J C Brown Constable, OC 'D' Company

2nd Lt. R A Brown, 'A' Company

2nd Lt. H A Coxon[iii], 'B' Company

2nd Lt. W E F Curror, 'B' Company

2nd Lt. D Kerr, 'C' Company

---

[i] The Official History has the figures as 14 officers and 602 other ranks.
[ii] 69% of the total complement of the London Scottish.
[iii] 2nd Lt. Herbert Archibald Coxon, 1/14th London Regt. (London Scottish), was born on 5th May 1884, the fourth son and ninth of eleven children of Alfred and Elizabeth Elliott Coxon of Ingleside, Pelham Road, Gravesend. He was educated at St Lawrence College in Ramsgate and was a financial agent. After returning from Victoria in British Columbia he lived at 5, St Phillips Road, Surbiton. His next of kin was his sister, Mrs P Lovell of The Manor House, Durrington near Worthing. He attested 3115 Private in the Reserve battalion of the London Scottish on 3rd September 1914. Promoted sergeant in the 3/14th Battalion he was commissioned into this battalion in October 1915. He went to France on 3rd April 1916. His body was never found and his name is inscribed on the Thiepval Memorial, Pier and Face 9C and 13 C. [*Additional Sources:* Pam & Ken Linge, Thiepval Project]

Died of wounds:

2ⁿᵈ Lt. P T L Hunterⁱ, 'D' Company, died of his wounds on 19ᵗʰ July at the St John's Ambulance Brigade Hospital in Etaples.

Wounded:

Maj. C J Low D.S.O., OC 'C' Company, was wounded by a bullet in the arm and suffered two shrapnel wounds to the left leg, one of which broke his leg and the other entered his thigh. He was evacuated to No. 3 General Hospital at Le Treport before being evacuated to England. He returned to the battalion in May 1917.

Capt. J H Glover, RAMC

2ⁿᵈ Lt. B E Gavinⁱⁱ, 'A' Company, did not return to the battalion.

2ⁿᵈ Lt. R S Greig, 'D' Company, received a gun shot wound to the left arm on 1ˢᵗ July and was evacuated to England, arriving at the Queen Alexandra Military Hospital, Millbank, London where he spent eight weeks recovering from his wounds. He then developed tetanus which kept him in hospital for another two months. After recovering from his wounds he was appointed Acting Adjutant in the Royal Flying Corps for a period before rejoining the battalion.

2ⁿᵈ Lt. G W Prebble, 'D' Company, was evacuated from Le Havre on 6ᵗʰ July suffering from a machine gun bullet wound to the right foot which caused comminuted fractures of the 4ᵗʰ and 5ᵗʰ metatarsals and considerable tissue damage. He was admitted to the Princess Henry of Battenberg's Hospital for Officers at 30, Hill Street in Mayfair where he was subjected to three operations over six weeks. He returned to the battalion and was wounded again in the abdomen in May 1918. He survived.

2ⁿᵈ Lt. A A Speak M.C., 'B' Company

2ⁿᵈ Lt. C Woodcockⁱⁱⁱ, 'D' Company

Maj. Ward-Jackson, who had dined with Maj. Lindsay and several other officers from the London Scottish just a few days before the battle, was greatly saddened by the battalion's appalling losses. The officers and the men had made a great impression on him and the deaths of so many were a source of depression. His journal entry of the 4ᵗʰ July is almost a requiem for the regiment:

"I was dreadfully sorry to hear that Lindsay and nearly all the other fellows of the London Scottish with whom I dined the night before they went up are killed. I think out of the seven officers there is only one unwounded... There was something not exactly apprehensive but resigned about them and that sentiment was justified as they had a bad time... They certainly were the finest and highest class of men I have ever seen in the war."

---

i 2ⁿᵈ Lt. Percy Talbot Langley Hunter, 1/14ᵗʰ London Regt. (London Scottish), was born on the 19ᵗʰ September 1892. He was the son of William Pettingell and Elizabeth Hunter of Bath House, 50, Mall Road, Hammersmith. Educated at St Paul's School he was a barrister. He attested 3078 Private on 3ʳᵈ September 1914. He was promoted to Lance Corporal in November 1914 and was twice admitted to hospital in 1915 suffering from frostbite and measles. He was commissioned into the 3/14ᵗʰ Battalion in June 1915. He is buried at Etaples Military Cemetery I. B. 38.

ii 2ⁿᵈ Lt. Bertram E Gavin, 1/14ᵗʰ London Regt. (London Scottish), was born on 3ʳᵈ August 1877 in Lee, Kent. He was educated at Falcon Hall, Edinburgh Married, he and his wife lived 158a, Sinclair Road, West Kensington. He was a general merchant. He was commissioned into the 3/14ᵗʰ battalion on 3ʳᵈ November 1915 and was later promoted to Captain. He was later attached to the 2ⁿᵈ Gordons and made commandant of a Prisoner of War camp at Littleport near Ely.

iii 2ⁿᵈ Lt. Cecil Woodcock, 1/14ᵗʰ London Regt. (London Scottish), attested as 1365 Private in the London Scottish and was later promoted to Captain.

I was dreadfully sad about Lindsay. His widow has a little boy of four years old or thereabouts and a baby girl born last month. I said to Thorpe, G.S.O.1 of the 46th (Division) who is the widow's cousin, that I had noticed something weird and uncanny about the London Scottish as they went up and that I could not make out quite what it was... and Thorpe replied. "If you were a Highlander you would not make that remark, they <u>know</u>."

...I do not know that anything has made me feel in that sort of way so depressed as the death of my friend and all those splendid young fellows, the finest type of English [*sic*]. I can see them now, with their pipers playing a wild skirl as they marched through this French town. The pipers with their bonnets and black cock feathers set at a jaunty angle... squaring their shoulders and swinging their kilts so that even the little French gamin fell in on either side to keep step. And behind them a whole company of young men, clean and workmanlike with their heads a little down but their expressions brave; with a smile for all the girls and their friends amongst the crowd but just a little unmistakable droop at the corners of their mouths. They made me feel sad then."[10]

No. 8 Platoon of 'B' Company, led by 2nd Lt. W E F Curror, had a group photograph taken just before the attack in which forty one NCOs and men joined their officer to grin into the camera. On the back, someone, a survivor perhaps, recorded the fates of them all: 13 came back unwounded; 13 were wounded; seven, including 2nd Lt. Curror, were known to have died; eight were missing; and one was wounded and a prisoner of war. In all, 69% of the platoon were casualties (N.B. all of the missing were later confirmed as dead).

Pte R K Flint – safe	Pte D Collins – wounded	Pte S E Mackenzie – safe
Pte J A Simpson – wounded	Pte H Billington – safe	Pte J L Milne – missing
Pte J H Keys – wounded	Pte J T Moss – killed	Pte J H Young – wounded
Pte F Clare – safe	Pte E Wells – wounded	Pte A G Clayden – wounded
Pte E T Horsman – safe	Pte A E Godfrey – safe	Pte P S Henderson – killed
Pte J F Boyes – safe	Pte F Clipstone – missing	Pte L H Pullen – wounded and POW[i]
Pte E C Mills – safe	Pte W Coutts – missing	L/Cpl W W Jones – wounded
Pte O Robertson – wounded	Pte A Collie – missing	L/Cpl A Douglas – missing
Pte J Sartain – missing	Pte R Nimmo – safe	L/Cpl H T Smith – safe
Pte T Halley – wounded	Pte C J S Claypoole – killed	Cpl D J Vernon – killed
Pte A W Beaty – safe	Pte G W Benbow – killed	Sgt A R Smith – wounded
Pte R J Giddings – safe	Pte S CH Pitts – wounded	Sgt R Ferguson – killed
Pte H W Hance – missing	Pte A J Butler – safe	Sgt L H B Phillips – wounded
Pte E Burgess – missing	Pte G Cropper – wounded	2nd Lt. W E F Curror – killed

Table 16 Fate of men of No. 8 Platoon, London Scottish

The Rangers, the other lead battalion of the 168th Brigade in the attack, went into action with 23 officers and 780 other ranks. At roll call, 6 officers and 280 other ranks answered their names. Over the next few days, another 53 men who had been caught in No Man's Land or otherwise detached from the battalion returned to the ranks. In all, the battalion lost 17 officers and 447 men – 58% of

---

[i] It is believed that Pte Pullen died of wounds on 1st July 1916 whilst in German hands, however, his body was never found and his name is inscribed on the Thiepval Memorial.

the battalion strength. The Rangers' post-battle report gave the following numbers for unwounded men of the four Companies:

'A' Company – 1 officer and 49 other ranks

'B' Company – 57 other ranks

'C' Company – 63 other ranks

'D' Company – 46 other ranks.

This gave a total of one officer[i] and 215 unwounded men remaining from the 23 officers and 780 men who had gone into action at 7.30 a.m. on 1st July. The officer casualties were:

Killed:

Capt. R L Hoare, OC 'C' Company

Maj. L F Jones, OC 'D' Company

Lt. R E K Bradshaw[ii], 'A' Company was reported missing.

2nd Lt. W R Davey, 'D' Company

2nd Lt. J Josephs, 'C' Company

2nd Lt. A W Taplin, 'B' Company

2nd Lt. W H Tucker[iii]

2nd Lt. D S Ward[iv]

Wounded:

Capt. H W Wightwick M.C., OC 'B' Company, was wounded twice.

Capt. G M G Wyatt, OC 'A' Company, was evacuated from Le Havre on 6th July on board the hospital ship *'Salta*[v]. He had been hit by two machine gun bullets, one in each shoulder, suffering a comminuted fracture of the left scapula.

Lt. A G Hine[vi] suffered from a gun shot wound to the left forearm and was evacuated from Le Havre on 2nd July. The bullet passed from the inside to the

---

[i] The other five officers who were at roll call were members of the headquarters contingent, e.g. C.O., the Bombing Officer, etc.

[ii] Lt. Richard Edward Kynaston Bradshaw, 1/12th London Regt. (The Rangers), was aged 21. He was the son of William Graham Bradshaw and Dora Sophia Bradshaw of Down Park, Crawley Down, Sussex. He studied at Cambridge University where he was a member of the OTC and was commissioned straight into the battalion. His body was never found and his name is inscribed on the Thiepval Memorial, Pier and Face 9 C.

[iii] 2nd Lt. William Henry Tucker, 1/12th London Regt. (The Rangers), was born on 20th October 1881. He was educated at All Saints Residents Choir School and was an accountant. Married to Gladys A Tucker, they lived at 4, Woodbury Grove, Finsbury Park, London. He had attested 2504 Rifleman in the 16th London Regt. (Queen's Westminster Rifles) on 31st August 1914. His brother was a Captain in The Rangers and, in November 1915, Col N F Leese, CO 3/12th London Regt. wrote to Col. Shoolbred of the Westminsters asking that Rfn Tucker might be commissioned into his brother's battalion. The last sighting of 2nd Lt. Tucker was soon after he had been hit in the knee during the attack. His body was never found and his name is inscribed on the Thiepval Memorial, Pier and Face 9 C.

[iv] 2nd Lt. Dacre Stanley Ward, 1/12th London Regt. (The Rangers), was aged 33 and lived at Highfield, Ravensbourne Park, London, SE. He was the son of Alfred and Alice Ward, of 67, Westcombe Park Rd., Blackheath, London. He married Marion Ethel Greenwood, later of 16, Alexandra Court, Queen's Gate, Kensington, London, at St George's, Perry Hill on 16th June 1915. He attested 4689 Private in the Inns of Court OTC on 8th July 1915. He was commissioned into The Rangers on 27th November 1915. Killed in action on 1st July 1916, his body was never found and his name is inscribed on the Thiepval Memorial, Pier and Face 9C.

[v] *HMHS Salta* was sunk by a mine on 10th April 1917 with 5 officers, 9 nurses and 37 RAMC personnel being drowned. The mine had been laid the previous day by the UC 26. She was built in 1911 by Forges & Chant. de la Méditerranée, La Seyne for the Soc. Générale de Transports Maritimes à Vapeur, Marseille. Memorials to the men lost on this ship can be found in St Sever Cemetery, le Havre.

[vi] 2nd Lt. Algernon George Hine, 1/12th London Regiment (The Rangers), was born on 9th August 1886 and attested 1579 Private in the Inns of Court OTC on 6th October 1914. He was commissioned into The Rangers and was promoted Lieutenant on 1st June 1916. In November 1916 he was attached to the 9th (Reserve) Battalion, London Regiment in Exeter. In February 1917 he was declared fit for general service, having been seconded to the Railway Transport Department for several months. He was disembodied from the Army on 18th April 1919. He lived at Whitegates, Howells Birch, Woking.

outside of his forearm (from the ulna to the radial aspect) causing no damage to the bones but large and ragged entry and exit wounds.

Lt. J A R Reeves[i]

2nd Lt. E G D Liveing, 'B' Company, suffered a severe bullet wound which entered the front of, and exited through the rear of, the hip leaving a two inch exit wound. He did not return to the battalion.

2nd Lt. C F Monier Williams was hit by a shell splinter which entered the front of his right thigh and exited through the rear and outer side. He was also wounded in the right wrist. The thigh wound became septic. He was evacuated from Le Havre on board the *'Salta'* on 5th July. He did not return to the battalion.

2nd Lt. A J Reincke[ii] suffered a shrapnel wound in the back and was sent to No. 1 General Hospital in Etretat. He was then evacuated from Le Havre on 2nd July on the hospital ship *'Lanfranc'*. He was admitted to the Queen Alexandra Military Hospital, Millbank on 7th July where he remained for six weeks.

2nd Lt. H Rochford[iii], 'B' Company, was evacuated from Le Havre on board the *'Marama'*[iv] on 17th July. A shell explosion so damaged his left arm that it was necessary to amputate it at the elbow. He was fitted with an artificial arm in March 1917 at the Red Cross Hospital for Officers in Brighton.

Prisoner of War:

2nd Lt. W G Parker, 'A' Company

***

THE 1/4TH LONDONS, WHO HAD THE JOB of supporting The Rangers in front of Nameless Farm, suffered only slightly less. Before the attack they numbered 32 officers and 890 other ranks of which 9 officers and 115 men were detached as 'battle surplus' or were with the transport and another 75 were detailed as brigade carriers. This left 23 officers and 700 men available to go into action. On 2nd July, 7 officers and 356 men of those committed to the attack answered their names. The battalion suffered casualties of 16 officers and 344[11] men – 50% of those that went into action. 'A' Company lost all of its officers and all

---

i 2nd Lt. John Arthur Ramsay Reeves, 1/12th London Regt. (The Rangers), was later promoted Captain. He went to France with the battalion on 2nd February 1915.

ii 2nd Lt. Arthur Julius Reincke, 1/12th London Regt. (The Rangers), was born on 10th January 1891. He was the son of Leopold Reincke of Albis Lodge, 5, Champion Hill, Denmark Hill, London and was educated at Dulwich College (where he was in the Cadet Corps) and University College (where he was in the OTC Artillery). He attested 1706 Private in 28th County of London Regt. (Artists' Rifles) on 7th August 1914 before being commissioned into The Rangers. After being wounded on 1st July he was sent to the 9th (Reserve) Battalion, London Regt., at Fovant Camp at the end of October 1916. He was still declared unfit for General Service in February 1917. On 4th June 1923 he married Catherine Jeffrey, second daughter of Francis Bell of Bangor, County Down. During World War II he served as a Lieutenant in the Intelligence Corps. [*Additional sources:* Dick Flory: Dulwich College War Record, 1914-1919; Dulwich College Register, 1619-1926; Dulwich College War List, 1939-1945]
His older brother (and also an Old Alleynian), Capt. Leopold Frederick Reincke, 11th Duke of Wellington's (West Riding) Regt. attached 48th Squadron RFC was killed on patrol on 17th August, 1917. He was buried in Zuydcoote Military Cemetery, grave I. A. 5.

iii 2nd Lt. Harry Rochford, 1/12th London Regt. (The Rangers), was born on 22nd April 1890 and was the son of Thomas and Mary Anne Agnes Rochford of Twinford Hall, Broxbourne, Herts. He was educated at Ampleforth and was a nurseryman. He attested 2192 Private in the Honourable Artillery Company on 8th September 1914, being promoted Corporal, before he was commissioned into the 2/12th London Regt. (The Rangers).

iv HMNZHS *Marama* was built for the Union Steam Ship Co. of New Zealand in 1907. She displaced 6,497 gross tons. She was converted to a hospital ship in 1915 capable of carrying a Medical/nursing staff of 9 medical officers, 66 other ranks and 27 nurses. It could carry 592 cot cases. The ship spent some time in the Eastern Mediterranean before moving to Southampton to be used for cross-Channel evacuataions from the Western Front. After the war *Marama* returned to civilian service until being laid up in 1937.

but 18 men. The two platoons of 'B' Company that went forward suffered badly with both officers wounded and only about ten men making it back to the British lines. 'C' Company, of which only two platoons got over, lost all of its officers and the remains of the Company was brought out of action by C.S.M. Davis. Casualties for 'D' Company, which stood all day under the most tremendous bombardment from the German guns, are not recorded.

The officer casualties were:

Killed:

Capt. A R Moore M.C., OC 'A' Company

2nd Lt. F R C Bradford, 'C' Company

2nd Lt. F C Fanghanel, 'A' Company

2nd Lt. T Moody, 'C' Company

Wounded:

Maj. W R Moore, OC 'B' Company

Capt. J T Sykes, OC 'C' Company

Lt. R L Herring[i], Adjutant, was buried by a shell and, although listed as a casualty, carried on until 18th September when he was sent to hospital suffering from neurasthenia or Shell Shock. He suffered from stress, memory loss and headaches and was evacuated to England on the 26th September from Le Havre. He did not return to the battalion.

2nd Lt. L R Chapman, 'B' Company, suffered a machine gun bullet wound to the left arm. The bullet entered the front of the arm and exited near the elbow without damaging the bone. He was evacuated from Le Havre on 2nd July on board the *'Lanfranc'*. He spent two months in the Queen Alexandra Military Hospital at Millbank in London.

2nd Lt. V C Donaldson was evacuated from Le Havre on board the *'Lanfranc'* on 2nd July suffering from a gun shot wound to the right wrist and was admitted to the Queen Alexandra Hospital, Millbank after evacuation. He did not return to the battalion.

2nd Lt. A S Ford, 'B' Company

2nd Lt. H G Hicklenton, 'B' Company, was sent to hospital at Le Treport before being evacuated on the *'Maheno'* [ii] from Le Havre on 5th July suffering from shell shock. In England he was sent to the 2nd Southern General Hospital in Bristol before being transferred to the Prince of Wales's Hospital, Marylebone. A year later he was still suffering from symptoms which included loss of all sensation in his legs.

---

i 2nd Lt. Ralph Lennox Herring, 1/4th London Regt. (Royal Fusiliers), was born on 2nd November 1893, the son of Stephen and Rose Hester Herring of Leyton. He was educated at the City of London School where he was a member of the OTC and lived with his parents at 'Branketre', St Mary's Avenue, Wanstead. On leaving school he became an articled clerk to a solicitor and he also enlisted in the 1st (City of London) Field Ambulance (T.F.) as 1130 Driver on 30th October 1911. He was commissioned into the 4th Londons on 4th July 1914. During 1915, he was, for a time, a Staff Captain with the Ferozepore Brigade to which the 1/4th Londons were attached and, after his recovery from shell shock, he successfully applied for a commission in the Indian Army.

ii *HMNZHS Maheno* was built for the Union Steam Ship Co. of New Zealand by Wm. Denny & Bros in Dumbarton in 1905. She displaced 5,282 gross tons. She was converted to a hospital ship in 1915 and could carry a Medical/nursing staff of 7 medical officers, 59 other ranks and 10 nurses. She had a capacity of 340 cot cases. After the war she returned to passenger service before being sold to Miyachi K.K.K., of Kobe and Osaka, Japan for scrap in 1935. On the 19th July 1935 she was hit by a cyclone off the Queensland coast and the towline parted. The *Maheno* was driven ashore on to Fraser Island, Queensland, where its wreck remains today as a tourist attraction.

2nd Lt. H Jones[i]

2nd Lt. W H Webster, 'D' Company, suffered from shell fragment wound to the face and was evacuated from Le Havre on 5th July. He returned to the battalion and was killed on 10th February 1917.

2nd Lt. B F L Yeoman[ii], 'D' Company, was buried by a shell explosion and knocked unconscious. He was evacuated on the *'Lanfranc'* from Le Havre on 2nd July suffering from shell shock and was sent to 4th London General Hospital. So severe were his symptoms that he occasionally lapsed into semi-consciousness for several weeks afterwards and suffered pain in his legs, back and arms. He was declared fit for light duties in February 1917.

Wounded and Prisoner of War

2nd Lt. A G Blunn[iii], 'A' Company, was wounded in both legs by bomb fragments and made a prisoner of war. He was sent to a camp at Gütersloh.

***

THE LAST BATTALION, THE KENSINGTONS, had committed some men as a clearing party behind the London Scottish and others were involved in the doomed attempt to dig the communications trench across No Man's Land. The rest of the battalion stood under heavy and sustained artillery fire for more than nine hours or made several forlorn efforts to reinforce and re-supply the attacking battalions. 24 officers and 525 men went into action on the morning of 1st July and 7 officers and 215 men came out – a casualty rate of 59%.

The officer casualties were:

Killed:

Capt. F H Ware, OC 'C' Company

2nd Lt. N O C Mackenzie, 'A' Company

2nd Lt. W G Mager, 'D' Company

2nd Lt. H B Pilgrim, 'D' Company

2nd Lt. C B Sach

Wounded:

Capt. E O Taggart, OC 'D' Company

Lt. H E Holland M.C.

Lt. W A Penn, 'B' Company, was severely wounded in the left arm by a rifle bullet which shattered his humerus. The arm was amputated at No. 3 General Hospital, Le Treport on 17th July. He was evacuated from Le Havre on 3rd August on board the *'Gloucester Castle'*[iv]. He was still in hospital, at the Queen

---

i Lt. Harry Jones, 1/4th London Regt. (Royal Fusiliers), died on 15th May 1918. Aged 42, he was the son of Walter and Mary Jones, of Hastings, Sussex; husband of Frances Amy Jones, of 528, Alexandra Park Rd., Wood Green, London. He was buried in Aldershot Military Cemetery, grave AG. 371.

ii 2nd Lt. Bryan Frank Lawson Yeoman, 1/4th London Regt. (Royal Fusiliers), was born in 1897 and was the son of Capt. Ernest W and Clara Yeoman of 'Lauriston', 80, Burnt Ash Road, Lee, Kent. He was the third of seven children. He was educated at Highfield College, Leigh-on-Sea. On August 5, 1914, he joined the 4th London Howitzer Brigade. He was commissioned into the 2/4th London Regt. with which he served in Gallipoli and Egypt. He joined the 1/4th Londons on 14th May 1916. After recovering from shell shock he was sent to the 3rd Reserve Battalion, London Regt. and was declared fit for General Service in May 1917. He was evacuated to England with Trench Fever in August. On recovery he joined the RFC and was killed in a flying accident at Witney, Oxfordshire on 11th May 1918 when he overshot the airfield and stalled his aircraft before crashing. He was buried in Witney Burial Ground, grave P. 3269.

iii 2nd Lt. Achbigh G Blunn, 1/4th London Regt. (Royal Fusiliers), joined the battalion from the 2/4th London Regt. on 22nd March 1916. He enlisted as 2957 Rfn. in the 1/16th London Regt. (Queen's Westminster Rifles) before being commissioned into the 4th Londons.

iv *HMHS Gloucester Castle*, 7,999 tons, was built in 1911 by Fairfield Shipbuilding and Engineering Co. at Glasgow for the Union Castle Steamship Co. On 24th September, 1914 she was commissioned as a 410 bed hospital ship and in

Alexandra Military Hospital at Millbank, in June 1917. He did not return to the battalion and was fitted with an artificial arm in July 1919.

2nd Lt. S A Ball, OBE, was hit by a shell fragment which entered the left side of his face, exiting on the right and causing compound fractures to both sides of his jaw and the loss of several molars. The wounds required three operations, including a tracheotomy necessitated by a pharyngitis infection. The tracheotomy wound became infected and he also developed an abscess in the maxillary region. He was not repatriated to England until 10th July because of the operations and he was still unable to eat properly in December 1916. He did not return to the battalion.

2nd Lt. G A Beggs M.C. M.M., 'D' Company, suffered from a gun shot wound and was evacuated from Le Havre on board the *'Marama'* on 13th July. He was sent to the 4th London General Hospital at Denmark Hill for eight weeks.

2nd Lt. G P Bryer was evacuated from Le Havre to Southampton on board the hospital ship *'Lanfranc'* on 2nd July and was sent to the 2nd Western General Hospital in Manchester. He had been hit by three fragments from a German trench mortar bomb. He had two minor wounds, one to the neck and another where shrapnel had to be surgically removed from the back of his neck. A third fragment had pierced his ear and embedded itself near the mastoid bone (at the base of the skull behind the ear) and, as a result, he complained of deafness in one ear. He did not return to the battalion.

2nd Lt. J P Clark[i] was evacuated on board the *'Lanfranc'* on 2nd July. He had been blown up and then buried by the explosion of two shells, suffering from concussion and severe shell shock. He was sent to No. 4 London General Hospital and did not return to the battalion.

2nd Lt. H W Hankins[ii] was evacuated from Le Havre on the 6th July on board the *'Lanfranc'*. A shell burst near to him on the parapet and, although he carried on for half an hour, he started to feel "stiff and funny". He was suffering from severe shell shock and concussion to the back and to the nerves of the left eye and ear and was sent to the 4th London General Hospital. He then went to the Officers' Convalescent Home at Osborne on the Isle of Wight[iii] in January 1917 still suffering from memory problems, sleeplessness and back pain. He eventually relinquished his commission on 4th April 1919 not having returned to the battalion.

2nd Lt. N E Parry, 'D' Company, was wounded by shell fragments that entered his groin. One piece lodged in his pelvis and another pierced his bladder. After

---

April 1915 took part in the Dardanelles campaign. On 30th March 1917, although clearly identified as a hospital ship, she was torpedoed by UB-32 in the English Channel. It took two weeks to tow the ship to safety for repair. In April 1919 she resumed commercial operations until 1939 when she was laid up at Netley in Southampton Water. On 21st June 1942 she sailed from Birkenhead and on 15th July, off the Ascension Islands, was shelled and sunk by the German surface raider *'Schiff 28, Michel'*. Out of 154 people on board 82 crew members, 6 women, 2 children and 3 male passengers were killed. The surviving 57 crew members, 2 women and 2 child passengers were taken aboard the German supply ship *'Charlotte Schliemann'* and taken to Japan for internment. The commander of the *'Michel'*, Von Ruckteschell, was found guilty of war crimes and imprisoned at Spandau in 1946. [*Source:* The Red Duster, web site of the Merchant Navy Association]

i 2nd Lt. John Pullen Clark, 1/13th London Regt. (Kensingtons), lived at 69, Bensham Manor Road, Thornton Heath, Surrey and worked for Thomas Cook and Sons, Ludgate Circus. He attested 1758 Private in the 21st County of London Regt. (1st Surrey Rifles), on 7th August 1914 and was commissioned in February 1916 into the Kensingtons.

ii 2nd Lt. Harold William Hankins, 1/13th London Regt. (Kensingtons), who was not quite 20 years old on 1st July, lived 26, Goldhurst Terrace, South Hampstead, London, NW6. He joined the battalion in France on 4th March 1916 and was later promoted Captain.

iii Where he may have met the author's grandfather who was Camp Commandant at Osborne for a period in 1917.

an operation to remove the fragment in his bladder he suffered a slight infection, lost weight and became of a highly nervous disposition. He was evacuated on 28th July on board the *Panama*[i] and was sent to the Sussex Lodge Hospital, Regent's Park. He did not return to the battalion.

2nd Lt. H E Paterson

2nd Lt. J P Williams

Prisoner of War

2nd Lt. P R Pike, 'C' Company, was unwounded and was made a Prisoner of War and sent to an officer's camp in Marienberg. He was later interned in Holland and repatriated on 22nd November 1918[ii].

***

THE OFFICERS OF THE 168TH BRIGADE'S Trench Mortar Battery were unscathed, but two officers of the Machine Gun Company were amongst the casualties:

Killed:

Lt. F S Thomson (London Scottish)

Wounded:

2nd Lt. S L Vincent[iii] (Kensingtons) was evacuated from Le Havre on 5th July on board the *'Salta'* suffering from shell shock and shrapnel wounds to the right foot and left arm. He returned to France in May 1917 and later served in Salonika with the 82nd Company, Machine Gun Corps. He was murdered by the IRA in 1921.

---

[i] *HMHS Panama*, 5980 tons, was built by Fairfield in 1902 for the Pacific Steam Navigation Company. She became a hospital ship in 1914. In 1920 she was bought by the Admiralty as a hospital ship for the Mediterranean Fleet. As the oldest hospital ship afloat she was given the number '1' when the Second World War was declared in 1939. She was paid off in February 1947 and broken up at Barrow.

[ii] 2nd Lt. (later Capt.) Pike found himself in serious trouble after his repatriation. Whilst interned in Holland from May 1918 onwards he, and several other officers, cashed cheques at various Dutch banks. Pike's nineteen cheques totalled £369, 3 shillings and two pence. There are various ways of calculating the value of this money in today's terms. Using the Retail Price Index it comes to £17,400 and using the growth in average earnings it comes to some £97,000! Unfortunately, all of Pike's cheques bounced and he was pursued by the banks through the War Office. Pike initially denied the cheques were his but this was shown to be untrue. He then blamed another officer who had since gone to South America and was uncontactable. Having finally accepted that the cheques were his he declared that his father would cover the sums owed but needed further information before paying up. When this did not transpire Pike stated that his uncle, currently in China, would cover his debts on his return to England. By August 1919, however, the game was up and Pike wrote to the War Office from his home at 10, Percy Road, Shepherd's Bush, saying that his wife had left him, his three children were in a home and that he could not afford to repay the money. The War Office then washed their hands of the matter and told the Dutch banks they could do nothing more to help. By 1921 he was reduced to driving petrol tankers for the RAF.

[iii] 2nd Lt. Seymour Lewington Vincent, 1/13th London Regt. (Kensingtons), was born in 1890 and lived in Loughton, Essex. He was seconded to the 168th Machine Gun Company on 16th March 1916. He died in strange circumstances in May 1921. He had been transferred to the 2nd Brigade, RFA, in December 1920 and had been serving at Fermoy, a small town in County Cork. He had applied for a transfer to the Army Educational Corps, before the war he was a teacher, and had then asked to resign his commission. He then disappeared without trace on 23rd May 1921. It was not until an anonymous letter was sent to the British Government in June 1924 containing details of the burial of a British officer in Lenihan's Bog, Glenville, Co. Cork, owned by one Dan Hickey, "the notorious reble (sic) farmer", that further investigations took place. At the time of his disappearance the Colonel commanding the 16th Infantry Brigade based at Fermoy basically accused Vincent of lying about his intentions of going on leave but, within a week, another report, regretting several errors in the first, was issued which noted that Vincent had appeared somewhat disorientated before going on (approved) leave. It went on to report that five days after he left, three members of the 2nd Brigade of the IRA raided Fermoy Station and, breaking into the office there, had stolen various items from Vincent's luggage, including a service revolver. Although the Royal Irish Constabulary were informed nothing was ever discovered about his whereabouts. It is thought that he, and possibly another man, were murdered by the IRA and buried at Lenihan's Bog. Vincent's body was later re-interred in Glenville Church.

In addition, 25 men of No. 1 Section, 2/2nd Field Company, Royal Engineers accompanied the London Scottish across during the attack – six came back. Amongst the Pioneers attached to the attack, 'C' Company, 1/5th Cheshires, (O.C. Capt. E M Dixon) lost 1 officer wounded and 22 other ranks.

***

ON THE LEFT FLANK, CASUALTIES amongst the battalions of the 169th Brigade had, with the exception of the London Scottish, been even more severe. On the far left, the London Rifle Brigade had started the day with 23 officers and 803 other ranks, a total of 826 men i.e. after battle surplus, transport, band and Quartermaster's Department have been discounted. Casualties were 19 officers and 569 other ranks[12] - 71% of those that had actually been involved in the attack. The majority of these casualties occurred within the ranks of the three attacking companies, 'A', 'C' and 'D' and the details were recorded in a post battle report by Lt. Col. Bates:

	Officers	Coy A	Coy B	Coy C	Coy D	Total ORs	Total all ranks
Killed/DoW	7	14	13	21	17	65	72
Wounded	10	63	44	67	68	242	252
Wounded & Missing	1	18	3	22	16	59	60
Missing	-	67	24	68	44	203	203
Missing believed killed	1	-	-	-	-	-	1
Total	19	162	84	178	145	569	588
Wounded returned by 23rd July	10	7	11	13	41	72	82

Table 17 London Rifle Brigade casualties

Assuming that the three assaulting companies were of roughly equal size, i.e. about 210 officers and men, the casualty rate in each company was: 'A' Company 79%, 'C' Company 88% and 'D' Company 72%.[i]

The officer casualties were:

Killed:

Capt. B S Harvey, OC 'C' Company

Capt. J R Somers-Smith M.C., OC 'B' Company

2nd Lt. C V Balkwill[ii]

---

[i] There is some debate about the accuracy of these figures and the number of officers and men actually involved in the attack on Gommecourt. Lt. Col. Bates reported to Brig. Gen. Coke at 00.50 hours that 23 officers and 803 men were in the assembly trenches. Writing some time after the war Capt. F H Wallis gave the numbers involved as 23 officers and 627 men. If Wallis was correct it means that the entire battalion suffered 90% casualties. This writer believes that Wallis may have been referring only to the three attacking companies, A, C and D Companies as B Company was not involved in the assault but were to clear Gommecourt Park later. Even if this is true, however, it does mean these companies were smaller than suggested and suffered a significantly higher proportion of casualties than given above.

[ii] 2nd Lt. Charles Vince Balkwill, 1/5th London Regiment (London Rifle Brigade), was killed on 1st July 1916. He was born on 17th April 1885, the son of Francis and Mary Vince Balkwill. His father was a foreign fruit merchant of 6, Garlies Road, Forest Hill. He was educated privately by Mr. J O Boyes at 45 Houston Road, Forest Hill before attending St Dunstan's College where he was Captain of the Rugby 1stXV and Lacrosse 1st XII and a member of the Cricket 1st XI. On leaving school in 1901 he played cricket for Old Dunstonians and Forest Hill and rugby for Catford Bridge. He played rugby for Kent for six seasons and was a member of Blackheath Harriers. A clerk with the East Indian Railway Co., he attested as 125 Private in August 1914, joining H Company. He was promoted Sergeant in December 1914 and was severely wounded at Ypres in April 1915. He was commissioned into the 3/5th London Rifle Brigade on 8th December 1915 and returned to the battalion on 27th May 1916. His body was never found and his names is inscribed on the Thiepval Memorial, Pier and Face 9D. His older brother 2nd Lt. John Balkwill, 1/6th Royal Warwickshire Regt, also died on 1st July 1916, aged 33. He is buried in Pargny British Cemetery, grave III.E.36. [*Sources:* Pam and Ken Linge of the Thiepval Project, Tony Sharp and David Collett, St. Dunstan's College Roll of Honour 1914-19 and The War Record of the Northern Assurance Co. Ltd 1914-1918]

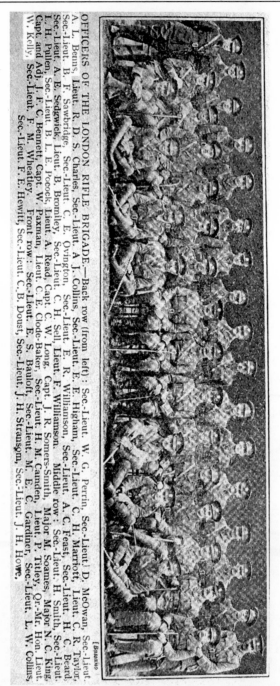

OFFICERS OF THE LONDON RIFLE BRIGADE.—Back row (from left): Sec.-Lieut. W. G. Perrin, Sec.-Lieut. D. McOwan, Sec.-Lieut. A. L. Beans, Lieut. R. D. S. Charles, Sec.-Lieut. A. J. Collins, Sec.-Lieut. E. E. Higham, Sec.-Lieut. C. H. Marriott, Lieut. C. R. Taylor, Sec.-Lieut. B. F. Sawbridge, Sec.-Lieut. C. E. Ovington, Sec.-Lieut. E. R. Williamson, Sec.-Lieut. A. C. Feast, Sec.-Lieut. H. C. Beard, Sec.-Lieut. A. E. Sedgwick, Lieut. B. Bromley, Sec.-Lieut. C. H. Sell, Lieut. F. Williamson. Middle row: Sec.-Lieut. H. Smith, Sec.-Lieut. I. H. Pullen, Sec.-Lieut. B. L. E. Pocock, Lieut. A. Read, Capt. C. W. Long, Capt. J. R. Somers-Smith, Major M. Soames, Major N. C. King, Capt. and Adj. J. F. C. Bennett, Capt. W. Paxman, Lieut. C. E. Clode-Baker, Sec.-Lieut. H. M. Camden, Lieut. P. Titley, Qr.-Mr. Hon. Lieut. W. Kelly, Sec.-Lieut. F. M. Wheatley. Front row: Sec.-Lieut. E. S. Bauloff, Sec.-Lieut. M. E. C. Gardiner, Sec.-Lieut. L. W. Collins, Sec.-Lieut. F. E. Hewitt, Sec.-Lieut. C. B. Doust, Sec.-Lieut. J. H. Stransom, Sec.-Lieut. J. H. Howe.

[Bassano]

Plate 57 Officers of the 3/5th London Rifle Brigade at Tadworth, late 1915
Highlighted officers were with the 1/5th L.R.B., or the 169th Brigade Trench Mortar Battery or Machine Gun Company in Summer 1916

426

2nd Lt. A L Benns[i], 'C' Company

2nd Lt. G E Clode-Baker, 'B' Company

2nd Lt. C B Doust, 'A' Company

2nd Lt. I R Pogose[ii], 'D' Company

2nd Lt. A Warner

Wounded:

Capt. G H Cholmeley, OC 'A' Company

Lt. G G Boston DCM, OC Battalion Bombers, was evacuated from Le Havre on 30th July on the *'Gloucester Castle'*. He was wounded in the left shoulder with compound fractures of the scapula and the neck of the humerus. He was in hospital until September 1917 and did not return to the Battalion.

Lt. B L E Pocock, 'A' Company, suffered a grenade fragment wound to the left hand and, on 3rd July, was evacuated back to England on board the *'Lanfranc'* where he spent five weeks at the Queen Alexandra Military Hospital, Millbank, London. The fragment broke his 3rd metacarpal and ruptured several tendons and required two operations. He returned to the battalion in the Spring of 1917.

Lt. P B B Oldfield, 'B' Company[iii], suffered a bullet wound to the back of the skull resulting in a depressed fracture which required a trepanning operation. He was evacuated from Le Havre on board the *HMHS Panama* on 28th July and was sent to the Officers' Hospital at Millbank. He did not return to the Battalion, suffering from visual disturbances and occasional blindness.

2nd Lt. R F Lydall[iv] was evacuated to England on 6th July from Boulogne on board the *'St Denis'*[v]. He had suffered a shrapnel wound to the back and was affected by shell shock. The shrapnel bullet was removed from near to his spine at the M.D.S. at Couin. Whilst he was recovering he went to the cinema to see

---

[i] 2nd Lt. Arthur Lionel Benns, 1/5th London Regt (London Rifle Brigade), was killed on 1st July 1916. Aged 24, he was the son of Roger William and Eliza Benns of 45, Bonsfield Road, New Cross. He was educated at Haberdashers Aske's, Hatcham School and Christ's Hospital, where he was in the OTC, and was a shipping clerk with the Commonwealth and Dominion Line. He played rugby for Old Blues and was assistant secretary of the Old Blues Swimming Club. He attested 9148 Private on 28th April 1910. Promoted Lance Corporal on 12th May 1915 he was wounded at Ypres in March 1915. He was commissioned into the 3/5th London Rifle Brigade on 28th September 1915 joined the battalion on 5th March 1916. His body was never found and his name is inscribed on the Thiepval Memorial, Pier and Face 9D. [*Additional Sources:* Pam & Ken Linge, Thiepval Project]

[ii] 2nd Lt. Ivor Reginald Pogose, 1/5th London Regt. (London Rifle Brigade), died of wounds on 2nd July 1916. Born on 28th May 1895, he was the son of Nicholas Marcar Pogose of Flat 2, 2, Acre Lane, Brixton, London, & the late Margaret Pogose. He was educated at Arlington Park College, Chiswick. A railway clerk he lived at 27, Princes Square, Kennington Park Road. He attested 687 Rifleman in the 10th King's Royal Rifle Corps on 5th September 1914 and was commissioned into the 1/5th London Rifle Brigade on 26th July 1915. He was buried in Couin British Cemetery I. C. 4

[iii] Lt. Percy Bertram Boyd Oldfield, 1/5th London Regt. (London Rifle Brigade), was educated at Radley and lived at 33, Collingham Road, Kensington. He was commissioned on 7th February 1915 and joined the 1/5th London Rifle Brigade on 1st May 1915. He was promoted Lieutenant on 1st June 1916 and was severely wounded on 1st July 1916. He later became an instructor with No. 16 Officer Cadet Battalion and relinquished his commission on the grounds of ill-health on 23rd May 1919.

[iv] 2nd Lt. Robert Francis Lydall, 1/5th London Regt. (London Rifle Brigade), was born on 18th May 1896. He was educated at the Borough Polytechnic and South London College, Dulwich and was a shipping clerk, living at 44, South Croxted Road, Dulwich. He joined the London Rifle Brigade on 22nd January 1914 as 9690 Private ('P' later 'C' Company) and went to France in November 1914. Having been promoted Lance Sergeant in November 1915, he was commissioned on 24th January 1916, rejoining the battalion on the 9th June 1916. Promoted Lieutenant on 24th July 1917, he joined the 2/5th London Rifle Brigade in December 1917 and was later transferred to the 3/5th Battalion as Brigade Bombing Officer of the 1st London Reserve Brigade. He was demobilised on 3rd February 1919 but re-enlisted with the Regiment in 1920 and was still serving in 1933.

[v] *HMHS St Denis* was built in 1908 for the Harwich to Hook of Holland service of the Great Eastern Railway, displacing 2,570 gross tons. Originally named the *'Munich'*, she was renamed on the outbreak of war when she was converted to a hospital ship. She kept the name after the war. She was caught in Amsterdam harbour when the Germans invaded in 1940 and was scuttled. Raised by the Germans she was eventually scrapped in 1950.

the recently released film of the Battle of the Somme, an experience which badly disturbed him, causing a recurrence of neurasthenia. He did not return to the Battalion in France.

2ⁿᵈ Lt. R E Petley, 'D' Company, was wounded in the shoulder and the knee. He embarked from Le Havre to Southampton on board the hospital ship *'Asturias*[i]. Recovering from his wounds, he rejoined the battalion on the 8ᵗʰ September 1916.

2ⁿᵈ Lt. E W Rose[ii], 'C' Company, was hit in the right thigh by a large shell fragment. He rejoined the battalion and was killed on 28ᵗʰ March 1918.

2ⁿᵈ Lt. B F Sawbridge[iii] was evacuated from Le Havre on 2ⁿᵈ July on board the *'Lanfranc'* suffering from a gun shot wound to the right wrist. He rejoined the Battalion in France in August 1918 and was wounded again the following month.

2ⁿᵈ Lt. H Smith, 'D' Company. He rejoined the battalion and was killed on 8ᵗʰ October 1916.

2ⁿᵈ Lt. E G Thomas[iv] was shot in the arm and head being left completely blind. He was sent to the 43ʳᵈ Casualty Clearing Station and then to the 1ˢᵗ General Hospital where he arrived on 5ᵗʰ July. He was evacuated to the Queen Alexandra Military Hospital, Grosvenor Park, Millbank, London where he arrived on the 6ᵗʰ July. On the 27ᵗʰ July he was discharged to Templeton House, Roehampton for further treatment but he was discharged from the Army in 1917 totally blind.

Prisoner of War:

Capt. A T B de Cologan, OC 'D' Company, was initially reported missing but later confirmed as a Prisoner of War. He was sent to a camp at Gütersloh.

---

i *HMHS Asturias*, 12,015 gross ton, was built by Harland & Wolff, Belfast, for the Royal Mail Steam Packet Co. and was launched on 26ᵗʰ September 1907. On 1ˢᵗ August 1914 she was requisitioned and converted to a Naval hospital ship but was taken over by the Army who fitted her to carry 1,700 wounded. On the night of the 20ᵗʰ/21ˢᵗ March 1917 she was torpedoed off Start Point. 35 lives were lost and most of her stern was blown away. She was beached near Bolt Head and was declared a total loss. The government salvaged her and she became a ammunition hulk at Plymouth for two years. Re-purchased by Royal Mail Steam Packet Co. after the war, she was towed to Belfast where she rebuilt as a cruise liner and renamed Arcadian. The slump of the early 1930s hit luxury cruising and in October 1930 she was laid up at Southampton until 1933 when she was sold to Japanese shipbreakers. [*Source*: Sea Breezes Magazine, March 1955]

ii 2ⁿᵈ Lt. Eric Wollaston Rose, M.C., 1/5ᵗʰ London Regt. (London Rifle Brigade), was born on 9ᵗʰ July 1896, the son of the Rev. Percy Wollaston and Isabel Katherine Rose, of 'Highwood', Ridgeway Rd., Redhill, Surrey. He was educated at St. Edward's School, Oxford. He attested 2142 Private in the 2/1ˢᵗ Sussex Yeomanry on 2ⁿᵈ October 1914 and was commissioned into the 2/5ᵗʰ London Rifle Brigade on 3ʳᵈ April 1915. He joined the 1/5ᵗʰ London Rifle Brigade in France on 22ⁿᵈ July 1915. He rejoined the battalion on 8ᵗʰ November 1916 and was killed in action on 28ᵗʰ March 1918. His body was never found and his name is inscribed on the Arras Memorial, Bay 9.

iii 2ⁿᵈ Lt. Bartle Frere Sawbridge, 1/5ᵗʰ London Regt. (London Rifle Brigade), born on the 2ⁿᵈ November 1883, the son of John Sikes and Elizabeth Tudor Sawbridge. His father was the Rector at Thelnetham, a small village between Diss and Thetford on the Norfolk/Suffolk border. He was educated at Winchester, where he was in the Rifle Corps, and University College, Oxford (1902-06) and was Chemist to Messrs. Whitbread & Co. from 1912. He was an Associate of the Institute of Chemistry, 1908, and a Fellow in 1911. He attested 3515 Private in the Inns of Court O.T.C. on 6ᵗʰ May 1915. He was commissioned into the 3/5ᵗʰ London Rifle Brigade on 11ᵗʰ July 1915, joining the 1/5ᵗʰ Battalion on 6ᵗʰ May 1916. On his recovery in September 1916 he was sent to join the 3/5ᵗʰ London Rifle Brigade at Fovant Camp. In December 1916 he was appointed Commandant of No. 6 Area Gas School, Southern Command and he was promoted Acting Captain on 1ˢᵗ July 1917. He rejoined the battalion on 2ⁿᵈ August 1918 and was wounded again on 12ᵗʰ September 1918 with a gun shot wound to the right thigh. He was married in April 1927 to Kathleen Frances, daughter of Prof. Edward Iles, Royal Academy of Music. [*Additional source*: Dick Flory: Winchester College Register, 1884-1934; Wykhemist War Service Roll, 1918]

iv 2ⁿᵈ Lt. Edward George Thomas, 1/5ᵗʰ London Regt. (London Rifle Brigade), was born on 17ᵗʰ September 1893 in Ramsgate, the son of Mr and Mrs J Thomas later of Station House, Sevenoaks, Kent. He was educated at the Wesleyan School, Deal and was a clerk. He attested 457 Rfn. in the 2/5ᵗʰ London Rifle Brigade on 4ᵗʰ September 1914 and, having been promoted Corporal, was commissioned on 4ᵗʰ September 1915 into the 2/5ᵗʰ L.R.B. He was transferred into the 3/5ᵗʰ Battalion and was sent to the 1/5ᵗʰ London Rifle Brigade on 27ᵗʰ May 1916, arriving with the battalion on 2ⁿᵈ June.

***

ON 30TH JUNE, THE QUEEN VICTORIA'S RIFLES counted 27 officers and 671 men in the assaulting waves. At roll call on the 2nd July there were 11 officers and 142 men remaining – casualties of 16 officers and 529 men. It must be assumed from the Official History's total of 448 other ranks casualties, that a number of men found their way back over the next day or two but, even allowing for this, the battalion had suffered 66% casualties. Of the three leading Companies, 'A', 'B' and 'C', all fifteen officers were either killed or wounded and only 64 men returned, many wounded. There were just three unwounded men in No. 1 Platoon. The War Diary recorded:

	Killed	Wounded	Missing	Total
Officers	5	5	5	15
Other Ranks	51	290	188	529
Total	56	295	193	544

Table 18 Queen Victoria's Rifles' casualties

The officer casualties were:

Killed:

Capt. R W Cunningham, OC 'A' Company

Capt. P S Houghton, OC 'B' Company

Capt. H E Leys Cox, OC 'C' Company

Lt. C P Fleetwood, 'C' Company

2nd Lt. R H Cary, 'B' Company[i]

2nd Lt. F W Fielding, 'C' Company[ii]

2nd Lt. O T Mason, 'B' Company

2nd Lt. N A Meeking, 'B' Company

2nd Lt. P G Simmonds, 'A' Company

Wounded:

Lt. W Goodinge[iii], 'B' Company, suffered wounds from shell fragments to both legs, the left buttock and the right shoulder. The latter wound resulted in temporary paralysis in his right arm and a fragment of shell lodged in his leg caused pressure on the popliteal nerve making walking difficult. He was evacuated from Le Havre to Southampton on 5th July. He did not return to the Battalion.

Lt. W S Stranack, 'B' Company

2nd Lt. C V Davis, 'B' Company

---

i 2nd Lt. Richard Harry Cary, 1/9th London Regt. (Queen Victoria's Rifles), was killed on 1st July 1916. Born on 6th March, 1894, he was the son of Mrs E Cary of 3, Darlington Road, West Norwood. He was educated at the Western High School, Washington, DC and was a commercial traveller with N S Croker and Co. He attested 2857 Private in the 13th London Regt. (Kensingtons) on 2nd September 1914 and was commissioned into the QVRs on 19th November 1915. His body was never found and his name is inscribed on the Thiepval Memorial, Pier and Face 13C.

ii 2nd Lt. Francis Willoughby 'Jack' Fielding, 1/9th London Regt. (Queen Victoria's Rifles), was killed on 1st July 1916. Born on 8th October 1892, he was the second son of the late Harry and Letitia Elizabeth Fielding, of Stoneleigh House, Thame, Oxon. He was educated at Taunton School and was an aeronautical engineer. He went to France in 1914 as a despatch rider with the Oxford Hussars (Yeomanry) having joined on 1st November 1909 as 1522 Private. He was commissioned into the 3/9th battalion in July 1915. He had been initiated into the Victoria Rifle's Masonic Lodge, No. 822, in January 1916. He is buried in Gommecourt British Cemetery No. 2, III. D. I

iii Lt. Wallinger Goodinge, 1/9th London Regt. (Queen Victoria's Rifles), He lived at 28, Exeter Road, Brondesbury, London. He attested 1534 Private in the Inns of Court OTC on 6th October 1914. After recovering from his wound he joined the 9th Reserve Battalion, London Regt. in March 1917. In August 1917 he was seconded to the Ministry of Munitions. He was declared permanently unfit for General Service in January 1918.

2ⁿᵈ Lt. F G Garsideⁱ, 'C' Company. He was killed in action on 27ᵗʰ August 1918.

2ⁿᵈ Lt. J S Hunter, 'A' Company
Wounded and Prisoner of War

2ⁿᵈ Lt. R Bennett, 'C' Company, wounded by a bullet wound in the front of the right thigh and was only prevented from bleeding to death by a tourniquet. He was made a Prisoner of War and was sent to Ohrdruf Hospital, part of the Langensalza Prisoner of War Camp.

***

THE QUEEN'S WESTMINSTER RIFLES, the battalion with the most difficult task – that of taking and holding the Quadrilateral behind Gommecourt village – suffered 73% casualties amongst the men called to action. The Official History erroneously gives totals of 28 officers and 661 men involved (the regimental history gives a figure of 750 in total) of which *every* officer and 475 men became casualties. The actual figures for officer casualties is eighteen, however, confusion has been caused by the fact that some of the officers who had recently joined the Westminsters from other regiments are given as casualties for their original regiment rather than their new one. It should be noted that nearly one third of the men who went into action with the Westminsters had recently come from the disbanded 2/2ⁿᵈ London Regiment. The officer casualties were:

Killed:

Capt. G E Cockerill, OC 'B' Company, Died as a Prisoner of War

Capt. H F Mott M.C., OC 'C' Company

Capt. F G Swainson M.C., OC 'A' Company

2ⁿᵈ Lt. E H Bovill, 'A' Company

2ⁿᵈ Lt. F A Farley, 'D' Company

2ⁿᵈ Lt. J A Horne, 'B' Company

2ⁿᵈ Lt. A G Negus, 'C' Company

2ⁿᵈ Lt. W F Strange, 'B' Company

2ⁿᵈ Lt. C A Stubbs, 'D' Company

2ⁿᵈ Lt. A G V Yates, 'C' Company

Wounded:

Capt. P M Glasier D.S.O., OC 'D' Company was evacuated to the Queen Alexandra Hospital, Millbank, London where he spent two weeks recovering from a bullet wound to the backside.

2ⁿᵈ Lt. J Daniel, 'A' Company, suffered from a compound, comminuted fracture of the right humerus caused by a machine gun bullet wound to the shoulder and also lost the top of his left thumb. He was evacuated from Le Havre on board the *'Panama'* on 28ᵗʰ July. Having lost a lot of muscle and movement it took over a year to recover sufficiently for him to pursue his desire to become a pilot in the RFC.

ⁱ Lt. Frank Gerald Garside, 1/9ᵗʰ London Regt. (Queen Victoria's Rifles) was born on 21ˢᵗ August 1888, the son of Edwin Samuel and Katherine Jane Garside of 250, Amhurst Road, West Hackney. He was educated at the Grocers' Company School, Hackney. A chartered accountant, he lived at 8, Park Mansions, St John's Wood and was married to Marjorie Swinford Garside later of Minster Lodge, Ormskirk, Lancashire. He attested 4147 Private in the Inns of Court OTC on 10ᵗʰ June 1915 and was commissioned into the 3/9ᵗʰ London Regt. in October 1915. He was killed on 27ᵗʰ August 1918 whilst attached to the 7ᵗʰ Royal Fusiliers. He was buried in Beaulencourt British Cemetery, Ligny-Thilloy, grave I. F. 24.

2nd Lt. C C Iveson[i], 'D' Company, was knocked unconscious and buried by a shell explosion. He was evacuated on 4th July from Le Havre on board the *'Maheno'* suffering from severe shell shock. His symptoms included: numb legs, involuntary knee jerks, headaches, nightmares and tremors. He did not rejoin the battalion.

2nd Lt. E H Jarvis[ii], 'A' Company

2nd Lt. H Luscombe, 'B' Company, was evacuated from Le Havre on board the *'Asturias'* on 4th July. Knocked unconscious by a shell explosion, he had also suffered severely bruised ribs from the impact of a shrapnel bullet, concussion and had a septic heel. In England he was diagnosed as suffering from tremors, insomnia and an inability to concentrate, i.e. neurasthenia or shell shock. He was declared fit for General Service on 10th November 1916. He was killed in action on 11th April 1917.

2nd Lt. F S Thomas, 'B' Company, was evacuated from Le Havre on 13th July on board the *'Marama'* suffering from gun shot wounds to both hands and to the back, neck and groin. The wounds became septic and an operation was needed to remove bone fragments from his left hand. He was sent to the 4th London General Hospital where he recovered slowly. A Medical Board in January 1917 found him still receiving treatment with the thumb, index and middle fingers of his left hand showing little improvement being both stiff and cold and 'practically useless'. He did not return to the battalion, still suffering from problems with his hands in 1920.

Wounded and Prisoner of War

Lt. P Spencer-Smith, 'B' Company, was wounded in the left forearm by a gun shot which fractured the radius and he was made a Prisoner of War. He was sent to Ohrdruf Hospital and then the Langensalza Camp before being interned in Holland.

2nd Lt. D F Upton M.C., 'B' Company, Prisoner of War

***

THE 1/2ND LONDONS, WHO HAD STRIVED so gallantly to take ammunition and bombs across to their beleaguered colleagues in the German trenches, suffered heavily. The precise numbers of men involved are not available though the complete battalion strength was 40 officers and 949 men on 1st July, broadly the same as the Q.W.R.. It would not be unreasonable, therefore, to assume that a similar number of men were involved in the battle, i.e. about 700. Their regimental history gives a casualty list of 12 officers and 241 men – or 36% of a battalion of which it is believed only a party of 21 men carrying mortar bombs ever got into the German lines. These casualties were heavily concentrated in two Companies and, after the attack, Pte Clements recorded that only 16 men out

---

i 2nd Lt. Cyril Charles Iveson, 1/16th London Regt. (Queen's Westminster Rifles), was born on 16th July, 1895, the son of C W Iveson, Glencairn Park Crescent, Church End, Finchley. He was educated at Christ's College, Finchley. A bank clerk, he was married to Dorothy Iveson and they lived at Carn Bica, 17, Warwick Road, Ealing. He was commissioned on 14th December 1915 and arrived in France on 4th March 1916. He was promoted Captain and appointed Adjutant of the 16th (Reserve), London Regt. in December 1918.

ii 2nd Lt. Ernest Henry Jarvis, 1/16th London Regt. (Queen's Westminster Rifles), joined the battalion on 1st June 1916. Later promoted Lieutenant Colonel, he was seconded to the Imperial War Graves Commission after the war.

of 260 from 'C' Company came back unwounded and from 'A' Company just 12 out of 260[i].

Officer casualties were:

Killed:

Capt. J R Garland, OC 'A' Company

Capt. P J A Handyside, OC 'C' Company

2ⁿᵈ Lt. B R Buxton[ii]

2ⁿᵈ Lt. J S Grainger, 'C' Company

2ⁿᵈ Lt. H C Gosnell[iii], 'C' Company

2ⁿᵈ Lt. A M Thorman[iv]

Wounded:

Lt. H W Everitt[v] was evacuated to Southampton on 4ᵗʰ July from the 3ʳᵈ General Hospital at Le Treport via Le Havre on board the *'Maheno'*. He had suffered a shrapnel wound above the left eye and severe contusions on the right forearm. He returned to the battalion in July 1917 but was sent home again soon after.

Lt. G B Henderson[vi] recovered from his wounds to join the 2/2ⁿᵈ Londons in France. He was killed on 16ᵗʰ June 1917.

---

i The numbers Pte Clements gives for each Company probably relate to the numbers before the battle surplus and other non-combatants were excluded and a figure of about 180 men actually involved per Company is a more likely figure.

ii 2ⁿᵈ Lt. Bertie Reginald Buxton, 1/2ⁿᵈ London Regt. (Royal Fusiliers), was born on 1ˢᵗ December 1891 in Hanley, Staffordshire, the son of Henry Samuel and Harriet Buxton. He was the second youngest of seven children. On the outbreak of war he enlisted in the 4ᵗʰ Seaforth Highlanders T.F., serving with them for a year, and was commissioned into the 2/2ⁿᵈ London Regt. on 3ʳᵈ November 1915. He joined the 1/2ⁿᵈ London Regt., in February 1916. He was killed on 1ˢᵗ July 1916. His body was never found and his name was inscribed on the Thiepval Memorial, Pier and Face Pier and Face 9 D and 16 B. [*Additional Sources:* Pam & Ken Linge, Thiepval Project]

iii 2ⁿᵈ Lt. Harold Clifford Gosnell, 1/2ⁿᵈ London Regt (Royal Fusiliers), died on Saturday, 1ˢᵗ July 1916. Born on 6ᵗʰ January 1890, he was the fourth of five children of Herbert Clifford Gosnell and the late Alice Augusta Gosnell of Highbury New Park. He was educated at Surrey House, Edgard Road, Margate in Kent. He attested as 1768 Private in the 7ᵗʰ Londons on 5ᵗʰ August 1914 being wounded at Festubert and fighting at Loos. He was commissioned into the 2ⁿᵈ Londons on 15ᵗʰ November 1915 whilst with the former battalion in France. He joined the 4/2ⁿᵈ London Regt. in England in December 1915. He joined the 1/2ⁿᵈ Londons from the 4/2ⁿᵈ Londons in March 1916. His body was never found and his name is inscribed on the Thiepval Memorial, Pier and Face 9 D and 16 B. His younger brother 2ⁿᵈ Lt. Vernon Clifford Gosnell served with the 1/28ᵗʰ Londons. [*Additional Sources:* Pam & Ken Linge, Thiepval Project]

iv 2ⁿᵈ Lt. Alan Marshall Thorman, 1/2ⁿᵈ London Regt (Royal Fusiliers), died on Saturday, 1ˢᵗ July 1916. Born on 23ʳᵈ July 1895, he was the third of four children of John Marshall Thorman and Eleanor Reed Thorman of Witton Castle, Witton-le-Wear, Co. Durham. He was educated at Charterhouse School and enlisted in the Public Schools Battalion, Middlesex Regt. Before the war he was a coal exporter. He was commissioned into the 2/2ⁿᵈ Londons on 16ᵗʰ January 1915, serving in Malta, Gallipoli and Egypt before joining the 1/2ⁿᵈ Londons in June 1916. His body was never found and his name is inscribed on the Thiepval Memorial, Pier and Face 9 D and 16 B. [*Additional Sources:* Pam & Ken Linge, Thiepval Project. Dick Flory: Charterhouse Register, 1872-1931; The Cross of Sacrifice]

v 2ⁿᵈ Lt. Harold William Everitt, 1/2ⁿᵈ London Regt. (Royal Fusiliers) was born on 2ⁿᵈ June 1894. Educated at St Francis Xavier's College in Bruges he was a stationer and lived at The Birches, Epsom, Surrey. He was commissioned into the 2ⁿᵈ Londons in April 1913 and promoted Lieutenant on 29ᵗʰ August 1914. He served with the battalion in France from January 1915 as a platoon commander. On his return to the battalion in July 1917, and having been promoted Captain, his seniority gave him command of a Company, however his CO, Maj. Sneath, did not believe him competent for such a command and requested his removal. It was later discovered that he had lied about his age when joining the Army and was two years younger than declared. He was sent home for further training in September 1917 where he joined the 32ⁿᵈ London Regiment and then the 1ˢᵗ Reserve Battalion, London Regt. In January 1918 he was court martialled for conduct prejudicial to good order and military discipline, i.e. he was found to have drunk with NCOs in the Sergeants' Mess and that he was improperly found in the bar of the Portobello Hotel in Walton on the Naze. He was found guilty on all charges and severely reprimanded. He was later attached to the 3ʳᵈ Royal Sussex Regt. based at Rugeley, Staffs., and was discharged from the Army in May 1919.

vi 2ⁿᵈ Lt. Graeme Bonhôte Henderson, 2/2ⁿᵈ London Regt. (Royal Fusiliers), was the son of Mr and Mrs John Henderson of 11, New Court, Lincoln's Inn, London. Born on 30ᵗʰ July 1883 he was educated at Mr Draper's School, Hemel Hempstead and Winchester College. He was a clerk in Union Discount Company of London. He enlisted in the 7ᵗʰ Londons and was commissioned into the 3/2ⁿᵈ London Regt. on 16ᵗʰ January 1915. He joined the

Plate 58 2nd Lt. Graeme Henderson, 2/2nd London Regt. wounded 1st July 1916

2nd Lt. H F Blows[i]

2nd Lt. N F Perris[ii] recovered from his wounds to join the RFC in May 1917. He was killed on 20th July 1918.

2nd Lt. J W Sanders[iii], 'A' Company

2nd Lt. A E Wiggs[iv] was knocked unconscious by a shell explosion in the trenches and was evacuated from Le Havre on board the *'Maheno'* suffering from shell shock. His symptoms included headaches, insomnia, nightmares, tremors of the hands and knees and an inability to concentrate.

***

1/2nd Londons in at Ypres in July 1915. After recovering from his wounds he joined the 2/2nd Londons in France. He was killed in action on 16th June 1917. His body was never found and his name was inscribed on the Arras Memorial, Bay 9. [*Additional source:* Dick Flory: Winchester College Register, 1884-1934; Wykhemist War Service Roll; Wykehamists Who Died in the War, 1914-1918, Volume I]

i 2nd Lt. Harold Frederick Blows attested 2386 Private in the Honourable Artillery Company before being commissioned into the 2nd London Regt. He later transferred into the Royal Engineers and was promoted Captain.

ii 2nd Lt. Noel Felix Perris, 1/2nd London Regt. att 143rd Squadron, RAF, was killed on 20th July 1918 at the age of 24. Lt. Perris was killed during an anti-Gotha patrol on 20th July 1918 in SE5a C1809. This aircraft collided with another SE5a, C1831, piloted by 2nd Lt. T Wright. Both were killed. C1809 went down out of control and crashed in flames. He had earlier served with 50 Squadron in home defence duties. Perris was born on 25th December 1893 and was the son of Mary Annie Perris, of 4, Wellington House, Eton Rd., Hampstead, London, and the late George Herbert Perris. He is buried in the South East part of Detling (St. Martin) Churchyard neard Maidstone, Kent. Educated at Dulwich College, he enlisted in the 3/2nd London Regt. in October 1914 and was commissioned into the 2/2nd Londons in June 1915. He served in the Dardanelles and Egypt before joining the 1/2nd Londons in France in May 1916. After recovering from his wounds he was seconded to the RFC, becoming a Flying Officer, and was promoted Lieutenant on 1st July 1917. [*Source:* Trevor Henshaw for the details of the accident]

iii 2nd Lt. John William Sanders, 1/2nd London Regt., (Royal Fusiliers), was later promoted Captain.

iv 2nd Lt. Albert E Wiggs, 1/2nd London Regt., (Royal Fusiliers), lived at 54, Aytoun Road, Brixton. After recovering from his wound he reported for duty to the 1st Reserve Battalion, London Regt., at Fovant on 10th September 1916. At the end of March 1917 he was admitted to the 1st London General Hospital following a disciplinary investigation into his departure from his unit then based at Torquay to visit Brixham in the company of an unknown 'lady'. Wiggs tried to cover his tracks by making up a story about taking a Miss Balfour, the 15 year old daughter of family friends, to meet some brother officers in Brixham but, after a complaint from the young lady's father, Wiggs admitted that all of his stories were false and designed to protect the identity of the actual woman in his company. An attempt was made by his battalion CO, Brigade GOC and Maj. Gen. L G Drummond, Commanding Southern Reserve Centre, to have Wiggs returned to the ranks however this was rejected by Lord French as officers could only be removed as a result of inefficiency and not matters of discipline and a court martial was suggested. This did not take place and he returned to France with the 2/2nd London Regt. in the summer of 1917. He was evacuated in September suffering from 'Pyrexia – unknown origin' (possible trench fever). He later joined the RFC/RAF before being returned to the Army as 'unfit for flying' in March 1919.

IN ADDITION, THE BRIGADE MACHINE GUN and Trench Mortar Batteries all contributed the long casualty list. The officer casualties were:

169th Brigade Machine Gun Company
Killed
2nd Lt. J S Engall (1/16th Londons)
2nd Lt. K M C Fradd[i] (1/2nd Londons)
Wounded
2nd Lt. R J Mackay

169th Brigade Trench Mortar Battery
Killed
Lt. E A J A Lane (1/9th Londons)

According to Rfn. R J Manning of the Queen Victoria's who was attached to the Machine Gun Company only five of the 38 officers and men who had gone across with the guns managed to return to the British lines and, as Manning was wounded, this represented a casualty rate of at least 90% within this unit.

***

AMONGST THE 1/5TH CHESHIRE REGIMENT men who either went over with the attacking waves or were given various tasks in the British lines losses were severe. 'A' Company, which followed the 169th Brigade over, lost every platoon commander, two dead and two wounded. In total, the company lost 4 officers and 113 men – certainly well over half the number that had gone into action. In 'B' and the platoon of 'D' Company involved the losses were one officer dead and 37 men dead, wounded or missing. In total, the Cheshires lost 6 officers and 172 other ranks. The strength of the 1/5th Cheshires on 30th June was 37 officers and 1,034 men.

The officer casualties were:
Killed:
Lt. P B Bass, 'A' Company
2nd Lt. G S Arthur, 'A' Company
2nd Lt. F A Davies, 'B' Company
Wounded:
2nd Lt. E J Andrews, 'A' Company
2nd Lt. H R Leigh, 'C' Company. His right arm was blown off two inches above the elbow. The remains of his arm were amputated the same day and he was evacuated to England on the 13th July, arriving in Southampton on the hospital ship *HMNZHS 'Marama'*. An artificial arm was fitted in 1917.
2nd Lt. H C H Simpson, 'A' Company

***

THE 167TH BRIGADE which, with the exception of the 1/1st and 1/3rd Londons, had played little part in the day's events still suffered losses. The 1/3rd Londons, who had attempted the impossible job of digging a trench across No Man's Land whilst under machine gun and artillery fire, were the worst hit.

---

i 2nd Lt. Kingsley Meredith Chatterton Fradd, 1/2nd London Regt. (Royal Fusiliers) was born on 24th August 1897, the son of Mrs Ada Mary Fradd. His father separated from his mother in 1906 leaving her to look after her son and two daughters. He was educated at All Saints' School, Bloxham, Oxfordshire where he was in the OTC, leaving in July 1914. He lived at 41, Fitzroy Street, Fitzroy Square, London. He was commissioned into the 4/2nd London Regt. in November 1915. He was killed on 1st July 1916 and is buried in Hebuterne Military Cemetery, grave IV. A. 10

Reporting to the 56th Division's Adjutant, their roll calls showed one officer, 2nd Lt. R J A Lidiard, dead, three wounded and one missing and 19 other ranks dead, 124 wounded and another four missing. The number of fatalities was soon to grow. 2nd Lt. Calder-Smith, the missing officer, was later shown to have been killed and Lt. D W L Jones succumbed to his wounds at Warlincourt Halte. Amongst the men, the list of dead grew to thirty three, with three of the wounded dying and another six of them being killed or fatally injured on 2nd July. Amongst the other three battalions one officer was killed and another died of wounds, seven more were wounded. Thirty six other ranks were killed or died of wounds and nearly 130 were wounded. The officer casualties were:

1/3rd Londons
Killed:
2nd Lt. R A Calder-Smith[i]
2nd Lt. R J A Lidiard[ii]
Died of Wounds:
Lt. D W L Jones[iii]
Wounded:
Capt. E V Noel was evacuated on board the Hospital Ship 'Oxfordshire'[iv] from Le Havre on 3rd July suffering from shell shock.

1/1st Londons
Missing believed killed:
2nd Lt. H W Cundall[v]
Wounded:
2nd Lt. J A Freeman[vi], 'D' Company, was wounded in the right knee by a shell fragment and, after being sent to hospital at Le Treport, was evacuated from Le

---

[i] 2nd Lt. Raymond Alexander Calder-Smith, 1/3rd London Regt. (Royal Fusiliers), was aged 26. He was one of five children of Mrs. Ramona Calder-Smith of Santona, Madrid, Spain, and the late Robert Calder-Smith of Manila, Philippine Islands. His body was never found and his name is inscribed on the Thiepval Memorial, Pier and Face 9 D and 16 B.

[ii] 2nd Lt. Richard John Abraham Lidiard, 1/3rd London Regt (Royal Fusiliers) was born on 4th May 1895. He was the younger son of Mr Herbert & Mrs Kate Mary Lina Lidiard, 114 Westbourne Terrace near Hyde Park, London. He was educated at St George's School, Windsor and was an articled clerk to his father, a solicitor. He was commissioned into the 2/3rd Londons in September 1914 and served with the 86th Brigade, 29th Division at Suvla Bay, Gallipoli being evacuated with jaundice after a bout of malaria. He had been recommended for a permanent commission in the Regular Army by Brigj. Gen. C J Percival, GOC 86th Brigade in March 1916. He is buried in Hebuterne Military Cemetery II. P. 1

[iii] Lt. David William Llewellyn Jones, 1/3rd London Regt. (Royal Fusiliers), died of wounds on 2nd July 1916. Aged 21, he was the son of the Rev. Canon David Jones and Katharine Edwards Jones, of Tregarth, Penmaenmawr, Caernarvonshire. He died at No 43 Casualty Clearing Station and was buried at Warlincourt Halte British Cemetery, grave II. D. 2.

[iv] HMHS *Oxfordshire* was built for the Bibby Line in 1912 by Harland & Wolff at Belfast with a displacement of 8648 gross tons. She was the first ship to be requisitioned for war service on 2nd August 1914 and she was converted to Naval Hospital Ship No.1 with 562 beds. She served in the Eastern Mediterranean, Persian Gulf and German East Africa before being used in the Channel and, by the end of the war, had carried more casualties than any other ship. She resumed commercial service in 1920 and in 1939 became Hospital Ship No. 6 serving in West Africa, the Mediterranean, Adriatic, Australia and the Phillipines. By the end of the war she had, again, carried more casualties than any other ship. Having been used to repatriate casualties and PoWs from Hong Kong she was involved in carrying casualties, troops, evacuees and pilgrims in the Indian Ocean and Mediterranean. She was sold to the Pan-Islamic Steamship Co. of Karachi in 1951 and re-named the *Safina-el-Arab*. She was broken up at Karachi in 1958. [*Source:* The Red Duster web site]

[v] 2nd Lt. Hubert Walter Cundall, 1/1st London Regt. (Royal Fusiliers) was aged 24. He was the son of Florence and the late John Hubert Cundall of 20, St George's Mansions, Causton Street, Westminster. His body was never found and his name is inscribed on the Thiepval Memorial, Pier and Face 9 D and 16 B.

[vi] 2nd Lt. Jesse Alfred Freeman, 1/1st London Regt. (Royal Fusiliers), was born on 15th March 1895, the son of C A Freeman of Betham House, Greenford, Middlesex. He was educated at Acton County School and Springfield College, Acton. He attested 3770 Private in the Inns of Court OTC on 27th May 1915. He was commissioned into the 2/1st London Regt., on 15th November 1915, going with them to Egypt in December. On the battalion's return

Havre on 5th July on board the *'Salta'*. He returned to the battalion in early 1917 being wounded again in May 1917.

2nd Lt. A J de Vall[i] was evacuated from Le Havre on board the *'Oxfordshire'* suffering from shell shock. He returned to the battalion in 1918 to be wounded again in August.

In all, the 56th Division had suffered just over 4,300 casualties, 1,300 of whom had died on the 1st July or would succumb to their wounds in the days and weeks ahead[ii].

***

IN SPITE OF THEIR APPALLING CASUALTIES, the work of the Division was not done – and nor was there any end to their losses. The Queen's Westminsters were marched back to Bayencourt in the late afternoon of the 2nd July. As they entered the village a short, sharp strafe came down and, with savage irony, one shell, landing in the middle of the street, killed three men who had come safely through the carnage of the previous day. The battalion's C.O., Lt. Col. Shoolbred, concluded that Bayencourt was not a safe enough place for his exhausted men so, as shrapnel shells exploded in a tearing roar of black smoke overhead, the officers hurried them to the far side of the village where they bivouacked in the open. The officers sought out a dugout in the village where some were reduced to sharing a tent such was the congestion. 2nd Lt. Moy, now recovered from his concussion, shared with a friend with whom he had trained in Richmond Park only a short time before:

"Poor Bill Thurston[iii] felt the loss of his friends even more than I did, that night he cried himself to sleep. I felt very sorry for him but soon tiredness overcame us both and we slept heavily."[13]

The London Rifle Brigade suffered in an identical fashion to their Brigade colleagues with one man killed and two more wounded when they were shelled as they entered Bayencourt on the afternoon of the 2nd July. Rfn. Jacobs was one of the wounded and his description shows the arbitrary way of death and survival on the Western Front:

"Next day we went back to Bayencourt about four or five miles behind the line and went in billets there. The Germans sent one over there occasionally just on the chance, of course, perhaps half a dozen during the day. Well, after tea I proposed a stroll down the street with a chap I knew and we started. Scarce had we gone twenty yards when we heard a

---

he joined the 1/1st Londons on 6th May 1916. After recovering from his wound he reported for duty to the 1st Reserve Battalion, London Regt., at Fovant on 19th September 1916 and was declared fit for General Service on 15th December 1916. On 13th May 1917 he was evacuated home after being wounded and also suffering from Trench Fever. He was seconded to the Ministry of Shipping in August 1917.

i 2nd Lt. Albert James de Vall, 1/1st London Regt., (Royal Fusiliers) was born on 10th January 1894. He was the son of James de Vall, a Superintendent in the Post Office. He lived at 5, Ashbourne Mansions, Finchley Road, Golders Green. He was a student at the Holloway branch of Clarks College between 1908 and 1910. He joined the Army on 9th January 1914 and was commissioned on 25th December 1915. He was still nervous and anaemic in October. He was sent to Fovant Camp to join the 1st (Reserve) battalion, London Regt., where, in December 1916, an accident with some explosives brought a return to his nervousness and insomnia. He was declared recovered in April 1917 and in July applied for a commission in the Indian Army. This application was rejected when it was found that he had brought back from France something rather more unpleasant than insomnia and he was sent to the Connaught Hospital for treatment. He returned to the battalion in 1918 and was wounded and suffered shell shock on 24th August at Croisilles and evacuated three day's later.

ii For a detailed account of the Division's casualties see Appendix 5.

iii Capt. N T Thurston was to win the M.C. twice and was Mentioned in Despatches.

shell coming and stopped and waited to see where it was going. Then there was a bang and I stopped what I've got at present. The poor chap I was with was killed and I must have had a marvellous escape. But I thought I had got it properly then. However I was at once seen to and taken off to the Dressing Station where I got a dose of morphia. I got hit in the foot, the thigh and the neck and some other places slightly."[14]

But, even as the horrors of war continued miles behind the lines, earlier that afternoon occurred an event remarkable even by the standards of this extraordinary war. Accounts vary but the principle of the action remains the same. In the regimental history of the 2nd Londons it is stated that:

"About 12.30 p.m. Cpl. A B Jones went out to assist a wounded man near the parapet and was hit by a sniper[i]. But a man who went out to the corporal was not fired on; and shortly afterwards the enemy was seen in Ferret showing a white flag. With Br Gen. Coke's permission, Capt. Maxwell Ramsay, the Medical Officer of the 1/2nd Londons, in company with the Medical Officer of the L.R.B., then went down the Gommecourt road with stretchers and brought in about 45 wounded... Many of the wounded lying near the enemy's wire paid a tribute to the Germans, who, they said, had come out to them during the night and given them coffee."[15]

Another account[16] has it that at about 2 p.m., Germans were seen to be gathering in their front line trenches and an alert went out in expectation of an imminent attack. Instead, however, a large Red Cross flag was displayed and it became clear that the enemy were offering a truce so that both sides could retrieve the hundreds of wounded men still lying in No Man's Land. Through this action, most (though not all) of the wounded were brought in and their suffering eased. 3254 Sgt. Bisgood was one of the men who went out to help bring in the wounded:

"As may be imagined the sight out there was terrible, there were men in every attitude, dead mostly, many blown to fragments. Most of the wounded we found in shell holes, I found three chums in one hole all unable to move but cuddled together and it was a hard job to persuade one to leave alone, they decided that age should settle it and the youngest left first. The look of amazement and relief on the poor devils' faces when they saw us peering over the shell hole was good to see. One boy could not believe it and asked me amid sobs if he was dreaming. I am glad to be able to write and say that we got all our wounded in. The dead we could do nothing for, as time would not permit I covered over a few of the most hideous cases and returned to the line sick, sad and very fatigued."[17]

This was not to be the last chivalrous action of the 2nd Guard Reserve Division. A few days later, a German aircraft flew low over the British lines and a complete list of the men captured in the battle was dropped. With some small pleasure one can report that this act of kindness to men and their frantic relatives was reciprocated some time later in a similar fashion.

On the 3rd July, some of the battalions continued to the rear, with the London Rifle Brigade marching to St Amand passing their Divisional commander, Maj.

---

[i] Cpl. Jones survived.

Gen. Hull, on the way. Their War Diary records the pathetic numbers that now represented their proud battalion:

"'A' Company numbered about 23, 'B' about 60, 'C' - 40, and 'D' Coy about 50. These figures included the 85 who had rejoined from the Nucleus Personnel."[18]

Remarkably, within a day some battalions, the 1/2nd Londons amongst them, were back in the front lines but this time not only were they occupying the sections in front of Hebuterne they had worked and died in since early May, they were now asked to take over the trenches of the 46th Division to the north. By some strange logic, the division that had suffered worst and achieved most, was asked to take the place of the division that had suffered least. Those battalions that did move into the area in front of Foncquevillers were quickly acquainted with the problems that had beset the North Midlanders when they found the trenches knee and sometimes thigh deep in water and virtually impassable. They would get no respite with their next turn in the trenches and for another six weeks they took their turns in manning the front lines, sending out regular raiding parties and maintaining consistent pressure on the German defences. That they could do this after everything they had been through speaks volumes for their morale, the leadership of the junior officers and the type of men they all were.

***

IN SPITE OF THE ENORMOUS CASUALTIES and the shambles of the entire main attack north of the River Ancre, praise was heaped upon the men of the 56th Division in recognition of their steadfast bravery. Lt. Gen. Snow was the first to pass on his thoughts:

"VII Corps G.C.R. 237/140   56th Division, S.G. 121/19

56th Division,

The Corps Commander wishes to congratulate all ranks of the 56th Division on the way they took the German trenches and held them by pure grit and pluck for so long in very adverse circumstances.

Although Gommecourt has not fallen into our hands, the purpose of the attack, which was mainly to kill and contain Germans, was accomplished thanks to a great extent to the tenacity of the 56th Division.

F Lyon, Brigadier General

3rd July 1916   General Staff, VII Corps"

On its way to the brigades and battalions, Snow's message passed through Maj. Gen. Hull's hands and he added his own comments to the Corps commanders words:

"The General Officer Commanding the 56th Division wishes all ranks to know how proud he is of the splendid way in which they captured the German trenches and of the way they held onto them until all their ammunition and grenades were exhausted. He is satisfied that the main task of the Division in containing and killing Germans was most thoroughly accomplished."

Last came the message from the C-in-C passed on via Allenby's Third Army Headquarters. Haig's message was a continuation of his subordinate's theme:

"Third Army S.G.R. 46/2   56th Division. S.G. 121/96
VII Corps G.C.R. 233/162

General Officer Commanding, Third Army

The Commander-in-Chief directs me to confirm in writing the verbal message already delivered by an ADC to Gen. Snow, conveying his appreciation of the gallant efforts made at Gommecourt on 1st and 2nd July by the 46th and 56th Divisions of the VII Corps.

While deeply deploring the losses suffered by these divisions, he is glad to be able to assure them that their vigorous and well-sustained attack has proved of material assistance to the success of the general plan of operations.

                         L E Kiggell, Lt. Gen.
13th July 1916   Chief of the General Staff"

Some days later Gen. Allenby inspected the men of the 56th Division and gave them a rousing speech:

"I can find no words to express my opinion of the splendid way you have fought. The great accumulation of German forces on your particular front – the accumulation of nearly 100 German batteries – and the Reserve of the Prussian Guard, made your task a desperate one; but you seized all points designated as your objectives, and your achievement will stand out and compare favourably with any fight in history. It has been the foundation of the success further south, and of the triumphant battle, the sound of which is now dinning in our ears."[19]

The view, assiduously propagated throughout the B.E.F., was that the sacrifice of the two divisions had not been in vain. In the days following their great sacrifice, however, some battalion officers started to question the need for the attack and to question whether the ends had justified the means. Capt., later Lieutenant Colonel, Ferdinand Wallis of the London Rifle Brigade was one such. Wallis was not just some disgruntled war-time volunteer officer with a gripe. Wallis had joined the L.R.B. in 1899 and served continuously in the ranks from March, 1909. He went to war in November 1914 and was promoted to 2nd Lieutenant in February 1915 and Lieutenant in June 1916. He served continuously with the battalion until March 1918 being appointed Adjutant twice and commanded the battalion at various times being appointed (Temp.) Lieutenant Colonel in August 1917 for four months. He went on to command the 1/13th Kensingtons at the end of the war. He was awarded two bars to his Military Cross. This was a man of vast experience and no little talent, who led from the front but always had the best interests of his men at heart. Nevertheless, he wrote later:

"…a reaction after the strain had set in; the losses seemed to have been out of all proportion to the ends gained. We felt something was wrong, was the failure due to the 46th Division? We reached our objective, why had they not joined up with us? Or was the failure due to having no reserve Division? This feeling was not improved when our few survivors were inspected and personally congratulated by the Corps Commander General Snow. In the course of his speech he stated "and when I heard that you had been driven back, I did not care a damn. It did not matter whether you took your objective or not. Our attack was only a feint to keep the German Guards Divisions occupied whilst the main attack was being made down South". It seemed a most tactless thing to say to the men who had been through Hell and whose best friends had been deliberately sacrificed."

But, for Wallis and many other officers and men of the 56th Division there was to be one, last insult to the men who died in front of Gommecourt:

"And now, once again the Staff Officers at the Base came in for great criticism. The L.R.B. was reinforced by men from 18 different Battalions in spite of the fact that 500 L.R.B. men were at the same Base Camp. In their lack of interest or lazy stupidity they would not take the trouble to reinforce Battalions with their own men. On getting orders for reinforcements it appeared as if they took the first row of tents and said these for X Batt'n regardless of a man's esprit de corps. We had London Scottish men in kilts and the London Scottish had L.R.B. men and we were prohibited from transferring them to their own Battalions. With L.R.B. men, numbering over 400, sent to different Battalions in the Division we received 544 men of the 2/7 Middlesex, excellent in every way but NOT L.R.B."

This complaint was echoed by nearly every battalion in the Division. Maj. Grey wrote in the regimental history of the 2nd Londons:

"The whole system of reinforcing regiments at the front was the cause of considerable heart-burning and evoked strenuous protests from all sides… it was discouraging to see men of a regiment going to other units in the same division. Such a disregard of esprit de corps could not but have a bad effect both on the battalion itself and on the reinforcements, who had been imbued with their own regimental tradition."[20]

Plate 59 Lt. Col. V W F Dickins, Queen Victoria's Rifles

The 2nd Londons were to be reinforced by 66 N.C.O.s and men of the 21st London Regt. (First Surrey Rifles) and 138 men of the 22nd London Regt. (The Queens). The Queen Victoria's Rifles accepted men from nine battalions

Pro Patria Mori - The 56th (1st London) Division at Gommecourt, 1st July 1916

between the 4th and 16th July: 1st, 3rd, 4th, 8th, 10th, 14th and 20th Londons and the 7th and 9th Middlesex, leading Col. Dickins to remark to Maj. Gen. Hull that 'he was commanding 17 regiments'.[21] One of the reasons for this 'dilution' of front line battalions with men from other regiments was the dreadful casualties suffered by the Pals battalions. In many towns, villages and communities, especially across the North of England, the scale of the local casualties, once they became known, devastated streets and neighbourhoods where young men had joined up, served and now died together. To prevent such potentially demoralising concentrated grief re-occurring it was decided to mix up battalions with drafts of men from a variety of regiments. Why this process was applied to the London battalions is somewhat difficult to understand as there were no genuinely community-based battalions from the capital. But, whatever its justification, the decision caused great resentment within the 56th Division as it recovered from the mauling it had received at Gommecourt.

Congratulatory messages were not just reserved for the men of the 56th Division. On the other side of the wire the defenders of Gommecourt were receiving the accolades befitting the victors. 2nd Guard Reserve Division rather pompously reported:

> "The 1st July ended in a complete victory for 2. G.R.D.; every member of the division was proud of this result and was glad of the success achieved. The western-most point of the Western Front remained firmly in our hands. Full of confidence, the brave troops maintained their watch with the same fortitude and tenacity to thwart any new attempted attack, wherever it might occur."

But it was the performance of the artillery that had guaranteed success and the performance of the 20th Reserve Field Artillery Regiment, both buy itself and as the overall co-ordinator of all of the artillery defences surrounding Gommecourt that deserved the greatest praise. This they received from the commander of the 52nd Infantry Division's artillery whose men in the 170th and 15th Reserve Infantry Regiments they had so materially assisted in the re-taking of the threatened position:

> "The 52nd Field Artillery Brigade expresses is warmest gratitude to the artillery of 2. G.R.D., which, under the command of Oberstleutnant Hohnhorst in July 1916, supported our batteries in such an outstanding and comrade-like manner in the defence of the attack by the British against the positions of 52. I.D.
>
> Signed: Körner, Generalmajor and Commander
> 52. Feldartillerie-Brigade"

ENDNOTES:
1 Bisgood, 3254 Sergeant Thornton Henry, 1/2nd Battalion, London Regiment (Royal Fusiliers). Unpublished diary. He went on to rise to the rank of Lt. Col. and was awarded the MBE and M.M.
2 Moy, 2nd Lt. C E, Unpublished papers, Liddle Collection, Leeds University.
3 Ibid.
4 Macdonald, Lyn, Somme, Page 68
5 VII Corps message to H.Q. 56th Division, NA WO 95/2931
6 Ibid
7 3rd Army memorandum SGR Z/1, Allenby to G.H.Q, dated 1st July 1916. NA WO 95/360
8 169th Brigade report to 56th Division. NA WO 95/2957
9 Bryden, Pte W M, Papers, IWM.
10 Ward-Jackson Maj. C L, VII Corps, IWM.
11 324 according to the Official History (Page 473).
12 535 according to the Official History (Page 473).
13 Moy, 2nd Lt. C E, Unpublished papers, Liddle Collection, Leeds University.
14 Jacobs, Rfn F W Hackney and Stoke Newington Recorder, 28th July 1916
15 Gray, Maj. W E, 2nd City of London Regiment (Royal Fusiliers) in the Great War, 1929
16 The History of the London Rifle Brigade 1859-1919, 1921
17 Bisgood, op cit.
18 LRB War Diary, NA WO 95/2961
19 Wheeler-Holohan, Capt. A V & Wyatt, Capt. G M C Wyatt, The Rangers Historical Records: From 1859 to the conclusion of the Great War, 1921
20 Gray, Maj. W E, 2nd City of London Regiment (Royal Fusiliers) in the Great War, 1929
21 Keeson, Maj. C A C, Queen Victoria's Rifles,1792-1922, 1923

15. PRISONERS OF WAR

"In the late evening of July 1st 1916 at Gommecourt when the remnants of a London Regiment who had been unfortunate enough not to get back to their own lines were paraded in a German dugout, a German officer called for an interpreter. When I stepped forward, he said to me: 'Will you please tell your comrades that they have today fought like British gentlemen.' He then saluted us."

Rfn. S Holyfield,
London Rifle Brigade

FOR THE SURVIVORS OF GOMMECOURT there was just the prospect of more work and more fighting to come. For the wounded there would be time in hospital, for some just briefly before a return to the ranks, for others with a 'Blighty' it might mean an extended stay, repeated operations, months and longer of pain, perhaps a medical discharge as medically unfit. For the dead there might be, sooner or later, a decent burial but for too, too many there would just be the long wait before their name was inscribed on the Thiepval Memorial to the Missing. But, for one small group who fought at Gommecourt, the British prisoners of war, the following years would be ones of acute deprivation, desperate hunger and, in some cases, brutal treatment at the hands of their gaolers and it would not be until the survivors of Germany's Prisoner of War Camps came home that the truth of the severity of their conditions was laid bare.

All officers and men were interviewed and hundreds of these interviews survive in the records of the National Archives at Kew[1]. They paint a graphic picture of the conditions endured by not just the British PoWs but also those of their French, Russian, Rumanian and Italian Allies. In the main, it seems as though the British prisoners were better treated than the Russians and Italians who, anecdotally from the reports, were harshly and sometimes savagely treated. Here the British system of food parcels from home helped take the edge of the gnawing hunger the men experienced day in and day out. They also give an interesting insight into the rapidly deteriorating social conditions within Germany as the British naval blockade brought the economy to a standstill and as food supplies dwindled affecting the Armed Forces and civilian population alike. It was these conditions that led to the political collapse of the country, undermined the will to resist of the German Army on the Western Front and eventually helped end the war.

The rules governing the treatment of Prisoners of War were laid down in a convention governing the 'Laws and Customs of War on Land' (Hague IV) ratified on 18th October, 1907 on neutral territory at The Hague. The provisions of the Hague Convention came into force on 26th January 1910. This Convention was itself a revision of a previous Hague Convention (Hague II) which had been brought into international law in July 1899. Hague IV was made up of nine Articles governing the application of the Convention and an Annex of 56 Chapters which contained the detailed provisions under a wide variety of headings. The Articles governed the terms and conditions under which the laws within the Annex were to be applied. Article 4, for example, made it clear that the provisions of Hague II still applied to any signatory to that convention which did not subsequently sign up to those contained within Hague IV. Within the Annex, it was Articles 4 to 20 in Chapter 2 'Prisoners of War' which contained the detailed provisions for the way in which all prisoners should be treated. The key provisions which directly affected those men kept prisoner by an enemy are listed below (some men were repatriated for reasons of permanent disability as a result of, for example, loss of a limb, blindness, etc., though this was not necessarily a swift process):

Article 4.

1. Prisoners of war are in the power of the hostile Government, but not of the individuals or corps who capture them.
2. They must be humanely treated.
3. All their personal belongings, except arms, horses, and military papers, remain their property.

Article 5.

1. Prisoners of war may be interned in a town, fortress, camp, or other place, and bound not to go beyond certain fixed limits, but they cannot be confined except as in indispensable measure of safety and only while the circumstances which necessitate the measure continue to exist.

Article 6.

1. The State may utilize the labour of prisoners of war according to their rank and aptitude, officers excepted. The tasks shall not be excessive and shall have no connection with the operations of the war.
2. Prisoners may be authorized to work for the public service, for private persons, or on their own account.
3. Work done for the State is paid for at the rates in force for work of a similar kind done by soldiers of the national army, or, if there are none in force, at a rate according to the work executed.
4. When the work is for other branches of the public service or for private persons the conditions are settled in agreement with the military authorities.
5. The wages of the prisoners shall go towards improving their position, and the balance shall be paid them on their release, after deducting the cost of their maintenance.

Article 7.

1. The Government into whose hands prisoners of war have fallen is charged with their maintenance.
2. In the absence of a special agreement between the belligerents, prisoners of war shall be treated as regards board, lodging, and clothing on the same footing as the troops of the Government who captured them.

Article 8.

1. Prisoners of war shall be subject to the laws, regulations, and orders in force in the army of the State in whose power they are. Any act of insubordination justifies the adoption towards them of such measures of severity as may be considered necessary.
2. Escaped prisoners who are retaken before being able to rejoin their own army or before leaving the territory occupied by the army which captured them are liable to disciplinary punishment.

3. Prisoners who, after succeeding in escaping, are again taken prisoners, are not liable to any punishment on account of the previous flight.

Article 9.

1. Every prisoner of war is bound to give, if he is questioned on the subject, his true name and rank, and if he infringes this rule, he is liable to have the advantages given to prisoners of his class curtailed.

Article 14.

1. An inquiry office for prisoners of war is instituted on the commencement of hostilities in each of the belligerent States, and, when necessary, in neutral countries which have received belligerents in their territory. It is the function of this office to reply to all inquiries about the prisoners. It receives from the various services concerned full information respecting internments and transfers, releases on parole, exchanges, escapes, admissions into hospital, deaths, as well as other information necessary to enable it to make out and keep up to date an individual return for each prisoner of war. The office must state in this return the regimental number, name and surname, age, place of origin, rank, unit, wounds, date and place of capture, internment, wounding, and death, as well as any observations of a special character. The individual return shall be sent to the Government of the other belligerent after the conclusion of peace.

2. It is likewise the function of the inquiry office to receive and collect all objects of personal use, valuables, letters, etc., found on the field of battle or left by prisoners who have been released on parole, or exchanged, or who have escaped, or died in hospitals or ambulances, and to forward them to those concerned.

Article 15.

1. Relief societies for prisoners of war, which are properly constituted in accordance with the laws of their country and with the object of serving as the channel for charitable effort shall receive from the belligerents, for themselves and their duly accredited agents every facility for the efficient performance of their humane task within the bounds imposed by military necessities and administrative regulations. Agents of these societies may be admitted to the places of internment for the purpose of distributing relief, as also to the halting places of repatriated prisoners, if furnished with a personal permit by the military authorities, and on giving an undertaking in writing to comply with all measures of order and police which the latter may issue.

Articles 10 to 13 covered the issue of parole of prisoners and anyone, journalists, civilian, etc., who might captured at the same time as soldiers and Articles 16 to 20 issues such as free postage of parcels and letter, religious freedom, wills and death certificates, repatriation when peace was declared, etc. As will be seen later, the German authorities were routinely to infringe both the spirit and the law of Articles 4, 6, 14 and 15. This is, perhaps, of no great surprise given the haste with which they ignored (and presumably must have been planning to ignore for some time) the first provision of Article 23 in Section II, Chapter 1, 'Means of Injuring the Enemy, Siege and Bombardments', which read:

"In addition to the prohibitions provided by special Conventions, it is especially forbidden - To employ poison or poisoned weapons"

The chlorine gas that was first employed to cause death, panic and acute suffering[i] to the Allied soldiers around Ypres was released on 22nd April 1915 and had clearly been in an experimental stage some time before that; leading to the inevitable conclusion that the Imperial German Army had little intention of adhering to the more inconvenient aspects of the Hague Conventions from early in the war if not before. If so on poison weapons, why not the same with prisoners? As a result, the first provision of Article 6 was the one most routinely infringed both by ignoring the word 'excessive' and then by steadfastly ignoring the phrase that work done "shall have no connection with the operations of the war." Indeed, by the end of the war there were no less than 57 Franzosen Kommandos, 26 Englander Kommandos, 38 Rumanien-Kommandos, 22 Italiener-Kommandos and 2 Portugiesen-Kommandos (i.e. French, English, Rumanian, Italian and Portuguese forced labour units. Kommando was an abbreviation of Arbeits (i.e. work) Kommando) working in hideous conditions at or near the German front line on the Western Front, sometimes within range of - and occasionally killed by - Allied guns.[2]

But more of these issues later.

***

BY THE END OF 1ST JULY, the Germans would claim 22 officers and 410 other ranks as prisoners of war (although the British Official History cites figures of 8 officers and 230 other ranks). On the other side of No Man's Land, 189 German officers and men were in the cages[ii] with the exception of fifty wounded men who were being treated by the medical teams. In the German lines, one by one and in small groups the men left in their trenches were being rounded up as the German re-occupied their shattered trenches. Some British soldiers were lucky to survive their capture. In Fir trench on the edge of Gommecourt Park, L/Cpl. Tom Short, an L.R.B. Lewis gunner who had been active around Point 94 all day, was only saved from being bayoneted by the curt order of a German officer who, in perfect English, told Short and his colleagues:

> "You've done enough for one day. Get down this dugout before you get hit."[3]

Some men were taken back into dugouts and others led into the ruins of the houses in Gommecourt. One of these prisoners, 2437 Rfn. Stanley Holyfield of the L.R.B., was reported later in the London Evening News:

> "In the late evening of July 1st 1916 at Gommecourt when the remnants of a London Regiment who had been unfortunate enough not to get back to their own lines were paraded in a German dugout, a German officer called for an interpreter. When I stepped forward, he said to me: 'Will you please tell your comrades that they have today fought like British gentlemen.' He then saluted us."[4]

---

[i] And, therefore, which might be deemed to have infringed another provision of Article 23, that belligerents should not: "employ arms, projectiles, or material calculated to cause unnecessary suffering"
[ii] They were made of: 170th Regt., 131 and 5 from the Machine Gun Company; 74th Machine Gun Marksman Section 11; 52nd Minenwerefe Company 5; 55th Reserve Infantry Regt. 35; and 260th Searchlight Section 1. In addition it was estimated that between 60 and 80 German prisoners were killed trying to cross No Man's Land on the 169th Brigade's front.

Plate 60 The ruins of Gommecourt after the battle
(Photograph courtesy of Imperial War Museum, Q4904)

The forty year old 2nd Lt. Parker of the Rangers, who had gallantly led a motley group of men from five battalions in their defence of a small stretch of Fall and then Fate trenches, evaded various parties of Germans before he was at last cornered and forced to surrender. He would spend the rest of the war in a POW camp in Germany. So would Capt. Bernardo de Cologan[i] of the London Rifle Brigade. He had decided to check a German front line dugout for signs of any wounded men who might escape back to the British lines when the order of 'every man for himself' was given. De Cologan emerged from the dugout to find himself at the wrong end of a German rifle. Outraged at his bad luck he was led away with some other men of the L.R.B. into captivity. Basil Houle, another captured member of the London Rifle Brigade, later recalled that de Cologan's temper and a rather precious desire to stand on his dignity nearly got the better of him, with potentially dire consequences for the other men waiting to be taken off to the German 'cages':

"When we arrived there was a loud argument proceeding between one of our officers and the German sergeant in charge. The Captain, a hot headed

---

[i] Capt. Arthur Thomas Bernardo de Cologan, 1/5th London Regt. (London Rifle Brigade), was born on 8th December 1890, the son of the late Alberto and May de Cologan of Loch Rosque Lodge, Achnasheen, Ross-shire. He was the adopted son of the late Sir Arthur Bignold and had recently succeeded to the Ross-shire estates of Achanalt and Strathbarn. He was educated at the Oratory School, Edgbaston and Queen's College, Oxford where was Captain of Boats. He was in the Oxford University O.T.C. between October 1909 and January 1912. In 1912 he applied for a Regular commission in the Royal Scots Fusiliers but he was repeatedly rejected because of poor eyesight. His mother, who had married Capt. Maddick, 5th Lancers, (died on Lemnos of Typhoid on 1st November 1915), continually wrote to leading figures, amongst others Herbert Asquith, the Prime Minister, in an effort to get him a Regular commission. He joined the London Rifle Brigade as a 2nd Lt. on 2nd April 1913 being promoted Lieutenant on 9th April 1914. He was appointed the Assistant District Commissioner, Somaliland Protectorate between 3rd July 1914 and 30th May 1915 being attached to the Somaliland Camel Corps in the Spring of 1915. On his return to England he went to France in January 1916. He was promoted Captain on 9th August 1915, having joined the 1/5th London Rifle Brigade on 18th July 1915. De Cologan was taken prisoner on 1st July 1916 and spent the rest of the war in a German Prisoner of War Camp. He tried again after the war to obtain a Regular commission without success.

447

Irishman[i], furious that he had been caught in a dugout without the opportunity to fire a shot, was insisting on walking in front of us, while the Jerry sergeant wanted him in the ranks with the other prisoners. Eventually – and just when we were wondering if he would get us all shot with his silly argument – he got his way and we proceeded in a slow moving, straggling disorder to their headquarters where the wounded were examined by a doctor and injected against tetanus."[5]

Eventually, the men were loaded into farm carts or onto the small trucks of the light railways that served the front and sent away to one of the German hospitals in places like Le Cateau, before being moved onto one of the many Prisoner of War camps that dotted the German countryside. For Houle and many of his L.R.B. chums it was to be Minden in Westphalia. To various other destinations would go 2ⁿᵈ Lt. Blunn of the 1/4ᵗʰ Londons, 2ⁿᵈ Lt. Bennett[ii] of the Q.V.R.s, 2ⁿᵈ Lt. Pike (Kensingtons) and Lt. Spencer Smith and 2ⁿᵈ Lt. Upton of the Q.W.R.s and dozens of wounded rank and file. Some failed to make it far, however, and their names can now be found in cemeteries stretching back from small villages like Vaulx-Vraucourt to major towns such as Cambrai and Le Cateau.

1495 Rfn. Ernest Evanson[6], another L.R.B. man, had gone over with the battalion's fourth wave and had fought his way into the German third line in front of Gommecourt where, as the day wore on, his group had been surrounded. Assailed on either flank by German bombing parties and continuously sniped from the front and then, more worryingly, from the rear they were slowly reduced to some 30 relatively fit men. With night now falling and the sounds of battle slowly fading it was decided that a withdrawal to their own lines was essential and, rather than a mass break, it was agreed that a movement by small groups would be best, with each one trying to keep its predecessor in view. It was also agreed that, if any party ran into trouble, the others should by-pass them and try to make good their own escape. Evanson was one of the earliest to leave but almost immediately ran into a German patrol. His watching colleagues, seeing the confrontation, opened fire wounding a couple of the enemy and giving Evanson a chance to slip away. Finding himself alone he worked his way across the German 2ⁿᵈ line but, with what was left of the trenches here amply justifying their name of The Maze, it was all too easy to be confused. Evanson came to a trench which, by now, he believed had to be the front line and so started with the intention of clambering down and climbing out and away into No Man's Land. But, once in the base of the trench he realised that this was a communication trench and that what he now presumed was the front line lay at its end. Moving slowly to the junction Evanson was about to peer around the corner when he was roughly grasped from the rear. His luck had run out and he had been taken prisoner by a German patrol about to go out into No Man's Land themselves.

---

i De Cologan was actually of Italian/Scottish parentage.
ii 2ⁿᵈ Lt. Bennett was first sent to Ohrdruf Hospital, part of the Langensalza Camp. He was sent to Holland after the Armistice where he volunteered to stay on repatriation duty at one of the twn posts set up on the Dutch-German border. Here he worked under Brig. Gen. Bruce at the Repatriation Commission in Rotterdam. He embarked from Rotterdam for Hull on 6ᵗʰ January 1919 did not rejoin the battalion until 23ʳᵈ March 1919 after taking leave. He was demobilised a week later and given the honorary rank of Lieutenant on 1ˢᵗ July 1919.

Plate 61 56ᵗʰ Division prisoners of war being questioned by German officers
(Photograph courtesy of Paul Reed)

Evanson was taken to the nearby dressing station in the cellar in Gommecourt. There he was confronted by a somewhat over-wrought German officer who, spying that he had not been relieved of his bayonet by his captors, grabbed it and threatened him, at the same time complaining bitterly in broken English about the damage done by the British heavy guns. Thankfully, no blood was drawn and soon Evanson was being taken by cart, hands tied, to the rear. With him went two wounded men of the L.R.B. lying in the bottom of the cart and, when the British guns opened up as they passed some German batteries and the driver set his horses to a gallop, the injured were badly jarred as they bounced over ruts and holes. Evanson was eventually unhitched from the cart at a chateau where he was taken into the cellars to be interviewed in excellent English by a German officer. Spying his shoulder tag the officer immediately identified him as a London Rifle Brigade man. He then enquired as to his pre-war profession, asking whether he worked in the City. Evanson worked for an accountants and the officer genially chatted about his work with a large London firm of accountants when he had been involved with a German bank and lived in London for several years before the war. But the disarming chat had a more sinister purpose as the officer moved discussions to matters more military. Trench maps were laid out and Evanson probed for useful military information. His refusal to comment led to a sudden cooling of the superficially warm atmosphere and Evanson was led away with the comment that: "There will be more along later who will tell me more".

Evanson awoke on Sunday, 2ⁿᵈ July, to find a score of British prisoners along side him and, when they were moved to a nearby church late in the morning, they discovered some 200 wounded British soldiers, amongst them some battalion colleagues such as Capt. de Cologan and a particular chum of Evanson's, Rfn. Frederick Crisfield. Trips to other churches swelled the crowd of prisoners to nearly 500, by Evanson's estimate, and then the ragged and bloodied crowd was led to a level crossing where a train waited to take them off to Cambrai to start their long and dismal period of imprisonment.

449

Plate 62 London Scottish prisoners of war

Note the soldier from another London regiment right and the German guard wearing a Pickelhaube helmet.
(Photograph courtesy of Paul Reed)

Their interlude at Cambrai was an unpleasant experience for all concerned. Consigned to a filthy barracks, possibly the Chateau de Selles, with no working sanitation for fourteen days their conditions rapidly degenerated causing distress to the wounded and disgust to the more healthy occupants. Medical treatment was completely absent, although, to be fair, Evanson had failed to report himself wounded to the German authorities, and food was restricted to a small ration of bread and vegetable soup apparently prepared by the nearby residents of the town. On the first day a field kitchen was set up in the square outside the barracks at midday and the men were ordered to parade for food – what turned out to be some bread and disgusting vegetable soup. As most men had not eaten since the issue of pea soup and, for some, a bacon sandwich in the early hours of Saturday morning, the able bodied did not need to be asked twice. The problem that then presented itself was that there were no bowls for the soup and no knives, forks or spoons. Those lucky few that had retained their Brodie helmets rapidly set to ripping out the lining and the upturned helmets were transformed into improvised 'field tureens' (Army: for the use of). The scalding soup was then allowed to cool before the tin hats were passed from man to man although, undoubtedly, some unlucky blighters missed out from time to time.

To add to their disgruntlement about their treatment, no-one was allowed to write home so that, had it not been for the charitable behaviour of someone at a higher level who arranged the air drop of a list over the British lines giving the names of the men now prisoner, frantic relatives at home stood little chance of finding out the whereabouts and circumstances of their men folk. It was with great relief, therefore, that, after two long weeks in these appalling conditions, the men were marched off to the railway station, packed into a closed cattle truck and sent on their way to one of many dedicated Prisoner of War camps within Germany. For Ernest Evanson his new home would be a camp at the small town of Dülmen near Münster in Westphalia. He would be a Prisoner of War in Germany for the next twenty months before becoming one of the small number to successfully escape.

The only PoWs who had a chance to write to their anxious relatives were those sufficiently seriously wounded to be immediately evacuated to a hospital in Germany. 2881 L/Cpl Claude Tucknott[i] of the Queen's Westminsters had been moved rapidly to No. 5 Reserve Lazarett at Hannover and was able to write home on 6th July:

"Dear Ma and Pa,

Just a few lines to let you know I am wounded and have been made a prisoner of war in Germany, but all the same for that you don't want to worry yourselves the slightest bit as I am quite comfortable and content in hospital. I was wounded before I was captured so I was helpless, but I am quite well. I went over the top with our boys in the morning but I am sorry to say that there are very few of us left.

Now, dear people, I should like you, as soon as you get this letter, to write and send a parcel off straight away of cigarettes and eatables. We are allowed to write two letters and four postcards a month, so you will hear from me now and then, but you can write as often as possible and don't forget to send plenty of parcels.

All we have to wait for now is the day when the end comes and we can all return. We are being treated jolly decent and I have nothing to grumble about and let me ask you again not to worry as I am quite safe and sound and content. I am with one of the boys from our company so we are quite happy together.

When you send money, don't send too much at a time and send an International Order through the Post Office. I am sorry I cannot write to everybody but you must tell them everything they enquire. I have a nice comfortable bed to sleep on and it is good – much better than being in the trenches. I cannot write much as this is all the paper I have but I will write at every opportunity. Wait patiently, dear people, and good luck. Love and kisses to you all and remembrance to kind inquirers.

P.S. Please send soap.

Parcels would soon loom large in the minds of all new prisoners and worried parents and friends would besiege the Prisoners of War Help Committee at 39, Russell Square from which special labels could be obtained. These labels allowed parcels of anything from 11lbs to 40 lbs in weight, all marked 'comforts', to be sent free of charge from any railway station in the United Kingdom to a British PoW in Germany. 2103 Rfn. Ronald Morris of 'C' Company of the L.R.B. had also been wounded and taken prisoner and was now enjoying the relative comforts of the Lazarett, or hospital, at Minden Prisoner of War Camp. Luckily for him his wounds were not serious and his recovery was rapid and he found time to write a quick letter home in mid-August. Apart from advising his family in Oakfield Road in West Croydon of his relative health and enquiring as to the

---

[i] 2881 L/Cpl Claude W Tucknott, 2/2nd London Regt., att. 1/16th London Regt. (Queen's Westminster Rifles), enlisted in the 3/2nd London Regt., on 17th September 1914 and saw service in Malta, Gallipoli and Egypt with the 2/2nd London Regt. before the battalion was disbanded on its return to France. His parents lived at 103, Bowes Road, Palmer's Green.

health of his brother Reg who had gone into the attack along side him, his main concern was to establish a steady flow of parcels:

"Tell everybody my address and ask them to write or send parcels. There is no limit to the number or size we may receive… write often."

He gave a list of his priorities for the parcels' contents: bread, plenty of plain chocolate, 100 fags, hard biscuits, jam or butter and tinned meats were the order of the day. For 2227 Rfn. Edward Job of The Rangers the list of 'eatables' sent to his parents at 104, Graham Road in Dalston comprised: bread, dripping, pipe tobacco, cigarettes, cakes and chocolate "and anything else you can think of". The only things not allowed were newspapers.

Plate 63 2103 Rfn. Ronald Morris, London Rifle Brigade, prisoner of war

***

84 L/CPL. GEORGE CARLE[i], another L.R.B. man, had been slightly wounded in the left foot and was captured with a colleague, 2802 Rfn. Ernest Martin, in a sap head near the German front line, he thought the time was about 4 p.m.[7] As the fighting was still raging, he and Martin were ushered into a German dugout, put under guard and kept there for two hours or more. They were then transported to another dugout towards the rear where they were interrogated in a rather half-hearted manner by a German officer. Their journey to the rear then continued and they were taken to a village and put in a church where they were given some bread and coffee substitute and cross-examined again. The following day, they marched some 15 kilometres to a station where they were embarked on a train to Cambrai. Carle had little to say about his experience at Cambrai but it broadly bears out the description given by Evanson, i.e. poor conditions and little food. His estimate of the rations was a fifth of a loaf of bread, about 250-300 gms in weight, a small quantity of vegetable soup and some coffee substitute. To his mind, the 600 or so British prisoners were essentially being starved for the two weeks the men were held in the town.

On 13th July Carle and others were packed into railway cattle trucks and sent into Germany. Like Evanson, Carle's destination was the camp at Dülmen where they eventually arrived on 15th July. He was there for just over a month when, on 17th August, he was sent to another camp close to the Danube, Lager Heuberg

---

[i] Aged 19 at the time of his capture, George Carle lived at 113, Wanstead Park Avenue, Wanstead, Essex. Before the war he had been a student at London University studying civil engineering. He enlisted on 7th August 1914 and was assigned to 'G' Company. He went to France with the original 1/5th L.R.B. on 4th November 1914. Carle was born at Plaistow, Essex in 1898 or 1899 and was a 2 year old in the 1901 Census making it apparent that he joined up and went overseaes under age. George Carle died in 1945. [*Source:* Chris Rippingale]

near the village of Stetten in Baden. Another Dülmen inmate to make the journey was 5764 Pte. Richard Edward Thompson of the London Scottish[8]. Thompson had been a pre-war officer in the Indian Army and had enlisted in the ranks on the outbreak of war and he had been taken prisoner unwounded during the attack. Now he, Carle and the rest were packed into Fourth Class carriages and given a piece of bread before setting off on a two day journey to the new camp in the south west of Germany. Thankfully, there were two or three stops for food along the way. Lager Heuberg had been built in 1910 as a training camp for the XIV Corps of the Imperial German Army and was converted for use as a Prisoner of War camp soon after the outbreak of war[i]. It was a huge establishment which, by 1917, housed some 15,000 PoWs but, whilst Carle was there, he estimated that the camp was only half full and only 300 of the prisoners were British. The camp was commanded by the 50 year old Oberst Freiherr von Plettenberg and his 'kingdom' was a vast encampment of shoddily built 120-man huts perched some 1,000 metres up on top of a hill. Cold and draughty, its one saving grace was the sanitation though the lack of beds, straw palliases were the only available bedding, was a major drawback. The bedding problem was eventually solved with the assistance of some Russian PoWs whose carpentry skills were employed making dozens of pine bedsteads.

The men were set to work constructing a road near the village of Stetten and those men so employed received payment of 30 pfennigs a day. This could be used to buy items from the camp canteen but, with the 'pay' so minimal, it was not every day that a prisoner could indulge themselves with a purchase from the limited range available:

"All that we could get there were cigarettes, matches, lemonade and an inferior kind of apple cider which was passed off as wine. Cigarettes were a penny each, matches 60 pfennigs a box, lemonade tuppence a bottle and cider 1½ marks per glass."

Even these limited and inferior 'luxuries' were denied the men unfit for work on the road. They were still forced to clean the camp and deal with the rations but for this they received no allowance. This was an important issue for the men at Heuberg as the rations were restricted in both variety and volume:

"The food supplied to us was wholly inadequate for the men to work upon. We used to get a loaf weighing 1500gms which had to last us five days[ii] and in the summer when bread was short I have known this ration to be made to last 6½ days. At midday we always had the same food, viz. the vegetable soup, and at night we were given coffee substitute and sometimes a small quantity of potatoes. We had no other food whatever, except that on Tuesdays and Fridays we had salt fish boiled up in the soup. It did not improve the flavour of the soup and I never use to eat it after I got my parcels. I have seen cheese served out, a very small piece once a week or so."

---

[i] Lager Heuberg became the first concentration camp in Württemberg/Baden in 1933, being in use for nine months. It was taken over by the Wehrmacht in the following year and in 1940 was passed over to the Reichsarbeitsdienst, the Reich Labour Service. It was, at various times, the home of a number of collaborationist units such as the Indische Legion (the Free India Legion), Division Italia (the 29th Waffen Grenadier Division of the SS), the 2nd Division of the Russian Army of Liberation and the Militia of Vichy

[ii] Thompson reported that the black bread was made up of some flour, sawdust and mashed potatoes.

Food and clothing parcels from home were, therefore, essential to the effort of keeping together body and soul. Carle had been given a white cotton shirt and some flannel squares which were supposed to be socks but which baffled every effort at putting them on. As a result, he was forced to wear his filthy, bloody and, undoubtedly, lice ridden uniform for some two months before his first clothing parcel arrived. His conditions eased somewhat thereafter, when his parcels provided food and clothing extras which just about made life bearable. The parcels and letters arrived at seemingly arbitrary intervals, with letters tending to turn up on a Thursday and Sunday and parcels as and when. Sometimes the parcels turned up every alternate day but, in January 1917, nearly a month went by between the arrival of these indispensable packages. All items were opened by the authorities and all letters passed under the nose of the local censor at a town called Immendingen, a small town nearby. Some items never found their way through, although quite why mustard joined paper and newspapers on the banned list is a mystery. Tins of food were opened by the Germans in the presence of a small committee of N.C.O.s who were then responsible for the fair allocation of their contents amongst the men, the empty tins being taken away no doubt to be recycled for the war effort.

The men were allowed to exercise between the rows of huts and football and boxing were popular pastimes. A mitt and ball were also conjured up from somewhere and, with the use of a stick, rough and ready games of baseball were enjoyed from time to time as well as more rather more cerebral games such as chess and cards. Otherwise, the men walked, talked and smoked when not at work or trying to sleep. And they wrote letters and postcards home. There were strict restrictions on the number of such communications, two letters and four postcards per month being the limit, but the letters sent and received preserved a vital link between the soldiers and their loved ones which must have helped them survive the rigours and hardship the their imprisonment.

Discipline in the camp was strictly enforced but Carle could not report any incidents of cruelty or abuse of prisoners within the camp itself. Just once, when on a working party, a Russian prisoner was bayoneted, a flesh wound Carle believed, when he got into an argument with an impatient guard. Otherwise he had no complaints about his treatment at the camp. Otherwise, as long as one kept one's nose clean and respected the regulations a man could keep out of trouble. There was a scale of punishments for those that did not. Failing to salute a German officer or attempting to escape drew 14 day's imprisonment. Striking a civilian attracted the same punishment but there was a scale of penalties for assaulting a soldier, the higher the rank the longer the term. Damage to German property was, however, the worst offence and, technically, it carried the death penalty. Having said that, Carle never saw such a sanction applied. And one never approached the wire. Anyone thought too close was given three verbal warnings by a guard and then they opened fire and the neared the wire the more accurate would be the attempted aim.

Sometimes men were sent on working parties to more remote areas where they were kept in secure accommodation locally. It was called going 'on commando' and was a mixed blessing. On the one hand the contents of one's parcels often failed to follow on but on the other the accommodation was often better and the food a slight improvement. You were, however, put in the charge of just a few guards and it was their attitude towards the prisoners which decided how pleasant or not the 'commando' turned out. Carle was sent 'on commando' on 24th April 1917 to a village called Todtnau, a village in the Black Forest twenty miles south of Freiburg. The party was of mixed nationalities: 11 English, 14 Russia and six French men and they were to work on wood chopping under the control of two Landstürmann. The work was hard but the accommodation, a disused garage, was alright and the food was good. Thompson, soon after, was sent 'on commando' at Adelhausen where he and sixteen others were sent to help a farmer getting early crops in. The seventeen men, 13 Russians and four English, were accommodated in a single room with one small window and, to get from one bed to another, it was necessary to clamber from bed to bed. The heat was oppressive and the bedroom riddled with fleas making sleep a near impossible exercise. The hours, by anyone's standards, were excessive – anything from 14 to 17½ hours a day and, although they were given five meal breaks and the food was better than in the camps, he found the work more than he could handle. Representations to the farmer and the Lager Heuberg commandant were rebuffed and when they complained to the local Burgomaster through a French interpreter the response was to threaten the Frenchmen with prison. Anglo-Russian solidarity, however, in the form of a threatened strike prevented the Burgomaster's intimidatory tactics from being implemented. Thompson's stint in the countryside was brought to an end by an attack of bronchitis. The illness saw him sent north to hospital in Freiburg, the nearest large town, where the treatment was good, the food acceptable but meagre, but medicines in short supply and the bandages all made of paper. Fit again, Thompson was sent back to work but he had been laying plans for escape and now it was just necessary to find an opportunity.

The outdoor life, better rations and exercise for the men 'on commando' made some of the men fitter and stronger and it was not long before Carle took advantage of this improvement. On 11th May Carle made his first escape attempt. It lasted four days and when he was recaptured he was sentenced to ten day's solitary on bread and water back at Heuberg. Perplexingly, on his release he was returned to Todtnau and, on 28th July, he escaped again. His time on the run was brief, a bare two days and this time it was eleven day's solitary on bread and water but this time in the local gaol in Todtnau. In between, Thompson made his first bid for freedom. Somehow he had managed to buy a compass at Heuberg and whilst at the farm he had 'liberated' a map from a child's atlas. Adequately prepared he and a mate then set off in mid-July but they were caught near Stetten. A few days spent in the local prison were but the preface to a more severe punishment at Heuberg. They were made subject to a 'Massen Arrest', a Bavarian version of the Black Hole of Calcutta. One hundred men, 90% escapees and the balance men refusing to work, were squeezed into a room about 12 by 7 metres. The windows had been blocked and with them went the ventilation. Outside the sun was beating down on the thin roof making the conditions for the near naked men inside unbearable. They were kept on bread and water for five days before being given some biscuits to supplement these starvation rations. The only time they were allowed out was to collect water but Thompson found these outings counter-productive as returning the foetid atmosphere afterwards was too much to take, so he stayed in doors and made the best of a very bad job. On his release Thompson was sent out to Carle's old stamping ground at Todtnau and there be planned his next getaway.

Just two week's after Carle's release in mid-August he 'had it away on this toes' once more this time with Thompson and one other as accomplices. They tasted freedom for just three days before it was back solitary at Heuberg for a week with an additional 18 day's confinement and hard labour. The hard labour was digging out tree stumps with crow bars, shovels and axes for thirteen hours a day and, at the end of it, they were despatched to Mannheim camp where they were set to work in a straw compressing plant near a railway line just outside the town. It was grinding work made worse by the absence of any food parcels from home for over a month and a reduction in bread ration to make it worse which forced them to scrounge for stolen carrots and turnips. They were kept there until 22ⁿᵈ December 1917 as part of the extended punishment for their repeated escape attempts. They were then returned to Heuberg. But Carle and Thompson were not to be denied. On 5ᵗʰ March 1918 Carle was sent with a working party to the village of Ippingen near Donaueschingen in the south of the Black Forest. Thompson was not supposed to have been on the working party but just joined the others as they were leaving the camp and no-one seemed to notice. And he went equipped with his map and a replacement compass bought in exchange for a bar of soap. At Ippingen the housing was positively luxurious with proper beds and proper sheets and the single Landstürmann who looked after them seemed affable and relaxed. So relaxed, in fact, that he would go back to his barracks to sleep at night leaving the prisoners on their own in the houses of their employers. The temptation was too much for Carle and Thompson and, on 12ᵗʰ March 1918, joined by one another, they made their final and successful breaks for freedom. Having travelled sixty miles in two days they crossed the Swiss-German border at Stuhlingen having to swim the Danube in the process. They then travelled onto Schleitheim where a Swiss hotel keeper treated them to a free dinner to celebrate their hard-earned freedom.

Carle was reputedly one of six men from the London Rifle Brigade who successfully escaped from a German Prisoner of War Camp during the war and half of these came from amongst those captured at Gommecourt. Two were men captured at Cambrai in November to December 1917 and who were held close to the front lines at Douai before escaping. They evaded capture thanks to the help of a selfless Belgian doctor. One escapee remains unidentified and the other two were the previously mentioned 1495 Rfn. E Evanson and 345 Rfn. Clifford Rippengal[i] who were both wounded and taken prisoner at Gommecourt and who both escaped, though at separate times, from Minden Camp.

Rippengal's[9] experience was somewhat different from Carle, his battalion colleague. Rippengal had suffered a shrapnel wound to his right thigh fairly early in the day and had been carried into a German dugout whilst the battle raged around him. In the evening, when the few remaining men of the 169ᵗʰ Brigade flung themselves into No Man's Land in their desperate effort to escape, Rippengal's safe haven became an inescapable trap. Because of the nature of his wound it was decided that Rippengal could not be moved immediately and it was not until Monday, 3ʳᵈ July that he was carried out of the dugout and taken to a

---

[i] Clifford Rippengal lived at 11, Kelsey Park Road, Beckenham, Kent and had been a clerk in the City before the war.

dressing station for treatment. He was then evacuated and housed in a church where his wound was dressed and they were fed with coffee, bread and jam. So far Rippengal was quite content with his treatment but affairs were to take a sharp down turn once he progressed further to the rear. On the 4th July he was evacuated by ambulance to another hospital where there were, he thought, some two hundred marquees laid out in the grounds. His uniform was taken away to be fumigated and not returned but otherwise the treatment there was extremely poor. So overcrowded was the hospital that Rippengal and some 200 other wounded men were given a blanket and told to lie out in the open as the marquees were all full. Overnight it rained and the men, many suffering from loss of blood and shock, got very cold and wet. For one or two of the more serious cases this was enough to finish them off. After a drink of coffee substitute and some black bread they were taken off to a railway station where they were put on board a train of Third Class carriages. There was no evidence of specific maltreatment but a number of the wounded were in no state to travel and, with no provided, they were weakening rapidly to the extent that, on the first stage of the journey, two men in the compartment next to Rippengal died and he saw one the bodies being removed at the first stop. Now they were transferred to cattle trucks for the next phase of their long journey but, at least, they were given food, more of the staple coffee, bread and jam.

Rippengal had no head for names and places and had no idea where the train ended up after two day's sedate chugging along the clogged railway system in occupied France. All he knew was that the new hospital was decent and clean, the German doctors and nurses efficient and the French girls who helped around the wards assisted the men discreetly in any way they could. One thing they could not help with was the problem that Rippengal's uniform had not been returned to him after it was taken away for fumigation and, consequently, when the time came for another move, on 10th July, he had only a vest to wear. There were several men in the same situation and those that could walk, which did not include him, were able to go off to the stores to draw clothes and boots. Rippengal and the other men unable to move then suffered the undignified experience of being carried semi-naked out of the hospital and down to the station where they were loaded onto another cattle truck for a further move east. This journey was, blessedly, only relatively brief – a few hours – and then they were all transferred to a proper ambulance train and placed in beds. Those that needed it had their wounds dressed but, again, there was no food – and the journey to Minden, their final destination, would take 28 hours. The train arrived at Minden station on 12th July and the prisoners had then to make their way to the camp which was some way out of the town. Unless unable to walk, everyone was forced to march to the camp which lay some considerable distance away. Rippengal was one of the apparently lucky ones and he was laid on a bed of straw in the back of a large van but the wounded men soon found that their vehicle's suspension was non-existent and they suffered agonies as they were bounced around on the rough track that led to the camp. At the gates, he was hoisted onto the back of another prisoner and led into the camp where he was to live for the foreseeable future.

Rippengal was sent initially to the camp hospital and placed in one of the 60-man huts that it comprised. He was to be there for nearly seven weeks and, as far as he could later recall, the bed sheets were not changed once. Medical help was supplied by men from the Russian Red Cross and, at least, medication and dressings were in reasonable supply. Food as ever was the problem. Their daily hospital diet was:

Breakfast – black bread and coffee substitute (made from barley and acorns)

11.30 a.m. – soup ("I cannot say what it was made of, terrible stuff")

2.00 p.m. – more coffee

Dinner – more soup of a generally better quality with, twice a week, a small piece of fish and some potatoes.

Shortly after their arrival – this was the first of a series of large influxes to the camp – the able bodied men in the camp proper, both British and French, made a collection of food from their parcels and this was sent into the hospital to supplement the patients' meagre fare. For some it would not be enough and Rippengal related in his interview that several men in the hospital died from malnutrition

On 25th August Rippengal was at last discharged from the hospital. He was given a suit of clothes and sent off to the camp proper. The accommodation was in large wooden huts with wooden bunk beds, mattresses of straw and two blankets. The blankets would prove essential as, with autumn drawing near, the two fireplaces in the huts would not prove up to the job of heating the space. Rippengal was initially employed on light duties around the camp, acting as a carpenter, but the main task of the able bodied men was to unload stones from barges tied up in a nearby canal. Whilst her was at the camp a party of men came who had been working at another site. The rumour was that they had been working in a munitions factory, jobs which soldiers strenuously resisted being employed on but, as Rippengal said afterwards:

"... as far as we possibly can we will not allow ourselves to be forced into this kind of work, but it is not always possible to do, and sometimes – much against our will – we have to give in."

Apart from the food, and this improved once he started to receive his Red Cross parcels, Rippengal had relatively few complaints about the regime in the camp. Although it got progressively colder as the year drew in this, at least, had the benefit of improving the condition of the bread sent to the camp which, in warmer conditions, had often arrived mouldy. The authorities also supplied him with an overcoat as the temperatures fell and a football was provided at his behest which added some interest to their other exercise of walking around the camp. Their spiritual needs were seen to by a Capt. Wilkins, a Canadian chaplain who led a service every Sunday and who was seen around the camp almost daily talking to his 'flock'. In addition, Wilkins[i] persuaded the commandant to allow a stage to be erected so that the men might entertain themselves with concerts from time to time.

In spite of the restrictions on food and the paltry sums paid for those working by the canal there were still some men who managed to become drunk on a fairly regular basis. 'Wine' could be bought from the camp canteen but for some this was not enough and they started to bribe some of the guards to bring alcohol

---

[i] Capt. Wilkins also ministered to the needs of the occupants of the officers' camp at Gütersloh.

into the camp for them. Soon it became apparent that a problems was developing as men 'silly' from drink could be seen staggering around the camp and the Germans, perhaps unaware of their guards' activities, issued wine cards which were needed to buy 'wine' that had previously been unrestricted. This acted as no block to the drunkards in the camp as they now begged or stole from other inmates or simply threatened those less able to defend themselves. Mental health problems seemed not, however, to have been widespread and Rippengal reported only one man who was taken away for treatment. He returned but continued to act strangely, if less so.

If the men at Minden had no real complaints then a party that arrived there in December certainly had. These were some of the men (see also the story of Rfn. Dorsett below) who had been kept behind the German lines to work as forced labourers. Here, the treatment of prisoners had been appalling and was a deep stain on the reputation of the German Army. These men, not quite working within range of Allied guns, had been starved and abused almost systematically in a grim harbinger of German conduct to come in 25 year's time. Emaciated and exhausted, they reported that their mates had been dying daily under the barbarous treatment:

"They were forced to work, had been given hardly any food, and when they fell down from sheer exhaustion they were kicked until they got up again, and it was not until one absolutely could not get about that he was sent back… The men so employed behind the lines are not allowed to write letters or, even if they are they are not sent out of the country, and none of these men received letters or either parcels."

It is the purest speculation as to how many names of the men who died in these circumstances now appear on Memorials to the Missing. If there is but one then it is an indictment of the policies pursued by the new Western Front 'management team' of Hindenburg and Ludendorff who, even if they knew nothing of the specifics of this treatment, were morally and legally responsible for the disgraceful conduct of their juniors[10].

On 6th March 1917, Rippengal and some 260 other British PoWs, including the aforementioned Basil Houle and Edmund Evanson, were transferred by train to a new camp at Westerholt. Westerholt was a satellite 'working' camp attached to another at Friedrichsfeld, designated Camp J.O. 32., which lay between Mannheim and Heidelberg. The accommodation, treatment and discipline here were all considerably worse than at Minden with Rippengal describing the camp commandant as a 'violent man'. This violence was on display from the time they arrived. As the new arrivals paraded near the camp gates a number of longer term occupants spilled out of their huts to greet them. Rippengal and Houle watched in amazement when the guards within the compound immediately set upon these men with rifle butts and boots to drive them back indoors. A mini-riot ensued when the new men joined in the mayhem and it took some time for the guards to restore order, but the tone had been set and it would not improve.

The camp actually seems to have been run by an unter-offizier who seemed to have the commandant under this thumb and who delighted in making life miserable for the British and Russian prisoners who occupied the place. The beds comprised coconut mats hung like hammocks and they were crammed together into the huts giving little living space. The Russians, who lived on the other side of a thin partition, helped out from time to time making extra tables and stools, carpentry being something which they happily turned their hand to in a number of camps, but the unter-offizier took a perverse delight in finding any excuse to have them removed and destroyed. Punishments here were more regular too and, although the commandant was nominally responsible for their imposition, their implementation was in the hands of his junior without whom, Rippengal believed, they would have had a far better time, describing him as:

"An absolute brute (who) would get men punished for the most trivial offences."

Work here was down a mine and the sanitary facilities were of importance to the men, but here they were described as 'vile'. When the men arrived they were immediately paraded for a medical check, the pretext being to winnow out from the group those medically unfit to work in the pit. Only six out of the 260 men were deemed unfit, and they were suffering very badly from their wounds, but this was of no relief to the men concerned. They were immediately put on half rations and, after a few days, were told that must now either go to the hospital or do 'light' duties on the surface at the mine. Apparently, the hospital was an even worse prospect than these supposed 'light duties' and so the men elected this option but this rapidly was revealed to have been Hobson's choice as the work was gruelling – digging and shovelling – and just as hard as anything down the pit. Meanwhile, though, these men remained on half rations. After a few days of this treatment the men refused to work and they were immediately hauled off to prison and put in cells through which ran hot water pipes. The temperature in these cells was so excessive that the men were forced to remove all of their clothes and lie on the stone floor but still, according to those so treated, the sweat ran off them in rivers. Basil Houle was one of the men dealt with in this way and he and twenty others, angered by their treatment, decided upon an escape attempt. A tunnel was started but, after a few weeks of digging, the tunnel was betrayed by a man who claimed to be a member of the Queen Victoria's Rifles and who had acted as an interpreter down the mine. More time in the punishment cells followed before Houle and the others were sent down the mine.

Rippengal was one of the men employed down the mine. In all they were underground for 56 hours a week, four days on an eight shift and two on a twelve hour shift, but, with the 3 hours it took each day to get to and from the mine and clean up afterwards, this 'working time' extended to 71 hours. Their task was to shovel coal and stones onto wagons and then to pull and push them onto and off the lifts to the surface. They were supplied with a thin suit of blue material and clogs when working underground and there were washing facilities at the pit head for cleaning this kit. The mines were overseen by civilians, known as 'Steigers', and their behaviour and discipline was erratic; some were quite reasonable but Rippengal testified that, on occasions, men returned to the surface 'black and blue' from the beatings given out by the 'steigers'. For this arduous work the men were 'paid' between one and ten marks a week though there was no hourly rate and no-one ever knew why people were paid the amount they actually received. The unter-offizier, anyway, found almost any disciplinary pretext to fine the men and so any money earned was quite often denied them for reasons often unknown. So exhausted were the men by their work that other forms of recreation, though nominally available, were hardly ever undertaken. There was a football and men could walk around the compound but rest was their main need.

On their first day at the mine an effort was made by the men to refuse to work. A pile of clogs was nearby and they were ordered to pick up a pair in readiness to go underground but the men refused to move. This insubordination threw the unter-offizier into a rage and a man was grabbed by guards and beaten with rubber piping and kicked towards the clogs. When he still refused to select his clogs he was kicked again so severely that he, and the others, eventually gave in. Discipline generally was applied to everyone irrespective of the numbers involved in the breach. An escape, even if unsuccessful, resulted in the withholding of every inmates' food parcels for between one and four weeks and the escapee was sentenced to fourteen days in the cells. Other punishments would be the banning of smoking and the stopping of all forms of entertainment. A particularly popular form of punishment, for the guards that is, was called the 'Stillystand'. Here men were forced to stand on parade for anything from two to eight hours. After one attempted escape the men, on their return from an exhausting shift down the pit, were made to stand on parade from mid-day to 1.30 a.m. the following morning. They were then woken at 5 a.m. and their huts and persons searched by the guards, a process that had them standing on parade again until 1.00 p.m. Throughout this time, that is from mid-day on the first day until one in the afternoon on the following day, they were not fed.

Medical care in the camp hospital was under the control of a civilian doctor who was clearly cut from the same cloth as the commandant and his junior. Men reporting sick were invariably forced back to work immediately and the treatment that was provided was performed in ways as painful to the patient as possible. Rippengal recalled a man with a badly swollen thumb that clearly needed lancing. This the doctor achieved with the use of his own thumb nail pressed hard into the skin. The men rapidly became run down and suffered from boils and rashes, as did Rippengal himself, but still they were not treated and it was only in the event of serious illness that the men were properly treated but this required evacuation to the hospital in Friedrichsfeld

About the only improvement over Minden that the quality and quantity of the food was better, presumably because even the commandant and his crony realised that starving men would be useless down the mine and that, if production faltered, questions might be asked about their regime. There was more and better bread and soup, every PoW camp staples, and the canteen supplied luxuries such as apples, golden syrup and cigarettes but the prices were so steep, no doubt helping to keep both commandant and unter-offizier in the manner to which they had become accustomed, that few could afford to buy much with which to supplement their standard issue fare.

The stopping of parcels and letters was used at Westerholt as another form of punishment and once they were held for four weeks after it was found that some of the men had indulged in a bit of sabotage in the mine. At the same time, to add to the men's misery, the bread ration was stopped and was instead sold off to a local pig farm, further lining the pockets of the unter-offizier. When parcels were allowed they were, in the main, provided complete although the cardboard and string were kept by the authorities for some purpose or other. Rippengal, given the state of some of the bread, became quite fond of the Huntley and

Palmer's lunch biscuits that were a regular item in the parcels but, after his escape and return to England, he suggested that more salt was included in the packages as a means of improving the run down condition of the men. The contents of the prisoners' food parcels were, however, a source of wonder to the civilians with whom they had dealings at the mine. Rippengal remembered having conversations after parcels arrived when he told the astonished German workers that he had received rice and butter amongst other treats:

> "Invariably I heard the same comment: 'Rice! Why I haven't seen any for about two years'. The civilians are undoubtedly not receiving enough to eat and I noticed that one with whom I worked brought sandwiches of bread with boiled potatoes and apple in the centre... I heard from the civilians of a food riot a Buer in July of this year (1917) and firing went on in the streets."

The food shortages felt by the civilians inevitably filtered through to the camps and the men started to experience a dramatic decrease in both the quantity and quality of their rations. In May and June of 1917 the soup was reduced to a practically inedible mix of flour and water, the loaves slowly reduced in size and by October the twice weekly supply of meat had been halved. It was just as well for the health and well-being of Rfn. Rippengal that he successfully escaped from Westerholt on 20ᵗʰ October 1917, by the rather unusual expedient of just walking away from the mine in the company of a Canadian called Scott, but it is of interest to note that during his de-briefing on 15ᵗʰ November 1917 by a Col. B L Anstruther, that the interviewer remarked:

> "This man is well educated but seemed rather the worse for his experiences... when speaking of the specially harsh treatment and conditions prevailing at Westerholt."

These experiences would undoubtedly stay with men like Clifford Rippengal for the rest of their lives. His reward, if reward it be, was the award, along with his fellow escapers Evanson, Carle and Thompson, of the Military Medal. Evanson won his when, after a failed attempt with another L.R.B. man, 2198 Rfn. Herbert Sidwell, he got away from Westerholt with an Australian called Gardiner. The two men simply hid down the coal mine and then walked out with the German miners when their shift ended. The two of them then made their way to Holland, taking a tram ride in the process, and, travelling at night and crossing a large bog, they crossed into Holland in February 1918. Evanson made contact with the Rotterdam branch of the firm of accountants for which he had worked pre-war. The men were repatriated and Evanson spent the rest of his war as the RQMS in the 3/5ᵗʰ Battalion at Blackdown Barracks[i] near Chobham in Surrey.

As his mates made it home, Basil Houle spent a much happier time working for an elderly farmer in rural Westphalia. It was a bucolic idyll with the food plentiful and time available to cycle from village to village enjoying the hospitality of the local inns. It was as good a way to end a war as most and, when he heard that the Armistice had been declared, he returned to the main camp at Friedrichsfeld where anarchy reigned. The German officers had fled leaving the camp under the nominal rule of some N.C.O.s and de-mob happy, cigarette smoking guards. The British inmates were keen to leave but, without transport,

---

i Now the somewhat notorious Deepcut Barracks.

this proved difficult. After a few day's chaos it was decided that some pressure was in order so the 'authorities' were told that the camp would be burnt down if transport west was not made available. Some days later a train arrived which pottered off towards the Dutch border carrying a cheerful crowd of men from all parts of the Empire. The men were dropped a mile short and happily marched the short remaining distance to their freedom. Basil Houle was back with his family for Christmas and Tom Short, the Lewis gunner nearly bayoneted at the end of 1st July arrived home on New Year's Eve.

4734 Rfn. Walter Herbert Dorsett[11] was a member of the 1/16th London Regt. (Queen's Westminster Rifles) and his initial experiences seemed to have been marginally better than those of George Carle. Pre-war Dorsett had been a bank clerk and, aged 19, he lived at 46, Valentines Road, Ilford. During the attack he was wounded in the shoulder and, having been taken prisoner whilst lying in the German lines, he was taken into the aid post in Gommecourt where he was treated. Later in the evening he was moved to the rear and, at another aid post, he was given what was presumably an anti-tetanus injection. He was then taken by cart to a barn where he and other prisoners spent the night. On Sunday morning a group of prisoners were taken by an overcrowded lorry, seriously wounded and able bodied alike having to stand, to the grounds of a chateau. Here they were given some bread and coffee and were told they would sleep out doors on straw pallets. Two days later Dorsett was moved by train to Le Cateau and again the transport was overcrowded and the men were given no food or water. On his arrival at Le Cateau, however, his story diverges from that of Carle. Given the nature of his wound he was separated from the uninjured and slightly wounded and taken to a hospital which he described as:

"… very good and the doctors kind; we were put in proper beds and given good food. I was allowed to write a card home but it did not arrive till September. Here my arm was put in plaster of Paris."

Dorsett was kept in hospital for eighteen days and, on the 22nd July, he was sent on an ambulance train with beds to the large hospital at Ohdruf, a town in Thuringia[i]. This place had a capacity of some 1,200 prisoners and, although the doctors were 'decent', the hospital itself was in a poor condition, with the badly built accommodation huts being both leaky and draughty.

After two months at Ohrdruf, Dorsett started to receive his parcels from home, the contents of which provided a major improvement in the diet, which was both monotonous and sparse. Indeed, so bad was the food supply in the early days that Dorsett was forced to sell his wrist watch to a Frenchman for forty five biscuits. From September onwards, however, the arrival and distribution of the parcels seemed to work smoothly for most of the time and, with the exception of a couple of weeks in April 1917 when the German authorities withheld them when the French prisoners were suspected of receiving poisoned cigarettes, the parcels were regularly distributed amongst the inmates. All, that is, except for the string that bound the parcels - this was kept by the Germans.

---

[i] There was a concentration camp at Ohrdruf in World War Two. It was part of the Buchenwald complex and was the first camp liberated by US troops (on 4th April 1945). The discoveries there prompted a visit by Supreme Allied Commader, Dwight D Eisenhower, accompanied by Generals Patton and Bradley. The conditions were so bad Patton refused to enter some areas for fear of being sick.

The camps were subject to intermittent and, apparently random, inspections by representatives of the Red Cross and neutral diplomats who, until their entry into the war, were invariably men from the United States Embassy. One such visit took place in January in 1917 and Dorsett took the opportunity to lobby the American about the reliability of letters from home and the delivery of parcels and, for a time, some improvement was experienced. But, as the war wore on, there was a general deterioration in conditions, not only for prisoners but for the guards, principally old men and youngsters, and their families too. Given their close proximity, it was inevitable that there would be contact between prisoners and gaolers and some of older men on occasion gave an insight into the harsh life being led by the average German non-combatant by 1917. Dorsett reported on his return to England how a German sergeant had been given two month's leave to look after his seriously ill wife. When the man returned to the camp he told Dorsett about her condition. His wife, he said:

"...had been taken very ill owing to standing for hours in the snow waiting for food. When he came back he said that his children were quite changed – lifeless and run down owing to lack of food."

There were rumours of food riots and political upheaval with the arrests of socialist activists, but nothing concrete as far as Dorsett could report.

With the blockade biting increasingly hard it was inevitable that the prisoners would suffer serious food shortages in parallel to the ordinary German citizen. To make matters worse, the cooking facilities for the prisoners were very poor. Each barracks hut had only a small kitchen so most men resorted to cooking whatever was available on small fires outdoors using wood bought from the canteen. The sanitary facilities were equally poor. The water supply to the camp was inconsistent and was often off for hours on end. As a result, with nothing to flush out the latrines, they would get blocked and the resulting stink would be all pervading. Inevitably the conditions led to sickness and, in September and October 1917, a serious outbreak of dysentery swept through the camp. Dorsett later estimated that deaths amongst the Russians and Rumanians, whose conditions seemed generally far worse than those of the British and French, were running at the rate of ten a week as a result.

Although the Germans appeared to treat their Eastern European prisoners more harshly than the British and French their most aggressive behaviour seemed reserved for the Italians. Dorsett recalled that, at some point in 1917, 250 wounded Italians arrived at the hospital in a fleet of furniture vans. An English camp orderly named Sidebottom (KOYLI) witnessed their treatment and described it to Dorsett:

"He said the Italians were very roughly handled particularly by one young German orderly. I do not know his name. The wounded were dragged out one over the other and they were groaning and crying out with pain. They were packed into the transport which was terribly overcrowded. I saw them afterwards in the hospital and they looked very thin and wretched. The French were selling food to them for their watches and rings. We gave them food and cigarettes."

At the end of 1917 Dorsett's health made him a candidate for repatriation and, on 5th December, he was transferred first to Langensalza camp, which he described a 'very dirty', and then on to Mannheim two days later. This latter journey was by train and took twenty hours during which time they were given no food and had to sit on wooden boards throughout. Dorsett, at least, had some leftovers from a food parcel so was not completely starved during this unpleasant train ride. The relief was, however, that the hospital at Mannheim was more comfortable and the food better. The down side was that the quality of medical care from the staff was worse. Dorsett's stay at Mannheim was restricted to just three weeks and, on 28th December 1917, he was put on a typically uncomfortable, cold and draughty train to Aachen. From there he was sent home through Holland, being well treated on the way, arriving back in England in early January 1918. He was then interviewed by a Capt. Theodore Byard at Tooting Military Hospital on 12th January 1918 who concluded that Rfn. Dorsett was "... well educated and intelligent. I should say very truthful."

Not every prisoner coped with the stresses and privations of the camps and Dorsett told Capt. Byard about a Cpl. Taylor of the Lancashire Fusiliers. He arrived at the end of the Battle of the Somme and, although he seemed fine at the time, swiftly deteriorated mentally. By Christmas 1916 he was clearly insane and in February he was removed to a special hospital which Dorsett thought was near the town of Cassel in Hesse, central Germany. Dorsett also reported on the appalling condition of able bodied British prisoners who had been retained by the German Army to act as forced labourers behind the German lines in France:

> "At Ohrdruf were a lot of our men who had been working behind the German lines at Cambrai, Valenciennes and other places. They looked very ill indeed and a number died as a result of frost bite, consumption and general neglect. I spoke to Private Stevenson (HLI) who said that the lack of food was awful behind the German lines and that he had been struck several times for stepping out of the ranks to get a root to eat."

There was widespread international outrage when the treatment of these men and their employment close to the front lines became well known. It was a policy which had started with the extensive use and abuse of Russian prisoners captured in huge numbers during their disastrous campaign in East Prussia which encompassed such catastrophic defeats as those at Tannenberg and the Masurian Lakes. But the pressures on the German Army to employ these men in direct contravention of the Hague Conventions grew ever greater so that, by August 1916, 253,000 (16%) of the 1.6 million PoWs were being used in this way. Matters reached a head in the early summer of 1917 after many French and British prisoners had been employed in the construction of the Hindenburg Line and in preparing for the scorched-earth policy which accompanied the German withdrawal to these positions. In June, however, a tripartite agreement between the three governments ensured that all prisoners were withdrawn from close proximity to the battle zone. The Germans, though, then started to form organised Labour companies, the Arbeitskommandos, from amongst British and French PoWs to join the existing Russian, Serb, Rumanian and Italian kommandos already in existence. These units were employed in rear areas but were still, again employed in contravention of the Hague Convention, working directly towards the German war-effort and, by 1918, so desperate was the German High Command (OHL) for the labour they provided that is estimated that 400,000 PoWs were employed thus. The agreement that they should not be used close to the lines also rapidly went by the board as the pressures on the German Army grew to breaking point. At the time of the German March 1918 Offensive OHL decreed that, effectively, PoWs could be used as operational needs dictated and there is plenty of evidence that the kommandos were brought within Allied artillery range again and used directly in military activities such as loading and unloading artillery shells onto transports. If men refused such work then beatings and threats of execution followed swiftly on. The senior officers attempted to cover their backs from any post-war retaliation by issuing guidelines on appropriate forms of treatment for these men but they were honoured more in the breach and there was no formal system for their application nor were concerted efforts made to discipline junior officers and N.C.O.s who abused the PoWs under their direct operational control. The resulting physical and mental abuse and severe malnutrition must, inevitably, have led to the deaths of hundreds of Allied prisoners, many of whom will have had no known grave.

After the Armistice, the German Army basically drove the remaining prisoners towards Allied troops as a report from the French 10th Army described:

"The lamentable state of physical misery of the French and British prisoners whom the Germans have driven into our lines. These unfortunates are in a terrifying state of thinness and of exhaustion. The Germans have left them without food. A great number of them have not even had the strength to reach our lines and lie in ditches along the roads in front of our front line."[12]

The Hague Conventions had proved powerless to defend the vulnerable prisoners of the Allied nations who were systematically abused in their tens of thousands by an increasingly desperate enemy. The leaders of the Imperial German Army, not least Field Marshal Hindenburg and Chief of Staff Ludendorff, connived and conspired at, encouraged and sometimes ordered and organised these flagrant breaches of international agreements in place for only a few years and which their Government had freely ratified. The harsh militaristic attitudes which led to these abuses were deeply entrenched within the German Army and would be brought to their peak of brutality and efficiency in barely three decade's time but this time with civilians being brought within their barbarous grip. And again, no international Conventions would save them.

ENDNOTES:
1 They can be found in the WO161 series. Not all interviews were recorded but the names of those interviewed are listed. They are listed in a somewhat arbitrary system and some patience is needed to find the correct interview..
2 Hermann Cron, Geschichte des deutschen Heeres im Weltkriege, 1914-1918 (Berlin: 1937)
3 Short L/Cpl T, 1/5th London Rifle Brigade, Papers, IWM
4 Holyfield, 2437 Rfn S, 1/5th London Rifle Brigade, Papers, Liddle Collection, Leeds University
5 Houle, Rfn. B, 1/5th London Rifle Brigade, 'Black as a Pit: a true account of an experience of a PoW in German hands during the 1914-18 war' quoted in K W Mitchinson 'Gentlemen and Officers', page 125.
6 Evanson, Rfn E, 1/5th London Rifle Brigade, 'My Twenty Months' Captivity in Germany', IWM, LRB L47.
7 Carle, Rfn. George, 1/5th London Rifle Brigade. WO 161/100/136 Pages 2651-2656
8 Thompson, Pte Richard Edward, London Scottish WO 161/100/137. Pages 2656-2657
9 Rippengal, Rfn. Clifford, 1/5th London Rifle Brigade. WO 161/99/179 Pages 2095-2102
10 A detailed, and horrifying, article about the use of Prisoner of War Labour Companies by the Germans, 'The final logic of sacrifice? Violence in German prisoner of war labor companies in 1918,' was published in 'The Historian' on 22nd December 2006. It was written by Dr Heather Jones, Lecturer in the Department of History, School of Histories and Humanities, Trinity College, Dublin. It clearly shows how the treatment of PoWs by the German Army on the Western Front was a precursor to the inhumane attitudes towards both civilians and PoWs, especially of Eastern European origin, that was all pervasive in World War Two.
11 Dorsett, Rfn. W H, 1/16th London Regt., WO 161/99/233. Pages 2306-2307
12 SHAT 16 N 2380, Novembre 1918, GQG, 2e Bureau, Message telephonique recu de la Xe Armee. 16.11.18.

16. CASUALTIES

> *"The battlefield over which our battalions had so recently charged was
> dotted with prone figures, many of them beyond assistance. Near the
> enemy trenches the fighting had been more terrible and grey figures
> mingled with brown. Over all of this the sun burned; the rough shell
> broken terrain was bright with grasses and summer flowers; the
> troublelesssky seemed to deny the sad evidence of the battle."*

From 'The 2/2ⁿᵈˢ In France'
2/2ⁿᵈ London Field Ambulance

MEDICAL SERVICES TO THE 56ᵀᴴ DIVISION were supplied by three second-
line Territorial London Field Ambulances: the 2/1ˢᵗ, 2/2ⁿᵈ and 2/3ʳᵈ.
These three Field Ambulances had been formed by men left over from their first
line units (i.e. 1/1ˢᵗ, 1/2ⁿᵈ and 1/3ʳᵈ) and from men recruited from August 1914
onwards. Recruitment had taken place at the R.A.M.C. Territorial Depot, 1ˢᵗ
London Division at the Duke of York's Barracks, Chelsea. All three units then
left Chelsea at the end of December 1914 for further training in Sussex. In the
mid summer of 1915 they moved to East Anglia where they became attached to
the 58ᵗʰ Division and there they continued their training. On the 21ˢᵗ February,
1916 all three units went by train to Southampton where they boarded the paddle
steamer *'Mona's Queen'* and sailed for Le Havre. After a rough crossing they
landed in the morning of the 22ⁿᵈ February and rested there for 36 hours before
being ushered on board several cattle trucks for the journey to Pont Remy from
which they marched to their initial host villages – Airaines, Huppy and Brucamps.
They were now part of the newly formed 56ᵗʰ Division.

For the next two months, the Field Ambulances familiarised themselves with
the equipment they were to use. In addition, parties of all three units were
temporarily attached to either the 15ᵗʰ or 43ʳᵈ Field Ambulances or used as
stretcher bearers in order to gain some first hand experience of life in an active
Field Ambulance. Then, in early May, they joined the 56ᵗʰ Division's exodus
south to their new positions at Hebuterne. The men were immediately set to
work to augment the existing medical facilities. 'A' and 'C' Sections of the 2/1ˢᵗ
led, by Lt. Col. C S Brebner, were initially billeted in Souastre but they moved to
Couin where, with the help of elements of the other two Field Ambulances, they
started work on creating the Main Dressing Station (M.D.S.). This camp of huts
and tents was constructed in fields of corn and clover next to a large farm on the
edge of the village. Meanwhile, 'B' Section went to Sailly and Hebuterne. In
Sailly the men occupied some new dugouts known as 'The Rendezvous' whilst
those in Hebuterne built, with the help of men from the R.E., the Advanced
Dressing Station (A.D.S.) at a farmhouse near the centre of the village.

The 2/2ⁿᵈ had been sent to St Amand where they were billeted near to a farm
building that was being used as a dressing station. On May 15ᵗʰ a party was sent
up to Hebuterne to help the detachment of the 2/1ˢᵗ. They were billeted in the
village's cellars, one of which, 'The Grotto', was also used for church services.
The job of this party was to build extra dug outs in the garden behind the A.D.S.,
near to where a cemetery was growing all too fast[1]. At the same time, a party

went to Bayencourt where a small dressing station was built for the heavy artillery in the village. On June 18th the unit moved to open country between Souastre and Couin where they prepared for the forthcoming attack. Throughout this time the 2/3rd sent sections to help at Couin, Sailly and Hebuterne.

Plate 64 Lt. Col. E C Montgomery-Smith DSO, 2/2nd London Field Ambulance
(*Source:* The Second Seconds in France, Spottiswoode, Ballantyne & Co Ltd 1920)

During the last few days of June, Lt. Col. Montgomery-Smith led 'A' and 'C' Sections of the 2/2nd up to Hebuterne to take over the A.D.S., 'B' Section remaining at the M.D.S. at Couin where the majority of the 2/1st and the 2/3rd were also based. Motor ambulances were distributed at various locations along the route from Hebuterne to Couin and, on the evening of 30th June, some of them went on their last run up to the A.D.S. to collect any casualties from the day's work. Arthur Atkinson, a member of the Motor Section of the 2/3rd London Field Ambulance, came back along the route being used by the attacking battalions as they marched towards the frontline:

"On our return we met columns of marching troops – the 12th London Rangers and 14th London Scottish moving up to their positions for the attack the next morning. It was a most moving and unforgettable sight – the comparatively quiet, almost peaceful evening and all these men – many mere young boys singing as they marched, very many to witness for the last time a sunset and the fields in all their summer glory!"[2]

The men of the London Field Ambulances would not have long to wait before they saw at first hand the consequences for the human body of being wounded by intense artillery and machine gun fire. The first casualties to arrive in the early hours of 1st July were the men caught by the German artillery retaliation to the bombardment that was harrying their progress into the assembly trenches. Hurried down the congested communication trenches by regimental stretcher bearers, they were met in the centre of the village by men with wheeled stretchers and taken to the dug outs in the A.D.S. to await treatment and evacuation. Pte H L Chase of the 2/1st London Field Ambulance was one of the men waiting to assist the wounded and he had been in position since the early hours:

"Dozed off from about 10.30 to 12.15 and reported at 12.30 (a.m.) Two of us sent off to wait at the end of Welcome Street communication trench. There we stood behind a wall while both sides chucked over a lot of heavy stuff, though fortunately none of them came very near us. We waited from about 1.30 till 3.45 and then cleared off down to the A.D.S. with a walking case. Left again and went up Welcome Street to the Kensington and Scottish Aid Post where we found things very busy and got our first stretcher case. Had a simply wicked job getting him down through an awful trench with plenty of stuff coming over. Got back however and then got another squad to come up and help us. This was about 6.45."[3]

As the day wore on, the flow of casualties turned to a flood. So great was the demand for stretcher bearers and ambulances that the men and motors of all three Field Ambulances were called up to the A.D.S. in a desperate attempt to move people out of danger to a place where their wounds could be inspected and treated properly. And even then, the medical and evacuation resources were overwhelmed, leaving men who should not have walked at all struggling down the road to Sailly au Bois, past the batteries of 18pdrs dug in alongside the road whose crews, bare-chested and sweating, were firing with increasing ferocity in a desperate effort to help the men now trapped in the German trenches.

In the A.D.S. a small band of doctors and orderlies worked feverishly in the foetid gloom of the dugouts in desperate efforts to save men mutilated by shards of metal or pierced by machine gun and rifle bullets. The wounds presented were many and various. Across the whole front many of the injuries were shell or shrapnel wounds such was the pounding their positions were receiving. On the left flank, however, machine guns had done great execution to troops attempting to re-supply the faltering attack and some of the wounded would have fallen into or would have been dragged back into the trenches.

Shrapnel balls or shell fragments were relatively slow moving and rapidly decelerating objects. The effects of being hit by such a projectile were a matter of luck and a function of the size and speed of the fragment. Large, fast-moving shards of the shell's casing could kill instantly. In such cases, decapitation, disembowelment, bisection and the removal of limbs led to instant mutilation and death. For others, small, irregular pieces caused jagged wounds into which material from the uniform and other debris could be drawn. These wounds were survivable but needed urgent attention to clean the wound and prevent infection setting in. Finally, came the minor wounds and contusions caused by a very slow moving piece of shrapnel or shell. Often, contact with almost anything, helmet, uniform, equipment, was enough to so slow the fragment as to render it all but impotent.

The effect of a shrapnel shell very much depended on the height at which it exploded. Too high, and the deceleration of the shrapnel balls and the associated fragments of the shell casing, the fuse and the base plate, meant that casualties might be spread over a wide area but the wounds caused would be minor. For the attacking British troops, it was now that they came to appreciate the heavy, unventilated, uncomfortable and ill-balanced Brodie helmet. The helmets had only become widely available in the spring and early summer of 1916 and, initially, the men had regarded them as a cumbersome irritant. But, made of hardened manganese steel and weighing 2lbs, they had been designed to withstand a shrapnel ball travelling at 750 feet per second. Now, as the German shrapnel shrieked and cracked high above their heads, the men's instinctive reaction was to tilt their heads in the direction of the explosion and hope that the helmet would do its job. In many cases, it did; head wounds declined by as much as 75% after their introduction. If a shrapnel shell was set to explode low, however, its effects would be dramatically different. Initially accelerated by the explosive charge set behind the shrapnel balls, the 300 ten gram bullets from a German 77mm field gun or the 500 bullets contained in a 10.5cm field howitzer shell, swept forward in a dense and deadly cone of fire. Fired at a range of 3,000 metres, the balls from this shell would, at such close range, be travelling in excess of 900 feet per second, more than the Brodie was designed to resist. Hitting the body, the balls acted more like those fired by muskets from wars in the eighteenth and earlier centuries. They would cause large but not deep injuries, known as 'cul-de-sac wounds' because the ball would stay in the body. The ball was often accompanied by fabric from the man's uniform and other detritus, all of which was liable to cause infection if not quickly cleaned and disinfected.

Of course, the Brodie helmet did not protect a man's face. It had been apparent from the late assaults of 1915 that while the helmet protected the skull – and thus reduced the risk of fatal wounds to the brain – the incidence of facial injuries had increased. If major blood vessels were damaged then survival was unlikely, but the effect of shell fragment or bullet hitting bones in the face, when they then tumbled and spun about, could be horrific. Injuries to the jaw could damage the attachments of the tongue, so if a man was laid flat the tongue would fall back into the throat and suffocate him.

But, even with the protection of his helmet, a man could be killed or severely wounded by the air pressure generated by the nearby explosion of a high explosive shell. L/Cpl. Reginald Davis of the Queen Victoria's Rifles was in the German front line when:

"... I felt a pressure of tons upon my head. My right eye was sightless, with the other I saw my hand with one finger severed, covered in blood. A great desire came over me to sink to the ground, into peaceful oblivion, but the peril of such weakness came to my mind, and with an effort I pulled myself together. I tore my helmet from my head, for the concussion had forced it tight down. The man in front bandaged my head and eye. Blood was pouring into my mouth, down my tunic... I made my way slowly – not in pain, I was too numbed for that."[4]

For those hit by a rifle or machine gun bullet the problems were different. If they were lucky, the bullet went through flesh without hitting either a major organ or artery or striking a bone. The entry and exit wounds might be neat little holes, surrounded by bruising caused by ruptured blood vessels. The exit wounds would be apparently larger than the entry wound but this was because the skin had been stretched and distended before it perforated and the bullet exited. Bullets that had ricocheted off another object would tend to lodge in the wound carrying with it cloth fragments and anything else picked up by the bullet on its path. Then there were enfilade wounds, ones where the man was hit through a limb and then the torso by a bullet from the side, or others when, perhaps, the soldier was lying down and a bullet through the shoulder passed down through the body into the leg or buttock. However, if the bullet struck a bone then it would start to spin and tumble through the body, causing massive internal injuries and often a large, explosive exit wound. To the effects of the bullet would then be added those of the splintered bone. Fragments driven deep into the surrounding area increased the area of damaged tissue. Finally, the impact of a high velocity round could drive fluids away from the path of the projectile with such force that yet further damage to the body could occur.

Hit in head, hand or foot, areas with a concentration of nerve endings, the wounded man would be aware of immediate and acute pain. Hit elsewhere, after the initial shock of the impact, a strange numbness would take over, sometimes leaving the man unaware of the severity of the injury. Gun shots to the head, abdomen and major arteries were invariably fatal and sometimes swiftly so. For wounds to the lungs and abdomen, early surgical treatment was vital if the patient was to have any chance of survival but even then the likelihood of recovery was slim. Figures for the 19th Casualty Clearing Station in May showed that, of fourteen men needing surgery for an abdominal wound, only five survived the immediate shock of the operation long enough to be transferred on to a Base Hospital. Wounds to the chest, arms and legs presented a better prognosis, and it was with injuries such as these that the wounded arrived in the Regimental Aid Posts in ever increasing numbers as the day drew on.

The stretcher-bearers' priorities when dealing with a wounded man were threefold of which two were, by nature, a compromise of one another. Keeping the patient warm was regarded as, perhaps, the most important function. Shock and blood loss, the former partly a function of the latter, meant that body temperature could plummet dangerously such that, by the time the patient arrived at the A.D.S., cold could be their most pressing concern. In some circumstances, surface body temperature could fall as low as 90°. In this parlous state, the movement of the injured man could add increased pain and anxiety and so still greater stress to his condition. The stretcher-bearers had, therefore, to carry their burden as gently as possible, the more so if their patient had suffered fractures or severe limb injuries perhaps requiring later amputation. On the other hand, severe external or internal blood loss caused by such injuries required urgent transmission to the A.D.S. and beyond. The responsibilities on the stretcher-bearers were, therefore, manifold. As they struggled down the pandemonium of the communication trenches, themselves the targets of machine gun fire, high explosive and shrapnel, they had, at the same time, to hasten their wounded man towards medical attention with the greatest delicacy lest, in their rush, they inflict increased injury. Under the merciless pressure of 1st July speed of delivery must have understandably become the priority as the stretcher bearers were asked to make the impossible choice between a slow transfer of their current patient and the needs of the hundreds of others flowing in a steady torrent into the Regimental Aid Posts. Pte Chase of the 1/2nd London Field Ambulance and his mates were being kept more than busy:

"Had another journey up to the Aid Post during the morning and was by then pretty done. By some miracle, none of us was hit. By the middle of the morning casualties were coming down in hundreds, many of the very bad cases walking. I stayed at the ADS... helping to load cases. The chaplain stood outside directing all walking cases on and sending bad cases inside. In the afternoon I went up Wood Street but it was apparently too hot for we were stopped and sent back."

At the Dressing Station the hard-pressed medical officers and orderlies could do little here other than patch up and pass on. The men themselves had probably already made use of their Field Dressing, having first poured the little bottle of iodine into the wound. Those that could walk or stagger were sent off down the lines to the Advanced Dressing Station under their own steam. Those that could not were carried, helped, given piggybacks - got back to the A.D.S. by whatever means possible. Once they had arrived at the broad main street that ran through the middle of Hebuterne, there were wheeled stretchers on to which those that could no longer walk were placed. But, however fast the stretcher-bearers struggled and scrambled down the communication trenches to the A.D.S., the journey could take as long as an hour, such was the congestion and chaos.

Plate 65 The Advanced Dressing Station, Hebuterne
Taken before the battle (*Source:* The 2/1st London Field Ambulance, Morton, Burt & Sons, 1924)

Four Medical Officers and 110 men of the 2/2nd London Field Ambulance manned the A.D.S. in Hebuterne. It was located on the right hand side a few metres up the road to Sailly-au-Bois from the centre of Hebuterne. Turning through an archway and into a courtyard the casualty would see a heavily sandbagged cottage. In the courtyard were the sand-bagged entrances to two Elephant dug outs, each connected to the cottage's cellar. The dug outs had a planned capacity of 50 lying and 200 sitting cases. They were soon full to overflowing. Trenches led into the dug out entrances and these were now full of the walking wounded waiting to be assessed and treated. Slumped against the trench walls, a bloody field dressing pressed against the wound some drew heavily on a Woodbine and all shuddered at every heavy nearby shell blast. Orderlies from the R.A.M.C. moved from man to man. Those with a wound that could be simply dressed were dealt with as quickly as the numbers allowed and prepared for swift evacuation. Others, particularly those suffering heavy blood loss, were, after the wound was dressed, encouraged to sip a warm drink in order to keep up body temperature and replace body fluids. The favourite drink administered was hot, sweet tea giving what was then thought to be an ideal combination of warmth, fluid and, from the sugar, some easily absorbed carbohydrate. That the caffeine was a diuretic was not regarded, at least at the time, as a heavy consideration; neither was it realised then that too much warm fluid would both open up the circulation, encouraging further bleeding, and would compromise the giving of an anaesthetic.

Plate 66 The Advanced Dressing Station, Hebuterne
Taken later in the campaign (*Source:* The 2/1st London Field Ambulance, Morton, Burt & Sons, 1924)

Every few minutes the cry would go up to 'make room' and a white-faced casualty, unusually quiet and still, tunic sodden and dark with blood, would be rushed through the silent throng on a stretcher into the gloom of the dugouts. Many observers commented on how it was those with the worst injuries who were the quietest, the most phlegmatic, with a resigned cheerfulness. Often, these were the ones without a limb or with a serious and deep penetrating wound. They were the ones rushed down the steps to the operating area of the A.D.S. deep under the now full courtyard. Inside, it was like a subterranean abattoir. By the dim light of electric light, lamps and candles, the doctors of the Field Ambulance worked feverishly to administer morphine, assess and where necessary clean wounds, staunch with tourniquets pulsing arterial flows and keep the gravely wounded clinging to life until they could reach the better equipped Main Dressing Station and the Casualty Clearing Stations ranged behind the lines. Operations were conducted only in cases of utmost urgency, life threatening haemorrhage and the amputation of irretrievably ruined limbs, otherwise men were made ready for onward transmission to the M.D.S. and the properly equipped operating theatres of the Casualty Clearing Stations where the majority of operations took place.

Lt. Col. H M W Gray, a leading consultant surgeon with the B.E.F., gives a graphic description of an Advance Dressing Station during a major attack:

"It is beyond the power of words to convey anything but the feeblest impression of the conditions under which surgical work is carried on at a very advanced unit during a big 'push'.... The dimly lit dugout dressing station, the dust, the wet, the mud, the blood, the noise, the bustle, the numbers of wounded, the appalling wounds, the hopeless shock... Here is no brilliantly lighted and fully equipped theatre, here his patients do not come before him in spotless apparel, here he has not unlimited skilled assistance, here he must be content with very simple things. And through it all he must keep cool, he must hurry, he must be thorough, he must be gentle and careful in every possible way. His is the responsibility to make or mar a man for life."[5]

Lt. Col. E C Montgomery Smith R.A.M.C., C.O. of the 2/2ⁿᵈ Londons and officer in charge of medical arrangements in Hebuterne, had already called up parts of the 2/1ˢᵗ London Field Ambulance and had brought up all of the men from the other 2/2ⁿᵈ London A.D.S. at Sailly[i]. Several volunteer doctors from other units had also arrived to do what good they could. But it was clear that the A.D.S. could not cope with the overwhelming numbers of men arriving every minute. When the A.D.S. had been built, it had been designed to cope with a throughput of 1,000 casualties in a period of 96 hours but, in the event, the M.D.S. at Couin received nearly 1,200 wounded from Hebuterne in just the first twelve hours of the attack.

To make matters worse German shells were also dropping with increasing frequency in the vicinity of the station, further wounding or killing the wounded waiting so patiently to be treated. It was decided that the only course of action was to keep the village as clear of the wounded as possible. Initially, three ambulances from the 3ʳᵈ Motor Ambulance Company[ii] were based in the village, there to transport wounded to the M.D.S. at Couin but they were now obviously inadequate. Ambulances and any other motorised vehicle that could carry the wounded were ordered to drive up the road from Sailly to the rear of the village, something that would never normally have been risked in daylight. But the congestion in the A.D.S. was so severe that urgent action was needed if more casualties were not to be caused amongst those awaiting treatment.

Some of the casualties wore field grey, German prisoners wounded by their own machine guns or artillery as they were sent helter-skelter across No Man's Land to the waiting 'cages' behind the lines. 2ⁿᵈ Lt. Liveing, newly arrived at the A.D.S., recalls seeing a German medical orderly, a red-cross armband on his sleeve, carefully tending his wounded enemies:

"Here were our men attending to the German wounded and the Germans attending to ours. Both sides were working so hard now to save life. There was a human touch about that scene in the ruined village street which filled one with a sense of mingled sadness and pleasure. Here were both sides

---

[i] Originally manned by 2 M.O.s and 25 men. This A.D.S. had a capacity of 20 lying and 45 sitting casualties.
[ii] 3ʳᵈ Motor Ambulance Company was formed at Grove Park on 1ˢᵗ November 1914. Commanded by Capt. R A Preston R.A.M.C. they were based at the Divisional Rest Station at Mondicourt.

united in a common attempt to repair the ravages of war. Humanity had at last asserted itself."[6]

Liveing had been transported to the A.D.S. on board one of the wheeled stretchers that were being used to get the more seriously hurt from the end of the communication trenches down to the dugouts on the Sailly road. Before this part of his tortuous journey had begun, however, his wound had been examined by an RAMC orderly at an Aid Post in Cross Street:

"After about five or ten minutes an orderly slit up my breeches.

"The wound's in the front of the hip," I said.

"Yes, but there's a larger wound where the bullets come out, sir."

I looked and saw a gaping hole two inches in diameter.

"I think that's a Blighty one, isn't it?" I remarked.

"I should just think so, sir!" he replied.

"Thank God! At last!" I murmured vehemently, conjuring up visions of the good old homeland."[7]

Liveing was then loaded onto his ambulance for the journey to the Dressing Station. The first man he saw was one of the Battalion 'padres' directing traffic. Capt. Julian Bickersteth was one of three 56ᵗʰ Division chaplains[i] who were trying to make some organisational sense out of the flood of injured men who threatened to overwhelm the creaking medical systems. They had started on the road outside the A.D.S., identifying those that needed urgent help and those that might wait awhile. Depending on the nature of the wound, they would help a man with a drink or, if suffering from a stomach or abdomen injury, gently explain that taking fluids was not possible until the doctors had examined them. A few days later, Bickersteth wrote down his recollections of the day in his diary:

"Downstairs in the two dug-outs, the doctors were working hard, but could not keep pace with the numbers. They began to arrive in ever increasing numbers, staggering along the main village street or being carried on stretchers by faithful stretcher bearers. Never was nobler work done that day than by those who went up to the trenches to bring down wounded."[8]

Dressing the wounds of the increasing flood of casualties swiftly became impossible and staunching the flow of blood was all they could achieve. Ambulances were called up to entrance to the A.D.S. itself and then set off down the road to Sailly with various loads, either four lying and four sitting or eleven sitting cases with the priority being the more serious lying cases. Otherwise, Bickersteth was given a variety of tasks by Lt. Col. Montgomery Smith. The walking wounded were patched up and sent on their way along the tracks to the rear; the ambulances and other vehicles commandeered for the transport of the injured and their human cargoes were organised and despatched; those in need of fluids were given either 'Oxo' or hot tea to help with the effects of shock and blood loss; and two out of the way dugouts now filled with wounded were cleared and the men sent onwards by foot or by ambulance.

The 1ˢᵗ July was the first truly hot day of this French summer and Bickersteth now found his thoughts turning to the wounded lying under a blistering sun

---

[i] The other chaplains were Rev Kenneth Northcote Crisford who had been attached to the 1/5ᵗʰ London Rifle Brigade on the 23ʳᵈ November 1915, and Rev Reginald Palmer.

amidst the carnage of No Man's Land and, briefly, he turned to prayer for their safe keeping. But the mortuary was soon full and Bickersteth set to organising a space next to the A.D.S. to be used to lay out the dead. But that was all that could be done for these men with the needs of the wounded being so pressing.

By mid-day, the German artillery began to lengthen their range and shrapnel started to crack and whine over the village centre and explosions shook the roads and houses near the A.D.S. The road outside was now an unhealthy place to be and dealing with the wounded lying and milling around the A.D.S. became a more difficult and dangerous task. Through luck, though several of the ambulances were struck by shrapnel balls, none of the casualties lying or sitting ready for transport to the rear were further injured.

The improvised fleet of vehicles took as many casualties as they could along narrow, undulating lanes through Sailly, Bayencourt and Souastre to the Main Dressing Station by the large, solidly built, redbrick Ferme de la Voieirie just outside Couin, four kilometres away. To get there, they passed 2ⁿᵈ Lt. Moy and his colleagues waiting for news in the village of Souastre:

> "At 1.00 motor ambulances started flying through the village; one caught glimpses of the mangled heaps lying on stretchers. In one I saw Glasier, with ghastly face and bloody uniform. Walking wounded came trudging painfully, singly and two and two, arms dangling, heads bandaged. When questioned they all made the same reply "all killed, everybody dead.""[9]

On the other side of No Man's Land a great many of the 56ᵗʰ Division's dead and wounded lay in the trenches of the German positions. Here, as with the German prisoners in Hebuterne, they were assisted with the same care and concern as the doctors and orderlies showed to their own men. The Germans had prepared for the assault by setting up two dressing stations in dug outs within Gommecourt village. Dugout 'A', the larger of the two, was manned by three medical officers and Dugout 'B' had one. Dugout 'B' was to be used to check and pass on casualties to the bigger dressing station where they had capacity for 30 lying and up to 60 sitting cases. During the hurricane bombardment in the last hour before the assault, the battalion H.Q. of I/55ᵗʰ R.I.R. was destroyed and the officers and men were forced to move into Dugout 'A', itself under heavy attack. Thanks to reinforcement of its upper levels, however, the dugout survived although its upper cellar had to be evacuated after several direct hits blocked the entrance and threatened to collapse the roof.

As the fighting continued Dugout 'A' was used to treat both German and British casualties. Walking wounded were sent to Essarts and Bucquoy by foot whilst the more severely injured were carried by soldiers to the rear areas as the medical personnel had insufficient stretchers. Next port of call for the badly wounded was the Main Dressing Station at Courcelles. During the day, 739 cases were admitted of which 157 were captured English. To get to Courcelles, walking wounded were collected at the Medical Company's dug out at Bucquoy and then sent by trench tramway to the M.D.S. The more severely wounded were collected from Essarts by ambulance. Once treated at Courcelles, the wounded were moved by ambulance on to the 45ᵗʰ Field Hospital at Vaulx-Vraucourt and the 17ᵗʰ Field Hospital at Fremicourt, sometimes stopping at the rest stations at Mory and Ervillers. Not all survived. A number of German dead are buried under their stark black crosses in the out of the way cemetery at Achiet

476

le Petit. Further back, all the way to places like Cambrai, the names of London Division men who failed to survive can be found on the ranks of white headstones in the Commonwealth War Graves Commission cemeteries that litter this part of northern France.

***

AT COUIN THE M.D.S., commanded by Lt. Col. Brebner, manned by the 2/1st and reinforced by elements of the 2/2nd and 2/3rd London Field Ambulance, had a capacity of 600 and, within hours, these beds and more were filled although by how many casualties is a matter of some dispute. According to a Third Army report published on 24th July, the numbers admitted to the M.D.S. for the 36 hours between 6 a.m. on 1st July and 6 p.m. on the 2nd July were[10]:

Period	Officers	Other ranks	Prisoners of War	Total
1st July 6 a.m.-6 p.m.	60	1,090	19	1,169
6 p.m. – 6 a.m., 2nd July	6	273	3	282
2nd July 6 a.m. – 6 p.m.	9	159	3	171
TOTAL	75	1,522	25	1,622

Table 19 Casualties admitted to Main Dressing Station, 1st-2nd July 1916

Plate 67 Lt. Col. C S Brebner, 2/1st London Field Ambulance
(*Source:* The 2/1st London Field Ambulance, Morton, Burt & Sons, 1924)

The War Diary of the 2/1st London Field Ambulance records another set and significantly higher set of figures, suggesting that 65 officers and 1,758 men were admitted on the 1st July alone with another 9 officers and 214 men coming in on the 2nd July. Their total of 74 officers and 1,972 men admitted over the two days seems to be the more likely figure of the two though why the Third Army's report should be so at odds with the figures provided by the doctors 'on the ground' is odd. The Diary goes on to give figures for those subsequently evacuated and for those who made it no further:

Evacuated to Casualty Clearing Stations: 71 officers and 2,114 other ranks[i]
Sent to the Divisional Rest Station: 119 other ranks

---

[i] The discrepancy between the figures of other ranks admitted, 1,972, and the figures evacuated, 2,114, is explained by the movement of men admitted to the M.D.S. prior to 1st July. For example, 176 officers and men were admitted on the 30th June and only 55 men discharged or evacuated.

Died: 1 officer and 19 other ranks
To duty: 3 officers and 2 men

The unit history of the 2/1st London Field Ambulance recalls the scene (again at odds with the Third Army's 'official figures'):

"Wounded men lying on stretchers covered the whole area of the camp – the huts could only contain a fraction of the cases that poured in – and in 24 hours more than 2,000 wounded were dealt with and evacuated to the Casualty Clearing Stations."[11]

Pte. Clements had been wounded in the jaw when 'C' Company of the 1/2nd Londons had tried in vain to reinforce the London Rifle Brigade in front of Gommecourt village. He was taken by ambulance to Couin for treatment:

"The crowd of wounded was like a Bank Holiday crowd at Blackheath. We were inoculated for lockjaw and then laid down on the grass, glad of some rest at last."[12]

Couin was also a meeting place for those still able to talk as Edward Liveing discovered. Shortly after passing a man with a lung wound who was "vomiting blood freely" he came across the servant of a friend, an officer in the London Scottish. The officer, identified only as 'E---', had been evacuated ill shortly before the attack and was now writing letters home for the wounded and he dashed off two postcards to Liveing's family to tell them he was wounded but alive. While he waited, and as a Medical Officer first labelled him 'GSW back' and then ordered him to be taken to the Officers' hut, Capt. Wyatt was brought in with a machine gun bullet in each shoulder to be followed soon after by 2nd Lt. Hine with a wounded arm. Tea was brought round but Wyatt demanded bread and jam instead; Liveing meanwhile enjoyed large quantities of both. Soon after, with an inflatable rubber ring giving him some relief from his wound, he was sitting back enjoying a read of the newest edition of *'The Tatler'* but, at the other end of the hut and a universe away, three young men were dying in agony from untreatable stomach wounds. Then came a clutch of young officers with varying degrees of shell shock: one from the Kensingtons who had been blow up in the forlorn attempt to dig the communication trench across No Man's Land; a second weeping uncontrollably and imploring anyone who would listen that he should not be sent back to the trenches; a third half-heartedly arguing with an RAMC orderly over his name before giving up; and a fourth, also swathed with bandages, who thought he was still fighting in the trenches and who was loudly encouraging both his men and himself to stick to the task, stick to the task.

Those with minor injuries, the 'walking wounded', were patched up and moved onwards, mainly to the Divisional Rest Station at Mondicourt being run by the 2/3rd London Field Ambulance or another facility at Henu where they had room for 1,000 such cases. The Rest Station at Mondicourt was commanded by Maj. A W French who had only been appointed C.O. of the 2/3rd Field Ambulance two days earlier. In the early afternoon two of his officers, Capts Thompson and Bell, were ordered to go up to help at M.D.S. at Couin. This left French only one other doctor, Capt. McHattie, and the unit Quartermaster to run the rest station. By 2 a.m. on 2nd July they had accepted 400 injured and shell-shocked cases and every hut and tent was crammed full. Overall, the Rest Station evacuated 1,600 cases by motor ambulance convoy.

At Couin, however, a strict triage system was in operation, learned by hard experience of war. The less severely injured were sent straight on to one of the Casualty Clearing Stations at Warlincourt Halte, transport allowing. The more seriously wounded that could be saved were dealt with as a matter of urgency. Some might already have been operated on at the A.D.S., especially those with chest and abdomen injuries, wounds that demanded urgent surgical attention. Others might require a bullet or shrapnel wound to be cleaned and fragments removed, a novel procedure known as 'debridement'.

'Debridement', from the word 'debris', was introduced as a medical technique in 1915 after some initial explorations by the French Medical Officer Dr P. Riche in October 1914 supported by independent work done by an Australian M.O., Major E. T. C. Milligan, and the previously mentioned Lt. Col. H M W Gray[13]. Early in the war, it became clear that non-fatal wounds were often made fatal by infection caused by soil, micro-organisms, pieces of uniform and shell or bullet fragments remaining in the wound. Various antiseptic solutions had been in use, such as hydrogen peroxide, Eusol[i] and Carrel-Dakin solution[ii], but, although these killed any micro-organisms in a wound, they did not deal with the problem of dead tissue surrounding the wound in which infection could breed. As a result, wounds were surgically enlarged with the excision of all dead tissue and the removal of all foreign bodies and this technique of 'debridement' which cleared and cleaned the damage tissue was, until the introduction of antibiotics in 1943, a soldier's best hope of avoiding the often fatal perils of 'gas gangrene'. Wounds to the buttocks and the thigh were especially prone to the onset of infection. The loss of blood flow to the damaged muscle led to a rapid degeneration of the tissue surrounding the wound and the swift onset of gangrene was the likely outcome unless urgently treated in the manner prescribed above.

For injuries to the limbs the use of tourniquets was a mixed blessing for although they might help stop the patient from bleeding to death, a prolonged period of severely restricted blood flow to the affected area might quickly have other, equally fatal, side effects. Experience showed that for any limb subject to a tourniquet for more than three hours there was a 4 in 5 likelihood of it being amputated as a result of severe infection. So, for some, the only early surgical option was amputation and, for the hard-pressed Medical Officers at Couin (and beyond at the C.C.S. in Warlincourt and Doullens), if it was case of saving life against the loss of one limb or more then the argument was brief in the extreme. Anaesthetic, the saw and knife were much in use that day.

But for some, the long and painful journey to Couin would be their last. The triage system demanded hard and swift decisions from the doctors. Would this man live with treatment, were his chances slim, were his chances zero? The greater the pressure on the medical services, the more likely some marginal case would slip down the priority order. Those that failed to get the MO's nod for instant surgery or the dressing of wounds, were carried gently to another part of the Dressing Station, a tent, set somewhat apart from the rest, where nurses hurried quietly from one recumbent figure to another. Here, the men were given

---

i Eusol stands for Edinburgh University solution of lime, a calcium hypochlorite solution.
ii A sodium hypochlorite solution devised by the French Nobel Prize winner Alexis Carrel and biochemist Henry D. Dakin which was applied to wounds every three or four hours. The application was very complicated utilising tubes and syringes.

large doses of morphine. Those that could drink might be lifted gently and a cup of water pressed to their lips. In the dim recesses of the softly lit marquee, they would be washed and made comfortable by patient, tender nurses. Those that cried out would be comforted. Those that thrashed and cursed in their agony or delirium would be restrained and sedated more heavily. But no doctors moved from bed to bed, assessing wounds and marking men for further treatment. For this was the 'moribund' ward - a place where wounded soldiers came to die[i].

For those that survived and yet still needed further intensive treatment, the route lay towards Warlincourt Halte, a stop on the main Arras-Doullens railway that lay just south of the long straight Roman between the two towns. Transport, via the ambulances of No. 3 Motor Ambulance, took these men to the two Casualty Clearing Stations, Nos. 20 (46th Division) and 43 (56th Division), that had been established between the village of Saulty and No. 8 Squadron R.F.C.'s base at La Bellevue. Here 16th Motor Ambulance Company shipped men to the waiting trains at Warlincourt Halte. Pte Clements of the 1/2nd Londons gave a graphic description of the scenes at the newly built railway platform:

> "We had tea, names were taken and we went down to the siding to wait for the train. Here I met Dan, Charlie and John. We stuck together all the way after this. As night fell we could hear the incessant roar of the shells and the sky was lit up with the flashes. The crowd at the train reminded one of the time we were at Woolwich and tried to get on a train as the Arsenal was emptying. At last, in the train we had comfortable seats but I couldn't sleep. I kept on dozing and dreaming of the attack."[14]

Edward Liveing arrived at No. 43 Casualty Clearing Station in the company of a young subaltern from the Kensingtons. He had chattily announced on the ambulance ride from Couin that he'd taken a bullet in the pit of the stomach whilst out in No Man's Land attempting the forlorn enterprise of the new communication trench. He believed he would recover and had seemed remarkably cheery on the journey, probably helped through the pain by a generous dose of morphine but, once at the C.C.S., he seemed to quieten and then, without real warning, he groaned and rolled off his stretcher. A passing doctor swiftly examined the apparently innocent little hole in his abdomen and, equally swiftly, the young man was hurried off to the operating theatre located behind a screen at the end of the room[ii]. Liveing, again left to his devices, resorted to his favoured pastime of a spot of afternoon tea with more bread and jam while he waited for his turn on the operating table.

The Rev M A Bere was a priest attached to the 43rd Casualty Clearing Station and his letters home reveal the strains of dealing with the flood of casualties that had threatened to overwhelm the medical services in the days after the attack:

"3rd July

I was sorry to send only a field card yesterday but we have been having a heavy time. I suppose a C.C.S sees the worst of it. No other link in the chain for evacuating the wounded can have to deal with quite the same thing. Saturday night and Sunday I will

---

[i] Those soldiers who died of their wounds at the M.D.S. from May to July 1916 are buried in Couin British Cemetery on the south side of the Couin to Souastre road. Couin New British Cemetery on the north side contains the graves of men killed in 1917 and 1918.

[ii] It must be presumed that the anonymous officer of the Kensingtons survived as no officer of the battalion died of his wounds at Warlencourt Halte or at a hospital further to the rear.

not attempt to describe, nor the bad wards as they are today nor the funeral this evening. How to use myself to advantage I hardly knew. I spent my time doing odds and ends, little services for the poor men – small things that are no-one's business in particular. A few prayers in the wards and seeing the MOs and nurses were fed during the night, taking them soup, coffee and sandwiches at intervals.

4th July

Today I have had some more funerals but considering the numbers we have dealt with there have been very few losses. The surgery must have been excellent. I hear the machine guns again and during dinner the Boche start dropping shells quite close. We have had only a very few patients today so I have spent some time with about half a dozen dear boys. One can really do something when there are only a few and I have written several letters on their behalf. Nobody could put on paper the whole truth of what happened here on Saturday and during Saturday night and no-one can read of it, and, if he did, without being sick.'[15]

But for Rev. Bere the fifth day after the attack was a melancholy one. He was left with the sad task of informing the next of kin of the death of their beloved sons, brothers or husbands, soon to be buried in the fast growing cemetery at Warlincourt Halte:

"6th July

I have just written four letters to three mothers and one wife on the paper you sent me."

Those not immediately treated at the two C.C.S at Warlincourt would be shipped onwards to Doullens and the four Casualty Clearing Stations waiting there. Those that survived further surgery or the onset of infection would then be loaded onto trains for transport to the Base Hospitals near one of the Channel Ports: Le Treport, Etretat and Le Havre. Some would be sent back to England to one of the many hospitals scattered across London and the South East for further treatment, rehabilitation and, for those that needed them, the fitting of prosthetics. All of these hospitals had one thing in common irrespective of their size, location and facilities. Wherever there was a military hospital, so there was a military cemetery, and their harvest of crosses was to grow fast this summer and autumn.

Eight Ambulance Trains were called into action to transport the wounded to the Channel ports over the period between 1st and 5th July. Two days before the attack the G.O.C. VII Corps, Lt. Gen. Snow, had inspected one of the trains to be used and had come away with a very favourable impression:

"I went, this morning, over a hospital train. It is really a Great Eastern train and was very well done up with kitchens, sculleries, pantries, operating rooms, etc., Three nurses on the train and any assortment of medical officers."[16]

Not all of the men carried on these trains from the Warlincourt, Frevent and Doullens C.C.S were from the Third Army. So overwhelmed were the medical systems of the Fourth Army to the south that casualties were diverted from the planned routes to the already over-burdened facilities designed to support VII Corps. In total, the trains carried 7,449 men to the three ports being used to ship men back home.

No. of train	Date and time of collection		Source of casualties	Port taken to	Totals moved
23 AT	1.7.16	1100	Warlincourt	Etretat	446
24 AT	1.7.16	1740	Warlincourt	Le Treport	599
16 AT	1.7.16	2154	Warlincourt	Le Havre	691
26 AT	2.7.16	0130	Warlincourt	Le Treport	453
4 AT	2.7.16	0630	Warlincourt/Doullens	Le Treport	364
15 AT	2.7.16	1045	Doullens	Etretat	382
17 AT	2.7.16	1115	Frevent/Doullens	Le Havre	573
12 AT	2.7.16	1310	Warlincourt/Doullens	Le Treport	403
26 AT	2.7.16	2240	Doullens	Etretat	413
4 AT	3.7.16	0600	Frevent/Doullens	Le Treport	603
23 AT	3.7.16	?	Doullens	Le Havre	361
16 AT	3.7.16	1920	Doullens	Le Havre	386
12 AT	3.7.16	1930	Doullens	Le Havre	320
4 AT	4.7.16	1100	Warlincourt/Doullens	Etretat	438
17 AT	4.7.16	1415	Frevent/Doullens	Le Havre	356
15 AT	4.7.16	1415	Doullens	Le Havre	295
16 AT	5.7.16	?	Frevent/Doullens	Rouen	366
					7449

Table 20 Ambulance Trains used: dates and routes

Given the nature of the French railway system allied to the need for reinforcements, supplies, ammunition and other supplies to be moved to the front, the journeys of these trains was often a slow and laborious process. The first train to arrive at Warlincourt Halte, 23 Ambulance Train, left its base at Doullens at 7.30 a.m. on 1st July but it took 3½ hours to arrive at Warlincourt, a distance of just 16 kilometres along the single track line towards Arras. Loading typically took anything between 1 and 2 hours so one can assume that Train No. 23 left Warlincourt at about 1 p.m. It took twelve long hours to travel the 190 kilometres to Etretat where was located No. 1 General Hospital.

Journeys to Le Havre took even longer with some trains taking 18 hours and more to reach the town with its hospitals[i] and waiting ships. Some of these journeys only served to add insult to injury to the men being carried. No. 17 Ambulance Train had started collecting men at Aubigny at 7.45 a.m. on the 2nd July. More collections were made at Frevent and then Doullens where it arrived at 2.45 p.m., five hours later. Unfortunately, another train (No. 15) was already there taking on its own load of wounded so No. 17 couldn't start to entrain its 373 passengers until 3.15 p.m., a process that took 2 hours and 20 minutes. Ten minutes later the train pulled away from Doullens station en route to Abbeville where it arrived at 8.30 p.m. Doctors on the train had, by this time, identified ten men too ill to travel further so they were put off the train and taken to one of the two hospitals in the town (either No. 2 or 5 Stationary Hospital). By the time they left Abbeville it was 9.15 p.m. and the first 112 men taken on at Aubigny had been on the train for some 13½ hours. Their journey was not yet half-way done. At Serquex the train stopped again from 3.15 a.m. (now 3rd July) to 4.30 a.m. while Coach No. 550 was removed. This coach had contained 70 casualties and now they had nowhere to sit. No 17 Ambulance Train's War Diary reports:

---

[i] No. 2 General Hospital and Nos 9 and 52 Stationary Hospitals.

"Patients, 70, had to be turned out and, as the train was already packed, the only room was standing in the corridors. Slow journey on account of the amount of traffic on the line."[17]

Just how slow is revealed by the fact that the train did not arrive at Le Havre until 1 p.m., some 29¼ hours after they left Aubigny. Even then, it took another hour and a half to evacuate the train. But No. 17 Train's problems were not at an end. As it shunted out of the harbour it collided with a handcart damaging two coaches and delaying its departure for Frevent until 9 p.m. that night. No. 17 was to repeat the journey over the 4th and 5th of July and, on their departure from Le Havre on the evening of the 5th the War Diary records:

"Much congestion and delay at Havre, the whole place being filled with stretcher cases, trains unloading and boats loading at the same time."

Such scenes were to be witnessed day by day over the coming months as the Somme battle built in savagery and futility.

Accommodation on the trains was split between lying and sitting cases with sitting normally being for those with relatively minor injuries. In these pressing circumstances, however, casualties were put where there was room, as the War Diary of the No. 26 Ambulance Train reports:

"Many of the cases taken on as sitting were of such a nature that, in a less strenuous time, they would have been lying cases…. All the cases on the train were severely wounded. Many had been lying out for several hours before being dressed. Every case required re-dressing at least once on the train, many required it more than once, these being the cases that had been operated on and had some form of drain in the wounds."[18]

Thankfully, owing to the skill and dedication of the doctors and nurses on the trains, very few men are recorded as having died in transit. One such was a man from the 1/7th Middlesex, a battalion that, ironically, had played little part in the actions of 1st July. L/Cpl. William Edward Moore[i] of 'B' Company, a resident of Enfield, succumbed to his wounds at 2.15 a.m. on the morning of the 4th July as No. 23 Ambulance Train carried its pathetic load from Doullens to Le Havre. He was laid to rest amongst the ranks of more than 3,000 of his colleagues who lie in St Sever cemetery at Rouen.

For some of the men on the trains, however, it was a place as close to heaven on earth as they ever came as Rfn. Russell of the L.R.B. soon found:

"I do not remember much about the train except for one thing. I looked up in a sort of half coma to see a Red Cross nurse looking down at me. I was never to forget this because I have always though of it as the most beautiful sight I have ever seen in my life. I never saw this girl again and I only know that her name was Miss Jones, which does not leave me much chance of ever identifying her."[19]

2nd Lt. Liveing of the Rangers was, by some estimates, closer to heaven still. He had been taken up front to the officers' carriage where he met his battalion colleague, 2nd Lt. Claude Monier Williams. Liveing had last seen him in the

---

[i] 2534 L/Cpl William Edward Moore, 1/7th Middlesex Regt., died on Tuesday 4th July 1916. Aged 20, he was the son of David and Elizabeth Ellen Moore of 102, Percival Rd., Enfield, Middx. He is buried in St Sever Cemetery, Rouen Seine-Maritime, France, grave A. 22. 18.

middle of the night as 'B' and 'A' Companies had struggled up the shell-battered communication trenches to their assembly positions.   Since then, Monier Williams had been hit in the leg and wrist and, Liveing noted, he had a somewhat flushed appearance which might have been a sign of the early sepsis that was to affect his leg wound in the coming days.   As the two officers swapped stories and, as their 'Officers''carriage filled, out of necessity, with both officers and other ranks, an M.O. appeared and, to their amazement, asked what they wanted to drink with dinner.   The choices were whiskey and soda, beer or lemonade (the first two thoroughly unsuitable for the wounded).   Sensibly Liveing stuck to the non-alcoholic drink and, as he gazed out of the window at an aeroplane being shelled by someone's 'Archie', he was taken off up the line towards the base hospitals and, for all intents and purposes, out of the war.

***

AT THE HOSPITALS ON THE COAST, beds soon ran out.   These large well-equipped hospitals had sprung up along the coast of northern France as the war progressed with the first, Nos. 1, 2 and 3 General Hospitals, being set up in Rouen and Le Havre, the port where the majority of cross-channel shipping berthed in the opening months of the year.   Steadily more and more opened and, as they did, they appeared at an increasing number of ports and coastal towns such as Etretat, Le Touquet, Etaples and inland at major railway junctions such as Abbeville.   Most of the hospitals were in purpose built huts but others, in the more fashionable resorts towns, occupied the large hotels that overlooked the beaches formerly the haunt of happy holiday makers.

No. 26 General Hospital was typical of the large 'purpose built' establishments that sprung up in the first year of the war.   Located at Etaples, it consisted of 35 wards and a hut for twelve psychiatric patients and occupied thirty huts for patients, accommodation huts for the doctors, nurses and other staff, two operating theatres and an x-ray department.   There was running water and electricity connected to the French supply.   When the hospital opened on 28th July 1915 it was staffed by 39 officers (mainly Territorials), 204 N.C.O.s and men and 73 sisters and staff nurses.   It was to facilities like these that the men were steadily evacuated in the early days of July but in numbers that few had anticipated and none wished to see.

Some hospitals moved to new sites as the need for bigger premises grew.   One such was No. 3 General Hospital which set up in the huge Trianon Hotel[i] on the clifftops overlooking Le Treport at the mouth of the Canal D'eu La Mer.   Spread over five floors (including the basement), there were beds for 500 patients with two operating theatres, an x-ray room and a pathology laboratory on the first floor.   The west wing of the top floor was given over to officers with dining and sitting rooms and the east wing provided accommodation for 53 nursing sisters. The rest of the hotel was made up mainly of surgical wards with the restaurants, billiard rooms, bar and other rooms turned into wards and a dining room seating 100 available to the 'other ranks'.   About a quarter of the beds were in medical wards with specialist small wards for cases of tuberculosis, scabies and venereal disease.   When space ran out in the building a small village of huts and marquees

---

[i] The Trianon Hotel no longer exists.   It was blown up by the Germans in World War Two to make room for coastal defences.   Just the foundations now remain.

was built within the spacious grounds and by the summer of 1916 there were 20 marquees, four barrack huts (for 100 RAMC other ranks), five 30-bed hospital huts, a 12-bed hut for mental patients, one for 18 nursing sisters and another for 10 officers. Two of the marquees were used for operations. Under the direction of Lt. Col. Septimus Fairrie, RAMC, 1st July was mainly spent in preparing the beds and surgical facilities for the anticipated surge in patients and in discharging or evacuating existing patients, with 150 officers and men being moved out by late in the day. The first Ambulance Train to arrive was No. 24 at 2 a.m. on the morning of Sunday, 2nd July and its complement of 24 sick and 274 wounded officers and men were soon unloaded and allocated a bed.

Plate 68 No. 3 General Hospital at the Trianon Hotel, Le Treport
Showing the entrance to the hotel. The cliffs and the sea are on the far side and the huts were to the left

Plate 69 Hospital and Barracks huts at No. 3 General Hospital, Le Treport
Shows the five 30 bed hospital huts and two of the barracks huts for RMAC personnel
(*Source:* National Archives file WO 95/4075)

L/Cpl. Reginald Davis of the Q.V.R.'s Battle Police had been severely wounded by the concussion from a nearby high explosive shell and by shell fragments, one of which had lodged in his skull. The fragment had caused a horrifying wound, entering just above his right eye, it had exposed his brain and opened up his sinuses. Having been unconscious for a day, he came round in the operating theatre of a Casualty Clearing Station just as he was being lifted onto the operating table. A short time later, his right eye was removed under anaesthetic and it was another 24 hours before he 'came to' on an Ambulance Train as it rumbled through the French countryside towards the base Hospitals on the Channel coast. His left hand had also been shattered by shell fragments with the top of his fourth finger having been left in the German front lines. Another finger was later amputated at a hospital at le Treport, perhaps No. 3 General. But this was not the end of his travails. The shell fragment in his head had to be removed by magnet as its proximity to the brain meant the knife was too dangerous a tool to use. Davis spent another five days in hospital before it was thought safe to send him home and even then his mother had been sent a telegram advising that his condition was critical. Incredibly though, Davis was writing postcards home within hours of the operation to remove the metal splinter in his head. The third card went to his former employer:

"4ᵗʰ July 1916

Have unfortunately fallen victim to the Hun shell in the last attack. I am not sure to what extent I am damaged. The wounds are the right eye, side of face and left hand. They hope to save my eye and I have only lost one finger on hand.

I will write again, sir, when I arrive in England. At present am near Dieppe.[20]"

The doctor who attended him in the Le Treport hospital wrote:

"It is wonderful how these fellows who have been fighting for us exhibit such a marvellous fortitude."[21]

L/Cpl. Davis survived his injuries to return to work, though with a glass eye, a metal plate in his head and a special glove on his left hand.

Henry Russell was sent to a hospital at Etaples where he was placed in a ward crammed with seriously wounded men. One by one they were wheeled into the operating theatres:

"I must pay tribute to the surgeons who carried out this difficult job. They continued day and night without rest, dealing with wounds of the most dreadful kind in all parts of the body. It must have been both exhausting and distressing for these surgeons, particularly as they knew that the number of casualties was so great that they could see no end to their work for a long time… Surgical attention to me took place probably three days after I was wounded and after a few days on the ward I was sent back to England on a hospital ship."[22]

Rfn. Hawkings of the Queen Victorias had been sent by train to Etretat, arriving sometime on 2ⁿᵈ July. There, pressure on the beds was so severe that the less seriously wounded were put on the beach, the weather being warm and dry but, later that evening, several charabancs arrived and 200 or so of these men were taken by road to Le Havre. By midnight, they were lined up on the quay as a hospital ship, the *'Egypt'*, attempted to tie up. Her pilot failed to negotiate the dockside waters in the dark and the *'Egypt*[1] caused yet another delay to the embarkation of the wounded by crashing into the pier head and stoving in her bows. Hawkings and his wounded mates were eventually embarked on the *'Lanfranc'*, arriving in Southampton on the evening of 3rd July where the returning men were greeted by cheering crowds who were, as yet, ignorant of the tragedy that was unfolding just across the Channel.

Plate 70 Pte Donald Wood, London Scottish, died 18th July 1916, buried at Netley

The *'Lanfranc'* was to be kept busy throughout the weeks ahead. In June she had made four trips to and from Le Havre and back to its main port of Southampton. The last of these had started on 29th June and a total of 26 officers and 331 other ranks started to be disembarked at 9 a.m. on the morning of 1st July at the quay at Southampton ready for the short train journey to Netley on the eastern shore of Southampton Water where lay the Royal Victoria, or Netley, Hospital. With accommodation for some 2,000 patients, some in the impressive red and white brick building started in 1856 and others in the Red Cross hutted accommodation to the rear, this would be the first port of call for many men evacuated from France. From there they would be entrained for distribution to the numerous military hospitals the length and breadth of Great Britain. Not every man would survive to be sent far away from Netley, however, and, by the end of the war, some 636 men who died of their wounds or of disease were buried in the cemetery attached to the hospital. One of the men to be so buried was 22-year old Pte Donald Campbell Wood of the London Scottish. He had been transferred to the University War Hospital in Southampton[ii] and lingered on for just over two weeks before he passed away. He was brought back to Netley to be buried amongst his comrades on the 18th July[iii].

i HMHS *Egypt* was built in 1897 for the P&O Line by Caird & Co. of Greenock. On 20th May 1922, her unlucky life came to an abrupt end. Stopped in thick fog off Ushant she was rammed by the French ship *'Seine'*, sinking in 20 minutes with the loss of 15 passengers and 71 crew. Although six times larger than the *'Seine'*, the smaller ship had a reinforced ice-breaker bow which sliced through the *'Egypt'* and sent her to the bottom. Along with her went £1 million of gold (c. £40 million at current prices) which was eventually salvaged in 1933

ii The University War Hospital, Southampton occupied new buildings in Greenfield Lane which had just been opened (on 20th June 1914) as the new premises of the Hartley Instution which became a University College in 1902. It was renames Hartley University College in 1919 and then Southampton University College. It gained its Royal Charter in 1952.

iii 5182 Pte Donald Campbell Wood, 1/14th London Regt. (London Scottish) was born on 21st September 1894, the son of Walter Thomas and Mary Wood, of 38, Buckleigh Rd., Streatham, London. He was educated at Dulwich College from where he joined the Admiralty having passed theCivil Service Second Division Examination. He

Plate 71 Royal Victoria Hospital, Netley

The enormous Royal Victoria Hospital seen from the end of the special 170 yard pier built for the unloading of patients in 1865. Water was insufficiently deep for the hospital ships of 1914-18, however, and patients were unloaded at Southampton Docks and taken by train on a special railway spur which ran into the hospital grounds. The buildings were badly damaged by fire in 1963 and demolished in 1966 except for the chapel. [*Source:* Sue Light]

By 10.45 a.m. the wounded had all been removed and, with orders to return to Le Havre having arriving at midnight, the beds were changed, the ship cleaned and disinfected – all at the highest speed. At 7.00 a.m. on the morning of Sunday, 2nd July the *'Lanfranc'* cast off and sailed down to Cowes Roads where they waited for their escort and, at 8.10 a.m. they set off the Channel towards the mouth of the Seine. After a 12½ hour crossing they made fast alongside the quay in Le Havre at 9.40 p.m. and were ready to take on patients 50 minutes later. It took nearly six hours to load the 56 officers and 673 other ranks, one of whom was Rfn Hawkings, who were waiting patiently on the dockside. Barely a third of the wounded, 225 patients, were placed in the available cots and the rest of the men had to find a berth wherever one could be found. With time being of the essence, just fifteen minutes after embarkation was complete, the *'Lanfranc'* was casting off and heading out through the mine-cleared channel towards the Isle of Wight. This time the crossing was swifter, 8½ hours but, although they anchored off Netley at 1.00 p.m. on the Monday, it was not until 6.30 p.m. that they finished tying up and disembarkation could start. This task was completed at 9.00 p.m. and, by midnight, the ship was heading out to sea again to pick up another cargo of wounded. This would now be the ship's routine, with trips to and from Le Havre taking place every three days throughout July and beyond as the Somme battle wore on[i].

enlisted in the London Scottish in September 1915 and went to France in January 1916. He died from wounds on 18th July 1916 and was buried in Netley Military Cemetery, grave C.E. 1816.

i *HMHS Lanfranc* was built by the Caledon Shipbuilding & Engineering Co., Dundee for the Booth Line in 1906. Displacing 6287 tons it was commissioned as a hospital ship on 6th November 1915 with accommodation for 403 wounded. It was sunk without warning by the German submarine the UB-40 on the 17th April 1917 when bound for Southampton with the loss of 17 British and 17 German patients. On the same day *HMHS Donegal* was also sunk by the same submarine, again without warning, with the loss of 29 wounded and 12 crew. The Hospital Ships *Asturias* and *Gloucester Castle* had also been sunk without warning in March 1917 as a result of an accusation by the German Government that British troops and supplies were being transported by hospital ships. The British

With severe pressure on the evacuation routes, other men were kept at hospitals in France pending their evacuation. 3694 L/Cpl. Sidney Appleyard, another Queen Vic, had arrived by train at Le Treport at 2 a.m. on the morning of 3rd July. His diary entry for the next day described the scene:

"Convoys of wounded still arrive and every bed in the hospital is occupied – even temporary beds have been erected on the floor. Some of the patients, all of them walking cases, have already gone to embark for Blighty."[23]

The following days were spent waiting for news of evacuation and in treating his arm and leg wounds:

"5th July

We were awakened at 4 a.m. for washing and bed making. Breakfast 7 a.m.... My wound is getting on quite well... and the nurses are extracting all kinds of refuse from it such as pieces of khaki and lead water bottle. My arm is painful and inflamed from inoculation.

6th July

Another day spent in wondering whether I shall get to Blighty or not... If I don't get home it will break my heart for after 14 months of continuous trench warfare one is inclined to get fed up."

7th July

Everything as yesterday and if this lasts much longer I shall feel inclined to break bounds. My leg has been very painful during the night but Sister says it is getting nice and clean. I am off to Blighty at 4.30 p.m."

Having got his wish, Appleyard departed at 7.30 p.m. for Le Havre arriving at 11 a.m. after a veritable crawl along the French railway system. By mid-day on the 8th July, he was happily ensconced on the hospital ship *'Salta'* and was embarked on a gentle Channel crossing to Southampton on a millpond-like sea.

Of the four ports used, Le Havre saw the largest number of medical evacuations in the days after 1st July (see Table 21 for details). Over half of the casualties that were sent back to 'Blighty' in the immediate aftermath of the opening of the Somme battle went through the port furthest from the front with Southampton being their destination. As this sorry procession progressed from hospital to port and then to sea, the same number again, another 24,000 men, were being evacuated to the Base and General Hospitals in France from the Casualty Clearing Stations cluttered behind the front lines.

Date	Boulogne	Rouen	Le Havre	Calais	Totals
1st July	367	660	0	209	1236
2nd July	761	666	957	219	2603
3rd July	898	377	3,732	602	5,609
4th July	2,745	740	4,119	745	8,349
5th July	2,409	0	4,000	602	7,011
Totals	7,180	2443	12,808	2377	24,808

Table 21 Ports from which casualties evacuated by ship 1st-5th July 1916

subsequently removed the Red Cross markings from such ships. Several other hospital ships, such as *HMHS Salta* lost on 10th April 1917, were sunk by mines laid in and around the channel into the mouth of the Seine.

From Southampton, the wounded were distributed far and wide as the pressure for beds became acute. 2361 Sgt. Gilbert Telfer of 'A' Company, Queen Victoria's Rifles, who had spent ten hours lying out in No Man's Land with bullet wounds to the thigh and back, was evacuated from a Canadian Hospital at Le Treport all the way to the South National Red Cross Hospital in Glasgow. 'A' Company's C.S.M. and about thirty others were sent to Rugby and L/Cpl. Packer, who had so splendidly rushed across the open to bomb Fell trench, ended up in Torquay, a somewhat more attractive destination than his mates'. Appleyard ended up at the Croesnewydd Military Hospital in Wrexham and on the 9ᵗʰ July he was happily enjoying his best dinner since he left London in early 1915. As he finished off his roast beef, potatoes and peas and contemplated his rice pudding the pain of a Blighty wound must have seemed very worthwhile.

Rfn. Henry Russell's painful journey ended in a rather more significant event than just a decent dinner. After landing at Southampton, he was sent off to recuperate at the Bevan Military Nursing Hospital at Sandgate near Folkestone. After a few days, the cause of an alarming rise in temperature was traced by the doctor to a mouldy piece of uniform that been lodged in his scrotum by the shell explosion that had nearly emasculated him. Once removed his general health improved slowly, though an open wound in his shattered arm took months to heal. He was then transferred to a small 42-bed VAD hospital in the Vestry Hall in Cranbrook, a Kentish village about twenty miles west of Folkestone. This was run by a Miss D P Adams who, in short order at the beginning of the war, had stepped in to set up two hospitals in the village: one in the Vestry Hall, part of the Town Hall, and another in the Drill Hall of the local Territorials. So struck was Russell by her energy, efficiency and, no doubt, various characteristics of a more uniquely feminine nature that he married Miss Adams soon after the end of the war and they lived happily together for some thirty five years.[i]

***

BACK AT HEBUTERNE the work of the doctors, orderlies and stretcher bearers went on unceasingly until the evening of 2ⁿᵈ July when, at last, they were granted an opportunity for rest from tending to the wounded. Pte. Chase of the 1/2ⁿᵈ London Field Ambulance was back at work having survived a very near miss only hours before:

"In the evening we were sent to our billets from about 7.30 till 10. At 9.30 when I was sleeping a shell came through our billet and Harvey was hit. I woke at the sound of a frightful crash and clouds of smoke coming down the steps of the cellar. I though we were done for. Two of them went upstairs and brought Harvey down, dressed him and carried him round. At 10.30 I heard bearers were wanted and reported to A.D.S. Worked there for an hour or so taking cases down the road to the Elephant dugout and taking messages etc., and then tried to get some sleep.

2ⁿᵈ July

Hauled out about 2 am to go up to the trenches again with a 2/2ⁿᵈ Corporal and went to Wurzel Street dugout to clear cases. Apparently we were seen for the Boche machine guns started on us like hell. However we

---

[i] Henry Russell records that his wife was awarded the Associate Royal Red Cross Medal for her work in the war.

cleared several and then went off at 5. I slept until 9.30 and then started again. Worked till nearly three at the Elephant and then went back to the A.D.S."[24]

The Field Ambulances had suffered casualties too. Two men had died early on the 1st July as they did their work amongst the wounded and dying and Pte Chase recalled how both men were buried in Hebuterne Cemetery on Monday 3rd July:

"Slept till 12 noon and then went up to the ADS. In the afternoon we dug two graves for Hocking[i], whose body had been found, and for Giles[ii], the 2nds man, and they were buried, about 30 of our fellows were present and an officer and the service was as decently conducted as possible."

Another RAMC man, Pte William Tanter[iii], succumbed to his wounds at Warlincourt Halte the next day and five more were wounded but survived. But, even now, their work was not done. Still lying out in No Man's Land were hundreds of dead and injured men and as the sun rose on the morning of 2nd July their shrieks, groans and imprecations still filled the air, replacing the thump of artillery and the crack and whine of machine bullets. It is an encouraging statement about the innate humanity of men who only a few hours before had fought and killed with all the strength at their disposal that a truce was organised during the afternoon at the suggestion of the Germans. For an hour the medical staff and stretcher bearers of both sides moved across No Man's Land bringing aid to those still alive. The scene that greeted them was shocking even to men used to dealing with the badly injured on a daily basis:

"The battlefield over which our battalions had so recently charged was dotted with prone figures, many of them beyond assistance. Near the enemy trenches the fighting had been more terrible and grey figures mingled with brown. Over all of this the sun burned; the rough shell broken terrain was bright with grasses and summer flowers; the troubleless sky seemed to deny the sad evidence of the battle. There was little time, however, for thoughts such as these, every ounce of energy being needed to help the men who were not beyond all aid. The German bearers were equally busy, carrying away all the wounded they could get into the greater safety of their trenches. It was difficult to be enemies with such work on. In one particular case some Germans called over a squad of our men to take away two wounded infantrymen who had been badly hit near the enemy trenches. These Germans had given drink to the helpless men and done what they could to make them easy."[25]

Unhappily for the men not yet rescued, this joint mission of mercy was brought to an untimely halt by the firing of the British artillery. And yet, the

---

[i] 678 Pte Leslie Harold Hocking, 2/1st London Field Ambulance, died on 1st July 1916. Aged 19, he was the son of William John Hocking, C.V.O., C.B.E., and Agnes Hocking of Bristol House, Danbury, Essex. Born in London. He is buried in Hebuterne Military Cemetery, grave II. N. 1

[ii] 722 Pte Alex Giles, 2/2nd London Field Ambulance, died on 1st July 1916. Aged 19 he was the son of David and J. M. Giles of 3, Canning Rd., Highbury, London. He is buried next to Pte Hocking in Hebuterne Military Cemetery, II. N. 2

[iii] 408 Pte William Laurence Tanter, 2/1st London Field Ambulance, died of his wounds on 2nd July 1916. Aged 25, he was the son of William H. and Bertha L. Tanter of 66, Malvern Rd., Leytonstone, London. He is buried in Warlincourt Halte British Cemetery, Saulty, II. D. 6. His younger brother was wounded but survived.

Germans still honoured their truce, giving the men in No Man's Land ten minutes to return to the trenches before hostilities resumed as Pte Chase later testified:

"... was immediately sent up Yiddish Street as there was supposed to be a two hour armistice on. Several of the boys went right up and over the top and spoke to the Germans who behaved very well and bandaged up our fellows. Unfortunately I missed that through staying at Yiddish Street to evacuate from there by the order of a 2/2nd Sergeant. In a quarter of an hour the order came through to pack up. Our artillery had not stopped firing and this apparently annoyed the Boche who gave us about ten minutes to clear. About this time I met Hugh's pal Jack Hawken, one of only three LRB bombers left. After this things quietened down though they started to village in the evening. Turned in at 11 pm for the first proper night since Wednesday."[26]

It is not clear if the firing was as a result of a deliberate choice by someone at Corps or Army level to prevent an extended armistice or whether it sprang from an unfortunate break down in communications at some level or other. Whatever the cause, it left men to suffer, some for days on end, and others to die alone and untended, men who might have otherwise survived. Over the next few days a trickle of men crawled in from the shattered and bloody landscape of No Man's Land - men such as 23 year old 2nd Lt. Edward Thomas of the London Rifle Brigade who had been shot in the right arm and head and blinded. For three days he had survived in the horrors of No Man's Land before he was eventually found crawling about trying to find his way home. He survived but never regained his sight.

For some of the wounded the rescuers wore Field Grey. Pte. Frederick Glanville had joined the Queen's Westminster Rifles from the newly disbanded 2/2nd London Regiment in May. He had formed part of the 2nd wave of the attack and as they had arrived near the German wire it was clear that the men in front were struggling to get through the gaps in the wire. Whilst they waited their officer had ordered them to lie down some 20 to 30 yards from the wire. As he lay in the firing position Glanville was struck by a machine gun bullet in the top of his left leg. The bullet exited his left and leg and smashed into his other one, coming out half way down right leg. In spite of the severe pain, Glanville had managed to fire four or five fruitless shots at a machine gunner on the German parapet but then shock and loss of blood took their toll and he took no further part in the battle and he lay out amongst the wounded, dying and dead for the rest of the day and throughout the night. On the Sunday morning during the truce an officer came across him and called for stretcher bearers but no-one came and Glanville, unable to move was again left out in No Mans Land. Injury was now added to the insult of being abandoned and, as the artillery resumed remote hostilities, he was hit by three bits of shrapnel in his chest. Concerned that another wound might be in the stomach and, therefore, fatal, Glanville painfully managed to roll over onto his front. His efforts were vindicated when he was almost immediately hit again in the hip by another piece of shrapnel. Lying face down near the German lines Glanville now faced another day and night out in No Man's Land. On Monday, at about midday, a couple of Germans crept out to search amongst the bodies and debris. Glanville had managed to hold onto both his rifle and one Mills bomb and now, worried lest the enemy might regard him as a threat, he hastily threw them both away so that he was unarmed. But his luck had changed and the Germans dragged him in and laid on the fire step. From there he was taken first to a German Field Hospital and then, on 17th July, he arrived at the Hospital in St Quentin. From there he was shipped onwards to the Prisoner of War Hospital at Ohrdruf and finally, once recovered, onto the camp at Langensalza where he spent the rest of his war.

4189 Rfn. Edward Hall[i] of the Queen Victoria's had nearly been caught in the front line by a party of German bombers and scrambled over the parapet in an effort to escape. Wounded in the hip as he went, he was forced to lie out in No Man's Land waiting for help. Like Glanville it was on the Monday that a German patrol found him and brought him in but not before, in an uncanny replica of Glanville's troubles, he was hit by shrapnel right leg and the right elbow. He was given food and drink and his wounds were dressed before he was shipped off to a German hospital for an operation to remove the bullet and the shrapnel. By September he was writing home from the Dülmen Camp, though left handed, to his mother in Lambeth giving the cheerful information that his wounds were healing well.[27]

One man out in No Man's Land, whose selfless act rightly earned him the DCM, was 2855 Rfn. Dominic Hegarty of 'C' Company, The Rangers. Although seriously wounded, he stayed with some other men, more seriously wounded still. By day they sheltered in a shell hole, by night Hegarty crawled about the charnel house that was No Man's Land fetching food and water from the haversacks and water bottles of the dead. For three nights Hegarty kept his friends and himself alive until, on the fourth, he determined that rescue was the only answer. Weak through loss of blood, he crawled into the British lines but, before receiving treatment himself, he led a rescue party out into No Man's Land to find and bring in his wounded chums. His much merited award for his devotion to his mates was posted in the London Gazette on 22nd September 1916[ii].

But the most extraordinary story of survival must be that of Pte A Matthews of the 1/4th London Regiment who survived an astonishing thirteen days wounded and embedded in mud before being rescued. Matthews had gone over with one of the waves supporting The Rangers when his Company commander ordered him and a Pte Cabel to accompany some German prisoners back across No Man's Land. Cabel led the way while Matthews herded the PoWs from the rear with his bayonet. He had not gone fifty yards when a bullet smashed through his water bottle and into his right thigh and, while Cabel and the prisoners hurried across the shell-swept No Man's Land unawares, Matthews was left behind in a bloody heap. An officer in a nearby trench heard his cries and dragged him into its shelter, he then applied his field dressing and gave him a drink but then left him to move forward with a small group of men waiting with him. Matthews was now stranded. It would later be found that he was suffering from a compound fracture of the femur, a wound that was often fatal as a result of shock and haemorrhage, but the severity of the injury meant Matthews found

---

i 4189 Rfn. Edward Stanley Hall, No. 7 Platoon, B Company, 1/9th London Regt. (Queen Victoria's Rifles) was wounded on Saturday, 1st July 1916. He was the son of Mrs Hall, 161, Mitre Street, Waterloo Road, Lambeth. He was exchanged in December 1916 and evacuated to the Queen Alexandra Hospital, Millbank.

ii 2855 Rfn. Dominic Philip Biddalph Hegarty was later also awarded the Russian Cross of St George, 4th Class (London Gazette 15th February 1917).

it almost impossible to move. For hours he was left to his own devices, sheltered from the storm of high explosive crashing down around him by the trench but also hidden from the view of any potential rescuers. Later in the day, a Company runner passed him by, generously taking the time to leave him his water bottle, an act one hopes did not cost the man dear, but otherwise Matthews was on his own and unable to move. At length night drew in and his was one of just hundreds of voices crying out for help – but his voice was not heard.

On Sunday morning Matthews investigated what resources he had available to him: a few cigarettes, which he proceeded to smoke, the water bottle left by the charitable runner and his haversack containing his iron ration – five hard biscuits and a 12 ounce tin of bully beef. These he started to consume sparingly as there was no certainty that his discovery was imminent or even likely. Every now and then he roused himself to shout but he attracted no attention and now night came and then day and then night again. On the fourth night he was roused by the sounds of men approaching and he shouted out for help. At last some faces peered over the edge of the trench, one of whom he recognised as a member of his own Company, a man called Wrightson, and he explained his plight. But, sympathetic though this group of Fusiliers, Rangers, Westminsters and Victorias were, these men were unable to help directly. They were all wounded themselves and had also been lying out in No Man's Land trying to find their way home. They did, however, collect iron rations and as much water as possible from dead men nearby to help keep body and soul together before setting off for the British lines with promises to send a rescue party as soon as they were able. An hour or two passed when Matthews heard more footsteps. Hopes of an end to his suffering were briefly raised and then dashed when it proved to be the same group of men, still completely lost in the shambles of No Man's Land. They now set off in another direction, again assuring him that a stretcher party would be sent out just as soon as they reached safety but, astonishingly, twenty four hours later they were back, still lost and in an increasingly desperate state. Pte Wrightson, wounded in the leg and hand, was reduced to crawling on his hands and knees but still the party persisted in their efforts to find their lines, but not before they collected some more food and water to keep Matthews fed and watered.

On the morning of the sixth day Matthews awoke from a deep and exhausted sleep to discover that a nearby shell burst had covered him with earth and that he was now partly buried. Having cleared some of the soil away he found, to his dismay, that his biscuits were now buried and that a shell fragment had pierced his water bottle, emptying it. Completely unable to move and with neither food nor drink Matthews' future was extremely bleak and, for the next two days, he lay trapped. Then, on the ninth day it rained. Some drinking water was eagerly caught in his upturned helmet and, when that ran out, he lapped like an animal from nearby puddles. With lips parched and throat dry even shouting for help became an agony and Matthews slipped into a delirium in which his mates came to rescue him only for the full horror of his position to return when he came briefly to his senses. A clutch of letters from home were read and re-read in an effort to retain some sort of sanity but hope and life was nearly gone when Matthews was aware of the sound of feet nearby and a desperate croak for help faintly passed his lips.

It was now the night of the 13th/14th July and 'B' Company of the London Scottish were holding the old front line trench between Wood Street and Whiskey Street that had been in use before the end of May. It lay some three hundred yards behind the trenches dug over those three nights between the 25th and 27th May and which had since been abandoned. Towards midnight, 2nd Lt. R White, accompanied by Sgt. S E Mackenzie, Cpl. Scott and L/Cpl. Nimmo set off from the end of Woman Street towards the advanced front lines in order to investigate the activities of German patrols in No Man's Land. The night was pitch black though illuminated from time to time by the shimmering white glare of Verey lights. German machine guns were playing on the trenches and so, when the patrol approached the old front line, they took to the shallow shelter of the old Boyau de Service to avoid the scything bullets. White had just clambered from the bottom of one shell hole to the top of another and slithered down to its muddy bottom when a pair of filthy, bony hands grabbed his kilt and a ghostly voice whispered, "Scottish".

Once White had recovered from the shock of this apparition, he quickly questioned Matthews who was able to give his name, rank and number as well as a muttered, " wounded 1st July". Matthews was understandably desperate to be taken in straight away but White had a patrol to complete and, leaving him some chocolate and water, promised to return with a team of stretcher bearers as soon as possible. White and his men then completed their work and returned to Company headquarters where the new O.C. of 'B' Company, Capt. Ellis, was informed of the situation. A new patrol, again led by 2nd Lt. White but this time accompanied by Sgt. S E Smith, Sgt. Fox and Cpl. Peachey[i], set out to find Matthews and put an end his misery. This time the patrol carried no weapons, their only burdens being two shovels and a stretcher. Following the same route they soon found the young Private and set to the task of freeing him. It was no easy matter. The earth around him was now solid from his waist down and White and the men had to dig him out in one complete block of earth. He was then rolled onto the stretcher and the job of carrying him in began. In the meantime, more than just some German machine gunners had got restless and shells were now dropping on either side of No Man's Land and it was decided to bring him in through 'D' Company's wire. Taken to the Company Sergeant Major's dugout he was fed, cleaned and his wound dressed and then, later in the morning, he began the long journey back to England and to health.

Amazingly, the wound, though serious, had not turned septic and, after two weeks in a Base Hospital, he was evacuated to England where he spent a year recovering, some of which was spent in Manchester. Remarkably, while he was there, Cpl. Scott, who had been a member of the first patrol which found him, having been wounded himself was evacuated to the same hospital and he and Matthews resumed their acquaintance. In September 1917 Matthews was sent to the London Command Depot at Sleaford, sporting a right leg three inches shorter than the left. He would soon be fitted with a surgical boot and, some time later, was discharged from the Army as medically unfit for further service.

---

i 511386 Sgt. Archie Randolph Peachey, M.M., 1/14th London Regt. (London Scottish), was killed on 11th May 1917. Aged 28, he was the brother of Mrs. Gertrude Pressland, of The Croft, London Rd., Hampton-on-Thames, Middx. He is buried in Bailleul Road East Cemetery, St. Laurent-Blangy, grave III. E. 31.

But Matthews' story was unique and many men, too injured to move or too far away from help to attract attention, died where they lay out in the wasteland between the two front lines or were killed by subsequent British and German bombardments. How many might have been saved it is impossible to say. John Keegan, in his book *'The Face of Battle'* makes a highly educated guess. According to his calculations perhaps as many as a third of those eventually recorded as killed or missing might have survived had medical aid been swiftly available to them. On either flank of the Gommecourt salient it means that over 900 men might have been saved. Along the whole length of the front line on 1st July 1916, the figure would have been close to 7,000.[28]

One such tragic case was 4302 Rfn. Jonathan Brandon of The Rangers. Brandon had been badly wounded in the ankle and, unable to move, had rolled into a shell hole and there waited for help. Nearby, another wounded Ranger, 4436 Rfn. George Hall, was lying in another shell hole suffering from a wound to the arm. There they stayed all day Sunday unaware of one another's presence until, on Sunday night, Hall heard someone groaning nearby and, under cover of darkness, he decided to search for the wounded man. Hall soon found Brandon, whom he recognised as they were both members of No. 6 Platoon. He was helpless and unable to move, and after giving him some water, Hall stayed in the shell hole with him. The water seemed to perk Brandon up and, after a while, they agreed that Hall should go and look for help but a sudden strafe from some guns put a stop to that and they both pressed themselves into the earth and hoped not to be hit by shrapnel. When the guns were quiet Hall set off across No Man's Land and through the battered wreckage of the recently dug trenches until he stumbled into a position being held by men from the 1/3rd London Regt. Having reported Brandon's condition and given a vague idea as to where he might be found, Hall was hurried off to the A.D.S. for treatment. A search party was sent out but it was all to easy to get lost amidst the wreckage of the new trenches and No Man's Land and finding one wounded soldier lying in a shell hole at night was like finding the proverbial needle in a hay stack. Tragically Jonathan Brandon was not found that night. Indeed, he was never found. His only memorial is the name inscribed on the Portland stone of Face C on Pier 9 of the Thiepval Memorial to the Missing of the Somme.

***

While the likes of Glanville, Hegarty and Matthews hung on grimly out in No Man's Land for the men of 2/3rd London Field Ambulance there was still work to be done. At night, volunteers were called for and sent out into No Man's Land to bring in any not yet dead and to bury the remains of those that were. On successive nights thirty men of 'B' and 'C' Sections led by a Cpl. Challis undertook this dangerous and unpleasant task.

"'B' Section were called out one night and put on parade, and volunteers asked to go out and collect the dead (no married men allowed). We went to the front line through trenches up to our waists in water – then over the top into No Man's Land. It took us some time to get the bodies out of the mud.

Next night 'C' Section were asked to volunteer for the same duty of bringing in the bodies, after which they buried them in the front line trenches – it was a horrible job. The men all returned very wet and muddy but very proud of having carried out their task."[29]

In spite of these efforts, many of the dead remained lying out in No Man's Land for months to come. Although no more serious fighting was to take place around the Gommecourt salient, it was still not possible to recover their bodies and, as the battle to the south ground on through the summer and autumn, here the unrecovered bodies of the dead rotted until all that was left were their bones and a litter of equipment. In early 1917 the Germans withdrew as part of a complete realignment of their front and it was at long last possible for the battlefield to be cleared and for the dead to be buried in one of four battlefield cemeteries. But, even after these remains had been collected and given their last rites, hundreds of the missing could not be found. The extraordinary concentration of German artillery fire that had swept No Man's Land for some fourteen hours on 1ˢᵗ July 1916 took with it the mortal remains of many men, their bodies obliterated and their names later to be recorded on the great Memorial to the Missing on the hill at Thiepval. Capt. Sparks of the London Scottish, who had led the defence of the Farmer-Farmyard strongpoint with such remarkable bravery, visited the battlefield again in 1917. He later wrote in his diary:

"I had never been able to appreciate the large number of attempts which had been made to get through bombs and ammunition to us, but I appreciated something of what had been done during this visit, finding a number of boxes of bombs still in No Man's Land with the remains of our fellows who had tried to bring them over."[30]

***

Over the weeks, months and years ahead the visible scars of battle would heal. They might yet be painful and damaging to the health of the man involved but they were understandable wounds with an attributable cause and effect. But for many tens of thousands of men their wounds were invisible, their causes still broadly unknown to medical science and their symptoms and side effects a distressing mystery to sufferer and relatives alike. It would not be for another fifty years and more that research into the psychological effects of battle on US troops returning from Vietnam would eventually coin the phrase 'Post Traumatic Stress Disorder' (PTSD) and with it came official recognition that the extraordinary stresses of battle could have long term effects on the mental health of the men involved. In World War One, however, the terms used to describe the deterioration in the psychogical condition of officers and men after battle were 'shell shock' and 'neurasthenia'.

Neurasthenia was a word first used by an American doctor, George Miller Beard, in 1869 and was used to describe a mental state created by the increasing pressures of urban living. Amongst its symptoms were: fatigue, anxiety, headache, impotence, neuralgia and depression. When officers and men started to report to their Medical Officers in increasing numbers with these symptoms, and others such as tremors, knee shakes, temporary blindness, nightmares and insomnia, then it was natural for the doctors to whom these cases were referred to group them conveniently under the heading of 'neurasthenia'. Broadly, officers were treated more sympathetically than other ranks when these conditions were reported in part, perhaps, because Beard and others had associated the condition with the middle and upper classes when faced with the pressures of business and of being in authority. Siegfried Sassoon and Wilfred Owen are probably the Great War's most famous 'neurasthenics' and they were just two of 1,700 or so officers sent to the Craiglockhart War Hospital in Edinburgh, every one of whom was diagnosed with neurasthenia.

In 1915 the British Army declared that there was a distinct difference between officers and men suffering from these various symptoms. The paperwork of those affected by a shell explosion were labelled with a 'W' for wound but those for which there was no obvious cause were marked with an 'S' for sick. This latter categorisation could lead, especially in the case of other ranks, to the suspicion that these men were, at best, malingerers and, at worst, cowards. Cowardice in the face of the enemy was a capital offence and many young men suffering from what would now be diagnosed as severe PTSD were court-martialled and shot in consequence[i]. Officers were more sympathetically treated and, once home, were subject to regular medical boards at which their cocktail of symptoms were reviewed. Anecdotally, if the evidence from the officers of the 56th Division is indicative, those who had actually been blown up faced greater difficulties in returning to the front than those suffering from the cumulative stresses of active service. Obviously, this may well have been because actual neurological damage had been caused to the officer concerned to which could be added the psychological damage of the event itself.

It is possible to identify twelve officers involved on 1st July 1916 who were sent home as a result of 'shell shock', although some suffered clear physical wounds as well. Of these twelve, seven did not return to active service on a war front. The seven officers concerned were:

Lt. R L Herring, Adjutant of the 1/4th Londons. He had been buried by a shell but had carried at the front until 18th September when he was sent to hospital suffering from stress, memory loss and headaches.

2nd Lt. H G Hicklenton, 1/4th Londons. Twelve months later his Medical Board was still reporting severe symptoms which included the loss of all sensation in his legs.

2nd Lt. J P Clark, Kensingtons, was blown up and buried by two shells, suffering from concussion and severe shell shock.

2nd Lt. H W Hankins, Kensingtons, started to feel "stiff and funny" thirty minutes after a shell burst near to him. Seven months later he was still suffering from memory problems, sleeplessness and back pain.

2nd Lt. R F Lydall. L.R.B., suffered a shrapnel wound to the back but was also seriously affected by shell shock such that, when he went to the cinema to see the recently released film of the Battle of the Somme, it brought about a return of all of his previous sysmptoms.

2nd Lt. C C Iveson, Q.W.R.s, was knocked unconscious and buried by a shell explosion. His symptoms included: headaches, numb legs, involuntary knee jerks, nightmares and tremors.

Capt. E V Noel, 1/3rd Londons, was evacuated suffering from shell shock. He had previously been shot and was reported as behaving badly during the attack

---

[i] 306 British soldiers were shot in WW1 for cowardice. In the light of modern advances in psychology and mental health the UK Government gave them all a posthumous conditional pardon on 7th November 2006.

on 1st July. He did not return to the battalion having disciplinary problems in the UK.

Of the officers that did return to duty three died in violent circumstances:

2nd Lt. B F L Yeoman, 1/4th Londons, had been buried by a shell explosion and knocked unconscious. His symptoms were so acute that he lapsed into semi-consciousness for several weeks afterwards and suffered pain in his legs, back and arms. He was declared fit for light duties in February 1917 but was killed in a flying accident in May 1918.

2nd Lt. S L Vincent, Kensingtons, suffered from shell shock and shrapnel wounds to the right foot and left arm. He returned to France in May 1917 and later served in Salonika. He was murdered in strange circumstances by the IRA in 1921 at Fermoy near Cork.

2nd Lt. H Luscombe, Q.W.R.s, was knocked unconscious by a shell explosion and suffered from tremors, insomnia and an inability to concentrate. He was declared fit for General Service on 10th November 1916 and was killed in action on 11th April 1917.

2nd Lt. A E Wiggs, 1/2nd Londons, was knocked unconscious by a shell explosion, his symptoms including headaches, insomnia, nightmares, tremors of the hands and knees and an inability to concentrate. He had disciplinary problems in England and, although he returned to the front with the 2/2nd Londons, he later joined, and was then rejected by, the RAF.

2nd Lt. A J de Vall was evacuated suffering from shell shock. He was still suffering from nervousness and insomnia in December when a training accident with some explosives at Fovant caused a relapse. He returned to the battalion in 1918 to be wounded again in August.

It is interesting to note that two of these officers, Noel and Wiggs, went on to have disciplinary issues after suffering from shell shock. It is, of course, quite possible that these problems would have occurred whatever the circumstances. To be fair to these two officers, and to others who had similar lapses, one must mention that the combination of potential neurological damage caused by the shell explosions and the psychological damage of the event may well have caused personality changes which then led to these disciplinary and, sometimes, serious legal problems. There are, for example, several cases of shell shocked officers from the 46th Division who went on to have more or less serious disciplinary or legal problems subsequent to their evacuation home, for example:

2nd Lt. Alexander Michie, 1/8th Sherwood Foresters, who was reprimanded and then court martialled for drunkenness. His sentence of dismissal from the service was commuted to forfeiture of rank due to his mental condition.

2nd Lt. George Collis, 1/6th North Staffordshires, who was later sent to Wormwood Scrubs for obtaining money under false pretences.

2nd Lt. Douglas Robinson, 1/6th South Staffordshires, who was later dismissed from the RAF for using a forged document and impersonating another officer. A plea of insanity supported by his M.O. was rejected by the Court. He had been left 'deaf and dumb' by a shell explosion on 1st July 1916.

These cases are clearly no more than anecdotal evidence of the long term psychological effects of shell shock and do no more than hint at the possibility that some of these men might have undergone such severe personality changes that, as a result, their behaviour changed out of all recognition. Recent research, since the acceptance of PTSD to the *Diagnostic and Statistical Manual of Mental Disorders'* in 1980, has shown how such traumatic events affect emotion, cognition, social interaction and behaviour. A paper by Daniel Neller and John Fabian for the Centre for Crime and Justice Studies set out how these factors can be influenced[31]. The impact on emotion includes: anxiety, depression, hostility, anger management difficulties and callousness. The effects on cognition span: pessimism, attention and concentration difficulties, problems with verbal skills and 'dysfunctional thought patterns'. The results can be severe in terms of social interaction: distrust, detachment, social rejection and mis-reading others' intentions. Lastly, the effects on behaviour tend towards engaging in 'high risk' actions such as heavy drinking, drug taking and anti-social/criminal acts with an increased tendency towards rash and impulsive conduct and the possibility of violence. In mitigation of the officers named above it can be seen that various of these conditions manifested themselves in their 'post traumatic' behaviour. They would not have been alone. There were, undoubtedly, tens of thousands more cases such as these, mainly undetected, undiagnosed and untreated, which placed a curse on these men and their families for years to come – their 'invisible wounds' a crippling hidden legacy of the Great War.

ENDNOTES:
[1] Now Hebuterne Military Cemetery.
[2] Atkinson, Arthur 2/3rd City of London Field Ambulance 1914-18 London soldiers – unarmed comrades.
[3] Chase, Pte H L, 1/2nd London Field Ambulance, Papers, IWM.
[4] Hodder, Williams J E (editor), One Young Man
[5] Gray, Lt. Col. H M W, The Early Treatment of War Wounds.
[6] Liveing Edward G, Attack
[7] Ibid.
[8] Bickersteth, John (editor), The Bickersteth Diaries.
[9] Moy, 2nd Lt. C E, Unpublished papers, Liddle Collection, Leeds University.
[10] Lt Gen Snow's report to Third Army, 24th July 1916. Third Army report SGE 47/1. NA
[11] The 2/1st London Field Ambulance, H L Chase.
[12] Clements Pte (later Lt.) H T, 1/2nd London Regiment, Diary, IWM.
[13] Reported in Major E T C Milligan 'The Early Treatment of Projectile Wounds by Excision of Damaged Tissues' in the British Medical Journal, 26th June 1915; and Lt. Col. H M W Gray 'Treatment of Gunshot wounds by Excision and Primary Suture' in the Journal of the Royal Army Medical Corps, June 1915.
[14] Clements Pte (later Lt.) H T, 1/2nd London Regiment, Diary, IWM.
[15] Bere Rev M A, 43rd Casualty Clearing Station, Letters, IWM.
[16] Snow, Maj. Gen Sir Thomas D'Oyly, entry in personal diary 29th June 1916, IWM
[17] No 17 Ambulance Train War Diary. NA WO95/4135
[18] No 26 Ambulance Train War Diary. NA WO95/4138
[19] Russell, Rfn H, 1/5th London Regt. (London Rifle Brigade). Papers, IWM.
[20] Hodder, Williams J E (editor), One Young Man
[21] Ibid.
[22] Russell, Rfn. H op. cit.
[23] Appleyard Rfn S W, 1/9th London Regt (Queen Victoria's Rifles), Papers, IWM
[24] Chase, Pte H L, op. cit.
[25] The 'Second Seconds' in France.
[26] Chase, Pte H L, op. cit.
[27] Territorial Service Gazette, 9th September 1916, page 133.
[28] Keegan, John, The Face of Battle.
[29] Atkinson, Arthur 2/3rd City of London Field Ambulance 1914-18 London soldiers – unarmed comrades.
[30] Lindsay, Lt. Col. J H, The London Scottish in the Great War.
[31] Neller, Daniel J and Fabian, John M. 'Trauma and its contribution towards violent behaviour', Criminal Justice Magazine, Centre for Crime and Justice Studies, Winter 2006/7 pages 6-7.

17. THE AFTERMATH

"A forlorn endeavour... it is not clear that a single German was 'diverted'"

John Terraine
Haig: The Educated Soldier

GIVEN THE SCALE of the casualties, the general lack of progress and the strength and resilience of the German resistance along most of the front line the reaction of the senior officers to the relentless roll-call of setbacks is somewhat perplexing. As late as 16th June Haig had still been talking about the possibility of shifting the focus of the British Army's attack away from the Somme to Messines. Indeed, on 5th June he advised Rawlinson that the attack would be closed down in favour of the Messines ridge if his offensive met with 'considerable opposition'. It might have been thought that the complete and bloody failure of the attack from Gommecourt to La Boiselle would have been grounds enough to warrant closing down the offensive according to Haig's earlier criteria as, across that whole length of line, what little that was left of the attacking battalions was back in their own trenches. And then there was the sheer scale of the casualties suffered by the infantry wherever they went 'over the top'. Whilst it is appreciated that, in the confusion after 1st July, it would have taken some time to ascertain the full extent of the disaster that had befallen the majority of the attacking battalions, it could easily be argued that losing 60,000 men in the space of a few hours constituted '(meeting) considerable opposition'. And, in any case, the Adjutant-General, Lt. Gen. Fowke, had indicated on 2nd July that the initial casualties were likely to be a minimum of 40,000. A figure close to the actual final total must have been available within a few days as returns from the battalion roll calls filtered up through the system to G.H.Q. Indeed, it is almost certain that these estimates would have exceeded the final accurate figures as many men who had been recorded as missing were, in fact, stranded in No Man's Land or in some other way separated from their unit. In other words, provisional figures given to Haig should have been even worse than the 59,000 casualties that later proved to be correct. Yet, in spite of these horrific statistics, Haig still decided that the 4th Army attack had not met sufficient 'considerable opposition' to warrant closing down the offensive and shifting the emphasis northwards. This all begs the questions: why?

As has been shown, Haig's optimism about the probable success of the offensive had grown to envisage a complete breakthrough with a wide ranging cavalry exploitation. This turn around in thinking occurred barely two weeks after he had issued his warning to Rawlinson about the possible closing down of the Somme battle. Furthermore, in spite of the shambles of 1st July, Haig continued to hold on to the idea that a breakthrough on the Somme was a realistic proposition until mid-September. It was only when the modest performance of the new war-winning weapon, the tank, at long last forced him to moderate his views that he retreated into advocating Joffre's (and Rawlinson's) original concept of the battle of attrition. Interestingly, shortly after the battle had finished, Haig wrote a despatch describing the totality of the Battle of the

Somme. Published on 23rd December 1916 it was somewhat disingenuously entitled *'The Opening Of The Wearing-Out Battle'* and covered the campaign from its initial planning through to its muddy end in November. The objectives of the Somme, as set out in the despatch, were:

"1. To relieve the pressure on Verdun.
2. To assist our Allies in the other theatres of war by stopping any further transfer of German troops from the Western front.
3. To wear down the strength of the forces opposed to us."[1]

The title and the insertion of objective three are a remarkable transformation of Haig's perspective in June and for several months thereafter. A 'wearing out battle' was the concept Rawlinson and Joffre had argued for in the Spring of 1916, but Rawlinson's modest 'bite and hold' plan had been overturned by Haig who had, progressively, transformed the nature of the offensive into one involving a total rupture of the German line then exploited by massed cavalry. By the end of a battle that moved the front line but seven miles at its maximum point in five long and bloody months, however, it appears that 'wearing out' the enemy had been Haig's objective all along. How things change. For years after the Field Marshal's death in 1928 some of Haig's acolyte's such as Kiggell, his Chief of Staff, and Charteris, his chief Intelligence officer, argued post-war and post-mortem as far as Haig was concerned, that he had always accepted the likelihood of the Somme developing into a battle of attrition *before* the battle had started. Quite what one is to make of such statements expressed as they were in Charteris's book *'At G.H.Q.'* published in 1931 and in a series of increasingly desperate letters written by Kiggell in the 1930s in an attempt to influence Brig. Gen. Edmonds, the author/overseer of the Official History of the War, is unclear. By this time the anti-war sentiments fuelled by the Great War authors and poets and by officer/historians such as Liddell Hart were rampant and Haig's reputation was under increasing pressure.

There are, however, two contemporaneous statements that sum up the fundamental differences between Rawlinson's 'Bite and Hold' and Haig's expansive approach to the coming offensive. Rawlinson justified his original limited plan thus:

"It does not appear to me that the gain of 2 or 3 more kilometres of ground is of much consequence... Our object rather seems to be to kill as many Germans as possible with the least loss to ourselves."

In response, Haig wrote in his dairy on Wednesday, 5th April:

"I studied Sir H Rawlinson's proposals for attack. His intention is merely to take the Enemy's first and second system of trenches and 'kill Germans'. He looks upon the gaining of 3 or 4 kilometres or less of ground immaterial. I think we can do better than this by aiming at getting as large a combined force of French and British across the Somme and fighting the Enemy in the open!"

Throughout April, May and June, Haig pushed harder and harder for the offensive to reflect his views as expressed on 5th April. It is impossible to accept, as his friends and supporters have earnestly tried to portray, that his was a commitment to a 'wearing out' battle where killing Germans was the priority. The attack on 1st July was designed to further reflect his concerns. For Haig to entitle his end of battle despatch as *'The Opening Of The Wearing-Out Battle'* is as blatant a piece of back covering as one could wish to see. All along, Haig had planned for a breakthrough battle, one which would return the Western Front to fluid fighting found in open fields. In this analysis Winston Churchill concurs:

"It is easy to prove that rapid progress was in fact contemplated and resolutely bid for. The use by Haig of his artillery indicates the immediate ambitions which were in view. Instead of concentrating the fire on the first lines which were to be assaulted, the British artillery were dispersed in its action over the second and remoter lines and on many strong points far in the rear, the hope clearly being that these would be reached in the course of the first day's or two day's fighting. The position of the British and French cavalry in close proximity to the front also reveals indisputably the hopes and expectations of the commanders."[2]

Nowadays it is popular to attack critics of Haig's conduct of the Somme as viewing history through spectacles most magically equipped with 20:20 hindsight. These issues seem, at least to this writer, to be arguable matters of opinion – there is no right or wrong though some of the leading characters were more wrong than others! However, Haig's own words do seem to suggest that there was considerable confusion in his own mind about the objectives of the battle. On 15th June he wrote in his diary that the objectives of the attack were:

"1. To gain the line of the Pozieres heights... then

2. (a) if the enemy's defence breaks down, to occupy the enemy's third line... push detachment of cavalry to hold Bapaume and work northwards with the bulk of cavalry and other arms so as to widen the breach in enemy's line and capture the forces in the re-entrant south of Arras...

(b) If enemy's defence is strong and fighting continues for many days, as soon as the Pozieres heights are gained, the position should be consolidated... while arrangements will be made to start an attack on the Second Army front (i.e. Messines)."[3]

As the Pozieres heights were still being fought over in August one wonders what happened to the plan to consolidate and close down the Somme action in favour of Messines? The Battle followed no obvious plan expounded by Haig at any time prior to its opening. One concludes that, as much as the German Army at Verdun, the B.E.F. was sucked into an ill-conceived venture from which they could not escape until the weather and the ground brought all possible action to a muddy end in November.

John Terraine is, perhaps, the leading supporter of Field Marshal Haig's performance throughout the war. As such, he finds it nearly impossible to criticise Haig for the clear muddle at the heart of the planning of the Battle of the Somme and, in his seminal work *'The Educated Soldier'*, he leaps through several hoops to show that Haig's strategic and tactical over-view of the Battle was fundamentally correct. Terraine, it seems, wants his cake and eat it too. On the one hand he quotes from Haig's Diary from Wednesday, 29th March 1916:

"...consequently it is possible that the War will not end this year. Lord K(itchener) wished me for that reason to beware of the French, and to husband the strength of the British Army in France. I said that I had never had any intention of attacking with all available troops except in an emergency to save the French from disaster, and Paris from capture."[4]

And then, eight pages later, Terraine is attempting to justify the Somme in the following words:

"It is very easy to understand Haig's mind, if one is disposed to... The British effort must be made with the maximum strength, aiming at the maximum result – the defeat of the German Army in the field. On this reasoning, which had clarified in him by the middle of March, Haig abandoned all thoughts of other major diversions on his front... and ordered all resources to be concentrated on the Somme."[5]

As G.H.Q.'s own papers show clearly in April, May and even June, Haig was a long way from 'abandoning all thoughts of other major diversions' and as late as early June he was still considering switching his reserves and effort north towards Messines. And how does one square Haig's stated intention of 'husbanding his strength' in case the war dragged on into 1917 against Terraine's conviction that Haig, at the same time and with the same breath, had determined to take his maximum strength into a life or death struggle with the German Army?

There was, however, one over-riding reason why Haig stood and fought on the Somme. This was, simply, that Joffre would not countenance any other form of action. The early French advances had been highly successful and Joffre and Foch wished to push their advantage. This could not conceivably have been done if the British Army had stopped fighting and then painstakingly moved key resources, most notably the heavy artillery, north to Messines. It is also clear that given the military and political relationship between Britain and France Haig would have found it impossible to disengage, leaving his allies exposed on either bank of the Somme. But these facts were clear well before 1ˢᵗ July 1916 and begs the question as to why Haig ever thought it possible that he might be able to switch his focus of attack away from the Somme without the agreement of Joffre – an agreement that was never likely to materialise given that the Somme had always been Joffre's preferred location for the great joint Allied offensive of summer 1916. It is difficult, therefore, to fathom the precise nature of Haig's thinking in the weeks before the opening of the Somme campaign. Many have tried and none, yet, to this author's satisfaction.

***

BUT WHAT OF THE PLANNING AND CONDUCT OF THE ATTACK ITSELF?

Terraine recites the tantalising, if wholly misleading, claim that 'The Battle of the Somme was lost by three minutes' (i.e. the time it took the men to get across No Man's Land before the Germans could man the trenches and mount their machine guns). It is, of course, the case that in many parts of the line, the attacking troops managed to get into the German front lines but, in all areas except for those on the southern edge of the advance, they were rudely and bloodily expelled for many other reasons that a simple failure to get across No Man's Land within a restricted time frame.

He then excuses Haig because: "G.H.Q. simply did not know what it was up against", the 'it' being the complex and secure German dugouts and strongpoints that littered the front line. As has been made clear, Rawlinson had commented on the German dugouts in use at Givenchy in June 1915 in a report made to his senior officer – Sir Douglas Haig. Again, in January 1916, a report had been circulated as to the strength and depth of dugouts at Ovillers La Boisselle. And then, on 8th June 1916, a detailed report with attached sketches of the design and layout of a typical dugout had been sent from III Corps to Fourth Army who had published it in their Intelligence Report which one must assume had been forwarded to Charteris at G.H.Q,. How could Haig have failed to see these reports? And, if he saw them, why were they not acted upon? Or did his Intelligence Officer, Charteris, deem them to be of insufficient importance for him to bother his boss with them?

Terraine's litany of excuses then touches upon the lack of sufficient heavy artillery stating that there were not enough heavy guns per yard of line and that this had then been exacerbated by the poor quality of a large proportion of the hurriedly supplied shells. This latter point is undoubtedly true but Haig himself bears a heavy responsibility for the inadequate weight of shell delivered per yard of front. After all, it was his demand at the beginning of April that the line to be attacked should be extended and the depth of the attack should be twice as deep as suggested that played a significant role in diluting the power of the available British guns.

Terraine admits to certain errors by G.H.Q. and, by definition, the man there with whom the buck stopped, Sir Douglas Haig. G.H.Q. apparently did not know the strength of the German defences (whereas in fact they had a very good idea as has been shown); G.H.Q. allowed the British heavy artillery to be placed evenly along the line rather than be concentrated against areas of specific importance (certainly *not* the case at Gommecourt where the heavy and super-heavy howitzers were concentrated on key positions and, as far as one can see, not the case anywhere else. Rather it was Haig who extended and deepened the area to be attacked with the consequent diminished impact of the concentration of shell fire); and G.H.Q. 'overlooked the outstanding lesson of Verdun' that men and weapons could survive the heaviest of bombardments and still provide effective resistance (but was it not Haig whose own analysis of the opening of Verdun stated that "The result of the combination of surprise and an overwhelming artillery preparation was that the infantry appear to have had little more to do in their first advance than to take possession of ground already practically won by the artillery"? And it was he who imbued senior officers with the confidence to believe nothing could stand in the way of their artillery); and lastly, Gen. Foch was apparently to blame for prolonging the preparatory bombardment by two days 'with consequent dilution of its effect' (in fact, although Foch had requested this, it was the weather that forced the two-day delay on the Allied commanders who were unanimous in their decision to postpone. A greater 'dilution of effect' must surely have come from Haig's demand, made on the 20th June, for a reduction in the intensity of the bombardment, something to which Rawlinson felt obliged to agree).

But all good excuses require scapegoats and the first fall guy in Terraine's analysis is Gen. Sir Henry Rawlinson and his Fourth Army *Tactical Notes'* issued on 17th May. These are the notes that contain such infamous lines as:

"…nothing could exist at the conclusion of the bombardment in the areas covered by it" and, "…the assaulting columns must go right through above ground to the objective in successive waves or lines."

There are several problems with this analysis. Foremost amongst them is that it was Douglas Haig who believed the artillery preparation more than adequate to the task - the artillery would conquer and the infantry occupy. Hardly surprising then that the Rawlinson 'monkey' happily parroted the words of the chief organ grinder when describing the anticipated impact of the bombardment. On the issue of serried ranks of inexperienced British soldiers marching stolidly to their doom, something Terraine tries to illustrate with an emotive if highly localised eyewitness account by Sir Edward Spears, this is simply not true. Prior and Wilson's recent book *'Somme'* comprehensively de-bunks the widely held idea that the British Army walked to its death on 1st July 1916. Tactics employed at a Divisional, Brigade and even Battalion level varied hugely as did the results. Some followed the tactical advice, others ignored it completely. Some crept out to the German wire, others employed Russian saps to get men forward under cover, some were helped by excellent moving shrapnel barrages fired by the Royal Field Artillery and, at Gommecourt, they employed a dense smoke screen. The methods used were many and various and to blame the failures and casualties on Rawlinson's 31-page advisory pamphlet seems absurd at any level.

The next herd of scapegoats appear to be almost every General commanding a Corps or Division. They are held responsible for their failure to report upwards the complete picture on their fronts before 1st July. It is suggested that reports of uncut wire, especially on the VIII Corps' front north of the Ancre, failed to reach Charteris at G.H.Q. It is extraordinary to think that such information was not passed upwards and one wonders how Charteris and his Intelligence Department could preside over such an unintelligent system of reporting. But then, that Haig appeared to rely solely on the verbatim reports of his Corps commanders given during flying visits to their Corps' headquarters on the 29th and 30th June seems equally extraordinary. These officers knew there was no prospect of any additional delay in the timetable and, if their Army commander, Rawlinson, had felt it impossible to argue against the wishes of the Commander-in-Chief for the expansion of the front in April, and against a reduction in the intensity of the bombardment in June, then it seems highly unlikely that these officers would have felt able to argue for another delay in the attack because the wire was not properly cut as such admissions would have immediately met with stern enquiries as to the reasons for this failure. It was not in the nature of the rigidly hierarchical system of command in the B.E.F. for subordinates to query the opinions, or otherwise get on the wrong side, of their commanders. Those that did found themselves marked men, as Sir Horace Smith-Dorrien had found with Field Marshal Lord French and Maj. Gen. Stuart-Wortley discovered almost within hours after the failure at Gommecourt.

Of course, Terraine is not the only biographer of Haig who is expert at 'passing the buck' to cover Haig's back. Philip Warner in 1991 repeated many of Terraine's excuses for the failure of the 1st July, again blaming nearly everyone except the Commander-in-Chief for the failures (but now pointing the finger at Brigade commanders for good measure!). One small section alone suggests that the facts were not to be allowed to get in the way of a good story. First, Warner holds Joffre responsible for the delay from the 29th June to 1st July, conveniently ignoring the fact that the poor weather was the cause of a delay agreed by all parties. Second, he states that, as a result, the attacking troops:

"had to wait an extra forty-eight hours in their own trenches, being deafened by gunfire and drenched with torrential rain."[6]

This ignores the inconvenient facts that the majority of the British troops earmarked for the attack were advised of the postponement well before they reached their jumping off trenches and spent most of the 29th and 30th behind the lines and secondly, it barely rained at all on these days with a meagre 0.7mm of rain on the 29th and none whatsoever on the 30th. The trenches may not have been in great condition because of earlier rain but there is no suggestion that the assaulting units spent 48 hours in pouring rain and cramped trenches before they attacked. But, there again, Terraine and Warner leave no excuse unused when it comes to exculpating their chosen subject.

Lastly, Duff Cooper, in his 1935 biography *'Haig'*, justifies the Somme in the following sweeping, and inaccurate, sentence:

"All military writers are agreed that the Battle of the Somme saved Verdun and if no further justification were forthcoming that alone would suffice."

As has been shown, the crisis at Verdun had passed when the offensive on the Somme started. Petain, by this time, was confident not only that the position was stable but that opportunities to inflict casualties and tactical reverses on the German troops were growing. That these occurred and that the Somme carried on in its relentless and formless way gives the lie to Duff Cooper's claim. Certainly, the Somme stretched German resources which must have aided the French Army engaged at Verdun but, by this time, they were considering counter-attacks rather than a continuation of solely defensive operations. Indeed, it could well be argued that, had Haig switched the point of attack to Messines after the initial Somme attack, then German resources would have been stretched still further. And, of course, up to 4th June Haig was actively considering this option even to the exclusion of the Somme and on 16th June he wrote to his Army Commanders, when considering the possibility that a breakthrough on the Somme might not prove possible, that the:

"… most profitable course will probably be to transfer our main efforts rapidly to another portion of the British front."[7]

Duff Cooper's suggestion that the Somme saved Verdun is, therefore, nonsense and yet another feeble attempt to excuse Haig for the Somme stalemate, and his comments about the opening of the battle itself defy belief:

"Even Germany could produce no finer soldiers than the men who manned them. Yet after a bombardment such as they had never imagined they found themselves driven at the point of the bayonet out of positions they had believed impregnable."

Setting to one side the fact that the majority of the German divisions on the Somme were Reserve divisions, many resting from hard fighting elsewhere, and by far the cream of the German Army the idea that these men had been 'driven at the point of the bayonet out of positions they had believed impregnable' is just not supported by the facts of the battle.

***

APPORTIONING RESPONSIBILITY for the debacle of 1st July 1916 is one thing, explaining why the battle continued apace is quite another.

In early July, and for many weeks after, the popular view amongst senior officers was that the enemy was severely and possibly fatally damaged. An insight into the mindset of these British officers can be gained from the entries in Lt. Gen. Snow's personal diary written on and after 1st July. On the day he wrote:

"I don't think the Boche are very plentiful, indeed I think there are very few in front of us but they have plenty of guns both big and machine.... Things seem to be going alright. We are killing a lot of Boche and we know there are not many in front of us."[8]

This entry indicates significant degrees of both complacency and muddled thinking, i.e. the two things 'the Boche' were recognised as 'having plenty of' were the two weapons responsible for the vast majority of casualties in the war: artillery and machine guns! And the complacency sprang from the conviction that they so far outnumbered the Germans that they must be overrun whatever the British casualties. This, in spite of the fact that his divisions had suffered casualties at a ratio of 5:1 and had been unable to hold on to any of their objectives. Of course, Snow and Haig could have little idea about the size of the German casualty list in the early days of the battle. Assumptions were clearly made based on those areas where an advance had been achieved and where trenches and dugouts could be checked for evidence.

A lot of reliance was still placed on the assumed success of the seven-day bombardment in causing heavy casualties amongst the Germans manning the forward defensive positions. Looking at the casualties caused to the French at Verdun it almost seems as though Allied staff and intelligence officers had formulated some sort of simple-minded equation about the likely numbers of casualties caused by the delivery of a certain weight of shell within a defined area. If so, they had got it wildly wrong, as the casualty returns of the front line companies of the 55th Reserve Infantry Regiment at Gommecourt show. Whatever their own casualties, the British High Command and, indeed, many ordinary soldiers, remained convinced that the German defenders must have suffered equally severely. In spite of the evidence that the deep dug outs had remained largely unaffected, they were certain that losses through the bombardment must have been considerable. On both counts they were hopelessly wrong. The War Diary of the 55th Reserve Infantry Regiment shows that losses throughout the bombardment amounted to only four dead and forty-four wounded. Interviews with prisoners of war from the 170th Infantry Regiment elicited figures for three out of the four companies manning the front two lines. These were: 8 dead and about 20 wounded. We also know from the 15th Reserve Infantry Regiment's history that in two strafes they lost 10 dead and 16 wounded and that some more were lost in other artillery strikes on the rear villages. But the numbers are not large and are substantially lower than those suffered by the British infantry occupying the trenches opposite.

On the British side, in the first five days of the bombardment, the 1/7th Middlesex alone had lost 148 men, 100 of them battle casualties. There is no reason to believe that any of the other German regiments affected by the bombardment suffered any more than the ones mentioned above. Assuming this to be true (and some were only partially involved in the bombardment) then it might be reasonable to guess that some 200 German soldiers were either killed or wounded throughout that seven days. The casualties of the 56th Division alone were more than twice as heavy and the 46ᵗʰ Division lost about 370 men in the same period. In other words, there was a casualty ratio of nearly five British for every one German dead or wounded along the whole of the VII Corps' front during the pre-attack bombardment. The daily casualty figures for the 56ᵗʰ Division were:

	Officers				Other ranks				Total casualties
	Killed	Wounded	Missing	Total	Killed	Wounded	Missing	Total	
U Day	0	I	0	I	2	6	0	8	9
V Day	0	3	0	3	12	54	0	66	69
W Day	3	6	0	9	23	95	19	137	146
X Day	I	7	0	8	18	113	4	135	143
Y Day	0	2	0	2	5	50	I	56	58
YI Day	0	I	0	I	4	58	2	64	65
Totals	4	20	0	24	64	376	26	466	490

Table 22 56ᵗʰ Division casualties notified to Divisional Adjutant 24ᵗʰ-29ᵗʰ June 1916

Similar figures can be provided for German units further to the south. For example, Ralph Whitehead has produced fatal casualty details for the 26ᵗʰ and 28ᵗʰ Reserve Divisions. The 26ᵗʰ defended Thiepval and Beaumont Hamel and the 28th defended the sector from north of Ovillers to east of Mametz (and, therefore, included some areas towards Montauban, where the preparatory bombardment was a considerable success). Total fatalities for the period 24ᵗʰ – 30ᵗʰ June were:

26ᵗʰ Reserve Division: 126 officers and men
28ᵗʰ Reserve Division: 84 officers and men.

This gives a total for the two divisions defending the line from Redan Ridge in the north to opposite Carnoy in the south of 210 fatal casualties. Facing these divisions were elements of ten British divisions and, if the numbers given below for the casualties of the 56ᵗʰ Division during this period are in any way representative, then it is reasonable to assume that British dead and died of wounds were upwards of three times heavier. But true or not, the fact is that the figures suggest that the bombardment had relatively little impact on the defenders in terms of casualties and the tenacious way in which they defended their lines suggest it had little impact on their morale either.

The disparity in casualties suffered by the opposing armies at Gommecourt on 1ˢᵗ July 1916 was even more marked, with the attacking units suffering losses at 5½ to every one defensive loss. One wonders what would have happened to the whole Somme battle had these relative figures, and those of the other units involved the length of the front line, been generally known to the Army, politicians and public at an early date. According to the British Official History the 1ˢᵗ July casualty figures for the attack on Gommecourt were as follows:

British Casualties					
56ᵗʰ Division	Killed	Wounded	Missing¹	Prisoners	Total
Officers	53	107	17	6	183
Other Ranks	1,300	2,248	356	227	4,131
Total	1,353	2,355	373	233	4,314
46ᵗʰ Division					
Officers	50	71	14	2	137
Other Ranks	803	1,340	172	3	2,318
Total	853	1,411	186	5	2,455
Total	2,206	3,766	559	238	6,769

German Casualties					
2nd Guard Reserve Division					
Officers	3	10	0	0	13
Other Ranks	182	372	24	0	565
Total	185	382	24	0	578
52nd Division					
Officers	9	20	0	0	29
Other Ranks	233	252	136	0	621
Total	242	272	136	0	650
Total	427	654	160[2]	0	1,241

Table 23 British and German casualties at Gommecourt
[1] The majority of the Missing were killed in action or died of wounds
[2] Some of the Missing will have been Prisoners

Similar numbers of men were supposed to have been committed to the assault on the village by the two attacking divisions, however, the 56th Division lost 64% of the casualties suffered on the day. Along the whole Somme front, only five divisions suffered a higher number of casualties than the 56th Division and some of these, for example 4th Division north of Beaumont Hamel, had committed elements of all three brigades to the attack. The 56th Division's casualties were mainly confined to the two attacking brigades.

On the 2nd July, by which time Snow must have had some idea as to the scale of the casualties suffered by VII Corps, he was still ploughing the same furrow, i.e. whatever level of casualties his divisions had suffered the enemy had suffered much more heavily (although whether relatively or absolutely is not clear). The only difference now was that the Germans were military conjurors, able to pull well-armed rabbits out of pickelhaubes whenever necessary:

"We did not do all I wanted to do yesterday but the powers that be seemed quite content… It is quite certain there are not many Boche about and I never thought that there were but they are wonderfully good at producing them at the required places."[9]

By 3rd July, as his staff must have been digesting the uncomfortable statistics of the failure at Gommecourt, Snow was off in a world of make believe:

"I tell you the Boche is done in. He may attack or meet our attacks and will do so as long as he lives but he is beat and he knows it. His men are wonderfully good still and his machines excellent but he can't stand his losses which are perfectly enormous every day."[10]

As VII Corps was no longer actively involved in the offensive, one can only imagine that Snow's statement was based on information being fed down the line by higher authorities, i.e. G.H.Q.. Although the northern half of the front had been closed down and, with the exception of Montauban in the south, every first phase objective of the *first day* was still being contested, Snow was now privately convinced that the Germans were beaten. One could understand this message being put out for public consumption, especially as a means of bolstering the morale of his own shattered battalions, but as the private and considered view of a very senior officer it is, frankly, extraordinary. That this was not an over-reaction to the setback on his own front was confirmed by his entry on 4th July. Indeed, losing nearly 7,000 men was clearly not even regarded as a setback:

"I was quite content with my show … I think if things are kept humming on all fronts like they are now that the war cannot last long. The Boche losses must be colossal and they can't last much longer."[11]

Haig, too, had the clear impression that there were few German troops opposite them and that they were finding reserves hard to come by. On 3rd July, he wrote to his wife:

"Things are going quite satisfactorily for us here, and the Enemy seems hard pushed to it to find any reserves at all."[12]

And yet, in spite of this apparent lack of men the Germans - days, and even weeks, later - were still successfully defending positions Haig had expected to take in the first rush on the morning of Saturday, 1st July. This ability to persuade oneself that successful results were being achieved in spite of the evidence before their eyes is commented upon by Lloyd George in his post-war 'War Memoirs'. Commenting on the Somme he states how:

"western strategists… worked themselves into a belief that the Germans were so pulverised by these attacks that they had not the men, the guns, nor the spirit to fight anywhere much longer… This is no exaggeration of their illusions."[13]

There is a relentless complacency amongst senior commanders about the results of the opening of the Battle of the Somme that makes one wonder about the quality of information they were being given about German casualties and morale. It was either self-deception or they were being misled by Staff officers who were themselves either misinformed, misguided or incompetent. Whatever it was, Haig and his Army commanders persuaded themselves that the battle was going well and that the Gommecourt 'diversion' had contributed significantly to the 'successes' gained on the 1st July.

And even in this last thought they were wrong. The attack on Gommecourt was designed to divert attention and resources away from the main thrust of the offensive. The very obvious preparations for the attack, made so at the instruction of G.H.Q., certainly did attract reserves to the area, reserves which *might* possibly have been diverted to another part of the Somme front. The only problem here is that, whilst the Gommecourt assault was designed to be obvious, the attacks further south were not. Except for the bombardment, scaled down versions of which occurred well beyond the areas to be attacked, the attacks to the south were kept, as far as was possible, 'under wraps' in order that there might be some element of surprise. One of the effects of this was that, in certain places, the attacking battalions had to advance across a breadth of No Man's Land wider still than was in place in front of Hebuterne in May, i.e. *before* the new front line and assembly trenches were dug in order to reduce the distance the men had to move in the open. The consequence of this secrecy was that nowhere on the German front line was reinforced to anything like the same degree as Gommecourt. This might appear to justify the diversionary attack by itself were it not for the fact that, with the exception of the areas around Montauban, Mametz and, to a lesser extent, Fricourt, the British attack was bloodily repulsed along the entire length of the *unreinforced* German line. But what, say, if the 2nd Guard Reserve Division had been put in place near Montauban instead of Gommecourt? Then the only genuine success of the day might too have been defeated. But there was no chance of this. If the German High Command was caught napping anywhere on the Somme battlefront it was in the areas where the French attacked and where the French and British line joined. The view of the German staff was that the French would be unable to launch any serious attack because of their losses at Verdun. So, when the French 6ᵗʰ Army and the men of the XIII Corps swept over the German front lines from Foucaucourt in the South to beyond Montauban in the North, the local German forces were both unprepared as well as shocked by the weight of the combined French and British bombardment.

But, the explanation for the lack of reinforcements on the main part of the Somme front goes far deeper than anything achieved by the Gommecourt 'diversion'. It is rooted in the persistent and widespread delusion at the German Supreme Command, O.H.L., that the big Allied push of Summer 1916 was to take place in Alsace-Lorraine and that any action in the Picardy-Artois area would be against the German 6ᵗʰ Army's front and not that of the 2ⁿᵈ Army astride the Somme. The 6ᵗʰ Army, commanded by Crown Prince Rupprecht, covered an area from two miles north of Gommecourt to St Eloi, just south of Ypres, and it was here that Falkenhayn became convinced that the hammer blow would fall. He was so convinced that, in April, he suggested to the Crown Prince that a pre-emptive strike might be in order. Lacking either the men or the artillery to do so, Rupprecht was unable to comply but Falkenhayn still kept a close eye on this sector and even appeared to ignore the local intelligence of both 6ᵗʰ and 2ⁿᵈ Armies that an attack was to be mounted further south. Gen. Fritz von Below, commanding 2ⁿᵈ Army, was still concerned about British preparations on his front and made repeated requests for reinforcements but, with the exception of some labour battalions and a few captured 15cm Russian howitzers, what Falkenhayn gave him with one hand, he took away with another. The 2ⁿᵈ Guard Reserve Division was put at his disposal but, at the same time, the 11ᵗʰ Bavarian Division, currently 2ⁿᵈ Army's general reserve, was sent to Galicia to aid the Austrians. Von Below continued to voice his concerns to the extent that he suggested first one and then another pre-emptive attack in the Somme sector. To help, O.H.L. sent him just one artillery regiment from general reserve.

By late May, von Below had become increasingly confident that attacks could be expected against the Gommecourt salient and Fricourt and on 6ᵗʰ June he sent O.H.L. a report highlighting the preparations in the Serre-Gommecourt area. On the whole though, he seemed more concerned about the weakness of his divisions south of the Somme but these had been weakened by his own actions when, in the first week of June, the 10ᵗʰ Bavarian Division was withdrawn from this sector and used to reinforce the line north of the Somme, some of the artillery going to help the defence of Gommecourt. In the second week of June more intelligence and espionage reports came in suggesting heightened activity north of the Somme around Albert and even a date for the offensive: the week beginning Monday, 19ᵗʰ June. In spite of this evidence, Falkenhayn clung on to his belief that Alsace-Lorraine would be attacked (because it was German territory) and that major offensives in Northern France were unlikely as the French would not want to lay waste to their own country. A subsidiary attack near Lens, on the 6ᵗʰ Army's front, was the best assessment of O.H.L.'s Operations Section.

Intelligence continued to flow in throughout June, all of it pointing to a late June offensive astride the Somme. Rupprecht, whose army O.H.L. was convinced would be attacked, concluded on the 25th June that the left flank of the attack would be at Gommecourt, i.e. 2nd Army's front, and that there were no signs of an attack on 6th Army's front. Two days later, 2nd Army, noting 14 observation balloons aloft along the British front north of the Somme (one for each of the British divisions in the front line) concluded that large scale attacks were to be made at Gommecourt and Fricourt with, perhaps, some attacks in between. Nothing south of Fricourt was expected because of the assumed weakness of the French Army caused by Verdun. To counter this, the only division given to the 2nd Army, the 2nd Guard Reserve Division, had already been sent to Gommecourt.

The obsessively delusional nature of the thinking at O.H.L. is most clearly exposed with their reaction to the news of the attack on 1st July. In the afternoon, when heavy fighting had been going on for several hours and when the British and French troops either side of the Somme had swept over the positions of the 2nd Army, O.H.L. released three divisions as reserves. The only problem was that the 3rd Guards, 11th and 12th Reserve Divisions were put at the disposal of the 6th Army, whose front had remained untouched all day. Two days later, Maj. Gen. Tappen of the Operations Section at O.H.L. telephoned a bemused Crown Prince Rupprecht to advise him of an imminent attack against the 6th Army. It took Falkenhayn several days to accept that the new crisis on the Western Front was north of the River Somme and that reserves should be directed accordingly.

In short, the German Supreme Command never had any intention of sending reinforcements to the 2nd Army front north of the Somme, consequently, there were no additional troops to divert. Ironically, had Allenby's suggestion of a diversionary attack at or near Vimy been accepted, it is highly likely that this would have moved significant quantities of resources to that sector; firstly because it was tactically important of itself; and secondly because it would have fitted in perfectly with O.H.L.'s mystifying interpretation of the situation on the B.E.F.'s front. Even if, after the initial diversionary attack, the German High Command had realised that the Somme was the site of the main offensive it would have taken some time to extricate the reserves committed to Vimy and send them south. And even that could have been made more difficult still by a continuation of the threat to Vimy spread over several days.

Overall, in spite of the evidence to the contrary, G.H.Q. and the Third Army's commanders stubbornly clung to the idea that the Gommecourt 'diversion' had been successful although whether they actually believed this is another question. Indeed, in Sir Douglas Haig's Despatch of the 23rd December 1916, somewhat misleadingly entitled *'The Opening Of The Wearing-Out Battle'*, the myth of the success was again alluded to, although in the briefest of references:

> "The subsidiary attack at Gommecourt also forced its way into the enemy's positions; but there met with such vigorous opposition that as soon as it was considered that the attack had fulfilled its object our troops were withdrawn."[14]

It is difficult to conceive of a more inaccurate summing up of the action at Gommecourt and extraordinary that it should come from the pen of the

Commander in Chief. The survivors of the 56ᵗʰ Division were only eventually extricated when their position had become untenable. They were not *ordered* to withdraw, they were forced to withdraw. If the objective had been to divert attention away from Serre then the total and early failure of the attack on that village clearly rendered the Gommecourt diversion pointless - and yet the last men were still in the German front lines over ten hours after the remnants of the 31ˢᵗ Division opposite Serre had long since been reduced to cowering in their shattered trenches by the appalling German artillery fire. Haig's Despatch as it refers to Gommecourt is, therefore, wrong in three particulars:

1. The 46ᵗʰ Division's attack was almost completely repulsed and no effective bridgehead was achieved in the German lines;
2. The 56ᵗʰ Division, after its initial success, was cut-off and methodically destroyed by German artillery and infantry counter-attacks. The troops were not withdrawn, they were defeated; and
3. The attack did not fulfil its objective as the entire left wing of the Somme offensive was repulsed all the way down to the Albert-Bapaume Road.

John Terraine, one of Haig's leading apologists, describing the 'purely... diversionary' attack on Gommecourt as a 'forlorn endeavour' goes on to say that:

"...it is not clear that a single German was 'diverted'."¹⁵

This is clearly not wholly accurate. It is obviously the case that the local prominence given to the preparations for the attack brought substantial reinforcements to an area of already great strength, i.e. a new division and a considerable quantity of guns. What Terraine was presumably referring to was that the 'diversion' did not have the most beneficial possible effect of diverting resources away from the main front to be attacked. This is certainly true, but it is not the only reason why, as a diversion, the attack on Gommecourt was a costly tactical failure with an impact well beyond its own boundaries. By attracting more men and artillery to Gommecourt the German defences that were part of, or near to, the left wing of the main British attack were also considerably strengthened. In short, the reinforcement of Gommecourt helped significantly strengthen the defences of Serre, the village that was to be the hinge of the great advance in July, Redan Ridge and even Beaumont Hamel.

The attacks on Serre and the ridges to the south were a key component of the overall offensive plan. The attack here was supposed to take the entire spur of high ground that ran SE from Serre towards Miraumont, a village in the Ancre valley some 2½ miles behind the German lines around Beaumont Hamel. This spur was then to act as the northern flank to the main drive over the Pozieres ridge to Bapaume. Apart from acting as a 'flank guard', the Serre-Miraumont spur also had the advantage of providing good observation over the German rear positions in the lower lying land to the North, East and South East. The success of this attack was, therefore of considerable importance. This success, however, was put at risk by the concentration of additional artillery and machine guns which was made possible by the strengthening of the German position at Gommecourt. The insertion of the 2ⁿᵈ Guard Reserve Division at Gommecourt allowed the 52ⁿᵈ Infantry Division to side step to its left but without any need to take over any additional frontage to the south. In other words, by reinforcing Gommecourt, the Germans also reinforced Serre and other parts of the front within reach of its artillery support with manpower, machine guns and artillery.

Furthermore, the newly arrived 20th R.F.A.R, which was given the task of leading the artillery defence of Gommecourt, allowed the artillery attached to the 52nd Infantry Division to concentrate their efforts on Serre and beyond and even then this effort was further reinforced by the arrival of elements of two Bavarian artillery regiments. The consequent effectiveness of the German artillery response to the attack on Serre can be gauged by the comments in the Official History:

> "The German batteries, heavy artillery from a hollow south east of Puisieux and field guns from about Serre... laid an accurate barrage on the British front trench, extending to fifty yards in front of and behind it... (the) barrage has been described as so consistent and severe that the cones of the explosions gave the impression of a thick belt of poplar trees."[16]

Of course, when the 31st Division's attack collapsed so disastrously on the barbed wire in front of Serre, this artillery was able to turn its guns on the men of the 56th Division by now stranded in the German trenches. By making the diversion so close to the actual attack it was inevitable that the extra men and guns brought in would be able to have an impact either on the main attack at Serre or on the diversion at Gommecourt or, as actually happened, on both.

It can be seen, therefore, that the concept of the diversion at Gommecourt was tactically flawed and could well have contributed to the shambles that occurred just to the south at Serre. It can also be argued that a far more sensible use of the resources available to the Third Army would have been to employ their enhanced heavy artillery presence in a properly co-ordinated and intense programme of counter-battery fire in the days before the attack and on 1st July itself. The infantry themselves need have done little except, perhaps, release smoke and use their massed machine guns, along with the Divisional 18pdr field guns, to interdict any German troops trying to move south the help defend Serre.

Interestingly, in his report to G.H.Q. dated 9th April in which he responded to G.H.Q.'s request for ideas for diversionary attacks, Allenby raised an issue which underlines the fact that attracting additional resources to Gommecourt was likely to have a damaging impact on the northern end of the main offensive. After an attack on Vimy Ridge, Allenby's secondary suggestion, enthusiastically received by Kiggell at G.H.Q., was for a diversionary attack between Monchy-au-Bois and Ransart, mainly targeted at eliminating the Monchy salient. Allenby cited as the 'chief advantage' of such an operation was the:

> "...direct assistance it can give to the Fourth Army by diverting the attention of the Adinfer batteries from the left of the main attack (i.e. Serre)."

At a distance of about 9,000 metres, Serre was within range of any 10 or 15cm guns (not howitzers) positioned within the confines of Adinfer Wood and certainly, the attack on Gommecourt prevented these guns from being used to help crush the attack by the 31st Division. But this could have been achieved by a direct attack on Monchy just as well. In addition, a significant proportion of the additional artillery attracted to Gommecourt, if it had been deployed between Monchy and Ransart instead, would have been either out of range of Serre or firing at extreme range. As it was, however, almost every field gun and howitzer brought into the Gommecourt salient could have fired at Serre if necessary and some of the additional guns certainly did so before being diverted onto the 56th Division. And, that they did so with little hindrance from a crucial part of the largest array of British artillery firepower ever seen is one of the keys to explaining the reason for the Germans' victory at Gommecourt.

***

THE USE, OR RATHER ABUSE, of the British heavy artillery before and on 1st July is an area that requires investigation. Only in front of Montauban did the artillery, with considerable French assistance, suppress the German defences sufficiently for the infantry to do their job and achieve their objectives. Nowhere else was this the case. There are various reasons for this. Firstly, the British artillery was not concentrated in areas of German strength, rather it was distributed evenly along the whole front. Secondly, the details of the artillery programmes to be used were decided by the local Corps commanders and the respective G.O.C., Heavy Artillery. Priorities were different everywhere but, in the main, one thing was absent – a sustained and effective counter-battery plan. Nowhere, except at Montauban, were German batteries identified and targeted in a methodical and effective manner and, at Montauban, the XIII Corps allotted considerable fire power to the *destruction,* not just neutralisation, of the German artillery. Four batteries of 60 pounders, one battery of 4.7 inch guns, one battery of 4.5 inch howitzers, one battery of 12 inch howitzers, and a section of 6 inch guns were given the task of destroying the German guns and great efforts were made to pre-register their targets. The results speak for themselves:

26th June, nineteen German batteries hit and silenced;

27th June, thirteen batteries were hit and many silenced (in spite of poor weather);

30th June, thirty-two enemy batteries were engaged.

The destruction of the German batteries and their ammunition in the valleys north of Mametz and Montauban were almost complete and the artillery of the 12th and 28th Divisions was all but wiped out. Nowhere else on the front was this success replicated, but nowhere else was such a plan with the necessary resources put in place. Elsewhere, the 'poor bloody infantry' suffered in consequence. It is the case, however, that the decisions of the local German artillery commander contributed significantly to the destruction of the guns defending this end of the front. North of the Albert to Bapaume Road, the basic principles of the various artillery plans had a common theme: they would only respond all out either when it was clear that a major assault was imminent or when a large scale gas attack was being mounted. Otherwise, the artillery plans at this end of the German front determined that the German guns should play a limited role in disrupting the British preparations and that any response to pleas for artillery assistance from the infantry should be limited and involve the use of as few batteries as possible. In this way, the German artillery commanders hoped to keep the presence of their guns a well guarded secret, allowing them to respond with a far greater weight of shell than expected by the attackers when the main assault went in and preventing the British observers from spotting the locations of the German guns, thus minimising the possibility of effective British counter-battery work. This policy was not adhered to, however, at the southern end of the British front. Here, requests for artillery support during the bombardment were more often than not agreed to and the German battery positions, also often less well constructed in this area, were spotted in greater numbers than elsewhere. The combination of an uncharacteristic lack of German discipline and an effectively organised and mounted Allied artillery plan was of great significance around Montauban and contributed hugely to the local success achieved there.

Elsewhere, the counter-battery programmes that were in place were then further hindered by the weather, which made R.F.C. aerial observation difficult, the inaccuracy of the inexperienced gunners, the high failure rate of the new ammunition - and the unreasonable behaviour of the defenders. The Germans insisted on moving their guns between the many positions they had built in the preceding months and concealed the true potency of their artillery by limiting the numbers of guns that fired before the attack proper started. As has been shown, the result of this was that British Intelligence had little real idea about either the location or extent of the German artillery arraigned against them. The consequences of this failure were predictable. German guns were relatively unaffected by the seven-day bombardment and, to make matters worse, there was little known about the whereabouts of these guns by 1ˢᵗ July. As a result, the attempts made on the day to disrupt the severe and destructive German barrage fire were of marginal utility and, as the British heavies also had little impact on the German dugouts, it can be seen that the huge expenditure of ammunition by this unprecedented concentration of British firepower had been largely wasted.

It is arguable that this lack of impact was a direct consequence of two things:

1. Haig's and other's misinterpretation of the effectiveness of the initial German bombardment at Verdun; and

2. The inexperience of all involved in mounting, monitoring and understanding the effects of such a huge and prolonged bombardment.

This was the biggest concentration of British firepower ever. The number of guns and the quantities of ammunition were unprecedented in British military history. No General before Haig had at their disposal so many heavy howitzers and so many field and long guns but also, so many inexperienced gunners new to their job and fresh out of training in the UK and so much ammunition, manufactured at such a pace that quantity had over-ridden quality on the factory floor. British artillery tactics were crude, with sheer weight of shell being expected to deliver the results required. The tactics were also inflexible, with little scope being given for either adapting the artillery plan to changed circumstances or for inter-unit co-operation. And British expectations as to the effectiveness of their new capability were, at least in the higher echelons, absurdly high and based on belief rather than experience. One would like to say that the experience of 1ˢᵗ July led to a radical re-think in the use of artillery and to significant improvements in both performance and results. Unfortunately, with one or two notable exceptions, such as Rawlinson at the Bazentin Ridges and Maxse at Thiepval, the application of the available artillery kept letting the infantry down as they flogged through the mud of the Somme. This was not through any fault of the hard-working gunners, but through the inept way they were employed and the persistent lack of co-ordination of infantry and artillery actions throughout a large part of the battle. The Somme would prove to be a steep learning curve for the Royal Garrison Artillery and for the generals who employed them.

***

BUT WHAT ABOUT THE USE OF ARTILLERY in the attack at Gommecourt? In a detailed post-battle report by the commander of the 2ⁿᵈ Guard Reserve Division, General Freiherr von Süsskind, in a section on lessons to be learned, made what seem to be extraordinary comments about the failures of the British artillery to effectively influence the outcome of the battle:

"Taking advantage of the fact that during the morning the enemy's batteries paid little attention to the ground in rear, the replenishment of (artillery) ammunition was begun as early as 10.30 a.m.; and, in spite of being in full view, was carried out without casualties and in accordance with the pre-arranged plan. Not one of the batteries of all the different calibres ran the least danger of exhausting its ammunition supply."

A reduction in the intensity of British artillery fire was noted by Lt. Büsing, an officer and regimental historian of Reserve Feldartillerie Regt No. 20. He wrote:

"A decline in enemy artillery fire had already been noticed in the morning…"

He put this down to the success of their gas shell bombardment which had been targeted on known battery positions. What is remarkable about this explanation, and indeed about the apparent failure of the British artillery on Z Day, is that throughout the preceding months, and on the day itself, British aircraft had continual air superiority. Von Süsskind's report of the seven-day bombardment repeatedly mentions the 'great activity' of enemy aircraft on most days. So, if any side's artillery should have mapped its targets adequately it should have been the British, not the Germans. Clearly, the German defensive barrage had the range of No Man's Land and the front lines measured to the metre and it was here that the majority of their shells fell. But how can they have been more effective in suppressing British artillery than the British were in suppressing German artillery on Z Day given their limitations in observing distant targets accurately? The fact is that Lt. Büsing's assumption seems to have been wide of the mark as there are no mentions of gas attacks on artillery positions on Z Day in British War Diaries and the German artillery spent very little time in identifying and targeting the British heavies or field artillery. Amongst the R.F.A. brigades attached to the 56ᵗʰ Division there were but eight casualties spread amongst three of the four brigades and it is thought that the majority of these were caused by concentrated fire dropped on known Observation Posts (O.P.s) by the Germans.

So, what was the artillery doing? They were certainly not taking on the German artillery particularly effectively. The 2ⁿᵈ Guard Reserve Division had some eighty pieces at their disposal on 1ˢᵗ July: 60 field guns and light howitzers and 20 heavy howitzers and guns[i]. Of these, three light howitzers, one field gun and one 9cm gun were put out action. Counter-battery fire, was, therefore, largely ineffective especially as far as the twenty heavy pieces available to 2ⁿᵈ Guard Reserve Division were concerned. The possibility that there would be a problem suppressing the German artillery was one already noted by at least one

---

[i] Excluding the support fire from the 111ᵗʰ and 52ⁿᵈ Infantry Divisions, the 2ⁿᵈ Guard Reserve Division had in use on 1ˢᵗ July 1916: forty 77mm field guns, twelve 10.5cm light field howitzers, eight 9cm guns, two 1914 pattern 10cm guns, four 1896 pattern 15cm howitzers, eight 1902/13 pattern 15cm howitzers, four captured Russian 15cm guns and two old pattern 21cm howitzers.

senior officer. On 4th June, Maj. Gen. Hull had issued a report, SJ6/5, under the name of the General Staff of the 56th Division. In it he stated bluntly:

"If there is a weak point in our organisation it is in the number of counter batteries available to deal with the enemy's guns."[17]

Of course, after Hull's prescient paper was written, the artillery defending Gommecourt had significantly increased, reducing still further the prospects of the VII Corps counter batteries overwhelming them.

But there was another reason why these batteries failed to inflict significant damage on the German guns - they were simply out of range of the majority of the guns supposedly earmarked for counter battery work. All of the 60 pdrs, the 6 in. howitzers and 4.7 in. guns just could not reach into the rear areas where these guns were located, leaving only the one 9.2 in. railway gun, the two to four 9.2 in. howitzers and the two 6 in. Mk VII guns able to disrupt their activities. Furthermore, equipment breakdowns did not just occur in the field artillery. Half way through the intense pre-assault bombardment, 116th Heavy Battery, the most modern of the four batteries permanently attached to 48th H.A.G., had two guns out of action because of damage to the breech loading mechanisms. The issue of inadequate range when comparing the performance of the British and German guns was one that persisted throughout the war. Maj. Gen. A G L McNaughton of the Canadian Corps was one of the leading counter battery exponents of the war and, writing in the 1930s, he explained the problem:

"German gun designers had an initial lead which we were never able to overtake, and at the end of the war their weapons still outranged ours on the average gun for gun by nearly 30 per cent."

Table 24 below shows the sometimes huge variations between the maximum ranges of the two Armies' artillery and was a factor which gave them a distinct advantage in their defensive battles to come.

German		British		Remarks
Type	Yards range	Type	Yards range	
10 cm howitzer	11,000	4.5 in. howitzer	7,200	Only medium, i.e. 6 in. howitzers broadly the same
15cm gun	25,000	6 in. gun	19,000	
35.5 cm gun	68,000	14 in. gun	34,000	
77mm gun	11,700	18 pdr	9,500	
15 cm howitzer	9,600	6 in. howitzer	9,500	
21 cm howitzer	11,000	8 in. howitzer	12,000	Advantage British

Table 24 Comparison of ranges of British and German artillery[18]

The War Diary of the 48th Heavy Artillery Group records some of the problems and mishaps that afflicted one of the two artillery groups dedicated to the task of destroying the German guns. The early morning weather, described in Sir Douglas Haig's diary as "...at first some mist in the hollows. This very favourable because it concealed the concentration of our troops..." did little to assist the British artillery to spot its early targets such as enemy observation posts. The C.O. of the 48th H.A.G. recorded: "The morning very hazy. Apart from smoke and bombardment it was almost impossible to see E(nemy's) O.P.s". From about 8.30 a.m. onwards, as previously concealed German batteries joined in the battle, the BE2cs overflying the salient sent down details of the new co-ordinates to bombard, however, because of the smoke and dust smothering the whole area, some of it caused by the lingering British smoke screen, it often proved impossible to observe the fall of shot on these new targets. As a result, it was not until 9.30 a.m. that the 48th H.A.G. diary was able to record its first battery as 'silenced'. In addition to the batteries on the 2nd Guard Reserve Division front there was also the problem of the many batteries hidden in Adinfer Wood. These had been the targets of the 4.5 in. howitzers of D/123 battery of 37th Division which had been attached to 48th H.A.G. throughout the preliminary bombardment. Just as the bombardment went in the battery had fired 190 rounds at a battery position on the southern fringe of the wood but, by 10.15 a.m., 46th Division was asking for more of the same and the battery spent the rest of the morning firing at a 'steady rate' at the original target and another within the confines of the wood. Nothing they, and the rest of the 37th Divisional field artillery firing independently, could do would suppress the terrible flanking fire of the Adinfer Wood batteries and any attempts at reviving the 46th Division's attack served only to bring down more fire from these guns.

As the day wore on, only the 116th Heavy Battery's 60pdr seemed capable of significantly damaging enemy battery positions. Three times during the day their targets were observed as having ceased firing but the effort needed to achieve this was considerable. One target, probably battery position 507, was eventually silenced after nearly 75 minutes had passed and 50 rounds had been fired. The other attached battery that might have done great execution was the 91st Siege Battery and its 9.2 in. howitzers, however, the two guns allocated to 48th H.A.G. each had a 100 round limit on 'Z' Day and this limit was reached just before 1 p.m. at a time when the 56th Division was embroiled along the length of its line and could have done with some help from the really 'heavy' artillery. In the afternoon, some other 'targets of opportunity' showed themselves and at 2 p.m. a concentration of German troops was seen moving towards the front between Essarts and Bucquoy. 116th Heavy Battery fired a few rounds under balloon observation but even here with very little reward the 48th H.A.G. diary reporting: "results unknown, probably not very successful." This comment by the author of the 48th H.A.G.'s war diary stands as an appropriate epitaph to the whole of the Gommecourt counter-battery programme and, indeed, to the heavy artillery performance as a whole. After the war, Lt. Col. J H H Jones, previously the Brigade Major of the VII Corps Heavy Artillery, wrote:

"The two Heavy Artillery Groups allotted to counter battery work received many locations from aeroplane observers; all, as far as I can remember, very indefinite, and many more outside the range of the 60pdrs and 6 in. howitzers of these groups. So indefinite were they that one group commander did not engage any enemy batteries and the other, though he fired, did not consider they could have produced much effect."[19]

General von Süsskind has already shown that attempts to disrupt ammunition supplies to the numerous battery positions were virtually non-existent. This is independently supported by British observers who remarked on seeing lorries loaded with ammunition driving up in full view to Rettemoy Farm which, on the 17th June, British Intelligence suspected being the site of at least one German battery (actually three). So re-supply was not affected by British artillery intervention nor, it appears, were attempts to interfere with infantry reinforcement any more successful. True, some field guns from the R.F.A. did try to break up visible concentrations of enemy troops but, it must be said, without much success and there are various accounts of German counterattackers moving with impunity across the open ground in the area around Rossignol Wood. The requests of Maj. Carrington (Adjutant, 1/5th Warwicks to the south) to both VIII and VII Corps artillery for action to break up bombing parties moving forward from the Bucquoy to Puisieux road foundered on a disagreement as to who was responsible. Certainly, the long communication trenches used by the Germans coming up from the rear were little affected by any part of the bombardment.

Another section of General von Süsskind's battle report described the condition of the trenches on 2nd July. Whilst certain parts, especially the major strongholds on either flank of the 56th Division's attack, had been more or less flattened, other key areas were far less damaged and it was from these or through these areas that German reinforcements proceeded to the counter-attack. Von Süsskind reports:

"1st Switch Line - Badly damaged by shells of all calibres, but still capable of defence.

2nd Switch Line - Less badly damaged and passable throughout. The dugouts in the 1st and 2nd Switch Lines are still habitable.

The Intermediate Line was not badly shelled, nor was Hebuterne Trench nor the network of trenches around Hill 147." (author's emphasis)

The importance of the last paragraph is significant. The Intermediate Line was the main communication trench up from the network of dugouts surrounding Point (Hill) 147 at which were located the 55th R.I.R.'s regimental H.Q., a key observation point for the Reserve Feldartillerie Regt. No. 20 and the most immediate reserves available, 10th Company, 55th R.I.R. Hebuterne Graben. It ran from almost the outskirts of Bucquoy and was one of the main thoroughfares used by the three reserve companies of the 55th R.I.R. and their 14 machine guns as well as by men of the 170th Regiment rushing to the aid of their comrades battling it out with the London Scottish in the Farmyard strongpoint. These locations should have been key targets in any artillery programme designed to cut off the German front lines from their supports. The fact is they were more or less untouched. It was a gathering of German reinforcements at the eastern end of Hebuterne Graben that was seen by Major Carrington and which neither the VII or VIII Corps artillery could be persuaded to bombard.

Finally, to add insult to injury to the attacking troops, when it became clear that the attack was close to collapse, the order was sent out to both the Heavies and the R.F.A. that they should conserve ammunition in case the Germans decided to launch their own attack across No Man's Land in an attempt to take advantage of the chaos in the British front lines. As a result, the defenders were able to take what might otherwise have been enormous risks such as, for example, rolling a field gun out into the open near Rossignol Wood, the better to bombard the London Scottish. What is extraordinary about the decision to withhold artillery support for fear of a counter-attack across No Man's Land is that, as far as research can tell, there was no previous case of such a counter-attack that might have acted as a precedent for this action. One can only assume that a degree of headless panic had set in at VII Corps H.Q. when they began to appreciate just how unexpectedly catastrophic the attack had been.

The table below shows the quantities of ammunition that VII Corps Heavy Artillery had kept in reserve for post-'Z' Day actions:

Type of gun	No of guns	Ammunition reserve/gun	Total reserve
4.7 in.	12	97	1,164
60 pdr	12	100	1,200
6 in. (26 cwt)	20	34	680
6 in. (30 cwt)	8	86	688
9.2 in. howitzer	24	0	0
12 in. & 15 in. howitzers	4	50	200
9.2 in. gun	1	50	50
6 in. Mk VII guns	2	60	120
		Total reserve ammunition	4,102

Table 25 Ammunition reserve for VII Heavy Artillery

What is notable here is the shortage of ammunition available for long range firing at the German heavy batteries and, because of this alone, it could be argued that keeping this reserve was a prudent thing to do. It is less easy to quantify the reserves available to the field batteries of the two divisions, however, the Artillery Plan published for the 56th Division indicates that there should have been in excess of 91,000 shells available as of 7.30 a.m. on 1st July and for the 46th Division 102,000. Of this total of 193,000 shells approximately 167,000 were 18 pdr shells and 26,000 4.5 in. howitzer shells. Precisely how many of these were used up on 1st July is impossible to say, however, one can make an educated estimate. The Southart Group, one of three supporting the 56th Division, fired just over 11,000 shells on 1st July. Assuming the other two groups fired a similar number this gives a total expenditure of 33,000 shells, leaving a balance of 58,000 shells available to the 56th Division. Given that the 56th Division field artillery had fired 8,300 before Zero hour the decision by VII Corps to suspend artillery support meant that they were holding in reserve 140% of the ammunition expended on 1st July which seems an excessive amount in the circumstances.

Of course, one of the reasons why there was this enormous surplus of ammunition was that the field artillery's guns were very nearly worn out by the constant firing that had gone on for nearly eight days. Neither the field nor heavy artillery guns were designed to sustain such wear and many gave out at a crucial time on the day of the battle. Here, the German decision to set limits on ammunition expenditure until the day of the attack reaped heavy dividends. The 'Gommecourt' artillery plan was that the artillery would only fire above and beyond pre-set limits in the case of two eventualities: the use of gas or an actual full scale attack. On two days in particular, the 26th and 27th ('W' and 'X' Days), smoke demonstrations of such a concentration were made that the infantry were convinced that a gas attack was in progress and, as a result, a considerable barrage was put down on the British trenches and front line villages. Beyond that, though, artillery expenditure was constrained by the dictums of the plan thus helping to both conserve guns and ammunition as well as keep concealed many of the well-hidden positions.

The ammunition expenditure of the 2nd Guard Reserve Division's artillery is given in Table 26 below:

Date	Field Guns & Light Howitzers			Heavy Guns and Howitzers					Total
	7.7cm Field Guns	10cm Light Field How.	9cm Guns	10cm Guns Model 14	15cm How. Model 96	15cm How. Models 02/13	15cm Russian Guns	21cm How. Model 99	Rounds Fired
No. guns	40	12	8	2	4	8	4	2	
24-Jun	528	223	211	8	80	138	42	17	1,247
25-Jun	1,105	313	452	214	178	357	154	102	2,875
26-Jun	3,806	621	651	385	79	953	74	67	6,636
27-Jun	4,518	468	208	70	152	664	260	68	6,408
28-Jun	664	210	173	0	38	404	39	32	1,560
29-Jun	751	69	108	126	141	247	67	6	1,515
30-Jun	548	90	0	0	31	25	52	0	746
1-Jul	11,698	4,429	3,873	609	481	2,821	258	252	24,421
Total	23,618	6,423	5,676	1,412	1,180	5,609	946	544	45,408
	35,717			9,691					

Table 26 Ammunition expenditure by 2ⁿᵈ Guard Reserve Division artillery U-Z Days

As can be seen, the total ammunition fired by the field guns and light howitzers by the 2ⁿᵈ Guard Reserve Division is broadly similar to that of the 56ᵗʰ Division alone. As the 46ᵗʰ Division's field artillery was firing a roughly similar number to that of the London gunners it would seem at first glance that the defensive fire was considerably less than that supporting the attackers. Three things need to be born in mind here:

1. The German artillery was firing to a strict plan, concentrating its fire in a strictly limited zone with one over-riding aim: to cut off the lead troops from their reserves and to destroy those reserves in their assembly trenches. This they did eminently successfully;
2. The German gunners were considerably assisted by their neighbours to north and south. To the north, the 111ᵗʰ Division's artillery joined in immediately helping to crush the 46ᵗʰ Division's attack and, to the south, that some of the 52ⁿᵈ Division's gunners were able to switch targets away from Serre and towards Gommecourt as soon as they were advised that the Serre position was secure; and
3. The British artillery had to follow its pre-ordained plan of timed lifts until the *certainty* of trouble persuaded Brig. Gen. Buckle and his staff that urgent adaptations were necessary. Then there was the issue of accurate observation, of who should fire at what, a conundrum they failed to solve all day, and lastly the 'need' to conserve ammunition against a German counter-attack into the British trenches.

So, whether the British artillery fired more shells than the Germans is rather academic. The point is that one side's artillery fired vastly more effectively than did the other. The Germans fired with the *certainty* of knowing that the British had to get men and supplies from Point A to Point B via one route. The British artillery fired in the *expectation* that their troops would succeed and be at Point B at time *x* and then Point C at time *x+10* and so on.

So, what was the British artillery doing on 1ˢᵗ July and why was the artillery plan for Z Day so much less effective than that of the Germans'?

Firstly it was a rigid programme based on an assumption of success. The artillery, both heavy and field, were given lines up to which they would 'walk' and which, at pre-defined times, would then move forward to another line. The infantry were given objectives which were also precisely timed. The consequence of any delay for the infantry was that the artillery barrage would quickly get further and further away from them leaving them open to infantry counter-attack. The lack of accurate information from the infantry, from the Forward Observation Officers (heavily targeted in the German artillery plan) and from the observers in the BE2c over-flying the salient, allied to the inexperience of the Staff in manipulating the artillery at their disposal and the rawness of the gunners themselves meant that redirecting the artillery was a real problem. No-one was entirely sure where to fire and what to fire at: infantry, artillery or both? Also, as the day wore on, overheating and wear on the barrels of the howitzers and guns would have increased resulting in a reduced rate of fire and decreased accuracy. Hitting any precise target, such as a heavily reinforced battery position, became more and more difficult, even assuming precise co-ordinates of their locations were known.

Brig. Gen. Loch, G.O.C. 168ᵗʰ Brigade, wrote a highly critical section of his post-battle report on the performance of the heavy artillery. Loch's first complaint was about the young and inexperienced artillery liaison officer attached to his H.Q. Although he appreciated the efforts he made to "get the assistance the infantry so desperately needed" Loch felt that the officer's requests lacked 'weight' when it came to ordering VII Corps artillery priorities. Communications were also poor in Loch's view. Any request for heavy artillery intervention had to be made through Division or Corps H.Q. and the telephone connections were very poor. Simply getting through took a long time and then, when contact was made, there was the problem of a young and inexperienced officer trying to persuade a more senior one of the urgency and importance of his requests. Loch was adamant that the only answer to the question about how to "neutralize the terrific and devastating fire to which the infantry (were) being subjected" was "effective counter battery work by heavy artillery." It was the plea of all infantrymen on both sides of the salient that day but, in great part, it was a plea left unanswered.

Apart from the inadequate counter-battery programme there was another considerable problem that diverted attention away from the predicament of the 56ᵗʰ Division. To a great extent any efforts of the heavy artillery to assist the 56ᵗʰ Division were compromised because they were constantly being asked to place a continuing bombardment of the NW flank of the Gommecourt salient in preparation for a renewal of the 46ᵗʰ Division's attack. This use of the heavies persisted long after there was any chance that the 46ᵗʰ Division would be able to mount a serious assault after the collapse of the initial advance.

The total chaos on the 46ᵗʰ Division's front cannot be over-estimated and, although one might have thought that such a day of disaster from Gommecourt south to La Boiselle might have generated intense official investigation, only the 46ᵗʰ's performance was the subject of any official Court of Inquiry[i]. It is interesting to note that, although the 46ᵗʰ Division suffered only 36% of the total

---

[i] Maj. Gen. Hon Edward James Montagu Stuart-Wortley CB C.M.G. M.V.O. D.S.O. had commanded the 46ᵗʰ Division in an attack on the Hohenzollern Redoubt on 13ᵗʰ October 1915, part of the Battle of Loos. There they had suffered their worst casualties of the war. They were the only division involved on the opening day of the Battle of the Somme for which 1ˢᵗ July 1916 was not the worst day of the war. Montagu Stuart-Wortley spent much of the rest of his life attempting, but failing, to clear his name. In 1919 he wrote to Lord French "I could not suffer a more ignoble and heart breaking fate had I been tried by Court Martial or had I committed some egregious blunder".

casualties in the attack on Gommecourt, the proportion of officers was higher amongst the North Midlanders casualties than in the London Division. Nearly 6% of all 46th Division casualties were officers against just over 4% for the Londoners. This might indicate that either the German defenders were better able to target officers amongst the 46th Division attackers or, in an effort to keep the attack going officers of this division exposed themselves to enemy fire in an even more reckless fashion than did those of the 56th Division. Whatever the reasons, such heavy losses amongst the officers of the attacking North Midland battalions can only have contributed still further to the chaos that overwhelmed the attack. Chaos that, the resulting Court of Inquiry suggests, was almost inevitable given the attack's poor planning, preparation and execution from early in the day. But one cannot criticise in any way the unfaltering bravery of the officers and men who attacked Gommecourt Wood that day. Only four under-strength[i] battalions had attacked the German lines and, whilst the men of the 1/6th North and 1/6th South Staffordshires suffered 41% casualties including two of their COs[ii] killed and one wounded, the two Sherwood Foresters battalions on the extreme left, the 1/5th and the 1/7th, lost nearly 80% of their men including both battalion COs, Lt. Col. D D Wilson[iii] and Maj. L A Hind[iv]. Nevertheless, the 46th Division suffered the lowest number of casualties of any of the divisions involved on the 1st July and this bare statistic was held against them by higher authorities for many months after the Battle of the Somme ended. Indeed, so poorly had they performed in the eyes of senior officers, that the division was withdrawn and played no further part in any of the battles of 1916 and 1917.

The reasons for the abject failure of the 46th Division's assault are not for this book. Suffice to say that the men and junior officers of the attacking battalions were grossly let down by the failings of the Commanding Officer and Staff of the Division and, as shall be shown later, for want of proper monitoring and control by the Commanding Officer and Staff of VII Corps. Brigadier-General Lyon, Chief of Staff at VII Corps, later described 'Eddy' Montagu Stuart-Wortley as "a worn-out man, who never visited his front line and was incapable of inspiring any enthusiasm[20]" and a member of his divisional staff, Lieutenant-Colonel A F Home, wrote of the division and its senior officers that "...the whole of this Division wants ginger putting into it from top to bottom!" The noted military historian, Col. J F C Fuller, was attached to the neighbouring 37th Division and, in a letter dated 5th June 1929 to Brig. Gen. Edmonds, the compiler of the Official History of the War, he stated: "Between ourselves, the command and the staff work of the 46th Division was shocking.[21]" There was even a story, whether

---

[i] The Official History gives the strengths of three of the four battalions: 1/6th S Staffs 500, 1/6th N Staffs 763 and 1/7th Sherwood Foresters 536.
[ii] Lt. Col Charles Edmund Boote, 1/6th North Staffordshire Regt died on 1st July 1916. Aged 41, he was the son of Richard and Sarah Anne Boote of Shallowford, Staffs; husband of Gertrude Ethel Boote of 62, St. Michael's Rd., Bedford. Served in the South African Campaign. He is buried in Gommecourt Wood New Cemetery, Foncquevillers, grave II. B. 12.
Lt. Col William Burnett D.S.O., 1/5th North Staffordshire Regt died of wounds on 1st July 1916. Aged 36, he was the son of Andrew and Mary E. Burnett of Burton-on-Trent and the husband of A. E. Burnett of Naunton, St. Cuthbert's, Bedford. He is buried in Warlincourt Halte British Cemetery, grave I.F.5.
[iii] Lt. Col D D Wilson, 1/5th Sherwood Foresters, formerly 17th Indian Cavalry, died on Saturday, 1st July 1916. His body was never found and his name is recorded on the Neuve Chapelle Memorial, Panel 6
[iv] Maj. Lawrence Arthur Hind M.C., 1/7th Sherwood Foresters, died on Saturday, 1st July 1916. Aged 38, he was the son of Jesse and Eliza Hind of Edwalton, Nottingham and husband of Eliza Montgomery Andrews of Ardara, Comber, Co. Down. His body was never found and his name is inscribed on the Thiepval Memorial, Pier and Face 10 C 10 D and 11 A.

true or apocryphal it is impossible to determine, that the staff of the 46th Division played tennis as their men were slaughtered on the wire in front of Gommecourt.[22]

It might have been thought that these problems would have alerted the Corps and Third Army staff to possible problems, however this did not happen. As a result, such was the shambles that the following day VII Corps commander, General Snow, sent a message to G.H.Q. stating:

"I regret to have to report that the 46th Division in yesterday's operations showed a lack of offensive spirit. I can only attribute this to the fact that its Commander, Major-General the Hon. E J Montagu Stuart-Wortley, is not of an age, neither has he the constitution, to allow him to be as much among his men in the front lines as is necessary to imbue all ranks with confidence and spirit... I therefore recommend that a younger man, and one more physically capable of energy, should be appointed to command the Division."

Stuart-Wortley was immediately and ruthlessly replaced by Haig who wrote to the War Office on the 4th July demanding his immediate recall to England, finishing with the comment that that he would not have him command another division on the Western Front. Whether Stuart-Wortley deserved such treatment is, perhaps, a matter of opinion but the severity of his treatment is odd when compared to that of other 'failures' on the 1st July. For example, Haig had already privately criticised the commander of VIII Corps, Lt. Gen. Aylmer Hunter Weston, describing him and his staff as "amateurs in hard fighting" in his diary and in his diary entry for 1st July he wrote angrily: "I am inclined to believe from further reports that few men of the VIII Corps left their trenches!"[23]. Any yet, neither Hunter Weston nor any of his divisional commanders were sacked or even disciplined. Conversely, Stuart-Wortley was removed expediently and his division the only one made subject of a Court of Enquiry.

One might wonder whether there was more to this than meets the eye. And the enquiring mind would be correct. Stuart-Wortley had severely irritated Haig and was a marked man. At the Battle of Loos in October 1915, the 46th Division had been ordered to attack a particularly strong part of the line, the Hohenzollern Redoubt and Fosse 8, and Stuart-Wortley had expressed concerns about the plan for this action. The assault had gone in and the Division had suffered 4,000 casualties. The man who ordered this disastrous attack was none other than Gen. Sir Douglas Haig, then G.O.C. First Army. In the previous months Stuart-Wortley, a man well connected at Court, had been writing on a weekly basis to the King, at the King's request, recounting the actions of the 46th Division. The reason for this was that the Division was the first complete Territorial Division to see active service on the Western Front and the King had taken a personal interest. Stuart-Wortley had asked permission from the then commander in chief of the B.E.F., Lord French, and French, a good friend of Stuart-Wortley, had agreed. These letters ceased after the Hohenzollern Redoubt fiasco because, as Stuart-Wortley later wrote, he would have felt it necessary to criticise his superiors for ordering the attack. However, Haig heard about these letters and was furious. Stuart-Wortley only found out that he was a marked man when his Corps commander, Gen. Haking, asked him whether he was in the habit of writing to the King. Stuart-Wortley later wrote:

"He then informed me that I had incurred the severe displeasure of a higher military authority, viz. Sir Douglas Haig, G.O.C. First Army."[24]

It is, of course, ironic that Sir Douglas Haig had spent several months assiduously courting the King and briefing against his predecessor, Lord French, through exploiting his own Court connections, i.e. his wife. Clearly here was a case that 'what was sauce for the Goose' was certainly not also sauce for the Gander.

After the war, Stuart-Wortley wrote to Winston Churchill, then in charge of the War Office, as part of his campaign for rehabilitation:

"For five months pressure had been brought to bear by superior authority on Generals Allenby and Snow to get rid of me; and the failure to take Gommecourt was finally decided upon as sufficient reason."[25]

Although critical of some elements of the 46th Division's performance, Brig. Gen. Archibald Home, who had been Division's G.S.O.1 from April to the end of June, supported the idea that Stuart-Wortley was a marked man. In his diary entry for 5th July 1916, Home wrote of his sadness at Stuart-Wortley's sacking:

"I am sorry for him as they meant getting rid of him and I suppose this was the opportunity."[26]

That Stuart-Wortley was already in Haig's sights can be confirmed from Haig's diary entry of 24th November 1915, not long after the Hohenzollern attack:

"I do not think much of Major General Stuart-Wortley as a Divisional Commander and have already spoken to G.O.C. XI Corps[i] on the subject."

The oddity in all of this is that of timing. Snow wrote to Allenby suggesting Stuart-Wortley's removal on 2nd July. Allenby concurred and forwarded the recommendation to Haig whose letter to the War Office was sent two days later. Stuart-Wortley clearly saw Snow's letter as, on the same day it was sent to Allenby, he had sent a rebuttal of its contents to Snow with the added complaint that neither Snow nor Allenby had yet seen a copy of his report on the attack. It is strange, then, that on the 3rd July, Brig. Gen. Lyon, General Staff VII Corps, sent out from Snow's headquarters a message to the Division that read:

"The Corps Commander wishes to congratulate the troops of the 46th Division for the manner in which they fought and endured during the fighting on 1st July. Many gallant acts both by units and individuals are to hand. Although Gommecourt has not fallen into our hands, the purpose of the attack which was mainly to contain and kill Germans was accomplished."[27]

It would appear that this message, sent out under Gen. Snow's name and presumably with his endorsement, went *down* the chain of command but not up. Of course, as shall be shown, there were critics of Snow's performance in high positions at Third Army H.Q. and, perhaps, there is an element of back covering in Snow's actions. It seems clear, however, that Stuart-Wortley was sacrificed by Haig out of personal spite and that the action was a settling of scores. After all, if the grounds for sacking were based purely on performance before and during 1st July, then Maj. Gen. Stuart-Wortley would not have been the only senior officer

[i] Lt. Gen. Richard Cyril Byrne Haking, later to make his 'reputation' as the overseer of the disaster at Fromelles.

making the sorry trip home in disgrace. Equally, though, there were many critics of Stuart-Wortley both personally and professionally and it is impossible to excuse him and his staff for the planning and conduct of the attacks.[28]

***

IT WAS CLEAR, at least at brigade level, that the 46th Division's attack had foundered more or less everywhere by 9 a.m., i.e. some 90 minutes after the attack had gone in. The 137th Brigade's attack had collapsed within the first few minutes whilst some men of the 139th Brigade had struggled into the German lines on the far left, there to be overpowered and either killed or captured in aggressive German counter-attacks. Headquarters at 46th Division, in consultation with VII Corps, somehow believed that the attack could be resurrected and attempts were made to re-organise the survivors and bring up fresh reserves (almost impossible given the state of the communication trenches which were thigh and sometimes chest high in water for hundreds of yards). Delay piled on delay until it was decided that the new attack could go over the top at 12.15 p.m. To facilitate this, Stuart-Wortley asked for and received support from elements of the Corps heavy artillery which was asked to put a barrage on the western edge of Gommecourt Wood and Village. 12.15 p.m. quickly became 1.15 p.m., then 2.45 p.m. and, eventually, 3.30 p.m. When it was given the go-ahead, the feeble attack finished before it started[i]. However, throughout these recurrent delays, significant parts of the available heavy artillery were either fruitlessly bombarding areas which were not to be attacked again or were awaiting instructions to bombard these self same places.

Messages from VII Corps H.Q. on 1st July, record the time and ammunition wasted in these futile exercises which went on as late as 4.25 p.m.:

"10.10 a.m. Gen. Buckle (Cmdg Corps Heavy Artillery) instructed to turn heavies onto SE corner of Gommecourt Wood at 10.30 for ten minutes.

10.55 a.m. Continue at slow rate of fire on SE corner of Gommecourt Wood and north end of village as attack will be made later. Heavy artillery will be informed to quicken rate of fire before this commences.

12 noon to 12.15 p.m. Heavy artillery to bring heavy fire to bear on West edge of Gommecourt Wood.

12.47 p.m. From 1 p.m. open on Foolery trench… til 1.15 p.m. From 1.15 p.m. til 1.30 p.m. continue to fire… on Foolery and Focus[ii].

2.10 p.m. Gen. Buckle instructed to shell again from 3.15 p.m. to 3.30 p.m. in support 46th Division artillery.

3.45 p.m. Situation as regards counter-battery work – ammunition difficult, batteries to keep 300 rounds 'til tomorrow.

4.25 p.m. Gen. Buckle to take fire off Minx and Might[iii] and keep a very slow rate of fire on western edge of Gommecourt Wood and SE corner of Wood."

It is instructive to see how precisely these orders affected one of the batteries involved. The C.O. of 68th Siege Battery, Lt. Col. Mayne, forwarded a detailed

---

[i] Tragically, twenty men of the 1/6th Sherwood Foresters left their trenches before the cancellation only for eighteen of them to become casualties within a few yards

[ii] German front line trenches to the west of Gommecourt village.

[iii] German support trenches running from the SE corner of Pigeon Wood (Reigel Stellung II)

report of his batteries activities on 1ˢᵗ July two days after the event. The constant switching of targets, cancellations and revisions of orders suggest such a state of confusion at VII Corps level that it is no wonder that many lower down the command 'pecking order' wondered what on earth the heavies were up to. 68ᵗʰ Siege Battery comprised four 30cwt 1896 pattern 6 in. howitzers split into a left and a right section both dug in around Sailly-au-Bois. After the attack went in, their targets were of importance to the 56ᵗʰ Division being Epte trench for the right section and Anna trench for the left. These two communication trenches were crucial to the 168ᵗʰ Brigade as Epte led to the boundary between the 168ᵗʰ and 169ᵗʰ Brigades on the left of their position and Anna ran straight from Rossignol Wood and Point 147 towards the Farmer-Farmyard stronghold on the right. Preventing German reinforcements from pouring down these two trenches would have been invaluable to all of the battalions involved. By 7.50 a.m. the guns were maintaining a slow rate of fire on these targets, slow but enough to make life uncomfortable for anyone trying to work their way down the trenches. At 8.44 a.m., however, under orders from 35ᵗʰ H.A.G., the left section was ordered to cease firing on Anna, thereby allowing men from the 170ᵗʰ I.R. unfettered access to the London Scottish's position. Their new target was to be the western edge of Gommecourt Wood, scene of the already failed attack of the 46ᵗʰ Division. For an hour these guns targeted the wood until 47ᵗʰ H.A.G. ordered them back onto Anna. From then onwards it was, as a result of a 'lack of clearness of the situation'[29], shoot-switch targets-shoot-switch targets as VII Corps desperately tried to flog the 'dead horse' of the 46ᵗʰ Division's attack back into action:

"10.15 a.m. 35ᵗʰ H.A.G. orders left section onto Gommecourt Wood

10.30 a.m. 35ᵗʰ H.A.G. orders left section onto Anna trench

11.45 a.m. 35ᵗʰ H.A.G. orders right section to lift from Epte and fire on Gommecourt Wood from noon to 12.25 p.m. (46ᵗʰ Division attack postponed)

12.25 p.m. 35ᵗʰ H.A.G. orders right section back onto Epte

12.35 p.m. 35ᵗʰ H.A.G. orders right section to resume bombardment of Gommecourt Wood at 1 p.m. (46ᵗʰ Division attack postponed)

1.25 p.m. Right section resumes shelling Epte

2.05 p.m. Both sections ordered to shell Gommecourt Wood from 3.15 to 3.30 p.m. then lift to Oxus trench in the rear of the Wood (46ᵗʰ Division attack postponed)

3.55 p.m. Both sections ordered to fire on Epte

4.42 p.m. Left section ordered to fire on Gommecourt Wood (46ᵗʰ Division attack cancelled)

5.07 p.m. One gun of right section ordered to fire on Etch

5.55 p.m. Lt. Col. Mayne reported right section again firing on Epte (76 rounds left) and left section still firing on Gommecourt Wood (36 rounds left)

6.10 p.m. One gun of right section ordered to fire on Etch

6.30 p.m. All guns firing on Epte

7.30 p.m. Ceased firing because FOO unable to observe anything because of intense enemy shell fire"[30]

Throughout this time the men of the 56th Division were grimly hanging on in the German trenches south of Gommecourt and requests for heavy artillery to mount effective counter-battery and interdiction fire were being, at best, responded to half-heartedly and, at worst, ignored. By the time 68th Siege Battery was able to concentrate the fire of its four howitzers on Epte trench it was too late to effect the outcome of the battle.

***

THESE DECISIONS were being made at VII Corps H.Q., one presumes by Lt. Gen. Snow and his G.O.C. Heavy Artillery, Brig. Gen. Buckle, and they were, at least, consistent with other similar decisions being made along the northern end of the front to 'reinforce failure' wherever it occurred and without thought to the consequences.

Lt. Gen. Snow's performance was already under scrutiny by the staff at Third Army H.Q. and, later, he was roundly criticised by Maj. Gen. S E Hollond[i] then a G.S.O.2 on Allenby's Staff. Hollond did not mince his words, stating his views bluntly after the battle:

> "Snow's arrangements for this attack were monstrously bad. He never co-ordinated the plan of his divisions, neither did he supervise their individual arrangements. He went on leave to England for ten days during the preparation and arrived back only a few days before the attack. I thought his supervisions so bad that I tried to get Allenby to degommer him (i.e. sack), but Allenby wasn't sure of getting G.H.Q. support."[31]

Snow was not a well man and eventually came home after Gen. Byng sacrificed him and several other Corps commanders on the altar of self-preservation after Cambrai, and he spent much of the rest of his life in a Bath Chair. The injury that caused him so much distress occurred when he was thrown from his horse during the retreat from Le Cateau. The resulting pelvic injury kept him at home for nearly two months but, in November 1914, he was rushed back to command the 27th Division. His visits home were often medically related and he was clearly a man in much discomfort. How much this might have distracted him in the run-up to the attack is impossible to say but to have been away for ten days shortly before the attack is extraordinary behaviour by anyone's standards and reeks of the complacency that had swept the B.E.F. in the last weeks of June. That Allenby felt it impossible to replace him sprang from Haig's long standing antipathy to Third Army's commander but it is hardly a healthy position to have a difficult attack being overseen by a General who had lost the faith of his superior but who could not be replaced because the C.in.C. has no faith in that superior officer.

In short, the attack was to be launched by an Army whose commander was disliked by, and who had little influence, at G.H.Q.; it was organised by a Corps commanders whose holiday arrangements and health worries were more significant than the fate of the attack; and against a position of enormous and

---

untested strength to which they were to draw yet more troops and artillery by means of their very public displays of preparation.

On 17ᵗʰ July, Maj. Gen. Hull forwarded a report on the attack to Snow and Allenby. It makes interesting reading as it combines a clear condemnation of the heavy artillery's counter-battery performance with a contradictory assessment that the main reason why the attack failed was the lack of hand grenades. Hull seemed convinced that, had the re-supply of bombs not been so totally disrupted, his men would have been able to hold onto their gains. He was also concerned that the efforts to use captured German bombs might not have been very well organised and, therefore, contributed to the failure. He takes no account of the failure of the 46ᵗʰ Division's attack or that, even with a reasonable supply of bombs, the 56ᵗʰ would have had only a tenuous hold on a dangerously exposed salient with no easy means of supply. It must surely be the case that the primary reason for the failure of the attack was the concentration and intensity of German barrage which prevented the re-supply of the attackers. Had the German artillery been neutralised then re-supply, though still costly, might have been sustainable. Then, and only then, would the quantity of bombs have become an issue. Hull tacitly accepted this point when he devoted one and a half pages of his report to the issue of the enemy's artillery. He put forward two means of dealing with enemy artillery - one of which was clearly never going to occur at Gommecourt:

1. Push the advance so far forward that the guns are overrun; or
2. Increase the artillery allotted to counter-battery work.

As the attack had clearly defined and limited objectives, the first method was never an option in this case. Option two, however, certainly was achievable had the resources been provided to achieve the intended objective. Hull wrote:

"I understand that on 1ˢᵗ July our counter-battery groups engaged a very large number of German batteries. *The results of the counter-battery work were not apparent* (author's emphasis)."[32]

Hull went on the complain about the number and calibre of guns used in the counter-battery programme and suggested that the heavy howitzers might be better used to destroy the enemy's guns. His suggestion for the use of the heavies after Zero hour seems commendably sensible:

1. The lighter guns in the H.A.G.s, i.e. the 4.7 in. and 60 pdr guns, should be used to barrage the roads and communications trenches being used to bring up reinforcements but which were outside the range of the Divisional field artillery;
2. The heavy guns, i.e. the 6 in. Mk VII and the 9.2 in. railway gun, should be used on barrage work as they were able to fire more quickly than the howitzers; and
3. The heavy howitzers should be used to silence hostile enemy artillery with their heavy calibre shells being more likely to collapse their emplacements and wreck the guns.

Hull then went on to comment on the German's use of effective counter-battery work at Verdun (something Haig's report in March did not mention) and how, at Gommecourt, they had not bothered with the British artillery, instead concentrating their efforts solely on cutting off and destroying the British infantry. He then commented on the preliminary bombardment stating that, in some ways, it did the attacking men no favours. Such was the damage in some of the strongpoints most heavily targeted that men either lost their way because they could not recognise the terrain (a problem made worse by the intensity and duration of the smoke screen) and others found themselves without adequate cover as the trenches had been flattened. As Hull confirmed that the heavies had a negligible impact on the deep dugouts as well as the morale of the defenders it is clear that he was not impressed by the seven day bombardment, however, he then makes a comment which suggests either that he had not really understood the reason for the attack or that he had a very short memory:

> "I am doubtful of the value of these very long bombardments, which give the enemy time to recognise the points selected for attack, and possibly relieve his troops, and to concentrate guns and bring up ammunition to the threatened points."[33]

Whilst this might be a valid criticism of the main attack to the south, as a comment on the Gommecourt action it is extraordinary. The whole point of a diversion is to attract enemy resources to a point of no particular importance to the main attack whilst, ideally, weakening the defences of the main position. The elaborate and lengthy preparations for the Gommecourt attack were designed to achieve exactly that and were then further reinforced by the heavy local bombardment. Had Hull been criticising the main attacks further south then, perhaps, his point might well have been valid but such criticism, when levelled at the diversion at Gommecourt, is plainly absurd.

Hull covered various other aspects of the attack complaining, for example, that the width of No Man's Land had proved a significant obstacle to reinforcing troops. The 56th Division's new front line trenches lay between 300 yards (opposite The Rangers) and 400 yards (on 169th Brigade's front) from the German lines. Further south, opposite Serre, Redan Ridge and Beaumont Hamel, these distances were between 100 and 200 yards and so, in that respect, Hull was absolutely correct, however, this was known for more than a month before the attack and should have been factored into any plan of attack. Again, the issue wasn't so much the distance reinforcements needed to travel across the open, it was the fact that the German barrage made movement within their own trenches and across No Man's Land next to impossible. The attempts at reinforcement usually foundered within a few yards of the British front lines under shell and machine gun fire and, for the most part, whether the trenches had been 100 or 800 yards apart was really immaterial.

Hull then returned to his theme of the lack of grenades and the organisation that was necessary in the enemy's trenches to ensure that the available bombs were collected and used in the most suitable places. His comment that: "...as many grenades as possible must be carried forward with the assaulting troops" must have raised an eyebrow or two with some of the battalion commanders especially Lt. Col. Bates of the L.R.B. who had to indulge in some special pleading for his men to be allowed to carry just three bombs each. So complacent had the likes of Hull and Snow been about the attack that they had viewed it as more akin to an occupation than a fight. Their conviction that the Germans would be unable to resist, their bodies and morale shattered by the bombardment, was so resolute that equipping the men to withstand a serious counter-attack was not high on their list of priorities. Digging in, reversing trenches, constructing and wiring strongpoints, establishing communications, digging trenches across No Man's Land, these were the tasks they felt the majority of the men would be involved in, that and a bit of mopping up where the few bombs supplied could be used to clear any undamaged dug outs.

Snow's report on the attack was finalised on the 24th July and was then forwarded to Allenby at Third Army H.Q. The report highlights some interesting areas but also skates over others. His conclusions broadly mirrored those of Hull except for Hull's conviction that with more bombs the position might have been held. But, when judging the overall success or failure of the attack, Snow conveniently ignored the fact that an operation designed to draw away enemy resources from the main attack had, in fact, concentrated artillery and infantry as much on the left flank of VIII Corps assaults on Serre and Redan Ridge as on the troops attacking Gommecourt. As a result, the failure opposite Serre had been even more conclusive than that of the two divisions further north. Interestingly, Snow's definitions of the objectives of VII Corps actually underline how badly the Gommecourt action *failed* to achieve its main intention of a diversion of enemy resources. Rather than talk about a diversion away from the Fourth Army's front in a general sense, Snow talked about diverting resources away from Serre specifically. He defined this objective as follows:

"To assist in the operation of the Fourth Army by diverting against itself the fire of artillery and infantry which might otherwise be directed against the left flank of the main attack at SERRE."[34]

As has been shown, the insertion of the 2nd Guard Reserve Division with its associated artillery along with the 20th Reserve Field Artillery, elements of the 19th Bavarian Field Artillery Regiment and the 10th Bavarian Foot Artillery Regiment had the effect of strengthening the defences of both Gommecourt, Serre and Redan Ridge. In that specific, therefore, it is impossible to agree with Snow's opinion (and that of all of his superiors) that the attack had contributed to the success of the main attack. Only by persisting with the myth of a successful diversion could these officers justify the destruction of two divisions one of which was, by common consent, the best Territorial division in France and Flanders.

Some of Snow's other comments reveal just how exposed the men involved in the attack were and how the lack of back up resources, such as labour battalions, made their position even worse. Apart from the exhaustion caused by the constant and gruelling workload imposed on the men due to lead the attack, which involved both digging new trench systems on both divisional fronts as well as bringing up supplies, laying roads and light railways, practising the attack, manning the trenches, etc., the limitations of the manpower available resulted in short cuts in the preparation of the attack. Crucially, the newly dug trenches were of little protection to the men expecting to re-supply and reinforce the leading waves of the attack as they were of flimsy construction with no decent dugouts or significant revetting. There just was not the time or manpower to do anything other than effectively dig an inter-connecting series of slit trenches which might protect a man from bullets but which were of little use when it came to protection from artillery and mortar shells. And even after all of the effort to dig and wire the new trenches, Snow agreed with Hull that they were still too distant from the German lines. Plans to push the trenches even further forward on the 56th Division's front were scuppered by the need to maintain the newly dug front line which was in danger of being eroded and undermined by the continuous rain throughout the middle of June and, again, it was the men earmarked for the assault who had to undertake this task.

But this lack of labour meant that another weapon that might usefully have been used in the attack was denied to them. Although the artillery had only a limited supply of gas shells, and those only SK tear gas shells, the infantry could have used ground released gas from canisters emplaced in the front trenches. With the wind having blown from the west throughout 1st July this might well have been highly useful especially if it had blown in sufficient concentrations into the woods and depressions behind the German lines where lurked their artillery. But, because of the strains placed on the men to achieve what they did there simply was not enough labour to dig the emplacements needed and to haul the gas canisters to the front. As a result, the only gas released on the VII Corps' front on 1st July came from 37th Division opposite Monchy as part of a fairly ineffective demonstration to the left of the main Gommecourt attack.

On the issue of counter-battery fire, Snow is brief but yet revealing. After listing the wholly inadequate number and weight of batteries available for the counter-battery programme he went on:

> "The results that they achieved cannot be estimated, but they were inadequate to deal with the large number of German batteries opposite our front.
>
> The batteries used as counter batteries were told to pay more attention to hostile batteries in the Southern area firing on the VIII Corps front than against those at Adinfer, as it was realised that it was more important to assist the attack on Serre than to succeed at Gommecourt. The amount of hostile fire which the VII Corps had to endure is in great measure attributable to this fact."[35]

It is probably just as well that this document was marked 'SECRET' and, therefore, had a necessarily limited circulation. Had the officers and men of the battalions sacrificed in front of Gommecourt known that there was a deliberate policy of *not* trying to destroy the artillery that killed and maimed so many of them then the disillusion that was fairly widespread in the ranks would have spread like wildfire. Of course, this policy, assuming it even existed as there is no mention of it in the numerous documents circulated covering the planning of the attack, failed lamentably. The attack on Serre was effectively over within minutes although various efforts were made until late in the evening to reorganise in order to mount further attacks. Thankfully for the men involved, these never materialised. The swift collapse of the attack on Serre did allow, however, the German command to switch their artillery onto the 56th Division's with a flexibility sadly lacking from those commanding VII and VIII Corps guns. But again, the unrealistically optimistic belief that the 31st Division's attack could somehow be revived lingered on until nearly 10 p.m. on Saturday night at VIII Corps' H.Q. in spite of the fact that Maj. Gen. Wanless O'Gowan, G.O.C. 31st Division, had informed Gen. Hunter-Weston at 6 p.m. that the attacking brigades were incapable of further action. These persistent delays in sensible decision making prevented any reciprocal action on the part of this Corps' heavy artillery.

After the distance between the trenches and the weight of the German artillery barrage, Snow's third main concern was the performance of the 46ᵗʰ Division whose commander was accused of 'faulty organisation', principally in allowing the follow-up waves to move up through the congested and flooded communication trenches rather than across the open using trench bridges as had been the case with the 56ᵗʰ Division. It must be said, however, that each division submitted plans for their assaults to VII Corps H.Q. and that 56ᵗʰ Division's plan to use trench bridges were explicitly set out. If they were missing from the 46ᵗʰ Division's plans then why was this not spotted by VII Corps staff and amendments demanded prior to 'Z' Day? The opinion of the Third Army staff officer, Hollond, that "Snow's arrangements for this attack were monstrously bad. He never co-ordinated the plan of his divisions, neither did he supervise their individual arrangements" seem in this respect at least to be borne out.

Allenby, Snow, Hull and their respective staffs made the cardinal error of relentlessly believing the most favourable reports of the effects of their plan. They believed religiously that the artillery would kill or demoralise every German in the salient. They accepted all the evidence pointing in that direction and rejected anything that contradicted it. They made no back-up plans in case anything should go wrong apparently being unable to conceive of such circumstances. Of course, these were not the only generals to make these mistakes before 1ˢᵗ July. Delusion and complacency ran rampant from G.H.Q. downwards affecting almost everyone except for the officers and men who were to take part in the attack. At that level, realism and cynicism reared its typically stubborn British head. From their own experience they knew that something would always go wrong or that the enemy would behave in a fashion that the senior officers found unreasonably unpredictable. And they knew that they would be the ones to pay the price.

Some time later, the 56ᵗʰ Division's attack on Gommecourt was the subject of a lecture, attended by Snow, Hull and other senior officers. The history of the attack, from the digging of the new trench system through to the end of the attack itself, was described and discussed. The usual complaints were rehearsed, the width of No Man's Land, the counter-battery issue, the use and supply of bombs, etc., but one new subject arose at the instigation of Maj. Gen. Hull and his comments were aimed at Company and Platoon commanders and senior N.C.O.s. Hull's words are the epitome of hypocrisy and they reek of buck-passing at its worst:

"...upon Platoon commanders in particular he would impress the importance of 'power to command' of leadership... it was easy to take a platoon to bathe in a river, but it was power to cope with a sudden and unforeseen emergency which was so essential – with the sudden arrival on the scene, let him suggest of a number of crocodiles. It was not enough to be able to deal with a definite job, every step in connection with which could be thought our previously. It was the power of quick thinking of quick decision in the face of an unexpected eventuality, which must be cultivated... It might be permitted to officers in a higher command to scratch their heads over a military problem, but the platoon commander must be, above all things, prompt. It might also be said that it was better to do something wrong than to do nothing."

As a gratuitous insult to the memories of the dozens of young company and platoon commanders who died in front of Gommecourt trying to deal with 'a number of crocodiles' Hull's words would take some beating. As a desperate attempt to divert attention away from the senior officers responsible for the sacrifice of the 56th Division it is despicable. And, if Haig, Allenby, Snow and Hull had given any thought at all to the possibility of 'the sudden arrival on the scene of 'a number of crocodiles' then, perhaps, they would not have had the deaths of nearly 1,700 young men resting heavy on their consciences.

The attack on Gommecourt is, perhaps, most succinctly summed up by post-war comment of Lt. Col. L A C Southam, D.S.O., T.D. who had commanded 280th Brigade R.F.A. and the Northern Group of the field artillery supporting the men of the 169th Brigade on 1st July 1916. He wrote:

"This tragic adventure resulted in the loss of thousands of splendid men, largely potential material for officers with no comparable enemy casualties and, in view of the complete failure at Serre, no advantage, however indirect."

In short, the men of the 56th Division had laid down their lives for nothing, their sacrifice predictable and pointless. Think of that as you trudge the fields around Gommecourt and bear witness to their deaths in the well-ordered cemeteries and on the many panels of the sombre Memorial to the Missing at Thiepval. And wonder at the Roman poet's oft quoted line[36]...

Dulce et Decorum est Pro Patria Mori.

ENDNOTES:
1 Boraston J.H., O.B.E., ed. Sir Douglas Haig's Despatches, Dec. 1915 - Apr 1919. 1919
2 Churchill, Winston, 'The World Crisis', page 737
3 Sir Douglas Haig's Diary, NA WO 256/11
4 Sir Douglas Haig's Diary and John Terraine, 'Douglas Haig: The Educated Soldier' page 193
5 Terraine, John, Haig: The Educated Soldier, 1990 page 201
6 Warner, Philp, Field Marshal Earl Haig, 1991 page 200.
7 G.H.Q. OAD 12, June 16th
8 Snow, Maj. Gen Sir Thomas D'Oyly, entry in personal diary, IWM
9 Ibid.
10 Ibid.
11 Ibid.
12 War Diary and Letters of Sir Douglas Haig, Haig Papers, National Library of Scotland.
13 Lloyd George, David, 'War Memoirs', 1931 page 322
14 Boraston J.H., O.B.E., ed. Sir Douglas Haig's Despatches, Dec. 1915 - Apr 1919. 1919
15 Terraine, John, Haig: The Educated Soldier, 1990, page 207.
16 Edmonds, Brig. Gen. Sir James E, Official History of the War: Military Operations, France and Belgium 1916, Volume 1 pages 442-3.
17 NA WO 95/2937, Commander, 56ᵗʰ Division Royal Artillery,
18 McNaughton, Maj. Gen A G L, 'The Development of Artillery in the Great War', The Field Artillery Journal, May-June 1930, page 258.
19 Letter from Lt Col J H H Jones D.S.O. dated 21ˢᵗ May 1929 commenting on a draft the Official History, CAB 45/135 National Archives.
20 CAB 45/135 NA
21 CAB 45/185 NA
22 From a letter written on 22ⁿᵈ June 1929 by Col G D Goodman CS, C.M.G., D.S.O. CAB 45/185 NA.
23 WO 256/11 NA
24 From Maj. Gen Stuart-Wortley's personal file WO 138/29 NA
25 Letter dated 4ᵗʰ May 1920 from Maj. Gen Stuart-Wortley's personal file WO 138/29 NA
26 Home, Brig. Gen Sir Archibald, The Diary of a World War One Cavalry Officer, 1985 page 113.
27 Copy in Maj. Gen Stuart-Wortley's personal file WO 138/29 NA
28 For a full description of the outcome of Stuart Wortley's sacking see this author's 'A Lack of Offensive Spirit? The 46ᵗʰ (North Midland) Division at Gommecourt, 1ˢᵗ July 1916', also by Iona Books.
29 War Diary 35ᵗʰ Heavy Artillery Group, NA WO 95/390
30 68ᵗʰ Siege Battery War Diary NA WO95/480.
31 Gardner, Brian, Allenby, Cassell 1965, pages 91-92.
32 WO95/2931 NA
33 Ibid.
34 Lt Gen Snow's report to Third Army, 24ᵗʰ July 1916. Third Army report SGE 47/1. NA.
35 Ibid.
36 From Horace's Odes (iii 2.13) but perhaps more famously known as the ending to Wilfred Owen's poem 'Dulce et Decorum Est'. Translated as "it is sweet and fitting to die for your country".

18. POSTSCRIPT

> *"My dearest Mother and Dad,*
>
> *I am writing this letter today before the most important moment in my life... The day has almost dawned when I shall do my little bit in the cause of civilisation.¹ "*

2nd Lt. Jack Engall
1/16th Queen's Westminster Rifles

FOR WEEKS AFTER THE ATTACK on 1st July 1916, battalion, company and platoon commanders spent many unhappy hours composing letters of condolence to the relatives of the men who had died that day. The bereaved would have already received the official telegram and now, in their anguish, they sought news of the manner of their son or husband's death. Where had he died? How had he died? Had he suffered?

John and Edith Engall of Acton in West London were the sad recipients of such a telegram. Their son, Jack, a 2nd Lt. in the Queen's Westminster Rifles was amongst the dead. John Sherwin Engall was just over 18 years of age when the war broke out. He had left St Paul's School in July 1914 after passing the preliminary examination of the Institute of Chartered Accountants and was articled to a City firm of accountants. He enlisted on 3rd September 1914 as a rifleman in the 16th County of London Queen's Westminster Rifles. Towards the end of the year he applied for a commission in the Queen Victoria's Rifles but, while the matter was under consideration, he was offered a commission in his own regiment, an honour which he highly appreciated. He was gazetted 2nd Lt. in the Queen's Westminsters on the 16th January 1915. In the Spring of 1916, as the 56th Division organised itself for the attack at Gommecourt, Jack Engall was plucked from the ranks of his battalion and seconded to the 169th Brigade Machine Gun Company. He would be one of ten officers in a company of just over 100 men and they soon set to the task of familiarisation with their Vickers machine guns and with one another.

The 169th Brigade MGC were to send men and guns over with the waves of the Queen's Westminster Rifles and Jack Engall's gun teams were given the task of helping to take, hold and fortify the Brigade's ultimate objective, the Quadrilateral, the rectangle of trenches behind Gommecourt village where the men of the 46th and 56th Division's would link up prior to the clearance of the village and park. Engall was immensely proud to have been selected for this job, believing it reflected well on him personally and on the men he led. When the attack went in, he and his men dragged their cumbersome guns, tripods, ammunition and water tins containing cooling water beyond the second line of the German position. Engall and some of his men fought one gun, being picked off until only Jack Engall and his spotter remained. He died from a bullet to the head somewhere in the German trenches.

Five day's after the attack, Mr and Mrs Engall were sent a letter from their son's superior in the 169th Brigade Machine Gun Company. Capt. J B Baber had also been seconded to the Machine Gun Company from the Westminsters and it fell to him to write the first official letter to the grieving parents.

From Capt. J Baber M.C.,
169ᵗʰ Brigade Machine Gun Company and Queen's Westminster Rifles
6ᵗʰ July 1916

Dear Mrs Engall,

By this time you will have received the official wire informing you of your son's death. I was not with him at the time of his death but from survivors I have heard the story. It is a very fine story. One section had to go forward into the German lines and your son went. He reached the third German line when he was killed instantly while getting his gun into action at close range. No doubt you would like to get confirmation of this and so I give you the name and address of the man who was with your son at that time and who afterwards fought the gun and by some strange chance lived to return that night. He is Cpl. Bolwell, Machine Gun Company, 169ᵗʰ Infantry Brigade. The death of your son deprived us of a very fine soldier. That is proved beyond question by the way his men followed him that day even if we had not known it before. We all miss him very much and, because we knew him, can sympathise all the more deeply with you.

I will see to it myself that all your son's kit is returned safely to you and finally enclose a letter which he left to be forwarded to you in the event of his death.

We have sympathy for you Mrs Engall but have only pride in your son with perhaps a little regret that he alone has been singled out for the highest honour and happiness.

Sincerely yours,

John Baber

Five day's later, the Westminster's C.O. committed his own feelings to paper.

From Lt. Col. Shoolbred C.M.G.
Commanding Officer, Queen's Westminster Rifles
11ᵗʰ July 1916.

Dear Mrs Engall,

I have been trying ever since July 1ˢᵗ to write to tell you how deeply I and all of us sympathise with you in your sad loss which is one which we also feel as our own in the loss of a tried and proved comrade. Your gallant boy died fighting his gun with the utmost gallantry leaving an example to the few of the Machine Gun Section who are left worthy of the highest traditions of the British Army.

I am, at any rate, able to give you the comfort of the assurance that he suffered not at all because, from what I am told, I am sure he must have been killed instantaneously. And in the pride and satisfaction of knowing that he was doing what must be the highest action of any soldier, setting up his gun in captured German trenches. There are not many of his comrades left but those of us who are will cherish his memory.

I hope you will accept our heartfelt sympathy at your loss which is very truly our own also. Believe me.

Yours sincerely,

N Shoolbred,
Lt. Col., Queen's Westminster Rifles.

The Engall's, determined to find out the circumstances of their boy's death, followed the suggestion of Capt. Baber and wrote to Cpl. Bolwell. On 16th July he wrote his own letter of condolence, one all the more poignant as he gave a detailed first hand account of their son's death.

From Cpl., now Sgt., J C Bolwell
Queen's Westminster Rifles, B.E.F.
Dear Mrs Engall,

In reply to your letter I am glad to be able to tell you of anything which may help you to bear the loss of your son. As you know we started the attack at 7.30 am when, under cover of smoke, we went forward from our own trenches. With your son leading the way we reached the German first line trenches with little resistance which we immediately crossed and advanced to their second line. Here the Germans were putting up a fight but as our chaps were rapidly clearing that trench we didn't wait long there but still went forward against their third line. As we went forward from the second line we were met with an awful fire from rifles, machine guns and artillery and here Mr Engall took the gun from my number 2 who was hit. When within 100 yards of the German third line we found it quite impossible to advance any further across the open so we took cover behind a bank by the side of a road. Indeed, we were lucky to have ever got so far as the fire was getting more intense every minute as the Germans were bringing to bear on us from other points. It was here that your son met his death. The Germans were but a very short distance from us and were pouring a perfectly deadly fire at this bank behind which we were yet your son, knowing this and quite aware of the danger, with the utmost sang-froid stood up and, seeing how things were, immediately decided to get his gun into action. This he did and stood up head and shoulders exposed firing at the Germans with good effect. Here, however, a bullet struck your son full in the forehead and he fell, death being instantaneous.

We who knew him as our officer feel very deeply his death. He was always very keen and, when off parade, would do anything in his power for his men. From the time we left the trenches to the time he met his death he had set a splendid example of pluck and coolness and we have nothing but admiration for him.

With regard to our attack there is little to tell, it being simply a fight against odds for the Germans were quite ready and prepared for us. We managed to get into the fourth line only to have to retire before superior numbers. Although we hung on in the German front line until nearly eight at night it was pretty hopeless as we had then, for some hours, been using German bombs. Finally we had to cut it back to our own lines. It was, however, not the empty defeat we thought it was as we had kept quite a large force of Germans in front of us and prevented them from being sent to where our men were making the real attack. We have since been complemented on the show we made by numerous commanders including General Haig.

I thank you for your good wishes and hope that these lines may be of some comfort to you.

With my deepest sympathy

Yours sincerely

J C Bolwell

Much though these letters must have meant to the broken-hearted parents, there was one other, forwarded with Capt. Baber's on 6th July, that would have been the most valued. On Wednesday, 28th June, the day before the originally intended attack, Jack Engall, like thousands of others, had written a letter home only to be posted if he failed to return. Engall's letter was entrusted to Capt. Baber and it was his sad duty to forward it with his own note a week later. The young subaltern had composed a letter of pride, patriotism, sentiment and quiet dignity. It has an overwhelming certainty in the rightness of his country's cause and of his God's support and love. It is an all too brief testament to one young man's too short life. It reads:

Wednesday 28th June 1916
My dearest Mother and Dad,

I am writing this letter today before the most important moment in my life. A moment which, I must admit, I have never prayed for, which thousands of others have, but a moment which, nevertheless, now it has come I would not back out from for all the money in the world. The day has almost dawned when I shall do my little bit in the cause of civilisation. Tomorrow morning I shall take my men, men who I have got to love and who I think have got to love me, over the top to do our bit in the first attack in which the London Territorials have taken part as a whole unit. I am sure you will be very pleased to hear that I am going over with the Westminsters. The old regiment has been given the most ticklish task in the whole of the division and I'm very proud of my section because it is the only section in the whole of the Machine Gun Company that is going over the top. And my two particular guns have been given the two most advanced and, therefore, most important positions of all - an honour that is coveted by many. So you can see that I have cause to be proud inasmuch as, at the moment that counts, I am the officer who is entrusted with the most difficult task.

I took my communion yesterday with dozens of others who are going over tomorrow and never have I attended a more impressive service. I placed my soul and body in God's keeping and I am going into battle with His name on my lips full of confidence and trusting implicitly in Him. I have a strong feeling I shall come through safely but, nevertheless, should it be God's Holy Will to call me away I am quite prepared to go. And, like dear Mr Lapeterell, I could not wish for a finer death and you dear Mother and Dad will know that I died doing my duty to my God, my Country and my King. I ask that you should look upon it as an honour that you have given a son for the sake of King and Country.

I wish I had time to write more but time presses. Give my fondest love to dear Marian, Walter and Frank, Auntie Milly, Miss Osmond and Auntie Lulu and dear Fred and Gerald, Auntie Katy and Noel and all my other relations who have been so kind to me since I have been out here. And remember me to all my many kind friends in Acton and elsewhere, especially the Boosteds, the Frees, Gladys Hart, Mr Paradise and others too numerous to mention.

I fear I must close now. Au revoir dearest mother and dad. Fondest love to all those I love so dearly especially to yourselves,

Your devoted and happy son,

Jack

2ⁿᵈ Lt. John Sherwin Engall was the son of John B. Sherwin Engall and Edith M. Engall of 62, Goldsmith Avenue, Acton, London. He was 19 years old when he died in front of Gommecourt on Saturday, 1ˢᵗ July 1916. Like thousands of others, Jack Engall's body was never found. His name is now inscribed in perpetual memory and with gratitude on the Thiepval Memorial, alongside those of over 70,000 of his comrades who died on the Somme in the summer and autumn of 1916. May he, his comrades from Britain and the Commonwealth and the German and French soldiers who died in those fields forever rest in peace.

ENDNOTES:
1 All quotations in the chapter from A subaltern's letters: The letters of Second Lieutenant J.S. Engall, 1915-16, IWM

19. Fallen at Gommecourt

This is a pictorial tribute to these men and to those whose likeness does not survive. Although the quality of some of the photographs is poor when it came to a choice between showing the pictures of these men or leaving them out simply because the quality was not perfect I decided that these men deserved to be seen.

The majority of photographs found below come from the 'Territorial Service Gazette' but I must also acknowledge the help of Simon Jervis and Chris Rippingale who have generously provided images from their collections and which appear below.

'We Will Remember Them'

1/2nd London Regt. (Royal Fusiliers)

Pte Arthur Borrie

Pte Percival Campbell

Pte Harold Dack

Pte Maurice Gale

Cpl Cecil King

Pte Alfred Lacey

543

1/5th London Regt. (London Rifle Brigade)

L/Cpl Douglas Adams

Rfn Bertram Alford

Rfn Edmund Allen

A/Sgt Wallace Austin

Rfn Arthur Baker

Rfn Edgar Baker

Rfn Eric Barton

Rfn William Batchelor

Rfn Harold Beard

L/Cpl Gerald Blake

Rfn Montague Brady

Rfn Wilfred Cantral

Rfn Eric Chambers

A/Cpl. Frank Chandler

Rfn Chapman

Rfn Norman Cowling

Rfn Gilbert Crockett

Rfn Henry Davison

Rfn Frederick Denham

Rfn. Leicester Dixey

Rfn Harold Dudley

Rfn Frank Dyer

Rfn Oswald Dykes

Rfn Julian Eburne

Rfn Daniel Evans

Rfn Archibald Fairs

Rfn Victor Gardiner

Rfn Barnet Griew

Rfn Samuel Hart

Rfn Charles Harris

Rfn Arthur Hill

L/Cpl Stanley Holden

Rfn Richard Hope

Rfn Sidney Howe

Rfn Archibald Johnson

Rfn Richard Johnson

Rfn Frank Johnston

Rfn Donovan King

Rfn Paul Kinnell

L/Cpl Henry Lilley

Rfn William Lydamore

Rfn Arthur Mardle

Rfn Norman Martin

Rfn Matthews

Cpl Edgar Middleton

L/Cpl Phillip Morris

Sgt Herbert Moulton

Sgt Robert Murphy

Rfn Victor New

Rfn Bertram Norton

Rfn Bertram Owen

Rfn John Park

Cpl H W Parslow

Sgt William Pascoe

Sgt Frank Phillips

L/Cpl Eric Poland

Rfn Donovan Poulter

Rfn Reginald Rand

Rfn Reginald Rapkin

Rfn Cecil Ravenscroft

Rfn Ernest Reeves

Rfn John Russell

Rfn Graham Seagrove

Cpl Alan Searle

Rfn Charles Shilson

Rfn Clifford Sinclair

Rfn Edward Smith

Rfn Alfred Snelling

Rfn Harry Spencer

Rfn Edward Stewart

Rfn Ernest Stone

Cpl Stanley Strutt

Rfn Victor Terrell

Rfn Walter Turner

Rfn Percy Wadsworth

Rfn James Watts

Rfn William Webb

Rfn Ronald Willimont

Rfn James Wingfield

Rfn Cyril Woodhouse

Rfn Stewart Yeomans

1/9th London Regt. (Queen Victoria's Rifles)

Rfn John Ashby

Rfn Sidney Atchison

Rfn William Baker

Rfn Stephen Bartlett

Rfn Henry Bassett, brother of...

Rfn Philip Bassett

Rfn Albert Beale

L/Cpl William Bettle

L/Cpl William Bezer

Rfn Charles Blackshaw

L/Cpl Lionel Brownscombe

Sgt Ernest Burley

Rfn Harold Candler

Rfn Reginald Card

Rfn Harold Cocks

Rfn Herman Cuthbert

Rfn George Cuthbert

Rfn Reginald Davey

L/Cpl William Deangate

L/Cpl Samuel Harrold

Rfn John Harvey

L/Cpl Edward Hatcher

Rfn Henry Hooker

Rfn Frank Jeeves

Rfn George Jessep

Rfn Reginald Larkin

Rfn Vivian Marchant

Rfn Arthur Measures

Rfn Frank Nash

Rfn Arthur Norman

Rfn Norman Poole

A/Cpl Frank Preece

Rfn Rowland Price

Rfn Norman Renwick

Rfn Henry Robinson

Rfn Reginald Shears

Rfn Walter Smith

Rfn Andrew Tait

L/Cpl George Tarrant

Rfn Albert Thornett

Cpl Edward Tozer

Cpl Richard Wigg

1/12th London Regt. (The Rangers)

Rfn Edward Baker

Pte Frank Bates (from 2/2nd Londons)

Sgt Henry Bennett

Pte Sidney Blackburn (from 2/2nd Londons)

559

Rfn John Brandon

Cpl Charles Brinkley

Rfn Joseph Burne

Rfn Charles Cole

Rfn Thomas Comber

Rfn Walter Davey

Rfn Victor Drury

Rfn Reginald Evans

Rfn Henry Foster

Rfn Arthur George

Sgt Harry Hines

Rfn Joseph Honer

Rfn William Hussey

Rfn Edward Johnson

Rfn Joseph Lacey

Rfn Henry Lacey

Rfn Percy Law

Pte William Lock (from 2/2nd Londons)

Rfn William Lucas

Rfn Thomas Mark

Rfn George Mendel

Rfn Alfred Moore, brother of ...

Rfn Harold Moore

Rfn Edward Parker

Rfn Albert Paxton

Cpl Arthur Prout

L/Cpl Alfred Smith

Rfn George Smith

Rfn Gordon Steer

L/Cpl Robert Stimpson

Rfn Albert Todd

Cpl Charles Walker (from 2/2nd Londons)

Rfn Reginald Walker

Rfn Leonard Wendon

Rfn Percy Whiting

Pte Ernest Wood (from 2/2nd Londons)

1/14th London Regt. (London Scottish)

Pte Arthur Alderton

Pte Bertie Anderson

Pte LeRoy Askey

Pte Frederick Budd

564

Pte Harold Busby

L/Cpl Alfred Charlton

Pte William Coutts

Pte Julius Dent-Young

Cpl William Dunn

Pte Walter Dunstone

Pte Walter Dutch

Pte Hubert Freeman

Pte Charles Gepp

Pte Sydney Goates

CSM James Hamilton

Pte Murray Hamilton

566

Pte David Hay

Pte Ernest Haywood

Pte Percival Henderson

Pte James Hepburn

Pte John Herring

Pte Alexander Johnson

Cpl Luther Kitson

Pte William Knight

Pte Frederick Larkin

Pte Reginald Lawrence

Pte Alexander McIntosh

Pte Alfred McLachlan

Pte John Miller

Pte Frederick Morgan

Pte Herbert Murdoch

Pte William Newham

Pte Lidell North

Pte Harold Noterman

Pte Gordon Panter

L/Cpl George Roberts

Pte Douglas Shuker

Pte Fred Skerton

Pte Anthony Smith

Pte Ernest Smith

Pte John Stacey

Pte Charles Stewart

Pte Herbert Tomasson

Cpl Frank Stewart

Sgt Alexander Torrance

Pte Frederick Trench
(served as Bloomfield)

Pte Frank Watson

Pte Ernest Webb

Pte Sidney Whitlock
1/16th London Regt. (Queen's Westminster Rifles)

Rfn Alfred Beer

Rfn Norman Bonser

Rfn Alfred Bowditch

Cpl Richard Brewer

Rfn Vivian Brocklesby

Rfn Maurice Bryon

Rfn Frederick Cooper

Rfn Victor Coventry

Pte Harold Crocker (from 2/2nd
Londons)

Rfn Jack David

Rfn Alfred Dexter

Rfn Joseph Eastwood

Rfn Graham Elmslie

Sgt Howard Fagan

Cpl Newton Gammon

Pte Maurice Fowler (from 2/2nd Londons)

Rfn Robert Gaskins

Pte Ewart Groves

Rfn Rodney Gudge

Rfn Stanley Hall

Rfn Stanley Hayes

Rfn George Hinds

574

Rfn Percy Hurst

Rfn Harold Jarrett

Rfn Percy Kentrzinsky

Rfn Frederick Lacey

Rfn Leonard Le Rossignol

Rfn Alfred Mabbott

Rfn Noel Masters

Rfn Arthur Norton

Rfn Robert Olive

Rfn Allen Parkhouse

L/Sgt Arthur Parsons (from 2/2nd Londons)

Rfn Charles Penn

Pte Thomas Proctor (from 2/2nd Londons)

Rfn Thomas Quinney

Rfn Charles Rodwell

Rfn Stanley Roser

Pte Sampford (from 2/2nd Londons)

Rfn Ernest Sharp

Rfn Albert Smith

L/Cpl Charles Soper (from 2/2nd Londons)

Rfn William Taffs

Pte James Thirkell (from 2/2nd Londons)

Rfn Richard Tebbutt

Rfn Charles Wagstaff

Rfn Arthur Waind

Rfn Arthur Williams

Pte Geoffrey Withers (from 2nd Londons)

Appendix 1 : British Order of Battle

Third Army
G.O.C.   Lt. Gen. Sir Edmund Henry Hynman Allenby KCB

VII Corps
G.O.C.   Maj. Gen. Sir Thomas D'Oyly Snow KCB

Royal Artillery
CRA   Brig. Gen. C M Ross Johnson

Heavy Artillery
G.O.C.   Brig. Gen. C R Buckle

19th Heavy Artillery Group
46th H.A.G. (Sub-group)

73rd (South African) Siege Bty R.G.A.	Maj. W Brydon	4x6 in. howitzers (26 cwt)
74th (South African) Siege Bty R.G.A.[i]	Maj. W H Pickburn	4x6 in. howitzers (26 cwt)
101st Siege Bty R.G.A.	Maj. G E Smart	4x6 in. howitzers (26 cwt)
102nd Siege Bty R.G.A.	Maj. W B Duncan	4x6 in. howitzers (30 cwt)
90th Siege Bty R.G.A.		4x9.2 in. howitzers
91st Siege Bty R.G.A.	Maj. W H Christian	4x9.2 in. howitzers
96th Siege Bty R.G.A.	Maj. C H M Sturgis	4x9.2 in. howitzers
45th Siege Bty R.G.A.	Maj. H M Kemble	1x9.2 in. gun
103rd Siege Bty R.G.A.	Maj. H D Hutchison	2x12 in. howitzers

35th Heavy Artillery Group   Lt. Col. H G Brett

47th H.A.G. (No. 3 Sub-group)	Lt. Col. Rumbold	
68th Siege Bty R.G.A.	Maj. H Mayne	4x6 in. howitzers (30 cwt)
88th Siege Bty R.G.A.		4x6 in. howitzers (26 cwt)
98th (Canadian) Siege Bty R.G.A.		4x6 in. howitzers (26 cwt)
No. 2 Sub-group	Maj. Twiss M.V.O.	
93rd Siege Bty R.G.A.		4x9.2 in. howitzers
94th Siege Bty R.G.A.		4x9.2 in. howitzers
95th Siege Bty R.G.A.	Maj. Twiss M.V.O.	4x9.2 in. howitzers
No. 1 Sub-group	Maj. A P Liston-Foulis	
No. 4 Howitzer, R.M.A.	As above	1x15 in. howitzer
No. 6 Howitzer, R.M.A.	As above	1x15 in. howitzer

39th Heavy Artillery Group

131st Heavy Bty R.G.A.		4x60pdr guns
135th Heavy Bty R.G.A.		4x60pdr guns
(74th (South African) Siege Bty R.G.A.	*Maj. W H Pickburn*	*4x6 in. howitzers)*
50th Siege Bty R.G.A.	Capt. R B Turbutt	2x6 in. Mk VII guns
(45th Siege Bty R.G.A.[ii]	*Maj. H M Kemble*	*1x9.2 in. gun)*

48th Heavy Artillery Group   Lt. Col. A J Pike

116th Heavy Bty R.G.A.	Maj. O R Swayne	4x60pdr guns
133rd Heavy Bty R.G.A.	Maj. R P Thompson	4x4.7 in. guns
1/1st Kent Heavy Bty R.G.A.		4x4.7 in. guns
1/1st Lowland Heavy Bty R.G.A.		4x4.7 in. guns
(91st Siege Bty R.G.A.[iii]		*4x9.2 in. howitzers)*

56th (1st London) Division

* = Killed in action or died of wounds, 1st July 1916,   † = wounded,   ‡ = prisoner of war.
Officers in italics not involved on 1st July 1916.   Officers emboldened died later in the war

G.O.C.   Maj. Gen. Charles Patrick Amyatt Hull CB

Artillery
CRA   T/Brig. Gen. R J G Elkington C.M.G., D.S.O.

---

[i] This battery switched between 19th HAG and 39th HAG depending on its targets.
[ii] This battery switched between 19th HAG and 48th HAG depending on its targets.
[iii] This battery switched between 19th HAG and 48th HAG depending on its targets.

280th Brigade R.F.A. (1/1st London Brigade R.F.A.)　　Lt. Col. L A C Southam
281st Brigade R.F.A. (1/2nd London Brigade R.F.A.)　　Lt. Col. C C Macdowell
　　　　　　　　　　　　　　　　　　　　　　　　Lt. N A E Massey †
282nd Brigade R.F.A. (1/3rd London Brigade　　　　　Lt. Col. A F Prechtel
R.F.A.)
　　　　　　　　　　　　　　　　　　　　　　　　Lt. M Sired †
283rd Brigade R.F.A. (1/4th London Brigade R.F.A.)　　Lt. Col. Wainwright
56th Divisional Ammunition Column　　　　　　　　　2nd Lt. L W Gee †
V56 (Heavy) Trench Mortar Battery　　　　　　　　　2nd Lt. J S Davies
X56 (Medium) Trench Mortar Battery　　　　　　　　Capt. Fripp
　　　　　　　　　　　　　　　　　　　　　　　　2nd Lt. A F R Quin †
Y56 (Medium) Trench Mortar Battery
Z56 (Medium) Trench Mortar Battery　　　　　　　　Lt. Wallace

Royal Engineers
CRE　　　　　　　　　　　　　　　　　　　　　　Lt. Col. H W Gordon D.S.O.
416th (1/1st) City of Edinburgh Field Coy, R.E.　　　　2nd Lt. S Angus *
512th (2/1st London) Field Coy, R.E.　　　　　　　　Capt. R Annan
　　No 1 Section　　　　　　　　　　　　　　　　Lt. H A Scott
　　No 2 Section　　　　　　　　　　　　　　　　Lt. E L Martin
　　No 3 Section　　　　　　　　　　　　　　　　Lt. J T F Henderson
　　No 4 Section　　　　　　　　　　　　　　　　2nd Lt. D E Clerk
513th (2/2nd London) Field Coy, R.E.　　　　　　　　Capt. A O Laird †
　　No 1 Section　　　　　　　　　　　　　　　　Lt. J E Villa
　　No 2 Section　　　　　　　　　　　　　　　　2nd Lt. W A R Bourne
　　No 3 Section　　　　　　　　　　　　　　　　2nd Lt. R O Beit
　　No 4 Section　　　　　　　　　　　　　　　　2nd Lt. C H R Dain
56th Divisional Signal Coy
No. 2 Company, 5th Battalion, Special Bde, R.E.　　　Capt. W Holland

Pioneer Battalion
1/5th Cheshire Regt (Earl of Chester's)　　　　　Lt. Col. J E G Groves C.M.G., T.D.
2inC　　　　　　　　　　　　　　　　　　　Maj. W A V Churton D.S.O. T.D.
Adjutant　　　　　　　　　　　　　　　　　*Lt. F Bishop M.C.*
MO　　　　　　　　　　　　　　　　　　　　Capt. F M Byrne (R.A.M.C.)
A Company　　　　　　　　　　　　　　　　Capt. C A Price
　　2nd Lt. E. T. Andrews †　　　　　　　　　2nd Lt. G. S. Arthur *
　　Lt. P B Bass *　　　　　　　　　　　　　2nd Lt. H. C. H. Simpson †
B Company　　　　　　　　　　　　　　　　Capt. H Caldecutt
　　Capt. E J Bairstow　　　　　　　　　　　2nd Lt. F A Davies *
　　2nd Lt. T L C Heald M.C.　　　　　　　2nd Lt. J D Salmon M.C.
　　　　　　　　　　　　　　　　　　　　　2nd Lt. W F Smith
C Company　　　　　　　　　　　　　　　　Capt. E M Dixon
　　Lt. A H Jolliffe M.C.　　　　　　　　　　2nd Lt. H R Leigh †
D Company　　　　　　　　　　　　　　　　Capt. O Johnson M.C.
　　　　　　　　　　　　　　　　　　　　　2nd Lt. H W Glendinning
Company unknown　　　　　　　　　　　　　*Capt. H L Churton*
　　Capt. G W C Hartley　　　　　　　　　*Capt. E S Heron*
　　Capt. H N Hignett　　　　　　　　　　*Capt. J H Rowlands*
　　Lt. B H Gregg　　　　　　　　　　　　*Lt. E B Morgan*
　　2nd Lt. S Clemence [i]　　　　　　　　*2nd Lt. W L Dingley* [ii]
　　2nd Lt. T O M Ffoulkes　　　　　　　　*2nd Lt. I Gledsdale* [iii]
　　2nd Lt. S A Harper [iv]　　　　　　　　*Lt. H E Ratcliffe*
　　2nd Lt. J S Spicer [v]　　　　　　　　*2nd Lt. K N Standish* [vi]

---

[i] 2nd Lt. S Clemence joined the battalion from the 3/5th Cheshire Regt. on 26th June 1916.
[ii] 2nd Lt. W L Dingley joined the battalion from the 3/5th Cheshire Regt. on 26th June 1916.
[iii] 2nd Lt. I Gledsdale joined the battalion from No. 1 Entrenching Battalion on 6th June 1916.
[iv] 2nd Lt. S A Harper joined the battalion from No. 1 Entrenching Battalion on 6th June 1916.
[v] 2nd Lt. J S Spicer joined the battalion from the 3/5th Cheshire Regt. on 5th June 1916.
[vi] 2nd Lt. K N Standish joined the battalion from the 3/5th Cheshire Regt. on 26th June 1916.

R.A.M.C.

2/1st London Field Ambulance
Maj. Sutherland
Capt. Jobson Scott

2/2nd London Field Ambulance
Capt. F Gibson
Capt. G W Miller

2/3rd London Field Ambulance
Capt. Bell
Capt. McHattie

Lt. Col. C S Brebner D.S.O.
Capt. Heddy
Capt. Rice-Oxley
Capt. Stewart
Lt. Col. E C Montgomery-Smith C.M.G., D.S.O.
Capt. H K Griffith
Capt. S Williams
Maj. A W French
Capt. Costello
Capt. Pollard
Capt. Thompson

Infantry

167th Brigade (Temp.) Brig. Gen. Frank Henry Burnell-Nugent D.S.O.

1/1st City of London Battalion, Royal Fusiliers
MO
Company unknown
2nd Lt. A J De Vall †

Lt. Col. D V Smith D.S.O., V.D.
Capt. J H Tomlinson (R.A.M.C.) †
Lt. H W Cundall *
2nd Lt. J A Freeman †

1/3rd City of London Battalion, Royal Fusiliers
MO
B Company
Company unknown
Capt. E V Noel †
Lt. D W L Jones *
2nd Lt. R J A Lidiard *

Lt. Col. F D Samuel D.S.O. T.D.
Capt. Graham (R.A.M.C.)
Capt. A Agius
Capt. Jones
Lt. Johnson
2nd Lt. R A Calder-Smith
2nd Lt. W A Thomas †

1/7th Middlesex Regt.

Adjutant
MO
A Company
B Company
C Company
D Company
Company unknown
Capt. H S Reeves
Lt. F B Carr
Lt. R Charlesworth M.C.
Lt. W G Kay
Lt. F Moxon M.C.
Lt. C Smith
2nd Lt. E A Brown
2nd Lt. R M Fry †
2nd Lt. T W Honeychurch
2nd D J Robbie
Lt. W A Whyman

Lt. Col. E J King C.M.G.
Maj. S King
Lt. P C Kay
Capt. Gibson R.A.M.C.
Lt. W G Woodroffe CdG
Capt. S H Gillett M.C. †
Capt. J K Tully
Capt. D W Hurd
Capt. C F Challen
Lt. C Ashby M.C. †
Lt. P Challen
Lt. P L Forbes
Lt. R M E King
Lt. A T Shipton M.C.
Lt. W W Tucker
2nd Lt. W E Edwards
2nd Lt. J W Higgs
2nd Lt. E A Jones
2nd Lt. G A Scutt

1/8th Middlesex Regt.
MO
Quartermaster
Company unknown
Capt. G W Tremlett
2nd Lt. A C Batho
2nd Lt. C V Burder
2nd Lt. J W Thorogood

Lt. Col. P L Ingpen D.S.O.
Lt. D M Clements R.A.M.C.
Lt. J D G Louch
Capt. T M Peake
Lt. C E Cox
2nd Lt. G R G Byham
2nd Lt. G A Challis †

167th Brigade Machine Gun Company

167th Brigade Trench Mortar Battery Capt. G Oliver

168ᵗʰ Brigade   (Temp.) Brig. Gen. Granville George Loch C.M.G.

1/4ᵗʰ City of London Battalion, Royal Fusiliers   Lt. Col. L L Wheatley
2inC   *Maj. H J Duncan-Teape*
Adjutant   Lt. R L Herring †
Asst Adjutant   *Lt. W J Boutall*
    2ⁿᵈ Lt. V C Donaldson †   2ⁿᵈ Lt. H Jones †
Works Officer   *Capt. R N Arnold (sick 27ᵗʰ June 1916)*
MO   Capt. A Hurd R.A.M.C.
Padre   Rev R Palmer
A Company   Capt. A R Moore M.C. *
    2ⁿᵈ Lt. A G Blunn ‡   2ⁿᵈ Lt. F C Fanghanel *
B Company   Maj. W R Moore †
    2ⁿᵈ Lt. L R Chapman †   2ⁿᵈ Lt. A S Ford †
        2ⁿᵈ Lt. H G Hicklenton †
C Company   Capt. J T Sykes †
    Capt. A L Long   2ⁿᵈ Lt. F R C Bradford *
        2ⁿᵈ Lt. T Moody *
D Company   Capt. H G Stanham
    2ⁿᵈ Lt. G H Davis   2ⁿᵈ Lt. W H Webster †
        2ⁿᵈ Lt. B F L Yeoman †
Company unknown   *Lt. H W Vernon* ⁱ
    Lt. J R Webster ⁱⁱ   *2ⁿᵈ Lt. C S G Blows* ⁱⁱⁱ
    2ⁿᵈ Lt. S Davis ⁱᵛ   *2ⁿᵈ Lt. N W Williams* ᵛ

1/12ᵗʰ (The Rangers), London Regt.   Col. A D Bayliffe C.M.G., T.D.
2inC   *Maj. A G E Syms*
Bombing Officer   2ⁿᵈ Lt. Higgins
A Company   Capt. G M G Wyatt †
    Lt. R E K Bradshaw *   2ⁿᵈ Lt. M L Harper
    2ⁿᵈ Lt. C F Monier Williams †   2ⁿᵈ Lt. W G Parker ‡
B Company   Capt. H W Wightwick M.C. †
    2ⁿᵈ Lt. E G D Liveing †   2ⁿᵈ Lt. H Rochford †
        2ⁿᵈ Lt. A W Taplin *
C Company   Capt. R L Hoare *
        2ⁿᵈ Lt. J Josephs *
D Company   Maj. L F Jones *
    2ⁿᵈ Lt. W R Davey *   2ⁿᵈ Lt. W H Tucker *
Company unknown   *Capt. S R Moss Vernon*
    Lt. F R How   Lt. J A Reeves †
    Lt. E S M Wellsman   *2ⁿᵈ Lt. H A W Backoff*
    2ⁿᵈ Lt. B G Coffin   2ⁿᵈ Lt. Down
    2ⁿᵈ Lt. E A Duncalf   2ⁿᵈ Lt. A G Hine †
    2ⁿᵈ Lt. L S Isbister   *2ⁿᵈ Lt. L H K Neil*
    2ⁿᵈ Lt. F W Osborne   2ⁿᵈ Lt. A J Reincke †
    2ⁿᵈ Lt. D S Ward *   *2ⁿᵈ Lt. F G White*
1/13ᵗʰ (Kensington), London Regt.   Lt. Col. W H Young
A Company   Maj. C C Dickens
    2ⁿᵈ Lt. Dawes   2ⁿᵈ Lt. N O C Mackenzie *
B Company   Capt. M R Harris M.C.
        Lt. W A Penn †
C Company   Capt. F H Ware *
        2ⁿᵈ Lt. P R Pike †

ⁱ 2ⁿᵈ Lt. H W Vernon joined on 14ᵗʰ May from the 2/4ᵗʰ London Regt.
ⁱⁱ 2ⁿᵈ Lt. J R Webster joined on 24ᵗʰ June from the 2/4ᵗʰ London Regt.
ⁱⁱⁱ 2ⁿᵈ Lt. Cyril Sydney George Blows joined on 7ᵗʰ May 1916 from 2/4ᵗʰ London Regt. The son of George Oliver and Elizabeth Jane Blows of The Briars, 131, Elm Road, Leigh on Sea, he was killed on 9ᵗʰ September 1916, aged 19. His body was never recovered and his name was inscribed on the Thiepval Memorial, Pier and Face 9 D and 16 B.
ⁱᵛ 2ⁿᵈ Lt. S Davis joined on 7ᵗʰ May 1916 from 2/4ᵗʰ London Regt.
ᵛ 2ⁿᵈ Lt. N W Williams joined on 14ᵗʰ May from the 2/4ᵗʰ London Regt.

D Company
2nd Lt. G A Beggs M.C. M.M. †
2nd Lt. N E Parry †
Company unknown
2nd Lt. S A Ball OBE †
2nd Lt. J P Clark †
2nd Lt. H E Paterson †
2nd Lt. R E F Shaw[i]

1/14th (London Scottish), London Regt.
MO
2nd Lt. H J Calder
Asst Adjutant
A Company
2nd Lt. R A Brown *
2nd Lt. A S Petrie
B Company
2nd Lt. H A Coxon *

C Company
2nd Lt. D Kerr *
D Company
2nd Lt. R S Greig †
2nd Lt. G W Prebble †

168th Brigade Machine Gun Company
Capt. J R Pyper M.C. & Bar (1/4th Londons)

168th Brigade Trench Mortar Battery

169th Brigade   (Temp.) Brig. Gen. Edward Sacheverell D'Ewes Coke C.M.G.

1/2nd City of London Battalion, Royal Fusiliers
Adjutant
MO
A Company

B Company
C Company
2nd Lt. J S Grainger *
D Company
Company unknown
Lt. B Attenborough
Lt. G Dearmer
Lt. G B Henderson †
2nd Lt. B R Buxton *
2nd Lt. L S Gray
2nd Lt. W H Sendall
2nd Lt. A J Whittle

1/5th (London Rifle Brigade), London Regt.
2inC

Capt. E O Taggart †
2nd Lt. W G Mager *
2nd Lt. H B Pilgrim *
Lt. H E Holland M.C. †
2nd Lt. G P Bryer †
2nd Lt. H W Hankins †
2nd Lt. C B Sach *
2nd Lt. J P Williams †

Lt. Col. B C Green C.M.G., T.D.
Capt. J H Glover (R.A.M.C.) †
Capt. F G Worlock
Lt. A G Douglas MC
Capt. H C Sparks
2nd Lt. B E Gavin †
2nd Lt. R White M.C. & Bar
Capt. F H Lindsay *
2nd Lt. W E F Curror *
2nd Lt. A A Speak M.C. †
Maj. C J Low D.S.O. †
Lt. H C Lamb D.S.O.
Lt. J C Brown Constable *
2nd Lt. P T L Hunter *
2nd Lt. C Woodcock †

Major M. W. Tait (1/14th Londons)
Lt. F S Thomson (1/14th Londons) *
2nd Lt. S L Vincent †

Capt. E D Alexander

Lt. Col. J Attenborough C.M.G. T.D.
Maj. Stacey
Capt. M Ramsay (R.A.M.C.)
Capt. J R Garland *
2nd Lt. J W Sanders †
Capt. J P Kellett
Capt. P J A Handyside *
2nd Lt. H C Gosnell *
Capt. R E F Sneath
Capt. A G Houlder
Lt. D L Childs
Lt. H W Everitt †
2nd Lt. H F Blows †
2nd Lt. J G Garthwaite
2nd Lt. N F Perris †
2nd Lt. A M Thorman *
2nd Lt. A E Wiggs †

Lt. Col. A S Bates D.S.O.
Maj. R H Husey D.S.O. & bar M.C.[ii]

---

[i] 2nd Lt. (later Lt. Col.) Robert Edward Frederic Shaw, M.C., 1/13th London Regt. (Kensingtons) was killed on 23rd August 1918. Aged 26, he was the son of the Rev. and Mrs. R. V. G. Shaw of Langleybury Vicarage, King's Langley, Herts. He was buried in Cabaret-Rouge British Cemetery, Souchez, grave VIII. N. 11.

[ii] Major (later Brig. Gen.) Ralph Hamer Husey, D.S.O. and bar, M.C., 1/5th London Regt. (London Rifle Brigade) was the son of C. Hubert Husey, of 65, Cornwall Gardens, Kensington, London and was educated at Marlborough and in Germany. He served in the Hertfordshire Yeomanry between 1901 and 1906. Commissioned into the London Rifle Brigade on 12th March 1906 he went to France as Captain, OC 'A' Company. He was wounded on 13th May 1915 and rejoined the battalion on 4th October 1915. He was the CO of the battalion between August 1916 and August 1917 when wounded, rejoining on 2nd December 1917. He temporarily commanded both 169th

Adjutant
Asst Adjutant
Quartermaster
2nd Lt. G H Ticehurst ii
Asst Intelligence Officer
Battalion Bombers
MO
Padre
A Company
    2nd Lt. F D Charles iv
    2nd Lt. W E M Gardiner v
B Company
    2nd Lt. G E Clode-Baker *

C Company
    2nd Lt. A L Benns *
D Company
    2nd Lt. F H Crews M.C. vii
    2nd Lt. I R Pogose *
Company unknown
    2nd Lt. F A Balls viii
    2nd Lt. B F Sawbridge †
    2nd Lt. E G Thomas †

Capt. F H Wallis M.C. & 2 Bars
2nd Lt. B Bromiley
Lt. W Kelly i
Lt. C W Long
2nd Lt. H J F Crisp M.M. iii
Lt. G G Boston DCM †
Capt. L Crombie (R.A.M.C.)
Rev K N Crisford
Capt. G H Cholmeley †
2nd Lt. C B Doust *
2nd Lt. B L E Pocock †
Capt. J R Somers-Smith M.C. *
2nd Lt. G H Howe vi
2nd Lt. P B B Oldfield †
Capt. B S Harvey *
2nd Lt. E W Rose †
Capt. A T B de Cologan ††‡
2nd Lt. R E Petley M.C. †
2nd Lt. H Smith †
2nd Lt. C V Balkwill *
2nd Lt. R F Lydall †
2nd Lt. C H Sell ix
2nd Lt. A Warner *

---

and 167th Brigades and appointed GOC, 25th Brigade, on 4th May 1918. He was wounded and taken prisoner on 27th May 1918, dying in enemy hands on 29th May, aged 36. He is buried in Vendresse British Cemetery, grave II. G. 1.

i Lt. William Kelly, 1/5th London Regt. (London Rifle Brigade) joined the Army on 9th January 1892. He was commissioned in October 1909. He retired in August 1914 but rejoined the 3/5th London Rifle Brigade on 8th January 1915. He joined the 1/5th London Rifle Brigade on 1st May 1916.

ii 2nd Lt. Gordon Harry Ticehurst, 1/5th London Regt. (London Rifle Brigade) the son of Gertrude M Ticehurst of 29, Guildersfield Rd., Streatham, London, and the late Harry A Ticehurst and.was educated at Battersea Polytechnic Secondary School. He served in the London University O.T.C. and was commissioned into the 2/2nd London Regt. on 14th July 1915 and served with them at Gallipoli and in Egypt. He was posted to the 1/5th London Rifle Brigade on 4th June. He was wounded on 9th September 1916 at Leuze Wood. He returned to France in March 1917 with the 2/5th London Rifle Brigade and was killed in action on 20th September 1917, aged 20. His body waa never found and his name is inscribed on the Ypres Memorial (Menin Gate), panels 52 and 54.

iii 2nd Lt. Harold John Francis Crisp, M.M., 1/5th London Regt. (London Rifle Brigade) was educated at Bournemouth School. He joined the LRB as a Private on 7th July 1911. He went to France in November 1914 and was promoted Sergeant before being commissioned on 23rd January 1916. He rejoined the battalion on 5th June and was appointed Assistant Intelligence Officer. He was wounded on 10th September 1916, later joining the 2/5th London Rifle Brigade and the 18th London Regt., before rejoining the battalion on 21st November 1918.

iv 2nd Lt. Frank Dallas Charles, 1/5th London Regt. (London Rifle Brigade) was educated at St Alban's School. He joined the London Rifle Brigade in 1910 and went to France in November 1914. He was commissioned in 1915 and was temporarily attached to the 187th Field Coy, R.E. during gas attacks at Loos in September 1915. He later served with the 3/5th London Rifle Brigade, 40th Pathans and the 1st Durham Light Infantry.

v 2nd Lt. William Edward Mansfield Gardiner, 1/5th London Regt. (London Rifle Brigade) was the son of Louisa Wills of Coaxden, Uxbridge, and the late William Mansfield Gardiner. He was educated at Forest School where he was in the O.T.C. He joined the Inns of Court O.T.C. on 6th May 1915 and was commissioned into the 3/5th London Rifle Brigade on 11th July 1915. He joined the 1/5th Battalion on 11th May 1916 and was killed in action on 19th July 1916, aged 20. He was buried in Hannescamps New Military Cemetery, grave F. 8.

vi 2nd Lt. George Hubert Howe, 1/5th London Regt. (London Rifle Brigade) was educated at Merchant Taylor's School and Guy's Hospital. He enlisted in the Artists' Rifles in 1911 and was commissioned into the London Rifle Brigade on 11th April 1915. He joined the battalion in France on 27th May 1916.

vii 2nd Lt. Frederick Howard Crews, 1/5th London Regt. (London Rifle Brigade), was educated at Eastbourne Municipal Secondary School. He attested at Private 9144 in April 1910 joining A Company. He went to France in November 1914 and was commissioned on 24th January 1916. He was given command of D Company on 2nd July 1916. He was awarded the M.C. for his actions on 8th October 1916.

viii 2nd Lt. Frank Aubrey Balls, 1/5th London Regt. (London Rifle Brigade), was educated at Tonbridge School. He joined the London Rifle Brigade in September 1909 and went to France in November 1914. He was commissioned into the 3/5th London Rifle Brigade on 20th October 1915 rejoining the 1/5th Battalion on 27th May 1916. He later returned to England and was seconded to the Labour Corps.

ix 2nd Lt. Charles Henry Sell, 1/5th London Regt. (London Rifle Brigade) enlisted in 1907 as Private 8298 in 'O' Company. He went to France in November 1914 and was wounded on 27th April 1915. He was commissioned into the 3/5th London Rifle Brigade on 28th September 1915 and rejoined the battalion on 17th January 1916. He was severely wounded on 22nd September 1916 and subsequently served with the 3/5th London Rifle Brigade.

1/9th (Queen Victoria's Rifles), London Regt.
2inC
Adjutant
MO
A Company
   2nd Lt. J S Hunter †
B Company
   Lt. W Goodinge †
   2nd Lt. R H Cary *
   2nd Lt. O T Mason *
C Company
   Lt. C P Fleetwood *
   2nd Lt. F W Fielding *
D Company
   Lt. T Hodgson
Company unknown

Col. V W F Dickins D.S.O., V.D.
Maj. S J M Sampson
Capt. C J Andrews
Capt. A B Clarke M.C. (R.A.M.C.)
Capt. R W Cunningham *
2nd Lt. P G Simmonds *
Capt. P S Houghton *
Lt. W S Stranack †
2nd Lt. C V Davis †
2nd Lt. N A Meeking *
Capt. H E Leys Cox *
2nd Lt. R Bennett †‡
2nd Lt. F G Garside †
Capt. R H Lindsey-Renton
2nd Lt. D A Ord-Mackenzie
Lt. S J Holloway

1/16th (Queen's Westminster Rifles), London Regt.
2inC
Adjutant
MO
A Company
   2nd Lt. E H Bovill *
   2nd Lt. E H Jarvis (10th Middlesex) †
B Company
   2nd Lt. H L Bell
   2nd Lt. H Luscombe (2/3rd Londons) †
   2nd Lt. C E Moy M.C.

C Company
   Lt. P Spencer Smith, †‡
   2nd Lt. N T Thurston M.C. & Bar

D Company
   2nd Lt. F A Farley (2/2nd Londons) *
   2nd Lt. A M Manson (2/2nd Londons)[i]

169th Brigade Machine Gun Company
2nd Lt. J S Engall (1/16th Londons) *
2nd Lt. R J Mackay †

169th Brigade Trench Mortar Battery
Lt. G G Nathan (1/9th Londons.)
2nd Lt. R G T Groves (1/2nd Londons)

Lt. Col. R Shoolbred C.M.G., T.D.

Maj. P E Harding
Capt. H S Price
Capt. A Ramsbottom (R.A.M.C.)
Capt. F G Swainson M.C. *
2nd Lt. J Daniel (2/3rd Londons) †
2nd Lt. J J Westmoreland
Capt. G E Cockerill *‡
2nd Lt. J A Horne *
2nd Lt. J H Martin
2nd Lt. W F Strange (2/2nd Londons) *
2nd Lt. F S Thomas †
Capt. H F Mott M.C. *
2nd Lt. A G Negus *
2nd Lt. D F Upton M.C. (2/2nd Londons) †‡
2nd Lt. A G V Yates *
Capt. P M Glasier D.S.O. †
2nd Lt. C C Iveson †
2nd Lt. C A Stubbs (2/2nd Londons) *

Capt. Baber M.C. (1/16th Londons)
2nd Lt. K M C Fradd (1/2nd Londons) *
2nd Lt. C E Ovington (1/5th Londons) [ii]
2nd Lt. W G Perrin (1/5th Londons) [iii]
Capt. P C Coote
Lt. E A J A Lane (1/9th Londons) *
2nd Lt. J B Pittman (1/2nd Londons)
2nd Lt. E R Williamson (1/5th Londons)

---

[i] 2nd Lt. Alexander Murray Manson, 2/2nd London Regt. att. 1/16th London Regt. (Queen's Westminster Rifles) was born on 1887 and lived at 35, Greyhound Road Mansions, West Kensington. Educated at Bedford Grammar School he was a clerk. He joined the 2nd London Regt. in 1909 and was commissioned on 29th September 1915.

[ii] 2nd Lt. Charles Edward Ovington, 1/5th London Regt. (London Rifle Brigade) was educated at Tottenham County School. He enlisted in October 1913 and went to France with the 1/5th London Rifle Brigade in November 1914. He was evacuated to England as a result of wounds suffered on 29th April 1915. He was commissioned on 5th August 1915 and returned to the battalion on 12th March 1916. He was seconded to the 169th Brigade Machine Gun Company in April 1916. He was awarded the M.C.

[iii] 2nd Lt. William Gordon Perrin, 1/5th London Regt. (London Rifle Brigade) enlisted in December 1909. He was commissioned on 28th September 1915, rejoining the 1/5th London Rifle Brigade on 16th March 1916. He was seconded to the 169th Brigade Machine Company on 17th April.

585

APPENDIX 2: GERMAN ORDER OF BATTLE

2ⁿᵈ Guard Reserve Division   General Freiherr von Süsskind

Divisional troops:
2ⁿᵈ Reserve Uhlan Regt   58ᵗʰ Flak Coy
4/10ᵗʰ Pioneer Battalion   260ᵗʰ Searchlight Section
2ⁿᵈ Guard Minenwerfer Coy.

Artillery:
20ᵗʰ Reserve Field Artillery Regt.   Oberstleutnant Hohnhorst
II/2ⁿᵈ Guard Foot Artillery Regiment   Hptm. Matschke
1/19ᵗʰ Bavarian Field Artillery Regt. (from 10ᵗʰ Bavarian Infantry Division)
2/52ⁿᵈ Foot Artillery Battalion (from 52ⁿᵈ Infantry Division)
Apel. Foot Artillery Battery   517ᵗʰ Foot Artillery Battery
692ⁿᵈ Foot Artillery Battery   706ᵗʰ Foot Artillery Battery
212ᵗʰ Foot Artillery Battery (½)   38ᵗʰ Flak Company

38ᵗʰ Reserve Infantry Brigade	Lt. Gen. von Etzel	
15ᵗʰ Infantry Regt.	Oberstleutnant Schwarz	Battalion MG Company
(2ⁿᵈ Westphalian)		662ⁿᵈ MG
I/15ᵗʰ I.R.		73ʳᵈ MG Marksman
1/15ᵗʰ		Section
2/15ᵗʰ		
3/15ᵗʰ		
4/15ᵗʰ		
II/15ᵗʰI.R.	Major Kiesel	
5/15ᵗʰ		
6/15ᵗʰ		
7/15ᵗʰ		
8/15ᵗʰ		
III/15ᵗʰ I.R.	Major Ritter	
9/15ᵗʰ		
10/15ᵗʰ		
11/15ᵗʰ	Leutnant Kaiser	
12/15ᵗʰ		
55ᵗʰ Reserve Infantry Regt.	Oberstleutnant von Laue	Battalion MG Company
I/55ᵗʰ R.I.R.	Major von Bothmer	663ʳᵈ MG
1/55ᵗʰ		
2/55ᵗʰ	Lt. of Reserve Dobberke	
3/55ᵗʰ	Hauptmann von Obernitz	
4/55ᵗʰ	Oblt. Graf von Matuschka	
II/55ᵗʰ R.I.R.	Hptm. Ldr. Minck	
5/55ᵗʰ	Rittmeister Straatmann	
6/55ᵗʰ	Oberleutnant von Trauwitz	
7/55ᵗʰ	Hptm Res. Brockmann	
8/55ᵗʰ	Lt. of Reserve Holländer	
III/55ᵗʰ R.I.R.	Maj. Tauscher	
9/55ᵗʰ	Hptm Res. Terberger	
10/55ᵗʰ	Leutnant Niediek	
11/55ᵗʰ	Lt. of Reserve Stolper	
12/55ᵗʰ	Hptm. Ldr. Winkelmann	
Pioneer Coy/55ᵗʰ		

26ᵗʰ Reserve Infantry Brigade   Maj. Gen. von Dresler und Scharfenstein

77ᵗʰ Reserve Infantry Regt.   Oberst Rücker   Battalion MG Company
331ˢᵗ MG
106ᵗʰ MG Marksman
      Section

91ˢᵗ Reserve Infantry Regt.   Oberstleutenant von Heynitz   Battalion MG Company
I/91ˢᵗ R.I.R.   Hauptmann von Eckartsberg   352ⁿᵈ MG
   1/91ˢᵗ
   2/91ˢᵗ
   3/91ˢᵗ
   4/91ˢᵗ
II/91ˢᵗ R.I.R.   Hauptmann von Beerfelde
   5/91ˢᵗ   Lt. Res Kluckhohn
   6/91ˢᵗ   Lt. Res Rittmeyer
   7/91ˢᵗ
   8/91ˢᵗ
III/91ˢᵗ R.I.R.   Major Lorenz
   9/91ˢᵗ
   10/91ˢᵗ   Lt. Res Overesch
   11/91ˢᵗ
   12/91ˢᵗ   Lt. Res Metzner
Pioneer Coy/91ˢᵗ

52ⁿᵈ Infantry Division   Lt. Gen. von Borries

Divisional troops:
4/16ᵗʰ Uhlan Regiment   103ʳᵈ Pioneer Coy
104ᵗʰ Pioneer Coy   103ʳᵈ Searchlight Section
52ⁿᵈ Minenwerfer Coy   1ˢᵗ Bavarian Pioneer Regiment
108ᵗʰ Flak Coy

Artillery:
52ⁿᵈ Field Artillery Brigade   Maj. Gen. Korner
   103ʳᵈ Field Artillery Regiment   Major Knorr
   104ᵗʰ Field Artillery Regiment   Major von Laer
   1, 2 & 3/7ᵗʰ Foot Artillery Regiment   Hptm. Dorn
   52ⁿᵈ Foot Artillery Battalion   Hptm. Haccius
II/19ᵗʰ Bavarian Field Artillery Regt. (from 10ᵗʰ Bavarian Infantry Division)
2/10ᵗʰ Bavarian Foot Artillery Regt. (from 10ᵗʰ Bavarian Infantry Division)
7/2ⁿᵈ Guard Foot Artillery Regiment (½)   471ˢᵗ Foot Artillery Battery (2/3)
472ⁿᵈ Foot Artillery Battery (½)   1ˢᵗ & 2ⁿᵈ/381ˢᵗ Bavarian Foot Artillery Battalion
10ᵗʰ Foot Artillery Battery   2/18ᵗʰ Ersatz Foot Artillery Regiment

104ᵗʰ Infantry Brigade   Maj. Gen. Lequis

15ᵗʰ Reserve Infantry Regt.   Oberstleutnant Schwarz
I/15ᵗʰ R.I.R.
II/15ᵗʰ R.I.R.   Major Kiesel
III/15ᵗʰ R.I.R.
66ᵗʰ Infantry Regt.   Major von Stoeklern zu   Battalion MG Companies
(3ʳᵈ Magdeburg)   Grunholzek   (2)

169ᵗʰ Infantry Regt.   Major von Struensee   Battalion MG Companies
(8ᵗʰ Baden)   (2)

170th Infantry Regt.	Major von Ihlenfeld	13th MG Company
(9th Baden)		74th MG Marksman
I/170th I.R.	Hptm. Wulff	Section
1/170th	Lt. Kremp	
2/170th	Lt. Bahl	
3/170th	Oblt. Res. Reinicke	
4/170th	Lt. Itt	
II/170th I.R.	Major Fischer	
5/170th	Hptm. Res. Mulhausen	
6/170th	Oblt. Res. Roser	
7/170th	Lt. Raapke	
8/170th	Oblt. Krumbiegel	
III/170th I.R.		
9/170th	Oblt. Schedl	
10/170th	Lt. Res Boelkle	
11/170th	Oblt. Ldr. Schillow	
12/170th	Oblt. Res. Buchner	
Pioneer Coy/170th		

APPENDIX 3: 56TH DIVISION CASUALTIES

The total losses of all units of the 56th Division involved on 1st July as supplied to the Division's Adjutant were as follows:

	Officers				Other Ranks				Total
	K	W	M*	Total	K	W	M	Total	
167th Brigade									
1/1 London	0	3	1 (1)	4	3	67	7	77	81
1/3 London	1	3	1	5	19	124	4	147	152
1/7 Middx	0	3	0	3	2	36	0	38	41
1/8 Middx	0	1	0	1	0	29	0	29	30
Total	1	10	2 (1)	13	24	256	11	291	304
168th Brigade									
1/4 London	2	8	3 (3)	13	28	178	56	262	275
1/12 London	0	8	9 (8)	17	28	250	220	498	515
1/13 London	3	11	3 (2)	17	34	184	82	300	317
1/14 London	3	8	3 (3)	14	47	234	263	544	558
168th MGC	0	0	1	1	0	18	4	22	23
168th TMB	0	0	0	0	1	4	0	5	5
Total	8	35	1 (16)	62	138	868	625	1631	1693
169th Brigade									
1/2 London	4	6	2 (2)	12	40	204	0	244	256
1/5 London	7	10	2 (1)	19	56	210	299	565	584
1/9 London	5	5	5 (4)	15	40	261	210	511	566
1/16 London	2	9	8 (7)	19	12	240	249	501	520
169th MGC	2	1	0	3	9	9	19	37	40
169th TMB	1	1	0	2	2	19	10	31	33
Total	21	32	0 (13)	70	159	943	787	1889	1999
Pioneers									
1/5 Cheshire	1	3	2 (2)	6	13	112	47	172	178
R.F.A.									
280 Bde	0	0	0	0	0	2	0	2	2
281 Bde	0	1	0	1	0	0	0	0	1
282 Bde	0	1	0	1	0	4	0	4	5
56 DAC	0	1	0	1	0	2	0	2	3
X56 TMB	0	1	0	1	0	0	2 (2)	3	3
Y56 TMB	0	0	0	0	4	0	1	5	5
Z56 TMB	0	0	0	0	0	1	0	1	1
Royal Engineers									
2/1 London	0	0	0	0	1	10	16 (11)	27	27
2/2 London	0	1	0	1	1	8	7 (6)	16	16
1/1 Edinburgh	0	0	1 (1)	1	4	10	1 (1)	15	16
5 Special R.E.	0	0	0	0	1	16	0	17	17
16 Lancers	0	0	0	0	0	1	0	1	1
R.A.M.C.									
2/1 London	0	0	0	0	1	3	0	4	4
2/2 London	0	0	0	0	1	6	0	7	7
TOTAL	31	86	40 (33)	157	347	2,242	1,497	4,086	4,243

Table 27 Casualties as notified to 56th Division Adjutant

* Figure in brackets is for those reported as 'missing' now known to have been killed.

The Official History increases these totals, rather surprisingly as usually the initial figures were reduced as men drifted back to their units as the chaos of the battle was resolved. The numbers given in the Official History underline why it has proved impossible to arrive at a definitive number of the dead, wounded and missing on the first day of the Battle of the Somme.

	Adjutant's figures*	Official History	Discrepancy
Officers			
Killed	63	53	-10
Wounded	86	107	+21
Missing (inc. PoWs)	8	23	+15
Total	157	183	+26
Other Ranks			
Killed	347	1,300	+953
Wounded	2,242	2,248	+6
Missing (inc. PoWs)	1,497	583	-914
Total	4,086	4,131	+45
Total	4,243	4,314	+71

Table 28 Comparison of 56th Division's and Official History's casualty figures
* Adjusted to include 'missing' now known as killed

The discrepancy in the numbers of officer casualties is most marked and perplexing. The 56th Division's Adjutant gives list of names for officer casualties and, in spite of the confusion about which officer belonged to which regiment (for example, two officers permanently attached to the Westminsters from the 2/2nd Londons are listed as 2nd London Regiment casualties on the Commonwealth War Grave Commission web site), the Official History's figures are significantly in error. By cross-checking War Diaries, regimental histories, the CWGC and Soldiers Died in the Great War the correct figures for officer casualties across every unit in the 56th Division appears to be: 68 dead, 86 wounded and 2 prisoners of war, a total of 156. Overall, therefore, a best estimate of the total casualties suffered on 1st July by the 56th Division is c. 4,300 with the numbers of dead being slightly higher than the 1,300 given to allow for men who died of wounds over the next few weeks.

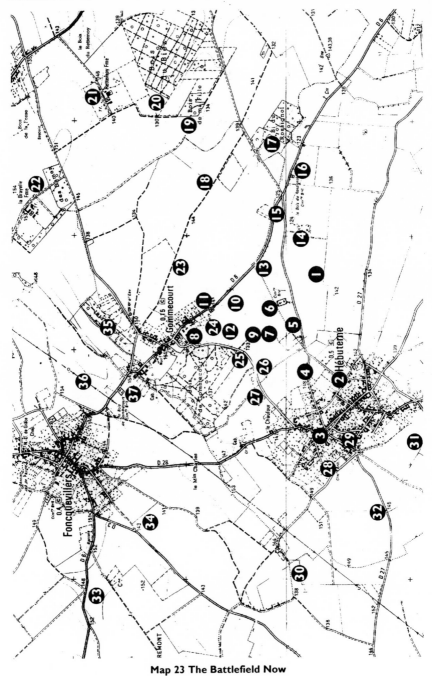

Map 23 The Battlefield Now
Numbers refer to location references in text of Appendix 4

APPENDIX 4: TOURING THE BATTLEFIELD & PLACES TO STAY

THE PAST TEN YEARS or so have seen an explosion of interest in the battles of the Great War and the recently opened Visitor Centre at the Thiepval Memorial is evidence of the fascination that these great battles now hold for the families of those who fought and died in the fields of Northern France and Belgium.

The Thiepval Memorial is, perhaps, as good a place as any to start if one wishes to visit Gommecourt and the other battlefields of the Somme. The quickest route from the Channel Ports is along the A26 autoroute from Calais to Arras and then south via the main Paris Road the A1. Exiting via the Bapaume turn-off, you drive through the town which was the main objective of Sir Douglas Haig's plan for the Somme offensive. Turning right and then left, following the signs to Albert, you leave the town on the Roman Road that runs for 20 kilometres to Albert and the famous land mark of its Golden Virgin atop the Basilica in the centre of the town. As you drive westwards you will pass through or by villages that were to become infamous in the Summer and Autumn of 1916: le Sars, Courcelette, Martinpuich and, lastly, Pozieres. Just before entering this last village you may wish to stop at the Memorial to the Tank Corps on the south side of the road. Opposite it, on the site of the old Pozieres windmill, lies the highest point on the Pozieres ridge, giving commanding views in all directions. It is here that hundreds of Australians soldiers gave their lives in the vicious struggle for this crucial position. Turning right in the centre of the village you may wish to pause at the memorial to the 1st Australian Division and contemplate the nearly 8,000 men from 'Down Under' who died in that Summer's fighting.

The road out of Pozieres takes you towards Thiepval on the north-west skyline but, in the depression between the two villages lies the site of Mouquet Farm. An opening day objective this farm eventually fell on 26th September after murderous fighting involving British, Australian and Canadian troops. After stopping at the relatively new memorials at the entrance to the farm, it is a short drive to Thiepval. At the village cross-roads you will get an excellent panorama of the area attacked with such panache by the Ulstermen of the 36th Division. On the left of the road down into the valley of the Ancre, just in front of Thiepval Wood, you will see Connaught Cemetery which lies on the front line from which the Ulster Division attacked. On the right, up the slight slope, can be seen first Mill Road Cemetery and the Ulster Tower which lie just behind and on the German front line trenches. On the slope behind them, in the fields opposite La Grande Ferme, was the Schwaben Redoubt, captured in the Ulstermen's gallant attack and only given up after hard fighting against overwhelming odds.

Following the signs, you will find the excellent Thiepval Visitor Centre with its audio-visual presentations, bookshop and exhibitions. It has taken over eighty years for a facility such as this to be provided for the burgeoning numbers of visitors to the battlefields but it is welcome in spite of the wait. Leaving the Visitor Centre you walk a short distance to the massive and forbidding Memorial to the Missing of the Somme. Designed by Sir Edward Lutyens and inaugurated by the Prince of Wales in 1932, its panels hold the names of over 73,000 men killed on the Somme but whose bodies were never found. At 45 metres in height, the Memorial can be seen from almost every part of the Somme battlefield and it stands in sombre remembrance of the men who gave their lives in the savage battles that scarred this now peaceful landscape.

The route to Hebuterne and Gommecourt now takes you across the Ulster Division's battlefield and across the marshlands surrounding the winding river Ancre. Following the signs to Hamel and then Auchonvillers you will pass by, and wish to stop at, the Newfoundland Memorial Park. This park, left still disfigured by shell holes and trenches, was bought by the Newfoundland Government after the war and recognises the sacrifice of the men of Newfoundland Regiment who were mown down in their hundreds as they advanced across the open in a vain effort to support an already failed attack. Some 700 men were killed or wounded in their tragic adventure and the great Caribou that stands at the peak of their memorial looks across the ground on which they suffered and died. Young Canadians now man the small centre there and they are relentlessly cheerful and informative in response to any question.

Further along the road on the right, a thicket of trees on the near horizon marks the area of the Hawthorn Ridge Redoubt under which 18 tons of explosive were detonated ten minutes before the start of the battle on 1st July 1916. The film of the explosion by Geoffrey Malins is one of the iconic images of the war but, like so much that happened on that day, it proved a false dawn to the hopes of the Generals and men of the 29th Division which suffered over 5,000 casualties in their failed attempt to take Beaumont Hamel and the ridges to the rear.

Auchonvillers was a British village and, on the left as you arrive, lies 'Ocean Villas', a guest house run by Avril Williams. Avril is something of an institution on the Somme and visits there have always been amusing, informative and stimulating. Ask her nicely and she will show you her trench and cellar used in 1916 as an Advanced Dressing Station by the men of the 29th Division.

The route to Hebuterne now lies to the north of Auchonvillers and the landscape to your right will show more of the VIII Corps' battlefield: Redan Ridge and Serre. Reaching the junction with the D919 Puisieux to Mailly Maillet road one can either go straight ahead to Hebuterne or, turning right, drive down past Serre Road Cemeteries Nos. 1 and 2 and the French Military Cemetery that holds the graves of the men killed in 1915. A bit further along on the left a farm track leads to the cemeteries of the 31st Division that attacked Serre at such cost.

Drive through Serre and into Puisieux and, in the centre of the village, a left turn takes you towards Hebuterne. Two thirds of the way between the two villages the opposing lines cut the road at right angles and it was here, and to the south, that the gap between the Gommecourt 'diversion' and the attack at Serre occurred. To the north of the road and away across the brow of the low ridge is the area attacked by the London Scottish (*see location 1 on map on page 591*).

As you enter Hebuterne an area of trees and bushes runs away from the road on the right hand side. Concealed in the undergrowth here, on the side of the village facing Gommecourt, were the two 18 pdr field guns of C/283 Battery, R.F.A. which were used to bombard the wire and trenches at the south-eastern corner of Gommecourt Park, otherwise known as Point 94 (*location 2*). At the first road junction in the village is the imposing church which, along with most of the village, lay in ruins even before the attack on 1st July. The road now bears around to the right and broadens out to encompass a triangular village green surrounded by lime trees (*location 3*). At the far end of the green was a pond and running north from every side turning on the right hand side of the road were the communication trenches that led to the British front line.

Take the right hand turn at the end of the green, where it is at its widest, and, at about 300 metres just before another lane joins from the right, you will be on the approximate position of the old British front line (*location 4 on map on page 591*). You get an excellent view from here across the area attacked by the 169th Brigade, the L.R.B. on the left towards the Park and the Q.V.R. and Q.W.R. straight ahead between the cemetery and the left hand edge of Gommecourt British Cemetery No. 2 the walls and trees of which are visible in a fold in the ground. Going past the junction you will be on the approximate position of the new British front line when you are half way between the junction and the entrance to the cemetery. You will be standing in the centre of the assembly trenches used by The Rangers (*location 5*). To your right along a slight rise in the ground, the left wing of the London Scottish attacked towards a small copse set in a depression in the middle of the fields.

Plate 72 Gommecourt British Cemetery No. 2
Taken from in front of the Great Cross of Sacrifice, looking north-west towards Gommecourt

Gommecourt British Cemetery No. 2 lies mid-way between the two front lines and on the line of the attack of 'C' and 'D' Companies of The Rangers (*location 6*). The cemetery contains the graves of 1,357 men, of which 682 are unidentified, most being men of the 56th Division. The village of Gommecourt was eventually occupied by British troops on the night of 27th-28th February 1917 after the Germans began their withdrawal to the Hindenburg Line. At this point it became possible to clear the 1st July battlefield and four cemeteries were created:

No. 1 Cemetery lay about sixty yards west of the existing cemetery (*location 7*);

No. 3 Cemetery was on the edge of Gommecourt village around the area of the Maze (*location 8*); and

No. 4 Cemetery was one hundred yards or so north west of the existing No. 2 Cemetery (*location 9 on map on page 591*).

Nos. 1 and 4 Cemeteries were in the area of No Man's Land across which the left of The Rangers, the Queen Victoria's and Queen's Westminster Rifles attacked. No. 3 Cemetery was the graveyard of the London Rifle Brigade. After the war, these cemeteries and some other isolated burials were concentrated in Gommecourt No. 2 Cemetery.

Plot I in the centre of the cemetery is the original No. 2 Cemetery and contains 101 graves of which 51 have been identified as men of the 56th Division. These graves represent the men who fought on or near the cemetery and they comprise:

30 men of The Rangers.

11 men of the 1/4th London Regiment;

8 men of the Queen's Westminster Rifles;

1 man of the Queen Victoria's Rifles;

1 man of the London Rifle Brigade.

Amongst the men buried here are Capt. Hoare and 2nd Lt. Josephs of The Rangers whose deaths are described in the text.

Plot II, which is on the left as you enter starting at the third row back (the first two rows are Plot VI), contains the known graves of 78 men of the 56th Division[i]:

19 men of the London Rifle Brigade;

18 men of the London Scottish;

16 men of the 1/2nd and 1/4th London Fusiliers;

7 men of the Queen Victoria's Rifles;

10 men of the Queen's Westminster Rifles;

4 men of The Rangers

2 men of the 1/5th Cheshire Regiment; and

1 man each of the 1/7th and 1/8th Middlesex Regiment (both killed on 26th June 1916).

Amongst those buried here are Sgt. Boardman of the Cheshires, Lt. Brown Constable (London Scottish), C.S.M. Froome (Queen's Westminsters) and Capt. Handyside (1/2nd Londons) whose deaths are described in this book.

Plot III, on the right of the cemetery as you enter starting at the third row back (the first two rows are Plot VII), contains the known graves of 97 men of the 56th Division:

27 men of the 1/2nd and 1/4th London Fusiliers;

24 men of the Queen Victoria's Rifles;

21 men of the London Rifle Brigade;

10 men of the Queen's Westminster Rifles;

7 men of the 1/5th Cheshire Regiment;

4 men of the London Scottish;

3 men of The Rangers; and

1 man of the Royal Engineers.

---

[i] It also includes the grave of an officer of the 46th North Midland Div. Ammunition Col, RFA.

Amongst those buried here are Lt. Davies and 2nd Lt. Arthur of the Cheshires, 2nd Lt. Fielding (Queen Victoria's) and Capt. Garland (1/2nd Londons) whose deaths are described in this book. Also to be found in this plot are the graves of brothers Philip and Henry Bassett of the Queen Victoria's Rifles who lie side by side in graves III.B.12 and 13.

Plots IV, V, VI and VII contain the graves of 13 men of the 56th Division:
8 men of the London Scottish;
2 men of the 1/2nd and 1/4th London Fusiliers; and
1 each from the London Rifle Brigade, The Rangers and the Royal Engineers.

Amongst those buried here are 2nd Lt. Curror (London Scottish) and 2nd Lt. Davey (The Rangers) whose deaths are described in this book.

Ranged against the north wall of the cemetery, are a series of Special Memorials for men believed to be buried in the cemetery. Fifteen of these relate to men of the 56th Division:
6 men of the London Rifle Brigade;
3 men of the Queen Victoria's Rifles;
2 men of the 1/2nd and 1/4th London Fusiliers;
2 men of the Queen's Westminster Rifles; and
1 man of The Rangers.

Amongst those remembered here are 2nd Lt. Horne (Queen's Westminsters) and Lt. Clode-Baker (London Rifle Brigade) whose deaths are described herein.

The rest of the cemetery is filled with the graves of men who died in 1917 as the Germans withdrew from the area or from 1918 when the great German Spring offensive reached its high water mark nearby in Rossignol Wood.

The cemetery gives an excellent view of the area attacked by the 56th Division. From the rear of the cemetery (at the opposite end to the Great Cross of Sacrifice) you will gaze across the area attacked by the 169th Brigade (*location 10 on map on page 591*). Across the fields about 100 yards away the Westminsters and Victorias attacked from left to right and swept over the two sets of German lines which lay this side of the Gommecourt-Puisieux Road. Held up on the road they eventually carried the third German line which ran a few yards beyond and parallel to the road.

In the distance looms Gommecourt Park and, 250 yards to the right, the low trees that surround Gommecourt Cemetery (*location 11*). The area between was the objective of the London Rifle Brigade and it was from the front line trench a 100 yards in front of the cemetery that the few remaining men tried to make good their escape from the German lines in the evening of 1st July (*location 12*).

Looking north, or to the right, as you enter the cemetery you will see the area attacked by The Rangers. The battalion's front straddled the cemetery road and its objective was the German third line just behind the Gommecourt to Puisieux Road. If you stand behind the War Stone, in front of Row B of the Special Memorials, and look towards the road you may notice a slight bend. At this point and on this side of the road was the location of Nameless Farm of which nothing now remains (*location 13*). It was the machine gun fire from this strongpoint that helped destroy The Rangers and the 1/4th London Regiment who had been tasked with the capture of the farm.

Returning to the entrance to the cemetery, looking east, you will notice that the land on the far side of the sunken road rises gently away to the south east.

Immediately on the far side of the road 'A' Company of The Rangers attacked and beyond them, the London Scottish. Here the front line bends away to the south and disappears from view but, nearly straight ahead, is a small clump of trees in the middle of the fields. This lies behind the Farmer-Farmyard stronghold that was the objective of the London Scottish (*location 14 on map on page 591*). If you leave the cemetery and turn left away from Hebuterne you will come to a track on the right that leads to these trees. It is negotiable with care and will give you a good view of the 168th Brigade's area of attack.

Go back to the road and continuing away from Hebuterne. You will first come to an area on the left used to collect rubbish. It is here that local farmers leave the unexploded shells that are dug up on a regular basis for the French Army Bomb Squads to deal with (*location 15*). **These shells are potentially lethal and should not be touched or moved.** Even now, people are killed and maimed as a result of explosions or gas leaks caused by these unstable munitions.

A few yards further on the Hebuterne to Bucquoy Road crosses the Gommecourt to Puisieux Road. A hundred yards to the right on the Puisieux Road lies Rossignol Wood Cemetery (*location 16*) which is of interest to anyone interested in the 56th Division's attack as Plot II on the left contains a number of German graves, several of which are of men of the 170th Infantry Regiment who died defending their trenches on 1st July. Turning your back on the cemetery and looking across the road and up the slope you will see Rossignol Wood (*location 17*) through which many German communication trenches ran which were used to send men to counter-attack The Rangers and London Scottish. The Hebuterne to Bucquoy Road runs up the slope and passes the western edge of the wood and, within its confines can still be seen the evidence of trenches.

Plate 73 Achiet le Petit German Cemetery

If you carry on down this road to Bucquoy and go straight through the village following the signs to Achiet-le-Petit you will find, tucked away in a quiet lane on the far side of the village, a small German cemetery which contains a number of graves from 1916. It was along this route that casualties were sent to the rear hospitals to the east of Bapaume.

Returning to the battlefield, fifty yards beyond the north-western corner of Rossignol Wood a metalled track runs off to the left and across the top of the ridge back into the rear of Gommecourt. Three hundred yards along this track lies Hill 147, the point used by the German infantry and artillery observers (*location 18 on map on page 591*). This location gives a perfect panorama over the entire 56th Division front and, to the south, above the trees that fringe Hebuterne you will just see the top of the village's church spire. Along this ridge ran the Garde Stellung and it was along this major trench artery that men of the 55th Reserve Infantry Regiment were sent to launch counter-attacks against the 169th Brigade. If you look to your right (north) you will see one small and one large wood – Square (*location 19*) and Biez Woods (*location 20*) – and, to their left, the tall trees surrounding Rettemoy Farm (*location 21*). Further left and surrounded by trees is La Brayelle Farm (*location 22*). Artillery batteries were dug in around and in these locations while the heavier guns were positioned further east along the Puisieux-Bucquoy-Douchy les Ayettes road.

Two thirds of the way along this track and just to its left (between the track and Gommecourt cemetery) lies the area of trenches known as the Quadrilateral (*location 23*). It is here that the 56th and 46th Division's were due to meet, however, only briefly did a small party of Westminsters led by 2nd Lt. Arthur of the Cheshires occupy this objective before being expelled by German bombing parties.

Follow the track into the village and, at the first cross-roads turn left and, after 100 yards, left again. Drive out of the village (on the Puisieux road) and stop at the cemetery. Between the cemetery and Gommecourt British Cemetery No. 2 in the middle distance is the area attacked by the Victorias and Westminsters. The road then was significantly below the level of the fields to your left and it was along the northern (left hand) bank of the road that the men of the two battalions re-grouped before taking the third German line. A small group of Westminsters bombed their way up these trenches to the cemetery early in the day.

Turning right reveals the London Rifle Brigade's area of attack. From the corner of the cemetery away towards the edge of Gommecourt Park ran Eck trench in which 2nd Lt. Petley and his men fought their battle. The Maze was a group of trenches about mid-way between the cemetery and Park to the right of the line of Eck Trench (*location 24*). Returning to the village you should take the first left, signposted Hebuterne. This takes you along the eastern fringe of the Park, the Maze now to your left, and, at the point where the edge of the Park leaves the road, you will be on the German front line at the junction of Fir and Fen trenches. Fir runs along the edge of the Park whilst Fen, the German front line, runs away to the left of Gommecourt British Cemetery No. 2. The place at which the edge of the Park turns sharp right away from the road is Point 94 where Gerfreiter Füchte and 2nd Lt. Doust met their ends (*location 25*).

The road now bends away to the right and about half way up the gentle slope opposite were the assembly trenches of the London Rifle Brigade (*location 26*).

On the opposite, right hand, side of the road the Z Hedge ran parallel to the road for about 50 yards before turning right and then left after a similar distance (*location 27 on map on page 591*).

Plate 74 Hebuterne Military Cemetery
The photograph shows the scattered nature of the burials in what used to be an orchard.

The road now runs into the western end of Hebuterne where it meets the Foncquevillers road at a T-junction. Turn left back into the village until you come to the elongated village green. At the near end a right hand turn directs you towards Sailly-au-Bois. Drive down this road until the road bends to the right and here, on the right, a farm track leads past a large barn to Hebuterne Military Cemetery (*location 28*). As you walk up the short path to the entrance to the cemetery on your right are some farm buildings which were the location of the Advanced Dressing Station started by the Field Ambulances of the 48th (South Midland) Division in the summer of 1915 and taken over by the 56th Division in May 1916 (*location 29*). The cemetery contains 735 graves of which all but a few carry names. This cemetery was an orchard in the summer of 1916 which goes some way to explain the rather random distribution of the graves; they are, however, reasonably grouped together by unit. The 56th Division's casualties are in Plots II, III and IV at far end of the cemetery in front of the War Stone and, in Row M of Plot IV, sixty one men who died on 1st July 1916 are buried in a mass grave with each headstone carrying the name of two or three men.

Amongst the graves are those of Lt. J J B Ball R.F.A., Lance Sergeant Buffham (1/1st Londons), 2nd Lt. Fradd (1/2nd Londons), Sapper Leuchars (R.E.), 2nd Lts. Mager and Pilgrim (Kensingtons), Lt. Meo and 2nd Lt. Phillips (The Rangers), 2nd Lt. Price (1/7th Middlesex) and Sgt Redgell (Queen Victoria's) whose deaths are described in this book.

Plate 75 The mass grave of London casualties in Row M, Hebuterne Cemetery

Returning to the Sailly road (the D27), turn right and drive across the plain to the village. In the fields on both sides of the road the guns of the 56th Division's field artillery were massed to prepare for and support the attack (*locations 30 & 31 on map on page 591*) and it was on tracks parallel to this road that the men marched into and out of Hebuterne. It was along this route that the battalions involved in the attack marched on the evening of 30th June (*location 32*). Just before you enter Sailly, two more field batteries were positioned on either side of the road near to the football ground, C/281 on the left and B/283 on the right. Driving straight through the village, past the church on the right, you will find Sailly-au-Bois Military Cemetery. Started in May 1916 it was the first port of call for casualties being evacuated from villages to the south and only a handful of men here, mainly from the R.F.A. and R.G.A., were involved in the activities of early Summer 1916.

Just past the cemetery, a left turn will be signposted Coigneux. This road runs along a valley, one of several known as 'Happy Valley', which eventually becomes the head of the River Authie. Sheltered from view this was a major route for supplies and an evacuation route to the Main Dressing Station at Couin, the next village after Coigneux. A right turn at a cross-roads will take you into the village of Couin. Towards the end of the village, past the chateau on your right, will be a turning signposted Souastre and 200 yards along this road, past La Ferme de la Voierie on your left, you will come to two war cemeteries, Couin British Cemetery on your right and Couin New British Cemetery on your left. The

M.D.S. was started here in May 1916 by the 48th (South Midland) Division Field Ambulances which were shortly after joined by those of the 56th Division. The casualties of 1916 are all in Couin British Cemetery which contains 401 British and three German graves. Scattered amongst plots I and II, which run down the centre of the cemetery are some thirty casualties from the 56th Division who include 2nd Lt. Pogose of the London Rifle Brigade and Capt. Galloway Smith of the 416th (1/1st City of Edinburgh) Field Coy RE.

On leaving Couin British Cemetery return the short distance to the junction which is signposted Henu. The drive is short, up and over a slight hill, and, on the far side you reach the eastern edge of the village. Go across the first cross-roads and turn left at the next one. On the left hand side you will soon spot the small church. At the side of the church is a small cemetery and at its rear there are a series of British and French graves. Amongst them you will find the grave of Capt. Bernard Christmas, 1/3rd Londons, killed in a skirmish in No Man's Land in mid-May. Follow the road another hundred yards or so and on the right, just before a junction, is the long avenue that leads to the chateau that served as H.Q. for the 56th Division in the Summer of 1916.

Now is the time to undertake that most tricky manoeuvre on any French road – the U-turn. Retrace your steps through the village but stay on the road to St Amand. Go straight over the crossroads with the D23 and after two hundred yards you will find St Amand British Cemetery. Opened in April 1916 it contains just under twenty men of the 56th Division whose graves lie in Plot I, three rows back from the entrance gate. A small Aid Post was started here by the London Field Ambulance and the casualties are pre-1st July. St Amand was one of the villages which harboured the great howitzers of the Heavy Artillery and one of the huge 12 in. railway mounted howitzers lurked in the orchards around the village (the other two railway mounted pieces, a 9.2 in. gun and the other 12 in. howitzer, were positioned at Humbercamps, a village a kilometre or more up the D26 to the north.

Return to the cross-roads with the D23 and turn left into St Amand, then follow the signs to Souastre. More guns were located at Souastre but it was also one of the villages used to billet troops and hundreds of men took shelter in the large barns that still stand in the quiet lanes of the village. On the evening of the 30th June, columns of men marched out of Souastre south towards Bayencourt and then to Sailly-au-Bois there to begin the trek across the plain to Hebuterne and the assembly trenches. Instead of taking this route, however, follow the D6 towards Foncquevillers and the area of the 46th Division's attack. Threequarters of the way along this road more batteries of the 56th Division's field artillery were positioned (*locations 33 & 34 on map on page 591*), firing to take the trenches and wire opposite Hebuterne in enfilade.

When you reach the centre of Foncquevillers follow the D6 and the signs for Gommecourt and Puisieux. As you leave the eastern edge of the village you will see, on the left hand side of the road, a wood stretching from right to left for perhaps 600 yards. This is Gommecourt Wood (*location 35*) and the German front lines were just in front of the wood. Before you reach the wood a line of electricity pylons cuts across the road, parallel to the wood (*location 36*). This is approximately on the line of the British forward trenches. Set between the two lines, Gommecourt Wood New Cemetery sits squarely in the middle of No Man's

Land (*location 37*). It is across the ground on the opposite side of the road that the North Midlanders attacked and were bloodily repulsed. The body of one of the three battalion C.O.s who died during the attack, Lt. Col. C E Boote of the 1/5th North Staffordshires, lies in the cemetery along with the remains of another 738 men who died in the years 1916-18.

Straight ahead is the village of Gommecourt. On the right as you enter is the new chateau which replaced the one destroyed in the war. You have now returned to the area over which the 56th Division attacked, the completion of your battlefield journey.

Places to stay

There has been significant growth in the amount of accommodation available on the Somme as well as in places to eat and drink. I can only recommend one place to stay as it is the only one I have stayed at so please don't think that the other places mentioned are anything other than welcoming and comfortable.

Ocean Villas, the guest house and tea rooms at Auchonvillers, run by Avril Williams is something of an institution on the Somme. Every guest has some interest in the Great War and some have considerable expertise. Conversation over dinner and breakfast, therefore, is sure to be interesting and stimulating unless, of course, you have no interest in the war in which case you may be bored rigid! The cellar of the guest house was an Advanced Dressing Station in the war and, over the years, enthusiasts have reconstructed a trench leading into the cellar which Avril will show off on request. Food is simple but ample and the atmosphere is relaxed. Lunch and snacks are available at the new Tea Rooms. The stay at Avril's has always been a highlight of my battlefield tours.

Contact details: 'Ocean Villas', Auchonviller, Tel: 33 322 76 23 66; web site: http://www.oceanvillas-tearooms.com/Avril/

Other places to stay:
Auchonvillers:
    Les Galets B&B (Julie Renshaw 33 3 22 76 28 79 or www.lesgalets.com)
Albert:
    Hotel de la Basilique (Tel: 33 3 22 75 04 71 or contact@hoteldelabasilique.fr)
    Hotel De La Paix (Tel: 33 3 22 75 01 64)
    Le Relais Fleuri (Tel: 33 3 22 75 08 11)
    Hotel Best Western Royal Picardie (Tel: 33 3 22 75 37 00 or reservation@royalpicardie.com)
    B&B Evelyne & Jackie (Tel: 33 3 22 75 63 28 or www.ensomme.net/liensg/eveanglais.htm)
Combles:
    Orchard Farm (Martin Pegler 33 3 22 86 56 72 or www.martinpegler.com)
Courcelles au Bois:
    La Martinierre B&B (http://membres.lycos.fr/lamartinierre/)
Flers:
    Otago View B&B (Peter & Hilary Smith 33 3 22 85 47 23 or hilary.smith@wanadoo.fr)
    Dinnaken House Gite (Rory Newsome 07791 545 214 or www.dinnakenhouse.plus.com)
Hardecourt aux Bois:
    Les Alouettes B&B (Vic & Diane Piuk 33 3 22 85 14 56 or www.lesalouettes.net)
    Chavasse Farm – Battlefield Gite (Jonathan/Richard 0785 585 0889 and
    www.chavasseferme.com)
Longueval:
    Rose Cottage Gite (Jeannie Alexander Tel: 0121 430 5348 or battletour@aol.com)
Montauban:
    Bernafay Wood B&B (Jean-Pierre Matte 33 3 22 85 02 47 or bernafaywood@aol.com)
Le Sars B&B (Mme Danièle Roussel 00 33 3 21 070 501 or www.memorysomme.com)

Appendix 5: Contemporary Newspaper Reports of the Attack

John D. Irvine, Daily Express, wrote:

"I AM ABLE TO GIVE first-hand information concerning the part which has been played by certain of our famous London regiments. These regiments, which include the Rangers, the Queen Victoria's Rifles, the London Rifle Brigade, the London Scottish and the Queen's Westminsters were assigned certain objectives near Gommecourt, towards the northern end of our original line of advance, where, owing to the extraordinary preparations made by the enemy, we did not fare so well as we have done and continue to do further south.

The London regiments, who fought with magnificent gallantry and tenacity, did in fact, accomplish their primary objects, but, owing to circumstances beyond their control they subsequently had to retire to a line which nearly corresponded to that they occupied before the battle began. It certainly represents no surrender of territory; the enemy is fully contained and is kept busy night and day, with the result that he can send neither guns nor men to assist his hard-pressed troops within the zone of our continuous penetration of his lines.

When the regiments received the order to leave their trenches at 7.30 on the morning of July 1st, a gap of from 250 to 300 yards in a valley separated them from the first line trenches of the enemy. At the given signal they leapt across their parapets, and with magnificent steadiness, advanced in the open under cover of smoke which had been sent up with the object of screening their movements from the enemy. Within half an hour they were in possession of the main objective. Immediately afterwards the enemy started to set up a terrific barrage fire, which almost pulverised the front line trenches from which our men originally started, and, what was of graver consequence, stopped all efforts to send up supports and carrying parties bearing munitions essential to the continuance of our advance.

The most gallant attempts were made to establish communication, and a series of enterprises characterised by desperate bravery involved us in heavy losses. Out of one party of fifty-nine which started across the shell-swept valley, one only reached his comrades and but three returned to our lines.

Reports sent back shortly before this showed that our artillery had succeeded in smashing up the German parapets and barbed wire entanglements, but had failed - as has been the experience everywhere - to crumple up the deep dug-outs in which it is the habit of the Boches to sit down and bide their opportunity. So when our men entered the enemy trenches, they were confronted by crowds of these cave-dwellers armed with bombs, and a series of hand-to-hand conflicts, in which we succeeded in killing many and capturing some Germans, ensued. A certain number of the Boches showed a readiness to surrender, but they were influenced by more courageous comrades, who assured them that the English could not send up supplies, and that very soon they would have to go back to their own territory. The Londoners did succeed in capturing about 200 unwounded or slightly wounded Germans, but as these hapless individuals were being sent across to our lines they came under the fire of their own artillery.

In bombing, during the time they were in the trenches, the Londoners easily out throw the Germans, and all along they were getting the best of the fight when the enemy succeeded in working partially round our flanks, cutting off communication with the units of another division. The London Scottish on the right flank put up a great fight, and further towards the left, superb gallantry was displayed by the Queen's Westminsters, the L.R.B. and the 'Vics.' Owing, however, to the fact that our of bombs and other ammunition had now reached the point of exhaustion, and that it was impossible to send up fresh supplies, our men had no option but to fall back, which they did with extreme reluctance, though in perfect order. A chapter of accidents robbed them of what would have been a fruitful victory."

Phillip Gibbs, the Daily Telegraph:

"WHEN THE FOUR LEADING BATTALIONS left their trenches near Gommecourt at 7.30 after the great bombardment of the German positions, they had a long way to go before they reached the enemy's front lines. No Man's Land was a broad stretch of ground, 400 yards across in some parts, and not less than 200 yards at the narrowest part. It was a long, long journey in the open, for fifty yards, or twenty, are long enough to become a great graveyard if the enemy's machine-guns get to work. But they advanced behind dense smoke-like clouds, which rolled steadily towards the German trenches and kept down the machine-gun fire, and their chief risk was from the barrage of shell fire which the enemy flung across No Man's Land with some intensity. But the Londoners started forward to this line of high explosives, and went on, and through, at a quick pace in open order.

On the left was the London Rifle Brigade, in the centre came the 'Vics.' and Rangers, on the right the London Scottish, and behind the Queen's Westminsters and Kensingtons, who were to advance through the others. Men fell across the open ground, caught by flying bits of shell or buried by the great bursts of high explosives which opened up the earth. But the others did not look back, afraid to weaken themselves by the sight of their stricken comrades, and at a great pace, half walking and half running, they reached the German line. It was no longer a system of trenches. It was a sea of earth with solid waves. Our heavy guns had annihilated parapet and parados, smashed the timbers into matchwood, strewed sandbags into rubbish heaps and made a great wreckage. But German industry below ground was proof against all this shell-fire, and many of the dug-outs still stood. They were full of Germans, for the line was strongly held, and many of these men came up with their machine-guns and bombs to resist the attack. But the Londoners sprang upon them, swept over them, and captured the front network of trenches with amazing speed.

It was not a steady-going business, slow and deliberate. The quick mind of the London man spurred him to quick action. He did not linger to collect souvenirs or to chat with English speaking Germans. 'London leads' was the shout of the Victorias and Westminsters. The London Scottish were racing forward on the right with their brown kilts swinging across the broken ground. But the officers kept their heads and as much order as possible at such a time. They held back enough men to clear the dug-outs and collect prisoners - the best kind of souvenirs. Two hundred of them were captured in the dug-outs and brought up and sent back over the place that had been No Man's Land and now, for a time, was ours. At least 200 came back, but there were many more who never got back, though they started on the journey under armed guard. The enemy's artillery was increasing the density of the barrage upon our old front-line trenches and the ground in front of it. He made a wall of high explosives through which no living thing could pass. The escorts and their prisoners tried to pass - and failed. The German gunners must have seen their grey-clad men going back, but they obeyed the laws of war and did not give them a chance, because if they passed back other British soldiers could pass forward, and it was for the guns to stop them.

At the time the London men fighting forward did not think of the barrage behind them. They were eager to get on, to be quick over the first part of their business before taking breath for the next. And they got on with astonishing speed. In less than the time it has taken me to write this narrative, No Man's Land had been crossed, the trenches had been taken, the prisoners collected and sent back on their way, and German strongholds and redoubts behind the first system of trench work had been seized by London regiments. It would have taken them longer to walk from Charing Cross to St. Paul's Churchyard with no Germans in the way. It was the quickest bit of work that has been done by any freemen of the City. The riflemen had swarmed into a strong point on the left, knocking out the machine-guns, and on the right the London Scots were holding a strong redoubt in a very ugly corner of ground. Everything had been won that London had been asked to win.

Before some hours had passed these London soldiers knew that they were in a death-trap, and cut off from escape, owing to the great strength of the enemy to the right and left of the position, where they had concentrated masses of guns, and where the ground was more difficult to carry. The troops on either side of the Londoners, in spite of heroic courage and complete self-sacrifice, had not advanced so far. The London men had therefore thrust forward a salient into the German lines, were enclosed by the enemy. Behind them, on the way to their own lines, the enemy's barrage was steadily becoming more violent. Having stopped the other attacks to the north and south, he was now able to concentrate the fire of his guns upon the ground of the London area, and by the early afternoon he had smashed our trenches and communication trenches while still flinging out a line of high explosives to prevent supports coming up to the men who were in the captured salient. They were cut off, and had no other means of rescue but their own courage.

Desperate efforts were made by the comrades behind to send up supplies of ammunition and other means of defence. The carrying parties attempted again and again to cross No Man's Land, but suffered heavy casualties. One party of sixty men with supplies of hand-grenades, set out on this journey, but only three came back. Single men went on with a few grenades, determined to carry some kind of support to the men in front, but fell dead or wounded before they reached their goal. In the meantime, as the day lengthened, the enemy organised a series of counter-attacks. Their grenadiers showed a great courage and daring, working down their communication trenches under heavy fire from our artillery and even crossing on top of the trenches in small groups until they were close enough for bomb throwing. Other parties came down on the left of the Londoners from the northern position, and from this direction also very heavy machine-gun fire began to enfilade our riflemen....

It is a tragic narrative but the London battalions who went out there beyond No Man's Land, did as well as any soldiers could, and the brave hearts which beat once to the pulse of London's great tide of life should be remembered on the long roll-call of honour which stretches back through the history of our great old town. 'London leads!' was the cry of these men."

Mr. Beach Thomas, correspondent of the Daily Mail:

"OUR ATTACK AT GOMMECOURT, the northern end of the long fronted battle, was as heroic as anything in the war. I know the trenches there well and happen to have intimate personal acquaintance with some of those engaged. I had played cricket with them, and football. The other day I was up in their trenches, and among other curious experiences put my head over the parapet - for all was dull and quiet - and stared at the silent and thorny German lines. But in spite of appearances the Germans (who held a sharp salient in Gommecourt Wood) were known to be both forewarned and forearmed.

At 7.30 a.m., and earlier, on July 1st, their guns - closely concentrated and of full calibre - set up a triple barrage (fire curtain). Through all these three barrages of intense fire our men marched quite steadily, as if nothing was in the way, as if they were under review. At every step men fell; and our trenches here are very far apart from the German. The gap was still wide, though a little while before the fighting we had built a completely new trench nearer the enemy in the course of a single night. When these steady, steadfast soldiers, true to the death, paraded in more than decimated numbers through and across the third barrage, the enemy - in their turn heroic - left their trenches, erected machine guns on the parapets, and the two parties fought one another in the open.

I have not the hardihood to write more. Heroism could no further go. Our men died; and in dying held in front of them enough German guns to have altered the fate of our principal and our most successful advance in the south.

THEY DIED DEFEATED, BUT WON AS GREAT A VICTORY IN SPIRIT AND IN FACT AS ENGLISH HISTORY OR ANY HISTORY WILL EVER CHRONICLE."

APPENDIX 6: ROLL OF HONOUR OF THE 56TH (1ST LONDON) DIVISION

The details contained in the Roll of Honour are published with the permission of, and with thanks to, the Commonwealth War Graves Committee (Visit their web site at http://www.cwgc.org/). It contains the details of the men killed and died of wounds from the 56th (1st London) Division and associated VII Corps units as a result of action on 1st July 1916.

All casualties are killed in action on 1st July 1916 unless an alternative date for died of wounds is given.

1/1ST LONDON REGIMENT (ROYAL FUSILIERS)
All casualties listed as Thiepval Memorial are on Pier and Face 9 D and 16 B
D COMPANY
No. 13 Platoon
  Cole 4832 Pte Bertram Archibald Son of Mrs Cole of 47, Ley Street, Ilford Thiepval Memorial
Company and Platoon not known
  Bailey 2413 Pte Ernest Thiepval Memorial
  Bean 2661 Pte Frederick Aged 20 Son of Mrs Minnie Bean of 141, Ossulston St., Euston Rd., London. Thiepval Memorial
  Bruce 4828 Pte William George Thiepval Memorial
  Chandler 3527 Pte Albert E Aged 19 Son of James & Ada Chandler of 3, Oval Place, Clapham, London. Hebuterne Military Cemetery IV. B. 2.
  Cundall 2nd Lt. Hubert Walter Aged 24 Son of Florence & the late John Hubert Cundall Thiepval Memorial
  Edwards 2981 Pte Walter Thiepval Memorial
  Horner 2753 Pte Charles Thiepval Memorial
  Maby 2679 Pte Charles A Thiepval Memorial
  Morton 2980 Pte James Thiepval Memorial
  Shaw 3355 Pte Charles Thiepval Memorial
  Skipp 5182 Pte Alfred Thiepval Memorial
2nd July 1916
  Harris 4756 Pte Arthur Son of Mrs A Harris of 6, Skipton Street, Southwark Warlincourt Halte British Cemetery, Saulty II. D. 10
  Wood 1951 Pte Henry George Hebuterne Military Cemetery II. H. 1
3rd July 1916
  Bowtle 4274 Pte Frederick Brother of Mr S M Bowtle of 35, Granville Rd., Hoe St., Walthamstow, London Couin British Cemetery I. C. 13.
  Yates 1320 Pte Charles Wilfred Aged 23 Son of Samuel & Esther Rose Yates of Little Brickhill, Bletchley, Bucks. Ste. Marie Cemetery, Le Havre Div. 19. HH. 4.
4th July 1916
  Smart 4296 Pte Henry John Couin British Cemetery II. A. 8.
5th July 1916
  Champion 5162 Pte Harold Aged 26 Son of Frederick William & Harriet Champion Doullens Communal Cemetery Extension No.1, IV. C. 2.
7th July 1916
  Bassam 5453 Pte James Stanley Brother of Mr F H Bassam of 30, Jeffreys St., Kentish Town, London Couin British Cemetery II. A. 11.
  Couldstone 2779 Pte William Son of Mrs J F Couldstone of 4, Hermes St., Pentonville Rd., King's Cross, London Couin British Cemetery II. A. 10.
9th July 1916
  Harris 2797 Pte F J Aged 23 Elder son of the late George Frederick Harris, F.G.S., & Mary Ann Mullens Harris of London. Le Treport Military Cemetery Plot 2. Row M. Grave 4C

1/2ND LONDON REGIMENT (ROYAL FUSILIERS)
All casualties listed as Thiepval Memorial are on Pier and Face 9 D and 16 B
A COMPANY
  Allen 2545 Pte Albert Gabriel Thiepval Memorial
  Bayston 2544 Pte John William Thiepval Memorial
  Brown 3555 Pte John Aged 18 Son of Benjamin & Mary Ann Brown of, 3, Manner's St., York Rd., Lambeth, London Gommecourt British Cemetery No. 2, Sp. Mem. B. 12

Garland Capt. James Richard Aged 23 Son of Richard Edmund & Olive May Garland of 162, All Souls Avenue, Willesden, London Gommecourt British Cemetery No. 2, III. H. I

Ilsley 2748 L/Cpl Cyril Vincent att. from 2/2nd London Regt. Aged 24 Son of Charles & Sarah Ann Ilsley of 11, Rochford Rd., Basingstoke, Hants. Thiepval Memorial

Lane 3124 Pte Arthur James Robert Gommecourt British Cemetery No. 2, III. F. 20

Monypenny 3301 Pte Anthony Aged 18 Thiepval Memorial

No. 1 Platoon

Cook 1767 Pte Frederick Percy Aged 18 Son of George & Elizabeth Cook of I, Renaldo St., High Rd., Balham, London Thiepval Memorial

Stacey 4782 Pte William Aged 18 Son of Mrs L Stacey of 230, The Grove, Hammersmith, London Thiepval Memorial

No. 2 Platoon

Austin 1909 Pte Richard Aged 23 Son of Richard & Eliza S Austin of 60, Walnut Tree Walk, Kennington Rd., London Thiepval Memorial

No. 3 Platoon

Gale 4485 Pte Maurice Aged 17 Son of William & Mary Gale of 129, Brook St., Kennington, London Thiepval Memorial

No. 4 Platoon

Cheeseman 4775 Pte George Husband of Mrs Cheeseman of 5, Oak Place, Clarence Street, Rotherhithe Thiepval Memorial

Cohen 3600 Pte Henry Aged 19 Son of Henry & Sarah Cohen of 84, Credon Rd., Camberwell, London Thiepval Memorial

Fenner 4479 Pte Alfred Hebuterne Military Cemetery IV. B. 6

LEWIS GUN TEAM

Dack 3483 Pte Harold Son of Mrs Dack of 73, College Road, Willesden Gommecourt British Cemetery No. 2, II. H. 18

Flatt 4601 Pte Arthur James Thiepval Memorial

B COMPANY

Myers 2626 L/Cpl John Frederick Aged 28 Son of Mrs L Myers of 12, Tennyson Rd., Willesden Lane, London; husband of Hilda May Myers of 67, Clarendon Rd., Putney, London Thiepval Memorial

Stopford 1466 Pte Charles John att. from 2/2nd London Regt. Aged 20 Son of Mr & Mrs Stopford of 5, Aylesford St., Pimlico, London, formerly of 25, Pulford Street, Pimlico Hebuterne Military Cemetery IV. J. 8

No. 5 Platoon

Dunkley 3973 Pte John Carrington Aged 17 Son of Eliza Lina Dunkley of 41, Eversleigh Rd., Battersea, London, & the late Charles Dunkley, formerly of 55, Motley Street, Battersea Thiepval Memorial

C COMPANY

Ballantine 2856 Pte Cecil William Henry Aged 19 Son of Mrs E E Ballantine of 224, Elmshurst Mansions, Elmhurst St., Clapham, London Thiepval Memorial

Gosnell 2nd Lt. Harold Clifford Aged 26 Son of H. Clifford Gosnell, & the late Alice Augusta Gosnell Thiepval Memorial

Grainger 2nd Lt. John Scott Aged 27 Son of Thomas Alexander & Marion Grainger of 122, Main St., Tweedmouth, Berwick on Tweed Thiepval Memorial

Handyside Capt. Percy James Alexander Aged 37 Son of James Handyside; husband of Dorothy Handyside (nee Hampshire) of Redcourt, Pyrford, Surrey Gommecourt British Cemetery No. 2, II. L. II

Meadows 3040 Pte Sidney Cecil att. from 2/2nd London Regt. Aged 20 Son of William Albert & Edith Minnie Meadows of 17, Ranelagh Grove, Ebury Bridge, London Gommecourt British Cemetery No. 2, I.A.II

No. 9 Platoon

Campbell 2676 Pte Percival William Charles Aged 21 Son of Mrs M A Campbell of 1, Amner Rd., Clapham Common, London Thiepval Memorial

King 3233 Cpl. Cecil Robert att. from 2/2nd London Regt. Aged 21 Son of Charles & Ellen King of 24, Longlands Park Crescent, Sidcup, Kent Thiepval Memorial

No. 10 Platoon

Lacey 4719 Pte Alfred William Aged 27 Son of William & Joan Lacey; husband of Louisa Annie Lacey of 41, Bayston Rd., Stoke Newington, London, formerly of 1, Hale Street, Islington Born at Islington Gommecourt British Cemetery No. 2, II.J.18

Mills 4567 Pte Harry Leslie Aged 21 Son of Henry James & Harriett Mills of 25, Summerfield Avenue, Brondesbury, London Gommecourt British Cemetery No. 2, II. E. 24

D COMPANY

No. 14 Platoon

Walsh 2978 A/Sgt. Michael Joseph Aged 32 Son of Andrew & Catherine Walsh (nee McHugh) of Carrokeel, Turlough, Castlebar, Co. Mayo Thiepval Memorial

ATTACHED TO 169TH MACHINE GUN COMPANY

Borrie 2971 Pte Arthur Lawrence att. 169th Machine Gun Company Thiepval Memorial

Fradd 2nd Lt. Kingsley Meredith Chatterton att. 169th Machine Gun Company Hebuterne Military Cemetery IV. A. 10

Company and Platoon not known

Annall 5057 Pte John Henry George Thiepval Memorial

Atkins 3241 A/Cpl. Arthur John Aged 23 Son of William Henry & Maria Anne Atkins of 101, Battersea Bridge Rd., Battersea, London Thiepval Memorial

Ball 3379 Pte Alfred E Hebuterne Military Cemetery IV. M. 9

Beams 2705 L/Cpl Albert Henry Aged 24 Son of Elizabeth Mary Beams of 19 Adelphi Rd., Epsom, Surrey, & the late Thomas Beams Thiepval Memorial

Biddle 4474 Pte John Thiepval Memorial

Boyce 4460 Pte Henry William Aged 19 Son of John & Eliza Boyce of 27, Barnardo St., Stepney, London Gommecourt British Cemetery No. 2, III. B. 10

Boyce 3466 L/Cpl Harry Gommecourt British Cemetery No. 2, II. J. 20

Brier 1626 Pte Edgar Cecil Aged 19 Son of William Thomas & Emily Brier of 8, Viceroy Rd., Wandsworth Rd., South Lambeth, London Gommecourt British Cemetery No. 2, I.D.10

Brooks 4675 Pte George Walter Aged 17 Son of George & Priscilla Lack Thiepval Memorial

Bunting 4292 Pte Joseph Gommecourt British Cemetery No. 2, Sp. Mem. B. 13

Buxton 2nd Lt. Bertie Reginald Thiepval Memorial

Caley 3628 Pte John Cyril Gommecourt British Cemetery No. 2, III. D. 24

Card 1641 Cpl. John William Aged 20 Son of John William & Elizabeth Card of 5, Moreton Place, Westminster, London Gommecourt British Cemetery No. 2, II. F. 20

Chapman 3434 Pte Charles Thiepval Memorial

Clifford 2862 Pte Ernest Reginald Thiepval Memorial

Cole 2128 L/Cpl Walter Alfred Gommecourt British Cemetery No. 2, III. F. 5

Connell 4908 Pte John Thiepval Memorial

Cormack 4725 Pte Henry Aged 19 Son of George Cormack of 60, Lower Rd., Rotherhithe, London Thiepval Memorial

Cox 2916 Pte Thomas Lea Aged 22 Son of James Lea Cox & Camilla Eliza Cox of 'Westholme', Chestnut Avenue, Esher, Surrey Gommecourt British Cemetery No. 2, III. F. 30

Craft 4612 L/Cpl Harry Alfred Gommecourt British Cemetery No. 2, III. F. 4

Cridland 5182 Pte George Charles Aged 24 Son of James Edward Cridland of 5, Odessa St., Rotherhithe, London Thiepval Memorial

Crook 2431 Pte Arthur Henry Gommecourt British Cemetery No. 2, I. A. 20

Dean 2617 Pte William George Thiepval Memorial

Deane 1907 Pte Henry Russell Hebuterne Military Cemetery IV. B. 1

Devenish 1627 Pte Thomas William Thiepval Memorial

Dewell 2614 Pte Reginald Horace Aged 19 Son of William Baylis Dewell & Annie Dewell of 83, Beechdale Rd., Brixton Hill, London Thiepval Memorial

Donhue 2823 Pte John Knightly Aged 18 Son of John & Mary Donhue of 9, Hook Rd., Epsom, Surrey Thiepval Memorial

Edmonds 4466 Pte John Thiepval Memorial

Foster 2781 Pte Herbert Thiepval Memorial

Fowler 2086 Pte George Ezra Thiepval Memorial

Fraser 2849 Pte Alexander Thiepval Memorial

Gardner 2525 Pte Percy Aged 23 Son of Mr M R & Mrs F Gardner of 107, Fosterwood St., Deptford, London Thiepval Memorial

Gilbert 4421 L/Cpl Sidney Gommecourt British Cemetery No. 2, III. G. 3

Gillson 4307 Pte Edward Gommecourt British Cemetery No. 2, III. H. II

Godwin 2493 Pte Alfred Ernest Aged 20 Son of Thomas Frederick Godwin of 46, Sturgeon Rd., Walworth, London Gommecourt British Cemetery No. 2, I. B. 21

Good 2637 Pte Frederick Thomas Aged 32 Son of Arthur Frederick & Mary Ann Good of 41, Sutherland Rd., Bow, London Thiepval Memorial

Gornall 1211 Pte William Gommecourt British Cemetery No. 2, III. C. 26
Green 5136 Pte Charles Thiepval Memorial
Gregory 3640 Pte Frederick Covey Aged 19 Son of Mrs Elizabeth Gregory of 43, Winchester Rd., Basingstoke, Hants Thiepval Memorial
Griffin 4686 Pte George Thiepval Memorial
Groom 4185 Pte Arthur James Gommecourt British Cemetery No. 2, II. K. 20
Hastings 4403 Pte Albert Gommecourt British Cemetery No. 2, III. C. 11
Hedley 2934 Pte Cyril William Aged 19 Son of Mr F R & Mrs F E Hedley of 86, Mayfield Rd., Sanderstead, Surrey. Also served at Gallipoli Thiepval Memorial
Henderson 1301 Pte Robert Francis Aged 22 Son of George John & Amelia Henderson Hebuterne Military Cemetery IV. M. 38
Hewitt 4220 Pte Harry Thiepval Memorial
Hogg 2964 Pte Frank Reginald Aged 23 Son of Mrs A E Hogg of 33, Myrtle Rd., Sutton, Surrey Hebuterne Military Cemetery IV. J. 7
Hornsby 2710 L/Cpl John Bert Aged 22 Son of Richard & Sarah Hornsby of Greens Norton, Towcester, Northants Thiepval Memorial
Hull 2747 A/Cpl. Horace Bright Thiepval Memorial
Hunt 4304 Pte Henry Edward Gommecourt British Cemetery No. 2, III. H. 23
James 3326 Pte Leslie John Aged 20 Son of Elizabeth Davis James of 40, Pulteney St., Bath, & the late John James Thiepval Memorial
Jones 4577 Pte Albert Edward Aged 21 Son of Mrs Sarah Jane Jones of 48, Parr Rd., East Ham, London Thiepval Memorial
Jones 2965 Pte Harold Britton Thiepval Memorial
Jones 3751 Pte William Frederick Thiepval Memorial
Jopling 3047 L/Cpl Albert Edward Thiepval Memorial
Kay 3882 Pte Stanley Arthur Aged 20 Son of Arthur & Annie Kay of 9, Ropery St., Bow, London Thiepval Memorial
Keeble 4781 Pte George Thiepval Memorial
Kirby 1818 Pte James Aged 26 Son of the late Coles & Elizabeth Kirby Thiepval Memorial
Klyen 2669 Pte Edward Thiepval Memorial
Loates 37 C.S.M. John Aged 38 Son of William & Barbara Loates; husband of Alice Loates of 46, Altenburg Avenue, West Ealing, London. Born at Waltham Abbey Gommecourt British Cemetery No. 2, III. J. 10
Lomas 1202 Dmr. Charles Thiepval Memorial
Loring 1438 Pte Henry Thomas Gommecourt British Cemetery No. 2, III. C. 21
Lovely 2509 L/Cpl James William Aged 22 Son of James & the late Annette Lovely. Born in Ireland Gommecourt British Cemetery No. 2, I. B. 15
Lyon 2245 L/Cpl Edward Frederick Thiepval Memorial
Macdonald 2204 Pte Edward Francis Thiepval Memorial
Mann 2182 Pte Charles Aged 25 Son of William & Annie Mann of Isleworth, Middx Gommecourt British Cemetery No. 2, III. F. 28
March 3084 Pte Henry Stanley Aged 22 Son of James William & Elizabeth Mary March of Riverside, The Quay, Christchurch, Hants Thiepval Memorial
Martin 1542 Pte John Thiepval Memorial
Maskell 2763 Pte George Aged 28 Son of Mrs. Caroline Maskell of Downside, Cobham, Surrey Thiepval Memorial
Maxsted 1785 Pte George Thiepval Memorial
McGowan 1920 Pte Rutherford Gommecourt British Cemetery No. 2, II. B. 6
McInnes 2568 Cpl. Roy Gommecourt British Cemetery No. 2, II. E. 23
Mills 1809 Pte Alfred Edward Thiepval Memorial
Mogg 4625 Pte William Aged 18 Son of William John & Rose Mogg of 107, Ely Terrace, Mile End, London Gommecourt British Cemetery No. 2, III. H. 25
Money 1057 Pte Victor Evan Thiepval Memorial
Newman 2236 Pte John Charles Aged 23 Son of Mr & Mrs E C Newman of 161, Elsenham St., Southfields, London Gommecourt British Cemetery No. 2, II. H. 21
Padley 2972 Pte Robert Alexander Aged 22 Son of Frank Robert & Hannah Padley of Wooler, Northumberland Thiepval Memorial
Parslow 2392 Pte C. F. Gommecourt British Cemetery No. 2, III. H. 15
Patience 4315 Pte Frederick William Aged 23 Son of Clara Patience of 9, Bessborough St., Westminster, London, & the late William Patience Thiepval Memorial

Peaceful 3288 Pte Henry James Percy Gommecourt British Cemetery No. 2, I. C. II

Potter 4537 Pte William George Aged 25 Brother of Alfred Charles Potter of 4A, Peabody Estate, Orchard St., Westminster, London Thiepval Memorial

Quarterman 3206 Pte Leonard Thiepval Memorial

Riddle 4843 Pte Robert Walter Thiepval Memorial

Roberts 1243 Pte Albert Edward Aged 20 Son of Jabez David & Annie Roberts of 19, Claremont Avenue, New Malden, Surrey Gommecourt British Cemetery No. 2, III. G. 19

Roffey 3606 Pte Frank Aged 22 Son of Mrs Sarah Roffey of 5, Byegrove Rd., Merton, London. Gommecourt British Cemetery No. 2, III. D. 9

Rowe 2746 Cpl. Leonard Edward Aged 20 Youngest son of the late Arthur Rowe of 12, Franconia Rd., Clapham, London Gommecourt British Cemetery No. 2, II. G. 12

Schofield 2304 Pte Frank Bienvillers Military Cemetery, XXI. J. 6

Seth 1183 Pte Thomas Aged 19 Son of the late Mr & Mrs E Seth Born in London. Gommecourt British Cemetery No. 2, II. G. 14

Sheldrick 3953 Pte John Aged 17 Son of Mr & Mrs Sheldrick of 31, Stanswell St., Lower Marsh, Lambeth, London Gommecourt British Cemetery No. 2, III. G. I

Sinclair 2129 L/Cpl Philip Charles Aged 18 Son of Archibald & Helen Elizabeth Sinclair of 47, Grotto Rd., Twickenham, Middx Thiepval Memorial

Smith 4899 Pte William Thiepval Memorial

Stagg 2897 Pte Arthur Walter Robert Aged 26 Son of Walter & Alice Mary Stagg of 46, Sunnyside Rd., Ilford, Essex Gommecourt British Cemetery No. 2, I. C. 6

Stewart 3104 Pte Kenneth Alexander Aged 20 Son of Marianne Phillips Stewart of Garlton, Bedford, & the late Alexander Petrie Stewart Thiepval Memorial

Sumner 2599 Sgt. Charles Gerard Aged 28 Son of John J Sumner of 24, Hood St., Manchester Thiepval Memorial

Tarbox 2093 Pte Reginald Thiepval Memorial

Taylor 1667 L/Sgt. Walter Aged 20 Son of Walter & Mary Taylor of 23, Horseferry Rd., Westminster, London. Thiepval Memorial

Thorman 2nd Lt. Alan Marshall Aged 20 Son of John Marshall Thorman & Eleanor Reed Thorman of Witton Castle, WittonleWear, Co. Durham Thiepval Memorial

Tombs 2882 Sgt. William John Husband of Lydia Annie Tombs of 'The Anchorage', Vanburgh Hill, Blackheath, London Thiepval Memorial

Tomes 1945 Pte James Wilfred Aged 21 Only son of John I & Catherine Ellen Tomes of 88, Claverton St., Pimlico, London. Gommecourt British Cemetery No. 2, IV. A. 3

Townsend 5138 Pte William Aged 18 Son of Mr & Mrs F Townsend of 14, Sutherland St., Pimlico, London Thiepval Memorial

Turner 1834 L/Cpl Charles James Aged 26 Son of Mrs R Turner of 87, Royal Rd., Kennington Park, London. Born at Lambeth, London Hebuterne Military Cemetery IV. M. 61

Urry 2255 L/Cpl Leopold Thiepval Memorial

Warner 4248 Cpl. Frederick Stevens Aged 22 Son of Louis George & Dorothy S. Warner. Born at Clifton, Cincinnati, Ohio, U.S.A Bienvillers Military Cemetery, XXI. G. 9

Waters 1689 L/Cpl Thomas Aged 23 Husband of Lilian Gertrude Waters of 8, Bonsor St., Camberwell, London Thiepval Memorial

Winfield 3152 Pte George Thiepval Memorial

2nd July 1916

Hart 1190 Pte Charles Aged 20 Son of William Charles, & Mary Christina Hart of 59, Paris Gardens, London, S.E.I. Couin British Cemetery, II. A. 7

3rd July 1916

Bentall 2843 Pte Arthur Eldred Aged 24 Son of William & Emily M. Bentall of Southchurch Wick, Southend-on-Sea, Essex. Born at Southchurch. In German hands. Douchy-Les-Ayette British Cemetery, III. F. 17

Patrick 3157 Pte Alfred Aged 29 Son of George William & Annie Patrick of Stanion, Thrapston, Northants. Native of Brigstock, Thrapston. Warlincourt Halte British Cemetery II.E.2

Starling 3234 Pte Nathan Son of William & Jessie Starling of Poplar, London; husband of Rebecca Starling of 3, Woollett Street, Poplar. Abbeville Communal Cemetery IV. C. 5

4th July 1916

Collins 3368 Pte Edward Le Treport Military Cemetery Plot 2. Row L. Grave 3A.

6th July 1916

Egan 4413 Pte Phillip Edward Aged 23 Son of Edward William & Annie Egan of London Le Treport Military Cemetery Plot 2. Row N. Grave 2.

Fisher 4219 Pte Leonard Aged 24 Etretat Churchyard II. D. 19A.

Jones 2887 Pte Percy John In German hands. St. Souplet British Cemetery III. AA. 14

11th July 1916

Stratford 2908 Pte Frederick Ernest Aged 21 Son of Mr C & Mrs K Stratford of 25, Gordon St., Heslington Rd., York. In German hands Caudry Old Communal Cemetery A. 13

12th July 1916

Beer 2194 Cpl. Henry John Aged 23 Son of James & Fanny Beer of 48, Essex Rd., Barking, London. Etretat Churchyard II. D. 6A.

Callaby 2122 L/Cpl Walter Samuel Aged 19 Son of Samuel & Emily Bessie Callaby of Westminster, London. Mont Huon Military Cemetery, Le Treport I. E. I.

19th July 1916

Smith 3243 Pte Major Ralph Mont Huon Military Cemetery, Le Treport II. D. 12

20th July 1916

Thorn 2580 Pte Alfred Aged 20 Son of Mr & Mrs S Thorn of 72, Gladstone Rd., Watford. In German hands. St. Souplet British Cemetery III. AA. II.

1/3ʀᴅ LONDON REGIMENT (ROYAL FUSILIERS)
All casualties listed as Thiepval Memorial are on Pier and Face 9 D and 16 B
A COMPANY

Andrew 4264 L/Cpl. Arthur Edward Benjamin Aged 23 Son of Arthur Samuel & Charlotte Andrew of 37, Wanstead Park Rd., Ilford, Essex Gommecourt British Cemetery No. 2, III. C. 25

Chexfield 2284 Pte Frederick Henry Thiepval Memorial

No. 3 Platoon

Fox 2475 Pte Basil George att. from 2/3ʳᵈ London Regt. Son of Mrs Fox of 'The Cottage', Cricklewood Lane Thiepval Memorial

C COMPANY

Eaton 1879 Pte Henry Thiepval Memorial

Smith 4049 Pte Frederick Aged 21 Son of John Charles & Emma Elizabeth Smith of 48, Morpeth St., Bethnal Green, London Thiepval Memorial

No. 12 Platoon

Sutton 4557 Pte Harold Frank Aged 19 Son of Samuel & Mary Sutton of 5, Enmore Avenue, South Norwood, London Thiepval Memorial

D COMPANY

No. 15 Platoon

Wright 3689 Pte William George Edward Aged 20 Son of the late Albert Edward & Lucy Emily Wright Thiepval Memorial

Company and Platoon not known

Barnes 2772 Pte Ernest John Gommecourt British Cemetery No. 2, III. B. II

Brentley 5086 Pte George William Hebuterne Military Cemetery IV. B. 11

Calder-Smith 2ⁿᵈ Lt. Raymond Alexander Aged 26 Son of Mrs. Ramona Calder-Smith of Madrid, Spain, & the late Robert Calder-Smith of Manila, Philippine Islands. Thiepval Memorial

Corbell 3838 Pte Frank Aged 17 Son of Mrs. Emma L Corbell of 45, Erskine Rd., Walthamstow, Essex Hebuterne Military Cemetery II. Q. 9

Goldsmith 4772 Pte Jack Thiepval Memorial

Greeno 4886 Pte Albert Aged 31 Husband of Dorothy Greeno of 193, Prince of Wales Rd., Kentish Town, London, formerly of 87, Queen's Crescent, Kentish Town Hebuterne Military Cemetery II. P. 6

Howes 4799 Pte Charles Frederick Hebuterne Military Cemetery II. P. 2

Jolley 2270 Pte William Harold Thiepval Memorial

Lidiard 2ⁿᵈ Lt. Richard John Abraham Aged 22 Younger son of Mr & Mrs Herbert Lidiard, 114 Westbourne Terrace. Hebuterne Military Cemetery II. P. 1

Loomes 4600 Pte Joseph George Thiepval Memorial

Macdonal 3289 Pte Alexander Hebuterne Military Cemetery IV. M. 1

Raven 4576 Pte George Thiepval Memorial

Rickett 3451 Pte William George Aged 21 Son of William & Esther Rickett of 91, Valetta Rd., Acton Vale, London Hebuterne Military Cemetery IV. E. 1

Roberts 4243 Pte John Francis Aged 40 Husband of A Roberts of 23, Bellair St., Toronto, Canada Hebuterne Military Cemetery IV. M. 36

Rogers 4816 Pte Ernest Albert Thiepval Memorial

Scoble 4363 Pte William Thiepval Memorial

Wilmott 4879 Pte Ernest Aged 26 Son of William & Isabel Willmott of 68, Nuly St., Old Kent Rd., London. Hebuterne Military Cemetery II. Q. 10.

Wright 3944 Pte John Henry Aged 18 Son of the late Albert Edward & Lucy Emily Wright Thiepval Memorial

Young 2343 Pte Alfred Charles Aged 37 Son of Alfred & Anna Elizabeth Verity-Young of 3, College St., Camborne, Cornwall. Couin British Cemetery I. C. 5.

2nd July 1916

Boyes 4954 Pte Thomas Aged 21 Son of George & Caroline F. Boyes of 212, Chatham Avenue, Nile St., Hoxton, London Hebuterne Military Cemetery II. P. 4

Fincken 2174 Pte William Henry Hebuterne Military Cemetery II. P. 5

Jones Lt. David William Llewellyn Aged 21 Son of the Rev. Canon David Jones & Katharine Edwards Jones of Tregarth, Penmaenmawr, Carnarvonshire Warlincourt Halte British Cemetery, Saulty, II. D. 2

Palmer 5044 Pte Frederick Sidney Hebuterne Military Cemetery IV. E. 2.

Sanguinetti 4532 Pte Leonard St John Aged 21 Son of Haughton & Jessie Louise Sanguinetti of Jamaica Hebuterne Military Cemetery II. P. 3

Spearing 4502 Pte Arthur Ernest Son of Mrs E Spearing of 111, Cambridge Rd., Kilburn, London Couin British Cemetery, I. C. 10

Wood 2478 Pte William E Aged 19 Son of Mr W T & Mrs A M Wood of 66, Woodsome Rd., Kentish Town, London. Hebuterne Military Cemetery IV. M. 20

3ʳᵈ July 1916

Child 3812 Pte Arthur Stanley Aged 19 Son of Joseph Child of Holloway Le Treport Military Cemetery, Plot 2. Row N. Grave 1

4ᵗʰ July 1916

Brown 3776 Pte Walter Edward Warlincourt Halte British Cemetery, Saulty, II. E. 1

6ᵗʰ July 1916

Barrett 3962 Pte Harold Edward Aged 23 Son of Edward William & Elizabeth Amelia Barrett Le Treport Military Cemetery, Plot 2. Row L. Grave 35

20ᵗʰ July 1916

Flavell 2840 Pte Ernest George Aged 20 Son of William Edward & Emmeline Flavell of 64, Sixth Avenue, Queen's Park, North Kensington, London. Kensal Green (All Souls') Cemetery 213. 5. 15. (Screen Wall.)

1/4ᵀᴴ LONDON REGIMENT (ROYAL FUSILIERS)

All casualties listed as Thiepval Memorial are on Pier and Face 9 D and 16 B

A COMPANY

Fanghanel 2ⁿᵈ Lt. Frederick Charles Aged 26 Son of Paul G A & Clara A Fanghanel of 'Ravendale', Shaa Rd., Acton, London Thiepval Memorial

Moore Capt. Arthur Robert Aged 32 Son of Sir John Moore, M.D., F.R.C.P.I., D.L., Physician to H.M. The King in Ireland, & Lady Moore of 40, Fitzwilliam Square, Dublin. M.A., University of Dublin; Barrister-at-Law; Gazetted Aug., 1914 Thiepval Memorial

No. 2 Platoon

Delgaty 4221 Pte Wallace Cadman Gommecourt British Cemetery No. 2, I. A. 6

No. 4 Platoon

Coan 4366 Pte William Thiepval Memorial

B COMPANY

No. 6 Platoon

Watson 3415 L/Cpl. Frederick Essie Gordon Aged 24 Son of Frederick & Edith Ann Watson of Alexandra Rd., Chapel Croft, Chipperfield, Herts Thiepval Memorial

C COMPANY

Bradford 2ⁿᵈ Lt. Frederick Reith Campbell Aged 19 Son of Archibald Campbell Bradford & Clara Sophia Bradford of 'Alverstoke', 68, Derby Rd., Woodford, Essex Thiepval Memorial

Cousins 3203 Pte Frederick William Aged 19 Son of Richard Ralph & Mary Ann Cousins of 51, Crouch Hill, London Thiepval Memorial

Moody 2ⁿᵈ Lt. Thomas Thiepval Memorial

No. 12 Platoon

Bowley 4746 Pte Oliver Son of Mr A A Bowley of Flora Villas, Henfield, Sussex Thiepval Memorial

LEWIS GUN TEAM

Matthews 4146 Pte Ernest Son of Mrs Mathieu of 21d, Botsham Street, Hackney Thiepval Memorial

D COMPANY

Symes 3284 Pte Percy James Aged 20 Son of Mr & Mrs A P Symes of 55, Wynndale Rd., South Woodford, Essex Thiepval Memorial

No. 13 Platoon

Edney 3033 Pte Samuel Thomas Husband of Mrs Edney of 29, Hereford Street, Lisson Grove, Marylebone Thiepval Memorial

No. 16 Platoon

Spencer 1930 Pte Henry George Son of Mrs. Rachel Spencer of 86, Brunswick St., Hackney Rd., London Bienvillers Military Cemetery, XXI. F. 7

Company and Platoon not known

Allport 2906 Pte Walter Ernest Aged 22 Son of Charles Ambrose Allport & Emma Mary Allport of 7, Watling St., Radlett, Herts Thiepval Memorial

Ashkettle 4721 Pte David Hebuterne Military Cemetery IV. B. 7

Bearman 3448 Pte William Aged 23 Son of Harry & Louisa Maria Bearman of 'Belvedere', Station Rd., New Barnet, Herts. Also served at Gallipoli, Malta and in Egypt Thiepval Memorial

Botwright 2548 Pte William John Gommecourt British Cemetery No. 2, III. C. 1

Brown 3473 Pte Albert Aged 30 Son of Robert & Esther Victoria Brown of Jays Green, Harleston, Norfolk Thiepval Memorial

Brown 2553 Pte Henry Richard Aged 19 Son of Mrs M R Lloyd (formerly Brown) of 20, New Houses, Taffs Well, Cardiff, & the late G. Brown Thiepval Memorial

Collinge 4080 Pte Sidney William Hebuterne Military Cemetery IV. M. 44

Cooper 1303 Pte Stanley Augustus Aged 22 Son of William Cooper Hebuterne Military Cemetery IV. M. 28

Daintry 2883 L/Cpl. Sydney Gommecourt British Cemetery No. 2, V. B. 10

Davidson 4522 Pte Sydney Leonard Thiepval Memorial

Faulkner 4467 Pte Walter Walley Thiepval Memorial

Freed 2428 Pte John Thiepval Memorial

Hale 3474 Pte William John Hebuterne Military Cemetery IV. B. 10.

Hebberd 4786 Sgt. Reginald Clifford Aged 23 Son of Richard Henry & Eleanor Louise Hebberd of Stafford House, St. Mark's Rd., Bangalore, India Hebuterne Military Cemetery IV. M.50

Hensman 2524 Pte Walter Cornelius Aged 18 Son of Walter & Elizabeth Hensman of 12, Kingsland Rd., London Thiepval Memorial

Hill 4339 Pte Richard Thiepval Memorial

Hillman 2459 Pte Walter Not found on CWGC

Holmes 1187 L/Cpl. Seymour Thiepval Memorial

Keep 2788 Pte Albert Edward Thiepval Memorial

Kinsey 2291 Pte Cecil Major Hebuterne Military Cemetery IV. M. 47

Mean 3374 L/Cpl. Percy Edward Aged 26 Son of Frederick Mean of 'Crosby', Red Down Rd., Coulsdon, Surrey Thiepval Memorial

Mills 3467 Cpl. Arthur Aged 23 Son of Arthur & Jessie Eliza Forehead Mills of 1, Woodside Cottages, Mugswell, Chipstead, Surrey Thiepval Memorial

Mills 4674 Pte George Samuel Hebuterne Military Cemetery IV. B. 4

Millward 2693 Pte Claude Thiepval Memorial

Montague 3053 Pte Harold Aged 19 Son of Mr & Mrs Charles Montague of 46, Falconer Rd., Bushey, Herts Thiepval Memorial

Morris 2523 Pte Frederick Aged 19 Son of Mrs Morris of 145, Pennington St., St. George in the East, London Hebuterne Military Cemetery IV. M. 40

O'Hanlon 3346 Pte Sidney Phillip Thiepval Memorial

Ovenden 3679 L/Cpl. Stanley Aged 17 Son of John & Charlotte Ovenden of 13, Gloucester Rd., Edmonton, London Thiepval Memorial

Pierce 4397 L/Cpl. Thomas Hebuterne Military Cemetery IV. M. 29

Powe 3188 Pte Ernest John Aged 20 Son of George John Powe of 21, Billiter St., Leadenhall St., London Thiepval Memorial

Rogers 2096 Pte John Thiepval Memorial

Scaggs 3482 Pte Ernest George Aged 23 Son of Louisa M Scaggs, of 25, Bolton Rd., Stratford, London. Hebuterne Military Cemetery IV. M. 39.

Shaw 4873 Pte Charles Alfred Thiepval Memorial

Shinkfield 3329 Pte Leonard Charles Aged 21 Son of Henry J & Julia A. Shinkfield of 6, Gilkes Crescent, Dulwich, London Thiepval Memorial

Toms 2475 Pte Geoffrey Gibbs Aged 20 Son of Charles Frederick & Sarah Amelia Toms of 855, Forest Rd., Dalston, London. Enlisted in 1914. Also served at Gallipoli Thiepval Memorial

Warne 2817 Pte Alfred Ernest Thiepval Memorial

Webster 4289 Pte Frank Thiepval Memorial

Williams 4688 Pte Arthur Alexander Thiepval Memorial

Wingrove 2519 Pte Arthur Aged 21 Son of George & Rachael Wingrove of 13, Great Chart St., Hoxton, London Hebuterne Military Cemetery IV. M. 7

2ⁿᵈ July 1916

Chapman 4290 Pte Thomas W Le Treport Military Cemetery, Plot 2. Row L. Grave 75

4ᵗʰ July 1916

Burwood 3752 Pte Ralph E G Aged 20 Son of Mr & Mrs Ralph Burwood of 99, Old Gravel Lane, St.George-in-the-East, London. Born at Wapping. City Of London & Tower Hamlets Cemetery Screen Wall

6ᵗʰ July 1916

Beesley 4743 Pte Frank William George Aged 27 Son of Mrs Florence Beesley of 3, Markhouse Avenue, Markhouse Rd., Walthamstow, Essex Newport (St. Woollos) Cemetery, Monmouthshire, United Kingdom 8 "C." 168

7ᵗʰ July 1916

Maskell 3392 Dmr. Thomas James Aged 24 Son of Mrs Emily H. Maskell of 28, Maidstone St., Hackney, London. Served in Malta, Gallipoli, Egypt and France Manor Park Cemetery, Essex 128. 472

11ᵗʰ July 1916

Burford 3490 Pte Donald Marten Aged 34 Son of George & Emma Burford of Peckham; husband of Ivy Burford of 50, Stondon Park, Forest Hill, London. Etretat Churchyard II.D.11

12ᵗʰ July 1916

Sambidge 2812 Pte A H Aged 34 Son of Henry & Mary Ann Sambidge; husband of Mrs. Sambidge of 207 Pentonville Rd., Kings Cross, London. (A/C Screen Wall) Cemetery: City Of London Cemetery 235. 19A

Mills 4420 Pte Alfred George Mont Huon Military Cemetery, Le Treport I. H. 12.

20ᵗʰ July 1916

Chipps 3294 Pte Sidney Ewart Aged 21 Son of Bertie Edward & Annie Chipps of 'Ringaskiddy', 11, Beech Grove, New Malden. Enlisted Nov., 1914. Served on Gallipoli and in Egypt and France. Kingston-Upon-Thames Cemetery D. 2309.

1/5ᵗʰ LONDON REGIMENT (LONDON RIFLE BRIGADE)

All casualties listed as Thiepval Memorial are on Pier and Face 9 D

HEADQUARTERS COMPANY

Gordon 2520 Rfn. Myer Aged 19 Son of Abraham Lazarus Gordon & Judith Gordon of 16, Marine Avenue, Westcliff-on-Sea, Essex Thiepval Memorial

Kemp 2107 Rfn. Thomas John Thiepval Memorial

BOMBERS

Chambers 2199 Rfn. Eric Leonard Son of Mrs Chambers of 'Welldene', Hayes End, Middlesex Thiepval Memorial

Hockaday 1358 Rfn. Walter Herbert Thiepval Memorial

Russell 1896 Rfn. John Aged 22 Son of Millicent Russell of 7, Rydal Rd., Streatham, London, & the late Oliver Lambert Russell Thiepval Memorial

Sheppard 1547 Rfn. Hubert Adley Aged 25 Son of Herbert Edward & Susan Sheppard of 1, Bath Villa, Weydon Hill Rd., Farnham, Surrey Thiepval Memorial

Stewart 1167 Rfn. Edward Henry Cecil Son of Mrs Stewart of 202, Stanstead Road, Forest Hill Thiepval Memorial

LEWIS GUN SECTION

Shilson 2445 Rfn. Charles Sidney Aged 26 Son of Edith Shilson of The Gables, Banbury, & the late Charles Johnson Shilson, formerly of Moorside, Esher Thiepval Memorial

SIGNAL SECTION

Mahon 1707 Rfn. Arthur Thomas Aged 19 Son of the Rev. E B Mahon & Agnes Catherine Mahon of 163, Harlaxton Rd., Grantham Thiepval Memorial

Waldren 2110 Rfn. George Augustus Aged 23 Son of the late George & Esther Waldren Thiepval Memorial

SNIPERS

Carew 604 Rfn. Arthur George Aged 31 Husband of Dora Mary Carew of 53, London Rd., Forest Hill, London Thiepval Memorial

Rand 9589 Rfn. Reginald Hays Aged 22 Son of Alfred Peter & Kate Emily Rand of 53, Willoughby Lane, Tottenham, London, formerly of 3, Bodney Road, Hackney Downs Thiepval Memorial

A COMPANY

Adams 1325 Rfn. Ralph Ewart Stretcher bearer Aged 20 Second son of Mrs L J Adams of 174, Greenvale Rd., Eltham, London Thiepval Memorial

Baker 349 Rfn. Edgar Cecil Aged 31 Son of William & Mary Baker of 5, Cranwich Rd., Stamford Hill, London Thiepval Memorial

Cowlin 1176 Cpl. Horace Thiepval Memorial

Crabb 2796 Rfn. Norman Frank Aged 26 Son of Thomas & Martha Crabb of 72, Parchmore Rd., Thornton Heath, Surrey Thiepval Memorial

Dixey 2127 Rfn. Leicester Albert Aged 23 Son of Gilbert G Dixey of I, Lansdowne Place, Hove, Sussex Thiepval Memorial

Doust 2nd Lt. Charles Bowden Thiepval Memorial

Gibbs 2792 Rfn. William Alexander Aged 25 Son of Alexander Henry & Agnes Emma Gibbs of 123, Revelstoke Rd., Wimbledon Park, London Thiepval Memorial

Goff 255 Rfn. Percy William Son of Mrs Goff of 63, Cheesham Road, Clapham Thiepval Memorial

Gosling 1924 Rfn. Eric Alfred Gommecourt British Cemetery No. 2, III. C. 22

Jennings 3049 Rfn. Edward Frederick Gommecourt British Cemetery No. 2, II. L. 16

Lilley 859 L/Cpl. Henry John Son of Mr J H Lilley of 22, Redcross Street, London, EC Thiepval Memorial

Middleton 272 L/Cpl. Herbert Harry Husband of Mrs Middleton of 96, Somers Road, Walthamstow Thiepval Memorial

Poulter 2987 Rfn. Donovan Aged 23 Son of Mr & Mrs Douglas Ford Poulter of Wallington, Surrey, formerly of 7, Borough Road, Isleworth Bienvillers Military Cemetery XXI. H. 14

Reeves 3062 Rfn. Ernest Edward Aged 25 Son of William & Mary Elizabeth Reeves of 21, Cissbury Rd., Hove, Sussex Thiepval Memorial

Ridder 890 Rfn. Bertram Thomas Thiepval Memorial

Slaughter 2043 L/Cpl. Herbert Nathaniel Aged 19 Son of Richard & Jane E. Slaughter of 21, Frayne Rd., Ashton Gate, Bristol. A student at the Westminster Training College Thiepval Memorial

Sowby 2202 Rfn. Ernest Perrin Thiepval Memorial

Squires 1501 Rfn. Arthur James Thiepval Memorial

Terraneau 945 Cpl. Stanley Aged 27 Son of A C Terraneau of 'Daughue', Sheen Common Drive, Richmond, Surrey, & the late Ernest Terraneau Thiepval Memorial

Terry 1339 L/Cpl. Walter Thiepval Memorial

Williams 2281 Rfn. Cecil James Thiepval Memorial

Yeomans 1315 Rfn. Stewart Coulthard Aged 31 Son of the late Montague & Phoebe Yeomans Thiepval Memorial

No. 1 Platoon

Brett 1985 Rfn. Cyril James Aged 17 Son of Edgar & Julia Jeannette Brett of 5, Burns Rd., Harlesden, London Thiepval Memorial

Boucher 2952 Rfn. William Henry Thiepval Memorial

Chapman 2097 Rfn. Harold James Sidney Stockwell Aged 22 Son of George S & Gertrude S Chapman of 160, Tufnell Park Rd., Holloway, London Thiepval Memorial

Coughtrey 1462 Rfn. Joseph Edward Aged 20 Son of Joseph William Henry & Rachael Louisa Coughtrey of 46, Broadwater Rd., Bruce Grove, Tottenham, London Gommecourt British Cemetery No. 2, II. K. 12

Evans 2407 Rfn. Daniel Rowland Son of Daniel & Mary Evans of Trego Isaf, Cemaes Bay, Anglesey Thiepval Memorial

Fairs 2958 Rfn. Archibald Aged 26 Son of Mr. & Mrs. Samuel William Fairs of Old Ford, Bow; husband of Gus Fairs of 2, Wendon St., Old Ford, Bow, London Gommecourt British Cemetery No. 2, III. G. II

Gardiner 2534 Rfn. Victor Henry Thiepval Memorial

Gillbard 2409 Rfn. Vernon Whitford Aged 19 Son of Richard & Ada Gillbard of 36, Dean Rd., Willesden Green, London Thiepval Memorial

Hope 2705 Rfn. Richard A Aged 28 Son of Paul & Emily Hope of 9, Davenport Rd., Catford, London Gommecourt British Cemetery No. 2, III. B. 6

Johnson 3050 Rfn. Richard Sargent Son of Mrs Johnson, Aberdeen House, Dyne Road, Brondesbury Thiepval Memorial

Marshall 2759 Rfn. Hugh Gommecourt British Cemetery No. 2, II. K. 17

Park 1662 Rfn. John Frederick Aged 21 Son of the late Robert & Janet Margaret Park of 107, Thackeray Avenue, Tottenham. Born in London Gommecourt British Cemetery No. 2, III. E. 26

Pipe 682 Rfn. Eric Francis Charles Aged 20 Son of Florence Pipe of 75, Goldhurst Terrace, South Hampstead, London, & the late Francis William Pipe Thiepval Memorial

Owen 2966 Rfn. Bertram George Aged 23 Foster son of Katherine Tucker of 5, Hornsey Lane Gardens, Highgate, London Gommecourt British Cemetery No. 2, III. F. II

Parslow 763 Cpl. H W Aged 27 Son of William Henry Parslow of 'Kingswood', 9, Kingston Hill, Surrey; husband of Edith Gertrude Parslow of 106, Howarth Rd., Plumstead, London Thiepval Memorial

No. 2 Platoon

Birch 1494 Rfn. William Leonard Aged 19 Son of Mr & Mr. Birch of 14. Osborne Rd., Kingston-on-Thames Thiepval Memorial

Corbett 2090 Rfn. Algernon James Aged 21 Son of Arthur James & Alice Maud Corbett of 70, Comeragh Rd., Barons Court, London. Gommecourt British Cemetery No. 2, III. E. 10

Hart 9521 Rfn. Samuel Aged 22 Son of Matilda Hart of 33, Anson Rd., Cricklewood, London, & the late Emanuel Hart Thiepval Memorial

Hidden 2610 Rfn. Cyril Robert Aged 19 Son of Herbert Charles & Emily Hidden of 51, Mayfair Avenue, Ilford, Essex Thiepval Memorial

Jones 2919 Rfn. Cedwin Thiepval Memorial

Peile 2166 Rfn. Henry Allason Aged 20 Son of Gertrude Peile of 62, Wodeland Avenue, Guildford, Surrey, & the late Walker Peile Thiepval Memorial

Phillips 9488 Sgt. Frank Gommecourt British Cemetery No. 2, I. B. 20

Reynolds 2173 Rfn. David Aged 18 Son of Mr & Mrs Reynolds of 7, Comus Place, Old Kent Rd., London Thiepval Memorial

Walker 2058 L/Cpl. John Humphrey Aged 22 Son of John and Alice Walker of 128, Iffley Road Hammersmith Worked at the Board of Trade Gommecourt British Cemetery No. 2, II. K. 18

No. 3 Platoon

Austin 2950 Rfn. Vincent John Aged 19 Son of Vincent J & Rebecca Austin of Hatfield, Herts Gommecourt British Cemetery No. 2, II. H. 2

Barton 2599 Rfn. Eric Forrest Aged 20 Son of Henry Thomas & Jessica Elizabeth Barton of 'Barlbro', 10, Elm Way, Worcester Park., Surrey. Bienvillers Military Cemetery XVIII. G.4

Cantral 2907 Rfn. Wilfred Herbert Aged 21 Son of Mrs S Cantral of 22, Pembury Rd., Clapton, London, previously of 85, Downs Road, Clapton Thiepval Memorial

Eburne 2139 Rfn. Julian Reginald Aged 23 Son of Edward George & Emily Eburne of 40, Carholme Rd., Forest Hill, London Thiepval Memorial

Harris 2129 Rfn. Charles John Aged 22 Son of Frederick W & Mary J Harris of 155, Clarence Rd., Clapton, London Thiepval Memorial

Hillman 1656 Rfn. Richard Edward Thiepval Memorial

Holden 1037 L/Cpl. Stanley Philip Aged 24 Son of Mrs A G Holden of 100, Osbaldeston Rd. Stoke Newington, London, & the late P. S. Holden. Thiepval Memorial

Matthews 9923 Rfn. Frederick Montague Leslie Aged 19 Only son of F C Johnson (formerly Matthews) of Edwalton, Nottingham, & the late Frederick Matthews of Culford Hall, Bury St Edmunds, Suffolk Born at Bury St. Edmunds Gommecourt British Cemetery No. 2, II. A. 19

Mead 1955 Rfn. Gordon John Aged 23 Son of Henry & Frances Mead of 12, The Square, Wimborne, Dorset Thiepval Memorial

Mulligan 2939 Rfn. Frederick Herbert Son of Mrs Mulligan of 39, Talbot Road, Tottenham Thiepval Memorial

Murphy 365 Sgt. Robert Sidney Son of Mrs Murphy of 52, Chesilton Road, Munster Park, Fulham Thiepval Memorial

Noble 3058 Rfn. George Aged 22 Son of George & Isabel Emma Noble of 23, Ermine Rd., Lewisham, London Gommecourt British Cemetery No. 2, II. K. 19

Sinclair 2750 Rfn. Clifford Howard Son of Mr and Mrs Sinclair of 'Bodrean', Nether Street, North Finchley Thiepval Memorial

14th October 1918

Ward 2998 Rfn A J In German hands Niederzwehren Cemetery, II. N. 8.

No. 4 Platoon

Butcher 2604 Rfn. Clifford Hugh Thiepval Memorial

Davis 2751 Rfn. Arthur Thiepval Memorial

Klein 2741 Rfn. Frederick Henry Thiepval Memorial

Martin 4116 Rfn. Norman Victor Aged 19 Son of Henry Reeler Martin & Florence Elizabeth Martin of 'Glen Allen', 77, Mayfield Rd., Sanderstead, South Croydon, Surrey Thiepval Memorial

Middleton 555 Cpl. Edgar Stewart Aged 25 Son of Mr & Mrs A G Middleton of 83, Pearl Rd., Walthamstow, Essex Thiepval Memorial

Newton 2140 Rfn. Percy Thiepval Memorial

Norton 2132 Rfn. Bertram Harrison Aged 26 Son of David Norton of 'Hazelmere', 48, Upper Walthamstow Rd., Walthamstow, Essex, & the late Louisa Constance Norton Thiepval Memorial

Pascoe 9697 Sgt. Wiliam John Son of Mr W J Pascoe of 71, Kimberley Avenue, East Ham Thiepval Memorial

Ravenscroft 2812 Rfn. Cecil Hugh Strode Aged 19 Son of Catherine Ann Gwillym Ravenscroft of 94, Mount Pleasant Rd., Lewisham, London, & the late Byfleet Charles Ravenscroft Hebuterne Military Cemetery IV. M. 10

Wheeler 594 Sgt. Charles Alexander Thiepval Memorial

6ᵗʰ July 1916

Ford 339 Cpl. Lachlan Mclean Aged 29 Son of John & Elizabeth Ford of Ilford. Essex. In German hands Le Cateau Military Cemetery, IV. A, 4

B COMPANY

Clode-Baker Lt. George Edmund Aged 22 Son of George & Winifred Clode-Baker of Holmfields, Reigate, Surrey. Born in London Gommecourt British Cemetery No. 2, Sp. Mem. C.6.

Coombs 549 Rfn. Frank Morris Thiepval Memorial

Cue 9615 Rfn. Douglas Aged 25 Son of Thomas E & Emma Cue. Born in London Gommecourt British Cemetery No. 2, Sp. Mem. B. 15

Davison 2163 Rfn. Henry Herbert Son of Mrs Davison of 79, Cranfield Road, Brockley Thiepval Memorial

Dean 206 L/Cpl. William Godfrey Aged 21 Son of William T Godfrey Dean & Annie Frances Dean of 'Wayside', Claygate, Surrey. Gommecourt British Cemetery No. 2, II.G.19

Gwyther 2717 Rfn. Stanley Victor Aged 19 Son of William & Elizabeth Gwyther of 4, Judkin St., East Ferry Rd., Cubitt Town, Poplar, London. Hebuterne Military Cemetery IV.M.57

Horning 2192 Rfn. Percy Louis Thiepval Memorial

Hyland 2714 Rfn. William Thomas Aged 22 Son of William Andrew & Minnie Elizabeth Hyland of 29, Coleridge Rd., Crouch End, London Thiepval Memorial

Johnston 1196 Rfn. Frank Aged 21 Son of Thomas & Caroline Mary Johnston of 38, Clarence Rd., West Green, Tottenham, London Thiepval Memorial

Keighley 2239 Rfn. John Edward Thiepval Memorial

Moulton 9059 Sgt. Herbert Aged 26 Husband of Tacy E Moulton of 26, Old Southend Rd., Southend; son of Mr. & Mrs. Moulton of 3, Wesley Rd., Southend Thiepval Memorial

Rapkin 9722 Rfn. Reginald Samuel Vincent Lived at 22, Valentine Road, Ilford, Essex Thiepval Memorial

Sims 2747 Rfn. Charles William Aged 26 Son of Henry James & Ellen Chester Sims of Lower Edmonton; husband of Eveline Maria Sims of 36, Millbrook Rd., Lower Edmonton, London Gommecourt British Cemetery No. 2, II. J. 19

Somers-Smith Capt. John Robert Thiepval Memorial

No. 5 Platoon

Langham 2222 Rfn. Harold Johnston Son of Mr W Langham of 'The Cottage', Dunton Bassett, Leicestershire Thiepval Memorial

Mardle 2965 Rfn. Arthur Joseph Sidney Aged 20 Son of Joseph & Elizabeth Emily Mardle of 122, Hainault Rd., Leytonstone, London Gommecourt British Cemetery No. 2, III. D. 10

Rawlins 2511 Rfn. Ernest Leslie Aged 18 Son of George & Sarah Ann Rawlins of 9, Leswin Rd., Stoke Newington, London. Enlisted July, 1915 Thiepval Memorial

Strutt 1250 Cpl. Stanley Aged 30 Son of the late William & Phoebe Ann Strutt of 23, East Crescent, Bush Hill Park, Enfield Gommecourt British Cemetery No. 2, II. G. 18

Whitehead 127 Cpl. Charles James Lewis Aged 21 Son of James & Jessie Whitehead of 2, Waverley Rd., Crouch End, London Gommecourt British Cemetery No. 2, II. H. 3

No. 6 Platoon

Austin 9978 A/Sgt. Wallace George Stanley Aged 27 Son of Frederick James & Laura Austin of 196, Mount Pleasant Rd., Tottenham, London Thiepval Memorial

Golding 2218 Rfn. George Son of Mrs M Peppercorn of 1, Victoria Villas, Victoria Road, New Barnet Thiepval Memorial

Hill 1227 Rfn. Arthur G L Son of Mrs Hill of 51, Cricketfield Road, Clapton Gommecourt British Cemetery No. 2, III. H. 5

Hooke 2191 Rfn. Thomas Aged 20 Son of Thomas & Marion Hooke of 'Moy Mir', 18, Carew Rd., Wallington, Surrey Gommecourt British Cemetery No. 2, II. H. 8.

Rolfe 2123 Rfn. Arthur Henry Sissons Thiepval Memorial

Swan 2148 L/Cpl. George James Thiepval Memorial

Writer 26 Cpl. William Cecil Aged 21 Son of Thomas Augustus Writer of 69, Seymour Gardens, Ilford, Essex Gommecourt British Cemetery No. 2, III. B. 21

No. 7 Platoon

Barnes 2589 Rfn. Harold Agate Son of Mr and Mrs Barnes of 3, Minet Avenue, Harlesden Gommecourt British Cemetery No. 2, III. J. 5

Dodson 2507 Rfn. Frank James Aged 23 Son of Mrs M A Dodson of The Lodge, Approach Rd., Victoria Park, London Thiepval Memorial

No. 8 Platoon

Alford 2205 Rfn. Bertram Charles Husband of Mrs Alford of 42, Westbourne Park Villas, London W Thiepval Memorial

Crockett 2415 Rfn. Gilbert Victor Husband of Mrs Crockett of Lower Granard Lodge, Putney Park Lane, Putney. Thiepval Memorial

Snow 2469 Rfn. William Albert Son of Mrs J Snow of 13, Stanmore Road, West Green, Tottenham Gommecourt British Cemetery No. 2, III. C. 24

LEWIS GUN TEAM

Eaton 1007 Rfn. Paul Charles Aged 24 Son of the late Charles Eaton & Margaret Eaton of 20A, Milton Avenue, Westcliff-on-Sea, Essex Thiepval Memorial

C COMPANY

Atkins 9567 Cpl. Harold Broadley Aged 27 Son of Thomas Broadley Atkins of 77, Brighton Rd., Stoke Newington, London Thiepval Memorial

Bee 2141 Rfn. Francis Stanley Thiepval Memorial

Benns 2nd Lt. Arthur Lionel Educated Christ's Hospital and Aske's School. Worked for Commerce and Dominion Line. Thiepval Memorial

Brunt 1720 Rfn. Robert Alfred Edmund Aged 24 Son of Mary Brunt of 30, Norfolk Louise Rd., Streatham, London, & the late Henry John Brunt. Thiepval Memorial

Chapman 3000 Rfn. George Robert Aged 27 Son of Henry & Jeanne Victorine Chapman of 25, Rue D'Hauteville, Paris; husband of Monica Mary Chapman of 9, Brisbane Avenue, Merton Park, Wimbledon, London Thiepval Memorial

Harvey Capt. Bernard Sydney Aged 27 Son of Walter Sydney & Florence Harvey of 9, Vale Court, Maida Vale, London Thiepval Memorial

Hember 8838 Sgt. Hugh Victor Aged 27 Son of Gilbert & Eliza Hember of 9, Carleton Rd., Holloway, London Thiepval Memorial

Ingram 2626 Rfn. Francis Wilton Thiepval Memorial

Levitt 3005 Rfn. Douglas Alfred Thiepval Memorial

Lloyd 9585 Sgt. Leonard Thiepval Memorial

McGrath 2692 Rfn. Joseph Martin Aged 24 Son of Maria Norman McGrath of Alwyn House, Finchley Lane, Hendon, Middx., & the late Joseph Michael McGrath Thiepval Memorial

McRoberts 2244 Rfn. Alan Aged 29 Son of William McRoberts of 22, Eastlake Rd., Camberwell, London Thiepval Memorial

Meakin 2168 Rfn. Frank Moss Aged 26 Son of Mr J H Meakin of 327, Stanley Rd., Bootle. Lancs Thiepval Memorial

Norris 1498 Rfn. Archibald William Aged 22 Son of Henry & Annie Norris of 'Elmslie', Bourne End, Bucks Gommecourt British Cemetery No. 2, Sp. Mem. B. 17

Phelps 2388 L/Cpl. Arthur Ernest Gommecourt British Cemetery No. 2, II. L. 15

Pring 249 L/Cpl. Victor Stoodley Thiepval Memorial, Addenda Panel

Robbins 9900 Rfn. Gilbert Arthur Aged 25 Son of Samuel Arthur Robbins of 'Heatherdene', The Grove, Slough, Bucks, & the late Melinda Jane Robbins Thiepval Memorial

Robertson 2904 Rfn. Ernest Brother of Mr W Robertson of 9, Wortley Rd., Plashet Grove, East Ham, London Thiepval Memorial

Stone 2030 Rfn. Ernest George Son of Mrs Stone of 15, Linden Grove, Sydenham Gommecourt British Cemetery No. 2, III. B. 25

Terrell 2134 Rfn. Victor James Aged 28 Son of Walter R. & Annie E Terrell of 116, Albany Rd., Luton, Chatham. A teacher at St. Mary's School, Rotherhithe, London Thiepval Memorial

Tindley 2499 Rfn. William Frederick Thiepval Memorial

Webber 2721 Rfn. Arthur Morris Aged 20 Son of Amy Elizabeth Webber of 'Riverston', 69, Eltham Rd., Lee, London, & the late Leonard Fred Webber Thiepval Memorial

No. 9 Platoon

Adams 521 L/Cpl. Douglas George Aged 20 Son of Charles & Louie Adams of Cromer Lodge, 2, Herne Hill, London, formerly of 39, Holmdene Avenue, Herne Hill Thiepval Memorial

Baker 2492 Rfn. Arthur Augustus Aged 18 Son of Charles W & Marie Baker of 28, Rembrandt Rd., Lee, London, formerly of 47, Alloa Road, Deptford Park Thiepval Memorial

Blake 8457 L/Cpl. Gerald John Aged 30 Son of John & Saima Blake of 11, Weltje Rd., Ravenscourt Park, London. Proceeded to France Oct., 1914 Thiepval Memorial

Clapp 9546 L/Cpl. Alfred Cecil Son of Mrs Clapp of 'Griffen House', Griffen Street, Deal Thiepval Memorial

Colbert 2902 Rfn. Walter James Son of Mrs M A Colbert of 7, Albert Road, Dalston Thiepval Memorial

Cook 830 Rfn. Alfred Aged 24 Resident of Islington. Worked for the LCC Education Department Thiepval Memorial

Cowling 2106 Rfn. Norman Vivian Son of Mr R J Cowling of 68, Copleston Road, East Dulwich Thiepval Memorial

Hucksted 1529 Rfn. Herbert Aged 19 Son of Mrs E R Hucksted of 22, Geoffrey Rd., Brockley, London Thiepval Memorial

Marlborough 1067 L/Sgt. William George Aged 24 Son of Florence Phillis Marlborough of 157, Thorold Rd., Ilford, Essex, & the late William James Marlborough Gommecourt British Cemetery No. 2, III. C. 13

Rowlatt 658 Rfn. William Henry Aged 37 Son of the late Henry William Napier Rowlatt & Susan Martha Rowlatt. Resident of Putney. Worked for the Buenes Aires and Pacific Rail Company Thiepval Memorial

Searle 2850 Cpl. Alan Ernest Aged 23 Son of Mrs Searle of 'The Mount', Widford, Herts Resident of Ware. Worked for City and Midland Bank Thiepval Memorial

Sheppard 2269 Rfn. William Charles Aged 18 Son of Mr W T & Mrs M J Sheppard of 15, Webster Rd., Bermondsey, London, formerly of 152, Jamaica Road, Bermondsey Thiepval Memorial

Turner 2736 Rfn. Walter Aged 19 Son of Walter Alfred Turner of 12, Prittlewell Square, Southend-on-Sea, & the late Emily Jane Turner, formerly of 4, The Hill, Northfleet, Kent Thiepval Memorial

Triggs 2677 Rfn. Joseph Brother of Mrs F J Jarvison of 57, Lewisham Rd., Windsor, Victoria, Australia Thiepval Memorial

No. 10 Platoon

Dudley 2460 Rfn. Harold Putnam Aged 29 Son of James Robert & Charlotte Dudley of 298, South Lambeth Rd., London Thiepval Memorial

Harrison 3002 Rfn. William Joseph Thiepval Memorial

Upton 2135 Rfn. Sydney John Aged 19 Son of Herbert Edward & Amelia Upton of 68, London Rd., Southwark, London Thiepval Memorial

Tumber 9830 Sgt. Edward Frederick Son of Mrs Tumber, 112, Manor Park, Lee Thiepval Memorial

No. 11 Platoon

Coulson 1943 Rfn. William Henry Aged 19 Son of Elizabeth Coulson of 102, Rosendale Rd., Dulwich, London, & the late G. Coulson. Gommecourt British Cemetery No. 2, III.E.16

Davies 2180 Rfn. Reginald William Aged 29 Son of Stephen & Eleanor Davies of 7, St. Paul St., Chippenham, Wilts Gommecourt British Cemetery No. 2, III. B. 22

Dyer 2897 Rfn. Frank Edward Aged 23 Son of Mrs H M Dyer of 145, Bentham Rd., South Hackney, London, & the late E. H. Dyer Thiepval Memorial

Fearn 2489 Rfn. Claude Douglas Thiepval Memorial

Shackleford 2784 Rfn. Edward John Aged 34 Son of Mrs Shackleford of 160, Bow Road, London; Husband of Amy M. Shackleford of 38, Torquay Drive, Leigh-on-Sea, Essex Thiepval Memorial

Wallis 2422 Rfn. Edward Henry Thiepval Memorial

Webb 2487 Rfn. William Son of Mrs Webb of 40, Pearcroft Road, Leytonstone Gommecourt British Cemetery No. 2, Sp. Mem. B. 16

Willimont 2427 Rfn. Ronald Harry Aged 17 Son of Mr H C & Mrs A S Willimont of 24, Inderwick Rd., Crouch End, London Thiepval Memorial

No. 12 Platoon

Batchelor 2031 Rfn. William Harold Aged 17 Son of Albert & Helena Frances Batchelor of 25, Revelon Rd., Brockley, London Thiepval Memorial

Beard 2859 Rfn. Frederick Percival Son of Mr W J Beard of 'Trevons House', Preston Road, Westcliff on Sea, Essex Thiepval Memorial Addenda Panel 5, Front Terrace.

Chandler 9 A/Cpl. Frank Denison Aged 23 Son of Gibbs William Chandler of 23, Vanbrugh Park, Blackheath, London. An employee of Lloyd's, Royal Exchange, London Thiepval Memorial

Dykes 2142 Rfn. Oswald Jas. Aged 21 Son of Reuben & Emma Jane Dykes of 53, Harpenden Rd., Wanstead Park, Essex Thiepval Memorial

Hale 2609 Rfn. Arthur Leonard Thiepval Memorial

Linforth 2482 Rfn. Stanley Ernest Thiepval Memorial

Redlich 2594 Rfn. Norman Kingsley Aged 24 Son of Frederick James & Venetia Margaret Redlich Thiepval Memorial

Sanders 2790 Rfn. William Duncan Aged 27 Son of the late Henry William & Adeline Sanders Gommecourt British Cemetery No. 2, II. H. 24

Spencer 2748 Rfn. Harry Varnals Aged 21 Son of Frederick & Emily Spencer of 66, Dalkeith Rd., Ilford, Essex. A clerk at the Ilford Gas Coy Thiepval Memorial

D COMPANY

Arthur 3028 Rfn. Richard James Gommecourt British Cemetery No. 2, II. H. 6

Austin 1703 Sgt. Henry Thiepval Memorial

Biddle 3030 Rfn. Edgar Thiepval Memorial

Burgess 2462 Rfn. Ebenezer Septimus Aged 21 Son of Henry T & Fanny Burgess of Rose Cottage, Baltonsborough, Glastonbury, Somerset. Born at West Norwood, London Gommecourt British Cemetery No. 2, Sp. Mem. B. 18

Eagle 1653 Rfn. Percival Charles Thiepval Memorial

Ebbetts 784 Cpl. Sidney Arthur Aged 25 Son of Charles Frederick & Harriett H. Ebbetts of 30, Wormholt Rd., Shepherd's Bush, London. Worked for the LCC Education Department Thiepval Memorial

Gillman 2186 Rfn. Ernest Henry William Aged 19 Son of Mr E F & Mrs M A Gillman of 276, Liverpool Rd., King's Cross, London . Gommecourt British Cemetery No. 2, III.E.15

Harvey 1329 L/Cpl. Frederick George Thiepval Memorial

Holdron 2276 Rfn. Harold Douglas Aged 23 Son of George & Priscilla Holdron of 'Raveloe', Stevenage, Herts Thiepval Memorial

Jarvis 2974 Rfn. Frederick Thomas Aged 19 Son of Thomas & Annie Louisa Jarvis of 5, Pretoria Rd., Chingford, Essex Thiepval Memorial

King 951 Sgt. Gerald Zephaniah Aged 42 Son of Zephaniah & Clarissa King of Norwich. Enlisted Aug., 1914. Thiepval Memorial

Marsh 3505 Rfn. Harold William Aged 18 Son of Elijah & Emily Harriett Marsh of 6, Woodland Rd., Loughton, Essex Thiepval Memorial

New 2761 Rfn. Victor Frederick Thiepval Memorial

Pogose 2ⁿᵈ Lt. Ivor Reginald Aged 21 Son of Nicholas Pogose of Flat 2, 2, Acre Lane, Brixton, London, & the late Margaret Pogose Couin British Cemetery I. C. 4

Robinson 9931 Sgt. Stanford Lawson Thiepval Memorial

Stapleton 680 L/Cpl. William Thomas Aged 22 Son of John & Elizabeth Stapleton Thiepval Memorial

Warden 2729 Rfn. Charles Percy Thiepval Memorial

Watson 2157 Rfn. Leonard Claude Thiepval Memorial

Weiner 2538 Rfn. Joseph Davis Thiepval Memorial

2ⁿᵈ July 1916

Hefford 2128 Rfn. William Hickman Aged 19 Only son of John P & Alice Hefford of 33, Albany Rd., Camberwell, London. A civil servant Couin British Cemetery I. C. 12

No. 13 Platoon

Gibbins 2477 Rfn. Sidney William Thiepval Memorial

Griew 1398 Rfn. Barnet Son of Mrs Griew of 171, Amhurst Road, Hackney Thiepval Memorial

King 188 Rfn. Donovan Hugh Vosper Aged 24 Son of Clara Ellen King of 50, Castle Boulevard, Nottingham, & the late Fred Arthur King, formerly of 182, Algernon Road, Lewisham Thiepval Memorial

No. 14 Platoon

Allen 2906 Rfn. Edmund Aged 30 Son of John Edmund & Mary Ann Allen; husband of Elsie Maud Allen of 31, Mount Pleasant, Tunbridge Wells. Born at Tunbridge Wells Gommecourt British Cemetery No. 2, III.B.5

Bean 2622 Rfn. Luke Alfred Addenda Panel, Thiepval Memorial

Bleaden 690 Rfn. Leslie Arthur Aged 20 Youngest of seven children of John & Elizabeth Mary Bleaden of 71, Northbrook Rd., Ilford, Essex. Worked for the Board of Trade Patent Office. His brother was killed seven days later serving with the Royal Fusiliers. Thiepval Memorial

Cooke 2003 Rfn. Harry Thiepval Memorial

Dennis 400 L/Cpl. Arthur George Frederick Aged 23 Son of Arthur & Elizabeth Dennis of 73, Boleyn Rd., Forest Gate, Essex Gommecourt British Cemetery No. 2, II. K. 14

Gudgeon 2992 Rfn. Percival Richard Aged 29 Son of Henry & Emma Gudgeon of 71, West St., Weedon, Northants Thiepval Memorial

Hooke 1657 Rfn. Edward Arthur Son of Mr E Hooke, 47, Bramfred Road, Wandsworth Thiepval Memorial

Kinnell 1688 Rfn. Paul Stuart Aged 22 Son of Mrs E R Kinnell of Church Hill, Epping, Essex, formerly of 1, Marine Terrace, Folkestone Thiepval Memorial

Poland 2911 L/Cpl. Eric Henry Thiepval Memorial

Smith 3014 Rfn. Edward Son of Mrs Smith of 2, St Stephen's Road, Bow Thiepval Memorial

Snelling 1850 Rfn. Alfred Aged 22 Son of William & Alice Emma Snelling of 85, Blondel St., Battersea, London Thiepval Memorial

No. 15 Platoon

Brady 1997 Rfn. Montague John Eugene Aged 28 Son of Mr. & Mrs J E Brady of 13, Brown Rd., Walthamstow, Essex Thiepval Memorial

Brooks 1998 Rfn. Douglas Robert Orris Aged 21 Son of Robert & Naomi Brooks of 146, Grange Rd., Plaistow, London Thiepval Memorial

Gasston 3037 Rfn. Thomas Sidney Aged 18 Son of Thomas George & Sarah Ann Gasston of 25, Addison Rd., Wanstead, London. A Civil Servant at the War Office Thiepval Memorial

Seagrove 2867 Rfn. Graham Alston Son of Mrs Seagrove of Lingfield Green Lane, New Eltham Gommecourt British Cemetery No. 2, III. B. 29

Sweeting 689 L/Cpl. Roberson George Blackmore The eldest son of William and Catherine Sweeting, born Lambeth March 1892 Thiepval Memorial

Whatmough 2768 Rfn. Frank Joseph Aged 29 Husband of Annie Whatmough of 2, Sherston Place, Bexley Heath, Kent Gommecourt British Cemetery No. 2, III. G. 12

Woodhouse 2328 Rfn. Cyril Aged 26 Son of James & Anna Woodhouse of 117, Kyverdale Rd., Stamford Hill, London Thiepval Memorial

14th July 1916

Hollingham 2099 Rfn. Frank Vincent In German hands Caudry Old Communal Cemetery A.14

No. 16 Platoon

Denham 1478 Rfn. Frederick William Aged 19 Son of George William & Nellie Denham of 29, Madeira Rd., Margate, previously 2, Hitherfield Road, Streatham Thiepval Memorial

Jones 1695 Rfn. Alfred Thomas Aged 19 Son of Alfred John & Ellen Mary Jones of 'Sunningdale', 31 Coleshill Rd., Teddington, Middx Thiepval Memorial

Scoones 2067 Rfn. Henry William Aged 28 Son of Edward H. & Kate M. Scoones of 5, Forest Rise, Walthamstow, Essex Gommecourt British Cemetery No. 2, II. H. I

Strivens 1728 Rfn. Edward Albert Thiepval Memorial

Wadsworth 2908 Rfn. Percy Aged 23 Son of Mr & Mrs T A Wadsworth of 16, Woodland Way, Palmer's Green, London, formerly of 64, Fox Lane, Palmer's Green Thiepval Memorial

Watts 1480 Rfn. James Frederick Thiepval Memorial

Whittard 2467 Rfn. Gordon Hedley Aged 24 Son of the late Alfred Henry & of Charlotte Elizabeth Whittard, now of 1, Hillside Avenue, Friern Barnet, London Thiepval Memorial

Wingfield 2405 Rfn. James Frederick Aged 30 Son of Mr & Mrs J P Wingfield; husband of A. Gertrude Wingfield of 32, Burnt Ash Rd., Lee, London Thiepval Memorial

Company and Platoon not known

Balkwill 2nd Lt. Charles Vince Thiepval Memorial

Betts 2546 Rfn. Charles George John Aged 26 Son of Charles Betts of 47, Olive Rd., Great Yarmouth. Thiepval Memorial

622

Bexley 1532 Cpl. Stanley Aged 27 Son of Thomas Charles & Ada Jane Bexley of 29, Forest Gardens, Bruce Grove, Tottenham, London Thiepval Memorial

Bishop 2472 Rfn. Horace Edgar Thiepval Memorial

Blake 2694 Rfn. Paul George James Aged 23 Son of Rosa Blake of St. Sebastiano 30, Palermo, Italy, & the late George Blake. Born at Naples Gommecourt British Cemetery No. 2, IV. E. 5

Browne 2395 Rfn. Harry Compton Aged 25 Son of the late Harry William & Amy Marion Browne Thiepval Memorial

Burden 2152 Rfn. Leonard Guy Thiepval Memorial

Causby 2927 Rfn. Lawrence Aged 28 Son of Frank & Charlotte Causby of 'Tendring', Leighton Avenue, Leigh-on-Sea, Essex Hebuterne Military Cemetery IV. M. 3

Clifford 600 Rfn. Charles Thiepval Memorial

Cooke 2253 Rfn. George Edward Thiepval Memorial

Cooper 571 Cpl. Frederick Charles Thiepval Memorial

Cossens 2956 Rfn. Maurice George Thiepval Memorial

Davis 2112 Rfn. Herbert Victor Thiepval Memorial

Davis 2167 Rfn. Hubert Edward Aged 24 Son of Charles Edward & Edith Agnes Davis of 'Yentoi', 16, Purley Park Rd., Purley, Surrey. Gommecourt British Cemetery No. 2, III.E.14

Dean 1607 Sgt. Harold Aged 26 Son of William & Mary Dean of 30, College Rd., Leyton, London Gommecourt British Cemetery No. 2, II. L. 14

Demuth 2780 Rfn Norman Frank Not found on CWGC

Dickins 2548 Rfn. Gilbert Collingwood Aged 20 Son of Florence C. Dickins of 'Belmont', Skinners Lane, Ashstead, Surrey, & the late John Martin Dickins Thiepval Memorial

Dods 9814 Rfn. Harry Aged 29 Son of Mrs. Laura Mary Dods of 14, De Crespigny Park, Denmark Hill, London Thiepval Memorial

Ellis 2925 Rfn. Philip Leslie Thiepval Memorial

Evans 2393 Rfn. Edwin Harry Aged 23 Son of Edwin John & Eveline E. Evans of 13, Lind St., Ryde, Isle of Wight Thiepval Memorial

Ewings 1002 L/Cpl. Harold Walter Handy Aged 23 Son of Walter A & Hannah J Ewings of Oak Cottage, 15, Fryston Avenue, East Croydon, Surrey, formerly of Westcliff-on-Sea, Essex Thiepval Memorial

Fenton 1496 Rfn. Ernest Alfred Aged 23 Son of Annie Fenton of 58, Park Lane, Stoke Newington, London, & the late Alfred John Fenton Thiepval Memorial

Francis 3011 Rfn. Sidney Llewellyn Aged 26 Son of Annie Francis of 39A, Balaclava St., St. Thomas, Swansea, Glam., & the late John James Francis Thiepval Memorial

Fuller 1986 Rfn. Albert Henry Thiepval Memorial

Gibling 2478 Rfn Robert V Not found on CWGC

Gooch 1970 Rfn. Kenneth William Aged 19 Only son of L & E Gooch of 78, Sangley Rd., South Norwood, London Thiepval Memorial

Gregory 2461 Rfn. Victor William Aged 19 Son of Thomas & Leonora Gregory Thiepval Memorial

Hanchett 2479 Rfn. Richard Aged 18 Son of Edward & Maria Kate Hanchett of Horseheath, Linton, Cambs Thiepval Memorial

Havard 2491 Rfn. Frank George Thiepval Memorial

Hollingsworth 2611 Rfn. William Leonard Aged 18 Son of Frederick William & Maria Jane Hollingsworth of 1, Riverdale Rd., Plumstead, London Thiepval Memorial

Howe 2891 Rfn. Sidney Ernest Aged 17 Son of Ernest Septimus Howe & Emily Louise Howe of 70, Warham Rd., Hornsey, London Thiepval Memorial

Johnson 141 Rfn. Archibald Brown Aged 22 Son of Mrs. Elizabeth Johnson of 112, Choumert Rd., Peckham, London. Worked for the Colonial Bank Thiepval Memorial

Lawrence 2224 Rfn. Walter Bunyon Thiepval Memorial

List 405 L/Cpl. Ronald Henry Aged 24 Only son of Robert & Lydia Ann List of 18, Harrow View, Harrow, Middx Thiepval Memorial

Llewellyn 1950 Cpl. Willam Alfred Peter Aged 39 Son of John & Alice Llewellyn of Haverfordwest, Pembrokeshire; husband of Amy E. Llewellyn of 6, Hillmarton Rd., Holloway, London Thiepval Memorial

Lydamore 2258 Rfn. William Fraser Aged 24 Son of William & Agnes Lydamore of 233, Balfour Rd., Ilford, Essex Thiepval Memorial

Matthews 301706 Rfn. Reginald Gilbert Aged 24 Son of Mrs Bessie Sarah Griffin (formerly Matthews) of 38, Wingfield Rd., Stratford, London Thiepval Memorial

Moss 2494 Rfn. Percy Clarence Aged 24 Son of Frank & Blanche Isabella Moss of 42, Fairlop Rd., Leytonstone, London Gommecourt British Cemetery No. 2, III. E. II

Oates 1487 Rfn. Sydney Ernest Thiepval Memorial

Phipps 2155 L/Cpl. Harold Montague Aged 23 Son of William John Henry Phipps of Kilkhampton, Holsworthy, Devon, & the late Mary Catherine Phipps. Resident of Finchley. Worked for the British and Dominion Insurance Company Thiepval Memorial

Pitt 1667 Rfn. Ernest Samuel Thiepval Memorial

Potter 2803 Rfn. William Henry Aged 20 Son of William Godfrey Potter & Mary Pyne Potter of 29, Warnborough Rd., Oxford Thiepval Memorial

Radford 2858 L/Cpl. William Henry Thiepval Memorial

Rawlings 2092 Rfn. Frank Thiepval Memorial

Rawlings 2866 Rfn. Sidney Aged 22 Son of William & Emma Rawlings of 462, Archway Rd., Highgate, London Thiepval Memorial

Read 9619 L/Cpl. Walter Simmonds Thiepval Memorial

Reeve 1419 Rfn. Clarence Stanley Charles Aged 21 Son of Clarence R O & Edith Blanche Reeve of 169, Grangehill Rd., Eltham, London Thiepval Memorial

Richards 2389 Rfn. William Steward Aged 21 Son of William Hodge Richards & Lillie Richards of 6, Gleneagle Rd., Plymouth Thiepval Memorial

Richardson 1959 Rfn. Percy Thiepval Memorial

Sanders 781 Rfn. William Frederick Aged 24 Resident of Harlesden. Worked for Willesden Education Department. Thiepval Memorial

Searle 2537 Rfn. Walter Stanley Aged 19 Son of Walter & Amy Amelia Searle of 14, Grove Hill, Woodford, Essex Gommecourt British Cemetery No. 2, Sp. Mem. B. 14

Stapleton 1314 L/Cpl. William John Aged 24 Son of Joseph John & Bessy Jane Stapleton of 190, Grove Green Rd., Leytonstone, London. Gommecourt British Cemetery No. 2, II.K.16

Symonds 2203 Rfn. Beaumont Augustin Patmore Thiepval Memorial

Taylor 1793 Rfn. Henry William Aged 19 Only son of Henry James & Rose Annie Taylor of 46, Bromley Crescent, Bromley, Kent Thiepval Memorial

Wagstaff 473 L/Cpl. Stanley Jarvis Aged 20 Son of Mr and Mrs Wagstaff of 30, Hampton Road, Forest Gate Thiepval Memorial

Walker 2233 Rfn. John Aged 41 Son of John & Anna Maria Walker of Tewkesbury, Glos Hebuterne Military Cemetery IV. M. 56

Warner 2849 Rfn. Albert Henry Thiepval Memorial

Warner 2nd Lt. Archibald Aged 32 Son of John Warner of Waddon House, Croydon; husband of Norah E. Marriage (formerly Warner) of The Parsonage, Broomfield, Essex. Served as Pte. in 3rd Bn. Artists' Rifles Hebuterne Military Cemetery IV. D. 7

Wontner 1921 Rfn. Harold Leslie Thiepval Memorial

2nd July 1916

Dodsworth 2305 L/Cpl. Edmund Francis Aged 41 Son of the late Lt.-Col. Edmund Dodsworth & Ruth Dodsworth Doullens Communal Cemetery Extension No.1, I. B. 10

Eves 1456 L/Cpl. Sidney Arnold Warlincourt Halte British Cemetery, Saulty, II. D. 8

Horman-Fisher 3047 Rfn. Robert Blake Son of Mrs E Horman-Fisher of 14, Trafalgar Square, Peckham Park Rd., London Couin British Cemetery I. C. 7

Morris 180 L/Cpl. Phillip Dudley Aged 22 Son of G J Morris of St., Dunstan's, Hendon, London Warlincourt Halte British Cemetery, Saulty, II. D. 5

Parsons 1873 Rfn. Philip Ernest Aged 21 Son of Harry Bartlett Parsons & Rose Flora Parsons of Barn Cottage, Bow, Devon. Native of Hanwell, Middlesex. Euston Road Cemetery, Colincamps III. N. 9.

3rd July 1916

Procter 4312 Rfn. William Tyernan Fovant (St. George) Churchyard II. A. 10.

6th July 1916

Butt 1721 Rfn. Frederick Claude In German hands Le Cateau Military Cemetery, IV. A. 1

7th July 1916

Clark 2872 Rfn. Percy John Aged 21 Son of John & Isabel Clark of Bexley Heath, Kent Le Treport Military Cemetery, Plot 2. Row N. Grave 2C

Hudson 647 Rfn. Charles Henry Aged 22 Son of Charles Ernest & Ellen Hudson of 28, Norwich Road, Forest Gate Le Treport Military Cemetery, Plot 2. Row L. Grave 6

Rumsey 100 L/Cpl. John Crook Aged 21 Son of Annie Rumsey of 'Broomfield', Queen Mary's Avenue, Carshalton, Surrey, & the late William Edward Rumsey Etretat Churchyard, II. D. 19

8th July 1916
Shipham 2147 Rfn. Edward In German hands Le Cateau Military Cemetery IV. A. 6.
9th July 1916
Fraser 2818 Rfn. Aubrey Aged 18 Son of Israel & Fanny Fraser of 14 Argyll Place, Regent Street, London W1. In German hands Deutz Jewish Cemetery 1660. Near the east side
12th July 1916
Johnson 1610 L/Cpl. Edward Vincent Aged 24 Son of Albert and Isabella Johnson, of London. Doullens Communal Cemetery Extension No.1, IV. D. 18.
16th July 1916
Gardner 2490 Rfn. George Aged 20 Son of Alfred & Elizabeth Gardner of Ivy Cottage, Runfold, Surrey. Native of Seale, Surrey Mont Huon Military Cemetery, Le Treport I. F. 1.
Mogford 1553 Rfn. Rowland Aged 21 Son of Edwin Mogford of 43, Lancaster Rd., East Ham East Ham (St. Mary Magdalene) Churchyard A/C Memorial Plaque
Soar 1934 Rfn. Owen Laurence Aged 21 Son of Arthur Burgess Soar & Clara Soar of Holly Lodge, 49 Station Rd., Hendon, London Bristol (Canford) Cemetery Sec. V. Grave 4842.
18th July 1916
Olorenshaw 88 L/Sgt. Sydney Harold Aged 27 Husband of Muriel Olorenshaw of 'Northcote', Woodlands Avenue, Rhos-on-Sea, Colwyn Bay. In German hands Le Cateau Military Cemetery IV. A. 10
Pearman 401 L/Cpl. Gerald Vokins Aged 19 Son of E W & Mary Pearman of 22, Woodhouse Terrace, Grove Rd., North Finchley, London. Worked for British and Dominion Insurance Co. Aldershot Military Cemetery AF. 2001.
24th July 1916
Calvert 2387 Rfn J N Aged 19 Son of James T and Annie Calvert, of Sunderland. Mont Huon Military Cemetery, Le Treport II. C. 2.
27th July 1916
Tookey 4092 Rfn. Harold James Aged 26 Son of W H & Mrs M E Tookey of 11, Willoughby Lane, Tottenham, London. In German hands Caudry Old Communal Cemetery A.4
16th August 1916
Adams 1684 Rfn W Aged 33 Son of William and Jane Adams; husband of Eleanor E. Green (formerly Adams), of Mansel Lacy, Hereford. Born at Whitchurch, Bucks. Willesden New Cemetery, Screen Wall. M. 666.
17th October 1917
Gibbons 1149 Rfn J R Thames Ditton (St. Nicholas) Churchyard, New. N. 5.

1/9TH LONDON REGIMENT (QUEEN VICTORIA'S RIFLES)
All casualties listed as Thiepval Memorial are on Pier and Face 13 C
A COMPANY
Bastin 4642 Rfn. Sidney Horace Thiepval Memorial
Booth 3753 Rfn. Albert Aged 26 Son of George Thomas Booth of 200, Canbury Park Rd., Kingston-on-Thames; husband of Mary Ann Booth (nee Smith). Bienvillers Military Cemetery VII. D. 12
Cunningham Capt. Robert William Aged 24 Son of the late Robert & Mary Cunningham Thiepval Memorial
Larkin 2890 Rfn. Reginald Harry Aged 22 Son of the late Mr F J Larkin of 'Villeurbanne', Kingston Rd., New Malden, & 'Jesmond Dene', Avondale Rd., South Croydon, & of Mrs. B. Larkin of 'Colonsay', Presburg Rd., New Malden, Surrey. In German hands Arras Road Cemetery, Roclincourt II. D. 18
Norman 3483 Rfn. Arthur Louis Aged 17 Son of William Bates Norman & Fanny Norman of 70, Chatsworth Gardens, Acton Hill, London Thiepval Memorial
Simmonds 2nd Lt. Percy Grabham Aged 30 Born at Southend-on-Sea. Son of Harry & E Mary Simmonds of Clacton-on-Sea Thiepval Memorial
Watson 363 Sgt. William Francis Husband of Mrs Watson of 58, York Road, Copper Mill Lane, Walthamstow Thiepval Memorial
Wormall 4153 Rfn. William Arthur Aged 22 Son of C E Wormall of 72, Weymouth Avenue, South Ealing, London, & the late Charles Henry Wormall Thiepval Memorial
No. 1 Platoon
Birtles 3575 Rfn. William Robert Thiepval Memorial
Cocquerel 3934 Rfn. Marcel Thiepval Memorial
Hayman 3754 Rfn. Harold Watts Thiepval Memorial

Leverington 4577 Rfn. James Aged 36 Son of George & Maria Leverington of Suton, Wymondham, Norfolk; husband of Elizabeth A. Leverington of 34, Herbert Rd., Stockwell, London Thiepval Memorial

Long 4137 Rfn. Arthur Henry Aged 28 Son of Henry & Minnie Lambert Long of Diss, Norfolk Thiepval Memorial

Newbold 1698 Rfn. William Thiepval Memorial

Price 4567 Rfn. Rowland Llewellyn Husband of Mrs R Price of 5 Kildoran Road, Brixton Thiepval Memorial

Rowland 1807 Rfn. William George Aged 20 Son of George & Ellen Rowland of 56, Norland Gardens, Notting Hill, London Thiepval Memorial

Sewell 5028 Rfn. William Thiepval Memorial

Snelling 4746 Rfn. Harold Measday Thiepval Memorial

Tymms 5025 Rfn. Christopher Henry Albert Gommecourt British Cemetery No. 2, III. H. 19

Wigg 1560 Cpl. Richard Edward Brother of Miss Minnie Wigg of 12, Ingelow Road, Queen's Road, Batteresea Thiepval Memorial

No. 2 Platoon

Allen 3123 Cpl. Sydney John Son of Mr and Mrs Allen of 83, Langdale Road, Thornton Heath Thiepval Memorial

Cox 969 Cpl. Frederick Geoffrey Aged 24 Son of the late Mrs. Agnes Mary Cox of 98a, Tremadoc Road, Clapham Thiepval Memorial

Davey 3511 Rfn. Reginald James Thiepval Memorial

Frost 4819 Rfn. Alexander William Son of Mrs Frost of 71, Somers Road, Walthamstow Thiepval Memorial

Harrold 4513 L/Cpl. Samuel Henry Husband of Mrs Harrold, 66, Latchmere Road, Batteresea Thiepval Memorial

Marchant 3373 Rfn. Vivian John Barker Aged 26 Son of John B & Florence Ino Marchant of Athelington House, Athelington, Suffolk Thiepval Memorial

No. 3 Platoon

Burley 2829 Sgt. Ernest Leonard Aged 27 Son of Edmund & Hannah Burley of 5A, Fieldhouse Rd., Balham, London. Enlisted Aug., 1914, proceeded to France May, 1915 Thiepval Memorial

Clarke 3194 Rfn. Stanley Percival Thiepval Memorial

Cuthbert 3625 Rfn. Henry Albert Son of Albert Edward & Amelia Cuthbert of 24, Ridley Rd., Harlesden, London Thiepval Memorial

Hazzard 1613 Rfn. Reginald Stephen Thiepval Memorial

Hodnett 3801 Rfn. Edwin Roy Thiepval Memorial

Taylor 3504 Rfn. Herbert Arthur Thiepval Memorial

4th July 1916

Edmondson 3347 Rfn. Edward Tepper In German hands Favreuil British Cemetery I. D. 6.

No. 4 Platoon

Atchison 3227 Rfn. Sidney John Lyell Lived at 92, Branksome Road, Brixton Hill Thiepval Memorial

Atkins 4915 Rfn. Leslie Not found on CWGC

Bassett 3912 Rfn. Henry Edward Aged 25 Brother of Mrs Jean Pichon of 28, Rue Vauquelin, Paris, & of Miss Mary Bassett of 90, Cambridge Road, Kilburn Gommecourt British Cemetery No. 2, III. B. 13

Beaumont 3777 Rfn. George Thiepval Memorial

Cuthbert 4805 Rfn. George Richard Aged 20 Son of Edward Charles & Kate Florence Cuthbert of 6, Cloudesley Mansions, Cloudesley Place, London, N Gommecourt British Cemetery No. 2, III. B. I

Gretton 2401 Rfn. Douglas Wilfred Aged 20 Son of Ernest Edward & Minnie Gretton of 'St. Omer', Herschell Rd., Leigh-on-Sea. Born at Goodmayes, Essex. Gommecourt British Cemetery No. 2, Sp.Mem.A.4

Taylor 4772 Rfn. John Ernest Aged 23 Son of John Robert & Lily Noami Taylor of 52, Lower Montlake Rd., Richmond, Surrey Gommecourt British Cemetery No. 2, II. E. 26

B COMPANY

Card 2433 Rfn. Reginald Oscar Aged 25 Husband of Frances Emily Card of 139, Brookscroft Rd., Hoe St., Walthamstow, Essex, brother of Miss Elsie Card of 230, St John's Road, Forest Road, Walthamstow Gommecourt British Cemetery No. 2, III. H. 6

Cary 2nd Lt. Richard Harry Aged 22 Son of Ellen Cary of 3, Darlington Rd., Knights Hill, West Norwood, London & the late Henry Cary Enlisted Sept. 1914. Gazetted Nov Thiepval Memorial

Cooper 1592 Rfn. Harry Aged 20 Son of Robert George & Sarah Ann Cooper of 8, Watcombe Rd., South Norwood, London. Native of Fulham, London Couin British Cemetery I. C. 11

Fielding 2111 Rfn. George Henry Victor Aged 19 Son of George & Emily Fielding of 8, Mead Flat, Willesden, London Thiepval Memorial

Hannam 4528 Rfn. William Alfred Aged 23 Son of Mr.H & Mrs M A Hannam of Rose Farm, Buckhorn Weston, Wincanton, Somerset Gommecourt British Cemetery No. 2, III. F. 18

Houghton Capt. Philip Squarey Thiepval Memorial

Kettle 2435 Rfn. William George Burnet Son of Mrs Kettle of 146, Lynton Road, Acton Thiepval Memorial

Mason 2nd Lt. Overton Trollope Son of Louis Henry & S A Mason of 565, Musgrave Rd., Durban, Natal, South Africa. Also served in South Africa, 1914, and German South West Africa, then came Overseas and joined O.T.C Thiepval Memorial

Matthey 1004 L/Cpl. Ernest Aged 26 Son of Mr Albert & Mrs Fanny Matthey of 21, Westmoreland Rd., Bayswater, London Thiepval Memorial

Meeking 2nd Lt. Norman Arthur Thiepval Memorial

Ridler-Rowe 1666 Rfn. Wallace Robert Buffett Aged 23 Son of William Robert & E Ridler Rowe of Harford House, Stogursey, Bridgwater, Somerset Gommecourt British Cemetery No. 2, Sp. Mem. B. 20

Thornett 4116 Rfn. Albert Valentine Aged 29 Only son of Lizzie Thornett of 'Kynares', 21, West Avenue, Hendon, London, & the late Albert James Thornett, formerly of 11, Dartmouth Road, Hendon Thiepval Memorial

Williams 2996 Rfn. Stanley George Aged 23 Son of George Davison Williams & Edith Mary Williams of 6, Alexandra Avenue, Wood Green, London Thiepval Memorial

No. 5 Platoon

Ashton 3655 Rfn. Frederick Henry Only son of Mr and Mrs Ashton of 79, Sayer Street, Walworth Thiepval Memorial

Bartlett 1236 Rfn. Stephen Harold Husband of Mrs Bartlett of 100, Netherwood Road, West Kensington Park Thiepval Memorial

Bassett 4963 Rfn. Philip James Aged 20 Brother of Mrs Jean Pichon of 28, Rue Vauquelin, Paris, & of Miss Mary Bassett of 90, Cambridge Road, Kilburn Gommecourt British Cemetery No. 2, III. B. 12

Bettle 1672 L/Cpl. William Henry Aged 23 Son of the late T Bettle; brother of Miss Bettle of 4, Agnes Road, Northampton Thiepval Memorial

Biggs 4637 Rfn. Sydney Son of Mrs Biggs of 10, South Island Place, Brixton Thiepval Memorial

Curths 2864 Rfn. Herman Morton Aged 21 Son of Capt. J V Curths & Mary Ellen Curths of 43, St. Mary's Grove, Chiswick, London Thiepval Memorial

Froment 4280 Rfn. Archibald Walter Son of Mrsd Froment of 7, Begnold Road, Forest Gate Thiepval Memorial

Saddleton 3004 Cpl. Sydney Gommecourt British Cemetery No. 2, III. G. 16

Shears 2919 Rfn. Reginald Aged 28 Son of William & Dora Shears of 'Oban', Blackness, Crowborough, Sussex, formerly of 38, Anerley Road, Westcliff on Sea, Essex Enlisted Sept., 1914. A.R.I.B.A. Employed by the London County Council Thiepval Memorial

No. 6 Platoon

Atkins 2333 Cpl. Frederick Robert Aged 21 Son of Mr & Mrs F R Atkins of 7, Monnery Rd., Highgate, London Thiepval Memorial

Davies 2984 Rfn. Kenneth Middleton Aged 24 Son of Mr W M & Mrs H Davies of 70, Revelon Rd., Brockley, London Thiepval Memorial

Kerr 2790 Rfn. Oliver John Whiston Gommecourt British Cemetery No. 2, III. E. I

Marlow 4662 Rfn. Alexander George Gommecourt British Cemetery No. 2, Sp. Mem. C. I

Renwick 2866 Rfn. Norman Thiepval Memorial

Robinson 4549 Rfn. Henry Alfred Son of Mrs Robinson of 2, Burr Road, Merton Road, Southfields Thiepval Memorial

No. 7 Platoon

Atkins 4188 Rfn. Frederick Charles Thiepval Memorial

Conquest 3982 Rfn. Louis Joseph Aged 18 Son of Joseph & Annie Conquest of 37, Oxhey St., Watford Thiepval Memorial

Dann 4209 Rfn. Frederick William Son of Mrs Dann of 35, Eaton Place, London SW Thiepval Memorial

Marsh 3977 Rfn. Harold Belsey Gommecourt British Cemetery No. 2, III. E. 12

Smith 4558 Rfn. Walter James Aged 33 Son of the late Jabez & Mary Ann Smith of 8, Ivy Terrace, Oldchurch, Romford Thiepval Memorial

Tozer 2527 Cpl. Edward Gidley Aged 25 Son of William Tozer of 'Roborough', South Rd., Chorley Wood, Herts, formerly of 60, Avenue Road, Highgate Thiepval Memorial

No. 8 Platoon

Ashby 4769 Rfn. John Stanley Son of Mrs Ashby of 58, Mountgrave Road, Highbury Gommecourt British Cemetery No. 2, III. H. 22

Bayley 4757 Rfn. Felix Guy Aged 25 Son of Nathaniel Robert & Ruth Bayley of 6, Egmont St., New Cross, London Thiepval Memorial

Butler 3779 L/Cpl. Walter John Thiepval Memorial

Cole 4875 Rfn. Reuben Garrett Gommecourt British Cemetery No. 2, I. A. 12

Gibbons 3993 Rfn. Frederick Arthur Thiepval Memorial

Maidment 8422 Cpl. Alfred Sydney Son of Mrs Maidment of 27, Lanark Villas, Clifton Road, Paddington Thiepval Memorial

Measures 3914 Rfn. Arthur Richard Aged 38 Son of Richard & Mary Ann E Measures of 'Rockleigh', Streete Court Rd., Westgate-on-Sea Thiepval Memorial

Tarrant 3835 L/Cpl. George Frederick Aged 22 Son of George & Maria Theresa Tarrant of 68, Station Rd., Bexhill-on-Sea, Sussex, foermely of 56, Lea Road, Bexhill Thiepval Memorial

LEWIS GUN SECTION

Bezer 2425 L/Cpl. William Dudley Son of Mrs Bezer of 'Ferncote', Marine Parade, Leigh on Sea, Essex Husband of Mrs Bezer of 36, Brandram Road, Lee Thiepval Memorial

C COMPANY

Jolley 1960 Sgt. Leslie Harold Thiepval Memorial

Walker 2080 Rfn. Arthur Alfred Aged 21 Son of Frank William & Jennie Walker of 79, Fernlea Rd., Balham, London Thiepval Memorial

No. 9 Platoon

Blackshaw 4794 Rfn. Charles Frederick Son of Mrs Blackshaw of 7, Chalton Place, Islington Thiepval Memorial

Collis 4343 Rfn. Leonard Alfred Aged 26 Son of Mr & Mrs C W Collis; husband of Mary Edith Hallifax (formerly Collis) of 47, Geraldine Road, Wandsworth Common, London. Born at Wandsworth, London Gommecourt British Cemetery No. 2, III. C. 19

Furse 3101 L/Cpl. Maurice Aged 27 Son of William John & Elizabeth Furse of 28, High St., Crediton, Devon Thiepval Memorial

Goodfellow 4121 L/Cpl. Arthur Thiepval Memorial

Jefferies 3610 Rfn. Walter Henry George Aged 20 Son of Walter & Ellen Jefferies of 41, Bramston Rd., Harlesden, London, formerly of 74, All Souls Avenue, Willseden. Born at Paddington Gommecourt British Cemetery No. 2, III. E. 30

No. 10 Platoon

Baker 2133 Rfn. William Godfrey Aged 25 Son of Walter & Mary Emma Baker of 80, New King's Rd., Fulham, London Thiepval Memorial

Brownscombe 2679 L/Cpl. Lionel Aged 21 Son of Henry & Georgina Brownscombe of Chapel Plaister, Box, Wilts. formerly of 81, Butler Road, Harrow Born at Harrow, Middx Gommecourt British Cemetery No. 2, II. F. 11

Everest 2238 Rfn. Albert Son of Albert & Signe Evelyn Everest of 51, Clarendon Rd., Putney, London Gommecourt British Cemetery No. 2, II. A. 20

Hatcher 3442 L/Cpl. Edward William Husband of Mrs Hatcher of 'Oakley', 20, Catisfield Road, Milton, Portsmouth Thiepval Memorial

Hindry 4043 Rfn. Albert William Thiepval Memorial

Hooker 4488 Rfn. Henry Arthur Husband of Mrs Hooker of 19, Tudor Road, Southall, Middx Thiepval Memorial

Smith 4004 Rfn. Walter Sidney Aged 32 Son of David Charles & Eleanor Smith of 26, Newman St., London Thiepval Memorial

Wandby 4033 Rfn. Alfred Robert Thiepval Memorial

No. 11 Platoon

Beale 3861 Rfn. Albert James Aged 22 Son of Mr A J Beale & Mrs M A Beale of 156, Selwyn Avenue, Highams Park, Chingford, Essex Thiepval Memorial

Brewer 4407 Rfn. Alfred Verney Aged 26 Son of John & Maud Brewer of 26, Keyberry Park, Newton Abbot, Devon Thiepval Memorial

Cocks 3848 Rfn. Harold Hornsby Aged 22 Son of John & Ellen Cocks of 171, Cemetery Road, Ipswich Born at Ipswich Gommecourt British Cemetery No. 2, III. H. 3

Elms 1370 Rfn. Frederick Gilbert Aged 21 Son of James & Alice Elms of 15, Shieldhall St., Abbey Wood, London. A clerk. Mobilized Aug., 1914 Thiepval Memorial

Gabriel 3540 Rfn. Herbert Henry Aged 24 Son of Thomas & Eliza Gabriel Gommecourt British Cemetery No. 2, III. J. 19

Harvey 2967 Rfn. John Delby Alexander Thiepval Memorial

Jeeves 4062 Rfn. Frank Cyril Aged 20 Son of the late Charles & of Ann Selina Jeeves of 17A, Caldecote St., Newport Pagnell, Bucks Thiepval Memorial

Jennings 3542 Rfn. George Henry Thiepval Memorial

Nash 3827 Rfn. Frank Branch Son of Mrs Nash of 7, Woodford Road, Watford, Herts Thiepval Memorial

Poole 3863 Rfn. Norman Son of Mrs J Poole of 5, Moray Road, Tollington Park, London N Thiepval Memorial

Vizard 4442 Rfn. Thomas Aged 24 Son of Clara Matilda Vizard of 44, Ilbert St., Queens Park Estate, Milburn, London, & the late Thomas Vizard Thiepval Memorial

No. 12 Platoon

Bailey 4433 Rfn. Frederick James Thiepval Memorial

Jessep 3472 Rfn. George Davie Son of Mrs Jesspep of 112, St George's Avenue, Tufnell Park Thiepval Memorial

Parsons 3172 Sgt. Frederick William Aged 27 Son of Mary Jane Parsons of 36, Eastwood Rd., Streatham, London, & the late Samuel Parsons Thiepval Memorial

Reed 3900 Rfn. Alfred Richard Thiepval Memorial

D COMPANY

Cox Capt. Harold Edward Leys Aged 29 Son of Edward William Cox of 28, Madeley Rd., Ealing, London Thiepval Memorial

Fielding 2nd Lt. Francis Willoughby Aged 22 Son of Harry & Letitia E. Fielding of Stoneleigh, Thame, Oxon Gommecourt British Cemetery No. 2, III. D. I

12th July 1916

Fleetwood Lt. Cyril Percy Aged 33 Son of George & Mary Fleetwood. In German hands Le Cateau Military Cemetery III. B. 3

LEWIS GUN SECTION

Candler 3969 Rfn. Harold Cornell Aged 21 Son of Emma Webster Greeves (formerly Candler) of 24, St. Margaret's Mansions, Lillie Rd., Fulham, London Gommecourt British Cemetery No. 2, II. K. 15

Deangate 3408 L/Cpl. William Thiepval Memorial

ATTACHED TO 169TH MACHINE GUN COMPANY

Claridge 3223 Rfn. Arthur Henry Aged 27 Son of the late John H & Emily Claridge of St. Dunstan's House, Fetter Lane, London Thiepval Memorial

Langston 3949 Rfn. Leslie Charles Thiepval Memorial

Mitchell 2175 L/Cpl. Harold Hildige Thiepval Memorial

Parsons 1782 Rfn. Frederick Charles Son of Mrs Parsons of 56, Lodge Drive, Palmers Green Thiepval Memorial

Preece 1894 A/Cpl. Frank John C Company Aged 21 Son of Mrs. Sarah Anne Preece of I, Edith Cottage, Stanley Rd., Twickenham, Middx Thiepval Memorial

ATTACHED TO 169TH TRENCH MORTAR BATTERY

Lane Lt. Edward Alfred Joseph Aiden Thiepval Memorial

Company and Platoon not known

Abbs 4010 Rfn. James Arthur Hebuterne Military Cemetery IV. M. 6

Astill 2010 Rfn. Reginald Ediedeneí, Woodstock Road, Carshalton Thiepval Memorial

Baggarley 1394 Rfn. Ernest Sidney Thiepval Memorial

Bell 3480 Rfn. Robert Morton Thiepval Memorial

Bignall 1645 Rfn. Charles John Aged 18 Son of John & Nellie Bignall of 'Wistaria', Church St., Chiswick, London Gommecourt British Cemetery No. 2, III. H. 4

Billington (alias Pannett) 4591 Rfn. Joseph Aged 17 Served as Pannett Thiepval Memorial

Bishop 2838 Rfn. Sidney Aged 25 Son of Abraham & Emily Bishop of 72, Treen Avenue, Barnes, London Thiepval Memorial

Boggis 3149 L/Cpl. Herbert Frank Aged 24 Son of Mr & Mrs H A Boggis of 5, The Leys, Witney, Oxon Thiepval Memorial

Bond 2486 Rfn. Harold Thiepval Memorial

Breed 3616 Rfn. Albert Thiepval Memorial

Buckett 4732 Rfn. Robert Frank Aged 22 Son of Mrs M A Buckett of 45, King's Rd., Henley-on-Thames Thiepval Memorial

Buckland 2222 Cpl. Richard Julian Thiepval Memorial

Bull 3614 Rfn. Charles Aged 23 Son of Edward & Emily Bull of Great Hormead, Buntingford, Herts Thiepval Memorial

Burt 2825 Cpl. John Alexander Gommecourt British Cemetery No. 2, III. C. 23

Clark 3217 Rfn. Charles Clifford Thiepval Memorial

Cooper 3437 Rfn. Frank Thiepval Memorial

Cooper 2043 Cpl. William Aged 20 Son of William Henry & Anne Clara Cooper of 'Bradstow', Birchington, Kent Thiepval Memorial

Cox 3849 Rfn. Ronald Owen Harvey Aged 19 Son of George Hatherly Cox & Alma Cox of 48, Freshfield St., Brighton Thiepval Memorial

Cross 2900 Rfn. Charles Sidney Aged 24 Only son of Sidney Charles & Jessie Cross, late of 5, Crown Court, Pall Mall, London Thiepval Memorial

Davies 1925 Rfn. Bertrand Thiepval Memorial

Dawkes 1358 L/Cpl. Albert Edward Thiepval Memorial

Downie 3040 Rfn. Hubert Barrett Aged 21 Son of Frederick William & Ada Jane Downie of 'Ferndale', Moss Lane, Pinner, Middx (previously 50 Rutland Park Mansions, Brondesbury) Thiepval Memorial

Drake 4720 L/Cpl. Henry Alfred Aged 27 Son of George Alfred & Sarah Drake of Chilbolton, Stockbridge, Hants Thiepval Memorial

Dullam 1731 Rfn. Reginald William Aged 23 Son of Joshua & Ellen N. Dullam of Langstone, Llangarren, Ross, Herefordshire Thiepval Memorial

Earthy 4329 Rfn. Wilfred Thiepval Memorial

Easton 4749 Rfn. Claude Edgar Thiepval Memorial

Edwards 1863 Rfn. Thomas Thiepval Memorial

Farquharson 3723 Rfn. Stanley James Aged 22 Son of Frederick Robert & Alice Farquharson of 5, Crescent Place, Fulham Rd., London Thiepval Memorial

Felton 4036 Rfn. Edwin Gommecourt British Cemetery No. 2, II. H. 5

Fielder 1231 W.O. Cecil Budder Aged 28 Son of Mrs H Fielder of 58, Manor Park Rd., East Finchley, London Thiepval Memorial

Fuller 2781 Rfn. Herbert William Thiepval Memorial

Gilders 3110 L/Cpl. Clifford Edward Thiepval Memorial

Glover 4632 Rfn. Frederick Thiepval Memorial

Green 1945 L/Cpl. John Arthur Aged 24 Son of Arthur Templeman Green & Edith Green of 52, Roxborough Park, Harrow, Middx Thiepval Memorial

Gregory 3871 Rfn. Albert James Thiepval Memorial

Gunnell 2760 Rfn. Arthur Revely Williams Aged 26 Son of Frances H Gunnell of 20, Beverley Rd., Chiswick, London, & the late Arthur W. Gunnell Thiepval Memorial

Hagen 4070 Rfn. Charles Macdonald Thiepval Memorial

Hairby 3844 Rfn. Frank Aged 23 Son of Alfred & Mary A Hairby of 38, Saltoun Rd., Brixton, London Thiepval Memorial

Harman 1655 Rfn. Reginald John Thiepval Memorial

Harrington 2716 Rfn. Henry Charles Thiepval Memorial

Harris 4810 Rfn. Delme Alfred Aged 22 Son of the late John James & Sarah Harris of Devizes, Wilts Gommecourt British Cemetery No. 2, III. E. 7

Harris 2830 Rfn. Gilbert Norwood Aged 22 Son of Albert James & Emily Alice Harris of 62, Brentham Way, Ealing, London Thiepval Memorial

Harris 4867 Rfn. Reginald Thiepval Memorial

Hassett 2565 Sgt. Ernest Edwin Gommecourt British Cemetery No. 2, III. C. 12

Hedges 4460 Rfn. Arthur James Gommecourt British Cemetery No. 2, II. E. 25

Hickman 2117 Sgt. Frank Henry Charles Aged 28 Son of Mr H W & Mrs G Hickman of 'Harberton', 2, Carew Rd., Eastbourne, Sussex Gommecourt British Cemetery No. 2, III. H. 9

Hilburn 4387 Rfn. Geoffrey Aged 21 Son of Mrs Alice Thornton Hilburn of 32, Duke's Avenue, Chiswick, London Thiepval Memorial

Hook 3352 Rfn. Henry Preston Aged 20 Son of Mrs Kate Hook of 1, Pincott Rd., Bexley Heath, Kent Gommecourt British Cemetery No. 2, III. B. 27

Hunter 3998 Rfn. Frederick Charles Thiepval Memorial

Kight 4347 Rfn. Douglas Thiepval Memorial

Lahee 1984 Cpl. Terence Aged 27 Son of Edward & Alice Elizabeth Lahee of Enfield, Middlesex; brother of Hylda Skinner of 30, Cliff Parade, Leigh-on-Sea, Essex. In German hands Canadian Cemetery No. 2, Neuville - St. Vaast 14. A. 7

Laycock 4575 Rfn. Benjamin Herbert Aged 22 Brother of Mr A E Laycock of 2, Loder Gardens, Worthing, Sussex Thiepval Memorial

Leveson 3272 L/Cpl. David Edward Aged 27 Son of Mr & Mrs Leveson of 135, Roslyn Rd., South Tottenham, London Thiepval Memorial

Lewis 2513 L/Cpl. Richard Frank Thiepval Memorial

Lewis 3822 Rfn. Victor Hudson Thiepval Memorial

Lewsey 4541 Rfn. George Aged 26 Son of Frederick & Elizabeth Lewsey; husband of Mabel Elizabeth Lewsey of 44, Nightingale Buildings, St. John's Wood, London Thiepval Memorial

Little 4825 Rfn. Herbert John Albert Aged 21 Son of Mr & Mrs Herbert Little of 23, Ashbourne Rd., Mitcham, Surrey Thiepval Memorial

Lucas 3300 L/Cpl. Frederick Thiepval Memorial

Mandy 4969 Rfn. William George Thiepval Memorial

Matthey 1875 Cpl. Archibald Henry Aged 23 Son of Charlotte Matthews of 132, St. Ann's Rd., Notting Hill, London, an William Matthews Thiepval Memorial

Mercer 4045 Rfn. Burvill Aged 28 Son of Burvill Holmes Mercer & Annie Mercer of 11, Winterstoke Gardens, Mill Hill, London Thiepval Memorial

Mogford 2734 Rfn. Leslie Wells Aged 20 Son of George D & Hannah M A Mogford of 128, Walne Lane, Cricklewood, London Thiepval Memorial

Morris 3335 Rfn. George Edward Aged 20 Brother of Miss F E Morris of 31, Bradley Gardens, Ealing, London Gommecourt British Cemetery No. 2, II. G. 20

Murray 1460 Sgt. Alexander Bolton Aged 23 Son of Mrs A M Murray of 5, Beaufort Gardens, Ilford, Essex, & the late F. Murray Thiepval Memorial

Mussenden 1646 L/Cpl. Leonard Lawson Aged 19 Thiepval Memorial

Myall 3087 Rfn. Edward Henry Thiepval Memorial

Newton 4263 Rfn. Russell Thiepval Memorial

Patey 2955 L/Cpl. Sydney Edward Thiepval Memorial

Pavord 3985 Rfn. Arthur Aged 27 Son of A C & Matilda Pavord of Barrington, Somerset Hebuterne Military Cemetery IV. I. 1

Peagam 2759 L/Sgt. Walter Ernest Aged 25 Son of David E. & Matilda Peagam of 60, Waller Rd., New Cross, London. Thiepval Memorial

Penney 2814 Rfn. George Arthur Aged 19 Only son of Louisa Edith Smith (formerly Penney) of 13, Halford Rd., Hillingdon, Middx., & the late Arthur James Penney Thiepval Memorial

Perrott 3186 L/Cpl. Alfred George Aged 26 Son of Mrs Mary E Perrott of 58, Lausanne Rd., Peckham, London Thiepval Memorial

Ramus 1599 Cpl. Ernest Isaac Aged 25 Son of Mr A & Mrs E Ramus of 23, Park Drive, Harrogate, Yorks Thiepval Memorial

Regal 4861 Rfn. Frederick Thiepval Memorial

Riley 3776 Rfn. Clifford Aged 30 Son of William Henry & Alice Riley of 1, Lark St., Burnley Gommecourt British Cemetery No. 2, III. J. 20

Rudge 3699 Rfn. Frank Percy Thiepval Memorial

Shilston 1427 Rfn. Christopher Thomas Aged 26 Son of Thomas & Fanny Shilston of 35A, Winchester Rd., Swiss Cottage, London Thiepval Memorial

Smith 3707 Rfn. Cecil Winterton Aged 20 Son of Horace Alfred & Isabel Smith of 20, Bell Lane, Hendon, London Thiepval Memorial

Smith 4373 Rfn. Walter Leslie Aged 20 Son of Walter Henry & Mary Ann Lorking Smith of 59, High St., Bexley, Kent Thiepval Memorial

Spooner 3214 Rfn. Tom Clifford Thiepval Memorial

Stephenson 3784 Rfn. John Alfred Aged 29 Son of Mr & Mrs W H Stephenson of 121, Boston Rd., Brentford Thiepval Memorial

Stevens 3787 Rfn. Arthur Mayo Aged 23 Son of Joseph & Emily Stevens of 42, Cranley Gardens, Palmers Green, London Hebuterne Military Cemetery IV. H. 1

Stilwell 4380 Rfn. Arthur James Hebuterne Military Cemetery IV. E. 10

Syrett 2943 Rfn. Harold Charles Thiepval Memorial

Tait 4143 Rfn. Andrew Duncan Aged 19 Son of Andrew & Alice Tait of 60, Seymour St., Portman Square, London Thiepval Memorial

Tapping 4379 Rfn. William George Aged 26 Son of William Thomas & Sarah Emily Agnes Tapping of School Green, Shinfield, Berks Thiepval Memorial

Taylor 2414 L/Cpl. Lionel William Aged 30 Only son of Mr J W & Mrs M E Taylor of 30, Florence Rd., Wimbledon, London. Embarked for France 1914 Thiepval Memorial

Terry 1858 Rfn. Leslie Eaton Aged 21 Son of Thomas & Edith Eliza Terry of 177, Broomwood Rd., Clapham, London Thiepval Memorial

Thompson 1907 L/Cpl. Frank Lovell Thiepval Memorial

Tompson 4540 Rfn. Charles Robert Aged 20 Son of James Hammond & Emily Tompson of 25, Salisbury Rd., Watford Thiepval Memorial

Trussell 4462 Rfn. Alan Lionel Gommecourt British Cemetery No. 2, III. B. 26

Tulley 4865 Rfn. William Aged 19 Son of Ada Sherwood (formerly Tulley) of Sandford, Hessle, Yorks, & the late William Henry Tulley Thiepval Memorial

Walden 4183 Rfn. George Gommecourt British Cemetery No. 2, III. G. 25

Walker 4964 Rfn. Herbert William Thiepval Memorial

Wells 2380 L/Cpl. Douglas Edward Aged 24 Son of Fanny Marian Wells of 46, Chelsham Rd., Clapham, London, & the late Creswell Wells, M.V.O Thiepval Memorial

White 4533 Rfn. Charles Albert Thiepval Memorial

White 4573 Rfn. Herbert William Aged 21 Brother of Edward John White of 5, Brooklands St., Wandsworth Rd., London Thiepval Memorial

Whitehouse 3116 Rfn. Sidney Charles Thiepval Memorial

Wickens 2576 Rfn. George Edward Thiepval Memorial

Willows 3399 Rfn. William Peter Thiepval Memorial

2nd July 1916

Hall 4601 Rfn. Charles James Howard Aged 23 Husband of Elizabeth F Turner (formerly Hall) of 4, Charles Lane, St. John's Wood, London Couin British Cemetery I. C. 8.

Hodson 4678 Rfn. George Frederick Husband of A Hodson of 58, York Rd., East Ham, London. Couin British Cemetery I. C. 3.

Hook 4678 Rfn. George Frederick Not found on CWGC

Kempe 3319 Rfn. Charles Brett Warlincourt Halte British Cemetery, Saulty II. D. 9

4th July 1916

Barnes 2738 Rfn. Sydney George Aged 22 Son of James Quick Barnes & Phyllis Barnes of 27, Endymion Rd., Brixton Hill, London Warlincourt Halte British Cemetery, Saulty I.G.14

5th July 1916

Bangs 3963 Rfn. Leonard Edward Aged 21 Son of William H & Susan Bangs of 9, Waltheof Avenue, Lordship Lane, Tottenham, London. Etretat Churchyard II. D. 21

6th July 1916

Graham 3734 Rfn. Sydney Harold In German hands Le Cateau Military Cemetery IV. A. 3

10th July 1916

Dix 4824 Rfn. I C Etretat Churchyard II. D. 12

South 3473 Rfn. G R S Aged 26 Son of William John & Louisa South of 33, Mercers Road, Upper Holloway, London Le Treport Military Cemetery Plot 2. Row N. Grave 3A

15th July 1916

Calder 3859 Rfn. Roy Grant In German hands St. Souplet British Cemetery II. AA. 1.

17th July 1916

Peirce 3994 Rfn. William Alec Aged 20 Son of William & Emily Harriet Peirce of 54, Warham Rd., Harringay, London. In German hands Le Cateau Military Cemetery IV. A. 8

20th July 1916

Layland 1871 Rfn. George James In German hands Brother of Miss M Layland of 4, Eustace Road, Fulham St. Souplet British Cemetery III. AA. 9.

1/12TH LONDON REGIMENT (THE RANGERS)

All casualties listed as Thiepval Memorial are on Pier and Face 9 C

SIGNAL SECTION

Hough 2380 Rfn. Michael Son of Mr. M. and Mrs. E. Hough, of 7, Livonia St., Soho, London Thiepval Memorial

A COMPANY

Bradshaw Lt. Richard Edward Kynaston Aged 21 Son of William Graham Bradshaw and Dora Sophia Bradshaw, of Down Park, Crawley Down, Sussex Thiepval Memorial

Dawe 1979 L/Cpl. Harry Edward Thiepval Memorial

Law 4335 Rfn. Percy Aged 23 Son of Edmund and Alice Marion Law, of 59, Olive Rd., Cricklewood, London, formerly of 112, Hallam Street, London, W. Thiepval Memorial

Scrivener 3300 Pte Basil Ernest att. from 2/2nd London Regt. Aged 22 Youngest son of Mrs. Euphemia Scrivener of 52, Limerston St., West Brompton, London. Thiepval Memorial

Walter 2787 Rfn. Reginald Frederick Aged 23 Son of Ernest and Flora Annie Walter, of The Haven, Cedars Avenue, Rickmansworth, Herts., previously of 'Homeleigh', Talbot Road, Wembley Thiepval Memorial

13ᵗʰ September 1916

Law, 4291 Rfn. Edmund Son of Edmund and Alice Marion Law, of 59, Olive Rd., Cricklewood, London In German hands Niederzwehren Cemetery, grave IV. D. 10.

No. 1 Platoon

Burfitt 2757 Cpl. Thomas Henry att. from 2/2ⁿᵈ London Regt. Son of Mrs Burfitt, 81, East Street, Epsom Thiepval Memorial

Hanna 3084 Sgt. William Archibald Thiepval Memorial

Hodgson 2822 Pte Leonard William att. from 2/2ⁿᵈ London Regt. Thiepval Memorial

Jarvis 4441 Rfn. Edward Charles Aged 20 Son of Clara Jarvis, of 62, Hilda Rd., Canning Town, London, and the late Walter Edward Jarvis Thiepval Memorial

Johnson 4170 Rfn. Edward Lionel Wayland Aged 18 Son of Sarah Ann Johnson, of 'Ottery', Uplands Park Rd., Enfield, Middx, and the late Henry Johnson. Thiepval Memorial

Mark 4183 Rfn. Thomas McKinley Aged 18 Son of James L and Christian C Mark of 8, Granville Rd., Wimbledon, London. Thiepval Memorial

Whiskerd 2704 Pte George Walter att. from 2/2ⁿᵈ London Regt. Aged 20 Son of Walter David & Louisa Eliza Whiskerd of 15, Cottage Rd., Ewell, Epsom, Surrey Thiepval Memorial

No. 2 Platoon

Burne 3760 Rfn. Joseph Daniel Son of Mrs Burne of 15, Chilworth Mews, Craven Road, Padington Gommecourt British Cemetery No. 2, I. A. 9.

Todd 4298 Rfn. Albert Charles Aged 18 Son of Albert E and Georgina A Todd, of 43, White Rock, Hastings Thiepval Memorial

Whiting 4455 Rfn. Percy Masters Aged 28 Husband of Winifred Daisy Whiting, of High St., Epping, Essex, formerly of 4, Hemnall Street, Epping Thiepval Memorial

No. 3 Platoon

Bulling 3090 L/Cpl. William Chambers Aged 27 Son of Mr and Mrs John Bulling, of 9, Crown St., Bury St. Edmund's. Thiepval Memorial

Ellis 1953 Rfn. Edward George Aged 19 Son of Thomas Henry Ellis, of 20, Tooting Bec Gardens, Streatham, London. Three times wounded. Thiepval Memorial

Goodwin 3912 Rfn. Sidney Aged 18 Son of the late George and Elizabeth Goodwin. Thiepval Memorial

Mayer 2505 Rfn. George Aged 22 Son of Herbert Henry and Emma Mayer, of 111, Mansfield Rd., Gospel Oak, London Thiepval Memorial

Smith 2827 L/Cpl Harry att. from 2/2ⁿᵈ London Regt. Son of Mrs A L Smith of 5, Wotton Road, Cricklewood Thiepval Memorial

No. 4 Platoon

Barnes 4253 Rfn. William Charles Aged 32 Son of Mrs Fanny Barnes, of 30, Beach Rd., Southsea, Hants, and the late Charles O. Barnes, formerly of 4, Chichester Street, Paddington Thiepval Memorial

Bowyer 1831 Rfn. Ernest Thomas Aged 19 Son of James Bowyer, of 17, Mitcham St., Lisson Grove, London Gommecourt British Cemetery No. 2, I. D. 7

Gandar 3878 Rfn. William Gustave Thiepval Memorial

Panter 2449 Rfn. John Wadwell Son of Mr and Mrs Panter of 'Court House', Ashley Road, Epsom Thiepval Memorial

Parker 4387 Rfn. Edward Aged 21 Son of Mrs Mary Parker, of 31, Colonnade, Russell Square, Bloomsbury, London. Thiepval Memorial

Stimpson 2809 L/Cpl. Robert Thiepval Memorial

Young 3008 Pte Albert Victor att. from 2/2ⁿᵈ London Regt. Aged 24 Son of David Turner Young & Henrietta Eliza Young of 63, Leslie Rd., Leytonstone, London Thiepval Memorial

B COMPANY

Hussey 2041 Rfn. William Henry Brother of Miss N Hussey of 19, Milton Avenue, Highgate Gommecourt British Cemetery No. 2, II. G. 13.

Taplin 2ⁿᵈ Lt. Albert William Aged 24 Son of William James and Sarah Taplin, of 12, North Side, Paddington, London Thiepval Memorial

Walker 3164 Cpl. Charles Alfred att. from 2/2ⁿᵈ London Regt. Thiepval Memorial

No. 5 Platoon

Bainbridge 3348 Pte William att. from 2/2ⁿᵈ London Regt. Gommecourt British Cemetery No. 2, II. D. 16

Shimmell 1986 Sgt. Thomas Aged 32 Son of Frederick Shimmell, of 92, Overstone Rd., Hammersmith, London; husband of Caroline Elizabeth Pauline Caterer (formerly Shimmell), of The King's Head, West Drayton, Middx. Thiepval Memorial

Smith 1801 Rfn. Kenneth Roger John Aged 18 Son of George R and Rosa L A Smith, of 14, Nigel Buildings, Bourne Estate, Holborn, London. Thiepval Memorial

No. 6 Platoon

Baker 2538 Rfn. Edward James Thiepval Memorial

Bennett 3751 Rfn. Roy Douglas Thiepval Memorial

Brandon 4302 Rfn. John William Aged 28 Son of Henry Levi Brandon and Charlotte Brandon, of Marylebone, London; brother of Miss Brandon of 5, Stalbridge Buildings, Lumley Street, Grosvenor Square Thiepval Memorial

Glassborow 4329 Rfn. Leonard Victor Lee Aged 19 Son of William Henry and Emily Sarah Glassborow, of 21A, Montpelier Crescent, Brighton Thiepval Memorial

Lacey 2260 Rfn. Joseph Edward Thiepval Memorial

Paxton 3514 Rfn. Albert Aged 19 Son of George and A Paxton, of 3, Sydney Rd., West Ealing, London. Thiepval Memorial

Steer 3687 Rfn. Gordon Wilfred Aged 21 Son of George and Lydia Steer, of 40, Staverton Rd., Brondesbury Park, London. Born at Willesden. Gommecourt British Cemetery No. 2, I. B. 18.

10th July 1916

Carter 4292 Rfn. Edwin George Aged 27 Son of Hannah Louisa Carter, of 5, Vera Rd., Fulham, London, and the late Edwin George Carter. In German hands Caudry Old Communal Cemetery A. 11.

No. 7 Platoon

Evans 4342 Rfn. Reginald Gommecourt British Cemetery No. 2, I. B. 14.

Lucas 4488 Rfn. William Charles Aged 28 Son of Mrs Josephine Lucas, of 106, Offord Rd., Barnsbury, London. Thiepval Memorial

Thickbroom 3813 Rfn. Sydney Son of Mr and Mrs Thickbroom of 118, Russell Avenue, Wood Green Thiepval Memorial

9th August 1916

Loker 3001 Cpl Bertram Horace Alfred att. from 2/2nd London Regt. In German hands Aged 28 The son of Joseph and Elizabeth Ann Loker, of 12, Portman Buildings, Lisson Grove, Marylebone, London. Porte-De-Paris Cemetery, Cambrai grave I. A. 30.

No. 8 Platoon

Dauncey 4047 Rfn. Reginald Arthur Aged 24 Son of the late Mr and Mrs Silvanus Dauncey. Born in London. Gommecourt British Cemetery No. 2, I. A. 19

Coffey 2600 Pte Wilfred Mortimer att. from 2/2nd London Regt. Thiepval Memorial

Schwartzburg 3810 Rfn. Moses Thiepval Memorial

Young 4511 Rfn. William Aged 24 Son of William and Lizzie Young, of 12, Alexandra Rd., Hendon, London. Thiepval Memorial

C COMPANY

Bennett 2420 Sgt. Henry Edward Thiepval Memorial

Brooks 4477 Rfn. Ezra Gommecourt British Cemetery No. 2, III. B. 8.

Fittin 1129 Cpl. John att. from 2/2nd London Regt. Son of Mrs Fitton of 119, Priory Park Road, Kilburn Thiepval Memorial

Hickman 3922 Rfn. Sidney Gommecourt British Cemetery No. 2, I. C. 2.

Hoare Capt. Richard Leonard Aged 33 Son of Laura Hoare, of Summerhill, Benenden, Cranbrook, Kent, and the late William Hoare. Born at Staplehurst, Kent Gommecourt British Cemetery No. 2, I. C. I.

Jordan 1942 Rfn. Herbert Charles Aged 24 Son of Mrs Henrietta Jordan, of 217, Farringdon Road Buildings, Clerkenwell, London Thiepval Memorial

Josephs 2nd Lt. Joseph Aged 19 Son of David and Sabina Josephs, of 206, Willesden Lane, London Gommecourt British Cemetery No. 2, I. C. 4.

Taylor 2866 Rfn. Herbert William Aged 18 Son of Mrs Jane Taylor, of 549, Manchester Rd., Poplar, London Thiepval Memorial

No. 9 Platoon

Arnold 4389 Rfn. Richard Frank Aged 20 Son of Mrs Emily Arnold, of 61, Shrubland Rd., Dalston, London Thiepval Memorial

Blackburn 3016 Pte Arthur att. from 2/2nd London Regt. Aged 23 Son of William & Helen Blackburn of 66, Fordel Rd., Catford, London Thiepval Memorial

Drury 3945 Rfn. Victor Charles Gommecourt British Cemetery No. 2, I. A. 14

6th July 1916

Blackburn 2493 Pte Sidney John att. from 2/2nd London Regt. Aged 19 Son of Samuel Joseph & Rachel Annie Blackburn of 48, Colonial Avenue, Whitton, Twickenham, Middx. Couin British Cemetery II. A. 9.

No. 10 Platoon

Allen 4215 Rfn. Leonard Thiepval Memorial

Lee 1931 Rfn. William Hendley Aged 19 Son of William Thomas and Mary Jane Lee, of 41, Rathcoole Avenue, Hornsey, London. Thiepval Memorial

Newman 1786 Pte Alfred Gregg att. from 2/2nd London Regt. Gommecourt British Cemetery No. 2, I. C. 10

Wendon 4088 Rfn. Leonard Ralph Son of Mr H Wendon of 99, Ravensbury Road, Earlsfield Thiepval Memorial

Whitley 3195 Pte Edward att. from 2/1st London Regt. Thiepval Memorial

No. 11 Platoon

Gobell 1465 Rfn. Frederick John Aged 25 Son of Mr and Mrs Gobell, of 23, Bamford Rd., Barking, Essex. Gommecourt British Cemetery No. 2, II. C. 6.

Levoir 3996 L/Cpl. Thomas Charles Gommecourt British Cemetery No. 2, I. D. 5.

Jenkins 4064 Rfn. William Edward Aged 21 Son of W H and Mary Jenkins, of 18, Babbacombe Rd., Bromley, Kent Thiepval Memorial

Mendel 3845 Rfn. George Son of Mrs Mendel of 106, Farringdon Road Buildings, Clerkenwell Gommecourt British Cemetery No. 2, I. A. 15.

Wood 3324 Pte Ernest att. from 2/2nd London Regt. Son of Mrs M S Wood of 20, Lesbia Road, Clapton Thiepval Memorial

No. 12 Platoon

Brown 4320 Rfn. George Frederick Thomas Thiepval Memorial

Honer 4378 Rfn. Joseph Son of Mrs Honer of 11, Lansdowne Gardens, South Lambeth Gommecourt British Cemetery No. 2, I. D. 6.

Morris 1617 Rfn. Arthur Charles Aged 19 Son of Charles Rochester Morris and Anna Sarah Morris of 64, Randolph Rd., Custom House, London Gommecourt British Cemetery No. 2, I D 9

Prout 2593 Cpl. Arthur Stanley Son of Mar A P Prout of 'Kenmore', 23, Grove Road, Denmark Hill Thiepval Memorial Pier and Face 9

Shepherd 4450 Rfn. Edwin Isaac Gommecourt British Cemetery No. 2, I. B. 19

Wheeler 4465 Rfn. William Henry Aged 25 Son of Mrs Wheeler of 2, Little Elm Place, Chelsea, London. Thiepval Memorial

D COMPANY

Davey 2nd Lt. William Roy Aged 19 Son of William Henry and Jessie F. L. Davey. Gommecourt British Cemetery No. 2, VI. A. I.

Jones Maj. Lewis Farewell Aged 31 Son of the late George Farewell Jones and Anna Louisa Jones, of Brenley, Mitcham, Surrey London Cemetery and Extension, Longueval Joint grave 9.J.12

Marks 4122 Rfn. Victor Harold Son of Mrs M A Marks, of 30, Anlaby Rd., Teddington, Middx. Thiepval Memorial

Moore 3422 Rfn. Alfred Filby Aged 25 Son of George and Mary Ann Moore, of 241, South Park Rd., Wimbledon, London. Gommecourt British Cemetery No. 2, I. A. 7.

Moore 3483 Rfn. Harold George Aged 27 Son of George and Mary Ann Moore of 241, South Park Rd., Wimbledon, London. Thiepval Memorial

Terry 4504 Rfn. Charles William Aged 21 Brother of Henry A. Terry, of 24, Stork Rd., Forest Gate, Essex. Thiepval Memorial

Warren 2707 Pte Ernest Cecil att. from 2/2nd London Regt. Aged 23 Son of Sarah Matilda Warren of 8, Ordell Rd., Bow, London, & the late Henry Stephen Warren Thiepval Memorial

No. 13 Platoon

Comber 4433 Rfn. Thomas Herbert Edward Son of Mr J Comber of 34, Whittingstall Road, Fulham Gommecourt British Cemetery No. 2, I. C. 9.

Davis 3707 Rfn. Alfred William Son of Mr G W F Davis, of 26, Banyard Rd., Bermondsey, London. Gommecourt British Cemetery No. 2, I. D. 4.

Foster 3943 Rfn. Henry Oliver Philip Aged 20 Son of Thomas Arthur and Annie Caroline Foster, of 12, Cromwell Rd., Luton Thiepval Memorial

Lacey 2238 Rfn. Henry William Son of Mrs Lacey, 29, King's Square, Goswell Road, London EC Thiepval Memorial

Pitt 3726 Rfn. Alfred Dreaton Aged 20 Son of William James and Amelia Pitt, of 102, Grayshott Rd., Battersea, London. Thiepval Memorial

Schaffrath 4283 Rfn. Frank Thiepval Memorial

Tucker 2ⁿᵈ Lt. William Henry Thiepval Memorial

No. 14 Platoon

Ashley 3811 Rfn. George Frederick Aged 22 Son of Mrs C F Ashley, of 96, Broke Rd., Dalston, London Gommecourt British Cemetery No. 2, I. C. 8.

George 2450 Pte Arthur Henry att. from 2/2ⁿᵈ London Regt. Aged 23 Son of John Daniel & Elizabeth George of 82, Wandsworth Rd., London Gommecourt British Cemetery No. 2, II H 23

Hines 1392 Sgt. Harry Aged 23 Son of Harry and Lucy Hines of 30, Tollington Place, Tollington Park, Holloway, London, previously of 483, Caledonian Road, Holloway Thiepval Memorial

Smith 4282 Rfn. George Ernest Aged 19 Son of George and Sarah Jane Smith, of 80, St. James's Road, Croydon, Surrey Thiepval Memorial

Ward 1457 L/Cpl. Robert Stanley Thiepval Memorial

No. 15 Platoon

Back 3775 Rfn. George Henry Son of Robert Henry Richard and Clara Emily Bache, of 18, Carlingford Rd., West Green, Tottenham, London. A Great Northern Railway Coy. employee Thiepval Memorial

Liddiard 4489 Rfn. Frederick John Thiepval Memorial

Murcutt 3208 Pte Ernest Henry att. from 2/2ⁿᵈ London Regt. Son of Mr T Murcutt of 92, ROundwood Road, Willesden Thiepval Memorial

Sterritt 2648 Cpl. David John Aged 22 Son of John and Elizabeth Sterritt, of 2, Raphael St., Knightsbridge, London Thiepval Memorial

No. 16 Platoon

Barrett 4174 Rfn. Richard Walter Aged 19 Son of Henry George and Mary Jane Barrett, of 65, Western Rd., Plaistow, London. Thiepval Memorial

Bedford 4101 Rfn. Cecil Thomas Gommecourt British Cemetery No. 2, III. F. 6

Cole 2175 Rfn. Charles Arthur Aged 23 Son of Simeon and Georgina Cole, of 5, Channel View Terrace, Plymouth. His brother, 3837, Pte. W. E. Cole, 1st/7th Bn. Worcestershire Regt., fell in August, 1916, on the Somme. Gommecourt British Cemetery No. 2, Sp. Mem. C. 3

Cole 3057 L/Cpl Gordon William att. from 2/2ⁿᵈ London Regt. Aged 19 Son of John Henry & Elizabeth Cole of 58, Palmerston Rd., Walthamstow, Essex Thiepval Memorial

Cole 2927 Pte Sidney Ernest att. from 2/2ⁿᵈ London Regt. Aged 22 Son of Walter & Kate Louise Cole of 22 Cunningham Park, Harrow, Middx, formerly of 32, Harrow View, Harrow Thiepval Memorial

Meyer 2620 Pte John Edward att. from 2/1ˢᵗ London Regt. Thiepval Memorial

Ronayne 4030 Rfn. William Aged 17 Son of the late William and Emma Ronayne. Thiepval Memorial

LEWIS GUN SECTION

Smith 3847 L/Cpl. Alfred William Son of Mr and Mrs Smith of 31, Manor Park Road, East Finchley Thiepval Memorial

Davey 2583 Rfn. Walter Aged 19 Son of Henry and Mary Ann Davey,brother of Mrs Broomes of 6, All Saints Avenue, Harlesden Thiepval Memorial

ATTACHED TO 168ᵀᴴ MACHINE GUN COMPANY

Lamb 4083 Rfn. Edward D Company Thiepval Memorial

Company and Platoon not known

Amey 2570 Rfn. Vernon Maxwell Aged 22 Son of Louisa Amey, of 28, Queen's Crescent, Haverstock Hill, London, and the late Richard Amey Hebuterne Military Cemetery IV.M.32

Bannister 3998 Rfn. Walter Aged 23 Son of William and Clementina Bannister, of 8, Inkerman Rd., Kentish Town, London. Thiepval Memorial

Bates 1779 Pte Frank Edward att. from 2/2ⁿᵈ London Regt. Aged 19 Son of Mrs. Mary S. Bates of 12, Paulton's St., Chelsea, London, formerly of 52, Bromar Road, Denmark Park Thiepval Memorial

Bickerton 4073 Rfn. Samuel Thomas Leslie Aged 18 Son of the Rev. Thomas Henry Bickerton and Isabella Ann Bickerton (nee Phillips), of 56, Westover Rd., Wandsworth, London Thiepval Memorial

Boatman 3950 Rfn. Thomas Charles Aged 21 Son of Mr T C and Mrs E M Boatman, of 18, Park Rd., Leyton, London. Thiepval Memorial

Boland 1941 Rfn. Frederick James Aged 21 Son of Chrissy Boland, of 54, King's Cross Rd., London, and the late Thomas W. Boland. Thiepval Memorial

Booth 4267 Rfn. Stanley Gordon Aged 27 Son of Mrs Mary Ann Booth, of 133, Grovenor Rd., Forest Gate, Essex. Thiepval Memorial

Boyle 2665 Sgt. Percy Robert Aged 28 Son of Robert and Jane Emily Boyle, of 'Tryst', Westborough Rd., Westcliff-on-Sea, Essex. Thiepval Memorial

Bradford 2031 Cpl. Sidney Aged 27 Son of Mr C F and Mrs S G Bradford, of 38, Belgrave Crescent, Bath. Born at Cambridge Gommecourt British Cemetery No. 2, II. F. 9

Brinkley 2023 Cpl. Charles Aged 21 Son of Charles T and Esther Brinkley, of 24, Alfred Rd., Paddington, London, previously of 7, Woodfield Place, Paddington Thiepval Memorial

Clayton 4266 Rfn. Walter Thiepval Memorial

Cole 2176 Cpl. Robert Thomas Aged 23 Son of Mrs Mary Kirchin (formerly Cole), of 72, Dover Rd. East, Northfleet, Kent Gommecourt British Cemetery No. 2, III. G. 20

D'Arcy 4356 Rfn. Charles Edward Aged 23 Son of Kate D'Arcy, of 29, Dawes Rd., Fulham, London, and the late John D'Arcy Thiepval Memorial

Dennison 1791 Rfn. Charles William Aged 19 Son of Henry John and Emma Jane Dennison, of 151, Osborne Rd., Forest Gate, Essex Thiepval Memorial

Dowling 3880 Rfn. Harry Thomas Aged 25 Son of Elizabeth Kate Hodgkins (formerly Dowling) and Robert Edward Hodgkins (Step father), of 200, Blackhorse Lane, Walthamstow, Essex. His elder brother also fell. Thiepval Memorial

Draper 3889 Rfn. Donald Stewart Aged 19 Son of Ellen Draper, of 13, Friendly St., Lewisham, London, and the late Charles Draper. Thiepval Memorial

Dutton 3900 Rfn. Francis Joseph Thiepval Memorial

Eldred 4213 Rfn. Charles Sydney Aged 20 Son of Robert and Phoebe Eldred, of 40A, Wingford Rd., Hill, Brixton, London Thiepval Memorial

Fatherly 4115 Rfn. Herbert Stanley Aged 22 Son of Henry James and Emily Rebecca Fatherly, of 63, Estcourt Rd., Woodside, South Norwood, London Thiepval Memorial

Feilder 2780 Rfn. Herbert Daniel Aged 24 Son of Jeremiah Alfred and Emma Lucy Feilder. Hebuterne Military Cemetery IV. M. 2

Ferris 4118 Rfn. Walter Lloyd Gommecourt British Cemetery No. 2, I. C. 7.

Furzer 3915 Rfn. Arthur James Gommecourt British Cemetery No. 2, I. B. 17.

Gowers 3881 Rfn. Spencer Allen Thiepval Memorial

Hales 3701 Cpl. Walter Sidney Aged 29 Son of Walter Charles and Jane Maria Hales, of 98, St. Stephen's Avenue, Shepherd's Bush, London Thiepval Memorial

Haswell 4192 Rfn. John Mavin Aged 20 Son of Elizabeth Haswell, of 103, Judd St., King's Cross, London, and the late Alfred Haswell. Thiepval Memorial

Hennell 3592 Rfn. Sidney Arthur Thiepval Memorial

Henwood 4321 Rfn. John Sinclair Aged 20 Son of William Hall Henwood and Fanny Henwood, of 'Maycroft', 97, Monkhams Avenue, Woodford Green, Essex. Gommecourt British Cemetery No. 2, I. A. 10

Holder 3634 Rfn. William Gommecourt British Cemetery No. 2, I. A. 16.

Howard 4036 Rfn. Oscar Edward Aged 18 Son of Mr. and Mrs. Howard, of Holborn, London. Gommecourt British Cemetery No. 2, I. A. 5

Hunt 2378 Rfn. William Henry Aged 32 Brother of Mrs M L Hutchinson, of 9, Canada Rd., North Acton, London Thiepval Memorial

Hunter 3618 Rfn. William James Aged 19 Son of G W and Mary Elizabeth Hunter, of 47, Clarence Rd., Walthamstow, London. Hebuterne Military Cemetery IV. M. 26.

Jee 2189 Rfn. Thomas Davidson Aged 23 Son of Edward and Eveline Jee, of 35, Institute Rd., Chatham, Kent Gommecourt British Cemetery No. 2, I. D. 10

Jones 4026 Rfn. George Frederick Thiepval Memorial

Kerner 4177 Rfn. George James att. to 56th Divisional Transport ASC Aged 21 Son of George and Hannah M Kerner, of 16, Radnor Terrace, South Lambeth Rd., London. Thiepval Memorial

Kibble 2015 A/L/Cpl. William .James Aged 28 Son of Mrs H M Kibble, of 156, Eswyn Rd., Tooting, London. Gommecourt British Cemetery No. 2, I. C. 3.

Lane 3930 Rfn. Cecil James Aged 18 Son of James and Elizabeth Lane, of 10, Carlingford Rd., Hampstead Heath, London. Gommecourt British Cemetery No. 2, II. C. 7.

Lee 3086 Rfn. James Garnett Thiepval Memorial

Lock 3291 Rfn. William att. from 2/2nd London Regt. Aged 22 Son of the late Mrs S Lock of 10, Randall St., Battersea, London Thiepval Memorial

Mendel 3845 Rfn. George Gommecourt British Cemetery No.2 I. A. 15.

Marcus 2216 Rfn. Dudley Harold Aged 21 Son of Julius and Ida S. Marcus. Born in London Gommecourt British Cemetery No. 2, I. A. 21.

Marriner 4445 Rfn. Archibald James Aged 27 Son of Arthur William and Amelia Eliza Marriner, of 225, Shirland Rd., Maida Hill, London Thiepval Memorial

Martin 2263 Rfn. George Albert Aged 27 Son of Mr B W Martin and Mrs. R. Martin, of 99, Alpha House, Alpha Rd., Cambridge Thiepval Memorial

Martin 2463 Rfn. John Godfrey Aged 23 Son of F M Martin, of 11, Oxford Avenue, Southampton, and the late John Hadlow Martin. Thiepval Memorial

Mayhew 4312 Rfn. Henry Clement Brother of Miss Mayhew, 60, Colegrave Road, Stratford Thiepval Memorial

Mower 1799 L/Cpl. Cecil Sandiford Aged 19 Son of Mary Elizabeth Mower, of 'The Cabin', Chalfont Common, Chalfont St. Peters, Bucks, and the late Robert Edward Mower. Native of Brondesbury, London. Hebuterne Military Cemetery IV. M. 34

Phillips 2155 Rfn. Herbert William Aged 20 Son of Mr J W and Mrs M A Phillips, of 8, Bristol Park Rd., Walthamstow, London. Couin British Cemetery I. C. 2.

Place 3822 Rfn. William Anson Coxon Thiepval Memorial

Pool 3815 Rfn. Leonard Rossiter Aged 21 Son of T R and Rose Emma Pool, of 1, Parkstone Avenue, Parkstone, Dorset. Hebuterne Military Cemetery IV. M. 35.

Popple 2834 Sgt. George Arthur Thiepval Memorial

Rhind 2097 Rfn. William John Cameron Aged 22 Son of the late W M Rhind, of 252, Fulham Rd., London. Thiepval Memorial

Riley 4447 Rfn. Frederick Aged 18 Son of the late Fred Riley and Clara Emily Potter (formerly Riley), of Alsager, Cheshire. Gommecourt British Cemetery No. 2, I. A. 17.

Rovery 1786 Sgt. Walter Charles Thiepval Memorial

Seabrook 2701 Pte Frederick John att. from 2/2nd London Regt. Aged 24 Son of Walter & Elizabeth Seabrook of 9, Eland Rd., Lavender Hill, London. Clerk to the Battersea Borough Council. Also served in Malta, Egypt and at Gallipoli Thiepval Memorial

Sherring 4097 Rfn. Arthur Frederick Aged 19 Son of Frederick Augustus and Edith Sarah Sherring, of 72, Foulser Rd., Upper Tooting, London. Thiepval Memorial

Shirtclippe 2842 Rfn. Frederick Clinton Aged 24 Brother of Mrs. Ethel Brand, of 45, Egerton Gardens, Hendon, London Hebuterne Military Cemetery IV. B. 12

Skipper 4452 Rfn. Claud Stanley Aged 21 Only son of Mrs A E Skipper, of 7, Chester Rd., Canning Town, London. Thiepval Memorial

Smeeton 2576 Rfn. Frederick John Aged 24 Son of Frederick Herbert and Alice Smeeton, of 1, Tottenham St., North Kensington, London. Native of Hornsey, London. Hebuterne Military Cemetery IV. E. 8

Smith 4501 Rfn. Percy Real name G S Jekyll Thiepval Memorial

Smith 4138 Rfn. Sydney Arthur Aged 19 Son of Frederick and Mary Ann Smith, of 72, Beresford St., Camberwell, London. Born at Kennington Gommecourt British Cemetery No. 2, I. A. 4.

Snooks 3789 Rfn. Thomas William Thiepval Memorial

St. Claire 3907 Rfn. John Bell Aged 20 Son of Emma Freeman (formerly St. Claire), of 34, Hewitt Avenue, Wood Green, London, and the late Alfred Joseph St. Claire. Couin British Cemetery I. B. 20.

Taylor 3975 Rfn. Thomas Gommecourt British Cemetery No. 2, I. D. 3.

Thomas 3970 Rfn. William Alfred Thiepval Memorial

Townsend 2459 Pte Herbert Harry att. From 2/2nd London Regt. Son of Mrs Townsend of 50, Fontarabia Road, Lavender Hill Bienvillers Military Cemetery, XIX. J. 14

Ward 2nd Lt. Stanley Dacre Aged 33 Son of Alfred and Alice Ward, of 67, Westcombe Park Rd., Blackheath, London; husband of Marion Ethel Ward, of 16, Alexandra Court, Queen's Gate, Kensington, London Thiepval Memorial

Webster 3322 Pte Cyril Victor att. from 2/2nd London Regt. Aged 18 Son of Mr J W Webster of 35A, Charlwood St., Pimlico, London Thiepval Memorial

Wright 1752 Rfn. Arthur Frederick Hebuterne Military Cemetery IV. B. 9.

2nd July 1916

Batter 4232 Rfn. Frank Edwin Aged 19 Son of Frank Charles and Mary Batter, of 1C, Grand Parade, Harringay, London. Warlincourt Halte British Cemetery, Saulty II. D. 7.

Kirkman 4399 Rfn. Henry James Warlincourt Halte British Cemetery, Saulty II. D. 4.

3rd July 1916

Lapham 3886 L/Cpl. James Candy Aged 25 Son of Tom Edwin and Martha Lapham, of 1, Albany Terrace, Trowbridge Rd., Bradford-on-Avon, Wilts. Native of Dinder, Wells, Somerset Warlincourt Halte British Cemetery, Saulty II. D. 13

Taylor 2653 L/Cpl. Francis James Aged 23 Son of Mr. and Mrs James B. Taylor, of 3, Station Rd., Tadcaster, Yorks Couin British Cemetery II. A. 6.

Ward 1921 Rfn. Arthur In German hands Bihucourt Communal Cemetery 1

8th July 1916

Mathie 3882 Rfn. Frederick Wigram Aged 33 Son of James and Elizabeth Mathie Le Treport Military Cemetery Plot 2. Row M. Grave 4A

10th July 1916

Barnett 4349 Rfn. William George Aged 26 Eldest son of George and Charlotte Barnett, of Windsor Le Treport Military Cemetery Plot 2. Row N. Grave 3C

15th July 1916

Cox 3392 Rfn. Douglas Son of Mrs Cox of 69, Gallmoor Gardens, Wimbledon In German hands Caudry Old Communal Cemetery B. 8.

Martin 3991 Rfn. Herbert Elton Aged 25 Son of Edward and Susan Martin, of Cyrus St, Clerkenwell; husband of Laura Martin, of 49, Clerkenwell Green, London (A/C Screen Wall) City of London Cemetery 339. 42489

Turnham 2054 Rfn. William Thomas Aged 21 Son of Robert and Emily Turnham, of 23, Beresford Rd., Hornsey, London Etretat Churchyard II. D. 3A

17th July 1916

Studd 4499 Rfn. Charles Henry Aged 20 Son of Edward and Ada Ruth Studd, of 67, St. James's Rd., Bermondsey, London. In German hands Douchy-Les-Ayette British Cemetery III. G. 3

1/13TH LONDON REGIMENT (PRINCESS LOUISE'S KENSINGTON)
All casualties listed as Thiepval Memorial are on Pier and Face 9 D, 9 C, 13 C and 12 C
SNIPERS

Law 3554 Pte Percival Charles Aged 27 Son of Emily Law of 86, Wellmeadow Rd., Catford, London & the late Charles Law Thiepval Memorial

BOMBERS

Reader 1617 Pte Edwin Frederick Aged 25 Son of Mrs Annie Reader of 35, Hurley Rd., Lower Kennington Lane, London, formerly 66, Redcross Street, Borough, London. Thiepval Memorial

A COMPANY

Battiscombe 2498 L/Cpl. Cyril Guy Aged 32 Son of the Rev. William C & Mrs Battiscombe, late of Warehorne Rectory, Ashford, Kent Thiepval Memorial

Mackenzie 2nd Lt. Noel Olliffe Compton Son of W O C Mackenzie & Geraldine Oliffe Augusta Mackenzie of 36 Park Village East, Regent's Park, NW1. Thiepval Memorial

No. 3 Platoon

Ferris 2744 Pte Arthur Charles att. from 2/1st London Regt. Aged 20 Son of Mr & Mrs C W Ferris of 16, Midland Brent Terrace, Cricklewood, London Gommecourt British Cemetery No. 2, II. D. 15

No. 4 Platoon

Sarle 2590 L/Cpl. Richard Albert att. from 1/4th London Regt. Brother of Mrs Pring of 40, Church Road, Tottenham Thiepval Memorial

Sheldrake 4446 Pte Hugh Albert Aged 23 Son of Charles Sheldrake of 18, Oaklands Grove, Shepherd's Bush, London. Thiepval Memorial

B COMPANY

Burns 4434 Pte Albert Victor Aged 23 Son of the late Mr & Mrs F W Burns of 3, Esmond Rd., Kilburn, London. Thiepval Memorial

No. 5 Platoon

Wilson 4219 Pte Montague James Thiepval Memorial

No. 8 Platoon

Price 4122 Pte Thomas Son of Mrs Price of 35, Seaton Street, King's Road, Chelsea Thiepval Memorial

C COMPANY

Ware Capt. Francis Henry Single & lived at 5, The Pryors, East Heath Road, Hampstead. Thiepval Memorial

No. 9 Platoon

Alexander 4115 Pte Thomas William Son of Mrs Alexander, 251, Portnall Road, Paddington Thiepval Memorial

Skinner 2139 Pte Sidney Thiepval Memorial

No. 11 Platoon

Newland 3051 Pte Albert att. from 2/1st London Regt. Husband of Mrs A Newland of 163, Shakespeare Crescent, East Ham Thiepval Memorial

No. 12 Platoon

Brougham 4303 Pte Ernest Arthur Aged 18 Son of Arthur & Alice Brougham of 5, Colonial Avenue, Whitton, Twickenham, Middx Thiepval Memorial

D COMPANY

Mager 2nd Lt. William George Hebuterne Military Cemetery IV. M. 51.

Pilgrim 2nd Lt. Henry Bastick Aged 22 and single, he was the son of Mrs Fanny Pilgrim of 277 Norwood Road, SE24 and Albert Ezra Pilgrim. He is buried in Hebuterne Military Cemetery, grave IV.B.14

Smith 4198 Pte Alfred George Aged 32 Son of Mrs Smith of 26, Lochaline Street, Fulham Palace Road, Hammersmith, husband of Elizabeth Smith of 24, Hampden St., Harrow Rd., Paddington, London Hebuterne Military Cemetery IV. M. 60.

No. 13 Platoon

Power 2933 Pte Ernest att. from 2/1st London Regt. Aged 19 Son of Enoch John & Elizabeth Ann Power of 75, Tynemouth Rd., South Tottenham, London Thiepval Memorial

No. 16 Platoon

Sharp 2820 Pte John George att. from 2/1st London Regt. Thiepval Memorial

Company and Platoon not known

Aikman 1227 Sgt. Thomas Hebuterne Military Cemetery IV. M. 45.

Baker 4320 L/Cpl. Edward Thomas Thiepval Memorial

Baldwin 4146 Pte Charles Thiepval Memorial

Beebee 1843 L/Cpl. Frank Alfred Aged 24 Son of the late John Beebee & of Sarah Beebee of 5, Nightingale Rd., Harlesden, London. Thiepval Memorial

Blows 1754 Pte Norman Woodgate Joseph Aged 21 Son of Arthur & Kate Mabel Blows of 398A, Richmond Rd., Twickenham, Middx. Native of Richmond, Surrey. Hebuterne Military Cemetery IV. M. 11.

Boadle 4625 Pte Frank Chambers Thiepval Memorial

Braddon 2027 Pte William Claude Thiepval Memorial

Brook 1375 L/Cpl. Arthur Thiepval Memorial

Brown 1512 Pte Thomas Henry Aged 20 Son of George Brown of 30, Herries St., Queen's Park, Paddington, London. Thiepval Memorial

Bryant 2467 Pte Charles Marrable Aged 22 Son of Charles & Kate Bryant of 7, Windmill Rd., Brentford, Middx. Thiepval Memorial

Budge 3428 Pte Arthur George Aged 21 Son of John & Harriett Budge of 30, Crabtree Lane, Fulham, London. Thiepval Memorial

Butterworth 3598 Pte William Edward Aged 21 Son of Mr & Mrs R Butterworth of 64, Lansdowne Rd., Dalston, London. Thiepval Memorial

Clarke 3404 Pte George Kenneth Bruce Aged 19 Son of George Bruce Clarke & Blanche Clarke of 14, Mercer Row, Louth, Lincs. Warlincourt Halte British Cemetery II. D. 14.

Cozens 3883 L/Cpl. Walter Ernest Thiepval Memorial

Crutchley 4355 Pte Edgar Aged 18 Son of Joseph & Emily Crutchley of 97, Malvern Rd., West Kilburn, London. Hebuterne Military Cemetery IV. M. 49

Dunn 4411 Pte Ernest James Hebuterne Military Cemetery IV. M. 14.

Dunt 4048 Pte Charles Robert Aged 28 Son of Charles & Alice Emily Dunt of Shotesham, Norwich. Native of West Kensington, London. Hebuterne Military Cemetery IV. E. 6

Feakes 4415 Pte Arthur Sidney Hebuterne Military Cemetery IV. M. 17.

Geeson 3470 Pte Frank Leonard Aged 22 Son of Frank & Clara Beatrice Geeson of Penge Villa, St. Ives, Hunts. Enlisted, 1914. An employee of Messrs. Hitchcock Williams of St. Paul's Churchyard, London. Thiepval Memorial

Green 4294 Pte Charles Thiepval Memorial

Green 3983 Pte James Hebuterne Military Cemetery IV. M. 37.

Gubbins 4167 Pte Walter Charles Aged 19 Son of Charles & Alice Gubbins of 25, Henry St., Vauxhall, London. Thiepval Memorial

Ham 2077 Cpl. Philip James Aged 25 Son of George Ham of 40, Fabian Rd., Fulham, London, & the late Emma Ham Thiepval Memorial

Harris 2105 Pte John William Thiepval Memorial

Ide 2409 Pte Frank Ernest Thiepval Memorial

Lewis 2101 Pte Albert Henry Lawrence Aged 21 Son of Albert Edward & Alice Louise Lewis of 33, Cedars Rd., Clapham Common, London. Thiepval Memorial

Lewis 4342 Pte Frederick Thiepval Memorial

Macey 1732 Pte Harold Thiepval Memorial

Markwell 1527 Pte Reginald Walton Aged 24 Son of Arthur & Amy Markwell of 50, Park Rd., Chiswick, London Thiepval Memorial

Owen 1607 Cpl. Alfred Aged 22 Son of Thomas & Emma Owen of 11, Burton Rd., Brixton, London Thiepval Memorial

Parslow 4174 Pte James Thiepval Memorial

Perrin 3852 Pte Horace Reginald Thiepval Memorial

Plummer 4148 Pte George Robert Thiepval Memorial

Price 4227 L/Cpl. Sidney Newcomb Aged 23 Son of Amelia Annie Price of 380, High Rd., Chiswick, London, & the late John William Price. Hebuterne Military Cemetery IV. M. 46.

Prime 4262 Pte William Thiepval Memorial

Rogers 4200 Pte Harold Augustus Aged 22 Son of Alfred & Elizabeth Rogers. of 25, Aldridge Rd Villas, Notting Hill, London. Thiepval Memorial

Sach 2nd Lt. Charles Burleigh Aged 19 Son of Charles Frederick & Emily Hannah Sach of 155, Victoria St., Westminster, London. Thiepval Memorial

Scull 1502 Cpl. Albert Hebuterne Military Cemetery IV. M. 27.

Spracklan 3458 Pte Reuben Henry Aged 21 Son of Henry & Charlotte Spracklan of 7, Harmood Place, Chalk Farm, London. Thiepval Memorial

Stonestreet 3460 Pte Alfred John Aged 22 Son of Benjamin John & Sarah Emily Stonestreet of Myrtle Cottage, High Rd., Southall, Middx. Couin British Cemetery I. B. 19.

Sully 2045 Pte Richard Arnold Aged 22 Son of Gilbert & Lilian Sully of 1, Bank Place, Falmouth, formerly of 57, St Mary's Grove, Chiswick Born at Cheltenham. Hebuterne Military Cemetery IV. B. 5.

Trice 2939 Pte Frederick Aged 19 Son of William & Esther Trice of 18, Glenwood Rd., Catford, London. Hebuterne Military Cemetery IV. M. 52

Ward 4332 Pte Stanley Son of Mr F Ward of 31, Bravington Rd., Maida Hill, London, Couin British Cemetery W.G. I. B. 14

Warford 3880 Pte Reginald George Charles Aged 17 Son of George William & May Jane Warford of 16, Stratford Rd., Kensington, London. Thiepval Memorial

3rd July 1916

Monk 4316 Pte Henry Alfred Aged 19 Son of Frederick William & Sarah Ann Monk; of 4, Martin St., North Kensington, London. Warlincourt Halte British Cemetery II. D. 11

7th July 1916

Oliver 4517 Pte George William Aged 42 Son of Mrs G R Oliver of 26, Sussex St., Pimlico, London. In German hands Caudry Old Communal Cemetery B. 4.

8th July 1916

Tibble 2103 Pte James Son of James & Harriet Tibble of Onslow Dwellings, Chelsea, London Abbeville Communal Cemetery V. A. 5

9th July 1916

Anderson 3873 Pte Ernest Charles Epsom Cemetery K. 101

12th July 1916

Mexson 4527 Pte Ronald Le Treport Military Cemetery Plot 2. Row L. Grave 4c

1/14TH LONDON REGIMENT (LONDON SCOTTISH)

All casualties listed as Thiepval Memorial are on Pier and Face 9 C and 13 C

SIGNAL SECTION

Weatherston 4922 Pte Sidney Bowler Aged 25 Son of John Thomas & Clara Weatherston of 78, Sandmere Rd., Bedford Rd., Clapham, London. Enlisted March, 1915. A Bank Clerk Thiepval Memorial

A COMPANY

Brown 2nd Lt. Ralph Adair Aged 21 Son of George T & Mary A Brown of Manor Hurst Palmerston Rd., Bowes Park, London. Thiepval Memorial

No. 1 Platoon

Dutch 6498 Pte Walter Sharp Thiepval Memorial

Whitlock 6500 Pte Sidney Charles Aged 20 Son of Sidney Herbert & Annie Elizabeth Whitlock of Wood Vale, Forest Hill, London, formerly of 24, Woolstone Road, Catford Thiepval Memorial

No. 2 Platoon

Bourchier 5296 Pte Claude Walter Thiepval Memorial

Hamilton 6280 Pte Murray Aged 17 Son of Frederick William & Jane Hamilton of 'Stonehaven', Orchard Way, Wickham Rd., Shirley, Surrey, formerly of 183, Manwood Road, Crofton Park, London SE Thiepval Memorial

Harris 5271 Pte Ernest Aged 21 Son of Mrs Grace Iddiols of 71, Becket House, Great Dover St., Borough, London. Thiepval Memorial

Johnston 3804 Pte Herbert Victor Thiepval Memorial

Nicholson 1601 Pte Phillip Henry Hamling Thiepval Memorial

Smith 5001 Pte Ernest James Aged 23 Son of Mr W C & Mrs S S Smith of 47, Grosvenor Rd., Westminster, London Thiepval Memorial

No. 3 Platoon

Gibbens 4959 Pte Henry Robert Thiepval Memorial

McGregor 5460 Pte Thomas William Thiepval Memorial

Senior 5603 Pte Albert Thiepval Memorial

No. 4 Platoon

Smith 4660 Pte Anthony Spurgeon Aged 23 Son of George Anthony Smith of 17, Benefield Rd., Oundle, Northants, & the late Jane Smith, previously of Inkerman West Street, Oundle Thiepval Memorial

LEWIS GUN SECTION

Howse 5094 Pte Frank Aged 24 Son of John & Ann Howse of The Entrance Lodge, Mostyn Rd., Merton Park, London Thiepval Memorial

B COMPANY

Coxon 2nd Lt. Herbert Archibald Aged 32 Thiepval Memorial

Lindsay Maj. Francis Howard Aged 40 Son of W A Lindsay Esq, K.C., Clarenceux King of Arms, & Lady Harriet Lindsay; husband of Helen Margaret Lindsay of 7, Emperor's Gate, South Kensington, London Thiepval Memorial

Morrison 6612 Pte James Gommecourt British Cemetery No. 2, V. A. I.

No. 5 Platoon

Curtis 6432 Pte Henry James Aged 19 Son of Mrs Sarah Ann Curtis of 106, Brunswick Rd., Poplar, London Thiepval Memorial

McKichan 5120 Pte Allan Archibald Thiepval Memorial

No. 6 Platoon

Bailey 3157 Pte William Lionel Aged 21 Son of Arthur John & Frances Bailey of 2, Christchurch Avenue, Teddington, Middx. Gommecourt British Cemetery No. 2, II. D. 21.

Black 5101 Pte George Felix Aged 24 Son of George Gow Black & Florence Marie Black of 31, Rodenhurst Rd., Clapham Park, London. Thiepval Memorial

Busby 6921 Pte Harold Wycliffe Camden Brother of Miss E O Busby of 14, Feversham Crescent, York Thiepval Memorial

Dicks 3382 Cpl. Thomas Ernest Aged 21 Son of Thomas Nelson Dicks & Florence Harriet Dicks of 59, Leppoc Rd., Clapham Park. London. Thiepval Memorial

Hall 4869 Pte William Spencer Aged 24 Son of the late William Carpenter Hall & Clara Maria Hall Thiepval Memorial

McLachlan 3766 Pte Alfred Devers Aged 18 Son of Charles Alexander & Lily Ann McLachlan of 29, Fairlawn Avenue, Chiswick, London Thiepval Memorial

Moxley 4745 Pte Gerald Archibald Charles Aged 22 Son of Gerald Douglas & Adelaide Moxley of 56, Beechcroft Rd., Upper Tooting, London; husband of Evelin Howles (formerly Moxley). A Clerk, London County Council Thiepval Memorial

Tanner 5103 Pte Cecil Allen Aged 23 Son of Mrs Caroline Tanner of 215, Kingston Rd., Merton Park, London Thiepval Memorial

No. 7 Platoon

Darling 1605 Pte George Aged 24 Son of Mrs J E Darling of 204, Shirland Rd., Paddington, London. Thiepval Memorial

McIntosh 5082 Pte Alexander William Son of Mrs McIntosh of 22, Woodbine Grove, Penge Thiepval Memorial

Mitchell 6617 Pte William James Son of Mrs Mitchell of 56, Ingelow Road, Queen's Road, Battersea Thiepval Memorial

No. 8 Platoon

Benbow 5566 Pte George Morris Aged 20 Son of William George & Elizabeth Jane Benbow of 5, Regent St., Bletchley, Bucks Thiepval Memorial

Burgess 5625 Pte Edgar Gommecourt British Cemetery No. 2, III. K. 10

Claypoole 5607 Pte Cyril George Stuart Aged 21 Son of George & Emily Claypoole of 20, Haven Bank, Boston, Lincs Thiepval Memorial

Clipstone 6200 Pte Frederick Aged 23 Son of John Clipstone of Great Oakley, Kettering, Northants. Gommecourt British Cemetery No. 2, II. D. 6

Collie 5637 Pte Alexander Aged 38 Son of Alexander Collie of Liverpool; husband of Beatrice C
E Collie of 9, Bishops Court, Bishops Avenue, East Finchley, London. Came from Honolulu,
Hawaiian Isles to enlist. Thiepval Memorial

Coutts 5645 Pte William Aged 34 Son of Francis & Elizabeth Coutts of 280, Great Western Rd.,
Aberdeen Thiepval Memorial

Curror 2nd Lt. William Edwin Forrest Gommecourt British Cemetery No. 2, V. C. I.

Douglas 511050 L/Cpl. Archibald Thiepval Memorial

Ferguson 3862 Sgt. Robert Aged 21 Son of Elizabeth Ferguson of 82K, Portland Place,
Marylebone, London, & the late James Tait Ferguson. A British volunteer from Latin America
Gommecourt British Cemetery No. 2, II. C. 16

Hance 6609 Pte Henry William Thiepval Memorial

Henderson 5193 Pte Percival Storey Aged 20 Son of Priscilla S. Henderson of Grange Gardens,
Cardiff, & the late R. S. Henderson Thiepval Memorial

Milne 5247 Pte John Leighton Thiepval Memorial

Moss 5369 Pte John Thomas Aged 19 Son of Herbert & Helen Moss of 5, Farcliffe Terrace,
Manningham, Bradford, Yorks, and Middlewich, Cheshire Thiepval Memorial

Pullen 5186 Pte Lewis Harold Thiepval Memorial

Sartain 5355 Pte John James Aged 24 Son of the late Edwin Davis Sartain & Rose Emma
Sartain Thiepval Memorial

Vernon 510722 Cpl. David John Aged 21 Son of Mrs Elizabeth Harris of Blacklands, Creetown,
Kirkcudbrightshire Thiepval Memorial

C COMPANY

Kerr 2nd Lt. Donald Aged 25 Son of James John & Anne Kerr of 140, Albert Rd., Crosshill,
Glasgow Thiepval Memorial

Mahoney 5022 Pte Joseph James Aged 28 Husband of Ethel Elizabeth Mahoney of 71,
Millbrook Rd., Brixton, London Thiepval Memorial

Mason 6471 Pte John Aged 20 Son of Mr & Mrs John Mason of Yarrow Cottage, Alva,
Clackmannanshire. Employee of National Bank of India, Bishopsgate, London Thiepval
Memorial

Milne 2360 Pte Campbell Aged 22 Son of Florence Charlotte Milne of 24, Dulwich Rd., Herne
Hill, London, & the late George Torrence Milne Thiepval Memorial

No. 9 Platoon

Askey 5500 Pte LeRoy Sidney Aged 21 Son of Esther Askey of 191, Hale End Rd.,
Walthamstow, Essex, & the late A. H. Askey. Thiepval Memorial

Morgan 5195 Pte Frederick Charles Thiepval Memorial

Roberts 3706 L/Cpl. George Albert Victor Son of Mrs Emily Roberts of 246, Stanstead Rd.,
Forest Hill, London Thiepval Memorial

Tomasson 5734 Pte Herbert Hugh Aged 32 Son of Mrs Hannah Tomasson of 20, Rutland
Park, Sheffield Thiepval Memorial

Watson 3059 L/Cpl. Francis Edward Aged 21 Son of Mr & Mrs James Watson of 51, Chestnut
Rd., West Norwood; husband of Ethel Ida Watson of 128A, Sternhold Avenue, Streatham Hill,
London. Thiepval Memorial

No. 10 Platoon

Wallis 5585 Pte Ernest Player Thiepval Memorial

No. 11 Platoon

Dunn 3721 Cpl. William Simpson Aged 21 Son of William & Harriett S Dunn of 35, St. Albans
St., Kennington Rd., Lambeth. London. Thiepval Memorial

Harwood 5425 Pte Benjamin Son of Mr B Harwood of 116, Landcroft Road, East Dulwich
Thiepval Memorial

Hay 5397 Pte David Telfer Aged 20 Son of William John & Mary Hay of 38, Church Lane,
Hornsey, London Thiepval Memorial

Knight 4747 Pte William Aged 25 Son of Mrs Mary Knight of 48, New St., Newport, Isle of
Wight Thiepval Memorial

Larkin 4664 Pte Frederick Edward Aged 21 Son of Frederick & Lavinia Ellen Larkin of 43,
Manor Park Rd., Harlesden, London Thiepval Memorial

Southgate 5313 Pte Wilfrid Reginald Aged 20 Son of Arthur M & Caroline Southgate of 166,
Barry Rd., East Dulwich, London Gommecourt British Cemetery No. 2, II. D. 3

Thompson 5399 Pte Ernest Edward Son of Mr and Mrs Thompson of 'Hondene', Couldson,
Surrey Thiepval Memorial

No. 12 Platoon

Atter 5301 Pte Harry John Aged 19 Son of Alice Atter of 118, Manor Grove, Richmond, Surrey, & the late Robert Atter. Thiepval Memorial

Carter 5419 Pte Ivor George Thiepval Memorial

Panter 5311 Pte Gordon Malcolm Aged 19 Son of Albert E & Ada Elizabeth Panter of 2, Glebeland, Hatfield, Herts Thiepval Memorial

Shuker 6248 Pte Douglas Aged 20 Son of John Frederick & Hannah Shuker of Woodside, Audlem, Cheshire Gommecourt British Cemetery No. 2, II. K. 3

Wills 6029 Pte Charles Walter Thiepval Memorial

LEWIS GUN TEAM

Brewster 5046 Pte Harry Edward Thiepval Memorial

Broadway 5328 Pte Edward William Albert Thiepval Memorial

Carr 3154 Sgt. George Henry Aged 26 Son of Henry Carr of 64, Medcalf Rd., Enfield Lock, Middx., & Sarah Jane Carr (Stepmother). Thiepval Memorial

Haywood 4952 Pte Ernest Henry Villiers Aged 18 Son of Tom & Lizzie Haywood of Ropery House, Wivenhoe Cross, Colchester Thiepval Memorial

Norton 3102 Pte George Charles Hebuterne Military Cemetery III. H. 2

Prior 5298 Pte Ernest Cecil Stephen Aged 20 Son of William Henry & Susannah Prior of 3, May Terrace, Sandgate, Kent Thiepval Memorial

Smith 5071 Pte Frederick James Aged 20 Son of Mrs A Wellesley Smith of 'Jhansi', Oxford, Rd., Carshalton, Surrey Thiepval Memorial

Tough 5014 L/Cpl. Robert Henry Aged 24 Son of Robert & Elizabeth Tough of 259, Union St., Aberdeen Thiepval Memorial

D COMPANY

Brown-Constable Lt. John Cecil Aged 26 Son of the Rev. Albert Edward & Clara Emily Brown Constable of "Greet," Mottingham, London. Gommecourt British Cemetery No. 2, II. G. 26 *19ᵗʰ July 1916*

Hunter 2ⁿᵈ Lt. Percy Talbot Lungley Aged 23 Son of William Pettingell Hunter & Elizabeth Hunter of Hammersmith, London. Barrister-at-Law. Etaples Military Cemetery I. B. 38.

No. 13 Platoon

Andrews 8138 Pte Raymond Gibson Aged 23 Son of Gibson Andrews of 3, High St., Woburn, Beds., & the late Emma Andrews. Thiepval Memorial

Craigie 4881 Pte James Alexander Aged 23 Son of William & Isabella Craigie of 34, Monteagle Avenue, Barking, Essex. Born at Kirkwall, Orkney Gommecourt British Cemetery No. 2, V C 19

Goates 6566 Pte Sydney Son of Mrs Goates of Mill Place, Brigg, Lincs Thiepval Memorial

Kitson 2640 Cpl. Luther Brother of Mrs Elizabeth McGillivray of Strathnairn, Clarkston, Glasgow Thiepval Memorial

Macbeth 4311 Pte Hubert Sidney Son of Mrs Macbeth of 26, Beecholme Road, Upper Clapton, London Thiepval Memorial

Stewart 5777 Pte William Barclay Thiepval Memorial *21ˢᵗ July 1916*

Heywood 6221 Pte Reginald Charles In German hands St. Souplet British Cemetery III AA 10.

No. 14 Platoon

Charlton 5504 Pte Alfred William George Aged 20 Son of George Charlton of 15, Hercules Rd., Holloway, London. Gommecourt British Cemetery No. 2, II. D. 4

Freeman 6211 Pte Hubert Harold Son of Mrs Freeman of 97, Cleveland Street, Great Portland Street, London W Thiepval Memorial

Newham 3764 Pte William John Aged 29 Son of Robert & Emma Newham of 142, Ramsden Rd., Balham, London Thiepval Memorial

No. 15 Platoon

Smith 5584 Pte Thomas Henry Thiepval Memorial

ATTACHED TO 168ᵀᴴ MACHINE GUN COMPANY

North 3984 Pte Lidell Peverley Gommecourt British Cemetery No. 2, II. D. 7

Robertson 5124 Pte James Richard Alan Aged 27 Only son of Louise B. Robertson & the late James Matheson Robertson Thiepval Memorial

Thomson Capt. Frederick Stanley Aged 34 Son of the late W E S Thomson (Admiralty Registry and Treasury). A Civil Servant. (Admiralty Registry). Thiepval Memorial

Company and Platoon not known

Adams 6454 Pte Richard Aged 21 Son of William & Katherine Adams of 10, Radstock St., Battersea, London. Bienvillers Military Cemetery XXI. J. 11.

Airey 8109 Pte Thomas Arthur Aged 21 Son of Thomas & Fanny Airey of Moorthwaite, Barbon, Westmorland Thiepval Memorial

Alderton 4949 Pte Arthur Aged 34 Son of James & Elizabeth Alderton of 18, Gibbon Rd., Kingston, Surrey Hebuterne Military Cemetery IV. M. 48

Allan 5168 L/Cpl. Alfred John Rettie Aged 27 Son of William & B C Allan (nee Rettie) of 11, Dickens St., Port Elizabeth, South Africa. Thiepval Memorial

Anderson 4608 Pte Bertie George Glover Aged 18 Son of Charles & Lizzie Anderson of The Nest, North Stoke, Wallingford, Berks. Thiepval Memorial

Atkin 6666 Pte Mark Aged 18 Son of Amos & Jane Elizabeth Atkin of West Cliffe Lodge, Denby Dale, Huddersfield. Thiepval Memorial

Bain 3548 Cpl. William Aged 25 Son of J P Bain of 'Ortinola', Maracas Valley, St. Joseph, Trinidad, British West Indies, & the late Mrs. M. R. F. Bain. Thiepval Memorial

Barrie 5067 Cpl. Charles David Ogilvie Aged 35 Son of Alexander Ogilvy Barrie & Mary Barrie of Strathview, Kirriemuir, Forfarshire; husband of Mary Letitia Barrie of 87, Lonsdale Rd., Barnes, London. Thiepval Memorial

Barton 5128 Pte Arthur Keith Aged 20 Son of Lt. Col. A E Barton of Maison Manera, Menton Garavan, Alpes-Maritimes, France. Thiepval Memorial

Beeching 5415 Pte Douglas Hampden Aged 20 Son of Walter & Clara Maude Beeching of 'Home', Connaught Avenue, Chingford, London. Thiepval Memorial

Benstead 5592 Pte John William Aged 26 Son of Arthur John & Elizabeth Eleanor Benstead of 51, Argyle Rd., Brighton Gommecourt British Cemetery No. 2, III. A. 17

Blaver 6455 Pte Joseph Henry Aged 19 Son of William Edward & Selina Blaver of 51, Kirkham St., Plumstead, London. Thiepval Memorial

Bradley 5322 L/Cpl. John Elder Gommecourt British Cemetery No. 2, III. K. 8.

Bremner 6547 Pte Huntley William Bruce Aged 35 Son of the late William Bremner & of Diana H. Bremner of 3, Kents Terrace, Torquay, Devon. Thiepval Memorial

Brett 5594 Pte George Webster Aged 22 Son of Adelaide Elizabeth Brett of The Tent, Imperial Rd., Feltham, Middx., & the late George Webster Brett. Thiepval Memorial

Briggs 4604 Cpl. Robert Cecil Thiepval Memorial

Bryden 5644 Pte Richard Edgar Cecil Thiepval Memorial

Budd 5202 Pte Frederick Charles Aged 33 Son of James & Mary Anne Louisa Budd Thiepval Memorial

Campbell 3425 L/Cpl. Andrew Craig Thiepval Memorial

Carlton 6501 Pte Edwin Arthur Aged 21 Son of Edwin Arthur & Caroline Carlton of 12, Oakwood Lane, Roundhay, Leeds Gommecourt British Cemetery No. 2, II. D. 26

Charlton 4281 L/Cpl. Alfred Douglas Aged 19 Son of Frank & Hannah M. Charlton of 246, North Main St., Riverside, California, U.S.A. Thiepval Memorial

Clappen 2688 Pte Percival George Aged 18 Son of Edward Smith Clappen & Florence May Clappen of 'Westholme', The Cliffs, Westcliff-on-Sea, Essex. Enlisted Sept., 1914. Thiepval Memorial

Clark 2604 L/Cpl. William George Aged 22 Son of George Clark of 56, Stockwell Park Rd., Stockwell, London. Thiepval Memorial

Clark 4776 Pte William Wallace Thiepval Memorial

Cleghorn 6630 Pte Thomas Arthur Aged 26 Son of the late George & Elizabeth Davidson Cleghorn. Curate at St. David'S, Scotstoun, Glasgow. Thiepval Memorial

Coleman 5248 Pte Bert Thiepval Memorial

Cooper 5169 Pte Henry Albert Gommecourt British Cemetery No. 2, VII. A. 19

Day 4119 Pte George Edward Thiepval Memorial

Dent-Young 4121 Pte Julius Henry Aged 20 Son of Jules & May Dent-Young of 55, Lyncombe Hill, Bath Thiepval Memorial

Digby 4856 Pte Edward Thiepval Memorial

Dodd 5580 Pte Percy Edward Aged 23 Son of William & Lois Ellen Dodd of 24, Clarence Place, Gravesend, Kent Thiepval Memorial

Downs 6177 Pte Charles William Thiepval Memorial

Drane 6769 Pte Frank Charles Williams Thiepval Memorial

Dungey 5446 Pte William Aged 19 Son of Mr W H & Mrs E R Dungey of 65, St. Mary's Rd., Faversham, Kent Thiepval Memorial

Eckford 5337 Pte Harold John Wynn Aged 22 Son of Edwin & Margaret Elizabeth Eckford of 39, Foulser Rd., Tooting, London Thiepval Memorial

Fieldgate 5541 Pte Bernard Samuel Gommecourt British Cemetery No. 2, V. C. 18

Filshie 4940 Pte Robert Malcolm Thiepval Memorial
Findlay 5609 Pte Malcolm Hebuterne Military Cemetery IV. M. 4
Fluck 6115 Pte Clissold Graham Aged 27 Son of Alice Jane Frederica Fluck of 22, Conway Rd., Southgate, London & the late Theodore Graham Fluck. Gommecourt British Cemetery No. 2, II. J. 7
Gaze 3516 Sgt. Harold Stanley Thiepval Memorial
Gepp 6496 Pte Charles Thiepval Memorial
Gibson 5493 Pte James McLintock Aged 21 Son of Dr & Mrs Gibson Thiepval Memorial
Giles 5032 L/Cpl. Sidney Herbert Aged 22 Son of Herbert & Martha Giles of 40, Fawnbrake Avenue, Herne Hill, London. Thiepval Memorial
Graham 4815 Pte George Hugh Thiepval Memorial
Gravestock 6505 Pte William Aged 24 Son of Samuel & Lizzie Emma Gravestock of 146, Wellesley Rd., High Rd., Chiswick, London. Native of Fulham, London. Hebuterne Military Cemetery III. G. 6
Gray 5906 Pte Thomas Dyet Thiepval Memorial
Gurney 4611 Sgt. Edward Ernest Thiepval Memorial
Hamilton 1968 C.S.M. James Leckie Aged 20 Son of Matthew & Mary Hamilton of 24, Blackhall St., Paisley Thiepval Memorial
Hammett 3351 L/Cpl. James McDonald Bernard Thiepval Memorial
Harper 4528 L/Cpl. Harold Sanders Aged 24 Son of Albert & Emily Louisa Harper of 9, St. Mary's St., Bedford. Thiepval Memorial
Harrington 5458 Pte William Charles Gommecourt British Cemetery No. 2, II. D. 2
Hayter 5704 Pte Alfred Thomas Aged 19 Son of Tom & Ellen Hayter of Sway Rd., Brockenhurst, Hants Gommecourt British Cemetery No. 2, III. K. 7
Heath 5653 Pte Harold Griffin Thiepval Memorial
Hellyer 4960 L/Cpl. Albert Edward Aged 19 Son of Albert Edward & Eliza Jane Hellyer of 30, Dumont Rd., Stoke Newington, London. Thiepval Memorial
Hepburn 4030 Pte James Douglas Thiepval Memorial
Herring 6615 Pte John Henry Aged 21 Son of Mr H L & Mrs E J Herring of 44, Wellesley Rd., Gunnersbury, London Gommecourt British Cemetery No. 2, V. C. 5
Hoare 5617 Pte Leonard William Aged 23 Son of Ada Hoare of 22, Hercules Rd., Holloway, London, & the late Henry Stovell Hoare Hebuterne Military Cemetery IV. J. 10
Horsman 7732 Pte Thomas Herbert Johnstone Aged 19 Son of Alfred Herbert & Jane Frances Buchanan Horsman of The Bungalow, Condette, Pas-de-Calais, France Thiepval Memorial
Horspool 51052 L/Cpl. Henry James Aged 22 Son of Mr J R M & Mrs A I Horspool of 70, Truro Rd., Wood Green, London Thiepval Memorial
Horton 5320 Pte Ernest Claude Aged 39 Son of the Rev. E V Horton of Bude, Cornwall; husband of Adele Horton of 40, Norfolk Rd., Brighton Thiepval Memorial
Hunter 5444 Pte Alfred Aged 27 Son of Charles & the late Jemima Hunter; husband of Lillian Marion Hunter of The Firs, Lee Mill Bridge, Ivybridge, Devon Thiepval Memorial
Isaacs 5835 Pte Alexander Thiepval Memorial
Jackson 5384 Pte William Ernest Aged 20 Son of the late William H. & Annie Jackson Gommecourt British Cemetery No. 2, V. C. 4
Johnston 6224 Pte Alexander Davidson Aged 33 Son of Alexander Davidson Johnston of 'Braeside', 16, Urfa Terrace, South Shields. An employee of Henry Simons Ltd., Manchester Gommecourt British Cemetery No. 2, II. B. 24
Key 6535 Pte William Wilson Thiepval Memorial
Lambton 5572 Pte George Edward In German hands London Cemetery and Extension, Longueval 10.J.47
Lane 5990 Pte Alexander Henry Thiepval Memorial
Latham 3286 Sgt. Carl Stanley Thiepval Memorial
Lawrence 5774 Pte Reginald Thomas Gommecourt Wood New Cemetery, Foncquevillers IV. B. 15
Leggat 4946 L/Sgt. Robert Aged 28 Son of James Leggat of 'Duncarnock', Dumbreck, Glasgow. Thiepval Memorial
Lepper 5257 Pte Charles Thiepval Memorial
Lord 5436 Pte Joseph Toby Not found on CWGC
Lowe 5428 Pte Harry Edward Aged 20 Son of Mrs Alice A Lowe of 63, Nelson Square, Blackfriars Rd., Southwark, London Couin British Cemetery I. B. 15

Macdonald 2310 Cpl. Alexander Aged 29 Son of Mrs Ann Macdonald of 'Rockhill', Kenmore Rd., Aberfeldy, Perthshire. Thiepval Memorial

Macfarlane 6449 Pte George Thiepval Memorial

Maclean 4343 Sgt. Alexander Aged 34 Son of Mrs F Maclean of 32, Blackford Avenue, Edinburgh Thiepval Memorial

Manson 6492 Pte William Braithwaite Aged 20 Son of William & Mabel Manson of Sydney, New South Wales, Australia Thiepval Memorial

Maplesden 5175 Pte George Richard Aged 19 Son of Charles & Ellen Maplesden of 20, Brigden St., Brighton Thiepval Memorial

Marlow 3947 L/Cpl. Sidney John Thiepval Memorial

Marshall 6527 Pte Sidney Thiepval Memorial

Mather 5241 Pte Myles William Walker Thiepval Memorial

McMillan 5133 L/Cpl. Daniel George Aged 24 Son of Alexander & Margaret McMillan of East London, Cape Province, South Africa Gommecourt Wood New Cemetery, Foncquevillers III B 4

Metherell 5432 Pte Charles Aged 34 Son of the late Mr & Mrs J Metherell Thiepval Memorial

Michie 5110 L/Cpl. Harry Duncan Aged 31 Son of the late James Clark Michie & Mary Kilgour Thomson Michie Thiepval Memorial

Miller 3090 Pte Frederick John Bursey Aged 20 Son of Mabel Miller of 60, Fillebrook Rd., Leytonstone, London, & the late Fredric William Miller Thiepval Memorial

Miller 5850 Pte John Philip Aged 36 Brother of Mrs J A P Moncur of 28, Baronscourt Terrace, Edinburgh Thiepval Memorial

Miller 5487 Pte Leslie Austin Aged 25 Son of the late Mr C B Miller of Graaff-Reinet, Cape Province, South Africa Hebuterne Military Cemetery III. G. 2

Murdoch 5612 Pte Herbert Muir Aged 30 Son of George J Murdoch; husband of Florence E. Murdoch of 29, Richmond Terrace, Clifton, Bristol. Born in Scotland Gommecourt British Cemetery No. 2, II. D. 17

Nethercott 6483 Pte Walter Jacob Aged 27 Son of William Nethercott of 24, Alpha St., Heavitree, Exeter; husband of R. L. Nethercott of 87, Burrows Rd., Kensal Rise, London Thiepval Memorial

Noterman 6003 Pte Harold Aged 18 Son of Alphonse & Emma Noterman of 101, Frithville Gardens, Shepherds Bush, London Thiepval Memorial

Parker 5233 Pte Frederick Alfred Thiepval Memorial

Parker 1660 Pte Sidney Alexander Thiepval Memorial

Pinkerton 5665 Pte Stanley Aged 21 Son of Mr & Mrs Pinkerton of 1, Airedale Rd., Balham, London Thiepval Memorial

Popay 5666 Pte James Edwin Thiepval Memorial

Pratt 6306 Pte Ernest Alfred Thiepval Memorial

Pringle 5136 L/Sgt. Ronald Lockhart Rennie Aged 22 Son of Robert Henry & Enid Pringle of Clifton, Craig Rennie, Bedford, Cape Province, South Africa Thiepval Memorial

Ritchie 6643 Pte William Jacks Aged 28 Son of Mr & Mrs Alexander James Ritchie of Annavilla, Saltcoats, Ayrshire Thiepval Memorial

Saunders 4235 Pte William Kelly Thiepval Memorial

Savings (alias Smith) 5018 Pte Albert Aged 29 (Served as Smith). Son of Mrs Rose Helen Savings of Wytham, Oxford. Thiepval Memorial

Shaw 5479 Pte Edward Stuart Aged 20 Son of Edward John & Margaret Stuart Shaw. Born at Croydon Gommecourt British Cemetery No. 2, II. D. 25

Skerton 6557 Pte Fred George Aged 23 Son of Walter & Kate Skerton of Lypiatt Villa, Eastcombe, Stroud, Glos Thiepval Memorial

Stewart 6158 Pte Charles Edward Aged 21 Son of Mrs Sarah Jessie Stewart of 2, Devorgilla Terrace, Maxwelltown, Dumfries Thiepval Memorial

Stewart 2901 L/Cpl. Frank Aged 24 Son of Philip Christopher & Jane Stewart of 219, Felsham Rd., Putney, London. Gommecourt British Cemetery No. 2, II. D. 5

Stewart 5198 Pte James Todd Thiepval Memorial

Stroud 6253 Pte Thomas Benjamin Walker Aged 21 Son of Mr F J & Mrs E L Stroud of 32, Priory Rd., Tonbridge, Kent. Born at Woolwich, London Gommecourt British Cemetery No. 2, II. G. 24

Strutt 6579 Pte John Jordan Aged 22 Son of the late Mr & Mrs Strutt Thiepval Memorial

Studd 6160 Pte Archibald Charles Ellis Thiepval Memorial

Sutherland 3816 Pte Alexander Aged 24 Son of Christina Sutherland of Holmes Cottage, Rosemarkie, Fortrose, Ross-shire, & the late John Sutherland Thiepval Memorial

Sutherland 5255 Pte Peter Aged 24 Son of W J & Barbara Sutherland of 46, Milton St., Edinburgh Thiepval Memorial

Swaine 5870 Pte Bruce Thiepval Memorial

Sykes 40985 L/Cpl. Frederick Aged 25 Son of Samuel & Annie Sykes of 38, Maybank Rd., South Woodford, Essex. Thiepval Memorial

Theobald 4397 Pte William Oswald Thiepval Memorial

Thomson 6783 Pte James Wilfrid Aged 23 Son of James Yule Thomson & Annie Thomson of 12, Westborough Rd., Westcliff-on-Sea, Essex Thiepval Memorial

Torrance 3691 Sgt. Alexander Beggs Aged 26 Son of J Torrance of The Calcutta Inn, Whithorn, Wigtownshire, & the late Alexander Beggs Torrance Thiepval Memorial

Trench (alias Bloomfield) 5746 Pte Frederick Charles Aged 38 (served as Bloomfield). Son of Henry Bloomfield Trench of Huntington, Portarlington, King's Co.; husband of Catherine Anne Swetenham MacManaway (formerly Trench), M.B.E. of Greystone Hall, Limavady, Co. Londonderry, Ireland. Thiepval Memorial

Turner 6523 Pte John William Thiepval Memorial

Waddell 5153 Pte F Austine Hebuterne Military Cemetery IV. J. 9

Walker 4914 L/Cpl. Harold Duncan Aged 21 Son of the late James & Sarah Ann Walker Gommecourt British Cemetery No. 2, IV. A. 5

Walpole 5215 Pte Ronald Orford Spencer Aged 26 Son of Harry Orford Calibut Walpole (Solicitor) of The Croft, 63, Fornham Rd., Bury St. Edmund's, Suffolk, and the late Henrietta Walpole. An Insurance clerk Thiepval Memorial

Watson 5015 Pte Frank Alexander Thiepval Memorial

Watson 5673 Pte Frederick Thomas Aged 21 Son of Richard Charles & Rosetta Watson of 72, Whitefriars Avenue, Wealdstone, Harrow, Middx Thiepval Memorial

Watts 5011 Pte Stanley James Thiepval Memorial

Webb 6406 Pte Ernest Aged 27 Son of Frederick & Annie Elizabeth Webb of 19, Edith Rd., Oxford Thiepval Memorial

White 6874 Pte Richard Thiepval Memorial

Williams 4743 Pte Edwin Arthur Aged 23 Brother of Capt. W H Williams of 'Rockleaze', 100, Hampstead Rd., Brislington, Bristol Thiepval Memorial

Williams 4941 Pte George Henry Aged 21 Son of George Henry & Caroline Williams; husband of Amelia Williams of 14, Braintree St., Devonshire St., Mile End, London Thiepval Memorial

Williams 2490 L/Cpl. Harold Aged 23 Son of William Williams, a Chief Officer with the L.C.C. in the Botany Department at Avery Hill, and lived at 72 Davisee Road, Eltham. He was the brother of Alfred Williams, also educated at the Woolwich Polytechnic Secondary School, and killed in action in the war. Thiepval Memorial

Wilson 5480 Pte Archibald Thiepval Memorial

Wood 3173 L/Sgt. William Aged 24 Son of Richard & Jane Dawson Wood of 134, Onslow Drive, Glasgow. Thiepval Memorial

Yates 4777 Pte Arthur Edmund Aged 21 Son of Arthur Du Pasteur Yates & of Clare Yates of 595, Fairholme Rd., West Kensington, London Thiepval Memorial

Young 5804 Pte William Aged 32 Son of James & Isabel Young of Aberchirder, Banffshire; husband of Mary Adams (formerly Young) of 8, Church Rd., Battersea, London Gommecourt British Cemetery No. 2, II. J. 10

2nd July 1916

Buchanan 4313 Pte Robert Archibald Aged 22 Son of Robert & Allison Young Buchanan of 1057, Avenida Argentina, Antofagasta, Chile, South America. Native of Slamannan, Stirlingshire. Volunteered at Valparaiso, Chile 1914., Couin British Cemetery I. C. 1

Dunstone 6209 Pte Walter Frederick Aged 26 Son of Alfred William & Annie Elizabeth Dunstone of Hurstpierpoint, Sussex Doullens Communal Cemetery Extension No.1, IV.B.7

Parker 3409 L/Sgt. Herbert Octavius Gommecourt British Cemetery No. 2, II. C. 17.

4th July 1916

Nevison 4008 Pte George Robert Aged 23 Son of James & Margaret Jane Nevison of 140, Portnall Road, Paddington, London Le Treport Military Cemetery Plot 2 Row N Grave 1C

11th July 1916

Stacey 6252 Pte John James Aged 28 Son of William & Susannah Stacey of 61, Beaconsfield Rd., Croydon, Surrey. Born at Cobham, Surrey. Etretat Churchyard II. D. 8

18th July 1916

Wood 5182 Pte Donald Campbell Aged 21 Son of Walter Thomas & Mary Wood of 38, Buckleigh Rd., Streatham, London Netley Military Cemetery C.E. 1816

27th July 1916

Wainwright 6650 Pte Verner In German hands   Caudry Old Communal Cemetery A.3

1/16TH LONDON REGIMENT (QUEEN'S WESTMINSTER RIFLES)
All casualties listed as Thiepval Memorial are on Pier and Face 13 C
SIGNAL SECTION
Brocklesby 3138 Rfn. Vivian Geoffrey Pearson Aged 24   Son of the late Harry Pearson Brocklesby & Ada Clara Hope   Thiepval Memorial
Chamberlin 2040 Rfn. John   Thiepval Memorial
A COMPANY
Bodenham 3892 Rfn. John Edward Cyril   Thiepval Memorial
Bovill 2nd Lt. Edward Henry   Thiepval Memorial
Clarke 2185 Rfn. Albert Josiah Aged 28   Eldest son of Mr & Mrs Josiah Clarke of 2, Court Lane Gardens. Dulwich, London   Thiepval Memorial
Luscombe 2142 Rfn. Robert Aged 24   Son of William & Mary Irena Luscombe of 1, The Broadway, West Norwood, London   Gommecourt British Cemetery No. 2, I. B. 9
Minuto 4680 Rfn. Theodore Joseph Aged 23   Son of Theodore B & May E Minuto of 27, Hoppingwood Avenue, New Malden, Surrey   Thiepval Memorial
Swainson Capt. Francis Gibbon Aged 21   Younger son of Mrs E P Swainson of 'Rosebank', Knowsley, Prescot, Lancs, & the late G A Swainson   Thiepval Memorial
Paling 2828 Rfn. Allan Clayton Aged 22   Son of Francis & Margaret Paling of 142, Westbourne Grove, Notting Hill, London   Thiepval Memorial
Rush 2841 Cpl. Edgar Wilfred Aged 28   Son of the late James Walker Rush of 9, Silverdale Avenue, Westcliff-on-Sea, & Rose S. Rush (stepmother).   Thiepval Memorial
Wing 288 Sgt. Bertie   Gommecourt British Cemetery No. 2, III. J. 18
No. 1 Platoon
Bounds 3964 Rfn. Herbert Aged 28   Son of George & Louisa Bounds of 98, Alexandra Rd., St. Leonards, Sussex   Gommecourt British Cemetery No. 2, I. D. I
Cornish 3614 Rfn. Frederick Victor Aged 21   Son of Frederick J Cornish; husband of A E Cornish of 39, Coleridge Avenue, Manor Park, Essex   Gommecourt British Cemetery No. 2, I A I
Coventry 4590 Rfn. Victor Cornelius Aged 19   Son of George Herbert Coventry of 18, Essex Rd., Enfield, Middx., formerly of 627, High Road, Tottenham   Thiepval Memorial
Dornan 4392 Rfn. Harold Ernest Aged 20   Son of James & Annie Dornan of 'Gartmorn', Brighowgate, Grimsby   Thiepval Memorial
Hayes 4585 Rfn. Stanley Frank Aged 25   Son of Lindsay & Jane Hayes of 42, Aubert Park, Highbury, London.   Gommecourt British Cemetery No. 2, II. A. 24.
Lacey 4443 Rfn. Frederick Henry   Gommecourt British Cemetery No. 2, Sp. Mem. C. 2
Love 4234 Rfn. Vincent James Aged 28   Husband of Edith Florence Dew (formerly Love) of 26, Maison Dieu Rd., Dover, previously of 40, Granville Road, Wandsworth Common, London. Thiepval Memorial
Masters 2562 Rfn. Noel George Aged 20   Son of Mrs Masters of 51, Alderney Street, London SW   Gommecourt British Cemetery No. 2, II. B. 7
Miles 3875 Rfn. Albert Aged 31   Son of Enos Miles; husband of Sarah Harriet Miles   Gommecourt British Cemetery No. 2, III. F. I
Perry 4244 Rfn. Edwin Charles Aged 36   Son of Henry & Annie Perry of Quendon Street, Quendon near Newport, Essex   Born at Quendon, Essex   Gommecourt British Cemetery No. 2, I. D. 2
Roper 4068 L/Cpl. Harry Ernest Aged 23   Son of Henry Charles & Kate Roper of 16, Lammas Park Rd., Ealing, London   Thiepval Memorial
Sears 2619 Pte Frank   Thiepval Memorial
Thirkell 3295 Pte James Charles William att. from 2/2nd London Regt. Aged 20   Son of Mrs M E Thirkell of 69, Tantallon Rd., Balham, London.   Thiepval Memorial Pier and Face 9 D and 16 B
Young 4649 Rfn. Percival Robert   Thiepval Memorial
No. 2 Platoon
Armitage 2472 Rfn. William Henry Marshall   Gommecourt British Cemetery No. 2, I. A. 18
Bonser 4560 Rfn. Norman   Son of Mrs Bonser of 99, Brudenell Road, Upper Tooting   Gommecourt British Cemetery No. 2, I. A. 2
Fickling 2559 Pte Arthur Stanley att. from 2/2nd London Regt.   Thiepval Memorial
Heath 4393 Rfn. John Edward Aged 26   Youngest son of Mr & Mrs S G P Heath of 29, Routh Rd., Wandsworth Common, London, formerly of 39, Schubert Road, East Putney   Gommecourt British Cemetery No. 2, I. A. 8.

Hughes 4442 Rfn. Maxted Beadle Brother of Mrs Seager, 45, Guildford Road, Greenwich Thiepval Memorial

Parsons 4507 Rfn. Herbert Aged 41 Son of George Henry & Catherine Parsons of Maytrees, South Ealing; husband of Florence Edith Parsons of 14A, Northcote Avenue, Ealing, London Gommecourt British Cemetery No. 2, I. B. 16

Smith 3981 L/Cpl. Alan Rossyn Aged 21 Son of G E & Edith Smith of The Little House, Hindhead, Surrey, formerly of 44, Prentis Road, Streatham Thiepval Memorial

Williams 2179 Rfn. Arthur Victor Aged 19 Son of Arthur W & Georgina Williams of The Rectory Cottage, Trowbridge, Wilts Thiepval Memorial

No. 3 Platoon

Bolt 4214 Rfn. Arthur James Aged 20 Son of William & Mary Bolt of 30, High St., Wimbledon, London Thiepval Memorial

Bowditch 4209 Rfn. Alfred Ernest Thiepval Memorial

Cooper 4242 Rfn. Frederick George Aged 25 Son of Frederick George & Annie Priscilla Cooper of 3, Poynder Villas, 380, London Rd., Isleworth, Middx Thiepval Memorial

Kyte 2639 Pte Frederick James att. from 2/2nd London Regt. Brother of Miss Kite of 27, Southwark Bridge, London, SE Thiepval Memorial

Palmer 2747 Rfn. John Aldred Brother of Miss Palmer of 13, Kingsfield Road, Oxhey, Watford Thiepval Memorial

No. 4 Platoon

David 4180 Rfn. Jack Son of Mr T David of 123, Evering Road, Stoke Newington Thiepval Memorial

Harris 4060 Rfn. Shirley Woodbine Son of Mr F Harris of 11, Sidney Avenue, Bowes Park, London Thiepval Memorial

Olive 4453 Rfn. Robert Edward Aged 27 Son of George Edward Olive of 133, Lansdown Rd. Tottenham, London, & the late Elizabeth Ann Olive Thiepval Memorial

Straker 4049 L/Cpl. Stanley Charles Aged 31 Youngest son of John Henry & Caroline Straker of 75, Sotheby Rd., Highbury, London Thiepval Memorial

Tenbroeke 4704 Rfn. Quentin Larpent Brother of Miss Tenbroeke of 46, Warwick Road, Earl's Court Gommecourt British Cemetery No. 2, III. B. 28

LEWIS GUN SECTION

Harley 4548 Pte Arthur Henry William att. from 2/2nd London Regt. Aged 18 Son of Henry John & Ellen Harley of 173, Eardley Rd., Streatham, London Gommecourt British Cemetery No. 2, III. E. 8

B COMPANY

Horne 2nd Lt. James Anthony Aged 23 Son of the Rev. Joseph White Horne & Katherine Grace Horne of 8, Stradmore Gardens, Kensington, London Gommecourt British Cemetery No. 2, Sp. Mem. C. 5

Lambert 2129 Rfn. Reginald William Aged 21 Son of William Henry & Susan Lambert of 144, Church Rd., Canonbury, London Thiepval Memorial

Le Rossignol 3021 Rfn. Leonard Aged 29 Son of Pauline E Le Rossignol of 'Pendower', Oxhey Drive, Northwood, Middx., & the late F Le Rossignol, formerly of 'Argyle House', The Avenue, Surbiton Hill, Surrey Thiepval Memorial

Parkhouse 3924 Rfn. Allen George Son of Mrs M Parkhouse of Ingatestone House, Essex Thiepval Memorial

Strange 2nd Lt. William Frederick att. from 2/2nd London Regt. Thiepval Memorial

3rd July 1916

Cockerill T/Capt. George Edward Aged 38 Son of George Edward & Edith Cockerill of London. In German hands Vaulx Hill Cemetery I. C. 15

No. 5 Platoon

Bennett 4328 Rfn. Douglas Bradford Aged 27 Son of Frederic & Maria Bennett of 39, Birdhurst Rd., Merton, London Thiepval Memorial

Crocker 3163 Pte Harold Hutchings att. from 2/2nd London Regt. Aged 30 Son of Thomas William Crocker of 'Moorgarden', Brock Hill, Wickford, Essex, & the late Charlotte Crocker formerly of 9, Atherton Road, Forest Gate Thiepval Memorial

Fea 2776 Rfn. Allam Son of Mr W C Fea of 73, Tannsfield Road, Sydenham Gommecourt British Cemetery No. 2, II. H. 17

Hinds 3896 Rfn. George Aged 27 Son of Mrs William Hinds of 3 Queens Rd. Ealing, Middx, & the late William Hinds, brother of Miss Hinds of 8, Corfton Road, Ealing Thiepval Memorial

Lazzell 4194 Rfn. Stanley Francis Thiepval Memorial

Quinney 4190 Rfn. Thomas Edward Albert Aged 29 Son of Thomas William & Leonie Sarah Quinney of 323, Upper Richmond Rd., East Sheen, London Thiepval Memorial

Taffs 4186 Rfn. William Clifford Son of Mrs Taffs of 50, Queen's Road, Leytonstone Thiepval Memorial

Waller 2327 Rfn. Charles David Son of Mr D Waller of 18, Warrington Road, Croydon Thiepval Memorial

No. 6 Platoon

Barker 4752 Rfn. Harold Charles Aged 19 Son of Charles & Clara Sarah Ann Barker of Astrope House, Puttenham, Tring, Herts., formerly of 26, Wathen Road, Dorking, Surrey Thiepval Memorial

Dexter 4408 Rfn. Alfred Keyte Aged 20 Son of Annie Dexter of 107, Loyd Rd., Northampton, & the late Fred Dexter and brother of Mrs Purdue, 14, Bowerdean Street, Fulham Thiepval Memorial

Divall 3251 Rfn. Reginald Born on 6th June 1896, son of Thomas George, a bricklayer, and Emily Divall of The Green, Ringmer Gommecourt British Cemetery No. 2, III. F. 2

Elmslie 4402 Rfn. Graham Beversham Aged 36 Son of Jane A Elmslie of 9, Carlton Mansions, West End Lane, West Hampstead, London, & the late Graham Elmslie Thiepval Memorial

Gammon 2377 Cpl. Newton Edwin Aged 32 Son of the late Edwin B & Hetty Gammon of 37, Hollingbourne Rd., Herne Hill, London Thiepval Memorial

Gaskins 2801 Rfn. Robert William Aged 23 Husband of Edith Gaskins of 'Bohemia', The Crescent, Belmont, Sutton, Surrey Bailleul Road East Cemetery, St. Laurent-Blangy II. M. 18

Hall 2255 Rfn. Stanley Son of Mrs Hall, 15, Church Road, Brixton Hill Thiepval Memorial

Harvey 4207 Rfn. Theodore Stuart Thiepval Memorial

Hurst 4278 Rfn. Percy Haslewood Aged 30 Son of Samuel Hurst of 81, Cambridge Rd., Seven Kings, Essex; husband of Geraldine Hurst of 18, Teddington Park Rd., Teddington, Middx Thiepval Memorial

Jarrett 3383 Rfn. Harold William Son of Mrs Jarrett of 'Eschol', Lower Ham Road, Kingston on Thames Thiepval Memorial

Morgan 4274 Rfn. Arthur John Aged 29 Son of George Gerrard Morgan & Margaret Morgan of Walworth, London Thiepval Memorial

Penn 4373 Rfn. Charles William Son of Mrs Penn of 564, Bristol Road, Northfield, Birmingham Butler to Sir Maurice & Lady de Bunsen Thiepval Memorial

No. 7 Platoon

Dando 1985 L/Cpl. John Edward Aged 21 Son of the late John & Alice Mary Anne Dando of 102, Peckham Rye, London Thiepval Memorial

Dyson 3280 Rfn. Augustus Sydney Aged 30 Son of Annie Maria Dyson of 46, Lambert Rd., Brixton Hill, London, & the late Joseph Dyson Thiepval Memorial

Fowler 2970 Pte Maurice Henry att. from 2/2nd London Regt. Aged 26 Son of Henry & Mary Clementina Fowler of 'Innisfallen', Sulkington Avenue, Worthing, Sussex, formerly of 108, Palmerston Road, Bowes Park Thiepval Memorial

Ives 2555 Rfn. Vincent George Aged 25 Son of Vincent & Emily Ives of 201, Abington Avenue, Northampton Thiepval Memorial

Johns 3959 Rfn. Lionel Aged 21 Son of Thomas & Kate Johns of 27, Grandison Rd., Clapham Common, London Gommecourt British Cemetery No. 2, II. H. II

Kench 3862 Rfn. Richard William Aged 27 Son of Richard & Mary Ann Kench of 9, Cecil Rd., Ilford, Essex Thiepval Memorial

Manning 4427 Rfn. John Jack Samuel Aged 20 Son of Arthur Richard & Bessie Ann Manning of 34, Parsons Green, Fulham, London Thiepval Memorial

Newham 2402 Rfn. Howard Frank Aged 25 Son of the late Frank Noyce Newham & Edith Newham Thiepval Memorial

Pocock 4100 Rfn. Martin William Son of Mrs Pocock, 9, Bickerton Road, Upper Holloway Thiepval Memorial

Rodwell 4261 Rfn. Charles Alfred Aged 41 Son of Mr & Mrs Rodwell of Berkhamsted; husband of Marion Elizabeth Rodwell of Grange Lodge, Ashley Rd., Walton-on-Thames Thiepval Memorial

Sharp 4432 Rfn. Ernest Granville Aged 20 Son of Ernest Alfred & Louisa Jane Sharp of 115, Queen's Road, Brighton Gommecourt British Cemetery No. 2, II. J. 15

Winter 2485 Pte Claude Reginald att. from 2/2nd London Regt. Aged 21 Son of Arthur Sidney & Bertha Winter of 135, High St., Ponders End, Middx Thiepval Memorial

No. 8 Platoon

Brett 4056 Rfn. Leonard Gloyn Aged 26 Son of William Charles & Elizabeth Susan Brett of 56, Rodenhurst Rd., Clapham, London Thiepval Memorial

Eastwood 4773 Rfn. Joseph Edward Thiepval Memorial

Mawson 4527 Rfn. Walter Fox Hebuterne Military Cemetery IV. J. 4

Nicholls 4744 Rfn. William Miles Thiepval Memorial

Parr 3539 Cpl. James Thiepval Memorial

Restall 4018 Rfn. Frederick Aged 22 Son of Lydia Restall of 19, St. Paul's Rd., Canonbury, London, & the late George Restall Thiepval Memorial

Ridley 2869 Rfn. Cyril Edward Aged 22 Son of the late Edward John Ridley & of Minnie Louise Ridley of 55, Tivoli Crescent, Dyke Rd., Brighton, formerly of 130, Warwick Road, Thornton Heath Born in London Gommecourt British Cemetery No. 2, II. H. 12

Small 4431 Rfn. Reginald Robert Thiepval Memorial

C COMPANY

Hughes 1969 Rfn. Alfred Edgar Aged 25 Son of the late Alfred & Phoebe Jane Hughes Thiepval Memorial

Mott Capt. Hugh Frederick Aged 22 Son of Alfred Fenwick Mott & Katherine Mary Mott of The Holt, Reigate, Surrey. Educated at Marlborough College and Oriel College, Oxford Thiepval Memorial

Negus 2ⁿᵈ Lt. Arthur George Thiepval Memorial

Sampford 2718 L/Cpl Frank Mynott att. from 2/2ⁿᵈ London Regt. Son of Mr and Mrs Sampford of 12, Norwood Road, Herne Hill Thiepval Memorial

Withers 2713 Pte Geoffrey Carrington att. from 2/2ⁿᵈ London Regt. Aged 24 Son of the late F & M Withers of36, Elm Road, East Sheen Thiepval Memorial

Yates 2ⁿᵈ Lt. Arthur Gerald Vavasour Aged 29 Son of Hercules Campbell Yates & Annie Yates of The Lower Beech, Tytherington, Macclesfield Thiepval Memorial

No. 9 Platoon

Fellows 3345 Rfn. William Blyth Thiepval Memorial

Norton 2384 Rfn. Arthur Aged 28 Son of the late John & Mary Ann Norton of 137, Milton Avenue, East Ham; husband of Elsie Emily May Moore (formerly Norton) of 23, Churchfield Rd., Acton, London Thiepval Memorial

Oldham 3543 Rfn. Henry Leicester Aged 22 Son of James & Mary Oldham of 2, Mysore Rd., Battersea, London Thiepval Memorial

Smith 2770 Rfn. Albert George Aged 22 Son of Esther Catherine Smith of 7, Hampden Rd., Hornsey, London, & the late John D Smith. Educated at Stationers' School, Hornsey, London Thiepval Memorial

Waind 4225 Rfn. Arthur Aged 31 Son of the late Frederick Waind; husband of Edith M Waind of The Gables, New Earswick, York Thiepval Memorial

No. 10 Platoon

Allen 3348 Rfn. Clarence Rayton Thiepval Memorial

Bryon 4609 Rfn. Maurice Clare Son of Mrs Bryon of 104, High Street, Hampton Hill, Middx Thiepval Memorial

Martin 2715 Rfn. John Gordon Thiepval Memorial

Wallis 2588 Pte John att. from 2/2ⁿᵈ London Regt. Aged 27 Son of Jane Wallis of Pipe Gate, Market Drayton, Salop, & the late John Wallis, formerly of 'Westholme', Woore, Crewe, Cheshire Thiepval Memorial

No. 11 Platoon

Haselton 4352 Rfn. Frank Douglas Thiepval Memorial

Nelson 4306 Rfn. Joseph Aged 25 Son of Margaret Nelson of 143, Church Rd., Hove, Sussex, & the late Joseph Nelson Thiepval Memorial

Proctor 2458 Pte ThomasWalter att. from 2/2ⁿᵈ London Regt. Aged 24 Son of Emily A. Proctor of 31, Bexhill Rd., St. Leonards on Sea, & the late T W Proctor, formerly of Church Far, Tendring, Essex Thiepval Memorial

Tebbutt 4066 Rfn. Richard Son of Mr and Mrs Tebbutt, 9, Rossington Street, Upper Clapton Thiepval Memorial

No. 12 Platoon

Drown 4345 Rfn. Norman Frank Aged 23 Son of Frank & Fanny Amelia Drown of 44, Selsdon Rd., West Norwood, London Thiepval Memorial

Kentrzinsky 4625 Rfn. Percy Walter Darragon Aged 23 Son of Kate A Kentrzinsky of 'Darragon', Townshend Rd., Richmond, Surrey, & the late Henry Hermon Kentrzinsky Thiepval Memorial

Pomeroy 2915 Rfn. William George Aged 24 Son of Frank Louis Pomeroy & Annie Louise Pomeroy of 64, Maybank Rd., South Woodtord, Essex Thiepval Memorial

Soper 2939 L/Cpl Charles Edward att. from 2/2nd London Regt. Aged 19 Son of Mrs Rhoda Soper of 222, Roundwood Rd., Willesden, London, & the late T H Soper Gommecourt British Cemetery No. 2, III.F.19

D COMPANY

Farley 2nd Lt. Frederick Albert att. from 2/2nd London Regt. Aged 25 Son of Arthur Albert & Frances Eleanor Farley of 11, Warleigh Rd., Brighton, Sussex Thiepval Memorial

2nd July 1916

Stubbs 2nd Lt. Cecil Arthur att. from 2/2nd London Regt. Aged 22 Son of Arthur & Martha Ann Stubbs of 26, Grafton Rd., Worthing, Sussex Warlincourt Halte British Cemetery, Saulty, II. D. 1

No. 13 Platoon

Newton 2549 L/Cpl. Douglas Thiepval Memorial

No. 14 Platoon

Benton 2759 Rfn. Samuel Westwood Gommecourt British Cemetery No. 2, III. E. 24

Parsons 2527 L/Sgt. Arthur Johnathan att. from 2/2nd London Regt. Aged 19 Son of Johnathan & Alice L Parsons of 16, Nelson Rd., Hornsey, London, formerly of 74, St Thomas Road, Finsbury Park Enlisted in 1914 Also served at Gallipoli Gommecourt British Cemetery No. 2, III.H.14

No. 15 Platoon

Billing 3085 L/Cpl Stuart Morrison att. from 2/2nd London Regt. Husband of G M Billing of 55, Chelsham Rd., Clapham, London Gommecourt British Cemetery No. 2, I. C. 5

Groves 3049 Pte William Ewart att. from 2/2nd London Regt. Aged 18 Son of Margaret Fanny Ruse (formerly Groves) of 6, Dacre Rd., Upton Manor, London, & of Charles Ruse (stepfather). Thiepval Memorial

No. 16 Platoon

Hargreaves 4409 Rfn. Reginald Percy Thiepval Memorial

Mabbott 4343 Rfn. Alfred Leonard Son of Mr J F Mabbott of 58, Portland Road, South Norwood Thiepval Memorial

NO. 1 LEWIS GUN TEAM

Heyworth 4184 Rfn. Herbert Harold Aged 26 Brother of Edward Heyworth of 'Fernlea', Rainhill Rooks, Barnoldswick, Colne, Lancs Thiepval Memorial

ATTACHED TO 169TH MACHINE GUN COMPANY

Durden 3298 Pte Leonard Stanley C Company att. from 2/2nd London Regt. Fillievres British Cemetery, B. 8

Engall 2nd Lt. John Sherwin Aged 19 Son of John B Sherwin Engall & Edith M. Engall of 62, Goldsmith Avenue, Acton, London Thiepval Memorial Pier and Face 5 C and 12 C

Fairclough 2714 Rfn. Leonard Aged 29 Son of Abraham & Emily Fairclough of 14, Rumsey Rd., Stockwell, London Gommecourt British Cemetery No. 2, III. J. 17

Loynes 4201 Rfn. Edward Francis Aged 26 Son of Edward Arthur & Florence Jane Loynes of Church Lane, Wroxham, Norwich Thiepval Memorial

Roser 2382 Rfn. Stanley Gordon Aged 22 Son of G J & Emily Roser of 1, Bridge Rd., East Ham, London Thiepval Memorial

ATTACHED TO 169TH TRENCH MORTAR BATTERY

Graham 3793 L/Cpl. Keith Forster Aged 26 Son of Joseph Forster Graham & Charlotte Rose Graham of The Chase, Beechwood Rd., Sanderstead, Surrey. Thiepval Memorial

Wagstaff 3841 Rfn. Charles Edward Aged 21 Son of John & Harriet Wagstaff of Pertenhall, Beds Gommecourt British Cemetery No. 2, II. E. 27

Company and Platoon not known

Abrahams 2278 Rfn. Stanley Aged 27 Son of Joseph & Caroline Abrahams of 1, Riffel House, Riffel Rd., Cricklewood, London Thiepval Memorial

Argles 8817 L/Cpl. Seymour Thiepval Memorial

Baily 3875 Rfn. Harold Thiepval Memorial

Beer 3995 Rfn. Alfred James Son of Mr S W Beer of 40, St Andrew Street, Wandsworth Road Thiepval Memorial

Beer 40240 Rfn. David Stanley Aged 21 Son of Henry & Mary Beer of St. Mary's, Ely, Cambs Thiepval Memorial

Bennett 4542 Rfn. Sidney Francis Aged 20 Son of Francis Richard & Florence Alice Jane Bennett of West Norwood, London; husband of Doris Maud Bennett of 42, Rosendale Rd., West Dulwich, London Hebuterne Military Cemetery Sp. Mem. II

Blasby 4335 Rfn. Jonathan Llewellyn Hebuterne Military Cemetery IV. E. 5

Boughey 4321 Rfn. Frederick Wiliam Dudley Aged 22 Son of Walter Samuel & Charlotte Jane Boughey of 12, Hampstead Gardens, Golders Green, London. Thiepval Memorial

Brant 4544 Rfn. Robert Digby Gommecourt British Cemetery No. 2, II. B. 8

Brewer 2795 Cpl. Richard Leslie att. from 2/2nd Londons. He served in Malta, Egypt, Gallipoli and France. Gommecourt British Cemetery No. 2, Hebuterne, I. A. 3

Brookman 1853 L/Cpl. Henry George Wm. Thiepval Memorial

Burgess 4732 Rfn. Frederick Nelson Thiepval Memorial

Burrough 4357 Rfn. Harold John Gommecourt British Cemetery No. 2, III. B. 30

Butler 2591 Rfn. William George Aged 21 Son of Mr & Mrs Butler of 18, Beatrice St., Plaistow, London Gommecourt British Cemetery No. 2, Sp. Mem. B. 19

Cooper 4608 Rfn. Herbert Henry Aged 18 Son of Mr F H & Mrs F Cooper of 153, Herne Hill, London Thiepval Memorial

Cornish 1810 Rfn. Reginald Alfred Son of Herbert Stockbridge Cornish & Ellen Eliza Cornish of 6, Wing Rd. Terrace, Linslade, Leighton Buzzard, Beds Thiepval Memorial

Couper 3672 Rfn. William Alfred Aged 31 Son of Edwin Alfred & Alice Couper Thiepval Memorial

De Voil 2730 Rfn. Benjamin Thomas Aged 27 Son of Benjamin & Henrietta De Voil of 'Woodside', Harrow Rd., Dorking, Surrey. Gommecourt Wood New Cemetery, Foncquevillers IV. B. 24.

Deakin 1481 Cpl. Stanley Aged 21 Son of Charles & Elisa Deakin of 'Salcombe', Avenue Rd., Southgate, London Thiepval Memorial

Dear 1476 L/Cpl. Gerald Arthur Aged 24 Son of Francis George & Georgina Dear of 77, Arcadian Gardens, Wood Green, London Thiepval Memorial

Edwards 1842 L/Cpl. William Hargreaves Aged 23 Son of John & Sarah Edwards of 14, Derby Place, Hoole, Chester Thiepval Memorial

Froome 24 C.S.M. Charles William Aged 44 Son of Charles William & Catherine Mary Froome; husband of Fanny Elizabeth Froome of 26, Raymond Avenue, West Ealing, London Gommecourt British Cemetery No. 2, II. H. 27

Gissing 4620 Rfn. Walter Leonard Aged 24 Son of the late George & Edith Gissing Thiepval Memorial

Glenister 4349 Rfn. Vernon Howard Aged 26 Son of Charles Lawrence & Elizabeth Glenister of 81, Milward Rd., Hastings Serre Road Cemetery No. 2, XLI. M. 1

Green 3935 Rfn. William Thiepval Memorial

Green 3511 Rfn. William Joseph Thiepval Memorial

Gudge 4337 Rfn. Rodney Christopher Aged 21 Son of Mr & Mrs W J B Gudge of 67, Guilford Avenue, Surbiton, Surrey Thiepval Memorial

Hammond 4441 Rfn. John Westbrook Thiepval Memorial

Handley 3907 Rfn. William Hebuterne Military Cemetery IV. B. 3

Harrison 4586 Rfn. Sydney Edward Thiepval Memorial

Hughes 4109 Rfn. Frederick Arthur Aged 21 Son of Ernest Gladstone Hughes & Mary Alice Hughes of Warrington, Lancs Gommecourt British Cemetery No. 2, III. F. 15

Kemp 2708 Rfn. William Aged 21 Son of Mr W Kemp M.B.E., & Mrs S Kemp of 11, Carew Rd., Thornton Heath, Surrey Thiepval Memorial

King 1640 Sgt. Leonard Frederick Thiepval Memorial

Langdale 2565 Rfn. William James Aged 31 Son of the late Edward Fuller Langdale & Margaret Ann Langdale Thiepval Memorial

Lloyd 2583 Rfn. Robert Carey Aged 24 Son of William Charles & Emily Lloyd of 212, Condercum Rd., Benwell, Newcastle-on-Tyne Gommecourt British Cemetery No. 2, III. C. 21

MacGillivray 3849 Rfn. John Ruxton Aged 19 Son of Mr & Mrs W MacGillivray of Banchor, Newtonmore, Inverness-shire Thiepval Memorial

Malcolm 4407 Rfn. John Paterson Thiepval Memorial

Marsh 1497 Cpl. Arthur Leonard Aged 23 Son of Joseph William & Alice Martha Marsh of 6, Claremont Avenue, Woking, Surrey Thiepval Memorial

Masson 26 C.S.M. Herbert Montgomery Thiepval Memorial

Moore 3234 L/Cpl. Stanley Aged 29 Son of Alfred Moore of 15, Boot Trades Institution, Mortlake, London, & the late Florence Northover Moore (nee Lenthall). Thiepval Memorial

Nelhams 3634 Rfn. Stuart Cyril Thiepval Memorial

Newby 3850 Rfn. John Rupert Trevor Aged 27 Son of the late John Alfred & Alice Maria Newby Thiepval Memorial

Oldham 2308 Rfn. Frederick Thiepval Memorial

Pangbourne 4272 Rfn. George Aged 26 Son of the late George Lewis Pangbourne & Elizabeth Pangbourne Thiepval Memorial

Potter 1019 Sgt. Archibald William Thiepval Memorial

Reeves 4249 Rfn. Albert Walter Aged 32 Son of Edmund & Emma Reeves of Plumtrees, Headcorn, Kent Thiepval Memorial

Reynolds 4416 Rfn. Edward William Ernest Son of Ernest James & Emma Edith Reynolds of 30, Elm Grove, Rye Lane, Peckham, London Gommecourt British Cemetery No. 2, II. G. II

Rogers 3099 Cpl. Frank Austin Aged 26 Son of Frank A. & Lillie Rogers of Oxford and Cambridge Mansions, London. B.Sc. (University College, London.) Thiepval Memorial

Ross 4564 Rfn. Charles William Aged 27 Son of John & Christian Ross (nee Stenhouse) of 29C, London Rd., Forest Hill, London Thiepval Memorial

Salt 2361 Rfn. Howard Thiepval Memorial

Scott 3899 Rfn. Frederick James Aged 25 Son of John William & Annie Scott of 30, St. Martin's Rd., Canterbury, Kent Thiepval Memorial

Sims 2961 Rfn. Melvin Harry Maurice Aged 23 Son of Emily A Sims of 30, Kingswood Avenue, Kilburn, London, & the late Harry William Sims Gommecourt British Cemetery No. 2, III. C. 2

Stebbings 4584 Rfn. Henry George Thiepval Memorial

Taylor 4504 Rfn. Reginald Edmund Aged 19 Son of Henry & Rosetta Taylor of Parsons Farm, Faygate, Horsham, Sussex Thiepval Memorial

Tompkins 3963 L/Cpl. Harry Thiepval Memorial

Trace 2863 Rfn. James att. from 2/2nd London Regt. Thiepval Memorial

Tucker 2173 Sgt. Thomas John Aged 30 Son of Mr & Mrs Henry Tucker of 17, Sketty Rd., Swansea. Enlisted, Aug., 1914 Thiepval Memorial

Tuckey 4110 Rfn. Henry Victor Aged 21 Son of Harry John & Alice Emma Tuckey of Fullers Lane, Woolton Hill, Newbury, Berks Thiepval Memorial

Tyler 2996 L/Cpl. Leonard John Thiepval Memorial

Weller 1060 Rfn. Charles George Aged 19 Son of the late David Weller & of Maud Weller (stepmother) of 6, Rutley Gardens, Kennington Park, London Thiepval Memorial

West 3904 Rfn. Arthur Henry Thiepval Memorial

Williams 4714 Rfn. Ernest Stanley Aged 19 Son of Edward Albert & Rosa Susan Williams of 9, St. Helen's Rd., Westcliff-on-Sea, Essex Hebuterne Military Cemetery IV. J. 6

3rd July 1916

Cavell 4745 Rfn. John Reginald Aged 24 Son of John & Martha Cavell of 22, Broad Street, Whittlesea, Cambs Boisguillaume Communal Cemetery I. E. 4

Lambert 2854 Pte Leonard att. from 2/2nd London Regt. Aged 18 Youngest son of Samuel Stephen & Kezia Lambert of 104, Kilmorie Rd., Forest Hill, London.. He served in Malta, Egypt, Gallipoli and France. Etretat Churchyard II. E. 8

5th July 1916

Webb 4571 Rfn. Arthur Charles William Aged 30 Son of Arthur Edward & Louisa Webb of 15, Beverley Rd., Barnes, London Etretat Churchyard II. D. 20

6th July 1916

Noble 3967 Rfn. Ralph Edgar Aged 23 Son of William Henry & Mary Noble of 82, Fernlea Rd., Balham, London. In German hands Le Cateau Military Cemetery IV. A. 5

8th July 1916

Holroyd 4381 Rfn. Cyril Bernardine Aged 20 Son of Rosaline Holroyd of 2, Beechwood Drive, Jordanhill, Glasgow, & the late Frederick William Holroyd. In German hands St. Souplet British Cemetery III. AA. 17.

McKenna 2333 L/Cpl. Neil McCarthy Aged 29 Son of George Frederick Neil McKenna & Florence McKenna of 52, Lower Sloane St., Chelsea, London. Born at Tonbridge, Kent Abbeville Communal Cemetery V. A. 11

9th July 1916

Latreille 3996 L/Cpl. Arthur York City of London Cemetery 254. 85152

Waterson 4051 Rfn. Eric Aged 22 Son of Andrew & Emily Waterson of London Le Treport Military Cemetery Plot 2. Row N. Grave 4A
13ᵗʰ July 1916
Gosling 3620 Rfn. Albert Stanley Mont Huon Military Cemetery, Le Treport I. F. 12.
21ˢᵗ July 1916
Fagan 1474 Sgt. Howard Alec M.M. Aged 18 Son of Mr and Mrs Fagan of 2, Briarwood Road, Clapham Mont Huon Military Cemetery, Le Treport, grave I. E. 3.
6ᵗʰ August 1916
Jones 2150 Sgt. Hector Stanley Aged 25 Son of James and Rosina Jones of 30, Belvoir Road, Dulwich, London. On the staff of Messrs. I. and R. Morley, of City of London. Mont Huon Military Cemetery, Le Treport, grave II. D. 9.

1/7ᵀᴴ MIDDLESEX REGIMENT
All casualties listed as Thiepval Memorial are on Pier and Face 12 D and 13 B
2ⁿᵈ July 1916
Cox TF2991 Private F C Hebuterne Military Cemetery II. L. 3.
Reeves TF1696 Private Gerald Leslie Aged 20 Son of Charles Skinner Reeves & Eleanor Rosa Reeves of 333, Kentish Town Rd., Kentish Town, London Hebuterne Military Cemetery II. L. 6.
4ᵗʰ July 1916
Moore TF2534 Private William Edward Aged 20 Son of David & Elizabeth Ellen Moore of 102, Percival Rd., Enfield, Middx St. Sever Cemetery, Rouen A. 22. 18

1/8ᵀᴴ MIDDLESEX REGIMENT
All casualties listed as Thiepval Memorial are on Pier and Face 12 D and 13 B
Clark TF4744 Pte William Thiepval Memorial
Croxon TF2424 Pte Sydney Thomas Aged 19 Son of Thomas & Florence S. Croxon of 126, Ealing Rd., Brentford, Middx Hebuterne Military Cemetery IV. M. 15
Gray TF3509 Pte John Edwin Aged 22 Son of James Edwin & Louisa Gray of Mount Ash, Chartridge Lane, Chesham, Bucks. Thiepval Memorial
Harrison TF1970 L/Sgt. Sidney W Aged 38 Husband of Rose A Harrison of 20, Station Rd., Hanwell, Middx Thiepval Memorial
Laflin TF2957 Pte Edward William Aged 20 Son of William John & Rosanna Laflin of 25, Trent Avenue, Ealing, London Hebuterne Military Cemetery IV. M. 12
Matthews TF1486 Pte Richard Aged 19 Son of James & Annie Matthews. Thiepval Memorial
Poole TF3806 Pte William Henry A Company Son of Mr and Mrs Poole of 'The Clair', Percy Road, Hampton on Thames Thiepval Memorial
Rudd TF2643 L/Sgt. Ernest Henry John Thiepval Memorial
Seabrook TF3744 Pte Frederick William Aged 19 Son of Margaret Ann Fairley (formerly Seabrook) of 3, Creswell Gardens, Hounslow Heath, Middx., & the late William Seabrook Thiepval Memorial
Smith TF1311 Pte Ernest Palmer Son of Albert & Elizabeth Jane Smith of 1, St. Mary's Cottages, Stanwell, Staines, Middx. Enlisted 1911 Thiepval Memorial
2ⁿᵈ July 1916
Allen TF3464 Pte Albert Etretat Churchyard II. E. 18
12ᵗʰ July 1916
Hedges TF3517 Pte John Ste Marie Cemetery, Le Havre Div. 19. JJ. 8

1/5ᵀᴴ CHESHIRE REGIMENT (EARL OF CHESTER'S)
All casualties listed as Thiepval Memorial are on Pier and Face 3 C and 4 A
Ackerley 1343 L/Cpl. Charles Thiepval Memorial
Allen 1891 Pte. Sydney Thiepval Memorial
Arthur 2ⁿᵈ Lt. George Stuart Aged 32 Son of Samuel & Louisa Arthur of 24, Heath Crescent, Halifax Gommecourt British Cemetery No. 2, III. C. 15
Atherton 3754 Pte. John Thiepval Memorial
Atkin 3421 Pte. John Aged 19 Son of William & Anna Atkin of 2, Dinting Lane, Glossop Thiepval Memorial
Bass Lt. Phillip Burnet Aged 21 Son of Col. P de S Bass, C.M.G., & Mrs Bass of 8, Madeley Rd., Ealing, London Thiepval Memorial
Bennett 2972 Pte. Charles Henry No. 2 Platoon, A Company Aged 29 Son of the late Charles & Margaret Davison Bennett Thiepval Memorial
Blackburn 2822 Pte. Charles Thiepval Memorial

Boardman 1244 Sgt. Edwin Aged 24 Son of Edward & Edith Boardman of 7, Broom Rd., Hale. Cheshire Gommecourt British Cemetery No. 2, II. K. 13

Boardman 1868 Pte. John William Aged 22 Son of Edward & Edith Boardman of 7, Broom Rd., Hale, Cheshire Bienvillers Military Cemetery XXI. H. 13

Boulger 1988 Pte. John William Thiepval Memorial

Broadribb (alias Perry) 2430 Pte. Norman Randolph Son of William & Eliza Broadribb of 13, City Rd., Chester Thiepval Memorial

Brocklehurst 1736 Pte. Vivian Aged 20 Son of Henry & Ada Mary Brocklehurst. Proceeded to France in Feb.1915 Thiepval Memorial

Buchanan 3611 Pte. Robert Thiepval Memorial

Carter 3900 Pte. William Aged 18 Son of Martha Evernden (formerly Carter) of 20 Back, Queen St., Chester Thiepval Memorial

Cash 1628 Pte. Albert Aged 20 Son of T W Cash & Annie Cash of 3, White Bear Yard, Knutsford, Cheshire Thiepval Memorial

Clarke 1779 Pte. Arthur Hebuterne Military Cemetery II. C. 7

Clarke 3123 Pte. Arthur Edwin Hebuterne Military Cemetery Sp. Mem. A. 3

Clifford 1527 Pte. John Thiepval Memorial

Davenport 3821 Pte. Harry Aged 25 Son of Charles & Kate H. Davenport of 15, Oakfield Rd., Altrincham, Cheshire Thiepval Memorial

Davies 2ⁿᵈ Lt. Frank Arnold Gommecourt British Cemetery No. 2, III. B. 7

Dutton 3732 Pte. Neville Aged 18 Brother of Mrs E M Lloyd of 4, St. Andrew's Avenue, Timperley, Cheshire. Born at Altrincham, Cheshire Gommecourt British Cemetery No 2, III E 22

Edge 1413 Pte. George Thiepval Memorial

Fletcher 1460 L/Cpl. Robert Thiepval Memorial

Gayter 3679 Pte. Harry Thiepval Memorial

Hinchliffe 3471 Pte. William Aged 25 Husband of the late Clara Hinchliffe of 4, Bank St., Heaton Lane, Stockport Gommecourt British Cemetery No. 2, III. H. 2

Jones 3192 Pte. George Frederick Hebuterne Military Cemetery II. C. 6

Jones 2351 Pte. John Hebuterne Military Cemetery II. C. 9

Kendall 1979 Pte. John Aubrey Aged 21 Son of Alice Maude Lamb (formerly Kendall) of 239, Lea Rd., Wolverhampton, & the late Joseph Kendall Gommecourt British Cemetery No. 2, III. E. 17

Large 1820 Cpl. Jack Hebuterne Military Cemetery IV. M. 41

Lear 4487 Pte. George Percy Aged 22 Son of George & Kate Lear of 238, Muslin St., Newton, Hyde, Cheshire Thiepval Memorial

Martin 3980 Pte. John Aged 23 Son of John & Phoebe Martin of 43, Askeridge St., Runcorn, Cheshire Thiepval Memorial

Mattimore 1564 Pte. Leo Aged 19 Son of Peter & Mary Ann Mattimore of 3, Princess St., West Bollington, Macclesfield, Cheshire Thiepval Memorial

Minshall 1595 Pte. James Gommecourt British Cemetery No. 2, III. B. 4

Moores 3743 Pte. Joseph Aged 20 Son of William & Jessie Moores of 4, Stone St., Runcorn, Cheshire Thiepval Memorial

Mugan 2736 Pte. John Thiepval Memorial

Peirce 2297 Sgt. Phillip Hugh Aged 31 Son of John & Emily Peirce of 'Glenhurst', Shipton-under-Wychwood, Oxford Hebuterne Military Cemetery II. C. 8

Poole 3591 Pte. William Gommecourt British Cemetery No. 2, III. C. 18

Rackstraw 1920 Pte. William Aged 21 Son of Joseph & Sarah Ann Rackstraw of 80, Welcomb St., Hulme, Manchester Thiepval Memorial

Rees 3795 Pte. W A Warlincourt Halte British Cemetery, Saulty II. D. 12

Shaw 2553 Pte. Harry Aged 21 Son of John & Annie Shaw of 63, Park Rd., Hale, Altrincham, Cheshire Thiepval Memorial

Sutcliffe 1728 Dmr. Herbert Aged 22 Son of Mr & Mrs Sutcliffe of Altrincham, Cheshire Gommecourt British Cemetery No. 2, II. F. 15

Thomas 2376 Cpl. Harry Aged 19 Son of William Henry & Ellen Thomas of 13, Heyes St., Altrincham, Cheshire Thiepval Memorial

Turner 1657 Pte. Frank Aged 21 Son of the late John Turner of 67, Mill St., Congleton, Cheshire Thiepval Memorial

Wakefield 3320 Pte. John William Aged 20 Son of Mr & Mrs Joseph Wakefield of 4, Loch St., Runcorn, Cheshire Thiepval Memorial

Walker 240094 Pte. Frank Thiepval Memorial

Walker 240591 Pte. Frank Thiepval Memorial
Whitney 3015 Pte. Herbert Hebuterne Military Cemetery II. B. 2
Yarwood 1062 Pte. Joseph Hebuterne Military Cemetery II. B. 1
2nd July 1916
Kinsey 2050 L/Cpl. William Aged 30 Son of Mrs J Kinsey of Ship St., Frodsham; husband of W Kinsey of 12, Moreton Terrace, Frodsham, Warrington Doullens Communal Cemetery Extension No.1, Somme, France I. B. 13
Silver 3161 Pte. William Aged 20 Son of Thomas & Margaret Silver of 12, Smith's Court, Northwich, Cheshire Couin British Cemetery I. C. 9
White 2667 Pte. Frank Aged 17 Son of William & Jane White of Churton, Chester Warlincourt Halte British Cemetery, Saulty, II. D. 3
4th July 1916
Parker 1651 Pte. William Aged 22 Son of Fred & Alice Parker of Frodsham Le Treport Military Cemetery, Seine-Maritime, France Plot 2. Row N. Grave 1A
5th July 1916
Shaw 3072 Pte. William Aged 21 Son of Thomas & Martha Shaw of Tiverton, Tarporley, Cheshire Boulogne Eastern Cemetery, VIII. C. 98
14th July 1916
Watkinson 4218 Pte. Willie Isaac Aged 20 Son of Isaac & Martha Watkinson of 6, Heyes Terrace, Heyes Lane, Timperley, Cheshire. Birmingham (Lodge Hill) Cemetery B10 5 404A

ROYAL ENGINEERS
All casualties listed as Thiepval Memorial are on Pier and Face 8 A and 8 D
416th (1/1st City of Edinburgh) Field Coy RE
Angus 2nd Lt. Stewart Aged 25 Son of Mary Wilson Angus of 9, Muswell Rd., London, & the late David Angus, M. Inst. C.E. A.M.I.C.E., B.Sc. (Engineering) Edinburgh University. On engineering staff of Buenos Aires Great Southern Railway, Argentine. Thiepval Memorial
Glover 2012 2nd Cpl Robert Thiepval Memorial
Hogg 1858 L/Cpl. George Allan Aged 28 Son of the late John & Barbara Hogg; husband of Jane Hogg of 9, South Elgin St., Edinburgh Serre Road Cemetery No. 1, I. B. 58
Leuchars 1409 Spr. William Aged 21 Son of Alexander & Georgina Leuchars of 24, Colville Place, Edinburgh Hebuterne Military Cemetery IV.M.59
Purves 1721 A/L/Cpl. George Aged 33 Son of George & Margaret Purves of 2, Elm Row, Luth Walk, Edinburgh; husband of Jessie Boyd Purves of 8, Sunnybank Terrace, Edinburgh Thiepval Memorial
Reid 422599 L/Cpl. John Thomas Aged 46 Son of John & Agnes Reid of 194, Rose St., Edinburgh Thiepval Memorial

512TH (2/1ST LONDON) FIELD COY RE
Calvert 1906 Spr. John Thomas Aged 38 Husband of Rosa Florence Calvert of 167, Devonshire St., Mile End, London Thiepval Memorial
Everitt 2245 Spr. Victor Thiepval Memorial
Gardner 546605 Spr. Frederick Thiepval Memorial
Ives 2401 Spr. Henry George Aged 32 Son of the late Henry George Ives Thiepval Memorial
Jones 1955 Spr. Reginald Husband of the late A. Jones Thiepval Memorial
Merrin 1957 Spr. William Aged 34 Son of George & Ellen Merrin, (nee Blackborough) of 34 Derbyshire Street, Bethnal Green; husband of Jane Merrin of 5, Taylor's Place, Stepney, London. His brother Thomas Samuel also fell Thiepval Memorial
Reynolds 2221 Spr. Horace John Aged 29 Son of Richard & Sarah Reynolds of 35, Kilravock St., Queen's Park, London Gommecourt British Cemetery No. 2, III. E. 2
Sewell 1826 Spr. George Thiepval Memorial
2nd July 1916
Wilson 3508 Spr. William Francis Aged 27 Son of James & Mary Wilson of Chapel Lane, Garforth, Leeds. Couin British Cemetery I. C. 6
3rd July 1916
Fenner 1901 L/Cpl. Richard Husband of Mrs Fenner of 67, Cleveland Street, Mile End Doullens Communal Cemetery Extension No.1, I. B. 20
11th July 1916
Cox 3455 Spr. Dudley Farr In German hands Caudry Old Communal Cemetery A.12

513TH (2/2ND LONDON) FIELD COY RE

Brown 2084 Spr. Frederick George   Aged 19   Son of Mrs Amelia Brown of 21, Cambridge Place, Paddington, London   Gommecourt British Cemetery No. 2, V. C. 6

Rate 2376 Spr. Robert Arthur   Thiepval Memorial

Rose 2377 Spr. Thomas Arthur   Thiepval Memorial

Shipton 2116 2nd Cpl Charles William   Aged 31   Son of Frederick & Isabella Shipton of Bow, London; husband of Ethel Georgina Shipton of 17, Candy St., Bow, London   Sailly-Au-Bois Military Cemetery, I. C. I

Strong 1827 A/2nd Cpl W A   Son a Mr A E Strong of Green Man, Cambridge Road, London, N   Thiepval Memorial

Trant 3262 Spr. George   Thiepval Memorial

Williams 2219 Spr. Sidney Herbert   Aged 38   Husband of L J Williams of 3, Wilton Terrace, Melton Mowbray   Serre Road Cemetery No. 2, I. H. 24

ROYAL FIELD ARTILLERY

56th Div. Ammunition Col., Royal Field Artillery

James 19964 Drvr William   Hebuterne Military Cemetery, IV. M. 55

Lynch 569 Gnr John   Thiepval Memorial, Pier and Face 1 A and 8 A

Parry 4764 Gnr Albert Brindley   Aged 20   Son of William Alfred & Elizabeth Parry of 2, Coal Yard Terrace, Blaenavon, Mon   Hebuterne Military Cemetery, IV. M. 13

Williams 70934 Gnr John   Aged 22   Son of Ellen Williams of 11, Tai Newydd, Brynsiencyn, Llanfairpwllgwyngll, Anglesley, & the late John Williams   Hebuterne Military Cemetery, IV. M. 8

Y 56th Trench Mortar Bty

Saunders 1633 Gnr Christopher William Herbert   Aged 20   Son of Mr and Mrs C M Saunders, of 23, Gladstone Avenue, Manor Park, Essex.   Thiepval Memorial, Pier and Face 1 A and 8 A

ROYAL ARMY MEDICAL CORPS

2/1st London Field Ambulance

Hocking 678 Pte Leslie Harold   Aged 19   Son of William John Hocking, C.V.O., C.B.E., & Agnes Hocking of Bristol House, Danbury, Essex.   Born in London   Hebuterne Military Cemetery, II. N. 1

2nd July 1916

Tanter 408 Pte William Laurence   Aged 25   Son of William H & Bertha L Tanter of 66, Malvern Rd., Leytonstone, London   Warlincourt Halte British Cemetery, Saulty, II.D.6

2/2nd London Field Ambulance

Giles 772 Pte Alec   Aged 19   Son of David & J M Giles of 3, Canning Rd., Highbury, London   Hebuterne Military Cemetery, II. N. 2

ROYAL GARRISON ARTILLERY

2nd July 1916

Hall 66277 Gnr Edmund   101st Siege Bty   Son of Mrs A A Morris of 93, Bennett's Lane, Bolton   Bienvillers Military Cemetery, VI. B. 2

Watson 67543 Gnr John   68th Siege Bty   Aged 22   Son of William & Elizabeth Ann Watson of Hocket, Alnwick, Northumberland   Sailly-Au-Bois Military Cemetery I. C. 2

11th July 1916

Baumber 61423 Gnr John William   88th Siege Bty   Aged 23   Son of William & Sarah Baumber of Helpringham, Lincs.   Le Treport Military Cemetery Plot 2. Row N. Grave 3

APPENDIX 7: PRISONERS OF WAR

The list of Prisoners of War below is not an exhaustive one but is based on information gleaned from various sources, in particular the *Territorial Service Gazette* for the period August to December 1916. The exception to this proviso is the list of London Rifle Brigade PoWs which has been provided by Chris Rippingale. As far as is known, this list is complete.

1/2nd London Regt.

2580	Thorn, Pte Alfred	DoW 20.7.16 probably at St Quentin
2843	Bentall, Pte Arthur Eldred	DoW 3.7.16 at Douchy-Les-Ayette
2887	Jones, Pte Percy John	DoW 6.7.16 probably at St Quentin
2908	Stratford, Pte Frederick Ernest	DoW 11.7.16 at Caudry

1/4th London Regt.

	2nd Lt. A G Blunn	Gütersloh Camp
125	Edwards, H W C.S.M.	
1666	Ebeling, Cpl. Albert A Company	Wounded
	Knight, R Sgt.	
	Dunn, Pte.	
	Barr, Pte.	

1/9th London Regt. (Queen Victoria's Rifles)

	2nd Lt. R Bennett	
	Lt. Cyril Percy Fleetwood	DoW 12.7.16 at Le Cateau
1487	Gittens, Cpl Walter R C Company	
1636	Symons, Rfn. Barnett B V	Wounded in both arms and back Lazarett Minden
1676	Walter, Rf. R 8 Platoon	Wounded in the hand Minden Camp
1871	Layland, Rfn. George James	DoW 20.7.16 at St Quentin
1984	Lahee, Cpl. Terence	DoW 1.7.16
2073	Payne, Sgt. H	Wounded No. 5 Reserve Lazarett, Hannover
2262	Caunt, Rfn. E E 9 Platoon	
2421	Springate, Rfn. S P	Minden Camp
2475	Courteen, Rfn. Harry	Langensalza Camp
2603	Woodland, Cpl E F	
2647	Cane, Rfn. Walter G	Slightly wounded Langensalza Camp
2731	Cheesman, Rfn. R J 6 Platoon	Initially reported killed
2810	Gibson, Cpl	Wounded No. 5 Reserve Lazarett, Hannover
2836	Small, Rfn. A R	Hannover Camp
2840	Heronimas, Rfn. J	Ohrdruf Camp
2890	Larkin, Rfn. Reginald Harry A Company	DoW 1.7.16 at Roclincourt
3141	Davies, Rfn. C O	Lived at 70, Revelon Road, Brockley Hannover Camp
3347	Edmondson, Rfn. Edward Tepper 3 Platoon	DoW 4.7.16 near Bapaume
3398	Sutton, L/Sgt A C	Reserve Hospital, Minden Camp
3475	Clark, Rfn. James 10 Platoon	Son of Mr and Mrs Clark,20, Alexandra Road, Finsbury Park Dülmen Camp
3734	Graham, Rfn. Sydney Harold	DoW 6.7.16 at Le Cateau
3859	Calder, Rfn. Roy Grant	DoW 15.7.16 probably at St Quentin
3994	Peirce, Rfn. William Alec	DoW 17.7.16 at Le Cateau
4189	Hall, Rfn. E S 7 Platoon	Son of Mrs Hall, 161, Mitre Street, Waterloo Road, Lambeth Wounded right arm Dülmen Camp and exchanged December 1916 and evacuated to Queen Alexandra Hospital, Millbank

4367	Atkinson, Rfn. J L 12 Platoon	Wounded in left hand and arm
4465	Robertson, Rfn. Lester D 6 Platoon	
4466	Day, Rfn. William J 6 Platoon	Dülmen Camp
4622	Spencer, Rfn. J H	Hannover Camp
4684	Child, Rfn. J R 5 Platoon	
4798	Odell, Rfn. L C	Slightly wounded
4994	Thoms, Rfn. W F 12 Platoon	Wounded
	Prince, L/Sgt George	Son of E P Prince, 25, Heathville Road, Crouch Hill, London N
		Wounded
	Morris Rfn.	

1/12ᵗʰ London Regt. (The Rangers)

	2ⁿᵈ Lt. W G Parker	
1921	Ward, Rfn. Arthur	DoW 3.7.16 at Bihucourt
2227	Job, Rfn. Edward W 14 Platoon	Lived at 104, Graham Road, Dalston
		Dülmen Camp
3001	Loker, Cpl B H A att 2/2ⁿᵈ Londons 7 Platoon	DoW 9.8.16 at Le Cateau
3392	Cox, Rfn. Douglas	DoW 15.7.16 at Caudry
3416	Harvey, Rfn. William G 10 Platoon	Son of Mrs Harvey, 50, Church Street, Edgware Road, London W
4184	Alleman, Rfn. Leonard D 14 Platoon	Lived at 22, Euston Square
		Dülmen Camp
4209	Taylor, Rfn. Charles W	Son of Mr Taylor, 22, Offord Street, Barnsbury
		Wounded
		Lazarett Gottingen
4291	Law, Rfn. Edmund	Lived at 112, Hallam Street, London, W
		Wounded in the leg
		Died of wounds 13.9.16
		Ohrdruf Camp
		Brother Rfn. P Law killed 1.7.16
4292	Carter Rfn. Edwin George	Lived at 5c, Vera Road, Fulham
		Wounded left leg and foot
		DoW 10.7.16 at Caudry
4328	Bailey, Rfn. William 14 Platoon	Ohrdruf Camp
4499	Studd, Rfn. Charles Henry	DoW 17.7.16 at Douchy-les-Ayettes

1/13ᵗʰ London Regt. (Kensingtons)

	2ⁿᵈ Lt. P R Pike	Marienberg Camp
4517	Oliver, Pte George William	DoW 7.7.16 at Caudry

1/14ᵗʰ London Regt. (London Scottish)

3003	Bros, Pte Henry L	Ohrdruf Camp
4257	Faulkner, Sgt. Howard B	Dülmen Camp
4509	Goodall, Pte John	Minden Camp
4865	Meggy, Cpl Robert C	Dülmen Camp
4936	Tynemouth, Pte Angus M	Son of Mr Tynemouth, 4, Beechhill Road, Eltham
	C Company Lewis Gun Section	Minden Camp
4983	Sim, Pte Alexander G	Dülmen Camp
5084	Crosby, Pte Reginald J 2 Platoon	Wounded
5113	Fullagar, Pte Alfred J	Minden Camp
5114	Gear, Pte Bernard H	Minden Camp
5117	Hutcheson, Pte Thomas G	
5119	Bradshaw, Pte Frederick J	Giessen Camp
5143	Barrett, Pte William R	
5158	Livesey, Pte Reginald G	Wahn Camp
5186	Pullen, Pte L H	DoW 1.7.16
5292	Newington, Pte David J	Dülmen Camp
5437	Phillips, Pte Henry A	Dülmen Camp
5509	Head, Pte Reginald V	Wahn Camp

5764	Thompson, Pte Richard Edward	Lager Heuberg and Adelhausen
		MM for escaping
5572	Lambton, Pte George Edward	DoW 1.7.16
5626	Barnett, Pte John R	Minden Camp
5681	French, Pte Frederick W	Dülmen Camp
5726	Meakins, Pte Charles E	Wahn Camp
5764	Thompson, Pte Richard E	Dülmen Camp
5775	Robertson, Pte Alexander J	Son of Mrs Robertson, Lochnagar
		Lodge, Cavendish Gardens, Illford
6221	Heywood, Pte Reginald Charles	DoW 21.7.16 probably at St Quentin
6450	Miller, Pte Albert E	
6546	Robertson, Pte George	Minden Camp
6578	Grant, Pte. William J 7 Platoon	Wounded in the leg
6594	Westwood, Pte Alfred	Dülmen Camp
6650	Wainwright, Pte Verner	DoW 27.7.16 at Caudry
6782	Bennett, Pte George S P	Dülmen Camp

1/16th London Regt. (Queen's Westminster Rifles)

	Capt. G E Cockerill	DoW 3.7.16 at Vaulx
	Lt. P Spencer Smith	
	2nd Lt. D F Upton M.C.	
1681	Mockett, Rfn. W E	Giessen Camp
2380	Warrilow, Cpl James F A Company	
2456	England, L/Cpl W J 6 Platoon	Slightly wounded in head and shoulder
		Minden Camp
2566	Glanville, Rfn. Frederick D	Langensalza Camp
2668	Lanham, Pte B att. from 2/2nd Londons	Lived at 7, Warmington Road, Herne
		Hill, London
2815	Clarke, Rfn. Albert Josiah A Company	Shell wound to the back
		Lazarett, Le Cateau
2881	Tucknott, L/Cpl C W H att. from 3/2nd	Lived at 103, Bowes Road, Palmer's
	Londons	Green
		Wounded
		No. 5 Reserve Lazarett, Hannover
2907	Jones, Rfn. Albert S 11 Platoon	Lived at 7, Broadhurst Gardens, South
		Hampstead
		Dülmen Camp
3084	Nicholls, Rfn. G H	Langensalza Camp
3967	Noble, Rfn. Ralph Edgar	DoW 6.7.16 at Le Cateau
4365		Lived at 56, Tremadoe Road, Clapham
		Wounded in the chest and thigh
		Lazarett Wahn and Ohrdruf Camp

	Lovis, Rfn. F C 10 Platoon	
4381	Holroyd, Rfn. Cyril Bernardine	DoW 8.7.16 probably at St Quentin
4734	Dorsett, Rfn W H	Ohrdruf Camp
	Jones, Rfn P H	
	Hughes, Rfn.	

512th Field Company, R.E.

T2627	Larkin, Spr. William G	Husband of 71, Glenarm Road, Clapton
		Wounded
T3455	Cox, Spr. Dudley Farr	DoW 11.7.16 at Caudry

I am indebted to Chris Rippingale for the list of the men from the London Rifle Brigade who were taken prisoner at Gommecourt on 1st July 1916. In 1916 the Army embarked on a renumbering system with soldiers being given a six digit number. Soldiers who were prisoners of war and also those who were missing and not confirmed as dead were renumbered as part of this process and the list below includes the old and the new numbers where applicable. Several men from the London Rifle Brigade attempted to escape and those that succeeded, Messers Carle, Rippengal and Evanson, were subsequently awarded the Military Medal.

1/5th London Regt. (London Rifle Brigade)

Army No. 1	Army No. 2	Name	
		Capt. A T B de Cologan	Gütersloh Camp
4	300250	Burn, A	
84	300217	Carle, C G	Lager Heuberg
			MM for escaping
339		Ford, L McI 4 Platoon	DoW at Le Cateau 6.7.16
345	300351	Rippengal, C G 4 Platoon	Wounded
			MM for escaping
			Minden Camp
1157	300710	Brown, L A	Minden Camp
1334	300822	Colvin, F	Lived at 71, Pennard Road, Shepherd's Bush
			Hannover Camp
1377	300847	Icke, Percy A E 11 Platoon	Son of Sgt M T Icke, 1st Essex Volunteer Regt., of 56, Devonshire Road, Stratford
			Wounded
			Repatriated via Switzerland January 1917
1425	300881	Icke, Rfn. S G 11 Platoon	Dülmen Camp
1459	300901	Bates, W G	Shrapnel wound in the lower back
			Lazarett CL2, Ohrdruf
			Died 21.1.19
1475	300916	Wells, A E	Son of Mrs Wells, 27, Almond Road, Park Lane, Tottenham
			Wounded
			Minden Camp
1495	300931	Evanson, E	Wounded
			MM for escaping, Minden Camp
1518	300944	Crisfield, F S	Wounded
1538	300957	Richardson, L H	
1644	301015	Cause, S A	
1721		Butt, F C	DoW 6.7.16 at Le Cateau
1744	301077	Pratt, W C	
1773	301096	Brans, P C 12 Platoon att C Company Lewis Gun Section	
1865	301152	Whitehouse, W L	Minden Camp
1883	301166	Dean, F E	Minden Camp
1922	301194	Wood, E	
1988		Olerenshaw, S H	DoW 18.7.16 at le Cateau
2012	301250	Houle, B	Wounded
			Minden Camp
2072	301291	Sheval, L/Cpl A J	
2198	301385	Sidwell, H C	Wounded
			Minden Camp
2025	301259	Preston, C M	
2049	301275	Hoddinott, E H	Minden Camp
2099		Hollingham, F V 15 Platoon	DoW 14.7.16 at Caudry
2103	301312	Morris, Rfn. Ronald Victor Samuel 10 Platoon	Son of Mr F W Morris, 39, Oakfield Road, Croydon
			Wounded
			Minden Camp

2113	301320	Grundon, Harold S	Son of Mr and Mrs Grundon of Chapel House, Osborne Road, Forest Hill Chest wound and a bomb wound right arm Repatriated via Switzerland January 1917
2147		Shipham, E	DoW 8.7.16 at Le Cateau
2177	301368	Grigg, W H	
2183	301372	Bassett, J I 14 Platoon	Minden Camp
2214	301399	Farren, A T	
2236	301412	Woodward Rfn. Reginald F 2 Platoon	Son of Mr and Mrs Woodward, 72, Denman Road, Peckham Wounded Minden Camp
2417	301559	Holliday, C E 11 Platoon	Slightly wounded Giessen Camp
2419	301561	Lankester, A W	Son of Mrs Lankester of 13, Regnold Road, Forest Gate
2428	301567	Gough, H F 3 Platoon	
2437	301572	Holyfield, S F M	
2455	301586	Short, T	
2458	301589	Thom, A G	
2517	301632	Eckworth, Rfn. S G 3 Platoon	Son of Mr and Mrs Eckworth of 107, Westcliff Park Drive, Westcliff-on-Sea
2528	301641	Yeomans, S	
2607	301701	Drake, H G	
2700	301776	Hyslop, J	
2703	301778	Aarons, S L 11 Platoon att C Company Lewis Gun Section	Wounded in the arm and leg Lazarett Ohrdruf
2744	301804	File, H	
2793	301838	Rayfield, A F 2 Platoon	Lived at 169, Ballspond Road, Islington Dülmen Camp
2802	301843	Martin, E A	
2813	301851	Sharman, E A	
2817	301855	Clayton, A E A Company	
2818		Fraser, A	DoW 9.7.16 at Cologne (Deutz)
2824	301859	Potter, A E	
2994	301954	Ward, A J	Died 14.10.18 at Niederzwehren
2949	301921	Ault, F W	Wounded right shoulder
2996	301952	Moore, H E	
3003	301959	Homersham, F J	Wounded Lazarett Ohrdruf
3004		Kimber, Rfn. Charles Lyddon	Unconscious for five days, wounded in thigh and stomach Ohdruf Camp
3006	301961	Paine, C A 10 Platoon	
4092		Tookey, H J	Wounded in the arm DoW 27.7.16 at Caudry
5025	303066	Bowden, B G	
9553	300125	Morgan, E G H	
9868	300214	Avery, C W	

APPENDIX 8: ROLL OF HONOUR OF THE 2ND GUARD RESERVE INFANTRY DIVISION

Ranks:
Lt. der Res: Leutnant der Reserve – Reserve Lieutenant
Offz Stellv: Offizier Stellvertreter – Warrant Officer
Vzfeldw: Vizefeldwebel - Sergeant
Utffz: Unteroffizier – Corporal
Gefr: Gefreiter – Lance Corporal (Sanit Gfr – Medical Lance Corporal)

Casualties of the 55th Reserve Infantry Regiment (Courtesy of Ralph Whitehead)

5th Company	Town of Birth	Military District	Nature of casualty
Ltn Walter Doess		Seigburg	Killed
Uttfz Friedrich Sadermann		Dusseldorf	Severely wounded
Gefr Johann Schiffels		Elberfeld	Severely wounded
Gefr Martin Gropper	Hövelhof	Paderborn	Slightly wounded
Gefr Friedrich Klemme	Lage	Lippe-Detmold	Severely wounded
Gefr Martin Tepper	Westenholz	Paderborn	Severely wounded
Franz Gockel	Elsen	Paderborn	Severely wounded
Leopold Geisler	Beckandorf	Danzig	Slightly wounded
Johann Borutta	Osterwein	Osterode	Wounded
Rickard Neumann	Ostritz	Zittau	Slightly wounded
Johannes Reuter	Atteln	Buren	Wounded
Josef Farke	Ahden	Buren	Wounded
Wilhelm Asbeck	Wald	Solingen	Slightly wounded
Wilhelm Eickmeier		Herford	Slightly wounded
Walter Haussels		Solingen	Killed
Matthias Back		Dusseldorf	Killed
Ernst Tillmann	Holzwickede	Horde	Killed
Fabian Brenineck	Wilhelmsruh	Fraustadt	Severely wounded

6th Company			
Uttfz Heinrich Tunsmeyer	Bentfeld	Buren	Slightly wounded
Gefr Heinrich Vollmer	Steinhausen	Buren	Slightly wounded
Gefr Heinrich Schluter	Wersen	Herford	Killed
Gefr Martin Dierks	Thule	Buren	Slightly wounded
Gefr Heinrich Meverring		Lubbecke	Severely wounded
Gefr Josef Igges	Etteln	Buren	Killed
Johann Maaskerstingiost	Westerloh	Paderborn	Severely wounded
Heinrich Voss	Legden	Ahaus	Severely wounded
George Ridermeyer		Paderborn	Slightly wounded
Theodor Winkels		Herne	Slightly wounded
Heinrich Bovermann	Barop	Hurde	Slightly wounded
Wilhelm Tappe	Schwarzenmoor	Herford	Slightly wounded
Erich Darkow		Bielefeld	Slightly wounded
Bernard Steinbicker	Osterwick	Koesfeld	Severely wounded
Franz Niedworok	Czarnowanz	Oppeln	Slightly wounded
Anton Flamme	Leiberg	Buren	Slightly wounded
Erich Kuhlmann	Schildesche	Bielefeld	Killed
Peter Blatzheim	Kreuzau	Duren	Slightly wounded

7th Company			
Feldw Lt. Heinrich Backenecker	Weitmar	Bochum	Slightly wounded
Offz Stellv Hermann Ridder	Deutsch Krone		Killed
Uttfz Jozef Rolte	Lütgeneder	Warburg	Slightly wounded
Uttfz Franz Hocker	Hövelhof	Paderborn	Severely wounded
Uttfz Wilhelm Huffschmidt	Stolberg	Aachen	Killed
Gefr Wilhelm Friedhof	Senne	Schötmar	Killed

Gefr August Arnold		Dusseldorf	Killed
Gefr Wilhelm Linnemann	Salzuflen	Schötmar	Killed
Gefr Wilhelm Janv		Breslau	Missing
Gefr Paul Kehl		Elberfeld	Missing
Sanit Gefr August Bruseke	Neuhaus	Paderborn	Missing
Freiderich Lehmann	Altenhagen	Springe	Slightly wounded
Hermann Uhlmeyer	Brockhagen	Bielefeld	Slightly wounded
Gustav Neermann	Polle	Bielefeld	Slightly wounded
Gustav Przvgodda	Liebenberg	Ortelsburg	Slightly wounded
Johann Stockhorst	Kellen	Cleve	Severely wounded
Heinrich Koch		Herford	Slightly wounded
Martin Buchwald	Klein Galonski	Pleschen	Slightly wounded
Ernst Boing	Witten	Ruhr	Slightly wounded
Albert Berfuch	Neuteichsdorf	Marienburg	Slightly wounded
Gustav Kunkel	Wlozlawek	Russland	Slightly wounded
Johann Kusszta	Borbeck	Essen	Wounded
Heinrich Hoppe	Bagersehn	Leer	Wounded
Heinrich Beine	Dossel	Warburg	Wounded
Franz Brinkmann		Dusseldorf	Slightly wounded
Karl Lucking	Oberhauerschaft	Lubbeke	Slightly wounded
Erwin Kleiner	Schweidnitz	Breslau	Severely wounded
Peter Himmelmann	Barmen		Severely wounded
Peter Wakowski	Neu Allenstein		Killed
Adam Fugen	Steiningen	Daun	Killed
Wilhelm Riederbremer	Bieren	Herford	Killed
Erich Kaltenvoth		Essen	Killed
August Thomas	Asernissen	Schötmar	Killed
Theodor Erzeflad	Livie	Kempen	Killed
Johann Bohning		Luneburg	Killed
Freidrich Apke I	Niederbecksen	Minden	Slightly wounded
Freidrich Apke II	Solterwisck	Herford	Missing
Paul Sadler		Barmen	Missing
August Muller		Elberfeld	Missing
Johann Balsliemke	Sende	Wiedenbruck	Missing
Wilhelm Lubbeke	Hannover		Missing
Wilhelm Spanner	Wewelsburg	Buren	Missing
Franz Eichler	Mauche	Bomst	Killed
Gerhard Bilchof	Rhede	Borken	Killed
Bernhard Jansen	Crefeld		Severely wounded
Franz Stammschroer	Wadersloh	Beckum	Slightly wounded
Wilhelm Meier	Ostsilver	Herford	Slightly wounded
Konrad Jurgens	Hovelhof	Paderborn	Slightly wounded
Wilhelm Schulz	Pieckarn	Posen West	Missing
Wilhelm Fischer		Bielefeld	Missing
Johannes Bentler	Katernberg	Essen	Missing
Nikolaus Gross		Muhlhausen	Missing
Karl Lesermann	Blomberg	Detmold	Slightly wounded
Robert Kurten	Dorst	Solingen	Slightly wounded
Karl Finck	Wilhelmsburg	Hamburg	Slightly wounded
Josef Brechmann	Hovelhof	Paderborn	Slightly wounded
Hyazinth Chlopeck	Neudorf	Meseritz	Slightly wounded

8th Company

Lt. der Res Otto Weil	Homburg	Bavaria	Slightly wounded
Lt. Gustav Jeger			Slightly wounded
Vzfeldw Wilhelm Edelbrock	Styrum	Oberhausen	Missing
Vzfeldw Gustav Riesv	Schwartzenmoor	Herford	Killed
Utffz Friedrich Schonlau	Oberntudorf	Paderborn	Slightly wounded
Utffz August Muller	Meerhof	Paderborn	Slightly wounded
Utffz August Koch	Meinberg	Detmold	Slightly wounded
Utffz Eduard Otto	Ovenhausen	Hoxter	Killed

Utffz Josef Muss	Osterwiese	Wiedenbruck	Killed
Utffz Herman Gieselmann	Enger	Herford	Killed
Utffz Friedrich Strangboner		Herford	Killed
Utffz Johann Rohde	Cuersen	Hoxter	Killed
Uttfz Heinrich Weickers	Alternbeerse	Warburg	Killed
Utffz Wilhelm Hamer		Hamburg	Slightly wounded
Utffz Ferdinand Drenkelfutz	Ovenhausen	Hoxter	Missing
Utffz Wilhelm Schmidt	Hegensdorf	Buren	Missing
Gefr Karl Jobmann	Sporl	Detmold	Killed
Gefr Friedrich Pabmeier	Gidinghausen	Minden	Killed
Gefr Heinrich Kampeter	Kobinghausen	Herford	Missing
Gefr Ernst Witz	Rielasingen	Konstanz	Severely wounded
Gefr Josef Knies	Delbruck	Paderborn	Severely wounded
Gefr Franz Kempe	Auenhausen	Warburg	Severely wounded and missing
Gefr Josef Canisius		Dusseldorf	Severely wounded
Gefr Heinrich Hortsmann	Oberbauerschaft	Lubbeke	Slightly wounded
Gefr Hugo Weber	Werne	Bochum	Slightly wounded
Gefr Friedrich Arning	Talle	Brake	Slightly wounded
Gefr Georg Meischl	Ernestgrun	Tirschenreuth	Missing
Gefr Heinrich Langehenke	Enthausen	Paderborn	Missing
Johann Sieberg	Erfeln	Hoxter	Killed
Johannes Thiele	Meerhof	Buren	Missing
Ignaz Gistwitski	Grabau	Lobau	Missing
Clemens Kaub		Witten	Killed
Heinrich Kober		Duisburg	Killed
Hermann Buckert		Gevelsburg	Killed
Wilhelm Baumbach	Urdenbach	Bemrath	Killed
Max Langenberg	Ohligs	Solingen	Killed
Josef Lucas II	Engelskirchen	Gummersbach	Killed
Simon Ostmann	Pivitsheide	Detmold	Killed
Hermann Motzkau	Liebstadt		Killed
Johannes Duker	Udendorf	Gelsenkirchen	Killed
Anton Riggemeyer	Rosebeck	Warburg	Killed
Franz Tobat	Kray	Essen	Killed
Josef Plata	Wirowen-Kalisch	Berent	Killed
Wilhelm Steinkamp	Unterwusten	Schotmar	Killed
Michael Mikolajczak	Szczevankovo	Samter	Killed
Emil Moslein		Dusseldorf	Killed
Johann Rudolf	Tondorf	Schleiden	Killed
Otto Ballmann		Dusseldorf	Killed
Paul Lehmann		Juterbog	Killed
Wilhelm Servatius	Langenfeld	Solingen	Killed
Wilhelm Roth	Marbach	Reckarkreis	Killed
Anton Dellbosen	Blerichen	Bergheim	Killed
Friedrich Tekutsch	Schalke	Gelsenkirchen	Killed
Franz Brinkmann		Hagen	Killed
Wilhelm Krimer	Bocholt	Essen	Killed
Hermann Strakelfahn	Spenge	Herford	Killed
Karl Brinkmann	Grotzenmarpe	Blomberg	Severely wounded
Heinrich Mets	Fischeln	Crefeld	Severely wounded
Heinrich Bles	Styrum	Mulheim	Killed
Gustav Studemann	Tollenbeck	Bielefeld	Severely wounded
Eduard Volfmann	Ummeln	Bielefeld	Severely wounded
Gustav Tolle	Schweicheln	Herford	Severely wounded
Gustav Rebse	Kochheide	Schotmar	Severely wounded
Heinrich Schlomann	Huder-u-Aschen	Herford	Slightly wounded
Gustav Funke	Wulser	Schotmar	Slightly wounded
Wilhelm Goke	Hontruv	Detmold	Slightly wounded
Max Lichtenauer	Penzberg	Weilheim	Slightly wounded

Justus Botzel	Roddenau	Frankenberg	Slightly wounded
Friedrich Adam		Olpe	Slightly wounded
Josef Grundmann	Lobberich	Kempen	Slightly wounded
Walter Weide		Hagen	Severely wounded
Wilhelm Melchior	Bieren	Herford	Slightly wounded
Anton Lobige	Dahl	Paderborn	Slightly wounded
Adolf Sielemann	Augustdorf	Detmold	Slightly wounded
Gustave Dresel	Silschede	Hagen	Slightly wounded
Johann Meter	Dalhausen	Hoxter	Slightly wounded
Hermann Mebmaier	Melbergen	Herford	Slightly wounded
Fritz Fabri	Hollweisen	Herford	Slightly wounded
Anton Muller	Merlsheim	Hoxter	Missing
Lorens Tepel	Rustelberg	Brilon	Slightly wounded
Wilhelm Arnold	Buggingen	Lorach	Severely wounded
Johann Grimberg	Assinghausen	Solingen	Severely wounded
Heinrich Hagen	Erle	Redlinghausen	Slightly wounded
Alfred Hendriks	Iserlohn	Hagen	Killed
Hermann Lucking		Herford	Killed
Eugen Machelett	Eggenscheid	Altena	Killed
Reinhard Eisenbach	Krimm	Lennep	Killed
Wilhelm Schelberg	Ammenhausen	Kreis der Twiste	Killed
Albert Goluke	Eilversen	Hoxter	Killed
Richard Erbmann		Braunschweig	Killed
Emil Menke		Bielefeld	Killed
Heinrich Steinkamp	Westerenger	Herford	Missing
Georg Kretzer		Duisburg	Missing
Aler Kipp	Neviges	Mettmann	Missing
August Maes	Materborn	Cleve	Missing
Josef Burke	Handrup	Lingen	Missing
Franz Besse	Dalhausen	Hoxter	Missing
Paul Schuster	Neuzulzendorf	Nimptsch	Missing
August Hilgenstobler	Horste	Detmold	Severely wounded and missing
Heinrich Mube	Dobren	Hannover	Missing
Paul Ulrich		Herford	Missing
August Enbrulat	Draweningken	Stalluponen	Missing
Wilhelm Eickmeier	Grimminghausen	Herford	Slightly wounded
Heinrich Kramer	Koppenbrugge	Hameln	Severely wounded
Christof Buschlep	Hausen	Worbis	Killed
Karl Antholz		Crefeld	Killed
Bernhard Goffart		Aachen	Slightly wounded
Lorenz Justus	Bonenburg	Warburg	Missing

9th Company

Offz Stellv Johann Hau	Munchweis	Ottweiler	Severely wounded
Utffz Alfred Dee		Elberfeld	Slightly wounded
Utffz Wilhelm Wortmann	Wobbel	Lippe-Detmold	Slightly wounded
Utffz Albert Lingemann	Kamen	Hamm	Slightly wounded
Gefr Friedrich Blomberg	Linderhofe	Lippe-Detmold	Severely wounded
Gefr Georg Wolf		Minden	Slightly wounded
Gefr August Gnade	Talle	Lippe-Detmold	Slightly wounded
Gefr Friedrich Pfordt		Ottweiler	Slightly wounded
Friedrich Bruns I	Sabbenhausen	Lippe-Detmold	Killed
Paul Deus		Solingen	Slightly wounded
Heinrich Hagermeier	Borninghausen		Slightly wounded
Otto Ast	Schonfeld	Stendal	Severely wounded
Josef Pohlmann	Monheim	Solingen	Slightly wounded
Karl Kruger I	Rehme	Minden	Slightly wounded
Heinrich Theben		Borken	Severely wounded
Hermann Resa		Hagen	Killed
Bernhard Lefting	Sudlohn	Ahaus	Slightly wounded

Friedrich Knickmeier	Oberlubbe	Minden	Slightly wounded
Josef Muller III	Schlebusch	Solingen	Slightly wounded
Heinrich Rolfsmaier	Gohfeld	Herford	Slightly wounded
George Krautz	Eschenstruth	Cassel	Slightly wounded
Lorenz Warden		Dusseldorf	Slightly wounded
August Henke	Bunde	Herford	Slightly wounded
Johann Agatz		Gelsenkirchen	Slightly wounded
Wilhelm Buscher		Dusseldorf	Slightly wounded

10th Company

Lt. der Res August Keifer	Eving	Dortmund	Slightly wounded
Offz Stellv Gustav Besecke	Vilshofen	Passau	Slightly wounded
Utffz August Holschbach	Grafrath	Solingen	Severely wounded
Utffz August Frickmann	Ehrsen	Schotmar	Severely wounded
Utffz Fritz Artschwager		Essen	Slightly wounded
Utffz Gustav Wernecke	Gross Germersleben	Wanzleben	Slightly wounded
Gefr Gustav Eickmeier	Unterwusten	Lippe-Detmold	Killed
Gefr Wilhelm Beyer	Neumunster	Holstein	Killed
Gefr Johann Freitag	Sassanfahrt	Bavaria	Killed
Gefr Johann Siekmann	Schildesche	Bielefeld	Killed
Gefr Heinz Schneider	Limburg	Wiesbaden	Slightly wounded
Gefr Franz Krings	Wurselen	Aachen	Severely wounded
Gefr Johannes Keusgen		Gelsenkirchen	Severely wounded
Heinrich Werner		Duisburg-Melberich	Killed
Gottbils Kienzle	Klein Villars	Maulbronn	Killed
Gustav Kuhlmann	Eickum	Herford	Killed
Isidor Dranga	Altenbammer	Lauenberg	Killed
Christian Pennigroth	Kutenhausen	Minden	Killed
Josef Bickschafer		Dusseldorf	Killed
Felix Milenz		Honigfeld	Killed
Johann Geerkens	Bocholt	Geldern	Killed
Gerhard Nierocks	Weeze	Geldern	Slightly wounded
Johann Theizsen		Cleve	Slightly wounded
Gustav Schroder	Eilshausen	Herford	Severely wounded
Robert Schwanitz	Eisleben	Magdeburg	Severely wounded
Otto Unger	Blumbergerbruch	Landsberg	Slightly wounded
Robert Eckenbach	Borde	Schwelm	Severely wounded
Herman Heidbrebter		Bielefeld	Slightly wounded
Stephan Misslaf	Bolechowo	Posen	Slightly wounded
Hermann Muller		Elberfeld	Severely wounded
Franz Dombrowski	Neuhof	Dirschau	Slightly wounded
Paul Freitag	Rodewisch	Zwickau	Severely wounded
Bernhard Diedenhofen		Cleve	Slightly wounded
Kuno Biedebach	Sudberg	Mettmann	Severely wounded
Rudolf Huts		Elberfeld	Slightly wounded
Franz Morch		Remscheid	Severely wounded
Wilhelm Schroder	Eilshausen	Herford	Severely wounded
Wilhelm Baak	Stollhammerdeich	Butjadingen	Severely wounded
Ernst Hutter	Friederichshoh	Solingen	Severely wounded
Hugo Siekmann	Cronenberg	Mettmann	Severely wounded
Paul Hotze		Halle	Severely wounded
Josef Franke	Sonnern	Hamm	Severely wounded
Willhelm Braus		Duisburg	Slightly wounded
George Friedrichs	Apen	Oldenburg	Slightly wounded
Fritz Bohe		Elberfeld	Killed
Wilhelm Herrler		Merseburg	Killed
Josef Peters	Ottmarsbocholt	Ludinghausen	Severely wounded
Dietrich Husmann	Hamminkeln		Severely wounded
Wilhelm Hagemann	Werne	Ludinghausen	Severely wounded

Hinrich Bauer	Backemoor	Leer	Died of wounds at Res. FeldLazarett 45
Ernst Frose	Schwerte	Horde	Severely wounded
Heinrich Gobel		Dillenburg	Severely wounded
Erich Matthias	Lichtenburg	Neiderbayern	Severely wounded

11th Company

Vzfeldw Martin Besser	Voigtsdorf	Hirschberg	Slightly wounded
Utffz Franz Fleitmann	Ostenland	Paderborn	Slightly wounded
Gefr Berhard Vorwold		Paderborn	Severely wounded
Gefr Hermann Scheuer		Mulheim	Slightly wounded
Gefr Kaspar Vehige	Westenholz	Paderborn	Severely wounded
Karl Kobler	Obermatzfeld	Meiningen	Killed
Karl Lesch		Gelsenkirchen	Killed
Emil Liefland	Nierbhaben	Hamm	Killed
Ludwig Grobski		Gostyn	Killed
Anton Tochtrov	Benninghausen	Lippstadt	Killed
Friedrich Lebnert	Barop	Dortmund	Severely wounded
Wilhelm Wolf	Neiderganbern	Gottingen	Slightly wounded
Paul Gapp		Mulheim-Speldorf	Slightly wounded
Hugo Sander	Hombruch	Dortmund	Slightly wounded
Friedrich Weeke	Pivitsbeide	Detmold	Slightly wounded
Hermann Raabe		Gelsenkirchen	Slightly wounded
Paul Coch		Rawitsch	Slightly wounded
Heinrich Gross-Albenhausen	Schonnebeck	Essen	Slightly wounded
Ernst Osper	Kronenberg	Mettmann	Killed
Karl Kohn		Barmen	Missing
Heinrich Nachtigall	Rhedebrugge	Borken	Severely wounded
Friedrich Urbach		Lengefeld	Killed
Ernst Schopp	Berghofen	Horde	Killed
Wilhelm Lueg	Duren	Bochum	Killed
Wilhelm Kollmeier	Langerfeld	Schwelm	Died of wounds at Res. FeldLazarett 45
Franz Trentmann		Paderborn	Slightly wounded
Mar Missing		Duisburg-Meiderich	Slightly wounded
Georg Siempelkamp		Duisburg	Severely wounded
Gerhard Focking	Rhedebrugge	Borken	Slightly wounded
Wilhelm Zoller		St Goarshausen	Severely wounded

12th Company

Utffz Karl Bruckner	Dose	Hamburg	Slightly wounded
Utffz Wentzel Boland	Mehrhoog	Rees	Severely wounded
Utffz Otto Schumann	Ochtrup	Steinfurt	Killed
Gefr Adolf Otting	Schildeische	Bielefeld	Killed
Gefr Ignatz Czarczynski	Buin	Schrimm	Slightly wounded
Gefr Fritz Kruger	Barkbausen	Minden	Slightly wounded
Gefr Gerhard Tebart	Winnekendorf	Geldern	Killed
Ignatz Berus	Kunowo	Schrimm	Slightly wounded
Wilhelm Dahm	Zabna	Wittenberg	Slightly wounded
Gustav Plies		Bielefeld	Slightly wounded
Hermann Tiemann	Dreven	Herford	Slightly wounded
Gerhard Meisters	Hochelten	Rees	Slightly wounded
Jacob Karell	Buschhausen	Dinslaken	Slightly wounded
Albert Josef Wachowski		Essen	Slightly wounded
Karl Helig	Losgebnen	Friedland	Severely wounded
Anton Horbach		Mulheim	Slightly wounded
Theodor Althaus	Haspe	Hagen	Severely wounded
Willi Schneider		Gelsenkirchen	Slightly wounded
Erich Burk	Herne	Redlinghausen	Severely wounded
Hermann Becker	Hamborn	Neumuhl	Severely wounded

| Josef Mederer | Walddorf | Kelheim | Slightly wounded |
| Wilhelm Eickenhorst | Huddestorf | Stolzenau | Severely wounded |

15th Reserve Infantry Regiment

Leutnant Stollberg	Wounded
Feldwebel Piepertz	Killed
Vizefeldwebel Strohmeyer	Wounded

77th Reserve Infantry Regiment

Gefr Eduard Grunwald	3rd Company	Killed
Res Peter Salchert	10th Company	Killed
Musk Wilhelm Hilker	11th Company	Died of wounds at Res Feldlazarett 63

19th Field Artillery Regiment

Utffz Joseph Kuchler	3rd Battery	Died of wounds at Res Feldlazarett 45
Kann Ortmeier	3rd Battery	Wounded
Gefr Wimmer	3rd Battery	Wounded
Utffz Maas	3rd Battery	Wounded
Vize-Wachmeister Hafner	3rd Battery	Wounded
Lt. der Res Adam	4th Battery	Wounded
Kann Karl Bock	4th Battery	Killed

20th Field Artillery Regiment

Kann Schnurhuis	1st Battalion	Killed

APPENDIX 9: DETAILS OF CEMETERIES & MEMORIALS MENTIONED

The details below are published with the permission of, and with thanks to, the Commonwealth War Graves Committee

Name	Location
Abbeville Communal Cemetery, Abbeville, Somme.	Abbeville is on the main road from Paris to Boulogne (N1), about 80 kilometres south of Boulogne. The communal cemeteries are located on the left hand side of the road when leaving the town in a north-east direction for Drucat. Enter the Communal Cemetery by the left hand side main gate and follow CWGC signs within the Cemetery.
Agny Military Cemetery, Pas De Calais.	Agny is immediately south of Achicourt. The Military Cemetery is NW of the main part of the village across the River Crinchon. It is 4.75 kms SSW of Arras Railway Station.
Bavincourt Communal Cemetery, Pas De Calais.	Bavincourt is 250 metres north of L'Arbret on the N25 between Arras and Doullens.
Bronfay Farm Military Cemetery, Bray-Sur-Somme, Somme.	Bray-sur-Somme is 8 kilometres SE of Albert. Bronfay Farm is 3 kilometres NE of the village on the road to Maricourt and the Cemetery is on the SE side of the road opposite the farm.
Cabaret-Rouge British Cemetery, Souchez, Pas De Calais.	Souchez is a village 3.5 kms north of Arras on the main road to Bethune. The cemetery is about 1.5 kms south of the village on the west side of the D937 Arras-Bethune Road.
Caudry Old Communal Cemetery, Nord.	Caudry is 12 kilometres east of Cambrai on the south side of the main road to Le Cateau (N43). From the Cambrai to Le Cateau road take the dual carriageway into Caudry. Follow road for 1.10 kms to some traffic lights. Turn right and right again on to Rue Aristide Briand approximately 220 metres later. Follow road for approx. 300 metres and the cemetery entrance is on the right hand side just after the junction with Rue de Dunkerque on a small road (D164).
Combles Communal Cemetery Extension, Somme.	Combles is 13 kms south of Bapaume. From Bapaume take the N17 towards Peronne. After the village of Sailly Saillisel, take the D172 to Combles. The Extension is at the back of the Communal Cemetery which is on the right just before the village.
Couin British Cemetery, Couin, Pas de Calais.	Couin is a village 15 kilometres east of Doullens. Follow the main Doullens to Arras road, N25, as far as the crossroads with the D23. Follow the D23 to Souastre, then the D2 to Couin. Couin British Cemetery and Couin New British Cemetery are at the side of the road just before entering the village.
Delville Wood Cemetery, Longueval, Somme.	Longueval is a village 11 kms east of Albert. Delville Wood Cemetery is east of the village and on the south side of the road from Longueval to Ginchy.
Doullens Communal Cemetery Extensions Nos. 1 & 2, Somme.	Doullens is approximately 30 kms north of Amiens on the N25 road to Arras. The Communal Cemetery and Extensions lie on the southern side of the town, about 270 metres SE of the road to Arras.
Etretat Churchyard, Etretat, Seine-Maritime.	Etretat is a small seaside town about 26 kilometres north of Le Havre. The churchyard is on the D.940 from Fecamp.
Gommecourt Cemetery No. 2, Hebuterne, Somme.	Gommecourt is a village 19 kilometres SW of Arras. The Cemetery lies just off the road between Gommecourt and Puisieux (D6). A CWGC signpost indicating the directions to the site is situated at the junction 2 kilometres along this road. Access can also be made from the village of Hebuterne where a CWGC signpost indicates the way from the main square.
Grove Town Cemetery, Meaulte, Somme.	Leave Albert heading SE on the D329, through Meaulte towards Bray-sur-Somme. 2.5 kms down the road turn right towards Etinehem (C6). Follow the C6 for 0.8 kms and then the CWGC signpost indicating a right turn down a dirt track. Go down the dirt track for 0.4 kms and Grove Town British Cemetery is on the left.

Guillemont Road Cemetery, Guillemont, Somme.	Guillemont is 12 kilometres east of Albert. From the D929 direction Bapaume-Albert take the 2nd turning for Martinpuich, continuing along the D6 for 5 kilometres until the crossroads in Longueval. Follow D20 until you leave Guillemont on the D64 direction Montauban. The Cemetery is 500 metres on the right as you leave Guillemont.
Harlebeke New British Cemetery, West Vlaaderen, Belgium	Harlebeke New British Cemetery is located 32 kilometres east of Ieper town centre on a road leading from the N8 Meenseweg, connecting Ieper to Menen, Wevelgem, Kortrijk and Zwevegem.
Hebuterne Military Cemetery, Hebuterne, Somme.	Hebuterne is a village 15 kilometres north of Albert (Somme) and 20 kilometres SW of Arras. Using the D919 from Arras to Amiens you will drive through the villages of Bucquoy, Puisieux then Serre (approximately 20 kilometres south of Arras). On leaving Serre, 3 kilometres further along the D919, turn right following the signs for Hebuterne. Hebuterne Military Cemetery lies to the west of the village and a CWGC signpost clearly indicates the way from the village green to the cemetery.
Henu Church Cemetery, Somme.	Henu lies on the D6, 16km east of Doullens to the south of the N25, the main road between Doullens and Arras.
Le Treport Military Cemetery, Seine-Maritime.	Le Treport is a coastal town approximately 30 kms NE of Dieppe. The Military Cemetery lies to the south of the town next to the town's Communal Cemetery on the D940.
London Cemetery and Extension, Longueval, Somme.	From the D929 direction Bapaume-Albert take the 2nd turning for Martinpuich and continue along the D6 direction Longueval, for 2 kms. London Cemetery and Extension will be found on the right hand side of the road.
Louvencourt British Cemetery, Somme.	Louvencourt is a village 13 kms SE of Doullens on the road to Albert (D938). The Cemetery is on the SE side of the village.
Rue Petillon Military Cemetery, Fleurbaix	Fleurbaix is a village 5 kilometres south-west of Armentieres on the D22. Rue-Petillon Military Cemetery will be found by taking the D175 from Fleurbaix towards Fauquissart, then the D171 towards Petillon. The cemetery is on the south side of the road from Petillon to La Boutillerie.
Sailly au Bois Military Cemetery, Pas de Calais.	Sailly-au-Bois is a village between Arras and Amiens. The Military Cemetery is western of the village, on the south side of the road (D23) leading to Bayencourt and Souastre. Access to this road can be taken from the main road (N25) from Doullens to Arras leading to Gaudiempre and St Amand (D23).
St Amand British Cemetery, Pas De Calais.	St. Amand is a village in the southern part of the Department of the Pas-de-Calais, 17 kilometres east of Doullens. The British Cemetery is on the northern side of the village.
Ste Marie Cemetery, Le Havre, Seine-Maritime.	Ste. Marie Cemetery is one of the town cemeteries, but it is actually situated in the commune of Graville-St. Honorine. It stands on the ridge overlooking Le Havre from the north and is north of the N.182.
St Sever Cemetery, Rouen, Seine-Maritime.	St. Sever Cemetery and Extension is situated about 3 kilometres south of Rouen Cathedral and a short distance west of the road from Rouen to Elbeuf.
Sebourg British Cemetery, Nord.	Sebourg is a village in the Department of the Nord, about 9.5 kms east of Valenciennes. The British Cemetery stands on the high land east of the village, about 140 metres north of the road to Roisin.
Thiepval Memorial, Somme.	The Thiepval Memorial will be found on the D73 off the main Bapaume to Albert road (D929).
Vaulx Hill Cemetery, Pas De Calais.	Vaulx-Vraucourt is a village in the Department of the Pas-de-Calais, 6 kms north-east of Bapaume. Vaulx Hill Cemetery is sign-posted from the village. Take the RD36, direction Lagnicourt, up the hill and the Cemetery can be seen at the road side 1 kilometre from Vaulx-Vraucourt

Villers Hill British Cemetery, Villers-Guislain, Nord.	Villers-Guislain is a village 16 kms SSW of Cambrai and 4 kms east of Gouzeaucourt, which is a large village on the main road from Cambrai to Peronne. Villers Hill British Cemetery is one kilometre SE of the village.
Vis-en-Artois Memorial	Vis-en-Artois and Haucourt are villages on the straight main road from Arras to Cambrai about 10 kms SE of Arras. Within the grounds of Vis-en-Artois British Cemetery, which is west of Haucourt on the north side of the main road, will be found the Vis-en-Artois Memorial
Warlincourt Halte British Cemetery, Saulty, Pas de Calais.	Warlincourt and Saulty are villages on either side of the main road (N25) between Arras (22 kms) and Doullens (13 kms). Warlincourt Halte British Cemetery is situated just off the north side of the road.

BIBLIOGRAPHY

British Regimental and unit histories
56th (1st London) Division
Dudley Ward, Maj. C A, The Fifty Sixth Division 1914-1918, 1921
Brosnan, Matthew J, The Tactical Development of the 56th (London) Division on the Western Front 1916-18, MPhil Thesis, University of Birmingham 2005
1/2nd London Regiment
Gray, Maj. W E, 2nd City of London Regiment (Royal Fusiliers) in the Great War, Headquarters of the Regiment, 1929
1/4th London Regiment
Grimwade, Capt. F Clive, The War History of the 4th Battalion, The London Regiment (Royal Fusiliers), Headquarters of the 4th London Regiment, 1922
1/5th London Regiment (London Rifle Brigade)
The History of the London Rifle Brigade 1859-1919, Constable and Co. 1921
Mitchinson, K W, Gentlemen and Officers, Imperial War Museum 1995
The L.R.B. Record - various years
1/9th London Regiment (Queen Victoria's Rifles)
Keeson, Maj. C A C, Queen Victoria's Rifles,1792-1922, Constable and Co.1923
1/12th London Regiment (The Rangers)
Wheeler-Holohan, Capt. A V & Wyatt, Capt. G M C Wyatt, The Rangers Historical Records: From 1859 to the conclusion of the Great War, Harrisons and Sons Ltd, 1921
1/13th London Regiment (Princess Louise's Kensington Regiment)
Bailey, Sgt O F & Hollier, Sgt H M, 'The Kensingtons', 13th London Regiment, Regimental Old Comrades Association, 1936
1/14th London Regiment (London Scottish)
Lindsay, Lt. Col. J H, The London Scottish in the Great War, Regimental Headquarters, 1925
Lloyd, Mark, The London Scottish in the Great War, Pen and Sword, 2001
The London Scottish Gazette – various years
1/16th London Regiment (Queen's Westminster Rifles)
Henriques Maj. J Q, The War History of the First Battalion, Queen's Westminster Rifles 1914-1918, Medici Society 1923
1/7th Middlesex Regiment
King, Col. E J, The History of the 7th Battalion, Middlesex Regiment, Harrison and Sons, 1927
1/5th Cheshire Regiment (Earl of Chester's)
Churton, Lt. Col. W A V, The War Record of the 1/5th (Earl of Chester's) Battalion, The Cheshire Regiment August 1914-June 1919, Phillipson and Golder 1920
Royal Army Medical Corps
G Blair, Dr J S, 'In Arduis Fidelis', Centenary History of the Royal Army Medical Corps 1898-1998, Scottish Academic Press 1998.
The 2/1st London Field Ambulance, Morton, Burt and Sons, 1924
The Second-Seconds in France, Spottiswoode, Ballantyne and Co Ltd., 1920
Atkinson, Arthur, 2/3rd City of London Field Ambulance 1914-18 London soldiers – unarmed comrades, privately published 1977.
Royal Artillery
Farndale, Gen. Sir Martin, History of the Royal Regiment of Artillery, Western Front 1914-18, Royal Artillery Institution, 1986

German Regimental histories
Büsing, Georg „Das Reserve-Feldartillerie-Regiment Nr. 20 im Weltkriege 1914-18" Göhmann, Hannover 1932
Forstner, Kurt Frhr. v. „Das Königlich – Preussische Reserve-Infanterie-Regiment Nr. 15" Sporn Zeulenroda 1931
Kümmel, Alfred „Reserve-Infanterie-Regiment Nr. 91 im Weltkriege 1914-1918" Stalling, Oldenburg 1926
Nörr, Hermann „Das K. B. 19. Feldartillerie-Regiment" Schick, München 1930
Wohlenberg, Alfred „Das Reserve-Infanterie-Regiment Nr. 77 im Weltkriege 1914-18" Gerstenberg, Hildesheim 1931

Official accounts
Edmonds, Brig. Gen. Sir James E, Official History of the War: Military Operations, France and
    Belgium 1916, Volume 1 and Maps and Appendices
Jones, H A, The war in the air : being the story of the part played in the Great War by the Royal Air
    Force. Volume 3.
Somme Nord Vol 1, Reichsarchiv, Oldenburg 1927

Personal accounts
Bickersteth, John (editor), The Bickersteth Diaries Leo Cooper 1995
Dolden, A Stuart, Cannon Fodder, Blandford Press 1980
Hawkings Frank, From Ypres to Cambrai, The Elmfield Press 1973
Hodder, Williams J E (editor), One Young Man, Hodder and Stoughton, 1917
Liveing Edward G, Attack, MacMillan 1918, republished by Strong Oak Press 1986
Smith, A, Four Years on the Western Front, Naval and Military Press 1999
Wolff, Anne, Subalterns of the Foot, Square One, 1992

General accounts
Cave, Nigel, Gommecourt, Battleground Europe Series, Pen and Sword, 1998
Churchill, Winston, The World Crisis,
Farrar-Hockley, Gen. Sir A H, 'The Somme', B T Batsford 1966
Hart, Peter, The Somme, Weidenfeld and Nicholson, 2005
Keegan, John, The Face of Battle, Penguin, 1976.
Macdonald, Lyn, Somme, Michael Joseph 1983 and Papermac 1984
Middlebrook, Martin, The First Day on the Somme, Penguin 1971
Prior R & Wilson T, The Somme, Yale University Press, 2005
Sheffield, G, The Somme, Cassell, 2003
Sheldon, J, The German Army on the Somme 1914-16, Pen and Sword 2005

Biographies and Diaries
Boraston J.H., O.B.E., ed. Sir Douglas Haig's Despatches, Dec. 1915 - Apr 1919. J. M. Dent; 1919
Duff Cooper, Haig, 1935
Gardner, Brian, Allenby, Cassell 1965
Home, Brig. Gen. Sir Archibald, The Diary of a World War One Cavalry Officer, Costello, 1985
Lloyd George, David, War Memoirs, 1931
Prior R & Wilson T, Command on the Western Front: The Military Career of Sir Henry Rawlinson
    1914-18, Blackwell Publishers 1992
Savage, R, Allenby of Armageddon, Bobbs-Merrill, 1926
Sheffield G & Bourne J, Douglas Haig, War Diaries and Letters, Weidenfeld and Nicholson, 2005
Terraine, John, Haig: The Educated Soldier, Leo Cooper, 1990
Warner, Philp, Field Marshal Earl Haig, Bodley Head, 1991

Weapons and Equipment
Hogg I V & Thurston L F, British Artillery Weapons and Ammunition 1914-18, Ian Allan, 1972
Jager, H, German Artillery of World War One, The Crowood Press, 2001
Marble, S, 'The Infantry Cannot Do with a Gun Less' The Place of the Artillery in the B.E.F., 1914-
    1918, Gutenberg-e, Columbia University Press, 2005

Miscellaneous
Gray, Lt. Col. H M W, The Early Treatment of War Wounds, Oxford Medical Publications 1919
Pelling, H, Social Geography of British Elections 1885-1910, MacMillan, 1967
German Military Terms, Imperial War Museum

Periodicals
Territorial Service Gazette, July 1916 to April 1917

REFERENCES

Imperial War Museum

VII Corps — Snow, Lieutenant General Sir Thomas D'Oyly (IWM 7274 76/79/1)
Ward-Jackson, Major C L A (IWM 6792 78/22/1)

168th Brigade HQ — Neame, Maj. P (IWM Sound 48/15)
1/2nd London Regiment — Clements, 2nd Lieutenant H T (IWM 3413 86/76/1)
Williams, Lieutenant D J, M.C. M.M. (IWM 6764 78/15/1)

1/3rd London Regiment — Agius, Captain A J J P, M.C. (IWM 8589 99/70/1-3)
Newman, S A (IWM 7076 77/83/1)
Wallace, Captain W G (IWM 11463 86/9/1)

1/4th London Regiment — Payne, 2nd Lieutenant H S, DCM (IWM 196 90/1/1)
Senyard, F G, M.M. (IWM 7953 98/28/1)

London Rifle Brigade — Baker, A G (IWM 8576 01/6/1)
Borrett, H G (IWM 6660 79/35/1)
Hangar, Lance Corporal (IWM 5586 Misc 187 (2818))
Horsley-Smith, Reverend C J (IWM 5601 96/38/1)
Houle, Captain B E (IWM 4637 81/35/1)
Marlborough, W G (IWM 2780 86/48/1)
Russell, H (IWM 7312 76/119/1)
Schuman, A (IWM 4326 82/1/1)
Wass, A E (IWM 12763 03/29/1)
Williams, H G R (IWM 11514 PP/MCR/86)
Woodward R F (IWM 10397 Misc 91 (1354))
London Rifle Brigade Collection Files:
Operational Orders (L64)
Epehemera (L138)
F H Wallis (L168)

Queen Victoria's Rifles — For his friends: Letters of 2nd Lt. P.G. Simmonds of Mansfield College, Oxford, who was killed in action on the Somme, July 1st, 1916 (IWM 90 / 2259)
Appleyard, S W (IWM 7990 82/1/1)
Fitch, J P, M.M. (IWM 7074 77/81/1)
Hawkings, Lieutenant F, RNVR (IWM 7529 75/113/1 & DS/MISC/25)
Lowe, L V (IWM 2793 86/51/1)
Newman, C T (IWM 12494 03/5/1)
Stockman, R (IWM 1337 87/8/1)

The Rangers — Meacham, A G (IWM 6631 79/29/1)
Kensingtons — Lane, S A A, M.M. (IWM 6450 97/10/1)
Mundy, P D (IWM 4862 80/43/1)

London Scottish — Bryden, R E C (IWM 13262 05/8/1)
Bryden, W M (IWM 13263 05/7/1)
Low, Major C J, D.S.O. T.D. (IWM 6702 79/54/1)
Ross, R (IWM 8274 99/22/1)
White, Capt. R (IWM 15175 06/88/1)
Yarnall, G S W (IWM 4576 81/13/1)

Queen's Westminster Rifles — A subaltern's letters: The letters of Second-Lieutenant J.S. Engall, 1915-16 (IWM 8640)
Bunting, Lieutenant D G (IWM 5888 Con Shelf)
Clarke, A O (IWM 3409 86/71/2)
Glanville, F D (IWM Sound 14720/2)
Farley, R (IWM 4510 81/1/1)
Jones, P H (IWM 12253 P246)

1/7th Middlesex Regiment — Atkins, A L (IWM 10767 P267 & Con Shelf)
1/8th Middlesex Regiment — Franklin, W F (IWM 4332 82/3/1)
1/5th Royal Warwickshire Regiment — Carrington, C Maj. (IWM Sound 4057/1)

102nd Siege Battery R.G.A.   Wise, P A   (IWM 1131 90/7/1)
16 Ambulance Train   (IWM 12668 Misc 234 (3333)
    Horner, L W (IWM 7825 Con Shelf)
2/1st London Field Ambulance   Chase, H L (IWM 14996 06/54/1)
2/2nd London Field Ambulance   Kimbel, W C (IWM 1649 87/51/1)
2/3rd London Field Ambulance   French, Major A   (IWM 6521 79/1/1)
283rd Brigade R.F.A.   Darlington, Lieutenant A F D, M.C. (IWM 3968 84/34/1)
43rd Casualty Clearing Station   Bere, Reverend M A   (IWM 12105 66/96/1)
168th Brigade Machine Gun Coy   Orchard, W (IWM 6672 79/41/1)
169th Brigade Trench Mortar Battery   Fripp S T (IWM 10562 PP/MCR/5)

National Archives

G.H.Q
General Staff WO 95/3-5   Medical Services WO 95/45
3rd Army
Gen. Staff WO 95/360   Deputy Dir Ordnance WO 95/383
Adjutant and QMG WO 95/376   Deputy Dir Supply & Transport WO 95/384
Artillery WO 95/387-397   RE Cdr WO 95/383
VII Corps
Staff WO 95/804   Adjutant and QMG WO 95/809
Cdr, Royal Engineers WO 95/815   Dpty Dir Medical Services WO 95/814
Asst Dir Ordnance Services WO 95/815   Cdr R.A. WO 95/811
Corps Heavy Artillery
Cdr Heavy Artillery WO 95/813
19th Heavy Artillery Group WO 95/217   35th Heavy Artillery Group WO 95/390
39th Heavy Artillery Group WO 95/391   48th Heavy Artillery Group WO 95/225
45th Siege Battery (Right section) WO 95/304   50th Siege Battery (Left section) WO 95/476
68th Siege Battery WO 95/480   73rd Siege Battery WO 95/542
88th Siege Battery WO 95/297   91st Siege Battery WO 95/477
93rd Siege Battery WO 95/474   94th Siege Battery WO 95/470
96th Siege Battery WO 95/231   101st Siege Battery WO 95/227
102nd Siege Battery WO 95/227   103rd Siege Battery WO 95/393
116th Heavy Battery WO 95/478   131st Heavy Battery WO 95/299
133rd Heavy Battery WO 95/391   135th Heavy Battery WO 95/388
1/1st Lowland Heavy Battery WO 95/230   No 4 RMA WO 95/327
No 6 RMA WO 95/231
56th Division
Staff WO 95/2931   Adj & QMG WO 95/2936
Cdr R.A. WO 95/2937
280th Bde R.F.A. WO 95/2940   281st Bde R.F.A. WO 95/2940
282nd Bde R.F.A. WO 95/2941   283rd Bde R.F.A. WO 95/2941
Cdr RE WO 95/2939
512 (2/1st London) Field Co RE WO 95/2942   513 (2/2nd London) Field Co RE WO 95/2942
416 (1/1st Edinburgh) Field Co RE WO 95/2942
Asst Dir Medical Services WO 95/2938
2/1st London Field Amb WO 95/2944   2/2nd London Field Amb WO 95/2944
2/3rd London Field Amb WO 95/2944
167th Brigade WO 95/2946,2949-50
1/1st London   1/3rd London
1/7th Middlesex   1/8th Middlesex
167th Brigade MGC   167th Brigade TMB
168th Brigade WO 95/2951, 2954-6
1/4th London   1/12th London (Rangers)
1/13th London (Kensington)   1/14th London (1st London Scottish)
168th Brigade MGC   168th Brigade TMB
169th Brigade WO 95/2957, 2960-1, 2963
1/2nd London   1/5th London (London Rifle Brigade)
1/9th London (Queen Victoria's Rifles)   1/16th London (Queen's Westminster Rifles)
169th Brigade MGC   169th Brigade TMB

Pioneers
1/5th Cheshire WO 95/2943

Royal Flying Corps
8 Squadron   AIR 1218/204/5/2634

Other
Diary of Field Marshal Earl Haig of Bemersyde   WO 256/7-11

Cabinet Papers
Correspondence with Sir James Edmonds,   CAB 45/132-8
compiler of the History of the Great War   CAB 45/183-188

Liddle Collection
1/1st London Regt. (Royal Fusiliers)   Miller W   GALL 062
1/5th London Regt. (London Rifle Brigade)   Barber H A   Western Front Recollections B4
                                             Holyfield S
1/12th London Regt. (The Rangers)   Mason R J   Western Front Recollections M13
1/16th London Regt. (Queen's Westminster   Mockett W   GS 1121
Rifles)   Moy, 2nd Lt. C E   GS 1149
2/1st London Field Ambulance   Boyd A   GS 0175
1/8th Middlesex Regiment   Batho, 2nd Lt. A   GS 0100
90th Siege Battery, R.G.A.   Eldridge, Sir J   GS 0514
94th Siege Battery, R.G.A.   Lush M   GS 0991

National Army Museum
1/5th London (London Rifle Brigade)   Jacobs F W

Privately Held
1/2nd London Regiment (Royal Fusiliers)   Bisgood T.H.

Officers' Personal Files (National Archives)
1/1st City of London Regt. (Royal Fusiliers)
2nd Lt. W S Campbell   WO 374/12186   2nd Lt. E G Johnson   WO 374/37643
Lt. H W Cundall   WO 374/17230   Lt. Col. D V Smith   WO 374/63270
2nd Lt. A J De Vall   WO 374/19386   Lt. G A Westlake   WO 374/73258
2nd Lt. J A Freeman   WO 374/25738
1/2nd City of London Regt. (Royal Fusiliers)
2nd Lt. B R Buxton   WO 374/11549   Capt. P J Handyside   WO 374/30736
Lt. H W Everitt   WO 374/23271   Lt. G B Henderson   WO 374/32582
2nd Lt. K M C Fradd   WO 374/25428   2nd Lt. J W Sanders   WO 374/60253
2nd Lt. H C Gosnell   WO 374/28211   2nd Lt. A M Thorman   WO 374/68526
2nd Lt. J S Grainger   WO 374/28514   2nd Lt. A E Wiggs   WO 374/74215
1/3rd City of London Regt. (Royal Fusiliers)
Capt. A Agius   WO 374/470   2nd Lt. R J A Lidiard   WO 374/42108
2nd Lt. R A Calder-Smith   WO 374/63714   Capt. E V Noel   WO 374/50779
Lt. D W L Jones   WO 374/38125
1/4th City of London Regt. (Royal Fusiliers)
2nd Lt. F R C Bradford   WO 374/8387   2nd Lt. T Moody   WO 374/48473
2nd Lt. A G Blunn   WO 374/7271   Capt. A R Moore M.C.   WO 374/48507
2nd Lt. L R Chapman   WO 374/13253   2nd Lt. J W Price   WO 374/55215
2nd Lt. V C Donaldson   WO 374/20252   Lt. W A Stark   WO 374/64907
2nd Lt. F C Fanghanel   WO 374/23539   2nd Lt. W H Webster   WO 374/72846
Lt. R L Herring   WO 374/32953   2nd Lt. B F L Yeoman   WO 374/77517
2nd Lt. H G Hicklenton   WO 374/33178
1/5th London Regt. (London Rifle Brigade)
2nd Lt. C V Balkwill   WO 374/3495   2nd Lt. B L E Pocock   WO 374/54500
2nd Lt. A L Benns   WO 374/5878   2nd Lt. I R Pogose   WO 374/54510
Lt. G G Boston   WO 374/7772   2nd Lt. E W Rose   WO 374/59076
2nd Lt. G E Clode-Baker   WO 374/14345   2nd Lt. B F Sawbridge   WO 374/60568

Capt. A T B de Cologan	WO 374/19048	Capt. J R Somers-Smith	WO 374/64106
2nd Lt. C B Doust	WO 374/20455	2nd Lt. A Warner	WO 374/71928
2nd Lt. R F Lydall	WO 374/43345	Lt. E R Williamson M.C.	WO 374/75210
2nd Lt. P B B Oldfield	WO 374/51269		

1/9th London Regt. (Queen Victoria's Rifles)

2nd Lt. R H Cary	WO 374/12760	Lt. W Goodinge	WO 374/27950
Capt. R W Cunningham	WO 374/17308	2nd Lt. J S Hunter	WO 374/35827
Col. V W F Dickins	WO 374/19591	Lt. E A J A Lane	WO 374/40631
2nd Lt. F W Fielding	WO 374/24168	2nd Lt. N A Meeking	WO 374/47208
Lt. C P Fleetwood	WO 374/24587	2nd Lt. P G Simmonds	WO 374/62402
2nd Lt. F G Garside	WO 374/26604		

1/12th London Regt. (The Rangers)

Lt. R E K Bradshaw	WO 374/8477	2nd Lt. W G Parker	WO 374/52222
2nd Lt. H G Brown	WO 374/9794	2nd Lt. A B Phillips	WO 374/53799
2nd Lt. W R Davey	WO 374/18019	Lt. J A Reeves	WO 374/56760
2nd Lt. A G Hine	WO 374/33618	2nd Lt. A J Reincke	WO 374/56911
Capt. R L Hoare	WO 374/33763	2nd Lt. H Rochford	WO 374/58714
Major L F Jones	WO 374/38381	2nd Lt. A W Taplin	WO 374/66975
2nd Lt. J Josephs	WO 374/38645	2nd Lt. W H Tucker	WO 374/69680
Lt. G B Meo	WO 374/47346	2nd Lt. D S Ward	WO 374/71727
2nd Lt. C F Monier-Williams	WO 374/48372	Capt. G M G Wyatt	WO 374/77305

1/13th London Regt. (Kensingtons)

2nd Lt. S A Ball	WO 374/3550	2nd Lt. W G Mager	WO 374/45549
2nd Lt. G A Beggs	WO 374/5392	2nd Lt. N E Parry	WO 374/52360
2nd Lt. G P Bryer	WO 374/10409	Lt. W A Penn	WO 374/53349
2nd Lt. J P Clark	WO/37413883	2nd Lt. P R Pike	WO 374/54147
Maj. C C Dickens	WO 374/19553	2nd Lt. H B Pilgrim	WO 374/54170
2nd Lt. H W Hankins	WO 374/30747	2nd Lt. C B Sach	WO 374/60006
Capt. M R Harris	WO 374/31284	2nd Lt. S L Vincent	WO 374/70654
2nd Lt. N O C Mackenzie	WO 374/44661	Capt. F H Ware	WO 374/71892

1/14th London Regt. (London Scottish)

2nd Lt. H J Calder	WO 374/11752	Capt. J H Glover	WO 339/14960
2nd Lt. W E F Curror	WO 374/17386	2nd Lt. P T L Hunter	WO 374/35840
Lt. A G Douglas	WO 374/20382	Maj. F H Lindsay	WO 374/42209
2nd Lt. B E Gavin	WO 374/26709	2nd Lt. A S Petrie	WO 374/53659
Lt. Col. B C Green	WO 374/28890	2nd Lt. G W Prebble	WO 374/55058
Capt. R S Greig	WO 374/29261	Lt. F S Thomson	WO 374/68379

1/16th London Regt. (Queen's Westminster Rifles)

2nd Lt. J Daniel	WO 374/17751	2nd Lt. C E Moy	WO 374/49421
2nd Lt. J S Engall	WO 374/22809	2nd Lt. A G Negus	WO 374/50134
2nd Lt. F A Farley	WO 374/23565	Lt. P Spencer Smith	WO 374/64459
Capt. P M Glasier	WO 374/27497	Lt. Col. R Shoolbred	WO 374/62148
Lt. L P Harrow DCM	WO 374/31516	2nd Lt. W F Strange	WO 374/66000
2nd Lt. J A Horne	WO 374/34734	2nd Lt. C A Stubbs	WO 374/66216
2nd Lt. C C Iveson	WO 374/36580	Capt. F G Swainson M.C.	WO 374/66577
2nd Lt. H Luscombe	WO 374/43305	Lt. M M Webb	WO 374/72718
Lt. A M Manson	WO 374/45927	2nd Lt. A G V Yates	WO 374/77439
Capt. H F Mott	WO 374/49303		

1/7th Middlesex Regiment

Lt. C Ashby	WO 374/2424	Capt. W G Woodroffe	WO 374/76648

1/8th Middlesex Regiment

Lt. L W Easman	WO 374/21713	Capt. H E Martin	WO 374/46423
Lt. J D G Louch	WO 374/42917		

1/5th Cheshire Regiment

2nd Lt. P B Bass	WO 374/4556	2nd Lt. F A Davies	WO 374/18258
Capt. H Caldecutt	WO 374/11742	2nd Lt. H R Leigh	WO 374/41599

1/1st City of Edinburgh Field Coy RE

2nd Lt. S Angus	WO 374/1873	Capt. D G Smith	WO 374/63263

INDEX

Alan MacDonald was born in London in 1951 and was educated at Dulwich College. His various careers as rock and roll musician, political organiser and director of a market research company were an imperfect preparation for writing books about the First World War, or any other book for that matter. Encouraged by his late brother, Ian MacDonald, to turn some rambling and half-hearted research into a book, he published the first edition of *'Pro Patria Mori – The 56ᵗʰ (1ˢᵗ London) Division at Gommecourt, 1ˢᵗ July 1916'* in June 2006. Somewhat carried away by the results he decided to research and write a companion volume about the involvement of the 46ᵗʰ (North Midland) Division at Gommecourt. The result, *'A Lack of Offensive Spirit?'*, happily took less time to write, although 170 pages longer. It was published in March 2007. In the meantime, various factors necessitated the withdrawal of *'Pro Patria Mori'* and this opportunity was used to considerably revise, update and expand the book.

Unlike his brother, who was a real writer, he is an enthusiastic amateur who probably won't do this again. Ian MacDonald, however, wrote several genuine gems, amongst them: *'Revolution in the Head'* which is in its third edition; and *'The New Shostakovich'*, recently re-published in its second edition. Real books for serious readers from a brilliant mind.

Alan MacDonald lives in South London with his wife, two children and four cats. A sports fan, he supports Wolverhampton Wanderers, Harlequins RFC and all teams Scottish. Like writing these books, supporting such teams is a genuine labour of love.

Printed in the United Kingdom
by Lightning Source UK Ltd.
132817UK00001B/200/P